# ROUTLEDGE ENCYCLOPEDIA OF LANGUAGE TEACHING AND LEARNING

# ROUTLEDGE ENCYCLOPEDIA OF LANGUAGE TEACHING AND LEARNING

Edited by Michael Byram

London and New York

First published 2000
by Routledge
11 New Fetter Lane, London EC4P 4EE

Simultaneously published in the USA and Canada
by Routledge
29 West 35th Street, New York, NY 10001

*Routledge is an imprint of the Taylor & Francis Group*

Typeset in Times by Taylor & Francis Books Ltd
Printed and bound in Great Britain by TJ International Ltd,
Padstow, Cornwall

*British Library Cataloguing in Publication Data*
A catalogue record for this book is available from the British Library

*Library of Congress Cataloging-in-Publication Data*
The Routledge Encyclopedia of Language Teaching and Learning /
Edited by Michael Byram, Christopher Brumfit *et al.*
Includes bibliographical references and index.
1. Language and languages – study and teaching – encyclopedias.
I. Byram, Michael. II. Brumfit, Christopher.
P51 .R66 2001
418′.0071–dc21  00-036626

ISBN 0–415–12085–3

# Contents

# Illustrations

# Editorial team

# List of contributors

**Dick Allwright**
University of Lancaster, UK

**Gunilla Anderman**
University of Surrey, UK

**Mark Atherton**
Regent's Park College, Oxford, UK

**Hugo Baetens Beardsmore**
Vrije Universiteit Brussel, Belgium

**Colin Baker**
University of Wales, Bangor, UK

**Jayanti Banerjee**
Lancaster University, UK

**Susan Bassnett**
University of Warwick, UK

**Rupprecht S. Baur**
Universität Gesamthochschule Essen, Germany

**Margie Berns**
Purdue University, Indiana, USA

**Carl S Blyth**
University of Texas at Austin, USA

**Lothar Bredella**
Justus-Liebig-Universität Giessen, Germany

**Mary Brennan**
University of Edinburgh, UK

**David Brien**
University of Durham, UK

**Geoff Brindley**
Macquarie University, Sydney, Australia

**Christopher Brumfit**
University of Southampton, UK

**Anne Burns**
Macquarie University, Sydney, Australia

**Wolfgang Butzkamm**
Universität Aachen, Germany

**Martin Bygate**
University of Leeds, UK

**Michael Byram**
University of Durham, UK

**Robin Cain**
Society for Effective Affective Learning, UK

**Antoinette Camilleri Grima**
University of Malta

**Kip A. Cates**
Tottori National University, Japan

**Ruth Cherrington**
University of Coventry, UK

**Caroline Clapham**
University of Lancaster, UK

**James A. Coleman**
University of Portsmouth, UK

**Jean E. Conacher**
University of Limerick, Ireland

**Vivian Cook**
University of Essex, UK

**Martin Cortazzi**
Brunel University, UK

**Alister Cumming**
Ontario Institute for Studies in Education, Canada

**Jim Cummins**
Ontario Institute for Studies in Education of the
University of Toronto, Canada

**John Daniels**
Berwick on Tweed, UK

**Claire-Lise Dautry**
Université de Franche-Comté, Besançon, France

**Graham Davies**
EUROCALLThames Valley University, UK

**Kees De Bot**
Katholieke Universiteit Nijmegen

**James Dickins**
University of Durham, UK

**Alan Dobson**
Oxford, UK

**Zoltán Dörnyei**
University of Nottingham, UK

**Peter Doyé**
Technische Universität Braunschweig, Germany

**Richard Duda**
CRAPEL, Université Nancy 2, France

**Gerd Egloff**
Technische Universität Darmstadt, Germany

**Mark Fettes**
Ontario Institute for Studies in Education, Canada

**Claudia Finkbeiner**
Universität Gesamthochschule Kassel, Germany

**Roland Fischer**
Universität Linz, Austria

**Michael Fleming**
University of Durham, UK

**Adrian Furnham**
University College London, UK

**Peter Garrett**
University of Wales, Cardiff, UK

**Claus Gnutzmann**
Technische Universität Braunschweig, Germany

**Walter Grauberg**
Nottingham, UK

**Rüdiger Grotjahn**
Ruhr-Universität, Bochum, Germany

**Peter Grundy**
University of Durham, UK

**Manuela Guilherme**
University of Durham, UK

**Xavière Hassan**
Open University, UK

**Silvia Haumann**
Karl Franzens Universität, Graz, Austria

**Gisela Hermann-Brennecke**
Martin-Luther Universität, Halle, Germany

**Frank Heyworth**
EAQUALS, Fribourg, Switzerland

**Randal Holme**
University of Durham, UK

**Gisèle Holtzer**
Université de Franche-Comté, Besançon, France

**Martina Huber-Kriegler**
Pädagogische Akademie des Bundes, Graz, Austria

**Werner Hüllen**
Universität Gesamthochschule Essen, Germany

**Motomichi Imura**
Tamagawa University, Tokyo, Japan.

**Carl James**
University of Wales, Bangor, UK

**Anne-Mieke Janssen-van Dieten**
University of Nijmegen, Netherlands

**Lixian Jin**
De Montfort University, Leicester, UK

**Richard Johnstone**
University of Stirling, Scotland

**Mika Kawanari**
Meikai University, Japan

**Friederike Klippel**
Universität München, Germany

**Paul Kotey**
University of Florida, USA

**Jürgen Kramer**
Universität Dortmund, Germany

**Richard D. Lambert**
National Foreign Language Center, Washington
DC, USA

**Judith E. Liskin-Gasparro**
University of Iowa, USA

**David Little**
Trinity College, Dublin, Ireland

**Shaozhong Liu**
Guangxi Normal University, Guilin, China, and
Wake Forest University, Winston-Salem, USA

**Michael Long**
University of Hawai'i at Manoa, Honolulu, USA

**William McClure**
Queens College and The Graduate Center, City
University of New York, USA

**Steven McDonough**
University of Essex, UK

**Kirsten Malmkjær**
Middlesex University, London, UK

**Gillian S. Martin**
Trinity College, Dublin, Ireland

**Ernesto Martín-Peris**
Universidad Pompeu Fabra, Barcelona, Spain

**Paul Meara**
University of Wales Swansea, Wales

**Péter Medgyes**
Eötvös Loránd University, Budapest, Hungary

**Birgit Meerholz-Härle**
Universität Leipzig, Germany

**Bernice Melvin**
Austin College, Texas, USA

**Meng-Ching Ho**
Open University of Kaohsiung, Taiwan

**Myriam Met**
National Foreign Language Center, Washington,
DC, USA

**Muriel Molinié**
E.N.S. de Fontenay/St Cloud, Paris, France

**Carol Morgan**
University of Bath, UK

**Bernd Müller-Jacquier**
Technische Universität Chemnitz, Germany

**Andreas Müller-Hartmann**
Justus-Liebig-Universität, Giessen, Germany

**Paul Nation**
Victoria University, Wellington, New Zealand

**Marietta Nedkova**
University of Sofia St Kliment Ohridski, Bulgaria

**Hilary Nesi**
University of Warwick, Coventry, UK

**Joan Netten**
Memorial University of Newfoundland, Canada

**Gerhard Neuner**
Universität Gesamthochschule Kassel, Germany

**David Newby**
Karl Franzens Universität, Graz, Austria

**Günter Nold**
Universität Dortmund, Germany

**Susan Norman**
London, UK

**John M. Norris**
University of Hawai'i at Manoa, Honolulu, USA

**Julie E. Norton**
University of Leicester, UK

**David Nunan**
University of Hong Kong

**Rebecca Oxford**
Teachers College, Columbia University, USA

**Norbert Pachler**
Institute of Education, London, UK

**Gloria Paganini**
E.N.S. de Fontenay/St Cloud, Paris, France

**Brian Page**
Leeds, UK

**Lynne Parmenter**
Fukushima University, Japan

**Alastair Pennycook**
University of Technology, Sydney, Australia

**Clive Perdue**
Université de Paris VIII, France

**Marjorie Perlman Lorch**
University of London, UK

**June K. Phillips**
Weber State University, Ogden, USA

**Yip Po-Ching**
University of Leeds, UK

**Karl-Heinz Pogner**
Copenhagen Business School, Denmark

**Christian Puren**
Institut Universitaire de Formation des Maîtres,
Université Paris-III, France

**Albert Raasch**
Universität des Saarlandes, Saarbrücken, Germany

**Marcus Reinfried**
Pädagogische Hochschule Erfurt, Germany

**Annette Richter**
Justus-Liebig-Universität Giessen, Germany

**Philip Riley**
CRAPEL, Université Nancy 2, France

**Karen Risager**
Roskilde University, Denmark

**Shelagh Rixon**
University of Warwick, UK

**Pauline Robinson**
University of Reading, UK

**Margaret Rogers**
University of Surrey, Guildford, UK

**Frédéric Royall**
University of Limerick, Republic of Ireland

**Phyllis Ryan**
Universidad Nacional Autónoma de México,
Mexico

**Kari Sajavaara**
University of Jyväskylä, Finland

**Yasuyuki Sakuma**
Fukushima University, Japan

**Serge Santi**
Université de Provence, Aix-en-Provence, France

**Sandra J. Savignon**
The Pennsylvania State University, USA

**Hanno Schilder**
Universität Duisburg, Germany

**Peter Schofer**
University of Wisconsin-Madison, USA

**Krista Segermann**
Friedrich-Schiller-Universität Jena, Germany

**Barbara Seidlhofer**
Universität Wien, Austria

**Elena Semino**
University of Lancaster, UK

**Lies Sercu**
Katholieke Universiteit Leuven, Belgium

**Monica Shelley**
Open University, UK

**Takashi Shimaoka**
Ibaraki Christian University, Ibaraki, Japan

**Richard C. Smith**
University of Warwick, UK

**Karl Sornig**
Karl-Franzens Universität Graz, Austria

**Marc Souchon**
Université de Franche-Comté, Besançon, France

**Hugh Starkey**
Open University, UK

**Ross Steele**
University of Sydney, Australia

**Douglas K. Stevenson**
Universität Essen, Germany

**Gé Stoks**
National Institute for Curriculum Development,
Enschede, Netherlands

**Michael Stubbs**
Universität Trier, Germany

**Jane Sunderland**
Lancaster University, UK

**Linda Thompson**
National University of Singapore, Singapore

**Makhan L. Tickoo**
National English Language Testing Service,
Hyderabad, India

**Renzo Titone**
University of Rome, Italy

**Loreto Todd**
University of Ulster, Coleraine, UK

**Richard Towell**
University of Salford, UK

**John L.M. Trim**
Cambridge, UK

**Claude Truchot**
Université de Strasbourg, France

**Erwin Tschirner**
Universität Leipzig, Germany

**Yuji Ushiro**
University of Tsukuba, Japan

**Jan van Ek**
Alkmaar, Netherlands

**Theo van Els**
Katholieke Universiteit Nijmegen, Netherlands

**Arthur van Essen**
Rijksuniversiteit Groningen, Netherlands

**Yu Weihua**
Guangdong University of Foreign Studies,
Guangzhou, China

**Henry Widdowson**
Universität Wien, Austria

**Gerard M. Willems**
University of Professional Education of Arnhem en
Nijmegen, Netherlands

**Claire Williams**
Oporto, Portugal

**Colin Wringe**
University of Keele, UK

**Zeng Yantao**
Guangdong University of Foreign Studies,
Guangzhou, China

**Roslyn Young**
Université de Franche-Comté, Besançon, France

**Geneviève Zarate**
E.N.S. de Fontenay/Saint Cloud, France

**Etienne Zé Amvela**
University of Douala, Cameroon

**He Ziran**
Guangdong University of Foreign Studies,
Guangzhou, China

# Introduction

## Purpose

At the turn of the twenty-first century, it has become a commonplace to remark how the world has become a village where people of many different places and origins encounter each other in real or virtual space, in ways which a generation ago would have seemed impossible. Encounters mean communication, and communication should lead to understanding and harmony, or at the very least a reduction of conflict. Yet communication depends above all on overcoming the barriers which languages can symbolise, especially for those who do not live in societies where a variety of languages are already part of their environment.

Language learning has become a necessity for everyone, even those whose first language is English, currently a dominant *lingua franca*, but whose future is unpredictable. Perhaps ironically, this current situation means that this encyclopedia can be published in one language, English, and be accessible to the largest number of readers, although we are acutely conscious that there are still limitations.

When the language(s) that are needed are not readily available in the immediate environment, learning becomes dependent on teaching, for, despite the ease and inevitability of first language(s) acquisition in early childhood, language learning of any other kind turns out to be a complex and difficult task. It is in these circumstances that, for over a century, language teaching has increasingly become a significant profession. At the same time, the complexity of the task of language learning, and therefore of teaching, has become more and more apparent. That complexity has been met with the ingenuity of learners and teachers to devise methods, to create environments, to understand the processes, to simplify and systematise, to find appropriate institutions, all of which is multiplied by the number of traditions which have developed at different times and places more or less independently of each other.

For those who are professionally engaged in language teaching – as teachers, as teacher educators, as inspectors and evaluators, as testers and assessors, as curriculum designers and materials producers – the field has become so complex that it is difficult to know. Like other professions, they need works of reference, those which describe the languages they teach, and those which describe the discipline which they profess. The former include grammars and dictionaries but also the encyclopedias of languages and linguistics which have become commonplace.

This encyclopedia is in the latter category. It provides an authoritative account of the discipline of language teaching in all its complexity. It does so in a way which makes that account readily accessible, whether for quick reference or as a means of gaining an overview and insight in depth of a particular issue. It also enables the language teaching professional to discover the relationship of language teaching to other disciplines. It can thus provide rapid help on a particular problem or be the basis for in-depth and wide-ranging study, as one entry leads to another through the use of cross-references in the text and after each entry, and lists of further reading.

## Readership

The encyclopedia has been created for the language teaching profession. Language teaching professionals – there is unfortunately no generic term to cover the different branches – are like those in other professions which draw upon a range of academic disciplines, pure and applied. They have their own knowledge and skills, and yet they also need to be familiar with other disciplines, such as psychology, sociology, linguistics. This encyclopedia therefore presents accounts both of professional knowledge and skills, and of the supporting or source disciplines.

Because language teaching as a modern profession is relatively young, having grown very quickly and in many different places in parallel, neither an agreed body of knowledge nor a defined and fixed terminology are widely available. Readers in one country may not be familiar with the advances and terminology of another, and the use of different languages for professional purposes makes the situation even more complex. We hope that this encyclopedia will help to bridge some of these inevitable gaps. It has been deliberately produced with as wide an audience as possible in mind, accepting that this itself creates difficulties. It would have been easier to create an encyclopedia of language teaching in a specific tradition – French, Canadian, Indian, Japanese, etc. – but it is precisely one of the aims of language teaching to create the conditions for increased understanding across linguistic and cultural borders, and to produce an encyclopedia which does not attempt to do the same for the profession would be a contradiction in terms.

We hope therefore that our readership will be international and will find the account of the discipline itself international. For, although Western traditions are dominant in this as in many other disciplines, compounded by the current dominance of English and English Language Teaching, authors have been deliberately sought as widely as possible, particularly from outside the ELT world, from Asia, from the whole of Europe, as well as from Britain and North America. This means that there are entries with headwords which are not English, because some terms and traditions are not translatable – as linguists are the first to recognise. It also means that the entries about individual people have been chosen to identify those who have been influential in various traditions of language teaching and learning, rather

than simply being a 'hall of fame' of great language educators.

Contributors have thus been encouraged to write from their own perspective, with as little editorial direction as possible once the general parameters had been set and agreed by the editorial team. If this means that there is not complete harmony within the text as a whole, that there are different views evident in different but related entries, that is a reflection of the discipline in its international character, not an error in production. Readers will be able to pursue topics and see their significance from these different perspectives.

## Contents and organisation

The main body of the encyclopedia contains entries of different lengths, from a few lines to major entries of 3,000 words. These entries are both analyses of the body of knowledge and skills of the language teaching profession, and related issues, and second, sources of information about professional matters, e.g. the meanings of acronyms, the origins and purposes of professional bodies. In the case of the former, authors provide references and suggestions for further reading. Many major entries lead on to other entries which provide further elaboration, and all entries have cross references marked within the text, and further suggested links at the end of texts. In the case of information entries, the dominant criterion has been that the item in question should be of international importance. It is not possible or helpful to include all national associations and institutions, but some exceptions have been made when they also have an international standing.

The entries are in alphabetical order in the main body of the text in order to facilitate access. There are also two other routes of access: a list of contents with all the main entries grouped by theme, and an index of key words, including those appearing either as headwords for entries or others within the texts of entries. In both cases, terminology is included which is not English for the reasons stated earlier.

There are entries on the teaching of specific languages and on the teaching of languages in specific countries. It is obviously not possible to be exhaustive in this any more than in other issues, and there will no doubt be readers who regret the absence of a particular language or country. The intention is as much to remind readers of the multiplicity of approaches to language teaching and learning as to portray the history of a particular language or country, and the choice was, though not arbitrary, largely a personal one. This reflects the nature of the endeavour: to include traditions other than the Anglo-American, important though this clearly is.

It is also a symptom of what an encyclopedia can be at the beginning of the twenty-first century. We have become aware that languages need to be understood in their cultural contexts, and this applies no less to teaching and learning processes. On the other hand we have also become aware that any attempt to be not only comprehensive but also exhaustive is doomed to fail. Development and change is constant and ever more rapid, and no publication, even in the new electronic media, can keep up with every change. Third, there can be no pretence that an encyclopedia is 'objective', neither in the sense of being the ultimate arbiter nor in the sense of being separated from the authorial and editorial presence of contributors and editor. The encyclopedia doubtless reflects to a large extent my own view of what is important in language teaching and learning, moderated by the advice and guidance of the editorial team. One result of this is the presence of entries on the cultural dimension of language teaching, on language education policy and on anthropology. On the other hand, I have not attempted to be comprehensive with respect to teaching methods, techniques and aids. There have been almost too many methods and certainly too many panaceas in the history of language teaching. Methods have been included which have been 'successful', in that they have become well known, but there is no attempt to provide a handbook of methods here.

There is therefore a tightrope to be negotiated stretching from 'comprehensive' to 'interpretative', and this is made all the more difficult in that the encyclopedia has to strike a balance between being an in-depth analysis of the field and a quick reference work, providing the services of a dictionary of terms. I have tended not to provide the latter, since dictionaries already exist.

A similar issue arises with respect to the multi-disciplinarity of language teaching. The sources on which language teachers draw are numerous, and the disciplines from which they come in their own education may be multifarious. Those teachers who were educated and trained specifically for the profession, acquiring knowledge of relevant disciplines as part of this, are probably still a minority. Yet it cannot be the task of an encyclopedia of language teaching and learning simultaneously to be an encyclopedia of linguistics, psychology, cultural anthropology, to mention only a few. We have tried none the less to provide those teachers unfamiliar with such disciplines with the necessary overview and further reading if they wish.

In short, there are many entries which are expected and, I hope, many which are not. I hope readers will find the encyclopedia useful, not only for quick reference but also to browse from one entry to another, via the cross-references in the text and the further references and readings at the end of each text.

## How to use

The organisation of the encyclopedia thus allows for different types of use. Readers who wish to know about a particular issue may look first in the thematic list of contents for the headword they have in mind. They may also go straight to the main body of the text and find the headword in alphabetical order. If the issue is not represented as a headword, they should turn to the index.

Readers who wish to pursue a particular topic or area of interest should use the thematic list of contents. They may wish to start with one of the major overview entries or go immediately to a more specific entry. In either case they will find further cross-references to other parts of the encyclopedia and suggestions for further reading. They will also find that there is some overlap between entries. This is deliberate and allows readers to gain different perspectives on the same topic from different writers.

## Endnote – on writing encyclopedias

There have appeared in recent years a number of encyclopedias on language, linguistics, educational linguistics and now on language teaching and learning. This is probably an indication that, after a century of teaching 'modern' languages, following the Reform Movement, we have reached a point where a degree of certainty exists about what is worth knowing about languages and language teaching and learning. The coincidence of the term 'modern' foreign languages – avoided in French *langues vivantes* and German *Fremdsprachen* – with 'modernism' is not entirely by chance, of course. On the other hand, we do not yet speak of 'post-modern' language teaching, despite the widespread critique of modernism.

None the less, it might appear as though we are out of step with the times to be offering an encyclopedia in a post-modern period, and it is important to acknowledge that what is contained in these pages is the state of an art which is constantly changing. On the one hand we must be aware of Umberto Eco's reminder that 'After all, the cultivated person's first duty is to be always prepared to re-write the encyclopedia' (*Serendipities. Language and Lunacy*, 1999: 21), and encyclopedia writing is never complete. On the other hand, as pedagogues know, there has to be laid down a foundation of knowledge, even if it is later to be challenged. This encyclopedia offers a contribution to that foundation for teachers and learners alike.

# Acknowledgements

Many people have contributed to this volume, but none more so than Susan Metcalf, without whose secretarial skills and personal interest and enthusiasm the encyclopedia would not have seen the light of day.

The second person to whom I owe a special debt of thanks is Ruth Cherrington who, by good fortune, was able to take the leading role in the preparation of texts for publication at a crucial time when my other duties threatened the time and effort I could devote to the encyclopedia. Ruth not only edited entries but also wrote a number herself, and thereby reduced another of my burdens.

Two others, Sally Wagstaffe and Meng Ching Ho, preceded Ruth for short but crucial periods, and I am equally grateful for their help. Furthermore, Sheena Smith was particularly helpful with secretarial support, as both Susan Metcalf and I appreciated.

I am extremely grateful to members of the editorial team, who were supportive throughout what became a long process. They responded to my calls for help, to my requests for comments and advice, and especially to my requests for comments on the major entries. Without their help, the encyclopedia would not have appeared and would certainly not have the qualities it has. For any errors or failings, however, I remain responsible.

Other people also responded to my requests for help. I am particularly grateful to Werner Hüllen, who not only wrote entries but suggested other authors. I also had helpful suggestions from Anne Burns, Caroline Clapham, Dagmar Heindler, Josef Huber, Gisèle Holtzer, Henry Widdowson and Claude Germain.

Sophie Oliver took over from her predecessor as my editor at Routledge and was always encouraging and helpful, especially when I sometimes did not see an end to the task. I am also particularly grateful to James Folan at Routledge for managing the complexities of contracts and my inefficiencies in this respect, and for taking over during Sophie's absence.

Two organisations provided me with financial and material help without which the encyclopedia would have taken many more months, if not years. The School of Education of the University of Durham provided financial support for secretarial help of a very substantial nature. Second, in January–March 1999, I was Adjunct Fellow at the National Foreign Language Center, Washington DC, during which time I had absolute peace and quiet to spend on nothing but the encyclopedia. I am very grateful to colleagues there, to David Maxwell, Betsy Hart and Elizabeth Camero, in particular.

That was one time of absence and there were many more, when I was isolated at my desk. My wife, Marie Thérèse, and my children, Alice and Ian, have always been long-suffering and indulgent towards my belief that being an academic is not a job but just a way of life. This encyclopedia is dedicated to them.

Last but not least, of course, are all those who wrote entries for the encyclopedia. Often they were asked to do so at short notice and in a busy timetable. The 'art' of writing to tight limits on length is something we have all had to learn. I hope that they think the finished product worthwhile, even though in some cases they have had to wait for a long time for their work to see the light of publication.

Michael Byram
Cossé en Champagne
December 1999

# Thematic list of entries

board drawing
*communicative language teaching
dictionaries
direct method
exercise types and grading
flashcard
grammar–translation method
group work
humanistic language teaching
intensive language courses
language laboratories
linguistic psychodramaturgy
literary texts
*materials and media
media centres
neuro-linguistic programming
overhead projector
poetry
proficiency movement
reading methods
reference works
silent way
suggestopedia
*teaching methods
total physical response
visual aids

## Curriculum and syllabus

area studies
*civilisation*
Common European Framework
*contrastive analysis
Council of Europe Modern Languages Projects
cultural studies
European Language Portfolio
graded objectives
*Handlungsorientierter Unterricht*
heritage languages
*Landeskunde*
*language for specific purposes
*le français fondamental*
*literary texts
mother tongue
*mother-tongue teaching
needs analysis
notions and functions
objectives in language teaching and learning
*planning for foreign language teaching
quality management

*syllabus and curriculum design
Threshold Level
US Standards for Foreign Language Learning

## Systems and organisation of Foreign Language Teaching and Learning

*adult language learning
Africa
Australia
Canada
Central and Eastern Europe
China
Common European Framework
*early language learning in formal education
European Language Portfolio
exchanges
France
*higher education
India
internationalisation
Japan
journals
language across the curriculum
large classes
linguistic imperialism
*primary education
*secondary education
study abroad
tandem learning
United States of America
*vocational education and training

## Languages

African languages
Arabic
Chinese
creoles
English
English for specific purposes
Esperanto
French
Japanese
lingua franca
pidgins
Portuguese
Spanish

## History and influential figures

history: the nineteenth century

history: from the Reform Movement to 1945
history: after 1945
Reform Movement

Bloomfield
Chomsky
Comenius
Gouin
Halliday
Hawkins
Hornby
Humboldt
Jespersen
Lozanov
Palmer
Rivers
Saussure
Stern
Sweet
Trim
van Ek
Viëtor
Widdowson

## Evaluation and research

action research
classroom observation schemes
classroom research
*evaluation
*research methods
*second language acquisition theories
*Sprachlehrforschung*

## Contexts and concepts

*anthropology
*applied linguistics
conversation analysis
cross-cultural psychology
discourse analysis

disorders of language
error analysis
gender and language
global education
human rights
intercultural communication
interlanguage
interpreting
language planning
lexicography and lexicology
*linguistics
*linguistique appliquée*
*literary theory and literature teaching
mental lexicon
motivation theories
neurolinguistics
non-verbal communication
politeness
pragmatics
*psychology
Sapir–Whorf hypothesis
schema and script theory
second language acquisition theories
*sign languages
*sociolinguistics
speech act theory
standard language
stereotypes
structural linguistics
stylistic variation
text and corpus linguistics
translation
*translation theory
universal grammar
untutored language acquisition

# Acculturation

Acculturation is the process an individual needs to go through in order to become adapted to a different culture. For this to take place there will need to be changes in both social and psychological behaviour. Where the target culture involves a different language, a key part of the acculturation process will involve language learning. Research has concentrated on the acculturation of immigrant workers to their host country. The fact that many of the learners in this category fail to master the target language is associated with their isolation and lack of social contact with the host population. This lack of progress and the **FOSSILISATION** of their language **SKILLS** has been linked to pidginisation (Schumann, 1976). Acculturation is not generally associated with foreign language learning because this can take place without any direct contact with the target country. Where pupils do have contact with the target language and culture, for example through a pupil **EXCHANGE**, some of the features of acculturation could be seen to have relevance for foreign language learning.

Acculturation requires the learner to adjust their social and psychological behaviour in order to become more closely integrated with the target culture. This distance which separates the learner from the target culture is a measure by which acculturation can be assessed. Byram (1989) talks about the outsider beginning to become an insider, and how critical the move is '... from noticing the boundary markers to appreciating the whole complexity of the way of life'. The initial contact in this process of adaptation may be associated with **CULTURE SHOCK** as the learner discovers that they need to accept differences in behaviour from those with which they are familiar from their own culture. The learner's **MOTIVATION** to become more closely integrated with the target culture will be associated with their individual **NEEDS**.

Acculturation theory originated with the ethnographic work of Linton (1960), who studied the changes Native Americans needed to make in order to become more integrated into mainstream American society. He identified the notion of the distance separating the two cultural groups and the social and psychological changes which would be necessary for closer integration to take place. Social distance would be associated with the actual contact which was available between the two cultures, while psychological distance represented the extent to which the learner wanted to become more closely adapted to the dominant culture. Where differences in language existed between the two cultures, language learning was clearly an important part of the acculturation process.

For Schumann (1978), acculturation theory provided an explanation for individual differences in second language learning and represented the causal variable in the second language **ACQUISITION** process. In his model of the factors determining social and psychological distance, Schumann established the positive and negative elements of acculturation. So, for example, the **ATTITUDE** of the learner to the target social group could be a positive or negative factor while, psychologically, **MOTIVATION** would be seen as a key factor. For him, the first stages of language acquisition are 'characterised by the same processes that are responsible for the formation of **PIDGIN** languages. When there are hindrances to acculturation – when social or psychological distance is great – the learner will not progress beyond the early stages and the language will stay pidginized' (McLaughlin, 1987). The learner's language will therefore fossilise due to the lack of contact with the target language group. Further research (Andersen, 1981), has described in more detail these characteristics, identifying a number of different stages in the process of pidginisation and creolisation (development of a more complex form of pidgin). So, nativisation 'involves assimilation as the learner makes the input conform to an internalized view of what constitutes the second language system', while denativisation represents the next stage when the learner adjusts this early language to external input. The first stage of second language learning involves, therefore, simplification and regression, while later learning is concerned with replacement and restructuring. McLaughlin (1987) describes nativisation as 'perhaps the most interesting aspect of Acculturation/ Pidginization theory as it relates to the mechanisms of learning'.

The theory of acculturation as developed by Schumann is proposed to explain the factors affecting **ADULT** second language **ACQUISITION** taking place without formal instruction, in naturalistic situations. As the theory stands, then, it would appear to have little to offer instructed second or foreign language learning (McLaughlin, 1987; Ellis, 1994). However, McLaughlin has pointed to the probable relevance of the notion of psychological distance for foreign language learning in the classroom. Attitude to the target culture and pupil motivation are likely to be key factors in classroom foreign language learning. Moreover, where pupils have the possibility of direct contact with the target country through a period of exchange or work experience abroad, they are in a situation where they will need to adapt to new and different cultural situations. The extent to which they are able to become integrated with the family with whom they are staying approximates, even for a limited period, the kind of changes emphasised by the acculturation theory. The theory provides, therefore, a useful means of assessing the adaptation of exchange pupils to their new environment which could be measured through the use of questionnaires.

Acculturation theory clearly matches, in a number of important areas, the fossilisation theory of Selinker (1972), which pre-dates it. Both theories seek to explain incomplete language learning and the fact that most learners do not achieve mastery of the target language. In their descriptions of simplified and reduced forms of speech not matching target language norms, they are describing similar phenomena. However, whereas fossilisation theory is based on a linguistic analysis of second language development as identified through examples of usage, acculturation begins with the notion of a single external factor – relationship to the target culture – which leads to these recognised limitations in learner **INTERLANGUAGE**. Acculturation, centred on the degree to which learners are in contact with the target culture, is largely, in contrast with the fossilisation theory, concerned with naturalistic and not instructed language learning. While they differ in the learning environment they describe, both theories have concentrated on the permanence of the language features identified. This is a point which McLaughlin takes up in his **EVALUATION** of the acculturation theory: '. . . relatively little attention has been given to the possibility of changes in individual motivation and attitude as they relate to second language acquisition' (McLaughlin, 1987). Changes in fossilisation theory have begun to address this problem and Selinker (Selinker and Lakshmanan, 1993), recognising the difficulties of identifying a point when language development stops, no longer sees the process as necessarily permanent and identifies the concept of 'plateaus in L2 learning rather than cessation of learning'.

The acculturation/pidginisation theory provides a powerful means for assessing a learner's involvement with the target culture. By extending the scope of the theory to include instructed language learning, it would certainly have, as McLaughlin (1987) suggests, '. . . something to say to teaching practitioners'.

**See also:** Cross-cultural psychology; Culture shock; Intercultural communication; Intercultural competence; Second language acquisition theories

## References

Andersen, R. (1981) 'Two Perspectives on Pidginization as Second Language Acquisition', in R. Andersen (ed.), *New Dimensions in Second Language Acquisition Research*, Rowley, MA: Newbury House.

Byram, M. (1989) *Cultural Studies in Foreign Language Education*, Clevedon: Multilingual Matters.

Ellis, R. (1994) *The Study of Second Language Acquisition*, Oxford: Oxford University Press.

Klein, W. (1986) *Second Language Acquisition*, Cambridge: Cambridge University Press.

Linton, W. (1960) *Acculturation in Seven American Indian Tribes*, Gloucester: Smith.

McLaughlin, B. (1987) *Theories of Second Language Learning*, London: Edward Arnold.

Schumann, J. (1976) 'Second Language Acquisition: The Pidginisation Hypothesis', *Language Learning* 26: 391–408.

Schumann, J. (1978) *The Pidginisation Process: a Model for Second Language Acquisition*, Rowley, MA: Newbury House.

Selinker, L. (1972) 'Interlanguage', *International Review of Applied Linguistics*, X: 209–30.

Selinker, L. and Lakshmanan, U. (1993) 'Language Transfer and Fossilisation: The Multiple Effects Principle', in S. Gass and L. Selinker (eds), *Language Transfer in Language Learning*, Philadelphia: Benjamin.

## Further reading

Aitchison, J. (1996) *The Seeds of Speech, Language Origin and Evolution*, Cambridge: Cambridge University Press.

JOHN DANIELS

# Achievement tests

Achievement tests follow a well-defined period of instruction and are designed to check the extent to which students have learned or absorbed what has been taught over a fixed period. This period can be very short, as in the case of an intensive course, or can extend to a whole year or longer. The content of achievement tests is chosen with reference to a clearly defined **SYLLABUS**, so only the material and skills on that syllabus are tested. The resulting scores reflect the amount the test-takers have learned. Indeed, it is important to remember that an achievement test could be demotivating for the students if it were designed to show up their deficiencies rather than to indicate how successful they had been at absorbing the material they had been taught. Henning (1987), therefore, stresses the importance of pitching the test at the appropriate level for the students concerned.

Achievement test results can be used to make decisions about students' readiness to begin the next stage in their learning; for instance, their readiness to progress from an intermediate to an advanced course. In this respect, achievement tests seem similar to **PROFICIENCY TESTS**, since the results from both are used for decision-making. However, an achievement test is distinct from a proficiency test because the latter does not select its material from a particular syllabus or teaching programme. So, while proficiency tests draw on the language used for a real-world purpose, achievement tests sample only from the language that the students have been taught.

Achievement tests can also be used to evaluate teaching programmes. In such cases, an individual student's score is not of primary interest. Instead, the focus is on the average performance of the group, and this information is used to decide whether changes (if any) need to be made.

**See also:** Assessment and testing

## Reference

Henning, G. (1987) *A Guide to Language Testing*, Boston, MA: Heinle and Heinle.

## Further reading

Davies, A., Brown, A., Elder, C., Hill, K., Lumley, T. and McNamara, T. (1999) *Dictionary of Language Testing*, Cambridge: Cambridge University Press.

Weir, C.J. (1993) *Understanding and Developing Language Tests*, Hemel Hempstead: Prentice Hall International.

JAYANTI BANERJEE

# Acquisition and teaching

When considering the relevance of **SECOND LAN-GUAGE ACQUISITION THEORIES** (SLA) to language teaching, in addition to the fact that theories are just theories, not 'the truth' about SLA, there is a question of focus. The scope of many SLA theories does not extend to the L2 classroom at all. Moreover, even the minority of SLA theories that aspire to classroom relevance focus on instructed SLA, not language teaching *per se*, which involves acquisition *plus* a number of situational variables, and so is far more complex. Furthermore, whereas the goal of most SLA theorists is to discover the least powerful theory that will handle the known facts, i.e., to identify what is *necessary* and *sufficient* for language acquisition, the language teacher and the language teaching theorist alike are interested in the most *efficient* set of procedures, the combination of conditions and practices that will bring about language learning fastest and with least effort, whether strictly necessary or sufficient or not.

Supporters of a current proposal for language *teaching* known as *focus on form* (not forms) (see, e.g., Doughty and Williams, 1998a; Long, 1998; Long and Robinson, 1998) advocate drawing students' attention to language as object – **GRAMMAR**, **VOCABULARY**, collocations, etc. – in context, with the linguistic sequence and timing determined by the students' internal **SYLLABUS**, not an externally imposed one, during otherwise meaning-based lessons of some kind, e.g., **TASK-BASED** or **CONTENT-BASED** classes. Their position is based not only on theoretical grounds but also on empirical findings (see Doughty and Williams, 1998b; Long and Robinson, 1998; Norris and Ortega, forthcoming; Spada, 1997), a growing number of researchers having reported intentional learning to be more efficient (e.g., to occur faster) than incidental learning.

This embryonic language teaching theory of which focus on form is a part is already more powerful than, say, Krashen's theory (e.g. 1981), because (among others) it has recourse to a mechanism, focus on form, to induce acquisition that **MONITOR** Theory does without. This would be important when evaluating the claims as part of a theory of SLA, but it is immaterial in the classroom context, since the relevant theories against which to

judge a theory of language teaching will be other theories of language teaching, not theories of SLA. A relevant comparison, for example, would be between a theory of language teaching that invoked focus on form, on the one hand, and on the other, one which claimed that such interventions were unhelpful, or one which held that an externally imposed linguistic syllabus, explicit grammar rules, **TRANSLATION**, structural pattern drills, etc., were either necessary or more efficient ways of inducing learning of some or all grammatical structures and lexical items.

Almost every theory ever invented in any field has turned out to be wrong, at least in part, and there is no reason to expect that current SLA theories will fare any better. That is not a license for so-called 'eclecticism' in language teaching, however. 'Eclectic methods' (sic) are usually little more than an amalgam of their inventors' prejudices. The same relative ignorance about SLA affects everyone, and makes the eclecticist's claim to be able to select the alleged 'best parts' of several theories absurd. Worse, given that different theories by definition reflect different understandings, the resulting methodological mish-mash is guaranteed to be wrong, whereas an approach to language teaching based, in part, on one theory can at least be coherent, and, subject to the previously discussed caveats, has a chance of being right. That said, theories are what people rely on in the absence of anything else. They are attempts to make sense of experience, and where data are lacking, as is massively the case in SLA and in SL teaching, they go beyond the putative facts of the matter, using logical inference, imaginative speculation and other ingredients. Therefore, while they are one potential source of crucial insights about language learning, which language teaching is trying to induce, SLA theories should always be treated with caution – as one or more theorists' current best shot at explaining language learning, never the truth about it – and with downright suspicion whenever advocated as a recipe for success in the classroom, which will always require consideration of other factors, not 'just' SLA, however important a component of a theory of language teaching that may be.

Most SLA theories, and most SLA theorists, are not primarily interested in language teaching, and in some cases not at all interested. So, while SLA theories may be evaluated in absolute terms and comparatively in a variety of ways – parsimony, empirical adequacy, problem-solving ability, and so on – it makes no sense to judge them solely, as some have suggested, or in some cases at all, on the basis of how useful they are for the classroom or how meaningful they are to classroom teachers. Theories of the role of innate linguistic knowledge in adult SLA, for instance, should be judged on their own terms, e.g., according to how well the predictions they make are borne out by empirical findings, not as to whether they say anything about how teaching should proceed (most do not). By the same token, even when not saying anything about how to teach, SLA theories may provide the classroom practitioner with useful new ways of thinking about, for instance, the varied socio-linguistic milieu learners inhabit outside the classroom, the need for negative feedback, and different *kinds* of structural differences between the learners' L1(s) and the L2. The theories themselves might not say anything to teachers about how to teach, but perhaps something about who and what it is they are trying to teach, e.g., about whether drawing students' attention to some contrasts is essential, facilitative, or not needed at all.

SLA theories may provide insight into putatively universal *methodological principles*, in other words, while saying little or nothing about the inevitable particularity of appropriate classroom *pedagogical procedures*, in which the local practitioner, not the SLA theorist, should always be the expert. An SLA theory might hold provision of negative feedback to be necessary or facilitative, for example, i.e. to be a universal methodological principle; but it will be up to the teacher to decide which pedagogical procedures, ranging from the most implicit corrective recasts to the most explicit forms of 'error correction', are appropriate ways of delivering negative feedback for a particular group of learners. Whatever the precise relationship, given that SLA theorists and language teachers share a common interest, L2 development, it would clearly be self-defeating for either group to ignore the other's work.

**See also:** *Didactique des langues*; Learning styles; Media centres; Second language acquisition theories; *Sprachlehrforschung*; Teaching methods

## References

Doughty, C. and Williams, J. (1998a) *Focus on form in classroom second language acquisition*, Cambridge: Cambridge University Press.

Doughty, C. and Williams, J. (1998b) 'Pedagogical choices in focus on form', in C. Doughty and J. Williams (eds), *Focus on form in classroom second language acquisition*, Cambridge: Cambridge University Press.

Krash, S. (1981) *Second language acquisition and second language learning*, Oxford: Pergamon.

Long, M.H. (1998) 'Focus on form in task-based language teaching', *University of Hawai'i Working Papers in ESL* 16, 2: 35–49.

Long, M.H. and Robinson, P. (1998) 'Focus on form: theory, research, and practice', in C. Doughty and J. Williams (eds), *Focus on form in classroom second language acquisition*, Cambridge: Cambridge University Press.

Norris, J. and Ortega, L. (forthcoming) 'A meta-analysis of research on type of instruction: the case for Focus on Form'. Paper presented at the AAAL Conference, Stamford, Connecticut, March 6–9, 1999.

Spada, N. (1997) 'Form-focused instruction and second language acquisition: a review of classroom and laboratory research', *Language Teaching Abstracts* 30: 73–87.

MICHAEL LONG

## Action research

Action research is part of a broader movement in education associated with the concepts of 'reflective practice' and 'the teacher as researcher'. It involves a self-reflective, systematic and critical approach to enquiry by participants who are also members of the research context. The aim of action research is to identify problematic situations or issues the participants consider worthy of investigation, and to intervene in those situations in order to bring about critically informed changes in practice. For example, researchers may decide to investigate particular aspects of **TEACHER TALK**, **TASK-BASED** learning, the classroom culture or **CLASSROOM LANGUAGE**. **RESEARCH METHODS** for collecting action research data are primarily qualitative and include, for example, **CLASSROOM OBSERVATION** and **JOURNALS**.

Several essential features distinguish action research from other forms of educational research. First, it is small-scale, contextualised and local in character, identifying and investigating teaching–learning issues within a specific situation. Second, it involves **EVALUATION** and reflection aimed at bringing about continuing changes in practice. Third, it is participatory, providing for communities of participants to investigate collaboratively issues of concern within their social situation. Fourth, it differs from the 'intuitive' thinking that may occur as a normal part of teaching, as changes in practice are based on systematic data collection and analysis. Finally, action research is underpinned by democratic principles; it invests ownership for changes in curriculum practice in those who conduct the research.

Action research typically involves four broad phases, which form a continuing cycle or spiral of research:

*planning*   a problem or issue is identified and a plan of action is developed in order to bring about improvements in specific areas of the research context;

*action*   the plan is put into action over an agreed period of time;

*observation*   the effects of the action are observed and data are collected;

*reflection*   the effects of the action are evaluated and become the basis for further cycles of research (based on Kemmis and McTaggart, 1988).

Action research has its roots in a complex mixture of educational and social reform movements reaching back into the nineteenth century. Amongst these influences are:

1   the Science in Education movement of the late nineteenth and early twentieth centuries which considered how scientific methods could be applied to educational problems;

2   progressive and experimentalist educational thinkers, notably John Dewey (1929), who argued that educational practices should be tested by inductive scientific methods of problem solving;

3   the Group Dynamics Movement in social **PSYCHOLOGY** and human relations of the 1930s and 1940s, which included social psychologists such as Kurt Lewin who was interested in the concept of action in group settings and stressed the importance of democratic and collaborative involvement in experimental enquiry;

4   the emergence of curriculum as a field of enquiry, in which the role of teachers as key participants in curriculum reform and the social organisation of learning were acknowledged by educational philosophers such as Schwab (e.g. Schwab, 1969);

5   the teacher as researcher (Stenhouse, 1975), and reflective practitioner movements (Schön, 1983), which gave prominence to the enquiry-based nature of teaching and the role of teachers in studying classroom practices as a way of identifying the problems and effects of curriculum implementation.

Lewin's contribution, in particular, is important, as he was amongst the first to construct a theory and develop descriptions of action research processes (1946). He is often credited with being the 'founding father' of action research, although there is evidence that the concepts and terminology were first used by Collier, the US Commissioner on Indian Affairs (1945).

Three broad phases of development characterise the application of action research in educational contexts. The first, a scientific-technical approach, emerged in the **UNITED STATES** in the 1950s championed in the work of both Stephen Corey (1953), and Taba and Noel (1957), as a way of involving teachers in large-scale curriculum design. This movement was rapidly overshadowed, however, by more scientifically oriented research and development models. The second approach grew from Lawrence Stenhouse's concepts of the teacher as researcher and adopted a practical orientation involving scrutinising personal practice and acquiring improved teaching **SKILLS** as the basis for curriculum development. Stenhouse's work in Britain through The School Council Humanities Curriculum Project (1967–72) and that of his successors, John Elliott and Clem Adelman, in the Ford Teaching Project (1972–5) represent major initiatives of this phase. A third phase, associated with the work of Carr and Kemmis in **AUSTRALIA**, Winter and Whitehouse in the UK and Fals Borda in Colombia, has taken an emancipatory-critical approach which proposes that action research has its base in social movement and political action, which must inevitably underpin collaborative movements for educational reform.

Criticisms of action research have generally focused on questions relating to its rigour and its recognisability as a valid research methodology. Corey's work soon suffered from comparisons with positivist experimental research which placed value on criteria of objectivity, rationality and generalisability. Hodgkinson, in a paper published in 1957, criticised action research for its 'sloppy' methodological approaches, the lack of research training by those who conduct it and its inability to contribute to theoretical developments. Others (e.g. Halsey, 1972) have pointed to the fundamental tension between 'action' and 'research' and to the differing, and inherently incompatible, orientations taken by teachers and researchers to educational questions. Winter (1982) and others have drawn attention to the lack of rigour in **INTERPRETATION** and the restricted nature of the data that characterise much action research. Issues of a more pragmatic nature highlight the resistance of teachers to becoming researchers, suspicion on the part of other staff and principals towards practitioners who adopt a research stance, the complexities of collaborative teacher–researcher partnerships and the risk that the research could be co-opted by academic researchers. The relative newness of action research in the language teaching field means that there is a limited literature and uncertain professional status associated with action research, so that its potential benefits as a research method and the ways in which it may contribute to professional development are yet to be fully understood.

However, the broad scope and flexibility of action research mean that its applications to the field of language teaching are potentially numerous (Crookes, 1993). They include:

- to provide an impetus for individual and group action and to elucidate immediate teaching or learning problems (Nunan, 1990; Wallace, 1998);
- to facilitate continuing professional development and **TEACHER EDUCATION** (Richards and Nunan, 1990; van Lier, 1996; Freeman, 1998);
- to underpin educational change and innovation (Goswami and Stillman, 1987; Markee, 1997);
- to play a role in the **EVALUATION** of teaching and learning programmes (Murphy, 1996);
- to stimulate school and organisational renewal (Elliott, 1991; Burns, 1999);
- to promote researcher and teacher partnerships (Somekh, 1994);
- to support broad educational trends towards school-based curriculum development (Hopkins, 1993).

As the research focus is on the classroom and on immediate practical concerns in teaching, action research holds promise as a site for building theories about language teaching which are potentially of value and interest to other teachers.

**See also:** Classroom language; Classroom observation schemes; Research methods; Teacher education; Teacher talk

## References

Burns, A. (1999) *Collaborative Action Research for English Language Teachers*, Cambridge: Cambridge University Press.

Collier, J. (1945) 'United States Indian administration as a laboratory of ethnic relations', *Social Research* 12, 3: 256–303.

Corey, S. (1953) *Action Research to Improve School Practices*, Columbia University, New York: Teachers' College Press.

Crookes, G. (1993) 'Action Research for Second Language Teachers: going beyond teacher research', *Applied Linguistics* 14, 2: 130–44.

Dewey, J. (1929) *The Sources of a Science of Education*, New York: Horace Liveright.

Elliott, J. (1991) *Action Research for Educational Change*, Milton Keynes: Open University.

Freeman, D. (1998) *Doing Teacher Research. From Inquiry to Understanding*, New York: Heinle and Heinle.

Goswami, D. and Stillman, P.R. (1987) *Reclaiming the Classroom. Teacher Research as an Agency for Change*, Portsmouth, NH: Heinemann Boynton/Cook.

Halsey, A.H. (ed.) (1972) *Educational Priority Volume 1: Educational Priority Area Problems and Practice*, London: HMSO.

Hodgkinson, H.L. (1957) 'Action Research – a

critique', *Journal of Educational Sociology* 31, 4: 137–53.

Hopkins, D. (1993) *A Teacher's Guide to Classroom Research* (2nd edn), Milton Keynes: Open University.

Kemmis, S. and McTaggart, R. (eds) (1988) *The Action Research Planner* (3rd edn), Deakin University, Victoria: Deakin University Press.

Lewin, K. (1946) 'Action research and minority problems', *Journal of Social Issues* 2, 4: 34–46.

van Lier, L. (1996) *Interaction in the Language Curriculum. Awareness, Autonomy and Authenticity*, London: Longman.

Markee, N. (1997) *Managing Curricular Innovation*, Cambridge: Cambridge University Press.

Murphy, D. (1996) 'The Evaluator's Apprentices. Learning to do evaluation', *Evaluation* 2, 3: 321–38.

Nunan, D. (1990) 'Action Research in the Language Classroom', in J.C. Richards and D. Nunan (eds), *Second Language Teacher Education*, Cambridge: Cambridge University Press.

Richards, J.C. and Nunan, D. (eds) (1990) *Second Language Teacher Education*, Cambridge: Cambridge University Press.

Schön, D. (1983) *The Reflective Practitioner: How Professionals Think in Action*, New York: Basic Books.

Schwab, J.J. (1969) 'The practical: a language for curriculum', *School Review* 78, 1: 1–23.

Somekh, B. (1994) 'Inhabiting Each Other's Castles: towards knowledge and mutual growth through collaboration', *Educational Action Research* 2, 3: 357–81.

Stenhouse, L. (1975) *Introduction to Curriculum Research and Development*, London: Heinemann.

Taba, H. and Noel, E. (1957) *Action Research: A Case Study*, Washington: Association for Supervision and Curriculum Development.

Wallace, M.J. (1998) *Action Research for Language Teachers*, Cambridge: Cambridge University Press.

Winter, R. (1982) '"Dilemma analysis": a contribution to methodology for action research', *Cambridge Journal of Education* 12, 3: 161–74.

**Further reading**

Burns, A. and Hood, S. (1995) *Teachers' Voices: Exploring Course Design in a Changing Curriculum*, Sydney: National Centre for English Language Teaching and Research.

Carr, W. and Kemmis, S. (1986) *Becoming Critical: Educational Knowledge and Action Research*, London: Falmer Press.

Edge, J. and Richards, K. (1993) *Teachers Develop Teachers. Research. Papers on Classroom Research and Teacher Development*, Oxford: Heinemann.

Nunan, D. (1989) *Understanding Language Classrooms*, London: Prentice Hall.

*Educational Action Research: An International Journal.*

*Networks: An Online Journal of Teacher Research* http://www.oise.utoronto.ca/~ctd/networks.

ANNE BURNS

# Adult language learning

Adult language learning (ALL) occurs either as an independently organised process – although still too rarely so – or in an institutional framework, for example in publicly accredited or private or work-based institutions. ALL attempts on the one hand to bridge the gap, large or small, between the outcomes of school learning and needs and wants in the world outside school, or on the other hand to build up the language competencies needed for the new challenges which appear in adult life, for example professional, social or cultural challenges.

Whilst in the following we shall consider such questions as 'Who learns languages in ALL?'; 'Who teaches languages in ALL?'; 'Where does ALL take place?'; 'What do people learn in ALL?', there are a number of points to bear in mind. Whereas discussion of the concept of ALL leads to consideration of the specificity of the language learning of adults, it should not lead to the isolation of this kind of learning but should rather take note of the links with the language learning of young people – or of senior citizens – in order to contribute to the aim of lifelong learning.

ALL has begun to play a more and more important role in the modern world, as shown by examples from **AUSTRALIA** (literacy programmes for immigrants), **CANADA** (social integration and cohesion of a bilingual country) and the Scandinavian countries (the importance of ALL in

Denmark, Sweden and Finland). In the **USA**, adult second language learning is most important in the teaching of **ENGLISH** to non-English speaking immigrants, who need some thirty hours of English instruction in order to qualify for citizenship. There is a similar case in the teaching of the Estonian language to Russians living in Estonia, who need language competence in order to be integrated in the vocational and social life of the country.

## Characteristics of the language learning of adults

In the light of current thinking it is not possible to define concepts of language learning which are uniquely adult in nature. It is more sensible to accept a degree of uncertainty, because one thereby gains a fruitful flexibility in methodological and didactic terms. This uncertainty is caused by the fact that various criteria more or less overlap with each other.

1 The distinction of **ADULT LEARNERS** is made partly in terms of age, although this criterion is only partly valid since learners in school are often of the same age as learners in adult education who have already left school for the world of work or for **VOCATIONAL TRAINING**. The distinction is better made in terms of:
2 the daily rhythm determined by professional life;
3 personal characteristics, which may be less developed in young people, such as independence, responsibility for one's own learning, cognitive insight, capacity for comparison, ability to self-evaluate;
4 social responsibilities, for example towards children, family, employer;
5 economic conditions, which for example oblige learners to acquire (additional) qualifications;
6 biographically based characteristics: for example **MOTIVATION** – for example a desire for social contacts through participating in a language course; previously acquired competencies such as languages acquired earlier; previous – positive or negative – experiences of the teaching and learning process, for example anxieties about learning;
7 adult-oriented learning resources as opposed to

learning conditions and aims which are determined by the school curriculum. The school should prepare the path from one phase to the other if it is to contribute to lifelong learning. This preparation for ALL is above all crucial in the area of **LANGUAGE AWARENESS** and in communicative and **CULTURAL AWARENESS**;
8 tourist, cultural and other interests, often in connection with planned activities such as travel;
9 professional demands, for example the acquisition of additional qualifications for applications for jobs or specific activities such as a sojourn abroad;
10 **NEEDS** which arise from particular social situations and which can influence the aims and contents of language teaching for adults in specific ways. A notable example is the opening of the Iron Curtain, which had political, economic, social and also cultural effects on the integration of Europe. Other examples are **INTERNATIONALISATION** and globalisation, which we shall return to later in this entry;
11 social, vocational and cultural integration of immigrants into the society of many countries, often in connection with literacy programmes;
12 the 'voluntary' participation of adults in a language course, as opposed to the largely obligatory teaching of language to school pupils – a central and difficult question. The problem lies in the question whether all or almost all of the criteria mentioned above are obligations, internal or external, which lead to participation in language courses.

These criteria are relevant for adult learners in different degrees and quantities, and it is this which creates increased demands on teachers in adult education. It is evident that the methodology of language teaching has to take into account the characteristics which have been listed here. There are certain consequences for teaching:

- on the one hand, teachers and institutions, i.e. those who offer languages, attempt to cater for the average, in order to serve as many learner groups as possible and to offer something for everyone;
- on the other hand, it is necessary to consider whether learners with specific characteristics

should be offered specific help, i.e. by differentiated teaching or through specific externally differentiated courses.

## Characteristics of language courses for adults

Language teaching for adults is organised in specific ways, although here, too, it is not possible to give a unique definition but rather to identify particular emphases.

1  From an institutional point of view, language learning for adults is basically designated as 'post-school', and is therefore institutionally part of further education.

   Language courses for adults which are organised outside school are offered by various providers. In certain countries there are evening schools that teach the secondary school programmes; in others there are citizens' and workers' institutes; higher education institutes often offer language courses to citizens (in their language centres); in the USA, most cities offer their citizens adult education programmes that include foreign languages. The market usually includes, in addition to public or publicly accredited providers and language courses internal to firms, a large, unquantifiable number of private institutions, although this is not the case in the USA, for example. This situation, which is characterised by multiplicity and competition, has been described for a specific region and is regularly up-dated.

   The difficulties of allocating this kind of learning to further education are evident and include the following:

   • there are pupils who take up language courses in further education whilst still at school;
   • certain forms of school-based course could in fact be described as adult education, for example teaching in vocational schools which may for institutional reasons be defined as 'school' courses.

2  The teaching and learning of languages in adult education have specific characteristics on account of the learner characteristics mentioned above, at least in theory. ALL is fundamentally characterised by the following facts:

• in adulthood there are possibilities, which scarcely exist in schools, of determining aims, methods and contents autonomously, taking into consideration the needs and wants of the learners and also the conditions of the institution;
• this basic premise is realised in various ways: for example by developing curricular approaches which are offered to learners to make their own choice. This is the case, for example, with the 'European Language Certificates' which are offered in the member countries of the 'International Certificate Conference'. The alternative is that in a particular language course specific learning programmes are agreed on the basis of the participants' interests.

   This independence with respect to learning content exists, however, in practice only to a limited degree, and has not existed for very long or indeed everywhere.

• The work of the **COUNCIL OF EUROPE** is closely linked to the publication of the **THRESHOLD LEVEL**, *Niveau seuil, Kontaktschwelle Deutsch* and so on, and the foundation of this work, besides the innovative ways of describing language, was above all the methodological description of needs and wants analysis. This was the basis for adult education to free itself from definitions of learning **OBJECTIVES**, determined by the curriculum and widely seen as imposed from outside. The difficulty of realisation in practice is less in the approach to the individuality of needs and wants – which is not a basic problem due to the nature of the analyses – but rather in the variability or dynamic of the results of analyses. These results have to be continuously updated on account of the unstable and scarcely predictable changeability of the needs situation, i.e. they have to be changed to fit a given constellation of factors. In practice, however, this goes beyond what is apparently feasible. Furthermore, the diagnosis which is possible on the basis of such analyses creates the need for another large step, namely the transfer into a 'therapy' of lesson planning and practice.
• The limitations in terms of content and

methodology include the fact that language teaching in adult education in the twentieth century has been very dependent for its methodological concepts on school-based language teaching. The exceptions are commercial schools which use only **NATIVE SPEAKERS**, just to mention one example of a very progressive approach, albeit of limited extent. The situation in further education began to change mainly in the 1960s and 1970s, partly through the work of the Council of Europe and also as a consequence of other influences such as learning theory, psycholinguistics, approaches to language description, vocational orientation, changes in the ways of thinking about language and education, and emphasis on practice. This has brought considerable success in the emancipation of adult education, and was the basis for further developments which in turn have influenced schools. None the less there remains a strong link between school and further education, particularly in language teaching, which for further education has been both fruitful and inhibiting. This difficulty is increased by the fact that many teachers in adult education simultaneously work in schools, although these numbers are falling, and they bring their school teaching approaches into adult education unless they are prepared and given the opportunity to acquire and experience the specificity of language teaching adapted to adults.

- Despite the realisation that linguistic competence is a necessity, it has not yet been possible to professionalise the training of teachers for ALL or to anchor it institutionally in academic activity. The widely used alternative of offering in-service instead of pre-service courses cannot provide the qualifications which are required for teaching and learning appropriate to adults.

## The science of language teaching for adults

### Institutional aspects

The systematic concern with language teaching and learning for adults is a scientific activity, but it cannot be said that a scientifically established discipline has emerged from this, which might for example have a place in **HIGHER EDUCATION**. To illustrate this from the Federal Republic of Germany, there have been considerable efforts on the part of the German Institute for Adult Education (*Deutsches Institut für Erwachsenenbildung* – DIE), although this is not a university-type institution, and the 'variety' of the higher education sector was described by Quetz and Raasch in 1982 and has not changed essentially since. In **FRANCE** the situation is different, although similar. There came significant developments from organisations such as **CRÉDIF** (until 1998) and **CRAPEL**, and from universities in more or less haphazard ways, for example on the basis of the founding of chairs in French as a Foreign Language at the Universities of Besançon, of Paris III etc., which train students in **FRENCH** as a Foreign Language (FLE – Français langue étrangère) and whose graduates in many cases later teach in ALL institutions. In certain countries (e.g. in France) the law obliges employers to organise courses for employees as part of their continuing education (or to pay for such courses organised by specialised institutions).

### Content and subject aspects

The important contributions of the scientific discipline of ALL to the discussion of foreign language teaching are in the following areas:

- **AUTONOMOUS LEARNING**
- **NEEDS ANALYSIS**
- **DISTANCE LEARNING**
- **QUALITY** assurance, quality control and auditing
- target group orientation
- modular courses
- certification of learning
- professional orientation of language teaching
- teaching **LANGUAGE FOR SPECIFIC PURPOSES**
- **PRAGMATIC**-functional language descriptions instead of emphasis on morpho-syntax
- development of international cooperation (e.g. **RELC** Singapore, the **EUROPEAN CENTRE FOR MODERN LANGUAGES**) in Graz (Austria).

Some of these can be described in more detail:

*Certification*   One of the interesting specific aspects

of ALL is the development and implementation of examinations and certificates. The statistics of the major examining bodies demonstrate the extent of the need; examples include the Cambridge English examinations, the DELF/DALF French examinations and the Goethe-Institut German examinations. The need that adults have to take examinations is doubtless largely attributable to the increasing requirement for professionally valid certificates, but this cannot be the only explanation. Self-motivation, self-discipline and learner autonomy are other explanations, and in the European context there is an approach to portfolio assessment at school level (the **EUROPEAN LANGUAGE PORTFOLIO**) which is being transferred into further education, together with the **COMMON EUROPEAN FRAMEWORK**. This approach gives a decisive impulse to lifelong, or life-accompanying, learning which is particularly characteristic for language learning. Certification is of great indirect significance for foreign language teaching and learning because it contributes to the development of modular forms of teaching, allows learning to be organised in approachable stages, sanctions what has been achieved, and thereby creates motivation to continue. These are some of the advantages of certification practices independent of the professional significance of certificates.

*Modular learning and definition of learning aims*   For professional purposes more than traditionally for learning which is independent of a professional purpose, it is important that the results of learning can be read concretely from the certificates of achievement. Both employees applying for jobs, and employers or personnel officers selecting from among the applicants, rely on this. Certification thus does not mean simply giving a mark, it should also provide a detailed account of what has been achieved. This produces a pressure on further education institutions to describe their courses in much more transparent ways than has hitherto been the case. It may also have some influence on schools. This transparency in the description of learning aims, which also of course has methodological implications, is an important step in the realisation of adult-specific learning, and corresponds to one of the most important demands characteristic of adults. It is the pre-condition for

the organisation of language courses according to target groups.

*Professional language courses*   A significant step in ALL is made through the professional orientation of language learning. What has been achieved here includes also, in part, vocational schooling, although the effect on general education and higher education language teaching is limited. In professional activity, it is not formal ('systemic') or educationally oriented competencies which are required, so much as capability for **INTERCULTURAL COMMUNICATION** abroad or with speakers of the target language. In this context there is a need for a theory of **CULTURAL STUDIES/ LANDESKUNDE** teaching oriented to adults which should take place in the following steps, each building on the previous ones:

1 knowledge about the culture of the target country and its inhabitants;
2 ability to compare knowledge of the target country with one's own culture;
3 capacity for accepting the other/the foreigner (empathy competence);
4 capacity to act together with others on the basis of the previous steps (**INTERCULTURAL COMPETENCE**) whilst taking into account the otherness of other cultures;
5 capacity to create, in common with other cultures, a new mutually organised and validated over-arching culture.

This progression leads to the pre-conditions for public political action as it is needed, for example, in Europe (integration of the European Union) or in South America (development of a free trade area 'Mercosur'/'Mercosul'). This kind of planning for cultural learning is particularly oriented to adults, i.e. to the challenges which adults in particular have to meet, whether in their professional life or in their ordinary life as responsible active citizens. In this theory of cultural learning, there is an assured place for contemporary language description (with an orientation to language for action) as the basis for methodology, including autonomous learning and open teaching. These aims are also especially served by attempts at innovative approaches which are the central aims of language developments by the European Union and its programmes such as LEONARDO and SOCRATES.

*Autonomous learning* Self-directed learning and **SELF-ACCESS** which can offer those in employment the necessary flexibility are not yet much developed in practice. The pre-conditions which determine self-directed learning above all are that, besides the theoretically adequate description of learning strategies, there should be practical realisations of these in the form of thoroughly concrete learner counselling by the teaching institutions, and learning materials, in an appropriate introduction to the use of these strategies, in the creation and use of user-friendly, comprehensive self-assessment processes. Since these pre-conditions are still largely absent, and furthermore are not visibly developed in school foreign language teaching, there is still in practice a lack of the desirable combination of institutional and self-directed learning. The corresponding expectations of technology, especially in software development (for example in multimedia courses and authoring systems) have so far been only partially fulfilled. In this sense, autonomous learning has not yet become a characteristic of ALL. What are today considered to be the priority communicative skills are in fact difficult to handle and have so far only been developed singly rather than as a comprehensive whole. It has to be emphasised that the development work needed for autonomous learning does not concern only technology, but is inseparable from psychological, psycholinguistic, linguistic and pedagogical-methodological aspects of self-directed learning. Until this work becomes a central concern of **RESEARCH**, rather than that of individual initiatives and publishing houses, the situation will not change fundamentally. One of the consequences is that language learning among adults cannot yet be differentiated from the school learning scenario.

## Conclusion

Language learning for adults has the opportunity through quality control and **QUALITY MANAGE-MENT** to make a major step forward.

Quality assurance is so far limited to organisations in adult education. This is explained by the fact that quality control has become usual in the economy. Schools have so far avoided these controls but many further education institutions, especially publicly accredited ones, are also holding back. Perhaps this is because of the fear-inspiring term 'control' which should be replaced by 'management' in order to gain more acceptance.

The pre-condition for quality assurance is to have an appropriate instrument. A model proposed here (see Figure 1) includes the various factors and their interrelationships. The model has eight 'corners' to which the factors are attached.

Teaching must always be seen in relation to other factors, and we have used this model as a basis for the presentation here and discussed all the factors, although not all equally. We have also shown that there lies around the model's octagon a circle which we can call 'society', and influences from this circle penetrate the system. These include, for example, changes in the integration of Europe or South America, or the professional situation of many people who need qualifications for certain activities, including qualification in linguistic competence. This becomes particularly clear through phenomena such as internationalisation – defined as intentional effort towards international cooperation; and globalisation – defined as unintentional, worldwide developments such as environmental catastrophes or uncontrolled movements of capital. Adults experience these developments either as opportunities or as threats or challenges, and it is here that language learning for adults has an increasingly important role. This task is a characteristic of ALL, although as yet a missing characteristic.

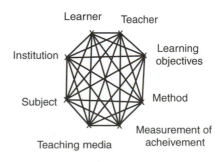

Figure 1   An appropriate instrument for quality assurance in ALL

**See also:** Age factors; Autonomy and autonomous learners; Central and Eastern Europe; Council of Europe Modern Languages Projects; Languages for specific purposes; Needs analysis; Notions and functions; Psychology; Self-access; Teacher education; Teaching methods

### References

Quetz, J. and Raasch, A. (1982) *Fremdsprachenlehrer für die Erwachsenenbildung*, Braunschweig.

Sprachenrat Saar (ed.) (1997f.) *Sprachlernatlas Saar*, Saarbrücken (http://www.phil.uni-sb.de/FR/romanistik/raasch/)

### Further reading

Burger, G. (ed.) (1995) *Fremdsprachenunterricht in der Erwachsenenbildung: Perspektiven und Alternativen für den Anfangsunterricht*, München: Hueber.

Eggers, D. (ed.) *Sprachandragogik*, Frankfurt am Main: Peter Lang.

van Hest, E. and Oud-de Glas, M. (1990) *A survey of techniques used in the diagnosis and analysis of foreign language needs in industry*, Brussels: Lingua.

Krashen, S.D. (ed.) (1982) *Accounting for child-adult differences in second language acquisition*, Rowley, MA: Newbury House.

Titmus, C.J. (ed.) (1989) *Lifelong Education for Adults. An International Handbook*, Oxford: Pergamon Press.

Vielau, A. (1997) *Methodik des kommunikativen Fremdsprachenunterrichts. Ein lernerorientiertes Unterrichtskonzept (nicht nur) für die Erwachsenenbildung*, Berlin: Cornelsen Verlag.

ALBERT RAASCH

# Adult learners

In general the capacities of adults to learn seem to remain relatively stable under conditions of continuous use and absence of diseases and time pressure. With respect to **SECOND LANGUAGE ACQUISITION** we find that **FOSSILISATION** is quite normal, although there appear to be adult second language learners who attain perfect performance. There are many factors that influence the success of second language **ACQUISITION**. In the case of adult migrants learning the language of the dominant community, sociopsychological factors play an important role.

## Adult learning in general

'The' adult learner does not exist. Capacity to learn is the result of personal **APTITUDE** and learning history and may differ from individual to individual (Bolhuis, 1995). This distinction reflects the distinction that has been made by psychometrists between fluid and crystallised intelligence. It is suggested that the former seems to decrease after the **AGE** of 20 while the latter continues to increase (Sternberg and McGrane, 1996). Fluid intelligence is neurophysiological in nature whereas crystallised intelligence depends on sociocultural influences, among which education plays an important role. All learning processes that adults have experienced are relevant for their actual learning.

The effects of physical and psychological changes with increasing age and the effects of sociocultural factors, let alone the interaction of these factors, are largely unknown. Physical changes that affect learning most are (brain) diseases. Prior knowledge and experience in learning are the dominant factors that influence cognitive changes (Merriam and Caffarella, 1991). Elderly learners are able to compensate for age-related declines in cognitive skills, such as the ability to retrieve information and the efficiency of information processing, by their expertise and knowledge in certain domains (Sternberg and McGrane, 1996). Sociocultural factors, such as social roles or ethnic differences, may affect development in adulthood as much as individual maturation. Participation in adult education is predominantly influenced by social status. The social environment may impede the act of learning and disuse of learning capacities is known to be of negative influence.

The major difference between child learning and adult learning is attributable to the larger extent of prior knowledge and learning experiences of adults, their mental models, which are socioculturally and historically determined. This prior knowledge influences the learning process at all stages. Prior knowledge seems to be rather resistant to new information and may consist of concepts as well as of misconceptions. In the case of language learners there may, for example, be ideas about what language is, how language should be learned, or previously learned language rules. Adults' mental models are generally more developed and more stably fixed than those of children. Adult learners seem to be particularly inclined to try to fit new information into existing models. In other words they strive more after cognitive assimilation, whereas children seem to be more inclined for cognitive accommodation, which is, in most cases, needed for effective learning. Prior knowledge may both benefit and hinder learning (Bolhuis, 1995). It can be concluded that age-related changes are no obstacle to learning, but that the learner's prior knowledge, self-perception and ideas about how to learn have strongly to be taken into account in adult education.

## Adult language learning

Does the above apply to the learning of all subject matters; in other words, are there any reasons to assume that language learning is different from other learning? Among linguists there does not seem to be much doubt that language learning is different where first language learning is concerned. They assume the existence of an innate language learning capacity, **CHOMSKY**'s Language Acquisition Device, later referred to as **UNIVERSAL GRAMMAR**, which seems to operate highly independently from general cognitive abilities. The question whether or to what extent this innate capacity plays a role in postpuberty second language learning is subject to much debate in Second Language Acquisition research.

Of more practical relevance are findings from research into **AGE FACTORS** and second language learning. The findings are far from conclusive, but in naturalistic settings a general tendency emerged: in the beginning, older learners outperform younger ones, but ultimately those who started learning a second language in childhood outperform learners who started later (Harley and Wang, 1997). 'The younger one starts, the better' seems to be the adage for native-like attainment of second language. Hypotheses about a critical or sensitive period for second language acquisition were countered by showing that non-natives with first

exposure to the target language after the critical period could not be distinguished from natives. Bialystok (1997: 134) concludes in a review that perfect mastery by late learners is possible when conditions are favourable. Nevertheless, it has to be born in mind that in the case of adult learners fossilisation is much more common than native-like mastery (Klein, 1996). Explanations for this phenomenon are manifold, and as yet rather speculative in nature, a rather straightforward one being that it may take many years of exposure and practice to gain skills necessary for the highest levels of performance.

## Adult migrant learners

The situation of adult immigrants, especially of immigrants with low social status, differs in many ways from that of adult learners learning a foreign language in their home country. Schumann (1978) draws attention to the fact that sociopsychological factors play a very important role in the acquisition of the language of the host country. Immigrants, for whom language and **ACCULTURATION** are the keys to success in the host country, find themselves in the paradoxical situation that they must both learn and use the language at the same time. Differences in social and linguistic behaviour often consolidate **STEREOTYPED** or sometimes racist ideas in the dominant language community. The perception of this behaviour may contribute to considering second language learners as persons with a low level of communicative **SKILLS**, socially inadequate behaviour and low intelligence. This, in turn, can lead to demotivation, low self-esteem and feelings of incompetence in migrant learners (Perdue, 1982). The vulnerability and powerlessness of migrants often makes them teacher-dependent learners, which in turn adds to their feelings of powerlessness. The best way to break this cycle is to tackle the linguistic and pedagogical dependency (Wajnryb, 1989). In most cases society in the host country expects high standards of language ability and does not allow much (educational) time to reach these standards. Therefore it is most important that migrants know or learn how to profit from the linguistic environment outside the classroom. Although Willing (1988) found that self-directedness is one of the least favoured learning preferences among migrant learners, he and Janssen-van Dieten (1992) consider '**LEARNING TO LEARN**' as important an educational target as language learning for this particular group.

**See also:** Acculturation; Adult language learning; Age factors; Attitudes and language learning; Culture shock; Learning styles

### References

Bialystok, E. (1997) 'The structure of age in search of barriers to second language acquisition', *Second Language Research* 3, 2: 116–37.

Bolhuis, S. (1995) *Leren en veranderen bij volwassenen (Learning and change in adulthood)*, Bussum: Coutinho.

Harley, B. and Wang, W. (1997) 'The critical period hypothesis: where are we now?', in A. de Groot and J. Kroll (eds), *Tutorials in bilingualism: psycholinguistic perspectives*, Mahwah, NJ: Lawrence Erlbaum.

Janssen-van Dieten, A. (1992) *Zelfbeoordeling en tweede-taalleren: Een empirisch onderzoek naar zelf-beoordeling bij volwassen leerders van het Nederlands (Self-assessment and second language learning: An empirical investigation into self-assessment by adult learners of Dutch)*, dissertation, Nijmegen: KUN.

Klein, W. (1996) 'Language acquisition at different ages', in D. Magnusson (ed.), *The lifespan development of individuals: behavioral, neurobiological and psychosocial perspectives: a synthesis*, Cambridge: Cambridge University Press.

Merriam, S. and Caffarella, S. (1991) *Learning in adulthood: a comprehensive guide*, San Francisco: Jossey-Bass.

Perdue, C. (1982) *Second language acquisition by adult migrants: a field manual*, Strasbourg: European Science Foundation.

Schumann, J. (1978) 'The acculturation model for second-language acquisition', in R. Gingras (ed.), *Second-language acquisition and foreign language teaching*, Arlington, VA: Center for Applied Linguistics.

Sternberg, R. and McGrane, P. (1996) 'Lifespan development: Intelligence', in A. Tuijnman (ed.), *International encyclopedia of adult education and training* (2nd edn), Oxford: Pergamon.

Wajnryb, R. (1989) 'Some reflections on learning and the learner', in C. Corbel (ed.), *Opinions in teaching English to adult speakers of other languages*, Geelong: Deakin University Press.

Willing, K. (1988) *Learning styles in adult migrant education*, Adelaide: National Curriculum Resource Centre.

### Further reading

Birdsong, D. (ed.) (1999) *Second language acquisition and the critical period hypothesis*, Mahwah, NJ: Lawrence Erlbaum.

Jarvis, P. (1995) *Adult and continuing education: theory and practice* (2nd edn), London: Routledge.

Schumann, J. (1978) 'The acculturation model for second-language acquisition', in R. Gingras (ed.), *Second-language acquisition and foreign language teaching*, Arlington, VA: Center for Applied Linguistics.

ANNE-MIEKE JANSSEN-VAN DIETEN

# Africa

The foreign languages most widely taught in Africa are **ENGLISH**, **FRENCH**, **PORTUGUESE**, **SPANISH**, Italian, and **GERMAN**. 'Foreign' in this context refers to languages that are not indigenous to sub-Saharan Africa. The teaching of these languages stems from the colonial era when the British, the French, the Belgians, the Portuguese and the Spanish had possessions on the continent (Spencer, 1971). The 1884–5 Berlin Conference stratified these possessions. The foreign language policies of the European powers placed emphasis on the **ACQUISITION** of the appropriate European language, which became the official language and the **MEDIUM OF INSTRUCTION** in the colonies. **TEXT-BOOKS** that were based on Latin **GRAMMAR** models were used as the primary tools of instruction. Language instruction began in elementary schools, continued in secondary schools and teacher-training colleges, and culminated at the university level.

## The social significance of language learning

Proficiency in the European language during the colonial period was seen as a measure of one's academic, professional and social advancement and sophistication. In fact, if a student passed all the subjects required for a particular diploma/certificate, but failed the required test in the relevant European language, that student did not earn the appropriate certificate or diploma. Conversely, passing the required test in the European language with distinction could yield a particular certificate/diploma without the need to pass all of the other subjects. While the assimilation policies of the French and Portuguese were aimed at making Africans acquire the phonetic proficiency of European **NATIVE SPEAKERS**, those of the British did not. This paralleled differing colonial policies, including policies for education, whereby **FRANCE**, for example, integrated its colonies into its administrative system and installed a French education system, whereas Britain did not tie its colonies as closely to the home administration, allowing each colony to evolve its own education system. The result was that anglophone Africans who achieved structural expertise in English did not necessarily acquire English phonetic proficiency to parallel the phonetic proficiency in French of their francophone counterparts. As colonial-influenced institutions taught the colonial language to one generation of African students, those students in turn became the instructors of future generations.

## The era of independence

The struggle for independence and the movements that followed in the 1960s saw radical changes in the various colonies. But changes in foreign language instruction lagged behind the changes that occurred elsewhere in society. Nationalist fervour called for a de-emphasis of European languages and a broadening of instruction of indigenous African languages. Instruction in the indigenous languages *was* broadened, but instruction in the colonial language remained very strong (Le Page, 1964; Whiteley, 1971; Bamgbose, 1991). A notable achievement was the successful replacement of English by Swahili as the official language of Tanzania. However, for the bulk of the continent, a European language remains the *de facto* official language.

The newly independent African nations continued the grammar-based approach to instruction in the official foreign language. Meanwhile, political calls for African unity in the 1960s also led to a greater emphasis on the instruction of European and non-European languages that were used in other independent African nations. Thus, Spanish, Portuguese, French and English, as well as Swahili and **ARABIC**, were taught in African nations where these languages were not commonly used. When independent African nations established close ties with **CHINA** and the Soviet bloc during the Cold War era, foreign language instruction in Russian and **CHINESE** also became available to Africans in Africa. With the end of the Cold War and the diminished influence of the Soviet Union, serious instruction of Russian and Chinese as foreign languages all but disappeared from the continent.

The advancement of modern pedagogical approaches to foreign language teaching and learning has not yet flooded foreign language instruction in Africa. Few institutions have the resources to provide learners with simple viable tape recorders, let alone **LANGUAGE LABORATORIES**, or sophisticated computer-based language laboratories and **MEDIA CENTRES** for interactive video and audio instruction. Foreign languages are still taught with a heavy orientation towards a grammatical structure-based approach. This emphasis sometimes slows proficiency in other aspects (e.g. **SPEAKING** and **LISTENING**) of the target language. With the exception of the official languages, instruction in a foreign language is still not mainly undertaken in that foreign language, but rather through another foreign language. Hence, in an English speaking area, most institutions teach French, Spanish or German by using English as the medium of instruction rather than the target language. At the university level, this handicap may be supplemented by sending selected learners for immersion in the target language in nations where the target language is predominantly used.

## African languages as official languages

Tanzania, Burundi and Rwanda are the only African nations that cite African languages as official languages (Mann and Dalby, 1987). In African nations, the period preceding independence was also a period of strong nationalist sentiments. Such surges of nationalism become dormant periodically; when they re-emerge, nationalism often manifests itself as a desire to replace the colonial official language with an indigenous African language (Bamgbose, 1991; Bokamba and Tlou, 1977). Those who argue for the retention of the *status quo* feel that the colonial language is widely used and accepted, and therefore that there is no need to replace it. Senegal, Burundi and Rwanda are often cited as examples of this pro-colonial language **ATTITUDE**. Over 80 per cent of the Senegalese population speak Wolof, but French is the official language of Senegal. Burundi 'uses' French and Kirundi as official languages, and Kirundi is spoken by 99 per cent of the population. In Rwanda, Kinyawanda – spoken by over 95 per cent of the population – and French are the official languages. In all three countries, French is not the **MOTHER TONGUE** of Africans, yet the language is so popular that citizens actually prefer to retain it as the official language.

Those who support the retention of the colonial language point out that the colonial language is an international **LINGUA FRANCA**, has international prestige, and that the choice of an African language will lead to unrest in nations like Nigeria where ethnic feelings are very strong (Arasanyin, 1998), and where the major languages have millions of native speakers. They also observe that replacing the colonial language with an African language will constitute **LINGUISTIC IMPERIALISM**: an African language will be imposed on those who do not know, use, or speak that language. Furthermore, they contend that it is not economically viable or practical to allocate scant national resources to the conversion and reproduction of national documents, textbooks, etc., into an African language at a time when the economies of African nations are suffering. The proponents of replacing the colonial language respond to these arguments by declaring that if an African nation has the will, that nation should begin **PLANNING** now to replace the colonial language eventually. They argue that a nation cannot truly be independent if it still depends on its colonial language for official deliberations, medium of instruction, language of government, and for official commercial transactions. An African language, they note, is capable of being as expressive as any Western language. But, should the appropriate scientific, legal or other useful terms be lacking, the void should be filled by the creation of new terminology (as Tanzania has done with Swahili), or the terminology should be borrowed from elsewhere, as other international languages have done. These proponents admit that, since many African nations have many different ethnic groups and many languages, it is indeed true that in some instances it would be difficult to agree on which African language should be selected. But then, they are also quick to point out, with proper preparation and education citizens will accept the language that is selected. The manpower and fiscal allocation for the selection and conversion to an African language should be part of a country's broad national economic development strategy.

The official language debate is not likely to lead to a resolution soon. But, hopefully, the technological advances in foreign language teaching and learning will soon saturate Africa.

**See also:** African languages; China; Lingua franca

### References

Arasanyin, O.F. (1998) 'Planning national language: the Hausa factor in language policy for Nigeria', in I. Maddieson and T.J. Hinnebusch (eds), *Language history and linguistic description in Africa*, Trenton, NJ: Africa World Press.

Bamgbose, A. (1991) *Language and the nation: the language question in sub-Saharan Africa*, Edinburgh: Edinburgh University Press.

Bokamba, E.G. and Tlou, J.S. (1977) 'The consequences of language policies of African states *vis à vis* education', in P.F.A. Kotey and H. der Houssikian (eds), *Language and linguistic problems in Africa*, Colombia, SC: Hornbeam Press.

Le Page, R.B. (1964) *The national language question: linguistic problems of newly independent states*, London: Oxford University Press.

Mann, M. and Dalby, D. (1987) *A thesaurus of African languages: a classified and annotated inventory of the spoken languages of Africa with an appendix on their written representation*, London: Hans Zell Publishers.

Spencer, J. (1971) 'Colonial language policies and their legacies', in T. Sebeok (ed.), *Current trends in*

*linguistics, Vol. 7: Linguistics in sub-Saharan Africa,*
The Hague: Mouton.

Whiteley, W.H. (1971) 'Language policies of
independent African states', in T. Sebeok (ed.),
*Current trends in linguistics, Vol. 7: Linguistics in sub-
Saharan Africa,* The Hague: Mouton.

### Further reading

Lewis, L.J. (1962) *Phelps-Stokes Reports on Education in
Africa,* Oxford: Oxford University Press.

UNESCO (1953) *The use of vernaculars in education.
UNESCO monographs on fundamental education 8,*
Paris: UNESCO.

PAUL KOTEY

# African languages

Interest in learning and teaching African languages
outside **AFRICA** pre-dates the colonisation of the
continent. This interest falls into three broad
phases:

1  the period prior to the 1884–5 Berlin Conference;
2  the period between 1885 and the end of World
War Two;
3  the Cold War era and its aftermath.

The first phase is characterised primarily by
early attempts to record aspects of African
languages. The second phase is marked by active
colonisation including missionary activity. Books on
African languages showed a greater appreciation
for the intricacies of the structure of those
languages. European powers increasingly involved
native Africans in missionary and governmental
activities. **PEDAGOGICAL GRAMMARS** were used to
teach and learn African languages.

During the third phase, i.e. the Cold War and its
aftermath, Africa offered an attractive set of
colonies, and later, a group of independent
countries, to be wooed by both the West and the
East. Citizens of Cold War powers went to Africa
to assist the emerging nations. As these citizens
learned African languages, their home governments provided support for such endeavours.

Linguists intensified their efforts towards understanding, describing, analysing and classifying
various African languages. In the early sixties, the
**AUDIOLINGUAL** and **AUDIO-VISUAL** methods were
used to teach African languages. Major strides in
research on **SECOND LANGUAGE ACQUISITION** were
made in the seventies and eighties. The nineties
have seen an expansion into computer-generated
interactive multimedia technology. The target in
the study of African languages is now the
acquisition of **COMMUNICATIVE** and performance
competency and proficiency.

### Earliest works on African languages

Moslem scholars used **ARABIC** to produce the
earliest known written records of African languages
between the tenth and twelfth centuries. During
the fifteenth century, as the Portuguese explored an
ocean route to **INDIA**, their contacts with Africa led
to the first European record of Karanga, a Bantu
language, in 1506. In 1624, *Doutrina Christaa,* a 134-
page Roman Catholic catechism attributed to
Mattheus Cardoso, became the first book to use
an African language, because, although the book
was written in Portuguese, it contained an interlinear **TRANSLATION** into Kongo. Portuguese success in contact with Africa caused other European
nations to undertake their own exploration of the
continent. The first known grammar of an African
language is the 98-page grammar of Kongo written
by the Italian Giacinto Brusciotto in 1659. The title
of this book is *Regulae Quaedam Pro Difficillimi
Congensium Idiomatis Faciliori Captu Ad Grammaticae
Norman Redactae.* Several other European publications on different African languages preceded, and
followed, this first grammar book (Sebeok 1971: 1).

The fifteenth-century Portuguese exploration of
Africa and the subsequent European interest in the
continent culminated in the 1884–5 Berlin Conference. This Conference partitioned the continent
primarily into British, French, Portuguese, Spanish,
Belgian, German and Italian possessions. The
solidification of colonial administration was accompanied by an intensification of missionary activities,
which led to a quest for orthographies to be used in
translating the Bible and other scriptures into
indigenous African languages.

## Learners of African languages

Learners of African languages outside Africa may be categorised into three main groups:

1 academic;
2 professionally driven;
3 neo-cultural.

*Academic learners* These learners are primarily associated with institutions of higher learning. Some institutions require students to take a certain number of hours in a foreign language prior to graduation. Some academic learners simply enjoy learning an African language without using it for an academic programme. Academic learners are mostly non-Africans. They may also be guided by a desire to undertake fieldwork in the area where the African language they study is used, or they may use their knowledge for research in **LINGUISTICS**.

*Professionally driven learners* Such learners study an African language to assist them in their professions (academic, governmental, religious etc.) in an African country. Professionally driven learners may have developed an interest in an African language as academic learners. They are also mostly non-Africans.

*Neo-cultural learners* Neo-cultural learners are those who have at least one African immigrant parent, or who are themselves African immigrants. As Africans migrate to Britain, the US, **CANADA**, Germany, **FRANCE** and other European countries, Westernised transplanted African ethnic communities have begun springing up in cities outside Africa. In an effort to maintain aspects of their culture, such communities encourage their offspring to learn their ethnic language. Adults who feel that they are forgetting their ethnic languages also make efforts to learn those languages.

## Languages taught outside Africa

Among the many African languages *regularly* taught in institutions of higher learning outside Africa are: Amharic, Bambara, Fulfulde, Hausa, Lingala, Shona, Somali, Swahili, Twi, Wolof, Xhosa, Yoruba and Zulu. One or more of these may be taught by one institution. Other languages are taught on demand coupled with the availability of instructors. Instruction at institutions is available at the **BEGINNER**, intermediate and advanced levels. The languages offered for professionally driven learners and neo-cultural learners depend on the requirements of the professions, and the **NEEDS** of the transplanted ethnic group.

Languages are taught by either fluent **NATIVE SPEAKERS**, non-native speakers who have acquired native speaker or near native speaker fluency, or instructors of limited fluency who know the structure of the language. If a fluent native speaker is available, such a person may assist the instructor of limited fluency by handling **SPEAKING** proficiency. This third group of instructors, understandably, has dominated instruction in African languages outside Africa.

## Language Materials

Computer-based interactive multimedia materials now point to the trend in the development of instructional materials for African languages. Efforts are being made to produce Africa-oriented *clip art* for language instruction, content of materials is being redesigned, and considerations are being made for **DISTANCE LEARNING**. This trend will enable language instruction materials to be more easily accessible anywhere in the world. The new emphasis is on the acquisition of speaking, listening, **READING** and **WRITING** proficiency. The aim is to empower the learner to acquire native or near native competency and proficiency. The seamless incorporation of **AUTHENTIC** cultural materials into the instructional materials, and the inclusion of native speaker-generated authentic samples of the language, are integral to this new emphasis. Learners are assessed on three proficiency levels: novice, intermediate and advanced; and appropriate **ASSESSMENT** tools are being devised to evaluate learner proficiency. Hard-copy-based instructional materials *still* dominate the market, however, in spite of the shift towards electronic media.

During the first part of the Cold War era, the US Foreign Service Institute published audio-lingual-based instructional materials on several African languages. Similar efforts were made in Britain, Canada and France. But some instructors still use pedagogical grammars to teach African languages. Language instruction in such cases emphasises grammatical knowledge.

## Institutions offering African languages

The US-based African Language Teachers Association (ALTA) plays a leadership role in teaching and learning African languages. ALTA has five Language Task Forces for Yoruba, Swahili, Hausa, South African languages and West African languages. ALTA organises annual conferences on African language teaching, and workshops for language teachers. It is affiliated with the National Council of Organisations of the Less Commonly Taught Languages (NCOLCTL), and produces its own newsletter, *Lugha*. ALTA members are affiliated with the various National Foreign Language Centers.

The US Federal Department of Education, through its Title VI programmes, has designated some institutions as National Resource Centers (NRCs) and Foreign Language and **AREA STUDIES** (FLAS) Fellowship Programmes. These institutions receive competitive three-year renewable grants. FLAS institutions include Boston University, Columbia University, Indiana University, Michigan State University, Ohio University, University of California at Berkeley and at Los Angeles, Stanford University, University of Florida, University of Illinois, University of Pennsylvania, University of Wisconsin at Madison, Yale University, and University of Maine. These institutions award post-bachelor degree fellowships to support the study of various African languages, and they serve as the focus of the bulk of African language instruction in the US.

The School of Oriental and African Studies (SOAS) in London has played a pioneering role in teaching African languages. Among other institutions that teach African languages are the University of Oslo, NTNU-University of Trondhjem, Norway, Norwegian Aid Agency (NORAD), Cambridge University, Britain, Goteborg University and Uppsala University, Sweden, the Institut National de Langues et Civilisations Orientales (INALCO – the National Institute of Languages and Oriental Civilisations) in Paris, the School of Oriental and African Languages at the University of Paris, and the Langage, Langues et Cultures d'Afrique Noire

(LLACAN – the Speech, Languages and Cultures of Black Africa) in Meudon, France, the Instituto Universitano Orientale, Italy, Warsaw University, Poland, Leiden University, The Netherlands, and McGill University, Canada. Several German institutions also teach African languages. Prominent among these are the University of Hamburg, University of Frankfurt, University of Köln, University of Bayreuth, University of Leipzig, Humboldt University of Berlin, and the University of Mainz. The German Foundation for International Development and Cooperation (DSE) at Bad Honnef also offers short-term intensive courses in African languages. The Osaka University of Foreign Languages at Kyoto, **JAPAN** also offers courses, as do Sydney University Language Centre and Melbourne University, Australia.

In addition to African language instruction outside Africa, some organisations send learners to Africa to be immersed in a language. For example, the US Department of Education, through its Fulbright-Hays Group Projects Abroad Program, provides grants for students to travel to Africa to take part in organised eight-week **INTENSIVE LANGUAGE COURSES** in Hausa (Nigeria), Yoruba (Nigeria), Swahili (Kenya and Tanzania) and Zulu (South Africa).

**See also:** Africa; Area studies; Study abroad

## Reference

Sebeok, T.A. (ed.) (1971) *Current trends in linguistics, Vol. 7: Linguistics in sub-Saharan Africa*, The Hague: Mouton.

PAUL KOTEY

# Age factors

It is popularly believed that the age at which an individual begins to be exposed to a language has a determining influence on how quickly and/or efficiently the **ACQUISITION**/learning (the terms will be used interchangeably here) of that language proceeds. The general assumption is that the earlier learning begins the more successful it will be. This notion has been explored within the language sciences under the heading of the critical age or critical period hypothesis, which in its strongest form posits that unless language acquisition gets under way within a particular maturational phase (usually thought of as ending around puberty) it will never take place. As far as L2 development – referring here to both second and foreign languages – is concerned, the somewhat weaker claim made by many SLA researchers is that L2 learning which begins after a particular age will typically fail to deliver native speaker levels of **COMPETENCE**.

There is widespread acceptance among language acquisition researchers that age is a factor in language development, although the strong form of the critical period hypothesis is treated more sceptically. One indicator of age playing a role is the way in which the major 'milestones' of normal L1 development appear to follow a maturational time-table (cooing beginning between 1 and 4 months, babbling between 4 and 8 months, 1-word utterances around 12 months, and 2-word utterances between 18 and 24 months, etc. – see Singleton, 1989: chapter 2). Another body of pertinent evidence comes from studies of **SIGN LANGUAGE** acquisition. The profoundly deaf are frequently deprived of access to an L1 in early childhood because, on the one hand, they are cut off from auditory stimuli and, on the other, owing to anti-sign language prejudice, they are often not provided with opportunities to learn sign language until later in life. Studies of later signers suggest that some aspects of sign language systems are typically not mastered unless exposure to sign language begins before age 6. Individuals who begin to acquire a sign language in their childhood years show marked advantages in terms of control of morphosyntax over those who start learning sign language in adulthood (see, e.g., Long, 1990: 258–9).

With regard to L2 acquisition, the balance of evidence favours Krashen et al.'s (1979) conclusion that in situations of 'naturalistic' exposure, while in the initial stages of learning, older **BEGINNERS** tend to outperform their juniors – at least in some respects – in terms of long-term outcomes. Generally speaking, the earlier exposure to the L2 begins the better. Support for the Krashen et al. position comes, for instance, from the research of Snow and Hoefnagel-Höhle (1978) on the learning of Dutch as an L2 by English speakers residing in the Netherlands. This provides clear evidence of

more rapid initial learning on the part of **ADULT** and adolescent subjects, but also of younger beginners catching up with and beginning to overtake the older beginners after about 12 months of L2 exposure.

As far as instructed L2 learning is concerned, the consistent finding (see, e.g., Burstall et al., 1974; Oller and Nagato, 1974) is that learners exposed to an L2 at **PRIMARY** school who then at secondary level are mixed in with later beginners do not maintain an advantage for more than a modest period over these latter. The apparent discrepancy between such evidence and the naturalistic evidence can probably be accounted for in terms of the de-motivating effect on children who have had some early experience of an L2 of being put into classes where most pupils are starting from scratch (see, e.g., Singleton, 1995; Stern, 1976), and also in terms of the vast differences in exposure time between naturalistic and instructed learning (see Singleton 1989: 121, 235ff.).

Whereas in recent years the question of age and language acquisition has been approached with a high degree of empirical rigour, discussion of this matter in the past was based largely on anecdote and assumption. For instance, the psychologist Tomb (1925) refers to hearing English children in Bengal (in the days of the British Raj) fluently conversing in English, Bengali, Santali and Hindustani, while their parents barely had enough Hindustani to issue instructions to the servants. Science appeared to loom larger in the 1950s, when the neurologist Penfield took an interest in the discussion (Penfield and Roberts, 1959). However, in fact, Penfield's advocacy of early L2 instruction owed much more to his personal experience of bringing up his own children than to his work as a scientist (see Dechert, 1995). Even the neurolinguist Lenneberg based part of his contribution to the age debate on folk wisdom rather than science. For Lenneberg the critical period was a by-product of the lateralisation process, by which one hemisphere of the brain (usually the left) was thought to become specialised for language functions, and which Lenneberg posited as ending at puberty. One of his arguments in this connection (1967: 176) was that after puberty L2 learning required 'labored effort' and foreign accents could not be 'overcome easily' – a claim for which he offered no hard evidence whatsoever.

To return to current research and thinking in this area, as has already been indicated the idea that age plays some kind of role in language acquisition is seen by most researchers in the field to be validated by the available empirical evidence, while absolutist versions of the critical age hypothesis are widely criticised. In relation to this latter point, the sign language studies mentioned above do not demonstrate that L1 acquisition is *impossible* outside of a putative critical period. Moreover, with regard to L2 acquisition, a number of researchers have reported on L2 learners whose first contact with their L2 was in adolescence or adulthood and who, despite their late start, succeeded in attaining to native-like levels of proficiency in various domains (see, e.g., Bongaerts *et al.*, 1997; Ioup, 1995). Nor is there any real consensus on how one might explain the influence of age on language acquisition, accounts on offer ranging from an age-related decrease in cerebral plasticity to a diminution with age of quality language input.

Clearly, the age issue is not something which is of academic interest only. It is a major element in the debate about the point at which L2 pro-grammes should be introduced into formal education. However, it is important to emphasise in this connection that age is not the *only* relevant issue. After all, the early introduction of mathematics in schools depends not on any notion of a critical period for numeracy acquisition but rather on the general idea that this is such an important area that it needs to be broached as soon as possible. On the other hand, the question of when an L2 compo-nent should begin to figure in the curriculum obviously cannot be divorced from that of the availability of resources (suitably qualified person-nel, appropriate materials, etc.).

**See also:** Acquisition and teaching; Gender and language learning; Planning for foreign language teaching; Psychology; Second language acquisition theories

### References

Bongaerts, T., van Summeren, C., Planken, B. and Schils, E. (1997) 'Age and ultimate attainment in the pronunciation of a foreign language', *Studies in Second Language Acquisition* 19: 447–65.

Burstall, C., Jamieson, M., Cohen, S. and Har-greaves, M. (1974) *Primary French in the balance*, Windsor: NFER Publishing.

Dechert, H. (1995) 'Some critical remarks con-cerning Penfield's theory of second language acquisition', in D. Singleton and Z. Lengyel (eds), *The age factor in second language acquisition*, Clevedon: Multilingual Matters.

Ioup, G. (1995) 'Evaluating the need for input enhancement in post-critical period language acquisition', in D. Singleton and Z. Lengyel (eds), *The age factor in second language acquisition*, Clevedon: Multilingual Matters.

Krashen, S., Long, M. and Scarcella, R. (1979) 'Age, rate and eventual attainment in second language acquisition', *TESOL Quarterly* 13: 573–82.

Lenneberg, E. (1967) *Biological foundations of language*, New York: Wiley.

Long, M. (1990) 'Maturational constraints on language development', *Studies in Second Language Acquisition* 12: 251–85.

Oller, J. and Nagato, N. (1974) 'The long-term effect of FLES: an experiment', *Modern Language Journal* 58: 15–19.

Penfield, W. and Roberts, L. (1959) *Speech and brain mechanisms*, Princeton, NJ: Princeton University Press.

Singleton, D. (1989) *Language acquisition: the age factor*, Clevedon: Multilingual Matters.

Singleton, D. (1995) 'Second languages in the primary school: the age factor dimension', *Teanga: The Irish Yearbook of Applied Linguistics* 15: 155–66.

Snow, C. and Hoefnagel-Höhle, M. (1978) 'The critical period for language acquisition: evidence from second language learning', *Child Development* 49: 1114–28.

Stern, H. (1976) 'Optimal age: myth or reality?', *Canadian Modern Language Review* 32: 283–94.

Tomb, J. (1925) 'On the intuitive capacity of children to understand spoken languages', *British Journal of Psychology* 16: 53–4.

### Further reading

Harley, B. and Wang, W. (1997) 'The critical period hypothesis. Where are we now?', in A. de Groot and J. Kroll (eds), *Tutorials in bilingualism: psycholinguistic perspectives*, Mahwah, NJ: Lawrence Erlbaum.

Singleton, D. and Lengyel, Z. (eds) (1995) *The age factor in second language acquisition*, Clevedon: Multilingual Matters.

DAVID SINGLETON

## AILA – Association Internationale de Linguistique Appliquée

AILA is an international federation of approximately thirty-five national or regional associations of **APPLIED LINGUISTICS**. The objectives of the association are to promote research and teaching dealing with all fields of applied linguistics, to disseminate the results of this research, and to promote international and interdisciplinary cooperation in these fields. In order to attain these objectives, the association does the following:

- ensures that a regular affiliate hosts a world congress of applied linguistics every three years;
- establishes and supports the work of scientific commissions (listed on the AILA website);
- facilitates scientific and professional cooperation among regular affiliates;
- collaborates with other organisations with related objectives and goals;
- oversees the dissemination of scientific publications by a variety of means including book publications, reviews, newsletters and use of computer-mediated communication.

AILA was founded in 1964 at an international colloquium on applied linguistics at the University of Nancy, **FRANCE**. This decision was the result of two years of preparatory work and discussion, with the financial support of the **COUNCIL OF EUROPE**.

The *Association* has two major publications. The *AILA Review* appears once per year, is guest edited and contains collections of papers around a common theme. In addition, an AILA newsletter, the *AILA News*, is published three times per year in an electronic version on the internet and in hard copy.

### Website

AILA's website is: http://www.brad.ac.uk/acad/aila

ANDREW D. COHEN

## ALA – Association for Language Awareness

The Association for Language Awareness was established in 1992, at the same time as the journal *Language Awareness* was launched at the First International Conference on Language Awareness at the University of Wales, Bangor. Conferences are held biennially. The Association aims to support and promote activities across the whole breadth of Language Awareness. These are conducted in different fields, for example **MOTHER TONGUE** learning, foreign language learning, **TEACHER EDUCATION**, language use in professional settings and in the community; at a variety of levels, for example primary, secondary and tertiary education, professional training and practice, community education programmes; and with objectives in a range of domains, for example effects on language performance, on **ATTITUDES** to language.

The ALA pursues this goal in a variety of ways: for example, by collecting and disseminating information on Language Awareness initiatives, promoting research into Language Awareness, arranging conferences and meetings for practitioners, theorists, and those with interests in Language Awareness.

MIKE SCOTT

## Alliance française

The *Alliance française* is the oldest French secular organisation whose purpose is to 'disseminate the **FRENCH** language in the colonies and abroad'. It was created in 1883 at a time of colonial expansionism, international competition and patriotic militarism, and was a response to several contemporary **NEEDS**: that of supporting the influence of French language and *CIVILISATION* outside **FRANCE**; that of re-establishing the international image of France which had been weakened by its defeat by Prussia in 1870; and that of being the secular and ecumenical counterbalance to the networks of missionaries existing outside France.

The *Alliance française* has existed since its foundation as an association because of its concern to remain independent from official and governmental organisations. Committees created in France and abroad recruit volunteers such as people influential in the economic, literary, publishing or diplomatic spheres. Outside France, each *Alliance* is anchored in the structures of the host country. However the *Alliance* has gradually formalised its relationships with the French State. It was present in the French pavilion at the universal exhibitions at the end of the nineteenth and beginning of the twentieth century. It gradually increased contacts with the Ministries for the colonies and foreign affairs, and with various French presidents, and Presidents of the current Fifth Republic are Honorary Presidents of the *Alliance*.

The educational activities of the *Alliance* began in 1894 with the creation of language courses designed for foreign teachers of French, followed by an *Ecole supérieure de langue française* in 1911, by the introduction of courses in French 'conversation', by the dispatching of lecturers across the world, and then by the founding in Paris of an *Ecole pratique* which offered courses for foreigners from 1919. Exhibitions, journals and international conferences followed and reinforced the initial developments which were based on the concept of the universality of French language and thought. The two World Wars of 1914–18 and 1939–45 forced the *Alliance* to reduce its activities, but were also the starting point for new work once they were over. The *Alliance* developed its own **TEXTBOOK** for teaching French which became familiar to thousands of learners throughout the world under the name of its author (Gaston) Mauger and by its red and blue cover.

The *Alliance* is currently represented in 137 countries and involves 1100 committees, with 1,000 centres for the teaching of French. It is particularly strong in Latin America (130,000 learners), in Asia, Europe and **AFRICA** (about 60,000 learners in each of these areas). It employs two types of teacher: 360 teachers are seconded from and paid by the French Ministry of Foreign Affairs, and 4500 are locally recruited and paid by each *Alliance* from its own resources at local rates. The *Alliance française* is one of the most important organisations among the many which serve French language policy, and has a tradition and a status which are widely recognised abroad.

**See also:** British Council; CIEP; CRÉDIF; France; French; Goethe-Institut

### Website

The website of the *Alliance française* is: http://www.paris.alliancefrancaise.fr

### Further reading

Bruezière, M. (1963) *L'Alliance française. Histoire d'une institution*, Paris: Hachette.
Greffet, P. (1984) 'Permanence de l'Alliance', in D. Coste (ed.), *Aspects d'une politique de diffusion du français langue étrangère depuis 1945. Matériaux pour une histoire*, Paris: ENS de St Cloud/Hatier.

GENEVIÈVE ZARATE

## Alternation hypothesis

A variant of **CONTRASTIVE ANALYSIS** specifically geared to making testable predictions about orders of **ACQUISITION** (cf. **DEVELOPMENTAL SEQUENCE**), elaborated by Jansen, Lalleman and Muysken (1981). The hypothesis, generally stated, is that when the language to be learned contains two (or more) structural possibilities, and the learner's L1 contains but one equivalent possibility, then this latter possibility is acquired first in the L2. The prediction was tested by a **CROSS-SECTIONAL**, **CROSS-LINGUISTIC** approach, of which the following is a simplified account. These researchers compare word order phenomena in the utterances of Turkish and Moroccan learners of Dutch, observing that, in Dutch, main verbs may 'alternate', occurring in the second or final position of the sentence, whereas Turkish is a verb-final language and Moroccan a verb-second language.

The prediction is, then, that learners will initially analyse the Dutch input for – and find – the structural possibility of their own language, and overgeneralise it. Jansen *et al.* looked at groups of learners of different proficiency levels and found that the **BEGINNERS** indeed overgeneralised as predicted, and that the more proficient the learner, the more the other structural possibility was used. Such a cross-linguistic methodology allows greater precision in characterising **TRANSFER** effects.

**See also:** Untutored language acquisition

### Reference

Jansen, B., Lalleman, J. and Muysken, P. (1981) 'The alternation hypothesis: acquisition of Dutch word order by Turkish and Moroccan foreign workers', *Language Learning* 31, 2: 315–36.

CLIVE PERDUE

# American Army Method

The Army Specialized Training Program (ASTP) or 'Army Method' was developed after the entry of the **UNITED STATES OF AMERICA** into World War Two and represented a significant shift in foreign language teaching and learning in America. Aimed at producing, with a degree of urgency, skilled **INTERPRETERS** and speakers, the programme moved away from the prevailing consensus in foreign language teaching methodology in the USA, which was largely oriented towards **READING** skills. This method, although relatively short-lived, contributed to the development of **AUDIOLINGUAL-ISM** which, by the mid-fifties, had become the main American approach to teaching English as a Second Language.

Until the war, foreign language teaching in the USA had set itself the fairly limited 'but more realistic goal of establishing a reading knowledge of the foreign language only' (Wilkins, 1990: 523). The influential Coleman Report of 1929 had concluded that this was the way forward for US foreign language teaching, and it was the context up until the war. Richards and Rodgers state that the reading-based approach 'emphasized teaching the comprehension of texts' (1986: 44).

**VOCABULARY** lists were introduced and some discussion of foreign language texts took place in English, with some stress on silent reading but very little on conversation.

American language teaching methodology was fairly traditional, according to Wilkins (1990: 524), and comparatively underdeveloped when compared to those being explored by applied linguists in Britain and Europe. Linguists there had already begun to look at language content more systematically with attempts to standardise vocabulary and **GRAMMAR** items and grade key stages in foreign language learning. There was not the same emphasis on producing skilled readers who were not very competent at actually speaking the target language.

The deficiencies became apparent when the US entered the war and the authorities saw the pressing need for fluent speakers of Japanese, **GERMAN** and the languages of occupied countries, especially in East Asia. Interpreters and translators in various government departments were urgently required who could do more than comprehend set texts. Rapid and systematic training was required to produce personnel with all the desired language abilities and **SKILLS**. This new situation led to the US government commissioning linguists at several universities to develop a foreign language programme suitable for military personnel.

Those involved in developing the new scheme looked for alternatives to the prevailing reading-based methods. They found one in the language training of anthropologists, linguists and other field-researchers intending to study cultures where the languages were often not written, such as Native American. As there were usually no **TEXT-BOOKS** in such cases, a different approach was taken to facilitate the required mastery of the languages of the target groups. Linguists such as **BLOOMFIELD** at Yale had been developing such programmes, and their methods were considered to possess the relevant requirements and outcomes.

This field-research preparation language training was sometimes referred to as the 'informant method' (Richards and Rodgers, 1986: 45), as it involved the use of a **NATIVE SPEAKER** (the informant). This person would provide phrases, vocabulary and sentences for imitation by the learners. Also involved in the training would be a linguist, not necessarily a native speaker, whose role was to elicit the basic structure of the language from the informant. They would be trained in these skills rather than the language and would supervise the drilling of the given phrases and sentences. The linguist and students together would participate in guided conversation with the native speaker and thus would learn the language as well as gain an understanding of basic rules of grammar, which were implicitly rather than explicitly introduced. Usually there were fifteen hours of drill with the 'informant', as well as private study of twenty to thirty hours, assisted by the linguist and spread over two to three six-week sessions.

Adoption of this field training method resulted in the ASTP in 1942, and by early 1943 fifty-five universities were involved in it (Richards and Rodgers, 1986: 44). It was a very intensive method, which together with the wartime context and the high **MOTIVATION** level of the learners accounts for much of its success. The students had specific goals linked not only to linguistic mastery but to assisting the war effort by carrying out military-related jobs and tasks. They studied for 10 hours a day, six days a week, as did the linguists and anthropologists in the model upon which the ASTP was founded. The drilling was also intensive, with mostly oral work, and there was 'only a minimum of explicit grammar' (Wilkins, 1990: 524). The Army usually chose mature students for the programme and teaching was in small classes, which also added to the high levels of success.

The programme lasted until the end of the war and was much discussed during this time as well as in the subsequent decade. Its novelty and high rates of success led to the consideration of its suitability for ordinary foreign language courses in the post-war situation. It failed to be widely adopted, however, for a number of reasons.

One reason was its lack of a well-developed methodological basis. Its success, as previously stated, was largely due to its intensity and the high level of motivation of the students. The linguists who helped develop the programme, secondly, were not particularly interested in language teaching *per se*, according to Richards and Rodgers (1986: 45). There was not much theoretical interest in this method to develop and, once the war was

over, linguistic interest in the 'Army Method' declined. Its lasting impact, however, lies in its contribution to the development of an intensive, oral-based approach in contrast to earlier predominantly reading-based methods. The results helped to persuade a number of leading American linguists who were interested in language teaching and learning to shift attention to this type of method and develop suitable theoretical and methodological foundations which were lacking in the 'Army Method'.

One linguist in particular to be influenced by the method was Fries (1945), and his proposals for EFL teaching had widespread impact on the teaching of languages in the USA and elsewhere (Wilkins, 1990: 525). The ideas of Fries were related to the intensity of the ASTP method and the notion that drilling with the spoken language was viewed as more important than the written. This led to the popularity of the audiolingual method of the 1960s.

The Army Method served its purpose during the war years and assisted the important shift from a fairly limited, reading-based approach to the audiolingual method.

**See also:** Audiolingual method; Behaviourism; Bloomfield; History: after 1945; Structural linguistics

### References

Fries, C. (1945) *Teaching and Learning English as a Foreign Language*, Michigan: University of Michigan Press.

Richards, J.C. and Rodgers, T.S. (1986) *Approaches and methods in language teaching: a description and analysis*, Cambridge: Cambridge University Press.

Wilkins, D. (1990) 'Second languages: how they are learned and taught', in N.E. Collinge (ed.), *An encyclopedia of language*, London: Routledge.

RUTH CHERRINGTON

# Anthropology

Anthropology refers to a domain which was constituted as a scientific discipline in the nineteenth century in the West. It responds to every society's need to know the culture or cultures of which it is composed and to know those which are foreign to it. In this sense, anthropology occupies a border position between two or more cultures. Although it takes a global perspective by sometimes seeing its task as bringing together all the disciplines in the study of man, its least controversial findings are those established on the basis of the study of primitive or rural societies. In the European context, this latter domain is sometimes termed ethnology.

## Anthropology and languages

Anthropology adopts a multi-disciplinary perspective and is related to the following domains: economics, history, politics, religion, and **LINGUISTICS**. Despite the diversity of these, they have methodological assumptions in common which underpin the field of study of anthropology and distinguish the anthropological approach from the sociological. Anthropology prefers restricted social units which are accessible to direct observation, and which are studied by qualitative analysis. This involves anthropologists at a personal level and requires of them the ability to overcome the effects of their own subjectivity. By explaining the functions of values which have been acquired implicitly by the individual in a given society, the anthropologist shows that behaviours which are experienced empirically as natural are not universal but the product of cultural learning. They are thus part of the identity of a community.

Countries which had a policy of foreign conquests (leading, for example, to the colonies of Ancient Greece, the Great Discoveries of the sixteenth century, colonialism in the nineteenth and twentieth centuries) created the foundations for the confrontation of different cultures, on the basis of military and economic interests and spheres of cultural influence. The Other was seen from the double perspective of threat and wonder (Greenblatt, 1991). The need to have access to the language of the foreigner was immediately recognised as being indispensable for military knowledge of the terrain, and for commercial exchange, to overcome the limitations of the simple language of gesture and exchange. **INTERPRETERS**, the conquerors who lived with indigenous women, or these

women themselves, were the first to experience the multiple functions of the linguistic and cultural intermediary, as was for example the case of Malinche, also called Doña Marina, the mistress of the Spanish conqueror Cortes, described by Diaz del Castillo in the sixteenth century.

In the face of linguistic difference in the field, anthropologists overcome their lack of language and check their data by using intermediaries who serve as guides, informants or interpreters, and ascertain the correctness of their assertions. (For an account of daily practices in the field, see the New Guinea journal of Malinovski which he kept from 1914 to 1915 and again from 1917 to 1918, and the work of his pupil Firth). Anthropologists thus developed skills focused on the relationship to the Other which can compensate for what, seen from a language teaching perspective, seems to be a linguistic handicap. In the course of the twentieth century it has been recognised that the competence of the anthropologist includes mastery of the language, but that this competence is not sufficient to guarantee the scientific value of their work. The skills of anthropologists do not consist only in the ability to suppress their subjectivity, which is inevitable, but also to recognise its existence, and to overcome the effects of exoticism, by becoming involved in the daily life of the society being observed. The complexity of the relationships between anthropologists and their field, in the continuum between the two poles of involvement and distancing, can be described as a paradox (Clifford, 1988) and the basis for the process of taking an objective view.

For those countries which during the nineteenth century developed a policy of disseminating their language abroad, linked to a policy of colonisation (Britain, Germany, Russia and the USSR, **FRANCE**, Italy etc.), the relationships between anthropology and education are influenced above all by the national interest of the colonisers. The dissemination of French and German cultures beyond their national frontiers reflects two different interpretations of national feeling, influenced by the three wars between these two countries in less than one hundred years (1870, 1914–18, 1939–45). German *Kulturkunde* incorporated the particularity of the German spirit (Elias, 1969), whereas the dissemination of the **FRENCH** language was linked to the dissemination of the **CIVILISATION** *française*, the bearer of universal values. These cultural models created a relationship of political, economic and cultural dependency in the countries where the language was disseminated. '**LINGUISTIC IMPERI- ALISM**' is linked with cultural imperialism (Phillip- son, 1992).

At the beginning of the twenty-first century, the recognition of cultural and linguistic diversity is one of the points on which there is agreement between the claims made on behalf of the findings of anthropology and those made in the name of politics. The concept of **HUMAN RIGHTS**, which is fundamental to a pluralist vision of democracy and concerned with minorities and the respect for cultural identity, plays a mediating role between the human sciences and educational and political interests. The use of the term 'ethnic group' provides for a positive categorisation of cultural diversity and the development of an official policy of multiculturalism, linked to the defining of identity and national citizenship. This is what happened in the 1970s in the USA, **CANADA** and **AUSTRALIA**, which recognised the role of indigen- ous minorities ('First Nations' in North America, and aborigines in Australia) in the definition of their national identity, although they did not recognise officially the linguistic pluralism which is its equivalent. The contrast between **MOTHER TONGUE** and culture and foreign language and culture is not deemed to be relevant in this case. The fundamentals of multi-ethnic education, in which reduction of prejudice, anti-racist education, **CULTURAL AWARENESS**, equality and equity of rights are relevant to language teaching, were institutionalised in the context of courses desig- nated as multicultural.

These approaches, also evident in Europe, ensure continuity between a pluralist interpretation of citizenship, the national identity of each European country, and the recognition of the multi-ethnic dimension of a society. One of the aims of the **COUNCIL OF EUROPE**, stated in 1949, is to 'favour the recognition and valuing of European identity whilst combating all kinds of intolerance'. The 1992 Treaty of the European Union uses for political purposes concepts borrowed from the field of anthropology such as cultural values and heritage. The development of the European dimension in education is related directly to the learning and the dissemination of the languages of the Union's Member States. The language field is seen, at the level of the whole education system, as being appropriate for the diffusion of a message of tolerance.

## Anthropology and language learners

As it was developed from the study of so-called primitive societies, anthropology initially focused on a naturalist approach to mankind in particular, based on the study of anatomic variation. This starting point, called physical anthropology and similar to the interests of archaeology, aimed to classify populations in terms of biological, cultural and sociological factors, and to measure physical differences by anthropometric classification. Today the description of the influence of physical factors on social factors is only a marginal aspect of the discipline. These theories were invalidated scienti- fically, after World War Two, by the recognition of symbolic systems, the attack on the reductive effects of cultural evolutionism based on a Western view of progress (Lévi Strauss, 1958), but also politically by the political fallout of racial ideology, decolonisation and the acceptance of humanist values by international organisations such as UNESCO and the Council of Europe. Anthro- pology rejected a unitary vision of the development of humanity, asserted the equality of cultures in the scientific approach to comparison, and contributed to the popularisation of its knowledge by attacking threats to identity and the ethnocentrism of prejudice towards foreigners. The implications of this for language teaching are important: the notion of the native, borrowed from anthropology and re-used in the expression **NATIVE SPEAKER**, neutralises the ambiguous and pejorative values contained in the term 'foreigner', especially when this notion was preceded by such notions as 'the barbarians', 'the bedevilled', 'the enemy' and 'the colonials'. However, the anthropologist relativises the ability of the native to describe the culture to which he/she belongs, giving him/her the status of informant, whereas in a traditional mode of thinking in language teaching, the native is generally an absolute model whom the foreigner is encouraged to follow.

In the context of the **INTERNATIONALISATION** of the economy, the requirements created by geographic mobility also make the debates and discussions in anthropology relevant to language teaching, in connection with expatriation and immigration. The issues of short- or medium-term residence abroad have arisen in different geographic contexts and structures according to the social categories involved. On the one hand there are managerial staff who have to leave their own country in order to export the technological know-how of their company. On the other hand, there are the migrant workers who bring their labour to countries richer than the ones where they were born. For example, as the US policy of economic expansion was established, work was developed to respond to the **NEEDS** of the commercial world. This had to take into consideration the constraints of efficiency and economic viability, whilst developing the skills of negotiation and persuasion of those sent abroad. It involved, for example, the raising of awareness of the unconscious models which in every culture structures the concepts of time (Hall, 1959) and space (Hall, 1966), of cultural misunderstandings which trouble communication between interlocutors socialised into different cultures, and of the effects of the length of the period of residence abroad, in particular the concept of **CULTURE SHOCK**.

A quite different direction was taken in the 1970s in Europe with the beginning of a common European linguistic policy, focused on **ADULT** and child migrants who needed to be educated in their host country. The response to this in linguistic terms was accompanied by a critical analysis of the concept of **ACCULTURATION**, which had direct implications for family structures, relationships between men and women, and the question of citizenship. For example, in France the terms 'integration', 'assimilation' and 'insertion' were used to designate the measures taken with respect to these groups, measures which devolved from the French conception of the universality of values, whereas in Britain the focus was on 'differentiation by class as opposed to differentiation by race' (Todd, 1994), and Germany preferred to maintain the identity of the ethnic groups it hosted, as the terms *Ausländer* or *Aussiedler* imply, designating respectively immigrant and foreigner with German forebears.

Language teaching attempts to systematise the description of the difficulties arising from the movement from one culture to another by using the term '**INTERCULTURAL COMPETENCE**', and is beginning to focus on the resolution of these difficulties. This term provides a common perspective on all those who are involved in the relationship between two languages: those who learn a language in which they have not been socialised, and those who belong to the culture whose language is being learned. The creation of European mobility programmes creates a new area of interest, in particular with respect to **EXCHANGES** of university and school students. The aim that every European should in the long run speak three languages of the European Union (European Commission, 1996) can be related to the globalisation of information, to flexibility in education and employment, and to the construction of a European identity.

Wherever such mobility exists, for example between North America and East Asian countries, it requires language teaching to recognise the reciprocity of identities and the valuing of linguistic and cultural pluralism. This means, for example, that in the context of a period of residence abroad, when they participate in new ways of life and become involved in a different education system, students should move beyond the status of a foreigner and not relate to the country as a tourist. Their position is comparable to that of the anthropologist.

## Anthropology and language teaching

The dissemination of anthropological knowledge in language teaching can be envisaged on two levels. On the one hand, there is the question of the nature of the information about the culture whose language is being taught. On the other hand, there are the processes used in anthropology which are relevant to teaching.

In the first case there is an obvious use for work related to the anthropology of the body – studies of the perceptions of illness, health, ill-luck and death – and historical anthropology which studies the evolution of mentalities in the form of a history of national emblems, of eating habits, of religious thought, of living conditions, of private life, of taste, of hygiene, of the family and of sexuality. A second source of interest are the accounts of discoveries and voyages, autobiographies of explorers and migrants, and travel diaries. These are important documents through which it is possible to study how over the course of the centuries an analysis of the relationship to the Other has been developed. On the basis of such documents it is possible to make explicit intercultural misunderstandings and to begin a process of analysing the notion of the universality of values which is unthinkingly experienced by learners as natural. The quality of the anthropological information in these areas is now beginning to influence the content of **TEXTBOOKS**.

There is a parallel and often complementary development linked to the ethnography of communication, which studies the social distribution of linguistic **SKILLS** and the linguistic variation evident in different societies. Here, anthropology sensitises the teacher to the social diversity in any group of learners, to the variety of cultural practices which co-exist in any educational environment. It also contributes to the raising of learners' awareness of the complexity of a culture which initially they often see in a reductive way.

The transfer of methods from anthropology to language teaching can contribute to the modernisation of the foundations of the teaching of languages which were established in the middle of the twentieth century. The anthropologist's purpose is to develop a description of the way of life and the system of values of a given cultural community. It is also to systematise a **RESEARCH METHOD** based on an inside knowledge of the society arising from long-term contact with the community being studied, and on the principle of openness to the Other which ensures the anthropologist's own independence of thought. The anthropologist's work is characterised by the collection of information on foreign cultural products and values, the comparison of this information with another cultural system, and the relationships between the known and the unknown. There is, then, a parallel between the anthropologist, the teacher and the learner.

Although teachers and learners are most often valued in terms of their linguistic **COMPETENCE**, they none the less share with the anthropologist their position of being on the borders between several cultural systems. The social role of the teacher, like that of the anthropologist, is to describe a foreign society in a way which is free of prejudice, which takes into consideration cultural distance between the society being described and the one producing the description, and which is part of the process of understanding of this distance. There are several theoretical models to underpin the process of comparison. First, use of the notion of the cultural bridge takes into account the issue of intercommunication between groups and the difficulties involved. Second, the analysis of mutual perceptions of two cultures in a specific domain – for example, the media or school textbooks – emphasises the possibility of changing these perceptions. Third, and more broadly, the study of images of the foreigner in different sections of a given society shows how the sense of proximity and distance between cultures depends on the way information is received, and on the international geo-political context. Fourth, the analysis of practical situations of language teaching, where the focus is on issues of mobility rather than strictly educational **OBJECTIVES**, is linked to the methodology of anthropology in so far as such analysis is concerned with relationships in the field and with confrontation with cultural Otherness.

The relationships between anthropology and language teaching are, however, surrounded by ambiguity, since they are both political and academic. The impact of anthropology on the field of language teaching varies according to the languages and culture in question, and according to the geographic and historical realities within each national context. The impact varies also according to the level of learning. There is anthropological awareness linked to early language teaching, but it is especially at university level that the discipline is taught in its own right. In the Anglo-Saxon context, this disciplinary domain contributes to the teaching of **CULTURAL STUDIES** or **AREA STUDIES**. In this case the name of the course is linked to a national designation (a course in German literature, for example) or to a linguistic area (French Studies, for example) which often includes several cultural areas. In fact, this kind of alignment is determined by academic requirements:

the same cultural area might be designated in one situation as 'Romance' or 'European', and in another as 'Cultural Heritage'. If there is explicit reference to anthropological terminology in the administrative organisation of university language departments, it is usually in parallel with linguistic terminology.

## Conclusion

In the expression of public opinion, the term 'language barrier' tends to be used indiscriminately to describe all the difficulties of communication with a foreign language and culture. Often, communication by gesture is seen as a simple but universal response, and cultural difference is spontaneously interpreted in terms of human progress, in a linear and ethnocentric perspective. This is especially so in a tourist context. When the findings of anthropology are transferred to the field of language teaching, they confirm the significance of the cultural dimension of language teaching by identifying the limitations of purely linguistic competence and performance in a foreign language. There are certain areas, otherwise marginalised by a strictly linguistic approach – **NON-VERBAL COMMUNICATION**, for example – or certain kinds of competence, such as attitudinal competence, which can be based on this and acquire academic legitimation. Contrary to the ideological discourses which idealise or reject the Other, the findings of anthropology offer a differentiated reading of difference, between universality and particularity (Geertz, 1973) and allow us to choose between several levels of interpretation – political, economic, historical, linguistic, educational – through which to approach a foreign culture.

**See also:** Area studies; Attitudes; *Civilisation*; Cultural awareness; Cultural studies; Culture shock; Exchanges; Linguistic imperialism; Stereotypes

## References

Clifford, J. (1988) *The predicament of culture*, Cambridge, MA: Harvard University Press.
Diaz del Castillo, B. (1908) *Historia verdadera de la conquista de la Nueva España (The true history of the conquest of New Spain)*, trans. G. García, London: Haklyut Society.
Elias, N. (1969) *Über den Prozess der Zivilisation (The civilizing process)*, trans. E. Jephcott (1982), New York: Pantheon Books.
European Commission (1996) *Teaching and learning. Towards the learning society*, Brussels: European Commission.
Geertz, C. (1973) *The interpretation of cultures*, New York: Basic Books.
Greenblatt, S. (1991) *Marvellous possessions. The wonder of the new world*, Oxford: Oxford University Press.
Hall, E.T. (1959) *The silent way*, New York: Doubleday.
Hall, E.T. (1966) *The hidden dimension*, New York: Doubleday.
Lévi Strauss, C. (1958) *Anthropologie structurale (Structural Anthropology)*, trans. C. Jacobson and B. Grundfest Schoepf (1963), New York: Basic Books.
Phillipson, R. (1992) *Linguistic imperialism*, Oxford: Oxford University Press.
Todd, E. (1994) *Le destin des immigrés. Assimilation et ségrégation dans les démocraties occidentales*, Paris: Editions Seuil.

## Further reading

Bourdieu, P. (1985) *Distinction*, London: Routledge and Kegan Paul.
Geertz, C. (1973) *The interpretation of cultures*, New York: Basic Books.
Greenblatt, S. (1991) *Marvellous possessions. The wonder of the new world*, Oxford: Oxford University Press.
Hall, E.T. (1959) *The silent way*, New York: Doubleday.

GENEVIÈVE ZARATE

# Applied linguistics

The role of applied linguistics as a source discipline for language teaching is not one which is easy to define. This is partly due to the fact that the term 'applied linguistics' has changed its meaning several times since it was first used in the 1940s as an academically respectable way of talking about language teaching theory. As a result of this, the relationship between applied linguists and language teachers has not been a stable one, and has itself undergone many changes. Nevertheless, it is possible to distinguish three main periods during which Applied Linguistics has impacted on language teaching.

## The emergence of 'applied linguistics'

The emergence of 'applied linguistics' as a formal discipline can largely be traced to World War Two. There was at the time considerable interest in teaching languages quickly and effectively, as part of military training, and many professional linguists became involved in this work, in both the US and the UK. Since many of these people had been involved in the development of **STRUCTURAL LIN-GUISTICS** in the 1930s, it was natural that they should attempt to use the insights that structural linguistics provided to inform the way they thought that languages should be taught. Linguists trained in structuralist techniques were able to produce good, usable descriptions of these languages, and were able to use these descriptions to make contrastive analyses of the target language and the learner's L1. These linguistic descriptions were soon linked together with training methods derived from behavioural **PSYCHOLOGY**, and teaching aids made possible by the rapid development of sound recording technology. The combination proved to be a very effective one, and underlies much of the **AUDIOLINGUAL** teaching methodology that emerged in the 1950s.

Of course, the combination of good linguistic descriptions, good teaching practice and exploitation of technological developments was not a new one: the best language teachers had been doing this long before the emergence of 'applied linguistics'. A good example of this would be the work of Harold **PALMER** (e.g. Palmer, 1922), who never described himself as an applied linguist but published work which would certainly be classed under that heading today (see Bongers, 1947, for a full description of Palmer's work).

Sridhar (1993) suggests that the growth of applied linguistics as a formal discipline owes much to the desire of language teachers to upgrade

their formal academic status by associating their work with Linguistics, which was considered at the time to be the most rigorous, and most successful, of the social sciences.

Applied linguistics in the United States is particularly associated with Charles Ferguson, and the work of the Center for Applied Linguistics in Washington (Ferguson, 1975). In the United Kingdom, the emerging discipline crystallised around a number of important figures, notably Pit Corder and Peter Strevens, who were influential in setting up university departments that specialised in 'applied linguistics'. In practice, these departments were mainly involved in advanced training for **ENGLISH** Language teachers, particularly teachers of English working outside the UK. Corder's views on the relationship between applied linguists, linguists and language teachers are explicitly laid out in his book *Introducing applied linguistics* (Corder, 1973), which is probably the classic text of this school of thought. Corder believed that there was a clear hierarchy of responsibility between three groups of people. Linguists produced descriptions of languages. The immediate consumer of these descriptions was the applied linguist, whose job was to mediate the work of the *linguist*, by producing **PEDAGOGICAL GRAMMARS**. These pedagogical grammars were turned into **TEXTBOOKS** and teaching **MATERIALS**, and eventually reached the *teachers* whose job it was actually to teach the language to *learners*. Corder's model allowed for little, if any, feedback from teachers to applied linguists, and little interaction between linguists and applied linguists; the information flowed only in one direction: 'The applied linguist is a consumer, or user, not a producer of theories' (Corder, 1973: 10). In practice, of course, this hierarchy was not as rigid as it may have been in theory. Many people worked as both linguists and applied linguists, many teachers moved into applied linguistics, and many people who thought of themselves as applied linguists also taught languages.

For many years, this relationship appears to have worked well, although inevitably there were tensions between linguists and applied linguists – Strevens refers to applied linguistics being 'tolerated' as long as it was narrowly interpreted as 'linguistic theory applied' (Strevens, 1992). In practice, this narrow definition was not closely adhered to, and 'applied linguistics' – at least as taught in British universities – soon came to encompass a lot more than the mere application of linguistic theory. A glance at the contents of the four volumes of the Edinburgh Course in Applied Linguistics (Allen and Corder, 1974; Allen and Davies, 1977) soon reveals how wide the boundaries of the discipline had begun to be. By this time, the scope of applied linguistics had come to include course design, practical phonetics and phonology, pedagogical grammar, **ERROR ANALYSIS**, content-analysis, language testing, **READING** and **WRITING**, **STYLISTICS** and experimental methods, as well as broader applications of educational technology in the form of **LANGUAGE LABORATORIES**, pro-grammed learning techniques and the use of audio-visual materials.

## A period of tension

Relationships between theoretical linguistics and applied linguistics began to become increasingly strained in the 1970s. At this time, linguistic theory, particularly the theories associated with the work of Noam **CHOMSKY** (e.g. Chomsky, 1965a) rapidly moved into a dominating position in academic linguistics. At first, these formal theories seemed to strengthen the position of applied linguistics. They were not easy for lay readers to understand, and needed to be interpreted before they could be used for practical purposes. This seemed to reinforce Corder's idea of the applied linguist as mediator, and a number of pedagogical grammars based loosely on Chomskyan linguistics appeared (e.g. Thomas, 1965). Chomsky himself, however, made it clear that he did not think his theories had anything to say about language teaching, and that he was 'rather sceptical about the significance, for the teaching of languages, of such insights and understandings as have been attained in linguistics and psychology' (Chomsky, 1965b). This made it increasingly difficult for applied linguists to argue that they were 'applying linguistics' in any obvious way. Gradually, theoretical linguistics became increasingly more formal, particularly after the development of Government and binding theory, and more recently of Minimalist theories of syntax, (cf. Radford, 1997), and, with these developments,

it became ever more difficult to argue this position with conviction.

Paradoxically, however, the complexification of theoretical linguistics seems to have increased the temporary importance of 'applied linguistics' as an academic discipline. As linguistics became increasingly closely identified with abstract syntactic theory, many researchers working in areas that lay outside this central field seem to have become disaffected, and applied linguistics seems to have provided a temporary home for them. Many people who identified themselves as linguists were not primarily concerned with the formal tenets of linguistic descriptions. These people shared a common belief in language as communication and interaction, rather than language as formal system, and, for a short time, applied linguistics served a sort of refuge discipline which provided a framework for these people to work in and a set of shared assumptions about the social function of language. Sridhar (1993) calls this 'extended linguistics'. It was not uncommon at this time to find meetings of applied linguists discussing a much wider range of topics than would have been common during the earlier period. Sociolinguists, speech therapists, child language specialists, translators, discourse analysts, lexicographers, neuro-linguists, as well as the traditional language teachers, would all have been considered active applied linguists at this time. When AILA, the *International Association for Applied Linguistics*, decided to organise its work through a series of scientific commissions, all these subject areas were considered to be part of its formal remit.

As a result of this broadening of boundaries, interactions between language teachers and applied linguists working in other areas seem to have been particularly fruitful at this time, and it is possible to see the benefits of this contact in a whole range of textbooks which appeared in the 1970s and 1980s. These texts dealt with the problems of teaching languages, but they were no longer constrained by narrow linguistic concerns – see, for example, Gardner and Lambert (1972), Krashen (1982) and Dulay, Burt and Krashen (1982). Paradoxically, perhaps, the result of this increased collaboration was that applied linguistics tended to lose its coherence as an area of study. The term came to be used as an umbrella description, distinguishing between a rather narrow view of language that built on Chomsky's ideas about linguistic **COMPETENCE**, and a broader view that focused on language as both text and interaction, or, more generally, on language as problem. The defining characteristic was, however, a negative one. Applied linguistics became a broad coalition that defined itself in negative terms – anything to do with language which wasn't theoretical linguistics. What it did not develop was a clear set of shared methodologies, or a shared set of theoretical assumptions of its own.

## Recent developments

Inevitably, this broad coalition has turned out not to be a very stable one. By 1980, one of the major figures in British applied linguistics was commenting: 'It is possible – even likely – that linguistics, as it is customarily conceived, may not be the most suitable source for a practical teaching model of language' (Widdowson, 1980). As areas of research developed their own bodies of theory, they tended to define themselves out of applied linguistics, or even in opposition to it. What became known as 'hyphenated linguistics' – socio-linguistics, psycho-linguistics, neuro-linguistics, computational linguistics, etc. – became increasingly **AUTONOMOUS** and independent. Language teaching, too, was affected by this fragmentation, as applied linguists interested in **SECOND LANGUAGE ACQUISITION** began to develop their own independent theories about how languages are learned. International learned societies specifically concerned with second language acquisition began to spring up in the late 1980s, and to run conferences separate from those of applied linguists. At the same time, SLA (second language acquisition) theory rapidly developed into a coherent set of theoretical ideas about language acquisition. Only a fraction of this work owed much to contemporary linguistic theory (e.g. White, 1989); most of it was much more broadly based in the psychology of perception and communication – see, for example, McLaughlin (1987), Ellis (1994) and Skehan (1998).

These ideas are beginning to affect the way languages are taught, or at least the way teachers are taught to teach languages. The irony here is that, as SLA develops, it becomes increasingly

technical, and – like the linguistic theories it replaced – increasingly difficult to explain to lay readers. What we have here is a sort of 'theoretical applied linguistics', more broadly based than the linguistic theories of the 1940s or the 1960s, but something that still needs interpretation and elucidation before it can be easily applied.

The current situation seems to be that few people expect modern theoretical linguistics to make a serious contribution to language teaching. Modern linguistics deals with language at an abstract level, and tends to ignore language as interaction or performance, and this means that the claims it makes have little immediate relevance and cannot be applied in any obvious way. However, the insights of structural linguistics – particularly contrastive linguistics – are still with us, and they still inform the way we teach languages. In a way, the enduring legacy of applied linguistics is that it has preserved, and continues to make use of, a body of knowledge about language which was in danger of being lost to mainstream linguistics. These ideas are no longer at the cutting edge of research, but they still form part of the basic training of most language teachers – particularly TEFL (English as a Foreign Language) teachers, though perhaps less so for teachers of other languages. In a way, the fact that these once-radical and innovative ideas are now part of basic training – a set of shared assumptions that professional language teachers and textbook writers can usually take for granted – is a measure of the impact that applied linguistics has made on language teaching.

## Conclusion

Mackey (1966) noted that: 'In one form or another, both language analysis and psychology have always been applied to the teaching of foreign languages. In fact, the history of language teaching could be represented as a cyclic shift in prominence from the one to the other, a swing from the strict application of principles of language analysis to the single-minded insistence on principles of psychology … today's interest in applied linguistics represents another swing toward the primacy of language analysis in language teaching.' The peak of this swing seems to have been relatively short-lived, but its legacy survives as what Sridhar (1993) describes as 'a common thread that runs through the various areas of research: a commitment to empirical data, a contextualised view of language, a functionalist emphasis, and an interdisciplinary openness'. Applied linguistics may no longer be a formally defined source discipline for language teaching, but the attitudes that developed during its heyday continue to influence language teachers in a fundamental way.

**See also:** Audiolingual method; Contrastive analysis; Linguistics; Pedagogical grammar; Second language acquisition; Structural linguistics

## References

Allen, J.P.B. and Corder, S.P. (eds) (1974) *The Edinburgh course in applied linguistics, Vols 1–3*, Oxford: Oxford University Press.

Allen, J.P.B and Davies, A. (eds) (1977) *Testing and experimental methods: the Edinburgh course in applied linguistics, Vol. 4*, Oxford: Oxford University Press.

Bongers, H. (1947) *The history and principles of vocabulary control*, Woerden: WOCOPI.

Chomsky, N. (1965a) *Aspects of the theory of syntax*, Cambridge, MA: MIT Press.

Chomsky, N. (1965b) 'Paper read at the Northeast Conference on the Teaching of Foreign Languages', in J.P.B. Allen and P. van Buren (eds), *Chomsky: selected readings*, Oxford: Oxford University Press, 1971.

Corder, S.P. (1973) *Introducing applied linguistics*, Harmondsworth: Penguin.

Dulay, H., Burt, M. and Krashen, S. (1982) *Language two*, Oxford: Oxford University Press.

Ellis, R. (1994) *The study of second language acquisition*, Oxford: Oxford University Press.

Ferguson, C.A. (1975) 'Applications of linguistics', in R. Austerlitz (ed.), *The scope of American linguistics*, Lisse: de Ridder.

Gardner, R. and Lambert, W. (1972) *Attitudes and motivation in second language learning*, Rowley, MA: Newbury House.

Krashen, S. (1982) *Principles and practice in second language acquisition*, Oxford: Pergamon.

Mackey, W.F. (1966) 'Applied linguistics: its meaning and use', *English Language Teaching* 20, 1: 197–206.

McLaughlin, B. (1987) *Theories of second language acquisition*, London: Arnold.

Palmer, H.E. (1922) *The principles of language study*, London: Harrap.

Radford, A. (1997) *Syntactic theory and the structure of English*, Cambridge: Cambridge University Press.

Skehan, P. (1998) *A cognitive approach to language learning*, Oxford: Oxford University Press.

Sridhar, S.N. (1993) 'What is applied linguistics?', *International Journal of Applied Linguistics* 3, 1: 1–16.

Strevens, P. (1992) 'Applied linguistics: an overview', in W. Grabe and R.B. Kaplan (eds), *Introduction to applied linguistics*, Reading, MA: Addison Wesley.

Thomas, O. (1965) *Transformational grammar and the teacher of English*, New York: Holt, Rinehart and Winston.

White, L. (1989) *Universal grammar and second language acquisition*, Amsterdam: John Benjamins.

Widdowson, H. (1980) 'Applied linguistics: the pursuit of relevance', in R.B. Kaplan (ed.), *On the scope of applied linguistics*, Rowley, MA: Newbury House.

## Further reading

Grabe, W. and Kaplan, R.B. (eds) (1992) *Introduction to applied linguistics*, Reading, MA: Addison Wesley.

James, C. (1993) 'What are applied linguistics?', *International Journal of Applied Linguistics* 3, 1: 17–32.

Rampton, B. (ed.) (1997) 'Retuning applied linguistics', *International Journal of Applied Linguistics* 7, 1 (special issue).

Rampton, B. (1998) 'Problems with an orchestral view of applied linguistics: a reply to Widdowson', *International Journal of Applied Linguistics* 8, 1: 141–5.

Sridhar, S.N. (1993) 'What are applied linguistics?', *International Journal of Applied Linguistics* 3, 1: 1–16.

Widdowson, H.G. (1998) 'Retuning, calling the tune, and paying the piper: a reaction to Rampton', *International Journal of Applied Linguistics* 8, 1: 131–9.

Widdowson, H.G. (1998) 'Positions and oppositions: hedgehogs and foxes', *International Journal of
Applied Linguistics* 8, 1: 147–51.

PAUL MEARA

# Aptitude for language learning

The concept of language aptitude has been
developed to explain differences among individuals
in language learning. It is considered to be a
capacity specific to language learning rather than a
general ability to learn, although there may be
some indirect links between the two, and it applies
to both first and subsequent language learning. In
foreign language learning, aptitude can be used as
a means of predicting achievement. However, the
degree to which success can be predicted on the
basis of a measure of aptitude alone is limited, but
not without significance.

The definition of language aptitude has evolved
slowly since the 1950s, when work was first
conducted by Carroll and Sapon to develop the
**MODERN LANGUAGE APTITUDE TEST**, because
research on aptitude has been limited. Carroll
defined aptitude in terms of an individual's
'phonemic coding ability' – their ability to identify
distinct sounds and to retain and associate them
with symbols; their sensitivity to grammatical
structures; their ability to learn items of a foreign
language by rote; their ability to infer rules about a
language from experience of the language. A more
recent proposal by Skehan (1998) suggests that
there are three components: auditory ability,
similar to Carroll's phonemic coding ability;
linguistic ability, combining Carroll's notions of
grammatical sensitivity and ability to infer rules;
and memory, further differentiated into what
learners do to assimilate or code new material,
how they store the memorised material in terms of
patterns and generalisations, and how they retrieve
material from memory.

If an individual's aptitude for language learning
is assumed to be stable and a given which cannot
be improved upon, the implications for pedagogy
appear to be discouraging. If teaching cannot
overcome low language learning aptitude, then
teachers may feel that their efforts are not

worthwhile. In so far as research has shown that
the predictive success of measures of aptitude is
high, teachers may feel justified, but since other
factors are also important – notably measures of
motivation – then teachers should not label
learners solely in terms of aptitude.

Furthermore, the identification of subcomponents of aptitude opens the possibility that learners
are not equally apt in each component. Their
aptitude can be described in terms of a profile of
different abilities, and this can be the basis for
differentiated teaching to cater for different
components and different **LEARNING STYLES** corresponding to them. Moreover, the definition of
aptitude refers to cognitive abilities rather than
**ATTITUDES** and affective dimensions of learning,
and it may be the case that aptitude measures can
predict achievement in cognitive language capacity
rather than ability to communicate on an interpersonal level (cf. Cummins's 'basic interpersonal
communications skills', and 'cognitive academic
language proficiency' – **BICS** and **CALP**). Nor does
language aptitude include reference to culture
learning and its implications for developing **INTER-
CULTURAL COMPETENCE** as a basis for communication with people of other cultural identities.
Such a capacity for interpersonal communication,
which may be the **OBJECTIVE** of some language
courses, will not necessarily be predictable by
measures of language aptitude as presently constituted. The use of aptitude tests for selecting
learners for courses should therefore be circum-
spect.

**See also:** Attitudes; Modern Language Aptitude
Test; Motivation

### Reference

Skehan, P. (1998) *A cognitive approach to language
learning*, Oxford: Oxford University Press.

### Further reading

Gardner, R. and MacIntyre, P. (1992) 'A student's
contributions to second language learning. Part 1:
Cognitive variables', *Language Teaching* 25: 211–20.
Parry, T.S. and Stansfield, C.W. (1990) *Language*

*aptitude reconsidered*, Englewood Cliffs: Prentice Hall.

MICHAEL BYRAM

Skehan, P. (1989) *Individual differences in second-language learning*, London: Edward Arnold.

JAYANTI BANERJEE

# Aptitude tests

Designed to capture an underlying ability to learn a language or acquire a skill, **APTITUDE** tests require students to perform a number of tasks, each of which is designed to tap a specific ability or aptitude. The results of such tests are generally considered to predict a student's success or failure on a language learning programme and they can be used as screening instruments.

While research into what general language aptitude might entail is inconclusive, it is generally assumed to include the following abilities:

- the knowledge of words and verbal reasoning;
- a short-term memory for the way words sound and look;
- the ability to distinguish between sounds, associate them to their spelling and to remember these connections;
- the ability to recognise grammatical regularities.

An example of an aptitude test is the **MODERN LANGUAGE APTITUDE TEST** (MLAT) which comprises five tape-recorded **EXERCISES** in either **ENGLISH** or **FRENCH** and covers number learning, phonetic script, spelling clues, structural understanding of sentences and memorisation of new words in an exotic language. Further research on the MLAT has indicated that it is not possible to train test-takers to perform well on the test. Indeed, research into aptitude testing in general has revealed that language aptitude cannot be learned or trained.

**See also:** Assessment and testing

## Further reading

Carroll, J.B. (1979) 'Psychometric approaches to the study of language abilities', in C.J. Fillmore *et al.* (eds), *Individual differences in language ability and language behaviour*, New York: Academic.

Cohen, A.D. (1994) *Assessing language ability in the classroom*, Boston, MA: Heinle and Heinle.

# Arabic

Arabic has been taught in the Islamic world since the early centuries of Islam; the central impetus for both the development of Arabic **GRAMMAR** and the teaching of Arabic was the desire to preserve the purity of the language of the Qur'an following the Islamic conquests and the subsequent mixing of Arabs with other peoples. Arabic is currently taught as a university subject in most Western countries, and as a religious language throughout the Islamic world. This article covers the historical development of Arabic, phonology and script, grammar, **VOCABULARY**, **STYLISTICS**, diglossia and trends in Arabic teaching.

## Historical development

The most widely held view among modern scholars is that in pre-Islamic Arabia there existed alongside a number of different tribal-based dialects a pan-Arabic *koiné* (cf. Holes, 1995: 7–24). This was used mainly for the composition of **POETRY**, which had a central place in pre-Islamic culture. The *koiné* is believed to have differed from the dialects in a number of ways. The most striking of these were its retention of ancient Arabic case endings for nouns and adjectives, and mood endings for verbs.

With the emergence of Islam, Qur'anic Arabic became the exemplar for formal written Arabic (hereafter referred to as Standard Arabic). The language of the Qur'an is essentially that of the poetic *koiné* with its case and mood endings. Throughout the Arab world, however, local dialects continued to develop, based largely on ancient Arabic dialects, and apparently lacking case and mood endings from the outset.

During the Ottoman period, Standard Arabic underwent an eclipse, Turkish being used as the language of administration and much non-religious culture in the Arab world. In the nineteenth century, however, Standard Arabic was revived. Today, it is the language of almost all formal communication – novels, poetry, formal **DRAMA**, newspapers, news broadcasts, academic **WRITING** and formal debates, etc. The colloquial dialects are used in informal contexts – everyday conversation, informal drama, some poetry, and sometimes for dialogue in novels.

Everyone in the Arab world speaks a local dialect as their **MOTHER TONGUE**. Standard Arabic is taught in schools, and different speakers have differing degrees of command of it depending on their level of education.

## Phonology and script

The phonology of Arabic may present problems for some learners. From the perspective of the English-speaking learner, for example, the best known among these are the emphatic phonemes. These are a series of pharyngealised phonemes (i.e. sounds involving constriction of the pharynx in the throat), contrasting with non-pharyngealised phonemes.

Arabic script is not difficult to learn, and is well fitted to the phonology of Standard Arabic. There are twenty-eight letters. The script is cursive, and most letters have variant forms, depending on their position in the word. Short vowels are not normally written, although they may be added as diacritics.

## Grammar

The morphology of Arabic is extremely rich. Words are derived from a combination of what are known as roots and patterns. This can be illustrated by the following examples: *kitaab* 'book', *katab* 'he wrote', *kitaaba* 'writing' (noun). These examples share the root *k-t-b* which has a general sense of 'to write/writing'. Affixed into and around this is a pattern; thus the pattern *i-aa* is combined with the root *k-t-b* to give the word *kitaab* 'book'. This type of morphology is sometimes called non-concatenative morphology (see Watson, forthcoming). Arabic also has a large amount of inflectional morphology, mainly involving suffixes.

Parts of speech are not problematic. For pedagogical purposes, it is possible to use traditional notions such as verb, noun, adjective, adverb, preposition and conjunction. Arabic has a high degree of agreement, and complex agreement patterns. Other syntactic features, however,

are relatively straightforward, and standard Western notions such as subject and object fit the language relatively easily.

## Vocabulary

Standard Arabic has an extremely large vocabulary, with a large number of synonyms and near-synonyms. Historically, this is partly due to the incorporation of words from different ancient Arabic dialects or from other languages into Standard Arabic. In the modern era, however, Standard Arabic (unlike the colloquial dialects) shows a strong and officially sanctioned tendency to avoid loanwords. Where such words have come into the language, an attempt is often made to replace them by neologisms formed from existing Arabic roots and patterns, or by existing Arabic words which are given an extended sense to cover the new meaning.

## Stylistics

Standard Arabic exhibits a number of stylistic features which differ markedly from those of **ENGLISH**. In particular, there is a tendency towards repetition of various kinds, such as the repetition of near-synonyms to provide emphasis. One frequently comes across phrases in Arabic such as *taḥallul al-qiyam wa-l-axlaaqiyyaat*, literally 'the dissolution of morals and values', where in English it would be more normal to restructure the doublet 'morals and values' into a noun-adjective phrase and perhaps add an element such as 'all' for additional emphasis, to give something like 'the dissolution of all moral values'.

## Diglossia

Diglossia, i.e. the co-existence of Standard Arabic and dialect throughout the Arab world, presents learners with a number of choices. If they require limited oral communication **SKILLS** for a particular area, they need only learn the dialect of that area. If they want to deal with official written communication, it is sufficient for them to learn Standard Arabic. Anyone who wants a general command of Arabic, however, needs to learn both Standard Arabic and at least one Arabic dialect. Here two general teaching strategies can be identified. The first involves teaching Standard Arabic and the chosen dialect separately. Students typically learn to read, write, listen and speak in Standard Arabic, and to listen and speak in a dialect. This engenders a number of register anomalies. For example, students learn to engage in everyday conversation in Standard Arabic – something which even highly educated Arabic speakers may not be able to do. The approach does, however, allow the four basic language skills to reinforce one another, and gives students a sense of confidence in using Standard Arabic.

The alternative strategy of teaching Standard Arabic and a dialect together has the advantage of allowing teachers and learners to reproduce register norms in Arabic directly. Students read a passage in Standard Arabic, but discuss it in a dialect. They also learn to develop a proficiency in mixing dialect and **STANDARD LANGUAGE** when appropriate. The potential disadvantages are two-fold. First, students may fail to get sufficient oral reinforcement in Standard Arabic, leaving them with a command of the language which is over-oriented towards the written form. Second, they are required to learn two languages at once, with a correspondingly greater likelihood of confusion.

## Trends in Arabic teaching

It is possible to distinguish three main phases in the development of **MATERIALS** for teaching Standard Arabic over the last thirty or forty years (Alosh, 1997: 88–90). During the first phase, Arabic language teaching was based around the **GRAMMAR–TRANSLATION METHOD**. A good example of this approach is *A new Arabic grammar of the written language* (Haywood and Nahmad, 1962). Each chapter in this book deals with one or more grammatical points, for which written practice is provided by translation sentences from and into Arabic. The second phase begins with the publication of *Elementary modern Standard Arabic* (Abboud *et al.*, 1968). Here, chapters are organised around a basic text, and a wide variety of **EXERCISES** are provided, including oral and aural exercises. The prevalence of substitution drills of various kinds strongly reflects the influence of the **AUDIOLINGUAL METHOD**. Most recently, there has been a shift to a more **COMMU-NICATIVE** approach to the teaching of Arabic,

making use of techniques adopted from ELT. One of the first books of this type was *Mastering Arabic* (Whightwick and Gaafar, 1990). A more recent book, adopting the same approach, is *Al-Kitaab fii Ta'allum al-'Arabiyya: A Textbook for Beginning Arabic* (Brustad *et al.*, 1995). It is striking that both *Elementary modern Standard Arabic* and the more recent communicatively-oriented works maintain a strong formal grammatical element. Given the complexity of Arabic morphology in particular, it is difficult to see how this could be avoided.

At the more advanced level, there has been something of a dearth of standard Arabic teaching materials. The first attempt at a comprehensive course was *Modern Standard Arabic: intermediate level* (Abboud *et al.*, 1971), which was designed to follow on from *Elementary modern Standard Arabic*. A revised version of this is currently being produced. A more recent work is *Standard Arabic: an advanced course* (Dickins and Watson, 1999), which adopts a topic-based structure.

Courses in colloquial Arabic dialects have been produced for many decades, initially mainly by academic publishers or for colonial authorities. Since the 1980s in particular, mainstream publishers have begun to publish colloquial courses.

**See also:** African languages; Area studies; Chinese; Japanese

## References

Abboud, P., Abdel-Malik, Z.N., Bezirgan, N., Erwin, W.N., Khouri, M.A., McCarus, E.N., Rammouny, R.M. and Saad, G.N. (1968) *Elementary modern Standard Arabic*, Michigan: Ann Arbor (reprinted by Cambridge University Press (1983)).

Abboud, P., Abdel-Massih, E., Altoma, S., Erwin, W., McCarus, E. and Rammouny, R. (1971) *Modern Standard Arabic: intermediate level*, Michigan: Ann Arbor.

Alosh, M.M. (1997) *Learner, text and context in foreign language acquisition: an Arabic perspective*, Columbus: Ohio State University.

Brustad, K., Al-Batal, M. and Al-Tonsi, A. (1995) *Al-Kitaab fii Ta'allum al-'Arabiyya: A textbook for beginning Arabic*, Washington, DC: Georgetown University Press.

Dickins, J. and Watson, J.C.E. (1999) *Standard*

*Arabic: an advanced course*, Cambridge: Cambridge University Press.

Haywood, J.A. and Nahmad, H.M. (1962) *A new Arabic grammar of the written language*, London: Lund Humphries.

Holes, C. (1995) *Modern Arabic: structures, functions and varieties*, London: Longman.

Watson, J.C.E. (forthcoming) *The phonology and morphology of Arabic*, Oxford: Oxford University Press.

Whightwick, J. and Gaafar, M. (1990) *Mastering Arabic*, Basingstoke: Macmillan.

### Further reading

Alosh, M.M. (1997) *Learner, text and context in foreign language acquisition: an Arabic perspective*, Columbus: Ohio State University.

Beeston, A.F.L. (1970) *The Arabic language today*, London: Hutchinson.

Holes, C. (1995) *Modern Arabic: structures, functions and varieties*, London: Longman.

JAMES DICKINS

# Area studies

Area studies is one of the terms for a complex domain of study also called **CULTURAL STUDIES**, *LANDESKUNDE* (German), *CIVILISATION* (French), and has been defined from various perspectives. It has its origin(s) in the developmental context of the national philologies of the nineteenth century and is part of the present state of affairs in which modern foreign languages are regarded as academic subjects in their own rights.

The field of area studies has been one of the most contentious ones in the debates around foreign language learning and teaching, because many (perhaps too many) prospectors have staked their claim to it: representatives of academic disciplines (first and foremost modern languages, but also political science, geography and sociology), specific courses of study (concerned with the training of teachers, businessmen, diplomats etc.), educational institutions (at almost all levels with different types of learners) and, last but not least, politicians, administrators, bureaucrats and jour-

nalists. Moreover, the always implicit – but most often also explicit – political nature of this field has added to its controversial status.

In systematic terms, area studies has been a part or a dimension of four different groups of disciplines/subjects/studies (see Figure 2).

## Modern (national) philologies and European languages

In the European context (Figure 2: 1), an interest in the study of modern languages and literatures and their establishment as academic disciplines developed more or less concomitantly with the rise of the nation states, the consolidation of their centralised political power structures and their production of nationally unified cultures in the nineteenth century. In most of the cases, the subjects of study, the theoretical and methodological frameworks and the human/social interests of these *modern (national) philologies* were modelled on those of the classics which set the standards of this part of the scientific community: historical linguistics, the editing of early **LITERARY TEXTS** and philological analysis were given precedence over the attainment of practical language **COMPETENCE**, the discussion of more recent (or even contemporary) texts and a comparative approach to the different cultures in question. Although the university departments of modern (foreign) languages were primarily set up to meet the growing need for professionally trained foreign language teachers, the actual training was more suitable for philologists concentrating on **LINGUISTICS** and/or literary criticism. Paradoxically, language practice and foreign language teaching methodology were regarded as secondary; and area studies came last, if it was taught at all.

Despite a number of educationally and politically motivated debates foregrounding the relevance of the study of culture, particularly towards the end of the nineteenth century and between the two World Wars, above all in Germany (see *Landeskunde*), but also in **FRANCE** (see *civilisation*) and other countries, this situation remained essentially unchanged until after World War Two, when, first for the **USA** (because of the conflicts arising from their military and political engagements in many parts of the world), and then in Europe (because of the beginning process of

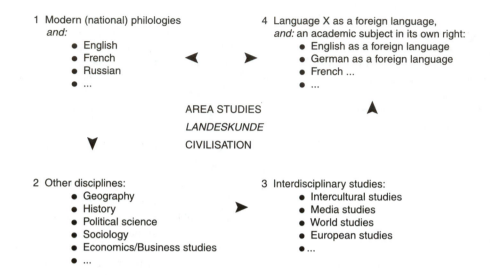

Figure 2   Area studies has been a part or a dimension of four different groups of disciplines/subjects/ studies

European integration, the growing influx of migrants, and the problems arising from these developments), the social, political and educational relevance of cultural differences could not be ignored any longer. They demanded a certain space and specific place in the training of those who had to deal with them for professional reasons: psychologists, social workers, teachers and, first and foremost, teachers of the indigenous and foreign languages. The slow and uneven but irreversible development of, for example, **CULTURAL STUDIES** in Britain, regarded first as a critique and later as a necessary enhancement of English studies, and *Interkulturelle Germanistik* in Germany, testifies to this transformation which soon spread to and included the respective foreign modern philologies. In Germany, for example, until the late 1980s *Landeskunde* (which was also called *Kulturkunde* or, more specifically, *Englandkunde* or *Frankreichkunde*) had either occupied a more (English studies) or less (Romance studies) marginal place in the university departments (of the Federal Republic of Germany) or been, at least to a certain extent, instrumentalised by party politics (in the German Democratic Republic). Since the early 1990s a discernible change of attitude in favour of area studies within the philologies has taken place: the cultural dimension of the modern national philologies is

in the process of being given the same status as the linguistic and literary ones (see Kramer and Lenz, 1994). As a consequence, these philologies are being transformed into studies of particular cultures. Similar developments can be observed in many other countries (cf. *British studies now*, 1992– present day; Byram, 1994; *Journal for the study of British cultures*, 1999).

The central objective of area studies in its modernised or reformed version (see Kramer, 1997) is to understand (to study, learn about, do research into) a particular culture and society and, by doing so, to learn to understand cultures in general. At the same time, it is intended that the process of understanding a culture which differs from one's own should also lead to a better understanding of one's own culture. In this context, a culture is understood as a 'particular way of life' (Williams, 1965: 57) in a society which is usually composed of a number of different ones. A culture includes elements of a society's relations of production (and, by implication, distribution and consumption), power and communication, as well as one or more of its ways of experiencing, structuring and making sense of them: a culture is socially produced and symbolically made sense of. If a culture that differs from one's own, particularly a *foreign* culture, is to be understood, it has to be reconstructed: its social reality and its symbolical interpretation have to be represented in one's own language (as do its concepts). Thus, from the very start, understanding a foreign culture implies making use of and, thereby, exposing and reflecting one's own culture while studying the other. This process entails comparing both cultures and, by doing so, transforming them and oneself.

## Other disciplines

In other academic disciplines (Figure 2: 2), which are not related to foreign language learning, the term 'area studies' has been used to characterise either primarily descriptive accounts of specific cultures and societies with an almost encyclopedic claim to completeness (as, for example, in geography or the political sciences), particular fields of specialisation within the discipline (as, for example, in history or sociology), or optional rather than constitutive elements of a discipline (as, for example, in economics or business studies). In most of these contexts, the chosen term has been 'area studies' (or, in German-speaking contexts, '*Landeskunde*'), while '*civilisation*' (or '*Kulturkunde*') has been associated with foreign language studies.

In recent years, a particular 'linguistic paradox of culture studies' (Seeba, 1996: 404) has developed in the United States and, to a certain extent, in **CANADA**: 'the more academic programs in the humanities' have embraced 'the cultural turn of their disciplines, with special emphasis on multicultural paradigms and intercultural approaches, the more they [have] tend[ed] to move away from the particular language whose instruction was their original raison d'être' (Seeba, 1996: 404). At the moment, it is not clear if this trend can be reversed (cf. Seeba, 1996: 405–6; Prokop, 1996), if the loss in foreign language competence can be offset against the relative gain in culture studies, or if a new theoretical integration of language practice and culture studies may prove to be a viable alternative (Michel, 1996; Altmayer, 1997).

## Interdisciplinary studies

Various kinds of interdisciplinary studies (Figure 2: 3), which may or may not be related to foreign

language learning (European, Asian, African Studies, Jewish Studies etc.), have defined their particular forms and functions of area studies by drawing on the concepts of either philologies or other disciplines depending on the nature and direction of their **OBJECTIVES**, theories and methods.

## Academic subjects in their own right

Over the past three or four decades three interdependent developments have led to the conceptualisation and institutionalisation of modern languages as foreign languages *and* academic subjects in their own right, whose objectives, theories and methods decisively differ from those of the related philologies and, consequently, entail a transformation of the traditional form of foreign-language teacher training. The three developments are as follows:

1 Increasing international cooperation and communication have made the expansion of foreign language learning at all levels a socially desirable goal: foreign language competence may not be able to guarantee a job, but in most contexts it is certainly regarded as an asset.

2 The expansion of foreign language learning at all levels has entailed a (related) transformation of the learner population. This has not only been a quantitative problem, but also a question of methodology and curriculum development: formulating attainable learning goals for groups of learners which may widely differ with respect to their **AGE**, ability and **MOTIVATION**, the fact that this particular foreign language is the first, second or third they are learning, and the context in which the language is learned and/or used, etc.

3 As the qualifications of foreign language learners left much to be desired and were in urgent need of improvement if learners were to be enabled to meet their most urgent communicative **NEEDS**, two paradigmatic shifts have taken place in the attempts at theorising foreign language learning and teaching since the 1960s.

The first shift was away from producing *linguistic competence* only, towards developing what was then called *communicative competence*. While the former was thought to be attained through the traditional teaching of **GRAMMAR**, syntax and semantics, the acquisition of the latter required that a great deal of attention be paid to either developing model phrases which then could be learned through imitation (as in the **AUDIOLINGUAL METHOD**) and/or establishing (and learning) certain utterances serving specific functions in particular situations/contexts (as in the **NOTIONAL–FUNCTIONAL APPROACH**). The model to which the learners were supposed to orientate themselves, before and after this shift, was the **NATIVE SPEAKER**.

The second shift was away from concentrating on speech patterns and/or situations in which the utterances of a foreign language are used, towards the people who use them as means of communication, negotiation and interaction. These latter terms already indicate the nature of the shift: instead of being seen as the relatively passive 'victims' of determining situations to which they have to adapt themselves (either through mimicking and memorising patterns or conforming to alien situations), the learners were envisaged as people who actively negotiate the meanings of their utterances within certain situations of which they and their interlocutors are in fact constitutive parts. The new focus was on the negotiation of meaning between speakers of different cultures. Moreover, rather than regarding these three accentuations of the linguistic, communicative and interactive/intercultural dimensions of the foreign language learning process as excluding each other, they have come to be seen as complementary: the need to develop the learners' **INTERCULTURAL COMMUNICATIVE** competence which enables them to understand what they need to understand and to say what they want to say (to each other and to their foreign interlocutors) in certain situations in relation to specific topics has become the central tenet of the foreign language learning process. As a consequence, the native speaker is no longer regarded as a model.

If foreign language learners have intercultural communicative competence, they should be regarded as 'heteroglossic language user[s]' (Nolden

and Kramsch, 1996: 64), or as intercultural speakers who are able 'to interact with people from another country and culture in a foreign language' and 'to negotiate a mode of communication and interaction which is satisfactory to themselves and the other' and 'to act as mediator between people of different cultural origins. Their knowledge of another culture is linked to their language competence through their ability to use language appropriately ... and their awareness of the specific meanings, values and connotations of the language' (Byram, 1997: 71).

These developments resulted in the necessary transformation of the traditional, philologically oriented form of foreign language teacher training. Put simply, the central (and transformative) insight was that the qualifications of philologists differ from those of foreign language teachers. Where the former focus on the critical analysis and balanced interpretation of texts, images, etc. of a foreign culture (which include, but do not necessarily foreground, the foreign language), the latter primarily concentrate on the initiation, implementation and **EVALUATION** of language learning processes of which the cultures involved form an indispensable part.

But what exactly *is* the character and function of area studies in the training of foreign language teachers and, by extension, in foreign language education? The following two models mirror the current state of affairs: one was developed in the context of **GERMAN** as a Foreign Language (GFL), emphasising the communicative aspect of language learning and the exemplary role of the native speaker; the other is a combination of ideas developed in the context of **ENGLISH** as a Foreign Language (EFL), stressing the intercultural dimension of language learning and introducing the intercultural speaker.

In the first model, the core of the discipline is defined as the theory and practice of teaching and learning GFL (see Henrici, 1994, 1996): the function of research is to steadily advance our knowledge and understanding of language learning processes, while that of teaching is to make what we already know as transparent as possible to future teachers so that they can build on it in their teaching practice. Of the many qualifications future teachers need, the most important ones are:

1 general and specific didactic (i.e. educational and methodological) know-how concerning the initiation, implementation and evaluation (observation, analysis/diagnosis and therapy) of language learning processes, media and **MATERIALS**;

2 the ability to apply this know-how in various contexts, taking into account their diverse (pre)conditions (cognitive, affective, social and other variables; institutional, medial factors, etc.) and thereby to teach, always in relation to particular contents (or subject matters), linguistic competence, **COMMUNICATIVE STRATEGIES**, knowledge about – and certain **ATTITUDES** towards – the foreign culture;

3 knowledge of the history of the discipline and the development of its particular profile.

In order to acquire these qualifications, students have to study and make interdisciplinary use of certain disciplines: basic; contents-related; and neighbouring. In this model, **SECOND LANGUAGE ACQUISITION** research, L2-**CLASSROOM RESEARCH** and **APPLIED LINGUISTICS** are regarded as the basic disciplines whose interests and results determine, at least to a certain extent, the ways and forms in which the contents-related disciplines (**LINGUISTICS**, literary criticism, *Landeskunde*) and the neighbouring disciplines (sociology, **PSYCHOLOGY**, education, etc.) are being made use of: the latter

two are functionally related (i.e., more or less subordinated) to the former.

In this model of GFL, area studies is present as one of the (three) component parts of the (modernised version of the) related philology (*Germanistik*), but in the language learning processes it is mainly reduced to the role of providing the contents of and information or subject matters for these processes. Although this function is not negligible (and is certainly more pertinent than simply supplying 'contextual' knowledge), it does not extend to the (inter)cultural character of the language learning processes themselves.

This problematic is foregrounded in a second model (Figure 3) which is here (re)constructed from suggestions for teaching EFL and, by implication, the training of professional teachers (cf. Vielau, 1997: 208–14; Zydatiß, 1998: 1–16), and complemented by ideas on **INTERCULTURAL COMPETENCE** (IC) and intercultural communicative competence (ICC) (see Byram, 1997). Although this model also subscribes to the relevance of Second language acquisition and L2-classroom research as well as Applied linguistics, it strikes a different balance between these three on the one hand, and linguistic and cultural competence on the other. Rather than letting the former functionalise the latter (as in the GFL model), it regards the former, together with the textual domain, as necessary links between linguistic and intercultural competence.

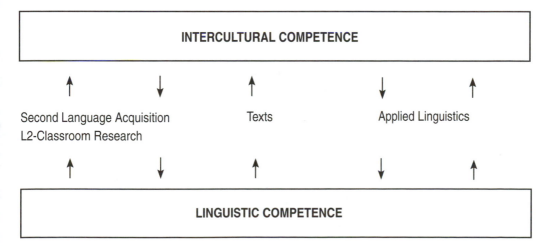

Figure 3    Intercultural competence in foreign language education

In this context, intercultural competence (IC) has to be understood as a complex combination of knowledge, **SKILLS** and attitudes held together by a critical engagement with the foreign culture under consideration and one's own (as sketched in Figure 4 below).

In this understanding, IC does not determine the contributions of the other factors but, rather, pervades or informs them. In doing so, IC selects and combines linguistic competence and communicative strategies as well as knowledge about the foreign language and culture, in such a way as to enable the learners to confront their communicative practice. In this practice, i.e. in their interaction with speakers of another culture, they have to negotiate the necessary communicative processes and their contexts and, thereby, become intercultural speakers, developing intercultural communicative competence (see Figure 5).

Area studies forms but a part, though an indispensable part, of IC. Its role cannot be reduced to providing the contents of, and information or subject matters for, language learning processes or knowledge about the foreign language and culture, but has to be understood in a more comprehensive way: as a complex, but flexible structure (or network) of culturally specific knowledge, skills and attitudes which enables learners of a foreign language to begin (and continue) to communicate with native or other non-native speakers of that language, mediate and negotiate between the two (or more) cultures in question (which always more or less 'interfere with' the area studies part of the learners' IC) *and* reflect these various processes in relation to their own culture(s). The nature of area studies in this model can be compared to a twine, i.e. a 'strong thread or string composed of two or more strands twisted together' (*Webster's Dictionary* 1989: 1530). Culturally specific knowledge, skills at negotiating or mediating communicative processes (geared to the cultures in question), and a mixture of attitudes including transcultural ones (e.g. interest in and tolerance of foreign cultures and their people) and culturally specific ones (e.g. preference of certain cultures or cultural traits) in their indivisible interaction are the components which together produce this twine.

**See also:** *Civilisation*; Cultural studies; Higher education; *Interkulturelle Didaktik*; *Landeskunde*; Study abroad

### References

Altmayer, C. (1997) '*Zum Kulturbegriff des Faches Deutsch als Fremdsprache* (On the concept of culture in German as a Foreign Language)', *Zeitschrift für Interkulturellen Fremdsprachenunterricht* (Online: http://www.ualberta.ca/~german/ejournal/altmayer3.htm), 2, 2: 25pp.

*British Studies Now* (1992–present day).

Byram, M. (ed.) (1994) *Culture and language learning in higher education*, Clevedon: Multilingual Matters.

| | Skills<br><br>interpret and relate<br><br>(savoir comprendre) | |
|---|---|---|
| **Knowledge**<br><br>of self and other;<br><br>of interaction:<br><br>individual and<br><br>societal *(savoirs)* | **Education**<br><br>political education;<br><br>critical cultural awareness<br><br>*(savoir s'engager)* | **Attitudes**<br><br>relativising self;<br><br>valuing other<br><br>*(savoir être)* |
| | **Skills**<br><br>discover and/or interact<br><br>*(savoir apprendre/faire)* | |

Figure 4    Factors of intercultural competence (IC) interacting in intercultural communication
Source    Byram (1997: 34).

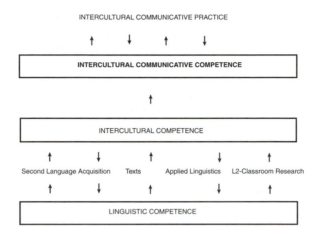

Figure 5   The development of intercultural communicative competence

Byram, M. (1997) *Teaching and assessing intercultural communicative competence*, Clevedon: Multilingual Matters.

Henrici, G. (1994) '*Die Kontur des Fachs Deutsch als Fremdsprache. Ein Vorschlag* (German as a Foreign Language. Suggestions for an outline)', in G. Henrici and U. Koreik (eds), *Deutsch als Fremdsprache (German as a Foreign Language)*, Hohengehren: Schneider.

Henrici, G. (1996) '*Deutsch als Fremdsprache ist doch ein fremdsprachenwissenschaftliches Fach!* (Foreign language research is a particular disciplinary field and also part of German as a Foreign Language)', *Deutsch als Fremdsprache* 33, 2: 131–5.

*Journal for the Study of British Cultures* (1999) Special Issue on 'British Studies: European Perspectives'.

Kramer, J. (1997) *British cultural studies*, Munich: W. Fink.

Kramer, J. and Lenz, B. (1994) 'Editorial', *Journal for the Study of British Cultures* 1, 1: 3–7.

Michel, A. (1996) 'Theory in German studies', in J. Roche and T. Salumets (eds), *Germanics under construction. Intercultural and interdisciplinary projects*, Munich: Iudicium.

Nolden, T. and Kramsch, C. (1996) 'Foreign language literacy as (op)positional practice', in J. Roche and T. Salumets (eds), *Germanics under construction. Intercultural and interdisciplinary projects*, Munich: Iudicium.

Prokop, M. (1996) 'A survey of the state of German studies in Canada', in J. Roche and T. Salumets (eds), *Germanics under construction. Intercultural and interdisciplinary projects*, Munich: Iudicium.

Seeba, H.C. (1996) 'Cultural versus linguistic competence? Bilingualism, language in exile, and the future of German studies', *The German Quarterly* 69, 4: 401–13.

Vielau, A. (1997) *Methodik des kommunikativen Fremdsprachenunterrichts (Communicative methodology in foreign language teaching)*, Berlin: Cornelsen.

*Webster's Encyclopedic Unabridged Dictionary of the English Language* (1989), New York: Gramercy Books.

Williams, R. (1965) *The long revolution*, Harmondsworth: Penguin.

Zydatiß, W. (1998) '*Leitvorstellungen einer zukunftsfähigen Fremdsprachenlehrerausbildung* (On the training of future foreign language teachers)', in W. Zydatiß (ed.), *Fremdsprachen-Lehrerausbildung: Reform oder Konkurs (The training of future foreign language teachers. Reform or bankruptcy)*, Munich: Langenscheidt.

**Further reading**

Buttjes, D. (ed.) (1981) *Landeskundliches Lernen im Englischunterricht (Cultural Learning in EFL)*, Paderborn: Schöningh.

Buttjes, D. and Byram, M. (eds) (1990) *Mediating languages and cultures*, Clevedon: Multilingual Matters.

Byram, M. (1989) *Cultural studies in foreign language education*, Clevedon and Philadelphia: Multilingual Matters.

Byram, M. (ed.) (1993) *Germany. Its representation in textbooks for teaching German in Great Britain*, Frankfurt: Diesterweg.

Doyé, P. (ed.) (1991) *Großbritannien. Seine Darstellung in deutschen Schulbüchern für den Englischunterricht (Great Britain. Its representation in textbooks for teaching English in Germany)*, Frankfurt: Diesterweg.

Kramer, J. (1983) *English cultural and social studies*, Stuttgart: Metzler.

Kramer, J. (1990) *Cultural and intercultural studies* Frankfurt: Peter Lang.

Kramsch, C. (1993) *Context and culture in language teaching*, Oxford: Oxford University Press.

JÜRGEN KRAMER

# Assessment and testing

The term 'assessment' is generally used to cover all methods of testing and assessment, although some teachers and testers apply the term 'testing' to formal or standardised tests such as the Test of English as a Foreign Language (TOEFL), and 'assessment' to more informal methods. In this entry, however, the terms 'assessment' and 'test' are used interchangeably.

## Recent history

In Britain, assessment of foreign languages was mostly conducted by means of traditional examinations until well into the twentieth century (Spolsky, 1995). However, in the **USA**, influences from the field of **PSYCHOLOGY**, together with concerns about the fairness of subjective **EVALUATIONS**, led to the wide use from the 1920s onwards of objectively marked tests. Such tests were ideally suited to the structural language **SYLLABUSES** of the 1950s and 1960s with their emphasis on the teaching of separate elements of language, and discrete point multiple choice questions became common in many parts of the world (Lado, 1961). Objective tests had many advantages: apart from being easy to mark, the internal **RELIABILITY** of the tests could be calculated, and item analysis could tell test constructors not only how difficult individual items had been for their examinees, but also how well these items discriminated between the strong and the weak students. (See Alderson, Clapham and Wall, 1995, for information about item analysis and reliability indices.)

In the 1970s, however, concerns that the answers to these discrete point items provided no evidence of students' more global linguistic **SKILLS** led to Oller's unitary competence hypothesis, and the wide use of integrative tests such as **CLOZE** and **DICTATION** to assess general linguistic proficiency (see Oller, 1979). Although Oller later concluded that language proficiency consisted of more than one underlying factor (Oller, 1983), and although cloze tests were later shown to be less valid and reliable than had originally been thought (Cohen, 1998), cloze tests have remained a popular method of testing around the world.

In recent years, the move towards the **COMMUNICATIVE** approach to teaching has encouraged testers to make their test items more integrated (less discrete), and the tasks more **AUTHENTIC** in both content and purpose. Interest has swung from reliability to validity, and more researchers are turning their attention once again to direct tests of **SPEAKING** and **WRITING** (see McNamara, 1996). In recent years, too, differing test philosophies have moved closer together: American test constructors are more concerned with test content than they were, while British examination boards use statistical procedures to analyse the validity and reliability of their tests.

## Theories of language testing

Test content is linked to theories of language learning and testing, and at present such theories relate to communicative principles. Canale and Swain (1980) included sociolinguistic and **STRATEGIC COMPETENCE** in their description of the domains of language knowledge, and Bachman (1990) added psychophysiological mechanisms. Bachman and Palmer (1996) elaborated on this model further to include both affective and metacognitive factors. This model of communicative language ability is used as the theoretical basis for tests such as the International English Language Testing System (IELTS) test, and also provides the theoretical basis for many current research projects. (See McNamara, 1996, for a discussion of recent language testing models.)

## Test purpose

The overall purpose of a test inevitably affects its contents. Tests where much is at stake for the examinee are generally based on a set of specifications (see Alderson, Clapham and Wall, 1995) which set out the main features of the test, and describe the test's aims, as well as describing its potential candidature, its content and the theory of language teaching on which it is based. The specifications vary according to whether they are designed to be read by students, teachers, item writers, or administrators, but in all cases these specifications state the test's overall purpose (whether it is to assess the students' linguistic **APTITUDE**, progress, achievement or proficiency, or whether it is to be used for placement or diagnostic purposes). The specifications also list other reasons for taking the test, such as the demonstration of an ability to communicate in a foreign language (for example, the International Baccalaureate language examinations) or to speak a language for a specific purpose (for example, the Finnish Foreign Language Diploma for Professional Purposes (FFLDPP)). Such Language for Specific Purposes (LSP) tests contain language and tasks similar to those the students will encounter in their future career (see Douglas, 1997, 2000).

## Test types

Test types, too, are affected by the test's purpose, and any detailed set of test specifications will describe the methods of assessment to be used (Alderson, Clapham and Wall, 1995). Since it is now accepted that students differ in the types of task in which they excel (Wood, 1991), test batteries generally include a range of test types, so that a test is not biased according to test method effect. Similarly, test constructors attempt to prevent their tests being biased against students according to factors such as **GENDER**, first language or background knowledge (Wood, 1991).

Discussions of different test types are given in Buck, 1997, Alderson, 2000, Fulcher, 1997, Hamp-Lyons, 1990 and Brindley, 1998a. One type of test which is widely used at present is the **C-TEST**, which is easy to construct and is supposed to assess a wide range of skills. However, it may have many of the

same weaknesses as the cloze test (see Jafarpur, 1995). (For useful descriptions of different test methods, see Heaton, 1988, and Weir, 1993.)

## Rating scales

With the increasing use of subjectively marked writing and speaking tests, rating scales have been devised to help raters assess students' performances. Examples of these are used in the Oral Proficiency Instrument (Lowe and Stansfield, 1988), and in the speaking and writing components of the English as a Foreign Language examinations of the University of Cambridge Local Examinations Syndicate (UCLES). Such scales may be 'holistic', where the assessor judges the student's performance as a whole, or 'analytic', where the performance is marked according to a range of separate criteria such as content, organisation, **GRAMMAR** and **VOCABULARY** (Weir, 1993; Alderson, Clapham and Wall, 1995). The validity of such marking scales may be questionable – few attempts have so far been made to design analytic scales using samples of actual performance (see, however, Fulcher, 1997) – but the accessibility of computer programs such as FACETS (see Cushing Weigle, 1998) have made it possible to assess how such scales work in practice. In addition, it is possible, using generalisability studies (Bachman, 1997) to investigate the reliability of the marking. How such scales work needs to be investigated because, in spite of training, raters do not always mark consistently and sometimes give marks that are not in line with those of other markers (Brindley, 1998b).

## Methods of test validation

Other advances in statistical analysis have enabled test researchers to use complex methods such as multiple regression, analysis of variance, factor analysis and structural equation modelling to assess the construct validity of their tests. Not all of Messick's (1989) theories about validity are universally accepted, but his views have had a profound effect on language testing. His 1989 article is long and complex, but many authors have explained his views more simply (see, for example, Moss, 1994, and Shepard, 1993). (For a more traditional view of test validity, see Alderson, Clapham and Wall, 1995.)

## Technological advances

So far, the expected impact of personal computers on language assessment has not materialised. Computer testing has tended to fossilise existing objective testing methods, because multiple choice items and gap filling tasks are straightforward to answer on the computer, and are easy to mark mechanically. However, the comparative ease with which videos and listening extracts can now be downloaded from the Internet, the increasing ability of the computer to recognise sounds and letters, and advances in the uses of language corpora for teaching and testing, are all steadily increasing the scope of computer-administered tests.

One project which has the potential to produce interesting tests which are easy to deliver and mark is DIALANG, a project supported by Lingua in Europe. This project aims to produce diagnostic tests in fourteen different European languages (DIALANG, 1997). Students will be tested on their grammatical knowledge and on their **READING**, **WRITING**, **LISTENING** and **SPEAKING** skills, and the tests will be computer adaptive, i.e. they will adapt to each student's level of linguistic proficiency. After taking their chosen test, students will receive instant diagnostic information about the strengths and weaknesses of their performance.

The fact that DIALANG will be able to adjust to the student's level is possible because of advances in test analysis. Unlike classical item analysis, which can only report the difficulty of an item for a particular group of test takers, Item Response Theory (see Bachman and Eignor, 1997) also takes account of the ability of the students, so that it is theoretically possible to report the difficulty of any test item regardless of the students on whom the item has been trialled. Items can therefore be banked according to their level of difficulty, and can be used as required in computer adaptive tests.

In addition, the increasing sophistication and ease of use of computer programs such as NUD*IST, the Ethnograph and ATLAS have made it more possible to analyse large amounts of qualitative data, and many researchers now use qualitative methods such as in-depth interviews

and verbal introspections and retrospections to investigate the validity of a test or a test method (Banerjee and Luoma, 1997).

## Alternative assessment

'Alternative assessment' refers to informal assessment procedures, such as writing-portfolios, learner diaries or interviews with teachers, which are often used within the classroom. Such assessment procedures may be more time-consuming and difficult for the teacher to administer than 'paper-and-pencil' tests, but they have many advantages. They produce information that is easy for administrators, teachers and students to understand; the tests tend to be integrated, and they can reflect the more holistic Teacher methods used in the classroom. One problem with methods of alternative assessment, however, lies with the reliability of such assessments. Their marking schemes may not have been validated, and raters have often not been trained to give consistent marks. As Hamayan (1995) says, such alternative methods of assessment will not be considered to be part of the mainstream of language assessment until they can be shown to be both valid and reliable.

It is difficult to draw a line between 'testing' and 'alternative assessment', and many test batteries include examples of each. However, it is perhaps fair to say that while 'tests' are often 'norm referenced', with the student's score being compared to that of other students, 'alternative assessment' is generally 'criterion referenced', with the student's performance being compared not to that of other students but to a set of performance **OBJECTIVES** or criteria. Similarly, it is often the case that teachers use 'tests' for 'summative assessment' at the end of a course or the school year, and 'alternative assessment' for 'formative assessment' that is carried out by teachers during the learning process, with the intention of using the information to decide what needs to be taught or reviewed in the next stages of a course.

## Impact and washback

In the last ten years there has been an upsurge of interest in the impact of tests on education, and the effect of tests on teaching (see Alderson and Wall,

1993; Wall, 1996). In their 1993 article, Alderson and Wall bemoan the lack of research into whether tests do actually affect teaching and, if they do, what form such 'washback' might take. Since then there have been many empirical studies into washback (Wall, 1997).

## Ethics and accountability

There is also increasing concern with issues relating to ethics and accountability in assessment. This concern relates partly to questions of fairness and equity, and partly to the uses that might be made of test results. Many testing organisations adhere to the AERA standards (American Educational Research Association, 1999) and ILTA (International Language Testing Association) has prepared its own Code of Ethics for language testers (ILTA, 2000) and is preparing its own Code of Practice. Other testing organisations, too, such as the Association of Language Testers in Europe (ALTE) and Educational Testing Service (ETS) in Princeton, New Jersey, have their own codes of practice. (For more about this, see Davidson, Turner and Huhta, 1997; Hamp-Lyons, 1997; and Norton, 1997.)

## Current trends

It seems likely that the competing requirements of test validity and financial practicality will maintain the distinction between tests which can be administered reliably to large numbers of students, and more holistic tests which can potentially reveal all aspects of the candidates' language proficiency. While testers are likely to experiment with complex and time-consuming methods of testing language, the expense of such methods will prevent many large testing organisations from adopting them. Current research in different areas of language assessment is discussed in Clapham and Corson (1997), and current concerns about language testing are described by Douglas (1995), Shohamy (1997), Bachman (2000) and Brindley (in press).

It is impossible to cover all aspects of language assessment in this entry, but the *Dictionary of language testing* by Davies *et al.* (1999) and the *Multilingual glossary of language testing terms* (ALTE, 1998) have concise explanations of most of the concepts related

to the field. In addition, the International Language Testing Association (ILTA) has produced twelve five-minute videos on the most frequently discussed aspects of language testing. These videos introduce the novice language tester to test specifications, item-writing, pre-testing, statistics, testing for specific purposes, validity, reliability, test impact and ethics, and the assessment of the skills of reading, writing, listening and speaking (ILTA, 1999).

**See also:** Aptitude tests; Cloze test; C-test; Diagnostic tests; Direct/Indirect testing; Discrete point tests; Evaluation; Integrated tests; Integrative tests; Placement tests; Proficiency tests; Progress tests; Reliability; Validity

## References

Alderson, J.C. (2000) *Assessing reading*, Cambridge: Cambridge University Press.

Alderson, J.C. and Wall, D. (1993) 'Does washback exist?', *Applied Linguistics* 14, 2: 115–29.

Alderson, J.C., Clapham, C. and Wall, D. (1995) *Language test construction and evaluation*, London: Longman.

ALTE (1998) *Multilingual glossary of language testing terms*, Cambridge: Cambridge University Press.

American Educational Research Association (1999) *Standards for educational and psychological testing*, Washington, DC: AERA Publications.

Bachman, L.F. (1990) *Fundamental considerations in language testing*, Oxford: Oxford University Press.

Bachman, L.F. (1997) 'Generalizability theory', in C. Clapham and D. Corson (eds), *Language testing and assessment, Encyclopedia of Language and Education, Vol. 7*, Dordrecht: Kluwer.

Bachman, L.F. (2000) 'State of the art article on language testing', *Language Testing*, 17, 1: 1–42.

Bachman, L.F. and Eignor, D.R. (1997) 'Recent advances in quantitative test analysis', in C. Clapham and D. Corson (eds), *Language testing and assessment, Encyclopedia of Language and Education, Vol. 7*, Dordrecht: Kluwer.

Bachman, L.F. and Palmer, A. (1996) *Language testing in practice*, Oxford: Oxford University Press.

Banerjee, J. and Luoma, S. (1997) *Qualitative approaches to test validation* in C. Clapham and D. Corson (eds), *Language testing and assessment*,

*Encyclopedia of Language and Education, Vol. 7,* Dordrecht: Kluwer.

Brindley, G. (1998a) 'Assessing listening abilities', *Annual Review of Applied Linguistics* 18: 171–91.

Brindley, G. (1998b) 'Outcomes-based assessment and reporting in language learning programmes: a review of the issues', *Language Testing* 15, 1: 45–85.

Brindley, G. (in press) 'Assessment', in R. Carter and D. Nunan (eds), *The Cambridge TESOL guide,* Cambridge: Cambridge University Press.

Buck, G. (1997) 'The testing of listening in a second language', in C. Clapham and D. Corson (eds), *Language testing and assessment, Encyclopedia of Language and Education, Vol. 7,* Dordrecht: Kluwer.

Canale M. and Swain, M. (1980) 'Theoretical bases of communicative approaches to language teaching and testing', *Applied Linguistics* 1, 1: 1–47.

Clapham, C. and Corson, D. (eds) (1997) *Language testing and assessment, Encyclopedia of Language and Education, Vol. 7,* Dordrecht: Kluwer.

Cohen, A. (1998) 'Strategies and processes in test taking and SLA', in L.F. Bachman and A. Cohen (eds), *Interfaces between second language acquisition and language testing research,* Cambridge: Cambridge University Press.

Cushing Weigle, S. (1998) 'Using FACETS to model rater training effects', *Language Testing* 15, 2: 263–87.

Davidson, F., Turner, C. and Huhta, A. (1997) 'Language testing standards', in C. Clapham and D. Corson (eds), *Language testing and assessment, Encyclopedia of Language and Education, Vol. 7,* Dordrecht: Kluwer.

Davies, A., Brown, A., Elder, C. and Hill, K. (1999) *Dictionary of language testing,* Cambridge: Cambridge University Press.

DIALANG (1997) 'DIALANG: A new European system for diagnostic language assessment', *Language Testing Update,* 21: 38–9 (website: http://www.jyu.fi/DIALANG).

Douglas, D. (1995) 'Developments in language testing', *Annual Review of Applied Linguistics,* 15: 167–87.

Douglas, D. (1997) 'Language for specific purposes testing', in C. Clapham and D. Corson (eds), *Language testing and assessment, Encyclopedia of Language and Education, Vol. 7,* Dordrecht: Kluwer.

Douglas, D. (2000) *Assessing language for specific purposes,* Cambridge: Cambridge University Press.

Fulcher, G. (1997) 'The testing of L2 speaking', in C. Clapham and D. Corson (eds), *Language testing and assessment, Encyclopedia of Language and Education, Vol. 7,* Dordrecht: Kluwer.

Hamayan, E. (1995) 'Approaches to alternative assessment', *Annual Review of Applied Linguistics,* 15: 212–26.

Hamp-Lyons, L. (1990) 'Second language writing; assessment issues', in B. Kroll (ed.), *Second language writing: research insights for the classroom,* Cambridge: Cambridge University Press.

Hamp-Lyons, L. (1997) 'Ethics in language testing' in C. Clapham and D. Corson (eds), *Language testing and assessment, Encyclopedia of Language and Education, Vol. 7,* Dordrecht: Kluwer.

Heaton, J.B. (1988) *Writing English language tests,* London: Longman.

ILTA (1999) *Frequently asked questions about language testing,* http://www.surrey.ac.uk/ELI/ilta/faqs/main.html

ILTA (2000) 'Code of ethics for ILTA', *Language Testing Update,* 27: 14–24.

Jafarpur, A. (1995) 'Is c-testing superior to cloze?', *Language Testing* 12, 2: 194–216.

Lado, R. (1961) *Language testing,* London: Longman.

Lowe, P. and Stansfield, C. (1988) *Second language proficiency assessment,* Englewood Cliffs, NJ: Prentice Hall Regents.

McNamara, T. (1996) *Measuring second language performance,* London: Longman.

Messick, S. (1989) 'Validity', in R.L. Linn (ed.), *Educational measurement,* New York: American Council of Education/Macmillan.

Moss, P. (1994) 'Can there be validity without reliability?', *Educational Researcher,* March: 6–12.

Norton, B. (1997) 'Accountability in language assessment', in C. Clapham and D. Corson (eds), *Language testing and assessment, Encyclopedia of Language and Education, Vol. 7,* Dordrecht: Kluwer.

Oller, J.W. (1979) *Language tests at school,* London: Longman.

Oller, J.W. (1983) 'An emerging consensus', in J.W. Oller (ed.), *Issues in language testing research,* Rowley, MA: Newbury House.

Shepard, L. (1993) 'Evaluating test validity', *Review of Research in Education* 19: 405–50.

Shohamy, E. (1997) 'Second language assessment',

in G.R. Tucker and D. Corson (eds), *Second language education, Encyclopedia of Language and Education, Vol. 4*, Dordrecht: Kluwer.

Spolsky, B. (1995) *Measured words*, Oxford: Oxford University Press.

Wall, D. (1996) 'Introducing new tests into traditional systems: insights from general education and from innovation theory', *Language Testing* 13, 3: 334–54.

Wall, D. (1997) 'Impact and washback in language', in C. Clapham and D. Corson (eds), *Language testing and assessment, Encyclopedia of Language and Education, Vol. 7*, Dordrecht: Kluwer.

Weir, C.J. (1993) *Understanding and developing language tests*, Hemel Hempstead: Prentice Hall.

Wood, R. (1991) *Assessment and testing*, Cambridge: Cambridge University Press.

## Further reading

Alderson, J.C. and Wall, D. (1993) 'Does washback exist?', *Applied Linguistics* 14, 2: 115–29.

Alderson, J.C., Clapham, C. and Wall, D. (1995) *Language test construction and evaluation*, London: Longman.

Bachman, L.F. (1990) *Fundamental considerations in language testing*, Oxford: Oxford University Press.

Bachman, L.F. and Palmer, A. (1996) *Language testing in practice*, Oxford: Oxford University Press.

Clapham, C. and Corson, D. (eds) (1997) *Language testing and assessment, Encyclopedia of Language and Education, Vol. 7*, Dordrecht: Kluwer.

McNamara, T. (1996) *Measuring second language performance*, London: Longman.

CAROLINE CLAPHAM

# Attitudes and language learning

Language does not consist only of forms, patterns and rules but is simultaneously bound up with the social, subjective and objective world, since it also carries the attitudes, habits and cultural characteristics of its speakers. The child already internalises in first language **ACQUISITION** the values of its environment, and identifies with those people who appear to it to be authorities. If it is confronted with an unknown sign system, this can undermine its ways of perceiving hitherto. As Wilhelm von **HUMBOLDT** says, this may be 'one of the best mental exercises' because 'on account of this, thought becomes more independent of one particular kind of expression, its true inner content appears more clearly, depth and clarity, strength and lightness meet each other in a more harmonious way' (Humboldt, 1907: 193).

The Humboldtian way of thinking has left its traces in the context of the justification and aims of foreign language teaching, as has that of the **SAPIR–WHORF HYPOTHESIS**, according to which belonging to a language community determines the mode of human perception (Sapir, 1970: 68).

It is for this reason that foreign language teaching sees its task, for educational, practical and political reasons, as that of leading pupils from primary age onwards out of its tried and tested conventions, with the help of a new language and its contents; of making them conscious of the limits of their own ways of seeing as determined by their **MOTHER TONGUE**. It aims thereby not only to teach the cultural context of the other language but also to create a certain distance from pupils' own culture. In this way it is hoped to establish an approach to the understanding of Otherness which will contribute to changes in attitudes, to the breaking down of prejudices and **STEREOTYPES**. Concepts such as **ACCULTURATION, CULTURAL STUDIES** and **INTERCULTURAL COMMUNICATION** are concerned at a theoretical level with the relationship between understanding of self and understanding of the Other. Empirical research into the connection between attitudes and language learning leads to two viewpoints, which as the resultative hypothesis and the **MOTIVATIONAL** hypothesis continue to be discussed in polarised terms, even though the data (here discussed selectively) and current theoretical work suggest a quite different interpretation.

## The resultative hypothesis

The resultative hypothesis is based on the assumption that experience of success influences attitudes to language, country and people. The first systematically collected data were provided by a study at the beginning of the 1940s of 11–15-year-old boys learning **FRENCH** in London (Jordan, 1941: 28–44). A survey of Welsh as a second language a few years later also showed that progress in learning goes hand-in-hand with improvements in attitudes (Jones, 1949: 44–52; 1950: 117–32). However, there was also evidence among all informants of a worsening of attitudes with increased age.

From the different studies it is possible to surmise possible reasons for this. Thus, at the end of an 18-week French course at an American college which had the purpose of evaluating the efficacy of different methods of teaching, it was suggested that 'it is achievement which influences attitudes towards French study ...' (Savignon, 1972: 63). However the dissatisfaction of the learners with the exercise in the **LANGUAGE LA-BORATORY**, which seemed so bereft of content, i.e. without information about the target language culture, could be an explanation for the fact that their attitudes deteriorated.

Even if the longitudinal study in Great Britain between 1964 and 1974 of approximately 17,000 8–16-year-olds learning French came to similar conclusions (Burstall, 1974: 244), the high number of dropouts among the 13-year-olds is cause for scepticism. The dropouts refer to difficulties in learning as their reasons. Examination of the data shows that boys give up French much more frequently than do girls, that the size of the school, insufficient individual attention and recognition in lessons, no opportunity to travel to **FRANCE**, also contribute to the resistance. Further, poor social environment also leads to a lack in confidence in one's own potential for achievement. A study of German informants shows how the way in which teachers and learners relate to each other accounts for 25 per cent of the total variance in foreign language achievement (Geisler, 1978: 254–5).

The assumed 'linear' relationship between learning success and attitudes seems to become entangled in a number of influence factors. As the comments on the efficacy of the language laboratory show, background knowledge is one of these. Language teaching without a conscious inclusion of information about the target language and its representatives apparently ends just as little in understanding of Otherness as it does in success in language learning. In a group of 750 German secondary school pupils aged 11–16, those in the

top third in the learning of **ENGLISH** had a number of differing opinions about the speakers of the target language (Hermann, 1978: 211). Either they prefer the English over other nations, or they value them to the same degree, or they even have negative views about them. On the other hand, those of the group who know a lot about English culture are positive towards it. The situation is different among the weakest third of the sample. Here it seems that failure has created such a rejection of everything English that Portuguese or Turks, who in social perceptions have very low status, are favoured much more highly. Lack of knowledge, in comparison, is not as destructive.

Those negative consequences of learning difficulties which are assessed are related statistically to other variables, as the results of a Franco-German study of 975 pupils in the eighth year of schooling show (Candelier and Hermann-Brennecke, 1993). As in other school contexts where data have been gathered, carefully prepared **EXCHANGE** programmes or ethnographic studies seem to have a particular significance for attitudes: 75 per cent of pupils in the lower streams of **SECONDARY EDUCATION** who see no purpose in English say they are disappointed that they cannot go to England at least once in their period of schooling. Their disillusionment transfers not only onto the speakers of the target language but also onto their interest in any other languages. Perhaps the destructive effect of failure in foreign language learning could be countered if those who have to struggle with it received more support from **TRANSLATION**, **DICTATIONS** and **VOCABULARY** tests, as they expect from their classes. As is evident from other research (e.g. Heuer, 1976), they would like more explanations in their mother tongue, i.e. less use of the target language only. The importance of comprehensible input, transparency and awareness raising in the process of language learning does not exclude for these same pupils the need for poems, myths, songs, games and 'interesting things', and underlines the link between cognitive and affective learning processes.

Despite the multiple variants on the relationship between attitudes and language learning which have become evident here – a summary of potential factors notes 200 individual variables (Geisler, 1987) – data collection and interpretation continue to be seen in a resultative way, and to be accepted as such in the scientific community (e.g. Crookes and Schmidt, 1991). This seems to be explicable only because of antagonism towards and a strong rejection of the motivational hypothesis.

## The motivational hypothesis

The motivational hypothesis switches the direction of influence. It is based on the belief that attitudes as stable, motive-like constructs decide how successful language learning will take place (Gardner and Lambert, 1972: 3). It is the *integrative* orientation or the interest in the other ethnic group for its own sake which is significant, as with the child who seeks communication with its environment and the assimilation of its ways of behaving. The *instrumental* orientation, or a concern with usefulness of a professional or subject-related kind, is considered to be a lesser motivating force.

Attempts to support this hypothesis empirically have met with problems since the beginning of the 1970s. When, among a group of Canadian pupils in their ninth, tenth and eleventh years of schooling, the integrative orientation increased among successful learners of French (a result which should not really happen, since it should remain the same from the beginning), the change was explained in terms of the reward-giving and strengthening effect of language acquisition. The fall in integrative orientation observed simultaneously among those who want to drop out of French and to reject French-Canadians is, however, not similarly accounted for in terms of unsatisfactory learning experiences (Gardner and Smythe, 1975).

The observation that, in the course of an exchange programme, on the one hand the participants' attitudes towards the French improve to a highly significant degree while on the other hand their integrative orientation lies much below that measured before their intercultural contact, this is described as 'paradoxical'. At the same time, contrary to all expectations, there occurs no significant change in the wish to learn French and in attitudes towards the target language (Gardner, 1974: 270–4). There is a lack of critical **EVALUATION** of the affective and cognitive processing of the experience of Otherness, even though there are sufficient indications that visits to the

target language community have to be well prepared from a geographic, historical, and contemporary political and everyday culture perspective if they are not to become a source of misunderstandings and disappointments, strengthening or even making worse existing attitudes (cf. Amir, 1969).

It seems to be just as problematic to maintain the priority of integrative over instrumental orientation. Indian Marati-speaking high school students learn English for utilitarian reasons above all, and report no need to identify with English-speaking compatriots (Lukmani, 1972), and Chinese students residing in the **USA** clearly have no intention to stay in the country longer than necessary, despite their excellent knowledge of English (Oller *et al.*, 1977).

The contradictory data led to a fundamental debate about the interrelation between success and attitudes, verbal intelligence and linguistic **COMPETENCE**. For the time being it ended in the socio-educational model. Clearly, motivation is still considered to be a central driving force whose social dimension mirrors the reactions of the individual to out-groups in general and to the target language country in particular. However, in the final analysis, it is still the attitudes of the learners to the target language community which count (Gardner, 1985: 146).

In comparison to the position taken by Gardner and Lambert in 1972, which has strongly been adhered to (e.g. Crookes and Schmidt, 1991: 469–512), this is more moderate and differentiated in so far as attitudes are no longer an unchangeable constant but can develop within a complex of factors. This emerging interactive view requires a closer look at the concept of attitudes itself.

## The holistic hypothesis

In social **PSYCHOLOGY**, two basic positions can be distinguished. One can be traced back to the **BEHAVIOURIST** approach and sees attitudes as learned stimulus–response relationships which correspond with a person's observed behaviour. The other refers to an intervening variable between stimulus and response, to a hidden inner psychological process, which cannot be observed and which influences behaviour in the form of a disposition to act. Attitudes as preconditions or readiness for behaviour can exist in all shapes and forms, from the most hidden traces of forgotten habits to the impulse which immediately provokes action.

The still-valid definition of attitude as ' . . . a mental and neural state of readiness, organized through experience, exerting a directive or dynamic influence upon the individual's response to all objects and situations with which it is related' (Allport, 1971: 13) raises similar issues to those raised by empirical research designs. To what extent are attitudes linked to learned experiences? Do they have a direct-cognitive, or rather a dynamic-motivational, influence? What organisation underpins them? Do they represent readiness to respond, or reactions? Do they belong to the mental or the neural system? Or do they represent a continuous system of motivational, emotional, perceptual and cognitive processes with respect to a quite specific aspect of the perceptual world of the individual? There are no conclusive answers to these, any more than to the question of a reliable measurement of this hypothetical construct.

Thus, existing methods of testing attempt, on the one hand, to measure the direction of attitudes as acceptance or rejection of an object (person, group or institution), and on the other to establish their intensity. Furthermore, those methods attempt to establish the status of attitudes within the personal hierarchy of values, their function within individual perception, their consistency with dominant collective opinions, and their susceptibility to social desirability. Moreover, they are multidimensional. They consist of three components: an affective, feeling-based evaluative component; a cognitive, epistemological component affecting beliefs; and a conative component affecting readiness for action. None the less they can only be justified in terms of belief statements and actions. Thus it cannot be said with absolute certainty to what extent they reflect temporary sets, or firmly anchored attitudes, to what extent they are self-determined or Other-determined, represent personal maxims for action or social role expectations, and whether they coincide with actual behaviour. Given the manifold content and multi-level integration of attitudes, it seems that the processing of them can only be holistic so that:

During a task its states of satisfaction, of disappointment, of enthusiasm, just as feelings of tiredness, exertion, boredom etc. play a role. At the end of a task, there can arise feelings of success or of failure, or even aesthetic feelings. There is no such thing as a purely affective state free of cognitive elements.

(Mandl and Huber, 1983: 17)

In the individual, who functions as a psychological unit, affective and cognitive processes are complementary to each other, as was already noted in Aristotle's *Rhetoric*. Piaget (1953) deals with this idea from a developmental perspective. Taxonomic research takes it over with respect to the debate about learning **OBJECTIVES** (Krathwohl, Bloom and Masia, 1967). In psychological, linguistic and anthropological research the 'cognitive turn' begun in the 1960s has given way to an increased interest in the role of the affective domain in group interactions, and in its place in feats of memory, expectations, self-evaluations and attributions. Meanwhile it has reached its apogee in the thesis of the inseparability of the rational and the emotional mind (Goleman, 1996: 10).

Either/or thinking, such as that which has dominated the research designs concerned with the interrelation between attitudes and language learning for decades, can only lead to a dead end. It should at last make way for an interdependent perspective, as was already suggested in 1980:

A pupil, starting with a foreign language at school, approaches his new subject with certain attitudes. In the course of his language study, his level of achievement and the acquisition process itself can have their repercussions on his attitudinal system, particularly if failure or success is involved. These attitudes, which need not remain affective but may overlap with the cognitive domain and may even become conative – thereby ceasing to be *set* only – could at the same time act as stimuli for certain phases within the learning process and thus function again as a kind of instantaneous orientation. Accordingly, it seems justifiable to argue that the development of real competence in a second language depends to a certain degree on a dialectic interrelationship between the acquisition process and permanent as well as short-term values.

(Hermann, 1980: 250)

The mutual dependence dynamic of attitudes and language learning requires, in its affective and cognitive synergy, a holistic interpretation. This affects the learner not only with respect to the processing of information and identification with people or groups, but also with respect to motives and the relationship between language and culture, and their place within the existing linguistic and cultural diversity. If the focus is on increasing one's knowledge, then it is to be expected that there will be changes in attitudes as a consequence of the need to understand relationships. If it is a question of adaptation, then it will be the avoidance of punishment and the desire to be rewarded which will be foregrounded. If the issue is self-assertion, then everything which makes the individual's feeling of well-being the centre of interest will tend to modify persuasions. If it is a matter of self-representation, then elements of knowledge which correspond with one's own beliefs, and thereby create a sense of satisfaction, are more likely to be accepted (Triandis, 1975: 254ff).

None of this happens without forms of social influence such as compliance, identification and internalisation (Kelman, 1970). Attitudes only have a chance of becoming permanent if cognitions are experienced as personally relevant and become a part of the personality, instead of getting stuck in the system of social role expectations. This kind of processing takes place at the level of internalisation, where affective and cognitive processes blend together and mark human action. Language and content are similarly inseparably interwoven. Communicative competence as the key to the understanding of Otherness presupposes familiarity with linguistic means, but also requires an intimate knowledge of genetic, territorial, linguistic, economic, religious, cultural and political entities. Each target language community can only be grasped in the context of cultural and linguistic diversity. This serves 'to make systems on the one hand more multifaceted and on the other hand more stable and less prone to disruption' (Huschke-Rhein, 1989: 219). The insight that, in the macrocosm and in the microcosm, everything is intertwined with everything else may help to escape an uncritical linguicism which falls prey only too easily to the dominant perception of English. It could also, in a multicultural language landscape, contribute to making the ambivalent relationship between attitudes and language learning less disruptive.

**See also:** Acquisition and teaching; Language awareness; Motivation; Motivation theories; Second language acquisition theories

## References

Allport, G.W. (1971) 'Attitudes', in K. Thomas (ed.), *Attitudes and behaviour*, Harmondsworth: Penguin.

Amir, Y. (1969) 'Contact hypothesis in ethnic relations', *Psychological Bulletin* 7: 319–42.

Burstall, C. (1974) *Primary French in the balance*, Slough: National Foundation for Educational Research.

Candelier, M. and Hermann-Brennecke, G. (1993) *Entre le choix et l'abandon: les langues étrangères à l'école, vues d'Allemagne et de France*, Paris: Didier.

Crookes, G. and Schmidt, R.W. (1991) 'Motivation: reopening the research agenda', *Language Learning* 41: 469–512.

Gardner, R.C. (1974) 'Bicultural excursion programs: their effects on students' stereotypes, attitudes and motivation', *The Alberta Journal of Educational Research* 20: 270–7.

Gardner, R.C. (1985) *Social psychology and second language learning. The role of attitudes and motivation*, London: Edward Arnold.

Gardner, R.C. and Lambert, W.E. (1972) *Attitudes and motivation in second-language learning*, Rowley, MA: Newbury Publishers.

Gardner, R.C. and Smythe, P.C. (1975), 'Motivation and second-language acquisition', *Canadian Modern Language Review* 31: 218–30.

Geisler, W. (1978) *Die Erforschung fremdsprachlicher Leistung mit statistischen Methoden und Verfahren der elektronischen Datenverarbeitung – dargestellt am Beispiel des Englischunterrichts Hauptschule*, Frankfurt, Bern, New York, Paris: Peter Lang.

Geisler, W. (1987) *Die anglistische Fachdidaktik als Unterrichtswissenschaft. Zur empirischen Erforschung der*

*Lernbedingungen und des Lernerfolgs im Englischunterricht*, Frankfurt/Main: Peter Lang.

Goleman, D. (1996) *Emotional intelligence*, New York: Bantam Books.

Hermann, G. (1978) *Lernziele im affektiven Bereich. Eine empirische Untersuchung zu den Beziehungen zwischen Englischunterricht und Einstellungen von Schülern*, Paderborn: Schöningh.

Hermann, G. (1980) 'Attitudes and success in children's learning of English as a second language: the motivational vs. the resultative hypothesis', *English Language Teaching Journal* 34: 247–55.

Heuer, H. (1976) 'Zur Motivation im Englischunterricht. Die Ergebnisse einer empirischen Untersuchung', in G. Solmecke (ed.), *Motivation im Fremdsprachenunterricht*, Paderborn: Schöningh.

Humboldt, W. von (1907) 'Über die Verschiedenheit des menschlichen Sprachbaus', in A. Leitzmann (ed.), *Wilhelm von Humboldts Werke*, Berlin: Behr's Verlag, Bd. VIII, 1. Hälfte.

Huschke-Rhein, R. (1989) *Systemische Pädagogik*, Bd. III, Cologne: Rhein-Verlag.

Jones, W.R. (1949) 'Attitudes towards Welsh as a second language: a preliminary investigation', *British Journal of Educational Psychology* 19: 44–52.

Jones, W.R. (1950) 'Attitudes towards Welsh as a second language: a further investigation', *British Journal of Educational Psychology* 20: 117–32.

Jordan, D. (1941) 'The attitude of central school pupils to certain school subjects, and the correlation between attitude and attainment", *British Journal of Educational Psychology* 11: 28–44.

Kelman, H.C. (1970) 'Three processes of social influence', in M. Jahoda and N. Warren (eds), *Attitudes*, Harmondsworth: Penguin.

Krathwohl, D.R., Bloom, B.S. and Masia, B.B. (1967) *Taxonomy of educational objectives. Handbook II: Affective domain*, New York: David McKay.

Lukmani, Y.M. (1972) 'Motivation to learn and learning proficiency', *Language Learning* 22: 261–72.

Mandl, H. and Huber, G.L. (1983) 'Theoretische Grundpositionen zum Verhältnis von Emotion und Kognition', in H. Mandl and G.L. Huber (eds), *Emotion und Kognition*, Munich: Urban und Schwarzenberg.

Oller, J.W., Hudson, A.J. and Fiu, P.F. (1977) 'Attitudes and attained proficiency in ESL: a sociolinguistic study of native speakers of Chinese in the United States', *Language Learning* 27: 1–29.

Piaget, J. (1953) 'Les relations entre l'intelligence et l'affectivité dans le développement de l'enfant', *Bulletin de psychologie* 1: 143–50 and 346–61.

Sapir, E. (1970) 'The status of linguistics as a science', in D.G. Mandelbaum (ed.), *Culture, language and personality*, Berkeley: University of California Press.

Savignon, S.J. (1972) *Communicative competence: an experiment in foreign-language teaching*, Philadelphia: Center for Curriculum Development.

Triandis, H.C. (1975) *Einstellungen und Einstellungsänderungen*, Weinheim: Beltz.

Whorf, B.L. (1978) 'Language, mind and reality', in J.B. Carroll (ed.), *Language, thought and reality. Selected writings of Benjamin Lee Whorf*, Cambridge, MA: MIT Press.

**Further reading**

Gardner, R.C. (1985) *Social psychology and second language learning. The role of attitudes and motivation*, London: Edward Arnold.

Goleman, D. (1996) *Emotional intelligence*, New York: Bantam Books.

Hermann, G. (1980) 'Attitudes and success in children's learning of English as a second language: the motivational vs. the resultative hypothesis', *English Language Teaching Journal* 34: 247–55.

GISELA HERMANN-BRENNECKE

# Audiolingual method

A method of language teaching developed in the United States and dominant in the 1960s, based on **STRUCTURAL LINGUISTICS** and **BEHAVIOURIST** psychology, audiolingual language teaching emphasised the learning of spoken language (it was initially called the aural–oral method) and the presentation of language in the order 'hearing–speaking–reading–writing'. The A-L method was associated with the introduction of the **LANGUAGE LABORATORY**.

The procedures of the A-L method typically involve (see Brooks, 1964; Rivers, 1964):

- the presentation of a short text, usually a dialogue, with a parallel text in the learners' language; this text is modelled by the teacher and repeated by the learners until memorised;
- learners are presented with drill **EXERCISES** or 'pattern practice', consisting of a number of sentences with the same grammatical structure but different lexical items, and they are required to repeat and modify these sentences, receiving immediately the correct version against which to compare their suggestion. These drills are often provided in the language laboratory;
- learners are provided with a substitution table where they can see the parallels in the sentences they have drilled and the underlying grammatical structure involved. This may also provide grammatical terminology;
- learners are invited to role-play dialogues similar to the original one, but they are required to modify the language they have memorised according to the circumstances of the role-play;
- exercises in **READING** and **WRITING** are introduced using the same grammatical constructions and lexis as they have been using in the spoken mode.

The origins of the A-L method are usually traced to the introduction of the 'Army Specialized Training Program' from 1943 in the United States, in response to the need in the armed forces to communicate with the Allies and other foreign peoples. The American school system had provided very little foreign language teaching and had concentrated on introducing learners to written texts rather than spoken language. The ASTP called upon well-known linguists, such as Leonard **BLOOMFIELD** (1942), who developed intensive courses in some fifteen languages taught to selected and highly motivated personnel in groups of ten over 9-month periods with fifteen hours of instruction a week. The methods used included, initially, twelve hours of oral work with **NATIVE SPEAKERS** and three hours of **GRAMMAR** work with professional linguists, with use of audio-visual aids. The success of 'the **AMERICAN ARMY METHOD**', as it came to be known, cannot be attributed only to the methods involved, which were in any case eclectic, but rather to the conditions of learning and the nature of the learners, whose **MOTIVATION** was high and who concentrated almost exclusively on language learning during the intensive period.

Interest in changing language teaching in the general education system began to develop in the early 1950s (Rivers, 1964: 3) but was given a major boost by the general response to the launching of the satellite Sputnik by the Soviet Union. This created a fear that the US education system was inadequate with respect to science and language teaching, and led to the National Defense Education Act which included the Language Development Program. The 'Army Method' served as a model with respect to the emphasis on the spoken language, the use of mechanical aids, the analysis of language in structuralist terms, and the reference to behaviourist psychology for a theory of language learning. Language teaching theorists, such as Brooks (1960 and 1964), promoted what became known as the A-L method, arguing that language is behaviour, that learning a language is learning how to behave rather than learning how to explain its grammar, that behaviour is best learned through the formation of appropriate habits which can be 'overlearned' to the point of becoming automatic by frequent *imitation* of the teacher or a recorded voice and *memorisation* of dialogues or key sentences. This was called the 'mim-mem' method. The language laboratory, being developed in the early 1960s, offered a useful means of providing 'mim-mem' exercises. Dialogues and key sentences were chosen to represent significant syntactic structures of the language, and to anticipate the structures which **CONTRASTIVE ANALYSIS** of the foreign language and the learner's own had shown to be difficult because different.

Criticisms of the A-L method by language teaching theorists focused on its psychological foundations. **RIVERS** published a review in 1964 which, whilst not rejecting the A-L method, argued against too much reliance on the behaviourism of B.F. Skinner, and advocated the introduction of the work of 'neo-behaviourists' such as Osgood and Mowrer, in order both to take account of learners' perceptions of their goals and ensure that language be learned in a rich cultural context, and 'to do justice to "meaning" in the foreign language as well as to manipulative skill' (Rivers, 1964: 139).

Rivers also suggested that there was little support for the taboo on the written word in the first stages of the learning process, imposed by the order of 'hearing–speaking–reading–writing'.

A much stronger criticism of behaviourism as represented by Skinner came from Noam **CHOMSKY** at a large meeting of language teachers in 1965, in which he dismissed the theories of language learning on which the A-L method was founded (Chomsky, 1966). Chomsky argued that behaviourist theory, with its explanation of language acquisition in terms of habit formation through stimulus from children's linguistic environment and reinforcement of correct response, could not possibly account for the ability to generate an infinite number of utterances from a finite grammatical **COMPETENCE**. Behaviourism could not account for the 'creativity' of human language.

Other criticisms of a more pragmatic nature were put forward: learners became bored with drills and pattern practice; the move from repetition and closely guided re-use of learned structures to spontaneous re-use of those same structures was not clearly specified; contrastive analysis did not anticipate and eradicate all the errors learners made; **MATERIALS** and the method itself appeared to provide only for the first few years of learning, and not for intermediate and advanced learners.

The influence of the A-L method beyond the United States was felt in Western European countries to differing degrees, and was modified by the parallel development in **FRANCE** of the **AUDIO-VISUAL** method, and the combination of the tenets of audiolingualism with other techniques and principles. In Britain, for example, the two methods are often treated as similar and related in procedures, whatever differences there might be in origins and theories of language and language learning (Bennett, 1974; Hawkins, 1987). The decline of the A-L method and of A-L **TEXTBOOKS** can be traced to the attacks on its psychological base in the mid-1960s, and the development of **COMMUNICATIVE LANGUAGE TEACHING** from the 1970s. The lasting influence of the A-L method can be traced, like that of other methods, in the rules-of-thumb handed down in the teaching profession, such as the order of presentation of new language, but no systematic use of the method is to be found any longer.

**See also:** Audio-visual language teaching; Behaviourism; Direct method History: after 1945'History: after 1945; History: after 1945; Intercultural competence;

## References

Bennett, W.A. (1974) *Applied linguistics and language learning*, London: Hutchinson.

Bloomfield, L. (1942) *Outline guide for the practical study of foreign languages*, Baltimore: Linguistic Society of America.

Brooks, N. (1960) *Language and language learning. Theory and practice*, New York: Harcourt, Brace and World.

Brooks, N. (1964) *Language and language learning. Theory and practice* (2nd edn), New York: Harcourt, Brace and World.

Chomsky, N. (1966) 'Address to the Northeast Conference', in J.P.B. Allen and S.P. Corder (eds), *The Edinburgh Course in applied linguistics*, Oxford: Oxford University Press.

Hawkins, E. (1987) *Modern languages in the curriculum*, Cambridge: Cambridge University Press.

Rivers, W. (1964) *The psychologist and the foreign language teacher*, Chicago: University of Chicago Press.

## Further reading

Brooks, N. (1960) *Language and language learning. Theory and practice*, New York: Harcourt, Brace and World.

Brooks, N. (1964) *Language and language learning. Theory and practice* (2nd edn), New York: Harcourt, Brace and World.

Puren, C. (1988) *Histoire des méthodologies de l'enseignement des langues* (History of language teaching methods), Paris: Clé International.

Rivers, W. (1964) *The psychologist and the foreign language teacher*, Chicago: University of Chicago Press.

Stack, E. (1960) *The language laboratory and modern language teaching*, New York: Oxford University Press.

MICHAEL BYRAM

# Audio-visual language teaching

Audio-visual language teaching is a method which is based on the coordinated use of visual and auditive technical media. It exists in 'strong' versions in which the simultaneous use of pictorial and auditive material is dominant, and in 'weak' versions in which pictorial and auditive materials are used only as a component within language instruction or, more frequently, with both elements dissociated from each other. The best-known implementation of the 'strong' variant is the *Méthode Structuro-Globale Audio-Visuelle* (SGAV) which was developed in the 1950s simultaneously at the University of Zagreb (under the direction of Petar Guberina) and at the École Normale Supérieure in Saint Cloud, France (in the institution which was predecessor to the **CRÉDIF**, under the direction of Paul Rivenc). The prototype is the audio-visual course *Voix et Images de France* (1961). This classical form of the audio-visual method is strictly **MONO-LINGUAL** and puts great emphasis on basic oral **SKILLS**, whereas **READING** and **WRITING** are only introduced after a considerable time delay. The choice of **VOCABULARY** and grammatical structures is based on **LE FRANÇAIS FONDAMENTAL**.

The audio-visual method is often linked to the audiolingual method because both methods use tape-recorders, work mainly with dialogues and were presented as scientifically-based methods during the 1960s. This affinity exists, however, only in a certain number of courses. Most SGAV methodologists reject pattern practice, and some even have a sceptical attitude towards the **LANGUAGE LABORATORY**. The A-V method not only has a closer relationship to the **DIRECT METHOD**, but it can even be seen as an offshoot of this approach. The common ground between the direct method and the A-V method consists not only in the use of visual media together with the monolingual principle, but also in similarities in the typical procedure of a particular teaching unit. There are none the less some differences. The direct method is, above all, descriptive, whilst the A-V method is oriented towards dialogues. The direct method frequently uses complex single pictures, whereas the A-V method uses sequences of pictures in which a single picture corresponds to

only one sentence or even to part of a sentence. Furthermore, the picture-based direct method is a relatively open methodological variant which can be complemented by real or artificial objects and by the reading of lesson texts, whereas the classic A-V method represents a closed method with precisely stipulated teaching techniques (Besse, 1985; Puren, 1988; Reinfried, 1992).

The typical procedures of the 'strong' version of the A-V method can be traced back to the prototype A-V course *Voix et Images de France* (CRÉDIF, 1961):

- Each teaching unit is introduced by a *presentation phase*, in which dialogue with approximately 30 pictures is presented twice to the learners. The pictures are projected onto a screen as slides for about one second before the corresponding verbal text. Then there can be a first repetition of parts of the text by the learners.
- In the following *explanatory phase* the pupils' general and incomplete understanding is deepened and improved by the teacher using monolingual semanticisation techniques (e.g., pointing at details of the picture, the use of mime and gesture, paraphrase). This should not be given just in the form of a presentation by the teacher but should be made as interactive as possible by taking the form of a classroom conversation. The lexical understanding of learners was made more difficult in the 1960s and 1970s because many audio-visual methodologists refused to give not only translations but even *analytical* monolingual explanation procedures.
- The tape-recorder is used again in an *imitation phase*. The learners repeat the passages of dialogue (singly or in chorus), and their **PRONUNCIATION** is corrected.
- During the *exploitation phase* the learners continue to absorb the dialogues. The teacher asks questions about individual pictures or the learners ask each other questions. Finally, the learners attempt to present the dialogue in role-play, during which the pictures are at first still used as stimuli.
- At the end of the teaching unit there is a *transposition phase*. The learners are supposed as

far as possible to use the language material in new situations. This can be, for example, free conversation or the creation of a new dialogue.

Shorter picture sequences with familiar vocabulary can be added for grammatical or phonetic **EX-ERCISES** (Renard and van Vlasselaer, 1976; Schiffler, 1973).

The linguist Petar Guberina (1964, 1984) developed approaches which were directed towards a structural–global learning theory. He starts with a concept of structure as developed in the first half of the twentieth century (especially in Germany and **FRANCE**) within the context of a holistic theory of language and the psychological *gestalt* theory. The act of linguistic understanding is for Guberina primarily a holistic process, from which the *valeur* of the individual structure is interpreted. At the level of expression, suprasegmental factors (intonation, prosody, intensity) become superimposed onto the phonological information, and, at the level of content, lexical meanings and sentence meanings are both complemented and modified by the context (speech situation, interpersonal relationships, mime, gesture). It is for this reason that the presentation of language should always have its starting point in the whole situation (including affective components) whereby the external speech context is conveyed by an illustration. This emphasis on globality applies to both the reception and the production of all the structures: linguistic units (whether sounds, lexemes or grammatical structures) should be presented to learners only in a situational or textual context, i.e. they should neither be isolated nor analysed in the classroom.

The principle of globality together with the monolingual approach can, however, hinder the processing of language. Empirical investigations of A-V courses have shown that a holistic, situation-related semanticisation is not sufficient to explain linguistic statements clearly. A correct understanding of the meaning was attained for only about a third of foreign language sentences, and elements which were missing or provided by the learners themselves were demonstrated in a further third, whereas gross distortions of meaning were found in the final third (Guénot, 1964: 133ff; Germain, 1976: 53ff). These results demonstrate the limitations of picture sequences as means of semantic transmission. In order to increase the semanticisation potential in the pictures, 'pictures within pictures' like speech bubbles were used in almost every second picture, even during the early period of A-V methods. Then, at the beginning of the 1970s, several language courses appeared with numerous coded pictures which were enriched with symbols or even took the form of picture puzzles. The A-V **FRENCH** course *Le français et la vie* (Mauger and Bruézière, 1971) represents the apex of this development. Thus, in the picture presented here (Figure 6), Henri on the left (who, as the speaker, is highlighted with a darker silhouette) asks Michel in the middle whether his wife works at the JAL company. The hammer is used here as a general symbol for work (though in fact Michel's wife is a typist), the schematic representation of the house symbolises the firm, and the rectangular shape of the 'speech bubble' symbolises the reference to the present in the verbal statement (there are other shapes of speech bubble used in the course for future and past). However, attempts of this kind to change pictures to ideograms were not successful in the longer term because they failed to improve on the comprehensibility of the verbal statements (Reinfried, 1990).

SGAV methods reached the peak of their international recognition in the 1970s. Empirical investigations of the CRÉDIF courses and other A-V courses were carried out in several countries to study their feasibility in state schools. The school experiments carried out in the Federal Republic of Germany came overwhelmingly to the conclusion that, despite some advantages in A-V methods, there were major disadvantages caused by the following four factors: the inadequate support of oral teaching by the lack of written materials; the exclusive limitation to dialogues in **BEGINNER** classes; the neglect of writing skills; and in part also the failure to develop grammatical awareness in learners. Furthermore, there were a number of critical voices raised against the rigidity of the sequencing of the courses, which left no room for creativity in learners and teachers (Firges and Pelz, 1976; Schiffler, 1976).

Some A-V methodologists reacted to this criticism by varying the sequencing, and no longer beginning the lesson with the A-V presentation phase but by encouraging pupils to express

*Henri*  Ta femme aussi travaille chez Jal?

Figure 6  'Coded' pictures in audio-visual language teaching
Source  Mauger and Bruézière, 1971: 88, fig. 19

hypotheses about the contents of the pictures. Moreover the **COMMUNICATIVE** revolution of the 1970s led to a structured progression based on communicative functions in A-V courses, and to a stronger emphasis on free expression. Role-play with physical actions was now introduced more often into A-V courses; writing as an independent skill was given greater value; and the purely oral phase of the course was reduced. In the 1980s, American alternative methods became an important influence on some A-V courses. The pressure on learners to express themselves from the very beginning of the first teaching units was rejected on the basis of the concept of delayed oral practice, and grammatical progression was made more flexible. Some A-V courses now recommended that the imitation phase should be abandoned and suggested instead the introduction of group activities, games and **TOTAL PHYSICAL RESPONSE**. Some methodologists also re-defined SGAV meth-

ods, in the context of these re-orientations, in constructivist and interactionist terms.

Despite all these efforts at reform, A-V methods did not manage, on the whole, to maintain their foothold in state schools. There is no doubt that in the 1970s they contributed significantly to the priority of dialogues over descriptive and narrative texts in newly published textbooks. Furthermore, many textbook publishers made an effort at the time to produce visual and audio media as additional and optional materials for foreign language teaching. However, on the whole, A-V methods in their 'strong' version were limited to intensive courses for all age groups and **ADULT** education. Courses following SGAV methods appeared in 13 languages.

In 1978, Paul Rivenc founded an international SGAV association which still organises seminars and methodology publications. Its members are mainly in France, Belgium, **AUSTRALIA**, Spain,

CANADA, Yugoslavia and Germany. Although the A-V method persists, it has disappeared from the centre of the methodology agenda. At the beginning of the twenty-first century, it exists only in a 'weakened' form in textbooks and courses, in which picture sequences and LISTENING dialogues no longer have a key role. Moreover, listening and visual material written for teaching purposes has been complemented by AUTHENTIC materials in A-V courses. The semanticising function of the picture has decreased in importance, whereas the intercultural–situational function of the picture and the creative verbal element with picture sequences has gained in relevance. Video films compete with static picture sequences. None the less, the A-V method in a developed form may yet experience a renaissance in the context of (CALL) COMPUTER ASSISTED LANGUAGE LEARNING.

**See also:** Audiolingual method; CRÉDIF; French; History: after 1945; Monolingual principle; Psychology

### References

Besse, H. (1985) *Méthodes et pratiques des manuels de langue*, Paris: Didier.

CRÉDIF (ed.) (1961) *Voix et images de France. Méthode rapide de français*, Paris: Didier.

Firges, J. and Pelz, M. (eds) (1976) *Innovationen des audio-visuellen Fremdsprachenunterrichts. Bestandsaufnahme und Kritik*, Frankfurt/Main: Diesterweg.

Germain, C. (1976) 'L'image dans l'apprentissage des langues', *Communication et langages* 29: 51–68.

Guberina, P. (1964) 'The audio-visual global and structural method', in B. Libbish (ed.), *Advances in the teaching of modern languages*, Vol. 1, Oxford: Pergamon Press, 1–17.

Guberina, P. (1984) 'Bases théoriques de la méthode audio-visuelle structuro-globale (méthode Saint-Cloud Zagreb). Une linguistique de la parole', in D. Coste (ed.), *Aspects d'une politique de diffusion du français langue étrangère depuis 1945. Matériaux pour une histoire*, Paris: Hatier.

Guénot, J. (1964) *Pédagogie audio-visuelle des débuts de l'anglais. Une expérience d'enseignement à des adultes*, Paris: S.A.B.R.I.

Mauger, G. and Bruézière, M. (1971) *Le français et la vie*, Vol. 1, Paris: Hachette.

Puren, C. (1988) *Histoire des méthodologies de l'enseignement des langues*, Paris: Clé International.

Reinfried, M. (1990) 'Bilder als Bedeutungsmittler im Fremdsprachenunterricht', *Lehren und Lernen* 16, 6: 45–80.

Reinfried, M. (1992) *Das Bild im Fremdsprachenunterricht. Eine Geschichte der visuellen Medien am Beispiel des Französischunterrichts*, Tübingen: Narr.

Renard, R. and van Vlasselaer, J.-J. (1976) *Foreign language teaching with an integrated methodology: the SGAV methodology*, Paris: Didier.

Schiffler, L. (1973) (2nd edn 1976) *Einführung in den audio-visuellen Fremdsprachenunterricht*, Heidelberg: Quelle und Meyer.

### Further reading

Besse, H. (1974) 'Signes iconiques, signes linguistiques', *Langue française* 24: 27–54.

Germain, C. (1993) 'La méthode SGAV', in C. Germain, *Evolution de l'enseignement des langues: 5,000 ans d'histoire*, Paris: Clé International.

Renard, C. and Heinle, C.H. (1969) *Implementing 'Voix et Images de France'*, Part I: *In American schools and colleges*, Philadelphia and New York: Chilton Books.

Renard, R. (1993) *Variations sur la problématique SGAV. Essais de didactique des langues*, Paris: Didier.

Rivenc, P. (1991) 'La problématique SGAV (Structuro-Globale Audio-Visuelle) aujourd'hui', *Revue de phonétique appliquée* 100/101: 121–32.

MARCUS REINFRIED

# Australia

Language teaching in Australia has been linked, since European settlement in 1778, with fluctuations in the political climate, and characterised by the country's geographical location, its cultural diversity, and inherent tensions between monolingualism and multilingualism (Lo Bianco, 1997). Clyne (1991) identifies four phases marking different periods of Australian language policy, whether implicit or explicit, and their concomitant implications for language education: the laissez-faire (up to the mid-1870s); the tolerant but restrictive (1870s to early 1900s); the rejecting (circa 1914 to circa 1970); and the accepting – even fostering (from the early 1970s). These phases encompass educational changes in **ENGLISH** as a second language for immigrant groups, Languages Other Than English (LOTEs), Aboriginal languages and Australian English. Language policy developments in Australia culminated in the publication of the National Policy on Languages (Lo Bianco, 1987) and The Australian Language and Literacy Policy (Department of Employment, Education and Training, 1991), both of which have had a major impact on language education in Australia in the 1990s.

## Phase 1: Up to the mid-1870s

Clyne (1991: 4), notes an 'accepting but laissez-faire' attitude during this period towards the use of languages other than English. The Australian colonies varied in the extent to which they perceived themselves as mono- or multilingual, but there was little political interference in the use of their own languages by different ethnic groups – **GERMAN**, **FRENCH**, Gaelic – for educational, business and cultural purposes. Such acceptance, however, did not extend to Aboriginal languages which were persistently viewed negatively (Fesl, 1988, cited in Clyne, 1991).

## Phase 2: 1870s–early 1900s

With the establishment in the latter part of the nineteenth century of English-medium schools, a 'tolerant but restrictive' (Clyne, 1991: 5) **ATTITUDE** towards the use of languages other than English emerged. Limitations placed on the teaching of languages in some states were paralleled by increasing Australian identification with English monolingualism, especially in the face of growing world political tensions.

## Phase 3: circa 1914–circa 1970

The aftermath of World War One brought a 'xenophobic' and 'rejecting' phase, during which an 'aggressive monolingualism' (Clyne, 1991: 5) was in evidence. Australia was intent on affirming its political status as a newly independent nation and part of the British Commonwealth. The

assimilationist 'White Australia' policies, which persisted throughout the periods of mass immigration post-World War Two and into the early 1970s, meant that non-English-speaking groups entering Australia during this time faced considerable restrictions on their ability to maintain and teach their own languages.

Lingering Education Act legislation dating back to World War One prevented **BILINGUAL** education in some states, while a pro-British bias sustained political and social preferences for monolingualism. Such languages as were taught in secondary schools, primarily French and German and, to a lesser extent, classical languages, were viewed as part of a liberal education modelled on the British system and as academic disciplines for the purpose of university entrance (Ozolins, 1993: 15). Little attempt was made to introduce the teaching of the languages of major immigrant groups and the language **SKILLS** they brought were largely overlooked. Large-scale facilities were, however, set in place for the learning of English by **ADULT** immigrants through the Commonwealth government-funded Adult Migrant English Program (AMEP), a national settlement programme established in 1949 which continues to the present time.

Clyne (1991) estimates that, of approximately 250 indigenous Aboriginal languages, 100 were lost during this period, which saw forced assimilation and 'a stolen generation' of Aboriginal children removed from their communities (National Inquiry into the Separation of Aboriginal and Torres Strait Islander Children from their Families, 1997).

## Phase 4: 1970–2000

This period saw a major shift away from assimilation to multiculturalism and the embracing of a growing Australian linguistic identity. The use of more than 100 'community languages', a term which emerged in 1974 (Clyne, 1991: 6; Kipp, Clyne and Pauwels, 1995) by various Aboriginal and immigrant groups was widely recognised at both government and community levels, and Australia increasingly regarded itself as a multicultural and multilingual society.

A telephone **INTERPRETER** service (TIS), the multicultural Special Broadcasting Service (SBS), and government and public ethnic radio stations were set up, reflecting the greater diversity and acceptance of multilingualism. In the 1990s, up to thirty-eight languages (including Australian **SIGN LANGUAGE** [AUSLAN] and Australian Indigenous Languages) were taught and examined at high school matriculation level, and twenty or more LOTEs at primary school level across different states (Clyne, 1997). The strong associations with Britain gradually eroded and the Australian variety of English was given credence through the work of linguists such as A.G. Mitchell and Arthur Delbridge. The Macquarie Dictionary, first published in 1981, legitimised this work and has provided the standard for Australian English since this time.

Seventeen 'transitional' bilingual Aboriginal programmes were also initiated in the Northern Territory (Fesl, 1988), providing instruction in Aboriginal languages as well as English up to Grade 5. Despite its widely acknowledged success, a political decision in 1999 saw the abolition of this programme by the Northern Territory government and, although pressures to reverse this decision continue, the development signals a broader movement back to monolingual values at the Commonwealth government level (Lo Bianco, 1999).

Accompanying this latter phase of multiculturalism from the mid-1970s was widespread support for a powerful push from ethnic, academic and educational groups for a national language policy which would reflect social justice, access and equity, cultural diversity, and 'ethnic rights'. Lobbying for a national policy accelerated throughout the 1970s through migrant education conferences, which gave rise to the Migrant Education Action Committee, the newly-established Ethnic Communities Councils and alliances of ethnic groups, academics, teacher organisations and trade unions (Clyne, 1991; Wren, 1997).

In response to this lobby, in 1982 the Commonwealth Government commissioned a bipartisan Senate committee to consider the need for a national language policy. The committee's report, A national language policy (Senate Standing Committee on Education and the Arts, 1984), established four guiding principles:

- competence in English for all;
- maintenance and development of languages

other than English, both community and aboriginal languages;
- provision of services in languages other than English;
- opportunities for learning second languages.

These principles laid the foundations for the National Policy on Languages (NPL) (Lo Bianco, 1987), which affirmed the pre-eminence of English while stressing the significance of other languages to Australia in terms of social justice, economic strategies and external relations, and cultural enrichment (Kipp, Clyne and Pauwels, 1995: 4).

While the NPL was underpinned politically and ideologically by responses to ethnic community concerns, the late 1980s saw a shift towards economic and vocational imperatives. The impact of the world recession in Australia was accompanied by a political realignment towards the growing economic power of the Asian region and Australia's location within this region (Nicholas *et al.*, 1993). Following a government review, funding for NPL initiatives ceased, and in 1991 a white paper, *Australia's language: the Australian language and literacy policy* (ALLP) (Department of Employment, Education and Training, 1991). The ALLP set directions for language policymaking, particularly in the teaching of languages in Australia, throughout the 1990s. While it is acknowledged as signalling 'Australia's ongoing commitment to a formally articulated language education policy' (Ingram, 1994: 77), it has also attracted continuing criticism and resistance from educators in comparison with the NPL.

A major criticism arises in relation to the realignment of language teaching towards short-term vocational and economic rationalist goals, which diminished the focus of the NPL on linguistic pluralism, multiculturalism and social equity as well as on economic arguments (Lo Bianco and Freebody, 1997; Ingram, 1994). Whereas the NPL gave broad recognition to community languages and 'languages of wider teaching' (Lo Bianco, 1987: 125), the ALLP required state/territory Ministries of Education to prioritise eight LOTEs from a list of fourteen, including Aboriginal languages, **ARABIC**, **CHINESE**, French, **GERMAN**, Indonesian, Italian, Japanese,

Korean, Modern Greek, Russian, **SPANISH**, Thai and Vietnamese (Clyne, 1997; Ozolins, 1993).

The ALLP also laid greater stress on English and, as its title implies, on literacy, a shift which is perceived as leading to decreased recognition of ESL and LOTE programmes and a diminution of funding to these programmes, particularly in the schools sector (Clyne, 1997; Kipp, Clyne and Pauwels, 1995; Wren, 1997). A change of Commonwealth government from 1996 increased the policy emphasis on (English) literacy and introduced benchmarking of literacy achievement in schools (see the papers in Burns and Hammond, 1999). Issues such as language maintenance, **BILINGUAL EDUCATION** and language services, foregrounded in the NPL, have increasingly been played down at the political level in the 1990s, while the relevance of language learning – particularly of Japanese, (Mandarin) Chinese, Korean and Indonesian – to the competitiveness of the business community is given prominence (Liddicoat, 1996).

Despite these criticisms, among English-speaking nations Australia is generally regarded as unique in developing a national policy that informs and gives official status to language education (Hamilton, 1996; Lo Bianco and Freebody, 1997; Ozolins, 1993; Romaine, 1991). Fishman (1988: 137) comments from a US perspective that 'We are a long way from a positive language policy, such as the one the Australians have … adopted calling for an active second language, either English or a Community Language Other Than English, for every Australian'; and Romaine (1991) regards Australia as leading the way in language policy development.

**See also:** Canada; Heritage languages; Language planning; Mother tongue; United States of America

### Websites

Language Australia: http://langoz.anu.edu.au
National Centre for English Language Teaching and Research: http://nceltr.mq.edu.au

### References

Burns, A. and Hammond J. (eds) (1999) *Prospect: a journal of Australian TESOL* 14, 2. Special issue on ESL and policy, Sydney: National Centre for English Language Teaching and Research.

Clyne, M. (1991) *Community languages: the Australian experience*, Melbourne: Cambridge University Press.

Clyne, M. (1997) 'Language policy in Australia – achievements, disappointments, prospects', *Journal of Intercultural Studies* 18, 1: 63–71.

Department of Employment, Education and Training (1991) *Australia's language: the Australian language and literacy policy*, Vols 1 and 2, Canberra: Australian Government Publishing Service.

Fesl, E. (1988) *Language policy formulation and implementation: an historical perspective on Australian languages*, Unpublished PhD thesis, Monash University.

Fishman, J.A. (1988) ' "English Only" – its ghosts, myths and dangers', *International Journal of the Sociology of Language* 74: 125–40.

Hamilton, J. (1996) *Inspiring innovations in language teaching*, Clevedon: Multilingual Matters.

Ingram, D.E. (1994) 'Language policy and planning in Australia in the 1990s', in R.D. Lambert (ed.), *Language planning around the world: contexts and systemic change*, Washington, DC: The National Foreign Language Center at the Johns Hopkins University.

Kipp, S., Clyne M. and Pauwels, A. (1995) *Immigration and Australia's language resources*, Canberra: Australian Government Publishing Service.

Liddicoat, A. (1996) 'Australia's changing language policy', *Babel* 31, 1: 4–7.

Lo Bianco, J. (1987) *National policy on languages*, Canberra: Australian Government Publishing Service.

Lo Bianco, J. (1997) 'English and pluralistic policies: the case of Australia', in H. Wren and W. Eggington (eds), *Language policy: dominant English, pluralist challenges*, Amsterdam and Melbourne: John Benjamins and Language Australia.

Lo Bianco, J. (1999) 'Policy word: talking bilingual education and ESL into English literacy', *Prospect* 14, 2: 40–51.

Lo Bianco, J. and Freebody, P. (1997) *Australian literacies: informing national policy on literacy education*. Canberra: Language Australia and Commonwealth of Australia.

National Inquiry into the Separation of Aboriginal and Torres Strait Islander Children from their

Families (1997) *Bringing them home: national inquiry into the separation of Aboriginal and Torres Strait Islander children from their families*, Sydney: Human Rights and Equal Opportunity Commission.

Nicholas, H., Moore, H., Clyne, M. and Pauwels, A. (1993) *Languages at the crossroads*, Report of the National Enquiry into the Employment and Supply of Teachers of Languages Other Than English, Canberra: National Languages and Literacy Institute of Australia.

Ozolins, U. (1993) *The politics of language in Australia*, Cambridge: Cambridge University Press.

Romaine, S. (ed.) (1991) *Language in Australia*, Cambridge: Cambridge University Press.

Senate Standing Committee on Education and the Arts (1984) *A national language policy*, Canberra: Commonwealth of Australia.

Wren, H. (1997) 'Making a difference in language policy agendas', in H. Wren and W. Eggington (eds), *Language policy: dominant English, pluralist challenges*, Amsterdam and Melbourne: John Benjamins and Language Australia.

## Further reading

*Australian Language Matters*, published quarterly by Language Australia.

Burns, A. (ed.) (1996) *Prospect: a journal of Australian TESOL*, 11. 2. Special issue on language policy and planning, Sydney: National Centre for English Language Teaching and Research.

Clyne, M. (1992) *Community languages in Australia*. Oxford: Oxford University Press.

Clyne, M., Fernandez, S., Chen, I. and Summo-O'Connell, R. (1997) *Background speakers: diversity and its management in LOTE programs*, Belconnen, ACT: Language Australia.

Moore, H. (1996) 'Language policies as virtual realities: two Australian examples', *TESOL Quarterly* 30, 3: 473–98.

ANNE BURNS

# Authenticity

The interest in the use of authentic **MATERIALS** for language teaching developed during the late 1970s and the early 1980s under the influence of applied linguists such as **WIDDOWSON** (1978), Candlin and Edelhoff (1982) and Breen (1985). The most prominent feature of authenticity is the quality of the language data which is studied or which is used as the core of an activity. Most often this is interpreted to imply the selection for teaching purposes of a text (written or spoken) which was first conceived as a way of communicating amongst **NATIVE SPEAKERS** of a particular language, with no intention on the part of its originators for it to be used as an instrument for teaching that language to learners. The advantage of this approach is felt to lie in the fact that, in authentic texts, the language data is genuine and may be expected to embody characteristics that specially-devised teaching materials often fail to capture or which they distort. This is particularly marked in the area of **LISTENING** comprehension in which the phonological phenomena of natural speech are a factor to be considered along with the choice of words of the speaker or speakers. Where the use of authentic written texts is concerned, a related dimension is the visual means that were originally employed to present the text, so that layout, typeface and headings are considered an integral part of the message as well as any accompanying pictorial or diagrammatic material. Discourse structure is felt to be another important aspect of communication that can best be studied through the use of authentic texts, both spoken and written.

From the outset it was emphasised by innovators in this area that authenticity lay not only in the genuine nature of the texts selected, but also in the relationship of the learner with the text. Thus, using an authentic newspaper article for a purpose far removed from its original intention – which might have been to amuse, inform or shock – by, for example, requiring learners to underline and analyse all the noun-phrases would by many be thought to render the experience inauthentic. Others would say that, provided the first contact with the text had reflected its real-life purpose, it would be legitimate then to use it as an object of study so that the learner could consciously discover the linguistic as well as other means by which the intended effects were conveyed. The analysis of the linguistic features of texts has been much facilitated by the growth of corpus-based computer studies, and a methodological dimension has been opened by the incorporation into **CALL (COMPUTER AS-SISTED LANGUAGE LEARNING)** of corpus-based investigations of authentic texts by learners themselves.

A fundamental issue with the use of authentic texts lies in the quantity of unfamiliar language that they can put before the learner, which is often seen as a measure of difficulty. This has led in some cases to a reluctance to use authentic texts with learners below a certain level of language attainment. An opposite view has been that learners can benefit from contact with texts that are considerably above their attainment level, and that the teacher should grade the task rather than the text, so that a relatively impenetrable text can be given an extremely easy task. Swan (1985a, 1995b) satirised the extremes to which this view has occasionally been taken by both coursebook writers and classroom teachers.

Authenticity is an area in which it is necessary to distinguish the considered contributions of applied linguists and the more thoughtful methodologists from the often diluted or crude interpretations that have been used as the idea has become widely diffused. Publishers of teaching materials have often been accused of distortions of the term, possibly because, for a period in the 1980s, the notion of authenticity became very closely associated with the central tenets of **COMMUNICATIVE** approaches. 'Authentic' became a desirable term to see in the publicity material for new materials, and hybrid and – to many people – self-contradictory terms such as 'semi-authentic' or 'near-authentic' were often used in the descriptions of teaching materials, especially where listening comprehension was concerned. These loose terms often obscured the respectable aims of recording techniques, such as the use of semi-scripted stimuli for speakers, which aims to elicit a stream of speech that reproduces or closely approximates the phenomena of spontaneous speech even though the content and the language of the recording are to a considerable extent pre-planned and controlled. A related issue is whether an authentic **READING** text remains authentic if it is slightly adapted to lessen expected barriers to comprehension. The issue of the quantity and nature of realism in language data is thus a lively one when communicatively-based language learning is under discussion.

A possible resolution to the debate over how to render authentic materials accessible to learners lies in the recognition that not all authentic texts are of equal difficulty, in that there is often a balance between linguistic or discourse unfamiliarity and sources of comprehension support to be found within the same text. It could be legitimate to put major effort into the selection of texts so that the level of challenge they present to a particular class is at a reasonable rather than an unfeasible level. Criteria for judging the level of challenge in relation to particular learners are therefore an issue for teachers and teacher trainers, as well as for applied linguists.

**See also:** Native speaker; Non-native speaker teacher; Study abroad; Teacher thinking

### References

Breen, M. (1985) 'Authenticity in the language classroom', *Applied Linguistics* 6, 1: 66–70.

Candlin, C. and Edelhoff, C. (1982) *Challenges: teacher's handbook*, Harlow: Longman.

Swan, M. (1985a) 'A critical look at the communicative approach (1)', *ELT Journal* 39, 1: 2–12.

Swan, M. (1985b) 'A critical look at the communicative approach (2)', *ELT Journal*, 39, 2: 76–87.

Widdowson, H. (1978) *Teaching language as communication*, Oxford: Oxford University Press.

SHELAGH RIXON

# Autonomy and autonomous learners

Autonomy in language learning depends on the development and exercise of a capacity for detachment, critical reflection, decision making and independent action (see Little, 1991: 4); autonomous learners assume responsibility for determining the purpose, content, rhythm and method of their learning, monitoring its progress and evaluating its outcomes (see Holec, 1981: 3). In **SELF-ACCESS** language learning this may entail learners devising their own learning programmes to suit their particular **NEEDS**; in classrooms it is likely to be a matter of teachers helping learners to become reflective managers of their own learning within the constraints imposed by official curricula and public examinations. Pedagogical measures calculated to foster the development of learner autonomy have much in common with those adopted by collaborative learning and **HUMANISTIC** methods.

Autonomy is the means by which learners in any domain transcend the limitations and constraints of their immediate learning environment. In the case of foreign language learning, this means that autonomous learners are able to apply their learning **SKILLS** in contexts beyond the classroom or other environment in which learning has taken place, but also that they are able to deploy their target language knowledge and skills in autonomous target language use. In other words, the development of autonomy entails the development of a capacity for independence in language use as well as in language learning. In principle these two capacities should interact with one another in a mutually enhancing way.

Learner autonomy engages the metacognitive but also the affective domain. The pedagogical procedures by which its development is fostered give sustained attention to the metacognitive processes of planning, monitoring and evaluating the performance of individual learning tasks and the progress of learning overall. Yet at the same time the learner is engaged affectively, since learning is repeatedly reflected upon and evaluated in terms of individual needs, interests and capacities. Positive **MOTIVATION** is thus central to the development of learner autonomy.

As a general pedagogical concept, learner autonomy accommodates a wide range of teaching and learning techniques. Nevertheless, language pedagogies that are intent on fostering the development of learner autonomy tend to have certain practices in common. For example, to the extent that they recognise the importance of autonomy in language use as well as language learning, they use the target language as the principal channel of teaching and learning. Similarly, their concern with reflection and critical evaluation means that they tend to assign a central role to learner journals and group discussion.

The ideas that cluster around the concept of learner autonomy have also been promoted under other banners – for example, 'humanistic language teaching', 'collaborative learning', 'experiential learning', 'the learning-centred classroom'. What distinguishes 'learner autonomy' from these terms is the fact that it necessarily implies a holistic view of the learner as an individual. It thus reminds teachers that learners bring to the classroom a personal history and personal needs that may have little in common with the assumed background and implied needs on which the curriculum is based. It also reminds them that the ultimate measure of success in second or foreign language learning is the extent to which the target language becomes a fully integrated part of the learner's identity.

Learner autonomy is never absolute. The freedom it entails is always constrained by the interdependence that in part defines the human social condition and thus the nature of human learning. Learners can only ever be autonomous to the extent that their achieved knowledge and skills permit. The capacity for autonomous learning behaviour inevitably varies according to context and task, and learners exercise their autonomy with varying degrees of conscious awareness.

Autonomy was first introduced into discussion about language teaching and learning by Henri Holec's *Autonomy and foreign language learning*, published by the **COUNCIL OF EUROPE** in 1979 (cited as Holec 1981). Holec took his immediate inspiration from the Council of Europe's work in **ADULT** education, which emphasised the importance of equipping adult learners with the knowledge and confidence to participate in the democratic process: 'From the idea of man "product of his society", one moves to the idea of man "producer of his society" ' (Janne, 1977; cited in Holec, 1981: 1). The general educational arguments that lie behind Holec's treatment of autonomy in foreign language learning have much in common with radical theories of education current in the 1970s (e.g., Illich, 1971; Freire, 1972).

A second source of ideas important for the development of thinking about learner autonomy is work on language and communication in the classroom undertaken in the UK in the 1970s. Douglas Barnes's *From communication to curriculum* (1976) is representative of this movement. Although it fits into the same general political picture as Holec's Council of Europe report, the immediate sources for Barnes's book are psychological. Essentially, he argues that if schooling is to have long-term benefits, pupils must be fully engaged in the learning process; this can happen only if they can make connections between the knowledge presented to them in the classroom ('school knowledge') and the knowledge by which they lead their lives outside the classroom ('action knowledge').

A closely similar concern with the relation between learning and forms of discourse arises in studies of child language **ACQUISITION**, especially those that emphasise the social-interactive dimension (see Tizard and Hughes, 1984; Wells, 1985). This encourages the thought that autonomy is central to the process and the outcome of developmental learning; it also provides support for the argument that autonomy develops out of social interaction and interdependence. The exploration of the socio-historical psychology of Vygotsky by educational psychologists is another rich source of insight into the processes that underlie the development of learner autonomy (see, e.g., Tharp and Gallimore, 1988; Moll, 1990).

The concept of learner autonomy is subject to two widespread misinterpretations. First, it is often taken to be a synonym for self-instruction or self-access learning. This is due partly to the historical conjunction of self-access and autonomy in discussion about language learning, and partly to the common-sense assumption that autonomy means independence and independence means learning without a teacher. The second misinterpretation is that autonomy requires learners to work in isolation from one another; this arises in discussion of autonomy in relation to both classroom and self-access language learning.

Perhaps the most frequently voiced criticism of learner autonomy as a general goal in foreign language learning is that it derives from liberal traditions in Western education and thus may be inappropriate in non-Western educational cultures. Attempts to respond to this criticism appeal at once to the universal and the relative in human culture and society, arguing that autonomy is a hallmark of all truly successful learning, but that the discursive

practices by which it is developed are culturally conditioned and thus endlessly variable.

As a general educational ideal, learner autonomy has a long history that has rarely moved far from the liberal mainstream. Perhaps under the impact of radical educational theories, the 1980s saw an increasing tendency for national and regional curricula to include the development of learner autonomy among their core goals, though terms like 'independent learning' and 'critical thinking' are more often used than 'autonomy' itself. Yet the development of learner autonomy is among the most acute challenges that teachers can face, and its thoroughgoing pursuit is likely always to remain a minority interest.

**See also:** Attitudes; Learning to learn; Motivation; Psychology; Self-access

## References

Barnes, D. (1976) *From communication to curriculum*, Harmondsworth: Penguin.

Freire, P. (1972) *Pedagogy of the oppressed*, London: Sheed and Ward.

Holec, H. (1981) *Autonomy and foreign language learning*, Oxford: Pergamon (first published 1979, Strasbourg: Council of Europe).

Illich, I. (1971) *Deschooling society*, New York: Harper and Row.

Little, D. (1991) *Learner autonomy 1: Definitions, issues and problems*, Dublin: Authentik.

Moll, L.C. (ed.) (1990) *Vygotsky and education. Instructional implications and applications of socio-historical psychology*, Cambridge: Cambridge University Press.

Tharp, R. and Gallimore, R. (1988) *Rousing minds to life. Teaching, learning, and schooling in social context*, Cambridge: Cambridge University Press.

Tizard, B. and Hughes, M. (1984) *Young children learning. Talking and thinking at home and at school*, London: Fontana.

Wells, G. (1985) *Language development in the pre-school years*, Cambridge: Cambridge University Press.

## Further reading

Barnes, D. (1976) *From communication to curriculum*, Harmondsworth: Penguin.

Dam, L. (1995) *Learner autonomy 3: From theory to classroom practice*, Dublin: Authentik.

Gremmo, M.-J. and Riley, P. (1995) 'Autonomy, self-direction and self-access in language teaching and learning: the history of an idea', *System* 23, 2: 151–64.

Holec, H. (1981) *Autonomy and foreign language learning*, Oxford: Pergamon (first published 1979, Strasbourg: Council of Europe).

Little, D. (1991) *Learner autonomy 1: Definitions, issues and problems*, Dublin: Authentik.

DAVID LITTLE

# B

## Beginner language learners

A term applied to language learners of any **AGE** in the initial stages of acquisition of a language other than their **MOTHER TONGUE**. A distinction can be made between 'absolute or real' beginners, who exhibit no knowledge of the language (what Stevick, 1986, terms 'pre-beginners') and 'false beginners', who may have experienced previous instruction, incidental exposure to the language, or be self-taught. Their knowledge is 'dormant'.

Beginner learners are by no means a homogeneous group but bring to the classroom diverse backgrounds and highly varied personal characteristics and learning factors. These include:

- the extent of previous experience of second/ foreign language learning;
- age at the time of learning;
- cognitive development;
- existing abilities and knowledge in first and second languages;
- **SPEAKING** and literacy;
- familiarity with the script of the language;
- **ATTITUDES** and expectations about the language and its culture;
- understandings about the 'distance' of the first from the second language;
- affective factors;
- existing **LEARNING STYLES** and **STRATEGIES**.

The learning context may also vary according to time, intensity and duration of the learning experience; location (in the home country or overseas, in second or foreign language settings); the requirement to follow prescribed **SYLLABUS** guidelines; and the demands for internal and external **ASSESSMENT** and examination.

Significant work in identifying the communicative needs of **ADULT** beginner learners was conducted through the **COUNCIL OF EUROPE** from 1971, resulting in **THRESHOLD LEVEL** (T-Level) specifications for **ENGLISH** (van Ek, 1975), French (1976), Spanish (1979), German (1980) and Italian (1981). T-level referred to the 'common core' of language items and functions which beginner learners would need to acquire before moving on to more advanced courses related to professional or personal goals.

**See also:** Age factors; Attitudes and language learning; Council of Europe Modern Languages Projects; Gender and language learning; Learning styles; Mother tongue; Psychology; Second language acquisition theories; Threshold level

### References

Stevick, E.W. (1986) *Images and options in the language classroom*, Cambridge: Cambridge University Press.

van Ek, J.A. (1975) *The Threshold Level in a European unit/credit system for modern language learning by adults*, Strasbourg: The Council of Europe.

### Further reading

Arthur, B.M. (1991) 'Working with new ESL students in a junior high school reading class', *Journal of Reading* 34, 8: 628–31.

Brumfit, C., Moon, J. and Tongue, R. (eds) (1995)

*Teaching English to children: from practice to principle*, London: Longman.

Burns, A. (1990) 'Genre-based approaches to writing and beginning adult ESL learners', *Prospect: A Journal of Australian TESOL*, 5, 3: 62–71.

Dam, L. (1996) 'The acquisition of vocabulary in an autonomous learning environment – the first months of beginning English', in R. Pemberton, E.S.L. Li, W.W.F. Or and H.D. Pierson (eds) *Taking control: autonomy in language learning*, Hong Kong: Hong Kong University Press.

Grundy, P. (1994) *Beginners*, Oxford: Oxford University Press.

Phillips, S. (1993) *Young learners*, Oxford: Oxford University Press.

Reilly, V. and Ward, S.M. (1997) *Very young learners*, Oxford: Oxford University Press.

ANNE BURNS

# Behaviourism

Behaviourism as a psychological theory can be traced back to the early twentieth century, and a basic premise is that most human behaviour is learned through a continual process of responding to stimuli. Reinforcement of stimulus and response patterns leads to repetitious behaviour or habits, which are to some extent predictable, based upon previous experience. Behaviourism's central notions were linked to a positivist view of the scientific method, which accepts only phenomena that are observable and measurable as worthy of serious attention. Empirical methods were the only creditable means of conducting research. This rather unequivocal view of science was a characteristic feature of behaviourism and, initially, an appealing one. Behaviourism became the dominant theory in American **PSYCHOLOGY** immediately before and after World War Two, and its influence extended into many academic fields, including **APPLIED LINGUISTICS**. Through the works of psychologists and linguists such as Watson, **BLOOMFIELD** and Skinner, the behavioural approach to the teaching of languages developed which then dominated American linguistics in the 1950s and 1960s.

Behaviourism developed a 'broad and diverse character' (Mann, 1983: 19) but this article will focus on the general notions and applications, its views on the nature of human behaviour, its scientific method and the application of behaviourist principles to language teaching theory and methodology. Behaviourism, often associated with **AUDIOLINGUALISM**, was subsequently heavily criticised, notably by **CHOMSKY** (1959). Other theories and related methods have since come to the fore, but behaviourism can be viewed as a key stage in the development of language learning and teaching methodology.

Behaviourism claimed to have found the key to human behaviour, which is viewed as no different to that of other, simpler, living organisms. Behaviour results from stimuli presented to us in our environment, including internal ones such as hunger, and can be observed as responses to these stimuli. If the result is positive, such as obtaining food to satisfy our hunger in a particular manner, it is reinforced and is likely to be repeated, eventually becoming a habit which is carried out unconsciously.

In behaviourism, we see the search for the understanding of stimuli and related responses and how reinforcement and the potential for controlled learning occurs. The early theorists built on the work of Pavlov, the Russian physiologist who looked at the process of stimuli and response in experiments on dogs. He focused on reflex mechanisms and how these can be turned into learned or conditioned behaviour. The result of the dogs being conditioned to salivate (response) to the ringing of a bell (stimulus) is a classic example of this early stimulus–response (S–R) psychology.

Behaviourism concentrated on the S–R in human behaviour and, at its most extreme, adherents claimed that any stated type of behaviour could be produced in an individual through the conscious manipulation of the process of stimulus, response and reinforcement or conditioning.

The work of J.B. Watson, the 'founder of the so-called "behaviourist" approach in psychology' (Lyons, 1991: 30) was central, and he and his followers did not feel the need to concern themselves with anything that fell outside the positivist, empirical framework. Objectivity was to be the key rather than subjective hypothesising about unobservable phenomena. The existence of the mind, for example, or the subconscious was not important, because these were considered as postulates which may or may not exist and were not directly observable. In this sense, behaviourism was a reaction against Freudian psychology and its notions of a submerged subconscious affecting, even controlling, our behaviour. Stimuli, responses and habits, on the other hand, were open to the empirical method. Speech could be observed directly, with thought being, in Watson's view, inaudible speech.

Watson's writings on behaviourism from 1913 onwards influenced the work of Bloomfield (who subsequently set up the ' "Bloomfieldian" tradition of "autonomous" **LINGUISTICS**') and his book *Language* (1935) contributed significantly to behavioural linguistics. Bloomfield 'explicitly adopted behaviourism as a framework for linguistic description' (Lyons, 1991: 30–1). He believed we could predict or hypothesise what might cause a person to speak and what they might say in certain circumstances. The more detail we obtain about a given situation, the more specific will be our prediction of the speech behaviour based upon knowledge about the stimuli and the previously observed patterns of language habits or behaviour.

The work of Skinner was also pivotal in this field. His influential, if not controversial, *Verbal behaviour* (1957) made the claim that language is no different to any other type of non-verbal behaviour and there is no need, therefore, for any new principles or theories to explain it. Behaviourism could be applied just as well to language learning as anything else.

It was accepted that second language (L2) learning had many similarities to first language (L1) learning, with foreign language instruction largely viewed as a process of 'imitation and reinforcement' (Crystal, 1987: 372). Just as suitable habits of speech have to be encouraged in children, so too is the case with second language learners. Listening to patterns and drills and repeating these, as with the audiolingual method, with correction when necessary, assists the development of good L2 habits. It was accepted that properties from L1 might lead to interference in L2, but these would have to be dealt with in order to promote the correct patterns. According to Crystal, 'the main aim of behaviourist teaching is thus to form new,

correct linguistic habits through intensive practice, eliminating interference errors in the process' (1987: 372).

Language behaviour, therefore, can be seen as a response to many stimuli, including communication **NEEDS**. Conversations may be based on this premise, or different stimuli may be seen, such as one person talking to another in a particular way. Ideas of positive and negative reinforcement enter the equation with certain behaviour more likely to be deterred by the latter, as with punishment. Reinforcement is central as it increases the chances of behaviour recurring and becoming a habit. Manipulation of stimuli can lead to different patterns of response and certain language habits can be produced with others changed. Drilling and repetition is considered as a key method for instilling L2 language behaviour patterns.

Behaviourism's dominance seemed to be appropriate for the post-war period, but it declined as its limitations became increasingly hard to suppress and new theories and methods were developed. Its restricted applicability was seen in language learning, which cannot always be reduced to drilling and patterned behaviour. It was also seen as failing to predict patterns of linguistic behaviour with other factors involved outside the S–R equation.

Its theoretical basis was criticised as it reduced human behaviour to a series of learned habits and had a problem in explaining creativity. It was also attacked for offering an extremely mechanistic and atomistic view of human behaviour with its implications of passivity and manipulation. Various refinements were made in order to counter the main criticisms, but these could not save the paradigm. The relegation of disputed phenomena such as the mind and the subconscious to the category of 'unscientific' was always problematic and became increasingly the subject of critical focus.

**CHOMSKY** provided both direct and indirect critiques, claiming that language is not a habit and that it may be free from stimulus–control. Differences between linguistic and other behaviour were recognised, with the implication that language learning and teaching required special consideration. Chomsky's theory of transformational **GRAMMAR** and the related view of innate cognitive and not just physiological abilities contributed to behaviourism's final demise. Human beings do not just react, but think, reflect and draw upon abilities that may not be learned but innate. These are difficult to account for within the empirical method. 'Sentences are not learned by imitation and repetition but "generated" from the learner's underlying "**COMPETENCE**" ' (Richards and Rodgers, 1986: 59 [editor's emphasis]). Such views gained favour from the 1960s onwards and, although behaviourism retained some importance in language theory and practice, its reign was over.

**See also:** Acquisition and teaching; Audiolingual method; Transfer; Universal grammar

### References

Bloomfield, L. (1935) *Language*, London: Allen and Unwin.

Chomsky, N. (1959) 'A review of B.F. Skinner's "Verbal Behaviour" ', *Language* 35, 1: 26–58.

Crystal, D. (1987) *The Cambridge encyclopedia of language*, Cambridge: Cambridge University Press.

Lyons, J. (1991) *Chomsky* (3rd edn), London: Fontana.

Mann, M. (1983) *Student encyclopedia of sociology*, London: Macmillan.

Richards, J.C. and Rodgers, T.S. (1986) *Approaches and methods in language teaching: a description and analysis*, Cambridge: Cambridge University Press.

Skinner, B.F. (1957) *Verbal behaviour*, New York: Appleton-Century-Crofts.

### Further reading

Chomsky, N. (1959) 'A review of B.F. Skinner's "Verbal Behaviour" ', *Language* 35, 1: 26–58.

Chomsky, N. (1966) 'Linguistic theory', in J.P.B. Allen and P. van Buren (eds), *Chomsky: selected readings*, London: Oxford University Press.

RUTH CHERRINGTON

# BICS and CALP

The acronyms BICS and CALP refer to a distinction introduced by Cummins (1979) between basic interpersonal **COMMUNICATIVE** skills (BICS) and cognitive academic language proficiency (CALP). The distinction draws attention to the very different time periods typically required by immigrant children to acquire conversational fluency in their second language as compared to grade-appropriate academic proficiency in that language. Conversational fluency is often acquired to a functional level within about two years of initial exposure to the second language, whereas at least five years is usually required to catch up to **NATIVE SPEAKERS** in academic aspects of the second language (Collier, 1987; Klesmer, 1994; Cummins, 1981a). Failure to take account of the BICS/CALP (conversational/academic) distinction has resulted in discriminatory psychological assessment of bilingual students and premature exit from language support programmes, such as **BILINGUAL EDUCATION** in the United States, into mainstream classes (Cummins, 1984).

Skutnabb-Kangas and Toukomaa (1976) brought attention to the fact that Finnish immigrant children in Sweden often appeared to educators to be fluent in both Finnish and Swedish but still showed levels of verbal academic performance in both languages considerably below grade/**AGE** expectations. Similarly, analysis of psychological assessments administered to minority students showed that teachers and psychologists often assumed that children who had attained fluency in **ENGLISH** had overcome all difficulties with the language (Cummins, 1984). Yet these children frequently performed poorly on English academic tasks as well as in psychological assessment situations. Cummins (1981a) provided further evidence for the BICS/CALP distinction in a reanalysis of data from the Toronto Board of Education. Despite teacher observation that peer-appropriate conversational fluency in English developed rapidly, a period of 5–7 years was required, on average, for immigrant students to approach grade norms in academic aspects of English.

The distinction was elaborated into two intersecting continua (Cummins, 1981b) which highlighted the range of cognitive demands and contextual support involved in particular language tasks or activities (context-embedded/context-reduced, cognitively undemanding/cognitively demanding). The BICS/CALP distinction was maintained within this elaboration and related to the theoretical distinctions of several other theorists, e.g. Bruner's (1975) communicative and analytic competence, Donaldson's (1978) embedded and disembedded language and Olson's (1977) utterance and text. The terms used by different investigators vary, but the essential distinction refers to the extent to which the meaning being communicated is supported by contextual or interpersonal cues, such as gestures, facial expressions, and intonation present in face-to-face interaction, or is dependent on linguistic cues that are largely independent of the immediate communicative context.

The BICS/CALP distinction also served to qualify Oller's (1979) claim that all individual differences in language proficiency could be accounted for by just one underlying factor, which he termed *global language proficiency*. Oller synthesised a considerable amount of data showing strong correlations between performance on **CLOZE TESTS** of **READING**, standardised reading tests, and measures of oral verbal ability, such as **VOCABULARY** measures. Cummins (1979, 1981b) pointed out that not all aspects of language use or performance could be incorporated into one dimension of global language proficiency. For example, if we take two monolingual English-speaking siblings, a 12-year-old child and a 6-year-old, there are enormous differences in these children's ability to read and write English and in their knowledge of vocabulary, but minimal differences in their phonology or basic fluency. The 6-year-old can understand virtually everything that is likely to be said to her in everyday social contexts and she can use language very effectively in these contexts, just as can the 12-year-old. Similarly, as noted above, in second language **ACQUISITION** contexts, immigrant children typically manifest very different time periods required to catch up to their peers in everyday face-to-face aspects of proficiency as compared to academic aspects.

Early critiques of the conversational/academic distinction were advanced by Edelsky and colleagues (Edelsky *et al.*, 1983) and in a volume edited by Rivera (1984). Edelsky (1990) later reiterated and reformulated her critique, and others were advanced by Martin-Jones and Romaine (1986) and Wiley (1996).

The major criticisms are as follows:

- The conversational/academic language distinction reflects an autonomous perspective on language that ignores its location in social practices and power relations (Edelsky *et al.*, 1983; Wiley, 1996).
- CALP or academic language proficiency represents little more than 'test-wiseness' – it is an artefact of the inappropriate way in which it has been measured (Edelsky *et al.*, 1983).
- The notion of CALP promotes a 'deficit theory' in so far as it attributes the academic failure of bilingual/minority students to low cognitive/academic proficiency rather than to inappropriate schooling (Edelsky, 1990; Edelsky *et al.*, 1983; Martin-Jones and Romaine, 1986).

In response to these critiques, Cummins (Cummins, 2000) pointed to the elaborated socio-political framework within which the BICS/CALP distinction was placed (Cummins, 1986, 1996). Underachievement among subordinated students was attributed to coercive relations of power operating in the society at large which are reflected in schooling practices. He also invoked the work of Biber (1986) and Corson (1995) as evidence of the linguistic reality of the distinction. Corson highlighted the enormous lexical differences between typical conversational interactions in English as compared to academic or literacy-related uses of English. Similarly, Biber's analysis of more than one million words of English speech and written text revealed underlying dimensions very consistent with the distinction between conversational and academic aspects of language proficiency. Cummins also pointed out that the construct of academic language proficiency does not in any way depend on test scores as support for either its construct **VALIDITY** or its relevance to education, as illustrated by the analyses of Corson and Biber.

The distinction between BICS and CALP has exerted a significant impact on a variety of educational policies and practices in both North America and the United Kingdom (e.g. Cline and Frederickson, 1996). Specific ways in which educators' misunderstanding of the nature of language proficiency have contributed to the creation of academic difficulties among bilingual students have been highlighted by the distinction. At a theoretical level, however, the distinction is likely to remain controversial, reflecting the fact that there is no cross-disciplinary consensus regarding the nature of language proficiency and its relationship to academic achievement.

**See also:** Age factors; Bilingualism; Cross-cultural psychology; Gender and language learning; Mother tongue

## References

Biber, D. (1986) 'Spoken and written textual dimensions in English: Resolving the contradictory findings', *Language* 62, 384–414.

Bruner, J.S. (1975) 'Language as an instrument of thought', in A. Davies (ed.), *Problems of language and learning*, London: Heinemann.

Cline, T. and Frederickson, N. (eds) (1996) *Curriculum related assessment, Cummins and bilingual children*, Clevedon: Multilingual Matters.

Collier, V.P. (1987) 'Age and rate of acquisition of second language for academic purposes', *TESOL Quarterly* 21, 617–41.

Corson, D. (1995) *Using English words*, New York: Kluwer.

Cummins, J. (1979) 'Cognitive/academic language proficiency, linguistic interdependence, the optimum age question and some other matters', *Working Papers on Bilingualism* 19, 121–9.

Cummins, J. (1981a) 'Age on arrival and immigrant second language learning in Canada: a reassessment', *Applied Linguistics* 2: 132–49.

Cummins, J. (1981b) 'The role of primary language development in promoting educational success for language minority students', in California State Department of Education (ed.), *Schooling and language minority students: a theoretical framework*, Los Angeles: Evaluation, Dissemination and Assessment Center, California State University.

Cummins, J. (1984) *Bilingualism and special education: issues in assessment and pedagogy*, Clevedon: Multilingual Matters.

Cummins, J. (1986) 'Empowering minority students: a framework for intervention', *Harvard Educational Review* 56: 18–36.

Cummins, J. (1996) *Negotiating identities: education for empowerment in a diverse society*, Los Angeles: California Association for Bilingual Education.

Cummins, J. (2000) 'Putting language proficiency in its place: responding to critiques of the conversational/academic language distinction', in J. Cenoz and U. Jessner (eds), *English in Europe: the acquisition of a third language*, Clevedon: Multilingual Matters.

Donaldson, M. (1978) *Children's minds*, Glasgow: Collins.

Edelsky, C. (1990) *With literacy and justice for all: rethinking the social in language and education*, London: Falmer Press.

Edelsky, C., Hudelson, S., Altwerger, B., Flores, B., Barkin, F. and Jilbert, K. (1983) 'Semilingualism and language deficit', *Applied Linguistics* 4, 1: 1–22.

Klesmer, H. (1994) 'Assessment and teacher perceptions of ESL student achievement', *English Quarterly* 26, 3: 5–7.

Martin-Jones, M. and Romaine, S. (1986) 'Semilingualism: a half-baked theory of communicative competence', *Applied Linguistics* 7, 1: 26–38.

Oller, J. (1979) *Language tests at school: a pragmatic approach*, London: Longman.

Olson, D.R. (1977) 'From utterance to text: the bias of language in speech and writing', *Harvard Educational Review* 47: 257–81.

Rivera, C. (ed.) (1984) *Language proficiency and academic achievement*, Clevedon: Multilingual Matters.

Skutnabb-Kangas, T. and Toukomaa, P. (1976) *Teaching migrant children's mother tongue and learning the language of the host country in the context of the sociocultural situation of the migrant family*, Helsinki: The Finnish National Commission for UNESCO.

Wiley, T.G. (1996) *Literacy and language diversity in the United States*, Washington, DC: Center for Applied Linguistics and Delta Systems.

## Further reading

Cline, T. and Frederickson, N. (eds) (1996) *Curriculum related assessment, Cummins and bilingual children*, Clevedon: Multilingual Matters.

Cummins, J. (2000) *Language, power and pedagogy: bilingual children in the crossfire*, Clevedon: Multilingual Matters.

JIM CUMMINS

# Bilingual education

Bilingual education has a wide range of meanings but is generally used where two languages are used to transmit the curriculum. 'Weak' bilingual education occurs when children are only allowed to use their home language in the curriculum for a short period, with a transition to education solely through the majority language. 'Strong' bilingual education occurs when both languages are used in school to promote **BILINGUALISM** and biliteracy. Language methodology in bilingual education concerns the way in which languages are kept separate (e.g., by subject, person and time allocations) or are integrated (e.g., concurrent use of both languages in a lesson).

Bilingual education would seem to describe a situation where two languages are used in a school. However, 'bilingual education' is a simple label for a diverse phenomenon. One important distinction is between a school where there are bilingual children and a school that promotes bilingualism. In many schools of the world, there are bilingual and multilingual children. Yet the aim of the school may be to ensure that children develop in one language only. For example, a child may come to school speaking a minority language fluently but not the majority language. The school may aim to make that child fluent and literate in the majority language only, with integration and assimilation of that child into mainstream society. Such 'weak' forms of bilingual education aim for a transition from the home culture and language to the majority culture and language.

In other types of schools, the aim may be to teach the children two languages, and through the **MEDIUM OF INSTRUCTION** of two languages, so that they develop full bilingualism and biliteracy. For example, in **HERITAGE LANGUAGE** schools, children may receive much of their instruction in the home language, with the majority language being used to transmit 20–90 per cent of the curriculum.

Alternatively, a child from a majority language background may go to an immersion school or a mainstream bilingual school and learn through a second majority (or minority) language. For example, in **CANADA**, an English-speaking child may go to a French immersion school where much of the curriculum will be taught through the medium of **FRENCH**. Such 'strong' forms of bilingual education aim for children to maintain their **MOTHER TONGUES**, their minority languages, and become culturally pluralist. The maintenance and enhancement of language, literacy and cultural **SKILLS** are a key part of the school's mission.

Bilingual education is a term that includes not only 'weak' and 'strong' forms but also trilingual or multilingual schools, where three or more languages are used (e.g. in the European Schools Movement, or Luxembourgish/German/French education in Luxembourg, or Hebrew/English/French in Canada).

Second language-medium teaching is different from second language teaching. In the former, a child may be taught curriculum areas through the medium of that second language. For example, in the European Schools, children in the middle years of **SECONDARY EDUCATION** may learn History, Geography and Social Sciences through a second language. If there is a useful demarcation, then bilingual education may be said to start when more than one language is used to teach curriculum content (e.g. Science, Mathematics, Social Sciences or Humanities).

## Language methodology in bilingual education

A teaching and learning methodology, separate from second language teaching methodology, has arisen in schools where both languages are used to transmit the curriculum. There are different dimensions of 'how' and 'when' two languages can be either separated and/or integrated in **BILINGUAL METHODOLOGY**, and these will be considered in turn.

In the allocation of two languages in the classroom and in the curriculum, the need for distinct separation and clear boundaries between the two languages is often advocated. The separation of languages can occur in school settings by reference to eight overlapping dimensions.

## Subject or topic

In elementary schools and high schools, different curriculum areas may be taught in different languages. For example, Social Studies, Religious Education, Art, Music and Physical Education may be taught through the minority language (e.g. **SPANISH** in the USA). Mathematics, Science, Technology and Computer Studies may be taught through the majority language (e.g. **ENGLISH**). In primary schools, the allocation may be by topic rather than by subject. A danger is that the minority language becomes associated with tradition and history rather than with technology and science. The minority language is thereby allocated a lower status and is seen as much less relevant to modern existence.

## Person

The use of two languages in a school may be separated according to person. For example, there may be two teachers working in a team-teaching situation. One teacher communicates with the children through the majority language, the other teacher through the children's minority language. There is a clear language boundary established by person. Alternatively, teachers' assistants, parents helping in the classroom, auxiliaries and paraprofessionals may function in the classroom as an alternative but separate language source for the children.

## Time

A frequently-used strategy in language allocation in schools is for classes to operate at different times in different languages. For example, in some US Dual Language schools, one day may be taught in Spanish, the next day in English. Other schools alternate by half-days. The separation of time need not be solely in terms of days, half-days or lessons. It may also valuably include a policy that varies by grade and age. For example, children may be taught through the minority language for the first two or three years of elementary education for 100 per cent of the time. During the primary school, an increasing amount of time may be allocated to the majority language inside the school.

## Place

A lesser used means of language separation in the classroom is via different physical locations for different languages. The assumption is that a physical location provides enough cues and clues to prompt the child to adhere to different languages in different places. In reality, the teacher and other students may be more crucial in influencing the choice of language. However, all informal events in the school contribute to the creation of the overall language experience of the school.

## Medium of activity

Another form of separation focuses on distinguishing between **LISTENING**, **SPEAKING**, **READING** and **WRITING** in the classroom. For example, the teacher may give an oral explanation of a concept in one language, with a follow-up discussion with the class in that same language. Then the teacher may ask the children to complete their written work in a second language. This sequence may be deliberately reversed in a second lesson. The aim of such a teaching strategy is to reinforce and strengthen the learning by children. What is initially assimilated in one language is transferred and reinterpreted in a second language. By reprocessing the information in a different language, greater understanding may be achieved. One danger of 'different medium' separation is that one language may be used for oracy and another language for literacy. Where a minority language does not have a written script this may be a necessary boundary.

A 'medium of activity' separation strategy tends to be used when – and only when – both the child's languages are relatively well developed. When this has occurred, the argument is that a child has to think more deeply about the material when moving between languages, comparing and contrasting, developing the theme of the material, assimilating and accommodating, transferring and sometimes translating in order to secure a concept and understanding.

## Function

In schools and classes where there are bilingual

children, teaching may be in the majority language while the management of the classroom occurs in the minority language. When the teacher is organising students, disciplining, informally talking with individual students or small groups, giving additional explanations, the minority language is used. Otherwise, the curriculum is delivered in the majority language.

### Student

Students themselves help define the language that is being used in a classroom. For example, if a pupil addresses the teacher, it may not be in the language that the teacher has used to deliver the curriculum. Students influence when and where languages are used, and affect boundary making.

### Language integration

In many bilingual classrooms, the frequent switching between two or more languages is customary. Jacobson (1990) has argued that, on occasions, the integrated use of both languages rather than language separation can be of value in a lesson. Four concurrent uses will now be considered.

### Randomly switching languages

Bilingual children may switch languages within short episodes. In many minority language groups, this is frequent both in the home and on the street as it is in the school, and is a sign of shift towards the majority language. For minority languages to survive as relatively distinct and standardised languages, few would argue for such a random practice to be encouraged in a bilingual classroom.

### Translating

In some bilingual classrooms, teachers will repeat in another language what they have previously said. For example, the teacher may explain a concept in French, and then repeat the same explanation in English. The danger is that children will opt out of listening when the teacher is transmitting in their weaker language.

### Previewing and reviewing

One strategy in a classroom is to give the preview in the minority language and then the fuller review in the majority language. That is, a topic is introduced in the child's minority language, for example, to give an initial understanding. Then the subject matter is considered in depth in the majority language. This may be reversed. While an extension and reinforcement of ideas occurs by moving from one language to another, there is sometimes also unnecessary duplication and a slow momentum.

### Purposeful concurrent usage

Jacobson (1990) proposed that equal amounts of time are allocated to two languages, and teachers consciously initiate movement from one language to another. This may strengthen and develop both languages, and reinforce taught concepts by being considered and processed in both languages. A use of both languages, it is suggested, contributes to a deeper understanding of the subject matter being studied.

**See also:** Bilingual method; Medium of instruction; Mental lexicon; Mother tongue; Mother-tongue teaching; Primary education

### Reference

Jacobson, R. (1990) 'Allocating two languages as a key feature of a bilingual methodology', in R. Jacobson and C. Faltis (eds), *Language distribution issues in bilingual schooling*, Clevedon: Multilingual Matters.

### Further reading

Baker, C. (1996) *Foundations of bilingual education and bilingualism* (2nd edn), Clevedon: Multilingual Matters.
Baker, C. (1998) *The encyclopedia of bilingualism and bilingual education*, Clevedon: Multilingual Matters.
Crawford, J. (1995) *Bilingual education: history, politics, theory and practice* (3rd edn), Los Angeles: Bilingual Educational Services.
Cummins, J. (1996) *Negotiating identities: education for*

*empowerment in a diverse society*, Ontario, CA: California Association for Bilingual Education.

Ovando, C.J. and Collier, V.P. (1998) *Bilingual and ESL classrooms. Teaching in multicultural contexts* (2nd edn), New York: McGraw-Hill.

COLIN BAKER

# Bilingualism

Who is bilingual or not is difficult to define and requires consideration of a person's ability in and use of two (or more) languages. Few bilinguals are equally proficient in both languages and tend to use their languages for different purposes in different domains or areas of language use. Thus, balanced bilinguals are rare. Bilinguals have been described as 'double semilinguals', but this is usually a function of social and economic circumstances and not of limits to a bilingual's linguistic or cognitive potential. Negative characterisations of bilinguals (the fractional view) are compared with holistic characterisations, of which codeswitching is one example.

## Individual bilingualism

Bilingualism and multilingualism are frequent phenomena in almost every country of the world. Estimates are that between 50 and 70 per cent of the world's population are bilingual – depending partly on how 'bilingual' is defined and the complex relationship between a language and a dialect. However, there is no simple definition of bilingualism (the term bilingualism is often used to include trilingualism and multilingualism) or classification of bilinguals; but the following central issues clarify the concept.

- There is a difference between ability in language and use of language, usually referred to as the difference between degree (proficiency or **COMPETENCE** in a language) and function (use of two languages). An individual's proficiency in each language may vary across the four language competencies of **SPEAKING**, **LISTENING**, **READING** and **WRITING**. An academic may use one language for conversation but switch to another language for reading and writing. Another person may understand a second language well, in its spoken and written form, but may not be able to speak or write it well. Such a person is said to have a passive or receptive competence in a second language.

- Few bilinguals are equally proficient in both languages. One language tends to be stronger than the other. This is described as the dominant language but it is not always the first or native language of the bilingual. Defining bilinguals as those who have native-like competence in both languages (**BLOOMFIELD**, 1933) is too restrictive and fails to reflect the reality of language life in bilinguals. The vast majority of bilinguals do not have native-like competence in both languages but still regularly use both languages.

- Few bilinguals possess the same competence as monolingual speakers in either of their languages. This is partly because bilinguals use their languages for different functions and purposes and with different people. Levels of proficiency in a language may depend on in which domains (e.g. street and home) and how often that language is used. Communicative competence in one of a bilingual's two languages is usually stronger in some domains than in others. For example, some bilinguals use one language at home, in religion and in the local community. They use another language at work and in meetings to do with their trade or profession. This explains why many bilinguals are not effective at **INTERPRETATION** and **TRANSLATION**. Bilinguals rarely have identical lexical knowledge in both languages.

  A particular case of a bilingual is a deaf person who uses **SIGN LANGUAGE** (e.g. British Sign Language, American Sign Language) and has oracy and/or literacy competence in a spoken majority or minority language (e.g. **ENGLISH**).

- A bilingual's competence in a language may vary over time and according to changing circumstances. Over time, the second language may become the stronger or dominant language. If a person loses contact with those who speak it, he or she may lose fluency in that language.

- Bilinguals are often expected to be balanced in their language competencies. This is rarely the case. A balanced bilingual is often regarded as someone who possesses **AGE**-appropriate competence in two languages. The term 'balanced bilinguals' is more of an idealised concept, as dominance in languages varies according to the contexts in which those languages are used.

- Another proposed (but much contested) category of bilinguals is 'semilinguals' or 'double semilinguals', regarded as having 'insufficient' competence in either language. A 'semilingual' is seen as someone with deficiencies in both languages when compared with monolinguals. Such a person is considered to possess a small **VOCABULARY** and incorrect **GRAMMAR**, consciously thinks about language production, is stilted and uncreative with both languages, and finds it difficult to think and express emotions in either language. The notion of semilingualism, or double semilingualism, has received much criticism (e.g. Skutnabb-Kangas, 1981). For example, if languages are relatively undeveloped, the origins may not be in bilingualism *per se*, but in the economic, educational, political and social conditions that constrain development. The danger of the term 'semilingualism' is that it locates the origins of underdevelopment in the individual rather than in external, societal factors that co-exist with bilingualism. Thus linguistic underdevelopment in bilinguals is typically a function of social and economic circumstances and not of limits to a bilingual's linguistic or cognitive potential. Indeed, there are cognitive advantages for bilingualism (e.g. creative thinking; see Baker, 1996).

Until recently, bilinguals have often been wrongly portrayed negatively (e.g., split identity, cognitive deficits, double semilingualism). While part of this is political (e.g., assimilating immigrants, majority language groups asserting their greater power and status), a misjudgement of bilinguals is often based on a failure to understand that bilinguals typically use their languages for different purposes, with different people and in different contexts. Bilinguals are increasingly understood in terms of their 'wholeness', their total language repertoire and language use.

Grosjean (1985) suggests two contrasting views of bilinguals. First, there is a fractional view of bilinguals, which perceives the bilingual as 'two monolinguals in one person'. For example, a bilingual's English language competence is typically measured against that of a native monolingual English speaker. Many bilinguals themselves feel they are not sufficiently competent in one or both of their languages compared with monolinguals, thus accepting and reinforcing the monolingual view of bilinguals. A second, holistic view argues that the bilingual is not the sum of two complete or incomplete monolinguals, but has a unique linguistic profile. Thus any **ASSESSMENT** of a bilingual's language proficiency should be based on a totality of the bilingual's language usage in all domains. In this viewpoint, the bilingual is a complete linguistic entity, an integrated whole.

Another misconception until recently was that there were coordinate bilinguals (who had two separate systems for their two languages), compound bilinguals (who had one integrated system for their two languages), and subordinate bilinguals. Language learners were often conceived as subordinate bilinguals who filter their second language through their first language (e.g. they interpret words in the second language through the first language). There is little evidence to support this triple classification, and the distinctions are generally regarded as too simplistic and invalid. Similarly, there is little confirmation as to whether bilinguals store their languages separately, interdependently, or have three stores (first language, second language, concepts).

Some children acquire two languages from birth. This is often called simultaneous bilingualism or 'bilingualism as a first language' as distinct from consecutive, sequential or successive bilingualism which result from informal or formal language learning in later years. Three years of age is generally regarded as an approximate borderline between simultaneous and consecutive bilingualism.

'Codeswitching' is the term used to describe the purposeful way in which bilinguals move between their two languages. Bilinguals codeswitch, for example, because they do not know a word or a phrase in one language or because they can express an idea more adequately or effectively in a second language. Codeswitching can also be used to mark relationships, signalling status and situation, deference and intimacy. Bilinguals often operate along a dimension from monolingual proceedings to frequent codeswitching with similar bilinguals, with many possibilities between these two.

The issues raised indicate that a distinction between a second language learner and a bilingual will be arbitrary and artificial. There is a multiple series of dimensions such that classification is dependent on self and other attribution as much as ability in languages. That is, labels are dependent on perception as much as on proficiency. Any language learner is an incipient bilingual. Any bilingual is or was a language learner.

**See also:** Attitudes and language learning; Bilingual education; Heritage languages; Mother tongue; Native speaker; Sign languages

### References

Baker, C. (1996) *Foundations of bilingual education and bilingualism* (2nd edn), Clevedon: Multilingual Matters.

Bloomfield, L. (1933) *Language*, New York: Holt.

Grosjean, F. (1985) 'The bilingual as a competent but specific speaker–hearer', *Journal of Multilingual and Multicultural Development* 6, 6: 467–77.

Skutnabb-Kangas, T. (1981) *Bilingualism or not: the education of minorities*, Clevedon: Multilingual Matters.

### Further reading

Baker, C. (1996) *Foundations of bilingual education and bilingualism* (2nd edn), Clevedon: Multilingual Matters.

Baker, C. (1998) *The encyclopedia of bilingualism and bilingual education*, Clevedon: Multilingual Matters.

Hoffmann, C. (1991) *An introduction to bilingualism*, London: Longman.

Ovando, C.J. and Collier, V.P. (1998) *Bilingual and ESL classrooms. Teaching in multicultural contexts* (2nd edn), New York: McGraw-Hill.

Romaine, S. (1995) *Bilingualism* (2nd edn), Oxford: Basil Blackwell.

COLIN BAKER

# Bilingual method

Bilingual method is a method of language teaching developed by C.J. Dodson (1967/1972) to improve the **AUDIO-VISUAL** method as advocated in the 1960s. Its architecture is best understood as a traditional three-phase structure of presentation – practice – production. A lesson cycle starts out with the reproduction/performance of a basic dialogue, moves on to the variation and recombination of the basic sentences (semi-free use of language), and ends up with an extended application stage characterised by the free, communicative exploitation of the previous work. Well-ordered activities take the students up to a conversational level in the shortest possible time. Examples given here are from the teaching of English to German students, but the method has been applied in a variety of bilingual concepts, including Welsh/English, Gaelic/English, English/Swedish, English/Polish, German/Japanese, etc.

In audio-visual courses, basic dialogues are presented and practised over several months on a purely oral basis. Dodson, however, proposed a well-tested procedure where the printed sentence is presented simultaneously to the oral utterance from the beginning. Teachers may read out the dialogue to the class just once with books closed, but as soon as they get the class to say the lines after them, books should be open and the class is allowed to glance at the text in between imitation responses as they listen to others, and look up when they speak themselves. Dodson showed that, provided the class is instructed to make the spoken sentence the primary stimulus, the imitation of sentences could be speeded up, without degradation of intonation and undue interference from the printed text. Having the printed word to glance at (whilst at the same time relying on the auditory image of the sentence just heard), pupils find it easier to segment the amorphous sound stream and retain the fleeting sound image. The mutual support of script and sound outweighs possible interference effects (e.g. where 'knife' would be pronounced with an initial 'k' sound by German learners of English).

Audio-visual **TEXTBOOKS** present dialogues with a picture strip on the left. The pictures (also available on slides) are designed to match closely the meaning of the dialogue sentences. It was claimed that at long last the necessary media (slides and audio tapes) had been made available to do justice to **DIRECT METHOD** principles and allow teaching without relying on the **MOTHER TONGUE**. Pictures and slides, along with the teacher's drawings and realia, should clarify the meaning of new words and structures.

Dodson, however, used oral mother-tongue equivalents at sentence level to convey the meaning of unknown words or structures. Interference from the mother tongue is avoided because the teacher says each dialogue sentence twice, with the mother tongue version sandwiched between:

*Teacher (or tape):* Night's candles are burnt out
*Teacher:* Die Nacht hat ihre Kerzen aus-
gebrannt
*Teacher:* Night's candles are burnt out
*Teacher points to pupil(s) to repeat the sentence after him.*

It is the direct succession of the (second) foreign language stimulus and the imitation response which prevents interference.

Not word, but utterance, equivalents are given – either whole utterances or meaningful parts of an utterance. The teacher chooses the closest natural equivalent which accomplishes what probably no other method of semanticising can do so directly and so sensitively, i.e. convey the precise communicative value of the utterance. Whereas an isolated word equivalent is neutral in terms of intonation, teachers can now show how the utterance is meant by using their voice and body (intonation, stress, gestures), both for the original sentence and for the equivalent. Moreover, natural, idiomatic translations include, for instance, typical German modal particles ('*denn*', '*doch*', '*schon*', '*ja*') which contribute to the full meaning of an utterance:

Wilt thou be gone? It is not yet near day.
Willst du *schon* gehen? Der Tag ist *ja* noch fern.

All in all, through these synergistic effects the teacher is able to create a total language event that immediately brings home to the pupils what and how an utterance is meant. This is very different from traditional bilingual word lists as well as from **AUDIOLINGUAL** parallel texts. The mother tongue

thus proves to be the ideal (and most direct) means of getting the meaning across as completely and as quickly as possible. Bringing the differences to light, contrasting and comparing, seems to be the most effective antidote to interference errors. Pupils who, on hearing the **FRENCH** '*anniversaire*' without *at first* linking it to 'birthday' would simply not understand. Dodson was able to show by controlled experiments that a combination of printed word, mother tongue equivalents and picture strip (for retention of meaning, not for meaning conveyance), can bring a class more quickly to a point where they can act out a basic situation as freely and naturally as possible.

Due to this technique of meaning-conveyance, authentic **LITERARY TEXTS** become available even to beginners – quite an important side-effect. There need not be the content vacuum that is so typical of beginners' **MATERIALS**.

The bilingual method proceeds step-by-step under careful guidance with continual feedback, ensuring that prerequisite sub- or part **SKILLS** are acquired (within a lesson cycle) before a final stage of free and spontaneous language use. Learners are led from knowing nothing about a language situation to complete mastery of this situation, from a mastery of one situation to a mastery of sentence variations and combinations, and from a mastery of known situation combinations to forays into new, unknown and unforeseeable communication situations. It is argued that free, message-oriented use of new language when attempted too early in the lesson cycle, and on too flimsy a basis, would only undermine the pupils' confidence.

## The Generative principle and communication

Learners create new sentences by interchanging words and structures already previously consolidated: **HUMBOLDT**'s idea that language is a way of 'making infinite use of finite means'. The teacher's cues for possible substitutions and extensions are given in the native language. This bilingual technique prevents pupils from giving 'empty' responses, and sentence variations become concept variations which exploit the communicative potential of a given structure. This is an important improvement on conventional pattern practice, whose sole focus was the automatisation of structures. It is syntactic *and* semantic manipulation at the same time, which prevents the process from becoming mechanical. Again, the teacher can use voice and body language to support meaning. Paradoxically, the new foreign language pattern is pressed home by using the familiar first language pattern. A literal and often ungrammatical **TRANS-LATION** – called *Spiegelung*/mirroring – may be added just once if the new structure is not transparent to the learner:

*Teacher:* Ich will ja nur eine Tasse Tee. (Alles ich will ist eine Tasse Tee.)
*Pupil:* All I want is a cup of tea
*Teacher:* Ich will ja nur eine Tasse Kaffee
*Pupil:* All I want is a cup of coffee
*Teacher:* Ich will ja nur eine ruhige Klasse
*Pupil:* All I want is a quiet class

Pupils are trained to take these linguistic leaps which are at the same time concept leaps. With the right type of substitutions, the teacher can help the students to perceive the structure as valid and relevant to their communicative **NEEDS**. Finally, students take over, make up their own sentences or chain sentences together, and may thus venture into new situations. The native language (and to some extent the teacher) is no longer needed, and the exercise becomes monolingual.

Dodson concentrates on a careful sequence of steps so that a growing command of words and structures gradually leads to message-oriented communication, where people exchange messages and mean what they say. If the practice stopped before that point, the students would be cheated. About one-third of the whole teaching time should be allocated to genuine communicative activities. For every lesson cycle, the transition must be made from role-taking to role-making, from bilingual **EXERCISES** to foreign-language-only activities, from guided use to free use, from studying the language to studying topics meaningful in their own way. Bilingual method techniques fit well into a modern communicative approach.

Dodson's seminal work dealt the death blow to the short-sighted notion of the mother tongue as nothing but a source of interference. It is, above all, a scaffold on which to build further languages. Teachers can banish the native language from the classroom, but cannot banish it from the students' minds. It would even be counterproductive, since it would mean trying to stop them thinking altogether. However, in spite of Dodson's experiments and subsequent confirmation by other researchers (see especially Meijer, 1974, a book-length study of a year-long experimental comparison of methods with Dutch pupils of French), in many countries orthodoxy still says that the mother tongue should be avoided except for occasional glosses of difficult words. The problem lies not in the new ideas, but in escaping from the old ones.

**See also:** Audio-visual language teaching; Direct method; Generative principle; Medium-oriented and message-oriented communication; Teaching methods; Textbooks

## References

Dodson, C.J. (1967/1972) *Language teaching and the bilingual method*, London: Pitman.

Meijer, T. (1974) *De globaal-bilinguale en de visualiserende procedure voor de betekenisoverdracht. Een vergelijkend mehtodologisch onderzoek op het gebied van het aanvangsonderwijs frans (The global-bilingual and the audio-visual approach to meaning conveyance. A comparison of two methods for first-year secondary French teaching)*, Amsterdam: Vrije Universiteit.

## Further reading

Alexander, L. and Butzkamm, W. (1983) 'Progressing from imitative to creative exercises. A presentation of the bilingual method', *British Journal of Language Teaching* 21: 27– 33.

Butzkamm, W. (1980) *Praxis und Theorie der bilingualen Methode (Practice and theory of the bilingual method)*, Heidelberg: Quelle and Meyer.

Caldwell, J.A.W. (1990) 'Analysis of the theoretical and experiential support for Carl Dodson's bilingual method', *Journal of Multilingual and Multicultural Development* 11: 459–79.

Ishii, T., Kanemitsu, Y., Kitamura, M. *et al.* (1979) 'Experiment on the acquisition and retention of sentence-meaning and the imitation performance', *Journal of the Kansai Chapter of the Japan English Language Education Society* 3: 52–9.

Sastri, H.N.L. (1970) 'The bilingual method of

teaching English – an experiment', *RELC Journal* 2: 24–8.

Walatara, D. (1973) 'An experiment with the bilingual method for teaching English as a complementary language', *Journal of the National Science Council of Sri Lanka* 1: 189–205.

WOLFGANG BUTZKAMM

# Bloomfield, Leonhard

b. 1 April 1887, Chicago, IL, USA; d. 18 April 1949, New Haven, CT, USA

Professor of Linguistics at various American universities, and from 1940 at Yale University

Bloomfield devoted his scholarly work to Germanic philology, indigenous American languages, and general methodology of **LINGUISTICS** which would later be called 'Bloomfieldean structuralism'. He was involved in practical language teaching during World War Two as (co-)author of **TEXTBOOKS** written after the **AMERICAN ARMY METHOD**, whose basic concepts linked Bloomfield's ideas about syntactic analysis together with ideas of psychological **BEHAVIOURISM** about learning.

Bloomfield influenced foreign language teaching indirectly, but strongly, by the method of linguistic analysis as explained in *Language* (published 1934, still in print). It is a strictly empirical and inductive approach, isolating phonemes, then moving on to morphemes, to immediate constituents (i.e. to syntactic groups below the phrase-level), phrases, clauses and sentences. Each higher level contains the lower ones as units and sub-units. The analysis of this structural framework, the so-called discovery procedure, was to be done bottom-up simply by observation of morphological (grammatical) markers (i.e. third person -s, plural -s, comparative -er, tense -ed, etc.) and the distribution of units. 'Distribution' pertains to the possible position(s) of units within the predetermined word order in sentences (e.g. front position of subject, position of indirect object between verb and direct object, etc.). Contrary to the opinion frequently mentioned in the secondary literature, Bloomfield did not exclude semantics altogether from his linguistic

deliberations. The 'discovery procedure', however, which was mainly meant as a guideline for the exploration of hitherto unscripted American languages, was indeed solely based on the observation of formal data, thus, as Bloomfield thought, ensuring strictness of scientific method for linguistics.

'Bloomfieldeanism' made a great impact on the development of phonology, word-based morphology and structuralist syntax, which was later called 'taxonomic'. Together with the behaviourist psychology which looked at learning as responses automatically triggered by stimuli if there was enough supporting reinforcement, it was made the base of teaching syntax in foreign language classes. The popular procedure was pattern practice, i.e., the manipulation of clauses (sentences) mainly by lexical variation (substitution tables). Its aim was to show the identity of syntactical structures while neglecting meaning. The technical devices of the **LANGUAGE LABORATORY** enhanced this technique of structure drills. A whole generation of textbooks, including those in **CONTRASTIVE** linguistics which compared the structures of two languages, appeared on the market. From today's point of view they exploited the ideas of Bloomfieldean structuralism and of behaviourism in rather a coarse way.

The impact of Bloomfieldean structuralism on foreign language teaching was particularly strong in the **USA**, and from there transferred to other areas of the world. The appearance of transformational **GRAMMAR** with its corollary, psychological mentalism, and of the concepts of communicative competence, occasioned what is called the communicative (or pragmatic) turn in language teaching methodology. Learning syntax lost its central importance for classroom teaching. Yet we thank Bloomfield for an unprecedented promotion of investigations in particular into **ENGLISH** syntax to which his distributionalism is much more easily applicable than to other languages. Almost all grammars, theoretical as well as applied to teaching, owe their present-day standard to the precision of Bloomfield's work.

## Further reading

Lado, R. (1964) *Foreign language teaching: a scientific approach*, New York: McGraw Hill.

Swiggers, P. (1996) 'Bloomfield, Leonhard', in H. Stammerjohann (ed.), *Lexicon grammaticorum. Who's who in the history of world linguistics*, Tübingen: Niemeyer.

WERNER HÜLLEN

# Board drawing

Board drawing is undoubtedly one of the oldest and most widely-used ways of adding a visual element to language classrooms. Often it is a messy, dusty process – the blackboard with chalk has ruined many a teacher's clothes! – but where available, more modern whiteboards with water-based coloured pens have made the process rather easier and cleaner.

At the very least, every language teacher has scribbled a word or two on a board at some point. With a little bit of practice and imagination the board can become the stage for a wide range of creative language experiences for learners. It is fair to say that most language teachers underexploit their classroom board.

Board planning is essential if words and pictures are to be an integral part of the lesson; it is often a good idea to stay behind after school and practise the production – of pictures in particular, but also of handwriting and overall layout. Equally, a good lesson plan should work through exactly *what* is to be put on the board, not just how and when. A teacher who fails to do this may end up by confusing learners.

In general, images need to be bold and clear, with strong single lines. For example, typical stick figures will suffice to represent humans; teachers can easily learn to produce them, even those with no artistic bent (see Wright 1984/1993). The teacher also needs to learn not to obscure the board for learners, although a certain amount of this is inevitable whilst writing or drawing. Colour adds interest to what is produced and can also be used to highlight key features of what is written or drawn, so it is a good idea for the teacher to invest in a box of coloured chalks, or a pack of coloured (dry-wipe) board pens.

A problem with board drawing is that, unlike the **OVERHEAD PROJECTOR**, the teacher must to some extent turn their back to the class whilst working; this can create discipline problems, and lead to a loss of rapport with the learners.

**See also:** Flashcard; Media centres; Self-access; Teaching methods; Visual aids

### Reference

Wright, A. (1984/1993) *1000+ pictures for teachers to copy*, Harlow: Addison Wesley Longman.

### Further reading

Mugglestone, P. (1981) *Planning and using the blackboard*, London: Heinemann.
Shaw, P. and de Vet, T. (1980) *Using blackboard drawing*, London: Heinemann.
Wright, A. and Haleem, S. (1991) *Visuals for the language classroom*, Harlow: Longman.

DAVID A. HILL

# British Council

The British Council was established in 1934, and incorporated by Royal Charter in 1940 (revised in 1993). Its purpose is to promote a wider knowledge of the United Kingdom as a forward-looking and dynamic democracy and to advance the use of the **ENGLISH** language.

The Council is a non-departmental public body, registered in England as a charity. In the late 1990s it operated in 109 countries around the world. Since 1993 the Central Bureau for Educational Visits and Exchanges (CBEVE), established in 1948, has been part of the British Council and promotes foreign language teaching and learning. Its programmes, funded by the UK government and the European Union, offer opportunities for **EXCHANGES** and placements abroad for pupils, students and teachers.

### English language teaching (ELT)

The Council works to enhance Britain's reputation as the world leader in ELT, and promotes English as the language of international communication. To achieve these aims, it runs a global network of teaching centres; supports public and private sector ELT; develops networks of professionals; and actively promotes British ELT services and **MATE-RIALS**.

English language teaching is a major British export, and the Council provides information about and access to the best of British expertise in all sectors (**HIGHER EDUCATION**, schools, teacher training, language schools, publishing, examination boards). The British Council runs the 'English in Britain' Accreditation Scheme, which inspects and accredits ELT provision in schools, colleges and universities.

The British Council works in partnership with Ministries of Education, teachers, teacher trainers, and publishers. For instance it supports collaborative **TEXTBOOK** development projects, and works with the BBC to encourage the use of broadcast materials on radio and television (including cable and satellite TV). The Council encourages the development of approaches which focus on learners and promote **MOTIVATION**. These include comparative **CULTURAL STUDIES** (and British Studies programmes), English for specific/special purposes (ESP), and 'English plus' courses, where the language is taught with another subject or activity. It encourages supported learning approaches, including **DISTANCE LEARNING**, **SELF-ACCESS** programmes and centres, and has developed CD-ROM and web-based on-line materials.

The British Council supports professional development by running many projects and courses for in-service and pre-service education and training (INSET and PRESET). It encourages the development of more practical approaches to pedagogy in higher education (for university teachers as well as those in schools) including postgraduate programmes in **APPLIED LINGUISTICS**, pedagogy and cultural studies. The Council encourages strong self-sustaining networks of professionals. It helped build an English Language Teaching Contacts Scheme (ELTECS) in Eastern and Central Europe

which was then developed further in Western Europe, central Asia, **CHINA** and Latin America.

The Council aims to stimulate professional debate. For example 'The future of English?' (Graddol, 1997) looked at how English and other languages might develop by the year 2050. It commissions surveys into the growth of Primary ELT, and research into key areas such as Landmark Reviews of ELT in China and Latin America and the possible impact on ELT from new technologies.

The head office of the British Council is at Spring Gardens in London.

**See also:** *Alliance française*; Camões Institute; Cervantes Institute; CRÉDIF; Goethe-Institut; Linguistic imperialism

## Website

The British Council's website is: http://www.britishcouncil.org/

## Reference

Graddol, D. (1997) *The future of English?*, London: The British Council.

## Further reading

The British Council's *Annual Report*.

## Publications

The following books/journals are published in association with the British Council:

*ELTJ* (*English Language Teaching Journal*), Oxford: Oxford University Press.

*ELT Review*, Harlow: Addison Wesley Longman.

*Language Teaching*, Cambridge: Cambridge University Press.

CAROLINE MOORE

# C

## CAL – The Center for Applied Linguistics

The Center is a private, non-profit-making organisation established in the USA in 1959, whose organisational headquarters are located in Washington, DC, with a regional office in Sarasota, Florida.

The Center's core purpose is to improve communication through better understanding of language and culture. To accomplish this purpose, CAL seeks to promote and improve the teaching and learning of languages, identify and solve problems related to language and culture, and serve as a resource for information about language and culture.

CAL staff have expertise in languages and **LINGUISTICS**, education, measurement and **EVALUATION**, **PSYCHOLOGY** and sociology. The organisation provides its services to schools, school districts, states, institutions of **HIGHER EDUCATION**, businesses and government agencies in the United States and around the world.

Specific services provided by the Center include curriculum and **MATERIALS** development, information collection and dissemination, language testing, **NEEDS** assessment, policy analysis, professional development, programme design and evaluation, research, technical assistance, and **TRANSLATION**. Languages covered are **ENGLISH** as a second or foreign language as well as dialects of English, and foreign languages both commonly and less commonly taught.

### Website

The website of the Center for Applied Linguistics is: http://www.cal.org

## CALL (Computer Assisted Language Learning)

CALL is an approach to language teaching and learning in which computer technology is used as an aid to the presentation, reinforcement and assessment of material to be learned, usually including a substantial interactive element. Early CALL favoured an approach that drew heavily on practices associated with programmed instruction. This was reflected in the term Computer Assisted Language Instruction (CALI), which originated in the **USA** and was in common use until the early 1980s, when CALL became the dominant term. Throughout the 1980s CALL widened its scope, embracing the communicative approach and a range of new technologies, especially multimedia and communications technology. An alternative term to CALL emerged in the early 1990s, namely Technology Enhanced Language Learning (TELL), which is felt to provide a more accurate description of the activities which fall broadly within the range of CALL.

Typical CALL programs present a stimulus to which the learner must respond. The stimulus may be presented in any combination of text, still images, sound and motion video. The learner responds by typing at the keyboard, pointing and clicking with the mouse, or speaking into a microphone. The computer offers feedback, indicating whether the learner's response is right or wrong and, in the more sophisticated CALL programs, attempting to analyse the learner's response and to pinpoint errors. Branching to help and remedial activities is a common feature of CALL programs.

The extent to which the computer is capable of analysing learners' errors has been a matter of controversy since CALL began. Practitioners who come into CALL via the disciplines of computational **LINGUISTICS**, natural language processing and language engineering – mainly computer scientists – tend to be more optimistic about the potential of **ERROR ANALYSIS** by computer than those who come into CALL via language teaching. Computer scientists have made enormous advances in the development of parsers and speech analysis software, but language teachers continue to be sceptical about the use of such tools. The controversy hinges on those who favour the use of artificial intelligence (AI) techniques to develop 'intelligent CALL' (ICALL) programs (Matthews, 1994) and, at the other extreme, those who perceive this approach as a threat to humanity (Last, 1989: 153).

Within the language teaching profession itself, there has been some degree of controversy about the teacher-centred, drill-based approach to CALL, as opposed to the learner-centred, explorative approach. The explorative approach is strongly favoured by teachers who advocate the use of computer-generated concordances in the language classroom – described as 'data-driven learning' (DDL) by Johns (Johns and King, 1991; see also Tribble and Jones, 1990).

CALL's origins can be traced back to the 1960s. Up until the late 1970s CALL projects were confined mainly to universities, where computer programs were developed on large mainframe computers. The PLATO project, initiated at the University of Illinois in 1960, is an important landmark in the early development of CALL (Marty, 1981).

The advent of microcomputers in the late 1970s brought computing within the range of a wider audience, resulting in a boom in the development of CALL programs and a flurry of publications in the early 1980s (Davies and Higgins, 1982, 1985; Kenning and Kenning, 1984; Last 1984; Ahmad et al., 1985). Many of the CALL programs that were produced in the early 1980s consisted of a series of drills, multiple-choice **EXERCISES** and **CLOZE TESTS**, focusing on **GRAMMAR** and **VOCABULARY**. This was out of tune with orthodox language teaching methodology, which by this time had embraced **COMMUNICATIVE LANGUAGE TEACHING**. There was initially a lack of imagination and skill on the part of programmers, a situation that was rectified to a considerable extent by the publication of an influential seminal work by Higgins and Johns (1984), which contained numerous examples of alternative approaches to CALL.

Early microcomputers were incapable of presenting **AUTHENTIC** recordings of the human voice and easily recognisable images, but this limitation was overcome by combining a 12-inch videodisc player and a microcomputer to create an interactive videodisc system, which made it possible to combine sound, photographic-quality still images and video recordings in attractive presentations. The result was the development of interactive videodiscs such as *Montevidisco* (Schneider and Bennion, 1984) and *Expodisc* (Davies, 1991), both of which were designed as simulations in which the learner played a key role. Inappropriate responses by the learner could result in failure to communicate the right message to the characters in the video recordings with, in *Montevidisco*, disastrous consequences.

The techniques learned in the 1980s by the developers of interactive videodiscs were adapted for multimedia personal computers (MPCs), which were in widespread use by the early 1990s. CD-ROM was established as the standard storage medium for MPCs, having being used initially in the 1980s to store large quantities of text and later to store sound, still images and video. By the mid-1990s a wide range of multimedia CD-ROMs for language learners was available, including imaginative simulations such as *Who is Oscar Lake?* (produced by Language Publications Interactive, New York). MPCs are more compact and cheaper than the interactive videodisc systems of the 1980s and, in combination with CD-ROM technology, they are capable of presenting photographic quality images and hi-fi audio recordings. The quality of video recordings offered by CD-ROM technology, however, has been slow to catch up with that offered by the older interactive video-discs. The Digital Video Disc (DVD), which offers much higher-quality video recordings, appears to point the way ahead.

In 1992 the World Wide Web (WWW) was launched, reaching the general public in 1993. The WWW is a system for finding and accessing resources on the **INTERNET**, the worldwide network of computers, and is playing an increasingly important role in language teaching and learning. Compared to CD-ROM-based CALL, however, the WWW lacks interactivity and speed of access, especially when downloading sound and video. It remains to be seen to what extent initial enthusiasm for the WWW as a delivery medium for language learning **MATERIALS** will be sustained: see Burgess and Eastham (1997), Schwienhorst (1997). There is no doubt, however, that the WWW is a remarkable source of information and means of communication.

CALL's influence extends into a wide range of language teaching and learning activities. A language **MEDIA CENTRE** is almost certain to contain a number of multimedia computers and to offer access to the Internet. CALL also plays an important role in **AUTONOMOUS LEARNING**, open and **DISTANCE LEARNING** (ODL), and **TANDEM LEARNING**.

CALL figures prominently in the activities of the Association for Language Learning (ALL), the **BRITISH COUNCIL**, the **COUNCIL OF EUROPE**, the **GOETHE-INSTITUT**, **FIPLV** and **IATEFL**.

Several professional associations are devoted to CALL and TELL, most publishing a regular journal (in brackets here). Among these are: EUROCALL, Europe (*ReCALL*); CALICO, USA (*CALICO Journal*); IALL, USA (*IALL Journal of Language Learning Technologies*); CCALL, Canada (regular conferences but no journal); ATELL, Australia (*On-CALL*); CALL Austria (*TELL&-CALL*). The main CALL and TELL associations are grouped together under WorldCALL, based at the University of Melbourne, Australia.

**See also:** Internet; Learning styles; Materials and media; Media centres; Self-access; Teaching methods

## Websites

*Language Learning Technology Journal* (*LLTJ*): http://llt.msu.edu

*Apprentissage des langues et systèmes d'information et de communication* (*ALSIC* – Language Learning and Information and Communications Technology): http://alsic.univ-fcomte.fr

## References

Ahmad, K., Corbett, G., Rogers, M. and Sussex, R. (1985) *Computers, language learning and language teaching*, Cambridge: Cambridge University Press.

Burgess, G. and Eastham, S. (1997) 'Cybertrash or teaching tool? Or untangling the Web: a critical look at using World Wide Web resources for foreign language teaching and learning', in J. Kohn, B. Rüschoff and D. Wolff (eds), *New horizons in CALL: Proceedings of EUROCALL 96*, Szombathely, Hungary: Dániel Berzsenyi College.

Davies, G.D. (1991) '*Expodisc* – an interactive videodisc package for learners of Spanish', in H. Savolainen and J. Telenius (eds), *EUROCALL 91: Proceedings*, Helsinki: Helsinki School of Economics.

Davies, G.D. and Higgins, J.J. (1982) *Computers, language and language learning*, London: CILT.

Davies, G.D. and Higgins, J.J. (1985) *Using computers in language learning: a teacher's guide*, London: CILT.

Higgins, J.J. and Johns, T. (1984) *Computers in language learning*, London: Collins.

Johns, T. and King, P. (eds) (1991) *Classroom concordancing*, special Issue of *ELR Journal* 4, University of Birmingham: Centre for English Language Studies.

Kenning, M.J. and Kenning, M.M. (1984) *An introduction to Computer Assisted Language Teaching*, Oxford: Oxford University Press.

Last, R.W. (1984) *Language teaching and the micro-computer*, Oxford: Blackwell.

Last, R.W. (1989) *Artificial intelligence techniques in language learning*, Chichester: Ellis.

Marty, F. (1981) 'Reflections on the use of

computers in second language acquisition', *System* 9, 2: 85–98.

Matthews, C. (1994) 'Intelligent Computer Assisted Language Learning as cognitive science: the choice of syntactic frameworks for language tutoring', *Journal of Artificial Intelligence in Education* 5, 4: 533–56.

Schneider, E.W. and Bennion, J.L. (1984) 'Veni, Vidi, Vici, via Videodisc: a simulator for instructional courseware', in D.H. Wyatt (ed.), *Computer assisted language instruction*, Oxford: Pergamon.

Schwienhorst, K. (1997) 'Modes of interactivity: internet resources for second language learning', in D. Kranz, L. Legenhausen and B. Lüking (eds), *Multimedia, Internet, Lernsoftware: Fremdsprachenunterricht vor neuen Herausforderungen?* (Multimedia, internet, learning software: new challenges to foreign language teaching?), Edition Volkshochschule 4, Münster: Agenda Verlag.

Tribble, C. and Jones, G. (1990) *Concordances in the classroom*, Harlow: Longman.

### Further reading

Blin, F. and Thompson, J. (eds) (1998) *Where research and practice meet: selected papers from EUROCALL 97*, special Issue of *ReCALL* 10, 1.

*CALL Journal*, Lisse, Netherlands: Swets and Zeitlinger.

Cameron, K. (ed.) (1998) *Multimedia CALL: theory and practice*, Exeter: Elm Bank Publications.

Korsvold, A.-K. and Rüschoff, B. (eds) (1997) *New technologies in language learning and teaching*, Strasbourg: Council of Europe.

Levy, M. (1997) *CALL: context and conceptualisation*, Oxford: Oxford University Press.

Liddell, P., Ledgerwood, M. and Iwasaki, A. (eds) (1998) *FLEAT III: Foreign Language Education and Technology: Proceedings of the Third Conference*, Victoria, Canada: University of Victoria.

GRAHAM DAVIES

# Camões Institute

The Camões Institute was set up in 1992 to replace the Institute for **PORTUGUESE** Language and Culture (ICALP: Insituto de Cultura e Lingua

Portuguesa), which had itself succeeded the Institute for High Culture (IAC: Instituto de Alta Cultura). Along the lines of the **BRITISH COUNCIL** and the **CERVANTES INSTITUTE**, the role of the Camões Institute is to promote the Portuguese language and culture both at home, in lusophone countries (through the Portuguese Schools in cities such as Luanda and Maputo), and abroad (through language courses and cultural centres). At first under the jurisdiction of the Portuguese Ministry of Education, in 1994 the Institute became a branch of the Ministry for Foreign Affairs.

The aims of the Institute include promoting Portuguese as a language for international communication, developing projects and programmes for the dissemination of Portuguese language and culture (such as **DICTIONARIES** and multimedia packages), coordinating the network of *leitores* (language lecturers/assistants) in schools and universities abroad, supporting cultural activities in conjunction with the Ministry of Culture, contributing to the organisation of international conferences, supporting the establishment of language courses for foreign students, and training both *leitores* and teachers of Portuguese as a Foreign Language (PLE: *Português como Língua Estrangeira*). It is involved in the development of an examination to recognise proficiency in Portuguese for foreign students and also participates in the European Association for the Promotion of the Languages of Community Countries.

The Institute has its own website with links to its cultural centres around the world and information about its activities, projects and publications. It is planning to open a Virtual Interactive Centre accessible to *leitores* and teachers of Portuguese, students and lusophiles.

**See also:** *Alliance française*; British Council; Cervantes Institute; CRÉDIF; Goethe-Institut

### Website

The Camões Institute's website is: http://www.instituto-camoes.pt

CLAIRE WILLIAMS

# Canada

In the Canadian federal system, education is constitutionally designated as being under provincial jurisdiction. However, the federal government exerts an influence, through federal/provincial agreements, on the teaching of **FRENCH** and **ENGLISH** and the aboriginal and immigrant languages.

Because the Official Languages Acts (1969, 1988) made French and English the two official languages, each province receives financial support for all children enrolled in public school courses teaching French as a Second Language (FSL) or English as a Second Language (ESL). In addition, the adoption of the Charter of Rights and Freedoms (1982) guarantees to all Canadians of French and English descent education in their **MOTHER TONGUE**, where numbers warrant. Quebec is francophone and all the other provinces and territories predominantly anglophone, which creates a distinction between majority and minority language schooling. Thus the minority language group in Quebec is anglophone, while elsewhere it is francophone. In order to ensure mother tongue education in the minority language communities, the federal government gives financial support to French and English-first-language schools. The Multiculturalism Acts (1971, 1988) also encourage the maintenance of all **HERITAGE LANGUAGES** (aboriginal and immigrant), and federal financial support is provided for heritage language programmes. While the money is distributed through federal/provincial agreements, the provincial governments control its use.

The three major groups of languages taught in Canada are aboriginal, colonial (English and French) and immigrant languages. Since twentieth century immigrants settled mainly in the westerly provinces, ethnic – and therefore linguistic – diversity increases from east to west. As a general pattern, English, French and the aboriginal languages are taught in the Atlantic provinces; in Quebec and Ontario, these same language groups in addition to several immigrant languages, particularly **SPANISH** and Italian, are taught. In the western provinces the number of immigrant languages taught increases dramatically, with a considerable emphasis on oriental languages ap-

pearing in the extreme west. In provinces such as Alberta and British Columbia, the priority on French as an official language is not as readily accepted as in eastern Canada.

Provincial departments of education take all the decisions pertaining to languages taught, curriculum, resources, number of hours of instruction and pedagogy, with some wide variations. Since each province (except New Brunswick, where school boards were eliminated in 1997) is divided into a number of school districts governed by boards or commissions, with considerable discretion in interpreting provincial guidelines, there is additional variation at the classroom level.

As a general rule, the teaching of ESL and FSL begins at grade 4 in the public school system. In English schools, FSL instruction is generally included in the regular curriculum until the end of grade 9; participation in FSL programmes from grade 10 to the end of secondary school (grade 12) is optional. In French schools, ESL instruction is usually continued to the end of secondary school. While participation in ESL and FSL programmes is encouraged, participation is compulsory only in some provinces, and then only at certain grade levels. Instruction in other second languages usually begins in the intermediate (grades 7 to 9) or secondary (grades 10 to 12) school. French, English or another second language is taught for approximately 40 minutes per day. This model describes the regular second language programme. For FSL, this is termed 'core French' and is the most widespread option. About 90 per cent of the total anglophone school population is enrolled in a core French programme, giving students who participate in such a programme from grade 4 to the end of grade 12 about 1200 hours of instruction in the second language. A similar percentage of francophone students participates in the regular ESL programme in Quebec.

The exceptions to this general pattern are the programmes designed for the teaching of ESL and FSL to immigrants. ESL instruction is offered on a non-graded basis, according to need, in anglophone schools; children attend regular classes while improving their English **SKILLS**. In Quebec, the learning of French, which is compulsory under provincial legislation for all immigrants, is addressed through special programmes, called *classes* *d'accueil* (welcoming classes), which are offered both within the public school system for children and through *centres d'orientation et de formation des immigrants* (COFI – Orientation and Language Learning Centres for Immigrants) for adults. A designated proficiency level is required before entering other programmes, as the language of instruction is French. The *classes d'accueil* have a dual purpose with cultural as well as linguistic goals.

For the teaching of FSL and ESL, models other than the core or regular programme have been developed. In the francophone schools of Quebec, where teaching subject matter in any language other than French is forbidden, intensive English was initiated. In this model, students are exposed to a concentrated period of study in English during one half of the academic year at grades 5 or 6. During the other half of the year the regular curriculum is offered in a compressed form. The increased exposure to English, about three to four times above the norm, occurs in a communicative situation, providing a mini-immersion experience without studying other content areas in English. This model was begun in the school district of Mille Iles, Quebec, in 1970. Newfoundland and Labrador have also experimented with intensive French.

In anglophone schools in all provinces and territories, various types of French immersion programmes are offered. These include: early immersion (EFI), beginning in kindergarten or grade 1; middle immersion (MFI), beginning in grades 4 or 5; and late immersion (LFI), generally beginning in grade 7. Programmes are based on a home–school language switch, and students study the regular content areas of the curriculum in French. In the EFI programme in the primary grades (1–3), 80 to 100 per cent of the curriculum is taught in French. English language arts are introduced at grade 3, and from grade 4 to the end of secondary school approximately 60 to 70 per cent of the curriculum is offered in French, with the rest in English. Students remaining in this programme to the end of secondary school receive about 5,000 hours of instruction in French.

In MFI and LFI, the first years are not given entirely in French, as some subjects can only be offered in English due to the specialities of available teachers. In general, a 60/40 division of subjects between those offered in French and those in English is desired, which decreases to 30 per cent in French in secondary school. Considerable variation exists from one programme to another, due primarily to teacher qualifications and time-table exigencies within a particular school situation. Subjects taught in French tend to be the social sciences, although some school districts offer natural sciences and mathematics. Students remaining in these programmes to the end of grade 12 reach approximately 3,000 hours of instruction in French. In Canada overall, about 10 per cent of the anglophone/allophone school population is enrolled in French immersion programmes.

The immersion model, initiated in 1965 in St. Lambert, Quebec, has been widely adopted throughout the world as a means of teaching a second language. It has also been adapted to the teaching of other second languages, such as the Inuit languages in northern Canada and the oriental languages in western Canada. Other models, less widespread and influential, have been developed for the teaching of FSL. These include bilingual programmes (50 per cent instruction in each of French and English); and extended (or expanded) core French, where one or two areas of the regular curriculum are taught in French in addition to the regular core French programme. These programmes normally commence at grade 10.

Traditionally, a **GRAMMAR–TRANSLATION** approach has been used in the teaching of second languages in Canada, followed by an **AUDIO-LINGUAL** one. However, since the 1970s, languages have been taught increasingly by a **COMMUNICA-TIVE** approach. The success of the French immersion model has had considerable influence in promoting **COMMUNICATIVE LANGUAGE TEACHING** in the core programme. The National Core French Study, initiated by **STERN** and undertaken from 1985 to 1990, gave support to this type of methodology. It proposed the adoption of a multidimensional curriculum for core French based on four components: linguistic, communicative/ experiential, cultural and general language education. **TEXTBOOKS** for the teaching of second languages in Canada tend to conform to this general framework.

Teacher certification is a provincial responsibility, and each province has its own **TEACHER**

**EDUCATION** programmes at university level. Language teaching qualifications vary, and teachers must obtain certification from the province where they seek employment.

Research in second language teaching in Canada is world-renowned. The French immersion phenomenon is the most researched of second language teaching alternatives. Theories such as the output hypothesis and the interdependence of languages, as well as theories on the importance of intensity, the components of communicative competence, the negotiation of form and the role of error correction, have been developed at Canadian universities.

**See also:** Australia; BICS and CALP; Bilingual education; Content-based instruction; Heritage languages; Mother tongue; United States of America

### Further reading

Edwards, J. (ed.) (1998) *Language in Canada*, Cambridge: Cambridge University Press.

Germain, C. (1993) *Le point sur l'approche communicative (State of the art: communicative approach)* (2nd edn), Montreal: Centre éducatif et culturel.

Gouvernement du Québec (1996) *Document d'information sur l'enseignement intensif de l'anglais, langue seconde au primaire (Information document on the intensive teaching of English as a Second Language in the elementary grades)*, Quebec: Ministère de l'Éducation.

LeBlanc, R. (1990) *The national core French study: a synthesis*, Quebec: The Canadian Association of Second Language Teachers and *M Editeur*.

Rebuffot, J. (1993) *Le point sur l'immersion au Canada (State of the art: immersion in Canada)*. Montreal: Centre éducatif et culturel.

JOAN NETTEN

# Central and Eastern Europe

The construction and, since the collapse of communism in the late 1980s, reconstruction of 'Central and Eastern Europe' (CEE) have important implications for foreign language education. The placement of some states into this area is geographically dubious – Prague, for example, is further west than Vienna (Eisenberg and Trapp, 1996) – therefore political as well as linguistic dimensions have to be considered.

The origins of the former communist 'bloc' lie in shared history as well as similarities in languages. After 1945, what was known as Eastern Europe, a largely political construction, represented the opposite of the West. From diverse geographical and cultural identities a common political one was to be forged, with clear implications for language education. Russian became the **LINGUA FRANCA** intended to emphasise a shared linguistic heritage as well as to promote unity. This policy was, however, embraced more enthusiastically by some states than others. In 'pariah' states such as Yugoslavia, Russian was never a compulsory school subject (Enyedi and Medgyes, 1998: 3). Bulgaria was relatively much closer to Russia than was the rest of CEE but established, during the communist era, middle schools where the emphasis was on Western language learning. Their selectivity meant that pupils were initially well placed after the fall of communism.

Internal linguistic variations may be masked if we consider all CEE states as a bloc, and ethnic minority languages need to be added to the equation. Language education may imply the dominant or official language of any given state being taught with **BILINGUALISM** and multilingualism features of many places. There have always been diversities amongst the original nine 'Eastern bloc' countries. Enyedi and Medgyes contest the policy of viewing countries in this region as 'lookalikes', and relate political changes to shifts in foreign language education (Enyedi and Medgyes, 1998: 1). Hall (1995) described how little Westerners knew about Eastern Europe before the fall of communism. 'In our stereotyped vision it was a single area of totalitarianism, industrial pollution, food queues, strong liquor, and people who won all the medals at international sporting events' (1995: 49). There were common trends but also divergences in language education linked to political and economic as well as cultural factors.

CEE has changed considerably since 1989. The original number of CEE states has 'more than doubled' since the 'cataclysm of 1989–90' (Enyedi and Medgyes, 1998: 1). The Baltic states were also formerly Soviet-dominated, and exhibited similar language teaching and learning trends as they passed into 'post-communism'. The general shift from Russian to **ENGLISH** and other Western languages involved the drastic reduction in the status of Russian. English moved 'from a low-bordering-on-subversive-status language to one whose popularity is matched only by that of **GERMAN**' (Gill, 1995: 66). The new demands entailed a multitude of requirements, from providing basic **MATERIALS** such as **TEXTBOOKS**, to adequate facilities, new curricula and examinations, together with teachers and trainers equipped with appropriate knowledge and skills. These were hard to meet all at once.

Many teachers of Russian, finding themselves unemployed, were targeted for retraining. Programmes were launched in many states with varying degrees of success. Participants 'were an unhappy lot' (Enyedi and Medgyes, 1998: 6), faced with the need to learn another language and new methods mid-career whilst still working full-time. The success of these schemes, such as in Slovakia, was 'at best limited' (Gill, 1995: 67).

The retraining of Russian teachers declined in the second half of the 1990s. In Poland in 1992, 42.9 per cent of language teachers were teaching Russian, but this fell to 31.2 per cent in 1994. The figures for English rose from 27.3 to 36.2 per cent in the same period: 'in 1994 the number of English teachers surpassed, for the first time, the number of Russian teachers' (Bogucka, 1995: 46). For German, the increase was from 22.8 to 25.8 per cent. As in other former CEE states, Russian used to be compulsory at primary and secondary schools, but there emerged an 'unprecedented demand for English and German' (Bogucka, 1995: 46).

Early shifts of direction were supplemented by further training courses to accompany the rapid expansion of foreign language teaching. 'Fast-track' degrees, where students study pedagogy alongside supervised practical teaching experience, were devised (Gill, 1995: 67). The number and variety of pre- and in-service courses also grew. Accompanying this was the spread of teacher and teacher trainer networks which assisted training and offered support to those in the profession.

In many countries the progress was impressive, but often demand, especially for English, out-stripped the supply of courses and teachers. Private language schools were established by local and foreign organisations that met some of the additional **NEEDS**. This sector was diverse, with differing standards across the region, but there was a degree of cooperation between the different providers. Fee-paying schools established in the 1990s could only expand as far as local economies could allow and some could not support a large private sector, having insufficient well-off people to use it. Cheaper options of non-state provision also sprang up. It is generally accepted that foreign-language students offer private tuition as a way of supplementing their own incomes and stipends.

Developments were assisted by organisations such as the **BRITISH COUNCIL**, **GOETHE-INSITITUT** and the *Institut Français*, as well as by EU-sponsored schemes. American organisations have a presence, with the Peace Corps, for example, sending young people to teach English. International assistance was linked to the nurturing of democracy in the former communist states. They provided materials, textbooks, low-priced books, and personnel at all levels from primary level to university. They also assisted with standards and accreditation in state and private sectors. The British Council during the 1980s and 1990s provided teacher as well as student education, supported various English Language Teaching projects, and set up nearly fifty Resource Centres 'from Tallinn to Tirana providing access to 30,000 teachers per year' (Marsden, 1994: 3).

Language **SYLLABUSES** were changed because, under communism, these had been fairly rigid and included political as well as linguistic objectives. The same was true for examinations. Oral examinations predominated, with an emphasis on rote learning. This began to change as links were made between new syllabuses, teaching methodologies and materials. In some places, however, old textbooks were retained because of lack of funds as well as inertia and conservatism.

Language conferences became a feature of the changing context, with local branches of international organisations such as **IATEFL** established. The production and distribution of language journals also increased, with local personnel producing their own. Newsletters were set up to further language teaching projects. **EXCHANGE** schemes with Western schools and colleges have also become increasingly popular.

All these developments, from the Baltic states to Albania, helped to raise the profile of language teaching, but still it retains low status and poor salaries. The transition from communism towards market economies has highlighted other areas of work, and financial uncertainties in the 1990s caused localised crises in education. People with language skills moved into private companies or went abroad. Just as Russian used to be a passport to a good job, a Western language became the post-communist equivalent. Bogucka noted that, in Poland, the majority of graduates in the early 1990s took positions at private language schools or in business (1995: 46).

The economic lead of some CEE countries is reflected in language provision as well as in links to the European Union, with some states in advance of others. English, French and German may be more common in the 'advanced' group. Growing gaps may be narrowed to some extent by international funding, training and materials, but the poorer countries are losing some of those best equipped to teach the next generation of language learners.

There will also be increased use of new technology as 'the role of computers in language instruction has now become an important issue confronting large numbers of language teachers throughout the world' (Warschauer and Healey, 1998: 57), with greater exploitation of computer assisted language learning (**CALL**). Other aspects of technology are already evident and the use of the **INTERNET** and on-line learning are certain to be expanded. Once again this will be determined by economic infrastructures. Relatively impoverished CEE states already struggling to supply basic textbooks will be disadvantaged. A two-tier system may be emerging, with the relatively more advanced countries like Poland, the Czech Republic and Hungary making greater progress.

**See also:** German; Language planning; Linguistic imperialism; Planning for foreign language teaching

### References

Bogucka, M. (1995) 'In-service teacher training in

Poland', in J. Greet (ed.), *ELTECS Fourth Annual Conference*, Manchester: The British Council.

Eisenberg, J. and Trapp, M. (1996) 'Introduction', *The Berkeley Guide to Eastern Europe*, New York: Fodor.

Enyedi, A. and Medgyes, P. (1998) 'ELT in Central and Eastern Europe', *Language Teaching* 31: 1–12.

Gill, S. (1995) 'Spotlight on Slovakia', *Modern English Teacher* 4, 1: 66–70.

Hall, M. (1995) 'Training teachers to do business: developing an INSETT model in a new context', in J. Greet (ed.), *ELTECS Fourth Annual Conference*, Manchester: The British Council.

Marsden, E. (1994) 'Opening remarks', in F. Banks (ed.), *ELTECS Third Annual Conference*, Manchester: The British Council.

Warschauer, M. and Healey, D. (1998) 'Computers and language learning: an overview', *Language Teaching* 31: 57–71.

### Further reading

Banks, F. (ed.) (1994) *ELTECS Third Annual Conference*, Manchester: The British Council.

Bolitho, R. (1995) 'Introducing the new textbooks: a time of change', *Together* 1, 1: 5–13.

Council of Europe (1997) *Working papers of the second annual colloquy of the European Centre for Modern Languages of the Council of Europe*, Graz: Council of Europe.

*Together: the Romanian Language Journal for Teacher Educators*, British Council, Romania, 1995–7.

RUTH CHERRINGTON

# CercleS – Confédération Européenne des Centres de Langues dans l'Enseignement Supérieur

CercleS – also known as the European Confederation of Language Centres in Higher Education and the *Europäische Konföderation der Hochschulsprachzentren* – was founded in Strasbourg in 1991. It is a confederation of seven independent associations and has a network of associate members throughout Europe in some eighteen countries. It brings together language centres and other institutions in **HIGHER EDUCATION** whose main responsibility is the teaching of languages.

CercleS aims to support language centres in the provision of language training, backed up by appropriate technological resources; to promote research in foreign language learning at international level; to encourage international and interdisciplinary cooperation between language centres to enable them to coordinate the pursuit of their objectives.

CercleS organises conferences, and issues publications and maintains a website. Institutional membership is open to all language centres and similar bodies in higher education in Europe.

## Website

The website of CercleS is: http://www.cercles.org

DAVID LITTLE

# Cervantes Institute

In 1991 the Spanish parliament passed legislation to allow the formation of the Cervantes Institute. This had a dual purpose. The first was to develop and extend the use of **SPANISH** as the main language of the Spanish-speaking community (and not just as the official language of Spain). The second purpose was to disseminate abroad, in conjunction with the other official state organisations, the culture of all Spanish-speaking peoples. So it was a similar institution to those of other countries which had been operating for some time, such as the **BRITISH COUNCIL** for the **ENGLISH** language and the **GOETHE-INSTITUT** for **GERMAN**.

The Cervantes Institute was established as an official public body (and therefore with independent legal status), attached to the Spanish government's Ministry of External Affairs. It has an administrative council presided over by the Secretary of State for International Cooperation, and has representatives from the Ministry for Education and Culture and the Treasury. The official patron of the governing body is the King of Spain. Among its members, as well as the Prime Minister and various other ministers, are prestigious representatives of the cultural life of Spain and Latin America.

The Institute's Director-General is appointed by the government. There are two main areas of activity, each under separate directors: the Academic Department (responsible for all activities connected with teaching Spanish as a Foreign Language, ELE) and the Cultural Department (responsible for the dissemination of cultural and scientific matters). The Academic Department also initiates research activities connected with the present state of the language and with the use and application of new technologies, and coordinates projects developed by universities and research bodies. In this connection it has set up the *Observatorio Español de Industrias de la Lengua*. In 1994 the Cervantes Institute published its curriculum, which was open, learner-centred, and laid down a communicative syllabus based on tasks.

The Institute also has a training programme for teachers of ELE. The Cervantes Institute manages the administration and organisation of the ELE Diplomas (Diplomas de Español como Lengua Extranjera) for the Ministry of Education and Science.

By the middle of the 1990s, the Cervantes Institute consisted of a network of thirty centres. There are none in Spain, each centre being in a foreign country. Throughout these centres there was a total number of 20,000 registrations on 2,000 language courses. At the same time, the libraries in the centres had some 70,000 registered readers.

In 1997, the *Centro Virtual Cervantes* website was created, accessible on the **INTERNET**. Among its contents are teaching **MATERIALS**, a discussion forum and a news bulletin.

**See also:** British Council; Camões Institute; CRÉDIF; Goethe-Institut

## Website

The website of the Cervantes Institute, *Centro Virtual Cervantes*, is: http://cvc.cervantes.es

ERNESTO MARTÍN-PERIS

# China

Since the birth of New China in 1949, the development of foreign language teaching can be divided into four periods. The first (1949–56) was one of full-scale extension of Russian education; the second (1957–65) was one of considerable expansion of English and other foreign language education; the third (1966–76) was a silent period in which foreign language teaching substantially ceased; the fourth (1978–present) is witnessing a full-scale, rapid and normal development of foreign language teaching.

## 1949–56

New China's recovery and development of economic construction urged the Chinese government and people to learn from the USSR. The first and foremost need was to teach people Russian. From 1952 on, seven Russian institutes, and Russian departments or sections in seventeen comprehensive universities and nineteen normal universities, were established. Russian courses were taught in most of the middle or secondary schools and some primary schools; and Russian colleges came into existence even in the Army.

An effort over nearly ten years saw the drawing-up of a Russian teaching programme, the compilation of Russian **TEXTBOOKS**, and extensive teacher recruitment and training, including some at postgraduate level. By the end of 1956, there were almost 2,000 teachers of Russian, and 13,000 graduates majoring in Russian.

Rapid development of Russian education, however, resulted in a surplus of Russian learners, which triggered reformation and regulation of foreign language teaching. Measures were taken to alter the teaching system, mobilise students to learn other foreign languages, and reduce the enrolment of students of Russian. By 1957, Russian education began to shrink in scale.

While great importance was thus attached to Russian, other foreign languages were largely ignored. This is because, first, most of the Western countries did not then establish diplomatic relations with China, while China's communication with Asian, African and Latin American countries was limited. Second, the authorities then respon-

sible for education failed to have a long-term programme and comprehensive view of foreign languages education.

China's participation in the Asian–African Conference in Bandung, Indonesia, symbolised a new page of China's diplomatic history. China began to have more and more communication with Third World countries, so there arose an increasing demand for people skilled in Asian and African languages. By 1956, English departments or sections had been set up in 23 universities, institutes or colleges, with even five French sections and four German sections having emerged.

## 1957–65

In 1959 the 'Great Education Revolution' was initiated. The guiding principle was that 'Education should serve proletarian politics and be combined with productive labour', and its aim was to change old educational thought, systems, methodology, etc. However, due to over-emphasis on politics, the textbooks, full of translated articles about politics but lacking lessons in the original, led to unidiomatic foreign language apprehension. Furthermore, due to over-emphasising cooperation between teachers and students in compilation, the teachers' expertise was not given full play. Theories of foreign language teaching were ignored. However, the central government realised these problems and, in 1961, a programme was drafted for the selection and compilation of liberal-arts textbooks for universities. A very popular, widely used English textbook was compiled by Xu Guozhang, and, at the same time, textbooks of other foreign languages were also published.

Following Premier Zhou Enlai's instructions, the Ministry of Education drafted the Seven-Year Programme of Foreign Languages Education in 1964. Four principles were defined: emphasising foreign language teaching for professional and general purposes; juxtaposing formal with informal foreign language education; defining English as the first foreign language and readjusting the allocation of hours for foreign language teaching in colleges; attaching special importance to the quality of foreign language education. These principles were not actually carried out, due to the so-called Great Cultural Revolution (GCR), but achievements in foreign language teaching were obvious. The number of foreign language departments or sections in higher or tertiary institutions increased to 78, more than double that of 1956. Foreign language students were up to 40,000, and altogether forty-two foreign languages were taught, which was four times the number in 1949.

## 1966–76

The GCR was disastrous for China's foreign language teaching, which actually stagnated. In the early 1970s, however, many countries established diplomatic relations with China, China won back its right to a seat in the UN, and US President Nixon visited China. The new international situation increased China's need for more and more specialists understanding foreign languages. Mao Zedong, Zhou Enlai and other leaders of the People's Republic showed particular concern for foreign language teaching. Thus, after 1971, recruitment to some universities and colleges recovered; some offered new foreign languages. Nevertheless the interference of the notorious 'Gang of Four' retarded the progress of foreign language teaching.

## After 1978

From 1978 to the present day, the policies of reformation and opening to foreign countries led China into international communication of unprecedented range and depth. Foreign language teaching has become full of vigour and vitality. In 1978, for the first time after the GCR, the Ministry of Education held a symposium to discuss overall PLANNING FOR FOREIGN LANGUAGE TEACHING. The delegates passed a resolution entitled 'A few remarks on strengthening foreign language teaching', which claimed: 'The high level of foreign language education is not only an important component for promoting the scientific and cultural standard of the whole Chinese nation, but also a necessary precondition of being an advanced country and race.' This understanding helped push foreign language teaching forward, raising as a whole its quality and standard, as shown by:

1 Raising the structural and professional level of the foreign language teaching contingent by improving their practical skills and sending teachers and students to STUDY ABROAD.
2 Strengthening communication with domestic and international foreign language teaching communities; sending scholars to attend domestic or international conferences on foreign language teaching; inviting foreign language teaching specialists from abroad to give lectures; encouraging schools to establish friendly intercollegiate relations with their counterparts or schools of similar nature abroad.
3 Combining foreign languages learning with politics, economics, and other background knowledge of the corresponding nations, thus improving foreign language teaching itself and widening learners' knowledge scope.
4 Enhancing the construction of foreign language teaching MATERIALS and modern teaching devices, improving the conditions and environment for foreign language teaching.

In the following twenty years, the scale of China's foreign language teaching expanded further. By the end of the 1980s, there were twelve foreign language institutes or universities (FLU), seven other related institutes or universities, and thirty comprehensive universities with foreign language departments or schools. The number of teachers in the FLUs alone was more than 13,000, and the number of students 35,000. By the mid-1990s, more than forty foreign languages were offered by FLUs of various types and levels.

The remarkable achievements in foreign language teaching during this period are also evident in other aspects:

- Scientific research developed. Teachers and researchers now take an active part in foreign language teaching research. Many monographs and papers on foreign language teaching have been published, covering a large range of subjects, including the developing strategies, principles, policies and system of China's foreign language teaching, methodology, subjects, etc.
- Symposiums have been sponsored and organised to discuss foreign language teaching in China. For instance, a symposium on Applied Linguistics and English teaching was sponsored

in Guangzhou in 1980, the first of such seminars since the birth of New China; the First and Second International Symposiums on foreign language teaching in China were held successively in Guangzhou in 1985 and in Tianjin in 1992; the First Conference of the China Association of Foreign Languages Audio-visual Education was organised in Beijing in 1985.

- All types of teaching programmes are offered, and textbooks of various languages compiled. The programmes offered include the 'First-stage Teaching Programme of College English Major'; the 'First-stage and Advanced-Stage Teaching Programme of College German Major'; and First-stage Teaching Programmes of Russian, Japanese, French, ARABIC, etc. More than 200 types of textbook have been published, which absorbed the merits and experience of traditional teaching material both at home and abroad. Advanced and professional textbooks prevail in cities. Textbooks of LINGUISTICS and literature have also become widely available.
- Testing devices have been utilised and perfected. A nationwide general purpose college English test has been conducted twice a year from 1987. Examinees have amounted to 800,000 each year in recent years.
- Modern technology is applied extensively. Language laboratories and AUDIO-VISUAL equipment have been installed in almost all tertiary institutions and most secondary schools. The application of computers in foreign language teaching is no longer limited to data retrieval and language testing, but rather it has been extended throughout the whole teaching process. In some universities, there are software libraries of considerable scale.

From the mid-1980s on, there has been a new tendency in the reformation of foreign language teaching, embodied in:

- A new rational structure of foreign language majors has been designed, in which foreign languages are combined with a variety of academic subjects so as to satisfy the domestic demand for new types of specialist.
- A multi-level school system and competitive mechanisms have been introduced into education management systems.

- Inter-school and inter-departmental cooperation makes it possible for the FLUs to make use of non-language specialists to train students with professional knowledge, and give impetus to remould old specialities and develop new, practical specialities.

Nevertheless, some problems have arisen with the progress of foreign language teaching in China. It is developing too rapidly, and lacks overall long-term planning, and current foreign language teaching cannot yet satisfy the all-round development of the society. In addition there is a shortage of funds. The teaching staff are ageing and many middle-aged, while young teachers are leaving the teaching force.

**See also:** Central and Eastern Europe; Chinese; Japan; Language planning; Planning for foreign language teaching

## Further reading

Fu Ke (1986) *The history of China foreign language education*, Shanghai: Shanghai Foreign Languages Education Press.

Lan Renzhe (1993) 'Running language colleges well in the condition of market economy', *Foreign Language World* 3: 6.

Qun Yi and Li Xinting (1991) *The development strategy of foreign languages*, Chengdu: Sichuan Education Press.

Wang Zuoliang (ed.) (1990) *ELT in China: Papers presented at the 1985 International Symposium on Teaching English in the Chinese Context*, Beijing: Foreign Language Teaching and Research Press.

Zhang Xuyi (1993) 'Stabilize teaching faculties and ensure teaching effectiveness', *Foreign Language World* 3: 3.

Zhuang Zhixiang and Shu Dingfang (1993) 'On the three aspects of foreign language research theory', *Foreign Language World* 3: 16.

HE ZIRAN AND ZENG YANTAO

# Chinese

Chinese is believed to belong to the Sino-Tibetan language family. It is the language spoken by the majority of the Chinese population, who are known as the Hans. Chinese is therefore also referred to, especially by the Chinese themselves, as *Hanyu*, 'the language of the Hans'. *Hanyu*, spoken presently by over a billion **NATIVE SPEAKERS** in a vast country covering an area of nearly 3,700,000 square miles, has a history of at least 4,500 years.

## The language

Chinese has gradually developed from its proto-typical form into today's eight major dialects: the northern, central, and western parts of the country are dominated by the dialect known in the Western world as Mandarin (a word originally used to refer to the Manchu officials of the Qing Dynasty and their officialese), and in the south-eastern regions of the country one encounters the other dialects – generally speaking, *Wu* in Jiangsu and Zhejiang provinces, *Gan* in Jiangxi, *Xiang* in Hunan, Northern and Southern *Min* in Fujian, *Hakka* (i.e. Kejia) in the north-east of Guangdong, and *Cantonese* (i.e. Yue) in Guangzhou and Hong Kong.

The principal differences between these eight dialects (each of which may, of course, be further divided into subdialects or local accents) lie in pronunciation and everyday **VOCABULARY**, which makes oral communication extremely difficult or sometimes impossible. Mandarin, for example, has only four tones, and two consonantal endings -n and -ng. Cantonese, on the other hand, may employ more than six tones, with consonantal endings like -m, -p, -t, -k, in addition to -n and -ng; and young speakers of Cantonese simply do not differentiate between initials n- and l- (for them, if they are not careful when they speak **ENGLISH**, 'nice' will always be 'lice'). The use of different vocabulary also presents difficulty in mutual understanding: for a Mandarin speaker, a fridge is *bingxiang* (literally 'ice-box'), while for a Cantonese speaker from Guangzhou or Hong Kong, where in fact snow never falls, it is *xutguai* (literally 'snow-cabinet'). However, despite such phonological and lexical differences, these dialects miraculously keep to a uniform script (e.g. rén 'person', kŏu 'mouth', etc., each being a combination of strokes confined to a squarish writing space and based on a monosyllable in speech), follow a similar disyllabification tendency in word-formation (e.g.

rénkŏu 'population', guójiā 'country', etc.) to offset endless homophonic clashes inherent in monosyllables, and adopt more or less the same grammatical rules (e.g. wŏ ài tā 'I love him' as opposed to tā ài wŏ 'he loves me') with comparable word order and few morphological features. It sounds almost legendary to say that, wherever immediate oral transmission fails, writing (either on paper with a pen or on the palm of one's hand with a finger) has always come in to rescue the situation and effect communication among the literate.

Nevertheless, to find a more permanent solution to such communication problems between different dialect speakers, endeavours have been made to unify the country's speech (as the first emperor of **CHINA** did to the country's writing over 2,000 years ago). In 1958 the Chinese government promulgated a new system of romanisation called *pinyin*, based on the version of Mandarin spoken in the Beijing area, and people all over the country were encouraged to learn to speak this standard dialect which is nationally referred to as *Putonghua* 'the common language'. *Putonghua* is variously called Mandarin in the West, *guoyu* 'national language' in Taiwan, and *huayu* 'the Chinese language' in Singapore. With its standardised pronunciation regulated in *pinyin* and essential grammatical features and conventions derived from **LITERARY TEXTS** of the twentieth century after the 1919 intellectual movement, *putonghua* is what is now commonly known as Modern Standard Chinese. It is one of the official languages of the United Nations and the principal form of Chinese taught or learned outside China. However, Cantonese, for historical reasons, is still very much the **LINGUA FRANCA** of Chinese-speaking communities in Europe and elsewhere in the world. Cantonese, as mentioned earlier, shares a similar script and writing practice with Mandarin. None the less, it is not surprising to find writings in the vernacular carried in popular journals and tabloids in Hong Kong, using *ad hoc* or established coinages of written characters representing part of the spoken dialect not found in the shared tradition.

## The study of Chinese as a Foreign Language

The earliest recorded contact with China made by Westerners seems to start with Marco Polo, a

Venetian merchant and traveller in the late thirteenth century, but the account of his experience in China served as no more than an eye-opener at the time. What really brought Europe to an intimate knowledge of Chinese thought and society were the seventeenth and early eighteenth century writings of Jesuit missionaries, such as Matteo Ricci, Adam Schall von Bell and Ferdinand Verbiest. Most of them, despite their sometimes difficult lives in China, were one-time favourites of Chinese emperors and held important offices. Though Jesuit and other Catholic missionaries travelled to China from virtually every part of Europe (including Russia), it was the French missionaries who, under the auspices of Louis XIV, collectively laid the foundation for sinological studies in the West.

However, the major breakthrough in the demand for learning Chinese had to wait till the latter half of the eighteenth century and the beginning of the nineteenth century, when the Industrial Revolution with its rapid advances in commercial production and scientific knowledge pushed Britain to the fore. All at once China found herself confronted not only by missionaries (now Protestant as well as Catholic) but also by merchants and traders from the West, first from Iberian countries and Holland and then from Britain, particularly through the East India Company. In this unprecedented period of imperialist expansion, diplomats were seen to follow in the footsteps of missionaries and traders and the Portuguese and the British were soon followed by the French, the Germans, the Americans and the Russians, vying for a foothold in China in order to exploit and divide up its vast potential market. Necessity certainly infused **MOTIVATION** into all branches of learning. By the time of the two Opium Wars, serious attempts were already being made to establish the discipline of sinology in Europe and America, as a better understanding of China was important in coercing her to open her closed doors. All over Europe and America, colleges and universities set up Chinese courses and, at the same time, appointed professors to teach them. In 1876, both America and Britain set up university chairs of Chinese, with Samuel Wells Williams at Yale and James Legge at Oxford, while similar appointments were being made at Paris, Leiden,

Munich and Berlin from the 1830s onwards. On the other hand, many missionary- or diplomat-turned-scholars like Robert Morrison (who translated the Bible into Chinese), James Legge (who translated Confucian classics into English), and Thomas Wade and Herbert Giles (who invented the Wade-Giles system of Chinese romanisation) were beginning to make their names known to the rest of the world in the field of sinology. Towards the end of the nineteenth century, sinology with its emphasis on the study of Chinese classics was a well-accepted discipline in the West.

It was, however, at the turn of the twentieth century, particularly during the years leading up to and following World War Two, that the study of Chinese saw its greatest advance in Europe and America, as the emerging political situation compelled these countries to see the need for training not only missionaries, **INTERPRETERS** for trade missions, diplomats, public servants and academics, but also large numbers of military personnel, and for orientating the study of Chinese towards more immediate and contemporary goals. As a result, text-based and classics-oriented sinology metamorphosed into or, to be more exact, gave way to so-called Modern Chinese Studies, with its emphasis on area studies relating to China as well as on the Chinese language itself. Very soon, motivated by these new orientations, America took over the lead from Europe.

With China gradually throwing open its doors to the rest of the world, the study of the Chinese language and disciplines related to China is gaining greater momentum, not only in Europe and America but also in **AUSTRALIA** and **JAPAN**. Japan has actually produced many distinguished sinologists, and boasts the best Chinese library holdings outside China. At present, the world is readier than ever to pursue the study of Chinese, and the Association of Asian Studies is an important umbrella organisation for Chinese and Asian Studies while the Association of Chinese Language Teachers likewise sponsors annual academic **EXCHANGES** among college and university teachers from America and publishes in its official journal contributions from its members. To add to the global effort for Chinese Studies, the International Society for Chinese Language Teaching was set up in Beijing in 1987 through Chinese initiative. The

Society, which has committee members from countries all over the world where Chinese is taught, organises a conference to discuss Chinese language teaching every three years in Beijing (or elsewhere in the world, as the latest Committee suggested) and publishes a quarterly journal called *Chinese teaching in the world*. In 1989, HSK (*Hanyu Shuiping Kaoshi* – Chinese Standard Examinations) was established by China's Leading Group for the Teaching of Chinese to Non-Native Speakers. HSK assesses different levels of achievement in Chinese and is for learners who are non-native speakers of the language.

Throughout the twentieth century, numerous **DICTIONARIES** and **TEXTBOOKS** have been produced by Western scholars to help students of Chinese master the language. The way these textbooks were written or compiled clearly reflects the pedagogical stance of their authors. The textbooks compiled by those who had themselves originally been missionaries and diplomats in China had two characteristics which stood out. First, they mostly seem to cater for the practical **NEEDS** of the would-be student, a potential diplomat or merchant who would want to be able to read official documents, civil contracts, or even shop signs so as to enable him to get around during his stay in China, and who would also want to be able to engage in everyday dialogue with his Chinese associates. Second, these textbooks, readers and **GRAMMARS** have an ample provision of **READING** passages or illustrative sentences, invariably with corresponding English translations, which, according to some of the authors, if learned by heart with their meaning fully understood, were supposed to save the student time and help him to think in ready-made idioms and quotations and thus achieve fluency in the language.

In contrast, the textbooks compiled by more academically-minded authors, who advocate more in-depth study of the language and its culture, insist on the reading of classics and good modern or contemporary literature and a thorough appreciation of the workings of the language.

The two different orientations have persisted till this day, and the future seems to be more of a compromise than a split. With the advent of computer facilities and more sophisticated aids to learning, methodology is bound to change in the

new millennium. Given the increasing involvement of Chinese nationals in Chinese Studies at universities throughout the world, there is little chance that teaching and learning Chinese will prove to be an exception.

**See also:** Arabic; China; Japanese

### Further reading

Barrett, T.H. (1989) *Singular listlessness – a short history of Chinese books and British scholars*, London: Wellsweep Press.

Europe Studies China (1995) *Papers from an International Conference on the History of European Sinology*, London: Han-Shan Tang Books.

Herbert, P.A. and Chiang, T. (1982) *Chinese studies research methodology*, Hong Kong: Chinese Materials Center.

Lo, Hsiang-lin (1963) *The role of Hong Kong in the cultural interchange between East and West*, Tokyo: Centre for East Asian Cultural Studies.

Mo, Dongyin (1949, reprinted 1989) *The history of the development of sinology*, Beijing: Peking Cultural Publisher.

Wang, Yanqiu (1982) *Library resources for Chinese studies outside China*, Taiwan: Resource and Service Centre for Chinese Studies.

YIP PO-CHING

# Chomsky, Noam

b. 7 December 1928, Philadelphia, PA, USA

After studies at the University of Pennsylvania, from 1955 Professor of Linguistics at the Massachusetts Institute of Technology, Cambridge, MA

As the instigator of transformational-generative linguistics and **UNIVERSAL GRAMMAR**, he is certainly the most debated and influential linguist of the second half of the twentieth century. Between *Syntactic Structures* (1957), his first publication, and *The Minimalist Program* (1995), he published 70 books and some 1,000 articles on linguistics, philosophy, cognitive science, **PSYCHOLOGY** and also politics. Indeed, with books like *American Power* *and New Mandarins* (1969), many people, above all in the USA, remember him better as a left-leaning political author rather than as a linguist.

Chomsky never reflected on the problems of any type of language teaching, and, on seeing the impact which his ideas made in this field, he even stressed that they were too abstract to be applied in a classroom. It was only in his influential review of B.F. Skinner's book *Verbal Behavior* (1959) that he came anywhere near the problems. Yet he influenced language **ACQUISITION** studies and language teaching programmes by the axiomatic principles of his linguistic views.

For Chomsky, language is located in a human-specific **COMPETENCE** of the mind which works according to abstract rules. These rules are the same for all languages extant, although they appear in different phonetic interpretations. In various grammatical models, he described this **GENERA-TIVE** process, giving syntax the leading part in it. At first, he assumed a 'deep' structure, i.e. an abstract syntactical framework of each sentence, which, by and large, consisted of the regularities of constituent structures, as for example **BLOOMFIELD** had explained them. By exactly defined transformations, which included lexical and phonetic concretisation, this 'deep' structure was made a 'surface' structure, i.e. a concrete act of performance. In various steps which dealt with problems arising out of these assumptions, Chomsky finally gave up the difference between 'deep' (abstract, syntactic) and 'surface' (concrete, semantic and phonetic) structure and spoke of universal principles organising all human languages. All this is meant to explain the working of the human mind as a genetically determined cognitive apparatus.

It is this anthropological background that stimulated scholars of linguistics to understand the data of language acquisition and of second/foreign language learning as signs of the working of the human mind whose processing is triggered, but not essentially influenced, by experience or by teaching. The general aim is to gear the methods of teaching to the predetermined order of learning and, by doing so, make them more effective. Many detailed investigations appeared in which the general rules of language acquisition were thought to be much stronger than, for example, the differences which are observable in the classroom between first language and second/foreign language lessons.

There are many language pedagogues who doubt that these analyses will lead to applicable results, in particular because Chomsky has always the 'ideal' speaker in mind, whereas teachers deal with concrete learners. But even where such doubts prevail, language learning and language competence is nowadays generally understood as the outcome of mental cognitive processes with their own strong, but not omnipotent, dynamism. It is the teacher's task to set this dynamism going. If their work is at all to be described in Chomskyan terms, teachers must accept the principles and try to influence the parameters of language learning, in addition to the behavioural conditions on much lower levels of human nature. Chomsky's general legacy is the cognitive mentalism of present-day language learning theories.

## Further reading

Barsky, R.F. (1997) *Noam Chomsky: a life of dissent*, Cambridge, MA: MIT Press.

Lyons, J. (1991) *Chomsky* (3rd edn), London: Fontana.

Newmeyer, F.J. (1986) *Linguistic theory in America. The first quarter-century of transformational generative grammar* (2nd edn), New York: Academic Press.

Newmeyer, F.J. (1988) *Linguistics. The Cambridge Survey*, vols 2 and 3, Cambridge: Cambridge University Press.

WERNER HÜLLEN

# CIEP – Centre international d'études pédagogiques

CIEP provides courses and information for people in charge of policies, administration and pedagogical matters in relation to the French education system. There are three departments: expertise and educational cooperation; academic exchanges and international teaching; and **FRENCH** language.

The French language department offers expertise and training and contributes to analyses of the language, organising an annual forum on the current status of the French language. There are modular training sessions and individually pre-pared courses for those in charge of programme development, for teacher trainers, for teachers of French as a foreign and second language, for teachers of French for Specific Purposes and for those teaching through the MEDIUM of French.

The CIEP also maintains links with those responsible for the promotion of the French language abroad, and with pedagogical profes-sionals of the Ministry of Education. There is a website for news of contemporary FRANCE, with MATERIALS for teachers and information about examinations.

The CIEP is the centre for the educational and administrative management of the DELF (*Diplôme d'Etudes de Langue Française*) and the DALF (*Diplôme Approfondi de Langue Française*), which were created in 1985.

## Website

The CIEP's website is: http://www.ciep.fr

# CILT – The Centre for Information on Language Teaching and Research

CILT was established in 1966. Its purpose is to collect and disseminate information on foreign language teaching and learning. Since 1986 this has been specifically interpreted to mean the promotion of greater national capability in lan-guages throughout the United Kingdom. In 1991 The Scottish Centre for Information on Language Teaching and Research (ScottishCILT) was estab-lished as a partnership between CILT and the University of Stirling, and in 1994 The Northern Ireland CILT (NICILT) was established at Queen's University Belfast.

CILT is a registered educational charity. It was originally a non-departmental public body, but in 1999 its status changed to that of a 'near to Government' body. It has a Board of Governors who are appointed for terms of up to six years, and who broadly represent the main constituencies served by CILT throughout the United Kingdom.

## Activities, resources, information

CILT receives an annual grant from the Depart-ment for Education and Employment as well as from the Scottish Parliament and the Welsh and Northern Ireland Assemblies. It also generates income from its programme activities.

CILT's Resources Library constitutes a unique collection of multimedia language teaching re-sources. In addition, it contains a wide selection of books and periodicals on language teaching methodology, policy and related issues. The library is open to the public throughout the year.

CILT collects and makes available information on a wide range of language related topics. CILT staff also offer advice and consultancy services. This information is made available in paper form, and online through the CILT website and the Lingu@net virtual resources centre.

## Projects and publications

CILT also supports developmental work through its projects on key issues relating to language teaching. These include European funded projects as well as major projects on such areas as Early Language Learning, Teacher Supply and Technology and Language Learning. It produces a regular review of current research into language teaching and learning.

CILT has an extensive conference and in-service training programme, both 'on-site' and throughout the UK. In a typical year, over 70 events are organised, ranging from training sessions on-site to major residential conferences in the UK and abroad.

CILT has an extensive list of publications on language teaching and learning and research. The organisation also publishes a wide range of informative literature, including bulletins aimed at most sectors of education.

## Networks and partnerships

In addition to the partnerships which have created Scottish CILT and NICILT, CILT is the centre of a major initiative in England and Wales – the network of regional COMENIUS Centres. These are regional resource, information and in-service training centres established in partnership with other national providers of services to language professionals, including the Central Bureau and the BBC and the cultural services of the main European embassies.

## Websites

CILT's website is: http://cilt.org.uk
Lingu@net can be found at: http://www.lingua-net-europa.org

## Further reading

*CILT Facts and Figures 1999*, London: CILT.
Hawkins, E.W. (ed.) (1996) *30 years of language teaching*, London: CILT.

## Civilisation

The concept of the French word *civilisation* has its roots in a discourse and ideology of colonialism. Its connotations include a sense of cultural superiority and its use in language teaching reflects the intention to convey a largely positive image of French culture and society to an external audience. It has survived to the beginning of the twenty-first century, however, as a term that is commonly used and readily understood in the context of teaching and learning **FRENCH** as a Foreign Language. The word is used to describe that part of a language course that includes sociocultural knowledge to complement and give context to the linguistic content. This opposition and complementarity is exemplified in the title of Mauger's bestselling *Cours de langue et de civilisation françaises*, written in the 1950s but still being reprinted in the 1980s.

Two points are particularly significant. First, the development of the teaching of *civilisation* is linked institutionally with the **ALLIANCE FRANÇAISE**. Second, there are difficulties in conceptualising the term adequately and in finding an appropriate pedagogy. Together these help to explain why the term has been gradually replaced since the 1980s by concepts incorporating the word 'culture' such as **CULTURAL STUDIES**, cultural anthropology and **INTERCULTURAL COMMUNICATION**.

Galisson and Coste (1988) give three definitions of *civilisation*, namely:

- the act of civilising;
- the characteristics of civilised societies;
- the characteristic features of a given society.

The first of these refers to the colonial ideology, based on a hierarchy of cultures, whereby the colonising power embarked on a mission to bring less developed cultures into modernity through imposing new institutional structures, including schools. The second definition, whilst potentially referring to any society, in fact is likely in a French context to take **FRANCE** as the model. French Republican values are considered by their proponents to be universal as well as national. *Civilisation* therefore has connotations of Frenchness.

The third definition is the one most closely associated with language teaching. Whereas education in general can be seen as a civilising process, and an understanding of the nature of civilisation is likely to be acquired through the study of history and the humanities, language learners need a knowledge of a range of cultural references in order to have a full understanding of texts in the target language. In this sense, *civilisation* can also be applied to the features of societies whose languages are studied by French learners, as in *civilisation britannique*.

The *Alliance française* was set up in 1884 to spread the use of the French language in the colonies and elsewhere overseas. The *Alliance* continues to recruit and train teachers to run classes or provide tuition, and it organises conferences and supports the production of teaching material. It thus has a strong institutional position in the teaching of French as a Foreign Language and has been influential in helping to define the cultural content of language courses. There is in fact a continuous link between language teaching from the colonial era to the present day, the unifying thread of which is the presentation of French *civilisation* in a broadly positive, uncritical light. For many years and in many places one of the main vehicles for the promotion of French was the *Cours de langue et de civilisation françaises* (Mauger, 1953), which combines the teaching of French **GRAMMAR** with a storyline based on a foreign family visiting France and discovering its everyday life and institutions.

Mauger, in his preface, situates the work as a contribution to the *Alliance française* (de Carlo, 1998: 27).

The France portrayed by Mauger is a single social entity, with a single, neutral or standard form of expression. French *civilisation* is presented as if it were the culmination of the Jules Ferry educational reforms of the 1870s, namely as a single nation with a single language. Regional and social variations are invisible. The institutions and monuments presented in the *Cours de langue et de civilisation françaises* are largely located in Paris and chosen to prepare students for an encounter with **LITERARY TEXTS** in the fourth volume. Thus one persistent tradition within French *civilisation*, strongly challenged since the advent of communicative methodology, was a monolithic view of language, culture and society aligned with a nation and a state.

Technical developments in sound recording and the availability of photographic images for classroom use led to the development of **AUDIO-VISUAL** courses, initially, as in *Voix et images de France* (produced in 1960 by **CRÉDIF**) still based on a specially written **STANDARD LANGUAGE**. The course content is dominated by linguistic necessities rather than by a real desire to transmit cultural knowledge. By the time of *C'est le printemps* (produced in 1976 by CLE), course writers had introduced a wider spectrum of characters and situations as well as a functional rather than grammatical **SYLLABUS**. However, further technical advances, together with the development of educational television and video and the availability of photocopying, enabled teachers to have access to a greater range of representations of France and the French language. The move to **COMMUNICATIVE LANGUAGE TEACHING**, with its stress on **AUTHENTIC** materials, paved the way for a reconsideration of what might be considered to be *civilisation*.

Whereas language learning in the tradition of the *Alliance française* aimed to initiate learners into a high and very literary culture, from the 1960s the purposes were increasingly instrumental and to do with tourism and commerce. Alongside high culture, courses started to contain elements of popular culture which widened the definition of *civilisation*. One reason for this is that communicative language teaching requires learners to respond and react, and so texts are chosen with this in mind. Another is that universal access to **SECONDARY EDUCATION** and foreign languages was thought to necessitate engaging with learners at their level, rather than inducting them directly into a high culture which might be doubly alienating as foreign and socially unfamiliar.

During the 1980s *civilisation* was the term for teaching about French and francophone culture in French as a Foreign Language (FLE) courses in France. The field developed rapidly, together with specialist teachers, conferences and journals.

Whereas coherent methodologies for teaching language have been developed following theoretical and empirical research on language **ACQUISITION**, no single approach to teaching *civilisation* has emerged. Beacco (1996) and Chalançon (1996) describe teachers lecturing to classes, enlivening them with personal anecdotes or, in an attempt to promote discussion, introducing themes around which there is public or media interest and often political controversy; these might include youth culture (including drugs), the development of multicultural societies, unemployment, the media. Given that the emphasis within foreign language classes has tended to be primarily on the linguistic potential of a stimulus document, students are likely to be asked comprehension questions in the foreign language or to translate or to summarise part of the text, however controversial the topic. There may be discussion, but this is likely to be constrained by the learners' linguistic competence and thus may not lead to an improved understanding of the topic. **STEREOTYPES** and unsustainable generalisations may even be reinforced during this process.

Two developments within the field of language learning have provided a framework for the development of a pedagogy able to integrate *civilisation* into a unified programme of language-and-culture teaching (Byram *et al.*, 1994). The first is a concern for **AUTONOMOUS LEARNING**, which emphasises investigation and research or *savoir-faire*. Students may learn to decode implicit assumptions in language material. The second is intercultural education, which uses insights from **CULTURAL STUDIES** and **ANTHROPOLOGY** and stresses a reflexive process involving making comparisons between cultural forms in an attempt to achieve a non-ethnocentric perspective. Le Berre (1998) maintains that the term *civilisation* was replaced in the 1980s by *anthropologie culturelle* . This may involve *objectivation*, constructing provisional knowledge through observing difference and oppositions, and contextualisation.

By the end of the twentieth century, the colonial connotations of *civilisation*, together with the development of increasingly multicultural nation-states and the lowering of national boundaries, made it a term that was used sparingly as language teachers increasingly saw their mission as teaching language and cultures rather than a single culture.

**See also:** Area studies; CIEP; Cultural studies; French; *Landeskunde*

### References

Beacco, J.-C. (1996) 'Enseignement de civilisation en classe de langue et méthodologie circulante (Teaching language and culture: problems of informal approaches)', *Echos* 78–9: 123–8.

Byram, M. *et al.* (1994) *Teaching-and-learning language-and-culture*, Clevedon: Multilingual Matters.

Chalançon, J.-P. (1996) 'L'enseignement de la civilisation en classe d'allemand (Teaching culture in the German language classroom)', in *Didactique de l'allemand*, Clermont-Ferrand: CRDP Auvergne.

de Carlo, M. (1998) *L'interculturel (Intercultural issues)*, Paris: CLE International.

Galisson, R. and Coste, D. (1988) *Dictionnaire de didactique des langues (Dictionary of language teaching)*, Paris: Hachette.

Le Berre, M. (1998) 'De la civilisation à l'anthropologie culturelle (From civilisation to cultural anthropology)', *Cahiers Pédagogiques* 360: 54–5.

Mauger, G. (1953) *Cours de langue et de civilisation françaises (French language and civilisation coursebook)*, vols I–IV, Paris: Hachette.

### Further reading

Porcher, L. (ed.) (1986) *La civilisation*, Paris: CLE International.

Zarate, G. (1993) *Représentations de l'étranger et didactique des langues (Representations of the Other in language teaching)*, Paris: Didier.

XAVIÈRE HASSAN AND HUGH STARKEY

# Classroom language

Classroom language refers to teachers' and learners' verbal behaviour in L2 classrooms. Language in this context is both the means for and the goal of instruction. Classroom language tends to be modified in form and function compared to language used in interactions between **NATIVE SPEAKERS** and non-native speakers outside the classroom.

### Development of studies of classroom language

Early studies of classroom language were conducted by means of interaction analysis. Based on this approach, **CLASSROOM OBSERVATION SCHEMES** were employed to record and quantify participants' verbal behaviour in predetermined sets of categories (see, e.g., Moskowitz, 1971). Although observation schemes have become quite sophisticated over their years of implementation, they still reduce complex interactions to rigid categories and fail to fully account for the co-constructions accomplished by conversational interactants.

Initially, studies on classroom language were mainly concerned with describing **TEACHER TALK** (see Allwright and Bailey, 1991). An increasing interest in the role of comprehensible input (Krashen, 1981), interaction (Long, 1983) and the production of comprehensible output (Swain, 1985) for successful second language **ACQUISITION** led researchers to take into account the interactional contributions of all classroom participants. Ethnographic (e.g. van Lier, 1988) and discourse analytic studies (e.g. Ellis, 1984; see also Long, 1980, for a discussion of methodological issues) have sought to provide more elaborate descriptions of classroom language based on observations and the analysis of transcripts of verbal interactions between learners and teachers.

## The special nature of classroom language

Kasper (1986), in the introduction to her book, stresses that the classroom environment entails a particular set of participant rights and obligations, as well as role relationships. Numerous studies have investigated the differences between language use in the classroom and language use in naturalistic conversations among native and non-native speakers. Some have commented on the range of conversational moves teachers and students perform, such as asking questions, responding, or requesting (e.g. Long and Sato, 1983; Ellis, 1997). Others have investigated turn-taking procedures as well as openings and closings of conversational interactions (e.g. Löscher, 1986; van Lier, 1988). Work describing turn-taking procedures in language classrooms is heavily based on studies completed in the field of ethnomethodology (Sacks, Schegloff and Jefferson, 1974). These studies explored turn-taking in naturalistic conversations and thus provided a baseline of comparison for analyses of talk in other contexts.

Discourse analytic studies of classroom interactions in general identified a specific sequence of moves to be basic to most teacher-fronted classroom contexts (Sinclair and Coulthard, 1975): Initiation (teacher) – Response (student) – Feedback (teacher), known as IRF. This structure was found to apply to the language classroom as well, with the possible addition of another response move by the student (IRF-R), such as for instance the repetition of the teacher's feedback (McTear, 1975). As Ellis states: 'Although IRF(R) exchanges tend to dominate [in the classroom], other kinds can be found' (1994: 575). Several approaches have aimed at providing more detailed descriptions of patterns of language use and interaction in the classroom. Ellis (1984), for example, proposes to identify the 'goal', i.e. the purpose, of an interaction, as well as the 'address', i.e. the interlocutor. Van Lier suggests identifying the relative amount of control which teachers hold over both topic (i.e., 'what the talk is *about*', 1988: 149) and type of activity (i.e., 'what is being *done* and *how* it is done', 1988: 149). Whether focusing on goals and address or on topic and activity, both Ellis (1984) and van Lier (1988) aim at analysing how language in the classroom is used, when, and by whom.

## Related factors

A number of studies have explored the relationship between classroom organisation and teachers' as well as learners' use of language. In particular, they compared teacher-fronted and group activities in terms of participant contributions and negotiated modifications of the input, such as clarification requests, comprehension checks, or rephrasings (Pica and Doughty, 1985; House, 1986). Pica and Doughty (1985) also suggest that, in addition to group structure, the nature of the task will influence the negotiation work which can be observed in the classroom. In the context of their study, they stipulate that the kinds of information exchange required among participants influences their use of language.

Some researchers have also studied classroom discourse based on a sociocultural framework. Antón (1999), for instance, explored how teachers within learner-centred classrooms used language to foster in learners the responsibility for their own learning. Language use from a sociocultural perspective is considered an important tool for learners' cognitive development.

A small number of studies have targeted still other aspects of language use, such as the role of cultural background (e.g. Sato, 1982), as well as learners' socialisation of discourse competence in language classrooms (Duff, 1995; 1996). Findings are difficult to generalise due to the different approaches used as well as the different groups studied. Despite these differences, most researchers seem to assign a central role to linguistic production and interaction for classroom second language acquisition, although the exact relationship between learners' use of language or interaction and actual language acquisition remains unclear (see, e.g., Gass and Varonis, 1994; Long, 1996).

**See also:** Classroom observation schemes; Classroom research; Communicative language teaching; Discourse analysis; Research methods; Teacher talk

## References

Allwright, D. and Bailey, K. (1991) *Focus on the language classroom: an introduction to classroom research*, Cambridge: Cambridge University Press.

Antón, M. (1999) 'The discourse of a learner-centered classroom: sociocultural perspectives on teacher–learner interaction in the second language classroom', *Modern Language Journal* 83: 303–18.

Chaudron, C. (1988) *Second language classrooms. Research on teaching and learning*, Cambridge: Cambridge University Press.

Duff, P. (1995) 'An ethnography of communication in immersion classrooms in Hungary', *TESOL Quarterly* 29: 505–37.

Duff, P. (1996) 'Different languages, different practices: socialization of discourse competence in dual-language school classrooms in Hungary', in K. Bailey and D. Nunan (eds), *Voices from the language classroom: qualitative research in second language education*, Cambridge: Cambridge University Press.

Ellis, R. (1984) *Classroom second language development*, Oxford: Pergamon.

Ellis, R. (1994) *The study of second language acquisition*, Oxford: Oxford University Press.

Ellis, R. (1997) *Second language acquisition research and language teaching*, Oxford: Oxford University Press.

Gass, S. and Varonis, E. (1994) 'Input, interaction, and second language production', *Studies in Second Language Acquisition* 16: 283–302.

House, J. (1986) 'Learning to talk: talking to learn. An investigation of learner performance in two types of discourse', in G. Kasper (ed.), *Learning, teaching and communication in the foreign language classroom*, Aarhus: Aarhus University Press.

Kasper, G. (ed.) (1986) *Learning, teaching and communication in the foreign language classroom*, Aarhus: Aarhus University Press.

Krashen, S. (1981) *Second language acquisition and second language learning*, Oxford: Pergamon.

Long, M. (1980) 'Inside the "black box": methodological issues in classroom research on language learning', *Language Learning* 30: 1–42.

Long, M. (1983) 'Linguistic and conversational adjustments to nonnative speakers', *Studies in Second Language Acquisition* 5: 177–93.

Long, M. (1996) 'The role of the linguistic environment in second language acquisition', in W.C. Ritchie and T.K. Bhatia (eds), *Handbook of second language acquisition*, New York: Academic Press.

Long, M. and Sato, C. (1983) 'Classroom foreigner talk discourse: forms and functions of teachers' questions', in H. Seliger and M. Long, *Classroom oriented research in second language acquisition*, Rowley, MA: Newbury House.

Löscher, W. (1986) 'Conversational structures in the foreign language classroom', in G. Kasper (ed.), *Learning, teaching and communication in the foreign language classroom*, Aarhus: Aarhus University Press.

McTear, M. (1975) 'Structure and categories of foreign language teaching sequences', in R. Allwright (ed.), *Working papers: language teaching classroom research*, Essex: University of Essex, Department of Language and Linguistics.

Moskowitz, G. (1971) 'Interaction analysis – a new modern language for supervisors', *Foreign Language Annals* 5: 211–21.

Pica, T. and Doughty, C. (1985) 'Input and interaction in the communicative classroom: a comparison of teacher-fronted and group activities,' in S. Gass and C. Madden (eds), *Input in second language acquisition*, Rowley, MA: Newbury House.

Sacks, H., Schegloff, E.A. and Jefferson, G. (1974) 'A simplest systematics for the organization of turn-taking for conversation', *Language* 50: 696–735.

Sato, C. (1982) 'Ethnic styles in classroom discourse', in M. Hines and W. Rutherford (eds), *On TESOL '81*, Washington, DC: TESOL.

Sinclair, J. and Coulthard, M. (1975) *Towards an analysis of discourse*, Oxford: Oxford University Press.

Swain, M. (1985) 'Communicative competence: some roles of comprehensible input and comprehensible output in its development', in S. Gass and C. Madden (eds), *Input in second language acquisition*, Rowley, MA: Newbury House.

van Lier, L. (1988) *The classroom and the language learner*, London: Longman.

**Further reading**

Allwright, D. and Bailey, K. (1991) *Focus on the language classroom: an introduction to classroom research*, Cambridge: Cambridge University Press.

Chaudron, C. (1988) *Second language classrooms. Research on teaching and learning*, Cambridge: Cambridge University Press.

Ellis, R. (1994) *The study of second language acquisition*, Oxford: Oxford University Press.

Ellis, R. (1997) *Second language acquisition research and language teaching*, Oxford: Oxford University Press.

Philips, S. (1983) *The invisible culture. Communication in classroom and community on the Warm Springs Indian Reservation*, Prospect Heights, IL: Waveland Press.

BIRGIT MEERHOLZ-HÄRLE
AND ERWIN TSCHIRNER

# Classroom observation schemes

A classroom observation scheme is an instrument for recording aspects of teaching and learning events in the classroom. Observation schemes generally consist of a number of specific categories, and are employed in **TEACHER EDUCATION**/development as well as for research purposes.

## Development

Classroom observation schemes or schedules (Allwright, 1988) started to gain acceptance in research on language learning in the mid-1960s. Researchers at the time were particularly interested in identifying the method most effective for language teaching. Based on their findings, they intended to prescribe to teachers the principal elements of good teaching. The main focus of these early observation schemes was on the language teachers' behaviour. Over the years, and with a change in research emphases and questions asked, the design of observation schemes has changed to include aspects of learner behaviours and learning processes.

One of the first observation schemes applied to language teaching was Flanders's (1970) 'Interaction Analysis'. This instrument consisted of ten categories (accepts feeling, praises or encourages, accepts or uses ideas of student, asks questions, lecturing, giving directions, criticising or justifying authority, student talk-response, student talk-initiation, and silence or confusion), and was originally developed for **CLASSROOM RESEARCH** in general. Moskowitz (1971) further modified Flanders's categorisation to fit the context of the language classroom. Her instrument, termed 'FLint' (Foreign Language interaction), was intended for use in research as well as in teacher development. Beyond designing a tool for teacher trainers, Moskowitz was also interested in providing the teachers themselves with a tool to observe and reflect on their own teaching. Another frequently cited observation scheme is FOCUS (Foci for Observing Communications Used in Settings), developed by Fanselow (1977) in the mid-1970s. Since Fanselow intended the scheme's application to go beyond the immediate language teaching context, FOCUS did not include separate categories for teacher and learner behaviour. Rather, it consisted of five general categories (source, medium, use, content and pedagogical purpose of a move) which could be adapted to a variety of settings and participants.

## Issues of objectivity and reliability

Since they were first introduced in classroom research, observation schemes have become quite sophisticated (Nunan, 1992). One example of such a well developed and complex scheme is COLT (Allwright, Fröhlich and Spada, 1984; Spada and Fröhlich, 1995), an instrument intended to rate classroom activities on their communicative potential. COLT consists of two parts, the first of which is designed to record information on activity type and content, participant organisation, **SKILLS** involved, and **MATERIALS** required. The second part, part B, addresses the communicative features (e.g. use of the target language, discourse initiation, etc.) employed by classroom participants.

Despite the growing sophistication of observation instruments, their respective degree of objectivity and reliability is still at issue. Allwright and Bailey state that 'the value of an observational schedule depends directly and exclusively on the reliability and **VALIDITY** of its categories' (1991: 13). As Chaudron (1988) claims, the reliability of most instruments has not been sufficiently proved (see also Allwright and Bailey, 1991). Since researchers tend to develop their own instruments rather than use pre-existing ones, and since they frequently use different categories to record similar aspects of behaviour, instruments as well as findings are hard to compare. Items assessing similar aspects also frequently differ on the degree of inference (see

Long 1980) required for their rating. Furthermore, as Nunan (1992) claims, researchers will always be informed by specific theories on language learning as well as on research. Nunan states that 'there is no such thing as "objective" observation ... what we see will be determined, at least in part, by what we expect to see' (1994: 98). Observation schemes, from this point of view, then, are bound to be subjective. Another point of criticism addresses the kind of rigid classification which observation schemes demand. Classroom situations contain complex events which might not be accounted for in a prefabricated list of categories. Comparing a selection of observation schemes, Chaudron states that 'no one scheme in fact includes all the potentially relevant dimensions of information about classroom interaction' (1988: 21). Researchers might therefore miss events crucial to the research question but not encoded in the scheme.

While there is considerable debate on the objectivity and reliability of observation schemes for research purposes, most researchers actually agree that the instruments can be beneficial for teacher training and development. Lightbown and Spada (1999), for instance, point out that observations can help teachers reflect on their teaching practices and the pedagogical assumptions informing these. Following Genesee and Upshur, 'classroom observations consist of a set of observational categories that directs teachers in their search for information, inferences, and explanations of teaching and learning' (1996: 95). Observation is thus considered a valuable tool which can assist teachers in their everyday classroom practice.

## Selection and design of schemes

When selecting an observation scheme, several design features have to be taken into account in order to ensure a fit between the instrument and the purpose of the observation (Chaudron, 1988): recording procedure, item type (high versus low inference items; see Long, 1980), possibilities of multiple coding for one event, real-time coding or post-event coding on a recording, as well as units of analysis employed (temporal, linguistic or pedagogical) have to be examined. It is, of course, also crucial to consider whether a particular scheme

was developed with research or teacher education purposes in mind (Nunan, 1992).

Genesee and Upshur (1996) provide guidelines for the design of original observation schemes. Similar to Moskowitz (1971), they envision teachers observing themselves and making use of their observations for those everyday decision-making processes required of them in the classroom. The design guidelines they suggest address the following issues: (a) identify the *what*, i.e. those aspects of the teaching and learning process intended for observation; (b) identify the *whom*, i.e. decide whether to focus on individual students or on group/whole class interaction; (c) decide *how often* and *when exactly* to observe; and (d) decide on the *how*, i.e. the form of record keeping (anecdotal records, checklists or rating scales). Since rating scales and checklists consist of predetermined categories, Genesee and Upshur advise beginning teachers/teacher researchers to use anecdotal records to develop appropriate categories.

**See also:** Action research; Classroom language; Classroom research; Research methods; Teacher talk

## References

Allwright, P., Fröhlich, M. and Spada, N. (1984). 'The communicative orientation of language teaching: an observation scheme', in J. Handscombe, R. Orem and B. Taylor (eds), *On TESOL '83*, Washington, DC: TESOL.

Allwright, D. (1988) *Observation in the language classroom*, London: Longman.

Allwright, D. and Bailey, K. (1991) *Focus on the language classroom. An introduction to classroom research for language teachers*, Cambridge: Cambridge University Press.

Chaudron, C. (1988) *Second language classrooms: research on teaching and learning*, Cambridge: Cambridge University Press.

Fanselow, J.F. (1977) 'Beyond "Rashomon" – conceptualizing and describing the teaching act', *TESOL Quarterly* 11: 17–39.

Flanders, N.A. (1970) *Analyzing teaching behavior*, Reading, MA: Addison-Wesley.

Genesee, F. and Upshur, J. (1996) *Classroom-based*

*evaluation in second language education*, Cambridge: Cambridge University Press.

Lightbown, P.M. and Spada, N. (1999) *How languages are learned*, Oxford: Oxford University Press.

Long, M. (1980) 'Inside the "black box": methodological issues in classroom research on language learning', *Language Learning* 30: 1–42.

Moskowitz, G. (1971) 'Interaction analysis – a new modern language for supervisors', *Foreign Language Annals* 5: 211–21.

Nunan, D. (1992) *Research methods in language learning*, Cambridge: Cambridge University Press.

Richards, J. (1998) *Beyond training: perspectives on language teacher education*, Cambridge: Cambridge University Press.

Spada, N. and Fröhlich, M. (1995) *The Communicative Orientation of Language Teaching (COLT) observation scheme: coding conventions and applications*, Sydney: National Centre for English Language Teaching and Research.

## Further reading

Allwright, D. (1988) *Observation in the language classroom*, London: Longman.

Allwright, D. and Bailey, K. (1991) *Focus on the language classroom. An introduction to classroom research for language teachers*, Cambridge: Cambridge University Press.

Chaudron, C. (1988) *Second language classrooms: research on teaching and learning*, Cambridge: Cambridge University Press.

Genesee, F. and Upshur, J. (1996) *Classroom-based evaluation in second language education*, Cambridge: Cambridge University Press.

Nunan, D. (1992) *Research methods in language learning*, Cambridge: Cambridge University Press.

BIRGIT MEERHOLZ-HÄRLE
AND ERWIN TSCHIRNER

# Classroom research

Classroom research looks into the classroom itself for an understanding of what happens there. It was already established in teacher training in the 1960s, with systematic **CLASSROOM OBSERVATION** being used as a feedback tool in teacher training when the failure of comparative method research to take classroom events sufficiently into account prompted the rapid development of academic classroom research on classroom processes. Classroom research studies learner behaviour and teacher behaviour, observable behaviour and unobservable behaviour (thoughts, **ATTITUDES** and opinions). For some time mainly associated with second language **ACQUISITION** studies as an academic research tool, it is now even more strongly associated with teacher-based research for teacher development, often in the form of **ACTION RESEARCH**, whereby teachers use classroom research procedures to investigate their own classrooms.

Classroom research can involve direct classroom observation, or less direct, and more obviously subjective, data collection procedures such as participant diaries, questionnaires and interviews. Classroom research thus lends itself to qualitative as well as to quantitative approaches to research design. Classroom observation is central to the tradition, however, with lessons recorded via audio- and/or videotape, and transcribed for analysis, typically via an observation schedule or category system that reduces data to quantifiable categories of classroom behaviour. Inferences are then made from the patterns of behaviour so revealed.

## Forty years of classroom research: origins and developments

Classroom observation has a long history in education, with teacher performance typically being evaluated this way, and a long history in initial teacher training, with observed classroom performance crucial to professional qualifications.

When 'interaction analysis' arrived (Flanders, 1960), both a research tool and a practical tool for teacher training with only ten categories and requiring only twelve hours of training, interest in classroom observation grew rapidly. In the **USA** (Moskowitz, 1968) and Europe (Wragg, 1970; Krumm, 1973) interaction analysis was adopted and adapted to represent the characteristics of language classrooms. Objective descriptions of classroom behaviour had arrived to replace subjective and prescriptive evaluations.

Also during the 1960s, US educational researchers (Smith, 1970) tried, by making direct comparisons between classes taught audiolingually and classes taught more traditionally, to establish the **AUDIOLINGUAL METHOD** as the one best method. The results were inconclusive, but one of the first critics (Clark, 1969) noted that they were uninterpretable, rather than inconclusive, since the study's classroom observation element was unable to demonstrate that the designated methods had been used systematically and exclusively. The 'inconclusive' results were most probably due to insufficiently different classroom practices. This prompted teacher trainers wishing to broaden their research, and people interested in classroom processes but not involved in teacher training, to move away from observation as a feedback tool and to focus instead upon what the 'objective' description of language classroom processes offered academic research (Allwright, 1975).

It was now possible to develop research techniques following academic research criteria, rather than according to training requirements, and so category systems could hope to represent the complexities of language classrooms. 'FOCUS' (Fanselow, 1977) was designed to get the best of both worlds with a system that, for academic research purposes, exhaustively categorised classroom language teaching and learning, but which could be used highly selectively by teachers in training for their more restricted purposes. Early in the 1980s, working outside teacher training, and more interested in investigating **COMMUNICATIVE LANGUAGE TEACHING**, researchers at **OISE** (Ontario Institute for Studies in Education) developed the extensive category system COLT (Communicative Orientation of Language Teaching – Allen, Fröhlich and Spada, 1984). Researchers could now also develop non-observational techniques, and make productive links with **SECOND LANGUAGE ACQUISITION** studies (SLA). SLA offered motivated research questions in a coherent theoretical framework (Long, 1981).

'Mentalistic' research techniques were also developed (Cohen and Hosenfeld, 1981) using diary studies (Bailey, 1980) or think-aloud procedures (Hosenfeld, 1979), for example, to elicit talk from teachers (and learners) about their experiences. This represented a major break with

tradition. Participants' subjective experiences were now potentially as important as anything which could be captured by observers (or audio/video-recording machines).

Academic classroom research had largely broken away from teacher training, then, and no longer saw direct observation as central (Allwright, 1987). It gained increasingly wide acceptance as a valid academic pursuit, drawing mainly on SLA for its research questions, and contributing to a growing body of published research. However, the link with SLA began to weaken, as teacher development via in-service (rather than pre-service) work developed fast as a rival source of ideas, influenced by overtly ideological concerns. The notion of the teacher as 'intellectual' was proposed (Giroux, 1988), replacing the teacher as mere 'delivery system' for other people's thinking. Teachers could now be expected to develop their own theories of teaching and learning, from experience and reflection.

At the same time, in spite of its obvious concern for the classroom, academic classroom research had further eroded relations between teachers and researchers. SLA-inspired research agendas appeared largely irrelevant to teachers, and the research procedures themselves were intrusive and time-consuming. Action research arrived (Carr and Kemmis, 1986; Nunan, 1989), proposing that the people to undertake classroom research were teachers, who would do research by taking action for change – research aimed at solving teachers' own immediate classroom problems, unhindered by abstract theoretical agendas. Action researchers, working for their own development, in their own classrooms, would keep on taking adaptive action until their problem had been solved. No control group was needed, nor was it necessary to hold everything else constant while an experimental action was tried out – major requirements of traditional experimental research. Otherwise, however, action research followed the academic repertoire of classroom research procedures.

## Some current problems and unresolved issues

None the less, the relationship between academic classroom research and its counterpart in teacher development is problematic. Can teacher-based research contribute to theory, or can it only contribute, at best, to practical problem-solving? Should teacher-researchers follow academic research practices, or should they re-invent classroom research, and find their own criteria for validity (see Nunan, 1997 and Allwright, 1997)?

Using action research to solve classroom problems is also problematic in practice, because of the heavy burden the procedures can place on teachers. 'Exploratory practice' (Allwright and Lenzuen, 1997) is designed to minimise such problems.

Academic acceptance of classroom research has countered the simplistic assumptions behind large-scale methodological comparisons. Also, classroom research has largely succeeded in finding a place on teacher training and **TEACHER EDUCATION** courses, and in teacher development work. On academic courses in **APPLIED LINGUISTICS** the full academic model typically predominates, whereas action research (and, more rarely, exploratory practice) is more common elsewhere.

However, one influential commentator has regretted that many published 'classroom' studies are really 'classroom-oriented' rather than 'class-room-based'. They do not involve 'investigating real behaviour in real classrooms' (Nunan, 1991: 260). It would be ironic if a too-broad interpretation of 'classroom research' brought about a neglect (Breen, 1985) of what was originally its central concern – what actually happens in classrooms.

**See also:** Action research; Classroom observation schemes; Evaluation; Research methods; Second language acquisition theories; Teacher education; Teacher talk

## References

Allen, J.P.B., Fröhlich, M. and Spada, N. (1984) 'The communicative orientation of language teaching', in J. Handscombe, R. Orem and B. Taylor (eds), *On TESOL '83*, Washington, DC: TESOL.

Allwright, R.L. (1975) 'Problems in the study of the teacher's treatment of learner error', in K.M. Burt and H.C. Dulay (eds), *On TESOL '75: New directions in second language learning, teaching and bilingual education*, Washington, DC: TESOL.

Allwright, R.L. (1987) 'Classroom observation: problems and possibilities', in B. Das (ed.), *Patterns of classroom interaction in Southeast Asia*, Singapore: SEAMEO/RELC.

Allwright, R.L. (1997) 'Quality and sustainability in teacher-research', *TESOL Quarterly* 31, 2: 368–70.

Allwright, R.L. and Lenzuen, R. (1997) 'Exploratory practice: work at the Cultura Inglesa, Rio de Janeiro, Brazil', *Language Teaching Research* 1, 1: 73–9.

Bailey, K.M. (1980) 'An introspective analysis of an individual's language learning experience', in S.D. Krashen and R. Scarcella (eds), *Research in second language acquisition*, Rowley, MA: Newbury House.

Breen, M.P. (1985) 'The social context for language learning – a neglected situation?', *Studies in Second Language Acquisition* 7: 135–58.

Carr, W. and Kemmis, S. (1986) *Becoming critical: education, knowledge, and action research*, London: Falmer Press.

Clark, J.L.D. (1969) 'The Pennsylvania Project and the "audiolingual vs traditional" question', *Modern Language Journal* 53: 388–96.

Cohen, A.D. and Hosenfeld, C. (1981) 'Some uses of mentalistic data in second language research', *Language Learning* 31: 285–313.

Fanselow, J.F. (1977) 'Beyond *Rashomon* – conceptualizing and describing the teaching act', *TESOL Quarterly* 11, 1: 17–39.

Flanders, N.A. (1960) *Interaction analysis in the classroom: a manual for observers*, Ann Arbor: University of Michigan Press.

Giroux, H.A. (1988) *Teachers as intellectuals*, South Hadley, MA: Bergin and Garvey.

Hosenfeld, C. (1979) 'Cindy: a learner in today's foreign language classroom', in W. Borne (ed.), *The foreign language learner in today's classroom environment*, Montpellier, VT: Northeast Conference.

Krumm, H.J. (1973) 'Interaction analysis and microteaching for the training of modern language teachers', *IRAL* 11, 2: 163–70.

Long, M.H. (1981) 'Input, interaction and second language acquisition', in H. Winitz (ed.), *Native language and foreign language acquisition*, New York: New York Academy of Sciences.

Moskowitz, G. (1968) 'The effects of training

foreign language teachers in interaction analysis', *Foreign Language Annals* 1, 3: 218–35.

Nunan, D. (1989) *Understanding language classrooms*, London: Prentice Hall.

Nunan, D. (1991) 'Methods in second language classroom-oriented research: a critical review', *Studies in Second Language Acquisition* 13, 2: 249–74.

Nunan, D. (1997) 'Standards for teacher-research', *TESOL Quarterly* 31, 2: 365–7.

Smith, P.D. (1970) *A comparison of the cognitive and audiolingual approaches to foreign language instruction; the Pennsylvania Project*, Philadelphia: Center for Curriculum Development.

Wragg, E.C. (1970) 'Interaction analysis in the foreign language classroom', *Modern Language Journal* 54, 2: 116–20.

## Further reading

Allwright, R.L. (1988) *Observation in the language classroom*, Harlow: Longman.

Allwright, R.L. and Bailey, K.M. (1991) *Focus on the language classroom: an introduction to classroom research for language teachers*, Cambridge: Cambridge University Press.

Chaudron, C. (1988) *Second language classrooms*, Cambridge: Cambridge University Press.

Long, M.H. and Seliger, H.W. (1983) *Classroom oriented research in second language acquisition*, Rowley, MA: Newbury House.

Nunan, D. (1989) *Understanding language classrooms*, London: Prentice Hall.

van Lier, L. (1988) *The classroom and the language learner*, Cambridge: Cambridge University Press.

DICK ALLWRIGHT

## Cloze test

The cloze test was invented by W. Taylor in 1953, who also coined the term 'cloze', linking it explicitly to the Gestalt **PSYCHOLOGY** term 'closure'. In its original form, a cloze test consists of a single passage of (**AUTHENTIC**) prose in which, after a short unmutilated lead-in, every *n*th word (*n* being usually a number between 5 and 10) is deleted leaving blanks. The candidate is requested to supply the missing words. The mechanical

deletion principle is intended to approximate random sampling of the language and to result in a content-valid test. As a rule, classical cloze tests are viewed as integrative or holistic tests of global proficiency in a first, second or foreign language. The cloze procedure is based on the theory of reduced redundancy testing. The number of correct restorations is seen as a measure of the efficiency of a global language processing **COMPETENCE** underlying both the receptive and productive use of language.

For a long time, cloze tests were viewed by many language testers as a particularly suitable instrument for measuring general language proficiency. However, there has been severe criticism, including the following:

1　Since cloze tests usually consist of only one longer text, there may be a bias due to text specificity.

2　The factors 'text', 'deletion rate' and 'starting point' affect **RELIABILITY** and **VALIDITY** coefficients.

3　If the exact method of scoring is used (only the original word present is viewed as correct), then cloze tests are often too difficult even for **ADULT** educated **NATIVE SPEAKERS**. If acceptable scoring is used, a large subjective component enters the scoring, and the tests are less reliable and marking more time-consuming.

4　The difficulty of cloze tests depends on the proportion of structure and content words deleted (different starting points and deletion rates result in different proportions).

5　Many of the cloze tests reported in the literature are much less reliable than was originally assumed.

6　Cloze tests measure primarily micro-linguistic **SKILLS** on the sentence level.

There have been several variations on the classical cloze procedure. In the multiple-choice cloze, options are provided for each blank on the basis of an empirical item analysis. The multiple-choice cloze does not assume **WRITING** competence on the part of the examinee, and it is easier than its classical counterpart. In the rational deletion cloze, specific words such as cohesive ties or 'important' grammatical structures are deleted. As a consequence, the rational deletion cloze is neither a test of reduced redundancy nor a measure of general language competence. Therefore, some authors consider it to be a specific gap-filling technique rather than a cloze test. A further, more recent variant of the cloze procedure is the **C-TEST**.

**See also:** Assessment and testing

### Further reading

Klein-Braley, C. (1997) 'C-tests in the context of reduced redundancy testing: an appraisal', *Language Testing* 14, 1: 47–84.

Oller, J.W. Jr and Jonz, J. (1994) *Cloze and coherence*, Lewisburg: Bucknell University Press.

RÜDIGER GROTJAHN

## Cognitive code theory

This theory can best be seen as a merger of two main areas. The first lies within the work of **CHOMSKY** on transformational grammar, while the second emanates from Carroll's application of cognitive psychology. Carroll's interest in foreign language teaching led him to assess the appropriateness of the prevailing methods in the **USA** during the early 1960s. He concluded that the predominant **AUDIOLINGUAL METHOD**, associated with the **BEHAVIOURIST** branch of psychology and learning theory, was 'ripe for major revision' (Carroll, 1966b: 105; and in Richards and Rodgers, 1986: 60). He suggested putting this method together with elements of the cognitive code learning theory which was gaining a great deal of attention at that time, as part of the Chomskyian 'revolution' (Lyons, 1991: 154). The resulting theory never replaced audiolingualism, however, in terms of 'prominence or pervasiveness' (Nunan, 1991: 232).

The term is also used to refer to teaching practice where a grammatical **SYLLABUS** is accompanied by learner activities, which allow for a degree of exploration and investigations, rather than didactic **TEACHER METHODS**. Wilkins writes that the label cognitive code 'captures both the nature of the mental operations involved and the focus on the language system' (1990: 521).

Cognitive code theory placed an emphasis on the mental processes involved in learning, and this was a departure from behaviourist views which outlined learning in terms of passive habit formation through drills and repetition. Chomsky posited that there are universal, innate abilities, which enable us, first as children, to learn a language long before any formal instruction takes place. The means by which children formulate rules, test them out and reformulate them, after being given limited numbers of examples, was evidence in Chomsky's view of innate cognitive abilities. It is not the case that we learn everything by example and practice or, in behaviourist terms, as response to stimuli. In this case, we would need many lifetimes 'to learn all the sentences of a language through a process of stimulus–response' (Nunan, 1991: 233). Instead, we work things out, basing new utterances upon examples and extrapolating the rules of **GRAMMAR**. We only formally learn the rules of grammar later on, if at all, during language education. Thus, cognitive code theory was another part of the rejection of behaviourism occurring in the 1960s, which was a watershed period in linguistics and language teaching. Cognitive code influenced many involved in the field, including Carroll.

Krashen, for example, writes of when he was a student of TESL and his acceptance as 'penetrating insight' Carroll's 'characterization of how language learning proceeds from the point of view of the then new "cognitive-code" school of thought' (1987: 83). He later went on to produce his own second language learning theory (**MONITOR MODEL**) which was also influential, and incorporated elements of cognitive code. Krashen emphasised the conclusion drawn from a number of studies and observations that not everything a second language learner knows is the result of conscious teaching. Language can be acquired through other means and sometimes appears as intuitive, before any structures or rules have been formally presented.

In practice, this implied the encouragement of learners to draw upon their innate abilities, even though involved in second language (L2) and no longer first language (L1) learning in the classroom. Language learning is viewed as active and rule seeking rather than rule remembering, and also as problem-solving with many **TASK-BASED** activities. Drilling and repetition were no longer emphasised but instead activities which necessitated active learning. It was believed that if teaching activities were planned appropriately, students would work out for themselves the underlying language rules of L2 and then practise them. Nunan points out that some cognitive courses, in fact, have language drills, but they have 'a different rationale and use from behaviourist drills' (1991: 233).

Rules are also important, but, with cognitive code, careful selection of rules will facilitate learners in working out many others. Not all rules have to be presented and learned in a rote manner. At the start of a typical cognitive code lesson, learners are encouraged to consider their previous knowledge with the assumption that new knowledge should always be linked to what has gone before, rather than being taught in a vacuum. This drawing upon previous knowledge would be considered a necessary preliminary. Active reflection and discussion about the target language is also to be encouraged.

New language items to be learned can be presented either deductively or inductively, with the former meaning that the item is 'embedded in a meaningful context' (Nunan, 1991: 233). With inductive learning, examples are given and then students have to work out the rule through guided learning and discovery. These techniques differ from audiolingualism, which it criticised on the ground that learners were not expected to use their cognitive abilities to work out rules. Again, there is the emphasis on the learner and what they can do for themselves, with the teacher becoming more of a facilitator and guide rather than a 'giver of knowledge'.

The status of errors in cognitive code learning is different to more behaviourist methods, with the suggestion the errors are part of the process of second language **ACQUISITION**. New rules are hypothesised from the information given and then tested out. Errors are not just to be corrected but can be indicative of cognitive processes in action.

Cognitive code theory attracted interest from language teaching theorists and practitioners, but 'no clear-cut methodological guidelines emerged, nor did any particular method incorporating this view of learning' (Richards and Rodgers, 1986: 60). It is probably the general view of the learner proposed by the theory that became important, together with its links with the general rejection of

behaviourist models. Cognitive code can be viewed as influencing the communicative approach, which does make use of some of the principles of that approach (Richards, Platt and Platt, 1992).

**See also:** Behaviourism; Chomsky; Communicative language teaching; Error analysis; Learning styles; Psychology; Second language acquisition theories

## References

Carroll, J.B. (1966a) 'Research in foreign language teaching: the last five years', in R.G. Mead Jr (ed.), *Language teaching: broader contexts*, Northeast Conference Reports on the Teaching of Foreign Languages: Reports of the Working Committees, New York: MLA Materials Center.

Carroll, J.B. (1966b) 'The contributions of psychological theory and educational research to the teaching of foreign language', in A. Valdman (ed.), *Trends in language teaching*, New York: McGraw Hill.

Chomsky, N. (1959) 'A review of B.F. Skinner's "Verbal Behaviour" ', *Language* 35, 1: 26–58.

Krashen, S. (1987) *Principles and practice in second language acquisition*, Hemel Hempstead: Prentice Hall.

Lyons, J. (1991) *Chomsky* (3rd edn), London: Fontana.

Nunan, D. (1991) *Language teaching methodology: a textbook for teachers*, Hemel Hempstead: Prentice Hall.

Richards, J.C. and Rodgers, T.C. (1986) *Approaches and methods in language teaching: a description and analysis*, Cambridge: Cambridge University Press.

Richards, J.C., Platt, J. and Platt, H. (1992) *Dictionary of stics*, Harlow: Longman.

Wilkins, D. (1990) 'Second languages: how they are learned and taught', in N.E. Collinge (ed.), *An encyclopedia of language*, London: Routledge.

## Further reading

Carroll, J.B. (1966b) 'The contributions of psychological theory and educational research to the teaching of foreign language', in A. Valdman (ed.), *Trends in language teaching*, New York: McGraw Hill.

Chomsky, N. (1959) 'A review of B.F. Skinner's "Verbal Behaviour" ', *Language* 35, 1: 26–58.

Lyons, J. (1991) *Chomsky* (3rd edn), London: Fontana.

RUTH CHERRINGTON

# Comenius, Johannes Amos (popular Latin form of Komenský, Jan Amos)

b. 28 March 1592, Nivnice, Moravia (today Czech Republic)
d. 15 November 1670, Amsterdam

Comenius was a priest of the Bohemian Brethren (a Hussite denomination), a theologian, philosopher, pedagogue and teacher. After studies in Germany followed by a short stay in his home country, the Thirty Years' War and the Counter-Reformation exiled him and forced him to live in various European countries (Poland, England, Sweden, Hungary, the Netherlands), all the time writing theological and pedagogical books, teaching at schools according to his own didactic programme, and exchanging letters with the great of his time.

For Comenius the sole aim of education was to make people pious and to show them their place in a world which exists after God's will and order. This is why he demanded that everybody should be made knowledgeable about everything, irrespective of his or her social standing. In his *Didactica magna* (1657), Comenius drew the guidelines for teaching: selection of realistic topics to be taken from the life-experience of learners, in particular inclusion of encyclopedic and scientific subjects; differentiation of teaching according to learning ability and age of children; using pictures for the sake of easy memorisation; preferring the useful to the traditional. These guidelines have been the stock of general pedagogy since then. Most of the *Didactica magna* is devoted to language teaching because, for Comenius, language teaching was the centre of education, language being the link between individuals in a society and between human beings and their God.

In accordance with the tradition of his polyglot home country, Comenius took it for granted that people learn more than one language. He distinguished between teaching the **MOTHER TONGUE** (more important than any other), the language of the neighbour (for Moravians, e.g., Hungarian or Polish), the nearest language of regional importance (for Moravians **GERMAN**), and a universal tongue (Latin, as long as no true universal language was available for mankind). Among other writings, he wrote two **TEXTBOOKS** for learning languages which, in the course of time, appeared in hundreds of editions in many languages all over Europe and even in the newly-discovered America. The first, *Janua linguarum reserata* (1631), is a collection of exactly 1,000 Latin sentences, broken down into a hundred sections. These follow the order of the world as it was commonly given in the traditional encyclopedias of Comenius's time: from God and the universe to the kingdoms of nature, to man and man-made reality, the sciences, and the arts. Each Latin sentence provides the definition of a word-meaning, so the whole is actually a topically ordered dictionary of definitions. In this book, Comenius adapted a similar project titled *Janua linguarum*, which had been published by the Irishman William Bathius (William Bathe, 1564–1614) as early as 1611. The second of Comenius's textbooks, *Orbis sensualium pictus* (1658), is a similar collection on a more modest scale and aimed at much younger learners, originally published in Latin and German. There are 150 sections in the traditional encyclopedic order of varying length (between five and twenty-five sentences). Its extraordinary success was stimulated by the ingenious woodcut illustrations that accompany each section and semanticise the words to be taught. With the combination of lexemes (sentences) and pictures referring to each other by numbers, the *Orbis sensualium pictus* became the archetype of a learning dictionary still in use today. Both textbooks are examples of Comenius's didactic principles that teaching must be meaningful and that language, in particular a foreign language, can only be meaningful if it refers to reality. Consequently, language teaching must go together with the teaching of reality.

In its tragic as well as its successful aspects, Comenius's life was a truly European one. Apart from details whose relevance even for present-day language teaching is evident, it is this European dimension that makes the Moravian bishop a most interesting historical figure.

### Further reading

Caravolas, J.-A. (1994) *La didactique des languages. Précis d'histoire I: 1450–1700 (Teaching languages. Conspectus of history I: 1450–1700)*, Montreal and Tübingen: Les Presses de l'Université de Montreal and Narr Publishers.
Hüllen, W. (1999) *English dictionaries 800–1700: the topical tradition*, Oxford: Oxford University Press.

WERNER HÜLLEN

# Common European Framework

The 'Common European Framework for language learning, teaching and **ASSESSMENT**' (CEF) was developed as part of the **COUNCIL OF EUROPE** (CE) Project 'Language learning for European citizenship' between 1991 and 1997, with a view to its general launch in 2001 (Council of Europe, in press). Its aims are:

- to promote and facilitate cooperation and mutual information among educational institutions in different countries;
- to provide a sound basis for the mutual recognition of language qualifications;
- to assist learners, teachers, course designers, examining bodies and educational administrators to reflect on their current practice and to situate and co-ordinate their efforts.

To realise these aims, the CEF needs to be *comprehensive*, specifying the full range of language use as well as the many kinds of knowledge and skill necessary to proficient use, so as to enable any of its users to describe their **OBJECTIVES** and achievements. It does not set out to be exhaustive – an impossible ideal – but rather to identify the major parameters and higher-level categories, with examples of their exponents. CEF must also be *transparent*, giving explicit and clearly formulated

information in a way comprehensible to its users; *coherent*, with all its parts harmoniously interconnected and free from internal contradiction; *flexible*, *open*, *dynamic* and *non-dogmatic*. The aim is not to prescribe how languages should be learnt, taught and assessed, but to raise awareness, stimulate reflection and improve communication among practitioners of all kinds and persuasions as to what they actually do.

## Structure of the CEF

To this end, the CEF provides:

- a descriptive scheme, presenting and exemplifying the parameters and categories needed to describe, first, what a language user has to *do* in order to communicate in its situational context, then the role of the *texts*, which carry the message from producer to receiver, then the underlying *competences* which enable a language user to perform acts of communication, and finally the *strategies* which enable the language user to bring those competences to bear in action;
- a survey of approaches to language learning and teaching, providing options for users to consider in relation to their existing practice;
- a set of *scales* for describing proficiency in language use, both globally and in relation to the categories of the descriptive scheme at a series of *levels*;
- a discussion of the issues raised for *curricular design* in different educational contexts, with particular reference to the development of *plurilingualism* in the learner.

## The descriptive scheme

The CEF provides descriptive categories for:

- the *context* of language use in terms of the locations, institutions, personal roles, objects, events, operations and texts which characterise situations which arise in the domains (personal, public, occupational and educational) in which social life is organised; the external conditions and constraints under which users communicate; and the mental context of the communicating parties;

- communicative *tasks and purposes*, not only practical transactions but also playful and aesthetic uses;
- *themes*, the topics which provide the content of particular acts of communication;
- *language activities*, classified as productive, oral or written; receptive, oral or written; interactive (e.g. conversation), in which the participants alternate as producer(s) and receiver(s); and mediating, in which the user acts simply as a channel of communication between two or more persons who for one reason or another cannot communicate directly;
- *language processes*, the actual sequence of skilled activities carried out by language users in planning, executing and monitoring their **SPEAKING**, **LISTENING**, **READING** and **WRITING**. This section also covers concomitant practical actions and paralinguistic actions (gesture, etc.);
- *texts*: This section deals with media and text-types, as well as with the nature and role of texts in relation to use;
- *the user/learner's competences*. The ability of human beings to communicate depends upon their having developed the necessary competences (knowledge, **SKILLS**, etc.). Whilst all human competences may be drawn upon in one way or another in the course of communication, the CEF distinguishes between those of a general character and those more closely related to language.
- *General competences* include: 'declarative' knowledge of the physical world, society and culture; practical and intercultural skills and knowhow; personality factors such as **ATTITUDES**, **MOTIVATIONS**, values, beliefs, cognitive styles and psychological type; general linguistic and **CULTURAL AWARENESS**, together with learning skills and heuristics.
- *Communicative language competences* include: *linguistic* **COMPETENCE**, i.e. knowledge of and skill in using the formal resources from which well-formed meaningful texts may be assembled and formulated, embracing lexical, phonological, morphological and syntactic elements, categories, classes, structures, processes and relations, and the relation of form and meaning (semantics); *sociolinguistic* competence, covering markers of social relations, **POLITENESS** conventions, popular sayings, register differences,

dialect and accent as social markers; and *pragmatic* competences, including knowledge and control of discourse structure, language functions (as in **THRESHOLD LEVEL**) and interactional schemata.

- *strategies*, the means exploited by language users to mobilise and balance their resources, to activate skills and procedures in order to maximise the effectiveness of the language activities: reception, production, interaction and mediation.

## Scaling and levels

This chapter of the CEF discusses the issues involved in adding a 'vertical' dimension to the Framework, and proposes descriptors for language proficiency at an ascending series of levels. A branching system is presented, allowing planners to subdivide learners into more homogeneous groups according to need. For most purposes, a series of six relatively broad levels appears adequate, and such a series is developed in detail in an Appendix of some sixty pages. Scales are provided for overall proficiency and also, so far as is practicable, for those particular activities, processes and competences set out in the descriptive scheme.

## The processes of language learning and teaching

Following the presentation of the descriptive scheme, this chapter of the Framework asks in what ways the learner comes to be able to carry out the tasks, activities and processes and build up the competences required for language communication; and how teachers, assisted by the various support services, can facilitate the process. After considering issues of principle, the chapter sets out methodological options for learning and teaching in relation to the descriptive scheme, dealing also with the role of teachers, including questions of the management of learning and attitudes to errors and mistakes.

## Linguistic diversification and the curriculum

This section of the CEF reflects the move away from 'all-or-nothing' approaches to language learning and explores the implications of accepting *plurilingualism* (an overall communicative competence within which varying degrees and directions of competence in a number of languages interact) as the overarching objective of language learning. The detailed description of the many components of language makes it easier to plan for *partial competences* rather than all-round proficiency, in the light of the **NEEDS**, Motivations, characteristics and prior experience of learners and of the available resources. A number of possible scenarios for language teaching in different educational environments is suggested. The **EUROPEAN LANGUAGE PORTFOLIO** (Schärer, 1999) provides a means of stimulating, recording and giving recognition to the development of plurilingual competences.

### Assessment

This chapter of the Framework defines and discusses different types of assessment in terms of thirteen polarities (e.g., achievement/proficiency, formative/summative, etc.) and the relation of assessment to scales of language proficiency. The use of the descriptive scheme as a resource for the development and/or description of assessment tools is briefly discussed. Finally, questions of feasibility are raised – a workable system cannot be too complicated – and alternative metasystems are presented.

### User guides

A user guide is available, designed to facilitate the use of the CEF by both general and specialised users (e.g., educational administrators, adult education providers, inspectors, examiners, **TEXTBOOK** writers, teacher trainers, teachers and learners).

The CEF's user guides are publicly accessible on the CE website. Following extensive field consultation and trialling, the CEF is in widespread use as a basis for reflection, planning and mutual exchange of information. As an open system it is expected to develop further in response to the needs and experience of users.

**See also:** Assessment and testing; European Language Portfolio; Threshold Level; Untutored language acquisition; Vantage Level; Waystage

### References

Council of Europe (in press) *A common European framework for language learning, teaching and assessment*, Cambridge, Cambridge University Press.

Schärer, R. (1999) 'European language portfolio', *Babylonia, 1/1999*. Comano, Fondazione Lingue e Culture.

### Further reading

Coste, D., North, B., Sheils, J. and Trim, J.L.M. (1998) 'Languages: learning, teaching and assessment. A common European framework of reference', *Language Teaching* 31, 3: 136–51.

JOHN L.M. TRIM

# Communicative language teaching

Communicative language teaching (CLT) refers to both processes *and* goals in classroom learning. A central theoretical concept in communicative language teaching is *communicative competence*, a term introduced into discussions of language use and second/foreign language learning in the early 1970s (Habermas, 1970; Hymes, 1971; Jakobovits, 1970). Competence is defined in terms of the expression, **INTERPRETATION** and negotiation of meaning, and looks to **SECOND LANGUAGE ACQUISITION** research to account for its development (Savignon, 1972, 1997). Identification of learner communicative needs provides a basis for curriculum design (van Ek, 1975).

### Origins and development

The origins of CLT can be traced to concurrent developments in both Europe and North America. In Europe, the language needs of a rapidly increasing group of immigrants and guest workers, and a rich British linguistic tradition that included social as well as linguistic context in description of language behaviour, led to the **COUNCIL OF EUROPE** development of a **SYLLABUS** for learners based on functional–notional concepts of language use. Derived from neo-Firthian systemic or functional linguistics that views language as meaning potential and maintains the centrality of context of situation in understanding language systems and how they work, a **THRESHOLD LEVEL** of language ability was described in terms of what learners should be able to *do* with the language (van Ek, 1975). Functions were based on assessment of learner **NEEDS** and specified the end result, the goal of an instructional programme. The term 'communicative' attached itself to programmes that used a functional–notional syllabus based on needs assessment, and the **LANGUAGE FOR SPECIFIC PURPOSES** (LSP) movement was launched.

Concurrent development in Europe focused on the *process* of communicative **CLASSROOM LANGUAGE** learning. In Germany, for example, against a backdrop of social democratic concerns for individual empowerment articulated in the writings of contemporary philosopher Jürgen Habermas (1970), language teaching methodologists took the lead in the development of classroom **MATERIALS** that encouraged learner choice (Candlin, 1978). Their systematic collection of **EXERCISE** types for communicatively oriented **ENGLISH** language teaching was used in teacher in-service courses and workshops to guide curriculum change. Exercises were designed to exploit the variety of social meanings contained within particular grammatical structures. A system of 'chains' encouraged teachers and learners to define their own learning path through principled selection of relevant exercises (Piepho, 1974; Piepho and Bredella, 1976). Similar exploratory projects were also initiated by Candlin at his academic home, the University of Lancaster, and by Holec (1979) and his colleagues at the University of Nancy (**CRAPEL**). Supplementary teacher resource materials promoting classroom CLT became increasingly popular in the 1970s (e.g., Maley and Duff, 1978), and there was new interest in learner **VOCABULARY** building.

Meanwhile, in the United States, Hymes (1971) had reacted to **CHOMSKY**'s characterisation of the linguistic competence of the ideal **NATIVE SPEAKER** and proposed the term 'communicative competence' to represent the use of language in social context, the observance of sociolinguistic norms of appropriacy. His concern with speech communities and the integration of language, communication and culture was not unlike that of Firth and

**HALLIDAY** in the British linguistic tradition (see Halliday, 1978). Hyme's communicative competence may be seen as the equivalent of Halliday's meaning potential. Similarly, his focus was not language learning but language as social behaviour. In subsequent interpretations of the significance of Hymes's views for learners, methodologists working in the **USA** tended to focus on native speaker cultural norms and the difficulty, if not impossibility, of **AUTHENTICALLY** representing them in a classroom of non-native speakers. In light of this difficulty, the appropriateness of communicative competence as an instructional goal was questioned (see, e.g., Paulston, 1974).

At the same time, in a research project at the University of Illinois, Savignon (1972) used the term communicative competence to characterise the ability of classroom language learners to interact with other speakers, to make meaning, as distinct from their ability to recite dialogues or perform on discrete-point tests of grammatical knowledge. At a time when pattern practice and error avoidance were the rule in language teaching, this study of **ADULT** classroom acquisition of **FRENCH** looked at the effect of practice in the use of coping **STRATEGIES** as part of an instructional programme. By encouraging them to ask for information, to seek clarification, to use circumlocution and whatever other linguistic and non-linguistic resources they could muster to negotiate meaning, to stick to the communicative task at hand, teachers were invariably leading learners to take risks, to speak in other than memorised patterns. The coping strategies identified in this study became the basis for subsequent identification by Canale and Swain (1980) of '**STRATEGIC COMPETENCE**' in their three-component framework for communicative competence, along with grammatical competence and **SOCIOLINGUISTIC COMPETENCE**. Test results at the end of the instructional period showed conclusively that learners who had practised communication instead of laboratory pattern drills performed with no less accuracy on discrete-point tests of grammatical structure. On the other hand, their communicative competence as measured in terms of fluency, comprehensibility, effort and amount of communication in unrehearsed communicative tasks significantly surpassed that of learners who had had no such practice. Learner reactions to the test formats lent further support to the view that even **BEGINNERS** respond well to activities that let them focus on meaning as opposed to formal features.

A collection of role plays, games and other communicative classroom activities was developed subsequently for inclusion in the adaptation of the French CRÉDIF materials, *Voix et Visages de la France*. The accompanying guide (Savignon, 1974) described their purpose as that of involving learners in the experience of communication. Teachers were encouraged to provide learners with the French equivalent of expressions like 'What's the word for ... ?', 'Please repeat ... ', 'I don't understand', expressions that would help them to participate in the negotiation of meaning. Not unlike the efforts of Candlin and his colleagues working in a European EFL context, the focus was on classroom process and learner **AUTONOMY**. The use of games, role play, pair and other small group activities has gained acceptance and is now widely recommended for inclusion in language teaching programmes.

CLT thus can be seen to derive from a multidisciplinary perspective that includes, at least, **LINGUISTICS**, **PSYCHOLOGY**, philosophy, sociology and educational research. The focus has been the elaboration and implementation of programmes and methodologies that promote the development of functional language ability through learner participation in communicative events. Central to CLT is the understanding of language learning as both an educational and a political issue. Language teaching is inextricably tied to language policy. Viewed from a multicultural intranational as well as international perspective, diverse sociopolitical contexts mandate not only a diverse set of language learning goals, but a diverse set of teaching strategies. Programme design and implementation depend on negotiation between policymakers, linguists, researchers and teachers. And **EVALUA-TION** of programme success requires a similar collaborative effort. The selection of methods and materials appropriate to both the goals *and* the context of teaching begins with an analysis of socially defined learner needs *and* styles of learning.

## Focus on the learner

By definition, CLT puts the focus on the learner. Learner communicative needs provide a framework for elaborating programme goals in terms of functional competence. This implies global, qualitative evaluation of learner achievement as opposed to quantitative **ASSESSMENT** of discrete linguistic features. Controversy over appropriate language testing persists, and many a curricular innovation has been undone by failure to make corresponding changes in evaluation. Current efforts at educational reform favour essay writing, in-class presentations, and other more holistic assessments of learner competence. Some programmes have initiated portfolio assessment, the collection and evaluation of learner poems, reports, stories, videotapes and similar projects, in an effort to better represent and encourage learner achievement.

Depending upon their own preparation and experience, teachers themselves differ in their reactions to CLT. Some feel understandable frustration at the seeming ambiguity in discussions of communicative ability. Negotiation of meaning may be a lofty goal, but this view of language behaviour lacks precision and does not provide a universal scale for assessment of individual learners. Ability is viewed, rather, as variable and highly dependent upon context and purpose as well as the roles and attitudes of all involved. Other teachers welcome the opportunity to select and/or develop their own materials, providing learners with a range of communicative tasks. And they are comfortable relying on more global, integrative judgements of learner progress.

An additional source of frustration for some teachers are second language acquisition research findings that show the route, if not the rate, of language acquisition to be largely unaffected by classroom instruction. First language cross-linguistic studies of developmental universals initiated in the 1970s were soon followed by second language studies. Acquisition, assessed on the basis of expression in unrehearsed, oral communicative contexts, seemed to follow a similar morphosyntactic sequence regardless of learner age or context of learning. Although they served to bear out the informal observations of teachers, namely that

**TEXTBOOK** presentation and drill do not ensure learner use of these same structures in their own spontaneous expression, the findings were none the less disconcerting. They contradicted both **GRAM-MAR–TRANSLATION** and **AUDIOLINGUAL** precepts that placed the burden of acquisition on teacher explanation of **GRAMMAR** and controlled practice with insistence on learner accuracy. They were further at odds with textbooks that promise 'mastery' of 'basic' French, English, **SPANISH**, etc. Teacher rejection of research findings, renewed insistence on tests of discrete grammatical structures, and even exclusive reliance in the classroom on the learners' native or first language, where possible, to be sure they 'get the grammar', have been in some cases reactions to the frustration of teaching for communication.

Moreover, the language acquisition research paradigm itself, with its emphasis on sentence-level grammatical features, has served to bolster a structural focus, obscuring pragmatic and socio-linguistic issues in language acquisition. In her discussion of the contexts of competence, Berns (1990) stresses that the definition of a communicative competence appropriate for learners requires an understanding of the sociocultural contexts of language use. In addition, the selection of a methodology appropriate to the attainment of communicative competence requires an understanding of sociocultural differences in styles of learning. Curricular innovation is best advanced by the development of local materials, which, in turn, rests on the involvement of classroom teachers.

## What about grammar?

Discussions of CLT not infrequently lead to questions of grammatical or formal accuracy. The perceived displacement of attention to morphosyntactic features in learner expression in favour of a focus on meaning has led in some cases to the impression that grammar is not important, or that proponents of CLT favour learner self-expression without regard to form.

While involvement in communicative events is seen as central to language development, this involvement necessarily requires attention to form. Communication cannot take place in the absence of structure, or grammar – a set of shared assumptions about how language works – along with a willingness of participants to cooperate in the negotiation of meaning. In their carefully researched and widely cited paper proposing components of communicative competence, Canale and Swain (1980) did not suggest that grammar was unimportant. They sought, rather, to situate grammatical competence within a more broadly defined communicative competence. Similarly, the findings of the Savignon (1972) study did not suggest that teachers forsake the teaching of grammar. Rather, the replacement of **LANGUAGE LABORATORY** structure drills with meaning-focused self-expression was found to be a more effective way to develop communicative ability with no loss of morphosyntactic accuracy. And learner performance on tests of discrete morphosyntactic features was not a good predictor of their performance on a series of integrative communicative tasks.

The nature of the contribution to language development of both form-focused and meaning-focused classroom activity remains a question in ongoing research. The optimum combination of these activities in any given instructional setting depends no doubt on learner age, nature and length of instructional sequence, opportunities for language contact outside the classroom, teacher preparation and other factors. However, for the development of communicative ability, research findings overwhelmingly support the integration of form-focused exercises with meaning-focused experience. Grammar is important; and learners seem to focus best on grammar when it relates to their communicative needs and experiences (Lightbown and Spada, 1993). Nor should explicit attention to form be perceived as limited to sentence-level morphosyntactic features. Broader features of discourse, sociolinguistic rules of appropriacy, and communication strategies themselves may be included.

## Sociolinguistic issues

Numerous sociolinguistic issues await attention. Variation in the speech community and its relationship to language change are central to sociolinguistic inquiry. Sociolinguistic perspectives on variability and change highlight the folly of describing native speaker competence, let alone non-native speaker competence, in terms of 'mastery' or 'command' of a system. All language systems show instability and variation. Learner language systems show even greater instability and variability in terms of both the amount and the rate of change. Sociolinguistic concerns with identity and accommodation help to explain the construction by bilinguals of a 'variation space' which is different from that of a native speaker. It may include retention of any number of features of a previously acquired system of phonology, syntax, discourse, communication strategies, etc. The phenomenon may be individual or, in those settings where there is a community of learners, general.

Sociolinguistic perspectives have been important in understanding the implications of norm, appropriacy and variability for CLT, and continue to suggest avenues of inquiry for further research and materials development. Use of authentic language data has underscored the importance of context – setting, roles, **GENRE**, etc. – in **INTERPRETING** the meaning of a text. A range of both oral and written texts in context provides learners with a variety of language experiences, experiences they need to construct their own 'variation space', to make determinations of appropriacy in their own expression of meaning. 'Competent' in this instance is not necessarily synonymous with 'native-like'. Negotiation in CLT highlights the need for interlinguistic, i.e. intercultural, awareness on the part of all involved (Byram, 1997). Better understanding of the strategies used in the negotiation of meaning offers a potential for improving classroom practice of the needed **SKILLS**.

Along with other sociolinguistic issues in language acquisition, the classroom itself as a social context has been neglected. Classroom language learning was the focus of a number of research studies in the 1960s and early 1970s. However, language classrooms were not a major interest of the second language acquisition (SLA) research that rapidly gathered momentum in the years that followed. The full range of variables present in educational settings was an obvious deterrent. Other difficulties included the lack of well-defined classroom processes to serve as variables and lack of agreement as to what constituted learning success. Confusion of form-focused drill with meaning-focused communication persisted in many of the textbook exercises and language test prototypes that influenced curricula. Not surprisingly, researchers eager to establish SLA as a worthy field of inquiry turned their attention to more narrow, quantitative studies of the acquisition of selected morphosyntactic features.

## What CLT is not

Disappointment with both grammar–translation and audiolingual methods for their inability to prepare learners for the interpretation, expression and negotiation of meaning, along with enthusiasm for an array of alternative methods increasingly labelled 'communicative', has resulted in no small amount of uncertainty as to what are and are not essential features of CLT. Thus, a summary description would be incomplete without brief mention of what CLT is not.

CLT is not exclusively concerned with face-to-face oral communication. The principles of CLT apply equally to **READING** and **WRITING** activities that involve readers and writers engaged in the interpretation, expression and negotiation of meaning; the goals of CLT depend on learner needs in a given context. CLT does not require small group or pair work. Group tasks have been found helpful in many contexts as a way of providing increased opportunity and **MOTIVATION** for communication, but classroom group or pair work should not be considered an essential feature and may well be inappropriate in some contexts. Finally, CLT does not exclude a focus on metalinguistic awareness or knowledge of rules of syntax, discourse and social appropriateness.

The essence of CLT is the engagement of learners in communication to allow them to develop their communicative competence. Terms sometimes used to refer to features of CLT include 'process oriented', '**TASK-BASED**', and 'inductive' or 'discovery' oriented. CLT cannot be found in any one textbook or set of curricular materials inasmuch as strict adherence to a given text is not likely to be true to the processes and goals of CLT. In keeping with the notion of context of situation, CLT is properly seen as an approach, a theory of Intercultural communicative competence to be used in developing materials and methods appropriate to a given context of learning. No less than the means and norms of communication they are designed to reflect, communicative **TEACHER METHODS** will continue to be explored and adapted.

**See also:** Council of Europe Modern Languages Projects; History: after 1945; Secondary education; Sociolinguistics; Teaching methods

## References

Berns, M. (1990) *Contexts of competence: English language teaching in non-native contexts*, New York: Plenum.

Byram, M. (1997) *Teaching and assessing intercultural communicative competence*, Clevedon: Multilingual Matters.

Canale, M. and Swain, M. (1980) 'Theoretical bases of communicative approaches to second language teaching and testing', *Applied Linguistics* 1: 1–47.

Candlin, C. (1978) *Teaching of English: principles and an exercise typology*, London: Langenscheidt-Longman.

Habermas, J. (1970) 'Toward a theory of communicative competence', *Inquiry* 13: 360–75.

Halliday, M.A.K. (1978) *Language as social semiotic: the social interpretation of language and meaning*, Baltimore: University Park Press.

Holec, H. (1979) *Autonomy and foreign language learning*, Strasbourg: Council of Europe.

Hymes, D. (1971) 'Competence and performance in linguistic theory', in R. Huxley and E. Ingram (eds), *Language acquisition: models and methods*, London: Academic Press.

Jakobovits, L. (1970) *Foreign language learning: a psycholinguistic analysis of the issues*, Rowley, MA: Newbury House.

Lightbown, P. and Spada, N. (1993) *How languages are learned*, Oxford: Oxford University Press.

Maley, A. and Duff, A. (1978) *Drama techniques in language learning*, Cambridge: Cambridge University Press.

Paulston, C.B. (1974) 'Linguistic and communicative competence', *TESOL Quarterly* 8: 347–62.

Piepho, H.E. (1974) *Kommunikative Kompetenz als übergeordnetes Lernziel des Englischunterrichts (Communicative competence as the overarching goal of English language teaching)*, Dornburg-Frickhofen: Frankonius.

Piepho, H.E. and Bredella, L. (eds) (1976) *Contacts. Integriertes Englischlehrwerk für klassen 5–10 (Contacts. Integrated English textbook for grades 5–10)*, Bochum: Kamp.

Savignon, S.J. (1972) *Communicative competence: an experiment in foreign language teaching*, Philadelphia: Center for Curriculum Development.

Savignon, S.J. (1974) 'Teaching for communication', in R. Coulombe *et al.* (eds), *Voix et visages de France: Level 1 Teachers' Guide*, Chicago: Rand-McNally. Reprinted (1978) in *English Teaching Forum* 16, 2–5; 9.

Savignon, S.J. (1997) *Communicative competence: theory and classroom practice*, New York: McGraw Hill.

van Ek, J. (ed.) (1975) *Systems development in adult language learning: the threshold level in a European unit credit system for modern language learning by adults*, Strasbourg: Council of Europe.

## Further reading

Breen, M. and Candlin, C. (1980) 'The essentials of a communicative curriculum in language teaching', *Applied Linguistics* 1: 89–112.

Byram, M. (1997) *Teaching and assessing intercultural communicative competence*, Clevedon: Multilingual Matters.

Canale, M. and Swain. M. (1980) 'Theoretical bases of communicative approaches to second language teaching and testing', *Applied Linguistics* 1: 1–47.

Holliday, A. (1994) *Appropriate methodology and social context*, Cambridge: Cambridge University Press.

Nunan, D. (1989) *Designing tasks for the communicative classroom*, Cambridge: Cambridge University Press.

Savignon, S.J. (1972) *Communicative competence: an experiment in foreign language teaching*, Philadelphia: Center for Curriculum Development.

Savignon, S.J. (1997) *Communicative competence: theory and classroom practice*, New York: McGraw Hill.

SANDRA J. SAVIGNON

# Communicative strategies

Communicative strategies in language teaching and learning are often known as language use strategies, i.e. the techniques that learners employ when attempting to use the target language for the purpose of communication. Communicative or language use strategies include retrieval strategies, rehearsal strategies, cover strategies, and so-called 'communication' strategies, each of which is defined and illustrated below.

## Terminology

As pointed out by Oxford (1990), the word strategy comes from the ancient Greek term *strategia*, which means steps or actions taken for the purpose of winning a war. The warlike aim of *strategia* has fallen away, but control and goal-directedness remain in the modern version of the word.

A plausible distinction can be made between communicative or language use strategies and language learning strategies. The latter are defined variously as: 'behaviors or thoughts that a learner engages in during learning that are intended to influence the learner's encoding process' (Weinstein and Mayer, 1986: 315) and 'the learner's toolkit for active, purposeful, and attentive self-regulation of mental processes [during learning]' (Kawai, Oxford and Iran-Nejad, forthcoming). One category of learning strategies is cognitive strategies for creating, strengthening and elaborating mental associations between the new and the known (e.g., using text features to understand the meaning, taking systematic notes using a T-line format, and breaking a word down into its root, prefix and suffix). Another learning strategy category is metacognitive strategies for planning, organising, evaluating and monitoring one's own learning and for understanding one's own learning processes (e.g., knowing one's favoured LEARNING STYLE, identifying necessary materials for a given language task, and monitoring mistakes during the task). Other forms of learning strategies, according to Oxford (1990, 1996), are affective strategies for controlling emotions and MOTIVATION and social strategies for learning with other people.

It could be argued that language use or communicative strategies frequently aid learning and should therefore be considered to overlap with language learning strategies. In fact, Oxford's (1990) taxonomy of language learning strategies includes a variety of communicative strategies under the rubric of compensation strategies, which serve to compensate for missing knowledge when the learner is engaged in a difficult language task. A possible reason for arguing that communicative strategies overlap with, or are part of, language learning strategies is that the former strategies allow learners to stay engaged longer in target language communication and thus enable learners to receive more of the language input and feedback that are needed for learning. In short, learning often results from employing communicative or language use strategies, even if learning is not the main objective.

However, it is true that the primary goal for employing communicative or language use strategies is not usually learning, and that such strategies do not always result in learning (Cohen, 1998), although they frequently do have learning as a by-product. It is helpful to remember the theoretical distinction between communicative or language use strategies on the one hand and language learning strategies on the other.

## Four types of communicative or language use strategies

Although many other theorists have contributed to the literature on communicative or language use strategies, Cohen (1998) has outlined the clearest taxonomy. The four aspects of Cohen's taxonomy are: retrieval strategies, rehearsal strategies, cover strategies, and 'communication' strategies. Another way to describe these four categories is: mnemonic strategies for retrieval, practice strategies, image-protection or masking strategies, and restricted-knowledge strategies.

### Retrieval (mnemonic) strategies

Retrieval strategies are those behaviours or techniques 'used to call up language material from [long-term mental] storage, through whatever memory searching techniques the learner can muster' (Cohen, 1998: 6). Retrieval strategies are frequently the mirror image of the language learning strategies initially used to encode the language material into long-term mental storage. The learner might have used a mnemonic learning strategy for initial encoding of the material in long-term memory storage. Employing the same strategy (or recalling the initial use of the strategy) helps the learner to retrieve the material when needed for live communication. For instance, various mnemonic techniques or strategies enable learners to retrieve information in an orderly string (e.g., acronyms), while other techniques create retrieval via sounds (e.g., rhyming), images (e.g., a mental picture of the word itself or the meaning of the word), a combination of sounds and images (e.g., the keyword method), body movement (e.g., **TOTAL PHYSICAL RESPONSE**), mechanical means (e.g., **FLASHCARDS**), or location (e.g., on a page or blackboard) (see Oxford, 1990, for details and multiple examples). When the technique is used for initial learning, it is clearly a learning strategy. However, technically speaking, when the same technique is used for retrieving language material for communicative use, this technique becomes a communicative or language use strategy.

## Rehearsal (practice) strategies

A second category of communicative or language use strategies can be called rehearsal or practice strategies. These strategies are employed for rehearsing structures in the target language. An example would be 'rehearsing the subjunctive form in preparation for using it communicatively in a request in Spanish to a boss for a day off' (Cohen, 1998: 6). Although language learning might indeed be involved in this process to one degree or another, the rehearsal of the subjunctive for real communication makes this a communicative or language use strategy. Cohen focuses on form-focused or grammatical rehearsal, but using strategies to rehearse specific pragmatic functions, **VOCABULARY** and **PRONUNCIATION** can also be important for successful communication.

## Cover (masking or image-protection) strategies

Cover strategies are 'those strategies that learners use to create the impression that they have control over material when they do not. They are a special type of compensatory or coping strategy which involves creating the appearance of language ability so as not to look unprepared, foolish, or even stupid' (Cohen, 1998: 6). Some examples given by Cohen are: using a memorised and partly understood phrase to keep the conversation going, producing simplified utterances, or producing overly complex utterances. In addition to these linguistically-based cover strategies, some social-psychological cover strategies are: laughing, joking, diverting the conversation partner, smiling, nodding, and appearing to be interested or fascinated by the conversation while not understanding what is being said (Oxford, 1995). Such social-psychological cover strategies are often known as masking or image-protection strategies in an anxiety-ridden communication situation. These terms can be employed to encompass linguistically-based cover strategies as well.

## 'Communication' (restricted-knowledge) strategies

The general term for the fourth group of communicative or language use strategies is 'communication' strategies. In a way this is an unfortunate term, because it is so broad and so confusingly similar to the larger category, communicative or language use strategies. However, the term communication strategies is deeply entrenched in the research literature (see, e.g., Bialystok, 1990; Cohen, 1998; Dörnyei, 1995; Dörnyei and Scott, 1997; Faerch and Kasper, 1983; Poulisse, 1990; Tarone, 1981). Communication strategies include overgeneralising a grammar rule or vocabulary meaning from one context to another where it does not apply, avoiding or abandoning a topic that is too difficult, reducing a message, switching to the native language temporarily (code switching), paraphrasing, or using circumlocution (Cohen, 1998; Oxford, 1990). In all these instances, the basic dynamic is to capitalise on the restricted amount that one knows while ignoring what one does not know, with the ultimate goal of conveying a meaningful message. Therefore the term restricted-knowledge strategies might be a useful synonym for communication strategies.

## Conclusion

This discussion has defined communicative or language use strategies and has distinguished them from language learning strategies, although learning sometimes occurs as a by-product of employing communicative strategies. Four types of communicative strategy include: retrieval (mnemonic) strategies, rehearsal (practice) strategies, cover (masking or image-protection) strategies, and so-called 'communication' (restricted-knowledge) strategies. Strategy instruction can address all of these types of strategy, just as it can address language learning strategies (Oxford, 1996).

**See also:** Communicative language teaching; Intercultural communication; Intercultural competence; Skills and knowledge; Sociolinguistic competence; Strategies of language learning

## References

Bialystok, E. (1990) *Communication strategies*, Oxford: Basil Blackwell.

Cohen, A.D. (1998) *Strategies in learning and using a second language*, London: Longman.

Dörnyei, Z. (1995) 'On the teachability of communication strategies', *TESOL Quarterly* 29 (55–85).

Dörnyei, Z. and Scott, M.L. (1997) 'Communication strategies in a second language: definitions and taxonomies', *Language Learning* 47, 1: 173–210.

Faerch, C. and Kasper, G. (eds) (1983) *Strategies in interlanguage communication*, London: Longman.

Kawai, Y., Oxford, R.L. and Iran-Nejad, A. (forthcoming) 'Learning strategies for internal self-regulation', *Brain and Behavior*.

Oxford, R.L. (1990) *Language learning strategies: what every teacher should know*, Boston: Heinle and Heinle.

Oxford, R.L. (1995) 'Language anxiety: A bane or a blessing?' Plenary speech presented at the annual meeting of Teachers of English to Speakers of Other Languages, Asunción, Paraguay.

Oxford, R.L. (ed.) (1996) *Language learning strategies around the world: cross-cultural perspectives*, Manoa: University of Hawaii Press.

Poulisse, N. (1990) *The use of compensatory strategies by Dutch learners of English*, Dordrecht: Mouton de Gruyter.

Tarone, E. (1981) 'Some thoughts on the notion of communication strategy', *TESOL Quarterly* 15, 3: 285–95.

Weinstein, C. and Mayer, R.E. (1986) 'The teaching of learning strategies', in M. Wittrock (ed.), *Handbook of research on teaching* (2nd edn), New York: Macmillan.

## Further reading

Cohen, A.D. (1998) *Strategies in learning and using a second language*, London: Longman.

Oxford, R.L. (ed.) (1996) *Language learning strategies around the world: cross-cultural perspectives*, Manoa: University of Hawaii Press.

Weinstein, C. and Mayer, R.E. (1986) 'The teaching of learning strategies', in M. Wittrock (ed.), *Handbook of research on teaching* (2nd edn), New York: Macmillan.

REBECCA OXFORD

# Community language learning

The origins of community language learning (CLL) lie in **PSYCHOLOGY**, and CLL can be viewed as the outcome of applying counselling learning techniques in the language classroom. The two are closely linked and will be dealt with together here. CLL, as a '**HUMANISTIC**' method with strong elements of Rogerian counselling theory, is associated with Charles Curran (1972, 1976), a professor of psychology and counselling specialist, and was developed by one of his students, La Forge.

Curran wanted to broaden the use of psychological methods, including that of taking a 'whole-person learning' approach. This recognises the multiplicity of factors that make up an individual, both affective as well as cognitive, with the idea that feelings and emotions are not necessarily put to one side upon entering the classroom. Humanistic techniques can 'blend what the student feels, thinks and knows with what he is learning in the target language', and also 'help to foster a climate of caring and sharing in the foreign language classroom' (Moskowitz, 1978: 2).

Curran's emphasis on the holistic approach was part of the break with previous views of the learner, particularly in **BEHAVIOURISM**, as passive and largely responding to stimuli. This atomistic view paid insufficient attention, in Curran's view, to creative abilities, with the intellect treated as a separate rather than an integral part of the whole person. In CLL, the learning process is described as an interaction which learners involve themselves in totally. The relationship between teacher and learner is redefined when compared to more traditional approaches.

By applying counselling learning, the teacher assumes the role of 'counsellor' while learners are 'clients' in the classroom rather than the consulting room. As counselling is about giving advice, support and encouragement to those with problems, there is a clear difference to the notion of the teacher as imparting knowledge to learner recipients. The 'problem' in this case is that of language, and the teacher has to involve the learners, drawing upon their senses as well as their experience. Sharing ideas and feelings can be viewed as a learner-centred approach, although the teacher needs ultimate control in directing the learning process. There has to be empathy with the learners, and communication of this whenever possible. It is also part of the teacher's role to provide a secure learning environment in which students can develop and grow in relation to the language being acquired.

Nunan writes of the anxiety a second language learner may have, and one of CLL's aims is to reduce this in order to maximise learning. By creating a supportive 'community', learners can move from dependence on the teacher to **AUTONOMY**. CLL is 'the method which focuses most assiduously on building trust' (Nunan, 1991: 236).

CLL utilises group learning, in small or large groups, and the group is the 'community'. The method generally assumes a group of homogenous language learners although it has been developed to teach more heterogeneous ones. The 'knowers' are those who are skilled in the target language, but this may only be the teacher in some circumstances. The learners first of all articulate what they want to say in the native language, perhaps by whispering to the teacher who then translates the learner's sentences into the target language. The learner repeats this to other group members or tape-records it, and this can subsequently be replayed. Students repeat and record more translated sentences. The use of tape recordings is an important part of CLL methodology. Unlike **AUDIOLINGUALISM**, practitioners do not normally use pre-recorded material but that produced by the learners themselves. It is also to some extent spontaneous, depending on what the learners wish to know and use during the session.

The learners usually sit in a circle where everyone can see each other, with the teacher on the outside. CLL learning activities include **TRANSLATION** and transcription, but most themes come from the participants. They are encouraged to pay attention to the 'overhears' they come across between other learners and knowers. La Forge believed that all members of the group should be able to understand what the others are trying to communicate, as they are in a relationship with all other learners and not just with the teacher. After the learning activities, participants reflect on their feelings and this feedback is central. The whole process is a group interaction as well as a total person one, and how people feel is important information to be shared. This assists the 'organic' growth of the learner and 'a new self of the learner is generated or born in the target language' (La Forge, 1983: 5).

There is a developmental theory of the learner in CLL. Stage one (the 'birth stage') compares the learner to an infant, one who is totally dependent on the knower for the new language and who has to ask for everything. In the next stage, there is a degree of independence gained, with learners beginning to find their own 'self' in the new language by employing the phrases and words they have heard and used. Stage three is described as the 'separate-existence stage', with more comprehension of the target language and less assistance required. There may even be some resentfulness when unsolicited help is given.

'Adolescence' follows, with a degree of learner independence, although the language level may still be fairly basic. The new role for the learner is to know how to gain the advanced level of linguistic knowledge from the knower. The final stage is that of independence, where the learners are refining their knowledge and can operate on their own. They may even act as counsellors to less advanced students.

At each stage of development there is not only linguistic input and skills but also cognitive and emotional tasks. These stages will involve crises for the learner, which need to be handled in cooperation with the teacher. There is also collaboration with other learners, as they all go through these sequential stages and can support each other, discussing their feelings and frustrations as well as their achievements. Without the feedback the frustration can deepen, and this may serve as a block to development as well as creating an atmosphere unconducive for learning.

There is little place in CLL for a conventional **SYLLABUS**, since what takes place emerges from teacher–learner interaction. A skilled practitioner, however, will be able to impose some degree of order by carefully monitoring what is happening and matching linguistic content to the level of the learners. Also, teachers must ensure that the required amount of learning is achieved as well as the sharing of feelings and feedback. The emergent syllabus is often compared to a learning contract. Similarly, there is minimal usage of set **TEXTBOOKS**. This would impose an order on the sessions that could impede the growth and interaction. Teaching **MATERIALS** often develop as the sessions evolve.

CLL can be seen as the cross-fertilisation of psychological, social and linguistic elements. Woodward writes of 'some very interesting underlying tenets' and of CLL being useful on teacher training courses because 'its differences point up very clearly the assumptions behind more mainstream methods' (Woodward, 1991: 44). The shortcomings, however, mean that it is not a widely used method.

It is not suitable for all learners, with some personality types unable to benefit from the sharing environment CLL attempts to promote. Not everyone wishes to be open about his or her own feelings and anxieties. Some may feel threatened by this approach, even though there is an emphasis on providing a secure, supportive environment. Richards and Rodgers point out that 'security is a culturally relative concept' (1986: 123). Many teachers who have worked in different countries would testify to the fact that methods accepted in the home country may cause anxiety and confusion elsewhere. CLL could provoke hostility, with some

learners wishing to have language training in a more familiar, traditional manner. La Forge, conversely, recognised that too much security was also a problem, and learning might be obstructed without some hint of insecurity. Some critics question the usefulness of the counselling **META-PHOR** and whether this is suitable in language training.

CLL clearly requires specialist training, with dangers in this approach if the teacher is insufficiently prepared. They have to be in control of a learning situation which emerges through interaction, and be able to impose basic aims and structures. They also have to show empathy and even to act as counsellors to assist learners through their successive stages and crises. These are heavy demands and probably require a particular type of personality as well as some skills in social psychology and language training.

Other limitations relate to the lack of syllabus with a problem of **EVALUATION**, since aims and **OBJECTIVES** are not set. CLL may only be suitable for particular types of language learning and with relatively small groups. Some of the techniques, however, have influenced other methods, and CLL illustrates very clearly how non-direct, communicative learning could occur in the language classroom.

**See also:** Acquisition and teaching; Attitudes and language learning; Humanistic language teaching; Motivation; Teaching methods

### References

Curran, C. (1972) 'Counseling–learning: a whole-person model for education', *TESOL Quarterly* 11, 4: 365–72.

Curran, C. (1976) *Counseling–learning in second language*, Apple River, IL: Apple River Press.

La Forge, P.G. (1983) *Counseling and culture in second language acquisition*, Oxford: Pergamon.

Moskowitz, G. (1978) *Caring and sharing in the foreign language class*, Rowley, MA: Newbury House.

Nunan, D. (1991) *Language teaching methodology: a textbook for teachers*, Hemel Hempstead: Prentice Hall.

Richards, J.C. and Rodgers, T.S. (1986) *Approaches and methods in language teaching: a description and analysis*, Cambridge: Cambridge University Press.

Woodward, T. (1991) *Models and metaphors in language teacher training*, Cambridge: Cambridge University Press.

## Further reading

La Forge, P.G. (1971) 'Community language learning: a pilot study', *Language Learning* 21. 1: 45–61.

La Forge, P.G. (1975) *Research profiles with community language learning*, Apple River, IL: Apple River Press.

La Forge, P.G. (1977) 'Uses of social silence in the interpersonal dynamics of community language learning', *TESOL Quarterly* 11, 4: 373–82.

Rogers, C.R. (1951) *Client-centred therapy*, Boston: Houghton Mifflin.

RUTH CHERRINGTON

# Competence and performance

The use of 'competence' and 'performance' as technical terms originates with **CHOMSKY** (1965: 4). 'Competence' refers to 'the speaker-hearer's knowledge of his language' and 'Performance' to 'the actual use of language in concrete situations'. Chomsky's primary goal has always been to provide a description of competence and the innate mechanism underlying it. Competence is minimally defined in so far as the notion covers only that knowledge which every normal adult **NATIVE SPEAKER** of a language has of it. From this perspective, 'The real difference between child L1 and adult L2 **ACQUISITION** is that in the former everybody ends up in the same place; in the latter... this is far from being the case' (Schachter, 1996: 86). Most of the extensive L2 learning literature which results from attempts to demonstrate and explain this difference agrees that L1 competence is achieved largely on the basis of innate properties of the language faculty. There is, however, considerable disagreement about the role of these properties in the learning of a second language after the so-called 'critical period' (see also **AGE FACTORS**).

The mature competence of a native speaker is the 'steady state' of their language faculty, reached, on the basis of its initial state which is genetically determined, after passing through a series of states in early childhood. The rate and route of this development is partially determined by the innate properties of the language faculty and partly by the typology of the language to which the person is exposed. The theory of the initial state is called '**UNIVERSAL GRAMMAR**' (UG), and the theory of the steady state is called '**GRAMMAR**' (Chomsky, 1995: 14).

Each state is a state of knowledge, a mental phenomenon, unavailable for direct inspection. In formulating both UG and grammar, the linguist is therefore forced to rely on speaker-hearer performance. However, competence would only be directly reflected in performance in the case of 'an ideal speaker-listener, in a completely homogeneous speech-community, who knows its language perfectly and is unaffected by such grammatically irrelevant conditions as memory limitations, distractions, shifts of attention and interest, and errors (random or characteristic) in applying his knowledge of the language in actual performance' (Chomsky, 1965: 3). In reality, what both a theorising linguist and a language acquiring child need to do is to extract from the varied examples of natural language use that they hear around them just those aspects that are relevant to the formulation of competence.

In this, the child is helped by the language faculty; UG determines the 'principles', or possible forms of human language, and also the 'parameters' within which it is possible for them to vary (Chomsky, 1981). In other words, UG restricts grammars powerfully, and 'the theory of language acquisition will be concerned with acquisition of lexical items, fixing of parameters, and perhaps maturation of principles' (Chomsky, 1995: 28). The linguist may be helped by various forms of experimentation, particularly native speaker judgements of the grammaticality of sentences.

From the point of view of the theory of second or foreign language (L2) teaching and learning, the interesting question raised by this view of first language (L1) acquisition is whether and to what extent **ADULT LANGUAGE LEARNERS** are able to access UG and use it in the development of a competence for L2. The answer might have implications for teaching methodology. UG might, for example, predispose a certain rate and route of learning of a second language, in which case it would make sense to structure teaching accordingly.

There are, as Mitchell and Myles (1998: 61) say, four major views on this issue. According to the 'No Access' or 'Fundamental Difference' hypothesis (Clahsen and Muysken, 1986; Bley-Vroman, 1989), adult language learners have no access to UG. In favour of this hypothesis, Bley-Vroman (1989: 43–9) points out that adult learners differ from child acquirers in failing to various degrees to become native-like; following different routes; using different strategies; having different goals; having unclear intuitions about grammaticality; benefiting considerably from instruction; and being susceptible to influence from affective factors. He argues that adults learn a foreign language, to the extent that they do, in reliance on the first language, which 'fills the role which Universal Grammar has in child language acquisition' (Bley-Vroman, 1989: 42), and on their general problem solving abilities.

According to the 'Strong Continuity' (Epstein, Flynn and Martohardjono, 1998) or 'Full Availability' (Gair, 1998) hypotheses, in contrast, L2 learners have and use the same type of access to UG as L1 learners do (Krashen, 1981). Adherents claim that this hypothesis offers the best explanation for the ability of learners to reset parameters to suit an L2 which has different parameter settings than L1 (Al-Kasey and Pérez-Leroux, 1998).

According to the hypothesis of 'Indirect Access', L2 learners access UG via their L1 knowledge. There are two versions of this hypothesis (White, 1989: 48). According to one, only those aspects of UG which are instantiated in L1 can be accessed, so parameter re-setting is impossible. According to the other, learners begin by assuming that L2 is like L1, but when they discover that this is wrong they can access UG to reset the parameters (White, 1986; Schwartz and Sprouse, 1994).

Finally, according to 'The Weak Continuity' (Vainikka and Young-Scholten, 1991, 1998), or 'Partial Access' hypothesis, only some aspects of UG are available to L2 learners. This position might help reconcile some of the conflicting data

procured by studies seeking confirmation or falsification of the remaining positions. However, as Mitchell and Myles remark (1998: 68), these data themselves tend to form the subject matter of the continuing debate concerning access to UG in L2 learning (see, e.g., Schachter, 1996), and the jury remains out on the question of the exact role of UG in second language learning.

**See also:** Age factors; Communicative language teaching; *Langue* and *parole*; Second language acquisition theories; Universal grammar

## References

Al-Kasey, T. and Pérez-Leroux, A.T. (1998) 'Second language acquisition of Spanish null subjects', in S. Flynn, G. Martohardjono and W. O'Neil (eds), *The generative study of second language acquisition*, Mahwah, NJ and London: Lawrence Erlbaum Associates.

Bley-Vroman, R.W. (1989) 'The logical problem of second language learning', in S. Gass and J. Schachter (eds), *Linguistic perspectives on second language acquisition*, Cambridge: Cambridge University Press.

Chomsky, N. (1965) *Aspects of the theory of syntax*, Cambridge, MA: MIT Press.

Chomsky, N. (1981) *Lectures on government and binding*, Dordrecht: Foris.

Chomsky, N. (1995) *The minimalist program*, Cambridge, MA: MIT Press.

Clahsen, H. and Muysken, P. (1986) 'The Availability of universal grammar to adult and child learners – a study of the acquisition of German word order', *Second Language Research* 2, 2: 93–119.

Epstein, S.D., Flynn, S. and Martohardjono, G. (1998) 'The strong continuity hypothesis: some evidence concerning functional categories in adult L2 acquisition', in S. Flynn, G. Martohardjono and W. O'Neil (eds), *The generative study of second language acquisition*, Mahwah, NJ and London: Lawrence Erlbaum Associates.

Gair, J. (1998) 'Functional categories in L2 acquisition: homegrown or imported? Commentary on Part I', in S. Flynn, G. Martohardjono and W. O'Neil (eds), *The generative study of second language acquisition*, Mahwah, NJ and London: Lawrence Erlbaum Associates.

Krashen, S. (1981) *Second language acquisition and second language learning*, Oxford: Pergamon Press.

Li, X. (1998) 'Adult L2 accessibility to UG: an issue revisited', in S. Flynn, G. Martohardjono and W. O'Neil (eds), *The generative study of second language acquisition*, Mahwah, NJ and London: Lawrence Erlbaum Associates.

Mitchell, R. and Myles, F. (1998) *Second language learning theories*, London: Arnold.

Schachter, J. (1989) 'Testing a proposed universal', in S. Gass and J. Schachter (eds), *Linguistic perspectives on second language acquisition*, Cambridge: Cambridge University Press.

Schachter, J. (1996) 'Learning and triggering in adult L2 acquisition', in G. Brown, K. Malmkjær and J. Williams (eds), *Performance and competence in second language acquisition*, Cambridge: Cambridge University Press.

Schwartz, B. and Sprouse, R. (1994) 'Word order and nominative case in non-native language acquisition: a longitudinal study of (L1 Turkish) German interlanguage', in T. Hoekstra and B. Schwartz (eds), *Language acquisition studies in generative grammar: papers in honour of Kenneth Wexler for the GLOW 1991 Workshops*, Amsterdam and Philadelphia: John Benjamins.

Vainikka, A. and Young-Scholten, M. (1991) 'Verb raising in second language acquisition: the early stages', *Theorie Des Lexicons* 4: 1–48.

Vainikka, A. and Young-Scholten, M. (1998) 'The initial state in the L2 acquisition of phrase structure', in S. Flynn, G. Martohardjono and W. O'Neil (eds), *The generative study of second language acquisition*, Mahwah, NJ and London: Lawrence Erlbaum Associates.

White, L. (1986) 'Markedness and parameter settings: some implications for a theory of adult second language acquisition', in F. Eckman, E. Moravscik and J. Wirth (eds), *Markedness*, New York: Plenum Press.

White, L. (1989) *Universal grammar and second language acquisition*, Amsterdam and Philadelphia: John Benjamins.

**Further reading**

Brown, G., Malmkjær, K. and Williams, J. (eds) (1996) *Performance and competence in second language acquisition*, Cambridge: Cambridge University Press.

Flynn, S., Martohardjono, G. and O'Neil, W. (eds) (1998) *The generative study of second language acquisition*, Mahwah, NJ and London: Lawrence Erlbaum Associates.

Hymes, D.H. (1971) *On communicative competence*, Philadelphia: University of Philadelphia Press.

Mitchell, R. and Myles, F. (1998) *Second language learning theories*, Chapter 3, London: Arnold.

Richie, W. and Bhatia, T. (eds) (1996) *Handbook of second language acquisition*, San Diego: Academic Press.

KIRSTEN MALMKJÆR

# Content-based instruction

This term describes a range of approaches to the integration of language and content. These approaches lie on a continuum, ranging from those which emphasise content learning through the medium of a second/foreign language, to those in which content is used as a vehicle for promoting language learning.

*Content-driven* approaches give primary emphasis to the learning of content. Language learning is important, but it is often viewed as an incidental by-product of content instruction. Similarly, subject matter courses taught through the medium of a second/foreign language are content-driven, in that learning content is a primary course outcome. These courses are commonly taught by content specialists, not language teachers.

At the centre of the continuum lie approaches with equal emphasis on both content and language. In these approaches students frequently learn the second/foreign language as a subject, often in a specific class or course. In addition, content is taught through the medium of the second/foreign language. Students are expected to demonstrate achievement of course outcomes in both language and content, and may be instructed by both content and language specialists.

At the other end of the continuum are *language-driven* approaches. In these, language learning is the primary course objective. Content is used by language instructors to make language learning more motivating, and to provide meaningful, **AUTHENTIC** topics about which to communicate. Language-driven approaches may or may not use content drawn from the school curriculum. Content may be a specific topic or theme related to the school curriculum, be multidisciplinary, or be drawn solely from learners' expressed interests.

## Content-driven approaches

One form of content-based instruction that lies at the content-driven end of the continuum is immersion. In immersion programmes, the second/foreign language serves as the **MEDIUM OF INSTRUCTION** for half or more of the school curriculum, with emphasis on content outcomes. In North America, immersion programmes are frequently deemed successful when students demonstrate content achievement at or above expected levels. Immersion programmes are also considered successful even when students demonstrate less than native-like productive **SKILLS**. Indeed, some North American programmes assess students regularly for content learning but only sporadically, if at all, for language learning.

Another form of content-driven instruction are 'sheltered' courses – content classes taught through the medium of a second/foreign language using linguistically sensitive instructional strategies that help make content accessible to learners with less than native-like proficiency. Frequently, all the students in a sheltered class are learners of the second/foreign language, distinguishing sheltered instruction from approaches in which language learners are instructed in content alongside students learning it in their **MOTHER TONGUE**. In the **USA**, sheltered content classes are commonly found in schools that help minority language students make academic progress while they are acquiring **ENGLISH**. Sheltered courses at the university level in the US serve a similar purpose. In contrast, sheltered courses in Canada have pioneered this approach for teaching **FRENCH** and psychology to speakers of the majority language, English.

Another content-driven approach found in a growing number of US universities are language enriched courses (Allen, Anderson and Narvaez, 1992; Krueger and Ryan, 1993; Snow and Brinton, 1997; Straight, 1994). Students enrol in a regular

university course taught in their mother tongue. Students may elect to take special modules or complete designated readings in their language of choice. While most students in the course will read course assignments in English, others will supplement course readings and experiences with **MATERIALS** from the target language or meet with native-speaking graduate students who assign readings and lead discussions in the target language. These graduate students are specialists in the discipline, and not in language instruction.

At the elementary school level, some US schools have chosen to introduce foreign languages by substituting second/foreign language instruction in one content area for instruction in the mother tongue. There are programmes, for example, in which mathematics is taught in **JAPANESE** or science in **SPANISH**.

## Shared emphasis: content and language

At the centre of the continuum of content-based instruction are programmes in which both language and content are of equal importance. In these, language classes or courses accompany subject matter courses taught through the medium of the second/foreign language. In school settings, these are most often found in US elementary schools or at the post-secondary level.

At the post-secondary level, several institutions report approaches that use the adjunct model (Brinton, Snow and Wesche, 1989; Snow and Brinton, 1997). Content and language instructors work collaboratively to ensure that students learn content and gain the language skills necessary for successful content learning. Another approach to integrating language and content are language courses for special purposes. Examples include courses with self-explanatory titles such as 'English for Academic Purposes', 'Business French' or 'Spanish for Hospital Workers'.

## Language-driven approaches

In language-driven approaches to content-based instruction, content is the vehicle for language learning (in contrast to content-driven approaches in which language is the vehicle for content learning). Theme-based courses at the university level have been reported in the US by Brinton, Snow and Wesche (1989) and Lafayette and Buscaglia (1985), and in **JAPAN** by Murphey (1997). Stoller and Grabe (1997: 83) suggest a theme-based approach to content-based instruction in which themes may be drawn from the academic content of the school or university ('Insects'; 'The solar system'; 'Demography'). Themes in language-driven approaches may be drawn from a single discipline, such as science, or may cross disciplines ('Our Roman Heritage'). Themes may be drawn from the culture of the language studied, such as its history, its geography, or its economic, social and political institutions. Themes may also be drawn from topics of interest to the students ('The Circus', 'How can we prevent violence?', 'Who are today's youth?').

At the far end of the content-based continuum are language-driven approaches that use content-based tasks and activities to serve the goals of **COMMUNICATIVE LANGUAGE TEACHING**. That is, if communicative language teaching strives to give learners authentic, meaningful and purposeful tasks for language use, then content can provide a rich source of such tasks. Here, content learning is not a course focus; neither teachers nor students are held accountable for content outcomes. Rather, language learning is the course goal, and content is an effective means for attaining it. Language practice activities and tasks are drawn from many disciplines, selected by the language teacher based on the degree to which they can help further the **OBJECTIVES** of the language curriculum (Met, 1991).

In the USA, making connections from language to other disciplines as a means of reinforcing language learning is one of the five major goals of the new National Standards for Foreign Language Learning (1996). Students not only have opportunities to connect to other disciplines in language courses, they are also expected to use their language skills to acquire information that may not be available to them in English.

## Rationales for content-based instruction

The diverse approaches to content-based instruction reflect varying priorities for language learning.

Content-driven programmes are frequently found in settings where students are regularly schooled in a language other than their mother tongue. These may be settings where students speak a minority language in the home, or where knowing languages in addition to the national language is an economic or political imperative. Content-driven programmes are also common where there is a perceived need for high levels of language proficiency and **INTENSIVE LANGUAGE LEARNING** is most likely to yield the desired results. Content-driven programmes, such as immersion, or programmes in which language and content courses are linked, are also time-efficient: students gain high levels of content and language skill more or less simultaneously, rather than separately.

Language-driven approaches reflect language learning priorities. Theme-based courses are likely to reflect students' vocational or leisure interests, preparing them to use their new language in the situations or contexts they are likely to encounter in their work or personal lives. Language-driven courses that draw tasks and activities from many disciplines are most likely to be found in standalone language courses where teachers are looking to engage students in meaningful, motivating and engaging language practice.

Research suggests that content-based approaches are likely to result in more successful language learning (Brinton, Snow and Wesche, 1989; Genesee, 1994; Snow, 1998; Wesche, 1993). Among the reasons for the success of such approaches may be the increased time spent in the target language, increased learner **MOTIVATION** that comes from meaningful communicative language use, increased learner attention to tasks that are cognitively engaging and demanding, increased learner motivation due to topics related to their personal interests, and increased learning due to the links between knowledge acquired in other disciplines and its connections to tasks in the language classroom.

**See also:** Bilingual education; Generative principle; Medium of instruction; Monolingual principle; Mother-tongue teaching; Teaching methods; US Standards for Foreign Language Learning

## References

Allen, W., Anderson, K. and Narvaez, L. (1992)

'Foreign languages across the curriculum: the applied foreign language component', *Foreign Language Annals* 25: 11–19.

Brinton, D., Snow M.A. and Wesche, M.B. (1989) *Content-based second language instruction*, Boston: Heinle and Heinle.

Genesee, F. (1994) *Integrating language and content: lessons from immersion*, Santa Cruz, CA: National Center for Research on Cultural Diversity and Second Language Learning.

Krueger, M. and Ryan, F. (1993) *Language and content: discipline- and content-based approaches to language study*, Lexington, MA: D.C. Heath.

Lafayette, R. and Buscaglia, M. (1985) 'Students learn language via a civilization course – a comparison of second language classroom environments', *Studies in Second Language Acquisition* 18, 3: 323–42.

Met, M. (1991) 'Learning language through content: learning content through language', *Foreign Language Annals* 24: 281–95.

Murphey, T. (1997) 'Content-based instruction in an EFL setting: issues and strategies', in M.A. Snow and D.M. Brinton (eds), *The content-based classroom*, New York: Longman.

National Standards for Foreign Language Learning (1996) *Preparing for the 21st century*, Yonkers, NY: National Standards in Foreign Language Education Project.

Snow, M.A. (1998) 'Trends and issues in content-based instruction,' in W. Grabe, C. Ferguson, R.B. Kaplan, G.R. Tucker and H.G. Widdowson (eds), *Annual review of applied linguistics*, New York: Cambridge University Press.

Snow, M.A. and Brinton, D.M. (eds) (1997) *The content-based classroom*, New York: Longman.

Stoller, F. and Grabe, W. (1997) 'A six-T's approach to content-based instruction', in M.A. Snow and D.M. Brinton (eds), *The content-based classroom*, New York: Longman.

Straight, H.S. (1994) *Language across the curriculum. Translation perspectives VII*, Binghamton, NY: Center for Research in Translation, State University of New York at Binghamton.

Wesche, M.B. (1993) 'Discipline-based approaches to language study: research issues and outcomes,' in M. Krueger and F. Ryan (eds), *Language and content: discipline- and content-based approaches to language study*, Lexington, MA: D.C. Heath.

### Further reading

Brinton, D.M. and Master, P. (1997) *New ways in content-based instruction*, Alexandria, VA: TESOL.

Hauptman, P.C., Wesche, M.B. and Ready, D. (1988) 'Second-language acquisition through subject-matter learning: a follow-up study at the University of Ottawa', *Language Learning* 38, 3: 433–75.

Johnson, R.K and Swain, M. (eds) (1997) *Immersion education: international perspectives*, Cambridge: Cambridge University Press.

Met, M. (1994) 'Teaching content through a second language,' in F. Genesee (ed.), *Educating second language children*, Cambridge: Cambridge University Press.

Met, M. (1998a) 'Curriculum decision-making in content-based second language teaching', in F. Genesee and J. Cenoz (eds), *Beyond bilingualism: multilingualism and multilingual education*, Clevedon: Multilingual Matters.

Met, M. (1998b) 'Making connections,' in J. Phillips (ed.), *Foreign language standards: linking research, theories and practices*, Lincolnwood, IL: National Textbook Company.

Snow, M.A., Met, M. and Genesee, F. (1989) 'A conceptual framework for the integration of language and content in second/foreign language programs', *TESOL Quarterly* 23, 2: 201–17.

MYRIAM MET

# Contrastive analysis

Contrastive analysis (CA) is an area of comparative **LINGUISTICS** which is concerned with the comparison of two or more languages or subsystems of languages to determine the differences or similarities between them, either for theoretical purposes or for purposes external to the analysis itself.

Comparison of languages has been a common practice since the first bilingual glossaries, early **GRAMMARS** in which languages were described against models from other languages, mostly Latin, and interlinear glosses on the pages of early manuscripts. Comparative historical linguistics is concerned with different stages in the development of a language or several languages; typological linguists look at the classification of languages on the basis of similarity or dissimilarity of features; and grammars and bilingual **DICTIONARIES** have always incorporated an element of comparison.

## Modern contrastive linguistics

After some pioneering studies with a primarily theoretical focus at the turn of the century, modern contrastive linguistics got its impetus from attempts, in the 1940s and 1950s in the United States, at working out effective and economical foreign language teaching **MATERIALS** (see, e.g., Fisiak, 1983, which is also a good source for early contrastive work). Contrastive analysis underwent a period of rapid development and expansion in the 1960s, particularly in the United States.

Throughout the 1970s and 1980s, however, contrastive analysis was extensively practised in various European countries, particularly in Eastern European countries (James, 1980: 205), and in the early 1990s there were clear signs of a renewed interest (see, e.g., Mair and Marcus, 1992). Since then, the rapid development of automatic data processing and information technology has opened up new prospects for contrastive approaches through the potential of large corpora.

Even after several decades of contrastive studies, the theoretical and methodological foundation of contrastive analysis has not been firmly established. The early proponents of contrastive analysis (see Fries, 1945) started from the general assumption that efficient language teaching materials could be produced by obtaining a scientific description of the language to be taught by means of its careful comparison with a similar description of the learner's first language. The underlying theoretical starting point was the idea, spelled out rather convincingly by Lado (1957), that the degree of difference between the two languages also correlated with the degree of difficulty. Later on, however, the analysts' attention was also drawn to similarities between languages, because language teaching was expected to benefit from such information.

At the heyday of American contrastive analysis

in the 1960s, a series of extensive contrastive linguistic analyses were undertaken between **ENGLISH** and a number of other languages (e.g. Stockwell and Bowen, 1965; Stockwell, Bowen and Martin, 1965; see also Di Pietro, 1971), and in Europe several contrastive projects were launched somewhat later (Fisiak, 1980). In many cases the interest faded away quite soon, because the applied objectives were never properly reached. In the United States the results of some analyses were never published, and what was left behind was a scepticism among a large body of linguists towards CA that has lasted up to the present day. The scepticism concerning the usefulness of contrastive studies derives mainly from the failure of the structurally oriented contrastive studies to cope with problems encountered in foreign language teaching, but it was also partly due to the fact that contrastive orientation had been linked with **BEHAVIOURISM**, mainly as regards the role of **TRANSFER** in language learning and language use. When the idea of transfer was given up, the idea of the influence of the **MOTHER TONGUE** on second languages could not be accepted either. In the United States, one more reason for the demise of CA in the 1960s was the rapid growth of **GENERATIVE** linguistics, which made linguists more interested in universals than in linguistic differences.

## Theoretical and applied contrastive linguistics

The experience derived from the early work with contrasts implies clearly that it is necessary to distinguish between two types of CA: theoretical and applied. A confusion between the aims of these two types of CA has often resulted in the **EVALUATION** of the results of theoretical research against applied objectives, or theoretical analysis has been performed for the purposes of, for instance, language teaching. The obvious result has been increased uncertainty about the usefulness of CA.

Theoretical contrastive studies produce extensive accounts of the differences and similarities between the languages contrasted. Attempts are also made at providing adequate models for cross-language comparison and at determining which elements in languages are comparable and how it should be done. The alignment of languages also adds to the information about the characteristics of individual languages or about linguistic analysis in general. No claims should, however, be made for the applicability of the results for purposes other than linguistic analysis. System oriented contrastive linguistics of this kind can take place on the basis of any type of data that is relevant. It can also make use of quantitative materials, which may be highly valuable for making probabilistic statements about items appearing in similar contexts in the two languages. We have never before been in a position of having access to large bodies of representative data in any number of languages.

The development of powerful computer tools makes it possible to carry out contrastive studies of language features in context through the use of large computerised corpora (see Aijmer *et al.*, 1996; Granger, 1998). In this way new insights can be expected into contrastive text linguistics, **DISCOURSE ANALYSIS**, rhetoric and **PRAGMATICS**. Many areas of syntax, semantics and lexis may also benefit from the availability of large parallel corpora. At the same time it may be possible to develop new theoretical approaches to contrastive analysis.

The target of applied contrastive studies is establishment of information that can be used for purposes outside the language domain proper, such as language teaching, **TRANSLATION**, **INTERPRETING** and **BILINGUAL EDUCATION**. Traditionally, this kind of contrastive analysis has been mainly concerned with the identification of potential trouble in the use of the language learner's target language.

Traditional contrastive analysis proceeds from the description of the same features or phenomena in the two languages (e.g., linguistic categories, rules or rule systems, realisations of semantic concepts, various functions of language, pragmatic categories, rhetorical issues) to their juxtaposition on the basis of translation equivalence as assessed by a bilingual informant. Normally a point of reference, often called *tertium comparationis*, is required outside the languages to be contrasted. It is possible to argue that there are no grounds for considering two texts in two languages as fully equivalent under any circumstances. All communication is culturally relative, and texts are the same because they are communicative events. This makes them relative also in another sense. It could,

for instance, be hypothesised that two highly specialised technical or medical documents are closer to each other than, for instance, a fictional text and its translation into another language. Even more problematic than this is the question of equivalence in spoken discourse. Under what circumstances would it be possible to assume a degree of equivalence? Or should equivalence be expressed in terms of statistical probabilities? Thus the implications of the concept of **GENRE** require careful consideration. What this means, in any case, is that we have to posit different types of equivalence and *tertia comparationis* for different environments and different purposes.

## Applied contrastive analysis

The main concern of early applied contrastive analysis was a reliable prediction of the learner's difficulties (James, 1980: 181–7). This was later to be called *the strong hypothesis of contrastive analysis* (Wardhaugh, 1970). It soon proved to be rather difficult to attest to the validity of such a hypothesis in terms of learning problems, mainly because similarities and differences between the languages were not the sole, or even the most important, cause of problems for the learner. The alternative approach that came to be offered instead was **ERROR ANALYSIS**. In error analysis, contrastive analysis was assigned an explanatory role, which was to be called *the weak hypothesis of contrastive analysis*. In many cases, however, the problem with error analysis was the same as with CA: it was difficult to ascertain what the reason for learners' problems really was – there were too many alternatives.

Despite continued criticism, contrastive analysis remains a useful tool in the search for potential sources of trouble in foreign language learning. It cannot be overlooked in **SYLLABUS** design, preparation of **TEXTBOOKS** and production of teaching materials. It is also a valuable source of information for the purposes of translation and interpretation. The scope of contrastive analysis has gradually widened, along with the expansion of researchers' interests beyond the confines of the sentence (see Fisiak, 1990), for instance, to **INTERLANGUAGE** pragmatics (Trosborg, 1995) or contrastive rhetorics (Connor, 1996).

Since many studies had resulted in the conclusion that the alignment and mapping of the language codes have proved to be insufficient for applied purposes, recent contrastive studies have introduced various psychological, sociological, and contextual factors alongside the purely linguistic ones. The learner had been almost totally forgotten in much of what had been written about the success – or mostly failure – of contrastive analysis from an applied viewpoint. It is quite evident that a straightforward setting alongside two linguistic systems – even irrespective of the level of analysis – is too simplistic and cannot easily produce information relevant for language teaching purposes. There is simply too much variation in learner performance for it to be accounted for by reference to linguistic phenomena alone. Language use is based on internalised categories of rules and structures and on various processes, and therefore speakers observe phenomena that they have learned, or choose, to observe. A student may hear, and thus also produce, a certain language feature differently from what is expected by the teacher because the student's perception is not governed by the patterning adopted for teaching from a theoretical or pedagogical perspective. It is impossible to understand learners' problems unless it is known how they feel, what they attempt to hear, what they actually hear, what the structures are that they perceive, and how these differ from the perceptions of **NATIVE SPEAKERS** in similar situations. This implies that true contrasts, at least from the learning point of view, lie inside each individual learner, i.e. in the interaction of various types of information relating to the second/foreign language, the mother tongue, and possible other languages. In addition, pedagogic contrastive studies should be concerned with phenomena characteristic of bilingual speakers using their second/foreign language as against the use of their first language, their reactions to native speaker speech or speech produced by other second/foreign language speakers, and native speaker reactions to their speech.

## New perspectives

Some prominent representatives of the research in this area have, however, voiced their doubts about the success of psycholinguistically oriented contrastive studies. Krzeszowski (1990: 243), for instance, is rather sceptical when he defines the key task of contrastive analysis as follows: 'For the time being, contrastive analysis must be limited to predicting potential errors, even if one builds it ... on psycholinguistic foundations. Actual performance still remains out of reach.'

A strong argument for new perspectives in contrastive linguistics, with a particular emphasis on its relevance for foreign language teaching, can be found, for instance, in Kühlwein (1990: 13), who argues for 'structurally limited contrastive linguistics' being redefined as 'processually opened contrastive linguistics via its growing recognition of performance/errors, universals, interlanguage, transfer, cognition and discourse'. It is important to remember that it is irrelevant at what level of language the analysis takes place if the analyst fails to recognise the interlinkage between the categories that he is dealing with and their role in the language-related communicative system. Analysis of specific details at the linguistic level makes sense only if their relevance as items in the receptive and productive message-processing systems is recognised and aspects of human communicative interaction are also taken into account. Such a holistic view is also necessary for us to be able to consider the role of the phenomena studied in the processes through which second/foreign languages are learned.

The equivalence between sociocultural phenomena depends on the match between the social environments and cultural factors. When transferred to the environment of another culture, some 'rules' will be valid as such, some will bring about desired outcomes although they appear to be out of place, and some will be completely wrong. The problem for the foreign language speaker is to know when it is possible to transfer L1 practices to L2. Cultural and social phenomena are difficult to perceive and categorise. This also results in difficulties in teaching. Subconscious knowledge derived from previous cultural and social experience makes it possible for people to carry out various social practices properly without paying too much attention to what they are doing and without being conscious of the factors that trigger appropriate behaviour. In their cultural behaviour people are more alike than different, which adds to the chances of success. Moreover, many of the assumed differences may actually be 'in the eye of the beholder', perceptions based on misguided experience, mere narrative, or stereotyping (for an example, see Sajavaara and Lehtonen, 1997). What is crucial is observation of other people's and one's own behaviour.

The question of what contrasts are essential is of importance here. How can we establish access to them? What has been said here implies that there is not a single type of contrast, or a single type of contrastive analysis, that can be expected to solve all possible problems, either in foreign language teaching, translation studies, or any other practically oriented field. It should also be evident by now that two types of approach are needed which are basically differentiated along the borderline between theoretical and applied research.

The theory and methodology adopted from linguistics has to be supplemented with those derived from sociology, **PSYCHOLOGY**, social psychology, neurology, **CULTURAL STUDIES**, ethnography, **ANTHROPOLOGY** and related disciplines for the analysis of pragmatic patterning, cognitive mechanisms and information processing systems involved. It is no longer necessary for the contrastive linguist to invent the examples in the way it used to be done. It is now possible to resort to corpora, where the relevant instances can be found by means of automatic searches. There is a wealth of information about the principles to be applied in the compilation of a unilingual text corpus, but there is much less information about parallel corpora. Since a bilingual parallel corpus is different from a unilingual one, it is to be assumed that the principles of its compilation are also different. It is evident that, within the next few years, we will have more information about this problem.

Applied contrastive linguistics is in a different situation, which is also evident from the rather depressing history of the field. Different objectives seem to require different methodological approaches. As has been pointed out repeatedly in this entry, the interlingual contrast is not housed directly in the two language systems but is mediated through the language learner (see Sajavaara and Lehtonen, 1980: 11), i.e. it is buried in the minds of bilingual language users. A distinction must defi-nitely be made between processes and products. The analogy that can be used to illustrate this is the existence of minute nuclear particles in physics. Products can be compared with the impact of some minute nuclear particle: the particle itself is never seen but it is known to exist because it leaves a mark. Processes take place in a similar fashion in the human mind, and the language products are their physical attestations. The way in which the product can be analysed from the process perspective is only indirect. This is why it is absolutely necessary to develop methodologies which make it possible to study languages in the production or reception process in real time. Here we enter an area where experimental research and qualitative research become essential, and perhaps less importance can be attached to purely quantitative work. Learner corpora may prove to be valuable resources in the future (see Granger, 1998). Such corpora can also be compared with parallel corpora, which may give added importance to corpus-based contrastive analysis for applied purposes.

**See also:** Applied linguistics; Error analysis; Linguistics; Pragmatics; Structural linguistics; Textbooks; Transfer

### References

Aijmer, K., Altenberg, B. and Johansson, M. (eds) (1996) *Languages in contrast*, Lund Studies in English 88, Lund: Lund University Press.

Connor, U. (1996) *Contrastive rhetorics*, Cambridge: Cambridge University Press.

Di Pietro, R.J. (1971) *Language structures in contrast*, Rowley, MA: Newbury House.

Fisiak, J. (1980) 'Some notes concerning contrastive linguistics', *AILA Bulletin* 27: 1–17.

Fisiak, J. (1983) 'Present trends in contrastive analysis', in K. Sajavaara (ed.), *Cross-language analysis and second language acquisition 1*, Jyväskylä Cross-Language Studies 9, Jyväskylä: University of Jyväskylä.

Fisiak, J. (ed.) (1990) *Further insights into contrastive analysis*, Linguistic and literary studies in Eastern Europe 30, Amsterdam: John Benjamins.

Fries, C.C. (1945) *Teaching and learning English as a Foreign Language*, Ann Arbor: University of Michigan Press.

Granger, S. (1998) *Learner English on computer*, London: Longman.

James, C. (1980) *Contrastive analysis*, London: Longman.

Krzeszowski, T.P. (1990) *Contrasting languages: the scope of contrastive linguistics*, Berlin: Mouton de Gruyter.

Kühlwein, W. (1990) 'Kontrastive Linguistik und Fremdsprachenerwerb: Perspektiven und historischer Hintergrund (Contrastive linguistics and foreign language learning: perspectives and background)', in C. Gnutzmann (ed.), *Kontrastive Linguistik*, Frankfurt am Main: Lang.

Lado, R. (1957) *Linguistics across cultures: applied linguistics for language teachers*, Ann Arbor: University of Michigan Press.

Mair, C. and Marcus, M. (eds) (1992) *New departures in contrastive linguistics 1–2*, Innsbrücker Beiträge zur Kulturwissenschaft, Innsbruck: University of Innsbruck.

Sajavaara, K. and Lehtonen, J. (1980) 'Prisoners of code-centred privacy: reflections on contrastive analysis and related disciplines', in K. Sajavaara and J. Lehtonen (eds), *Papers in discourse and contrastive discourse analysis*, Jyväskylä Contrastive Studies 5, Jyväskylä: University of Jyväskylä.

Sajavaara, K. and Lehtonen, J. (1997) 'The silent Finn revisited', in A. Jaworski (ed.), *Silence: interdisciplinary perspectives*, Berlin: Mouton de Gruyter.

Stockwell, R.P. and Bowen, J.D. (1965) *The sounds of English and Spanish*, Chicago: University of Chicago Press.

Stockwell, R.P., Bowen, J.D. and Martin, J.W. (1965) *The grammatical structures of English and Spanish*, Chicago: University of Chicago Press.

Trosborg, A. (1995) *Interlanguage pragmatics*, Berlin: Mouton de Gruyter.

Wardhaugh, R. (1970) 'The contrastive analysis hypothesis', *TESOL Quarterly* 4: 123–30.

**Further reading**

Eliasson, S. (1984) *Theoretical issues in contrastive phonology*, Heidelberg: J. Groos.

Fisiak, J. (ed.) (1981) *Contrastive linguistics and the language teacher*, Oxford: Pergamon.

Fisiak, J. (ed.) (1984) *Contrastive linguistics: prospects and problems*, Berlin: Mouton.

James, C. (1980) *Contrastive analysis*, London: Longman.

James, C. (1998) *Errors in language learning and language use: exploring error analysis*, London: Longman.

Kellerman, E. and Sharwood Smith, M. (eds) (1984) *Crosslinguistic influence in second language acquisition*, Oxford: Pergamon.

Odlin, T. (1989) *Language transfer: cross-linguistic influence in language learning*, Cambridge: Cambridge University Press.

Oleksy, W. (ed.) (1989) *Contrastive pragmatics*, Amsterdam: John Benjamins.

Trosborg, A. (1995) *Interlanguage pragmatics*, Berlin: Mouton de Gruyter.

KARI SAJAAVARA

# Conversation analysis

Conversation analysis (CA) emerged in the late 1950s and early 1960s from within the branch of sociology known as ethnomethodology. It is concerned with investigating discourse, or more specifically, as the name suggests, conversation, with a view to uncovering how interaction in everyday settings is organised and maintained by the interlocutors with reference to shared social knowledge. Unlike the deductive approach of **DISCOURSE ANALYSIS**, CA aims to reveal through inductive study the structures of naturally occurring interaction on the basis of detailed transcripts of audio or video-recordings. CA moves away from the single utterance as a focus of attention, characteristic of **SPEECH ACT THEORY**, and explores the sequential organisation of interaction and its basis in the turn-taking system. The influence of CA on other areas of study, most notably linguistics, psychology and cross-cultural communication scholarship, is growing. Its value to language teaching and learning lies in the manner in which it can reveal how meaning is mutually constructed and negotiated by interlocutors in both intra- and intercultural settings. Such insights have relevance for the fields of **PRAGMATICS** and for the development of **INTERCULTURAL COMPETENCE** amongst learners, including **INTERLANGUAGE** pragmatics.

## Development from ethnomethodology

Ethnomethodology explores the notion that members of a society use common-sense knowledge, which is based on a 'background of common understandings' (Garfinkel, 1967: 49), to interpret events and behaviour encountered in everyday social settings and thereby to organise their interaction on an ongoing basis. Central to the theory is the role of the so-called actors in constructing social meaning. In the 1950s this represented a new departure in sociological scholarship in its move away from deductively-based approaches.

CA builds on these assumptions and adopts an empirical approach to the study of interaction in real-life, everyday social activities. The focus is on the individual nature of the situations studied, their uniqueness being attributable to the role played by the actors in determining how events unfold. It attempts through extensive field study of naturally occurring interaction to learn about such activities from within, and eschews the establishment of general theories which detach interaction from the context in which it occurs. Experimental and other laboratory-generated data favoured by social-psychological research are rejected. Reliance on field notes as a record of observation, characteristic of ethnographic research, is questioned due to the inadequacies of memory. Thus, transcribed recordings of face-to-face and telephone interaction constitute the basis for analysis. They permit ongoing review of the data in the light of other research questions and as a means of comparison. A detailed transcription scheme developed by Jefferson (see Schenkein, 1978) incorporates aspects such as overlaps, pauses, voice volume and stress. It permits exploration of the sequential organisation of conversation in greater depth, including features such as repair, and results in a better understanding of interactional behaviour as it emerges from what is locally produced by the participants. The notation scheme also accommodates **NON-VERBAL** signalling. Essentially, CA interprets interaction by using the same sources of information available to the interlocutors.

Central to CA is the research carried out by Sacks, Schegloff and Jefferson (1974, 1977) into the organisation of conversation on a formal level by defining turn-taking mechanisms used by interactants to regulate and coordinate their interaction. It is claimed that the turn-taking system is 'context-free' and functions independently of the participants; yet to understand the contribution of a participant to a particular sequence requires reference to the local context, specifically the preceding utterance/s and, potentially, to the external context of the interaction, but only in so far as this is manifestly integrated into the interaction by the interlocutor. Similarly, interaction is 'context-renewing' (Heritage, 1989: 22); in other words, each contribution constitutes the context for the next or subsequent contributions to the sequence. The claim that the turn-taking system is 'context-free' suggests that it can be applied to intercultural settings with the proviso that there may be some variation in the sequential organisation of the discourse (Sacks, Schegloff and Jefferson, 1974: 700).

CA researchers have focused almost exclusively on conversation and on institutional settings where the principles of turn-taking are constrained by the situation; for example, interviews, courtroom settings and classroom interaction (Heritage, 1984: 238f.; Firth, 1995: 25). Recognition of the value of the methodology as a means of analysing institutional talk is growing (Boden, 1994); specifically, its ability to reveal how particular institutional contexts are reproduced in the talk of the interactants (Heritage and Atkinson, 1984: 15).

## Implications for teaching

CA has much to offer to the development of teaching resources, although its potential remains underexploited. It has been used in the analysis of classroom talk, specifically learner and **TEACHER TALK**, to investigate how negotiation of meaning might be optimised in the language classroom, in the context of growing interest in interaction and teacher research (van Lier, 1996). Employed in the foreign language classroom, CA can function as a diagnostic tool to reveal problems of discourse management and critical incidents encountered by learners through emphasis on how interlocutors make sense of each other's contribution. This notion of intersubjectivity diverges from the dominant concentration on speaker intention evident in speech act theory. CA can be used to promote interactively-based learning which moves away from the teaching of isolated language functions as product to focus on the process of interaction in intercultural settings. Thus, it is relevant to the field of cross-cultural pragmatics as a means of pinpointing misunderstandings in interaction and their resolution, the accomplishment of repair sequences, preferences for self as opposed to other correction, acceptability of simultaneous talk and cultural expectations in respect of **POLITENESS**. Critically, it also reveals how native and non-native interlocutors negotiate and review on an ongoing basis intercultural norms, thereby reinforcing the notion of interaction as a dynamic rather than a static phenomenon. Through attention to the micro details of interaction and inclusion of non-verbal features, the methodology allows access to a much wider range of potential sources of pragmatic failure. Contingent with the growing interest in the application of CA in institutional settings is its emergence within language for specific purposes (LSP) as a basis for investigating intercultural business meetings and negotiations, including the transfer of such insights to the development of interactively-focused teaching materials (Bolten, 1992) which draw on **TASK-BASED** learning. CA also offers access to how interlocutors reinforce particular organisational structures through their communicative practices, a neglected dimension of LSP research and materials design.

## Criticisms

Critics of CA argue that its focus on the cooperative basis of interaction is not sufficient to explain the linguistic basis of interaction (Gumperz, 1982). Linguistic knowledge affects interpretation of the various signalling mechanisms used by interlocutors; successful turn-taking relies on the participants knowing, *inter alia*, how to anticipate the end of an utterance and to differentiate between rhetorical and turn-relinquishing pauses (Gumperz 1982: 160). Discourse analysts claim that CA is inexplicit and that its adherents are confused about the conceptual categories which they use in analysis (Levinson, 1983: 287). More generally, CA has been criticised for being atheoretical: this **EVALUATION** refers to its

reaction to the focus within deductive approaches on pre-determined categories of analysis which may result in a neglect of the data (Heritage, 1989: 37f.). A further question relates to whether the principles of conversational organisation can be claimed to be universal in the absence of sufficient comparative research in non-European language settings (Levinson, 1983: 369f.). Whilst the methodology continues to grow in popularity, this question represents a continuing challenge to conversation analysts, particularly in respect of its potential implications for both child language acquisition and second language acquisition (SLA) research (Levinson, 1983: 368f.).

**See also:** Cross-cultural psychology; Discourse analysis; Non-verbal communication; Pragmatics; Sociolinguistics; Speech act theory; Text and corpus linguistics

## References

Boden, D. (1994) *The business of talk: organizations in action*, Cambridge: Polity Press.

Bolten, J. (1992) 'Interkulturelles Verhandlungsstraining' (Intercultural Negotiation Training), *Jahrbuch Deutsch als Fremdsprache* 18: 269–87.

Firth, A. (1995) *The discourse of negotiation: studies of language in the workplace*, Oxford: Pergamon.

Garfinkel, H. (1967) *Studies in ethnomethodology*, Englewood Cliffs, NJ: Prentice Hall.

Gumperz, J.J. (1982) *Discourse strategies*, Cambridge: Cambridge University Press.

Heritage, J. (1984) *Garfinkel and ethnomethodology*, Cambridge: Polity Press.

Heritage, J. (1989) 'Current developments in conversation analysis', in D. Roger and P. Bull (eds), *Conversation: an interdisciplinary perspective*, Clevedon: Multilingual Matters.

Heritage, J. and Atkinson, J.M. (eds) (1984) *Structures of social action: studies in conversational analysis*, Cambridge: Cambridge University Press.

Levinson, S.C. (1983) *Pragmatics*, Cambridge: Cambridge University Press.

Sacks, H., Schegloff, E. and Jefferson G. (1974) 'A simplest systematics for the organization of turn-taking for conversation', *Language* 50, 4: 696–735.

Sacks, H., Schegloff, E. and Jefferson G. (1977)

'The preference for self-correction in the organization of repair in conversation', *Language* 53, 2: 361–82.

Schenkein, J. (ed.) (1978) *Studies in the organization of conversational interaction*, New York: Academic Press.

van Lier, L. (1996) *Interaction in the language curriculum: awareness, autonomy, and authenticity*, London: Longman.

## Further reading

Boden, D. and Zimmerman, D. (eds) (1991) *Talk and social structure: studies in ethnomethodology and conversation analysis*, Cambridge: Polity Press.

Drew, P. and Heritage, J. (eds) (1992) *Talk at work: interaction in institutional settings*, Cambridge: Cambridge University Press.

Psathas, G. (1995) *Conversation analysis. The study of talk-in-interaction*, Thousand Oaks: Sage.

Schiffrin, D. (1994) *Approaches to discourse*, Oxford: Blackwell.

Wardhaugh, R. (1985) *How conversation works*, Oxford: Blackwell.

GILLIAN S. MARTIN

# Council of Europe Modern Languages Projects

The Council of Europe (CE) is an intergovernmental organisation which brings together forty pluralist democratic European states with the object of creating a united, free and democratic Europe based on HUMAN RIGHTS and cooperating in the treatment of common social issues. Its work in education, culture, youth and sport is conducted by the Council for Cultural Cooperation (CDCC) in the framework of the European Cultural Convention signed since 1954 by forty-seven states. Since 1961, when it called upon the CE actively to promote this aim, CDCC has organised a continuous series of medium term projects concerning modern languages.

1  1963–73. A ten-year Major Project covering all educational sectors and concentrating on the modernisation of teacher training and pioneering modes of inter-sector and international cooperation. The application of the findings of linguistic research to language teaching was promoted. AILA was set up and the AUDIO-VISUAL method developed by CRÉDIF was promoted.

2  1971–76. A working group investigated the feasibility of a European unit-credit scheme for foreign language learning by adults. In its early work it laid down the basic aims and principles based on the educational and political aims of the Council of Europe which have guided successive projects:

- to facilitate the free movement of people, information and ideas in Europe with access for all and to encourage closer cooperation by providing the linguistic means of direct interpersonal communication;

- to build up mutual understanding and acceptance of cultural and linguistic diversity in a multilingual and multicultural Europe, with respect for individual, local, regional and national identities, freely developing a common European identity based on shared values;

- to promote the personal development of individuals, with growing self-awareness and self-confidence, so that they may play an active role as socially responsible citizens in a pluralist democratic society

- to make the process of language teaching and learning itself more democratic, transparent and coherent by developing the necessary conceptual tools for the planning, conduct and EVALUATION of courses closely geared to the NEEDS, MOTIVATIONS and characteristics of learners and facilitating decision-making as close as possible to the point of learning.

These were elaborated in a series of studies (Trim *et al.*, 1980) on: needs analysis; the 'functional/notional' approach to the specification of OBJECTIVES; the 'Threshold' concept; an integrative view of language education as a lifelong process requiring the close cooperation of learners, teachers and other providers and users. The concepts were exemplified in THRESHOLD LEVEL descriptions for ENGLISH, FRENCH, GERMAN, SPANISH (and many other national and regional languages).

A draft unit-credit scheme was produced (Trim, 1980) but never implemented.

3   1977–81. In 'Project 4' (CDCC, 1981), the approach was applied in a series of experiments in lower secondary schools coordinated in a 'schools interaction network', in **ADULT** education, in provision for the learning of the host language and mother-tongue maintenance by migrants and their families, and in the use of mass media (especially the Anglo-German multimedia broadcast-led English course *Follow Me*). Following the positive evaluation of Project 4, the CE Committee of Ministers adopted Recommendation R(82) 18 to all member governments. Eighteen specific measures were recommended. In particular, governments were called upon:

1   To ensure, as far as possible, that all sections of their populations have access to effective means of acquiring a knowledge of the languages of other member states (or of other communities within their own country) as well as the **SKILLS** in the use of those languages that will enable them to satisfy their communicative needs, and in particular:

1.1   to deal with the business of everyday life in another country, and to help foreigners staying in their own country to do so;

1.2   to exchange information and ideas with young people and adults who speak a different language and to communicate their thoughts and feelings to them;

1.3   to achieve a wider and deeper understanding of the way of life and forms of thought of other peoples and of their cultural heritage.

2   To promote, encourage and support the efforts of teachers and learners at all levels to apply in their own situation the principles of the construction of language learning systems (as these are progressively developed within the Council of Europe 'Modern languages' programmes:

2.1   by basing language teaching and learning on the needs, motivations and characteristics and resources of learners;

2.2   by defining worthwhile and realistic objectives as explicitly as possible;

2.3   by developing appropriate methods and **MATERIALS**;

2.4   by developing suitable forms and instruments for the evaluation of learning programmes.

3   To promote research and development programmes leading to the introduction, at all educational levels, of methods and materials best suited to enabling different categories and types of student to acquire a communicative proficiency appropriate to their specific needs.

4   1982–87. Project 12 (Girard and Trim, 1988) was devoted to supporting the general implementation of R(82)18 in national reforms of curricula and examinations, in which the schools interaction network and the further development of threshold level descriptions played a part. Teacher trainers were identified as key personnel and a series of thirty-seven interactional workshops was held in fifteen countries, attended by 1,500 participants from twenty countries in which over 200 themes were introduced by 230 animators. The series played a significant part in developing a sense of common purpose in the language teaching profession across the continent.

5   1988–96. By this time national programmes for the reform of language teaching in the 11–16 age group were well advanced, and CDCC launched a Project 'Language Learning for European Citizenship' (Trim, 1997) directed towards other educational sectors: upper secondary, **VOCATIONALLY** oriented language learning (VOLL), advanced adult education, **PRIMARY EDUCATION**, and initial **TEACHER EDUCATION** and training. In each, as well as in lower secondary, new themes of growing interest and importance were taken up:

1   the enrichment of the specification of objectives. This led both to the updating of threshold level and **WAYSTAGE** and to the addition of a higher 'Vantage Level' specification. Furthermore, a **COMMON EUROPEAN FRAMEWORK** (CEF) for language learning, teaching and **ASSESSMENT** was drafted, with a view to the introduction of a **EUROPEAN LANGUAGE PORTFOLIO** (ELP);

2 use of new technologies;
3 the use of a second language as a medium of instruction in other curricular subjects, both in bilingual areas and in 'mainstream' education;
4 the integration of school links, visits and **EXCHANGES** into the Modern Languages curriculum in a whole-school perspective;
5 '**LEARNING TO LEARN**' and the promotion of learner independence;
6 the further development of modes of assessment. These sectors and themes were treated in a further series of thirty-one workshops, twenty-six of which were conducted as pairs linked by a two-year research and development programme.

Over this period, political changes in Central and Eastern Europe led to an increase in CDCC membership from twenty-four to forty-four states, and support was given to new member states in reorienting and modernising language teaching in accordance with Recommendation R(82)18. Following the endorsement of the Project's findings by an Intergovernmental Conference held in Strasbourg in 1997, a new Recommendation R(98)6 was adopted by the Committee of Ministers.

6 1998–2,000. A new project centred on the concept of European plurilingualism was launched, involving the field trialing of CEF and ELP for public launching in the European Year of Languages, 2001.

For the past forty years, the CE projects have provided a central focus for the transformation of modern languages in education from an aspect of the cultural formation of a social and intellectual élite to the provision of necessary international communication skills for all Europeans. The strength of the conceptual framework, the clarity of its formulation and the practical usefulness of its products, together with the determination and energy with which a long-term strategy was conceived and pursued, achieved a lasting consensus uniting the many independent agents in the language teaching profession, with understanding and support from their ministries, to produce a sense of enthusiasm, common purpose and at times excitement in carrying through the educational reforms demanded by the rapid evolution of European society in the late twentieth century.

**See also:** European Centre for Modern Languages; Notions and functions; Pedagogical grammar; Vantage Level

### References

Council for Cultural Cooperation (CDCC) (1981) *Modern languages programme 1971–81: report presented by CDCC Project Group 4, with a résumé by J.L.M. Trim, Project Adviser*, Strasbourg: Council of Europe.

Girard, D. and Trim, J.L.M. (eds) (1988) *Project no. 12: learning and teaching modern languages for communication. Final report of the Project Group (activities 1982–87)*, Strasbourg: Council of Europe.

Trim, J.L.M. (1980) *Developing a unit/credit scheme of adult language learning*, Oxford: Pergamon.

Trim, J.L.M. (ed.) (1997) *Language learning for European citizenship: Final report of the Project Group (1989–96)*, Strasbourg: Council of Europe.

Trim, J.L.M., Richterich, R., van Ek, J.A. and Wilkins, D.A. (1980) *Systems development in adult language learning*, Oxford: Pergamon.

### Further reading

Brumfit, C. (ed.) (1994) 'The work of the Council of Europe and second language teaching', *Review of English Language Teaching* 4, 2 (special volume).

Trim, J. (1996) 'Modern languages in the Council of Europe', *Language Teaching* 29, 2: 81–5.

van Ek, J.A. and Trim, J.L.M. (1984) *Across the threshold: readings from the modern languages projects of the Council of Europe*, Oxford: Pergamon.

JOHN L.M.TRIM

# CRAPEL – Centre de Recherches et d'Applications Pédagogiques en Langues

The Centre de Recherches et d'Applications Pédagogiques en Langues (Université de Nancy 2, **FRANCE**) was founded by Yves Châlon in 1969.

Originally a relatively informal group of language teaching enthusiasts, it has since acquired full status as a research and teaching institution or 'laboratory' working within the French system of **HIGHER EDUCATION**. None the less, the Centre still retains, and jealously protects, its intellectual and political independence. This is largely made possible by the fact that the Centre's twelve or so members, who are all language teachers in one of Nancy's tertiary institutions, are free to elect their Director, co-opt new members and plan future policy and activities with little outside interference. After Yves Châlon's tragically early death in a car crash in 1972, Henri Holec was elected Director, and he was regularly re-elected until his retirement in 1998, when Marie-José Gremmo was elected.

For members of the Centre, it is axiomatic that learners vary, as do the teaching/learning situations in which they find themselves. There can, therefore, be no question of an ideal or uniform methodology, so that the aim of research is to establish the principles and criteria on which specific language learning syllabi will be constructed. Research is carried out in sub-groups of three to five members. However, since any individual member may belong to more than one group, there are often eight to ten projects under way at any one time. As none of the members of the Centre are full-time researchers, there is a strong preference for relatively short-term, action-research projects rather than longitudinal or 'pure' studies. Research topics are identified and prioritised on the basis of problems and needs encountered in actual teaching/learning situations, rather than as ways of testing or developing theory. Certain problems, though, tend to recur, and experience and reflection are, to some extent at least, cumulative, which gives an overall consistency of approach to the Centre's work. The principal languages concerned are **ENGLISH**, **FRENCH** as a second or foreign language, and, to a lesser degree, **SPANISH** and **GERMAN**.

From its inception, two of the Centre's main areas of interest have been the **COMMUNICATIVE** approach and **AUTONOMOUS** or self-directed language learning. Both Yves Châlon and Henri Holec were members of the **COUNCIL OF EUROPE**'s panel of experts on modern languages. Members of the Centre work as consultants and trainers in language didactics and have contributed to the establishment of resource centres and self-directed learning systems in many countries, including Egypt, Finland, Hong Kong, Italy, Madagascar, Mexico and Spain. Other research projects have dealt with **INTERCULTURAL COMMUNICATION**, **LEARNING STYLES**, the development of specific approaches to and materials for the separate language skills, foreign languages in the primary school, languages for specific purposes (such as French for academic purposes and tourism), and the new technologies applied to language learning.

The Centre publishes language learning materials and its own journal, *Les Mélanges Pédagogiques*.

## Website

The Centre's website is: http://www.univ-nancy2.fr/RECHERCHE

PHILIP RILEY

# CRÉDIF – Centre de Recherche et d'Étude pour la Diffusion du Français

The CRÉDIF (1951–1996) was one of the main university institutions specialising in **FRENCH** as a Foreign Language. Being closely linked to France's Ministry of National Education and Ministry of Foreign Affairs, the CRÉDIF's main purpose was to contribute to the dissemination of French outside France.

The activities of the CRÉDIF fall into three categories: fundamental and applied research, the main object of research being the description of contemporary French; pedagogic research focused on contexts, **NEEDS**, teaching **OBJECTIVES** and the learning of French in **FRANCE** and abroad; training for people in the education system (students, researchers, teachers, teacher trainers, inspectors, experts in educational development) involved in French as a foreign or second language, and more generally in foreign language didactics. Throughout its history, the CRÉDIF published **REFERENCE WORKS** and edited several series on the teaching of French and of languages in general, such as *Cahiers du Français contemporain*, *Essais* and *LAL – Langues et*

*Apprentissage des Langues.* This was done in cooperation with various publishers in France, in particular Didier, and abroad. Then, in the 1990s, there were publications in partnership with other institutions: *Notions en Question – Rencontres en didactique des langues,* and *Triangle* (in cooperation with the **BRITISH COUNCIL** and the **GOETHE-INSTITUT**).

From 1959, the year of its official foundation, until 1996, the year of its administrative closure, the CRÉDIF was attached to the École Normale Supérieure de Saint Cloud (today the École Normale de Fontenay/Saint Cloud), in which the *Centre d'étude du français élémentaire* had been founded in 1951 with the support of the French Commission at UNESCO and under the patronage of eminent linguists and intellectuals. The purpose of this first institution was to analyse spoken French statistically in order to be able to identify the 'basic' elements, i.e. the most frequent **VOCABULARY** and grammatical forms. Following the example of 'basic English', 'elementary French' was intended to make the learning of French, with its reputation of being a difficult language, easier in order to promote international dissemination. In this simplified form, the French language was to be used for programmes of education and schooling supported by UNESCO, especially in African countries.

In 1959, the designation 'elementary French' was replaced by the term **LE FRANÇAIS FONDAMEN-TAL**, and the CRÉDIF took over from the *Centre d'Étude du français élémentaire.* It continued the research on the vocabulary and **GRAMMAR** of French, and then diversified its activities by turning to the production of learning **MATERIALS** and by introducing training programmes intended above all for future teachers of French abroad. CRÉDIF's courses and support services (a library specialising in the teaching of French, and an audio-visual centre) were to become a renowned location for training and the dissemination of publications, methods and practices in French as a Foreign Language.

The history of the CRÉDIF thus broadly coincides with the evolution of the teaching of French as a modern language. The early days of the Centre were notable for the development, in cooperation with the University of Zagreb, of the *méthode structuro-globale AUDIO-VISUELLE* (SGAV). This work was based on the theory of **STRUCTURAL LINGUISTICS** and led to two exemplary courses of the period: *Voix et Images de France* (1961) and *Bonjour Line* (1963). Parallel to this there were publications of the results of work on 'languages for specific purposes' (LSP), i.e. on scientific and technical vocabularies (*Vocabulaire général d'orientation scientifique*). Then, from the beginning of the 1970s, the teachers and researchers of the CRÉDIF turned their attention to the learning of French by 'migrants' to France and the education of the children of migrants.

In 1973, there came the publication of the English **THRESHOLD LEVEL** at the Council of Europe, and a team from the CRÉDIF was commissioned to develop the equivalent for French, published in 1976, entitled *Niveau Seuil.* The description of French was based on pragmatic theories of language, and emphasised communication and its functions, rather than grammar and vocabulary. The aim of language teaching was the acquisition of 'communicative competence'. The publications and courses produced by the CRÉDIF throughout the 1980s followed the so-called 'communicative' approach, including the course called *Archipel* (1982–87).

The final period was marked by new issues which reflected in teaching and research the recognition of **INTERNATIONALISATION** as a consequence of the increase in exchanges and partnerships, above all in the European context. The research and the products of the Centre thus widened to include **BILINGUALISM** and plurilingualism, the early learning of foreign languages, **LANGUAGE AWARENESS**, the use of new information and communication technologies, and the cultural and intercultural dimension in language learning.

The last publications by teachers and researchers at the CRÉDIF before its closure focused on the acquisition of 'plurilingual and pluricultural competence' in the context of the **COMMON EURO-PEAN FRAMEWORK** for language learning, teaching and assessment. The primary purpose of the Centre, the dissemination of French abroad, was deemed to be complete.

**See also:** Africa; *Alliance française*; British Council; *Didactique des langues*;   Early language learning; Linguistic imperialism; Pragmatics; Teaching methods

## Further reading

Coste, D. (ed.) (1984) *Aspects d'une politique de diffusion du français langue étrangère depuis 1945. Matériaux pour une histoire*, Paris: ENS de St Cloud/Hatier.

Porcher, L. (1987) *Champs de signes. États de la diffusion du français langue étrangère*, Paris: ENS de St Cloud/Didier.

GLORIA PAGANINI

# Creoles

A creole is a language that has developed from a **PIDGIN**. Creoles are found in multilingual areas of the world, such as parts of West **AFRICA** or the South Pacific, or in communities where a pidgin language has served as a useful **LINGUA FRANCA**. Because their speakers tend to have other languages at their disposal, pidgins can survive for lengthy periods with small vocabularies and simple **GRAMMARS**. Creoles, however, are often the sole language of a community and so they must be capable of fulfilling all their speakers' linguistic **NEEDS**. Thus, in being transformed into a creole, a pidgin's vocabulary is expanded and its structures made more subtle, more flexible and more precise.

Creoles always involve a language shift and are often brought about by the disruption of normal speech communities. The best-known examples came into being as a result of the Slave Trade. Between the sixteenth and nineteenth centuries, an estimated ten million Africans, speaking over 500 different **MOTHER TONGUES**, were sold into slavery. The Africans were obliged to relinquish their ancestral African languages and to communicate in a pidginised form of a European language, usually Dutch, **ENGLISH**, French, **PORTUGUESE** or **SPANISH**. Children born into slave communities learnt to use the pidgin for all their needs and, in doing so, they transformed it into a creole.

In the last half century, creoles have developed in urban communities in countries like Cameroon, Nigeria and Papua New Guinea. In such areas, many people have found that the pidgin lingua franca facilitates inter-group contact, and so it is employed for more and more purposes. Often, parents of different linguistic backgrounds use the pidgin as a home language and their children acquire it as a mother tongue.

The name 'creole' comes from either Spanish *criollo* or Portuguese *criolou*, originally meaning 'bred, brought up, domestic'. In the sixteenth century, when the term was first used in a colonial context, a 'creole' was a person of European ancestry born in the New World. Gradually over the next two centuries it was applied to children of mixed race and then to Africans who were born in the Americas. By the early 1800s, the word 'creole' could be applied to a language. Lady Nugent, the wife of the Governor of Jamaica at the beginning of the nineteenth century, has a diary entry in which she records that ' ... the Creole language is not confined to the negroes' (Nunn, 1966).

Creoles tend to develop differently depending on whether or not they co-exist in society with their lexical source language. The creole Englishes of Suriname are mother tongues in a country where Dutch is the **STANDARD LANGUAGE**. Since they have not been directly influenced by Standard English for over three centuries, they differ from the creole English in neighbouring anglophone Guyana in three main ways:

1 they have borrowed vocabulary from Dutch, e.g. *bromki, fro, nai* (*blommetje* 'flower', *vrou* 'woman', *naai* 'sew');

2 they often preserve archaic features, e.g. they often preserve the CVCV phonological patterning found in many West African languages. Thus, we find *bigi, koru* and *winti* from 'big', 'cold' and 'wind';

3 there is a clear linguistic cut-off between the creoles and Dutch.

In parts of the world where the creoles coexist with their lexical source languages, we tend to find the following features:

• continued borrowing from a source language such as English, so that dyads may exist, e.g. *fingafut*, but also 'toe', *man pikin*, but also 'boy', *wuman han*, but also 'left';

• newly borrowed prepositions – whereas a pidgin might have only two prepositions, one to indicate location and the other possession, creoles may gradually incorporate 'at', 'by', 'in', 'on', 'over' and 'under';

- grammatical nuances may be introduced, such as overt plural marking, some inflection and an extended range of pronouns, e.g. 'she come, take she two bags and she gone';
- the existence of a post-creole continuum. This means that there is a range of forms from the basilectal (i.e. deep creole) through mesolectal to the acrolectal standard. Most speakers are adept at using different varieties depending on such factors as the occasion (a wake or a wedding), the degree of intimacy between speakers (sisters or a minister and a member of the congregation), the region of origin (rural or urban), or the level of education.

The following examples give a simplified idea of the continuum:

| | | |
|---|---|---|
| *Basilectal* | A mi buk dat. | Na hu dei dei? |
| *Mesolectal* | Iz mi buk. | Hu dei? |
| | Dat mi buk. | Hu dere? |
| *Acrolectal* | That's my book. | Who is there? |

The features described are found in creoles generally and not just in creole Englishes.

The local idioms, **METAPHORS** and proverbs that characterised the original pidgin are often preserved in the creole. Thus, many Atlantic creoles continue to use African calques such as *ai wata*, 'tears', *corn stick*, 'cob', and *day clean*, 'dawn'. They also often show a strong preference for active structures, though passives can occur.

Whereas pidgins may be short-lived, and die if the conditions that brought them into being are removed, creoles are **MOTHER TONGUES** and are thus less linguistically vulnerable. They can, like any language, be given an orthography and they can be used for any purpose whatsoever. A good example of this is Afrikaans. This creole language developed in South **AFRICA** and is one of the official languages of a highly complex and technologically advanced society. If Afrikaans dies, it will not be because of any linguistic inadequacy, but rather because of its past political associations.

The study of contemporary creoles has indicated that the lifecycle of pidgin to creole may well be a feature of languages in contact. The Latin of the Roman Empire was probably pidginised as the legions moved throughout the known world. Some pidginised versions of Latin undoubtedly died out, but others were creolised into the related languages of French, Italian, Portuguese, Romanian and Spanish.

There is evidence, too, that today's Standard English may have undergone a process of pidginisation and creolisation because of the linguistic contacts, first with the Vikings and then with the Normans. Certainly, when compared with Old English, the English of Chaucer shows many features of pidginisation, including:

- a dramatic simplification of grammar. Nouns no longer have six cases; adjectives do not have to agree with nouns; verb endings have been reduced.
- the loss of grammatical **GENDER**. Old English had an illogical system where, for example, *wif*, 'wife or woman', was neuter, *wifmann*, 'woman', was masculine, and *hlaefdige*, 'lady', was feminine; or where the 'sun' and the 'earth' were feminine; where 'moon' and 'ground' were masculine; 'star' and 'land' were neuter. By about 1400, all inanimate nouns were neuter, and the sex of an animate noun determined whether it was referred to as 'he' or 'she'.
- the vocabulary shows a massive influx of words from both Norse and French. A modern estimate suggests that, of the 80,000 words in today's *Shorter Oxford Dictionary*, about 22.5 per cent are native Anglo-Saxon, 3.75 per cent are from other Germanic languages, mostly Old Norse, and 55 per cent are from French or Latin.

Creole languages are found in every continent today. Their existence helps us to speculate about linguistic change in the past.

**See also:** Acculturation; Bilingualism; Intercultural communication; Interlanguage; Mother tongue; Non-verbal communication; Pidgins

### Reference

Nunn, H.P.V. (1966) *Lady Nugent's journal of her*

*residence in Jamaica from 1801 to 1805*, Oxford: Blackwell.

## Further reading

Holm, J. (1988–89) *Pidgins and creoles*, Vols 1 and 2, Cambridge: Cambridge University Press.

Romaine, S. (1988) *Pidgin and creole languages*, London: Longman.

Sebba, M. (1997) *Contact languages: pidgins and creoles*, Basingstoke: Macmillan.

Todd, L. (1990) *Pidgins and creoles*, London: Routledge.

LORETO TODD

# Cross-cultural psychology

Cross-cultural psychology exists for a variety of reasons. It exists in part to test the generality of psychological processes in different societies to determine to what extent they are universal. For instance, at the beginning of the last century Malinowski tested Freudian ideas in the South Pacific, a very different society than Imperial Vienna, to see if such things as the oedipal complex was universal. Second, it exists to test the relationship between factors not found in one culture. Thus, to test whether patriarchal societies have a particular impact on social behaviour, one needs to look at comparable behaviours in matriarchal societies. Third, cross-cultural psychologists attempt to specify the frequency and intensity of certain behaviours and beliefs in different cultural groups within and between different countries. Typical issues for the cross-cultural psychologists are the constancy of gender differences across cultural groups, and the typical misunderstandings that occur between people from two different cultures who speak the same language (Berry, Poortinga and Pandey, 1997).

All cross-cultural psychologists take as axiomatic that culture shapes psychological functioning. That is, cultural values, beliefs and **ATTITUDES** both prescribe and proscribe particular behaviours which become normative and are outward signs of cultural differences.

Cross-cultural psychology is different from racial, national or cultural psychology. Cross-cultural psychologists typically use empirical methods – observation, interview, questionnaire and experiment – to test specific hypotheses about differences between specific population samples drawn from relevant ethnic groups. Though occasionally interested in racial characteristics or national differences, the focus is on culture and its artefacts. Cross-cultural psychologists use culture-level measures and concepts like individual–collectivism as well as individual-level measures and concepts like tolerance of ambiguity, to study behaviour between groups. Cross-cultural psychologists are interested in an impressive array of issues: language and thought, perception and memory, and social behaviour as well as the applicability of tests in different populations. A major difference between two schools of thought exists however.

Psychologists have contrasted what they call the *etic* and *emic* approach taken from the words phonetics and phonemics. Pike (1966) made the initial distinction:

1 One or many: The etic approach treats all cultures or languages (or selected groups of them) at one time. The emic approach, on the contrary, is culturally specific, applied to one language or culture at a time.

2 Units known in advance or discovered: Etic units and classifications are available in advance rather than determined during the analysis. These advanced etic units can be based on prior broad samplings or surveys. Emic units or categories must be discovered, not predicted, and are different for different cultures, which prohibits comparisons.

3 Creation or discovery of a system: The etic organisation of a worldwide cross-cultural system may be created by the researcher. The emic structure of a particular system must be discovered.

4 External or internal view: Etic descriptions or analyses are in some sense 'alien' with criteria external to the system. Emic descriptions provide an internal view, with criteria chosen from within the system, devised by one who knows how to function within it.

5 External or internal plan: An etic system may

be set up by criteria or a 'logical' plan whose relevance is external to the system being studied. The discovery or setting up of the emic system requires the inclusion of the criteria relevant to the internal functioning of the system itself.

6 Absolute or relative criteria: The etic criteria may often be considered absolute, and measurable empirically. Emic criteria are relative to the internal characteristics of the system, and can only be described or measured relative to each other.

7 Non-integration or integration: The etic view does not require that every unit be viewed as part of a larger setting. The emic view usually insists that every unit be seen as distributed and functioning within a larger structural unit or setting.

8 Evidence for differences: Two units are different 'etically' when instrumental measurements can show them to be so. Units are different 'emically' only when they elicit different responses from people acting within the system.

9 Partial or total data: Etic data can be obtainable early in analysis with partial information. Emic data require a knowledge of the total system to which they are relative and from which they ultimately draw their significance, hence take much longer to collect.

10 Preliminary or final presentation: Etic data provides access into the system – the starting point of analysis. They give tentative results and tentative units. The final analysis or presentation, however, would be in emic units. In total analysis, the initial etic description gradually is refined, and is ultimately – in principle, but probably never in practice – replaced by one which is totally emic.

The etic/emic methodological dichotomy and the respective concepts they use to guide research, the perspectives they advocate researchers to take and the number of cultures they aim to investigate, all these issues reflect the universalist/relativist orientation. Put simply:

The etic approach is clearly the approach of the biological, universalist, positivistic, transcultural psychologists. This approach, assuming the universality of mental disorders, uses concepts, methodologies and research instruments developed primarily in the West. The transcultural psychiatric school of thought has used standardised questionnaires and classification systems for researching distribution of symptoms and syndromes in different cultural settings. Therefore, the etic approach has focused on the collation of empirical comparative data. This contrasts with the emic approach, which is clearly a more anti-positive approach to research, stressing relativity, uses more interpretative methods (based on a hermeneutic philosophy), such as participant observation to focus on context. The new cross-cultural psychiatric school of thought has criticised

*Table 1*   The etic/emic approach to cross-cultural psychology

|  | *Etic* | *Emic* |
| --- | --- | --- |
| Perspective taken by the researcher | Behaviour of a culture is studied from the outside, by an outsider who is not familiar with that culture. | Behaviour of a culture is studied from within by an insider who is familiar with the culture. |
| Number of cultures studied | As many as possible – for statistical generalisation purposes. | Only one at a time – and generalisations not drawn across culture. |
| Structure of concepts guiding research | Constructs/structures created by the researcher, and the theoretical perspective adopted by the researcher, and are imposed onto the system being studied. | Constructs/structures are discovered by the researcher, when and if they manifest as important dimensions in one culture. |

the use of Western standardised questionnaires across cultures and advocated a more ethnographic or ethnomedical approach to research, which does not assume disorder categories. Such a methodology is often counter to the scientific rigour the universalists pride themselves in.

The problem with all cross-cultural comparisons, but particularly with the measurement of attitudes, is essentially the problem of *equivalence*. That is, all cross cultural comparisons made need to ensure that everything is equivalent except the cultural background of the participants, so as to rule out alternative explanations or plausible rival hypotheses. The major issues are:

1 Translation equivalence: ensuring that the translation and back translation process has picked up subtle and idiosyncratic differences. Is there conceptual equivalence across cultures?
2 Functional equivalence: Do the same behaviours (i.e. gift giving, initiation rites) fulfil the same or different behaviours across cultures?
3 Participant equivalence: ensuring that the two or more groups are not different on all possible salient variables like demographics (AGE, sex, education, socio-economic status) and psychographic (religion, politics, values) variables.
4 Scale equivalence: ensuring that the scale is used in the same way, and that problems of acquiescence, dissimulation and response sets are similar.
5 Test equivalence: Are test instructions and situations similar (experimenter effect). What does is mean to be a participant in the study?
6 Interpretational equivalence: What do cultural differences mean? Can generalisations be made across other groups?

Research in this area is very complicated, and the only way to ensure full understanding is to employ multitrait multimethods, to be certain that methodological errors are ruled out as much as possible; and to specify extensive and sensitive pilot work done by bicultural researchers with anthropological sensitivities.

Cross-cultural psychology remains a small but growing field with its own specialist journals, such as the *Journal of Cross-Cultural Psychology*, the *International Journal of Intercultural Relations* and the *International Journal of Psychology*.

**See also:** Acculturation; Culture shock; Disorders of language; Psychology; Research methods; Study abroad; Untutored language acquisition

### References

Berry, J., Poortinga, Y. and Pandey, J. (eds) (1997) *Handbook of cross-cultural psychology*, Needham Heights, MA: Allyn and Bacon.
Pike, K. (1966) *Language in relation to a unified theory of human behaviour*, The Hague: Mouton.
Smith, P. and Bond, M. (1998) *Social psychology across cultures*, London: Prentice Hall.

### Further reading

Brislin, R., Cushner, K., Cherric, C. and Yong, M. (1986) *Intercultural interactions: a practical guide*, Beverly Hills, CA: Sage.
Moghaddam, F., Taylor, D. and Wright, S. (1993) *Social psychology in cross-cultural perspective*, New York: W.H. Freeman.
Smith, P. and Bond, M. (1998) *Social psychology across cultures*, London: Prentice Hall.

ADRIAN FURNHAM

# Cross-linguistic analyses

The early psycholinguistic research on both first and second language ACQUISITION was confined to a limited number of languages, amongst which ENGLISH was predominant. The question soon arose, therefore, to what extent the results obtained were valid for the acquisition of other languages. The DEVELOPMENTAL SEQUENCE describing the acquisition of certain morphemes of English (plural, progressive, genitive, etc.) is representative of such early research: whereas the sequence is very robust for English (Brown, 1973), it is irrelevant as such for other languages because the descriptive categories used are specific to English. Subsequent research came more and more to examine the acquisition of many languages (and in the case of SECOND LANGUAGE ACQUISITION, the acquisition of an L2 by speakers of different L1s: cf. the ALTERNATION HYPOTHESIS) in an attempt to distinguish by means of *cross-linguistic comparisons* the general properties (or in Chomskyan terms the universal properties) of language acquisition from features specific to one (group of) language(s). The European Science Foundation's second language project, for example, was able to generalise over ten different L1–L2 pairings (Perdue, 1993).

Such research has to solve the methodological problem of comparability, and the associated problem of the degree of descriptive abstraction necessary to achieve comparability. Different theoretic approaches discover different types of generalisation which can be grouped under three main headings: psycholinguistic, structural and communicational. To give just one structurally-based example, Brown's developmental sequence can be recast more abstractly in terms of the distinction between lexical items (nouns, verbs, etc.), independent grammatical morphemes (or closed-class words: articles, prepositions, etc.) and dependant (derivational or inflexional) morphemes (the adverb suffix -ly, plural and past marking, etc.), which is then comparable to sequences from other languages couched in the same terms. One then sees that for at least Germanic and Romance languages, both first language and second language acquirers follow a fixed order of acquisition, starting with lexical items and ending with language-specific inflexional morphology.

**See also:** Research methods; Untutored language acquisition

### References

Brown, R. (1973) *A first language. The early stages*, London: George Allen and Unwin.
Perdue, C. (1993) *Adult language acquisition: cross-linguistic perspectives*, vol. I, Cambridge: Cambridge University Press.

CLIVE PERDUE

# Cross-sectional and longitudinal analyses

To characterise the language **ACQUISITION** process in a fixed amount of research time, a choice often has to be made between following a small number of language learners over time, testing them at frequent intervals ('longitudinal studies'), or testing, once, larger populations of different learners at different stages of development ('cross-sectional studies'). The advantages of longitudinal case studies is that they better capture the developmental path of the learner, but their results are not necessarily generalisable: how does one distinguish in the individual developmental path between what is specific to the particular learner and what is common to other learners? Cross-sectional studies, on the other hand, give generalisable results because they are designed for and amenable to standard statistical procedures on representative populations. The disadvantage of cross-sectional studies is, conversely, that they analyse the product of acquisition having-taken-place (translated into 'levels', such as 'intermediate' or 'advanced' learner), and cannot guarantee that learners at a homogeneous level of achievement reached that level along a comparable developmental path. Both methods therefore have advantages and disadvantages, and are complementary: ideally, they should be combined (Perdue, 1993: Chapter 5).

**See also:** Research methods; Untutored language acquisition

### Reference

Perdue, C. (1993) *Adult language acquisition: cross-linguistic perspectives*, vol. I, Cambridge: Cambridge University Press.

CLIVE PERDUE

# C-test

The C-test was introduced by Klein-Braley and Raatz in 1981 as a reaction to several shortcomings of the **CLOZE TEST**. The C-test is based on the same theoretical assumptions as the cloze, namely the principle of reduced redundancy testing, but has a different format. In order to ensure a greater degree of test fairness, and so that examinees with specialised knowledge will not be privileged, C-tests consist of several short texts, each of around seventy words in length. The texts selected should form one sense unit, should be appropriate for the target group, and should be maximally **AUTHEN-TIC**. To minimise problems connected with the choice of deletion rate, starting point and the ratio of deleted content words to deleted structure words, and to assure a sufficient number of items, not whole words but the second half of every second word is deleted, beginning with the second word of the second sentence of each text. Many proper names, and words which consist of only one letter, are ignored in the deletion process. The missing part of a word is indicated by a single unbroken underline. Sometimes, dashes are used to indicate the number of missing letters. The texts are ordered in increasing levels of difficulty. One point is given for each exact (in some few cases for each acceptable) reconstruction of the original word. Misspelled words are normally counted as wrong. The number of correct restorations is seen as a holistic measure of general language proficiency or, more specifically, of the efficiency of a global language processing **COMPETENCE** underlying both the receptive and productive use of language. A classic C-test usually consists of four to six texts, each with twenty or twenty-five deletions (items).

The C-test principle has been applied to various languages, and a number of modifications have been proposed to take specific linguistic aspects into account. To date, there has been a considerable amount of research into the C-test, especially into its construct validity, including investigations into the mental processes involved in C-test solving. C-tests have proved to be objective, highly reliable and very economical means for measuring global language proficiency. The time needed to administer a C-test with five texts is less than half an hour, and scoring takes around one to two minutes per text and subject. As a rule, C-tests correlate quite highly with much more time consuming tests of general language proficiency (e.g. the TOEFL). C-test results have been used for various purposes including decision-making, such as selection or placement. Volume 3 of Grotjahn (1992, 1994, 1996) contains a comprehensive C-test bibliography (224 entries) which is also available on the internet.

**See also:** Assessment and testing; Cloze test

### Website

Grotjahn's C-test bibliography is available at: http://www.slf.ruhr-uni-bochum.de/biblio/bibinfen.html

### References

Grotjahn, R. (ed.) (1992, 1994, 1996) *Der C-Test. Theoretische Grundlagen und praktische Anwendungen* (The C-test. Theoretical foundations and practical applications), 3 vols, Bochum: Brockmeyer.

Grotjahn, R., Klein-Braley, C. and Raatz, U. (2000) 'C-tests: an overview', in Coleman, J.A. (ed.), *University language testing and the C-test. Proceedings of a conference held at the University of Portsmouth in April 1995*, Portsmouth: University of Portsmouth, Institute for Language Learning, Teaching and Research.

Klein-Braley, C. (1997) 'C-tests in the context of reduced redundancy testing: an appraisal', *Language Testing* 14, 1: 47–84.

RÜDIGER GROTJAHN

# Cultural awareness

Cultural awareness (CA) is a concept which became popular within education in most anglophone parts of the world in the 1980s and 1990s, and it has near-synonyms in many languages. It is used especially in connection with languages, but, seen in a wider perspective, it is evident that the concept was born of the 'cultural turn' in the human and social sciences, and in the general social debate of the 1980s. Thus CA is closely linked with the development of post-modern society with its interest in cultural difference and the relationship to 'the Other', no matter whether the latter is different from a national, ethnic, social, regional or institutional point of view. An important dimension of CA is the concept of reflexivity, i.e. the idea that insight into or experience of the practices or systems of meaning of other cultures is of significance for the individual's cultural understanding of self and their own identity.

In education the concept is widely used in connection with a number of subjects, for example geography and social studies, which have both seen a prioritisation of the cultural dimension. In the subject history, it is also possible to see a parallel to CA in the concept of historical awareness, i.e. the consciousness of the differences in historical periods and of one's own historical identity. The concept is also sometimes used in connection with **MOTHER TONGUE** teaching, but it is in foreign and second language teaching that it is used most.

The fact that CA has acquired a relatively major significance in language teaching is related to its being linked with a wish for a broad and more explicit focus on ordinary language teaching's cultural content at all levels, including **BEGINNER** level. This does not mean that it was without importance in teaching before the 1980s, since language teaching has included work with literature and realia since the 1800s in varying degrees (see Buttjes, 1991), and thereby given a certain limited impression of the cultural and social context in target countries. Moreover, in connection with **COMMUNICATIVE LANGUAGE TEACHING**, there has always been an assumption that there has to be a content to communicate about.

However, it was not until the 1970s and especially in the 1980s that attempts were made to make explicit that part of cultural content which goes beyond literature (e.g. Byram, 1989; Zarate, 1986), and only in the 1990s has the question of **ASSESSMENT** of this dimension of learning come onto the agenda, and this in turn requires a much higher degree of explicitness. In this pedagogical development, CA is a key concept which emphasises both cultural insight and **ATTITUDE** and identity development.

Among the many other terms in this same semantic field, some of which emphasise the subject content, others the processes, others the outcomes, there are the following: **CULTURAL STUDIES** (English), *CIVILISATION* (French), *kulturelle Bildung*, **LANDESKUNDE** (German), *stranovedenie* (Russian), *kulturforståelse* (Danish), and 'realia'.

The understanding of what more precisely is contained in the concept of CA depends on which interpretation of culture it represents. There has not been a comprehensive theoretical discussion of the concept of culture itself in this field, but there are a number of themes which characterise the discussion. These themes are essentially developed from various conceptions of the aims of developing CA, and thereby reflect various priorities in the definition of culture:

- the reflexive role: How much emphasis should be given to understanding the culture and society of the target country, in relation to understanding one's own country? What role should be given to cultural comparison?
- the cognitive and the affective: How much emphasis should be given to the cognitive dimension (knowledge, insight, understanding) in relation to the affective (attitudes, representations, feelings)?
- the content of the cognitive dimension: Which cultural and social issues is it important to know about? What weight should be given to knowledge of facts in comparison to understanding of relationships?
- the relationship to the historical dimension and the historical awareness mentioned earlier: What emphasis should be given to historical as opposed to contemporary issues?
- the relationship to literature: Does CA also include the **LITERARY** content of a course?
- National versus other communities: Is CA concerned primarily with cultural content and cultural identity at the national/ethnic level, or does it also include multicultural communities and transcultural relationships and processes?
- the relationship to the linguistic dimension and **LANGUAGE AWARENESS**: In what sense is language awareness a part of cultural awareness, and in what sense not?
- the distance from target countries in foreign language teaching: Is it possible to develop CA at a distance? Some people differentiate between CA, which can primarily be developed in the school or the classroom, and cultural experience which is primarily developed during a stay in the target country (Byram, 1989; several articles in Byram and Fleming, 1998).

Furthermore, the concept CA is on a par with language awareness, which is also used in language teaching. Byram has developed a model for language and culture teaching which includes language learning, language awareness, cultural awareness and cultural experience (Byram, 1989).

In general the pedagogical discussion about

culture is much influenced by the American anthropologist Geertz's semiotic interpretative perspective on culture (Geertz, 1973). There are also examples of views inspired by **DISCOURSE ANALYSIS**, hermeneutics and post-modern thinking (Kramsch, 1993), or views inspired by theories of globalisation and the dissemination of culture, which are concerned with the cultural political significance of language teaching (Risager, 1998; Byram and Risager, 1999). Apart from the latter, there are very few approaches to what can be called critical cultural awareness (by analogy with critical language awareness, cf. Fairclough, 1992), i.e. a consciousness of the social and political dimensions of the cultural landscape, and of power and hegemonic relationships between various cultural practices and universes of significance.

As indicated earlier, one important aspect of CA is reflexivity. The development of CA is a development from ethnocentrism to relativity, including among other things an engagement with national **STEREOTYPES** (e.g. Zarate, 1986), or a development of the realisation that the world can be seen from many different perspectives, e.g. national perspectives (Byram, 1989). In this way two different disciplinary traditions are connected in the interpretation of CA: on the one hand the anthropological discussion of cultural representations and cultural relativism; on the other the social psychological discussion of prejudice, stereotypes and social cognition as a whole (see Tomalin and Stempelski, 1993, a practical handbook inspired by a mainly social psychological approach to cross-cultural interaction and communication).

CA is a concept which describes one of the aims of foreign and second language teaching. It thereby stands in a certain competitive relationship to another concept, **INTERCULTURAL COMPETENCE**. The latter refers to and supplements the concept of communicative competence, and therefore includes a **SKILLS** dimension. It is also a concept which is theoretically more developed and one which has been preferred in connection with the development of assessment criteria, including at the European level. In comparison to intercultural competence, CA is a more general, non-technical term liable to many different interpretations, which have to exist given the manifold nature of the

contexts and interests connected with the content dimension of language teaching.

**See also:** Acculturation; Area studies; *Civilisation*; Cross-cultural psychology; Cultural studies; European Language Portfolio; Intercultural competence; *Interkulturelle Didaktik*; *Landeskunde*; Native speaker; Objectives in language teaching and learning; Planning for foreign language teaching

## References

Buttjes, D. (1991) 'Culture in German foreign language teaching: making use of an ambiguous past', in M. Byram and D. Buttjes (eds), *Mediating languages and cultures*, Clevedon: Multilingual Matters.

Byram, M. (1989) *Cultural studies in foreign language education*, Clevedon: Multilingual Matters.

Byram, M. and Fleming, M. (1998) *Language learning in intercultural perspective*, Cambridge: Cambridge University Press.

Byram, M. and Risager, K. (1999) *Language teachers, politics and cultures*, Clevedon: Multilingual Matters.

Fairclough, N. (ed.) (1992) *Critical language awareness*, London: Longman.

Geertz, C. (1973) 'Thick description: toward an interpretive theory of culture', in C. Geertz, *The interpretation of cultures. Selected essays by Clifford Geertz*, New York: Basic Books.

Kramsch, C. (1993) *Context and culture in language teaching*, Oxford: Oxford University Press.

Risager, K. (1998) 'Language teaching and the process of European integration', in M. Byram and M. Fleming (eds), *Language teaching in intercultural perspective*, Cambridge: Cambridge University Press.

Tomalin, B. and Stempelski, S. (1993) *Cultural awareness*, Oxford: Oxford University Press.

Zarate, G. (1986) *Enseigner une culture étrangère*, Paris: Hachette.

## Further reading

Byram, M. (1989) *Cultural studies in foreign language education*, Clevedon: Multilingual Matters.

Kramsch, C. (1993) *Context and culture in language teaching*, Oxford: Oxford University Press.

Tomalin, B. and Stempelski, S. (1993) *Cultural awareness*, Oxford: Oxford University Press.

KAREN RISAGER

# Cultural studies

Cultural Studies is an umbrella term for multi- or interdisciplinary analyses of cultural phenomena (products, processes, problematics) which was first used and developed in Britain and has spread to many parts of the world over the last thirty years.

## Origins and development

The term was first used to characterise the works of Richard Hoggart and Raymond Williams, who continued the British tradition of cultural criticism (Matthew Arnold, T.S. Eliot, I.A. Richards, F.R. Leavis) and expanded as well as transformed it by democratising its concept of culture. The focus was no longer on a selective and élitist ('high') culture, but on the multiplicity of cultures within British society. This change of perspective was owed to a number of social, political and cultural transformations in post-war Britain. These included the expansion of the welfare state, the *embourgeoisement* of the working classes, the Labour Party in office, the decline of the British Empire, the increasing equality in educational opportunities, the coming into existence of a multicultural British society.

The rise, development and institutionalisation of British Cultural Studies was initiated by a number of foundational texts (such as Hoggart, 1957, Williams, 1958, 1961, and Thompson 1963) which tried to make sense of (some of) these transformations. It was implemented by the Centre for Contemporary Cultural Studies (CCCS) at the University of Birmingham, founded by Richard Hoggart in 1964 to carry out theoretical and empirical analyses of related problematics. Under Hoggart's directorship (1964–68) the CCCS concentrated on problems of literary and cultural sociology; under Stuart Hall's directorship (1968–79) questions related to the media, popular cultures, youth and working-class cultures, feminism, racism, as well as theory and ideology were added to the agenda. These studies subscribed to

more than one particular theoretical approach: French Structuralism (**SAUSSURE**, Levi-Strauss, Barthes), Marxism (Lukács, Althusser, Gramsci), the Frankfurt School and the specific British brand of Cultural Materialism (derived from Williams's work – see Williams, 1977: 5) were particularly influential. Until 1979, the CCCS was associated with the university's English Department. When Hall left to join the Open University, the Centre became an 'independent research and postgraduate unit in the Faculty of Arts' (CCCS, Eleventh Report – 1979–80) under Richard Johnson's directorship. In 1988 the Centre and the Department of Sociology were combined into a 'Department of Cultural Studies ... within the Faculty of Commerce and Social Science' (CCCS, Nineteenth Report – 1987–88).

Although other groups and institutions with similar interests came into existence in the 1960s and have produced a substantial output (e.g., the Centre for Television Research, Leeds, the Centre for Mass Communication Research, Leicester, the Glasgow Media Group), it is legitimate to equate the development of Cultural Studies in Britain with that of the CCCS until the late 1970s. Around 1980 the 'moment of autonomy' (Hall) came. Despite massive cuts in the tertiary sector, student demands led to the creation of a great diversity of Cultural Studies programmes and courses, first in the polytechnics and then in the universities. From 1982 to 1987 the Open University offered a course on 'Popular Culture' (U203) which was produced by a number of academics who, together with the graduates of the CCCS, were to decisively influence the further development of Cultural Studies in Britain (see Bassnett, 1997) and elsewhere.

Parallel to these developments, British Cultural Studies was received, assimilated to particular indigenous traditions and re-worked according to the specific **NEEDS** of its users in the United States (see Nelson and Grossberg, 1988; Grossberg, Nelson and Treichler, 1992), **AUSTRALIA** (see Turner, 1991, 1992), Taiwan (see Chen, 1992), Italy (see Baransky and Lumley, 1990), Germany (see Kramer, 1983, 1997) and other countries in Europe (see *Journal for the Study of British Cultures*, 1999) and the world (see *British Studies Now*, 1992–; *International Journal of Cultural Studies*, 1998–). Almost at the same time, Cultural Studies was introduced (in some cases also re-introduced) into the teaching of foreign languages (see Buttjes, 1981; Byram, 1989, 1994; Kramer, 1990) and other subjects (see Aronowitz and Giroux, 1991).

### Definitions and contemporary issues

But what exactly is Cultural Studies? The modern concept of culture (on which Cultural Studies is based) is composed of five different elements which have come into existence one after the other but which still inform our present understanding of the term. First, culture was used in the context of cultivating the land, crops and animals; later, this meaning was extended to the cultivation of the mind. Then, the meanings, values and ways of life of particular, highly regarded groups were seen as setting the cultural standard for society as a whole. Under the influence of J.G. Herder in the late eighteenth century, a process of relativisation set in which made it possible to speak of cultures (in the plural) as different ways of life within a particular society *and* between different societies. This idea led to the formation of the anthropological concept of culture. And finally, out of particular interest in the symbolic dimension, i.e. the signs and meanings a particular group shares, the semiotic concept of culture was developed.

This concept itself has undergone significant transformations. While structuralist approaches relied on the relative stability of meaning, post-structuralist approaches have confronted the fundamental instability of the relationship between signifier and signified. More recently, an interest in the production of knowledge and its relationship to social power structures has superseded the interest in meaning. Parallel to these developments a partial convergence of the anthropological and semiotic concepts of cultures has resulted in the fact that *signifying processes*, by and through which a particular social group represents, experiences and communicates itself, are no longer regarded as derived (as in traditional base–superstructure models) or as reflexive (as in traditional theories of ideology), but *as constitutive elements of the socio-cultural system.*

The central question of Cultural Studies – 'How, where, when and to what effect are the shared meanings of particular groups produced, circulated and consumed?' – can be demonstrated by a 'circuit of culture' and its five dimensions: representation, production, consumption, identity, regulation.

1 Representation: Meanings can only be produced because human beings possess two interdependent systems of representation. The first enables us to make connections between the 'things' of the world and our mental concepts; the second enables us to connect our mental concepts with particular signs or sign sequences. 'The relation between "things", concepts and signs lies at the heart of the production of meaning in language. The process which links these three elements together is what we call "representation" ' (Hall, 1997: 19).

2 Production – Consumption: Meanings are produced (and circulated) by individuals, collectives and social institutions; but they are also created in processes of consumption: people listen to a particular kind of music, read certain texts, watch specific films, wear certain clothes, attend particular events – and by doing so, they attach certain meanings to these cultural products which are constitutive of their identities.

3 Identity – Regulation: In and through producing shared meanings the members of a group create a sense of identity. These meanings can (and do) serve as a means of regulation: as they 'work' by including or excluding others, they regulate the identity of the group.

There is no consensus in Cultural Studies about the theories and methods to be applied in the concrete analyses of these questions; in the best studies a productive kind of eclecticism prevails, combining phenomenology, structuralism, post-structuralism, deconstruction, psychoanalysis, **GENDER**, feminism, queer theory, Marxism, new historicism, cultural materialism and post-colonial theory.

Although it is by no means clear why Cultural Studies in its diversity has experienced such an upturn and expansion, one may safely point to the truism that the need to debate culture arises when its meaning is no longer self-evident. In this sense the following reasons for the rise of Cultural Studies can be given without claiming to be exhaustive:

1 A growing interest in the social and political implications of the humanities made itself felt when the immediate after-effects of World War Two had worn off and the social and psychological resources had been filled again. This made it possible to reflect on, discuss and possibly transform those norms and values which had not been able to prevent Fascism and the war. In Europe (and other Western countries) these processes surfaced in the 'crisis of the humanities' (of the 1950s) and again in the student unrest and its related political and cultural transformations (of the 1960s). While the first problematic affected mainly the academic discourses, the second changed the political and cultural outlook of a whole generation.

2 The growing number of migrant workers that began to enter first Britain and then other European countries in the 1950s and 1960s at least implicitly influenced the debates around culture and politics, although they were hardly perceived and acknowledged as political or cultural factors in those days. This was to change decisively, when the second and third generations entered the schools and, even more importantly, the process of European integration intensified.

3 Similarly, 'the success of cultural studies in the United States coincided with the historical loss of the ability of that country to control the global economy and the increasing recognition that it can no longer dictate the terms of the "new world order", which, to a certain extent, has sustained the cohesion of American national identity' (Stratton and Ang, 1996: 376–7).

4 In a more global perspective it seems evident that a number of irreversible and transformative processes in the economy (globalisation, migration), politics (international integration, devolution, 'new' nationalisms) and culture (transnational communication, 'clash of cultures') have rendered *culture* a matter of necessarily constant debate.

**See also:** Acculturation; Area studies; *Civilisation*; Cultural awareness; Higher education; *Landeskunde*; Objectives in language teaching and learning;

Secondary education; Syllabus and curriculum design

## References

Aronowitz, S. and Giroux, H.A. (1991) *Postmodern education: politics, culture, and social criticism*, Minneapolis and Oxford: University of Minnesota Press.

Baransky, Z. and Lumley, B. (eds) (1990) *Culture and conflict in post-war Italy: essays in popular and mass culture*, London: Macmillan.

Bassnett, S. (ed.) (1997) *Studying British cultures*, London and New York: Routledge.

*British Studies Now* (1992–).

Buttjes, D. (ed.) (1981) *Landeskundliches Lernen im Englischunterricht* (Cultural Learning in EFL), Paderborn: Schöningh.

Byram, M. (1989) *Cultural studies in foreign language education*, Clevedon and Philadelphia: Multilingual Matters.

Byram, M. (ed.) (1994) *Culture and language learning in higher education*, Clevedon and Philadelphia: Multilingual Matters.

Chen, K.-H. (1992) *Media/cultural criticism: a popular-democratic line of flight*, Taipei.

Grossberg, L., Nelson, C. and Treichler, P. (eds) (1992) *Cultural studies*, New York and London: Routledge.

Hall, S. (1997) 'The work of representation', in S. Hall (ed.) *Representation: cultural representations and signifying practices*, London, Thousand Oaks and New Delhi: Sage.

Hall, S., Hobson, D., Lowe, A. and Willis, P. (eds) (1980) *Culture, media, language*, London: Hutchinson.

Hoggart, R. (1957) *The uses of literacy*, London: Chatto and Windus.

*International Journal of Cultural Studies* (1998–).

*Journal for the Study of British Cultures* 1/1999: Special issue on 'British studies: European perspectives'.

Kramer, J. (1983) *English cultural and social studies*, Stuttgart: Metzler.

Kramer, J. (1990) *Cultural and intercultural studies*, Frankfurt: Peter Lang.

Kramer, J. (1997) *British cultural studies*, Munich: W. Fink.

Nelson, C. and Grossberg, L. (eds) (1988) *Marxism*

*and the interpretation of culture*, Basingstoke and London: Macmillan.

Stratton, J. and Ang, I. (1996) 'On the impossibility of a global cultural studies: "British" cultural studies in an "international" frame', in D. Morley and K.-H. Chen (eds), *Stuart Hall: critical dialogues in cultural studies*, London and New York: Routledge.

Thompson, E.P. (1963) *The making of the English working class*, London: Victor Gollancz.

Turner, G. (1991) 'Return to Oz: populism, the academy, and the future of Australian studies', *Meanjin* 50 (Autumn).

Turner, G. (1992) ' "It works for me": British cultural studies, Australian cultural studies, Australian film', in L. Grossberg, C. Nelson and P. Treichler (eds), *Cultural studies*, New York and London: Routledge.

Williams, R. (1958) *Culture and society 1780–1950*, London: Chatto and Windus.

Williams, R. (1961) *The long revolution*, London: Chatto and Windus.

Williams, R. (1976) *Keywords: a vocabulary of culture and society*, Glasgow: Fontana/Croom Helm.

Williams, R. (1977) *Marxism and literature*, Oxford: Oxford University Press.

Williams, R. (1981) *Culture*, Glasgow: Fontana.

**Further reading**

Brantlinger, P. (1990) *Crusoe's footprints: cultural studies in Britain and America*, New York and London: Routledge.

During, S. (ed.) (1993) *The cultural studies reader*, London and New York: Routledge.

Hall, S. (1997) 'The centrality of culture: notes on the cultural revolutions of our time', in K. Thompson (ed.) *Media and cultural regulation*, London, Thousand Oaks and New Delhi: Sage.

Turner, G. (1990) *British cultural studies: an introduction*, London and New York: Routledge.

JÜRGEN KRAMER

# Culture shock

Dictionary definitions of the term culture shock are straightforward and succinct: culture shock is the psychological and social disorientation caused by confrontation with a new or alien culture. The anthropologist Oberg (1960) is the first to have used the term. In a brief and largely anecdotal article, he mentions various aspects of culture shock, though this analysis was fairly superficial.

Cleveland *et al.* (1960) offered a similar analysis, relying heavily on the personal experience of travellers, especially those at two extremes of the adaptation continuum: individuals who act as if they had 'never left home' and those who immediately 'go native'. These two extremes are well described, but the various possible 'intermediate' reactions were not considered. The work was typical of early case study approaches.

Researchers since Oberg have seen culture shock as a normal reaction, as part of the routine process of adaptation to cultural stress and the manifestation of a longing for a more predictable, stable and understandable environment (Furnham and Bochner, 1986). More recent research has tended to underemphasise the clinical problems associated with culture shock and examine how people adapt to, and learn, new, cultural repertoires (Ward, Bochner and Furnham, in press).

Others have attempted to improve and extend Oberg's definition and concept of culture shock. Guthrie (1975) has used the term *culture fatigue*, Smalley (1963) *language shock*, Byrnes (1966) *role shock* and Ball-Rokeach (1973) *pervasive ambiguity*. Different researchers have simply placed the emphasis on slightly different problems – language, physical irritability, role ambiguity – rather than actually helping to specify how, why or when different people do or do not experience culture shock.

Various themes pervade this literature. One is *bewilderment*, in which culture shock is primarily an emotional reaction that follows from not being able to understand, control and predict another's behaviour. When customary categories of experience no longer seem relevant or applicable, people's usual behaviour changes to becoming 'unusual'. Lack of familiarity with both the physical setting (design of homes, shops, offices) as well as the social environment (etiquette, ritual) have this effect, as do the experiences with, and use of, time.

Another theme is *alienation*. Researchers have often referred to individuals lacking points of reference, social norms and rules to guide their actions and understand others' behaviour. In addition, ideas associated with *anxiety* pervade the culture shock literature. Observers have pointed to a continuous general 'free-floating' anxiety, which affects normal behaviour. Lack of self-confidence, distrust of others and mild psychosomatic complaints are also common. Furthermore, people appear to lose their inventiveness and spontaneity and become obsessively concerned with orderliness.

A review of the writers in this field suggests that there are perhaps six facets of culture shock:

1 *Strain* due to the effort required to make necessary psychological adaptations.
2 *A sense of loss* and feelings of deprivation in regard to friends, status, profession and possessions.
3 *Being rejected* by and/or rejecting members of the new culture.
4 *Confusion* in role, role expectations, values, feelings and self-identity.
5 *Surprise, anxiety, even disgust* and indignation after becoming aware of cultural differences.
6 *Feeling of impotence* due to not being able to cope with the new environment.

Central to the concept of shock are questions about how people adapt to it, and how they are changed by it. Hence there exists an extensive literature on the U-curve, the W-curve and the inverted U-curve (Nash, 1991), referring to the adjustment of sojourners over time. Many (e.g. Torbiorn, 1982) are happy to interpret their data in terms of these curves, although there is a debate in the literature about the **VALIDITY** of this approach (Church, 1982). Indeed Nash (1991) compared a group of students studying abroad and a group who remained at home, looking at their manifest anxiety over the year. He found no evidence of the U-curve and even doubted its heuristic usefulness.

Most of the investigations of culture shock have been descriptive, in that they have attempted to list the various difficulties that sojourners experience and their typical reactions. Less attention has been paid to explaining who will find the shock more or less intense (e.g. the old or the less educated); what determines which reaction a person is likely to

experience; how long they remain in a period of shock; and so forth. The literature suggests that all people will suffer culture shock to some extent, which is always thought of as being unpleasant and stressful. This assumption needs to be empirically supported. In theory some people need not experience any negative aspects of shock; instead they may seek out these experiences for their enjoyment.

Mumford (1998) attempted to develop and validate a simple but useful measure of culture shock, as set out in Figure 7. It indicates in practical terms the theoretical dimensions discussed in this entry.

The questionnaire was validated on 380 British volunteer workers who had gone to twenty-seven different countries. External criterion validity was established by using the CDI (Culture Difference Index) (Babiker, Cox and Miller, 1980). It showed as predicted that the greater the cultural difference between Britain and the country visited, the greater the culture shock. It appears to be a simple, albeit fakeable, instrument to get a 'rough-and-ready' self-report with little difficulty.

Current thinking has moved away from the rather clinical culture shock concept to ideas of culture learning and adaptation integration which focuses on how, when and why migrants and sojourners learn ways of working in a new cultural environment (Ward, Bochner and Furnham, in press).

**See also:** Cross-cultural psychology; Cultural awareness; Exchanges; Intercultural communication; Intercultural competence; Study abroad; Untutored language acquisition

## References

Babiker, I., Cox, J. and Miller, P. (1980) 'The measurement of culture distance and its relationship to medical consultation, symptomatology and examination performance of overseas students at Edinburgh University', *Social Psychiatry* 15, 109–46.

Ball-Rokeach, S. (1973) 'From pervasive ambiguity to a definition of the situation', *Sociometry* 36, 3–13.

Byrnes, F. (1966) 'Role shock', *Annals of the American Academy of Political and Social Science* 368, 95–108.

A. 'Core' culture shock items

1  Do you feel strain from the effort to adapt to a new culture?

- ❏  Most of the time
- ❏  Occasionally
- ❏  Not at all

2  Have you been missing your family and friends back home?

- ❏  Most of the time
- ❏  Occasionally
- ❏  Not at all

3  Do you feel generally accepted by the local people in the new culture?

- ❏  Most of the time
- ❏  Occasionally
- ❏  Not at all

4  Do you ever wish to escape from your new environment altogether?

- ❏  Most of the time
- ❏  Occasionally
- ❏  Not at all

5  Do you ever feel confused about your role or identity in the new culture?

- ❏  Most of the time
- ❏  Occasionally
- ❏  Not at all

6  Have you found things in your new environment shocking or disgusting?

- ❏  Most of the time
- ❏  Occasionally
- ❏  Not at all

7  Do you ever feel helpless or powerless when trying to cope with the  new culture?

- ❏  Most of the time
- ❏  Occasionally
- ❏  Not at all

B.  Interpersonal stress items

1  Do you feel anxious or awkward when meeting local people?

- ❏  Most of the time
- ❏  Occasionally
- ❏  Not at all

2  When talking to people, can you make sense of their gestures or facial expressions.

- ❏  Most of the time
- ❏  Occasionally
- ❏  Not at all

3  Do you feel uncomfortable if people stare at you when you go out?

- ❏  Most of the time
- ❏  Occasionally
- ❏  Not at all

4  When you go out shopping, do you feel as though people may be trying to cheat you?

- ❏  Most of the time
- ❏  Occasionally
- ❏  Not at all

5  Are you finding it an effort to be polite to your hosts?

- ❏  Most of the time
- ❏  Occasionally
- ❏  Not at all

Scoring: First response = 2, second response = 1; third response = 0

If combined 12-item version is used it is recommended to alternate the items from sections A and B.

Figure 7   Culture shock questionnaire

Church, A. (1982) 'Sojourner adjustment', *Psychologist Bulletins* 91, 540–72.

Cleveland, H., Mangone, G. and Adams, J. (1960) *The overseas Americans*, New York: McGraw Hill.

Furnham, A. and Bochner, S. (1986) *Culture shock*, London: Melliven.

Guthrie, G. (1975) 'A behavioural analysis of culture learning', in R. Brislin, S. Bochner and W. Lonner (eds), *Cross cultural perspectives in learning*, New York: Wiley.

Mumford, D. (1998) 'The measurement of culture shock', *Social Psychology and Psychiatric Epidemiology* 33, 149–54.

Nash, D. (1991) 'The course of sojourner adaptation: a new test of the U-Curve hypothesis', *Human Organization* 50, 283–6.

Oberg, K. (1960) 'Culture shocks adjustment to new cultural environments', *Practical Anthropology* 7, 177–82.

Smalley, W. (1963) 'Culture shock, language shock, and the shock of self-discovery', *Practical Anthropology* 10, 49–56.

Torbiorn, I. (1982) *Living abroad: personal adjustment and personnel policy in the overseas setting.* Chichester: Wiley.

Ward, C., Bochner, S. and Furnham, A. (in press) *The psychology of culture shock*, London: Routledge.

## Further reading

Hofstede, G. (1991) *Cultures and organizations: software of the mind*, London: McGraw-Hill.

Trompenaars, F. (1993) *Riding the waves of culture*, London: Brealey.

Ward, C., Bochner, S. and Furnham, A. (in press) *The psychology of culture shock*, London: Routledge.

ADRIAN FURNHAM

# D

## DAAD – Deutscher Akademischer Austauschdienst

The DAAD is an organisation of the institutions of **HIGHER EDUCATION** and student bodies in the Federal Republic of Germany, founded in 1925 and re-founded in 1950. It is an institution for the promotion of international academic **EXCHANGES** and an intermediary for the implementation of foreign cultural and academic policy as well as for educational cooperation with developing countries. It is also the national agency for European Union programmes.

The DAAD provides information on the system of education and higher education in Germany, on courses of **STUDY ABROAD**, and on funding programmes and scholarships.

The DAAD also sponsors students, undergraduate and postgraduate, and academics from Germany and abroad. It funds scholarships for individuals, group programmes of study visits or university seminars, and the exchange of academics, guest lecturers and the placement of '*Lektors*' for the German language and German Studies at universities abroad.

Funding for the DAAD is provided mainly by different ministries, principally by the Federal Ministry for Foreign Affairs.

### Website

The DAAD's website is: http://www.daad.de

## Developmental sequence

Developmental sequences represent at first sight a descriptive generalisation to the effect that learners of a particular language (L1 or L2) learn features of that language in a particular order. The 'morpheme order' studies of Brown (1973) for L1 English (replicated for L2 by Dulay and Burt, 1974) represent the first such generalisation: Brown found that three young English-speaking children followed a particular order in supplying a set of fourteen morphemes of English in contexts where they are obligatory in adult English. Thus, for example, these children use the noun plural $-s$ before the possessive $-s$ before the third person singular $-s$. Such results turned out to be 'amazingly constant' (Brown, 1973: 272), so that the stronger hypothesis was formulated that **ACQUISITION** orders are constraining: learners *cannot avoid acquiring* certain elements of a language in another order – whatever the reason for this may be. The important criterion for establishing developmental stages is the ordering of acquired features on an implicational scale. Meisel *et al.* define such an implicational scale from their work on **SECOND LANGUAGE ACQUISITION**:

> ... if we find that all learners of L2 who have acquired rule $R_3$ also possess rules $R_2$ and $R_1$, but those who do not yet have $R_2$ do not use $R_3$ either, then we may assume that the three rules are ordered as $R_3 > R_2 > R_1$, and we can

furthermore hypothesize that each of these rules marks a new developmental stage.

(Meisel *et al.*, 1981: 33)

Applying this criterion to Brown's L1 study gives the scale: −*s* 3rd singular > −*s* possessive > −*s* plural.

The pedagogical implications for this type of result from untutored acquisition can be summed up in the question: Is it possible successfully to teach implicationally related elements of a language in a different order? Pienemann and his collaborators have addressed this question (see a summary of results in Pienemann, 1998: Chapter 6) and found that the answer is largely negative: learners tend to progress in the natural sequence regardless of the teaching schedule.

**See also:** Untutored language acquisition

### References

Brown, R. (1973) *A first language. The early stages*, London: George Allen and Unwin.

Dulay, H. and Burt, M. (1974) 'Natural sequences in child second language acquisition', *Language Learning* 24: 37–53.

Meisel, J., Clahsen, H. and Pienemann, M. (1981) 'On determining developmental stages in natural second language acquisition', *Studies in Second Language Acquisition* 3, 2: 109–35.

Pienemann, M. (1998) *Language processing and second language development*, Amsterdam: Benjamins.

CLIVE PERDUE

# Diagnostic tests

Designed with the purpose of identifying gaps in students' learning and their strengths and weaknesses, diagnostic tests can be set at any stage of a course and can have a number of different purposes. These can overlap with the purposes of other tests. For instance, a diagnostic test can aim to identify areas where remediation is necessary (as does a **PROGRESS TEST**) or to decide whether or not a student should be admitted to a particular course or level (as do **ACHIEVEMENT TESTS** and **PROFICIENCY TESTS**). Alternatively, a diagnostic test can

be used to group students of similar ability levels for teaching purposes (as do **PLACEMENT TESTS**). Given the considerable overlaps with other types of tests and the huge costs of test development (in time, money and other resources), it is rare that a test is designed specifically for diagnostic purposes. Instead, it is more common for diagnostic information to be drawn from the results of achievement and proficiency tests, even though such tests do not necessarily provide as much depth and precision of detail as a custom-designed diagnostic test.

**See also:** Assessment and testing

### Further reading

Anastasi, A. (1990) *Psychological testing*, New York: Macmillan.

Davies, A., Brown, A., Elder, C., Hill, K., Lumley, T. and McNamara, T. (1999) *Dictionary of language testing*, Cambridge: Cambridge University Press.

Henning, G. (1987) *A guide to language testing*, Boston, MA: Heinle and Heinle.

JAYANTI BANERJEE

# DIALANG

DIALANG is a project financed by the European Commission, coordinated at the University of Jyväskylä in Finland to develop diagnostic language **ASSESSMENT** tools in fifteen European languages, accessible through the **INTERNET**. The assessment materials cover all levels, from beginners to advanced. DIALANG is based on the ideas of the **COUNCIL OF EUROPE**'s **COMMON EUROPEAN FRAMEWORK** of Language Teaching and Learning, and supports the objective of proficiency in three community languages as raised in the European Commission's 1995 White Paper on education and training, *Teaching and learning. Towards the learning society.*

# Dictation

Both a teaching and test task, dictation is an **EXERCISE** in which a selected passage is read aloud (or played on an audio-tape) to students in carefully chosen chunks at a speed that is slow enough to allow them to copy it down. Sufficiently able students are expected to be able accurately to copy what they hear. It is an integrative task that measures a number of different **SKILLS**, including listening and grammatical knowledge.

However, the ways in which dictation is conducted can vary. For instance, the text may only be read once or may be read twice or more times. Students might be allowed to copy only on the second reading or might have no restrictions placed on them. The length of the pauses can also vary, as can the length of the chunks of text between each pause. On yet other occasions, students might not be required to copy what they hear verbatim but instructed simply to identify and write down the main points. In this case the task has more resemblance to a note-taking task.

Dictation is, therefore, a flexible task type as well as being easy to construct. Furthermore, it is able to distinguish well between students of different abilities. However, there are a number of problems associated with dictation, the first being the difficulties of devising an appropriate marking scheme. Even instructions that seem clear, such as those requiring markers to deduct one mark for misspelt words and two for words omitted or different from the original, are open to much interpretation. Indeed, it is not always possible to tell whether a word has been misspelt or is simply wrong. Also, as with other **INTEGRATIVE TESTS**, it is not easy to interpret dictation scores, and doubt has been cast on the confidence with which we can identify what dictation exercises measure.

**See also:** Assessment and testing

**Further reading**

Alderson, J.C., Clapham, C. and Wall, D. (1995) *Language test construction and evaluation*, Cambridge: Cambridge University Press.

Davies, A., Brown, A., Elder, C., Hill, K., Lumley, T. and McNamara, T. (1999) *Dictionary of language testing*, Cambridge: Cambridge University Press.

Lado, R. (1961) *Language testing*, New York: McGraw-Hill.

JAYANTI BANERJEE

# Dictionaries

Dictionaries are **REFERENCE WORKS** which provide linguistic information about words. They differ from encyclopedias in that they are more concerned with the meaning and behaviour of words than with the objective realities that the words refer to. The boundary between linguistic and factual information is not always clear, however, and most dictionaries include some encyclopedic elements. Dictionaries can be categorised according to the type of user for which they are intended, their coverage, their purpose, their organising principles, and the medium in which the information is presented.

Dictionaries provide information about the meaning, spelling, **PRONUNCIATION**, history, **GRAMMAR** and usage of words. Most dictionaries do not pay equal attention to all of these types of information, but apply different emphases according to the real or perceived requirements of their users.

The commonest type of dictionary, to be found in most literate households, is a **MONOLINGUAL** general purpose dictionary for adult **NATIVE SPEAKERS**. General purpose dictionaries aim to provide a comprehensive description of the whole language, and usually include all categories of word information. Other types of dictionary exist for children and language learners who lack the skills to use a general purpose dictionary efficiently, and for users seeking particular kinds of word information.

Dictionaries for children include only relatively frequent words or words children find interesting, and the information content is greatly reduced. The language of the entries is simplified, and pictures or examples are often used to explain word meaning. Dictionaries intended for non-native speakers (known as 'learners' dictionaries') also adopt a simpler defining style and have less extensive coverage than similarly sized general purpose dictionaries. Learners' dictionaries tend to provide more help with language production by giving detailed information about the pronunciation, grammar and contextual appropriacy of the most frequent words in the language, at the expense of historical description and information about less frequent words.

Many language learners at **BEGINNER** and intermediate level prefer to use bilingual dictionaries. These translate words from the target language for receptive use, and to the target language for productive use. Bilingual dictionaries intended for native speakers of either language are 'bi-directional' and give equal treatment to both wordlists. Most bilingual dictionaries are intended primarily for native speakers of only one of the two languages, however, and in these 'mono-directional' dictionaries more space may be devoted to information about target language words. 'Semi-bilingual' or 'bilingualised' dictionaries combine the features of a monolingual dictionary and those of a bilingual dictionary by using the target language for the entry word, definition, examples and grammatical information, together with a brief **TRANSLATION** in the user's **MOTHER TONGUE**.

Dictionaries which specialise in particular kinds of word information may deal with words outside the scope of a general purpose dictionary, or they may take an alternative approach to the treatment of standard words. Regionalisms, slang, new words, archaic words, proper names and technical terms are given only limited coverage in general purpose dictionaries, and are treated in separate word books. Many so-called dictionaries of specialised subject areas are primarily encyclopedic, however, and provide little linguistic information. There also exist productive dictionaries for spelling and pronunciation, and dictionaries of synonyms, antonyms, idioms and collocations. Alphabetical ordering in general purpose dictionaries often forces collocates and semantically related words apart, but these kinds of dictionary draw attention to the connections between words. (In alphabetically ordered learners' dictionaries, some semantic and collocational relations between words are indicated by means of cross-references, examples, usage notes and labelled pictures.)

'Thematic' or 'conceptual' dictionaries organise entries not alphabetically but in thematic groups. They enable users to find words via their meanings, rather than via their orthographic form, although many also contain an alphabetically ordered index. Individual entries in thematic dictionaries may contain the same types of information as entries in A–Z dictionaries, but some thesauruses and 'visual dictionaries' of labelled drawings, diagrams and photographs rely entirely on verbal or pictorial groupings to explain word meaning, and provide

no other linguistic information. Many alphabetically organised dictionaries contain thematically organised appendices, which list items such as units of measurement.

Spell-checkers and thesauruses within word processing packages, hand-held devices, terminology databanks and reference works on the **INTERNET** and on CD-ROM are all types of electronic dictionary. Although many such dictionaries are based on A–Z word lists which were originally published in book form, users are not usually restricted to alphabetic look-up procedures, but can search the entire database for any information category. Whereas large dictionaries in book form are cumbersome and expensive to produce, vast amounts of electronic dictionary information can be stored inexpensively in a tiny space. Thus electronic dictionaries are often able to expand by combining multiple sources, adding examples, or including audio and video material. Users may take control of the quantity of information that is revealed on-screen by opting for a short definition to confirm contextual guessing, or selecting more detailed information to aid language production (Nesi, 1996).

Although the prototypical dictionary for most people is the monolingual general purpose dictionary, truly monolingual dictionaries are a comparatively recent invention. In Europe the earliest dictionaries were bilingual or bi-dialectal glosses to Greek and Latin texts. These were followed by dictionaries of 'hard words', written for educational purposes, and eventually dictionaries that attempted to create a scholarly record of the standard form of an entire language. In the past, many users of English dictionaries (e.g., American immigrants) spoke the standard form as a second language or second dialect, but the distinction between monolingual dictionaries for foreign language learners and dictionaries for native speakers only became important in the second half of the twentieth century (McArthur, 1986; Béjoint, 1994).

The earliest dictionaries designed expressly for learners of **ENGLISH** as a Foreign Language were the *New Method English Dictionary* (1935) by M. West and J. Endicott, and *An Idiomatic And Syntactic English Dictionary* by A.S. **HORNBY**, E.V. Gatenby and H. Wakefield, first published in **JAPAN** in 1942 and reprinted as the *Advanced Learner's Dictionary Of*

*Current English* by Oxford University Press in 1948. Both of these drew on the work of H. **SWEET**, who thought that a learners' dictionary should provide detailed information about a limited number of words, with phonetic transcriptions, simple defining language and plentiful examples.

Grammatical information in the *Advanced Learner's Dictionary of Current English* included a coding system to indicate the syntactic patterns of verbs, which Hornby elaborated from the work of H. **PALMER**. Subsequent editions of the dictionary, now known as the *Oxford Advanced Learner's Dictionary*, have simplified the coding system but have increased the emphasis on information to aid encoding.

Further milestones in the development of learners' dictionaries were the introduction of a controlled defining **VOCABULARY** (based on the work of West) in the *Longman Dictionary of Contemporary English* (first published in 1978), the use of a computer-based corpus of English texts as a resource for *Collins COBUILD English Language Dictionary* (first published in 1987), the use of vast corpora of spoken and written English, including non-British varieties, to inform the production of the 1995 editions of the *Cambridge International Dictionary of English*, *Collins COBUILD English Dictionary*, *Longman Dictionary Of Contemporary English*, and *Oxford Advanced Learner's Dictionary*, and the adaptation of learners' dictionary material for use in electronic form (starting with the publication of the *Longman Interactive Dictionary* in 1993).

Developments in the analysis and description of language have brought about advances in the design of learners' dictionaries. In particular, computer analysis of **AUTHENTIC** text has enabled learners' dictionaries to provide much more information about the frequency, behaviour and use of everyday words, as an aid to appropriate language production. Studies show, however, that both native and non-native speakers usually use monolingual dictionaries to look up rare words, rather than common ones, and while reading, rather than while writing. There is also evidence to suggest that learners (and their teachers) have difficulty interpreting dictionary information, particularly the grammar codes (Béjoint, 1994: 140–54). If language learners are not making the best use of the dictionaries designed for them, one

solution is to provide better training in dictionary use. A number of workbooks exist for this purpose, but dictionary skills and dictionary skills training remain areas that are relatively neglected by educators and researchers. An alternative approach is to adapt dictionaries more closely to the requirements of learners. Every new edition aims for greater user-friendliness, but as the volume of information they contain continues to grow, paper-based dictionaries are also becoming increasingly unwieldy and structurally complex. Electronic dictionaries may ultimately prove more useful to learners by allowing fast access to highly specific information within a potentially vast database.

**See also:** Lexicography and lexicology; Materials and media; Reference works; Teaching methods; Visual aids

## References

Béjoint, H. (1994) *Tradition and innovation in modern English dictionaries*, Oxford: Clarendon Press.

Cowie, A.P. (1999) *English dictionaries for foreign learners: a history*, Oxford: Clarendon Press.

McArthur, T. (1986) *Worlds of reference*, Cambridge: Cambridge University Press.

Nesi, H. (1996) 'Review article: For future reference? Current English learners' dictionaries in electronic form', *System* 24, 4: 537–46.

## Further reading

Hartmann, R.R.K. and James, G. (1998) *Dictionary of lexicography*, London: Routledge.

Landau, S. (1984) *Dictionaries: the art and craft of lexicography*, Cambridge: Cambridge University Press.

HILARY NESI

# *Didactique des langues* (Language teaching methodology)

The terminology used in **FRANCE** to designate the discipline of foreign language teaching reflects the history of the field. Thus, since the beginning of the twentieth century, the general term 'pedagogy' has been used and the profession speaks of language pedagogy. The 1950s and 1960s were the period when the scientific approach to language teaching developed due to the influence of **LINGUISTICS** and **APPLIED LINGUISTICS**. The term *didactique des langues* ('language didactics') appeared in the 1970s, updating language teaching following the success of W.F. Mackey's book, *Language Teaching Analysis* (1965) which was translated into French in 1972 with the title *Principes de didactique analytique*. The creation of this new designation corresponded to a break with tradition: it expressed the will to have foreign language teaching recognised as an autonomous discipline with its own objectives. Michel Dabène, the then director of **CRÉDIF**, was one of the first in France to speak of 'language didactics' to cover a specific discipline that takes into account the nature and the finality of language teaching and not only the nature and functioning of language (Dabène, 1972: 10).

## Domination of French as a Foreign Language (*Français langue étrangère*)

Until the middle of the 1980s, research concerning the discipline was based on the teaching of **FRENCH** as a Foreign Language (FLE). This was a recent teaching area without a well defined pedagogical tradition, but it was rich in the diversity of its students throughout the world. FLE was the source of teaching innovations disseminated through the institutional overseas network (*ALLIANCE FRANÇAISE*, cultural centres, etc.). The specialised FLE teachers were trained in courses given by the CRÉDIF and the BELC (Bureau pour l'enseignement de la langue et de la civilisation françaises), emphasising audio-visual methodology and then the communicative approach. From 1983 university programmes were created for FLE teachers (Bachelor's and Master's degrees with majors in FLE) and provided the bases for the domination of FLE in language teaching research and practice.

Hindered by institutional lethargy and constraints and teachers trained in the more academic tradition, language teaching in schools in France became dependent on FLE and adapted its methodological principles to their situation

(**AUTHENTIC** documents, predominance of functional **OBJECTIVES**, communicative approach, etc.). FLE was developing an approach focused on one specific situation: teaching adults studying French in France (endolinguistic environment with **NATIVE SPEAKERS**). This situation differed greatly from the school environment, and explains the difficulty of transferring the situation, i.e. acclimatising the communicative approach to school situations.

## Cross-cultural trends

In the 1980s the situation evolved under the influence of political–institutional factors. One of the major phenomena was the development of a concerted approach to languages within the European Community where the question of languages and linguistic policies was a major issue. The action taken by authorities such as the **COUNCIL OF EUROPE** put language policy on an international plane (the proposals that were formulated applied to all the members of the Council) and across languages (the same teaching principles were applicable to all the member languages). The situation in France can only be analysed within these political movements, which tended to unify the learning/teaching concepts at a European level.

## Interaction between French as a native language and Foreign Language(s)

The learner is the natural meeting place between the **MOTHER TONGUE** and foreign language(s). However, in France, as in many other countries, mother tongue teaching and foreign language teaching had little in common. The interactions between French as a mother tongue (*Français langue maternelle* – FLM) and foreign languages (*langues étrangères* – LE) were progressively built up and stimulated by social factors. At the end of the 1960s, the presence within the French state school system of many children of foreign origin (approximately 800,000 Algerians, Portuguese, Moroccans, Yugoslavs and others) encouraged the links with FLE. The fight against school failures led the educational authorities to give priority to mastering oral and written French and developing a dialogue between FLM and FLE: 'The teaching of French, particularly in educational priority areas, can take its inspiration from the Teacher methods of French as a Foreign Language' (Education Department instruction, 1994). The generalisation in the 1990s of the teaching of foreign languages in primary schools created new links between FLM and LE. One of the objectives of 'early' foreign language teaching was to ensure the **ACQUISITION** of the basic skills which included mother tongue skills, to encourage 'better scholastic results' (Education Department instruction, 1989). It must be remembered that regional languages (Breton, Alsatian, Occitan, etc.) also had their place, even if it was a minor one, in these projects, and were part of the early **BILINGUAL EDUCATION** programme (approximately 110,000 students were attending regional language classes in 1996).

The interactions between FLM and LE could be associated with **HAWKINS**'s work on **LANGUAGE AWARENESS**. Research on the links between the native language and foreign languages and between foreign languages themselves was directed towards the development of a cross-cultural approach and gave a new impetus to comparative studies. A typical example was the work on the Romance languages, where French was associated with **SPANISH**, Italian and **PORTUGUESE** as a Foreign Language. Research was also carried out on the grammatical terminology used to describe the different languages. In these types of project, which were supported by the European institutions, the aim was to harmonise the grammatical metalanguage to facilitate interlanguage dialogue. These examples show that the barriers were being broken down, but the number of programmes still remained limited.

## Teaching foreign languages in schools

During the 1970s and 1980s, as the number of research projects on exolinguistic communication demonstrates, language research no longer focused on school institutions as a sector of observation, and instead went towards 'real-world' situations. However, in the 1990s, research returned to the school context. Language specialists in schools became aware of their own particularities and started to break away from the teaching of FLE. First, there were the specific educational objectives

that the teaching of French as a Foreign Language did not take into account. Thus, contemporary social issues (ensuring the coexistence of different communities in the global society) more than ever before called upon the teaching of foreign languages to play its role in the general education of the students (openness to the other, accepting differences). Another specific issue was the teaching/learning situation. The teaching of foreign languages in schools takes place in an exolinguistic environment with non-native teachers and 'captive' students whose **MOTIVATION** is often low. The idea that the teaching of different foreign languages is related to the same general question – the general didactics of teaching languages in schools – began to emerge. The creation in 1991 of the University Teachers' Training Colleges (*Instituts universitaires de formation des maîtres* – IUFM) provided an institutional framework that favoured this development.

## French as a second language

An overview of the French situation would be incomplete without taking into account the arrival in the 1980s of French as a second language (FLS). This ambiguous expression generally takes into account multilingual situations where French is taught as a Foreign Language, but has a preferential legal status (it can be an official language of the State), a social status (it is used in sectors of public life, such as the public service and the media, to varying degrees by all or part of the population) and finally an educational status (it is the language used in schools) (Cuq, 1991). The birth of French as a second language coincided with the rebirth of the idea of a French-speaking world (*la Francophonie*) symbolised by the creation in 1986 of the French Speaking States (*la Francophonie des Etats*). The awareness that the teaching of French as a second language was not part of the teaching of FLE began to be apparent in the middle of the 1980s. In many French-speaking countries, French was part of the psychological and cognitive development of the child as the language of education; it was the vehicle for the acquisition of knowledge, and corresponded to the notion of a plurality of linguistic usage (there was not just one French language, but several). Thus, the situation of French as a second language required a specific type of language teaching.

The teaching of foreign languages in France is an evolving sector which is seeking its way between a strong trend to highlight the specificities which distinguish three major areas: the teaching of French as a native language and as a foreign language (with the sub-area of French as a second language), the teaching of other foreign languages and a more recent cross-cultural trend based on the similarities across languages, i.e. between mother tongues and foreign languages or between foreign languages. A baseline has been developed to encourage the building of interrelations.

**See also:** Audio-visual language teaching; *Civilisation*; France; *Fremdsprachendidaktik*; Teacher thinking; Teaching methods

### References

Cuq, J.-P. (1991) *Le Français langue seconde*, Paris: Hachette.
Dabène, M. (1972) 'Le CRÉDIF en 1972', *Le Français dans le monde* 92: 8–13.

### Further reading

*Etudes de linguistique appliquée* (1998) 'La Didactique des langues en contexte scolaire', 111 (Special issue)
*LIDIL* (1997) 'Vers une métalangue sans frontières?' (Special issue 14 July 1997), Université de Grenoble III.

GISÈLE HOLTZER

# Direct method

The direct method of language teaching developed in Europe (mainly in France and Germany) in the late nineteenth century as a result of the **REFORM MOVEMENT** against the **GRAMMAR–TRANSLATION** method, and was dominant from the nineteenth century until World War Two. It was mainly based on such theories as linguistic principles of inductive analogy, experimental **PSYCHOLOGY** and naturalistic methods of education. The direct method imitated the way that children learn their first language, emphasising the avoidance of **TRANSLATION** and the direct use of the foreign language as the **MEDIUM OF INSTRUCTION** in all situations. Everyday **VOCABULARY** and structure of the language were used as the primary need. The method insisted on the introduction of phonetics and the spoken variety of the language. Concrete meanings of linguistic items are introduced through lessons involving objects, and abstract meanings are introduced through the association of ideas. Natural method, oral method, phonetic method and psychological method were some of the substitute names of the direct method.

- The procedures and main principles of the direct method typically involve:
- The use of the foreign language as a medium of instruction. Translation is totally avoided.
- Learning of a foreign language is similar to that of first language **ACQUISITION**. Imitation and an artificial language environment are needed in the classroom.
- Language teaching is focused on the sentence level with vocabulary of daily routine, oral communication and **GRAMMAR** learnt by induction.
- Oral communication **SKILLS** are built up in a carefully graded progression. They are organised around question-and-answer exchanges between teachers and students in small but intensive classes.
- New language points are to be introduced orally. Concrete vocabulary is taught through demonstration of objects and pictures; abstract vocabulary is taught through association of ideas and concepts.
- Both listening comprehension and **SPEAKING** ability are encouraged. And correct **PRONUNCIATION** and inductively acquired grammatical knowledge are insisted upon.

The teaching method adopted has the following axioms (Richards and Rodgers, 1986: 9–10):

- Never translate: demonstrate
- Never explain: act
- Never make a speech: ask questions
- Never imitate mistakes: correct them
- Never speak with single words: use sentences

- Never speak too much: make students speak much
- Never use the book: use your lesson plan
- Never go too fast: keep the pace of the students
- Never speak slowly: speak normally
- Never speak too quickly: speak naturally
- Never speak too loudly: speak naturally
- Never be impatient: take it easy

The name of the direct method came from one of the official documentary papers issued by the Ministry of Education of the French government in 1901. However, before the name was put forward, by the end of the nineteenth century educationists had shared a common belief that pupils learn a language by listening to it and also by speaking it. According to those beliefs, a child could acquire the foreign language in the same way as they learned their first language. Scholars (mostly French and German scholars at the first stage) believed that the learning of a foreign language was similar to that of first language acquisition. Direct association of foreign words by connecting them with the concepts of the outside world was emphasised in the method. The writings of **SWEET**, Viëtor and Passy, among several other reformists, explained how linguistic principles could be put into practice at the time of teaching a foreign language in a classroom situation. It was said that the impetus to the direct method can be partly attributed to practical unconventional teaching reformers who responded to the need for better language learning in a new world of industry and international trade and travel, such as Berlitz and **GOUIN** (Stern, 1984: 457). As a result, various 'oral' and 'natural' methods developed in this sense. All these methods advocated the learning of a foreign language by the direct association of foreign words and phrases by avoiding the native language.

In the following years, the influence of the direct method on theory and practice was deep-rooted and widespread. The method was first introduced in **FRANCE** and Germany by its supporters and later was recognised officially by the Governments of Germany, France and Belgium (1900–02). An international congress of modern language teachers was held in 1898 in Vienna and decided that the direct method should be used in all elementary teaching of foreign languages. Henness, Sauveur and Berlitz introduced the direct method in the United States where it was well received (Hawkins, 1987: 130). In Great Britain, a compromise policy, i.e. to adopt the direct method's emphasis on the spoken language and some other techniques, was recommended in the inter-war years (Stern, 1984: 457).

There are several criticisms of the direct method:

1 It is argued that, because of the absence of translation, the method makes it very hard to convey the semantics or to teach grammar. But this drawback is equally refuted by some scholars (Howatt, 1984) who state that semantics can be conveyed by gestures and objects. Similarly, progressing from the simple to the difficult, grammatical patterns can be built up in accordance with the learner's development.

2 It is argued that the direct method can be practised only in a classroom where the number of students is limited, because certain activities involved in the method are unlikely to be applicable to larger groups of learners. However, it is to be noted that the activity and its application to the learner group does not depend on the number of students in the group but the creative nature of the teacher who can divide the class and make it possible to engage all students.

3 The main drawback would be that for most of the time it is difficult to find a **NATIVE SPEAKER** to teach the foreign language. However, it can be argued that a language teacher who imparts foreign language instruction in a classroom should be able to imitate the native speaker as far as possible.

Other criticisms involved were as follows:

1 It was hard to believe that the learning conditions of the native language could be re-created in the foreign language classroom.

2 The method was only suitable for teaching younger pupils rather than **ADULTS**.

3 The method was too much dependent on the qualification of the teacher rather than on a **TEXTBOOK**.

4 It could not go beyond the intermediate level into academic study.

Whatever the criticisms, the direct method remained the biggest force for reform and progress and the dominant widespread method in the history of foreign language teaching during the nineteenth and the early twentieth century, after the grammar–translation method. Its emphasis on the use of the foreign language as the medium of instruction, and on oral and **LISTENING** communicative skills, and the use of simple words and associations to explain difficult concepts challenged the more traditional grammar–translation method to undergo some changes. It also had great impact on the later **AUDIOLINGUAL** and **AUDIO-VISUAL LANGUAGE TEACHING** methods. It is still possible to find some of its traces in today's foreign language teaching methods.

**See also:** Bilingual method; History: the nineteenth century; Jespersen; Monolingual principle; Teaching methods; Translation theory

### References

Hawkins, E.W. (1987) *Modern languages in the curriculum*, Cambridge: Cambridge University Press.

Howatt, A.P.R. (1984) *A history of English languages teaching*, Oxford: Oxford University Press.

Richards, J.C. and Rodgers, S.T. (eds) (1986) *Approaches and methods in language teaching*, Cambridge: Cambridge University Press.

Stern, H.H. (1984) *Fundamental concepts of language teaching*, Oxford: Oxford University Press.

### Further reading

Jespersen, O. (1961) *How to teach a foreign language*, London: George Allen and Unwin.

Palmer, H.E. (1929) *The oral method of teaching languages*, London: Harrap.

Richards, I.A. and Gibson, C. (eds) (1974) *Techniques in language control*, Rowley, MA: Newbury House.

Rivers, W.M. (1964) *The psychologist and the foreign language teacher*, Chicago: University of Chicago Press.

Sweet, H. (1964) *The practical study of languages: a guide for teachers and learners*, London: Oxford University Press (originally published in 1899).

West, M. (1962) *Teaching English in difficult circumstances*, London: Longman.

YU WEIUHA

# Direct/Indirect testing

Direct testing involves using tasks that are a direct reflection of the skill being tested. The **SPEAKING** and **WRITING** sections of the International English Language Testing System (IELTS) are good examples of direct test tasks, for they include simulated interviews, role plays, discussions of plans and aspirations, report writing and essay writing.

It is argued, however, that it is only possible to have direct tasks for speaking and writing, for these are productive **SKILLS**. The two receptive skills, **LISTENING** and **READING**, on the other hand, are not directly observable, so any measure of these two skills is necessarily indirect, i.e. it is an inference about the skill based on some observable behaviour.

Typical indirect tests generally contain more artificial tasks that are, at best, tenuously related to the skill they purport to measure. They are most popular in contexts where large numbers are being tested, e.g. dialogue completion as a measure of speaking in contexts where the candidature is too large to allow for face-to-face speaking tests. One example of an indirect test task is one of the tasks in the Test of English for Educational Purposes (TEEP), where students are given a text which contains a number of errors of **GRAMMAR**, spelling and punctuation with instructions to identify and correct all the errors.

Arguably this is a defensible test task, as it reflects a process that most writers in educational institutions have to go through when constructing their own texts. However, the task makes a number of unjustifiable assumptions. For instance, it is unclear whether students are as capable of identifying their own errors as they are of correcting others. Additionally, the task does not necessarily reflect the way people actually write. Finally, it is not clear how the resulting score can be interpreted, since this involves making an inferential leap from the students' task performance to their actual skill.

Indeed, it can be argued that if a direct test is not feasible it is possibly better, in many instances, not to test at all than to test inadequately. Certainly, direct tests have a higher face **VALIDITY** than indirect tests because it is easier for direct test users to see a relationship between the test performance and real-life language use. However, it is important to be aware of the very real risk of direct tests being accepted because they look valid when they might not necessarily be.

**See also:** Assessment and testing

### Further reading

Bachman, L.F. (1990) *Fundamental considerations in language testing*, Oxford: Oxford University Press.
Davies, A., Brown, A., Elder, C., Hill, K., Lumley, T. and McNamara, T. (1999) *Dictionary of language testing*, Cambridge: Cambridge University Press.
Weir, C.J. (1993) *Understanding and Developing language tests*, Hemel Hempstead: Prentice Hall International.

JAYANTI BANERJEE

# Discourse analysis

Activated language, i.e. language in use, manifests itself in texts. Verbal expressions cannot be understood without their context and co-text, which means they must be part of some textualised unit. Text as a term in **LINGUISTICS**, and as understood here, can be applied to any sequence of lingual structures that are connected by topical or semantic coherence, as distinguished from their grammatical cohesion (Halliday and Hasan, 1976). Textuality is one of the intrinsic and essential characteristics of any kind of language use. It not only contributes to its coherence but also to its acceptability (in a grammatical sense) and, above all, to its appropriateness for the actual communicative situation, i.e. its acceptance by the interactants/interlocutors. It is these aspects that can profitably be utilised when distinguishing one kind of textualised language item from others. Discourse analysis is concerned with identifying the characteristics of discourse, some of which are described here, and is of significance for language teaching in underpinning the development of learners' discourse competence in the target language.

Ever since the so-called pragmatic turning point in the late 1960s, interest in the analysis of language use has shifted from surface structures to the functions of language in actual communicative interactions. In accordance with these changing perspectives, linguistic units beyond the sentence level came into focus.

Texts differ both in length and consistency but above all in their intention. These features can distinguish between different types of texts, and a number of attempts at their classification have been proposed. One prominent feature is the difference between narrative, descriptive and argumentative **TEXT TYPES**. Their different semantic intentions have an effect on surface structures as well: whereas in narration verbal tenses are indispensable, they are not predominant in descriptions and are negligible in argumentative texts. These, on the other hand, need syntactic devices, e.g. causative and concessive clauses and the like. The consequences for teaching these structural differences are evident.

Another distinction is made between monologic texts and dialogues. Apart from monologic texts originating from one single person, there are many texts of dialogical interaction, the main characteristic of which is that there is more than one person with an active function who is responsible for the generation of the dialogue, its social consequences included. In fact, dialogues are, except for letter writing and the like, pre-eminently oral communicative interactions. These, though not the only means of communication, must certainly be acknowledged to be the most frequent ones. Whether they should be regarded as the primary target of learning and teaching depends on the teaching philosophy.

Of prominent importance in dialogues is their orientation towards the realisation of certain effects upon the addressee: it is not just illocution the speaker in a dialogue has in mind but rather the perlocutionary effect of what he/she is trying to get across, as described in **SPEECH ACT THEORY**. Actually, very few language items can be imagined without a recipient. Language would probably not come into existence without a recipient and it normally does not work just on its own. Texts that 'speak for themselves' are extremely rare. (This is also true of ancient inscriptions: even if we can read them, we may not understand their meaning as part of their situational and cultural setting.) Dialogues can be differentiated typologically according to various aspects, e.g. time and place of interaction, the number of participants, the role constellations among them, the topic dealt with, the spontaneity of the contributions, and the affective relationships among the participants. Categorisation can also concentrate on the various intentional and motivational elements, thus distinguishing interviews from consultations, reprimanding somebody from small talk, etc. Acts of suasion (persuasion) and their specific techniques can be allotted a category of their own, notwithstanding the fact that they have much in common with acts of deception, lies not excluded.

Textualised language items are, therefore, not just restricted to the sentence level. They are directed towards a recipient, more precisely the interlocutor, i.e. somebody who is expected to react, for example to answer a question, offer help when asked to, or perhaps, when confronted with a reproach, to come forward with something like an excuse. The ancients regarded it as an art (rhetoric) to know how to get along or rather to get one's way with one's contemporaries in everyday as well as in specific communicative situations. A modern branch of this can be seen in, among others, ethnomethodology and the ethnography of **SPEAKING**.

The main unit on an intermediate level of dialogue analysis is the turn, and the different modes and rules of turn-taking are of eminent importance for dialogue processing (Sacks, Schegloff and Jefferson, 1973, 1974). This is the reason why anything (including **NON-VERBAL** signals) the interlocutor does has its specific consequences. Back-channel behaviour may be just phatic and encourage the speaker to carry on, or it may consist of comments on the speaker's contribution. Another kind of response – contradictory steps – could claim to be a specific category in so far as the contradictory act – although it may threaten to jeopardise communicative equilibrium as far as its structural devices are concerned – may use the very same forms its adversary has used. This means that, for learners, it may be easy to contradict one's partner, and yet it may be dangerous to do so.

Interlocutors' communicative aims are usually not attainable within one single stretch of words, or even within the reach of one single speech act. Contrary to what has been postulated in speech act theory, a dialogue reaches its aim only by a series of steps, any of which will be responded to and could be contradicted by something the other interlocutor might say, as a contribution to the dialogue, either initiating or responding.

The steps of an interaction usually determine one another. This functions as a momentum of coherence. Common sequences are: greetings; question–answer; reproach–excuse/justification. Most frequent and **STEREOTYPED** among these are the initial and final stages of communicative interaction. Openings are phatic and have strong face-saving intentions and effects, which is why their topics are normally neutral. Opening up closes, on the other hand, are usually realised mutually and therefore consist of several (in any case more than one or two) steps. One-word sentences should be regarded and acquired as what they could be: cries for help, interjections, etc. Prefabricated texts, idiomatic routine formulas, should and can be a preliminary learning or teaching aim, but this is not sufficient for any productive (or **GENERATIVE**) use of the communicative and semantic devices provided in the language.

The different role constellations in **AUTHENTIC** conversation are something that can result in misunderstanding and conflict. Role constellations should complement each other, as exemplified by interactions between doctor–patient, teacher–student. Static roles that cannot be renounced or avoided (e.g. being a parent) need to be distinguished from roles with momentary, accidental relevancy (e.g. witness in a court of law). Mimetic roles are those where somebody tries to deviate from his/her usual behaviour.

Finally, indirectness, implied but not expressed knowledge and mutual understandings in a conversation, can produce an increase in familiarity, and for the expression and communication of emotional and affective elements non-verbal signals are used besides verbal ones. These may differ considerably from one cultural environment to another, and cause problems for the learner.

## Didactic consequences

Those attempting to acquire a language need to be aware of the fact that what appears 'foreign' to the foreigner may be just 'normal' for the native. Anybody learning a foreign language can only be motivated to proceed in their study if certain communicative transactions seem possible and conceivable. Problems of misunderstanding and failure, which have been relatively neglected in professional research, have become of increasing interest in linguistics. Full oral and dialogical competence cannot be acquired except by imitating active participation in genuine communicative behaviour which is something not usually possible nor feasible within the ordinary teaching environment and its amenities.

Teaching material, i.e. model texts and dialogues, should try to comply with maxims of cooperation and help to reduce the likelihood of failure in communicative interaction. (In case this happens, there are certain repair measures that can be regarded as part and parcel of any language learning kit.) There is one didactic problem with dialogical texts to be considered, especially when designing teaching material: it is usually not predictable what one's partner will do or say next. Therefore dialogical sequences cannot be planned or designed in advance. Neither can they be taught by some kind of premeditated dialogical input or textbook item.

Finally, silence gets very little attention in linguistics as well as in didactic research. Refraining from talking while nevertheless partaking in conversation, without pronouncing one's ideas, is not exceptional in everyday communication. Moreover, it has quite different consequences and it is ruled by different restrictions in various linguistic communities. The role of the mute participant may quite conceivably be the first communicative role a foreign language student is going to adopt and fulfil.

**See also:** Communicative language teaching; Conversation analysis; Linguistics; Speaking; Speech act theory; Text and corpus linguistics; Writing

## References

Halliday, M.A.K. and Hasan, R. (1976) *Cohesion in English*, London: Longman.
Sacks, H., Schegloff, E.A. and Jefferson, G. (1973) 'Opening up closings', *Semiotica* 8: 289–327.
Sacks, H., Schegloff, E.A. and Jefferson, G. (1974) 'A simplest systematics for the organisation of turn-taking for conversation', *Language* 50: 696–735.

## Further reading

Brown, G. and Yule, G. (1983) *Discourse analysis*, Cambridge: Cambridge University Press.
Edmondson, W. and House, J. (1981) *Let's talk and talk about it*, Munich: Urban and Schwarzenberg.
Farrington, O. (1981) 'The "conversation class" ', *English Language Teaching Journal* XXXV/3: 241–3.
Goffman, E. (1972) *Interaction rituals*, Harmondsworth: Penguin.
Goffman, E. (1981) *Forms of talk*, Oxford: Blackwell.
Henne, H. and Rehbock, H. (1982) *Einführung in die Gesprächsanalyse* (Introduction to discourse analysis), Berlin and New York: de Gruyter.
McCarthy, M. (1991) *Discourse analysis for language teachers*, Cambridge: Cambridge Language Teaching Library.
Stubbs, M. (1983) *Discourse analysis. The sociolinguistic analysis of natural language*, Oxford: Oxford University Press.
Tarleton, R. (1988) *Learning and talking. A practical guide to oracy across the curriculum*, London: Routledge.

KARL SORNIG AND SILVIA HAUMANN

# Discrete point tests

Such tests attempt to test knowledge of a language in decontextualised segments. Rather than assessing just one language skill at a time or one aspect of that skill, they assume the ability to isolate a particular grammatical form or a particular phoneme in pronunciation. They also assume that a test can comprise a large number of discrete items which, as a group, will cover all aspects of language ability. Consequently it can be argued that, while each item gives precise information about a test-taker's mastery of that aspect of the language, the candidate's total score describes their language ability as a whole.

A typical discrete syntactic item would test the ability to use the present-perfect form of a verb as in 'She _____ (live) in London since she started working for the bank'. Similarly, a discrete phonological item might involve providing a list of words and asking the test-taker to identify the odd one(s) out, as in the following example:

Which two words are the odd ones out? Consider the sound indicated by the underlined letters. (Choose *two* words)

b<u>oo</u>k
f<u>oo</u>d
c<u>oo</u>k
g<u>oo</u>d
sp<u>oo</u>n

Clearly, such tests represent a particular view of language ability where the focus is on accuracy of reproduction of isolated segments independent of context, rather than on the construction of meaning. Though this approach is helpful for the diagnosis of students' specific language difficulties, its usefulness for other purposes has been questioned in recent years.

**See also:** Assessment and testing

**Further reading**

Davies, A. (1990) *Principles of language testing*, Oxford: Blackwell.
Oller, J.W. Jr (1979) *Language tests at school*, London: Longman.

JAYANTI BANERJEE

# Disorders of language

Disorders of language are brought about by genetic, congenital and acquired brain dysfunction. Difficulties in verbal communication may also arise from sensory/motor, articulatory, perceptual and cognitive sources. These problems are set apart from language impairments, for which the term aphasia (or dysphasia, in Europe) is reserved. The linguistic, cognitive and therapeutic/educational aspects of both developmental and acquired language impairments have both theoretical import and practical implications.

Peripheral disorders such as hearing impairment and cleft palate will impact on language comprehension and production respectively. General disorders of learning, memory or thought may also be manifest in language, e.g. Down's syndrome, Alzheimer's disease, schizophrenia. The term aphasia is reserved for disorders of language which are not due to mental handicap or sensory/motor defects.

Aphasia typically refers to an acquired language disorder in a person with a previously intact language system suffering from brain damage rather than psychiatric problems. Developmental dysphasia involves language difficulties manifest in early childhood during the acquisition process.

Historically, the study of language disorder has been the primary focus of scientists and clinicians interested in describing the organisation of higher cognitive functions in the brain. During the nineteenth century in Western Europe, research on localisation of function in the brain was first detailed with respect to aphasic syndromes. The principle of hemispheric specialisation and left hemisphere dominance for language was detailed by Paul Broca in 1861. Broca reported on two patients with severe language production problems arising from left frontal lobe lesions in their brains. These represent the first significant case reports in the modern field of aphasiology. Over subsequent decades, detailed descriptions of language disorders and clinical/pathological correlations with autopsies were gathered for a variety of problems in naming, repetition, fluency, sentence formation, comprehension, as well as **READING** and **WRITING**. By 1900, the major aphasia types had been described, and several competing processing models had been developed. In the latter part of the twentieth century, new methods and technologies enabled advances in the investigation of language disorders in patients prior to autopsy.

In the second half of the twentieth century, the neurologist Norman Geschwind expanded on nineteenth-century (classical) descriptions of aphasia informed by advances in **PSYCHOLOGY** and **LINGUISTICS**. Imaging techniques such as Computerized Axial Tomography Scanning, Magnetic Resonance Imaging and Positron Emission Tomography developed in the 1970s and 1980s. These techniques permitted visualisation of brain damage and functional disorder for the first time in living subjects.

Greater precision in the linguistic and cognitive description of language disorders has been provided by advances in the theoretical and experimental methods in the respective fields of linguistics and psychology. Bedside examination and anecdotal descriptions of language disorders have been replaced by standardised **ASSESSMENT** procedures and experimental language elicitation tasks.

Eight classical aphasic syndromes have been recognised since the initial descriptions in the Wernicke–Lichtheim model of 1874. These language disorders have been classified with various terminological schemes but generally describe disorders according to the spared or impaired performance of auditory comprehension, verbal production, naming, and repetition. Other syndromes detail difficulties with the modalities of reading and writing. Certain language disorders are described with reference to the location of the brain damage rather than the characteristics of the verbal difficulties, such as aphasia arising from subcortical or right hemisphere lesions.

Research into language disorders has provided evidence of neural specialisation for linguistic behaviour. The modular organisation of subcomponents of communication is reflected in dissociations of spared and impaired performance on linguistic, speech (sensory and motor aspects), pragmatic and cognitive functions. The study of acquired disorders of reading (alexia) has been paramount in the development of accounts of the normal reading process. Aphasia in **BILINGUAL** speakers provides special insight into the neurolinguistic organisation of multiple languages.

**See also:** Bilingualism; Mental lexicon; Mother tongue; Native speaker; Neuro-linguistic programming; Neurolinguistics; Reading; Second language acquisition theories

## Further reading

Benson, D.F. and Ardilla, A. (1996) *Aphasia: a clinical perspective*, Oxford: Oxford University Press.
Code, C. (ed.) (1989) *The characteristics of aphasia*, London: Taylor and Francis.
Eckman, F.R. (ed.) (1993) *Confluence: linguistics, L2 acquisition and speech pathology*, Amsterdam: John Benjamins.
Goodglass, H. (1993) *Understanding aphasia*, New York: Academic Press.

MARJORIE PERLMAN LORCH

# Distance learning

Distance learning is an educational system in which learners can study in a flexible manner in their own time, at the place of their choice and without requiring face-to-face contact with a teacher (though some tuition may be available). The earliest form of distance learning, correspondence courses, is still widely used for teaching languages. However, although this has proved successful for teaching **TRANSLATION**, literature and formal **WRITING**, it is only comparatively recently that distance learning courses have been developed which include an element of interactive **SPEAKING**. The recent development of distance learning has been determined to a great extent by the potential of the various technologies available to support it. These technologies are becoming increasingly complex and offer an ever-increasing range of options to the language learner at a distance including – with the advent of CD-ROM and other multimedia platforms – interactive speaking.

Distance learning has frequently been linked to, and sometimes confused with open learning. Derek Rowntree of the British Open University summarises open learning as about 'opening up learning opportunities to a wider range of people and enabling them to learn more congenially and productively. This involves reducing barriers to access and giving learners more control over their own learning'. Distance learning, on the other hand, he defines as 'learning while at a distance from one's teacher – usually with the help of pre-recorded, packaged learning **MATERIALS**. The learners are separated from their teachers in time and space but are still being guided by them'. He concluded that all open learning involves some degree of distance learning, and that not all distance learning involves much openness – except perhaps of time, place and pace (Rowntree, 1992: 13, 29, 32). Although open and distance learning can mean different things, the one element they have in common is that they are both used in an attempt to provide alternative sources of high-quality education and training for those who cannot, or do not wish to, attend conventional, campus-based institutions or classes scheduled for particular times and places.

## History and current situation

While some scholars date the beginning of distance learning to St Paul's epistle to the Corinthians, distance education in the modern sense dates from the nineteenth century (Holmberg, 1989). The development of distance education, including the learning of foreign languages, has been described as falling into three stages which reflect different eras of industrialisation. This is outlined in theories advanced over a period of thirty years dating from 1965 by Otto Peters, the first Rektor of the Fernuniversität in Nordrhein-Westfalen, Germany, who concluded that 'The structure of distance teaching is determined to a considerable degree by the principles of industrialization, in particular by those of rationalization, division of labour and mass production' (Keegan, 1994: 124).

The first stage of development, facilitated by the invention of printing and the introduction of universal postal services, allowed distance education to reach individuals in their homes or places of work. 'These innovations came together in England in the mid 19th century and led quickly to the offering of courses by correspondence' (Daniel, 1996a: 48). The introduction of radio meant that schoolchildren in remote areas in **CANADA**, **AUSTRALIA** and New Zealand could be reached with correspondence tuition.

The second major stage, exemplified in the operations of innovators – for example the British Open University (founded in 1969), Deakin University in Australia (founded in 1974) and the Sukhothai Thammathirat Open University in

Thailand (founded in 1978) – was marked by new developments such as the enrichment of correspondence education by the integration of other media, beginning with television (asynchronous communication) and the use of telecommunications to link remote classrooms or tutor and student(s) (synchronous communication). **ASSESSMENT** schemes and contacts of different kinds with tutors were incorporated and proved crucial to progress and **MOTIVATION**. The development of large distance teaching institutions – described by Daniel (1996a) as mega-universities – was a major feature of this stage, as the governments of various countries saw them as a cost-effective solution to the unmet educational **NEEDS** of their citizens.

The third major stage of development combines computing and information technology, known variously as the knowledge media or third generation distance education technology. It has been suggested that use of the knowledge media may bring the correspondence and remote classroom traditions of distance education together. They are also, of course, being used in a variety of combinations with traditional face-to-face teaching, thus blurring the distinctions which have been accepted up till now.

Daniel and others have concluded that the development of distance education has been driven by technological development rather than by educational theory: a number of theoretical approaches have nevertheless been developed (summarised in Holmberg, 1995; Keegan, 1993, among others).

## Third generation technology and the language learner

The variety and interaction of media which are being used to support the language learner at a distance is constantly changing and expanding. CD-ROMs and the **INTERNET** offer the possibilities of text, pictures, sound and interaction. Electronic mail and computer conferencing are used for tutor–student communication or for students to communicate with each other. Electronic resources may supplement other learning materials. Since one of the particular challenges of learning languages at a distance is that of learning to speak and understand others speaking, synchronous interactive computer-mediated systems which facilitate spoken communication are of particular relevance and have been developed by distance teachers.

## Conclusion

A note of caution as regards the widescale acceptance of new learning technology has been struck by (among others) Daniel (1996b), when he reported on results of research which demonstrated that technology still ranks low when people are polled on their favourite methods of learning and that the early enthusiasm of some students may not be a good guide to the reactions of the majority. He concluded that, to attract the majority of students, it is essential to develop a 'whole product' which integrates course materials and tutorial support. This, of course, requires resources of finance, time and energy which may not always be available.

**See also:** Adult learners; CALL; Higher education; Intensive language courses; Internet; Learning styles; Teaching methods; Untutored language acquisition; Video

## References

Daniel, J.S. (1996a) *Mega-universities and knowledge media: technology strategies for higher education*, London: Kogan Page.

Daniel, J.S. (1996b) 'Implications of the technology adoption life cycle for the use of new media in distance education', in J. Frankl and B. O'Reilly (eds), *Lifelong learning, open learning, distance learning*, Proceedings of the 5th European Distance Education Network (EDEN) Conference, 1996, EDEN.

Holmberg, B. (1989) *Distance teaching of modern languages*, Hagen: Zentrales Institut für Fernstudienforschung, Fern-universität.

Holmberg, B. (1995) *Theory and practice of distance education* (2nd edn) London: Routledge.

Keegan, D. (ed.) (1993) *Theoretical principles of distance education*, London: Routledge.

Keegan, D. (1994) *Otto Peters on distance education: the industrialization of teaching and learning*, London: Routledge.

Rowntree, D. (1992) *Exploring open and distance learning*, Milton Keynes: The Open University.

## Further reading

Evans, T. and King, B. (1991) *Beyond the text: contemporary writing on distance education*, Geelong, Victoria: Deakin University Press.

Kischel, G. and Gottsch, E. (eds) (1999) *Wege zur Mehrsprachigkeit im Fernstudium* (Routes to multilingualism in distance learning), Hagen: Fernu-niversität.

Peters, O. (1998) *Learning and teaching in distance education: analyses and interpretations from an international viewpoint*, London: Kogan Page.

Porter, L. (1997) *Creating the virtual classroom: distance learning with the internet*, Chichester: John Wiley.

Richards, K. and Roe, P. (eds) (1994) *Distance learning in ELT*, London and Basingstoke: Macmillan for Modern English Publications and The British Council.

MONICA SHELLEY

# Drama

Drama in foreign language teaching usually involves students acting out make-believe scenarios in order to practise different uses of language. Often these take the form of simple functional role play (either scripted or improvised). The term 'drama' in this context is also used to embrace related activities including **EXERCISES**, games and simulations. In the 1990s, some writers recommended the adoption of a wider range of drama in education strategies which use the potential of the dramatic art form more fully in order to provide richer contexts for using and exploring language.

The possible categories of drama forms in language learning can be described as follows:

- *Typical exercises/warm-ups/games* might take the following form: in pairs students stand back to back and try to recall as much as they can about each other's appearance; everyone tries to shake hands and greet as many people as possible in the group; in small groups the class try to act out a scene which represents a time of day and the class try to guess in the target language what time is being represented.

- *Improvised role play* might involve the class

dividing into pairs to act out a spontaneous exchange between shopkeeper and customer.

- *Scripted role play* is based on similar situations with the dialogue written out for the participants in advance. As a variation, learners are not given access to each other's lines until the dialogue is enacted.
- *More extended drama simulations* might involve students in creating individual fictitious characters in a specific context (e.g. people living in the same country or village, or participants in a press conference) who speak and write to each other over a period of time or engage in problem-solving.
- *Drama in education techniques* include these types of activity but pay greater attention to the art form of drama, seeking for example to inject tension into enacted situations. Instead of a simple scenario of buying an article in a shop, the teacher might set up a richer context in which the two participants knew each other at school and were great rivals. Techniques might be used to explore inner thoughts and feelings, e.g. freezing the action and voicing inner thoughts, replaying the scene in different ways, repeating the same scene with different intonations.

Awareness of the potential for using drama in foreign language teaching derives from acknowledgement of the importance of child play as a valuable method of learning. In play children use language in imaginative ways in make-believe contexts with a high level of engagement and **MOTIVATION**. Even when students are simply repeating sentences or answering questions in the target language, it could be argued that they are using an embryonic form of drama because the intention is that they do so *as if* the situation is happening in real life. Drama provides the potential for developing the contexts in richer ways; if the language is embedded in action which has more genuine motivation, it is likely to be less mechanical and carry more emotional content and meaning.

In the 1970s there were considerable changes in both drama and foreign language teaching. In the latter case, the development of **COMMUNICATIVE LANGUAGE TEACHING**, the concern to increase motivation, lower inhibitions, encourage risk taking and promote collaborative learning paralleled

developments in the drama methodologies at the time. Here the focus was increasingly on process rather than product, on exploiting children's natural inclination for dramatic playing rather than emphasising theatrical production, acting skills or performance. Exponents of drama in the foreign language classroom emphasised creativity and imagination, developing activities intended to draw on 'the natural ability of every person to imitate, mimic and express himself through gesture' (Maley and Duff, 1978: 1).

The emphasis on natural imitation meant that spontaneous improvisation, either in groups or even as a whole class, was the dominant method in many drama classrooms. However, this approach required a fairly sophisticated level of language **COMPETENCE** and was not widely adopted as a method of teaching foreign languages. Instead, writers promoted the use of games, exercises and simple role plays which many drama specialists would argue hardly qualify as 'drama'. Another tension existed between the more specific **OBJECTIVES** required of language teaching and the much broader and more general aims of using drama in the same context. Games and simple role play exercises can be employed to target specific **SKILLS** (e.g. the use of a particular tense), but the nature of the dramatic enactment is thereby limited.

The introduction of drama in foreign language teaching was originally intended to produce more natural uses of language, but often its inclusion in the classroom meant that the results were no less stilted and false. This was partly because the make-believe contexts created were often highly functional, devoid of any real human interest or dramatic tension. Drama work with a theatrical/ performance orientation was explicitly rejected as being too stilted and unnatural, and the type of free-ranging expressive, creative work predominant in the drama classroom was not suitable for learning a foreign language.

Writers on drama have in recent years tended to look to the art form of theatre rather than child play as a theoretical underpinning for the subject and this has important consequences for the potential use of drama to teach foreign languages. The emphasis on theatre does not necessarily mean work which is oriented to production and performance, but places the focus more on understanding and exploiting the true nature of the art form. This change of emphasis has resulted in the development of a wider range of drama strategies in the 1980s and 1990s which have potential for the foreign language classroom.

The original emphasis on child play and natural imitation, rather than on theatre as a constructed art form, meant that drama (both in the specialist and foreign language classroom) tended to be seen as providing contexts which were a substitute for real experience. It was thought that activities such as visiting an airport, sitting with a family around the breakfast table or buying an item in a shop could be replicated through drama in the classroom as a substitute for the actual experience. However, drama has greater potential than simply seeking to replicate 'normal' real-life situations. It can be used to explore experiences in ways which are not possible in real life, e.g. freezing a moment in time, exploring subtexts, voicing characters' inner thoughts and intentions. The family around the breakfast table may actually be nervous about having a foreign visitor in their midst and the action can be frozen so that they can voice their thoughts.

In the drama classroom the exclusive use of spontaneous improvisation has given way to a wider range of techniques, including ones which slow the action down and explore underlying human tensions. These approaches have the advantage for the teacher of foreign languages that they do not require the same fluency in language because they do not always have to be spontaneous. They can still, however, have a strong emotional content and be just as engaging. Drama techniques such as 'teacher in role' (in which it is the teacher who adopts the fictitious role, perhaps using the target language), tableaux (in which groups create a still image to which can be added dialogue or thoughts), **QUESTIONING** in role (in which a fictitious character is questioned by the class to explore motivation) exploit the power of drama more fully.

Paradoxically it is the use of more crafted, stylised, theatrical devices which come closer to exploring human situations more realistically and in more depth. Language can be explored in human contexts in ways which go beyond the surface meaning of the words spoken. Drama of this kind can examine cultural contexts more explicitly and thus has greater potential for promoting **CULTURAL AWARENESS** in the context of foreign language teaching. The fictitious family around the breakfast table and the visitor can voice their inner confusions and misconceptions while replaying the scene with different outcomes. The more eclectic approach to drama opens up a wider range of methods: using unusual or absurd situations, experimenting with rhythm, sounds and intonation as well as working towards theatrical performance in the foreign language. The potential for using such techniques still needs to be developed and exploited more fully in the foreign language classroom.

**See also:** Acquisition and teaching; Intercultural competence; Literary texts and intercultural understanding; Poetry; Task-based teaching and assessment; Teaching methods; Total Physical Response

## References

Maley, A. and Duff, A. (1978, 1982) *Drama techniques in language learning*, Cambridge, Cambridge University Press.

## Further reading

Bolton, G. (1992) *New perspectives on classroom drama*, London: Simon and Schuster.

Butterfield, A. (1989) *Drama through language through drama*, Banbury: Kemble.

Byram, M. and Fleming, M. (eds) *Language learning in intercultural perspective: approaches through drama and ethnography*, Cambridge: Cambridge University Press.

Dougill, J. (1987) *Drama activities for language learning*, London: Macmillan.

Neelands, J. (1990) *Structuring drama work* (ed. T. Goode), Cambridge: Cambridge University Press.

Schewe, M. and Shaw, P. (eds) (1993) *Towards drama as a method in the foreign language classroom*, Frankfurt am Main: Peter Lang.

Wessels, C. (1987) *Drama*, Oxford: Oxford University Press.

MICHAEL FLEMING

# E

## Early language learning in formal education

Although the teaching at primary school of one or more languages additional to a child's first language was in evidence in many countries before the second half of the twentieth century, a major change took place in the 1960s stimulated by international policy-thinking in education.

The Hamburg conference in 1962 organised by UNESCO and subsequent international events generated an agenda eventually encapsulated in *Languages and the Young School Child* (Stern, 1969), in which it was claimed that, as a result of major changes in society, education at primary school was moving from a 'vernacular' unilingual, unicultural mode to one in which other languages and cultures were to be valued as fundamental to children's education. Among the issues identified as being of concern were:

- the optimum **AGE** for beginning another language at school;
- the effects of an early start on the subsequent learning of other (third, fourth) languages and on the development of the child's first or majority language;
- the measurement of children's emerging **ATTITUDES** to languages, language learning and other nations;
- the special **NEEDS** of bi/multilingual communities;
- the language-learning and broader educational needs of children from families of immigrants or minority groups;

- the use of the first or majority language in learning an additional language;
- the relative merits of experiential learning, drills or more cognitive processes;
- using the additional language as a **MEDIUM OF INSTRUCTION**;
- how to achieve 'continuation' within primary schools as children proceed from one year-group to another, and likewise 'articulation' with secondary schools when children's **PRIMARY EDUCATION** is completed;
- how to provide an adequate supply of appropriately trained and educated teachers.

'Early language learning at school' embraces a highly complex set of social, psychological and linguistic interrelationships. In many cases of course children's first language will be an official language of their country and, as additional language at primary school, they will learn either another official language of their country or a foreign language. Even here, however, the term 'first language' may carry a range of meaning, in that many children speak a social, regional or cultural variety of their first language that is very different from the more standard form that is taught in school, and so when studying their first language at school they may have to undergo a process akin to second-language learning. Overall, the languages involved may be: an official language of the country (possibly the majority language); another official language of the country (possibly spoken by a minority that may be large or small); an indigenous minority **HERITAGE LANGUAGE** that does not have official status; a more recent, non-indigenous minority heritage language that does not have official status; and a foreign language. Any of these languages could potentially be a child's first language or an additional language they are learning at primary school.

Since the mid-1960s a number of different models have been adopted in implementing early language learning at primary school. These vary according to particular combinations of key factors that include: 'time' available for learning and using the language (amount over the years and distribution within each week); 'intensity' (the extent to which the additional language is used in order to learn something else); 'starting age'; and 'language competence of the teacher'. There is not a clear divide between 'home' and 'primary/elementary school', and in many countries there are early language learning initiatives in kindergartens, playgroups and nursery schools. In some cases the aim is to introduce very young children to a foreign or second language, and in others to introduce them to a minority heritage language. Five models of language learning at primary school will briefly be discussed. Since their aims differ from each other, it is misleading to consider that one model is better or worse than another, even though they generate different levels of language proficiency.

## Models for the primary school

### Early total immersion

This has been implemented in several countries besides **CANADA**, where it first achieved prominence and where over the years high-quality research has confirmed a range of successful outcomes. For an account of immersion internationally, see Johnson and Swain (1997). Common to most early total immersion programmes at primary school is the teaching of subject-matter through the medium of the immersion language (which for some pupils may be a second or third language and for others a foreign language) by a teacher who is a native or highly fluent speaker. Among the conditions for their success appear to be their voluntary nature (with parents opting for this form of education for their children, rather than having it imposed upon them) and strong support for the child's first

language and culture through the home and by other means. Variants of the model include early or delayed total immersion, and early or delayed partial immersion (whereby children are taught some subject-matter through the immersion language and other subject-matter through what for most of them will be their first language but which for some may be a second or even third language, depending on their language background).

Given the large investment of faith made by parents, much immersion research has focused on what the different variants (early total, early partial, etc.) yield by the end of elementary and/or compulsory education. Parents need reassurance that the gain of acquiring a high level of fluency in another language will not be offset by losses in the learning of other subject matter or in their child's first or majority language. The results generally are consistent with the 'no disadvantage' hypothesis in relation to other subject matter. Regarding proficiency in the immersion language, early total immersion children generally achieve much higher levels of fluency than are achieved by children following non-immersion approaches but tend not to be indistinguishable from native speaking children in respect of their grammatical control and sociolinguistic range.

### Bilingual education

This implies the use of two languages for learning primary school subject matter. It may consist of 'early partial immersion' as already referred to, or may be based on 'two-way' or 'reciprocal' immersion whereby children who are speakers of one first language are educated alongside children with another first language, with the intention that each group will provide an important input and other forms of support for the other, so that bilingualism is achieved not only through input from a highly fluent teacher but also from peers.

Doyé (1997) provides an overview of bilingual primary school education in various European countries as well as a focused study of the Europa-Schule in Berlin which covered various bilingual combinations (**GERMAN** plus Russian, **FRENCH**, **ENGLISH**, **SPANISH**, Italian, Greek or Turkish). The study by Peltzer-Karpf and Zangl (1996) of the Vienna Bilingual Schools Project (VBS) involved children whose first language was German or English, with some others having a different first language. An indication of the huge difference on the 'time' factor between bilingual education and the more limited model of a 'foreign language at primary school' is given through a comparison of the 1,672 hours that VBS children received for their second language over Grades 1–4 against the 152 hours that children learning English as a Foreign Language at primary school received during these same four grades. Peltzer-Karpf and Zangl's study highlights the stages that the VBS children went through in developing their second language proficiency. Phrases that initially could be accurately reproduced were succeeded by a period of grammatical 'system turbulence' until eventually, by Grade 4, their **GRAMMAR** system had largely sorted itself out. A large-scale study of partial immersion in Spanish, Japanese or French in the United States by Thomas, Collier and Abbott (1993) showed the pupils to be slightly better than a controlled comparison group in Mathematics and much better in English language arts, and to be well above the mean average for their county. Those receiving partial immersion in Japanese did not seem disadvantaged in comparison with the other two language groups. A study by Clyne (1991) showed that children in **AUSTRALIA** receiving only a limited form of partial immersion in German made markedly more progress in the language than children on a non-immersion approach.

## Minority first language maintenance

This enables children who are speakers of a minority heritage language to receive some of their education through the medium of that language while also being educated through the country's majority language. Benefits accrue not only to the children concerned; the approach may also be indispensable in helping the minority language to stay in existence, particularly if it is in demographic decline, e.g. in the case of some if not all of the remaining Celtic languages. However, there is some evidence to suggest that a balanced bilingual model may not be strong enough for certain contexts, particularly where English is the majority language, since this may come to dominate if not obliterate the other language. Accordingly, in Scotland, bilingual Gaelic–English education has in some places given way to the stronger Gaelic-medium education whereby children are educated almost exclusively through the minority language, with English being gradually blended in later in their primary education. Children attending such classes tend to represent a mix of first language maintenance and second language immersion.

## Foreign languages at elementary school (FLES)

Also termed 'Modern languages at primary school' (MLPS), this implies relatively limited amounts of time per week, often from teachers who are far from being highly fluent, and with the aim of developing an initial competence in a particular foreign language that will be further developed at secondary school. This is by far the main model for early language learning across the European Union and has had a chequered career, with a collective trauma engendered by the negative **EVALUATION** of French in English primary schools (Burstall *et al.*, 1974), eventually being succeeded by new national initiatives beginning in many European countries in the 1990s and supported by both the **COUNCIL OF EUROPE** and the European Commission. A review by Blondin *et al.* (1998) of published research on MLPS within the European Union reveals that the question of whether MLPS pupils retain an advantage at secondary school over pupils who began at that stage remains largely unanswered, partly because relatively little research has been done on this aspect. The picture of progress within primary schools is more positive, with various studies indicating benefits to children not only in the development of an initial competence in a foreign language but also in the formation of positive attitudes towards their experiences.

## Metalinguistic awareness

Sometimes known as FLEX (in the United States), this is based in some studies on introducing children to several languages, including non-majority languages spoken in the local community (see, e.g., Charmeux, 1992). Among the aims are to awaken children to what language is, to stimulate respect for other languages and cultures including those in the locality, and to create a foundation for subsequent foreign language learning. Although the broad educational justification of this approach is clear, no research appears to have been published thus far concerning its impact on children's subsequent learning of a foreign language.

From the above it is evident that early language learning may serve very diverse purposes, including: the development of an initial, if modest, proficiency in a foreign language; bi-literate bilingualism, including an ability to use two languages for purposes of substantive learning of other subject-matter; maintenance of a minority heritage language, whether official or otherwise, indigenous or otherwise, and its associated cultures; awareness of, respect for and ability to learn from other cultures; metalinguistic awareness, including insight into what language is, what its component parts are, what it is used for and how languages are related; and conscious **STRATEGIES OF LANGUAGE LEARNING** and language use, on the grounds that it will not be possible to predict what languages an individual will need later in life.

## Debates about an early start

In the debate about early language learning, one of the most contested propositions has been that young **BEGINNERS** gain an advantage over older beginners in that their younger age makes them better equipped for language learning – see Harley (1986) and Singleton and Lengyel (1995). Contributing to the debate were Penfeld's 'brain plasticity hypothesis' which stated that, up to the age of roughly nine, 'a child can learn two or three languages as easily as one', after which 'for purposes of learning languages, the human brain becomes progressively stiff and rigid' (Penfeld and Roberts, 1959: 235–6), and the notion of a 'critical period for language **ACQUISITION**' deriving from Lenneberg (1967). Whatever the merits of these hypotheses, a review of international research conducted during the 1960s and 1970s (Burstall, 1978) demonstrated that in school conditions it tended to be older beginners who made quicker and more efficient progress.

Leaving aside the 'plasticity' and 'critical period' hypotheses, are there any other arguments that are relevant to the early start debate? Various researchers have identified characteristics that could be interpreted as benefiting older beginners. Ausubel (1964), for example, argues that older learners have acquired a complex network of concepts about the world and that they may be able to map their learning of a second language, e.g. its **VOCABULARY**, on to this, and also that older learners tend to be more able to make grammatical generalisations. Scarcella and Higa (1982) show that older learners tend to have developed a discourse structure for conversations that allows them to play an active role in negotiating and sustaining these, with the possible implication that this could be used in order to make the learning of another language more efficient. More generally, **ADULT LEARNERS** tend to have developed an array of general strategies for learning, and some, if not all, of these may be applicable to the learning of another language.

On the other hand, younger children seem able to pick up the sound system of another language very readily (see, e.g., Vilke, 1988). Also favouring an early start is the argument that the process of learning another language and of gaining insight into other cultures should be viewed as a profound formative educational experience. For example, in the European context the White Paper of the European Commission (1995) recommends that all children attending school should begin another language from the earliest possible point in their primary education or even earlier, with the objective of learning at least one further language, so as to leave secondary school with a good command of at least three of the EU's major languages. The White Paper argues its case against the backcloth of helping to form children's attitudes and competencies in a profound way so as to prepare them for active participation in the 'informational', 'knowledge-based' society and for 'mobility' within a very large community that defines itself as multilingual. Related to this may be a lowering of anxiety. Low *et al.* (1993), for example, found that 8-year-old MLPS beginners were less 'language-anxious' than their 11-year-old counterparts on the verge of adolescence.

One potential advantage of an early start about

which there is consensus is that it can offer more 'time'. Burstall concluded that 'the achievement of skill in learning a foreign language is primarily a function of time spent studying that language' (Burstall *et al.*, 1974: 123). Societal developments subsequent to Burstall demand a modification of her formulation from 'time spent studying that language' to 'time spent studying and using' it. Across the European Union, for example, there is huge variation in the extent to which children learning another language have opportunities for using it out of class. In many if not all countries, children learning English as a Foreign Language at primary school have opportunities for accessing this language through the media, allowing them to acquire a receptive vocabulary, a sense of the language's sound system and a **MOTIVATION** to learn it which can be complementary to what is provided through their primary school. Children in English-speaking areas, on the other hand, may have no such out-of-school exposure to the foreign language they are learning. The 'time' factor, therefore, embraces engaged time both at school and out of school.

By itself, however, 'time' may not make much impact. One of the lessons from many research studies is that, if the benefits of additional 'time' within an early start are to be realised, then this must be linked to other key factors, in particular 'continuity' of learning experience during primary education and into secondary and 'quality of teaching', which itself embraces a range of contributory factors such as language competence of the teacher, ability to provide appropriate input and interaction, ability to encourage reflection and to create an appropriate learning environment.

## The learning environment

Although the issues identified by **STERN** in the 1960s remain relevant and many questions remain unanswered, the international agenda has changed. It is no longer a question of experimenting in order to see if something will work. The debate now focuses on identifying and putting in place the conditions for making it work well. Video-conferencing, e-mail and the **INTERNET** have already demonstrated their rich potential for putting primary school children and their teachers

in regular touch with their counterparts in other countries, in ways that previously were inconceivable. The impact of these new technologies, not only on children's early learning of another language, including the particular language skills and information handling strategies they will need, but also on the culture of their schools, is a major area for future research investigation. The final recommendation of the Luxembourg conference on early language learning, marking that country's period of presidency of the EU, stated: 'The tendency to begin language learning earlier and earlier seems to be irreversible. This process will be successful provided that certain conditions are fulfilled' (Wengler, 1999: 35; translation).

**See also:** Age factors; BICS and CALP; Bilingual education; Medium of instruction; Monolingual principle; Mother-tongue teaching; Primary education; Second language acquisition theories

## References

Ausubel, D. (1964) 'Adults versus children in second-language learning: psychological considerations', *Modern Language Journal* 48, 420–4.

Blondin, C., Candelier, M., Edelenbos, P., Johnstone, R., Kubanek-German, A. and Taeschner, T. (1998) *Foreign languages in primary and pre-school education: a review of recent research within the European Union*, London: CILT.

Burstall, C. (1978) 'Factors affecting foreign-language learning: a consideration of some recent research findings', in V. Kinsella (ed.), *Language teaching and linguistic surveys*, Cambridge: Cambridge University Press.

Burstall, C., Jamieson, M., Cohen, S. and Hargreaves, M. (1974) *Primary French in the balance*, Slough: NFER Publishing.

Charmeux, E. (1992) 'Maîtrise du français et familiarisation avec d'autres langues (Mastery of French and familiarisation with other languages)', *Repères* 6: 155–72.

Clyne, M. (1991) 'Immersion principles in second language programs – research and policy in multicultural Australia', *Journal of Multilingual and Multicultural Development* 12: 55–65.

Doyé, P. (1997) 'Bilinguale Grundschulen (Bilingual

primary schools)', *Zeitschrift für Fremdsprachen-forschung* 8, 2: 161–96.

European Commission. (1995) *Teaching and learning. Towards the learning society. White Paper on education and training*, Luxembourg: Office for Official Publications of the European Commission.

Harley, B. (1986) *Age in second language acquisition*, Clevedon: Multilingual Matters.

Johnson, R.K. and Swain, M. (1997) *Immersion education: international perspectives*, Cambridge: Cambridge University Press.

Lenneberg, E.H. (1967) *Biological foundations of language*, New York: Wiley and Sons.

Low, L., Duffield, J., Brown, S. and Johnstone, R. (1993) *Evaluating foreign languages in primary schools*, Stirling University: Scottish CILT.

Peltzer-Karpf, A., and Zangl, R. (1996) *Vier Jahre. Vienna Bilingual Schooling: eine Langzeitstudie (Four years. Vienna bilingual schooling: a longitudinal study)*, Vienna: Bundesministerium für Unterricht und kulturelle Angelegenheiten, Abteilung 1/1.

Penfeld, W. and Roberts, L. (1959) *Speech and brain mechanisms*, Princeton: Princeton University Press.

Scarcella, R. and Higa, C. (1982) 'Input and age differences in second language acquisition', in S. Krashen, R. Scarcella and M. Long (eds), *Child–adult differences in second language acquisition*, Rowley, MA: Newbury House.

Singleton, D. and Lengyel, Z. (1995) *The age factor in second language acquisition*, Clevedon: Multilingual Matters.

Stern, H. (ed.) (1969) *Languages and the young school child*, Oxford: Oxford University Press.

Thomas, W., Collier, V. and Abbott, M. (1993) 'Academic achievement through Japanese, Spanish or French: the first two years of partial immersion', *Modern Language Journal* 77, 2: 170–9.

Vilke, M. (1988) 'Some psychological aspects of early second language acquisition', *Journal of Multilingual and Multicultural Development* 9, 1 and 2: 115–28.

Wengler, A. (ed.) (1999) *L'apprentissage précoce des langues … Et après?* Luxembourg: Ministère de l'éducation nationale et de la formation professionnelle.

**Further reading**

Blondin, C., Candelier, M., Edelenbos, P., John-stone, R., Kubanek-German, A. and Taeschner, T. (1998) *Foreign languages in primary and pre-school education: a review of recent research within the European Union*, London: CILT.

ERIC (1998) *K-12. Foreign languages education*. The ERIC Review, 6, 1. Educational Resources Informational Centre, National Library of Education, US Department of Education.

Johnson, R.K. and Swain, M. (1997) *Immersion education: international perspectives*, Cambridge: Cambridge University Press.

RICHARD JOHNSTONE

# EBLUL – European Bureau for Lesser Used Languages

The European Bureau for Lesser Used Languages was established in 1982. Its aim is to protect and promote the lesser used autochthonous languages of the European Union together with their associated cultures. It has member state commit-tees in each of the member states of the EU. The two working languages of the Bureau are **FRENCH** and **ENGLISH**. The Bureau publishes a newsletter called *Contact-Bulletin* three times per year in English and French, and a number of other publications on lesser used languages. Its head office is in Dublin, and there is an Information Centre in Brussels.

**See also:** Heritage languages; Mother tongue

**Website**

The Bureau's website is: http://www.eblul.org

# English

English is a subject that appears in the school curriculum in most parts of the world. Other languages, **FRENCH**, **SPANISH**, **CHINESE** and so on, figure as subjects too, though less frequently. Their occurrence is determined by considerations of local requirement. English is different: it appears practically everywhere because it is assumed to have a global relevance that other languages do not have. Whatever foreign language appears as a curriculum subject it is, of course, locally foreign in different ways in relation to the first language of the learners. But the very global status of English would seem to make it different from other language subjects.

The teaching of any language initiates learners into modes of knowledge and behaviour which characterise the community of its users. In many cases, the community is relatively well defined, and the language it uses is that which its members are socialised into through upbringing as '**NATIVE SPEAKERS**' and which as such it serves not only as a primary means of communication among its members, but as the expression of their social identity. The language in these cases can be said to be integral to a particular community and learning it a matter of conforming to its culture. Thus, in learning the Danish or Thai language, for example, one necessarily learns what it means to be a member of a native speaking Danish or Thai community.

But languages and cultures are not always so closely integrated within well-defined communities. It is not only the French who use French, or the Spanish who use Spanish as their first languages, their primary means of expression. When a language spreads to serve other communal requirements, it will naturally tend to be associated with different cultural values, and to vary accordingly. The extent of this variation will depend to a considerable degree on how far the emergent users will defer to the norms of the original user community. If emergent users are disposed to identify with this community, then variation will be held in check by exo-normative influence. If, on the other hand, they are inclined to independent identity, then language and culture will be realigned in relatively separate endo-normative development. The obvious problem for the teaching of these languages of wider communication and diverse communities is what norm should be set up as the appropriate one for learners to conform to.

This problem is particularly acute for English, for this language has spread to a prodigious extent. It has been adopted, and endo-normatively adapted, to serve the needs of communication and socio-cultural identity of different communities all over the globe. But not only has English dispersed into different primary varieties of first language in what Kachru has referred to as the Inner Circle (North America, Australia, the Caribbean and so on: Kachru, 1992), it has been taken up as a **LINGUA FRANCA**, a secondary means of international communication across a range of institutional purposes to do with commerce, diplomacy, science, technology and so on, with the consequent development of superposed varieties of the language which nobody acquires in the 'natural' course of socialisation in their primary culture. The vast spreading of the electronic web of global communication over recent years has both promoted, and been made possible by, the use of English as an international language. As a consequence, most of the people who now use English to interact with each other have not themselves acquired it as a first language.

In these rather remarkable circumstances, it clearly makes no sense to distinguish the community of users from foreigners who are aspiring to join them. The foreigners *are* the users. Nor does it make sense to talk about the language as belonging to such communities for the foreigners have appropriated it to their own purposes (see Widdowson, 1994). So it is not simply a matter of recognising that there is a problem of deciding which norm of primary 'native speaker' use one needs to adopt in deciding which English to teach – British or American or Australian or whatever. For these local national norms would seem to be superseded by those which develop to service the global institutional needs for the language. If the reason for having English as an obligatory subject on the curriculum is because of its status as an international language, then one cannot at the same time define that subject in terms of any particular community that happens to have it as a first language.

In spite of this, English is still generally conceived of as essentially the cultural property of its native speaking communities, and the subject defined accordingly. Such a conception concedes the authority of such communities to establish and maintain standard norms. In such a custodial role, it is argued, they protect the integrity of the language and prevent it from disintegrating into mutually unintelligible varieties. But this is to impose inappropriate *intranational* norms on an *international* means of communication, and so to deny the natural adaptive dynamic of the language whereby it necessarily diversifies to meet changing needs. The intelligibility of this varying language cannot be controlled by external fiat but will be internally regulated to the extent necessary for it to function as an effective means of international communication among its users (see Widdowson, 1997). The obvious point here is that the very international nature of the language acts as a guarantee of its continuing intelligibility, which the imposition of intranational controls would necessarily undermine.

One assumption that arises from the exclusive association of English with its communities of intranational users, then, is that these communities have the right and responsibility to control its development, and therefore the authority to determine how it should be defined as a subject to be taught. So it is that teachers are enjoined to teach only 'real' English (Sinclair, 1997); but this reality is defined in terms of what native users have actually produced, all other uses of the language being, by implication, unreal.

A second assumption arises from the notion that English must retain its intranational character no matter how international its use. This is so that emergent users of the language will necessarily have to subscribe to the socio-cultural values of its native speakers and so are effectively complicit in perpetuating their dominance, whether they realise it or not. In this respect, it has been argued, imperialism is inherent in the language itself, so its international spread constitutes the extension of its influence and the instrument of its policies (Phillipson, 1992). In this case, the teaching and learning of English are in some degree charged with ideological significance, and teachers, it is argued, should be critically aware of what socio-political implications underlie their apparently innocent practices. Language pedagogy and politics are inextricably entwined (Pennycook, 1994; Canagarajah, 1999).

These problematic issues about the definition of learning objectives and appropriate norms for the subject arise for the most part because the pedagogic implications of the international status of the language as a lingua franca have not been adequately examined. In a way this is not surprising. The reason why English has become

international is, historically, because of the political and economic power of its native speaker communities, and they have a vested interest in sustaining the illusion that the only real English is the one they provide. This being so, they are not disposed to recognise the contradiction that in so doing they in effect undermine the status of English as an international language, and remove the reason why it figures so prominently as a curriculum subject. There are signs, however, of a growing awareness of the need to identify the properties of English as an international lingua franca and to consider their pedagogic implications (Jenkins, 2000). There are signs, too, of a recognition that native users are no longer in a privileged position to pronounce on what needs to be taught in the name of English, or what the appropriate pedagogy should be for teaching it (Holliday, 1994; Medgyes, 1994; Seidlhofer, 1999). If such recent tendencies take hold, then it is likely that the teaching of English as a subject in the future will change, in some parts of the world at least, to correspond more closely with the global role of the language and the needs of its emergent users.

**See also:** Lingua franca; Linguistic imperialism; Non-native speaker teacher; Pronunciation teaching; Standard language

## References

Canagarajah, S. (1999) *Resisting linguistic imperialism in English teaching*, Oxford: Oxford University Press.

Holliday, A. (1994) *Appropriate methodology and social context*, Cambridge: Cambridge University Press.

Jenkins, J. (2000) *The phonology of English as an international language*, Oxford, Oxford University Press.

Kachru, B.B. (ed.) (1992) *The other tongue: English across cultures* (2nd edn), Urbana: University of Illinois Press.

Medgyes, P. (1994) *The non-native teacher*, London: Macmillan.

Pennycook, A. (1994) *The cultural politics of English as an international language*, London: Longman.

Phillipson, R. (1992) *Linguistic imperialism*, Oxford: Oxford University Press.

Seidlhofer, B. (1999) 'Double standards: teacher

education in the expanding circle', *World Englishes* 18, 2: 233–45.

Sinclair, J.M. (1997) 'Corpus evidence in language description', in A. Wichmann, S. Fligelstone, T. McEnery and G. Knowles (eds), *Teaching and language corpora*, London: Longman.

Widdowson, H.G. (1994) 'The ownership of English', *TESOL Quarterly* 28, 2: 377–89.

Widdowson, H.G. (1997) 'EIL, ESL, EFL: global issues and local interests', *World Englishes* 16, 1: 135–46.

## Further reading

Hedge, T. and Whitney, N. (eds) (1996) *Power, pedagogy and practice*, Oxford: Oxford University Press.

H.G. WIDDOWSON

# English for Specific Purposes

English for specific purposes (ESP) refers to the teaching and learning of **ENGLISH** for an instrumental purpose – work or study related – and embraces a great diversity of language teaching and learning situations around the world. A common means of identifying ESP groups is in terms of their specialist area of work or study ('the cement factory managers', 'the master's level economics students'). Various branches of ESP are identified, including EOP (English for Occupational Purposes), EAP (English for Academic Purposes) and EPP (English for Professional Purposes).

## Course design and rationale

Essential to course design is the analysis of students' needs and the tailoring of the design to fit those needs. Any **SYLLABUS** type and methodology may be employed, but, given the frequent shortage of study time and need for immediate use, a **TASK-BASED** and communicative approach may seem most appropriate. The ESP teacher is often also the course designer, **MATERIALS** writer and evaluator, and needs to acquire some familiarity with the specialist work or study area of the students.

Learners are typically adults and usually, although not always, highly motivated.

The rationale for ESP has always been that it is motivating for students to be in work- or study-related groups and to study material that in some way involves their specialist interest. The assumption is that such motivating courses will produce more efficient and more effective learning in a shorter time than an EGP (English for General Purposes) course. There are no studies, however, which have aimed to prove that such is indeed the case. Course **EVALUATION** has developed over the years, and ESP courses can be shown to yield a high degree of satisfaction, but this is not definitive proof that ESP is the necessary or only alternative for students in any particular case. Correspondingly, there is no 'theory of ESP', unless it is a theory of diversity: inherent to the notion of the specific purpose of each group of students is the idea that there will be different solutions to the problem of matching course design and approach to the students' needs.

ESP courses may be intensive or extensive. Examples of intensive courses are one-day or one-week courses on negotiating for business English students, one-month language and study skills courses for students about to study at English-medium universities. Extensive courses may be full- or part-time over several months. Courses are provided by private language schools and by universities and colleges. Some EOP courses are conducted at the workplace, for example courses which combine language and job training for immigrant workers.

**NEEDS ANALYSIS** can be seen as crucial to an ESP course, especially when the course is of limited duration. The analysis will be of the target situation: what do students need to be able to do in English as a result of the course (Target Situation Analysis or TSA)? Also important is Present Situation Analysis (PSA): what are the students' capabilities now; what are the features of the setting for the ESP course? Sources of information include the students themselves, past students, current and future employers or academic departments. The current employer will often be the sponsor – the person actually paying for the ESP course. In other situations, the sponsor may be a government ministry, a multinational company or organisation, the authorities of the university where the students are studying, or the students themselves – undertaking the course as a means of improving their employability and/or study abilities. A possible problem for the course designers is that sponsors and students do not agree about what the course should cover.

While lack of information may be a problem, the converse danger is too much data. For the actual course, some sort of balance must be found between what is ideal and what is possible. Swales (1989) refers to the 'opportunity cost' of course design, deciding, for example, what cannot be omitted from a course (in order to satisfy both sponsors and students) and what can be omitted without serious ill-effect. On a short course, especially, the syllabus is likely to be very restricted, with, for example, only **SPEAKING** skills being attended to, or with an exclusive focus on one kind of activity, such as oral presentations. Short EAP courses might focus on academic **LISTENING**, or the **WRITING** of examination answers.

The designer of an ESP course has to decide exactly how specific the language needs of the students are. For a general business English course, for example, potentially all the structural patterns of English need to be taught, using business rather than everyday **VOCABULARY**. Genres such as different types of letter, functions such as describing processes, checking facts and figures, requesting information will be practised. A more specific business English course will focus, for example, on finance, on importing and exporting, or on management, and particular types of document and communicative routine will be studied which may favour certain structural patterns over others. A very specific course will focus on the work and products of one particular company, taking into account its **STYLISTIC** preferences in writing and speaking.

ESP courses thus vary in terms of how the language is actually presented and where the focus is placed. Some students may be required to learn large amounts of terminology – in which case a lexical syllabus and the use of **CALL** may be appropriate. In EAP, the focus is often at the level of long complete texts, with more attention paid to features of textual organisation than structural accuracy.

## Materials and teachers

It is often assumed that each ESP course should have its own tailormade **MATERIALS**. However, there are increasing numbers of good published materials so that a course can be fitted around a course book. In business English, for example, there are a number of complete 'packages', and, in EAP, series of books, covering all the language **SKILLS**. In addition to sets of published materials, a language school or university language centre is likely to have banks of its own in-house materials, including worksheets exploiting **AUTHENTIC** materials, audio and video tapes, and CALL programs, many of which can be used for more than one type of course.

In some private language schools and university language centres, the ESP teachers may specialise, teaching only or mainly business English students, for example, or only students from the Faculty of Economics. Thus the ESP teachers may build up expertise in the subject area and in the culture of the discipline. They may also manage to develop good contacts with experts in the field.

## The relationship with EFL

The question is often posed as to whether ESP teachers are different from other teachers of EFL or ESL. A possible answer is that they need to be more flexible and more confident: able to deal with a wide age range and a wide range of ability, both in language and the specialist area. Confidence and negotiating skills may be needed to establish good relationships with specialist experts. New modes of teaching may be adopted – such as team teaching, with an ESP teacher and a specialist co-teaching a course.

While not fundamentally different from general Teaching English as a Foreign Language, ESP has often provided the opportunity to test out and develop innovations prior to their more general use: the use of needs analysis, task-based learning, the use of authentic materials, **GENRE** analysis, the teaching of language and content combined.

**See also:** Adult language learning; Adult learners; CALL; Communicative language teaching; Higher education; Languages for specific purposes; Needs analysis; Task-based teaching and assessment

## Reference

Swales, J.M. (1989) 'Service English program design', in R.K. Johnson (ed.), *The second language curriculum*, Cambridge: Cambridge University Press.

## Further reading

Dudley-Evans, T. and St. John, M. (1998) *Developments in ESP*, Cambridge: Cambridge University Press.

Ellis, M. and Ellis, C. (1994) *Teaching business English*, Oxford: Oxford University Press.

Hutchinson, T. and Waters, A. (1987) *English for Specific Purposes: a learning-centred approach*, Cambridge: Cambridge University Press.

Robinson, P.C. (1991) *ESP today: a practitioner's guide*, Hemel Hempstead: Prentice Hall.

PAULINE ROBINSON

# Error analysis

Error analysis (EA), a branch of **APPLIED LINGUISTICS** popular in the 1960s, looked specifically at **SECOND LANGUAGE ACQUISITION** (SLA) whereas previously there was no generally accepted view that first (L1) and second (L2) language learning differed significantly. EA differs from **CONTRASTIVE ANALYSIS** (CA) by proposing that learner errors are not just mistakes due to interference or **TRANSFER** from the first language but evidence of underlying, universal learner **STRATEGIES**. Errors were to be seen as patterned and the task was to collect error data and identify the main types. The results drawn from the data could provide feedback for language learning theory and teaching. EA was, therefore, multi-faceted, being an area of interest for language teachers and linguists, promising both practical and theoretical outcomes. The results obtained were illuminating but problems with conducting EA eventually led to its marginalisation. EA is also linked to the concept of **INTERLANGUAGE**. (Selinker, 1972, 1992).

The emphasis placed by EA on the learner's powers of hypothesis formation in the process of L2 acquisition was part of the trend towards a more student-centred approach (Candlin, 1984) and reaction against **BEHAVIOURISM**. The demise of behaviourism led to a period of 'flux and agitation' according to **CHOMSKY** (Richards, 1984: 20), and this 'apparent lack of a linguistic paradigm for second language research' was, possibly, a 'propitious occurrence' (Richards and Sampson, 1984: 3).

As Chomsky pointed to the possibility of innate language abilities, then EA postulated that, with sufficient data, the processes of SLA could be unravelled. Corder's seminal paper of 1967 (Selinker, 1992: 1) outlined many themes, and after this EA received much attention.

Wilkins places the shift of focus onto SLA within CA and its aim of predicting where 'difficulties would be likely to occur' (Wilkins, 1990: 530). In CA, errors are identified as largely the result of L1 interference with learners using familiar patterns, which cause incorrect L2 forms. CA made fairly complex predictions about potential errors and this progressed SLA theory, although it had limitations which EA claimed to deal with. Although CA was concerned with errors, the emphasis tended to be on predictions, not descriptions, of learner behaviour.

It is expected that learners will make errors, but it is the status of these and what they may indicate that are important in EA. For Corder, 'the study of learners' errors is part of the methodology of the study of language learning' (1973: 267), and he distinguished between 'mistakes' and true errors. The former are performance errors, such as slips of the tongue, the latter are markers of where the learner is in terms of L2 **COMPETENCE**. Mistakes are caused by many factors such as tiredness but, unlike genuine errors, are not indicative of the state of the learner's underlying knowledge of the language or 'transitional competence'. Corder also talked of the 'internal **SYLLABUS**' learners have in L2 learning (1973: 268), which can be accessed through EA since errors are usually systematic and related to underlying systems.

Errors can also be either interlingual or intralingual. The latter may be the result of faulty or partial learning of the target language such as over-generalisation and over-simplification. The former result from L1 interference. Richards collected samples of errors in L2 **ENGLISH** produced by learners with a variety of L1s and then identified common errors (1984: 181). He assumed that the error types largely excluded reference to the L1 and some were 'interlingual' and indicative of processes being worked out by learners.

Dulay and Burt found that around 80 per cent of errors could be explained without reference to L1 interference (Ellis, 1994: 19). Rather than comparing L1 with the target language, the latter could be compared to the actual performance of learners to see what systematic error patterns emerge. Another problem with citing L1 interference as the main obstacle, as CA does, is that it downplays target language interference.

The degree of emphasis on L1 interference differentiates CA from EA, but this can be viewed as a complementary rather than oppositional link with EA; 'an important source of corroboration to the contrastive linguistic analyses in their claims for predictability of errors' (Candlin, in Richards, 1984: Preface, x). Corder, however, reaffirmed that mother-tongue interference was not the cause, noting that most teachers often know where problems may occur. They also encounter errors not predicted by CA, which can help to locate areas of 'interlanguage interference', but not account for many of the errors made (Richards, 1984: 182).

Analysis of errors can assist the formulation of explanations about SLA as well as contributing to the refinement of **TEACHER METHODS**. Recognising that not all errors are due to L1 interference was a significant divergence and aimed to produce more accurate information about learning processes. In moving towards the mastery of L2, error analysts suggest that learners develop a series of 'transitional dialects' (Corder, 1971) which are linked to the concept of interlanguage (Selinker, 1972).

Criticisms came as EA proved to be 'an imperfect research tool' (Ellis, 1994: 19). By focusing only on errors, researchers failed to see the 'whole picture' (Larsen-Freeman and Long, 1991: 61). An overriding concern with errors also means insufficient attention to what learners do correctly. Problems with recognising errors additionally led to empirical problems with a lack of scientific **VALIDITY**. Teachers and researchers

collecting 'errors' might actually have been collecting different things. Corder, for example (1971), identified 'covert errors' – L2 forms produced by learners that are grammatically correct but do not actually mean to a **NATIVE SPEAKER** what the learner intended and are really errors. James points to this problem of EA failing to recognise covert errors but believes prior CA would assist in this by accurate prediction (James, 1980: 186).

It is also true that errors are caused not only by cognitive processes but by external factors. Teaching methods and **MATERIALS** may be unsuitable or faulty, for example, thus producing mistakes which have nothing to do with strategies of innate language learning. It could be argued, though, that rigorous EA would pick up these factors and cite them as extraneous variables. L1 interference, as well, certainly cannot be dismissed, nor physiological factors.

James sees CA as offering simpler and better explanations than EA, which is 'difficult, long-winded, and not plausible' (1980: 148). Certainly it was a time-consuming process to collect, collate and analyse error data. James also rejects the notion that common errors made by learners with different L1s are proof that they are non-contrastive errors. He claims that so-called 'universal' errors might be instances of interference errors (1980: 185–6). EA should not only be compared in usefulness, however, to CA, with little to be gained by taking 'an exclusive either-or approach' (1980: 187).

Larsen-Freeman and Long saw the faults of EA as 'too blatant for it to continue to serve as the primary mode of SLA analysis' (1991: 62). EA became more of a research tool for specific problems and was incorporated into overall performance analysis, which looks at the totality of learner language performance. By the late 1970s, the theory of interlanguage and more general SLA theory, to which EA contributed, prevailed.

**See also:** Contrastive analysis; Genre and genre-based teaching; Interlanguage; Learning styles; Psychology; Second language acquisition theories; Teaching methods; Transfer

## References

Candlin, C.N. (1984) 'Preface', in J.C. Richards,

*Error analysis: perspectives on second language acquisition*, Harlow: Longman.

Corder, S.P. (1971) 'Idiosyncratic dialects and error analysis', *International Review of Applied Linguistics* 92: 147–59.

Corder, S.P. (1973) *Introducing applied linguistics*, London: Penguin.

Ellis, R. (1985) *Understanding second language acquisition*, Oxford: Oxford University Press.

Ellis, R. (1994) *The study of second language acquisition*, Oxford: Oxford University Press.

James, C. (1980) *Contrastive analysis*, Harlow: Longman.

Larsen-Freeman, D. and Long, M.H. (1991) *An introduction to second language acquisition*, Harlow: Longman.

Richards, J.C. (1984) 'A non-contrastive approach to error analysis', *English Language Teaching* 25, 3: 204–19.

Richards, J.C. and Sampson, G.P. (1984) 'The study of learner English', in J.C. Richards (ed.), *Error analysis: perspectives on second language acquisition*, Harlow: Longman.

Selinker, L. (1972) 'Interlanguage', *International Review of Applied Linguistics* 10, 3: 201–31.

Selinker, L. (1992) *Rediscovering interlanguage*, Harlow: Longman.

Wilkins, D. (1990) 'Second languages: how they are learned and taught', in N.E. Collinge (ed.), *An encyclopaedia of language*, London: Routledge.

## Further reading

Corder, S.P. (1984) 'The significance of learners' errors', in J.C. Richards (ed.), *Error analysis: perspectives on second language acquisition*, Harlow: Longman.

Davies, A.C., Criper, C. and Howatt, A. (1984) *Interlanguage*, Edinburgh: Edinburgh University Press.

Dulay, H.C. and Burt, M.K. (1984) 'You can't learn without goofing : an analysis of children's second language errors', in J.C. Richards (ed.), *Error analysis: perspectives on second language acquisition*, Harlow: Longman.

Lado, R. (1957) '*Linguistics across cultures*', Ann Arbor: University of Michigan Press.

RUTH CHERRINGTON

# Esperanto

Esperanto is an international language designed for ease of learning and intended as a common, neutral second language for all. Launched in Warsaw in 1887 as 'the international language of Doctor Esperanto' (pseudonym of L.L. Zamenhof, 1859–1917), Esperanto is the only **PLANNED LANGUAGE** to have achieved relatively wide use; between five and fifteen million people are estimated to have studied it, although regular users probably do not exceed 1 per cent of this number. Most speakers live in Europe, but the movement has a long history in countries such as **CHINA**, **JAPAN** and Brazil, and active users can be found in most countries of the world.

## Form and structure

Esperanto uses a modified Latin alphabet of twenty-eight letters; its phonology is similar to that of Italian or Croatian. A unique morphological feature is its use of word endings to mark parts of speech: nouns end in -o, adjectives in -a, adverbs in -e; the simple past, present and future tenses of every verb end in -is, -as and -os respectively, without distinction of number, person or **GENDER**. Word roots are invariant and can be freely combined with each other as long as the result is meaningful, e.g. *vid-o* (sight), *vid-a* (visual), *vid-e* (by sight, visually), *vid-i* (to see); *ebl-o* (possibility), *ebl-a* (possible), *ebl-e* (possibly), *ebl-i* (to be possible); combining these roots yields *vid-ebl-a* (visible), *vid-ebl-i* (to be visible), etc. Most word roots are drawn from Western European languages, with a small number of Slavic and non-European elements. Word order in a sentence is relatively free, similar to Russian; cases other than the nominative are distinguished by the use of prepositions or the general-purpose marker -n. Richardson (1988) provides a straightforward introduction; Janton (1993) discusses some distinctive linguistic features; Jordan (1992) is a detailed reference guide for English speakers.

There is ample anecdotal and statistical evidence of Esperanto's relative ease of **ACQUISITION** for speakers of both European and non-European languages, although any level of mastery clearly demands greater time and effort from the latter.

Among the factors that appear to increase learnability are the close relationship between written and spoken forms, the productivity of the word-building system, the low frequency of irregularities and idiomatic expressions, and the relative openness of the speech community to new learners. Attempts at quantitative comparison have generally estimated the rate of progress in Esperanto as four to twelve times that of other second languages taught under classroom conditions. An early study was conducted by Thorndike *et al.* (1933), and later overviews are provided by Maxwell (1988), Fantini and Reagan (1992), and Corsetti and La Torre (1995).

Such research has also frequently reported a positive propaedeutic effect on the learning of other languages. For instance, English secondary school pupils who studied Esperanto for a year were subsequently found to achieve better results after three years of **FRENCH** than those who studied only French for four years (Williams, 1965). The effects were strongest for pupils who scored low on a range of intelligence tests (Halloran, 1952). Similar results have been reported for **NATIVE SPEAKERS** of Finnish (learning Esperanto followed by German), **GERMAN** (Esperanto/English), Japanese (Esperanto/English) and Italian (Esperanto/French; see overviews listed above). Esperanto study has also been found to improve students' performance on general (native) language tests (Wood, 1975; Piron, 1986), and to enhance various other kinds of **LANGUAGE AWARENESS** (Fettes, 1997).

## Teaching

For many language teachers, Esperanto is especially valuable in helping to establish contact with people of very diverse backgrounds, in contrast to the association of other foreign languages with one or two national cultures. By means of international correspondence between classes of similar ages, the language can help make geography and social studies more exciting and meaningful to the learners. Among the more long-lived initiatives of this kind are the Freinet school movement, where Esperanto has occasionally been used since the 1920s; the project *Grajnoj en Vento* (Seeds in the Wind), which functioned in a number of European countries in the 1960s; and the California-based network 'Children Around the World', which has

been in existence since the 1980s. The first **INTERNET**-based project of this kind, *Interkulturo*, opened a 'virtual school' in September 1999 with participation from schools in Europe, **AFRICA**, Asia and the Americas (the school, together with descriptions in several languages, is located at http://lps.uniroma3.it/kler/).

Formal school-based instruction of Esperanto is none the less relatively uncommon. Many active users are self-taught, while others learned the language in evening classes or intensive courses. There is a wide variety of teaching methods and **MATERIALS** for all of these situations, including some designed for international use. Two examples of the latter are the Cseh method, also known as the '**DIRECT METHOD**' because of its reliance on oral Esperanto without **TRANSLATION**, and the Zagreb method, which uses L1 translations to achieve rapid comprehension of a set collection of Esperanto texts and then trains learners in the active use of this core **VOCABULARY**. There is presently no international system of teacher certification or **ASSESSMENT**, but national systems exist in several countries, usually under the administration of the national Esperanto association or the national affiliate of the International League of Esperanto-Speaking Teachers (ILEI). The latter, an organisation in operational relations with UNESCO, also administers international examinations in Esperanto at two or three levels, testing oral and written communication **SKILLS** as well as linguistic **COMPETENCE** and knowledge of Esperanto culture. (Introductions to the latter can be found in Forster, 1982; Janton, 1993 and Richardson, 1988.)

At the university level, Esperanto is usually taught within departments of **LINGUISTICS**, often as part of a course or programme in interlinguistics; the programmes at Eötvös Lòrànd Technical University (Budapest) and Adam Mickiewicz University (Poznan) stand out among a few dozen courses worldwide. In North America the longest-running credit programme is the three-week summer workshop at San Francisco State University. Graduate theses on Esperanto have most often been written from a linguistic standpoint, but have also originated in such fields as history, comparative literature and sociology. A fairly complete overview of current publications appears in the section 'Auxiliary languages. International languages' of the MLA International Bibliography of Books and Articles on the Modern Languages and Literatures.

## Critique

Esperanto has been criticised on a number of grounds, although usually on the basis of *a priori* arguments rather than empirical studies. Its alleged lack of a cultural base, its European lexicon and phrase structure, and its perceived association with naive utopianism or a rootless cosmopolitanism have all been frequently cited (e.g. Mead and Modley, 1967). A more telling barrier to its wider use in education, however, is its lack of economic and demographic power and political recognition, which all but rule out its inclusion in the 'foreign language' curriculum in many countries. Teachers wishing to teach Esperanto in a classroom setting must therefore usually relate it explicitly to broader curricular goals such as multicultural education, social studies or language awareness. Works which could help to define or articulate such goals include Eichholz and Eichholz (1982), Piron (1994), Richmond (1993) and Tonkin (1997).

**See also:** Cross-cultural psychology; Cultural awareness; Lingua franca; Native speaker;Planned languages; Planning for foreign language teaching

## Website

Interkulturo, a virtual school: http://lps. uniroma3.it/kler

## References

Corsetti, R. and La Torre, M. (1995) 'Quale lingua prima? Per un esperimento CEE che utilizzi l'esperanto', *Language Problems and Language Planning* 19, 1: 26–46.

Eichholz, R. and Eichholz, V.S. (eds) (1982) *Esperanto in the modern world*, Bailieboro: Esperanto Press.

Fantini, A. and Reagan, T. (1992) *Esperanto and education: toward a research agenda*, Washington, DC: Esperantic Studies Foundation.

Fettes, M. (1997) 'Esperanto and language aware-

ness', in L. van Lier and D. Corson (eds), *Knowledge about language*, Encyclopedia of Language and Education, Volume 6, Boston: Kluwer.

Forster, P. (1982) *The Esperanto movement*, The Hague: Mouton.

Halloran, J.H. (1952) 'A four year experiment in Esperanto as an introduction to French', *British Journal of Educational Psychology* 22: 200–4.

Janton, P. (1993) *Esperanto: language, literature, and community*, ed. H. Tonkin, trans. H. Tonkin, J. Edwards and K. Johnson-Weiner, Albany, NY: SUNY Press.

Jordan, D. (1992) *Being colloquial in Esperanto: a reference guide for Americans*, Lanham: University Press of America.

Maxwell, D. (1988) 'On the acquisition of Esperanto', *Studies in Second Language Acquisition* 10: 51–61.

Mead, M. and Modley, R. (1967) 'Communication among all people, everywhere', *Natural History* 76, 12: 56–63.

Piron, C. (1986) 'L'espéranto vu sous l'angle psychopédagogique' (Esperanto from the standpoint of educational psychology), *Education et Recherche* 8, 1: 11–41.

Piron, C. (1994) *Le défi des langues: Du gâchis au bon sens* (The language challenge: from rummage to reason), Paris: L'Harmattan.

Richardson, D. (1988) *Esperanto: learning and using the international language*, Eastsound: Orcas.

Richmond, I. (ed.) (1993) *Aspects of Internationalism: language and culture*, Lanham: University Press of America.

Thorndike, E., Kennon, L. and Eaton, H. (1933) *Language learning: summary of a report to the International Auxiliary Language Association in the United States*, Division of Psychology, Institute of Educational Research, Teachers College, Columbia University, New York.

Tonkin, H. (ed.) (1997) *Esperanto, interlinguistics and planned language*, Lanham: University Press of America.

Williams, N. (1965) 'A language teaching experiment', *Canadian Modern Language Review* 22, 1: 26–8.

Wood, R. (1975) 'Teaching the interlanguage: some experiments', *Lektos: Interdisciplinary Working*

*Papers in Language Sciences*, Louisville: University of Louisville.

## Further reading

Forster, P. (1982) *The Esperanto movement*, The Hague: Mouton.
Maxwell, D. (1988) 'On the acquisition of Esperanto', *Studies in Second Language Acquisition* 10: 51–61.
Richardson, D. (1988) *Esperanto: learning and using the international language*, Eastsound: Orcas.

MARK FETTES

## EuroCLIC

EuroCLIC is an interactive European Network, funded in part by the European Commission, which aims to include as many players in the field of plurilingual education as possible, and to build on existing initiatives and networks. Plurilingual education includes situations where students learn other subjects through the **MEDIUM** of a foreign language, and is sometimes referred to as **BILINGUAL EDUCATION**.

EuroCLIC is coordinated by the European Platform for Dutch Education, in cooperation with the University of Jyväskylä in Finland and the Office Régionale du Bilinguisme in Strasbourg, **FRANCE**. It issues a bulletin three times per year and maintains a website with news, articles and teaching resources.

## Website

EuroCLIC's website is: http://www.euroclic.net

## European Centre for Modern Languages

The Centre is an institution of the **COUNCIL OF EUROPE** (officially designated as 'Le centre européen pour les langues vivantes' in French, and 'Europäisches Fremdsprachenzentrum' in German). It is situated in Graz, Austria, and was founded in 1994 by eight states of the Council of Europe as a forum in which educational policymakers can meet with specialists in language teaching methodology to discuss and seek solutions to tasks and challenges which play a decisive role in the process of European integration. Other states have joined and supported the work since then.

The aim of the centre is to offer, usually through workshops and conferences, a meeting place for officials responsible for language policy, specialists in didactics, **TEACHER EDUCATORS**, **TEXTBOOK** authors and other multipliers. It also organises and supports research and development networks.

The Centre concentrates on the investigation of innovative approaches and developments in language education, and on the implementation of language education policies. In this way it complements the work of the Modern Languages Project of the Council of Europe based in Strasbourg.

## Website

The centre's website is: http://culture.coe.fr/ecml

## European Language Council/ Conseil Européen pour les Langues

The ELC/CEL is a permanent and independent international association constituted under Belgian law. Its legal seat is in Brussels; its permanent secretariat is at the Freie Universität Berlin.

The association was officially launched in July 1997 by some fifty universities and associations with support from the European Commission. The founding of the association was one of the outcomes of the pilot project SIGMA Scientific Committee on Languages, which described and analysed the state of **HIGHER EDUCATION** language studies in fourteen European Union Member States, Norway and Switzerland, and proposed new measures to be taken at different levels.

The aim of the CEL/ELC is to promote linguistic and cultural diversity in Europe through transnational cooperation at higher education level. It seeks to contribute to the quantitative and qualitative improvement of knowledge of European languages and cultures. In this, it is guided by the conviction that an important aspect of European citizenship is a multilingual and **INTERCULTURAL COMPETENCE**, and that, because of this, the promotion of linguistic diversity has to be one of the main educational **OBJECTIVES** in an increasingly integrated Europe.

In pursuit of its general aim, the CEL/ELC seeks: to provide a forum for debate and joint policy development for institutions of higher education as well as for professional and academic organisations with a special interest in language studies; to initiate, launch and manage European projects in education, training and research designed to meet the cultural, social and professional needs of an integrated Europe; to represent the interests of its members in dialogue with European institutions as well as with other national and international organisations; to gather, exchange and disseminate information relevant to the field; to assess methods of teaching and research in language studies; to enhance the quality of language learning and language teaching.

Membership of the CEL/ELC is open to all institutions of higher education in Europe and to all pertinent international and national associations based in Europe. The activities of the CEL/ELC are coordinated by a Board and an Executive Committee. The CEL/ELC holds a major international conference every two years; it convenes task forces dedicated to key issues to conduct workshops, prepare policy papers and launch projects. It cooperates with the European Commission, the European Parliament and the Council of Europe. The CEL/ELC publishes an Information Bulletin twice a year.

The first major project launched from within the CEL/ELC was the Thematic Network Project (TNP) in the Area of Languages supported by the European Commission under the SOCRATES-ERASMUS Programme (1996–99). On the basis of the SIGMA pilot project, the TNP developed concrete proposals for language studies in higher education, to be exploited and disseminated in a project involving a large number of universities in Central and Eastern Europe. Other initiatives associated with the CEL/ELC include the **DIA-LANG** Project for the development of a testing system for fourteen European languages delivered via the **INTERNET**, and projects for the development

of European Masters courses in Conference **INTERPRETING** and in Clinical Linguistics.

## Website

CEL/ELC's website is: http://www.fu-berlin.de/elc

WOLFGANG MACKIEWICZ

# European Language Portfolio

The European Language Portfolio (ELP) is an initiative of the **COUNCIL OF EUROPE MODERN LANGUAGES PROJECT** and is closely linked to the **COMMON EUROPEAN FRAMEWORK**. The ELP is a means of **ASSESSMENT** which enables learners to keep a recognised record of all their language learning achievements both in formal education and training and outside these contexts. Pilots were begun in 1998 in fourteen member states and three non-governmental organisations with a view to the launch of the ELP in 2001.

The ELP is intended to be a personal document in which learners set out, within a standard, internationally recognisable format, their experiences of learning languages in successive stages of education and/or training. It provides learners with an opportunity to reflect on those experiences, and teachers and employers with evidence of them. It offers learners an opportunity to record and value their linguistic expertise and any intercultural experiences acquired beyond formal examinations and qualifications, such as the use of a **HERITAGE LANGUAGE** within their own community. The ELP therefore comprises three parts: a 'passport', recording formal qualifications; a language biography, describing in more detail both knowledge of specific languages and learning experiences, such as visits and **EXCHANGES** or work experience abroad; and a language dossier in which the learner may include samples of work or other evidence to support and illustrate the language biography. It follows that the ELP should be progressively updated by learners as their language learning develops and career transition points are reached, such as changing school or applying for a job.

The development of an ELP was first proposed at a Symposium in Rüschlikon in Switzerland in November 1991 to complement the **COMMON EUROPEAN FRAMEWORK** (CEF) (CCC, 1992). Following a feasibility study (1995–97), proposals for development were accepted by the Council of Europe in 1997 (CCC, 1997), and a pilot phase (1998–2000) agreed covering all stages from **PRIMARY EDUCATION** to **ADULT** education and training. This phase involved trials of various models in Austria, the Czech Republic, Finland, **FRANCE**, Germany, Hungary, Ireland, Italy, The Netherlands, Portugal, The Russian Federation, Slovenia, Sweden, Switzerland and the United Kingdom, and by three non-governmental organisations: the European Association for Quality Language Services (Eaquals), the European Languages Council (ELC) and the International Certificate Conference (ICC). In the case of some national trials, notably in Switzerland, the work continued experimentation which was already underway.

The aims of the ELP reflect those of the Council of Europe itself, such as promoting:

- the development of mutual understanding among European citizens;
- diversity of cultures, languages and ways of life;
- the development of the individual language learner;
- language learning as a lifelong process;
- the clear description of qualifications to promote mobility.

The main principles for the development of the ELP are that it:

- is the property of the learner;
- has both a learning and a reporting function;
- is based on the CEF and draws on it for its terminology and descriptors;
- serves, and is manageable by, a range of learners and users;
- is immediately recognisable across Europe.

The ELP venture is an ambitious one since it seeks to introduce an assessment document recognised in all phases of education and training and across more than forty member states.

To some extent, there is a tension between the ELP's learning function ('process') and its reporting function ('product'). For the former, it needs to be flexible in layout and length to meet the **NEEDS** of learners for reflection and self-**EVALUATION** and provide a source of **MOTIVATION**. For the latter, it needs to present information in a compact, manageable and immediately recognisable format for employers and other users. One means of resolving this tension is the use of a limited number of standardised 'hard sheets' (*pages dures*) to meet the reporting function, whilst promoting the learning function through the use of more flexible 'soft sheets' (*pages souples*) which may be selected and adapted to the needs of learners in different contexts.

The terminology to be used in the Portfolio raises another tension. The internationally comprehensible and rigorously drafted descriptors of language performance of the CEF are needed for comparison across national frontiers. However, these may not be immediately accessible, for example, for employers without a specialist background in language learning and teaching, and may not be 'user friendly' for younger or inexperienced learners. Some mediation by teachers or trainers may be necessary in such circumstances.

Portfolios have been used as assessment instruments in other fields of education, such as art where students have to present for assessment for qualifications and certification work completed over more extended periods than a timed examination. There is also experience in the United Kingdom of portfolio assessment across the wider curriculum in the development of the National Record of Achievement folder since the 1980s which shares similar features: for example, it is the property of the learner, and includes evidence beyond formal examinations, self-evaluation and a dossier. It has had some success, but has experienced some difficulty in gaining acceptance across a wide range of users, particularly with employers and **HIGHER EDUCATION**. The ELP will similarly have to establish itself as a currency among a wide range of users, but across national frontiers also.

**See also:** Assessment and testing; Council of Europe Modern Languages Projects; European Centre for Modern Languages; Non-verbal communication; Untutored language acquisition

## References

Council for Cultural Cooperation (CCC) (1992) *Transparency and coherence in language learning in Europe. Objectives, evaluation, certification. Report on the Rüschlikon Symposium*, Strasbourg: Council of Europe.

Council for Cultural Cooperation (CCC) (1997) *European Language Portfolio. Proposals for Development* (CC-LANG(97)1), Strasbourg: Council of Europe.

## Further reading

Council for Cultural Cooperation (CCC) (1997) *Report of the final conference of the project 'Language Learning for Citizenship'* (CC-LANG(97)7), Strasbourg: Council of Europe.

Department for Education and Employment (1997) *National record of achievement: report of the steering group*, London: Department for Education and Employment.

Office for Standards in Education (OFSTED) (1995) *Reporting pupils' achievements. A report from the office of Her Majesty's Chief Inspector of Schools*, London: HMSO.

ALAN DOBSON

# Evaluation

Evaluation is defined as the investigation of merit and worth, the first being measured 'against professional standards' and the second 'against institutional and societal needs' (Scriven, 1994). It involves a process of systematic and principled collection and communication of descriptive and/ or judgemental information about the entity of interest.

Evaluation is usually conceptualised in terms of several major dimensions: purposes for evaluating, the audience for an evaluation, evaluators, approaches, objects of evaluation, kinds of evaluative information, methods of data collection and criteria for judging merit and worth.

## Conceptualising evaluation

### Purposes

Evaluations can be conducted for a number of reasons, some of which are: with respect to courses, programmes and projects – to determine impact, identify strengths and weaknesses and suggest areas for improvement, or justify a decision that has been taken; with respect to teachers – to certify, select, raise awareness of possibilities for development; with respect to **MATERIALS** – to decide whether a **TEXTBOOK** should be adopted or retained. An evaluation can serve several purposes at the same time and these can be given different weighting and prominence. Some are official and overtly stated, others are tacitly supported and motivated by political considerations.

Broadly speaking, the variety of evaluation purposes can be reduced to several major groups: the formative function for improvement; the summative function for selection, certification or accountability; the psychological or socio-political function for motivation and increasing awareness; and the administrative function for exercising authority (Nevo, 1983: 119). Some authors in the field of second language education (Alderson and Beretta, 1992) and **TEACHER EDUCATION** (Raths, 1988) insist that evaluation should contribute to theory advancement by informing disputes about directions to be followed in the two fields.

Evaluation for improvement is a major tool for promoting professionalism. In language education it can significantly enhance both the teaching and learning processes. Rea-Dickins and Germaine (1992: 26) emphasise its potential for 'formalising and extending a teacher's knowledge about teaching and learning in classrooms'. Evaluation is therefore an important component of any **ACTION RESEARCH** cycle.

### The audience

The question 'who for?' has received a variety of answers, ranging from 'the client who has contracted the study', to 'all stakeholders', i.e. all those who are interested in or affected by the evaluated entity. Within this vast array of people, three broad classes are identified (Guba and Lincoln, 1989): agents (e.g. institutional authorities, teaching and administrative staff, decision-makers in regulatory bodies, future employers); beneficiaries (e.g. pupils, student teachers, parents); and victims (e.g. drop-outs of a course).

Interest in the audiences to be served by an evaluation has been largely dictated by concerns for the utilisation of the findings – still a problem in the field. Desire to facilitate use has led to the development of models and approaches where stakeholders are granted different measures of responsibility throughout the evaluation and play roles of varying importance.

## The evaluators

Discussions on this issue focus on two important distinctions – between 'insiders' and 'outsiders' on the one hand, and professional and amateur evaluators on the other.

The distinction 'insider–outsider' is well known in evaluation theory and practice. Internal evaluators are members of programme/project/institutional staff, and an external evaluator has no such connections. In general it is asserted that insiders have advantages for formative studies and outsiders for summative, even though the prevailing opinion is in favour of collaboration at all stages. Insiders are thought to have the advantage of possessing good knowledge of the evaluated entity and local context, of being less threatening to the participants in the educational endeavour, and of having the time to stay on and facilitate the utilisation of the findings. The price to be paid could be partiality and subjectivity.

External evaluators may provide a fresh perspective, they can have greater credibility to some of the stakeholders and be perceived by them as being objective. Some of the potential disadvantages are the hostility outsiders might encounter and their lack of in-depth knowledge about the evaluated entity. The choice between insiders and outsiders will depend on the purposes for the evaluation.

The second distinction is between evaluators who have had professional training in measurement and evaluation and those who are substantive

experts in other fields but have some on-the-job training in evaluation. Or sometimes none. Alderson and Beretta (1992) give an example within the field of language education, where frequently the fact that someone is a recognised figure is taken to be the sole criterion for his/her selection as an evaluator. The ideal would be a team comprising both kinds of experts.

Recently, participatory evaluation has been gaining ground. It involves collaboration between professional evaluators and groups of stakeholders. The idea of stakeholder involvement is associated with different rationales: facilitation of evaluation utilisation, empowerment of certain groups, and education as related to improved knowledge of the evaluated entity as well as the **ACQUISITION** of **SKILLS** for systematic inquiry. An approach which seeks to involve various groups of stakeholders is responsive constructivism (Guba and Lincoln, 1989), which regards them as equal partners in the design, implementation, interpretation and resulting action of an evaluation.

## Approaches

Approaches to evaluation are usually seen as dividing between the scientific and the naturalistic. Where a scientific approach is adopted, evaluation studies are characterised by reliance on experimental or quasi-experimental designs and insistence on the provision of scientific technical data. This approach once dominated the field, since it was considered that a study was accurate and valid only if it involved experimental and control groups, random assignments of participants and statistically analysable data. In language education, for example, programme evaluations in the 1960s and 1970s were basically comparisons of different teaching methodologies and materials through the use of experiments. Teacher evaluations in the 1970s were also affected by this way of thinking. They utilised instrumentation based on generic, easily obtained measures of teaching effectiveness and related direct observation of teacher process variables to pupil outcome measures.

A major shortcoming of evaluations premised on the scientific approach is that they cannot take into account the complexity of educational units and remain largely insensitive to the varied concerns of the different stakeholders. Hence, where the purpose is to describe and unravel this complexity, evaluators opt for naturalistic approaches. Naturalistic studies employ multi-faceted designs aimed at capturing the workings of the educational entities in their real-life settings and the subjective realities of classroom life, as well as presenting multiple viewpoints. Parlett and Hamilton's (1972) illuminative evaluation is a case in point. It is premised on the assumption that evaluation is similar to social **ANTHROPOLOGY** and the evaluator should therefore attempt to describe the culture evaluated via techniques such as documentation analysis, observation, interviews and questionnaires.

Whether the two types of approach are reconcilable is a major though rather controversial issue in evaluation theory and practice. Increasingly, an eclecticism is evident in current practices in both general and language education.

### Objects of evaluation

Typical evaluation objects in education are teachers, learners, courses, programmes, projects, **SYLLABUSES**, methods, instructional materials, institutions and administrative personnel.

### Kinds of evaluative information

The kinds of information that can be collected about the different evaluation objects depend on the purposes for the evaluation, the **NEEDS** and wishes of stakeholders, practical considerations, etc. For example, where the focus is on measuring gains, data about related criterial features can be gathered on entry to and exit from a project or programme.

Some basic sources of information are (current and former) learners, teachers, headteachers, inspectors, parents, administrative personnel, documentation, physical and social environment, etc.

### Methods of data collection

Methodological issues in evaluation are usually discussed within the dichotomy (disputed by some writers) between quantitative and qualitative methods. The former study educational entities in terms

of predetermined variables. They call for the use of standardised measures, which allow the variety of experiences, viewpoints and perspectives to be reduced to pre-specified categories which can then be quantified. Comparison across groups can thus be easily accomplished. For example, experiments, seeking to establish correlations and strength of relationships, and interaction analysis fall within this category. They generate data which are easily quantifiable and lend themselves to statistical analysis.

Qualitative methods are descriptive and discovery-oriented, allowing an in-depth analysis of selected issues. They are associated with open-ended interviews, direct observation, introspection and documentation review. Data yielded through qualitative methods are subject to interpretative analysis and are organised into 'readable narrative description with major themes, categories, and illustrative case examples' (Patton, 1990: 10).

Both groups of methods have their critics and ardent supporters. Some of the criticisms levelled at quantitative methods are that they may lead to a focus on easily measured aspects rather than the most significant ones, that side-effects may be overlooked, etc. Qualitative methods are usually criticised for being time-consuming and producing data which is subjective, anecdotal and unreliable. However, the prevalent view nowadays is in favour of a balance between the two types of method, which are seen as complementary, and their combination in some cases is desirable as they may serve different evaluation needs. In language education, as Rea-Dickins (1994) claims, there has been 'slower recognition (than in educational evaluation more generally) of the place for both'.

### Criteria

The sources of criteria could be substantive experts in the case of merit evaluations and the assessment of local needs and values where worth is the focus of interest. The criteria can be quantitative or qualitative and defined before the study – pre-ordinate – or can emerge in the process of work – responsive.

## Some foci for evaluation activity

### Evaluating programmes

Programme evaluation has received considerable attention in the literature on educational evaluation, where numerous models with a different degree of formalisation have been offered. In ENGLISH Language Teaching, however, the majority of publications focus on case studies rather than generalised models (but see, for example, Lynch, 1990).

Programme evaluation has a lot to offer to a wide variety of audiences – regulatory bodies, educational institutions, teachers, students, parents, etc. In language education evaluation, existing surveys of its historical development show that in the 1960s and 1970s the scientific perspective prevailed. The bulk of studies at the time were tightly controlled experiments of varied scope and scale, aimed at broad comparisons of TEACHER METHODS. Information was basically collected through tests and questionnaires, and post-test scores were used as a measure of programme effectiveness. A growing concern for what happens inside the programme and how it is implemented led to a shift in perspective. Evaluation studies began to appear which adopted a naturalistic approach and, through a variety of qualitative methods, attempted to present multiple perspectives and focus on programme process rather than outcome. Nowadays, despite the fact that summative, product-oriented evaluations are still prevalent in language education, more and more opinions are expressed to the effect that the scientific and naturalistic perspectives should be balanced.

The design of a programme evaluation premised on the scientific approach typically involves a comparison between an experimental and a control group on pre- and post-tests. Evaluations which do not employ this design can be based on the investigation of different focal points according to the purposes of the study and the needs, values and expectations of the parties involved. A number of frameworks seeking to organise the complexity of reality have been suggested in the literature. Patton (1990) offers a framework of sensitising concepts including context, goals, inputs, recruitment, intake, implementation, processes, outcomes, products and impacts. Sanders (1992, cited in Weir and Roberts, 1994) offers the following focal points for the evaluation of school programmes: programme needs assessment, individual needs assessment, resource allotment, and processes or strategies for providing services to learners, curriculum design, classroom processes, materials of instruction, monitoring of pupil progress, learner motivation, learning environment, staff development, decision making and outcomes of instruction.

Stake (1967) proposes a model which takes account of the important components of a programme focusing on both description and judgement. These components are Inputs, Process and Outputs, which are explored in two matrices, Description and Judgement. These are further subdivided into Intents and Observations, and Standards and Judgements respectively.

### Evaluating teachers

A number of different purposes for teacher evaluation have been identified in the literature. The two which are most frequently mentioned are accountability and professional growth (improvement).

The accountability purpose has to do with prescribed areas of performance and establishing the degree of achievement of minimum levels of competence. It typically serves the needs of the administrator, providing information for decisions such as selecting, hiring, firing, promoting, etc. This is also the type of evaluation that is found on courses leading to certification.

Evaluation for improvement aims at enhancing the professional development of teachers who are at least minimally competent. Research has identified three groups of variables affecting the conditions under which teacher evaluation is most likely to foster the professional growth of competent teachers – the characteristics of individuals, the characteristics of evaluation systems and the characteristics of the context in which evaluation takes place (Duke and Stiggins, 1990). Teacher self-evaluation, too, can be instrumental in bringing about improvement in practice.

The two purposes cannot be easily accomplished through the same teacher evaluation system and usually differ in terms of adopted standards of excellence and what counts as evidence –

standardised and externally defensible information in the case of accountability, and thick, descriptive and illuminative data when professional growth is the main concern.

Another possible aim in teacher evaluation is school improvement. A need is felt in the field to tie the evaluation of teachers to the larger context in which it occurs – the school, the faculty and the language programme. In pre-service and in-service teacher education, trainee evaluation can be used to assess programme quality and effectiveness.

Several aspects of teaching are usually evaluated – competency, competence, performance, and effectiveness (defined in Medley, 1982), which require different evaluation tools. Among these are teacher interviews, competency tests, **CLASS-ROOM OBSERVATION**, student evaluations, peer review, student achievement and portfolios. New trends of development are related to the use of techniques for assessing teachers' cognitions: direct and non-inferential ways of assessing teacher belief, methods relying on contextual analysis of teachers' descriptive language, taxonomies for assessing self-reflection and teacher cognition, and concept mapping (Kagan, 1990).

Scriven (1994) considers several major models of teacher evaluation. These are as follows:

- The 'inspector model' based mainly on class-room visits.
- Peer evaluation.
- Consumer rating models usually involving students but sometimes parents or employers.
- The interview model.
- Management by **OBJECTIVES** model.
- Competency-based approaches.
- Research-based teacher evaluation.
- The 'reflective teaching' model.
- Outcome models.
- The duties-based approach.
- Hybrid models involving a mix of several modes.

## *Evaluating materials*

Materials evaluation is an indispensable part of teachers' everyday work. They may be involved in both informal and formal assessment of textbooks, workbooks and teachers' guides, as well as **VISUAL AIDS**, tape and video cassettes, etc. (for conciseness this subsection will only be concerned with textbooks). Materials evaluation is also of interest to headteachers, teacher trainers, curriculum advisers, learners, textbook authors and publishers though these groups can have conflicting opinions about what makes a good textbook. It can lead to summative decisions concerning textbook selection or retention, formative decisions for improvement through supplementation or adaptation and it can sensitise teachers to their own teaching and learning situation.

As elsewhere in evaluation, evaluators here can be concerned with establishing both merit, the value of the materials as they stand, and worth, value considered in relation to actual classroom use. The distinction between the two is usefully captured by Rea-Dickins and Germaine (1992), who recognise three phases in materials evaluation: materials-as-workplan, materials-in-process and outcomes from materials. The first stage refers to theoretical value, the second is concerned with gathering information about the ways textbooks are used and responded to in the classroom and the third generates information about the achievements of learners. The three phases call for different procedures. Checklists and schedules, often commercially prepared, are usually used for defining merit. As Sheldon (1988) rightly observes, however, 'no one is really certain what criteria and constraints are actually operative in ELT contexts worldwide, and textbook criteria are emphatically local'. Information about the actual use of a textbook and the benefits from it can again be collected with the help of checklists but also through observation, teachers' logs, questionnaires, etc. Learners, too, can be involved in the evaluation through questionnaires and structured interviews, diaries, etc. The data gathered at stages one and two can then be complemented by details of learner outcomes obtained through appropriate test instruments.

**See also:** Assessment and testing; Materials and media; Needs analysis; Quality management; Research methods; Syllabus and curriculum design; Teacher thinking; Textbooks

## References

Alderson, J.C. and Beretta, A. (eds) (1992) *Evaluating second language education*, Cambridge: Cambridge University Press.

Duke, D. and Stiggins, R. (1990) 'Beyond minimum competence: evaluation for professional development', in J. Millman and L. Darling-Hammond (eds), *The new handbook of teacher evaluation*, London: Sage.

Guba, E.G. and Lincoln, Y.S. (1989) *Fourth generation evaluation*, London: Sage.

Kagan, D.M. (1990) 'Ways of evaluating teacher cognition; inferences concerning the goldilocks principle', *Review of Educational Research* 60, 3: 419–69.

Lynch, B.K. (1990) 'A context-adaptive model for program evaluation', *TESOL Quarterly* 24, 1: 23–41.

Medley, D.M. (1982) *Teacher competency testing and the teacher educator*, Charlottesville: Association of Teacher Educators and the Bureau of Educational Research, University of Virginia.

Nevo, D. (1983) 'The conceptualization of educational evaluation: an analytical review of the literature', *Review of Educational Research* 53, 1: 117–28.

Parlett, M.R. and Hamilton, D. (1972) *Evaluation as illumination: a new approach to innovatory programs*, Edinburgh: Edinburgh University Press.

Patton, M.Q. (1990) *Qualitative evaluation and research methods*, London: Sage.

Raths, J.D. (1988) 'Evaluation of teacher education programmes', in W.J. Gephart and J.B. Ayers (eds), *Teacher education evaluation*, The Hague: Kluwer.

Rea-Dickins, P. (1994) 'Evaluation and English language teaching', *Language Teaching* 27: 71–91.

Rea-Dickins, P. and Germaine, K. (1992) *Evaluation*, Oxford: Oxford University Press.

Scriven, M. (1994) 'Evaluation as a discipline', *Studies in Educational Evaluation* 20: 147–66.

Sheldon, L. (1988) 'Evaluating ELT textbooks and materials', *ELTJ* 42, 4: 237–46.

Stake, R.E. (1967) 'The countenance of educational evaluation', *Teachers College Record*, 68: 523–40.

Weir, C. and Roberts, J. (1994) *Evaluation in ELT*, Oxford: Blackwell.

## Further reading

Darling-Hammond, L., Wise, A.E. and Pease, S.R. (1983) 'Teacher evaluation in the organizational context: a review of the literature', *Review of Educational Research* 53, 3: 285–328.

Lynch, B.K. (1996) *Language program evaluation. Theory and practice*, Cambridge: Cambridge University Press.

Millman, J. and Darling-Hammond, J. (1990) *The handbook of teacher evaluation*, London: Sage.

Pawson, R. and Tilley, N. (1997) *Realistic evaluation*, London: Sage.

MARIETTA NEDKOVA

# Exchanges

Individual or class exchanges between students of different nations and cultures, **STUDY ABROAD** programmes of up to a year, and short study visits of a few days, have come to be central phases in the process of language and culture learning since the late nineteenth century. They form part of educational institutions and other contexts that promote personal exchanges, such as out-of-school youth exchanges. Attempting to strike a balance in the development of linguistic, communicative and **INTERCULTURAL COMPETENCIES**, they are organised in phases of preparation, follow-through and follow-up. The contact situation is characterised by a *pédagogie des échanges* (pedagogy of exchanges) (Alix and Bertrand, 1994) that defines **OBJECTIVES**, syllabi, and methods for an increased integration of learning in the field with classroom learning at home, the emphasis being on experiential and process-learning.

Exchanges of students and teachers began in the late nineteenth century, often having international correspondence exchanges as precursors to face-to-face exchanges. By 1919 a network of correspondence schools existed in Europe and the United States. After the two World Wars, one of the main motivations of international exchanges lay in the hope for reconciliation. It was assumed that it would be best to start with children to build lasting peaceful relations between nations, and schools were thus seen as playing a central role since political structures had failed during the wars.

While on a global level the founding of UNESCO in 1945 put exchanges back on the agenda, in the US programmes such as the Peace Corps (since 1961) led to an increase in cross-cultural education to prepare volunteers for contact in various cultures.

The increasing economic and political integration of European countries has led to a large number of associations and programmes that promote various kinds of exchanges, working towards the idea of a common European citizenship. What started with the *Deutsch–Französisches Jugendwerk* (German–French Youth Organization) in 1963 (promoting 2,500 school partnerships by 1990) has evolved into programmes such as SOCRATES since 1995, which continues programmes such as ERASMUS and **COMENIUS**. These are all geared towards facilitating exchanges on the level of universities and schools among European nations (Delahousse, 1996). Typical exchanges are reciprocal, but there is also the situation of one individual or group passing a certain amount of time in the host culture.

Exchanges are not only profitable for students, but also for teachers in pre- and in-service training, since the teacher's role in the exchange is a complex one which involves the organisation of the exchange, as well as the structuring of an often unpredictable learning process. This requires training.

In encounters with **NATIVE SPEAKERS**, students use the foreign language in real-life contexts. In opposition to classroom learning, language fluency is more important than accuracy, which means that the role of mistakes is downplayed. To attenuate fears and anxiety in the field, students need to extend their linguistic **COMPETENCE** as to the variety of sounds, speeds and registers they are going to encounter, such as the verbal play of adolescent language in group situations.

The interpersonal encounter situation involves not only cognitive aspects such as cultural knowledge of the participating cultures, but it is above all an emotional situation that involves affective and behavioural factors and thus calls for an experiential approach to learning. For example, having

elicited and worked with pre-existing views and **STEREOTYPES** of students in the preparatory phase, first-hand experience and the interaction in the field with native speakers is structured by collaborative methods – working on collective products, for example – which offer opportunities of finding out about the realities of the specific culture in question. Participant observation and investigative **AUTHENTIC** tasks such as exploring the place one visits, combined with various methods of collecting data, as through interviews, journals, and videos, allow for an ethnographic approach to the field, enabling students to become immersed in the daily culture, comparing and contrasting the respective cultures and possibly revising earlier preconceptions.

Apart from the principle of **TASK-BASED** collaboration between individuals or groups involved in the exchange, this dialogic form of encounter – as in **TANDEM LEARNING** – treats the participants as **AUTONOMOUS** subjects who should be allowed to accept responsibility on all levels of organisation. This helps to ensure an identification with the process and a deeper involvement with the other culture, thus facilitating intercultural learning.

Reflective phases during the exchange and especially the follow-up work at home are important aspects in analysing and interpreting the multiple experiences and gathered data to enhance a deeper understanding of one's own and other cultures.

In the context of exchanges, different models have been proposed to explain the process of intercultural learning. American models in the field of cross-cultural psychology have evolved from an assimilationist model of cultural adaptation to a more pluralistic model of cultural adaptation that takes into account the increasingly multicultural nature of modern societies. Byram has proposed a model of four savoirs that delineates the process of acquiring an intercultural competence in exchange situations. Based on a process model of learning, the traditional 'savoirs', i.e. information about the other culture, are enlarged by 'savoir être', the ability to give up ethnocentric **ATTITUDES** and thus change one's perspective, 'savoir apprendre', the ability to observe and analyse other people's cultures, and 'savoir faire' that highlights the ability to interact with people of another culture using the three other savoirs as a basis (Byram, 1997: 11–13). Ethnographic inquiry supports this process, leading to a reflection of the relationships between one's own culture, the foreign language, and the other culture.

On the organisational side, having clarified each side's expectations as to the outcome of the exchange, a clearly defined scenario, such as making a film about the foreign school, provides a coherent frame to visits abroad. In the realm of such projects, group identities can be formed and **MATERIALS** can be developed for further use in the home culture, thus allowing for the participation of other students in the experience who have not been involved in the exchange. For longer periods abroad, similar tasks of ethnographic inquiry may be developed.

The preparation phase needs to take into account the linguistic preparation of the participants, as well as instances of cross-cultural contact that can be practised through role play, simulations, or the study of critical incidents (Althen, 1994).

To support people in encounter situations and to minimise negative experiences such as **CULTURE SHOCK**, continuous counselling is necessary, especially during those phases of the exchange that are prone to frustrations, e.g. the frustration experienced once the first excitement about contact with a different culture is waning, or frustrations about differences in doing and seeing things, and when, prior to re-entry into the home culture, leavetaking becomes a crucial issue. In group exchanges the possibility of a space for retreat and reflection whilst in the foreign environment offers the necessary security of the monocultural home group and reflective stocktaking with the organisers of the exchange.

Apart from political and pedagogical aims, one major objective of exchanges is the attempt to increase foreign language proficiency. Research has produced conflicting results. While there are findings that informal out-of-class contact does not necessarily enhance **SECOND LANGUAGE ACQUISITION**, there is also evidence that learners gain a kind of global fluency, i.e. the ability to sound more native-like and to increase their rate of speech. While advanced learners show little change in structural accuracy, learners improve their oral skills, using a wider range of **COMMUNICATIVE STRATEGIES** (Freed, 1995: 3–33).

First findings of the European Language Proficiency Survey (since 1993) that covers 25,000 university students in eight countries involved in exchanges show that there is a persistent existence of stereotypes (Coleman, 1998: 59) which highlights the necessity of a 'pédagogie des échanges' that moves away from the tourist view to the sojourner who gets involved with the host culture.

**See also:** Acculturation; Acquisition and teaching; Attitudes and Language learning; Cross-cultural psychology; Internet; Learning to learn; Medium-oriented and message-oriented communication; Psychology; Study abroad; Tandem learning; Video

## References

Alix, B. and Bertrand, G. (eds) (1994) 'Pour une pédagogie des échanges, *Le Français dans le Monde*, Févr.–Mars, Numéro Spécial.

Althen, G. (ed.) (1994) *Learning across cultures*, Washington, DC: NAFSA.

Byram, M. (ed.) (1997) *Face to face. Learning 'language-and-culture' through visits and exchanges*, London: Centre for Information on Language Teaching and Research.

Coleman, J.A. (1998) 'Evolving intercultural perceptions among university language learners in Europe', in M. Byram and M. Fleming (eds), *Language learning in intercultural perspective. Approaches through drama and ethnography*, Cambridge: Cambridge University Press.

Delahousse, B. (1996) 'Socrates, un cadre européen dynamique (Socrates, a dynamic European frame)', *Les Langues Modernes* 2: 7–20.

Freed, B.F. (ed.) (1995) *Second language acquisition in a study abroad context*, Amsterdam: John Benjamins.

## Further reading

Association Européenne des Enseignants (1993) *European educational exchanges – a manual*, Paris: Hachette.

Fowler, S.M. and Mumford, M.G. (eds) (1995)

*Intercultural sourcebook: cross-cultural training methods*, Yarmouth, MA: Intercultural Press.

Snow, D. and Byram, B. (1997) *Crossing frontiers. The school study visit abroad*, London: Centre for Information on Language Teaching and Research.

Thomas, A. (ed.) (1984) *Interkultureller Personenaustausch in Forschung und Praxis (Reasearch and practices in intercultural exchange)*, Saarbrücken: Verlag Breitenbach.

Thomas, A. (ed.) (1988) *Interkulturelles Lernen im Schüleraustausch (Intercultural learning in student exchanges)*, Saarbrücken: Verlag Breitenbach.

ANDREAS MÜLLER-HARTMANN

# Exercise types and grading

Practice activities are at the heart of any learning process. Their aim is to consolidate learning and improve performance. Ideally, foreign language practice activities should help learners progress from strongly teacher-supported controlled exercise types to automatic and eventually autonomous reception and production of the foreign language they are learning. Throughout the history of foreign language teaching authors have tried to design exercise typologies that could meaningfully integrate a variety of exercise types into a coherent whole of progressive practice activities. Taking into account insights from educational **PSYCHOLOGY**, developmental psychology or **LINGUISTICS**, exercise typologies attempt to grade language learning.

## Exercise typologies

Exercise typologies organise exercise types into a systematic whole that holds the promise of grading the learning process in such a way that steady progress will be made, which will eventually lead to **AUTONOMOUS LEARNING** and the acquisition of a high level of knowledge, skill and competence. Exercise typologies are expected to be scientifically well founded, integrating insights from educational psychology and developmental psychology, and taking account of the state of the art of the subject's related disciplines.

Despite their aura of objectivity, presenting themselves as logical organising principles on which courses for teaching particular subjects can be based, exercise typologies have been much debated. Given the complex nature of the learning process, this should not surprise. Typologies not only tend to vary with **TEACHER METHODS** and approaches; they also appear to be in need of adaptation depending on the characteristics of the learner group and the learning situation. Factors as varied as **AGE**, **LEARNING STYLE**, degree of **MOTIVATION**, level of involvement, attitudinal development, prior knowledge, degree of assistance, etc., appear to affect the level of difficulty of particular exercise types. The relative degree of complexity of the contents that need to be acquired also affects the relative degree of translatability of particular exercise typologies into actual teaching practice.

## Principles underlying exercise typologies

Despite these reservations, when observing the principle of *meaningful learning* as defined by Ausubel (1977), observing De Corte *et al.*'s (1981) *taxonomy of cognitive OBJECTIVES*, and putting Craik and Lockhart's (1972) concept of *levels of processing* into practice, exercise typologies are helpful instruments for curriculum development and course **EVALUATION**, or for planning a sequence of practice activities.

According to Ausubel, materials can only promote learning when they are meaningfully related to what students already know, and when they contain cues and exercise types that help students process the new contents and relate them to the contents of their existing schemata (Ausubel, 1977; Ausubel *et al.*, 1978). It follows that exercise types which are too far above or too far below the learners' level of competence may be detrimental to the learning process, because they either do not challenge or overcharge them.

De Corte's taxonomy of intellectual operations is based on Guilford's 'structure-of-intellect-model' (Guilford and Meeker, 1969) and resolved some of the hierarchical problems inherent in Bloom *et al.*'s taxonomy of educational objectives in the cognitive domain published in 1956. It comprises seven categories which are ranked under two main headings, as is apparent from the displayed text below. The hierarchy's underlying principle is that of an increase in the complexity of cognitive operations and in the degree of independence in information processing envisaged. Exercise types observing this gradual progression from low to higher levels of involvement, from receptive to productive tasks, from teacher guided to learner independent learning can be assumed to make for graded consolidation and application of what is learnt.

> **Taxonomy of cognitive objectives (after De Corte, 1973)**
>
> I  Receptive–reproductive operations
>
> 1  Apperception
> 2  Recognition
> 3  Reproduction
>
> II  Productive operations
>
> 4  Interpretative production of information
> 5  Convergent production of information
> 6  Evaluative production of information
> 7  Divergent production of information

According to Craik and Lockhart (1972), who developed the notion of 'levels of processing', incoming information is processed by various operations which can be referred to as perceptual–conceptual analysis. The level of analysis reflects an individual's attention. If individuals deem incoming material worthy of long-term recall, they will analyse it differently from material they judge relatively unimportant. Whether the stimulus is processed at a shallow or a deeper level depends on the nature of the stimulus, i.e. the exercise type, or the time available for processing, but also on the subject's own motivation, attitudes, feelings, goals, and knowledge base. The operations performed during input thus determine the fate of the incoming information.

## Exercise types and grading in language learning

In foreign language teaching a large battery of exercise types has been developed over the years. In accord with developments in the concept of foreign language competence, the preference for particular exercise types evolved. Thus, pattern drill exercises and substitution tables can be said to have been characteristic of the **AUDIOLINGUAL** approach to language teaching, translations of the **GRAMMAR–TRANSLATION METHOD**, and exercise types geared towards the acquisition of the so-called four **SKILLS – LISTENING, SPEAKING, READING** and **WRITING** – of the **COMMUNICATIVE** approach to language teaching.

Exercise types can be classified according to a number of perspectives.

- First, it is possible to order them on the basis of their formal characteristics and, thus, to distinguish types, such as multiple choice, matching, classification, substitution, completion, transformation, etc., exercises.
- Content is a second principle according to which exercise types can be classified. Whereas with some exercise types the focus is on **PRONUNCIATION, GRAMMAR** or **VOCABULARY**, with others the focus will be on activating, consolidating or improving learners' listening, speaking, reading or writing skills. Still other exercise types may be classified as aiming at the learners' acquisition of independent learning skills, **INTERCULTURAL COMPETENCE** or compensation strategies, classifications which are still under development.
- A third perspective attempts to classify exercise types on the reception–reproductive–productive scale.
- A fourth one distinguishes between exercises that typically aim at either accuracy or fluency in language production.

It may be possible to apply still other criteria to classifying exercise types in use in foreign language teaching. It is important to realise that none of the criteria should be used in isolation. Whereas in some cases gap filling or completion may be considered reproductive exercise types, in other cases they have to be considered productive. Similarly, whereas, on the whole, the teaching of grammar, pronunciation or vocabulary can be considered to be accuracy-oriented, since it is interested in getting learners to construct their sentences in a way that sounds acceptable, in producing language that sounds right or in using appropriate words to express meaning, some vocabulary or grammar exercises may lead into exercises that aim at improving fluency. Vice versa, listening and reading exercises may be used for learning accuracy, and for the acquisition of grammar or vocabulary. Although with most classroom procedures a clear orientation one way or another is evident, a lack of awareness of the orientation of exercise types can lead to confusion and inefficient learning.

## Related issues

When intelligently used in the way described above, exercise typologies can be used as a basis for designing either tests or courses, or for evaluating course materials and **TEXTBOOKS**. Their degree of explicitness allows them to be used as a basis for these, highlighting which test types are better suited for testing fluency, which for accuracy, which for writing skills or which for the ability to reproduce lexical or grammatical items.

**See also:** Acquisition and teaching; Assessment and testing; Psychology; Questioning techniques; Syllabus and curriculum design; Text types and grading; Textbooks

## References

Ausubel, D. (1977) 'The facilitation of meaningful verbal learning in the classroom', *Educational Psychologist* 12: 162–78.

Ausubel, D., Novak, J. and Hanesian, H. (1978) *Educational psychology: a cognitive view*, New York: Holt, Rinehart and Winston.

Bloom, B.S., Engelhart, M.D., Furst, E.J. and Lavallée, M. (1956) *Taxonomy of educational objectives, the classification of educational goals. Handbook I: Cognitive domain*, New York: Longman.

Craik, F.I. and Lockhart, R.S. (1972) 'Levels of processing: a framework for memory research', *Journal of Verbal Learning and Verbal Behavior* 11: 671–84.

De Corte, E. (1973) *Onderwijsdoelstellingen: Bijdragen tot de didaxologische theorievorming en aanzetten voor het empirisch onderzoek over onderwijsdoelen (Educational objectives: contributions to the formation of a didaxological theory and impetuses for empirical research on educational objectives)*, Leuven: Leuven Universitaire Pers.

De Corte, E., Geerligs, C.T. and Lagerweij, N.A.J. (1981) *Beknopte didaxologie (Concise didaxology)* 5th rev. edn, Groningen: Wolters-Noordhoff.

Guilford, J.P. and Meeker, M.N. (1969) *The structure of intellect. Its interpretation and uses*, Columbus: Merrill.

## Further reading

Candlin, C. and Edelhoff, C. (1983) *The communicative teaching of English: principles and an exercise typology*, London: Longman.

Neuner, G., Krüger, M. and Grewer, U. (1985) *Übungstypologie zum kommunikativen Deutschunterricht*, Berlin: Langenscheidt.

Sheils, J. (1988) *Communication in the modern languages classroom*, Strasbourg: Council of Europe.

van Ek, J.A. (1990) *The threshold level in a European unit-credit system for modern language learning by adults*, Strasbourg: Council of Europe.

LIES SERCU

# F

## FIPLV – Fédération Internationale des Professeurs de Langues Vivantes

The World Federation of Language Teachers (FIPLV), founded in Paris in 1931, is the only international multilingual association of teachers of living languages. It has Non-governmental Organisation (NGO) and operational relations status with UNESCO.

Important among its many aims is the promotion of the teaching and learning of living languages in order to facilitate and improve communication, understanding, cooperation and friendly relations between all peoples of the world. Members of FIPLV include international monolingual associations, federations of language teachers and national multilingual associations. FIPLV organises a world congress every three years and produces three issues of the journal, *FIPLV World News*, each year.

The supreme authority of FIPLV is the World Assembly, which brings together the representatives of member associations every three years. The World Council meets annually, and the Executive Committee of the Federation meets biannually.

As a Non-governmental Organisation (NGO), FIPLV is frequently consulted by UNESCO and, in association with UNESCO, actively participates in initiatives of the International Linguapax Committee on the theme of the contribution of language teaching to Peace.

### Website

The federation's website is: http://www.fiplv.org

DENIS CUNNINGHAM

## Flashcard

A flashcard is a visual aid consisting of a piece of card or paper with a picture on one or both sides. The picture is usually of one object, and the card is used above all for the introduction, learning and recall of **VOCABULARY** items. In the simplest use, the card is held up by the teacher, for pupils to see, and accompanied by a question, the answer to which involves the item on the card. There are many variations, for example hiding or only partially revealing the card and guessing at the item, pupils manipulating cards themselves, using a number of cards to establish a sequence of actions, and so on.

The use of pictures is significant in the **AUDIO-VISUAL** method where they form part of a connected series to contextualise and explain a text, but flashcards usually function independently of each other. They have their origins in **COMENIUS**'s seventeenth-century book of pictures and names of 'all the chief things that are in the world', but the modern development of the use of pictures began in the late nineteenth century.

**See also:** Board drawing; Materials and media; Video; Visual aids

## Further reading

Bowen, B.M. (1992) *Look here! Visual aids in language teaching*, London: Macmillan.

Schilder, H. (1977) *Medien im neusprachlichen Unterricht seit 1880* (Media in modern language teaching since 1880), Frankfurt: Kronberg.

MICHAEL BYRAM

# Fossilisation

Fossilisation is the term used to describe incomplete language learning. This is identified by certain features of the learner's language being different from the speech of the target population, marking the point when progress in that aspect of the target language stops and the learner's language becomes fixed at an intermediate state. This is considered to occur because the learner's internalised rule system differs from that of the target system. Fossilisation can take a number of forms, such as fossilised accent or syntax, in which case it might approximate to pidginisation. Fossilisation would normally be judged in comparison with **NATIVE SPEAKER SKILLS** and would be seen as a permanent feature of the learner's language, although some authorities (Brown, 1980) describe it as 'relatively permanent'.

Second and foreign language learning, in clear contrast to first language learning, can generally be characterised by a lack of success, with few learners achieving complete mastery. The dynamics of language learning mean that the **INTERLANGUAGE** of the learner constantly needs to change as new **VOCABULARY** and structures are encountered and absorbed. Language development is marked by the learner's language becoming steadily more complex and sophisticated. However, the general lack of success of second and foreign language learners would lead us to anticipate that there is likely to be a point when this progress comes to a halt and learning stops. It is this point which is characterised as fossilisation.

Fossilisation is identified by comparing the learner's interlanguage to target language norms. In this way it is possible to identify language structures which differ from native speech. For example the learner may generalise past tense endings in English to include all verbs, and therefore come up with 'buyed' instead of bought. Such examples may well occur, too, in first language development, but the fact that here it is a transitional stage in their learning process, before correct forms are acquired, points to how the interlanguage of second and foreign language differs by being susceptible to fossilisation.

The **METAPHOR** of fossilisation clearly suggests the permanence of the process. We have seen that linguistically such features should represent only a temporary and intermediate stage in the language learning process, as they do in first language learning. If fossilisation is a permanent process, why and when does it occur? For the language teacher and learner these questions clearly have considerable importance. We would want to know what has to be done to try and avoid a process which, because it is linked to the general failure of learners to achieve native speaker competency, has wide implications.

The fossilisation theory is associated with Selinker and his work on interlanguage (Selinker, 1972). He identified five central processes associated with fossilisation: language **TRANSFER**, transfer of training, **STRATEGIES** of second language learning, strategies of second language communication, and overgeneralisation of target language material. For Selinker the 'combination of these processes produce what we might term entirely fossilised IL [interlanguage] competence' (Selinker *et al.*, 1975). Language development has therefore stopped.

Although initially fossilisation was identified with **ADULT** second language learning (Selinker, 1972), it was extended, as McLaughlin emphasises, to include child second-language performance, with the proviso that this took place 'when the second-language was acquired after the first language and when it occurs in the absence of native-speaking peers of the target language,' (Selinker *et al.*, 1975; McLaughlin, 1987).

Selinker, in his study of 7-year-olds in a French immersion programme in **CANADA**, found similar patterns of fossilisation as for adults. He identified three areas of error in the children's speech patterns, which were associated with the strategies pupils adopted in order to communicate effectively. These were: language transfer, overgeneralisation of target language rules, and simplification. So, an example of language transfer showing lexical confusion would be: *'Des temps'* (sometimes), of overgeneralisation: 'il a *couré* (he ran, instead of *couru*), of past tense endings, and the use of the infinitive for all tense forms demonstrated simplification (quoted by McLaughlin, 1987).

Ellis (1994) examined possible reasons for fossilisation and found no single cause, with both internal and external factors having an effect. Among the internal factors considered by him are: the **AGE** of the learner and the lack of desire for **ACCULTURATION**. For external factors he lists lack of learning opportunity, communicative pressure and the nature of the feedback available to the learner. Ellis suggested that there is a need to analyse the relative importance of these different factors and how they interact, but that we are still unable to do so. He also pointed to the fact that, with the exception of transfer, none of the other processes listed by Selinker as marking the cognitive dimension of fossilisation have been taken up by theorists.

Fossilisation is generally seen as a negative trait in foreign language learning, but, for Stevick: 'people acquire as much of a language as they really need for what they really want' (Stevick, 1988). This places a rather different emphasis on the concept by analysing the learner's **NEEDS** rather than the nature of their performance and how well it approximates to native speaker norms. Provided communication can take place satisfactorily, it may be relatively unimportant to the learner that they have a foreign accent or make some grammatical errors. This ability to communicate satisfactorily with reduced grammatical structure and vocabulary is illustrated by **PIDGIN** languages. Pidginisation is seen by Schumann to approximate fossilisation (1976). He points to the evidence suggesting that pidginisation might characterise all second language learning and that under certain conditions of social and psychological distance it persists; i.e. learning stops and fossilisation sets in.

The critical issue is at what point fossilisation occurs. While not requiring perfect mastery of the target language, which is achieved according to Selinker (1972) by only 5 per cent of learners, it is necessary to achieve a level of learning which enables adequate communication to take place.

We can see that, for the adult learner who has already spent a number of years using the second language in the target country, fossilisation would be likely to occur once an acceptable level of language skills, related to specific individual needs, had been achieved. This might be less evident for the child learner. The fact that Selinker has specifically included children's foreign language learning in the fossilisation process raises a number of interesting points in terms of the permanence of the phenomenon. Here, a change in linguistic environment or increased **MOTIVATION** might well lead to elements of language which had previously been fixed at an intermediate stage becoming fully acquired. In this situation, because the process is not permanent, fossilisation would be an unsuitable description. For language material which became reactivated following a stagnant period, 'dormancy' might be a more accurate description, with for example vocabulary dormancy referring to words which were only partially known becoming fully acquired. In this situation, learning has not stopped but is temporarily suspended unless, or until, there is a significant change in the linguistic environment.

The permanency of fossilisation has also now been questioned by Selinker (1992) who modifies 'the definition of fossilisation to an empirically more manageable concept of plateaus in L2 learning rather than cessation of learning.' He considers that 'it is impossible to show that a given individual has stopped learning'.

Fossilisation matches some of the characteristics of the acculturation, pidginisation theory of Schumann (1976). Both theories are concerned with incomplete language learning. Fossilisation, however, includes instructed language learning, while the acculturation, pidginisation theory is associated with natural language learning. However, the two theories are interconnected because we have seen that acculturation is described as a factor in fossilisation and the process of pidginisation has been identified by McLaughlin (1987) as the point at which 'the learner's development fossilises'.

Fossilisation is a recognised feature of second and foreign language learning. It is to be hoped that research will provide us with indications of how fossilisation can be avoided and the dynamic process of language development maintained.

However, for McLaughlin, the interlanguage theory and therefore fossilisation has had 'a relatively minor impact on pedagogy. Researchers have been primarily interested in describing learners' systems and little attention has been given to pedagogical concerns' (McLaughlin, 1987).

**See also:** Acculturation; Interlanguage; Learning styles; Pidgins; Psychology; Second language acquisition theories; Universal grammar; Untutored language acquisition

### References

Brown, H. (1980) *Principles of language learning and teaching*, Englewood Cliffs, NJ: Prentice Hall.

Ellis, R. (1994) *The study of second language acquisition*, Oxford: Oxford University Press.

Gass, S. and Selinker, L. (eds) (1993) *Language transfer in language learning*, Philadelphia: Benjamin.

McLaughlin, B. (1987) *Theories of second language learning*, London: Arnold.

Selinker, L. (1972) 'Interlanguage', *International Review of Applied Linguistics* X, 209–30.

Selinker, L. (1992) *Rediscovering interlanguage*, London: Longman.

Selinker, L. and Lakshmanan, U. (1993) 'Language transfer and fossilization: the multiple effects principle', in S. Gass and L. Selinker (eds), *Language transfer in language learning*, Philadelphia: Benjamin.

Selinker, L., Swain, M. and Dumas, G. (1975) 'The interlanguage hypothesis extended to children', *Language Learning* 25: 139–91.

Schumann, J. (1976) 'Second language acquisition: the pidginisation hypothesis', *Language Learning* 26: 391–408.

Stevick, E. (1988) *Teaching and learning languages*, Cambridge: Cambridge University Press.

JOHN DANIELS

# France

The situation for foreign language teaching in French secondary education appears to be much better than in other European countries, with, in principle, a wide range of languages on offer (approximately fifteen) and with a significant quantitative dissemination. Almost all students learn a first foreign language, 75 per cent a second and about 10 per cent a third. However, in practice there is a tendency which began in the 1990s towards 'all English' in the first foreign language, 'all Spanish' in the second and the reduction of the third. There are thus two paradoxical phenomena of interest: the increase in the number of students learning two foreign languages and, at the same time, the regression of 'linguistic diversity', i.e. the number of students learning different languages.

This negative evolution is the result of the absence of a proper national languages policy, whose objective would have to be the maintenance of linguistic diversity. There are three reasons for this. First, this linguistic diversity represents cultural wealth – and it would be unreasonable to allow the layers of competence in **ARABIC** and **PORTUGUESE** resulting from immigration to perish. Second, the languages learnt in a country inevitably reflect in part its political priorities and its economic realities – and it would be unreasonable to do nothing about the catastrophic reduction in students learning **GERMAN** as a first or second foreign language. Third, the diversity of languages learnt by citizens is one of the conditions of the future adaptation of their country to the largely unpredictable changes of the international environment – and it would be unreasonable to let the teaching of Russian regress or to maintain the teaching of Japanese and Chinese at a minimal level. Since language is an essential dimension of human life and the mastery of languages a vital factor, ecological concepts ought to be applied immediately to the linguistic policy of every country, and every modern nation ought to consider the protection and the management of its linguistic 'bio-diversity' as essential factors.

In the absence of a collectively defined and accepted linguistic policy, the fate of languages depends on the power relationships between different players, as a consequence of the different strategies they are obliged to use.

## Administrative strategies

The strategy of heads of educational institutions, upper and lower secondary, depends on two characteristics of languages as a subject. First, it is the subject which involves most individual options for students – three languages can be chosen at three different levels (first, second, third language) – and thus it creates the most organisational problems. One of the dominant strategies of heads of institutions is therefore, as a sound principle of administrative simplification, to reduce as much as possible the number of languages offered. Second, it is the subject which best allows one school to differentiate itself from another and/or to differentiate certain classes from others. It is thus an instrument for administrative strategies of attracting and keeping 'good students' and putting them in 'good classes'. Many heads of institutions thus use their margin of **AUTONOMY** to create courses likely to attract parents who have chosen the 'excellence' strategy (see below). This means offering languages which are prestigious and have the reputation of being difficult (Chinese, Japanese, etc.); unusual combinations of languages (including ancient languages such as Latin and Greek); special courses, for example with a second language from the beginning of secondary school; extra lessons, or even 'European classes' in which a language is used as the **MEDIUM OF INSTRUCTION**. On the other hand there are heads who manage to suppress the teaching of Arabic, probably because they think it gives their school a negative image in the eyes of parents.

These two administrative strategies can in theory be contradictory, but they co-exist without many problems in practice because they come from the same reasoning, which is not quantitative (how many languages are offered) but qualitative (which languages, with which courses).

## Parental strategies

Some parents adopt for their children an 'excellence' strategy, choosing languages less widely taught or considered difficult. This implies, on their part, a certain confidence in the ability of their child to be placed among the best or – perhaps more reasonably – a confidence in the beneficial effects for their child of being in a good learning environment, being with children from the same socially advantaged classes, and from a good teaching environment, the best teachers tending to choose the best classes.

However, the fact that the tendency in France is towards the rapid reduction of linguistic diversity is due to the most powerful strategy in the absence of a proper national languages policy, being a parental strategy which can be called 'safe', and which has the greatest effects. This means **ENGLISH** as first foreign language and **SPANISH** as second. None the less there are many other minority strategies in France which a true policy of managing 'linguistic biodiversity' could develop. In addition to the 'excellence' strategy mentioned above, there is the 'proximity' strategy, choosing the language of neighbours across the border (Dutch, German, Italian, Spanish), the 'culture of origin' strategy (either external, such as Arabic, Berber, Portuguese, Polish, Hebrew, Chinese, etc., or internal to France such as Breton, Basque, Occitan), a 'pre-professional' strategy (which can lead to a number of different languages in addition to English), a 'difference' strategy (a less widely taught language), or even a 'preference' strategy (a language chosen simply because it is interesting).

## Professional strategies

Strategies common to teachers, **MATERIALS** writers and inspectors are essentially defined in terms of the struggle of one language against the others in the educational 'marketplace' for languages. Until the 1960s in France, language teaching was characterised by very different tendencies, depending on functional, educational and pedagogic conceptions which were different and, sometimes, opposed to each other. These were, however, present in each language, and there were for example at that time **TEXTBOOKS** which were traditional, direct-method, or eclectic, and in German, English, Spanish and Italian. In the 1960s, the appearance of the **AUDIO-VISUAL** method provoked in lower secondary school language teaching the differentiation in the three main **OBJECTIVES** of language teaching (linguistic, cultural and educational) among the three main languages taught, English, German and Spanish.

The Anglicists adopted the new audio-visual method because it is well adapted to what they rightly considered the main characteristic of English at the time, i.e. English as the language of (international) communication. This is the same reason as for their adoption of the notional-functional approach in the 1980s.

The Germanists also adopted the new method because they were competing with English for being the first foreign language, whilst none the less maintaining paradoxically a very 'grammatical' tradition because it corresponds to their specific characteristic, i.e. the language chosen as first language by or for the best students because it has the reputation of being difficult.

The Hispanists, who are not in a position to compete with English and therefore play the second language card, did not choose the strategy of competition but that of being special. They therefore 'specialised' in the only characteristic still remaining in terms of the fundamental objectives of language teaching, i.e. culture. This is the reason why, in the official curricular guidelines for Spanish and in the textbooks for Spanish in the 1970s, there was the spread of the 'literature' option, and the LITERARY TEXT became from that time the main basis for teaching Spanish from the very beginning.

This positioning in terms of objectives led to bizarre effects in terms of contents and methods. The Anglicists sacrificed the cultural content to the teaching of language for everyday communication, just as the Hispanists sacrificed the teaching of language for everyday communication to rich and specific cultural content.

## Current developments

If the reduction of linguistic diversity continues, it is probable that the linguistic debate in France will be less about the languages taught and more and more about the courses taught. The current options under debate are very diverse: early language learning (from primary school); the personalisation of courses (each student deciding at what moment they will seek certification of the different levels defined for the language); modularisation of courses (with some more and some less intensive periods of learning, for certain years or periods of a year); the diversification of objectives

(some languages, for example, would be taught/learnt for comprehension purposes only); the specialisation of contents (adapted to the different orientations of the students: literary, scientific, economic, sociological, technological, etc.); the use of the language as medium, which can be internal to the education system (using the language as medium for another subject) or external (exhibitions, educational visits, correspondence, etc.); the diversification of approaches in comparison to the traditional collective, frontal teaching (**GROUP WORK**, project work, individualised learning, semi-autonomous learning in a resource centre, etc.); differentiation (variation of objectives, approaches, contents, learning aids, helpers, methods and intensity of teaching offered to each student according to their habits, or their learning profile, as a function of their level of proficiency, of their motivation, their interests, their objectives, their **NEEDS** and abilities); the consideration of the **INTERLANGUAGE** factor (work with students on transversal issues across all languages – for example, study skills, comparison of **TEACHER METHODS** and methods of learning, etc.).

**See also:** *Alliance française*; Attitudes and language learning; CRÉDIF; French; Language planning; Motivation; Planning for foreign language teaching; United States of America; Untutored language acquisition

## Further reading

Ager, D.E. (1997) *Language, community and the state*, Exeter: Intellect Books.

Ager, D.E. (1999) *Identity, insecurity and image. France and language*, Clevedon: Multilingual Matters.

Corson, D. (1990) *Language policy across the curriculum*, Clevedon: Multilingual Matters.

Herreras, J.C. (ed.) (1998) *L'enseignement des langues étrangères dans les pays de l'Union Européenne*, Louvain-la-Neuve: Peeters.

Marshall, D.F. (ed.) (1991) *Language planning*, Amsterdam: Benjamin.

Spolsky, B. (ed.) (1986) *Language and education in multilingual settings*, San Diego, CA: College-Hill Press.

Wodak, R. and Corson, D. (1997) *Language policy and political issues in education*, Dordrecht: Kluwer.

CHRISTIAN PUREN

# *Fremdsprachendidaktik*

*Fremdsprachendidaktik* (FD) is a term traditionally used in universities of German-speaking countries to refer to the scientific discipline that deals with foreign language learning and teaching in the context of instruction. In so far as foreign language learning is not exclusively restricted to this context, FD is also concerned with informal language learning.

The role of informal education has become more important as learners have become exposed to a greater amount and different types of foreign language input in the electronic media. In addition, in an increasing number of schools a language other than the native language is used as the **MEDIUM OF INSTRUCTION** in various school subjects. Such developments in formal education modify the predominant pattern of foreign language instruction and ultimately have an impact on FD. Such educational changes have broadened the scope of FD as a scientific discipline. It increasingly covers aspects of informal language **ACQUISITION**, in addition to foreign and second language learning and teaching (see Timm and Vollmer, 1993).

The specific selection of languages FD is concerned with is closely related to the kinds of foreign language that are taught in the primary, secondary and **VOCATIONAL** schools of a country or in various other institutions of **ADULT** education. In line with this emphasis on language learning in formal education, FD is divided into language-related fields of study such as the teaching and learning of English/**FRENCH**/**GERMAN**/Russian/**SPANISH**, etc. as a foreign language. In certain regions the languages of neighbouring countries, e.g. Dutch along the border between The Netherlands and Germany, can play a role in FD. Furthermore, immigrant languages, particularly the Mediterranean ones, may also become part of the school curriculum. Inevitably, such developments in formal education tend to affect the choice of languages dealt with in FD.

In the structure of the university FD is a fairly new scientific discipline. It has its roots, on the one hand, in pedagogy (including sociology) and learning **PSYCHOLOGY**, and, on the other hand, in the departments of modern languages that developed in German universities in the second half of the nineteenth century. FD was first established as an academic discipline in colleges of education in Germany after World War Two, when foreign language learning became an obligatory subject – mainly English – in almost all types of secondary school. Later, in the 1970s and 1980s, the demand for more professional teachers became a public issue and, as a result, most of the colleges of education were integrated into the universities in order to increase the academic standards of the teaching profession and especially to provide a greater range of job-related skills. In the course of these changes, FD became a firmly established scientific discipline, either in the language departments or the faculties of education in most universities with a tradition in **TEACHER EDUCATION**. At more or less the same time *Fremdsprachen-lehr- und -lernforschung* was developed in some universities in Germany to take the place of FD and, in addition, **APPLIED LINGUISTICS** was introduced so as to improve the practical relevance of linguistics for the language teaching profession.

Looking at the historical origin of FD, it becomes clear why different study and research domains are indispensable components of the subject of this scientific discipline. The pedagogical, psychological and sociological traditions are reflected in all the research projects that focus on the process of foreign language learning and the learner, on the teaching process and the role of the teacher and, above all, on the social context of language learning. Furthermore, there is a connection between FD and linguistics, especially in areas such as psycholinguistics and **SECOND LANGUAGE ACQUISITION** research, because the investigation of the mental processes involved is relevant to a deeper understanding of the network of factors that have an impact on the language learning process. Moreover, firm links with the study of literature and culture can be detected in all research where processes of textual comprehension and (inter-) cultural understanding are analysed. These relationships with pedagogical, psychological, sociological, linguistic, literary and cultural disciplines are characteristic of the interdisciplinary approach that is typical of FD as a scientific discipline (see Doyé, Heuermann and Zimmermann, 1988).

The **RESEARCH METHODS** used in FD match its range of research interests and objectives. The actual choice of a research method and design depends on the specific research objective and the subject that is to be investigated or analysed (see Geisler, 1987). The historical record shows a development here. In the early days of FD, hardly any real research was done. Although the publications written for teachers in the first half of the twentieth century mostly dealt with methodological questions, the recommendations that were given were only based on the personal experience of individual teachers or on sketchy information and unsystematic observation. As FD became a scientific discipline, this situation gradually changed. However, rapid changes in the general pattern of research eventually took place when proponents of the new discipline of **SPRACHLEHR- UND -LERN-FORSCHUNG** criticised empirical research projects done in FD on the grounds of insufficient quantity and poor quality (see Bausch, Christ and Krumm, 1995: 11). This criticism also coincided with a shift in the dominant research paradigm in the neighbouring sciences of empirical pedagogy, learning psychology, and applied linguistics. The focus of research in FD consequently moved from a **TEACHER METHODS** approach to an investigation of the learning and acquisition processes of the foreign language learner, while the teacher's role was defined relative to the foreign language learning and acquisition processes. Research methods reflected these changes. Since then, numerous research projects have investigated the complex network of factors involved in foreign language learning and teaching. The research methods of the social sciences, including both qualitative and quantitative designs, have been employed in this research. Recently qualitative research based on thinking aloud procedures, the **WRITING** of personal diaries, and systematic interviews has given greater weight to an analysis of internal processes (see Zimmermann and Plessner, 1998). This more diversified range of methods has become an essential element of empirical research in FD.

The firm relationship that exists between FD and the study of literature and culture explains why the research tradition of the humanities is also a characteristic feature of research in FD, especially in studies that deal with texts and the processes involved in communication. Older traditions in **LITERARY** studies and FD emphasise the importance of the structural aspects of texts. Accordingly, it is the role of FD to show how texts have to be analysed. FD has been regarded as a discipline that applies the findings of literary studies and develops a methodology of teaching literature. This concept of FD is no longer acceptable, because a new research paradigm has emerged that stresses the importance of the reader, who is now considered to be the centre of the process of interpretation. The reader makes sense of a text by constructing meaning. This focus on the reader has triggered off a great number of studies in FD that highlight the processes of meaning construction. At this point the hermeneutic research tradition of the humanities and the empirical research methods typical of the social sciences can be combined so as to analyse these processes of meaning construction more deeply and from different angles.

The future of FD as a scientific discipline will largely depend on the quality, scope and social relevance of its research. Moreover, research in FD has to be concerned with questions that are of importance to teachers and, more generally, to people who are interested in processes of instruction. In the past, studies such as the analysis and **EVALUATION** of **TEXTBOOKS** and the development of **SYLLABUSES** have been such relevant projects. It is now one of the central tasks of research in FD to find out to what extent and how foreign language learning processes can be supported rather than determined by textbooks, syllabuses and courses specially designed for learners. Furthermore, it is an essential aim to investigate the conditions and the learning processes that either facilitate or obstruct processes that are involved in understanding elements of a foreign culture.

**See also:** *Didactique des langues*; Goethe-Institut; *Handlungsorientierter Unterricht*; Research methods; *Sprachlehrforschung*; Teaching methods

# References

Bausch, K.-R., Christ, H. and Krumm, H.J. (eds) (1995) *Handbuch Fremdsprachenunterricht (Handbook on teaching foreign languages)*, Tübingen: Francke; (3rd edn 1991).

Doyé, P., Heuermann, H. and Zimmerman, G. (eds) (1988) *Die Beziehung der Fremdsprachendidaktik zu ihren Referenzwissenschaften (The relationship between 'Fremdsprachendidaktik' and related academic disciplines)*, Tübingen: Gunter Narr.

Geisler, W. (1987) *Die anglistische Fachdidaktik als Unterrichtswissenschaft*, Frankfurt a.M: Peter Lang.

Timm, J.-P. and Vollmer, H.J. (1993) 'Fremdsprachenforschung: Zur Konzeption und Perspektive eines Wissenschaftsbereichs (FL research: concepts and perspectives of an academic discipline)', *Zeitschrift für Fremdsprachenforschung* 4, 1: 1–47.

Zimmerman, G. and Plessner, H. (1998) 'Zum Zusammenhang von Lernstrategien, Wissensrepräsentationen und Leistungen beim Lernen mit Instruktionstexten im Fremdsprachenunterricht (The connection between learning strategies, knowledge representations and achievement when learning with didactic texts in an FL class)', *Zeitschrift für Fremdsprachenforschung* 9, 2: 265–90.

# Further reading

Hellwig, K.-H. and Keck, R.W. (1988) *Englisch-Didaktik zwischen Fachwissenschaft und Allgemeiner Didaktik (EFL teaching and learning – academic discipline or pedagogy?)*, Schriftenreihe aus dem Fachbereich Erziehungswissenschaften I der Universität Hannover, Band 18.

Henrici, G. and Riemer, C. (eds) (1996) *Einführung in die Didaktik des Unterrichts Deutsch als Fremdsprache (Introduction to the teaching and learning of German as a Foreign Language)*, Band 1. u. 2, Baltmannsweiler: Schneider-Verl. Hohengehren.

Jarfe, G. (1997) *Literaturdidaktik – konkret (Teaching literature – concrete)*, Heidelberg: C. Winter.

Stern, H.H. (1983) *Fundamental concepts of language teaching*, Oxford: Oxford University Press.

Timm, J.-H. (ed.) (1998) *Englisch lernen und lehren (Learning and teaching English)*, Berlin: Cornelsen.

Wendt, M. and Zydatiß, W. (eds.) (1997) *Fremdsprachliches Handeln im Spannungsfeld von Prozeß und Inhalt (Using a foreign language – focus on process and content)*, Bochum: Brockmeyer.

GÜNTER NOLD

# French

Although the designation *Français Langue Étrangère* (French as a Foreign Language) appeared in **FRANCE** in the 1960s, it was in the 1970s to 1990s that it became established at the national and international level with the widespread use of the acronym 'FLE'. This domain is different from that of French as a Second Language, which describes 'everything which was associated at different points in time with the dissemination policies and with the teaching of the French language in the French colonial empire, and in this sense is related to a historical complex of issues which are fundamentally different from those of FLE' (Vigner, 1998: 181; our translation). FLE has developed, together with teacher training and the dissemination of French abroad, since the end of World War Two, under the aegis of two French ministries: the Ministry of National Education (MEN) and the Ministry of Foreign Affairs (MAE). In order to understand the process of the institutionalisation of FLE it is therefore necessary to understand the cultural and linguistic policies of France abroad, and the way in which, after 1945, the MAE and the MEN established their roles as managers of the domain. Since it is linked into an interdependent world, this management has been closely related since 1992 both to the European policy of intercultural openness and of promoting plurilingualism, and to the values of the francophone world (*la Francophonie*). FLE is now attempting to adjust to its new role of being simultaneously 'a dimension of the Francophone world' (Coste, 1998: 75) and one of the guarantors of plurilingualism.

Following World War Two, French language and culture, until then closely linked as far as teaching is concerned, began a process of dissociation. French as a language was able less and less to depend on the dissemination of French culture abroad. On the other hand, new **OBJECTIVES** were set for French language activity in the post-war period. In order to attain these, the MAE gradually developed a foreign cultural programme thanks to its Department of Cultural, Scientific and Technical Relations (DGRCST), whose purpose was to support French as a means of access to knowledge and professional training by sustaining the teaching and dissemination of French within foreign structures: education systems, radio, television, etc. This policy of linguistic, educational and university cooperation involved 35 million learners and 250,000 teachers of FLE throughout the world. The MAE programmes were put into operation by 300 cultural and linguistic attachés and 600 teachers. The DGRCST was responsible for 133 Cultural Centres and Institutes, a thousand **ALLIANCE FRANÇAISE** committees (employing about 5,000 teachers), 255 secondary and primary schools, and used a media network whose principal operators were Radio France International, TV5 and Canal France International.

Two priorities, one quantitative and one qualitative, thus contributed to the progressive institutionalisation of FLE: the diversification of learner groups, and support for pre- and in-service training of teachers. Thus, in 1951, the MEN created the Centre for the Study of Elementary French so that it could carry out research on the linguistic elements necessary for communication in contemporary French. This had the aim of facilitating the widespread learning of *LE FRANÇAIS FONDAMENTAL* in developing countries. The results of the research helped in the development of the first **AUDIOVISUAL** method designed at the centre, which became in 1958 the **CRÉDIF**. The second priority was qualitative. It was necessary to modernise the practices of teachers of French. Two organisations in Paris played a crucial role in the production and publication of pedagogical **MATERIALS** used in the training of teachers: the CRÉDIF and, from 1959, the BEL (Bureau d'Etude et de Liaison) first headed by Guy Capelle before it became the BELC (later part of **CIEP**). Although FLE was first established in these two public bodies, there then came in 1961 the Centre de Linguistique Appliquée created at the University of Besançon by Bernard Quemada, the Centre de Didactique des Langues created in 1975 by Louise and Michel Dabène at the University of Grenoble, then the

CAVILAM in Vichy, the CRAPEL in Nancy, and so on.

The creation of the FLE sector also benefited from the energy of the publishers. Thus the publishers Hachette-Larousse began the journal *Le Français dans le Monde* in 1961, and the *Dictionnaire de Didactique des Langues* in 1976, in a series of **REFERENCE WORKS** begun in 1973 by André Reboullet. Other series of a similar kind began in 1976 and 1980: *Didactique des langues Étrangères* edited by Robert Galisson at Nathan-Clé International and *Langues et Apprentissages des Langues* founded by Daniel Coste and Henri Besse at Hatier.

The domain also developed through national associations (ANEFLE: Association nationale des Enseignants de Français Langue Étrangère in 1981, ASDIFLE: Association de Didactique du FLE in 1985), and through international associations. Thus in 1961 the AUPELF (Association des Universités Partiellement ou Entièrement Francophones) was created in Montreal. When in 1986 the first summit of Heads of States and Government of francophone countries prepared a programme for a scientific francophone world, the AUPELF adopted a plan to create the Université des Réseaux d'expression française. This became the AUPELF-UREF in 1990 and presided over the committee on **HIGHER EDUCATION** and research of the standing conference of the francophone world. There is also at the international level the FIPF (Fédération Internationale des Professeurs de Français) created in 1969.

Finally, at the beginning of the 1980s, work on the recent history of the domain led to the creation in 1987 of the Société Internationale pour l'Histoire du Français Langue Étrangère ou Seconde (SIHFLES). At the beginning of the 1980s the institutionalisation of FLE was complete in France. In fact, the Department of International Relations of the Ministry of National Education formed a commission whose work led to two proposals: the creation of national diplomas for French (the elementary diploma and the advanced diploma in French language: the DELF and the DALF), and the creation of university courses for FLE at first degree and Master's level. These courses have been popular with students, who continue to see work opportunities following them.

Since 1975, the work of the **COUNCIL OF EUROPE** has taken into consideration the problems of the learning of French as a foreign language by immigrant workers (Gardin, 1976). After the development of the **THRESHOLD LEVEL** in French (le Niveau Seuil), these problems were at the centre of research on **UNTUTORED LANGUAGE ACQUISITION**. In the educational context, these issues pose a crucial question for the school, that of its role with respect to the children of migrants. Opportunities for 'translation, mediation, interpretation' should help these children to make links between the languages and cultures of their parents and the language and culture of the host society (Mesmin, 1993: 142). So this theme of mediation between several languages and cultures is used to define a positive role for the school in an international context. In this context the school should promote plurilingual and pluricultural competencies, and these competencies are beginning to be defined. Thus, for the authors of *Plurilingual and Pluricultural Competence* (Coste, Moore and Zarate, 1997) 'to speak about plurilingual and pluricultural competence is to focus on the communication competence of social actors able to operate in different languages and cultures, to play the roles of intermediaries, of linguistic and cultural mediators, able too to manage and develop this plural competence in their course of their personal development' (Coste *et al.*, 1997: 9).

Thus it is possible to see how FLE at the turn of the century integrates European and francophone world issues, focuses on the understanding of complex competencies which have to be acquired in life-long learning, and is resolutely interdisciplinary.

**See also:** Africa; CRÉDIF; *Didactique des langues*; France; Languages for specific purposes; Linguistic imperialism; *Linguistique appliquée*; Spanish

### References

Coste, D. (ed.) (1984) *Aspects d'une politique de diffusion du français langue étrangère depuis 1945*, Paris: Hatier.

Coste, D. (1998) '1940 à nos jours: consolidations et ajustements', in W. Frijhoff and A. Reboullet (eds), *Histoire de la diffusion et de l'enseignement du français dans le monde, Le français dans le monde, Recherches et applications*, Paris: Hachette.

Coste, D., Moore, D. and Zarate, G. (1998) 'Compétence plurilingue et pluriculturelle', *Apprentissage et usage des langues dans le cadre européen, Le français dans le monde, Recherches et applications*, Paris: Hachette.

Gardin, B. (ed.) (1976) *L'apprentissage du français langue étrangère par les travailleurs immigrés, Langue Française no 29*, Paris: Larousse.

Mesmin, C. (1993) *Les enfants de migrants à l'école. Réussite, échec*, Paris: La pensée sauvage.

Vigner, G. (1998) 'Le français des colonies et des indépendances : pour une histoire du français langue seconde', in W. Frijhoff and A. Reboullet (eds, *Histoire de la diffusion et de l'enseignement du français dans le monde, Le français dans le monde, Recherches et applications*, Paris: Hachette.

### Further reading

Bremer, K., Roberts, C., Vasseur, M.T., Simonot, M. and Broeder, P. (1988) *Achieving understanding: discourse in intercultural encounters*, London: Longman.

Coste, D., Moore, D. and Zarate, G. (1997) *Plurilingual and pluricultural competence*, Strasbourg: Council of Europe.

Haut conseil de la francophonie (1994) *Etat de la francophonie dans le monde* (*State of Francophonie in the world*), Paris: La documentation française.

Porcher, L. (1995) *Le français langue étrangère* (*French as a foreign language*), Paris: Hachette-CNDP.

MURIEL MOLINIÉ

# G

## Gender and language

The term *gender*, in the phrase 'Gender and language', may refer either to gender in the social sense (it is used in this way in the entry on 'gender and language learning'), or to gender as a characteristic of language as an abstract system. It is this latter sense in which it is used here, to refer to a grammatical category.

Traditionally, languages have been described as having either 'natural' or 'grammatical' gender. Natural gender is 'semantic'. A language with natural gender requires that the gender of an animate noun or pronoun corresponds to the biological sex of the person or animal to which that noun refers. In this way, *woman* and *girl* in present-day English are feminine nouns, and *she* and *her* are feminine pronouns. Similarly, *ram* is a masculine noun and *ewe* is a feminine noun. Nouns like *star* and *museum* are neither feminine nor masculine, but rather 'neuter'. Despite a very few odd but well-known exceptions (a ship being sometimes referred to as *she*, for example), the English language is usually seen as having natural gender (but see below, and see Cameron, 1985, for a critique of the whole grammatical/natural gender dichotomy).

Grammatical gender, in contrast, is 'formal'. In languages with grammatical gender, all nouns, inanimate ones as well as those referring to humans and animals, have a gender. Whether a noun referring to an inanimate object is masculine, feminine or neuter is unlikely to be evident from the noun itself. In French, for example, *chaise* (chair) is feminine, hence *la chaise* (the chair), and *pain* (bread) is masculine (hence *le pain*). The determiner (in these cases, the definite article) indicates the gender. The gender of a noun in a language with grammatical gender has thus to be learned. (Although 'grammatical gender' can refer to a range of classes, many languages possess three: 'masculine', 'feminine' and 'neuter'.)

Some masculine nouns and pronouns in English and other languages supposedly have the potential to be 'generic' or 'sex-indefinite', i.e. have the capacity to include both males and females. Examples include *man* (and its compounds) and *he*, and familiar masculine animal forms such as *dog* and *lion*. So, in principle, it is grammatically correct to say to a class of male and female students: 'Everyone will get his homework back tomorrow.' But the fact that this utterance is possible means that gender in English is not entirely natural – rather, since *his* here includes females, gender in English is in part grammatical. (Having no such generic potential, the feminine forms, in contrast (*woman, she, bitch, lioness*), are then considered as the 'marked' forms. Feminine forms are 'marked' in many languages.)

The genericity of those masculine forms in English which can in principle also refer to 'humans' has, however, since 1970 been seriously challenged – one reason being that what may be intended as generic may not be so interpreted, and accordingly that women and girls may be effectively excluded by the use of these 'generics'. 'Generics' *man* and *he* have in particular been seen by feminist linguists as one form of 'sexist language'. They now have a somewhat old-fashioned ring to them, and, while not falling into disuse, are often substituted for by alternatives such as *people, he or she, s/he*, and 'singular *they*' ('Everyone will get their homework back tomorrow'), especially in spoken English. These alternatives are now included in many **PEDAGOGICAL GRAMMARS** (Sunderland, 1994) and **DICTIONARIES**, and 'inclusive language' is required by many academic journals and institutional Codes of Practice. (However, students are not – yet – recommended to use 'singular *they*' in examinations and tests of written English.) Other alternatives have been adopted for other languages, with different strategies being employed for languages with grammatical gender than for languages with natural gender (Pauwels, 1998).

Gender in the English language has thus undergone change in terms of alternatives to 'generic' masculine forms now available – something that is important for the teaching of English to speakers of other languages, and which has implications for **TEACHER EDUCATION** and **LANGUAGE AWARENESS**. For, while learners may or may not wish to adopt such forms as *s/he* and 'singular *they*', they are very likely to come across them.

**See also:** Error analysis; Gender and language learning; Grammar; Linguistics; Pedagogical grammar; Pragmatics; Speech act theory

### References

Cameron. D. (1985) 'What has gender got to do with sex?', *Language and Communication* 5, 1: 19–27.

Pauwels, A. (1998) *Women changing language*, London: Longman.

Sunderland, J. (1994) 'Pedagogical and other filters: the representation of non-sexist language change in British pedagogical grammars', in J. Sunderland (ed.), *Exploring gender: questions and implications for English language education*, Hemel Hempstead: Prentice Hall.

### Further reading

Corbett, G. (1991) *Gender*, Cambridge: Cambridge University Press.

Woods, E. (1994) 'Grammar and gender', in J. Sunderland (ed.), *Exploring gender: questions and implications for English language education*, Hemel Hempstead: Prentice Hall.

JANE SUNDERLAND

# Gender and language learning

Gender factors in language learning relate to the *people* involved in the learning/teaching process, and to the *language* itself. *People* include students and teachers as well as **TEXTBOOK** characters. Students' gender may relate to their **CLASSROOM LANGUAGE**, their **LEARNING STYLES** or **STRATEGIES** of learning, their **ATTITUDES** to languages and language learning, their proficiency in the language, and to their performance on different types of **ASSESSMENT**. As regards teachers, the distribution and nature of their teacher–student talk may be gendered, as may their perceptions. Textbooks and other teaching **MATERIALS** are gendered in the way they represent female and male characters.

Gender in the *people* sense refers broadly to the socially-shaped (as opposed to biologically-determined) characteristics of women and men, boys and girls. Recent post-structuralist thinking sees gender identities and relations as being shaped by, *inter alia*, language use, rather than language use being an effect *of* gender. Accordingly, gender identities and relations of language learners can be seen as being at least as much an effect of classroom processes as those processes are an effect of gender (see, e.g., Sunderland, 1995a).

### Learners and gender

As in other subject classrooms, in mixed-sex language classrooms it is boys who tend to contribute more than girls, and men more than women. In mixed-sex **GROUP WORK** – arguably a lynchpin of the **COMMUNICATIVE** approach – male students tend to dominate verbally (Gass and Varonis, 1986). However, there are exceptions (see, e.g., Sunderland, 1998), and it is important to remember that, even when there is evidence of male dominance, this is likely to come from a small subset of boys (French and French, 1984). In terms of the gendered *nature* of interaction, Sunderland (1996) found that boys were significantly more likely than girls to follow up the teacher's response to their academic question with another academic question, and Holmes (1994) that a greater proportion of questions asked by women than men in groupwork were 'response-facilitating' rather than 'response-restricting'.

Importantly, there is a large overlap in language learning styles and strategies used by female and male students. Some gendered *tendencies* have been found (Willing, 1989; Oxford, 1994), which might have implications for both teaching and testing. However, it is important to emphasise that there is no proof that these are innate or otherwise fixed.

Many more girls than boys elect to continue with languages when they have the choice. In all-boys schools, however, a greater proportion of boys continue with languages than in mixed-sex schools, suggesting that social reasons play a role (Loulidi, 1990). Studies in British secondary schools have found girls to be more positive about language learning than boys overall (Batters, 1986). In Batters's study this included girls being more positive about all type of activities – except for **SPEAKING**, towards which boys and girls were equally positive.

There is a prevailing view that boys tend to see French as a 'feminine' language, preferring **GERMAN**, but this is not borne out by evidence, and neither is the view that boys are put off language by the number of female teachers (Powell and Batters, 1986). However, studies in the US of *adults* learning a foreign language have either found only statistically insignificant gender differences in attitudes towards language study or no differences at all (e.g. Muchnick and Wolfe, 1992).

In the UK, girls do better than boys at languages at GCSE (see, e.g., Arnot *et al.*, 1996), and in some countries girls do so much better than boys that entrance requirements are lowered for boys applying to attend English-medium schools. Further, there is a 'common-sense' belief among some teachers that girls and women 'are' better foreign language learners than boys and men. However, in some mixed-sex schools, boys do better than girls (Cross, 1983), and those boys who do continue with languages to A-level perform very well (Arnot *et al.*, 1996). *Why* boys tend to perform less well than girls is a recurring theme (Clark and Trafford, 1995). Neurological evidence is unclear, suggesting that

potentially relevant male–female differences in the brain do exist, but that these differences may be too small to account for the differences in foreign language achievement (Klann-Delius, 1981).

Language tests have been shown to use stereotypical gender representation in the same way as textbooks (see below). Three forms of bias in foreign language and second language tests have been identified: content, task type and tester (Sunderland, 1995b). The content of a test item (e.g. one that draws on gender **STEREOTYPES**) may bias the outcome. As regards task types, male students tend to do better on certain types of item (i.e. multiple choice items), female students on others (i.e. extended **WRITING**). The tester may also influence the outcome in one of three ways: (a) if he or she marks female or male students preferentially; (b) if male and female testers have different standards from each other; and (c) if, on an oral test, students respond differently according to whether the tester/interlocutor is female or male (or of the opposite/same sex).

## Teachers and gender

Most language teachers in secondary schools in the UK (and many, though not all, other countries), and in language schools worldwide, are female (Powell, 1986). This is, however, decreasingly true of language teachers at tertiary level, and the majority of academics who teach **APPLIED LINGUISTICS** in universities are male.

Despite the sometimes-expressed belief that male teachers treat students differently from female teachers, there is little evidence of this. Female and male teachers may differentiate by student gender – but tend to do so in the same way. Many studies have found that teachers give more attention to male students – though, again, this tends to be to a small subset of males (see, e.g., Sunderland, 1996). This, however, is more likely to be a result of teacher–student 'collaboration' than teacher intention (Swann and Graddol, 1988). Importantly, a few studies (e.g. Yepez, 1994) have found no evidence of such differential teacher treatment. Further, this attention is not necessarily that which directly helps learning, but is more likely to be disciplinary in nature (see, e.g., Sunderland, 1996). In terms of teachers providing differential treatment which is likely to help learning, Sunderland (1996) in fact found that the girls were asked the more academically challenging questions.

As regards teachers' perceptions of gender, some teachers have suggested that it is writing that causes boys to fall behind in foreign languages (Powell, 1986).

There have been all-female teacher initiatives in the TEFL profession: the organisation 'Women in TEFL' existed from 1986 until 1995; in addition, in the late 1970s and early 1980s there was a magazine for women EFL teachers, *ETHEL*, which ran to at least seven issues. These clearly met a need felt by women teachers at the time.

## Teaching materials and gender

The many 'gender and textbook' studies of the 1970s and 1980s (which became far less frequent in the 1990s) overwhelmingly found textbooks to be populated by more male than female characters, and male characters to have the more interesting and positive personalities and more responsible occupations (see, e.g., Porecca, 1984). Gender bias of a similar nature was identified in **PEDAGOGICAL GRAMMARS** (see, e.g., Stephens, 1990) and **DICTIONARIES** (see, e.g., Kaye, 1989). In 1991 'Women in TEFL' produced *On Balance*, a guide for EFL publishers (reprinted in Sunderland, 1994). The situation may now have improved: one later study, which focused on dialogues in three very recent textbooks, found no evidence of gender bias (Jones *et al.*, 1997). The presence or absence of bias, however, indicates nothing about how a given text will be treated by teachers in class, nor how it will be interpreted by learners, and the same can be said of a 'progressive' text. Looking at textbook interpretation and use may accordingly be more fruitful than looking at the textbook alone.

## Language learning, gender, teacher education and change

Discussions of 'gender bias' found by studies of language classroom interaction and materials have not always been related to language learning, even speculatively. Doing so would make such findings much more relevant to discussions of gender on language **TEACHER EDUCATION** courses. There have, however, been suggestions for the teacher as regards remedial *action* for gender in the classroom. These include encouraging male students to be active listeners in groupwork (Holmes, 1994), and asking students to explore English 'opposites' such as *bachelor/spinster* and *man/wife* (Pugsley, 1991).

**See also:** Age factors; Attitudes and language learning; Classroom research; Gender and language; Learning styles; Materials and media; Strategies of language learning; Teaching methods

## References

Arnot, M., David, M. and Weiner, G. (1996) *Educational reforms and gender equality in schools. Equal Opportunities Commission research discussion series* No. 17, Manchester: EOC.

Batters, J. (1986) 'Do boys really think languages are just girl-talk?' *Modern Languages* 67, 2: 75–9.

Clark, A. and Trafford, J. (1995) 'Boys into modern languages: an investigation in attitudes and performance between boys and girls in modern languages', *Gender and Education* 7, 3: 315–25.

Cross, D. (1983) 'Sex differences in achievement', *System* 11, 2: 159–62.

French, J. and French, P. (1984) 'Gender imbalances in the primary classroom: an interactional account', *Educational Research* 26, 2: 127–36.

Gass, S. and Varonis, E. (1986) 'Sex differences in nonnative speaker–nonnative speaker interactions', in R. Day (ed.), *Talking to learn: conversation in second language acquisition*, New York: Newbury House.

Holmes, J. (1994) 'Improving the lot of female language learners', in J. Sunderland (ed.), *Exploring gender: questions and implications for English language education*, Hemel Hempstead: Prentice Hall.

Jones, M., Kitetu, C. and Sunderland, J. (1997) 'Discourse roles, gender and language textbook dialogues: who learns what from John and Sally?', *Gender and Education* 9, 4: 469–90.

Kaye, P. (1989) ' "Women are alcoholics and drug addicts", says dictionary', *ELT Journal* 43, 3: 192–5.

Klann-Delius, G. (1981) 'Sex and language

acquisition: is there any influence?', *Journal of Pragmatics* 5: 1–25.

Loulidi, R. (1990) 'Is language learning really a female business?', *Language Learning Journal* 1, 1: 40–3.

Muchnick, A. and Wolfe, D. (1992) 'Attitudes and motivations of American students of Spanish', *The Canadian Modern Language Review* 38: 274–6.

Oxford, R. (1994) '*La différence continue* … : gender differences in second/foreign language learning styles and strategies', in J. Sunderland (ed.), *Exploring gender: questions and implications for English language education*, Hemel Hempstead: Prentice Hall.

Porecca, K. (1984) 'Sexism in current ESL textbooks', *TESOL Quarterly* 18, 4: 705–23.

Powell, R. (1986) *Boys, girls and languages in school*, London: Centre for Information on Language Teaching and Research (CILT).

Powell, R. and Batters, J. (1986) 'Sex of teacher and the image of foreign languages in schools', *Educational Studies* 12, 3: 245–54.

Pugsley, J. (1991) 'Language and gender in the EFL classroom'. *The Teacher Trainer* 5, 1: 27–9.

Stephens, K. (1990) 'The world of John and Mary Smith: a study of Quirk and Greenbaum's *University Grammar of English*', *CLE Working Papers* 1: 91–107.

Sunderland, J. (1994) (ed.) *Exploring gender: questions and implications for English language education*, Hemel Hempstead: Prentice Hall.

Sunderland, J. (1995a) ' "We're boys, miss!": finding gendered identities and looking for gendering of identities in the foreign language classroom', in S. Mills (ed.), *Language and gender: interdisciplinary perspectives*, London: Longman.

Sunderland, J. (1995b) 'Gender and language testing', *Language Testing Update* 17: 24–35.

Sunderland, J. (1996) *Gendered discourse in the foreign language classroom: teacher–student and student–teacher talk, and the social construction of children's femininities and masculinities*, PhD dissertation, Lancaster University.

Sunderland, J. (1998) 'Girls being quiet: a problem for foreign language classrooms?', *Language Teaching Research* 2, 1: 48–82.

Swann, J. and Graddol, D. (1988) 'Gender inequalities in classroom talk', *English in Education* 22, 1: 48–65.

Willing, K. (1989) *Learning styles in adult migrant education*, Adelaide: National Curriculum Research Council.

Yepez, M. (1994) 'An observation of gender-specific teacher behaviour in the ESL classroom', *Sex Roles* 30, 1/2: 121–33.

**Further reading**

Clark, A. (1998) *Gender on the agenda: factors motivating boys and girls in MFLs*, London: CILT.

Ekstrand, L. (1980) 'Sex differences in second language learning?: empirical studies and a discussion of related findings', *International Review of Applied Psychology* 29: 205–59.

Good, T. Sykes, N. and Brophy, J. (1973) 'Effects of teacher sex and student sex on classroom interaction', *Journal of Educational Psychology* 65: 74–87.

Hennessey, M. (1994) 'Gender and pedagogic dictionaries', in J. Sunderland (ed.), *Exploring gender: questions and implications for English language education*, Hemel Hempstead: Prentice Hall.

Kunnan, A.J. (1990) 'DIF in native language and gender groups in an ESL placement test', *TESOL Quarterly* 24, 4: 741–6.

JANE SUNDERLAND

# Generative principle

The generative principle refers to the human ability to generate an infinite number of sentences from a finite grammatical **COMPETENCE**. It reflects the crucial feature of human language sometimes called compositionality. Meanings are built out of parts *and* from the way they are combined. A finite stock of words or word groups can be recombined again and again to produce numerous novel sentences. Human language as a sequential combinatorial system sparks off an explosion of possible meanings, due to which we will never run out of new ideas. Nothing like this can be found in animal communication. The most impressive formulation of the generative power of language is probably found in Wilhelm von **HUMBOLDT**'s philosophy of language. For him, the quintessential property of language was *energeia*, its productive potential or creativity:

> Denn sie (die Sprache) steht ganz eigentlich einem unendlichen und wahrhaft grenzenlosen Gebiete, dem Inbegriff alles Denkbaren gegenüber. Sie muss daher von endlichen Mitteln einen unendlichen Gebrauch machen, und vermag dies durch die Identität der Gedanken- und Spracheerzeugenden Kraft.
>
> (For it (language) is confronted with an essentially infinite and truly unbounded territory, the essence of everything which can be thought. It must thus make infinite use of finite means, and it achieves this through the identity of the power to produce both thoughts and speech.)
>
> (Humboldt, 1963: 477)

The fact that, as competence develops, learners often work with units larger than the word – sometimes called chunks – and do not generate all their sentences from scratch, as it were, does not devalue the generative principle. Learners should not be confused with mature speakers who may store and call into play entire phrases many words long.

Teachers at all times have sensed the importance of the generative principle and the necessity for learners to extrapolate underlying patterns from the sentences they hear and produce variations on them. They have tried to teach in ways so that word combinations turn into syntactic germ cells, and sentences become models for many more sentences. It has also been pointed out that children acquiring a first language play the analogy game, i.e. in phases of mere verbal play of an essentially non-communicative kind they vary words, phrases and ideas in ways reminiscent of pattern drills. However, teachers have also run into difficulties when using systematic conjugations not just of verbs but of lengthy sentences, or, as a modern variety of the same idea, pattern drills which often turned out to be mechanical and monotonous. There has always been the danger of working with isolated sentences at the expense of message-oriented communication. The problem remained as to whether successful practice on sentences and their variations could further communicative competence.

The problem seems to be that Humboldt's *energeia* is usually only familiar in its abbreviated formulation, 'making infinite use of finite means', and is interpreted in structuralist, or syntactic, terms only. This holds for linguists of the past, such as Prendergast (1864) and **PALMER**, who were well aware of the generative principle, as well as for twentieth-century advocates of pattern drills. To capture this aspect of language, Palmer (1968: 22) coined the term '*ergon*' and explained it in the following way: 'The number of sentences being infinite, recourse must be had to the study of their mechanism in order that, from the relatively limited number of lesser ergons, an infinite number of sentences may be composed at will.' He chided Berlitz for not realising 'the necessity for the pupil to mechanise type-sentences and to derive from these an unlimited number of subsidiary sentences and combinations' (Palmer and Palmer, 1925: 7).

The fact that Humboldt's *energeia* was not just about **GRAMMAR** but at the same time also about language as a thought crutch, even a thought organ, was consistently overlooked. Pattern drills, as well as substitution tables, aimed at the automatisation of structures. They were thought of as the manipulation of verbal elements, not the manipulation of ideas, and thus came into conflict with the communicative approach.

However, modern techniques have been devised where sentence drills have a dual focus, and lexical substitutions are not regarded as mere fillers. Structures are manipulated, but at the same time ideas are toyed with and the semantic potential of a given structure is explored (Butzkamm, 1993). For instance, German and French students need practice on the English question pattern 'Where does he live' because there is a tendency to say 'Where lives he'. Instead of merely consolidating the structure by listing indifferent habits or routines suggested by easy words that fill the slot, the teacher can personalise the structure by getting the students to produce variations which make particular sense to them. Students will spare more attention for the meaning of what they are saying and even identify with the ideas expressed:

- Where does he do his weight-training? (He looks like Mr Universe and is proud of it)
- Where does he go for his guitar lessons? (He is an excellent player)

- Where does she buy her wines? (She once treated us to a very good wine)
- Where does she get her good looks from? (Jane really feels good now)

Here, students will not only perform well in a drill, but are made aware of possibilities for communication. Sentence variations can be a stepping stone for free communication as the ultimate goal. At the same time pupils learn how far they can ride a given pattern, and know when it is safe. Even the simple and time-honoured practice of asking students to make up sentences of their own usually shifts the focus away from the grammatical point to the meanings expressed, and can be highly effective.

Although, as Howatt (1984: 149) points out, it is 'an ancient principle', the generative principle has been neglected because it has not been properly understood. It has been overlooked that a combining of words is not an end in itself but serves a combining of thoughts. If we are aware of the problem, the proper techniques can be found and a balance achieved between a powerful communicative principle and an equally powerful generative principle – as companions rather than as opposites.

**See also:** Audiolingual method; Behaviourism; Bilingual method; Direct method; Learning styles; Monolingual principle; Second language acquisition theories; Transfer; Universal grammar

### References

Butzkamm, W. (1993) *Psycholinguistik des Fremdsprachenunterrichts: Natürliche Künstlichkeit: Von der Muttersprache zur Fremdsprache* 2nd edn, Tübingen: Francke.

Howatt, A.P.R. (1984) *A history of English language teaching*, Oxford: Oxford University Press.

Humboldt, W. von (1963) *Werke in fünf Bänden*, in A. Flitner and K. Giel (eds), vol 3: 'Schriften zur Sprachphilosophie', Stuttgart: Cotta'sche Buchhandlung.

Palmer, H. (1968) *The scientific study and teaching of languages* (2nd edn), Oxford: Oxford University Press; (first published 1917).

Palmer, H.E. and Palmer, D. (1925) *English through actions*, London: Longman.

Prendergast, T. (1864) *The mastery of languages or the art of speaking foreign tongues idiomatically*, London: R. Bentley.

WOLFGANG BUTZKAMM

# Genre and genre-based teaching

The notion of genre as a framework for language instruction is relatively recent, emerging since the early 1980s. Formulated and investigated in research movements across different parts of the world, three distinct focal areas (Hyon, 1996) can now be identified. These are:

1 English for Specific Purposes (ESP);
2 Australian genre-based educational linguistics (also referred to as the Sydney School studies);
3 North American New Rhetoric studies.

To a greater or lesser extent, all three approaches involve analysis of the situational contexts or settings of spoken or written texts, as well as their communicative function and purpose within those settings. However, the approaches differ in the extent to which they attend to the formal structures and grammatical properties of texts related to different settings. Considerable differences are found in the degree to which applications for classroom instruction for both first and second language learners emerge from each approach, those from the Australian research being arguably the most fully developed.

## Definitions

The term 'genre' is conceived of rather differently in the three major approaches. ESP researchers (e.g. Bhatia, 1993; Dudley-Evans and St John, 1998; Flowerdew, 1993; Swales, 1990; Thompson, 1994), working with non-NATIVE SPEAKERS, have used genre as a tool for analysing the spoken and written texts required in post-secondary academic and professional settings. Their interest is in the common communicative purposes of particular kinds of genres (e.g. experimental research articles, university lectures, master of science dissertations, business letters, medical abstracts, legal case reports) within academic and professional discourse communities. Swales, a major figure in ESP research, defines genre as follows:

> A genre comprises a class of communicative events, the members of which share some set of communicative purposes. These purposes are recognised by the expert members of the discourse community, and thereby constitute the rationale for the genre. The rationale shapes the schematic structure of the discourse and influences and constrains choice of content and style ... In addition to purpose, exemplars of a genre exhibit various patterns of similarity in terms of structure, style, content and intended audience.
>
> (Swales, 1990: 58)

While the surrounding context of the genre is of interest to ESP researchers, the majority of ESP studies place emphasis on analysing the formal characteristics of genre rather than on the functions of texts in their social contexts.

Australian genre theory is grounded in systemic functional linguistics developed by Michael **HALLI-DAY** (1985) who, from his arrival in Sydney in 1975, greatly influenced work in educational linguistics, initially in first language and, more recently, in second language instruction. Systemic functional linguistics seeks to explain why and how people use language in social contexts and what language is required to *do* in those contexts of situation. Halliday based his systems of language function on the notion of *register*, constrained by three variables in the immediate context of situation (Halliday and Hasan, 1989): field (what is being done or talked about), tenor (the people involved and their relationships) and mode (the channel of communication and distance in time and space from events). The notion of genre, which concerns analysis of the structural patterns of whole texts within a systemic functional framework, was developed extensively by Martin (1984) – building on the work of Hasan (1978) – in educational applications. Martin's definition of genre as a 'staged, goal-oriented social process' is elaborated by Martin, Christie and Rothery (1987: 59):

> Most members of a given culture would participate in some dozens ... Australian examples include jokes, letters to the editor,

job applications, lab reports, sermons, medical examinations, appointment making, service encounters, anecdotes, weather reports, interviews and so on. Genres are referred to as *social processes* because members of a culture interact with each other to achieve them; as *goal-oriented* because they have evolved to get things done; and as *staged* because it usually takes mores than one step for participants to achieve their goals.

As this definition suggests, the focus of Australian genre studies is broad, including primary and secondary school genres, non-professional and professional workplaces, and community settings. Work conducted on written genres in primary schools (e.g. Callaghan and Rothery, 1988) has identified what are termed the *elemental* genres of procedure, report, explanation, discussion, exposition, recount and narrative. More recent work has highlighted the concept of 'macro-genres', texts which combine elemental genres in the more differentiated and specialised contexts of the secondary school and workplace (e.g. Iedema, Feez and White, 1994; Joyce, 1992), and has also shifted attention beyond written genres to spoken genres in casual conversation (Eggins and Slade, 1997).

While ESP and Australian genre studies draw primarily on linguistic analysis, New Rhetoric studies emphasise ethnographic description as their analytical base, as well as situational context and social action (Miller, 1984). New Rhetoric genre research, emerging from North American research, adopts humanist, social and cultural approaches, drawing on the disciplines of rhetoric, **SPEECH ACT THEORY**, cross-cultural **PRAGMATICS**, composition studies and professional **WRITING**. Freedman and Medway (1994:1) explain that recent analyses focus on combining notions of 'types' or 'kinds' of discourse with 'regularities in human spheres of activity'. Thus, genre is placed within 'the complex social, cultural, institutional and disciplinary factors at play in the production of specific pieces of writing' which leads to the 'unearthing of tacit assumptions, goals and purposes as well as the revealing of unseen players and the unmasking of others' (Medway, 1994: 2). Emphasis is also placed on social fluidity and institutional location, as in Schryer's description of genre as 'stabilized-for-now or stabilized-enough sites of social and ideological action' (Schryer, 1994: 108). Ethnographic approaches have been used to study genres in scientific research communities (Bazerman, 1988) and workplace settings (Devitt, 1991; Paré and Smart, 1994).

## Pedagogical implications

That genre studies is a growing theoretical area for first and second language teaching is reflected in the various genre conferences emerging since the 1980s. The 'Working with Genre' conferences (Sydney, 1989, 1991, 1993) originated by the Literacy and Education Research Network (LERN) in Australia and the 'Rethinking Genre' Colloquium (Ottawa, 1992) have highlighted both the rapidly developing and dynamic nature of this field as well as the heated controversies it engenders (Hyon, 1996; see also discussions in Reid, 1987). One area of dissent focuses on the extent to which language development is enhanced by the explicit teaching of the discourse structures and grammatical forms of genres (Berkenkotter and Huckin, 1993; Freedman and Medway, 1994; Watson and Sawyer, 1987; Widdowson, 1993). It is also argued that using text-based models of generic structures and forms, a particular feature of Australian and, to a lesser extent, ESP instructional approaches, results in prescriptive and derivative writing (Bhatia, 1993; Freedman and Medway, 1994) and in compliance with the discourses of dominant social norms (Freedman, 1993; Luke, 1996). Genre instruction is also seen as interventionist, leading to criticism that it overlooks what is known about natural processes of learning and learner creativity. Counter-arguments by Australian genre theorists define explicit instruction and the use of text models as a process of 'empowering' students by 'apprenticing' them into the established and influential genres required for success in educational and other social contexts (Hammond, 1987; Christie, 1991; Kress, 1993; Martin, 1993; Hasan and Williams, 1996). Australian proponents also criticise the imprecision, or even the virtual absence, of guidelines for teaching of the ESP and New Rhetoric theorists.

The pedagogical applications and influence of genre theory from the three areas, therefore, is highly varied. In New Rhetoric studies, genre theory has resulted in limited instructional proposals (but see, e.g., Bialostosky, 1994) in comparison with those in EAP where teaching has involved helping students understand the organisational and **STYLISTIC** features of professional and academic genres (e.g. Swales, 1990, Bhatia, 1993, Flowerdew, 1993). The instructional application of genre theory is most extensive in Australian contexts (Hyon, 1996), where theoretical and practical developments have centred especially on disadvantaged student groups in both **MOTHER-TONGUE** and literacy teaching in schools, as well as in **ADULT** ESL and basic education programmes. Central to Australian instructional applications are various versions of a 'teaching–learning cycle' consisting essentially of four phases: building the context (field); modelling the text; joint negotiation of text; and independent construction of text (Callaghan and Rothery, 1988; Hammond *et al.*, 1992; Rothery, 1996). The extent of the Australian influence of genre theory can also be measured by the fact that it has provided the basis for curriculum and **SYLLABUS** development in state-based school systems (e.g. New South Wales DET, 1998) and the Adult Migrant English Program (Hagan *et al.*, 1993; Feez, 1998, 2000) and to a lesser extent in EAP programmes (e.g. Drury and Webb, 1991). Further research and evolution of genre-based approaches are likely to focus on the impact of genre instruction on language learning (e.g. Hammond, 1996) and the interaction of genre-based teaching with critical pedagogy (Cope and Kalantzis, 1993; Benesch, 1993).

**See also:** Conversation analysis; Discourse analysis; Grammar; Language across the curriculum; Language awareness; Linguistics; Native speaker; Task-based teaching and assessment; Teaching methods; Text and corpus linguistics

## References

Bazerman, C. (1988) *Shaping written knowledge: the genre and activity of the experimental article in science*, Madison: University of Wisconsin Press.

Benesch, S. (1993) 'ESL, ideology, and the politics of pragmatism', *TESOL Quarterly* 27: 705–17.

Berkenkotter, C. and Huckin, T.N. (1993) 'Rethinking genre from a sociocognitive perspective', *Written Communication* 4: 475–509.

Bhatia, V.K. (1993) *Analysing genre: language use in professional settings*, London: Longman.

Bialostosky, D. (1994) 'From discourse in life to discourse in art. Teaching poems as Bakhtinian speech genres', in A. Freedman and P. Medway (eds), *Genre and the new rhetoric*, London: Falmer Press.

Callaghan, M. and Rothery, J. (1988) *Teaching factual writing: a genre-based approach*, Report of the Disadvantaged Schools Project, Sydney: Metropolitan East Disadvantaged Schools Program.

Christie, F. (1991) 'Genres as social processes', in *Working with genre: Papers from the 1989 LERN Conference, Working with Genre 111*, Sydney.

Cope, B. and Kalantzis, M. (eds) (1993) *The powers of literacy: a genre approach to teaching writing*, London: Falmer Press.

Devitt, A.J. (1991) 'Intertextuality in tax accounting: generic, referential, and functional', in C. Bazerman and J. Paradis (eds), *Textual dynamics of the professions*, Madison: University of Wisconsin Press.

Drury, H. and Webb, C. (1991) 'Literacy at tertiary level: making explicit the writing requirements of a new culture', in F. Christie (ed.), *Literacy in social processes*. Papers from the Inaugural Australian Systemic Linguistics Conference, Geelong: Deakin University.

Dudley-Evans, T. and St John, M. (1998) *Developments in ESP: a multidisciplinary approach*, New York: Cambridge University Press.

Eggins, S. and Slade, D. (1997) *Analysing casual conversation*, London: Cassell.

Feez, S. (1998) *Text-based syllabus design*, Sydney: NCELTR.

Feez, S. (2000) 'Heritage and innovation in second language education', in A. Johns (ed.), *Genres in the classroom*, Hillsdale, NJ: Lawrence Erlbaum.

Flowerdew, J. (1993) 'An educational, or process, approach to the teaching of professional genres', *ELT Journal* 47: 305–16.

Freedman, A. (1993) 'Show and tell? The role of explicit teaching in the learning of new genres', *Research in the Teaching of English* 27: 222–51.

Freedman, A. and Medway, P. (eds) (1994) *Genre and the new rhetoric*, London: Falmer Press.

Hagan, P., Hood, S., Jackson, E., Jones, M., Joyce,

H. and Manidis, M. (1993) *The certificates in spoken and written English*, Sydney: NCELTR and NSW AMES.

Halliday, M.A.K. (1985) *An introduction to functional grammar*, London: Arnold.

Halliday, M.A.K. and Hasan, R. (1989) *Language, context and text: aspects of language in a socio-semiotic perspective* (2nd edn), Oxford: Oxford University Press.

Hammond, J. (1987) 'An overview of the genre-based approach to the teaching of writing in Australia', *Australian Review of Applied Linguistics* 10: 163–81.

Hammond. J. (1996) 'Knowledge about language and genre theory', in G. Bull and M. Anstey (eds), *The literacy lexicon*, Sydney: Prentice Hall.

Hammond, J., Burns, A., Joyce, H., Brosnan, D. and Gerot, L. (1992) *English for social purposes*, Sydney: NCELTR.

Hasan, R. (1978) 'Text in the systemic functional model', in W. Dressler (ed.), *Current trends in textlinguistics*, Hamburg: Helmut Buske.

Hasan, R. and Williams, G. (eds) (1996) *Literacy in society*, London: Longman.

Hopkins, A. and Dudley-Evans, T. (1988) 'A genre-based investigation of the discussion sections in articles and dissertations', *English for Specific Purposes* 7, 113–21.

Hyon, S. (1996) 'Genre in three traditions: implications for ESL', *TESOL Quarterly* 30, 4: 693–722.

Iedema, R., Feez, S. and White, P. (1994) *Media literacy* (Write it Right; Literacy in Industry Research Project, Stage 2), Sydney: Metropolitan East Disadvantaged Schools Program.

Joyce, H. (1992) *Workplace texts*, Sydney: NSW Adult Migrant English Service.

Kress, G. (1993) 'Genre as a Social Process', in B. Cope and M. Kalantzis (eds), *The powers of literacy: a genre approach to teaching writing*, London: Falmer Press.

Luke, A. (1996) 'Genres of power? Literacy education and the production of capital', in R. Hasan and G. Williams (eds), *Literacy in society*, London: Longman.

Martin, J.R. (1984) 'Language, register and genre', in F. Christie (ed.), *ECT418. Children writing reader*, Geelong: Deakin University Press.

Martin, J.R. (1993) 'A contextual theory of

language', in B. Cope and M. Kalantzis (eds), *The powers of literacy: a genre approach to teaching writing*, London: Falmer Press.

Martin, J.R., Christie, F. and Rothery, J. (1987) 'Social process in education: a reply to Sawyer and Watson (and others)', in I. Reid (ed.), *The place of genre in learning: current debates*, Geelong: Deakin University Press.

Miller, C. (1984) 'Genre as social action', *Quarterly Journal of Speech* 70: 151–76.

New South Wales Department of Education and Training (DET) (1998) *K-6 English Syllabus*, Sydney: Board of Studies.

Paré, A. and Smart, G. (1994) 'Observing genres in action: towards a research methodology', in A. Freedman and P. Medway (eds), *Genre and the New Rhetoric*, London: Falmer Press.

Reid, I. (ed.) (1987) *The place of genre in learning: current debates*, Geelong: Deakin University Press.

Rothery, J. (1996) 'Making changes: developing an educational linguistics', in R. Hasan and G. Williams (eds), *Literacy in society*, London: Longman.

Schryer, C.F. (1994) 'The lab vs the clinic: sites of competing genres', in A. Freeman and P. Medway (eds), *Genre and the New Rhetoric*, London: Falmer Press.

Swales, J. (1990) *Genre analysis: English in academic and research settings*, Cambridge: Cambridge University Press.

Thompson, A. (1994) 'Frameworks and contexts: a genre-based approach to analysing lecture introductions', *English for Specific Purposes* 13: 171–86.

Watson, W. and Sawyer, K. (1987) 'Questions of genre', in I. Reid (ed.), *The place of genre in learning: current debates*, Geelong: Deakin University Press.

Widdowson, H.G. (1993) 'The relevant conditions of language use and learning', in M. Kreuger and F. Ryan (eds), *Language and content: discipline and content-based approaches to language study*, Lexington, MA: D.C. Heath.

### Further reading

Berkenkotter, C. and Huckin, T.N. (1995) *Genre knowledge in disciplinary communication*, Hillsdale, NJ: Lawrence Erlbaum.

Bhatia, V.K. (1996) 'The power and politics of genre', *World Englishes* 16, 3: 359–71.

Christie, F. and Martin, J.R. (1997) *Genre and institutions: social processes in the workplace and school*, London: Cassell.

Derewianka, B. (1990) *Exploring how texts work*, Sydney: Primary English Teachers Association.

Freedman, A. and Medway, P. (eds) (1994) *Learning and teaching genre*, Portsmouth: Boynton/Cook Publishers Inc.

Hammond, J. and Macken, M. (1999) 'Critical literacy: challenges for ESL classrooms', *TESOL Quarterly* 33, 3: 528–44.

Huckin, T. (1995/6) 'Cultural aspects of genre knowledge', *AILA Review* 12: 68–78.

Martin, J.R. (1993) 'Genre and literacy – modeling context in educational linguistics', *Annual Review of Applied Linguistics* 13: 141–72.

ANNE BURNS

# German

With approximately 92 million people speaking it as their **MOTHER TONGUE**, German is placed about eleventh among the languages of the world (Döcsy, 1986). It is found in a relatively enclosed linguistic space (Germany, Austria, parts of Switzerland and Liechtenstein) and, with a total of thirteen, has the most frontier neighbours in Europe. German as a foreign language is currently learnt on a global scale by approximately 18–20 million people.

### The demand for German

The interest in learning German has increased particularly in the countries of Eastern and Central Europe since the reunification of Germany and the break-up of the Soviet-dominated Eastern Bloc. It is estimated that about two-thirds of all learners of German live in these countries, approximately half of these being in Russia.

The German-speaking countries, except for Switzerland, are integral members of the European Union, and approximately a quarter of the people of the European Union speak German as their mother tongue. German is thus established within the European Union, beside **ENGLISH** and

FRENCH, as a language of commerce and documentation. In the European Union, the interest in learning German is, however, uneven. Whoever learns German often does so, especially as an adult, for pragmatic reasons, since knowledge of German can be useful for one's career and for commercial and economic links. The lack of interest in German or prejudices against Germans, on the other hand, are still based above all on historical memories (Germany as a former enemy) and on the mistrust of a too-dominant Germany. In the school systems, German often comes after English or French, but there is in some countries growing interest in introducing German as a subject in the secondary school sector (e.g. in Spain and Italy) or in the increase of German teaching in schools (e.g. Ireland) or in the non-school sector (e.g. Greece).

In countries beyond Europe the interest in German is often not only pragmatic but also directed towards German as a representative of a European region with a long-established cultural tradition in music, fine arts, literature, Romantic landscapes and castles etc., with a high standard of living and well functioning institutions such as the social system, the traffic system, political institutions, and education system. As such, it is seen as being untainted by a colonial and imperial past.

Third, there are in German-speaking countries currently about 10 million people whose mother tongue is not German, and who learn German as a second language or who grow up bilingual in the second or third generation. These are above all migrants seeking work from Southern, Southeast and Eastern Europe, but also asylum-seekers and political or war refugees. Their number is constantly growing. As one of the consequences of this migration and the interest of many Germans in spending their holidays in the south, German has developed in the last few decades as a kind of holiday LINGUA FRANCA around the Mediterranean.

## German as a school subject

German is established as the first foreign language in some regions adjacent to the German-speaking countries, for example in Italy, FRANCE, Poland, the Czech Republic, Hungary and Slovenia. This is also the case in a good proportion of further education schools and colleges in Russia, where there are advanced courses. In most countries in Europe and worldwide, however, German is offered as the second or third foreign language, especially following English as the first foreign language. For example, in general education schools in Central and Eastern Europe and in the CIS the distribution of foreign languages is as follows: English 40 per cent, German 30 per cent, French 11 per cent, Russian 10 per cent, others 3 per cent. In professional schools and colleges, however, German is the most popular foreign language (Goethe-Institut, 1998).

## German in adult education

There are many people who begin their German studies as adults after the end of schooling. This is due to the fact that people recognise the usefulness of German in the context of professional training. It is therefore characteristic of German teaching in ADULT education that there is a concentration on German from a professional perspective, for example German for Business. In many countries such as CHINA, JAPAN or Argentina, which are geographically distant from the German-speaking area, German is only occasionally taught in schools, and therefore its main location is in universities or other institutions of adult education such as the GOETHE-INSTITUT and in-country language institutions.

## Development of teaching methods

German as a Foreign Language has followed a similar development to other modern languages such as French and English in its TEACHER METHODS (Neuner and Hunfeld, 1993). In this development the GRAMMAR–TRANSLATION METHOD was dominant until the beginning of the twentieth century. Growing out of the teaching of the classical languages Greek and Latin, this concentrated on the transmission of the rules and GRAMMAR of the written, literary language and the art of TRANSLATION. The grammar–translation method is still today, especially in élite education, the leading method for the teaching of German as a Foreign Language in many parts of the world.

In contrast to the grammar–translation method, a number of methods were conceived – for example the **DIRECT METHOD** and the natural method – from the end of the nineteenth century. The most important of these was the **AUDIO-LINGUAL METHOD** developed in the **USA** in the 1940s and 1950s which became the **AUDIO-VISUAL** method in the 1960s. The latter was accepted in German as a Foreign Language in the 1960s because it had pragmatic **OBJECTIVES** – ability to communicate in everyday situations – and language **SKILLS** as opposed to the knowledge about language of the grammar–translation method.

These approaches were developed in **COMMU-NICATIVE LANGUAGE TEACHING** from the 1970s onwards. The results of research in **PRAGMATICS** were linked to a cognitive learning theory and a more consistent recognition of the **NEEDS** of the learners, and led to teaching which is focused on everyday communication and which attempts to engage learners actively in the lesson and take differences among individual learners into account.

In Germany, the debate on the evolution of the communicative approach was clearly influenced by general concepts of a pedagogical emancipatory nature. This can be traced back to the fact that foreign language learning was introduced for all learners in the German school system in the 1960s, and a rapidly increasing number of pupils of non-German mother tongue had to be integrated into the German school system. This led to the evolution of German as a Second Language, which in turn led to the intercultural approach in foreign language teaching. This is a learner-oriented development of communicative teaching. In foreign language learning, the world of the target language and the learners' own cultural world come face to face. The intercultural approach thus attempts particularly to focus on processes of understanding and the negotiation of meaning between other and own worlds.

## Institutions

There are many institutions dealing with German in the various German-speaking countries. The ones described here are a selection:

- the Goethe-Institut, which worldwide has more

than 150 branches and deals with language courses, **TEACHER EDUCATION**, cultural programmes (Goethe-Institut, 1998);

- the **DEUTSCHER AKADEMISCHER AUSTAUSCH-DIENST** (DAAD), whose focus is the development of scientific cooperation between institutions of **HIGHER EDUCATION** (Bode *et al.*, 1995);

- professional associations: Fachverband Moderne Fremdsprachen (Sektion Deutsch als Fremdsprache); Fachverband Deutsch als Fremdsprache; Internationaler Deutschlehrerverband;

- journals: *Deutsch als Fremdsprache*; *Fremdsprache Deutsch*; *Zielsprache Deutsch*; *Deutsch Lernen*; *Jahrbuch Deutsch als Fremdsprache*.

## Trends in German as a Foreign Language

One clearly discernible trend is an interest in learner-oriented concepts, evident in the development of the **PLANNING** of curricula and the production of **MATERIALS** specific to a particular region and target group (see Neuner, 1997). The focus is on the learner and the learning process, including learning **STRATEGIES**, individual **LEARNING STYLES** and types, and also holistic learning and an interest in helping learners to understand meaning. This is becoming the central interest of the development of teaching methods and learning processes. Learning of foreign languages at school is increasingly seen as preparation for lifelong learning, with the emphasis on **LEARNING TO LEARN** and the reinforcement of **AUTONOMOUS LEARNING**.

As a result of global socio-political developments at the end of the twentieth century, English has asserted itself as the world language of communication, and German is therefore becoming the language which is learnt after English.

**See also:** DAAD; Goethe-Institut; *Interkulturelle Didaktik*; Linguistic imperialism; Native speaker; Non-native speaker teacher; Quality management; Teaching methods

## References

Bode, Chr., Becker, W. and Klofat, R. (eds) (1995) *Universitäten in Deutschland*, Munich: Prestel.

Döcsy, G. (1986) *Statistical report on languages of the world as of 1985*, Bloomington: University of Indiana.

Goethe-Institut (1998) *Förderung der deutschen Sprache*, Munich: Goethe-Institut.

Neuner, G. (ed.) (1997) 'Trends 2000', *Fremdsprache Deutsch* Sondernummer II/1997.

Neuner, G. and Hunfeld, H. (1993) *Methoden des fremdsprachlichen Deutschunterrichts*, Munich: Langenscheidt.

## Further reading

Krumm, H.-J. (ed.) (1994) *Deutsch als Fremd- und Zweitsprache. Eine Übersicht über Studiengänge an deutschsprachigen Hochschulen*, Hamburg: Fachverband Moderne Fremdsprachen.

Raasch, A. (1997) *Sprachenpolitik Deutsch als Fremdsprache*, Amsterdam: Editions Rodopi.

GERHARD NEUNER

# Global education

Global education is an approach to education developed in the 1970s and 1980s which aims to promote students' knowledge and awareness of world peoples, countries, cultures and issues. As an approach to language teaching, it involves integrating a global perspective into classroom instruction through a focus on international themes, lessons built around global issues (peace, development, the environment, **HUMAN RIGHTS**), classroom activities linking students to the wider world and concepts such as social responsibility and world citizenship. Advocates of this approach see the foreign language as a window to the world and global education as a way to bring educational relevance to the classroom through meaningful content based on real-world topics. Interest in this field has led to a healthy debate about language teaching aims, to an increase in language teaching lessons, courses and materials designed around world themes, and to the formation of 'global issue' special interest groups in several language teaching organisations.

Global education arose out of new thinking in education and the social studies. It has been defined as education which 'promotes the knowledge, **ATTITUDES** and skills relevant to living responsibly in a multicultural, interdependent world' (Fisher and Hicks, 1985: 8) and as education which aims to bring about 'changes in the content, methods and social context of education in order to better prepare students for citizenship in a global age' (Kniep, 1985: 15). Global educators designate the fields of peace education, development education, environmental education and human rights education as the four component fields of global education.

The rationale for global education is that:

1 globalisation has led to growing interdependence and increased contacts with people from different countries;
2 our planet faces serious world problems which require international cooperation to solve;
3 surveys show that modern youth is often ignorant of world peoples, cultures and issues;
4 current education systems fail to prepare young people adequately to cope with these challenges due to traditional schooling based on rote memorisation, passive learning and examination pressures.

The goals of global education are divided into the four domains of knowledge, skills, attitudes and action:

1 knowledge about world countries and cultures, and about global problems, their causes and solutions;
2 skills of critical thinking, cooperative problem solving, conflict resolution, and seeing issues from multiple perspectives;
3 attitudes of global awareness, cultural appreciation, respect for diversity, and empathy;
4 action: the final aim of global learning is to have students 'think globally and act locally'.

While individual language instructors have long dealt with current events and international themes, serious interest in global education has only come about since the 1980s. One of the earliest publications to deal with global education and foreign language education was Conner (1981). A later definition describes global education as 'an approach to language teaching which aims at enabling students to effectively acquire and use a foreign language while empowering them with the knowledge, skills and commitment required by world citizens for the solution of global problems' (Cates, 1990: 3).

A number of figures have addressed the importance of global education for teachers of modern languages. **RIVERS** (1968: 262) questions whether international understanding has really been promoted by traditional language teaching focused on memorising foreign words, reciting irregular verb paradigms and deciphering foreign language texts. Maley (1992: 73) sees global education as a way to resolve the perennial problems faced by language teaching: the gulf between classroom activities and 'real life', the separation of language teaching from mainstream educational ideas, and the lack of a content as subject matter. Starkey (1988: 239) argues that the language class, by virtue of its focus on 'foreign' peoples, should really be the most global subject in the school curriculum.

Advocates of global education typically criticise the narrow focus of much traditional language teaching with its emphasis on linguistic form, trivial content (shopping, tourism, pop culture), its avoidance of controversial issues, and its **TEXTBOOK STEREOTYPES**. Global language teachers strive to design language lessons around world regions (e.g. **AFRICA**), social issues (e.g. AIDS), international themes (e.g. the Nobel Peace Prize), and global problems (e.g. landmines, tropical rainforests). They see e-mail and the **INTERNET** as ways to promote global awareness and **INTERCULTURAL COMMUNICATION**, and arrange overseas visits and **EXCHANGES** to promote international understanding.

Global education, through its emphasis on meaningful communication about real-world topics, has promoted interest in **CONTENT-BASED INSTRUCTION** and **COMMUNICATIVE LANGUAGE TEACHING**. It has also led language educators to reach out for teaching resources to global issue organisations such as Amnesty International, Oxfam and UNICEF, and to experiment with teaching ideas, activities and materials from such disciplines as peace education and environmental education. It has further led to new thinking about the social responsibility of the language teaching profession in a world of social inequality and **LINGUISTIC IMPERIALISM**.

The popularity of global education has led to the formation of special interest groups within several organisations, notably the Japan Association for Language Teaching (JALT) and **IATEFL** (International Association of Teachers of English as a Foreign Language). These have enabled language teachers involved with global education to receive funding, initiate projects, issue newsletters, hold workshops, obtain conference time and build networks in order to share their research, teaching experience and classroom ideas.

One initiative linking language teaching with global education is the **LINGUAPAX** project of UNESCO. This brought together representatives from **AILA** (the International Association of Applied Linguistics) and **FIPLV** (the World Federation of Modern Language Associations) to draw up a Linguapax Kiev Declaration entitled 'Content and Methods of Teaching Foreign Languages and Literature for Peace and International Understanding' (UNESCO, 1987). Further UNESCO meetings have generated additional Linguapax declarations and publications.

Global education has had its biggest impact with teachers of **ENGLISH**, who argue that the status of English as a global language (see Crystal, 1997) makes the EFL classroom ideal for global education. These teachers see English less as the language of **NATIVE SPEAKERS**, and more as a language for learning about the world and communicating with world peoples.

Critics of global education voice a number of concerns: that global issues are controversial and should be avoided, that global issues invite teacher bias and lead to 'preaching, not teaching', that language teachers don't have the specialised knowledge to properly teach complex global issues, that the curriculum is too full to add something new, and that language classrooms should focus on language and leave world affairs to the social studies. Defenders of global education respond that controversial topics can stimulate student **MOTIVATION** and **CLASSROOM** language use, that teachers can be 'neutral chairpersons' when dealing with controversy, that teachers can acquire a knowledge of global issues or explore issues with students as co-learners, that global education can be infused into language content, and that global education involves a global perspective across the curriculum.

The rapid growth of interest in global education within the field of language education has helped to stimulate the profession in many ways. It has encouraged a reconsideration of the basic aims of language teaching, sparked a debate about the mission of the profession, promoted a healthy discussion about meaningful content and educational relevance, spurred outreach efforts to other disciplines and to global issue organisations, provoked a sharing of classroom experimentation and research, resulted in new teaching materials on global issue themes, and led to the formation of special interest groups devoted to promoting global awareness through language teaching. The increasing globalisation and interdependence of the world in the twenty-first century makes it likely that interest among language teachers in the field of global education will continue to grow.

**See also:** Central and Eastern Europe; Common European Framework; Esperanto; Human rights; Intercultural communication; Intercultural competence; Internationalisation

### References

Cates, K. (1990) 'Teaching for a better world: global issues in language education', *The Language Teacher* XIV, 5: 3–5.

Conner, M. (ed.) (1981) *A global approach to foreign language education*, Skokie, IL: National Textbook Company.

Crystal, D. (1997) *English as a global language*, Cambridge: Cambridge University Press.

Fisher, S. and Hicks, D. (1985) *World studies 8–13*, New York: Oliver and Boyd.

Kniep, W. (1985) *A critical review of the short history of global education*, occasional paper, New York: Global Perspectives in Education.

Kniep, W. (1987) *Next steps in global education*, New York: American Forum for Global Education.

Maley, A. (1992) 'Global Issues in ELT', *Practical English Teaching* 13, 2: 73.

Rivers, W. (1968) *Teaching Foreign Language Skills*, Chicago: University of Chicago Press.

Starkey, H. (1988) 'Subject-based approaches to global education', in G. Pike and D. Selby, *Global teacher, global learner*, London: Hodder and Stoughton.

UNESCO (1987) *Kiev Linguapax Declaration*, Paris: UNESCO.

### Further reading

Classen-Bauer, I. (ed.) (1989) *International understanding through foreign language teaching*, Bonn: German Commission for UNESCO.

Conner, M. (ed.) (1981) *A global approach to foreign language education*, Skokie, IL: National Textbook Company.

Cunningham, D. and Candelier, M. (1995) *Linguapax V*, Melbourne: FIPLV/AFMLTA.

Elder, P. and Carr, M. (1987) *Worldways: bringing the world into your classroom*, New York: Addison-Wesley.

*Global Issues in Language Education Newsletter* (quarterly), c/o Kip Cates, Tottori University, Koyama-cho, Tottori City, Japan 680–8551.

KIP A. CATES

## Goethe-Institut

The Goethe-Institut, with its head office in Munich, is a worldwide organisation active in the promotion of the **GERMAN** language and culture, carrying out cultural **EXCHANGES** abroad on behalf of the Federal Republic of Germany.

Some 120 branches of the Goethe-Institut in over 70 countries implement cultural programmes together with a variety of partners in the host country, give information about Germany, teach German, and give further training to teachers of German. The aims of the Goethe-Institut are guided by two principles: partnership with the host country, introducing the German language and culture into the host country; culture understood in the widest sense, embracing everyday culture, technological culture – not just Beethoven, Goethe, Habermas, etc., but also politics, **HUMAN RIGHTS** or town planning.

There are also fifteen branches of the Goethe-Institut in Germany. The main focus of the branch in Weimar is on its cultural programmes; the remaining branches primarily teach language courses. 'Learn German – See Germany' is the motto of the Goethe-Institut in Germany.

The origins of the Goethe-Institut go back to 1925 when the 'Deutsche Akademie' was founded in Munich as an independent institution whose 'practical department' had the responsibility for German language and culture abroad. The first Goethe-Institut was created within the academy in 1932 with the main concern being the in-service training of foreign specialists in German in Germany and the sending of German university assistant lecturers abroad.

The misuse of the 'Deutsche Akademie' by the National-Socialist powers led to its being closed after 1945. The re-founding of the Goethe-Institut in 1952 was part of the democratic renewal and led eventually to the development of the Goethe-Institut of today.

## Website

The Goethe-Institut's website is: http://www.goethe.de

# Gouin, François

b. 1831, Normandy; d. 1896, Paris

Author of *The Art of Teaching and Studying Languages*

Gouin's fame rests chiefly on *The Art of Teaching and Studying Languages [ATSL]*, London: Philip and Son, 1892.)

He was educated at the College of Séez and became a classics teacher while continuing studies in literature and science at the university of Caen. Advised by his professors, he went to Germany to complete his philosophical studies, first to Hamburg, then to Berlin. He failed in his attempts to learn **GERMAN** in the classical (i.e. deductive) manner, which he carried to its extreme limits. Observing on this occasion his 3-year-old nephew during and after a visit to a watermill during the ensuing summer holidays he changed dramatically his view of language development, a change which would eventually lead him to write *ATSL*. Gouin returned to Berlin, becoming professor of **FRENCH** to the Berlin Court, and enjoying the friendship of Alexander von **HUMBOLDT**. In 1864 he became educational adviser to the Romanian government

and, following its overthrow, he went to England. He subsequently settled in Geneva, where he established a school and wrote *ATSL*. Later on he became Director of *École Supérieure* at Elboeuf, and professor of German at *École Supérieure Arago* in Paris. Here he also gave private tuition in Latin and Greek based upon his natural approach.

*ATSL* consists of five parts. Part One gives an account of the methods in vogue at the time and of Gouin's frustration at failing to learn German by 'the classical method, with its grammar, its dictionary, and its translations' (1892: 35) and at seeing the ease with which his nephew picked up his **MOTHER TONGUE**. Contrasting the latter's language development with his own, Gouin makes the discovery that the child, stunned by all that he had seen at the mill, shortly after 'manifested an immense desire to recount to everybody what he had seen' (1892: 37). The child could not be stopped telling his story over and over again. Later, he re-enacted the sequence of events in self-regulating talk and play, with numerous variants. This suggested to Gouin that: the child abstracts from the real events and orders his perceptions in succession of time, according to cause and effect; in the 'school of Nature' it is sentences (linked by 'and then ... '), not words, that are the primary units of verbal expression; and the verb plays a central role in the enactment and expression of events (1892: 50).

These observations led Gouin to develop in Part Two a psychology of language learning and teaching that permitted the selection of topics ('themes') from reality ('Nature') that were capable of analysis into constituent events ('acts' and 'facts') and of expression in at least two basic language functions. A typical **EXERCISE** would reflect the thematic unity ('Series') and look like this:

Theme 'Nursemaid'

'Walk, my pretty; That's it!
Go towards the door; That's very good!
Now you've got there; Bravo!
Lift up your little arm; Capital!
Take hold of the handle; That's the way!
Turn the handle; How strong you are!
Open the door; What a clever little man!
Pull the door open; There's a little darling!'

Note the simplicity of the interlinking sentences (most of which could be the starting-point of another Series), displaying a chronological order, and the centrality of the verb. The phrases to the left of the semi-colon represent 'objective language' (today mostly called the 'referential', 'propositional', 'cognitive', 'descriptive' or 'transactional' language function), those to the right of the semi-colon 'subjective language' (i.e. the 'emotive', 'expressive', 'attitudinal', 'interpersonal' or 'interactional' language function). Though strongly intertwined and developed simultaneously in natural language **ACQUISITION** (1892: 154), the teacher should begin by teaching the objective language, continue by teaching the subjective language, and finish by teaching the 'figurative [i.e. **METAPHORICAL**] language', which feeds on the objective language (He fell into the river – He fell into the trap).

Semanticisation took place by having learners enact and verbalise the series, first in their mother tongue and subsequently in the foreign language. Pictures might also be used. The ear being 'the master-organ of language' (1892: 127), much emphasis is placed on ear-training, with the teacher as the learners' model. Unlike other representatives of the **REFORM MOVEMENT**, Gouin made no use of the science of phonetics or phonetic transcriptions.

Part Three of *ATSL* deals with **GRAMMAR**, the morphology and syntax of spoken language, and mood, pride of place being given to the verb. Gouin favours an inductive approach: 'all that the teacher does is simply to aid or direct, it will be the class themselves who carry out this work' (1892: 262). Parts Four and Five treat the study of the Classics.

It has been observed that Gouin's method illustrates the problem faced by the language pedagogue who wishes to take into account the nature of language. Since no coherent theory of language was available to him at the time, he had to work out his own and to apply it (Stern, 1983: 153). Gouin's method was rather successful on the continent of Europe (especially in Germany and Holland) during the last decade of the nineteenth and the first three decades of the twentieth century, and in America during the early part of the twentieth century (see Howatt, 1984: 314). His distinction of a subjective and an objective

language function found its way into Deutschbein (1917) and Kruisinga (1932). As a language pedagogue, Gouin appears to have had little lasting influence.

### References

Deutschbein, M. (1917) *System der neuenglischen Syntax (The system of modern English syntax)*, Cöthen: Otto Schulze.

Gouin, F. (1892) *The art of teaching and studying languages*, London: Philip and Son, (*Exposé d'une nouvelle méthode linguistique*, *L'art d'enseigner et d'étudier les langues*, Paris: Fischbacher, 1880).

Howatt, A.P.R. (1984) *A history of English language teaching*, Oxford: Oxford University Press.

Kruisinga, E. (1932) *A handbook of present-day English. Accidence and syntax*, 3 vols, Groningen: Noordhoff.

Stern, H.H. (1983) *Fundamental concepts of language teaching*, Oxford: Oxford University Press.

ARTHUR VAN ESSEN

## Graded objectives

Graded **OBJECTIVES** in modern languages (GOML) are an essentially simple idea whose principles, philosophy and ideals are now commonplace, yet in the UK in the 1970s they were revolutionary. They arose from circumstances peculiar to the UK.

From 1944 onwards, **SECONDARY EDUCATION** (from age 11–16) was selective. Children deemed to be the most academically able (about 25–30 per cent) were sent to grammar schools, virtually the only schools where modern foreign languages (MFLs) were taught. The MFL course led to a national examination (available in several forms) taken at age 16. This mainly consisted of **TRANSLATION** with some free composition; the objective was to produce grammatically correct written sentences. There was no central direction of schools, and consequently the non-grammar schools began to teach MFLs (usually **FRENCH**) to their ablest learners and a new national examination was created for them – still aimed largely at grammatical accuracy.

A growing feeling among educationists that selection at age 11 was inefficient led in the 1960s to the creation of comprehensive secondary schools which accepted children of all abilities. By the early 1970s these were the norm. There, MFL teaching was expanded further down the ability range so that by the mid-1970s many more pupils were being taught a MFL. The only goal, however, was still the grammatically oriented national examinations, which were inappropriate for the new cohort of language learners. They became, along with their teachers, increasingly frustrated at their apparently unsuccessful language learning and abandoned it as soon as possible. Something had to change.

Teachers began to ask questions they had never asked before. If this course is not suitable for my learners, what course would be? What is French for, and why am I teaching it? The answers came surprisingly easily. A suitable course would be one that would engage the interests of the learners by being relevant to their lives and providing a reasonable hope of success. The purpose of French, as of any other language, is to enable human beings to communicate with each other in the everyday practical world. The purpose of language teaching should not be primarily the production of grammatically correct written sentences. The reason for teaching French was to offer insights into a different culture and into the nature of language and to provide a language **COMPETENCE** of practical use.

A suitable course would have to have characteristics markedly different from those currently on offer. Learners should not have to wait five years for official recognition of their success; the course should be divided into smaller steps, each of which would be rewarded. Existing examinations were defined purely by task with no indication of the range of language or grammatical complexity involved. The new course should define what learners would need to know in terms of language behaviours and exponents. Existing examinations were norm-referenced; they were devised to produce a rank order. The new tests were to be criterion-referenced, awarding marks for tasks successfully accomplished. The tasks themselves would mirror what is required of language users in the real world, and **MATERIALS** would be **AUTHEN-**

**TIC**. From these discussions came the main features of most GOML schemes:

- practical language to be used for everyday purposes;
- short-term objectives described in a series of levels;
- each level provides defined usable language and points forward to higher levels;
- authentic tasks and materials;
- criterion-referenced assessment; certificates awarded at each level state the language **SKILLS** acquired;
- ideally (though this is sometimes organisationally difficult) tests are taken when learners are ready and not at some predetermined time.

The dissemination of these ideas and the formation of groups of teachers who set up their own GOML schemes is an interesting example of how new ideas can achieve public recognition if the circumstances are favourable. As previously stated, there was no central direction of schools. It was because the system was highly decentralised that GOML schemes were able to grow and flourish.

The ideas were first expressed in two articles (Page, 1973; Harding and Page, 1974). These were taken up by headteachers, teacher trainers and language advisers (employed by local government to advise language teachers and organise in-service training). These would call meetings of teachers to discuss the ideas and set up working parties of serving teachers. In 1976 the first two groups were formed. Many more followed. The tasks the groups set themselves were formidable. They had to define **SYLLABUSES** at several levels, devise appropriate assessment instruments, and often create new teaching materials as those commercially available were geared to the old grammatical objectives.

Since they had never done anything like this before, they were learning as they went along. The earlier groups generously made their work available to the later ones, but many preferred to devise their own in response to local needs. A national coordinating committee was formed to disseminate ideas through a regular newsletter and organise an annual workshop. By 1987 there were 82 different schemes, many having very innovative and imaginative elements.

A course aimed at engaging the interest of

learners was completely novel in the school context. What does a young learner want to say to French speakers? This question introduced two new principles: first, the idea of basing syllabuses on assumed learner **NEEDS**; second, that language should be approached from a non-**NATIVE SPEAKER** point of view. The world over, native speaker families had for generations been the kernel of **GRAMMAR**-based courses – the Smiths, Greens, Schmidts, Duponts. It was now realised that the needs of non-native speakers had to be addressed.

The question also introduced the concepts of roles and settings: what social roles would our learners be playing and in what circumstances? Some groups based their early levels on these ideas. For example, learners on a school trip where accommodation and food are provided would need to buy ice creams, postcards, etc., whereas learners on a school **EXCHANGE** living with a French family needed to express likes, dislikes, exchange personal details, and so on. Those going independently to **FRANCE** with their families, for whom they served as **INTERPRETERS**, would have to obtain food, accommodation, understand public notices, etc. It can be seen that the choice of language at each level is driven by purely practical needs and not by the usual grammatical categories.

In the mid-1970s groups became aware of the work of the **COUNCIL OF EUROPE**'s MFL projects and particularly of **THRESHOLD LEVEL**. This expressed in detail many of the ideas groups had been working with. It was enthusiastically welcomed and informed much of the work thereafter. These now-commonplace ideas implied at that time an entirely new idea of what a language is and what language teaching/learning should entail.

All this required an enormous amount of work from teachers. Cooperation was essential. Groups would organise evening, day and weekend meetings where syllabuses and tests were devised and materials discussed and created. It was a huge self-help movement, the likes of which had not existed before, and it was invaluable in-service training. The results were excellent. In areas where GOML schemes operated, twice as many learners opted to continue MFL learning.

In the 1980s, the government decided to create a new national school-leaving examination amalgamating the two existing ones. Teachers in GOML schemes were well placed to offer advice, as they had several years' experience of devising new sorts of syllabuses and testing techniques. They had considerable influence on the debate and the new examinations introduced in 1988 aimed at the **ACQUISITION** of a practical language **COMPETENCE** and insisted on authenticity of materials and tasks. Unfortunately, they retained the five-year course before achievement was officially assessed.

In the 1990s, the government assumed more central control by introducing a National Curriculum that set out in some detail what was to be taught in each subject. This effectively squeezed out GOML schemes, and most gradually fell into disuse.

It is possible to claim that GOML changed completely the direction of MFL teaching in UK schools. In the world as a whole, MFL teaching was moving towards a more **COMMUNICATIVE** approach, but in the UK it was GOML that embodied the idea and showed it could be successful.

Some generally applicable lessons can be learnt:

- All teachers should be encouraged to ask themselves penetrating questions about what they are teaching and why, so as to become reflective practitioners.
- Teachers should be encouraged to cooperate with each other in institutions, cities/regions as well as nationally, to exchange ideas and materials and discuss language policy.
- Education systems should be flexible, encouraging effective practices and allowing innovative and imaginative teachers to experiment.

**See also:** Attitudes and language learning; CILT; Communicative language teaching; Motivation theories; Objectives in language teaching and learning; Proficiency movement; Threshold Level; United States of America; US Standards for Foreign Language Learning

### References

Harding, A. and Page, B. (1974) 'An alternative model for modern language examinations', *Audio-Visual Language Journal* 17, 3: 169–74.

Page, B. (1973) 'An alternative to 16+', *Modern Languages* 55: 1–5.

## Further reading

Page, B. (1985) 'Graded objectives in modern language learning', in V. Kinsella (ed.), *Cambridge language teaching surveys 3*, Cambridge: Cambridge University Press.

Page, B. and Hewett, D. (1987) *Languages step by step: graded objectives in the UK*, London: Centre for Information on Language Teaching and Research (CILT).

BRIAN PAGE

# Grammar

Despite the central role played by grammar in human communication and the large number of descriptions of it by linguists, it remains a difficult term to define since on the one hand the word 'grammar' can refer to a variety of phenomena and on the other, among grammarians, there is considerable disagreement concerning its nature. Discussions of grammar fall within three main areas: social, pedagogical and linguistic, which address the following general issues:

- What is to be regarded as standard grammar and what is the status and role of other varieties? (social)
- How is grammar learnt and how should it be taught? (pedagogical)
- What is grammar and how does it work? (linguistic)

The first question, often referred to as *usage*, is one that arouses considerable interest – and emotions – among the general public. The adjectives 'good' and 'bad' sometimes used in this connection reflect the fact that this is a social rather than a linguistic issue. In the past, reference grammars and 'guides to good usage' tended to take a largely *prescriptive* approach; in other words, authors would seek to impose their own, somewhat élitist, view of correctness upon language users (for example, in English, *I shall* instead of *I will*; avoiding 'split infinitives', etc.). Nowadays, however, grammarians are more likely to follow a *descriptive* approach: the sole criterion for correctness is whether a form corresponds to actual modern usage.

The second issue concerns the learning of grammar and is essentially a pedagogical question.

The third, and the most important area for students of language and **LINGUISTICS**, concerns attempts by linguists to explain the nature of grammar: its structure and function within the more general process of human communication. Although the history of grammatical description is thousands of years old, the last fifty years have seen not only an abundance of new theories but also considerable disagreement concerning the nature of grammar. Most descriptions are based on certain common premises: first, that grammar is at the very core of communication, the grammatical system representing an important way of both conveying and creating meaning; second, that grammar can be regarded as *rule-governed behaviour* and as a phenomenon operates in a highly systematic way. It is one of the main tasks of grammarians to explain the 'rules' which are the basis of both the form a language takes and of the systematic relationship that exists between form and meaning. It should be noted that the word 'rule' is to be understood purely as a synonym for 'regularity'. In doing so, grammarians will account for sentences which are *well-formed* or *grammatical* (formally correct), *acceptable* (meaningful) and, in some models, contextually *appropriate*.

It is often a source of confusion that the term 'grammar' is variously used to refer to a variety of phenomena. In linguistics in general it is usually stated to be one of four 'levels' of language, the others being phonology, lexis and semantics. According to this view, which sees grammar purely in terms of form rather than meaning, it can be further subdivided into *morphology*, which is concerned with the internal structure of words or morphemes, and *syntax* – the patterning of morphemes to form sentences. However, some linguists (e.g. Greenbaum, 1996) use syntax not in this particular sense but quite simply as a synonym of grammar in general. At the broader end of the scale, many linguists apply the word to other aspects of communication which operate systematically. Expressions such as 'text grammar', 'grammar of speech' or even the 'grammar of advertising' reflect this wider view.

A comparison of theories and models of grammar will show considerable differences, which derive from the respective theoretical orientation of the grammarian and which result in different areas of focus, categorisation and terminology. Whilst most grammatical theories will claim to be theories of language in general, they will nevertheless give particular emphasis to certain aspects of language. This may be: the forms of grammar and on the patterning aspect and relations between words (*formal* grammar); the human mind and on how thoughts are processed into grammatical form (*internal* grammar); the relationship between meaning and form within a broader network of human communication in general (*functional* grammar). The influences in modern grammatical description are most noticeable from the following sets of theories.

*Traditional grammar* is based not on a view of language as a process but on the external observation and analysis of the product, resulting in a form of classification begun by the Ancient Greeks. The most basic categories are *word classes*, also known as parts of speech such as noun and verb. These classes have largely survived in modern categorisation, with some terminological amendment and some additions such as 'determiners'. Well into the second half of the twentieth century, analysis based on 'parsing' of sentences was common school practice in first-language teaching.

*Generative grammar*, sometimes referred to as *transformational grammar*, was developed by **CHOMSKY**. Unlike previous structural approaches, which took as their starting point the form of grammar, Chomsky's various models of grammar begin with the mind of the speaker, or *internal* grammar. Essential to his view is the existence of a specific and innate language component in the brain, part of which is a **UNIVERSAL GRAMMAR**. The mechanism or unconscious knowledge which steers the use of language is referred to as ***COMPETENCE***, which is contrasted with *performance*, language in use. According to Chomsky, it is the task of the linguist to account for a speaker's competence, i.e. the mechanisms by which thoughts are stored and converted into sentences. These are specified in terms of a finite number of 'rules' by means of which an infinite number of sentences can be *generated*. Particularly in North America, both his

general ideas and the applications of the model, which renders itself open to a type of mathematical notation, has dominated linguistic analysis since the 1960s. Relatively undisputed is the psycholinguistic orientation of his initial premises. More controversial aspects are: his claim for a language-specific component in the mind; his claim for 'psycholinguistic reality' (that this is 'how language works'); and his focus on the sentence as the main unit of analysis at the expense of contextual and functional considerations.

*Systemic/functional grammar* was principally developed by M.A.K. **HALLIDAY** (1985). This has attracted more interest in Europe in particular. Functional grammar sees language 'as a system of communication and analyses grammar to discover how it is organised to allow speakers and writers to make and exchange meanings' (Lock, 1996: 1). These meanings are seen as a coherent network of meaning components, which can be combined in various ways to communicate messages. The term 'functional' has its own special meaning, differing from the usual narrow meaning of 'function' in language teaching. On the one hand, it has a pragmatic sense, referring to the behavioural, message-based aspects of language use; and on the other, it is formal in that it examines the internal function of language elements between themselves as part of a total linguistic system. The most comprehensive reference grammar of **ENGLISH** available, by Quirk *et al.* (1985), is broadly based on a functional view of grammar but also incorporates some categorisation from traditional grammar.

It follows from this that any definition of grammar must be seen in light of the respective orientation of the grammarian (see Woods, 1995: 14). Some examples of different ways of defining grammar are: from a formal perspective, 'the patterning of morphemes to make up sentences is generally described as the GRAMMAR of the language' (Allerton, 1979: 42); from an internal perspective, 'a set of rules which allow us to put words together in certain ways, but which do not allow others' (Leech *et al.*, 1982: 3); from a broad functional perspective, 'We refer to the structural or organising principles of language as grammar' (Jackson, 1990: 3).

**See also:** Acquisition and teaching; Dictionaries; Generative principle; Grammar–translation method; Language awareness; Linguistics; Pedagogical grammar; Reference works; Universal grammar

### References

Allerton, D.J. (1979) *Essentials of grammatical theory*, London: Routledge and Kegan Paul.

Greenbaum, S. (1996) *The Oxford grammar*, Oxford: Oxford University Press.

Halliday, M.A.K. (1985) *An introduction to functional grammar*, London: Edward Arnold.

Jackson, H. (1990) *Grammar and meaning*, London: Longman.

Leech, G., Deuchar, M. and Hoogenraad, R. (1982) *English grammar for today*, Basingstoke: Macmillan.

Lock, G. (1996) *Functional English Grammar*, Cambridge: Cambridge University Press.

Quirk, R., Greenbaum, S., Leech, G. and Svartvik, J. (1985) *A comprehensive grammar of English*, London: Longman.

Woods, E. (1995) *Introducing grammar*, Harmondsworth: Penguin.

### Further reading

Greenbaum, S. (1996) *The Oxford grammar*, Oxford: Oxford University Press.

Hudson, R. (1998) *English grammar*, London: Routledge.

Jackson, H. (1990) *Grammar and meaning*, London: Longman.

Morenberg, M. (1991) *Doing grammar*, Oxford: Oxford University Press.

Woods, E. (1995) *Introducing grammar*, Harmondsworth: Penguin.

DAVID NEWBY

# Grammar–translation method

A method of teaching a 'Modern Foreign Language' which was developed in Europe and dominant in the eighteenth till nineteenth century, the grammar–translation method was based on the method of studying Latin and Greek adopted by Europeans in the Middle Ages. The language teaching method emphasised the teaching of formal grammatical rules and translating foreign language written texts into one's **MOTHER TONGUE** with detailed grammatical analysis. It is the earliest and the traditional method of foreign language teaching, employed mainly when studying and reading academic literature. It was initially called the Grammar method and could also be called the Translation method, Classical method, Traditional method or Reading method.

The procedures of the Grammar–translation method typically involve:

- A summary of the main content of the text using the mother tongue so that learners can get a general idea of what they are going to learn. This is the first step of explaining, understanding, analysing and translating the foreign language text.

- Explain the language points and literal meaning of the difficult words and each sentence with grammatical analysis and translation into the mother tongue. Language teaching proceeds with rules of formal **GRAMMAR**, isolated **VOCABULARY** items (usually the new and difficult words and expressions), application of grammatical rules to the explanation, and analysis of the paradigm text and translation.

- Reading and translating the whole text into the mother tongue, and a final summary of the text also in the mother tongue.

- Questions and answers, **READING** and **WRITING** practice and **EXERCISES**. These mainly focus on the application of grammatical rules, the translation of the new and difficult words and expressions and typical sentence patterns into the mother tongue and, at the advanced level, vice versa.

- In the whole process of using the method to teach a foreign language, the mother tongue has always been used as a **MEDIUM OF INSTRUCTION**, emphasising the reading and writing aspects of the foreign language being taught without paying much attention to the **SPEAKING** and **LISTENING** (Richards and Rodgers, 1986: 3–4).

The Grammar–translation method was first adopted by Europeans in the Middle Ages when

Latin and Greek were learned and taught. In fact, Latin and Greek dominated the school curriculum at the time and this situation continued till the end of the eighteenth century. The actual purpose of language learning was to train the 'faculties' of the brain, and produce scholars. The learning of a foreign language was considered an intellectual discipline. People were of the opinion that Latin and Greek were the repositories of ancient civilisation. A major part of the curriculum and time in schools were devoted solely to achieving the goals of Latin/Greek teaching/learning. It was considered a matter of prestige to know the two languages.

Because the so-called 'superior' languages like Latin and Greek were taught through the Grammar–translation method only, it became very natural that, when students began to learn a modern foreign language and when the teaching/learning of a modern foreign language first became popular, the same language teaching method was imitated, since the basic goal was not communication but translation of the foreign language into the native language – or vice versa. Furthermore, there was no other foreign language teaching method generally known at the time (Howatt, 1984: 131). **TEXTBOOKS** were prepared to teach 'modern languages' on similar lines to those of Latin and Greek. In such books, grammar rules are introduced at the beginning, followed by written exercises and a bilingual vocabulary list. At the end of the vocabulary list, construction of sentences and later paradigm texts are taught with grammatical analysis, followed by translation. Each grammatical point is explained in detail and illustrations are given in plenty. The students are expected to memorise the rules of grammar (Rivers, 1972: 16).

Criticisms of the Grammar–translation method by language teaching theorists focus on its emphasis of the mental, intellectual, disciplinary and memorisation orientation while ignoring the speaking and listening communication aspect of the foreign language being learned/taught. **RIVERS** (1972: 17–18) observes that, in the Grammar–translation method, little stress is laid on accurate **PRONUNCIATION** and intonation. Communication **SKILLS** are neglected; there is a great deal of stress on knowing grammatical rules and exceptions, but little training in using the language actively to express one's own meaning even in writing. The language learned is mostly of a literary type, and the vocabulary is detailed and sometimes esoteric. The average student has to work hard at what he considers laborious and monotonous core vocabulary learning, translation and endless written exercises, without much feeling of progress in the mastery of the language and with very little opportunity to express themselves through it.

**STERN** (1984: 456) explains the reasons for the failure of Grammar–translation method and summarises four defects:

1 overemphasis of grammar rules;
2 limitations of practice techniques;
3 sheer size of the memorisation;
4 lack of coherence with language facts.

**HAWKINS** (1987: 129) mentions Ticknor, a professor of modern languages at Harvard, USA, who already criticised the Grammar–translation method during the course of his lectures on *The Best Methods of Teaching the Living Languages* in 1832 and who observed that spoken and active methods were best: they should begin in early childhood; and grammar should not be introduced until age 13.

In spite of vehement criticisms of the method, the very fact that it continued over a long period of time as a preferable way and is still being partly used by some foreign language teachers suggests that not only no alternative better than the Grammar–translation method was available to teachers, but it also has some valuable points we should learn from even today. It can increase reading comprehension and make the comparison of the differences between the foreign language being learned/taught and the mother tongue. It has a less strict requirement of the qualifications and competencies of the teacher to enable them to teach the foreign language. Large-size foreign language classes can be taught with the method. As support for the Grammar–translation method, Chastian (1971: 59) observes that Grammar–translation teaching satisfied the desires of the traditional **HUMANISTIC** orientation which placed primary emphasis on the belles-lettres expressed in the language.

In the early nineteenth century, notions about the view of language, language learning and language teaching were moving towards reform.

The Grammar–translation method, after a long period of domination, was challenged by the forces of reform at the end of the century, as a more rational and more practical approach (Howatt, 1984: 129). The Grammar–translation method itself also underwent many changes and improvements, combining some points from the other foreign language **TEACHER METHODS** such as the **DIRECT METHOD**. The **REFORM MOVEMENT** was the result of this. Foundations were laid for new approaches towards language teaching/learning methods. However, traces of the Grammar–translation method can still be found in the reading method and cognitive method.

**See also:** BICS and CALP; Grammar; History: the nineteenth century; Learning styles; Reform Movement; Teaching methods; Translation; Untutored language acquisition

### References

Chastian, K. (1971) *The development of modern language skills: theory to practice*, The Center for Curriculum Development, USA.

Hawkins, E.W. (1987) *Modern languages in the curriculum*, Cambridge: Cambridge University Press.

Howatt, A.P.R. (1984) *A history of English language teaching*, Oxford: Oxford University Press.

Richards, J.C. and Rodgers, S.T. (eds) (1986) *Approaches and methods in language teaching*, Cambridge: Cambridge University Press.

Rivers, W.M. (1972) *Teaching foreign language skills*, Chicago: University of Chicago Press.

Stern, H.H. (1984) *Fundamental concepts of language teaching*, Oxford: Oxford University Press.

### Further reading

Chastian, K. (1976) *Developing second language skills: theory to practice*, Chicago: Rand McNally.

Kelly, L.G. (1969) *25 centuries of language teaching*, Rowley, MA: Newbury House.

Mackey, W.F. (1965) *Language teaching analysis*, London: Longman.

Stern, H.H. (1970) *Perspectives on second language teaching*, Ontario: Ontario Institute for Studies in Education.

YU WEIHUA

# Group work

The interest in group work as a means of supporting foreign language learning developed in the early 1970s, and later became prominent as one of the methodological devices that typified many interpretations of **COMMUNICATIVE** approaches to teaching. In many countries the impetus came from experiences in mainstream schooling, particularly at **PRIMARY** level, and the early interest was simply in finding means of increasing student talking time. An issue that has always been prominent is that of how to control or to promote both the quantity and the quality of each group member's contribution (Long and Porter, 1985). An important distinction to be drawn is between working *in* a group and working *as* a group. Working in a group is mainly a matter of location. Students are sitting in a common area but can be pursuing independent activities, or can be working on the same task but with no impetus for everyone to participate. On the other hand, working as a group presupposes a task in common, some interaction amongst group members, and in the most powerful of cases a task which obliges each member to make a contribution. More refined accounts have been developed, investigating different types of challenge and interaction and the value that each has for learning (Long and Porter, 1985; Pica and Doughty, 1985; Foster, 1998).

Communication games and problem solving activities for groups of learners were created from the late 1970s onwards to set up reasons for oral interaction amongst students, and were seen by many as a particular hallmark of communicative teaching (Byrne and Rixon, 1979). Oral interaction is important in group work, in most cases at least, at some stages in an activity, but **SKILLS** other than speaking can also be exercised. For example, jigsaw listening activities depend on the individual efforts of members of the group to comprehend the content of a listening passage before they can discuss their results. The above devices, and many other successful group work tasks, depend upon an unequal distribution of information at the outset of the activity, resulting in an information gap which it is the responsibility of the group as a whole to resolve.

Another device related to the information gap is the opinion gap (Rixon, 1979). This depends on setting up good reasons for some group members to wish to disagree with others' arguments or points of view. Competition rather than cooperation within the group is thus the driving force. It can be used within the framework of a communication game if players can gain an advantage by arguing against another player's proposed move, but it is most commonly seen in role play and simulation activities in which the different role cards distributed to members of the group contain the seeds of a conflict of interest amongst group members. An example of this would be a role play activity for four participants in which three members play people who think they have booked the same table in a restaurant and the fourth plays the waiter who needs to resolve the situation.

Pair work is often seen as a subset of group work, but in fact differs from it in several important respects. It is normally much easier to execute in classroom management terms. Even in a classroom with large numbers and fixed desks it is usually possible to set up pair work by asking desk-mates or near neighbours to work together. It is also true that less sophistication is needed in pedagogical terms to make sure that interaction takes place between members of a pair. The obligation to contribute is much more strongly marked when only two people are involved, and to some extent MATERIALS need to be less cleverly constructed to ensure that activity of some sort takes place. It is, however, important to be very clear about the aims and the learning potential of the particular type of activity that is proposed for use in pairs, and as with group work it is by no means guaranteed as a path towards communicative interaction. For example, pair work lends itself more readily than group work to the sort of language repetition and controlled practice work that is not strongly associated with real communication and interaction. The repetition in pairs of exchanges in a learned or scripted dialogue long pre-dated communicative styles of teaching, and continues to be the major form of pair work in many countries. However, genuine interaction and exchange of information can take place in pairs, and the device of the information gap is also useful in the case of pair work.

**See also:** Beginner language learners; Large classes; Learning styles; Materials and media; Questioning techniques; Teaching methods

## References

Byrne, D. and Rixon, S. (1979) *Communication games*, Windsor: NFER/The British Council.

Foster, P. (1998) 'A classroom perspective on the negotiation of meaning', *Applied Linguistics* 19, 1: 1–23.

Long, M. and Porter, P. (1985) 'Group work, interlanguage talk and second language acquisition', *TESOL Quarterly* 19, 1: 115–23.

Pica, T. and Doughty, C. (1985) 'The role of groupwork in classroom second language acquisition', *Studies in Language Acquisition* 7, 2: 232–48.

Rixon, S. (1979) 'The information gap and the opinion gap', *English Language Teaching Journal* 33, 2: 104–6.

## Further reading

Nunan, D. (1989) *Designing tasks for the communicative classroom*, Cambridge: Cambridge University Press.

SHELAGH RIXON

# Halliday, Michael Alexander Kirkwood

b. 1925, Leeds

Linguist, applied linguist, educationist

The founder of systemic-functional linguistics, Michael Halliday pioneered the analysis of language in its social context. He convincingly re-established the centrality of meaning in understanding how language functions after the domination of linguistic research by **CHOMSKY**'s generative grammar model.

After studying **CHINESE** language and literature at London University, he studied linguistics in **CHINA** and completed his doctorate at Cambridge University. He taught at universities in the UK and the USA before being foundation Professor of Linguistics at Sydney University, Australia (1973–87). His huge publication output of over 150 books and articles and his many keynote addresses at conferences of linguists and language teachers brought him acclaim as a leading international scholar in the linguistic sciences.

Halliday's broad range of research interests are foreshadowed in the topics of his first three articles: 'Grammatical categories in Modern Chinese' (1956); 'The linguistic basis of a mechanical thesaurus' (1956); and 'Some aspects of systematic description and comparison in grammatical analysis' (1957). The Chinese language was to inspire numerous articles, including 'Analysis of scientific texts in English and Chinese' (1993). The 'mechanical thesaurus' topic evolved into machine **TRANS-**

**LATION** and the principles of translation in 'Towards a theory of good translation' (1998). The analysis of language produced his systemic-functional model. Other significant publication topics were to be intonation in English, child language development, the linguistic study of **LITERARY TEXTS**, scientific English, and the construction of knowledge.

Systemic-functional linguistics is derived from the work of Malinowski, Firth (Halliday's teacher), Hjelmslev and Whorf. For Halliday, language is not only *part* of the social process but also an expression of it. He analyses the relationship between the functional organisation of the linguistic system and the patterns of social use of its linguistic resources. Halliday's systemic-functional model posits a tristratal organisation of language consisting of a phonology, a lexico-**GRAMMAR** and a semantics. Each stratum is itself meaning-creating. Through a series of interlocking choices the language user activates the interrelations between strata to produce the desired meaning. The grammatical system, in addition to functioning as the realisation of the semantics, and through that of the context of situation, also functions directly as a form of social action in its own right.

Unlike most theoretical linguists, Halliday makes no distinction between linguistics and **APPLIED LINGUISTICS**, participating in applications of his theory of language use to educational practices. His interest in linking the linguistic sciences and both mother-tongue and foreign language teaching dates from a co-authored book (Halliday with McIntosh and Strevens, 1964). His systemic-functional model inspired the development of studies in classroom discourse, in language across the curriculum, in a semantically oriented approach to **ENGLISH** teaching, in **TEACHER EDUCATION**, and more broadly in educational linguistics and **SOCIOLINGUISTICS**, including the study of semantic variation.

### Reference

Halliday, M.A.K. (1994) *An introduction to functional grammar*, revised edn, London: Edward Arnold.

### Further reading

Halliday, M.A.K. (1975) *Learning how to mean: exploration in the development of language*, London: Edward Arnold.
Halliday, M.A.K. (1978) *Language as social semiotic: the social interpretation of language and meaning*, London: Edward Arnold.
Halliday, M.A.K., with Matthiessen, C.M.I.M. (1999) *Construing experience through meaning: a language-based approach to cognition*, London: Cassell.
Halliday, M.A.K., with McIntosh, A. and Strevens, P. (1964) *The linguistic sciences and language teaching*, London: Longman.

ROSS STEELE

# *Handlungsorientierter Unterricht* (Holistic and action-oriented learning and teaching)

Holistic, action-oriented learning and teaching (in German: *handlungsorientierter Unterricht*) are principles in schooling that take account of learners' undivided physical and psychological preconditions in the learning process as well as their inherent human drive to be actively involved in relevant actions. The teaching approach based on this presupposition considers that learners make active use of both hemispheres of the brain, thus including reason, intellect and consciousness on the one hand and feelings, emotions and **MOTIVATION** on the other. Furthermore, it includes learners' hearts, bodies and senses. As far as foreign language teaching is concerned this means that, far from regarding language use under purely

cognitive and instrumental aspects, one also focuses on the affective and emotional domain. The individuals thereby are considered as **AUTONOMOUS** personalities that are encouraged to take responsibility for their language learning and use.

Researchers and authors referring to this kind of approach originally focus on the importance of primary experiences and **AUTHENTICITY** in learning (van Lier, 1996). Language is the most important tool that allows human beings to initiate, be involved in, interfere and withdraw from any kind of actions. In this respect, language is the most important resource for primary experiences from an ontogenetic point of view: to express oneself and make oneself understood to others. Language and language related actions, therefore, are the most fundamental resource for a holistic, action-oriented way of foreign language teaching and learning.

### Brain research

Learning a foreign language is considered as a fully integrative and holistic process that involves all faculties, such as hearing, sight, smell, touch, taste, and an equilibrium when constructing meaning. Language processing, therefore, is based on the integrated activity of separately located faculties and body parts and thus of different areas of the brain. This is a very important hint as to linked and associated learning, but linking and association do not only take place within cognition. Rather, they occur with the feelings, interest and motivational state of each individual (Damasio, 1994). **MOTIVATION** and feelings which accompany the learning action are of fundamental importance, because parallel to the memorisation of the subject matter, the accompanying affective status is memorised too. Learners are usually not aware of the latter, as it usually happens in a more subconscious and implicit way. Therefore, one can talk about two sides of a learning matter, simultaneously processed, stored and recalled as two tightly connected representations: the content and the affective state.

To take an example from research (Finkbeiner, 1997): motivated **READING** in a foreign language includes deep processing, such as the formation of elaborations, **TRANSFER** and inference. Elaborations, for example, allow readers to link up new information to their cognitive and affective prior experiences, thus making meaningful personal associations. Elaborations are holistic, and even action-oriented, yet in an abstract way: they do not include actual but mental pictures, not actual but mental sounds and voices, not actual but mental actions, yet they include actual feelings. Thus, mental and actual experiences merge into each other and form a new kind of primary experience. Therefore, physiologically, motivated reading can have the same effect as the actual action itself. This does not happen with unmotivated reading, which happens on a superficial level where elaborations are not possible, but where rather translation in a relatively verbatim manner occurs. To sum up, abstract actions such as reading can be considered as a holistic, action-oriented kind of learning, when deep processing occurs. This perspective allows us to transfer the approach to a higher, more academic level, and thus to implement it also for **ADULT LEARNERS**.

## Origins and history

Teaching foreign languages according to holistic, action-oriented principles follows a **HUMANISTIC** view of the learner. To some extent this integrative teaching approach refers to principles from the history of pedagogy which can be traced back to **COMENIUS**, and from there to Pestalozzi, Dewey, Montessori and numerous other reform pedagogues. (It has to be mentioned that the reform pedagogues referred to in this context are pedagogues representing the Reform Pedagogy of the 1920s rather than the **REFORM MOVEMENT** in language teaching at the end of the nineteenth century.)

According to Comenius, for instance, teaching should be one wholly integrative, holistic and global process in which illustration, verbal representation and sensory-motor rehearsal and **EXERCISE** are linked to each other so that they lead to a new kind of order. Pestalozzi focuses on teaching as a fully bodily experience connecting all senses. According to his humanist concept of learning, social relationships are crucial for successful learning. The cooperative aspect makes peer tutoring possible. Dewey's (1933, 1997) philosophy of education and instrumentalism, which is also called pragmatism, points to learning-by-doing rather than rote learning and dogmatic instruction.

## Reasons for the revival and the future relevance of the approach

The renaissance of this approach can be explained with reference to the following aspects: socio-theoretical, anthropological, learning psychological, didactic and methodological (Gudjons, 1989).

### *Socio-theoretical aspect*

The rapid change of the world plays an important role in this consideration. Experiences are becoming increasingly abstract. Therefore, *handlungsorientierter Unterricht* is an attempt to support students in actively acquiring culture by means of pedagogically organised sequences of action.

### *Anthropological aspect*

Students are to become aware of the fact that they are able to solve conflicts and problems because they are able to think and act competently (Finkbeiner, 1995). The focus here is on the dialectic view of the individuals and their environment. Cognition and thinking are understood as results of action on the one hand and as most important factors regulating actions on the other. Consequently, holistic teaching must seek to organise active and transparent tasks in order to initiate actions that involve thinking rather than merely presenting facts and knowledge.

### *Learning psychological aspect*

The learning process is significantly supported and facilitated by means of practical experience and action with the object to be learned.

According to Leontjew's thesis (1982; see also Braun, 1982), the inner states of beings (the subject) transform via the outer world (the object) and thus develop and change. Galperin develops a dialectical entity of action and consciousness that concentrates on this view of subject and object: the consciousness is formed by means of action. In return, this consciousness exerts influence on the activity of the subject (Galperin, 1974). The formation of the consciousness through the internalisation of outer and material actions to intellectual and lingual actions is at the heart of Galperin's theory of action. This assumption is important for language learning because it focuses on the different stages in **ACQUISITION**. The first stage deals with the material and 'outer' actions, which are transformed into language in a second stage. In the third stage, the language has fully developed and is independent of the material object, i.e. it is able to exist without it. An internal language is created in the fourth stage. The learning process is complete when the individual is able consciously and independently to apply the internalised activity.

### Criteria and curriculum

The topics to be taught are selected from given curricula according to their exemplary value. Problem-solving becomes a process in which deep understanding of the subject matter and linking with prior knowledge are possible. Learning is discovery and does not focus on mere repetition of facts.

The following criteria play a decisive role:

- Transparency of aim, content, methods and learning **ASSESSMENT**.
- Students' interests and experiences.
- Individualisation.
- Sensory activity connecting mental and practical work.
- Students' activity and self-monitoring in planning, completing and evaluating their action.
- Focus on the social and emotional level.

### Summary

It has to be mentioned that, despite the relevance of *handlungsorientierter Unterricht*, a universally valid theory and definition of action does still not exist. That might be due to the fact that, so far, there are only very few empirical studies in the field (Finkbeiner, 1995). A further difficulty lies in the fact that the term 'action' is often used in a very colloquial and unreflected sense. To avoid misunderstandings: holistic, action-oriented learning and teaching – *handlungsorientierter Unterricht* – are not compatible with a reductionist teaching of factual and theoretical knowledge in school. Rather, this approach seeks to develop a well balanced and dialectic relationship of theory and practice as well as of reflection and production. Yet, the relationship of the scientific and theoretical content, and the orientation towards action and holism must be further elaborated, especially in consideration of the different school types and levels.

**See also:** Autonomy and autonomous learners; *Fremdsprachendidaktik*; Group work; Humanistic language teaching; Learning to learn; Reading; Strategies of language learning; Teaching methods

### References

Braun, K.-H. (1982) *Genese der Subjektivität. Zur bedutung der Kritischen Psychologie für die materialistische Pädagogik (Genesis of subjectivity. The impact of critical psychology on materialistic pedagogics)*, Studies of critical psychology, vol. 31, Cologne: Pahl-Rugenstein.

Damasio, A. (1994) *Descartes' error. Emotion, reason, and the human brain*, New York: Putnam's Sons.

Dewey, J. (1933) *How we think: a restatement of the relation of reflective thinking to the educative process*, New York: Touchstone.

Dewey, J. (1997) *Experience and education*, New York: Touchstone.

Finkbeiner, C. (1995) *Englischunterricht in europäischer Dimension: Zwischen Qualifikationserwartungen der Gesellschaft und Schülereinstellungen und Schülerinteressen. Berichte und Kontexte zweier empirischer Untersuchungen* (Teaching English in the European dimension: between demands of society on the one hand and students' attitudes and interests on the other), Bochum: Brockmeyer.

Finkbeiner, C. (1997) 'Zum Einfluß von Interessen auf das Verarbeiten von Texten. Bericht von einer empirischen Studie' (The influence of interest on text comprehension: report on an empirical study), in L. Bredella, H. Christ and M. Legutke (eds), *Thema Fremdverstehen* (Topic: Intercultural Understanding), Tübingen: Narr.

Galperin, P. (1974) *Die geistige Handlung als Grundlage für die Bildung von Gedanken und Vorstellung*, in P. Galperin and A. Leontjew (eds), *Probleme der*

*Lerntheorie* (Problems of learning theory), 4th edn, Berlin: Volk und Wissen.

Gudjons, H. (1989) *Handlungsorientiert lehren und lernen. Projektunterricht und Schüleraktivität* (Action-oriented teaching and learning), Bad Heilbrunn/Obb: Klinkhardt.

Leontjew, A. (1982) *Tätigkeit, Bewußtsein, Persönlichkeit* (Action, consciousness, personality), 2nd edn, Berlin: Volk und Wissen.

van Lier, L. (1996) *Interaction in the language curriculum. Awareness, autonomy and authenticity* (Applied Linguistics and Language Study), Harlow: Longman.

**Further reading**

Damasio, A. (1994) *Descartes' error. Emotion, reason, and the human brain*, New York: Putnam's Sons.

Dewey, J. (1997) *Experience and education*, New York: Touchstone.

Finkbeiner, C. (2000) *Interessen und Strategien beim fremdsprachlichen Lesen. Wie Schülerinnen und Schüer englische Texte lesen und verstehen (Interests and strategies in foreign language reading. How pupils read and comprehend English)*, Tübingen: Narr.

van Lier, L. (1996) *Interaction in the language curriculum. Awareness, autonomy and authenticity* (Applied Linguistics and Language Study), Harlow: Longman.

CLAUDIA FINKBEINER

# Hawkins, Eric William

b. 1915, Heswall, UK

Language teacher, headmaster, teacher trainer, educationist

Eric Hawkins has played a major role in most developments in language teaching in Britain since the 1950s, and is especially known for his advocacy of a new subject, **LANGUAGE AWARENESS**, to bridge 'the space between' **ENGLISH** and foreign languages.

A career in language teaching, begun in 1937 but interrupted by the war, led to the Headship of Oldershaw Grammar School (1949–53) and of Calday Grange Grammar School (1953–64).

Among many measures introduced in the latter to broaden the curriculum and 'open windows', were a scheme to send Sixth Form linguists to **FRANCE** and Germany for a term each, and an alternative French 'O' level syllabus in which candidates presented books of their choice for oral discussion.

Hawkins soon became known nationally. He chaired for six years the Schools Council Modern Languages Committee (1968–74), whose *Working Paper 28* produced in 1970 did much to liberalise existing language examinations.

In 1965, Hawkins was invited to head the new Language Teaching Centre at the University of York. There, too, he proved to be an innovator. Increasingly dissatisfied with the conventional one-period-a-day foreign language timetabling – 'gardening in a gale of English', as he called it – he explored ways of intensifying language teaching by encouraging older pupils to help **BEGINNERS**, and organising reciprocal courses in which matched groups of English and French teachers and Sixth Formers taught each other, using English and **FRENCH** on alternate days. In annual summer schools in Yorkshire towns, students helped Asian immigrant children and slower learners to develop their language **SKILLS**. Research projects were initiated on the characteristics of a good language teacher, the effectiveness of **LANGUAGE LABORATORIES** in schools and the foreign language **NEEDS** of industry and commerce.

Outside the language field, Hawkins served on the Plowden Committee on **PRIMARY EDUCATION** (1963–67), the National Committee for Commonwealth Immigrants (1965–68) and, after his retirement in 1979, on the Rampton Committee on the education of children from ethnic minorities (1979–81).

From these broad concerns with education and his own experience in teaching French in a local comprehensive school grew his proposal to introduce a progressive language awareness course in secondary schools, in which English and foreign language teachers would combine to 'light fires of curiosity' about language, and children would 'learn how to learn'. This proposal, first adumbrated in 1974 and elaborated subsequently, has been taken up nationally and internationally (*see also* Language awareness).

The inspirational contributions of Eric Hawkins to education and language teaching have been recognised with the award of academic honours and, in 1973, of the CBE.

## Bibliography

Hawkins, E.W. (1981, revised edition 1987) *Modern languages in the curriculum*, Cambridge: Cambridge University Press.

Hawkins, E.W. (1984, revised edition 1987) *Awareness of language – an introduction*, Cambridge: Cambridge University Press.

Hawkins, E.W. (ed.) (1996) *Thirty years of language teaching*, London: CILT.

Hawkins, E.W. (1999) *Listening to Lorca – a journey into language*, London: CILT.

## Further reading

Green, P.S. (1985) 'Eric Hawkins', in P.S. Green (ed.), *York Papers in Language Teaching – for Eric Hawkins*, York: University of York Language Teaching Centre.

WALTER GRAUBERG

# Heritage languages

Heritage language is a term that can be used to describe the language of an immigrant group or community when it differs from the official or dominant language(s). It is also a way of differentiating between the languages of indigenous (aboriginal) and non-indigenous minority languages. The use of this term can be found in countries such as **CANADA** and **AUSTRALIA**, where there are not only indigenous minorities with their own languages and cultures but many non-indigenous immigrant communities. It may be a preferable term to that of 'minority language', which may have negative connotations linked to low status and subordination to the dominant language.

The Canadian Heritage Languages Act, for example, positively defined heritage language as 'a language, other than one of the official languages of Canada, that contributes to the linguistic heritage of Canada' (languagestore: 1). An alternative term used is that of 'community language', which refers to a language used within a particular community, including languages spoken by ethnic minority groups.

In certain places where there are concentrations of immigrant communities, heritage languages may be found more frequently than the official languages. In some neighbourhoods in Toronto, for example, 'less than half of the people have **ENGLISH** as their first language' and instead are **NATIVE SPEAKERS** of **CHINESE**, Italian and **PORTUGUESE**, to name a few (languagestore: 1). This is not unusual in many large conurbations around the world which have attracted peoples from numerous countries and communities. Whilst it adds to the linguistic diversity and multiculturalism of a nation, there are also questions raised about how to retain heritage language use whilst at the same time encouraging the learning of the official or dominant language.

In the past, it may have been more the case that the official policy in many countries was to promote the official language, what can be termed monolingualism, at the cost of immigrants and their children losing touch with their own languages. Over a period of time this can lead to language shift to the dominant language, which then becomes the norm and 'takes over' from the immigrants' own **MOTHER TONGUE**. Indeed, one view is that heritage language use may have impeded the effective learning of the dominant language and hence the assimilation of immigrants into the new country.

It was often left to individual families or communities to provide special classes and courses of study in their own language for themselves and their children; for example, the Saturday morning classes in Cantonese for children of the Hong Kong community in London's Soho. A more extreme personal strategy would be to send children back to their home country for re-education in their own language. It was not often considered to be the duty of government, at national or local level, to provide such teaching. Gradually this position has changed in some countries.

A different approach has been taken by some governments in more recent times, however, which represents an attempt to foster **BILINGUALISM** by providing heritage language teaching programmes as well as teaching of the official language. Rather than assume that the official language must be learnt at the expense of the heritage language, there is more of a recognition of the value and key role played by language in any cultural community. In Canada, a number of Heritage Language teaching programmes have been set up throughout the country.

Within such programmes, questions about the most appropriate and effective methods are raised. McQuillan (1996) asked specifically about how heritage languages should be taught, and carried out research into the effects of a free voluntary reading programme (FVR) on heritage language maintenance. Experimental control groups were formed from students from two 'Spanish for Native Speakers' courses at a university, with the experimental group receiving FVR in addition to the normal course. It was discovered that FVR led to improved knowledge, more positive **ATTITUDES** to **READING**, and more reading in the long term. It was also viewed as a 'pleasurable, beneficial and motivating activity' (Johnstone, 1997: 155). The significance of this study is that it highlights the problem facing many representatives of minority groups who do not have a high level of literacy in their own heritage language and who are, as a result, susceptible to processes of language shift to the majority language. FVR, according to McQuillan's (1996) study, seems to offer some promise as a means of fostering heritage language literacy and thereby maintaining literate as well as spoken bilingualism.

Further research is needed, however, into how different policies of heritage language teaching are being implemented, what methods are being used and with what degree of success. It is still only a relatively recent development in some countries, such as Canada, that heritage languages have been viewed as worthy of investment and support, and this is still by no means the norm in an increasingly multilingual, multicultural world. The policy in some places may still be to foster the dominant language and bring about a shift away from the heritage language.

**See also:** Australia; Bilingual education; Canada; Bilingualism; EBLUL; Mother tongue; Mother-tongue teaching; Primary education

### References

Johnstone, R. (1997) 'Research on language learning and teaching: 1996', *Language Teaching* July, 149–65.

*LanguageStore.com* Language in Canada website.

McQuillan, J. (1996) 'How should heritage languages be taught? The effects of a free voluntary reading program', *Foreign Language Annals* 29, 1: 56–71.

RUTH CHERRINGTON

# Higher education

The place of language teaching and learning amongst the disciplines of Higher Education (HE) has been subject to a fundamental debate: is it the means to an end or is it an end in itself? If it is the means to an end, what is that end? And if it is an end in itself, then how is that end defined? When one has an answer to these questions, there are then further issues about the ways in which the **OBJECTIVES** can be achieved, both in terms of programme organisation and in terms of classroom delivery. Whilst these questions have been central since language teaching first had a role in HE, the answers have evolved over time and are still evolving.

### A means to an end

In the teaching of the precursor of modern languages, the classics, the role of language was clear: it was the means of access to great texts. This tradition carried over into the construction of early language **SYLLABUSES**: the emphasis was on knowing the **GRAMMAR**, knowing the **VOCABULARY**, in order to be able first to understand and then to appreciate great literature in the classic texts, the canon, of the language to be studied. Productive language use, in the form of written prose **TRANS-LATION**, was more a means of ensuring that the grammar was known than a means of communication with an audience. Oral language ability was largely irrelevant to the main objective to be achieved.

Within the same paradigm other models have replaced access to great texts with access to other kinds of knowledge about the particular country and its civilisation. One version of this replaces the **LITERARY** canon with **CULTURAL STUDIES**. This varies from the simple inclusion of another medium, e.g. the cinema as well as text-based literature, to a redefinition of culture to approximate that which a sociologist or an anthropologist might recognise as a definition of that term. A second domain which may be set up as the target for language learners is that of **AREA STUDIES**. Here the disciplines of geography, politics and economics provide the knowledge base which is to be accessed. A third approach is to define the area to be accessed as that of business in the country; this may be subcategorised into marketing, human resources, or accounting. A fourth area which has seen the recent introduction of several programmes of study enables students to gain access to the study of law in the country. A few programmes may even provide dual qualifications acceptable in each country. And, finally, more and more scientists and engineers wish to broaden their understanding of their discipline and to make their ideas available to a wider community by adding a linguistic ability to their scientific skills.

Most countries will now have within their HE system programmes of study where the language teaching curriculum will correspond to one or more versions of this overall pattern. The broadest range of courses is probably provided in **ENGLISH** as a Foreign Language. Other languages may only be studied in a smaller range of contexts. The decisions as to which languages will be taught in which context tend to relate more to how a particular country interprets the need and demand for modern languages rather than, for example, deciding that the languages which should be most widely taught should be those with the greatest numbers of speakers. Also, given the length of time needed to acquire a high-level command of a foreign language and the requirement for an existing teaching force, any changes in language policy (assuming a country has such a policy) take a long time to be implemented in practice.

Whilst this particular version of the paradigm which sees language learning as a means rather than an end is still present, it is no longer the only or even the dominant model.

## An end in itself

What, then, of the argument that language teaching is an end in itself? There are three main reasons why it may be considered so.

First, the object of the exercise may be seen as the ability to communicate effectively with the inhabitants of the country whose language is being studied. Whilst in the early stages of modern language teaching that communication would have been in writing, now it is just as likely to be oral, by telephone, via television, satellite links or face-to-face. Also, there are broad and narrow definitions of communication. A broad definition will require a sound background knowledge of the culture of the country. A narrow definition may limit the range of communicative functions that a learner may achieve to those which are required by the reasons for the learner visiting the country or by the professional activity to be undertaken. Some learners may also see their role as facilitating the communication of others by mediation between two or more languages as translators or interpreters. In many European countries there are specialist universities for the training of translators and **INTERPRETERS**. These have a particular kind of curriculum which is designed to provide a broad base of general knowledge as well as the high-level language skills required for linguistic mediation.

Second, the language may be the object of study for the sake of discovering how language and languages themselves function. This may take the form of a branch of **LINGUISTICS**: theoretical, descriptive, comparative, or historical. **SOCIOLINGUISTICS** and psycholinguistics combine linguistic study with sociology and **PSYCHOLOGY**. The process of language teaching and learning may also be the object of study in the disciplines of **APPLIED LINGUISTICS**, **SECOND LANGUAGE ACQUISITION** or applied language research.

Third, the learner may themselves intend to become a teacher of the language, perhaps at secondary level, and the subject matter of the teaching will be the language itself. This requires the learner to have explicit or declarative knowledge of language structure and the ability to explain that structure, as well as high-level oral and written language skills, given that almost all language teaching is now done in the foreign language.

Taking into account these various objectives, programmes of language teaching in higher education have the task of organising effective study to enable learners to achieve them. How is this now being done? A subdivision would be into three categories: programmes which aim to produce graduates whose main focus is on language(s) and cognate disciplines; programmes whose main focus is to add a linguistic ability to a student of another main discipline; programmes whose aim is to integrate the language study within the discipline which is the main focus. The first takes the form of language degrees which include within them a greater or lesser amount of education in one or more of the cognate disciplines, either in the foreign language or in the language of the host country. The second takes the form of Institution Wide Language Programmes (IWLP), in which staged progress towards a linguistic goal is made possible. The third seeks to teach much of the subject matter in the foreign language, often through extended periods of residence abroad. The first two are more widespread than the third.

Each of these models is then expressed through the standard modularised and semesterised organisational pattern which is present in many North American, British and, increasingly, European universities. Modules are normally taught and examined within one semester, normally of 15 weeks duration, with two semesters in each year.

One of the main aims of this model is to permit students to attain definable levels and to have those levels certificated before moving on to the next. For many years, **ENGLISH** as a Foreign Language has had a number of standard examinations (TOEFL, Cambridge Proficiency, etc.) which enable the qualifications gained to be recognised worldwide. For most other languages the system is less codified, although attempts are being made in Europe to encourage examiners to work within a more standardised framework. What is noticeable, however, is that the range of languages which can be studied in HE and the range of different starting and stopping levels has increased enormously.

With the possible exception of some universities in the **USA**, most degree programmes will offer or insist upon a period of residence in the country where the language is spoken. This may vary from a few months to a full year. The time may be spent as an **EXCHANGE** student, working as a language assistant in an educational establishment, or working for a company. The two former methods are more widespread than the latter. In the case of those programmes where the subject teaching is fully integrated with the subject, students may spend as much as two years studying the subject in the foreign country in order to obtain dual qualifications valid in each of the two countries.

## Teaching methods

How, then, will such programmes be delivered and what principles govern that delivery? It would be useful to be able to report that researchers are now able to give an account of the language learning process which is sufficiently well founded for teachers to derive the principles of their teaching from it. Unfortunately, despite the extremely healthy state of second language acquisition (SLA) studies, there is no consensus as to how learning happens. A major school of thought argues that linguistic knowledge must be related to an innate **UNIVERSAL GRAMMAR** (UG) which enables children to acquire their first language on the basis of inadequate evidence, and that, on the basis of an argument from parsimony, it is likely that UG has a role to play in the acquisition of a second language. Given, however, that a second language learner typically has far more nonsystematic variability in their L2, that their learning of the second language remains incomplete, that the influence of the L1 is frequently audible and visible, but that learners have none the less been shown to follow a systematic route in acquiring an L2, there is still a lot of research needed before it will be possible to state exactly what role UG may have in second language acquisition.

Other schools of thought would not attach such importance to UG but would rather emphasise the need for learners to be motivated through meaningful and contextualised language use in the classroom. They would argue that, whatever technical mechanisms are involved in the acquisition of the syntax, the essential requirement is for the learners to have a need and desire to use the language in a meaningful way: they will then find the means of developing the syntax they require to express their ideas. It is, however, probably fair to say that most SLA researchers would subscribe to a view which required learners to be exposed to as much naturalistic language as possible and also to be provided with clear explanations of the linguistic system where such explanation was helpful. Researchers would not expect either simple exposure alone or simple instruction alone to enable L2 learners to become fluent and accurate in the L2: both are needed, but exactly how and in what proportions remain matters for further research.

It is, therefore, not surprising that a variety of methodologies are in use in higher education, some of which stress the need for **AUTHENTIC** exposure and rely on the learner's ability to create the language in a way similar to L1 learning, and some of which stress the need to learn the grammatical rules of the language in a conscious and explicit way and rely on the learner to apply these rules in practice. Most, of course, do some of each. Depending on the choices made, courses will be sequenced in relation to functions of language, to topics to be covered and to the grammar to be presented. Exactly which of these takes the primary role will depend on the level, prior learning and objectives of the course.

In terms of what happens in language classrooms, again it is clear that variety is the order of the day. The **GRAMMAR–TRANSLATION** method is still used within degree programmes in higher education, particularly towards the end of the course. It often forms part of the final **ASSESSMENT**. Some institutions still believe that translation into the foreign language is the only skill which ensures precision in the use of specific structures. In order to inculcate knowledge of those structures, use will be made of grammar classes and grammar **EXERCISES** in the first years of the course and **STYLISTIC** exercises later on.

Others will place less emphasis on translation and certainly less on translation into the foreign language. Instead, they will emphasise the four skills of **READING**, **WRITING**, **LISTENING** and **SPEAKING**, and will organise the course in such a way as to develop these skills in the contexts in which the learners might have need for them. Oral classes, varying from conversation to advanced **INTERPRETING**, will also be a central feature of all university language programmes.

If the language being learnt is English, then separate courses may be offered for academic English, general English or even **ENGLISH FOR SPECIFIC PURPOSES**, including Business English. Most other languages, however, tend to offer more general courses, encompassing various areas, although all can, if required, produce the equivalent to specialised English courses.

The exact specification of skills, the amount of background knowledge, the amount of discussion of literature, etc., will depend entirely on the particular courses being followed. Specialist degree courses will stress more background knowledge, translation and written competence, whereas IWLP programmes will seek to develop the four skills in relevant contexts.

Most Western languages are also taught according to a **COMMUNICATIVE LANGUAGE TEACHING** methodology and will ensure that the language learners are required to make use of their language ability in a variety of communicative situations. This methodology will be present on both degree programmes and IWLP programmes, although the way in which communicative situations are defined will be different. The IWLP situations are likely to be closely determined in relation to the linguistic structures to be used in each of the four skills, whilst degree programme situations may be open-ended in terms of the language structures to be used in accomplishing various tasks.

The delivery of courses is increasingly being influenced by new technology. Computer-based instruction is playing an increasingly important role in the form of CD-ROM-based instruction, multimedia packages and locally networked **MATERIALS**. In some cases the use of high-band technology in the form of international networks has allowed live interaction in real time between students in different countries around a set of teaching materials. Even where such technology is not available, e-mail correspondence between students in classrooms in different countries is making an effective contribution to lifelong learning. The potential effect of the technology is enormous, but it still has a long way to go before it realises its maximum power for change.

**See also:** Area studies; CALL; Communicative language learning; Cultural studies; France; Interpreting; Japan; *Landeskunde*; Secondary education; Study abroad; Translation theory; United States of America

### Further reading

Coleman, J.A. (1996) *Studying languages: a survey of British and European students*, London: CILT.

Ellis, R. (1994) *The study of second language acquisition*, Oxford: Oxford University Press.

Evans, C. (1988) *Language people: an experience of teaching and learning modern languages in British universities*, Milton Keynes: Open University.

Freed, B. (1995) *Second language acquisition in a study abroad context*, Amsterdam/Philadelphia: Benjamins.

Hawkins, E. (1981) *Modern languages in the curriculum*, Cambridge: Cambridge University Press.

Hawkins, E. (ed.) (1998) *Thirty years of language teaching*, London: CILT.

Healey, F. (1967) *Foreign language teaching in the universities*, Manchester: Manchester University Press.

Kramsch, C. (1993) *Context and culture in language teaching*, Oxford: Oxford University Press.

Parker, G.P. and Reuben, C. (1994) *Languages for the international scientist*, London: AFLS/CILT.

Richards, J.C. and Rogers, T.S. (1986) *Approaches and methods in language teaching*, Cambridge: Cambridge University Press.

Stern, H.H. (1965) *Modern languages in the university* (2nd edn), London: Modern Language Association/Macmillan.

Stern, H.H. (1983) *Fundamental concepts of language teaching*, Oxford: Oxford University Press.

Thomas, G. (1993) *A survey of European languages in the UK 1992*, London: CNAA.

RICHARD TOWELL

# History: the nineteenth century

Two opposing currents may be seen in language learning between the Renaissance and 1800. The best educational practice in these centuries was along the lines of common sense, not yet infected by the virus of formal 'grammaticalism'; i.e., it was still common practice to teach languages by living contact with them, whether in their oral or their written form. The second trend in language teaching after the Renaissance had already begun to be formalised in a systematic teaching of **GRAMMAR** based on paradigms, tables, declensions and conjugations. One can easily agree with Mallinson about the cause of this deviation when he writes:

> When once the Latin tongue had ceased to be a normal vehicle for communication, and was replaced as such by the vernacular languages, then it most speedily became a 'mental gymnastic', the supremely 'dead' language, a disciplined and systematic study of which was held to be indispensable as a basis for all forms of higher education. Classical studies were then intended and made to produce an excellent mental discipline, a fortitude of spirit and a broad humane understanding of life. They succeeded triumphantly for the times in their objective. And when under the pressure of circumstance a modern foreign language had to be found a place in the school curriculum as a serious time-table subject, it was considered natural, right and proper that it should be taught along these patterned lines that had proved their worth.
>
> (Mallinson, 1957: 8)

Modern educational **PSYCHOLOGY** has discovered that a double fallacy lies in the traditional belief about the formative value of Latin as such and of the grammatical method as a means of mental training, especially since the concept of 'transfer of training' has become better understood. Latin has no unique value for mental discipline. This traditional belief may be explained by turning to the **TEXTBOOKS** used for so many decades by these teachers. They are probably the chief reason for perpetuating an opinion which today appears clearly contrary to common sense and science.

Nineteenth-century textbook compilers were mainly determined to codify the foreign language into frozen rules of morphology and syntax to be explained and eventually memorised. Oral work was reduced to an absolute minimum, while a handful of written **EXERCISES**, constructed at random, came as an appendix to the rules.

## The influence of textbooks

Of the many books published during this period, those by Seidenstücker and Plötz were perhaps the most typical and the most influential, since such compilations became the model for innumerable language textbooks during the nineteenth and first half of the twentieth century. Johann Heinrich Seidenstücker (1785–1817) intended, laudably, to offer only very simple material to the students. But he had an erroneous notion of simplicity. In his *Elementarbuch zur Erlernung der französischen Sprache* (1811), he reduced the material to disconnected sentences to illustrate specific rules. He divided his text carefully into two parts, one giving the rules and necessary paradigms, the other giving French sentences for **TRANSLATION** into German and German sentences for translation into French. The immediate aim was for the student to apply the given rules by means of appropriate exercises. Seidenstücker was closely imitated by Karl Plötz (1819–81), who dominated the schools of Germany even after his death. In his textbooks, divided into the two parts described above, the sole form of instruction was mechanical translation.

The manuals prepared by Seidenstücker and Plötz had all the material that was needed for a thorough drilling in the niceties of grammar and written French, but no pupil relying on these materials alone would ever have been able to converse with or understand a Frenchman.

In sum, it was 'a barren waste of insipid sentence translation', as Bahlsen put it. 'Committing words to memory, translating sentences, drilling irregular verbs, later memorizing, repeating, and applying grammatical rules with their exceptions – that was and remained our main occupation; for not until the last years of the higher schools with the nine-year curriculum did French reading come to

anything like prominence, and that was the time when free compositions in the foreign language were to be written' (Bahlsen, 1905: 10). Bahlsen is referring to his own painful experience. He had been a student of Plötz. He describes a situation still common today: having to write a letter or to speak in the foreign language would raise before his mind 'a veritable forest of paragraphs' and 'an impenetrable thicket of grammatical rules'.

The same defects can be found in other authors of the time, such as Johann Franz Ahn (*Französischer Lehrgang*, 1834) and H.S. Ollendorf (*Methode, eine Sprache in sechs Monaten lesen, schreiben und sprechen zu lernen*, 1783) (Bahlsen, 1905: 10). The main fault with the Ahn and Ollendorf method was the principle of constructing artificial sentences in order to illustrate a rule. 'The result', as H. **SWEET** later remarked,

> ... is to exclude the really natural and idiomatic combinations, which cannot be formed a priori, and to produce insipid, colourless combinations which do not stamp themselves on the memory, many of which, indeed, could hardly occur in real life, such as:
>
> The cat of my aunt is more treacherous than the dog of your uncle.
> We speak about your cousin, and your cousin Amelia is loved by her uncle and her aunt.
> My sons have bought the mirrors of the duke.
> Horses are taller than tigers.
>
> At one school where I learnt – or rather made a pretence of learning – Greek on this system, the master used to reconstruct the materials of the exercises given in our book into new and strange combinations, till at last, with a faint smile on his ascetic countenance, he evolved the following sentence, which I remembered long after I had forgotten all the rest of my Greek – *The philosopher pulled the lower jaw of the hen*. The results of this method have been well parodied by Burnand in his *New Sandford and Merton*, thus: *The merchant is swimming with (avec) the gardener's son, but the Dutchman has the fine gun.*
>
> (Sweet, 1964: 72–3)

This way of teaching foreign languages became the standard method during the first half of the nineteenth century, especially since the proliferation of textbooks modeled on the Plötz outline placed ready-made tools in the hands of many unskilled teachers.

## American influences

Fortunately, there were some exceptions to the invading and deviating trend in the first half of the nineteenth century. In both Europe and America a few great teachers felt that the right direction still lay in the natural approach, and they continued to teach languages in a living manner. One of these great educators who took the task of modern language teaching seriously was the American poet Longfellow (1807–82). James Geddes, who effectively commemorated Longfellow's unique contribution to the field of modern language teaching, writes:

> That Longfellow began his distinguished career by teaching modern languages has been so overshadowed by his poetical output throughout his life that his pedagogical production which followed upon assuming his duties of Professor of Modern Languages is practically unknown to the average reader. Finding the elementary treatises of the day poorly adapted to his course, he prepared no less than seven different textbooks. The fact that Longfellow brought out seven textbooks between 1830 and 1835 is in itself proof of his seriousness of purpose to teach French, Italian and **SPANISH** to the best of his ability. Some of these books were used for many years, a proof of their pedagogical worth and usefulness. They are all small books which, for **BEGINNERS**, Longfellow preferred to those treating the foreign languages *in extenso*.
>
> (Geddes, 1933: 26)

Longfellow treated languages as living languages, and therefore taught them as spoken idioms.

Another great American scholar, George Ticknor (1791–1871), deserves mention here. He was an example of the best in American culture in contact with European leaders, one of the first American scholars with an international reputation in the modern humanities. Ticknor's acceptance in 1816 of the newly established Smith Professorship of the French and Spanish Languages and

Literatures at Harvard induced him to spend much time in **FRANCE**, Spain, Portugal, and Italy. In 1819, after much preparatory work, he was ready to start his active career. His theories of instruction in the modern foreign languages were expressed in his *Lecture on the Best Methods of Teaching the Living Languages*, delivered in 1832. His main ideas can be summed up briefly as follows:

1 The primary characteristic of languages is their 'living aspect'. Ticknor's very first sentence in the lecture is a confession of faith: 'The most important characteristic of a living language – the attribute in which resides its essential power and value – is, that it is a spoken one ...'

2 Therefore, the easiest and best way to acquire a language is to 'reside where it is constantly spoken', and where it should be 'the minister to their hourly wants, and the medium of their constant intercourse', but since this is not possible for all students, the teachers must, 'while still endeavoring to teach it as a living and spoken language ... resort to means somewhat more 'artificial and indirect ... the best method within our power at home'.

3 'There is no one mode of teaching languages applicable 'to persons of all the different ages and different degrees of preparation who present themselves to be taught'. The method must be adapted to individual differences.

4 Teaching techniques must also be adjusted to different **AGE** levels. Ticknor does not agree with those who would have all learners follow the natural way, i.e. as a child learns his **MOTHER TONGUE**, because 'it is plain', he says 'that a method adapted to children seven or eight years old would be altogether unsuited to persons in the maturity of their faculties'. Therefore, the method should differ according to the various age levels; and while the oral approach and the inductive teaching of grammar may be advisable for younger learners, 'the mature students will choose to learn by the analysis of particulars from generals, rather than by the induction of generals from particulars'.

In his sense of balance and his affirmation of progressive principles, Ticknor closely approaches current trends in modern language methodology.

## Practical pioneers

While practice in teaching foreign languages was drifting among the vagaries of formalised grammar, and only a few great teachers managed to keep the main principles of sound tradition from total shipwreck, reform was slowly but surely getting under way. The reasserting of a more natural approach was not only the result of loyalty to a long-standing tradition that dated back to ancient civilisations and had been consciously affirmed, especially during the seventeenth and eighteenth centuries. It was more particularly the emergence of new ideas within the ranks of such newly born sciences as **LINGUISTICS** and psychology. Representative of the soundest portion of this educational heritage are such teachers as Heness, Marcel, Sauveur, and **GOUIN**. On the linguistic side, **VIËTOR** could be considered as the pioneer of a more scientific reform that arose toward the end of the nineteenth century.

The idea of the 'natural method', as opposed to the grammar-centred procedures introduced by Ahn, Ollendorf and Plötz, was strongly shared by Gottlieb Heness. Heness started a small private school of modern languages at New Haven, Connecticut, in 1866. His viewpoint was embodied in his text *Leitfaden für den Unterricht in der deutschen Sprache* (1867). Heness was soon joined by another capable teacher, L. Sauveur, the author of *Causeries avec mes élèves* and *Petites Causeries*. They founded a school in Cambridge, and opened summer schools of modern languages counting many outstanding personalities like Eliot, Longfellow and Gilman among their students.

The natural method as practised by Heness, however, may have lacked the systematic character demanded by effective teaching. To bring system and order into natural disorder was the aim of another great pioneer, Claude Marcel, who published *The Study of Languages Brought Back to Its True Principles, or the Art of Thinking in a Foreign Language* in 1867. The title was a very modern statement of purpose, psychologically speaking. Mastering a language was thought to consist not simply in the ability to manipulate forms, but more radically in the ability also to 'think' in the foreign language (what today we may call 'coordinate bilingualism'). However, the systematic character of

Marcel's method depended mainly on a restriction of scope by concentrating primarily on **READING**. The essential steps in the 'Marcel method' are the following:

1 The student's ear is trained by listening to the teacher reading extensively in the foreign language.
2 The student takes over by trying to read first simple, and, if possible, familiar material, followed by more and more difficult discourse as he progresses.
3 **SPEAKING** is then practised on the texts previously read.
4 **WRITING** is considered the least important ability.

Marcel avoids formal training in grammar or translation. Reading makes up most of the instruction, and grammar does not seem to help in improving reading comprehension. Dictionaries also are avoided, as they would hamper extensive reading. It can be easily understood how much Marcel's approach influenced the 'reading method' around 1920.

Heness, Marcel and Sauveur were European teachers who had left Europe (where Plötz was wielding a dominant influence) and had emigrated to the United States to find a more favourable educational climate. But another European was to exert a large influence in Europe and America. In 1880 the Frenchman François Gouin produced his *L'art d'enseigner et d'étudier les langues*, a work that was at the time completely neglected in France (the author had to have it printed at his own expense), but was a great success in Germany. It took England and America by storm and proved a happy source of inspiration for the later work of the 'direct-methodists'. In his book, Gouin tells of his fruitless attempts at learning **GERMAN** by some of the various grammatical methods then in vogue, and how one day his own son inspired him with the idea that was to become the basis of his method. Gouin conceived the idea of developing simple events for school use, known as the 'Gouin Series'. The new element that Gouin brought into the teaching of modern languages was intense activity through dramatisation of the sentences to be drilled. Language was no longer considered a construct of isolated pieces, something abstract to be anatomised and then pieced together again. 'Language is behaviour', Gouin could say today. Therefore, association, mimicry, memorisation constituted the pivotal activities of language learning. Furthermore, his ingenious classification of activities was meeting not only the child's need for activity, but also its need for concrete and familiar experiences. A third positive aspect to be found in Gouin's method is certainly represented by his use of complete sentences anchored in true-to-life situations instead of fragments of speech taken out of living context.

On the other hand, several methodological weaknesses tend to jeopardise the effectiveness of Gouin's approach. His opposition to phonetics, reading and written exercises, and his recommendation of a large **VOCABULARY**, not graded by difficulty or frequency, are both weaknesses in the light of modern **APPLIED LINGUISTICS**. Furthermore, unlike Comenius, Pestalozzi and more modern teachers, Gouin distrusted realia and pictorial representation and placed his faith instead in a vague intuitive awareness. Finally, the exaggerated analysis of speech and behaviour into 'micro-segments' and the excessive use of translation (especially in the early stages) endanger the positive effects of Gouin's main procedures. Gouin did, however, inaugurate a new era in language teaching by introducing a 'systematic psychological approach'.

## The influence of science

The practical innovations of such talented teachers as Heness, Sauveur, Marcel and Gouin did not impress the public until science stepped in to strengthen the appeal of the new methodology. In fact, the **REFORM MOVEMENT** came to be officially recognised only when noted linguists became enthusiastic spokesmen for the advancing trend. It was especially the new science of phonetics, 'the science of speech sounds and the art of pronunciation', as it was called by Henry Sweet, that supplied the first scientific basis for the reformed methodology. Alexander John Ellis had published his *Essentials of Phonetics* (1848), E. Bruecke his *Grundzüge der Physiologie und der Systematik der Sprachlaute* (1856), Alexander Bell his *Visible Speech* (1867) and his *Sounds and their Relations* (1882).

The new science of linguistics was basically reduced to descriptive phonetics; and it seemed that this science of sounds could promise intriguing new developments in the teaching of modern languages. Furthermore, deep changes in the fundamental structure of European society and in the whole economic outlook were creating new demands upon culture and school education. Germany and England had become industrial nations and strong colonial powers. Colonial exploitation and commercial enterprise depended not only on industrial undertakings but also on adequate foreign language training. The problems of that transitional period were similar to the ones confronting the post-World War Two generation.

In sum, the impact on language teaching came from two fronts, the economic and the scientific. The phoneticians – Sweet, Sievers, Trautmann, Helmholtz, Passy, Rambeau, Klinghardt and others – set themselves untiringly to develop this new science, so much so that it came to be considered an indispensable help in any language course. Archibald Sayce applied phonetics to the problems of language teaching. Wilhelm Viëtor (1850–1918) issued a pamphlet entitled *Der Sprachunterricht muß umkehren: ein Beitrag zur Überbürdungsfrage* (1882).

With withering sarcasm he denounced all the supporters of the Ploetz method and insisted that the spoken language become the basis of instruction; it is through the ear that the child learns its mother tongue, it is through the ear that a more mature person must begin the study of a foreign language. The teacher, therefore, must have a firm grasp of phonetics; and he must have resided long enough in the foreign country to have mastered and to be able to teach an exact **PRONUNCIATION**. Again, a language is not made up of isolated words, but of word-groups, of 'speech-patterns', of sentences that mean something. No more lists of words, therefore, to be learned laboriously by heart; no more meaningless snippets of sentences, void of all interest and real meaning; no more grammatical paradigms. Grammar is to be learned inductively, and translation, a most difficult exercise, is not to be used for the acquisition of new vocabulary, but as an art that requires considerable maturity of knowledge of the foreign tongue before it can profitably be indulged.

(Mallinson, 1957: 14–15)

Viëtor's appeal was heard all over Europe and also in America, especially after he started a review, *Die neueren Sprachen*, that popularised the new approach.

In Great Britain, one of Viëtor's disciples also made his voice heard. He was Walter Ripman, who belonged to a small band of English pioneers who had attended the first modern-language summer course at Marburg after the publication of Viëtor's pamphlet. He came away a convinced supporter, and in 1899 published his translation and adaptation of Viëtor's *Kleine Phonetik* (Elements of Phonetics) – a book that established itself as a classic in England.

In the same period, a Swiss by the name of Alge in 1887 started to use coloured wall pictures, introduced in 1885 by a Viennese, Holzel, to the teaching of modern languages. Thus the famous wall pictures of the seasons, of trades and occupations, and of village and town life, came into existence. Ripman, in collaboration with Alge, wrote his *First French Book* (1898). This was the beginning of a long collaboration between Ripman and his publishers, J.M. Dent and Sons, for whom he remained the general modern languages editor until his death in 1947.

The claims of the reformers were not, however, accepted peacefully. Reactions on the part of teachers and scholars arose, not only because of irrational attachment to old practices, but also because of the initial chaos caused by the unsystematic and rigid application of the new precepts to differing teaching situations and by enthusiastic but unprepared novice teachers. Lack of clear **OBJECTIVES** and flexibility was frequently the cause of students failing examinations or not managing to get a firm grasp of the language they were supposed to be studying. Consequently, teachers followed one of two courses: some reverted to the old grammar–grind tactics and to the Plötz approach; others tried some sort of compromise between the oral approach and the use of reading and grammar. It was a 'tamed' **DIRECT METHOD**. A final summing up of the controversy over the original direct method appeared in 1909. It read:

> The Reform has fulfilled its mission. It has laid the ghosts of the grammatical method, which made a fetish of the study of grammar with excessive attention to translation from and into the foreign language ... But what the grammatical method neglected, practical and correct use of the spoken language, the reform method has pushed to extremes. In making mastery of the spoken language the chief objective, the nature and function of secondary schools was overlooked, because such an objective under normal conditions of mass instruction is only attainable in a modest degree. The reform method requires not only a teacher who possesses a perfect mastery of the foreign language, but makes such claims on his nervous and physical energy as to entail premature exhaustion.
>
> Average pupils, not to mention weaker ones, do not justify the demands made by the oral use of the language; they soon weary, are overburdened and revolt. Early adherents of the new method, after their enthusiasm has been dashed by stern realities, have gradually broken away.
>
> (Breymann and Steinmuller, 1895–1909, cited by Buchanan and MacPhee, 1928: 19f)

**See also:** Direct method; Grammar–translation method; Humboldt; Materials and media; Monolingual principle; Reform Movement; Secondary education; Teaching methods

## References

Bahlsen, L. (1905) *The teaching of modern languages*, Boston: Ginn.

Buchanan, M.A. and McPhee, E.D. (1928) *Modern language instruction in Canada*, Toronto: University of Toronto Press.

Geddes, J. (1933) 'The old and the new', *French Review* VII, 1: ???–??.

Mallinson, V. (1957) *Teaching a foreign language*, London: Heinemann.

Sweet, H. (1964) *The practical study of languages*, Oxford: Oxford University Press; (first edition 1899).

## Further reading

Caravolas, J.-A. (1994) *La Didactique des Langues. Anthologie I. A l'ombre de Quintilien*, Montreal: Les Presses de l'Université de Montréal; Tübingen: Gunter Narr.

Caravolas, J.-A. (1994) *La Didactique des Langues. Précis d'Histoire I 1450–1700*, Montreal: Les Presses de l'Université de Montréal; Tübingen: Gunter Narr.

Hesse, M.G. (1975) *Approaches to Teaching Foreign Languages*, Amsterdam and New York: North Holland/Elsevier.

Howatt, A.P.R. (1984) *A history of English language teaching*, Oxford: Oxford University Press.

Jespersen, O. (1947) *How to teach a foreign language*, London: Allen and Unwin.

Kelly, L.G. (1969) *25 centuries of language teaching*, Rowley, MA: Newbury House.

Titone, R. (1968) *Teaching foreign languages: an historical sketch*, Washington: Georgetown University Press.

RENZO TITONE

# History: from the Reform Movement to 1945

## Europe

In most European countries the teaching of modern foreign languages was introduced into public sector schools in the course of the nineteenth century. In those days the living languages were predominantly taught according to the method used for the dead languages (i.e. Latin and Greek), i.e. by teaching grammar rules and bilingual wordlists, and by translating isolated, not seldom inane, sentences. Growing discontent over this approach was expressed throughout the early part of the nineteenth century (see Hawkins, 1987: 117), but did not come to a head until the last quarter of that century. When Viëtor's *Der Sprachunterricht muss umkehren!*, regarded by most historians of language education as the reformers' clarion call for innovation and change, came out in 1882 it therefore simply gave expression to ideas that had been in the air for some time, both in Europe and in America.

The **REFORM MOVEMENT** was induced by political and economic changes in Germany and fostered by the Neogrammarians' interest in the living languages and dialects (especially in their psycho-physiological side) for the purpose of explaining language change. Most, but not all, reformers were also phoneticians. From Germany the movement soon spread to the other German-speaking countries and to Scandinavia, where Francke and later **JESPERSEN** became its main protagonists. In **FRANCE** and England Passy (founder, in 1886, of *Le Maître Phonétique*) and **SWEET** gave an important boost to the movement.

Henry Sweet felt himself to be a phonetician in the first place and a linguist in the second. It is clear from Sweet's early writings where he situated his 'practical philology' (see Howatt, 1984: 189). It lies somewhere between 'living philology', which was based on phonetics and psychology, and the 'practical study of languages', which meant learning how to understand, speak, write and read a foreign language. In other words, 'practical philology' is the area where general linguistic principles are applied to the learning of other languages. Sweet's 'practical philology' came close to modern **APPLIED LINGUISTICS**. Its cornerstones were phonetics (1899: 4) and Herbartian associationism (1899: 40 and 103). He favoured an inductive presentation of grammar (i.e. one presenting sufficient examples for the learners to derive the rule themselves) (1899:117). Sweet was aware of the disadvantages of **AGE** (the older we are the less grow our powers of imitation and **MOTIVATION**) and of already knowing a language (one's own). For this reason he dismissed Gouin's 'natural' method (1899: 76). Nor did he approve of the view that the **NATIVE SPEAKER** teacher is the intrinsically better teacher (1899: 48).

The lasting impression after reading Sweet's book is one of emphasis on phonetic and linguistic principles. For the benefit of missionaries he had added a chapter which contained guidelines for the study of unrecorded, non-Western languages. The techniques described in this chapter, such as the use of native informants and linguistically trained instructors are really adumbrations of what the American linguist Leonard **BLOOMFIELD** was to propose for the language training of military personnel during World War Two (Bloomfield, 1942 and 1945).

Considerations of an educational nature are virtually absent from Sweet's book. His teachers and pupils are bloodless abstractions, and his style is that of learned discourse (Howatt, 1984: 188). How different is Otto Jespersen's book! *How to Teach a Foreign Language* came out in 1904 and has remained popular among language teachers ever since. Small wonder, for this is a book that both teachers and students can identify with, showing as it does their strong and weak points. Not only was Jespersen a phonetician and a linguist as famous as Sweet, but one with a mission as an educator at that. This is evident from almost every page of Jespersen's book, which shows a lively interest in teachers and pupils. His 'inventional grammar' is based upon his precept that one should 'never tell the children anything that they can find out for themselves' (1904: 127), a principle Sweet ridiculed (Sweet, 1899: 116). If Sweet focused on linguistics, Jespersen did so on pedagogy. In Jespersen's book one frequently comes across the expression 'from a pedagogical point of view'. It is Jespersen's pedagogical perspective which determines the choice of his subject-matter and the importance he assigns to the various language **SKILLS**. What was at issue for Jespersen was educating young people to become responsible world citizens. Jespersen was convinced that the modern humanities could play a big part in this (1904: 9). His book was influential in that it defined the principal aim of **READING** in terms of giving 'the pupils some insight into the foreign nation's peculiarity' as he called it (1904: 179). Since Jespersen wrote this, **LANDESKUNDE** has not been absent from European coursebooks and **TEACHER EDUCATION** programmes (van Essen, 1986). In the period under review its aims have varied from teaching just the realia to fostering a better understanding between peoples. Jespersen believed in the latter: 'language teachers all over the world', he writes, 'may ultimately prove more efficacious in establishing good permanent relations between the nations than Peace Congresses at the Hague' (1904: 180).

In foreign-language teaching, Jespersen argued, the language is not an aim in itself, it is a means to an end: communication (1904: 5). This was an encouraging noise, especially at a time when the **GRAMMAR–TRANSLATION** method was rife. What to the modern reader is not so much a novelty as a remarkable statement is the exclamation with which Jespersen concluded his chapter on grammar teaching: 'practise what is right again and again!' As far as I know, nobody has ever accused Jespersen of **BEHAVIOURISM** because of this.

In the period under discussion, nobody has contributed more to our field than the Englishman Harold E. **PALMER**. Palmer has left us a great many works, all of them of a practical, 'applied' nature. He was completely self-taught, and this may explain why he, of Sweet, Jespersen and himself, was the better language pedagogue. The lessons he taught to **ADULT** learners at Berlitz schools in Belgium have shaped Palmer as a language pedagogue. He taught according to the **DIRECT METHOD**, without recourse to the native language of his students. His teaching experiences found their way into a number of books, and it is the principles laid down in these books that have remained the core of Palmer's language pedagogy. In 1916 Palmer published his *100 Substitution Tables* (Palmer, 1916), a work with a **BEHAVIOURIST** slant.

In the same year, Palmer published *The Scientific Study and Teaching of Languages* (Palmer, 1917), based on an in-service course he had taught in London. It was the first time that the word 'scientific' in the title of a work on language pedagogy was explicitly associated with language education. This book contained so many idiosyncratic terms (e.g. 'ergonics') that it must have driven many a contemporary reader to despair.

Palmer's *Everyday Sentences in Spoken English* (1922a) embodies a first attempt at what in the 1970s was to be called the functional/notional **SYLLABUS**. Palmer's 'everyday sentences', arranged under such language functions as *Asking for Information*, *Giving Permission* and so on, meant a huge step forwards compared with the often absurd, isolated sentences that were still widely used in the grammar–translation coursebooks of the day. But at the same time they were a major step backwards compared with the connected texts of the reformers, as a context was wanting.

Habit-formation was the strongest pillar of Palmer's language pedagogy (Palmer, 1922b). But, just as with Jespersen and, later, Bloomfield, it would be wrong to attach too much importance to

Palmer's behaviourism. At most, Palmer was a proto-behaviourist (Howatt, 1984: 240). When Palmer wrote about habit-formation, behaviourism proper was still in its infancy. Palmer's use of isolated sentences conflicted with the precepts of *Gestalt* (i.e. 'pattern') **PSYCHOLOGY** which was just then coming into its own. It also put **NON-NATIVE SPEAKER TEACHERS** at a disadvantage, since they did not have at their disposal the whole range of sentences that a native speaker teacher potentially had (Palmer, 1922a). Just as Sweet had done, Palmer promoted the view that the teacher should command both the learner's mother tongue and the target language (Palmer, 1917: 163 and 173–4). When it came to using the learners' mother tongue in the classroom, Palmer made it clear that he was not against it as long as it was limited to the explanation of word meanings ('semanticisation'). This flexibility was probably due to Palmer's Japanese experiences, for Japanese teachers had a limited spoken command of **ENGLISH**, but it was really at variance with his views of a direct method.

After 1931, Palmer took great pains to provide his language pedagogy with a theoretical foundation. This he did with the aid of **SAUSSURE**'s teachings (Palmer and Vere Redman 1932: 72).

Palmer's language pedagogy is perhaps best characterised as 'eclectic', aimed at learning another language as efficiently as possible. If anything, his eclecticism meant pluralistic (Palmer, 1922b: 108). With his methodological pluralism Palmer was way ahead of his time. He anticipated a number of distinctions that have recently received renewed attention or have become topical issues in our field, like Krashen's unconscious **ACQUISITION** and conscious learning in the **MONITOR MODEL** (Palmer, 1922b; Krashen, 1982) and the presence of an incubation period in unconscious acquisition (Palmer 1917: 97) – similar to Krashen's 'silent period'.

The Reform Movement, with its emphasis on the primacy of speech, the use of connected texts, the **DIRECT METHOD** of teaching (i.e. banishing the mother tongue from the classroom) and an observational, inductive approach to grammar, did not lose its momentum until about 1910. Despite the fact that in Germany so many eminent scholars lent their names to the movement, it did not catch on there to the extent that it did in

France, where the direct method was introduced at least for English into the whole of education by ministerial decree in 1902 (Rombouts, 1937: 163). Besides Passy, France also had a reformer in **GOUIN**, who worked independently of the others and who was not a phonetician like the others (Gouin, 1880).

Gouin's impact on language teaching and learning in general education was bigger in Germany and Holland than in his own country, but even in the former it was marginal (van Essen, 1986: 285, 1989: 114). Today Gouin's name is associated chiefly with the natural method (i.e. imitating a child's language acquisition) and with the 'series' technique (i.e. describing all events in the real world – e.g., opening a door – in terms of some 'natural' order and sequencing a text in accordance with this, giving pride of place to the verb as the pivot around which each constituent sentence revolves).

From 1910 onwards the reform principles were increasingly coming under fire. The movement was criticised for its dogmatic exclusion of the mother tongue from the classroom, for its fixation on learning to *speak* the foreign language, whereas the majority of learners would never speak but would instead read or write it (Rombouts, 1937:130–1). While the value of *some* phonetics was not questioned, the value of a prolonged period of practising phonetic transcriptions was. And so was the artificial divorce of the spoken from the written language. This might be acceptable for commercial courses, taught by **NATIVE SPEAKERS**, but not for general education, which had formative pretensions.

In France, the direct method was abolished as abruptly as it had been introduced, by ministerial directive. France then entered upon a period of foreign-language instruction based upon the precepts of Henri Delacroix (1925), whose theory shows a striking resemblance to that put forward by some North American neurophysiologists in the 1960s: each time we learn a new language we establish a new, autonomous speech centre on the cortex (Penfield and Roberts, 1959). Typical of the *École française de l'enseignement des langues modernes* was the alternate use of the native and the foreign language during the lesson at elementary level. At intermediate level the translations were reintroduced. The way in which the words of a text were semanticised was new. The **TRANSLATION** of words was avoided by giving explanations in the foreign language. To make absolutely sure learners understood what they were reading, the mother tongue was used (Rombouts, 1937: 164). At the more advanced level, the teaching of literature became more important, while some attention was also paid to **CULTURAL STUDIES**. These were very much an intellectual affair.

In Germany the counter-reform was not as radical as it was in France, but then the reform had not been as radical as in France. The majority of German teachers opted for a method that combined what they thought were the best qualities of both the traditional and the reform methods (i.e. eclecticism). Characteristic of the German counter-reform was that it did not produce any leading figures. It rested on negative experiences with the direct method, on personal convictions, and on regional legislation. At the end of World War One almost everything in Germany had ground to a halt, and so had language teaching. It naturally took the Germans some time to get going again. And when they did, they retained in their coursebooks some phonetics and a very sparing use of phonetic transcription (usually of their own making, with a lot of diacritics). They also kept the connected text as the starting-point of the teaching–learning unit. In Germany, texts (a short story or a dialogue) remained the mainstay of foreign-language coursebooks throughout the inter-war period and long after. Their position within the unit shifted from the beginning to the middle, where they became sandwiched between introductory and exploratory **EXERCISES** (Butzkamm, 1973: 78ff.).

Where the German eclectics differed crucially from the reformers is the place they assigned to grammar. They were not content to deal occasionally with points of grammar, for example, as they occurred in the text; no, grammar was the ordering principle of the whole course! The treatment of grammar was not altogether retrograde, however. The text was used as a grammatical treasure trove, and any specimen found there was dealt with inductively. Anti-reform also meant the use of translations as did the deliberate use of the mother tongue. The most comprehensive account of the teaching methodology of the period from a German point of view is that given by Aronstein (1924).

What was true of Germany was true of many other European countries. In Belgium and Holland the situation was not essentially different (see van Essen, 1986). During World War Two the method debate in the professional journals of mainland Europe at first continued unabated but then stagnated, due to paper rationing or a ban by the Nazis.

## The United States

With the weaknesses of the reform method exposed, and not knowing what to do next, European language pedagogues began to look to the New World for guidance. But they gained little from looking at the United States. Rather the reverse was to be the case, as the following will make clear.

In the USA, foreign-language teaching had long been aimed not at learning to speak another language (there were no opportunities to do that anyway) but at learning to read one. For this reason the methodology of teaching the spoken language had badly lagged behind in compulsory schooling. It was not for nothing that commercial private language schools were booming in America.

In his publications of both 1914 and 1933, Bloomfield devotes a separate chapter to foreign-language education in the USA. In both books Bloomfield shows himself to be familiar with the works of Sweet, Jespersen, and Palmer discussed above. Indeed, in the final chapter of his *Language*, to which he gave the title 'Applications and outlook', Bloomfield pointed to the 'vastly greater success of foreign-language instruction in Europe' when it came to useful language mastery (1933: 504).

Therefore, when war came to the Pacific in 1941, the Americans found out to their cost that very few military personnel spoke any foreign languages. But now the armed forces were in need of people who, in addition to the more common foreign languages, also spoke the more exotic languages not taught at schools or universities. These people now had to be put through crash courses. In setting up such courses the trainers could make use of the experience American linguists had gained in the study of American Indian languages. Bloomfield (1945) described how he, like so many other linguists, had become involved in this **INTENSIVE LANGUAGE** programme. And earlier on in the war Bloomfield had produced a pamphlet setting out the guidelines for anyone wanting to undertake the study of a language for which there was no formal training available (Bloomfield, 1942). In writing this very practical pamphlet, whose title bore a strong resemblance to Sweet's (1899), Bloomfield had in effect made a liberal use of Sweet's, Palmer's and Jespersen's works. For anyone familiar with these works, Bloomfield's pamphlet contains very little that is new, not even his emphasis on habit-formation. But as it became required reading for the instructors in the intensive language programme, along with Bloch and Trager (1942), it soon became *the* model for any type of language learning, even after the war (Howatt, 1984: 266).

An important side-effect of the success of the **AMERICAN ARMY METHOD**, as it became known, was that the applied linguist had come to stay in language teaching and language research. In Bloomfield (1942) he emerged as the 'trained linguist'. This was someone who knew the ins and outs of the language, who instructed the informant, and so on. In short he was the person who knew how to process and re-work the raw materials supplied by the informant and make them ready for use in the classroom (Bloomfield, 1942, 1945).

Recent re-evaluations of the intensive language programme suggest that it may actually have hampered the war effort! (Spolsky, 1996).

**See also:** Australia; China; Japan; Non-native speaker teacher; Teacher education; Teacher thinking; Teaching methods

## References

Aronstein, Ph. (1924 [1926]) *Methodik des neusprachlichen unterrichts (The methodology of teaching modern languages)*, 2 vols, Leipzig/Berlin: Teubner.

Bloch, B. and Trager, G.L. (1942) *Outline of linguistic analysis*, Baltimore: Linguistic Society of America.

Bloomfield, L. (1914) *An introduction to the study of language*, London: Bell.

Bloomfield, L. (1933 [1935]) *Language*, London: Allen and Unwin.

Bloomfield, L. (1942) *Outline guide for the practical study of foreign languages*, Baltimore: Linguistic Society of America.

Bloomfield, L. (1945) 'About foreign language teaching', in C.F. Hockett (ed.), *A Leonard Bloomfield anthology*, Bloomington: Indiana University Press.

Butzkamm, W. (1973) *Aufgeklärte Einsprachigkeit (Enlightened monolingualism)*, Heidelberg: Quelle and Meyer.

Delacroix, H. (1925 [1930]) *Le langage et la pensée (Language and thought)*, Paris: Félix Alcan.

Gouin, F. (1880 [1894]) *The art of teaching and studying languages*, London: Philip.

Hawkins, E. (1981 [1987]) *Modern languages in the curriculum*, Cambridge: Cambridge University Press.

Howatt, A.P.R. (1984) *A history of English language teaching*, Oxford: Oxford University Press.

Jespersen, O. (1904) *How to teach a foreign language*, London: Allen and Unwin.

Krashen, S. (1982) *Principles and practice in second language acquisition*, London: Pergamon.

Palmer, H.E. (1916) *Colloquial English. Part 1. 100 substitution tables*, Cambridge: Heffer.

Palmer, H.E. (1917 [1968]) *The scientific study and teaching of languages*, London: Harrap.

Palmer, H.E. (1922a) *Everyday sentences in spoken English*, Cambridge: Heffer.

Palmer, H.E. (1922b [1964]) *The principles of language-study*, London: Harrap.

Palmer, H.E. and Vere Redman, H. (1932 [1969]) *This language-learning business*, London: Harrap.

Penfield, W. and Roberts, L. (1959) *Speech and brain-mechanisms*, Princeton: Princeton University Press.

Rombouts, S. (1937) *Waarheen met ons vreemde-talenonderwijs? (Which direction for foreign-language teaching?)*, Tilburg: RK Jongensweeshuis.

Spolsky, B. (1996) 'The impact of the Army Specialized Training Programme: a reconsideration', in G. Cook and B. Seidlhofer (eds), *Principle and practice in applied linguistics*, Oxford: Oxford University Press.

Sweet, H. (1899) *The practical study of languages*, London: Dent.

van Essen, A.J. (1986) 'Vijfenzeventig jaar grammatica in het vreemde-talenonderwijs (Seventy-five years of grammar in foreign-language education)', *Levende Talen* 411: 282–9.

van Essen, A.J. (1989) 'The continental European contribution to EFL, past and present', in C. Edelhoff and C.N. Candlin (eds), *Verstehen und Verständigung*, Bochum: Kamp.

### Further reading

Howatt, A.P.R. (1984) *A history of English language teaching*, Oxford: Oxford University Press.
Kelly, L.G. (1969) *25 centuries of language teaching*, Rowley, MA: Newbury House.
Stern, H.H. (1984) *Fundamental concepts of language teaching*, Oxford: Oxford University Press.

ARTHUR VAN ESSEN

# History: after 1945

This account of language teaching and learning since 1945 will point to various trends in language teaching around the world, focusing not only on *how* languages are taught (so-called methods) but also on *what* is taught, and *why*. In looking at what is taught and why, we shall focus on global trends in language use, and in particular five central themes: a new role for language in global politics and the growth of international languages, particularly **ENGLISH**; decolonisation and the struggle for new national languages; increases in formal education, and thus language learning occurring increasingly in school settings; large scale language death; and attempts to maintain language use within multicultural communities and to support threatened languages through language rights legislation. The second section will focus more on how languages are taught, and will look at another five principal themes: the history of language methods as a very particular and implausible history; the marketing forces that have driven particular trends and particular histories; the tendency to dismiss all other teaching practices that do not fit the category 'modern' as **GRAMMAR–TRANSLATION**; the need to understand language teaching practices as embedded in social and cultural contexts and changing according to different **NEEDS**; and the rapid changes being brought about with global changes in technology.

There are two kinds of problem in writing a history of language teaching from 1945 to the present: first, how to deal comprehensively with many languages across many contexts. Even book-length histories that have tried to give comprehensive overviews of language teaching limit themselves in crucial ways: Howatt's (1984) history of ELT deals only with **ENGLISH**, and does so almost entirely within Europe. He describes the history of English language teaching as dividing into two streams at the end of the eighteenth century, English in the Empire and English in Europe; it is the latter with which he deals. Kelly's (1969) impressive history of 2,500 years of language teaching, meanwhile, looks at the teaching of languages other than English but also remains entirely within the bounds of Europe and North America: 'We do not pretend to a world-wide coverage: only the countries whose intellectual traditions are derived from Greece are included' (1969: 2). The second problem is how to cover sufficient aspects of language teaching. The history of language teaching as it is commonly told within Europe and North America (e.g. Richards and Rogers, 1986; Titone, 1968) has been concerned predominantly with a history of **TEACHING METHODS**, viewed as a path of upward progress from method to better method. The approach here, however, will take a different direction.

## Global tendencies in a postwar world: what is taught and why?

1945 marked the end of an era of appalling death and degradation. The development of the European nation state (and **JAPAN**) – defined principally along linguistic and ethnic lines – had culminated in a bloodbath of unprecedented proportions. The year 1945 also marked the beginning of a series of significant global trends: the decolonisation of former European and Japanese imperial holdings; the establishment of the UN and other international bodies; a period of confrontation between the two 'superpowers', the **USA** and the USSR, followed by the emergence of the USA as the dominant international force; the rise of East Asian countries as major economic and political forces; and the development of transnational institutions such as international corporations, global media and tourism. The centrality of the nation state with its national language is being eroded in many parts of the world, to be replaced by centrifugal forces towards **INTERNATIONALISATION** and international languages, as well as centripetal forces towards language maintenance and language rights; there are major movements of people, whether business people flying from Frankfurt to Bangkok, tourists from Tokyo to Hawaii, or refugees from Kosovo to Helsinki; there are multi-channel TV networks operating across the world; transnational corporations manage the production of goods in one country and the selling of them in another without ever getting their hands dirty. These broad trends have had interrelated effects on languages, with concomitant effects on language learning and teaching.

Already in 1943 the British Prime Minister Winston Churchill declared that the sort of territorial warfare going on in Europe would be a thing of the past; the future would be a battle for people's minds, and the key tool in this battle would be language learning and, in particular, simplified languages such as BASIC English (Churchill in Ogden, 1968). Such comments signalled a major new strand in global politics. Whereas languages such as English had been rather haphazardly spread under colonialism, and often indeed withheld (see Pennycook, 1994), this new era was one of promotion of international languages as part of a new era of attempts to gain international political and economic hegemony. As a result, various major languages, and particularly English, were promoted like never before. It is evident from Phillipson's (1992) examination of 'English **LINGUISTIC IMPERIALISM**' that the spread of English has been very deliberately choreographed for economic and political gain. This process, he suggests, has led to the domination of certain linguistic and cultural forms and the death of others.

Decolonisation produced a shift in the language learning patterns of many former colonies, with new language policies favouring a local language over the former colonial language, and the development of new language teaching initiatives to strengthen the teaching of the new national language(s). Indeed, since education under colonial rule – especially British – had often followed the formula of limited primary vernacular education (aimed at creating a productive but quiescent workforce) and highly restricted **SECONDARY EDUCATION** in the colonial language, postcolonial education in local languages was part of a major restructuring of society and education. In Malaysia, for example, following independence in 1957, the strong promotion of Bahasa Malaysia as the national language significantly changed the language learning patterns for Malays, Chinese and Indians (Pennycook, 1994). In the Philippines, the years after 1945 saw a move away from English as a **MEDIUM OF INSTRUCTION** and an attempt to make Pilipino the main language of instruction. From 1974, however, a bilingual system with some subjects taught in English and others in Pilipino was introduced (Sibayan and Gonzalez, 1990). As in many former colonies, the colonial language – English, **FRENCH**, Dutch, **SPANISH**, **PORTUGUESE** – was used less as a medium of instruction and became increasingly a second or foreign language. This, then, links to the third theme, the growth of formal education, and the increased teaching of languages as second or foreign languages within school systems.

Once the early years of postcolonial optimism had passed, however, different patterns often emerged, a result of a mixture of influences including the emergence of local élites schooled in European languages, the dominance of the US and UK in postwar politics, the role English gradually came to play in global media, finance and politics, and the support for colonial languages through so-called development projects. In the long run, therefore, languages such as English ended up being far more widely taught than they had been under colonialism, albeit now as school subjects rather than as the medium of instruction. In former French colonies, decolonisation also saw changes in language policies in education, and attempts to shift from using French as a medium of instruction to a second language. Nevertheless, the former colonial languages have remained dominant, with French playing a significant role in Zaire (now the Republic of Congo), Mali, Niger, Guinea and other countries (Babault and Caitucoli, 1997). As Kamwangamalu asks: 'The question ... is why French, a foreign language with such limited social distribution, is used as the official language of a multilingual country such as Zaire; while indigenous languages, which have a much wider distribution, have taken the back seat' (1997: 72). There is also a trend amongst former French colonies such as Vietnam and Lebanon to join the global scrabble to learn English.

The fourth trend, a result of colonialism, the promotion and growth of dominant languages, and other economic and social changes, has been the rapid increase in language death. According to Dixon, it is estimated that 'of the 5,000 or so languages spoken in the world today at least three quarters (some people say 90 per cent or more) will have ceased to be spoken by the year 2100' (1997: 116–7). Taking **AUSTRALIA** as an example, it is estimated that as many as fifty indigenous languages have become extinct over the last 200 years, around 130 languages have less than fifty speakers and only remain in limited use by older speakers, about seventy languages have viable communities of speakers, and only about twenty-five of these have 250 or more speakers (Walsh, 1991). At the same time, a growing acknowledgement in many countries of their multilingual populations has led to various forms of support for 'community languages', while language learning as a communication-oriented educational goal appears to be growing (see Hawkins, 1996). Increasing pressure to encode 'language rights' within basic **HUMAN RIGHTS** recognised by international bodies such as the UN (see, for example, Phillipson and Skutnabb-Kangas, 1996; Skutnabb-Kangas, 1998) also shows some promise in promoting language diversity. Nevertheless, these recent trends will probably have more to do with promoting multilingualism and diversity over assimilationist policies, rather than actually halting the decline of many languages.

What does all this mean for language teaching? Clearly there are more people learning the dominant global languages, particularly English, than ever before, and people are doing so increasingly in formal educational settings, for formal school requirements and for utilitarian (particularly economic) purposes. (This is not to say that languages have not been learned – even created in the case of **PIDGINS** – for utilitarian purposes at other times, but rather that it is surely a dominant trend with the dominant international

language today.) The teaching and promotion of English, furthermore, is intertwined with other global trends towards global capitalist markets, global media and so on. The struggle to promote other languages as national, official or educational languages remains a tough, up-hill battle. Multilingualism continues as the world norm, both in informal settings and in formal educational contexts where multilingualism is officially recognised (**INDIA**, for example). Indigenous and minority languages, however, are increasingly under threat, and the total number of languages available to be learned as living instruments of communication will be massively reduced over the next one hundred years unless immense efforts are put into halting this decline. This may not mean either less language learning or teaching, but it will mean there are fewer languages to be learned.

## Methods and other histories: how languages are taught

The global spread of English and the dominance of Europe and the United States in global knowledge transfer has had many implications for language teaching. On the one hand, as discussed above, English is being learned by ever greater numbers of students around the world. On the other hand, the history of language teaching has been dominated by a Eurocentric version of the upward progression of teaching methods. The popular version of this myth is that much of language teaching prior to the twentieth century was conducted according to a so-called grammar–translation methodology, which was replaced by a revolution in language teaching that focused on the **DIRECT METHOD**. This was then followed by a series of methods, starting with **AUDIOLINGUALISM**, developed during and after World War Two and employing **STRUCTURAL LINGUISTICS** and behaviourist psychology. Following that we have various contenders for method status, including the **AUDIO-VISUAL** method, **COGNITIVE CODE**, a cluster of new methods that emerged in the 1970s including the **SILENT WAY**, **SUGGESTOPEDIA** and **TOTAL PHYSICAL RESPONSE**; and finally the modern era of **COMMUNICATIVE LANGUAGE TEACHING** and **TASK-BASED LEARNING**.

There are several problems with this version of the history of language teaching as an upward history of methods. First, it ignores large domains of language teaching, such as which languages get taught, as suggested above. Second, the whole status of methods is highly problematic: the very notion of a 'method' lacks any descriptive adequacy (in spite of attempts by Richards and Rogers, 1986, amongst others, to bring academic respectability to the area) and is clearly a very reductive way to think about language teaching (Pennycook, 1989). As Clarke (1983: 109) suggests, 'the term "method" is a label without substance'. Third, this history is in part precisely a product of the 'method boom' (Stern, 1985: 249) of the 1970s, an attempt to justify this faddish, market- and career-driven era in North America by attempting to locate it within an unfolding history. Fourth, to the extent that this history presents an upward path of development, from weaker methods to more modern teaching, it suggests a problematic progressivism, whereby whatever is happening now is presumed to be superior to what happened before. Such claims are often made by contrasting a modern 'scientific approach to the study of language and of language learning' with a past guided only by tradition (Richards and Rogers, 1986: 8). Yet, as Kelly's work suggests, the history of language teaching has been far more cyclical than linear: 'Nobody really knows what is new or what is old in present day language teaching procedures. There has been a vague feeling that modern experts have spent their time in discovering what other men [sic] have forgotten' (Kelly, 1969: ix).

This is not to say that there have not been many developments related to language teaching during this period. The notion of communicative competence (see, e.g., Canale and Swain, 1980), while tied for a long time to the waxing and waning of communicative language teaching, has provided a model that broadens the scope for thinking about what language use and language learning involve, and has led to important considerations in areas such as language testing (see, e.g., McNamara, 1996). The elaboration of the notional-functional **SYLLABUS** (Wilkins, 1976), though echoing various prior orientations, had an important influence on the development of language education through the Council of Europe in the 1970s and 1980s (Reeves, 1996), and has helped to orient syllabus

design more generally towards semantic rather than grammatical needs. Following from this, the development of language syllabuses for specific purposes (LSP, EAP, and equivalents in other languages) has made it possible to avoid the scatter-gun approach of general language courses and to target very specific populations and language domains. Developments in **SECOND LANGUAGE ACQUISITION**, contrastive rhetoric and contrastive **LINGUISTICS** and literacy have given language educators better tools for understanding the development of their students' language, differences in text organisation, and different ways in which students may take meaning from texts.

Focusing more on language teaching itself, a number of frameworks have also been developed that can take us beyond the method concept. These include Halliday, McIntosh and Strevens's (1964) and Mackey's (1965) attempts to present an overall conceptual framework for understanding language teaching, breaking the process down into processes of selection of **MATERIALS**, grouping and sequencing of materials, presentation, repetition and reinforcement through teaching, and **EVALUATION**. Other attempts, by Bosco and Di Pietro (1970) and Krashen and Seliger (1975) identify characteristics of teaching according to whether teaching approaches encourage categories such as discreet or holistic, inductive or deductive learning. **STERN**'s (1983) model of language teaching (embedded within a broader model of curriculum) suggests that teaching operates with three central pairs of options: cross-lingual versus intralingual (does it employ **TRANSLATION** or does it operate **MONOLINGUALLY**?); objective versus subjective (analytic versus experiential); and explicit versus implicit ('learning' versus '**ACQUISITION**'). More recently, Kumaravadivelu (1994) has suggested ways in which current thinking about language teaching can inform a 'postmethod concept'.

Certainly such frameworks allow us to understand language teaching in terms other than 'methods', and to look at language teaching in any context according to such categories. We are then able to consider the suggestion of Kelly's that 'the total corpus of ideas accessible to language teachers has not changed basically in 2,000 years' (1969: 363). This does not mean that nothing changes, but it does suggest that, in order to understand what configurations of choices teachers are making, we need detailed analyses of language teaching around the globe. As Holliday (1994) has remarked, such an analysis is still lacking. This leaves us with two broad questions: are there discernible trends in the teaching of the dominant languages such as English; and what can be said about the teaching of the many other languages around the world? The large-scale analyses of language teaching have suggested that teaching trends vacillate between a limited number of options: Howatt (1984) suggests that language teaching falls roughly into the natural or the rational camp, a distinction that echoes Mackey's (1965) image of a pendulum swinging between an extreme **GRAMMAR** focus on the one hand and total immersion in a language on the other. Kelly's vision of cyclic progressions emphasising different elements of the social (language as social, communicative behaviour), the artistic (language as a vehicle for creativity) and the philosophical (training in analytic techniques) gives us a further option.

In terms of global trends in language teaching connected to languages such as English, it is tempting to suggest a two-way distinction, following Tsuda (1994) and Phillipson and Skutnabb-Kangas (1996), between a diffusionist and an ecological perspective. From this point of view, recent developments in language teaching – audiolingualism, communicative and task-based – have more in common with each other and with the earlier direct method than they have significant differences. All emphasise oral language use and monolingualism, while proscribing **TRANSLATION**, **BILINGUALISM** and language analysis. As various commentators have suggested (Auerbach, 1993; Phillipson, 1992), such an emphasis needs to be seen in light of the global spread of English. The approach to English teaching advocated by the English-dominant nations has been driven largely by economic and political concerns, promoting new books with new methods, English-only teaching methods, and **NATIVE SPEAKER SKILLS** over non-natives, while guarding against the threats to this economic and ideological thrust by claiming that translation and language analysis should play no great role. It is only recently that a more critical approach to these issues has started to question these assumptions.

With respect to the diversity of practices elsewhere and in other languages, we are confronted by the reductionist and implausible description of all forms of language teaching before the twentieth century and outside Europe and North America as 'grammar–translation'. One of the problems with the way in which this history has been told is that an upward path of new and better methods is contrasted with a supposedly static body of 'traditional' approaches elsewhere. Of course, such a vision of a developing centre and a static periphery is one of the central tropes of colonial discourse (see Pennycook, 1998). To reduce all types of teaching that fail to fit some paradigm of 'modern' teaching to something called 'grammar–translation' is surely to do a disservice to the diversity of language teaching practices around the world. Such a position ignores change and diversity and alternative ways of teaching and learning. As critical approaches to literacy (e.g. Heath, 1983; Street, 1995) have shown, there is great diversity in how people use and understand texts. We are lacking what Canagarajah (1999) has termed 'ethnographies from the periphery', accounts not only of the global spread of English, the marketisation of methods and the homogenisation of **TEXTBOOKS** to ensure greater sales, but also accounts of resistance and appropriation, of local practices and changing practices. Without this, any history of language teaching is a very particular history.

For example, recent discussions of the Japanese teaching method known as *yakudoku* (Hino, 1988; Gorsuch, 1998) have shown how it simply cannot be reduced to a notion of grammar–translation but rather suggests a broader cultural orientation to text, literacy and translation. It is also clear from Tang Li-xing's (1983) overview of English language teaching in **CHINA** that it has changed and been influenced by many factors, from the Japanese, British and US influence in the early part of the twentieth century, through the post-revolutionary (1949) use of English to serve the New Republic, to the 'Russian Years' (1953–57), the subsequent oral emphasis from 1958–66, the banishing of English and then use of English to serve the cultural revolution (1966–77), and a return to more communicative goals in the late 1970s and 1980s. The teaching of other languages in China, such as

JAPANESE or French, has been influenced by similar changes as well as other changes more specific to the cultural relationships with JAPAN and French-speaking countries. This raises several important points:

- Language teaching has never been as static and traditional outside the English-dominant countries as is often suggested;
- Language teaching has not moved in some linear upward path but comes and goes with social, cultural, political and educational change;
- Language teaching tends to be influenced from many directions – there is no obvious 'traditional' or 'Chinese' way;
- An overview of language teaching needs to include not only so-called methods but also curricular and ideological content.

One trend, however, that is clearly discernible globally is the growth of new forms of technology. Kelly's (1969) history reports on the development of tape recorders, LANGUAGE LABORATORIES, radio, films, television and 'teaching machines'. Today we have a vast and expanding array of new technologies that are not only changing classroom practices but are shifting modes of communication around the globe. The arrival of word-processing changed the teaching of WRITING; e-mail is changing the nature of writing and the possibility of with whom and at what speed people can communicate; the INTERNET more generally is establishing new domains of communication (see Lankshear and Knobel, 1997). The effects of hypertext and the potential of electronic books are only just being considered. And finally the implications of widely available machine translation for language learning and teaching could be immense. There are still many questions to do with access to these new technologies around the world; but that they will have immense effects is surely in no doubt.

## Conclusion

It can be said that any understanding of language history from 1945 to the present has to take into account both large-scale global shifts in language use and local changes in language pedagogies.

More people are learning major languages such as English, while there are increasingly fewer languages to be learned. More languages are being learned in formal educational settings. We need to understand the spread of English, textbooks and methods as part of a massive marketing exercise. The development of a particular history of language teaching in terms of an upward path of methods emanating from the West is bound up with this diffusionism. The picture of the rest of the world as caught in a static 'grammar–translation' teaching methodology is part of this construction. In order to understand better what is going on in the world, we need ethnographies of classrooms around the world. Only then can we construct a history of language teaching.

**See also:** Central and Eastern Europe; China; Communicative language teaching; *Didactique des langues*; *Fremdsprachendidaktik*; Humanistic language teaching; Linguistic imperialism; Teacher education; Teaching methods

## References

Auerbach, E. (1993) 'Reexamining English only in the ESL classroom', *TESOL Quarterly* 27, 1: 9–32.

Babault, S. and Caitucoli, C. (1997) 'Linguistic policy and education in francophone countries', in R. Wodak and D. Corson (eds), *Language policy and political issues in education. Encyclopedia of language and education. Volume 1*, Dordrecht: Kluwer.

Bosco, F.J. and Di Pietro, R.J. (1970) 'Instructional strategies: their psychological and linguistic bases', *IRAL* 8, 1–19.

Canagarajah, A.S. (1999) *Resisting linguistic imperialism in English teaching*, Oxford: Oxford University Press.

Canale, M. and Swain, M. (1980) 'Theoretical bases of communicative approaches to second language teaching and testing', *Applied Linguistics* 1: 1–47.

Clarke, M.A. (1983) 'The scope of approach, the importance of method, and the nature of techniques', in J.E. Alatis, H.H. Stern and P. Strevens (eds), *Georgetown University round table on language and linguistics*, Washington, DC: Georgetown University Press.

Dixon, R. (1997) *The rise and fall of languages*, Cambridge: Cambridge University Press.

Gorsuch, G. (1998) '*Yakudoku* EFL instruction in two Japanese high school classrooms: an exploratory study', *JALT Journal* 20, 1: 6–32.

Halliday, M.A.K., McIntosh, A. and Strevens, P. (1964) *The linguistic sciences and language teaching*, London: Longman.

Hawkins, E. (ed.) (1996) *30 years of language teaching*, London: Centre for Information on Language Teaching and Research.

Heath, S.B. (1983) *Ways with words*, Cambridge: Cambridge University Press.

Hino, T. (1988) '*Yakudoku*: Japan's dominant tradition in foreign language learning', *JALT Journal* 10, 1 and 2: 45–55.

Holliday, A. (1994) *Appropriate methodology and social context*, Cambridge: Cambridge University Press.

Howatt, A.P.R. (1984) *A history of English Language Teaching*, Oxford: Oxford University Press.

Kamwangamalu, N.M. (1997) 'The colonial legacy and language planning in Sub-Saharan Africa: the case of Zaire', *Applied Linguistics* 18, 1: 69–85.

Kelly, L.G. (1969) *25 centuries of language teaching*, Rowley, MA: Newbury House.

Krashen, S.D. and Seliger, H. (1975) 'The essential contribution of formal instruction in adult second language learning', *TESOL Quarterly* 9, 2: 173–83.

Kumaravadivelu, B. (1994) 'The postmethod condition: (e)merging strategies for second/foreign language teaching', *TESOL Quarterly* 28, 1: 27–48.

Lankshear, C. and Knobel, M. (1997) 'Literacies, texts and difference in the electronic age', in C. Lankshear (with J.P. Gee, M. Knobel and C. Searle), *Changing literacies*, Buckingham: Open University Press.

Mackey, W.F. (1965) *Language teaching analysis*, London: Longman.

McNamara, T. (1996) *Measuring second language performance*, London: Longman.

Ogden, C.K. (1968) *Basic English: international second language*, (a revised and expanded version of *The system of Basic English*, prepared by E.C. Graham), New York: Harcourt, Brace and World, Inc.

Pennycook, A. (1989) 'The concept of method, interested knowledge, and the politics of language teaching', *TESOL Quarterly* 23, 4: 589–618.

Pennycook, A. (1994) *The cultural politics of English as an international language*, London: Longman.

Pennycook, A. (1998) *English and the discourses of colonialism*, London: Routledge.

Phillipson, R. (1992) *Linguistic Imperialism*, Oxford: Oxford University Press.

Phillipson, R. and Skutnabb-Kangas, T. (1996) 'English only worldwide or language ecology?', *TESOL Quarterly* 30, 3: 429–52.

Reeves, N. (1996) 'Does Britain need linguists?', in E. Hawkins (ed.), *30 years of language teaching*, London: Centre for Information on Language Teaching and Research.

Richards, J.C. and Rodgers, T. (1986) *Approaches and methods in language teaching*, Cambridge: Cambridge University Press.

Sibayan, B.P and Gonzalez, A.B. (1990) 'English language teaching in the Philippines: a succession of movements', in J. Britton, R.E. Shafer and K. Watson (eds), *Teaching and learning English worldwide*, Clevedon: Multilingual Matters.

Skutnabb-Kangas, T. (1998) 'Human rights and language wrongs – a future for diversity?', *Language Sciences* 20, 1: 5–28.

Stern, H.H. (1983) *Fundamental concepts of language teaching*, Oxford: Oxford University Press.

Stern, H.H. (1985) 'Review of J.W. Oller Jr and P. Richard-Amato (eds), *Methods that work: a smorgasbord of ideas for language teachers*', *Studies in Second Language Acquisition* 7, 2: 249–51.

Street, B. (1995) *Social literacies: critical approaches to literacy in development, ethnography and education*, London: Longman.

Tang Li-xing (1983) *TEFL in China: methods and techniques*, Shanghai: Shanghai Foreign Language Education Press.

Titone, R. (1968) *Teaching foreign languages: an historical sketch*, Washington, DC: Georgetown University Press.

Tsuda, Yukio (1994) 'The diffusion of English: its impact on culture and communication', *Keio Communication Review* 16: 49–61.

Walsh, M. (1991) 'Overview of indigenous languages of Australia', in S. Romaine (ed.), *Language in Australia*, Cambridge: Cambridge University Press.

Wilkins, D. (1976) *Notional syllabuses*, Oxford: Oxford University Press.

## Further reading

Canagarajah, A.S. (1999) *Resisting linguistic imperialism in English teaching*, Oxford: Oxford University Press.

Holliday, A. (1994) *Appropriate methodology and social context*, Cambridge: Cambridge University Press.

Howatt, A.P.R. (1984) *A history of English language teaching*, Oxford: Oxford University Press.

Kelly, L.G. (1969) *25 centuries of language teaching*, Rowley, MA: Newbury House.

Pennycook, A. (1994) *The cultural politics of English as an international language*, London: Longman.

Phillipson, R. (1992) *Linguistic imperialism*, Oxford: Oxford University Press.

Spolsky, B. (1995) *Measured words*, Oxford: Oxford University Press.

Stern, H.H. (1983) *Fundamental concepts of language teaching*, Oxford: Oxford University Press.

ALASTAIR PENNYCOOK

# Hornby, Albert Sidney

b. 1898, Chester; d. 1978, London

Lexicographer, journal editor, grammarian, teacher, materials writer, teacher trainer

A.S. Hornby is best known as a writer of **ENGLISH** language teaching **DICTIONARIES** and **REFERENCE WORKS**. He began his career in 1924 as an English teacher in Japan, and his early studies of lexis and syntax, influenced by the work of Harold **PALMER**, culminated in the publication of the *Idiomatic and Syntactic English Dictionary* in 1942. This was reprinted as *A Learner's Dictionary of Current English* by Oxford University Press in 1948, and retitled *The Advanced Learner's Dictionary of Current English* in 1952.

In the 1940s Hornby worked for the **BRITISH COUNCIL**, and started the journal *English Language Teaching* (renamed *ELT Journal* in 1981). He later became a full-time writer of dictionaries and textbooks. The Hornby Trust, established in 1961, funds training for overseas teachers in Britain.

## Bibliography

Hornby, A.S. (1954) *A guide to patterns and usage in English*, Oxford: Oxford University Press.

Hornby, A.S., with Cowie, A.P. and Windsor Lewis, J. (1974) *Oxford Advanced Learner's Dictionary of Current English*, (3rd edn), Oxford: Oxford University Press.

Hornby, A.S. and Ruse, C. (1978) *Oxford Student's Dictionary of Current English*, Oxford: Oxford University Press.

Hornby, A.S., Gatenby, E.V. and Wakefield, H. (1952 [1963]) *The Advanced Learner's Dictionary of Current English*, Oxford: Oxford University Press.

## Further reading

Cowie, A.P. (ed.) (1998) 'A.S. Hornby, 1898–1998. Commemorative Issue', *International Journal of Lexicography* 11, 4: 249–314.

Strevens, P. (ed.) (1978) *In honour of A.S. Hornby*, Oxford: Oxford University Press.

HILARY NESI

# Humanistic language teaching

Humanistic education, or the education of the whole person, has the fulfilment of human potential as its aim. As well as promoting 'self-actualisation', humane approaches to language teaching recognise the affective nature of the language learning experience. In contrast, scientific approaches give priority to empirical descriptions of the formal or functional properties of the language and to determining a method of instruction which enables the learner to gain control over them. This entry defines humanistic language teaching and discusses the contributions of Moskowitz and Stevick to humanistic methodology. The key principles of humanistic language teaching are then listed.

The study of language was regarded as a humane occupation from the European Renaissance until the early years of the twentieth century, when **SAUSSUREAN** structuralism first demonstrated the value of a scientific approach. According to Mackey, the term **APPLIED LINGUISTICS** was first used in the United States in the 1940s 'by persons with an obvious desire to be identified as scientists rather than as humanists' (1966: 197). The application of structural grammar based on the distributional properties of linguistic items and **BEHAVIOURISTIC** psychology to the practical problem of language teaching resulted in the first 'scientific' language teaching method, **AUDIOLINGUALISM**. It was against the background of audiolingual teaching with its emphasis on drills and error-free performance that humanistic approaches first began to be advocated in the field of language teaching.

Both Moskowitz (1978) and **STERN** (1983) state that the alienation which showed itself in the violent student uprisings of the late 1960s and early 1970s in the Western world resulted in more humane **TEACHER METHODS**. Certainly a considerable literature advocating humane methods appeared in the 1970s. This literature owed much to the pioneering work of two humanistic psychologists, Abraham Maslow and Carl Rogers.

In the field of language teaching, it is impossible to underestimate the influence of Gertrude Moskowitz's *Caring and Sharing in the Foreign Language Class* (1978). The two opening chapters of this book establish many of the most enduring principles of humanistic classroom management. These are followed by a chapter containing a hundred humanistic **EXERCISES** exhibiting ten crucial 'categories of awareness': Relating to Others; Discovering Myself; My Strengths; My Self-Image; Expressing My Feelings; My Memories; Sharing Myself; My Values; The Arts and Me; Me and My Fantasies. One of Moskowitz's classic exercises, a dialogue written between the right and left hands, gives a representative flavour of her work. One of the book's four appendices contains sixty-four 'Humanistic Quotes for the Foreign Language Class', the first two of which are 'The greatest discovery is finding yourself' and 'The most important ideas any man ever has are the ideas he has about himself'.

Moskowitz's book thus put before the language teaching world a series of humanistic principles with which it was largely unfamiliar. Equally important, she established the framework for what we now know as resource books for teachers, books containing supplementary **MATERIALS** written up in an easy-to-use recipe format. By the end of the twentieth century, teachers working in contexts where they were able to devise their own **SYLLA-** BUSES had come to rely more on resource books than on coursebooks. The content of many of these books also remains faithful to the humanistic example set by Moskowitz.

Another important figure responsible for bringing considered knowledge of humanistic methodology to a wide audience is Earl Stevick. In the second chapter of *Humanism in Language Teaching* (1990), Stevick brings together a wide range of different perspectives on humanism in education. Later in the book, he analyses the humanistic qualities of two alternative methods, **COMMUNITY LANGUAGE LEARNING** and the **SILENT WAY**, methods whose influence has been very great but whose practice has been limited to a small number of specialist centres. Stevick concludes that 'each emphasizes some *uniquely human attributes* of the learner, affirms and promotes human *freedom*, and contributes in some way to the human *dignity* of the learner' (1990: 131) [original author's emphasis]. Stevick goes on to measure other mainstream and alternative methods against these criteria.

The rise of generative linguistics and **UNIVERSAL GRAMMAR** in the latter half of the twentieth century continued the increasingly scientific study of language, but seen from a rationalist rather than an empiricist perspective. In the **GENERATIVE** model, language is regarded as an innate property of the human mind and thus as learnable rather than teachable. In this way, the generative account of language, despite its strict formalism, underscores the humanistic focus on the centrality of the learner in the language **ACQUISITION** process.

The cardinal principles of humanistic language teaching include:

- respecting learners as people, including fostering the individual learner's self-esteem, promoting mutual esteem among learners, and developing each learner's awareness of self and others;
- recognising the affective as well as the cognitive nature of the learning experience. This means working productively with the learner's emotional response to the foreign language and culture and to the learning situation, and may involve explicit **LEARNING TO LEARN** activities;
- respecting the learner's knowledge and independence. Accepting that willing learners know best and will learn in their own time means

recognising that only activities that students wish to engage in should be engaged in;

- recognising that teachers who manifest their authority by means of praise and blame undermine the **AUTONOMY** and independence of the learner and give the impression of being the sole determiners of what is right and wrong;
- respecting learner language and acknowledging the individual's entitlement to freedom from external correction and authority. This is much less challenging to traditional teacher-as-instructor values now that **SECOND LANGUAGE ACQUISITION THEORY** has shown that learner 'errors' are developmental and not evidence of insufficient application;
- rethinking traditional syllabuses and materials. Humanistic approaches encourage learners to express their own meanings rather than replicate model utterances. The methods used are person-related and the learner's personal experience and perspective are seen as the primary resource for both lesson content and language form and function. This contrasts with more traditional approaches which focus on language form and on declarative rather than procedural knowledge;
- teaching in an enabling way, including questioning the role of teachers as performers or entertainers who first determine and then fill the knowledge gap that exists between themselves and their learners. Humanistic approaches regard teachers not as instructors, but as enablers or facilitators who assist learners in self-discovery;
- questioning institutionalised norms and rejecting the kind of pedagogy which sets itself up as the artificial means to a natural end. Such pedagogy is evident in the use of terms like 'hour' to mean forty-five minutes, 'week' to mean five days, 'year' to mean thirty-six weeks, and 'course' to mean the amount of institutional time available for learning. Thus natural communication activities are preferred over artificial, form-dominated syllabuses.

Criticisms of humanistic approaches typically focus on the narrowness and intrusiveness of the attention on the person at the expense of understanding the empirical world and explaining it

satisfactorily. An early example of this criticism is provided by Francis Bacon (1605):

> ... error hath proceeded from ... a kind of adoration of the mind and understanding of man; by means whereof men have withdrawn themselves too much from the contemplation of nature, and the observations of experience ... and as it were invocate their own spirits to divine and give oracles unto them
>
> (Bacon, *The Advancement of Learning*, Book 1 V.6)

This criticism is repeated in a more even-handed way by Brumfit, who writes: 'it is dangerous to assume that intellectual analysis and description of events can be a substitute for experience. But it is equally dangerous to assume that experience, however sensitive, can be a substitute for analysis' (1982: 18).

**See also:** Applied linguistics; Audiolingual method; Autonomy and autonomous learners; Community language learning; *Handlungsorientierter Unterricht*; Learning styles; Learning to learn; Silent Way; Suggestopedia; Teaching methods; Total Physical Response

### References

Bacon, Francis (1605) *The advancement of learning*.

Brumfit, C.J. (1982) 'Some humanistic doubts about humanistic language teaching', in P. Early (ed.), *Humanistic approaches: an empirical view*, ELT Documents 113, London: The British Council.

Mackey, W.F. (1966) 'Applied linguistics: its meaning and use', *English Language Teaching* XX. 3: 197–206.

Moskowitz, G. (1978) *Caring and sharing in the foreign language class*, Rowley, MA: Newbury House.

Stern, H.H. (1983) *Fundamental concepts of language teaching*, Oxford: Oxford University Press.

Stevick, E. (1990) *Humanism in language teaching*, Oxford: Oxford University Press.

### Further reading

Arnold, J. (ed.) (1999) *Affect in language learning*, Cambridge: Cambridge University Press.

Rogers, C.R. (1961) *On becoming a person*, Boston: Houghton-Mifflin.

Rogers, C.R. (1968) *Freedom to learn: a view of what education might become*, Columbus: C.E. Merrill Publishing Corporation.

PETER GRUNDY

# Human rights

Human rights have been universally agreed, at government level at least, as a set of common values and aims. They are expressed in internationally recognised texts as a legal, ethical and moral framework for the regulation of relationships between states, between people and between states and people. The United Nations was established in 1945 to support international efforts to achieve justice, peace and freedom in the world through the promotion and protection of human rights. The basis for this is the fundamental belief in human beings as being endowed with inherent dignity. Human rights attach to all human beings equally, irrespective of origin, status, culture or language. Democracy and citizenship depend on an acceptance by governments and individuals of human rights.

Language teaching is a vehicle for transmitting knowledge and understanding of human rights and a policy instrument for promoting **INTERCULTURAL COMMUNICATION** in a spirit of human rights. New human rights instruments are being developed for the protection of cultural minorities, and these include specific reference to languages.

Human rights became adopted as the underlying principle of international law with the drafting of the Charter of the United Nations in 1945. They were first comprehensively defined in the Universal Declaration of Human Rights adopted by the General Assembly of the United Nations in 1948. In 1953, member states of the Council of Europe adopted the European Convention of Human Rights and Fundamental Freedoms which gives legal force to those rights and freedoms contained in it and provides a court to which individuals may take their cases. Although it does not have a court, the Convention on the Rights of the Child (1989) extended the acceptance of legal obligations to respect human rights to every country in the world. States report every five years

to the Committee on the Rights of the Child which monitors their progress in fulfilling obligations laid down by the Convention. Universal acceptance of human rights standards was further confirmed by states representing 99 per cent of the world's people in the Vienna Declaration of June 1993.

René Cassin, who helped draft the Universal Declaration of Human Rights, categorised the rights as:

- Personal rights such as: equality before the law and equal entitlement to rights; right to life, liberty and security of person; freedom from slavery, torture, arbitrary arrest; right of fair public trial and presumption of innocence.
- Rights in relationships between people, such as: right to privacy; freedom of movement; right to nationality; right to marry, have children, own property.
- Public freedoms and political rights, including: freedom of thought, conscience and religion; right to freedom of opinion and expression; right of peaceful assembly; right to elect a government.
- economic, social and cultural rights, including: right to work, rest and leisure; adequate standard of living for health, education, participation in cultural life (Osler and Starkey, 1996).

Human rights instruments include commitments to goals of education. Article 26 of the Universal Declaration of Human Rights states that: 'Education shall be directed to ... the strengthening of respect for human rights and fundamental freedoms. It shall promote understanding and tolerance amongst all nations, racial or religious groups'. The Convention on the Rights of the Child includes a commitment to provide education directed to 'the development of respect for human rights'.

Language teaching has a particular role to play in this education for human rights. Knowledge about human rights can be conveyed in the context of the study of a foreign language. A Council of Europe Recommendation (1985) suggests that this knowledge include 'an understanding of and sympathy for the concepts of justice, equality, freedom, peace, dignity, rights and democracy'. It specifies knowledge of 'the various forms of injustice, inequality and discrimination, including sexism and racism'.

Skills needed for the exercise of human rights are

also developed through language learning. The Council of Europe Recommendation lists these as: '**SKILLS** associated with written and oral expression, including the ability to listen and discuss and to defend one's opinions; skills involving judgement such as ... the identification of bias, prejudice, **STEREOTYPES** and discrimination; social skills, in particular recognising and accepting differences'.

Baumgratz (1985) identified two tendencies in cross-cultural communication, namely an instrumental approach and a human rights approach. The former stresses the usefulness of languages for trade and tourism. The latter seeks to use knowledge of foreign languages and cultures for improving relationships between people, both within and between countries.

Adopting a human rights approach to language teaching may provide a framework within which controversial issues can safely be examined. Acknowledgement of the essential dignity of human beings implies that debate is conducted showing respect for persons, particularly other interlocutors. The same principle also renders disparaging remarks about individuals or groups not present as inappropriate behaviour, and therefore unacceptable in an educational context. On the other hand, if respect for human rights is regarded as a standard, judgements can be made about the words or actions of individuals, governments or cultural groups. In this way uncritical cultural relativism can be avoided.

International organisations such as the United Nations or the European Union, which are founded with the explicit intention of advancing justice and peace in the world, promote human rights through their language education programmes. For instance, the programmes of the **COUNCIL OF EUROPE** 'have followed the philosophy underlying the doctrines of human rights central to the work of the Council of Europe' (Girard and Trim, 1988). At a global level, UNESCO initiated the **LINGUAPAX** project in 1987 to promote language policies for cultural and linguistic diversity, peace and tolerance. It has produced several reports (Linguapax, 1997).

Whereas human rights instruments outlaw discrimination on grounds of language and affirm the right to participate in the cultural life of the community, there is no fundamental right to have education provided in a specific language. Policies about which languages should be taught in schools and which should be used as the **MEDIUM OF INSTRUCTION** are legitimately determined by national or regional governments. On the other hand, governments are expected to protect all those who live within their jurisdiction, and some of the most recent human rights instruments, such as the European Framework Convention for the Protection of National Minorities, signed by thirty-seven member states by October 1998 and ratified by twenty-four of these, extend language rights. The Convention prohibits forced assimilation to the dominant culture, which usually involves a ban on the use of minority languages in public situations and in institutions. The Convention also binds its signatories to promoting the conditions for the preservation of culture, religion, language and traditions. This implies positive government measures which are likely to include the availability of teaching of – or in – the minority language.

**See also:** Cultural awareness; Gender and language learning; Global education; Intercultural communication; Intercultural competence; Internationalisation; Linguapax; Objectives in language teaching and learning; Syllabus and curriculum design

### References

Baumgratz, G. (1985) 'Transnational and cross-cultural communication as negotiation of meaning', in D. Sixt (ed.), *Comprehension as negotiation of meaning*, Amsterdam: Goethe-Institut.

Council of Europe (1985) *Recommendation (R(85)7) of the Committee of Ministers on Teaching and Learning about Human Rights in Schools*, Strasbourg: Council of Europe.

Girard, D. and Trim, J. (1988) *Final report of Project No. 12 'Learning and Teaching Modern Languages for Communication'*, Strasbourg: Council of Europe.

Linguapax (1997) *International seminar on language policies, Artaza 1996*, Bilbao: UNESCO ETXEA.

Osler, A. and Starkey, H. (1996) *Teacher education and human rights*, London: Fulton.

HUGH STARKEY

# Humboldt, Wilhelm von

b. 22 June 1767, Potsdam, Germany;
d. 8 April 1835, Tegel, Germany

Diplomat in the Prussian service,
philosopher, and linguist

Humboldt held various ambassadorial posts and, as minister, founded the University of Berlin (now bearing his name) according to a concept of 'research and teaching' which had a seminal effect on German and continental European university life after the Napoleonic Wars. In the same capacity and with the same success he planned the new *Preußisches Gymnasium* (together with Johann Wilhelm Süvern, 1775–1829), with its stress on education through, mainly, the classical languages. He was influenced by the philosophers Leibniz and Kant, by the Weimar classicists Schiller and Goethe, and by the French post-revolutionary philosophers the *Idéologues*.

Some Humboldtian ideas, in particular those on language origin, overlap with similar ones developed by the theologian and philosopher Johann Gottfried Herder (1744–1803). Many of Humboldt's writings remained unfinished. Others, such as sketches and **GRAMMARS** of indigenous Amerindian languages, are still unpublished. It was only towards the end of the nineteenth century that Humboldtian **LINGUISTICS** gained general acclaim. Some modern historiographers accuse him of leaning towards racist thinking because of his ideas about the superiority of inflectional languages.

Whereas it was the general aim of eighteenth-century **UNIVERSAL GRAMMAR** to show the partial identity of all languages by applying the categories of Latin to their description, it was Humboldt's endeavour to show their major differences as explainable by the fact that each language is expressive of the imagination, the worldview (*Weltsicht*), and the culture of the people that developed it in the course of its history. This makes it a storehouse of cultural concepts, an ideational unity (*ergon*), but also a means of permanently remodelling these concepts into a new unity (*energeia*). It is this idea about the interconnection between language and culture, as developed in *Über die Verschiedenheit des menschlichen Sprachbaus* (1836), the introduction to Humboldt's main work on Malayo-Polynesian languages (*Über die Kawi-Sprache*, 1836–39), which came to be debated and accepted as the centre of Humboldtian linguistic thinking. Its obvious consequence was that the study of any language in fact meant the study of the culture expressed by it, as was already common practice in classical philology. Although the abstract thinker Humboldt did not busy himself with the concrete intricacies of foreign language teaching and learning, he applied his main idea to it. He maintained that learning a foreign language in the right way was gaining a new viewpoint on one's own worldview and that this was the main reason for doing it at all.

In Germany, the introduction of modern languages into the curriculum of schools during the second half of the nineteenth century occurred in the light of Humboldtian thinking. **FRENCH** and then **ENGLISH** were taught as part of a general liberal arts education and not for practical purposes. Pedagogically this brought the modern languages into line with the ancient ones and reserved them for the intellectual bourgeoisie. In various ways, and frequently without any direct reference to Humboldt, the idea spread to other European countries, leaving purely practical language teaching to privately engaged house teachers or to schools like the one founded by Henri Berlitz.

In the twentieth century, Humboldtian ideas about language and culture were propagated in the so-called **SAPIR–WHORF HYPOTHESIS**. Although it is common opinion now that languages have to be taught in order to be spoken and written, the cultural dimension of language learning is seen as the general background of foreign language teaching. The general aim of **INTERCULTURAL COMPETENCE** is the present-day form of Humboldt's thoughts in language teaching pedagogy.

## Further reading

Davies, A.M. (1998) *Nineteenth century linguistics*, vol. IV, London: Longman.
Dilthey, W. (1894) 'Süvern', *Allgemeine Deutsche Biographie*, 37: 206–4; (reprint, Berlin: Duncker and Humblot, 1971).

WERNER HÜLLEN

# I

## IATEFL – International Association of Teachers of English as a Foreign Language

IATEFL was founded in 1967. Its mission is to link, develop and support **ENGLISH** Language Teaching professionals worldwide. The broad aims of IATEFL are:

- To benefit English language teachers all over the world and to raise the level of professionalism throughout ELT to provide teachers with opportunities for development.
- To enable the international network of ELT professionals to grow, for example by encouraging and fostering regional and local groupings, so that members can learn from each other.
- To encourage grassroots professionalism where all categories of members at whatever stage of their career can make significant contributions and continue to learn.
- To keep administration costs low so that financial resources can be deployed to the maximum advantage of members.

The association publishes newsletters and other publications, organises conferences, seminars and workshops, and has a number of Special Interest Groups.

### Website

The Association's website is: http://www.iaetfl.org

## IDV – Internationaler Deutschlehrerverband

The Internationaler Deutschlehrerverband is an association of associations of teachers of **GERMAN**, and of sections or groups of teachers and researchers at all levels in multilingual language teaching associations. Individuals may become members if there is no appropriate association in their country.

The aims of the IDV are to promote contact between associations, to support teachers of German in their professional work and in further or in-service training, and to further the development of German as a Foreign Language and the position of German in the world. The purpose is to promote German teaching which serves intercultural **EXCHANGE** and encounters with the cultures of German-speaking countries and regions.

The IDV was founded in 1968, and comprises more than seventy associations in approximately sixty states. It fulfils its aims by organising international meetings for teachers of German every three or four years on issues connected with German as a Foreign Language (*Deutsch als Fremdsprache*). It also organises seminars and expert meetings and publishes a newsletter and information sheet.

### Website

IDV's website is: http://www.wlu.ca/~wwwidv

# India

Language teaching in India is best viewed as part of India's multi-ethnic and multilingual character and the language policies laid down in the Constitution. India's several hundred languages (Census, 1961, found 1652 **MOTHER TONGUES**) belong to four language families. The Constitution (1950) gives every linguistic group the right to education through its own language, allows the minorities to open their own schools and enjoins governments to support them. Eighteen languages, whose speakers constitute about 96 per cent of the population, have received constitutional recognition as 'scheduled languages'. Between 1956 and 1966, state boundaries were redrawn on linguistic lines. As a result, twelve languages serve as official state languages. Hindi, which is spoken by 39.94 per cent of the country's population (Census, 1981), serves several states. What also stand out, however, are minority languages at every level – from administrative districts, to states, to India as a whole.

The Constitution made Hindi the country's official language and English its associate official language. The official policy on language use in education is known as 'the three language formula' (TLF). The TLF seeks to provide **PRIMARY EDUCATION** through the child's mother tongue and, in addition, to give every school-going child access to Hindi and English (or English and Hindi) as second and third languages. Not all the states have accepted the TLF; nor have all those that adopted it phased its teaching in schools to accord with the National Policy on Education (NPE – 1986). Failure to do so is a source of continuing concern in politics and education.

Languages in education number fifty-eight. They greatly differ, however, in status and role. The differences impinge on how much gets done and how well. At one end stand the majority-official languages that are used as instructional media from classes 1 to 12 and, in most cases, at the undergraduate stage as well. At the other are languages that serve as full or part primary-level media of instruction or as subjects in the primary school or a part thereof. Curricular languages differ in being first, second, third, etc., official or non-official, modern or classical, modern Indian or modern European, compulsory or optional subjects, and so on. They differ in the amount of time they are taught: from 1–3 hours a week for 2–3 years, to 4–6 or more hours for all the years of schooling. Each such difference raises hitherto unresolved issues in curriculum planning and implementation.

Inside the educational system, languages exist in a hierarchy. At the bottom stand minority (or 'majority-minority'; Tickoo, 1995) languages that may or may not be used even as subjects. Next come state or regional languages. Although Hindi is one such, in most states it is also an additional subject, as is English. Between the two there is a major difference, however. English is the language of postgraduate education and of science, technology and research. As the language of the Raj, it had a dominant place in most domains of life and learning. In contemporary India it is more central, as much to education as to every other important domain of public life.

There are a number of indications of the widespread belief in and dominance of English in education:

- the mushroom growth of English-medium schools;
- the mounting pressure on state governments to introduce English from Year 1, even in publicly funded schools;
- the central government initiatives that have made English full or partial medium for instruction in its own, better-provided, pace-setting Central Schools, Sainik Schools (armed forces) and Navodaya Schools (residential schools for the talented);
- the grant of university status to the Central Institute of English and Foreign Languages but not to the Central Institute of Indian Languages or the Central Hindi Institute.

Such dominance of English in education is viewed with concern by those who look at its long-term impact on Indian languages, their learners and users (e.g. Tickoo, 1993; Tully, 1997). It has not meant, however, that Indian languages have suffered neglect as instruments of learning. Over the years both Central and State governments have invested in making them viable instruments of literacy and learning. The coining of thousands of technical terms in Indian languages is a major achievement, as are efforts at standardising and modernising them. But, although results of such empowerment are seen in publications and, to some extent, in their use in education, problems that stand in the way of their becoming comparable sources of knowledge continue.

A major problem that surfaced early in **LANGUAGE PLANNING** is the failure of education systems to make Indian languages effective instruments of mass literacy. Especially in the case of the most-used Indian languages (e.g. Hindi, Telugu, Tamil), language standardisation has meant large infusions of classicalised and anglicised forms of language. As a result the language used in school **TEXTBOOKS** and teaching is far removed from everyday language (Khubchandani, 1997; Krishnamurti, 1998). The widening chasm between High and Low, Oriental and Modern, written and spoken varieties, has become a major roadblock which, in its extreme forms, makes acquiring one's mother tongue as difficult as learning another language.

Three other major concerns stand out in looking at the curricular goals and methodologies that govern first, second and foreign language teaching. These are:

- the failure to relate curricular **OBJECTIVES** to the functional roles and responsibilities of languages;
- the hold of established methodological practices;
- the belief in the superiority of English language teaching (ELT) methodologies.

Studies (e.g. Chaturvedi and Mohal, 1976) point to the absence of specific objectives for teaching languages. In most cases aims are not stated. Where they are, the stated aims do not distinguish between languages taught as mother and other tongues, as subjects and as media, for widely differing goals and at different levels, or between courses offered for markedly different periods of time.

The methods used are, in most cases, not informed by current thinking on language or learning. Pattanayak (1998: 13) provides an example. A grade 5 student 'read' a page in his mother-tongue textbook with the book open and also closed, but 'neither the teacher nor the learner found anything wrong in it'. Languages are treated much like content subjects, and teaching is

essentially transmissive. It is dominated by **TEACHER TALK**, the omniscient textbook ,and year-end tests of memorised matter. The system allows little room for learner–learner or learner–teacher interaction, for learner–text engagement or for learner efforts at gaining a personal voice.

One known reason is the hold of tradition, of the memory-based methods that characterised the still-valued Hindu and Muslim ways of learning. A second is the forty-year-long dominance of **LINGUISTICS** uninformed by educational concerns which has led to an almost total neglect of the basics of language teaching: its curricula and courses, methodology and **MATERIALS**, and, above all, language classrooms as learning environments. Mother-tongue teachers and teaching/learning have received very little attention in India's fifty-plus years of independence.

A powerful influence on language teaching has been the 'paradigm' shifts in ELT. India's ELT reforms have all along worked to adopt and to re-Christen imported methodological alternatives (Tickoo, 1990). Products of studies done first in North America and then in Western Europe, their strengths – real and claimed – have been vitiated in failures to relate them to the sociocultural, economic or linguistic constraints and compulsions that mark the differentness of Indian classrooms. But despite their having had mixed fortunes, these reforms serve as models for not only second and foreign language teaching but for Indian languages taught as mother tongues. Narrower aims, unsuitable methods and ill-fitting materials are the main result. The design and development of socioculturally appropriate methodologies remains a major unmet challenge.

**See also:** Africa; China; Heritage languages; Intercultural communication; Medium of instruction; Mother-tongue teaching

### References

Census of India (1961) Vol. l, part II-C, Language Tables 1964, New Delhi: Office of the Registrar General and Census Commissioner of India.

Census of India (1981) Series I India, Paper I of 1987. Households and Household Population by Language mainly spoken in the Household, New

Delhi: Office of the Registrar General and Census Commissioner of India.

Chaturvedi, M.G. and Mohal, B.V. (1976) *Position of languages in school curriculum in India*, New Delhi: National Council of Educational Research and Training.

Khubchandani, L.M. (1997) *Revitalizing boundaries: a plurilingual ethos*, New Delhi: Sage Publications.

Krishnamurti, Bh. (1998) *Language, education and society*, New Delhi: Sage Publications.

National Policy on Education 1986 (1992) New Delhi: University Grants Commission.

Pattanayak, D.P. (1998) *Position of languages in school curriculum in India*, New Delhi: National Council of Teacher Education.

Tickoo, M.L. (1990) 'Towards an alternative curriculum in acquisition-poor environments', in M.A.K. Halliday, J. Gibbons and H. Nicholas (eds), *Learning, keeping and using language*, Vol. 1, Amsterdam: John Benjamins.

Tickoo, M.L. (1993) 'When is a language worth teaching? Native languages and English in India', *Language, Culture and Curriculum* 6, 3: 225–39.

Tickoo, M.L. (1995) 'Kashmiri, a majority-minority language: an exploratory essay', in T. Skuttnab-Kangas and R. Phillipson (eds), *Linguistic human rights; overcoming linguistic discrimination*, Berlin: Mouton de Gruyter.

Tully, M. (1997) 'English: an advantage to India?', *ELT Journal* 51, 1: 157–64.

## Further reading

Pattanayak, D.P. (1998) *Position of languages in school curriculum in India*, New Delhi: National Council of Teacher Education.

Tickoo, M.L. (1995) 'Kashmiri, a majority-minority language: an exploratory essay', in T. Skuttnab-Kangas and R. Phillipson (eds), *Linguistic human rights; overcoming linguistic discrimination*, Berlin: Mouton de Gruyter.

MAKHAN L. TICKOO

# Integrated tests

Integrated tests take a view of language ability similar to **INTEGRATIVE TESTS**, in that a number of components of language ability are assessed at the same time. Integrated tests, however, are a subset of integrative tests. While the latter term can be applied to any test that assesses two or more language **SKILLS** or sub-skills (regardless of their specificity), an integrated test refers to an **ASSESS-MENT** of language ability in which two or more language skills are combined. The Carleton University Academic English Assessment (CAEL) is a very good example of an integrated test. Test-takers are required to read two articles and respond to questions based on their reading. They are also required to view a videotape and respond to a few questions on what they have seen and heard. Finally, they write a response to a **WRITING** task in which they are expected to draw on the information from their reading and **LISTENING**. This ensures that all the candidates have the same amount of information on a topic available to them and, theoretically, address the writing task with potentially the same level of background knowledge. Also, since each input section is timed separately, the risk is reduced of candidates taking longer on one task to the detriment of the other components of the test.

However, the primary difficulty of this approach to testing is the ease with which a candidate's performance on the writing task can be disentangled from their performance on the reading and listening tests. By including separate questions for the two reading texts and the listening **EXERCISE**, the CAEL Assessment goes some way towards being able to account for students' performances. However, even if it is able to disentangle reading from listening (and both these skills from writing), it still encompasses a number of different sub-skills within each language skill. Therefore, the reported scores are summaries of a number of processes that each candidate has gone through in order to complete the tasks.

**See also:** Assessment and testing

## Website

The Carleton Academic English (CAEL) Assessment is available at: http://www.carleton.ca/slals/cael1.htm

## Further reading

Lewkowicz, J.A. (1997) 'The integrated testing of a second language', in C. Clapham and D. Corson (eds), *The Encyclopedia of Language Education: Volume 7 – Language Testing and Assessment*, Dordrecht: Kluwer Academic.

JAYANTI BANERJEE

# Integrative tests

While **DISCRETE POINT TESTS** isolate the components of language **SKILLS** and test them separately, integrative tests claim to assess the test-takers' capacity to use a number of components of language ability at the same time. Consequently, integrative tests are considered to be a development on discrete point tests.

The components being tested can vary widely and operate at different levels of abstraction from the sub-skills involved. For example, a **CLOZE TEST** simultaneously tests grammatical knowledge and the ability to extract and predict meaning in a written text. A **WRITING** test such as an extended essay, on the other hand, tests the test-taker's grammatical knowledge, their ability to construct coherent discourse (a focus on meaning) and their ability to manage their language resources. At a more abstract level still are tests that involve two language skills such as **READING** an article and then writing a summary of the key issues raised. Such a test (which can also be termed an **INTEGRATED TEST**) integrates a number of language sub-skills such as grammatical knowledge, the ability to extract key information, lexical knowledge (and its sub-skills) and the ability to construct coherent discourse.

Integrative tests are usually preferred to discrete point tests because they reflect real language use more closely, and integrative items are commonly used in **PROFICIENCY TESTS**. However, one disadvantage of integrative tests is that the results are reported as a single score and, since the tasks combine different components of language ability, these scores are not always easy to interpret.

**See also:** Assessment and testing

## Further reading

Davies, A., Brown, A., Elder, C., Hill, K., Lumley, T. and McNamara, T. (1999) *Dictionary of language testing*, Cambridge: Cambridge University Press.
Oller, J.W. Jr (1979) *Language tests at school*, London: Longman.

JAYANTI BANERJEE

# Intensive language courses

Intensive language courses represent a concentrated period of foreign language study, usually of relatively short duration, which may contrast with traditional learning approaches. While a number of different methods exist for intensive language work, the term is characteristically associated with both adult and younger, school-based, learners. However, the use of the same term to describe both types of intensive work is not always satisfactory, given the largely different characteristics of each type of learner and the nature of the intensive courses designed for them. For the **ADULT** learner there is usually a specific goal to the learning with the need to achieve a level of language **COMPETENCE** quickly for business or leisure purposes. In contrast, for school-aged pupils, intensive work represents an alternative and complementary approach to normal language lessons with the emphasis on practical language work and the aim to improve language **SKILLS**. The increased need to communicate, due to the nature of the learning environment, provides the opportunity to acquire new material and perhaps, importantly, activate elements of language which have previously been only partially acquired.

### Courses for adults versus courses for younger learners

For adult learners the specific nature of business interests or holiday destinations will provide a context and focus for their learning. Intensive learning is also associated with the development of higher levels of language skill: 'If a higher level of competence is needed intensive study would be paramount' (CILT, 1998). The investment in time and energy required by participation in an intensive language learning programme means professional courses need to meet the specific requirements of the participants. This is made clear from a review of intensive courses at colleges of further and higher education: 'Short intensive courses may also be run, some designated specifically for business and professional people as well as company courses arranged to take place in-college and/or on company premises' (CILT, 1998).

A key to understanding intensive work for younger learners comes from identifying one of the characteristics of the courses designed for this target group: '... the use of the foreign language for some other purpose than merely learning it' (Perren, 1978: 2). Pupils are given the opportunity to use the language in practical situations. The target language is no longer being studied for its own sake but has become a necessary vehicle for communication. Pupils are involved in activities which require the use of the language but, unlike normal classroom procedures, the programme of activities, not the language itself, is the focus of attention. These activities are often based around a theme which may represent anything from 'secret agent training' to historical events in a target language country, and they provide the framework for the intensive experience. For this reason intensive work is often based outside the classroom, in special centres, to provide a different environment in which language work can take place. Language use becomes more realistic due to the practical activities in which pupils are involved. To provide more **AUTHENTICITY**, the intensive work may be situated in a target language country with easy access to the target language and culture. Intensive language opportunities of this kind could be included as part of the programme for short visits or **EXCHANGES** to the target country.

The differences in the nature of intensive courses provided for adults and children are explained by the different characteristics of each type of learner. Adults are likely to be more self-motivated, with a specific target for their learning

of the foreign language. They are often not already engaged in language learning and the intensive period may be their first encounter with the target language. The courses provide a concentrated period of exposure to the language, usually within a classroom setting. Increasingly, new technology will help this type of learner to access and interact with the target language. For younger, school-aged, learners who are already exposed to the foreign language through classroom learning, it will be important to provide a different approach.

## Links with immersion courses

Intensive language work is closely linked with the French *sections bilingues* and with the immersion work associated with Canadian pupils. However these learning systems typically represent traditional classroom-based learning. They are not limited in duration, but last for the whole school year. The foreign language is used as a vehicle for teaching either specific subject areas such as Geography or History, (*sections bilingues*) or, for younger children, the whole curriculum (immersion schemes). In this respect they share the characteristic of purposeful language use with typical intensive schemes. They differ because, while they extend the period of contact with the target language, they do not provide the short, concentrated period of exposure which might, as we will discuss below, have a specific role in increasing **MOTIVATION** and boosting language skills. Confusion over terminology means that intensive work and language immersion are often used synonymously.

## Historical precedents

Intensive language methods have historically been used to enhance and develop foreign language learning. This is a point emphasised by **HAWKINS** when he discusses Latin learning in England during the sixteenth century: '... there was the daily **GRAMMAR** class in which the structure of the language was expounded ... but this was supplemented by "level two" activity. Pupils were expected to use Latin for all purposes ... any boy caught using English, even in the playground, was to be beaten' (Hawkins, 1988: 4). As we shall see below, Hawkins distinguishes between **MEDIUM-ORIENTED AND MESSAGE-ORIENTED** ('level 1' and 'level 2') teaching. An appreciation that limiting contact of the target language to classroom lessons and not providing sufficient practical language use is evident even from this historical quotation. During the 1940s, intensive learning became associated with the development of the **AUDIOLINGUAL METHOD** of language teaching and the need to run intensive courses to provide military personnel with language skills.

While there is a clear historical precedent for intensive language work, this kind of activity does not fit readily into school-based foreign language learning today. A theoretical case has been made, however, in support of intensive work in schools. For **HAWKINS**, foreign language learning requires a two-level approach: activities focused on the form of language would concentrate on grammatical structure, **PRONUNCIATION** and the accuracy of language; while in 'message-oriented work', 'the learner concentrates on using the foreign language to transact meanings ... the most effective language learning involves a constant interaction between these two kinds of activity' (Hawkins, 1988: 3). This concept was based on the work of Dodson (1978) and Stevick (1976, 1988). Stevick associates learning with the involvement of the learner and the depth of learning which takes place: 'sentences are easier to learn if the student meets them in a meaningful context. One reason for this may be that the meaningful context permits more complex processing' (Stevick, 1976: 30). While Stevick does not deal specifically with intensive work, he considers the intensity of a learner's experience, identified as 'the vividness of exposure to an item', to be a key factor in language **ACQUISITION**.

## Significance of intensive courses

In a survey of intensive work in English schools, Hawkins (1978, 1988), found clear evidence for the enthusiastic response of participating pupils and teachers. What was less evident was research to show the extent to which exposure to this kind of experience not only increased motivation, but also improved language skills.

The importance of intensive language courses is related to their effectiveness in creating an environment in which access to the foreign language can be increased and language skills improved. While adult intensive work is a proven and accepted method of developing language skills, school-based initiatives remain unusual. Of more importance than increasing such intensive initiatives is contrasting language development during intensive work with normal classroom-based learning. We tend to examine foreign language learning for younger pupils from the perspective of classroom learning. It may be, however, that there are real lessons to be learnt from how pupils' foreign language skills can develop during intensive work, and the relevance of intensive methods to normal classroom practice should be investigated further.

We would expect that increased exposure to the target language, and pupil involvement in an experience when language is used in context, would lead to new items of language being acquired. Some of this **VOCABULARY** and these structures will be new to pupils, and will be specifically associated with the new environment in which they find themselves. However, what if some of the material acquired by pupils has been targeted for acquisition in the classroom but has remained only partially known until the intensive experience? This would suggest that there is a kind of 'vocabulary dormancy' operating for some language material in the classroom, and that it takes the catalyst of an intensive type of experience for this material to be activated and fully acquired (Daniels, in press).

**See also:** Acquisition and teaching; Exchanges; Medium-oriented and message-oriented communication; Study abroad; Task-based teaching and assessment

## References

CILT (1998) *Language courses for adults, a guide to part-time and intensive opportunities for learning languages*, Information Sheet 4, London: Centre for Information on Language Teaching.

Daniels, J. (in press) 'Intensive language work as a catalyst for classroom learning and an antidote for "Vocabulary Dormancy" ', *Language Learning Journal*.

Dodson, C. (1978) *Language teaching and the bilingual method*, London: Pitman.

Hawkins, E. (ed.) (1978) *Intensive language teaching in schools*, London: Centre for Information on Language Teaching.

Hawkins, E. (ed.) (1988) *Intensive language teaching and learning, initiatives at school level*, London: Centre for Information on Language Teaching.

Perren, G. (1978) 'Foreword', in E. Hawkins (ed.), *Intensive language teaching in schools*, London: Centre for Information on Language Teaching.

Stevick, E. (1976) *Memory, meaning and method*, Cambridge, MA: Newbury House.

Stevick, E. (1988) *Teaching and learning languages*, Cambridge: Cambridge University Press.

## Further reading

Ellis, R. (1984) *Classroom second language development*, Oxford: Pergamon.

Spolsky, B. (1989) *Conditions for second language learning*, Oxford: Oxford University Press.

JOHN DANIELS

# Intercultural communication

The interest in intercultural communication (IC) is an outcome of the ongoing globalization of academic studies, professional training and cooperation. Intercultural contacts become less intermittent and time-bound, demanding more and more specific communication strategies for mastering the processes of mutual adaptation, integration and mediation.

The term IC in its narrow sense was introduced into the foreign language and communication training literature in the 1970s (Samovar and Porter, 1972). IC denotes a peculiar communication situation: the varied language and discourse strategies people from different cultural backgrounds use in direct, face-to-face situations. As this term became more popular, it was also used to refer to studies in **TRANSLATION**, in contrastive **LINGUISTICS** (**PRAGMATICS**), in **READING** foreign literature or in comparative analysis of cultural meanings. In this broad sense the term IC faced some criticism, since similar studies had been

carried out before using the same methodological tools so that this labelling did not reveal important new issues to the respective fields. While this is certainly correct, research and its applications in the narrow sense of the term developed into a specific field of interest, namely the **DISCOURSE ANALYSIS** of communicative events, where people from different cultural backgrounds engage in face-to-face communication.

The current focus of IC is on how people handle differences in linguistic behaviour and its various effects. The analyses result in descriptions of culturally specific ways of expressing and interpreting the situated linguistic action of the coparticipants. Discourse analysis of this process of negotiation of meaning under multicultural conditions was supported by the development of low-cost and mobile video technologies, allowing researchers to record authentic IC and to work out micro-analyses of the specific rules of interaction under the conditions of multicultural influences. This research on discourse in intercultural situations has become increasingly important to the field of foreign language (FL) teaching, since the analyses have provided the linguistic grounds of the competencies FL learners need when they want to apply their acquired classroom knowledge in real intercultural communication situations.

This concept of 'intercultural situation/s' (IS) is tightly connected to intercultural communication because it indicates the framing activities coparticipants apply in order to build up a 'common' base of understanding. IS arise under the following conditions: speakers$_{1-n}$ from different cultures$_{C1-Cn}$. They communicate various 'things': i.e., while conversing they refer to *abstract concepts* (freedom, warm-heartedness, enjoyment, etc.), *concrete objects* (child, dog, apartment, etc.), *institutions* (school, café, etc.), or *perceptions* (pretty, unfriendly, extraordinary, etc.). According to their intentions they realise utterances, carrying out *speech acts* (promising, confirming, evaluating, presuming, etc.) in order to gain purposes like convincing, criticising, etc. Normally, the presence alone of an interlocutor from a foreign culture (as a coparticipant, not a bystander) determines sufficiently a situation as being intercultural. In an IS, coparticipants need to apply metacognitive thinking and master specific, non-face threatening actions to index or to monitor the mutual culture-specific production and reception of linguistic actions and knowledge bases.

However, intercultural situations are not simply the merging of different cultures. The IS are constituted by the coparticipants themselves by using various components of the given situation for setting third-cultural grounds and creating a 'situated talk'. For example, in a given situation, a group of people from Great Britain, France, Sweden and Germany meet in Frankfurt in order to discuss business arrangements. In this IS various cultural systems are involved that determine the situation consciously or unconsciously as being intercultural. In the given IS the following cultures can be used as common frames of interaction:

1  Culture$_{C1}$: Country of origin/cultural background of speaker$_{C1}$ (Great Britain);
2  Culture$_{C2}$: Country of origin/cultural background of speaker$_{C2}$ (France);
3  Culture$_{Cn-1}$: Country of origin/cultural background of speaker$_{Cn-1}$ (Sweden);
4  Culture$_{Cn}$: Country of origin/cultural background of speaker$_{Cn}$ (Germany);
5  Culture$_{CS}$: Cultural domain in which the speakers$_{C1-Cn}$ are currently interacting, i.e. the cultural domain of the current communication situation$_{CS}$ (Germany);
6  Culture$_{CM}$: Cultural domain of the foreign language being used as a medium of communication$_{CM}$, e.g. English, the form of expression of the cultural domains of Great Britain, the USA, etc.;
7  Culture$_{CN}$: Domain of an often neutrally perceived culture of the Anglo-American business world (CN).

The task of the participants in such an intercultural situation would be to negotiate, by means of implicit or explicit cues, a situationally adequate system of (inter-)cultural standards and linguistic rules of interaction. In practice, the grounds of this situation can be established within the following frames:

1  the above-mentioned cultural domain CS, i.e. the current communication situation ('We are having our meeting in Germany, and I propose we go the German way, establishing time limits for our discussion points and ... ');

2  using the cultural domain$_{C2}$ of one of the participants ('As a Frenchman I feel bad about this procedure and I propose to handle this problem as we always do in France, that is, to ... ');
3  the domain$_{CN}$ of the 'Anglo-American business world', often considered to be culturally neutral as an artificial cultural background when English is used as a **LINGUA FRANCA**;
4  a new cultural framework$_{IC}$, created *ad hoc* by the participants and including profitable aspects of several cultural domains for the benefit of the group, the situation and the communicative goals.

This last example shows a vision of intercultural understanding: the participants in IC situations are aware of the culture-bound character of meanings and try constructively, in the sense of the original meaning of the Latin *communicare*, to create for themselves a comprehension base for jointly defined frames, meanings, linguistic action and procedures. According to Koole and ten Thije (1994), this common knowledge and action practice can be called discursive interculture.

Sarangi (1994) and Clyne (1994) divide the attempts of analysing IC into three basic approaches: the 'cultural anthropological perspective' (where persons 'represent' different cultures and, therefore, cause various communication problems out of their different cultural background: e.g. Asante and Gudykunst, 1989; Brislin, 1981; Prosser, 1978); the 'cross-cultural pragmatic perspective' (looking for different realisations of predefined patterns of linguistic action: e.g. Blum-Kulka *et al.*, 1989; Kasper and Blum-Kulka, 1993); and the 'interactional sociolinguistic perspective' (providing data of IS that create culturally shaped communicative styles which might cause inter-ethnic misunderstanding: e.g. Gumperz, 1982; Scollon and Scollon, 1995). Some critical discourse analysts (Sarangi, 1994; Blommaert and Verschueren, 1991) question the tendency of all three schools to claim for the manifestations of miscommunication a culture-oriented reason. As can be seen in the data and in follow-up interviews, most coparticipants attribute them in this way and react correspondingly. Thus, in IC, the emerging situated discourse and its third-culture effects are not only determined by the composition of cultural backgrounds and linguistic behaviour of the coparticipants, but to a great extent by their (mis)interpretation and their attributions of linguistic action.

Any valuable research on IC, therefore, has to focus on how the participants perceive the linguistic manifestations of others, how they create 'new' meanings, adapted to be valid for the particular situation they are constituting. This means that persons do not rely entirely on their cultural norms but take into account other values and adapt eventually to what they assume to be the foreign cultural norms and actions that others orient their talk to. Any attempt, for example in the FL classroom, to improve IC not only depends on the amount of FL teaching input but on the **INTERCULTURAL COMPETENCE** of the coparticipants.

**See also:** Cross-cultural psychology; Cultural awareness; Intercultural competence; *Interkulturelle Didaktik*; Language awareness; Non-verbal communication; Skills and knowledge in language learning

### References

Asante, M.K. and Gudykunst, W.B. (eds) (1989) *Handbook of international and intercultural communication*, Newbury Park: Sage.

Blommaert, J. and Verschueren, J. (eds) (1991) *The pragmatics of intercultural and international communication*, Amsterdam/Philadelphia: John Benjamins.

Blum-Kulka, S., House, J. and Kasper. G. (eds) (1989) *Cross-cultural pragmatics: requests and apologies*, Norwood, NJ: Ablex.

Brislin, R.W. (1981) *Cross-cultural encounters*, New York: Pergamon Press.

Clyne, M. (1994) *Inter-cultural communication in the workplace: cultural values in discourse*, Cambridge: Cambridge University Press.

Gumperz, J. (1982) *Discourse strategies*, Cambridge: Cambridge University Press.

Kasper, G. and Blum-Kulka, S. (eds) (1993) *Interlanguage pragmatics*, New York/Oxford: Oxford University Press.

Koole, T. and ten Thije, J.D. (1994) *The construction of intercultural discourse. Team meeting of education advisers*, Amsterdam/Atlanta: RODOPI.

Prosser, M.H. (1978) *The cultural dialogue: an introduction to intercultural communication*, Washington: SIETAR.

Samovar, L.A. and Porter, R.E. (eds) (1972) *Intercultural communication: a reader*, Belmont: Wadsworth.

Sarangi, S. (1994) 'Intercultural or not? Beyond celebration of cultural differences in miscommunication analysis', *Pragmatics* 3, 409–27.

Scollon, R. and Scollon, S.W. (1995) *Intercultural communication. A discourse approach*, Oxford: Blackwell.

### Further reading

Asante, M.K. and Gudykunst, W.B. (eds) (1989) *Handbook of international and intercultural communication*, Newbury Park: Sage.

Samovar, L.A. and Porter, R.E. (eds) (1972) *Intercultural communication: a reader*, Belmont: Wadsworth.

Scollon, R. and Scollon, S.W. (1995) *Intercultural communication. A discourse approach*, Oxford: Blackwell.

BERND MÜLLER-JACQUIER

# Intercultural competence

Intercultural competence (IC) is the ability to interact effectively with people from cultures that we recognise as being different from our own. Cultures simultaneously share and differ in certain aspects, e.g. beliefs, habits and values. The so-called culture-general aspects are those they share, while the aspects in which they differ are usually reckoned as culture-specific (Brislin and Yoshida, 1994: 37–55). The fewer culture-general aspects shared and the more culture-specifics identified, the more we perceive a culture as being different.

Interacting effectively across cultures means accomplishing a negotiation between people based on both culture-specific and culture-general features that is on the whole respectful of and favourable to each. Smith, Paige and Steglitz (1998) provide a definition of 'effectiveness' and 'appropriateness' with respect to communication: 'Communication is *appropriate* when it meets contextual and relational standards (you did it right given the context); *effective* when it achieves desired ends or goals or provides satisfaction of both communicators' **NEEDS** and concerns.' (1998: 71–2).

Therefore, IC may have different meanings according to the type of relationship established between Self and Other. Either Self is expected to adjust to Other, or Self is expected to accomplish strategic goals on their or someone else's behalf with regard to Other, or Self and Other are expected to negotiate a cultural platform that is satisfactory for all parties involved (the preferable alternative). According to Byram, IC is more complex than Communicative Competence, precisely because it focuses on 'establishing and maintaining relationships' instead of merely communicating messages or exchanging information (Byram, 1997b: 3). Therefore, 'adequacy and flexibility' are, according to Meyer, abilities that should be developed among foreign language/culture learners because they help them to be aware of differences and able to deal with them (Meyer, 1990: 137).

The difficulty in achieving a successful intercultural interaction does not necessarily correspond to the gap between cultural backgrounds. There are several factors involved, not all of them cultural: e.g. personality. The linguistic element is also most important for developing and achieving IC. An intercultural interaction is generally accomplished in one language that may be either native or foreign to all speakers or simultaneously native for some and foreign for others. Therefore, Byram distinguishes between 'Intercultural Competence' as the 'ability to interact in their own language with people from another country and culture' and 'Intercultural Communicative Competence' which means performance in a foreign language (1997b: 70).

## The 'intercultural speaker'

Thus, the foreign language/culture learner is viewed by Byram and Zarate as an 'intercultural speaker', defined as someone who 'crosses frontiers, and who is to some extent a specialist in the transit of cultural property and symbolic values' (Byram

and Zarate, 1997: 11). The notion of an 'intercultural speaker' responds to contemporary theories of cultural identity as being socially constructed, always in the process 'of "becoming" as well as of "being" ' (Hall, 1990: 225).

The 'intercultural speaker' mediates between two or more cultural identifications. These include the criss-crossing of identities and 'the "positions" to which they are summoned; as well as how they fashion, stylize, produce and "perform" these positions' (Hall, 1996: 13–14). Therefore, the 'intercultural speaker' has to negotiate between their own cultural, social and political identifications and representations with those of the other, that is, they must be critical. The *critical* 'intercultural speaker' takes critical advantage of the world opened wide to them by appreciating the different narratives available, by reflecting upon how they articulate, how they are positioned and how their positions affect their perspectives.

An intercultural encounter encompasses an interaction between the multiple identities of social actors, their perceptions of each other's identities (Byram, 1997a: 56) and the fact that some are more dominant in particular circumstances (Byram and Fleming, 1998: 7). However, eventually the interaction is more than the sum of its parts because the intercultural encounter stretches the cultural identities involved and the exchange takes place 'in between' them, or at their extremities. This 'open country' where the extensions of our selves meet is identified by Bhabha (1994) as the 'Third Space', and described as 'unrepresentable in itself', a place where 'the meaning and symbols of culture have no primordial unity or fixity' and where 'the same signs can be appropriated, translated, rehistoricized and read anew' (1994: 37–8).

## Learning intercultural competence

The idea of the 'intercultural speaker' confirms the description of learners as 'border crossers' (Giroux, 1992), who make full use of the opportunities for establishing various, formal or informal, cross-cultural contacts that enable them to gather a variety of experiences. However, the 'intercultural speaker' is not a cosmopolitan being who floats over cultures, but someone committed to turning intercultural encounters into intercultural relationships. Therefore, the process of becoming inter-culturally competent is more complex than just realising that there is a 'They' and a 'We'. It entails awareness of the ever-evolving and struggling web of intra- and intercultural meanings. Accordingly, Byram and Zarate (1997) identify several factors/ '*savoirs*' – *savoirs, savoir être, savoir comprendre, savoir faire/apprendre* – for developing intercultural competence within foreign language/culture education. Furthermore, Byram distinguishes '*savoir s'engager*'/ critical **CULTURAL AWARENESS** as the centre of his model, which he describes as 'a rational and explicit standpoint from which to evaluate' (Byram, 1997b: 54). This is a world where identifications and representations are in constant contact and change and foreign language/culture has an important role to play in helping young citizens consciously to differentiate and mediate between competing identity loyalties.

## Teaching intercultural competence

The main target for the foreign language/culture learner/teacher is no longer to imitate a circum-scribed and standardised model of a **NATIVE SPEAKER** (Kramsch, 1993; Byram, 1997b; Byram and Zarate, 1997). Therefore, teachers need to discard their role as ambassadors of a foreign culture and the concept of a static, self-contained and strange culture. Instead, they must acknowl-edge the interactive nature and the social, political, and ethical implications of learning/teaching about culture. Such an understanding of foreign language/culture education has profound conse-quences for teacher development due to its effect on teachers' 'professional identity' (Byram and Risager, 1999: 79). Interdisciplinary research and **INTERCULTURAL TRAINING** are becoming more visible in teacher development programmes. Class-room-based and experiential learning are impor-tant and complement each other, since they prompt alternative cognitive, affective and beha-vioural outcomes. Therefore, integration of theory and practice – *praxis* – performed in an inter-pretive, reflexive, exploratory and pragmatic way in **TEACHER EDUCATION** is fundamental in order to induce teachers to promote it in their classes. Consistent preparation and follow-up to experien-tial learning have been achieved through the combination of 'home ethnography' and fieldwork abroad (Roberts, 1993). Teachers are not accultu-rated into the target culture, but instead develop a critical spirit towards foreign culture teaching/ learning, target and native cultures, intercultural interaction and **EXCHANGE** itself.

**See also:** Communicative language teaching; Cross-cultural psychology; Cultural awareness; Culture shock; Intercultural communication; *Interkulturelle Didaktik*; Non-verbal communication; Stereotypes

## References

Bhabha, H. (1994) *The location of culture*, London: Routledge.

Brislin, R. and Yoshida, T. (1994) *Intercultural communication training: an introduction*, Thousand Oaks: Sage.

Byram, M. (1997a) 'Cultural studies and foreign language teaching', in S. Bassnett (ed.), *Studying British cultures: an introduction*, London: Routledge.

Byram, M. (1997b) *Teaching and assessing intercultural communicative competence*, Clevedon: Multilingual Matters.

Byram, M. and Fleming, M. (eds) (1998) *Language learning in intercultural perspective*, Cambridge: Cambridge University Press.

Byram, M. and Risager, K. (1999) *Language teachers, politics and cultures*, Clevedon: Multilingual Matters.

Byram, M. and Zarate, G. (eds) (1997) *The sociocultural and intercultural dimension of language learning and teaching*, Strasbourg: Council of Europe.

Giroux, H.A. (1992) *Border crossings – cultural workers and the politics of education*, New York: Routledge.

Hall, S. (1990) 'Cultural identity and diaspora', in J. Rutherford (ed.), *Identity: community, culture, difference*, London: Lawrence and Wishart.

Hall, S. (1996) 'Introduction: who needs "iden-tity"?', in S. Hall and P. du Gay (eds), *Questions of cultural identity*, London: Sage.

Kramsch, C. (1993) *Context and culture in language teaching*, Oxford: Oxford University Press.

Meyer, M. (1990) 'Developing transcultural com-petence: case studies of advanced foreign language learners', in D. Buttjes and M. Byram (eds), *Mediating languages and cultures: towards an intercultural theory of foreign language education*, Clevedon: Multilingual Matters.

Roberts, C. (1993) 'Cultural studies and student exchange: living the ethnographic life', *Language, Culture and Curriculum* 6, 1: 11–17.

Smith, S.L., Paige, R.M. and Steglitz, I. (1998) 'Theoretical foundations of intercultural training and applications to the teaching of culture', in D.L. Lange, C.A. Klee, R.M. Paige, and Y.A. Yershova (eds), *Culture as the core: interdisciplinary perspectives on culture teaching and learning in the language curriculum*, Center for Advanced Research on Language Acquisition, Working Paper Series: University of Minnesota.

### Further reading

Bhabha, H. (1994) *The location of culture*, London: Routledge.

Brislin, R. and Yoshida, T. (1994) *Intercultural communication training: an introduction*, Thousand Oaks: Sage.

Byram, M. (1997) *Teaching and assessing intercultural communicative competence*, Clevedon: Multilingual Matters.

Byram, M. and Zarate, G. (eds) (1997) *The sociocultural and intercultural dimension of language learning and teaching*, Strasbourg: Council of Europe.

Hall, S and du Gay, P. (eds) (1996) *Questions of cultural identity*, London: Sage.

MANUELA GUILHERME

# Intercultural training

The connotations of the term 'training' reveal physical activities, and it is correct that, in general, trainees expect of intercultural training programmes (ICTs) not only a specific knowledge about a foreign culture, the linguistic and behavioural habits of its members, and/or of the dominant cultural values, but in the first place how to proceed in intercultural situations (Bennett, 1986). Perhaps because of these aspects of behavioural rehearsal, this kind of guided 'learning

of and about the foreign' is called intercultural training (ICT).

The history of Intercultural Training began shortly after World War Two (Mendenhall, 1996), stimulated by the still-ongoing diversity processes in the population and workforce. For example, the US American Foreign Service Institute hired anthropologists and linguists 'interested in studying the "out of awareness" aspects of communication (proxemics, paralinguistics, kinesics), as well as **LINGUISTICS**, and their training reflected this more holistic approach' (Paige and Martin, 1996: 40). Intercultural Training became increasingly popular with the worldwide exports of products, representing a necessary component in the actual phase of creating intercultural learning organisations.

ICTs are time-restricted learning units, varying from two days to several months; their participants, or trainees, are adults planning or currently practising intense professional and everyday interactions with persons from a different culture. All learning activities in pre-departure or in-service training are highly structured by a trainer/facilitator, often working with a native of the target culture as a cotrainer. In general, the objectives of Intercultural Training's concern interaction-relevant knowledge, conduct norms, and behavioural and linguistic strategies. The overall goal is often defined as 'to be able to function effectively in a foreign culture and/or in intercultural situations', which means that Intercultural Training influences three main areas: cognitive, behavioural and affective.

Gudykunst *et al.* propose a basic typology of Intercultural Training using the following distinctions: 'didactic versus experiential learning, and culture-general versus culture-specific content' (1996: 61). Concerning the content, the culture-general model demonstrates in various ways how culture influences human actions and the interpretation of actions. Culture-specific models apply to specific target cultures. In training seminars, a didactic approach uses lectures and discussions, videotapes, or critical incidents for elaborating similarities and contrasts between two cultures. Experiential approaches bring to bear empirical knowledge through simulations and games, resulting in explanations about how people tend to adapt to and analyse intercultural situations.

Brislin and Yoshida (1994: 24) summarise three general goals of present Intercultural Training. The first is concerned with awareness, knowledge and information about culture, cultural differences and the specific culture in which trainees will be living. The second one concerns the **ATTITUDES** related to intercultural communication. How people feel about others who are culturally different is included here with related notions of tolerance, prejudice or active enthusiasm about developing close relationships. Another aspect would be the possible emotional confrontation people might experience when dealing with cultural differences in everyday communication. The third area relates to the **SKILLS** or new behaviours that increase the possibility of effective communication when living and/or working with people from different cultural backgrounds.

The inherent critics of this kind of threefold Intercultural Training point to the ways anticipatory adjustment to the foreign is practised. It argues that, first, 'the foreign' is actually no longer a mono-cultural sphere demanding total adaptation but in many cases a multicultural unit, and that, second, the interdependence between culture-bound action and reaction lead to situational inter-cultures which often are left out in Intercultural Training. From this interactionists' point of view, the main problem of Intercultural Training is not the adaptation to the foreign culture nor to the values and the behaviour of its members, but the effects of foreign action and **INTERPRETATION**, resulting in a specific quality of 'discursive inter-cultures' (Koole and ten Thije, 1994). From a foreign language specialist's point of view, the basic problem with Intercultural Training lies in a general lack of communication analysis. Contrary to its origins, most actual procedures in Intercultural Training deal with the psychological consequences of interpersonal intercultural contacts, such as **STEREOTYPES**, stress, or anxiety/

nicative exchanges themselves. The latter have to be analysed carefully. Maladaptive interpretations of different (verbal and non-verbal, direct or indirect) expressions of cultural difference can lead to false attributions of the intentions and values of coparticipants, resulting in the negative psychological effects stated above, and not the differences

alone. Therefore, a primacy of linguistic analysis before the occurrence of any psychological attribution needs to be established. This kind of linguistic approach is important to foreign language teachers because it bridges the existing gaps between the foreign language classroom and the Intercultural Training seminar. This will be illustrated in more detail below.

### Critical incidents

Trainers present selected case studies, which allows multiple linguistically-based explanation hypotheses. Trainers offer different and alternative linguistic explanations and, at the same time, recapitulate latent tendencies to rashly attribute the observed differences to different attitudes on the part of individuals or to whole nations' mentalities, resulting in a first deliberate meta-linguistic reflection on intercultural situations. The trainees' own experiences are generally included in the meta-communicative attempts to describe and analyse intercultural situations.

### Relevant linguistic categories

Trainers introduce linguistic categories like 'meaning', '**SPEECH ACTS**', 'turn-taking', 'silences', or broader ones such as 'directness/indirectness, 'theme-construction' or 'register', using examples of critical incidents where these categories explain misunderstandings. Trainers must emphasise that the examples use contrast-cultures and that no attempt is being made to reach conclusions about the 'typical' communicative behaviour of members from either culture. Thus in this phase of training trainers are not concerned with how **AUTHENTIC** or typical certain forms of behaviour are. Rather, they are aiming at systematically working out a checklist of linguistic categories that represent a

intercultural situations. This list will enable them systematically to analyse intercultural situations in search of possible linguistic reasons for misunderstandings. At the same time they will acquire the necessary meta-linguistic basis for exchanging hypotheses about discourse features in intercultural situations.

## Discursive intercultures

Trainees discuss whether certain ways of behaving that are described as critical should possibly be considered a common product of the situation itself, i.e. seen as inter-cultural behaviour, rather than being considered typical of one culture or the other. This helps trainees systematically to move beyond comparative observations and develop the awareness that certain types of behaviour are reactions to the effects that the (foreign) behaviour of a coparticipant has.

## Evaluation

The goals of the linguistic approaches of Intercultural Training lie in mastering the method of analysis, and not in the ability to reproduce knowledge about typical behaviour of representatives of foreign cultures. In the evaluation phase, prepared critical interaction situations – supplemented by others reported by trainees during the course of the seminar – will be systematically interpreted according to the established checklist. This means that forms of behaviour illustrated in the case studies presented are to be identified as, e.g., problems of proximity, of different speech act realisations, of pause structure, or as problems of interpreting non-verbal signals. The generated hypotheses about possible reasons for communication problems are deliberately not put into a hierarchical order with regard to plausibility or frequency of occurrence in this first step. The reason for collecting all possible cause attributions as explanations is deliberately to develop a tolerance of ambiguity. Contrasting hypotheses are considered equally possible until one or the other receives more credibility from additional information. Only after this does the plenary discussion deal with the question of the plausibility of individual explanatory hypotheses.

## Conclusion

Training to improve the analysis of the important linguistic features of intercultural situations represents both a tool for discriminating linguistic and psychological approaches to Intercultural Training

and an ideal link between communication-oriented foreign language teaching and Intercultural Training programmes oriented towards cultural standards and values.

**See also:** Cultural awareness; Intercultural communication; Intercultural competence; *Interkulturelle Didaktik*; Internationalisation; *Landeskunde*; Language awareness; Stereotypes

## References

Bennett, J.M. (1986) 'Modes of cross-cultural training: conceptualizing cross-cultural training as education', *International Journal of Intercultural Relations* 10, 2: 117–34.

Brislin, R.W. and Yoshida, T. (eds) (1994) *Improving intercultural interactions: modules for cross-cultural training programs*, Thousand Oaks, CA: Sage.

Gudykunst, W.B., Guzley, R.N. and Bhagat, R.S. (1996) 'Designing intercultural trainings', in D. Landis and R.S. Bhagat (eds), *Handbook of intercultural training*, Thousand Oaks, CA: Sage.

Koole, T. and ten Thije, J. (1994) *The construction of intercultural discourse. Team discussions of educational advisers*, Amsterdam/Atlanta, GA: Rodopi.

Mendenhall, M.M. (1996) 'The foreign teaching assistant as expatriate manager', in D. Landis and R.S. Bhagat (eds), *Handbook of intercultural training*, Thousand Oaks, CA: Sage.

Paige, R.M. (1996) 'Intercultural trainer competence', in D. Landis and R.S. Bhagat (eds), *Handbook of intercultural training*, Thousand Oaks, CA: Sage.

Paige, R.M. and Martin, J.N. (1996) 'Ethics in intercultural training', in D. Landis and R.S. Bhagat (eds), *Handbook of intercultural training*, Thousand Oaks, CA: Sage.

## Further reading

Bhagat, R.S. and Prien, K.O. (1996) 'Cross-cultural training in organizational contexts' in D. Landis and R.S. Bhagat (eds), *Handbook of intercultural training*, Thousand Oaks, CA: Sage.

Kealey, D.J. and Protheroe D.R. (1996) 'The effectiveness of cross-cultural training for expatriates: an assessment of the literature on the issue', *International Journal of Intercultural Relations* 20, 2: 141–65.

BERND MÜLLER-JACQUIER

# *Interkulturelle Didaktik*
# (Intercultural didactics)

The term Intercultural Didactics (ID) was introduced in Germany in the mid-1980s (Gerighausen and Seel, 1987). It covers different approaches whose initial stages became significant as distinct ways of teaching foreign languages in the 1980s (Müller, 1992). Responding to new communicative **NEEDS** following the extensive internationalisation of business and everyday life, their common general objective was to expand the existing goals of the **COMMUNICATIVE LANGUAGE TEACHING** approaches using a specific progression. While the latter intended to build up a communicative competence aiming at the competence of a **NATIVE SPEAKER** or a near-native speaker, ID aims at a specific 'communicative competence for intercultural situations' (CCIS).

These two approaches partially overlap. The main difference is that ID emphasises systematic links between cultural backgrounds and linguistic behaviour and its situational effects, caused by the **INTERPRETATIONS** made by speakers with different cultural backgrounds. At the same time, ID aims at **STRATEGIC COMPETENCE** for dealing with direct interpersonal contact between native speakers and non-native speakers considered as social actors in and from a culture. This interaction becomes a process of negotiation of meaning related to culture-bound and situation-bound patterns of social relations. It is influenced by all coparticipants and by their ways of dealing with foreignness and non-understanding that results from interpretations, conceptualisations and reactions by all coparticipants.

This interactionist approach is intended to develop a **CULTURAL AWARENESS** of the effects of the native speaker behaviour as one of the 'foreign components' in intercultural situations. Its source disciplines are: cross-cultural functional **PRAGMATICS** (Blum-Kulka *et al.*, 1989), **DISCOURSE ANALYSIS** and **INTERLANGUAGE**.

## Objectives and curricula

The general objective of ID is to teach a communicative competence for interacting and, if necessary, mediating as coparticipants in intercultural situations. This requires specific **SKILLS** of interpreting intercultural situations according to general questions, such as: How do coparticipants express their intentions using culturally influenced rules of verbal and nonverbal interacting, of directness or indirectness, of problem solving, of ritualised behaviour, of taboos, etc.? How do they adapt to the behaviour of foreign coparticipants and to the intercultural context? By implementing these questions in various ways in the teaching process, ID demonstrates its concern systematically to introduce a foreign perspective to both the linguistic behaviour of the native (NS) and the non-native (NNS) speaker, considering possible cultural influences on them and the potentially different interpretations of these. This will be shown with regard to the learning **MATERIALS** as well as to classroom interaction. Thus, the foreign language (FL used in intercultural situations), foreign discourse conventions and foreign value orientations of the target language (TL) speakers are used to build up an analytic competence for dealing with various expressions of foreignness in general and for becoming a constructive coparticipant and a potential intercultural mediator in intercultural situations.

For ID to be realised as a distinct approach, all main subdivisions of didactics must be imbued with interculturalism: for the formulation of learning objectives at all levels; for the selection of teaching contents; for the preferred teaching and learning methods; and for the modes of **EVALUATION** of communicative competence.

More specifically, the objectives are to promote:

- the presentation of FL meaning as culture-bound (concrete and abstract **NOTIONS**, **SPEECH ACTS**, dialogues, texts, symbols and symbolic/ritual actions, politics/ideology, etc.),
- the presentation of intercultural interactions, combined with an analytic focus on the processes of **INTERCULTURAL COMMUNICATION** reflecting overlapping culture-bound perceptions and linguistic (re)actions of the coparticipants;
- the presentation of grammatical structures (e.g. comparatives, declaratives, negations, hedges,

and other linguistic tools for expressing general-ised views of the world) as they are used in intercultural situations; and the formulation of rules or even a **GRAMMAR** of interacting in intercultural situations in order to facilitate and coordinate understanding.

The approach calls for specific teaching and learning **STRATEGIES** (Byram, 1991). In order to lead its learners to develop an 'analytic mind', 'ethnographic competencies' (Roberts, 1995: 96) and finally a CCIS, ID uses methods that are 'interactive' in the sense that most of the content is not presented as static units to be learned; rather, **TEXTBOOK** authors and teachers present it using different cultural perspectives while students eval-uate it in specific classroom and outdoor activities. These procedures require special methods of evaluation (tests). Different ways in which the four didactic components can be developed within an ID will be illustrated with reference to the following approaches:

### Contact situation approach

A simple method of introducing ID to a foreign language classroom is to substitute intercultural dialogues for the common monocultural ones, integrating the interaction experiences of the learners in dealing with FL speakers inside and outside the native speaker country. The 'contact situation approach' proposes that a list of typical contact situations between non-native speakers and coparticipants from the target culture be compiled. This list of intercultural situations is to be used for designing communication settings, a progression of speech events and model dialogues.

### Intercultural cognitive approach

This approach links **LANGUAGE AWARENESS** and **CULTURAL AWARENESS** in teaching cognitive in-sights and then behavioural strategies for dealing with different representations of foreignness in intercultural situations. Its progression proceeds through major cognitive and linguistic domains, where conscious examination of native and foreign elements in linguistic interaction becomes relevant in three basic domains:

1 Cognitive basis of perception: parallel to the development of students' linguistic skills, special **EXERCISES** and outdoor observation assign-ments lead students to understand how their conceptualisation of foreign meanings is influ-enced by their own patterns of perception. This is intended to stimulate the development of adequate strategies for dealing with the foreign and to relativise common expectations that 'culture' can be learned by simple exposure to the foreign environment.

2 Reconstruction of foreign meaning: A number of semantic exercises devoted to showing that meanings are culture-bound, that they change historically and that they are cognitively orga-nised in a culture-specific web. The progression of these exercises helps students to develop conscious strategies for re- or deconstructing foreign concepts.

3 Relation between speaker intentions and cul-ture-bound linguistic expression: Special oral exercises systematically teach the students what speaker intentions are communicated by what linguistic means (including variation in register, use of clichés, etc.) and also how one can draw conclusions about speaker intentions from particular forms of expression. These exercises are in particular intended to dissociate the routinised and culture-bound establishment of links between speaker intentions and linguistic expressions, and to develop appropriate strate-gies to capture different conventions of convey-ing intentions of action. As constant features, the teaching and learning methods of this approach have been applied in the textbook 'Sichtwechsel' (Bachmann *et al.*, 1995); its progression intends to lead to language/culture awareness and conscious comparisons between native and target linguistic behaviour, thinking, **ATTITUDES**, value orientations, etc.

### Virtual contrast-culture approach

The dialogues rely on the following constellation: speakers of the TL interact with inhabitants of a fictional country who speak the FL and system-atically hint at culture-bound differences in acting and thinking between the TL speakers and themselves. They express their (virtual) foreign perspectives in the model dialogues indirectly or via metacommunication. In one realisation of this approach (Mebus *et al.*, 1987), special cartoon character commentators were added who question and point out specific evaluations of both TL and virtual culture rules, cultural facts and their situational effects on the ongoing interaction. Such a two-pronged constellation of virtual foreign perspective towards the foreign language behaviour is intended to stimulate the learners to bring in their own third perspective: what kind of interaction problems could they encounter with members of the TL? This underlying question provides a system of analytic tools for doing so, and generally avoids the stereotypical we–you confrontation.

All approaches have in common that they seek, by means of a continuous storyline, with selected exercises, themes, facts, ethnographic explorations (Byram and Esarte-Sarries, 1991: 186ff.) etc., to present FL structures, behaviours of the members of the TL culture, as well as information on the foreign culture, in a way that students can evaluate each interaction from a given – or, in multicultural classrooms, from different – foreign perspectives.

## Linguistic awareness of cultures approach

The approach arose from research in intercultural communication, especially the contextualisation hypothesis (Gumperz and Roberts, 1991): cultural differences are 'hidden' in linguistic manifestations. These expressions of cultural difference are found in all languages, and they can be found in different linguistic cues. All coparticipants present them in culture-specific explicit or implicit forms. If the interactors do not perceive these linguistic indicators or manifestations, they represent a constant source of misunderstanding. Therefore, this approach proposes to textbook authors and teachers a cumulative consideration of key linguistic problems. This framework of criteria for the analysis of intercultural communication situations can be applied to any teaching methodology, as it superimposes a parallel set of teaching objectives, contents and evaluations on the given progression.

The idea behind the technique is consciously to consider types of communication problems in intercultural contact (illustrated by different episodes, critical incidents or self-experienced situations of the learners) and teach strategies for solving them. In a first step, this framework applies to the following set of categories: lexicon (including culture-specific meanings, prototypes, culture-specific interrelations and their interpretations by different coparticipants); speech acts (culture-related preferences in form, condition, sequence, frequency and distribution); discourse conventions (conversation patterns, including the length of opening/concluding remarks, use of argument/counter-argument, routines of turn-taking related to the situational context); topics (different rules for the choice of topics and recognition of taboos); register (different functional varieties of speech, expressing interpersonal relations depending on the situation itself, the status, age, rank, or gender of the coparticipants); para-verbal phenomena (interpretation of prosody, rhythm, volume, pauses; **NON-VERBAL** expressions (facial expressions, gestures, proxemics, eye contact); communicative style (direct/indirect realisation of speech acts; degree of explicitness in **SPEAKING**; relationship of verbal and non-verbal expression; rules for interruption, simultaneous talk, self portrayal); culture-specific actions (including rituals) and action sequences (**STEREOTYPED** interpretation of actions like the wine-tasting procedure before a toast, the emitting of a laryngeal sound after taking a swig of beer, or other 'strange' forms of expression of courtesy or religion).

All these applications have in common that they do not merely hint at differences and describe them for various reasons, but focus on 'perceived' differences and their possible cultural sources. By means of a continuous storyline, contrast cultures, or a parallel awareness-oriented curriculum supplement, as well as selected exercises, or themes or facts, and the integration of the intercultural experience of the learners or of ethnographic excursions, etc., they try to establish a diversified strategy of building hypotheses about culturally determined behaviour and how it can be interpreted.

The integration of (non-, para-) linguistic behaviour in intercultural situations into the foreign language class leads to a complex teaching situation and raises questions which have to be resolved in the future:

The objectives of ID are diverse and can only be attained if the approach is completely directed at realising them. Therefore, if in an ID curriculum even one of the four didactic components mentioned above (see p. 303) is left out, one can hardly speak of an ID, because (inter)culture and those approaches which focus on the foreign language as if it can encode different cultural phenomena as a 'neutral' code, neutralise each other. The holistic effort of ID deliberately excludes all eclectic approaches that merely add some culture-contrast contents to their **GRAMMAR** and then focus on specific **VOCABULARY** issues at various stages of the teaching process.

## Teacher education and assessment issues

This does not exclude teachers experimenting with the various stages of intercultural work in the FL classroom. However, the continuous process of implementing ID in different teaching and learning settings calls for specific teacher-training methods for introducing specific exercise typologies (Müller, 1995), for applying new teaching strategies – or better: for adapted classroom interaction activities and a general raising of teachers' intercultural competence. It becomes obvious that teachers who have themselves acquired a linguistic and cultural awareness in intercultural situations are the ones who can handle them best in the diverse teaching/ learning activities. Therefore, ethnographic methods have been introduced to foreign language and culture studies and to teacher training.

Finally, particular efforts are needed to develop tools for the evaluation of the new intercultural skills. Students should not be taught intercultural competence and then be examined by grammar- and lexis-oriented tests. They should have the possibility of earning credit related to the intercultural goals of FL teaching (Kramsch, 1991) and – if necessary – compensate weaknesses in other areas.

The results of the (meta)cognitive practices of ID are not restricted to the systematic raising of language and culture awareness. The capacity consciously to analyse the rules of ongoing interactions can facilitate the culture-bound processes encountered in intercultural situations, e.g. through active cooperation with other participants or by acting as a mediator in complex interactions. By these efforts, students can show how effectively they handle the special risks and challenges of intercultural contacts. At the same time they are practising their intercultural experiences and giving assessors the evidence necessary to evaluate their intercultural FL competencies.

These two parts of ID, the raising of consciousness about the main components of interculturality in interaction and practical skills of cooperating and monitoring this kind of social intercourse, will have to be combined in future qualitative and quantitative research as well as in teacher training.

**See also:** Area studies; *Civilisation*; Cross-cultural psychology; Cultural awareness; Cultural studies; Intercultural communication; Intercultural training; Internationalisation; *Landeskunde*; Language awareness; Non-verbal communication

## References

Bachmann, S. Gerhold, S., Müller, B.-D. and Wessling, G. (1995) *Sichtwechsel Neu – Mittelstufe Deutsch als Fremdsprache*, vols 1–3, Stuttgart: Klett Edition Deutsch.

Blum-Kulka, S., House, J. and Kasper, G. (eds) (1989) *Cross-cultural pragmatics: requests and apologies*, Norwood, NJ: Ablex.

Byram, M. (1991) 'Teaching culture and language: towards an integrated model', in D. Buttjes and M. Byram (eds), *Mediating languages and cultures: towards an intercultural theory of foreign language education*, Clevedon/Philadelphia: Multilingual Matters.

Byram, M. and Esarte-Sarries, V. (1991) *Investigating cultural studies in foreign language teaching*, Clevedon: Multilingual Matters.

Gerighausen, J. and Seel, P.C. (eds) (1987) *Aspekte einer interkulturellen Didaktik*, Munich: Goethe-Institut/Iudicium.

Gumperz, J. and Roberts, C. (1991) 'Understanding in intercultural encounters', in J. Blommaert and J. Verschueren (eds), *The pragmatics of intercultural and international communication*, Amsterdam/Philadelphia: John Benjamins.

Kramsch, C. (1991) 'Culture in language learning:

a view from the United States', in K. de Bot and C. Kramsch (eds), *Foreign language research in cross-cultural perspective*, Amsterdam: John Benjamins.

Mebus, G., Pauldrach, A., Rall, M. and Rösler, D. (1987) *Sprachbrücke. Deutsch als Fremdsprache*, Munich: Klett.

Müller, B.-D. (1992) 'Grundpositionen einer interkulturellen Didaktik des Deutschen als Fremdsprache', in B. Krause, U. Scheck and P. O'Neill (eds), *Präludien. Kanadisch-deutsche Dialoge*, Munich: Iudicium.

Müller, B.-D. (1995) 'Steps towards an intercultural methodology for teaching foreign languages', in L. Sercu (ed.), *Intercultural competence. A new challenge for language teachers and trainers in Europe*, vol. I, Aalborg: Aalborg University Press.

Roberts, C. (1995) 'Language and cultural learning. An ethnographic approach', in A. Aarup Jensen, K. Jaeger and A. Loventser (eds), *Intercultural competence. A new challenge for language teachers and trainers in Europe*, vol. II, Aalborg: Aalborg University Press.

## Further reading

Aarup Jensen, A. Jaeger K. and Lorentsen, A. (eds) (1995) *Intercultural competence. A new challenge for language teachers and trainers in Europe*, vol. II, Aalborg: Aalborg University Press.

Knapp-Potthoff, A. and Liedke, M. (eds) (1997) *Aspekte interkultureller Kommunikationsfähigkeit*, Munich: Iudicium.

BERND MÜLLER-JACQUIER

# Interlanguage

Selinker (1972, 1992) is attributed with the development of the theory of Interlanguage (IL) in relation to **SECOND LANGUAGE ACQUISITION** (SLA). Coming after the demise of **BEHAVIOURISM**, IL was in line with the growing body of cognitive approaches in **APPLIED LINGUISTICS**. The focus was on the learner and how performance is indicative of underlying processes and strategies. IL was viewed as sequential and transitional, and best explained as a continuum which learners move along as they progress from knowing only L1

to gaining more skills in L2. Selinker introduced the concept of **FOSSILISATION** to explain errors which remain fixed in a learner's interlanguage.

A number of ideas come within this heading. Nemser wrote of 'approximate systems' (quoted in Ellis, 1985: 47), whilst Corder used the terms 'idiosyncratic dialects' and 'transitional competence' (Corder, 1973). Larsen-Freeman and Long pointed out how 'the term interlanguage ... entered common parlance, partly perhaps due to its neutrality of attitude' (1991: 60). There may be different emphases in these concepts but they are used, to some extent, interchangeably. IL also refers to 'interim **GRAMMARS** which learners build on their way to full target language **COMPETENCE**' (Ellis, 1994: 30). IL is closely related to the linguistic theories of **ERROR ANALYSIS** and **TRANSFER**.

IL posits that learners are involved in a continual process of hypothesis formulation and testing. As new elements of L2 are acquired, language is tested and assessed. L2 items are also constructed through analogy with items and rules already known. This may be carried out subconsciously, along with the processing of feedback and how this may or may not change the IL as the learner moves along the continuum. The changes may bring the IL closer to the desired L2 form, but not necessarily. With overgeneralisation, for example, the learner extends a newly acquired rule to a context in which it does not apply. Another is simplification of the target language. Error analysis helps to distinguish this system which, according to Corder, is 'not the system of the target language, but a system of some "other" language' (1973: 268).

Five main cognitive processes were identified by Selinker. The first was transfer or interference from L1, which he may have included in some deference to the prevailing contrastive approach of the time (Ellis, 1985: 48). The second was transfer of language training, and the third consisted of **STRATEGIES** of second language learning. The next item offers a key distinction from learning strategies, with strategies of second language communication identified. The way we learn L2 may not be the way we communicate with **NATIVE SPEAKERS**, and there are key differences that previously had not been paid much attention.

Finally, Selinker lists 'overgeneralization of target language material' (Ellis, 1994: 351) which might be a common feature of IL. Learners may make the learning task more manageable for themselves, according to their own learning SYLLABUS and strategies, even though this may lead to over-simplification and generalisation. Ellis points out that 'language transfer' and 'over-generalisation' could be considered as part of 'learning strategies' but overall they represented 'one of the first attempts to specify the mental processes responsible for L2 acquisition' (1994: 351). These points contributed to an IL agenda in terms of theory, research and teaching methodology.

Nemser proposed three assumptions concerning 'approximate systems which also contributed to IL theory' (Larsen-Freeman and Long, 1991: 60). There is the idea that a learner's speech is a patterned and systematic product, which is neither L1 nor L2 but is closer to one or the other, depending at which point on the IL continuum they have reached. Second, there is the notion of IL evolving in clear stages which, presumably, can be gauged with proper observation. This is linked to the final point that learners at the same stage of proficiency will exhibit similar features in their approximate systems with any major variations attributable to external factors such as different learning experiences. Basically, the IL should be similar, as it reflects innate processes, and again this can be tested through research of learners' performance, including their errors.

IL, then, is not a haphazard arrangement but is systematic, rule-governed and common to all learners. This was emphasised in Corder's (1973) work on the innate syllabus of learning and error analysis. The question then arises of the similarities and differences between the first and second language learning processes. It has to be asked how L2 learners, particularly adults, learn another language, since the original language learning device we use as children may be unavailable. Selinker suggested that adults do draw upon the underlying structures, which facilitates the transformation of UNIVERSAL GRAMMAR into that of another language. It is not always successfully reactivated, but it remains possible to acquire L2 through other learning mechanisms, which in turn raises the question of the nature of learning abilities of adults compared to children. Whether or not adults involved in SLA can successfully employ the latent language structure or have to resort to other means will affect the nature of their evolving IL.

The fact that the vast majority of L2 learners, perhaps as many as 95 per cent (Ellis, 1985: 48), do not reach target language (TL) fluency has to be considered. Fossilisation is the term used by Selinker to describe the phenomenon when learning ceases and the IL retains characteristics different from those of the TL. Fossilisation is a form of 'psychological mechanism' which underlies the production of fossilised items and is a 'major issue for which any description of IL must account' (Larsen-Freeman and Long, 1991: 60). Fossilised items may become 'ineradicable through learning or teaching' (McDonough, 1999: 3). Extended exposure to the language will not necessarily alter fossilised items, such as when people live in a country for many years yet their language fails to move beyond a certain level. Fossilisation can account for many errors made by speakers with years of L2 learning and a high degree of fluency.

Fossilised forms may be realised as errors, but they can also be equivalent to the TL form, which is clearly a preferable outcome. An incorrect form may still be intelligible to native speakers and does not necessarily interfere with communication. The key point is that, whether the equivalent or not, these are the result of the learner's own cognitive processes in SLA and not of simple copying. This makes fossilisation part of IL perspective. Some are more serious errors than others, but if a form interferes too much with communication, there is probably less likelihood of fossilisation.

It is not the case that learners are incapable of producing the correct L2 form, and in certain circumstances they may do so, but the IL form is their own 'norm' which they will resort to, especially when under pressure to produce L2 language or when the desire to communicate is strong. This is known as 'backsliding'. Fossilised forms may change, but where the correct form is not equivalent to the IL one, there is more tendency to backslide. That learners gravitate towards their own more familiar IL norm has been shown in a number of studies of learner performance (Ellis, 1994: 353).

The IL perspective furthered the development of SLA research and is now used 'by theorists of very different persuasions' (Ellis, 1994: 354). It promoted the examination and **EVALUATION** of learner's L2 performance with the key distinction between learning an L2 and communicating with it. Criticisms, however, include the view that the IL continuum may be an unnecessary postulate. It may be more fitting to discuss what has or has not been correctly learned, rather than resort to unobservable cognitive processes. Fossilisation can be similarly criticised as a disputed phenomenon, despite its explanatory powers. Fossilised forms could be persistent errors that were not addressed properly early on and became 'bad habits'. IL supporters would claim that the evidence points to a different conclusion, and the continuing use of IL themes stands in its favour.

**See also:** Contrastive analysis; Error analysis; Fossilisation; Grammar; Mother tongue; Native speaker; Second language acquisition theories; Untutored language acquisition

### References

Corder, S.P. (1973) *Introducing applied linguistics*, London: Penguin.
Ellis, R. (1985) *Understanding second language acquisition*, Oxford: Oxford University Press.
Ellis, R. (1994) *The study of second language acquisition*, Oxford: Oxford University Press.
Larsen-Freeman, D. and Long, M.H. (1991) *An introduction to second language acquisition*, Harlow: Longman.
McDonough, S.H. (1999) 'Learner strategies', *Language Teaching* January: 1–18.
Selinker, L. (1972) 'Interlanguage', *International Review of Applied Linguistics* 10: 209–31.
Selinker, L. (1992) *Rediscovering interlanguage*, Harlow: Longman.

### Further reading

Corder, S.P. (1967) 'The significance of learners' errors', *International Review of Applied Linguistics* 5, 4: 161–70.
Davies, A., Criper, C. and Howatt, A. (1984) *Interlanguage*, Edinburgh: Edinburgh University Press.
James, C. (1980) *Contrastive analysis*, Harlow: Longman.

RUTH CHERRINGTON

# Internationalisation

Responding to changes in society, internationalisation as an educational concept has been adopted from the wider political, economic and social spheres in which education systems exist. Still an ill-defined term, internationalisation within education signifies the policy and/or practice of developing the knowledge, competence and ways of thinking and seeing necessary to live in an international, intercultural and interdependent world.

Internationalisation in education has its origins in two separate domains. The first is in the societal context of education. From the 1970s, internationalisation and globalisation have become powerful forces in shaping the economic and political policies of individual nation states (Featherstone, 1995; Robertson, 1991). The rapid development of information technology has accelerated this process. As education is part of the society, and as education systems are increasingly perceived and structured as part of the economic and political capital of the society (Brown and Lauder, 1997), it is natural that internationalisation has become an issue of education. Within the education system, this 'economic-political source' of internationalisation joins with a second source domain. This second domain is in existing education for international understanding and knowledge. The traditional subject areas of world geography, world history, world religions and foreign languages are part of this second domain. They are supplemented by cross-curricular areas of education such as peace education, **GLOBAL EDUCATION**, **HUMAN RIGHTS** education and environmental education.

Drawing together these two separate domains, internationalisation in education is apparent in terms of policy and/or practice. Some countries, such as **JAPAN**, South Korea and Sweden, have officially adopted internationalisation as a national education policy. Internationalisation as a policy typically involves such measures as the development of an appropriate national curriculum and the establishment of **EXCHANGE** programmes and activities.

Internationalisation as a practice or process is a more localised phenomenon, and is not necessarily dependent on the existence of internationalisation as a policy. Internationalisation as a practice or process can be subdivided into three areas necessary for living in an international society; knowledge, competences and ways of thinking and seeing. The knowledge necessary for internationalisation includes knowledge of other countries, knowledge of the relationships between one's own and other countries in various spheres, and knowledge of international and global issues. The competence necessary for internationalisation include language competence, cultural competence and communication competence. Ways of thinking and seeing include the attitudes, values and identities involved in internationalisation.

Internationalisation is a cross-curricular issue within which language education plays a central role. Within foreign language education, internationalisation as a practice is similar in many ways to the development of **INTERCULTURAL COMMUNICA-TIVE COMPETENCE** (Byram, 1997). The role of foreign language education in developing cultural competence as well as linguistic competence (Damen, 1987; Byram, 1989) is increasingly acknowledged and is a vital part of internationalisation. Foreign language education may also contribute substantially to students' knowledge and understanding of foreign countries, people and cultures, if foreign language education incorporates **AREA STU-DIES**. Finally, the affective dimension – the development of students' ways of thinking and seeing – is an important part of foreign language education (Arnold, 1998). Whether it is done explicitly or not, foreign language education can influence students' **ATTITUDES** to other countries and their people, students' values regarding their own and other countries, and students' identities in the world. The responsibility of foreign language teachers to develop this affective dimension positively is a politically and ethically contested issue, but is also an essential aspect of internationalisation.

**See also:** Cultural awareness; Global education; Human rights; Intercultural communication; Japan; Syllabus and curriculum design

### References

Arnold, J. (ed.) (1998) *Affect in language learning*, Cambridge: Cambridge University Press.

Brown, P. and Lauder, H. (1997) 'Education, globalization, and economic development', in A.H. Halsey, H. Lauder, P. Brown and A.S. Wells (eds) *Education: culture, economy, and society*, Oxford: Oxford University Press.

Byram, M. (1989) *Cultural studies in foreign language education*, Clevedon: Multilingual Matters.

Byram, M. (1997) *Teaching and assessing intercultural communicative competence*, Clevedon: Multilingual Matters.

Damen, L. (1987) *Culture learning: the fifth dimension in the language classroom*, Reading, MA: Addison-Wesley.

Featherstone, M. (1995) *Undoing culture: Globalization, postmodernism and identity*, London: Sage.

Robertson, R. (1991) 'Social theory, cultural relativity and the problem of globality', in A.D. King (ed.), *Culture, globalization and the world-system*, Basingstoke: Macmillan.

### Further reading

Buttjes, D. and Byram, M. (eds) (1991) *Mediating languages and cultures*, Clevedon: Multilingual Matters.

Fennes, H. and Hapgood, K. (1997) *Intercultural learning in the classroom: crossing borders*, London: Cassell.

Iwane Shoten editorial committee (1998) *Kokusaika jidai no kyouiku* (Education in the age of internationalisation), Tokyo: Iwane Shoten.

Steiner, M. (ed.) (1996) *Developing the global teacher*, Stoke-on-Trent: Trentham Books

LYNNE PARMENTER

# Internet

The internet constitutes an important pedagogical tool which operates in an individualised and flexible learning and teaching environment. It fundamentally reorganises interactions amongst people and potentially necessitates a reappraisal of the various pedagogical methods, approaches or philosophies adopted by language learners and teachers. As an individualised environment, yet well situated within a social and communicative framework, it can be of great benefit, provided that certain principles are established and issues addressed at an early stage in the language learning and teaching phases. These principles and issues are based on both practical and pedagogical considerations.

The internet provides immediate, cost-effective and wide-ranging access to **AUTHENTIC** language-learning **MATERIALS**, irrespective of the level and location of language learners or teachers. This potentially promotes the democratisation of the learning process and allows those who would otherwise have little opportunity to visit the target country, or to immerse themselves in the language and culture, to do so from afar. The internet's flexibility, accessibility and user-friendliness mean that it can be used with care as an intrinsic element of self-directed learning and can also support, for example, **TASK-BASED** learning, **TANDEM LEARNING** or **GROUP WORK**. The retrieval of authentic materials and direct communication, both amongst learners in a classroom context and between them and **NATIVE SPEAKERS** at a distance, forms a new learning environment which is yet to be exploited to its full potential. The very flexibility and range of the internet has led to criticism that much time is wasted in the use of its various applications, and that much material on the internet is of little value. This criticism is less valid for language learners and teachers who, through internet use, gain access to a far wider range of up-to-date authentic materials which would not normally make their way into a **TEXTBOOK**. Furthermore, in the case of language learners, they have the opportunity to share more responsibility for their learning, as they have equal access to materials previously only available through their teachers.

This responsibility and ability for self-directed learning raises potential problems. Shared responsibility does not mean that learners are left free to 'surf the net' at will, although unstructured internet use may prove useful and advantageous at times. In order that long-term language learning and teaching **OBJECTIVES** do not suffer, language learners must be guided to use the internet in an effective way. They increasingly need to understand how they learn, what strategies they most generally adopt and how best they might exploit the materials they find for their own **NEEDS**. This pedagogical philosophy generates a more independent type of language learning, where language learners can work at their own pace and where teachers become more facilitators of learning than a conduit of knowledge.

The internet can be usefully described as a resource for information gathering purposes, and as a medium through which learning takes place. Language learners or teachers can exploit the many internet applications (discussion groups, e-mail, Usenet, the World Wide Web, etc.) to develop and enhance a wide selection of **COMMUNICATIVE STRATEGIES**. For example, students may access internet-based materials primarily to retrieve, adapt and present them: for content (as a basis for project or essay work); for linguistic or cultural value (text analysis, concordancing, specialist **VOCABULARY**); for language-learning **EXERCISES** (**GRAMMAR** drills, **CLOZE TESTS**); for interaction with other language learners (e-mail-based correspondence, virtual classrooms), etc. As a resource, the process of internet use is essentially one-way; as a medium, it may be two-way. Both processes are valid and of considerable benefit to language learners and teachers, but may not be equally simple to implement, due to pedagogical and practical issues which must be addressed.

If learners and teachers are to use the internet effectively to promote language learning, they should ideally take into consideration certain criteria. These criteria can provide an appropriate framework within which to measure the value of language learning or teaching activities and the possible, or desirable, levels of **AUTONOMOUS LEARNING**. Important issues to consider for resource-based, information gathering purposes are practical criteria such as the access, the use and the reliability of the hardware available, the technical support provided, the internet links used, the level of discourse, the type of register, etc. Of vital importance are also more medium-based pedagogical criteria, such as the choice of potential collaborators, the compatibility of computer systems, whether the internet-based activities provide an adequate learning stimulus, whether the activities fit within the general learning environment, whether the activities improve learning outcomes, and so on. For example, if teachers are required to work within the constraints of educational environments which do little to promote, encourage or enable a learning-centred approach, which do not allow for the development of autonomous learning, or which encourage and reinforce a traditional, didactic style of teaching, then internet use for language learning and teaching may be a largely futile exercise. Conversely, if language learners receive initial training sessions on **LEARNING TO LEARN** via the internet, and if those sessions are supported by constant monitoring (information sheets, questionnaires, formal and informal feedback sessions, etc.), then internet use for language learning can be of a considerable help in the language learning process and in the promotion of autonomous learning.

Language learners and teachers should also consider other issues of a more academic or ethical nature. For example, the accessibility of textual, graphic and audio materials on the internet raises important questions about ownership, copyright and plagiarism. While these questions are being addressed and guidelines are being established, caution must be exercised. Increasingly, internet providers are prohibiting website access to casual users and subscription systems are being introduced for web-based newspapers, magazines, journals, radio and television stations. These restrictions also alter the scope and type of materials which will be available to language learners and teachers in the future.

It is vital that language learners and teachers assess fully the potential of the internet, as a resource and as a medium, in order for language learning and teaching to take place in the best possible way and with the best results. The internet is an important pedagogical tool which operates in a highly flexible environment; the way in which it is applied to educational situations will ultimately determine the success of its contribution to language learning and teaching.

**See also:** CALL; Media centres; Video; Visual aids

## Further reading

Blin F. and Thompson J. (eds) (1998) 'Where research and practice meet, selected papers from EUROCALL 97', *ReCALL* Special Issue 10, 1.

Cameron, K. (ed.) ( 1998) *Multimedia CALL: theory and practice*, Exeter: Elm Bank Publications.

Gaspard, C. (1998) 'Situating French language teaching and learning in the age of the internet', *The French Review* 72, 1: 69–80.

Green, A. (1997) 'A beginner's guide to the internet in the foreign language classroom with a focus on the world wide web', *Foreign Language Annals* 30, 2: 53–264.

Horsfall, P. and Whitehead, M. (1996) 'The WWW in language learning and teaching', *Studies in Modern Languages Education* 3: 11–32.

JEAN E. CONACHER AND FRÉDÉRIC ROYALL

# Interpreting

The need for language specialists to help mediate spoken interlingual communication has been acknowledged from biblical times; St Paul is reputed to have advised the Corinthians to have recourse to interpreters (Herbert, 1977: 5). In today's world, however, the services of professional interpreters to transfer an oral or written message from a source language (SL) into an oral message in the target language (TL) not only help to further global communication but also serve a number of other purposes.

## Consecutive interpreting

The presence of specially designed interpreting booths at international conference venues indicates that the process of interpretation at multinational gatherings is now well established. Conference interpreting is, however, a relatively recent development. Historically, international meetings were held in **FRENCH**. During the negotiations following the close of World War One some of the high-ranking officers felt insufficiently conversant in French and, as a result, discussions were also conducted in **GERMAN** and **ENGLISH**. While the German army provided young officers with a good command of French and English to interpret into

German, the Allies recruited talented linguists to interpret from and into English and French. Later, during the conference on the Preliminaries of Peace in Paris, a dozen interpreters were engaged in consecutive interpreting with notetaking as we know it today (Herbert, 1977: 6). With the meetings of the International Labour Organisation and the foundation of the League of Nations, the need for professional translators rose sharply, and in 1941 the first School for Interpreters was created in Geneva, with the initial aim of training interpreters for the League of Nations. Today, more than half a century later, there are academic courses for the training of interpreters throughout Europe, often in conjunction with translators' training programmes.

The interpreter engaged in consecutive interpreting is usually seated at the same table or rostrum as the speaker addressing the audience and, after each contribution, interprets what has been said into the TL. It is also possible for the interpreter to be seated next to one or two participants at a meeting and, speaking in a whisper, convey into the TL the words of the speaker, a form of interpreting known as whispering interpreting or *chuchotage*. However, although whispered, there is the risk that the voice of the interpreter may interfere with the voice of the speaker. The method also has the added disadvantage that it is far from cost-effective; only a limited number of delegates are able to benefit from the interpreter's work.

## Simultaneous interpreting

The method whereby the interpreter conveys the information into the TL following the words of the speaker, as in consecutive interpreting, soon proved to be rather time consuming, and the need for a more efficient technique became evident. The answer came from simultaneous interpretation, a new mode of interpreting first used in Nuremberg, Germany, the seat of the 1945–46 War Crimes Trial following the end of World War Two (Gaiba, 1998). As the right of the defendants to a fair trial made it necessary for the proceedings to be interpreted into German, the services of interpreters were required and, as consecutive inter-

pretation would have taken an inordinately long time, simultaneous interpretation was introduced.

In simultaneous interpretation the interpreter, who is seated in a soundproof booth with a direct view of the meeting, listens to the speakers and interprets what they say into the TL. By means of a selector switch, listeners can choose one of a number of different language channels in order to hear either the original speech or the interpreted version in their own language. Having the interpreted version accompanying the speaker addressing the audience means a considerable time saving in comparison with consecutive interpretation and, as a result, the use of simultaneous interpretation now made it possible for multilingual conferences to be carried out at the same speed as one-language conferences.

At conferences and lectures, interpreters are also needed to interpret for the deaf, deaf–blind and hearing-impaired, using **SIGN LANGUAGE**, viewed as the native language of the deaf. In many countries, sign language interpreting enjoys public recognition as a branch on its own. Sign language interpreters may belong to professional organisations which, as a rule, are associated with societies of the deaf.

## Interpreting services

Interpreters are, however, also needed for other forms of interlingual communication. When required to mediate in face-to-face encounters between private individuals and officials of public institutions who do not speak each others' language, the services rendered are known as public service or community interpreting. Other terms in use are liaison or contact interpreting and, since it is often verbal exchanges that have to be interpreted, it is also referred to as dialogue interpreting (see, e.g., Niska, 1999). Once performed only by bilingual volunteers and family friends, this kind of linguistic assistance to members of ethnic communities has now developed into a profession, at present probably constituting the most frequently undertaken form of interpreting in the world at large (Wadensjö, 1998). Physical and mental health care, educational and social services and, in some countries, court interpreting are frequently given as subcategories of the wider and more general concept of community interpreting. Among these, court interpreting seems to be the kind which has, so far, been the most frequently described and explored in scholarly literature. Unlike conference interpreters, court interpreters are not usually isolated in booths while engaged in 'the oral interpretation of speech from one language to another in a legal setting' (Edwards, 1995: 1). Frequently, interpreted proceedings fall within the category of criminal law, but they may also include civil cases such as bankruptcy, divorce and child support.

## New technology and research

The services of interpreters may also be used in circumstances where they are themselves not physically present. Remote interpreting, also known as distance interpreting or tele-interpreting, is increasingly being used in community as well as conference interpreting. While tele-conferences rely on communication between participants in different places making use of the transmission of audio signals, video conferences, rapidly becoming accepted for brief meetings between busy executives, make use of video signals which convey the images of the participants. Distance interpreting, at least in its present stage of development, however, appears to increase fatigue and to provide inadequate feedback for interpreters to be able to perform to the same level as in face-to-face situations. Still, there is great interest among interpreters, who are well aware that the new technology is here to stay, for further research to be carried out in this branch of interpreting.

This is, however, not the only area of interpreting research that warrants scholarly interest. It has, for instance, been shown (Kurz and Pesche, 1995) that the type of brain activity involved in interpreting may be different from that used in the performance of other mental tasks, a proposal that would seem to point to the need for further, challenging interdisciplinary research. Interpreting research is still in its infancy, struggling to gain institutional status in academia. Nevertheless, although monolingualism may be viewed as the norm, at least in the Western world (Wadensjö, 1998: 10), simple observation reveals the global existence of multilingual communities, confirming the dual need for more trained interpreters and for increased efforts in promoting further interpreting research.

**See also:** Higher education; Languages for specific purposes; Skills and knowledge; Speaking; Translation; Translation theory

## References

Edwards, A. (1995) *The practice of court interpreting*, Amsterdam: John Benjamins.

Gaiba, F. (1998) *The origins of simultaneous interpretation. The Nuremberg Trial*, Ottawa: University of Ottawa Press.

Herbert, J. (1977) 'How conference interpretation grew', in D. Gerver and H. Wallace Sinaiko (eds), *Language interpretation and communication*, New York: Plenum.

Kurz, I. and Pesche, M. (1995) 'Interdisciplinary research – difficulties and benefits', *Target* 7: 1. Special Issue, 'Interpreting Research', 165–79.

Niska, N. (2000) 'Community interpreter training – past, present, future', in A.A. Lugris and A.F. Ocampo (eds), *Anovadores de nós, anosadores de vós*, I congresa internacional de estudios de traducción e interpretacvión, Vigo: Facultade de Filoloxia e Traducción.

Wadensjö, C. (1998) *Interpreting as interaction*, London: Longman.

## Further reading

Jones, R. (1997) *Conference interpreting explained*, Series Translation Theories Explained, vol. 5, Manchester: St. Jerome Publishing.

Mason, I. (ed.) (1999), *The Translator*, vol. 5.2, Special Issue, 'Dialogue Interpreting'.

Niska, H. (1999) *Text linguistic models for the study of simultaneous interpreting*, academic dissertation, Department of Finnish, Stockholm University.

GUNILLA ANDERMAN

# IPA – International Phonetic Association

The International Phonetic Association exists to promote the study of the science of phonetics and the applications of that science. The Association can trace its history back to 1886, and since that time the most widely known aspect of its work has been the International Phonetic Alphabet. The aim of the International Phonetic Alphabet is to provide a universally agreed system of notation for the sounds of languages, and for over a century the Alphabet has been widely used by phoneticians and others concerned with language.

The Association publishes the *Journal of the International Phonetic Association* (JIPA) twice per year. The journal contains many language descriptions, reports on the application of IPA principles to the transcription of languages and accounts of research into speech processes.

The *Handbook of the International Phonetic Association* (Cambridge University Press, 1999) is a comprehensive guide to the Association's International Phonetic Alphabet. It presents the basics of phonetic analysis so that the principles underlying the Alphabet can be understood, and exemplifies the use of each of the phonetic symbols comprising the Alphabet. The application of the Alphabet is then demonstrated by the inclusion of illustrations, concise analyses of the sound systems of more than twenty languages from all over the world, accompanied by a phonetic transcript of a passage of speech.

## Website

The Association's website is: http://www.arts.gla.ac.uk/IPA/ipa.html

# IVN – Internationale Vereniging voor Neerlandistiek

The International Association for Dutch Studies (Internationale Vereniging voor Neerlandistiek),

founded in 1970, is an organisation for people teaching Dutch Studies at foreign universities. Its most important aim is to promote the study of Dutch at universities outside the Netherlands and Flanders.

The IVN provides help with regular access to up-to-date information about academic, cultural and political developments in Belgium and the Netherlands. It organises the 'colloquium neerlandicum' every three years, alternately in the Netherlands and Flanders, specially focused on Dutch Studies outside the Netherlands and Flanders. It publishes the academic journal *Neerlandica Extra Muros* (NEM) three times per year with articles about the Dutch language, literature and culture in the Netherlands and Flanders, with a special focus on 'Teaching Dutch as a Foreign Language'. It produces a newsletter, *IVN-krant*, several times a year which is also available electronically.

The IVN receives a subsidy from the Dutch Language Union (Nederlandse Taalunie), an intergovernmental institution of the Dutch and Flemish governments, and in a joint venture produces three publications: a list of teachers of Dutch Studies outside the Netherlands and Flanders; a guide to Dutch studies inside the Dutch language area; a list of core texts for Dutch Studies.

## Website

The Association's website is: http://www.wxs.nl/-ivnnl

# J

## Japan

In characterising the teaching of foreign languages in Japan, three turning points in its history are important: the Meiji Restoration in 1868 to the end of World War Two (ending in 1945), where language teaching had practical and cultural purposes; the post-war period (1946–1980s), when the influence of the United States was particularly strong; and the current Heisei Period (1980s–1990s).

### The Meiji Restoration in 1868 to the end of World War Two

In the early Meiji Period, the purpose of teaching foreign languages was practical and cultural. Learning and understanding advanced Western culture and technology was an essential factor in the modernisation of Japan. **ENGLISH** was regarded as the most important language for the purpose of importing advanced Western civilisation. **GERMAN** and **FRENCH** were also among the foreign languages which could be taught at the advanced level of education. The Japanese government invited about 180 foreign specialists, mainly from Britain, **FRANCE**, **GERMANY** and the United States to teach a variety of specialities in their own language. The students made great efforts to understand the information through the **DIRECT METHODS** of learning these languages. A limited number of the young élite were also sent abroad, to Britain (107), the United States (98), Germany (41) and France (14), so that they could bring back the knowledge which they obtained as they mastered advanced language skills. They returned from these Western countries and subsequently taught the knowledge they had acquired to the general public, not in English, but in Japanese. **TRANSLATION** and **INTERPRETATION** techniques were essential means to disseminate information. Training in understanding the original words and expressions, **GRAMMAR**, and contextual meanings is a prerequisite in translation. Thus the **GRAMMAR-TRANSLATION** method became established in the public educational system.

As early as 1871, the fourth year of the Restoration, the government founded the Ministry of Education. In 1872, the Ministry enacted the law which initiated the nationwide educational system. Since getting into better high schools and universities was the key to success in their life, English was regarded as an important school subject in order to pass the entrance examinations. Middle schools required English instruction for six periods per week, and higher normal schools, following middle schools, taught English for seventeen periods per week. Even primary schools offered optional English instruction in 1884, but it was abolished later.

In 1922 Harold E. **PALMER**, a lecturer at the University of London, was invited as English teaching adviser to the Japanese Ministry of Education, and established the Institute for Research in English Teaching (later named the Institute for Research in Language Teaching). He created an 'Oral Method' based on his understanding of how babies begin to master their **MOTHER TONGUE**. His method was disseminated to a limited number of progressive schools, in Tokyo and some local cities. Unfortunately, however, because of World War Two, innovations introduced by Palmer were not fruitful and had to wait a long time before being implemented in the post-war period.

## The post-war period (1946–1980s)

After the war, the American occupation introduced a new structure into the Japanese school system: young people undertook six years at primary school, three years each at junior and senior high schools, and four years at college or university. The most salient feature is to offer equally and democratically the chances of education to the general public. English instruction was formally elective in the school curriculum, but in practice it became virtually obligatory. The influence of American English became stronger than that of British English, and the importance of **CROSS-CULTURAL** communication was emphasised.

The National Syllabus issued in 1947 revealed the influence of Palmer's Oral Method. Great emphasis on oral comprehension and **SPEAKING** skills rather than **READING** and **WRITING** was apparent. Most junior high schools offered English for four hours a week, and in senior highs for five hours or more.

In the 1950s and 1960s, the **AUDIOLINGUAL** approach became widespread among junior high schools in Japan. The English Language Education Council (ELEC), founded in 1956, took the initiative in disseminating information about this approach, which had been imported from Michigan University and some others. However, senior high school teachers as well as students were not receptive to the new method. The university entrance examinations put their main emphasis on grammar and translation, neglecting **LISTENING** and speaking. This bias has never changed significantly since the pre-war period. Thus high school English teaching in Japan was strongly influenced by the backwash effect of the characteristics of the university entrance examinations.

In 1960, the Ministry of Education established the Council for Improvement of English Teaching to review the directions of English language teaching in Japan. The Council proposed that English teaching put emphasis on language activities in terms of the four language skills. The Council was reconvened in 1975 and it made several more recommendations. However, the situation of English language teaching in Japan remained without much improvement over the following years. It was underscored by a reduction of English class hours to three per week at junior high school level in 1978.

The Ad Hoc Committee for Education Reform in 1984 concluded that the teaching of English in Japan was still not very effective in spite of the great efforts made by many people involved. The Ministry of Education held a conference in 1987 to decide on the curricula for primary and secondary schools. Under the revision of the National Syllabus, it was decided that the promotion of communicative ability for international communication as well as a positive attitude towards communication should be the ultimate goal, with much emphasis on the four basic language skills, and that international understanding should be one of the main objectives of high school English.

According to the National Syllabus, any language could be taught at junior and senior high schools. Only German and French are roughly regulated in its teaching guidelines. No other languages are regulated. However, in fact, English has been exclusively taught in 99 per cent of junior and senior high schools up to now.

The Japan Exchange and Teaching Program (JET) was launched in 1985 to improve student's communicative abilities and promote international understanding. It was a joint project of the Conference of Local Authorities for International Relations (CLAIR), assisted by the Ministries of Education, Home Affairs and Foreign Affairs. The purpose of the JET Program was to deepen mutual international understanding by inviting young natives as assistant language teachers to help Japanese teachers teach English and some other languages to high school students. Overall, the JET Program has been successful up to now.

## The current Heisei Period

Foreign language education policies in Japan today have been changing fairly rapidly. As today's society changed drastically in its economic, political, administrative, cultural and technological aspects at the approach of the twenty-first century, encounters with people in foreign countries increased for the general public in Japan. While English as an international language has become more widespread in international society, the average TEFL score of Japanese examinees in recent years was low relative to other Asian countries. It is apparent that the majority of people today feel it necessary to improve direct communication skills in English and other foreign languages, and it is time for a change from the traditional to the communication-centred approach in foreign language education. In colleges and universities, English remains dominant, but German and French have also been taught. However, **CHINESE** learners have increased recently, and it is estimated that in the near future Chinese will be learned as the second dominant foreign language.

According to the proposals of the University Council on Education Reform in 1991, colleges and universities were requested to try to make drastic revisions in their curricula and other educational and academic affairs. The distinction between speciality and liberal arts courses no longer exists. Colleges and universities can determine their own requirements regarding courses and credits. They can also decide whether credits should be given to the students who have passed some general tests of English proficiency (STEP, TEFL, TEIC). A self-evaluation system was introduced to allow colleges and universities to evaluate faculty research and teaching, and students evaluate the courses they have taken.

The proposals issued by the Government Commission on Foreign Language Policy Revision for the Twenty-First Century in 1993 included the introduction of structural change to improve the basic plans and policies on foreign language education in a number of concrete ways. They include numerous large-scale issues, such as a national **SYLLABUS**, overseas and domestic teacher training systems, assistant teacher projects, standardised public examinations, entrance examinations, international understanding and **EXCHANGE** programmes, more choice of foreign languages to be taught in the future, primary school foreign language teaching systems, and others. The Ministry officially declared that it would do its best to fulfil all the goals shown in the items.

Recently it was decided that, in 2002, the introduction of English teaching to the public primary school system would be voluntarily fulfilled as a part of integrated learning. The purpose of this is to improve students' communication skills in English. Instituting the teaching of English at an earlier stage seems to be a major trend in many other countries. In Japan there are a large number of difficult problems, such as training of teachers, developing the **TEACHING METHODS** and **MATERIALS** appropriate to young children, and need for a large amount of financial assistance by the government.

One of the highly authoritative academic organisations in this field is the Japan Association of College English Teachers. The nearly 3,000 members of this organisation represent a third of the total number of Japanese teachers of English in colleges and universities.

All in all, it is not easy for Japan to change its traditional grammar–translation approach to one that is communication-centred. It seems that the Japanese are in the middle of some drastic changes and that the most effective policies for communication need to be pursued. Revision of foreign language education is surely one of the important national goals.

**See also:** China; Higher education; India; Internationalisation; Japanese; Secondary education; Teaching methods

### Further reading

Hatori, H. (1992) 'A survey and history of English teaching', *Education for communication and language* 17: 8–217.

Koike, I. (1996) 'University foreign language education', *The Hiyoshi Review of English Studies* 28, 29: 1–22.

Koike, I. and Tanaka, H. (1995) 'English in foreign language education policy in Japan: Toward the twenty-first century', *World Englishes* 14, 1: 13–25.

Koike, I. *et al.* (1988) *A general survey of English language teaching: junior high school, senior high school and primary school education of Japanese children overseas: a research report*, Tokyo: Keio University.

Koike, I. *et al.* (1990) *A general survey of English language teaching in Japan: a research report*, Tokyo: Keio University.

Wada, M. (1992) 'Research data for English teaching', *Education for communication and language* 18: 1–403.

MIKA KAWANARI

# Japan Foundation

The Japan Foundation is **JAPAN**'s principal agent for cultural relations with other countries. It was established in 1972 as a special legal entity under the auspices of the Ministry of Foreign Affairs for the purposes of promoting mutual understanding and friendship on the international scene. In the late 1960s, amid the mounting need for cultural **EXCHANGES** between Japan and other countries, the groundwork was laid for the foundation of an organisation that would be dedicated to international cultural exchange, invested with a powerful system of policy implementation, and endowed with substantial funds.

It was the first specialist organisation for international cultural exchange in Japan, and it carries out a broad variety of cultural exchange programmes with personnel exchange as their basic premise, ranging from such academic pursuits as Japanese studies and Japanese language education to the arts, publication, audio-visual media, sports and general life culture. It does not work in the areas of science, technology and medicine. Its activities are financed by operation profits on government endowments, aid from the government (including ODA budget), and funding and donations from the private sector.

The Foundation coordinates its activities through its headquarters in Tokyo and its branch office in Kyoto, and is represented in seventeen countries overseas. Its offices overseas take the form of Japan Cultural Institutes, Japan Cultural Centres, Japanese Language Centres and Liaison offices. The promotion of the Japanese language is one of the Japan Foundation's core activities. A number of its annual grant programmes offer support to institutions worldwide to develop their Japanese language courses (including assistance for staffing and teaching **MATERIALS**) and Japanese language specialists are regularly dispatched overseas. Within Japan, the Japan Foundation Japanese Language Institute, Urawa, acts as a centre of research and information on Japanese language education, publishing regular academic journals and developing new teaching materials. It also provides short- and long-term training opportunities for teachers of Japanese, and surveys the number of learners of Japanese throughout the world on a regular basis. The more-recently formed Japanese Language Institute, Kansai, acts as a training centre for librarians, researchers and other specialists. It also administers the widely recognised Japanese Language Proficiency Tests. Outside Japan, the Foundation has set up seven Japanese Language Centres (in Sydney, Jakarta, Bangkok, Los Angeles, Kuala Lumpur, Sao Paulo and London) to provide additional help and training and to respond to local needs.

## Website

The Japan Foundation's website is: http://www.jpf.go.jp

STEPHEN MCENALLY

# Japanese

Japanese is the native language of approximately 125.5 million people, most of whom live in **JAPAN**, although there are communities of over 100,000 speakers in the United States, Brazil and Peru. Japanese is the eighth most-spoken language in the world after Mandarin **CHINESE**, **SPANISH**, **ENGLISH**, Bengali, Hindi, **PORTUGUESE** and Russian.

## History

Writing was introduced to Japan from **CHINA** in the sixth century, and the earliest studies of language within Japan date from the ninth century. However, these studies focus on the use of classical Chinese and on the development and organisation of the kana syllabaries, particularly as this relates to Sanskrit. The eighth century onwards saw sophisticated literary development, including the *Tale of Genji*. However, possibly because these works were written almost exclusively by women and not in Classical Chinese, Japanese itself was not treated as a scholarly subject until the rise of National Language Studies (*Kokugogaku*) in the eighteenth century. *Kokugogaku* focused primarily on the morphology and phonology of the earliest Japanese language, and it was part of a larger nationalistic movement seeking a supposedly untainted Japanese culture pre-dating Chinese influence. From such proto-nationalistic origins, *Kokugogaku* continues today as an active alternative to the Western linguistic tradition.

The first systematic study of colloquial Japanese was actually completed in **PORTUGUESE** between 1604 and 1608 by the Jesuit missionary João Rodriguez (*Arte de lingoa de Iapam*). A shorter related work, *Arte breve de lingoa Iapam*, was published in 1620. These were translated into French in 1862. Both books are based on traditional Latin **GRAMMARS** and include discussion of topics such as honorifics and regional dialects. However, Jesuit scholarship on Japanese was cut short by the expulsion from Japan of the Portuguese (which is to say the Catholics) in 1639. During the period of *sakoku*, or self-imposed isolation (1639–1854), only the Dutch maintained a significant European presence in Japan, and Dutch linguistic studies flourished until the late nineteenth century when **GERMAN** and English became more important. As a natural outcome of the continued contact between Japan and Holland, and paralleling the developments in Japan-based Dutch studies, Japanese studies in Europe began at Leiden in 1856. The Centre for Japanese and Korean Studies at Leiden continues this work today.

In the period between 1856 and the end of World War One, Japanese scholarship expanded in Europe with the creation of schools or institutes devoted to the study of non-Western civilisations. Examples include the Institut National des Langues et Civilisation Orientales in Paris (1868) and the Oriental University in Napoli (1903). The School of Oriental and African Studies in London was founded in 1917, although Japanese was first taught in England in 1903. Lesser-known programmes were also founded in nations such as Russia and Finland, motivated by direct contact

with Japanese. The Oriental Faculty at St Petersburg, for example, has existed since 1895, although the Japanese language was not taught until much later. Early grammars of Japanese published in Europe include *Introduction à l'étude de la Langue Japonaise* (Léon de Rosny, 1854) and *Japansche spraakler* (J.J. Hoffman, 1886). The earliest works written in English were published in Japan by diplomats and missionaries. These include *A short grammar of the Japanese spoken language* (William G. Aston, 1869); *A simplified grammar of the Japanese language* (B.H. Chamberlain, 1887) and *A handbook of colloquial Japanese* (B.H. Chamberlain, 1888). James C. Hepburn's Japanese–English dictionary was published in 1867. While Hepburn romanisation stands today as the most popular way to write Japanese in the Latin alphabet, systems based on the sounds of Portuguese, Dutch, German and French have all been used in the past. The romanisation currently taught in Japan (and used in this article) is known as *kunreisiki* and differs from Hepburn primarily in the representation of the *si*, *ti*, *tu* and *hu* sounds (which are *shi*, *chi*, *tsu* and *fu* in the Hepburn style).

Outside of Europe, Japanese language courses began simultaneously at Shanghai and at Berkeley in 1900, and at Sydney in 1917. As might be expected, the study of Japanese in Asia was promoted in tandem with the expansion of the Japanese empire, beginning with the incorporation of Taiwan in 1895. Japan was also the first country in Asia to undertake a systematic study of the West (from the end of the *sakoku* period), and to many Asian countries became a model for the successful infusion of Western technical, cultural and social practices. This pattern persists throughout Asia today, and is reflected in the tremendous increase in Japanese language programmes since 1970 focused on specific kinds of technical Japanese. The design of early Japanese Studies programmes in the United States was based on their European counterparts. Growth was slow until after World War Two, and only eight universities offered language instruction as late as 1934. In 1945, Yale University created the first Japanese **AREA STUDIES** programme in the United States with a focus on **COMPETENCE** in the language and first-hand experience in Japan. The language programme was directed by Bernard Bloch, a structural linguist who designed the course for the US government as part of the war effort against Japan. Bloch's own contribution to the understanding of Japanese linguistics is multiplied by the contributions of his students, including Eleanor H. Jorden, Samuel E. Martin and Roy Andrew Miller, all well known in their own right as scholars of the Japanese language.

As a rule, Japanese studies has been introduced at the highest levels of education before filtering downward. Nevertheless, the language has also been taught at the primary and secondary school levels since the end of World War Two, particularly in countries of the Pacific Rim. It has been a nationally tested subject in China since 1972, in Korea since 1973, and in Indonesia since 1984. While it does not usually rival English, it frequently competes as the second foreign language of choice. In **AUSTRALIA**, Japanese language study has been a federal priority since 1988 in order to expand economic opportunities and cross-cultural understanding in the Pacific region. Unusually, Japanese is offered at far more Australian schools than universities, and it holds its own against the traditional European languages as one of the most studied foreign languages in the country.

## The present

The **JAPAN FOUNDATION** figures (1998) estimate that some 2,090,000 people worldwide study Japanese. This is an increase of nearly 1,600 per cent from the 1979 figure of 127,000. Japanese is taught at just over 10,900 institutions, which employ approximately 27,600 teachers. Student numbers are highest in South Korea, Australia and China. Institution numbers are highest in South Korea, Australia and the USA. Teacher numbers are highest in South Korea, China and Australia. The most recent surveys also indicate that, in the United States at least, the number of students, institutions and teachers involved with Japanese has more or less stabilised, and Japanese is now the fourth most-studied language in American universities (after Spanish, French and German). New growth is found usually at the elementary and secondary school levels. Japanese studies has also broadened in appeal and interest as it has become a more normal part of the university curriculum.

**TEXTBOOKS** reflecting a variety of teaching methodologies are published in a dozen countries, and recent surveys list over 120 different texts currently in use. Japanese is also well represented in long-distance teaching and advanced technology projects as well.

From within Japan, the Japanese Ministry of Education, Science and Culture (*Mombusho*) takes a strong role in promoting initiatives in Japanese studies through the Japan Foundation. Professional organisations such as the Association of Teachers of Japanese or the recently founded Alliance of Associations of Teachers of Japanese serve an ever-growing membership, and there is increasing availability and recognition of standardised measurements of language ability such as the Japanese Language Proficiency Test (*Nihongo nooryoku siken*). Japanese is also offered by a great number of institutions within Japan, partially in response to demand from abroad and partially at the encouragement of the Japanese government in an effort to promote internationalisation. Such programmes are overseen by the Association of International Education, Japan (AIEJ). In 1992 there were over 48,000 foreign students in Japan, over 90 per cent of whom were from Asian countries, followed by the United States and Europe with just over 2 per cent each.

**See also:** Arabic; Chinese; Cross-cultural psychology; Higher education; Japan; United States of America

## References

Japan Foundation (1998) *Kaigai no Nihongo Kyooiku no Genzyoo (Survey report on Japanese-language education abroad)*, Tokyo: The Japan Foundation.

Sugimoto, T. and Iwabuchi, T. (eds) (1994) *Nihongogaku Ziten (New Japanese Linguistic Dictionary)*, Tokyo: Oohuu.

## Further reading

Daniels, F.J. (1967) 'Japanese', in *Word classes*, Amsterdam: North-Holland.

Jansen, M.B. (ed.) (1988) *Japanese studies in the United States: Part I, History and present condition*, Japanese Studies Series XVII, The Japan Foundation.

Available from the Association for Asian Studies, Ann Arbor.

WILLIAM MCCLURE

# Jespersen, Otto

b. 16 July 1860, Randers, Denmark;
d. 30 April 1943 Roskilde, Denmark

A philologist with interests mainly in phonetics, grammar and language teaching

In pursuit of linguistic studies, Otto Jespersen travelled extensively in Germany, **FRANCE** and England. Previous to his academic career he taught **FRENCH** and **ENGLISH** at secondary schools. From 1893 to 1925 he was Professor of English at the University of Copenhagen. His phonetic work included all major European languages and was based on strict observation of daily linguistic performance. It made him the promoter of a type of foreign language teaching which stressed communication and oral **SKILLS**. He was among the founding members of the Danish *Quousque tandem-* Society, called after Wilhelm **VIËTOR**'s influential publication. Furthermore, he took an active part in the development of an international artificial language, contributing to it with his own system called Novial.

Jespersen's academic work moved away from typical philology as was current most of all in Germany in the second half of the nineteenth century. He refuted the idea that sound laws were without exceptions, and demanded that a distinction be made between the change of sound and the change of meaning. Likewise he refuted the idea that languages had an organic life and that languages of the inflectional type were organically higher-developed than those of other types. Instead he looked at languages as a tool of expression and saw progress in the fact that some managed their communicative function with fewer morphological means than others. For Jespersen, this gave English the position of the most advanced European language, precisely because of its lack of inflectional morphology. His main work, the seven-volume *[M]odern English Grammar* (1912–49) was subtitled *on historical principles* but nevertheless envisaged a comprehensive synchronic **GRAMMAR** based on clearly defined syntactic concepts and terms. Besides being brimful with precise structural observations which find recognition even today, it is the first great example of grammars as they became popular later under the rubric of 'synchronic linguistics'.

Jespersen's ideas about foreign language teaching, laid down in *How to Teach a Foreign Language* (1904; Danish version *Sprogundervisning*, 1901) are a corollary of his ideas on philology. Twenty years after Viëtor's seminal pamphlet, it shows the progress that had been made in the meantime. The primacy of speech is unchallenged, and so is the priority of oral teaching techniques in the classroom. The sole aim of foreign language teaching is natural communication, and the semantically connected text is the centre of classroom work. In 1901 these principles of what was informally called the **DIRECT METHOD** were propagated by one of the most renowned European philologists, whereas in 1882 they had to be introduced by a relative outsider using a pen-name. Moreover, Jespersen himself wrote a number of **TEXTBOOKS** in English and French, not least among them his *Essentials of English Grammar* (1933, frequently reprinted).

Jespersen was a most successful scholar. In this role he holds an historically important position between nineteenth and early twentieth century philology and later twentieth century **LINGUISTICS**, even prefiguring **APPLIED LINGUISTICS**. He was also a most successful planner of foreign language teaching methodology. As the most eminent member of the **REFORM MOVEMENT** besides Henry **SWEET**, he again holds an historically important position between philologically dominated **TEACHER METHODS** and the teaching of foreign languages on linguistic principles, as was advocated in the second half of the twentieth century.

### Further reading

Henriksen, C. (1996) 'Jespersen, Jens Otto Harry', in H. Stammerjohann (ed.), *Lexikon Grammaticorum. Who's Who in the history of world linguistics*, Tübingen: Niemeyer.

Howatt, A.P.R. (1984) *A history of English language teaching*, Oxford: Oxford University Press.

Juul, A. and Nielsen, H.F. (eds) (1989) *Otto Jespersen: facets of his life and work*, Amsterdam: Benjamins.

WERNER HÜLLEN

# Journals

Journals of particular interest to those teaching and learning languages include academic journals that publish research into the literature and other aspects of the cultural life of the country whose language may be studied, journals in theoretical and **APPLIED LINGUISTICS**, and journals whose readership consists predominantly of practising language teachers, particularly those working at school level, which are often published by language teachers' associations themselves.

Many of the journals read by academics and university students in the languages field are devoted to research on **LITERARY** topics, but they may also include those specialising in linguistic studies and those devoted to the political, the economic and the social, cultural and artistic life of particular countries more generally. These are truly international journals in the sense that, though of necessity based and edited in one particular country, they are read and receive contributions from scholars in many countries and are held in university libraries worldwide. In both literary and linguistic fields, the five modern European languages which have traditionally been most widely studied in English speaking countries (particularly **FRENCH** and **GERMAN**, but also **SPANISH**, Italian and Russian) are well served both by journals produced within the country in question and also by those published by learned societies, often of many years standing, in the English-speaking world and in many cases containing articles mainly written in English. For an informative listing of even the most eminent of such journals, the reader must be referred to university, on-line and other catalogues, the following somewhat arbitrary selection being named for illustrative purposes only. The *Revue d'Histoire Littéraire de la France* has been published in Paris by the Société d'Histoire Littéraire de la France since the beginning of the twentieth century;

and the *Zeitschrift für Deutsche Philologie* based in Bonn has recently produced its 120th volume in which issues devoted to literary topics alternate with those devoted to linguistic studies of dialect and usage. The Modern Humanities Research Association, founded in Cambridge in 1918, produces the *Modern Languages Review* containing literary studies of works written in various European languages including English, as well as the *Review of Portuguese Studies* and the *Slavonic and East European Review*. In Britain, long established learned associations dedicated to French, German, Spanish, Italian and Slavonic Studies respectively all have journals wholly or largely devoted to studies of the relevant literatures. In America the State University of New York produces *Nineteenth Century French Studies*, the University of Wisconsin publishes *Monatshefte* with issues devoted to particular themes or authors as well as numbers devoted to German writers of all periods. *Modern Language Notes*, published by the University of Chicago (and often referred to simply as *MLN*), has four issues a year containing articles on French, German, Hispanic and Comparative Literature respectively. Those concerned with less widely studied languages and cultures will also find journals relevant to the study at various levels of Oriental, Asian, Middle Eastern, Celtic and Scandinavian languages and cultures.

Details of such journals may usually be accessed through specialist university departments and institutions, or through the relevant learned bodies or teachers' associations.

Though journals classified under the head of general or theoretical **LINGUISTICS** may be of academic interest to some teachers and learners of particular languages, their usefulness to practitioners is a matter of contention. Some, such as *Language* or the *Journal of Linguistics*, which take a broader view of the subject, may contain articles making useful and perceptive reference to major controversies regarding the nature of language and its **ACQUISITION**. Often, however, their content is technical and inaccessible to those whose interests are more practical, being concerned with detailed points of underlying linguistic structure or, as the case may be, minor – albeit sometimes fascinating – points of usage or semantic development in a variety of languages and dialects including some that must be considered esoteric. Some linguistics journals, notably those devoted to the detailed study of the French language, *Le Français Moderne*, *Langue Française*, *Journal of French Language Studies*, may seem to offer more appeal to teachers and learners of the language at the highest academic level but are of greater interest to those wishing to speak and write about the language rather than to speak and write the language itself.

Of somewhat greater relevance are academic journals devoted to research in **APPLIED LINGUISTICS**, which is often taken to be synonymous with the general theory and practice of second language teaching and acquisition, though it may also include first language acquisition and performance and its various pathologies. Journals in this category are widely quoted in some of the theoretical works on second and foreign language teaching and learning which have proved seminal in the subject. Periodicals whose titles include the expression 'Applied Linguistics' are legion. In addition to *Applied Linguistics* and the *Journal of Applied Linguistics* there exist both an *International Journal of Applied Linguistics* and an *International Review of Applied Linguistics*, as well as national journals or reviews of applied linguistics incorporating the names of the main English speaking countries, not to mention many countries where English is a principal medium of academic communication. In the case of most of these, the learning of English as a second language rather than the study of foreign languages commonly learned by English speakers themselves is the basis of most contributions. This is also true of the authoritative *Language Learning* as well, understandably enough, as of the very influential *TESOL Quarterly* (**TESOL** = The Teaching of English to Speakers of Other Languages).

Finally, there are journals specifically intended to be read by school and university teachers of languages other than English, including the bilingual *Canadian Modern Language Review/Revue Canadienne des Langues Vivantes* and *Le Français dans le Monde*, produced in Paris and containing short topical articles on French political, cultural and social life as well as detailed suggestions for classroom practice. The *Modern Language Journal* published by the University of Wisconsin Press for the American National Federation of Modern Language Teachers Associations is a refereed

journal devoted to research and discussion on the learning and teaching of foreign and second languages.

In Britain, *Modern Languages*, produced by the Modern Language Association (MLA), was for many years the principal journal for Modern Language teachers, though a number of affiliated associations of teachers other than French also had their own language-specific publications. In 1963, at the time of the so-called 'first language teaching revolution', the Audio-Visual Language Association produced the first issue of the *Audio-Visual Language Journal*, subtitled *The Journal of Applied Linguistics and Language Teaching Technology*. The Association subsequently became the British Association for Language Teaching (BALT) and the title of the journal was changed to the *British Journal of Language Teaching*. In 1989 the MLA, BALT and the various associations for the less-widely taught languages amalgamated to form the Association for Language Learning, producing the *Language Learning Journal* and five language-specific journals, as well as distributing *Dutch Crossing* for the Association for Low Countries Studies. Of these, the *Language Learning Journal* is an academic and professional journal of considerable international standing and readership, publishing contributions from academics and teachers from a number of countries.

Needless to say, many countries, particularly those of the European Union, have their own national language teaching organisations producing their own journals. The contents of these range from short theoretical or research articles and accounts of innovative teaching to reports of national language policies and items of Modern Language teaching news. Of these, *Langues Vivantes* and *Études de Linguistique Appliquée* may be regarded as achieving a measure of international recognition.

*FIPLV World News* is essentially the newsletter of the Fédération Internationale des Langues Vivantes but, in addition to useful information about international language teaching conferences and other events, it may also contain short articles of more general language teaching interest.

**See also:** African languages; Arabic; Chinese; French; German; Japanese; Portuguese; Spanish

COLIN WRINGE

# L

## Landeskunde/Kulturkunde

In Germany (and other German speaking countries) the terms *Landeskunde* (= **AREA STUDIES**) and *Kulturkunde* (= the study of culture/civilisation) have mainly, but not exclusively, been connected to the study of foreign languages since its institutionalisation in the second half of the nineteenth century. In relation to specific languages terms such as *Amerikakunde* or *Englandkunde*, *Frankreichkunde* etc. have also been used.

In Europe (and contexts influenced by European ideas and developments), the study of modern languages and literatures and their establishment as academic disciplines were modelled on the classics. Historical linguistics, the editing of early **LITERARY** documents and philological analysis were given precedence over the attainment of practical language **COMPETENCE**, the discussion of more recent texts and a comparative approach to the different cultures in question. Although the university departments were primarily set up to train foreign language teachers, the actual training was more suitable for philologists concentrating on **LINGUISTICS** and/or literary criticism because, paradoxically, language practice and foreign-language-teaching methodology were regarded as secondary; and *Landeskunde* (with an emphasis on realia, i.e. facts and figures) came last, if it was taught at all. Towards the end of the nineteenth century, a number of politically rather than educationally motivated debates (influenced by Germany's hostility towards France and its rivalry with Britain), foregrounded the relevance of the study of culture and led to a kind of *Kulturkunde*

(with an emphasis on the national character[s] of the foreign people[s]) which was not so much interested in understanding the foreign culture(s) as aimed at reinforcing the German identity of the learners. This development paved the way for the subordination of all *Landeskunde/Kulturkunde* to national-socialist educational policy from 1935 to 1945 (see Buttjes, 1990: 48–56; Kramer, 1997: 15–20).

After the defeat of Nazism and the end of World War Two, the two German states pursued different educational policies. The first response in the Federal Republic of Germany was 'to attempt to make *Landeskunde* value-free by emphasizing its subordination to the aim of acquiring the **SKILLS** of communication' (Byram, 1996: 185). However, values (such as democracy and international understanding) were soon reintroduced, first by the American politics of reeducation (which also supported the development of American Studies) and, later, as a consequence of the early Franco–German rapprochement (from which the evolution of Romance Studies benefited). In the 1950s and 1960s a number of avowedly value-free (or ideology-free) *Landeskunde* approaches existed in schools, universities and teacher training colleges which tried to square the circle of combining the provision of facts and figures, the mediation of positive (and, consequently, sometimes false) images of the target culture(s), and the political education of democratic German citizens.

It was not until the early 1970s that a number of social, political and cultural factors necessitated the re-**EVALUATION** of the status of *Landeskunde*. The intensifying process of European integration, the rising influx of migrants and the growth of transnational communication (as well as the problems arising from these developments) pointed to the educational relevance of cultural differences and demanded to be taken into account in the training of psychologists, social workers, teachers and, first and foremost, teachers of the indigenous and foreign languages. A long and intensive debate (see Buttjes, 1990: 56–61; Kramer, 1976, 1997: 20–7), which was decisively influenced by the reception of (British) **CULTURAL STUDIES**, by the early 1990s has resulted in a discernible change of attitude in favour of the cultural dimension of foreign language education. In the schools, *Landeskunde* is no longer reduced to its former ancillary status (providing background knowledge) but has attained a position in its own right in furthering the learners' intercultural competence (see Buttjes, 1986–87); in the universities, *Landeskunde* is in the process of being transformed into a kind of (American, British, Canadian, Australian, etc.) Cultural Studies (or *Civilisation Française*, etc.) equal in status with Linguistics and Literature (Kramer, 1997: 48–78).

In the German Democratic Republic a critique of pre-1945 *Kulturkunde* was complemented by a *Landeskunde* devised along Marxist–Leninist lines which closely followed the vagaries of GDR foreign policy (cf. Kramer, 1997: 27–34). In the first phase, which lasted from the foundation of the GDR to the building of the Berlin Wall (1961), *Landeskunde* was mainly used to distinguish between friends and foes by painting negative images of capitalist countries and positive images of socialist ones. During the second phase, between the early 1960s and the early 1980s, which witnessed the internal consolidation and international acceptance of the GDR, this position became more differentiated, but not fundamentally different. The more or less compulsive orientation towards the USSR (and the teaching of Russian) decreased; and German as a Foreign Language became the context in which *Landeskunde* was discussed. Finally, in the second half of the 1980s, the debate became more open-minded: approaches to intercultural learning (and communication) were received, discussed and partly integrated, and a number of fundamental questions related to the disciplinary character of *Landeskunde* were raised (see Kerl, 1990).

Today, although the term *Landeskunde* is still in use, it is in the process of being replaced by Cultural Studies (or *Kulturstudien, Kulturwissenschaft*). In universities, Cultural Studies aims at studying a particular culture and society and, by doing so, at learning to understand cultures in general, and at arriving at a better understanding of one's own. In schools, Cultural Studies aim at teaching a complex but flexible network of culturally specific knowledge, skills and **ATTITUDES** which enables learners of a foreign language to begin (and continue) to communicate with native or other non-**NATIVE SPEAKERS** of that language, mediate and negotiate between the two (or more) cultures in question and reflect these processes in relation to their own culture(s).

**See also:** Area studies; *Civilisation*; Cultural studies; German; Higher education; Intercultural competence; Stereotypes; Study abroad; Syllabus and curriculum design

### References

Buttjes, D. (ed.) (1986–87) *Panorama: English cultures around the world*, Dortmund: Lensing.

Buttjes, D. (1990) 'Culture in German foreign language teaching: making use of an ambiguous past', in D. Buttjes and M. Byram (eds), *Mediating languages and cultures: towards an intercultural theory of foreign language education*, Clevedon and Philadelphia: Multilingual Matters.

Byram, M. (1996) 'European cultural studies in Western Europe', in M. Payne (ed.), *A dictionary of cultural and critical theory*, Oxford: Blackwell.

Kerl, D. (1990) 'Area Studies in the German Democratic Republic: theoretical aspects of a discipline in evolution', in D. Buttjes and M. Byram (eds), *Mediating languages and cultures: towards an intercultural theory of foreign language education*, Clevedon and Philadelphia: Multilingual Matters.

Kramer, J. (1976) 'Cultural Studies vs. Landes-/Kulturkunde', in J. Kramer (ed.), *Bestandsaufnahme Fremdsprachenunterricht* (The state of the art of foreign language teaching), Stuttgart: Metzler.

Kramer, J. (1997) *British cultural studies*, Munich: W. Fink.

## Further reading

[Autorenkollektiv] (1989) *Landeskunde: Überlegungen zur Theorie und Methode*, Potsdam: PH 'Karl Liebknecht'.

Baumgratz, G. and Picht, R. (eds) (1978) *Perspektiven der Frankreichkunde II* (Perspectives of French Cultural Studies II), Tübingen: Niemeyer.

Bausch, K.-R. *et al.* (eds) *Handbuch Fremdsprachenunterricht* (A Handbook of Foreign Language Teaching) (with entries on 'Kultur- und Landeswissenschaften', 'Landeskunde-Didaktik und landeskundliches Curriculum', and 'Landeskundliches Curriculum'), Tübingen: Francke.

Buttjes, D. (ed.) (1981) *Landeskundliches Lernen im Englischunterricht* (Cultural Learning in EFL), Paderborn: Schöningh.

Frankel, M.A., Mackiewicz, W.W. and Wolff, D. (eds) (1995) *British Cultural Studies in higher education in Germany*, Cologne: The British Council and Freie Universität Berlin.

Höhne, R. and Kolboom, J. (eds) (1983) *Von der Landeskunde zur Landeswissenschaft* (Developing *Landeskunde* into an academic discipline), Rheinfelden.

Schröder, K. and Finkenstaedt, T. (eds) *Reallexikon der Englischen Fachdidaktik* (Encyclopedia of teaching English as a Foreign Language) (with entries on 'Amerikakunde', 'Englandkunde' and 'Kulturkunde'), Darmstadt: Wissenschaftliche Buchgesellschaft.

JÜRGEN KRAMER

# Language across the curriculum

The concept of 'language across the curriculum' (LAC) draws upon theoretical ideas from education, **SOCIOLINGUISTICS**, **SECOND LANGUAGE ACQUISITION** and **APPLIED LINGUISTICS** (Moon, 1991), extending across the broad rubric of 'educational linguistics' (Spolsky, 1978; Stubbs, 1986; Christie and Martin, 1997). The term *language across the curriculum* emerged from the work of British educationalists and refers to the fundamental role played by language in teaching–learning interactions across curriculum subject areas. **CONTENT-BASED INSTRUCTION**, immersion language programmes and adjunct or sheltered subject matter teaching are associated movements emerging from North America. LAC parallels other language-based educational developments, such as **LANGUAGE AWARENESS** (LA), and knowledge about language (KAL) in the UK and consciousness-raising (CR) in the **USA**, which position language as an explicit and focal object of teacher and learner study. The focus here is on LAC rather than content-based or immersion programme initiatives.

The LAC movement began in the 1960s with small-scale initiatives in a few British secondary schools to break down subject area barriers and develop an interdisciplinary curriculum. The centrality of language in processes of learning within the curriculum was highlighted by work carried out by the London Association of Teachers of English (LATE) in the early 1970s and *Language, the Learner and the School* (Barnes, Britton and Rosen, 1969). The Schools Council Programme in Linguistics and Language Teaching, and the resulting *Language in Use* **MATERIALS** (Doughty, Pearce and Thornton, 1971) also contributed. The Bullock Report, *A Language for Life* (1975), gave official recognition to LAC and stated that 'Every school should have an organised policy for LAC establishing every teacher's involvement in language and **READING** development throughout the years of schooling' (Principal Recommendation 4).

Educational concepts that have permeated the LAC movement include:

- Language is central to learning. It is the principal medium for processing and interpreting new concepts (Torbe, 1976; Marland, 1977).
- Language is the principal means of gaining new knowledge. Learners are assisted in this process when given opportunities to reflect upon and make sense of new ideas through talk and writing (Barnes, 1976).
- Language development is inextricably linked to the learning of subject areas and these provide context and purpose for language development (Messenger, 1980; van Lier, 1995).
- All teachers are language as well as subject teachers, as language is intertwined with all aspects of the curriculum and the discourses of the school (Christie, 1985/1989).

Some of the central assumptions of LAC

emerging from educational linguistics are captured in **HALLIDAY**'s (1980) tripartite description of the role of language in education: learning language, learning about language, learning through language.

Sociolinguistic influences emerge from theoretical concepts of register or functional variation in subject areas which hold that learning about the different disciplines is not merely a matter of learning the content with its technical 'jargon' or **VOCABULARY**. It is rather a matter of being 'apprenticed' into particular varieties of language, 'that is of learning the particular discourse patterns within which are encoded the various ways of working that are characteristic of the different subjects' (Christie, 1985: 37).

The language difficulties encountered in the specialist registers of school subjects have been a concern of classroom-based research in Britain, **AUSTRALIA** and the USA. These have focused both on **MOTHER TONGUE** (Barnes, 1976; Christie, 1985/1989; Hasan and Williams, 1996; Mercer, 1981) and second language medium education (Brinton, Snow and Wesche, 1989; Crandall and Tucker, 1990; Mohan, 1986). While initially associated with mother tongue primary and **SEC-ONDARY EDUCATION**, LAC has been applied to other contexts where learners use **ENGLISH** or other national/international languages as the **MEDIUM OF INSTRUCTION**. In particular, the central notions of LAC have been applied in **ENGLISH FOR SPECIFIC PURPOSES** settings (Bhatia, 1993; Swales, 1990).

In second/foreign language contexts, LAC promotes an integrated approach to language instruction where task, topics and texts are drawn from subject matter and the focus is on the development of the 'cognitive academic' language **SKILLS** (CALP) (Cummins, 1981) required for specific subject areas. The underpinning concept is that by focusing on meaning rather than form, and on subject-specific genres (Martin, 1993; Swales, 1990) required in the curriculum areas, language proficiency is enhanced through contextualised use (Kasper, 1997; Krashen, 1982; **WID-DOWSON**, 1978).

While the concept of LAC has generated innovative thinking about how language instruction can harness language and subject develop-ment, it has not achieved widespread acceptance in language education. Fillon (1985) attributes this to the characteristic structures of school organisation, especially at secondary level, which do not support cross-curricular development. He also sees a lack of clearly defined approaches or methodologies; the lack of research evidence that LAC makes a difference to learning; and the limited acceptance and knowledge by teachers and administrators of the basic concepts of LAC. That the central ideas embodied in LAC are complex, sophisticated and not easily understood or put into practice has been suggested by several studies, whose findings question the assumption that teachers are able to communicate content effectively and in such a way that language learning is enhanced (Ellis, 1984; Mumesci, 1996).

Kramsch suggests that an LAC/content-based approach 'runs the risk of reinforcing the skill vs. content distinction in language teaching and of upholding the illusion of the transparency of language' (1995: 48). An LAC approach also increases work for language teachers, whose lack of subject-specific knowledge may create difficulty in planning programmes or developing collabora-tive teaching relationships that focus on language development with subject teachers.

Perhaps the main impact of the LAC movement is in the attention drawn to the fact that language in the school curriculum is used for a wide range of situations and purposes, as well as to the impor-tance of talk as a tool for learning. Viewed from an LAC perspective, language becomes a medium of interpretation rather than transmission, as well as a process and vehicle *for* learning rather than a product *of* learning. Highlighting the expressive and exploratory functions of language renewed thinking about the essentially interactive nature of teaching and learning and the roles of teachers in mediating classroom interaction and, consequently, in making available the kinds of learning that take place. While the major concepts of LAC have been drawn from Western educational systems, they have influenced educational practices elsewhere. Some examples are the Molteno Project (*Bridge to English*, 1987) to prepare black South African primary children in learning science, mathematics and other subjects, and Bridging Courses for transition to secondary school in Tanzania. There have also been integrated language and subject teaching (e.g. *New Zambia Primary Course*, 1971) and topic/theme-based approaches through project work in primary schools in Botswana. Subject **TEXTBOOK** development has provided greater accessibility to content (e.g. UMSEPP project in Malaysia for tertiary materials).

The influence of LAC has been spasmodic and complex to sustain. Wells maintains that LAC 'is a slogan to rally the converted rather than a policy that is affecting the daily practice of the majority of teachers and administrators' (1991: 6). Numerous areas remain for further research and development (Crandall and Tucker, 1990) including **TEACHER EDUCATION**, student **ASSESSMENT** and programme **EVALUATION**, textbook and resource development, and studies of how language is used in subject areas texts and learning interactional processes.

**See also:** BICS and CALP; Content-based instruction; Genre and genre-based teaching; Language awareness; Research methods; Second language acquisition; Sociolinguistics

## References

Barnes, D. (1976) *From communication to curriculum*, Harmondsworth: Penguin.

Barnes, D., Britton, J. and Rosen, H. (1969) *Language, the learner and the school*, Harmondsworth: Penguin.

Bhatia, V.K. (1993) *Analysing genre: language use in professional settings*, London: Longman.

Brinton, D.M., Snow, M.A. and Wesche, M.B. (1989) *Content-based second language instruction*, New York: Harper and Row.

Bullock Report (1975) *A language for life*, Department of Education and Science, London: HMSO.

Christie, F. (1985) *Language education*, Geelong: Deakin University [Republished by Oxford University Press, 1989].

Christie, F. and Martin, J.R. (eds) (1997) *Genre and institutions. Social processes in the workplace and school*, London: Cassell.

Crandall, J. and Tucker, R.G. (1990) 'Content-based language instruction in second and foreign languages', in S. Anivan (ed.), *Language teaching methodology for the nineties* (Anthology Series 24), Singapore: SEAMEO Regional Language Centre.

Cummins, J. (1981) *The role of primary language development in promoting educational success for language minority students: a theoretical framework*, Los Angeles: California State University, Evaluation, Dissemination and Assessment Center.

Davies, F. (1991) 'Language varieties, genres and text-types across the curriculum', in *English Studies Information Update*, Issue 6, London: British Council.

Doughty, P., Pearce, J. and Thornton, G. (1971) *Language in use*, London: Edward Arnold.

Ellis, R. (1984) *Classroom second language development*, Oxford: Pergamon Press.

Fillon, B. (1985) 'Language across the curriculum', in *The International Encyclopaedia of Education*, vol. 5, Oxford: Pergamon Press.

Halliday, M.A.K. (1980) 'Three aspects of children's language development: learning language, learning through language, learning about language', in Y.M. Goodman, M.M. Haussier and D.S. Strickland (eds), *Oral and written language development research: impact on the schools*, Proceedings from the 1979 and 1980 Impact Conferences sponsored by the International Reading Association and the National Council of Teachers of English, Newark DE: International Reading Association.

Halliday, M.A.K. (1986) 'Language across the culture', in M. Tickoo (ed.), *Language across the curriculum* (Anthology Series 15), Singapore: SEAMEO Regional Language Centre.

Hasan, R. and Williams, G. (eds) (1996) *Literacy in society*, London: Longman.

Kasper, L.F. (1997) 'The impact of content-based instructional programs on the academic progress of ESL students', *English for Specific Purposes* 16, 4: 309–20.

Kramsch, C. (1995) 'The applied linguist and the foreign language teacher: can they talk to each other?', in G. Cook and B. Seidlhofer (eds), *Principle and practice in applied linguistics*, Oxford: Oxford University Press.

Krashen, S. (1982) *Principles and practice in second language acquisition*, Oxford: Pergamon.

Marland, M. (1977) *Language across the curriculum: the implementation of the Bullock Report in the secondary school*, Oxford: Heinemann.

Martin, J.R. (1993) 'Genre and literacy – modelling context in educational linguistics', *Annual Review of Applied Linguistics* 13: 14–172.

Mercer, N. (1981) *Language in school and community*, London: Edward Arnold.

Messenger, T. (1980) 'Language across the curriculum', in W.A. Gatherer and R.B. Jeffs (eds), *Language skills through the secondary curriculum*, Edinburgh: Holmes McDougall.

Mohan, B.A. (1986) *Language and content*, Reading: Addison Wesley.

Moon, J. (1991) 'Language across the curriculum in second language educational contexts: issues and problems', in *English studies information update*, Issue 6, London: The British Council.

Mumesci, D. (1996) 'Teacher–learner negotiation in content-based instruction: communication at cross purposes?', *Applied Linguistics* 17, 3: 286–325.

Spolsky, B. (1978) *Educational linguistics*, Rowley, MA: Newbury House.

Stubbs, M. (1986) *Educational linguistics*, Oxford: Basil Blackwell.

Swales, J. (1986) 'A genre-based approach to language across the curriculum', in M. Tickoo (ed.), *Language across the curriculum* (Anthology Series 15), Singapore: SEAMEO Regional Language Centre.

Swales, J. (1990) *Genre analysis: English in academic and research settings*, Cambridge: Cambridge University Press.

Torbe, M. (1976) *Language across the curriculum; guidelines for schools*, London: Ward Lock/NATE.

van Lier, L. (1995) *Language awareness*, Harmondsworth: Penguin.

Wells, G. (1991) 'Issues in language across the curriculum', in *English studies information update*, Issue 6, London: The British Council.

Widdowson, H. (1978) *Language teaching as communication*, Oxford: Oxford University Press.

**Further reading**

Bain, R., Fitzgerald, B. and Taylor, M. (eds) (1992) *Looking into language*, London: Hodder and Stoughton.

Brumfit, C. (ed.) (1995) *Language education in the national curriculum*, Oxford: Blackwell.

Carter, R. (ed.) (1990) *Knowledge about language and the curriculum: The LINC reader*, London: Hodder and Stoughton.

Corson, D. (1990) *Language policy across the curriculum*, Clevedon: Multilingual Matters.

Dixon, J. (1967) *Growth through English*, London: National Association for the Teaching of English.

James, C. and Garrett, P. (1991) *Language awareness in the classroom*, London: Longman.

Macken-Horarik, M. (1996) 'Literacy and learning across the curriculum: towards a model of register for secondary school teachers', in R. Hasan and G. Williams (eds), *Literacy in society*, London: Longman.

Vygotsky, L.S. (1978) *Mind in society*, Harvard: Harvard University Press.

Wells, G (1986) *The meaning makers: children learning language and using language to learn*, Oxford: Heinemann.

ANNE BURNS

# Language awareness

Language awareness (LA) is defined in the **ALA** (Association for Language Awareness) constitution as 'explicit knowledge about language and conscious perception and sensitivity in language learning, language teaching and language use'. This broad definition allows LA to extend into areas that include literature (e.g., Zyngier, 1994), medical contexts (Singy and Guex, 1997), folklinguistics (Preston, 1996), **TRANSLATION** (e.g., Faber, 1998); but we focus here on what is commonly regarded as the core, 'grassroots' LA, which is situated in language classrooms. LA is seen as a state of mind that emerges when we 'focus systematically on language' (van Lier, 1995: 4) and transcend our tacit understandings of language by focusing on representations that can be made explicit. LA implies having access to knowledge about one's (linguistic) knowledge. It thus counters the **BEHAVIOURIST** approach to language learning which proscribes teaching about language and emphasises learning language repertoires.

Traceable at least back to **HALLIDAY** (1971), LA gained impetus from the Bullock Report (DES, 1975), which highlighted poor standards among British school leavers amid increasing concern over underachievement in foreign languages (FLs). 'Reflective' teachers, frustrated by government procrastination, initiated local schemes for teaching pupils more about language and languages. Hence LA is rightly deemed a 'grassroots' movement, though institutional support soon followed through NCLE (National Council for Language in Education) working parties (1978) and national conferences (1981, 1985). **HAWKINS** (1981, 1984) laid some theoretical foundations, advocating LA as a bridge between **MOTHER-TONGUE** (MT) and FL education, and creating a new twentieth-century trivium: MT study plus LA plus FL study. Following a British Association for Applied Linguistics Seminar on LA in 1989, University of Wales Bangor held the First International Conference on LA in 1992, where the ALA and its journal *Language Awareness* were launched. A series of biennial international ALA conferences has followed.

LA's development is often, as above, identified with the UK, but others point to parallel progress in Europe and elsewhere, with various idiosyncrasies reflected in different labels. Sometimes optional labels convey subtle distinctions within a single country: in Germany, Gnutzmann (1997) refers to *Sprachbewußtsein, Sprachbewußtheit, Sprachbetrachtung,* and *Reflexion über Sprache*. English has also seen a proliferation of associated terms: e.g., consciousness raising (CR), from American applied linguistics. James (1996) suggests reserving LA for MT education and CR for FL education. A further term is Knowledge about Language (KAL), favoured in UK government publications on **ENGLISH** teaching (DES, 1988, 1989), and FL teaching (DES, 1991). Cameron (1993) questions this 'implied but inappropriate synonymy' of LA and KAL.

LA work is inductive and reflective (Schön, 1983). Learners typically undertake small-scale nontechnical investigations of language and language learning. Through reflection, they 'surface' their intuitions about how language works, what they need to learn, and how. One form of such awareness is identifying available learning **STRATEGIES** and judging their relative effectiveness for given tasks – a first step towards learner **AUTONOMY** (Little, 1997). Andrews (1993) provides a guide for teachers seeking LA activities for learners on a range of levels, while Wright and Bolitho (1993) and Borg (1994) exemplify approaches for **TEACHER EDUCATION**.

Benefits claimed for LA range across five dimensions: affective, social, power, cognitive and performance (James and Garrett, 1991). The affective dimension concerns **ATTITUDE** and **MOTIVATION**, endorsing Krashen's affective filter, which determines whether input to the learner becomes intake. LA aims to stimulate curiosity about language, thereby '... increasing receptivity to new linguistic experience' (Anderson, 1991: 133). This aspect is pivotal, for instance, to Hawkins's proposal for LA as a precursor to FL study in UK secondary schools, to remedy the poor FL achievements of most pupils.

The social dimension relates to social harmonisation in potentially divisive contexts of language variation and diversity. Some LA work aims at building '... better relations between all ethnic groups by arousing pupils' awareness of the origins and characteristics of their own language and dialect and their place in the wider map of languages and dialects used in the world beyond' (Donmall, 1985: 8). Similarly, for Anderson (1991), 'deepening understanding, fostering tolerance' are significant LA goals.

The power dimension focuses on how language is used for manipulation and oppression. Language education should ensure that citizens are sensitive to and able to counter commercial and political manipulation through subtle use of and assumptions about language that target the unaware mind. LA work with its prime focus on such empowerment of individuals is often called Critical LA (Fairclough, 1992).

The cognitive dimension of LA provides a powerful argument for its inclusion in the school curriculum. As Donmall (1985: 7) says, 'awareness of pattern, contrast, system, units, categories, rules of language' is what defines the concept. Relatedly, Hawkins (1984) suggests that the 'analytic competence' that was developed by learning Latin is generalisable beyond language learning contexts. Again, then, LA serves a more general mind training. The cognitive goals do not imply a return to '**GRAMMAR** grind', since the remit of the new language study also encompasses attention to functions, social **STEREOTYPES**, genres, verbal hygiene and the very processes of language learning and use. It is clear from this that there is inevitable overlap amongst these five dimensions.

The performance dimension asks whether knowledge accruing from LA leads to better language learning and use. Is there an interface from 'knowing that' to 'knowing how', from declarative to procedural linguistic knowledge? Arguably, of course, LA does not have to be justified in terms of improved proficiency, just as the study of biology need not lead to increased crop production to justify itself. Nevertheless, Hawkins (1984: 150) refers to 'a mass of research ... showing that insight into pattern lies at the root of successful FL learning and that it is also a key to efficient processing of verbal messages in the MT'. Ellis (1994) documents research showing the effectiveness of explicit language teaching, and there is a general shift in teaching from the communicative to the cognitive, motivated in part by a conviction that cognitive engagement in learning has positive results. Research by Andrews (1997) and Berry (1997) examines the efficacy with which language teachers frame explanations of language points that students find difficult.

Claims made for LA across these five dimensions are not uncontroversial: for example, see Alderson, Clapham and Steel (1997) on language performance, and Leets and Giles (1993) and Rampton (1995) on social tolerance. James and Garrett (1991) call for continuing **EVALUATION** of LA.

**See also:** Acquisition and teaching; Generative principle; Grammar; Grammar–translation method; Language across the curriculum; Learning styles; Linguistics; Monolingual principle; Teacher talk; Teaching methods

## References

Alderson, J., Clapham, C. and Steel, D. (1997) 'Metalinguistic knowledge proficiency, language aptitude and language proficiency', *Language Teaching Research* 1, 2: 93–121.

Anderson, J. (1991) 'The potential of language awareness as a focus for cross curricular work in a secondary school', in C. James and P. Garrett (eds), *Language awareness in the classroom*, London: Longman.

Andrews, L. (1993) *Language exploration and awareness*, London: Longman.

Andrews, S. (1997) 'Metalinguistic awareness and teacher explanation', *Language Awareness* 6, 2 and 3: 147–61.

Berry, R. (1997) 'Teachers' awareness of learners' knowledge', *Language Awareness* 6, 2 and 3: 136–46.

Borg, S. (1994) 'Language awareness as methodology: implications for teachers and teacher training', *Language Awareness* 3, 2: 61–72.

Cameron, L. (1993) 'Degrees of knowing', *Language Awareness* 2, 1: 3–13.

DES (Department of Education and Science) (1975) *A language for life: the Bullock Report*, London: HMSO.

DES (Department of Education and Science) (1988) *The Kingman Report*, London: HMSO.

DES (Department of Education and Science) (1989) *The Cox Report*, London: HMSO.

DES (Department of Education and Science) (1991) *The Harris Report*, London: HMSO.

Donmall, B.G. (ed.) (1985) *Language awareness*, London: CILT.

Ellis, N. (ed.) (1994) *Implicit and explicit learning of languages*, London: Academic Press.

Faber, P. (1998) 'Translation competence and language awareness', *Language Awareness* 7, 1: 9–21.

Fairclough, N. (ed.) (1992) *Critical language awareness*, London: Longman.

Gnutzmann, C. (1997) 'Language awareness: progress in language learning and language education, or reformulation of old ideas?', *Language Awareness* 6, 2 and 3: 65–74.

Halliday, M.A.K. (1971) 'Introduction to P. Doughty, J. Pearce and G. Thornton, *Language in use*, London: Edward Arnold.

Hawkins, E. (1981) *Modern languages in the curriculum*, Cambridge: Cambridge University Press.

Hawkins, E. (1984) *Awareness of language: an introduction*, Cambridge: Cambridge University Press.

James, C. (1996) 'A cross linguistic approach to language awareness', *Language Awareness* 5, 3 and 4: 138–48.

James, C. and Garrett, P. (eds) (1991) *Language awareness in the classroom*, London: Longman.

Leets, L. and Giles, H. (1993) 'Does language awareness foster social tolerance?', *Language Awareness* 2, 3: 159–68.

Little, D. (1997) 'Language awareness and the

autonomous language learner', *Language Aware-ness* 6, 2 and 3: 93–104.

Preston, D. (1996) 'Whaddayaknow?: the modes of folklinguistic awareness', *Language Awareness* 5, 1: 40–74.

Rampton, B. (1995) *Crossing: language and ethnicity among adolescents*, London: Longman.

Schön, D. (1983) *The reflective practitioner: how professionals think in action*, Aldershot: Ashgate.

Singy, P. and Guex, P. (1997) 'Scope and limits of medical discourse concerning AIDS prevention', *Language Awareness* 6, 4: 238–41.

van Lier, L. (1995) *Introducing language awareness*, Harmondsworth: Penguin.

Wright, T. and Bolitho, R. (1993) 'Language awareness: a missing link in language teacher education?', *English Language Teaching Journal* 47, 4: 292–304.

Zyngier, S. (1994) 'Introducing literary awareness', *Language Awareness* 3, 2: 95–108.

## Further reading

Aplin, R. (1997) *Knowledge about language and language awareness: an annotated bibliography*, Leicester: Leicester University School of Education.

Hawkins, E. (1984) *Awareness of language: an introduction*, Cambridge: Cambridge University Press.

James, C. and Garrett, P. (eds) *Language awareness in the classroom*, London: Longman.

van Lier, L. (1995) *Introducing language awareness*, Harmondsworth: Penguin.

PETER GARRETT AND CARL JAMES

# Language laboratories

These are systems of equipment, first introduced in the early 1960s, allowing learners to work individually on audio material supplied from a central control point from which the teacher maintains a monitoring role. The early popularity of language laboratories coincided with the **AUDIOLINGUAL METHOD**, and they were seen as a highly effective means of delivering the drill **EXERCISES** and 'pattern practice' and the highly controlled role play dialogues that typify that approach to teaching. As **COMMUNICATIVE LANGUAGE TEACH-ING** developed, new uses were found for the language laboratory, with greater focus on **LISTEN-ING** comprehension and the greater integration of laboratory work with 'live', face-to-face interaction among students.

The basic components of a language laboratory are a central control position (or console) linked to a set of student positions. Audio material is transferred to the student positions from the console, and the learners hear it through individual headphones to which a microphone is attached. This microphone is audio-active, meaning that sound entering it is channelled directly to the students' ears through the headphones, and thus they hear their own voices in a more objective way than is possible when bone-conduction is the main route for the sound to reach the ears. The normal source of language laboratory material is pre-recorded audio tape, although many laboratories (depending on their age) have facilities for using other sources such as live speech, radio, vinyl records or CD recordings. From the console, which is also equipped with headphones and microphone, the teacher can listen to individual students as they work, can open two-way communication with individuals, or speak to all the students.

The most effective language laboratories are Audio-Active Comparative (AAC). This means that, in addition to the headphones and micro-phone, each student position contains a recording device which allows the material transmitted from the console to be recorded on each student's equipment. This makes it possible for individuals to work at their own pace, playing, winding and rewinding the tape using student controls which are similar to those on conventional playback equipment. It is also possible for the teacher to control individual student machines from the console. Students can choose to record their own voices as they work, and later listen and review their attempts, comparing them with any model answers on the tape. This explains the 'Comparative' part of the label. The audio tape used in student machines has two tracks operating simultaneously. The lesson material is recorded onto the Master Track which cannot be erased by the student. The students' responses are recorded onto the Student Track which can be played back, but is erased when the machine is next in record mode so that successive attempts can be recorded and reviewed. When a new teaching programme is transferred from the console, previous material on the students' machines is erased.

The Audio-Active (AA) laboratory is much less versatile. The student positions have no recording device, and therefore learners must work in 'lockstep' at the pace of the teaching material as it comes from the console. They also cannot record and review their spoken responses to the material.

The 1960s period of audiolingual teaching represented the time at which the accepted methodology and the facilities offered by language laboratories were in the closest harmony. However, even during the late 1970s and the early 1980s when communicative teaching was gaining currency, language laboratories retained an important role as the medium for oral drill material. They were seen as a useful resource for providing language drills as part of 'controlled practice' in the Presentation, Controlled Practice, Free Practice ('PPP') model of a lesson. This 'weak' version of communicative teaching often made use of the same types of drill as audiolingual teaching and differed from it mainly in the greater attention given to the Free Practice stage. As more radical interpretations of communicative approaches became influential, the use of the language laboratory diminished in many institutions, but in others new ways of using it were being developed.

By the mid-1970s, growing attention was being given to training **LISTENING** comprehension as a skill in itself rather than using listening material merely as input for spoken performance. Extensive listening material could be as easily transferred to student positions from the console as oral drill material, and the language laboratory was recognised as a valuable resource for allowing students to work at their own pace with listening passages as they attempted to answer comprehension questions usually presented to them on worksheets. The change from reel-to-reel recording tape to audio cassettes in the late 1970s made tape handling more convenient, making it feasible for students to select their own tapes and place them in their machines by themselves. The creation of listening libraries (often using **AUTHENTIC MATERIALS**) was in step with those tenets of communicative approaches which stressed the importance of

allowing students choice and encouraging independent self-access work. This also fitted with the focus on meeting specific **NEEDS**, as the discipline of **ENGLISH FOR SPECIFIC PURPOSES** developed. For these types of listening work the full facilities of a language laboratory were not necessary, and the more portable and simpler to operate 'mini labs' became popular. Their main restriction was on the monitoring facilities on the teacher's console. Other institutions opted for good quality individual playback machines.

Significant changes in language laboratory architecture were driven by those aspects of methodology that focused upon the need for students to communicate among themselves and not only in response to the teacher. Until the late 1970s, the typical student position was a booth enclosed on three sides, preventing contact with other learners but usually allowing eye contact with the teacher. This privacy was at that time considered necessary to build confidence, encourage critical listening, and reduce distractions while the largely drill-type material was in use. Channels were kept open between teacher and learner because the teacher's ability to diagnose the sources of problems and give advice was felt to be an essential support to the learners' attempts to identify success or failure by listening to the fixed models supplied by the drill materials. From the late 1970s, many institutions began experimenting with a more open-plan arrangement of student positions, which allowed space for other types of work to take place in the teaching room with students moving in and out of the laboratory area according to the particular activity. The booth 'walls' also came down during this period, allowing face-to-face 'live' pair and **GROUP** work to take place. 'Jigsaw Listening', a type of jigsaw task technique developed by Geddes and Sturtridge (1978), made excellent use of such a remodelled language laboratory in order to promote communication amongst students based on the information gap principle. For this work, students use the information input from a number of slightly differing recordings as the basis for 'live' group discussions in which they try to piece together a complete story or solve a puzzle. Transferring the different recordings to different groups of positions in the laboratory is the most convenient way to set up such a lesson.

After the early 1980s, the faith of publishers and of many teachers in the value of drill-type oral exercises dwindled, to the extent that almost no coursebooks were supplied with sets of drill materials on tape intended specifically for use in the language laboratory. Language Presentation, Practice and listening comprehension materials continue to be published, but none of these necessitates the use of a language laboratory.

As with **CALL (COMPUTER ASSISTED LANGUAGE LEARNING)** it is true to say that the power of the technical equipment to promote learning depends mostly on the quality of the software or teaching material used with it. Even before the term 'communicative teaching' was in use, Dakin (1973) pointed out the absurdity of 'meaningless drills' and recommended many alternative activities that are still considered valuable. Other attempts to encourage the use of the language laboratory to support realistic use of language can be seen in books such as that by Ely (1984).

Much also depends on the training of both teachers and students to use the controls and facilities to the best effect, and this aspect should not be neglected.

Language laboratories require maintenance, and a technical assistant or a comprehensive maintenance contract are essential components of the budget for an institution which wishes to keep a laboratory in effective use.

A mini lab, or a bank of individual playback machines, are often the recommended options for many institutions which do not have an existing language laboratory.

**See also:** Audiolingual method; Audio-visual language teaching; Group work; Internet; Large classes; Listening; Materials and media; Media centres; Speaking; Video; Visual aids

### References

Dakin, J. (1973) *The language laboratory and language learning*, Harlow: Longman.

Ely, P. (1984) *Bringing the lab back to life*, Oxford: Pergamon Press.

Geddes, M. and Sturtridge, G. (1978) *Listening links*, London: Heinemann.

### Further reading

Ely, P. (1984) *Bringing the lab back to life*, Oxford: Pergamon Press.

SHELAGH RIXON

# Language planning

Language planning is usually defined as the totality of measures taken to influence or attempt to influence a language situation (Cooper, 1989). The situations in question are usually those of states, but linguistic measures may be taken in other contexts by a variety of agents, for example in regions, towns, institutions (international, cultural, scientific), or companies. In these different contexts, a language situation is defined in terms of a number of characteristics. These include: the languages and the language varieties present, the state of the languages, the status or level of institutional recognition of each of them, the relationships between different language communities, the social forces influencing language use, the ideologies determining the images of the languages or the **ATTITUDES** towards them.

The desire of human beings to influence language situations is as old as the relationships between languages and societies, but the development of a domain given the name 'language planning' is relatively recent. It was developed during the 1960s and 1970s, being linked to the emergence of **SOCIOLINGUISTICS**, and was an attempt to find solutions to societal language problems, especially those in newly independent countries. It was at this period that the principal concepts were developed and the methods defined on the basis of observations of different types of activity undertaken in several parts of the world. Many subsequent activities in language planning originated in these methodological and conceptual frameworks and contributed to their clearer definition.

All language planning takes place within a language policy and is the result of political choices which attempt to regulate the relationships between languages and societies. However, the term 'language policy' is also used to designate the wide domain which includes both language planning and the totality of the context into which it fits: the problems, the demands, the objectives, explicit or not, which are the motivation for a policy, the principles or values to which the social agents in question subscribe, and the ideologies from which they are derived, the public debate which is created by the policy, the decision processes used, the means of implementing them, and the social effects of language planning envisaged or subsequently established.

## Status planning

Status planning is the totality of measures taken to organise or modify the use of languages in a given situation. The choice by a state of one official language (Malay in Malaysia, English in Ghana) or of several official languages (eleven in South **AFRICA**), the attribution of institutional status to languages used in a country (in the Republic of Ireland, Irish is the national and official language and English is the second official language), are all obvious examples.

The foundations of status planning are derived from two concepts of rights: collective rights and the rights of the individual. Collective rights involve two principles, that of territoriality and that of nationality. It is the combination of these two principles which is most often the basis for the status of languages in national communities, whether state communities or not, as the examples mentioned above show. It is also true for most language policies of restoration or reinforcement of the use of a language: **FRENCH** in Quebec, Flemish in Belgium, **ARABIC** in the countries of North Africa. But the status of many languages is founded on only one of these principles. Thus it is on the principle of nationality that the recognition of many African and Amerindian languages is based. The recognition of the status of languages or language communities which are in a minority situation is often founded on the principle of territoriality. Thus the European Charter of Regional and Minority Languages adopted by the **COUNCIL OF EUROPE** in 1992 refers, above all, to criteria of territoriality.

However, many language demands made by groups of speakers of a language which is little or poorly recognised in a collectivity are based also on the rights of the individual, as derived from the Universal Declaration of **HUMAN RIGHTS** adopted by the United Nations or several state constitutions. This is particularly the case when these groups live scattered throughout a collectivity. Factors such as migration, the **INTERNATIONALISATION** of economic activity and mobility of people which these create, tend to scatter linguistic communities within collectivities whose linguistic statutes may be restrictive. The recognition by national collectivities of linguistic diversity is very unequal and takes different forms, but is tending to develop.

## Corpus planning

All activity which is intended to modify the structure of a language or its functions is known as corpus planning. The development of writing systems, alphabets and orthographies are the oldest and best-known activities in corpus planning. The writing systems of most languages are subject to reforms at greater or lesser intervals of time. Thus, in 1997, a reform of the orthography of **GERMAN** was adopted by all German-speaking countries. In the process of standardisation of a language, human intervention can have an effect on the choice of the language variety, on the definition or the imposition of norms for writing, lexis and **GRAMMAR**. This task can be given to an institution. The French Academy, created in 1634, is usually cited as the first example of such an institution. Many other languages have since been given academies, institutes, or councils charged with similar tasks. Other social agents can take charge of this too, in an influential but diffuse manner. Thus, no academy has ever been created for the English language, but it is generally agreed that this role has been taken by the great publishing houses. The development of specialist terminology, the treatment of borrowings (adopting words from another language, or, on the contrary, the transformation of borrowed terms to make them conform to the morphological rules of the language or to the purist intentions of its speakers), the updating of language use to follow social evolution (for example the feminisation of titles and functions in French) and in general the modernisation of a language, are the most frequent purposes of corpus planning.

In the planning and implementation of a language policy one can distinguish different domains of intervention in which planning measures are considered necessary. A typology of these domains would, for example, identify the use of language in legislation, administration, the exercise of justice, education, posting of information (urban and road signals, etc.), places of work, economic exchange, consumerism, culture, communication and the media, sciences, and technology.

## Language education policies

Whether they are considered as a domain of intervention or as a third element of language planning alongside status planning and corpus planning, language education policies always play a central role in language policies. They are part of all activities that develop or implement the decisions taken in status planning. Furthermore, the school is one of the main means of implementing corpus planning measures. In defining their role, the following can be distinguished: the teaching of the **MOTHER TONGUE** or first language, the use of languages as media of instruction, and the teaching of foreign or second languages. But these different aspects are closely interconnected. Thus, learning through a particular language as medium is increasingly seen as a means of in-depth **ACQUISITION** of the language. This is particularly the case in situations where the purpose for teaching the language is to maintain or restore its use in a collectivity.

Status planning, corpus planning and language education policies cover most of the activities that can be included in the framework of a language policy. Other elements are sometimes added, especially that of policy for spreading a language, involving for example the activities of semi-governmental organisations such as the **BRITISH COUNCIL**, the **GOETHE-INSTITUT**, or the *ALLIANCE FRANÇAISE*. These can also be considered to be language policy objectives where the measures undertaken are part of status planning (the presence of a language in international institutions, use of the language in information and communication technology), of corpus planning (diction-

ary making, the production of tools for the automatic handling of languages) and, above all, of language education policies.

**See also:** Dictionaries; History: after 1945; India; Linguistic imperialism; Mother-tongue teaching; Planning for foreign language teaching; Reference works; Secondary education; United States of America

## Reference

Cooper, R.L. (1989) *Languages planning and social change*, Cambridge: Cambridge University Press.

## Further reading

Calvet, L.-J. (1996) *Les politiques linguistiques* (*Language policies*), Paris: P.U.F.

Hamel, R.E. (1993) *Politicas y planificacion el langajue: una introduccion* (*Policies and language planning: an introduction*, Mexico: Iztapalapa.

Haugen, E. (1966) *Language conflict and language planning. The case of modern Norwegian*, Cambridge, MA: Harvard University Press.

Truchot, C. (ed.) (1993) *Le plurilinguisme européen. Théories et pratiques en politique linguistique* (European multilingualism. Theory and Practice in language policies), Paris: Editions Champion-Slatkine.

CLAUDE TRUCHOT

# Languages for specific purposes

The teaching of languages for specific purposes (LSP) involves a great range of teaching situations and methods, of languages and of purposes. The common factor is that, rather than focusing on the study of linguistic structure or creative literature, the language course is designed to help learners cope in a work or study situation. Thus, a course in Japanese for hotel employees in Guam, for example, or in French for Italian biologists participating in an international project, is likely to focus more on participants' immediate and particular **NEEDS** than on a systematic coverage of the language system. Work-related skills such as time and task management may be taught in addition to language. Participants in LSP courses are typically adults, often with a limited amount of time in which to study and a desire for quick results. Perceived relevance of **MATERIALS** and methods is thus normally important to students and to their sponsors (their employers or the educational authorities). Issues to consider are the degree to which work or study content is being taught alongside its linguistic realisation, and the extent to which an initial general linguistic **COMPETENCE** is required before addressing participants' special communicative needs.

## Which languages?

Any language may be studied and taught from an LSP point of view. By far the most popular language in this regard is **ENGLISH**, but other languages studied include **SPANISH**, **FRENCH**, **GERMAN**, Italian, Russian, **CHINESE**, **JAPANESE**, Korean and **ARABIC**. The perspective of those writing about LSP courses is most usually Anglophone or European, a major concern being to facilitate international business, but in principle LSP is of worldwide application.

## Rationale

The demand for LSP has a strong link with political and economic changes. As international mobility becomes easier (for example, following the collapse of the Soviet bloc, or upon the enlargement of the European Union), so opportunities expand for studying or working in other countries. As new markets develop (for example, the Pacific 'Tiger economies'), 'new' languages become important in the conduct of international business. Thus people wish to learn languages on a 'need to know' basis, often placing more importance on communication than on accuracy or on depth and breadth of knowledge. The theoretical rationale is that effective communication can indeed be achieved with a less than complete mastery of the language in question, and that degrees of effectiveness can be measured. LSP is additionally based on the linked premises that attention to learners' specific communication needs is motivating and that **MOTIVATION** leads to better learning. However, these premises have rarely, if ever, been empirically tested.

## The provision of LSP courses

LSP courses are offered in state education systems and by commercial language providers. Vocational secondary schools in many parts of the world may offer compulsory language classes (most often English) in technical or commercial 'streams'. The grammatical coverage may in fact be fairly general, but with technical or commercial **VOCABULARY** and topics. Technical high schools and colleges may offer a choice of languages and focus attention on discipline-specific **GRAMMAR** and texts. At university and college level we can find courses which combine a subject specialism (for example, engineering, economics) with a language. In addition, those who major in a language may be able to follow a business track, rather than the traditional literature or philology one.

For people in employment, classes may be organised at the workplace, at specialist training institutions (for example, at European trade union colleges, equipping trade unionists in transnational companies to participate in works councils), or at language schools – both private sector and those run by universities or colleges. Such courses are often part-time, or may be full-time over a short, concentrated period (for example, a two-day course in giving presentations, a one-week course in negotiating). A popular option is some form of 'open learning', involving a combination of self-study, small **GROUP** work and class sessions.

Funding for LSP courses may come from an industry or company, from regional or national government sources, or – in the case of secondary or tertiary level education in some countries – from the learners or their parents. In some situations, LSP courses are funded by aid agencies. In Europe, a number of international projects (Leonardo, Socrates, Erasmus, etc.) have promoted the mobility of students, researchers and employees, and funded the related language training, including the preparation of materials.

The teachers of LSP are likely to have a language degree and perhaps also some experience of a particular area of work. They may also have academic or professional training in a subject other than language (for example, in law, economics, science) and they may specialise in teaching a particular type of student (for example, business students, technicians, lawyers). A commonly identified problem, even so, is the difficulty of coping with the students' specialist content. As Myles points out, though, in relation to teaching French to engineers: 'the ultimate objective of the FSP teacher must be to teach French rather than engineering, whereas engineering in French (is) ... the goal ... of the students' (Myers, 1994: 128).

## Needs analysis

An essential component of LSP as an enterprise is the analysis of potential or actual needs. There are several different levels of needs analysis. At the highest level is the regional, national or international survey, which attempts to measure existing capability in terms of foreign language ability, and to estimate future requirements for language training. Such a survey may attempt to sample the entire workforce, or a particular sector – most usually the commercial sector. In the UK and USA, such surveys result from a concern that too few native English-speaking business people have a command of any foreign language. Data are most usually gathered by means of questionnaires, which may be supplemented by interviews of key personnel. Additionally, job advertisements may be studied, to see what is requested in terms of foreign language ability.

A lower level of needs analysis is at the company or institutional level. A company may undertake a 'language audit' in order to assess the likely cost and benefit of a language training programme. A university may investigate the establishment of an institution-wide language programme as a means of attracting more students. Language departments, experiencing falling rolls for language degree courses, may investigate the potential of business oriented programmes for language majors. Again, data may be gathered by means of questionnaires, and interviews with past and present students and staff.

Once an actual LSP course has been proposed, for example as a result of market research by a language school, or in response to a request by an employer, then a needs analysis of the intended participants should be undertaken. This will involve a Present Situation Analysis (PSA): finding out students' present level of competence, their aims and hopes regarding future proficiency, and details of their situation (for example, what time they have available). This is complemented by a Target Situation Analysis (TSA), looking at participants' jobs or studies: which of the language SKILLS has most priority, what do participants actually have to do in the foreign language, what more might they be enabled to do, what level of competence is required for success in work and study?

Such participant-specific needs analysis may involve observing participants in their place of work or study ('shadowing'), discussions with participants, their employers and supervisors or teachers, and the collection of AUTHENTIC documents and recordings. All of this may feed directly into the teaching materials, or be mainly used to inform the teaching staff, giving them an insight into the participants' world.

## Language analysis for LSP

The needs analysis should reveal typical routines of participants' work or study and typical written and spoken texts which are dealt with. From these, some idea may be gained of the linguistic forms most frequently used in the specialist area. However, any LSP utilises the same system or code as the Language for General Purposes (LGP). It can be argued that 'general language' does not in fact exist. The same stock of syntactic and morphological patterns, the same phonological system and most of the vocabulary of a language are found across the spectrum of work, study, leisure and survival. What is different in each situation is the terminology, the conceptual structure and the rhetorical organisation of the communication. Each situation has its preferred forms of communication (GENRES) and within these there may be niceties of style, deriving from regional variation, from the purpose of the communication, and from the relationship between producer and receiver. For example, business letters for use in Asian countries may differ STYLISTICALLY from those used in Europe and North America although their purpose is the same.

The LSP course designer has to decide where to locate the course on the continuum from very specialised to more general language. At one extreme there is the language pertaining to particular processes within a factory, business or organisation. An example of this is PoliceSpeak, which was prepared for use in the Channel Tunnel by British, French and Belgian police. It is described as 'a means of using natural language more efficiently in an operational context' (*Police-Speak*, 1993: 1). The manual and material thus focus on 'a number of more or less officially prescribed linguistic items and routines' together with 'many items and language routines which have become part of the linguistic repertoire of police officers by dint of constant usage, even though they have no official status within an officer's training' (*PoliceSpeak*, 1993: 11, 12).

Less specialised language will be found across a whole industry or business sector. The most general use of language belongs to the world of work in general, perhaps spilling over into social life. Co-workers in European transnational companies, for example, have some need to socialise in each other's languages, as well as to communicate about work issues. In their discussion of 'German as a business language', Bloch and Hahn make a point that applies to other 'languages for business'. 'The boundary between the business language and the more general colloquial usage within and external to businesses is at times indistinct … on another level Business German is a composite term which refers to related but distinct sub-languages of economics, banking, shipping, insurance, services industry and many others' (Bloch and Hahn, 1995: 3–4).

LSP course designers may carry out their own research into the language forms needed by their students, using, for example, a corpus concordancer to study the vocabulary and structures of representative situations. They may carry out **CONTRASTIVE ANALYSIS**, although this may focus on contrasts in behaviour (for example, regarding **POLITENESS** norms, or patterns of negotiation) rather than linguistic structures. Course designers may also make use of terminological studies. Important considerations are the contexts and purposes of the language in focus.

## Course design

The primary objective will be for students to use the target language effectively in certain specified situations, leading to a **SYLLABUS** usually expressed in terms of some combination of language forms, functions, skills and tasks. However, frequently there are additional aims, which are not linguistic in nature. The most common one is **INTERCULTURAL COMPETENCE**. Thus, activities which attempt to foster intercultural understanding and the ability to cope with other cultures and other work practices are built into the course design. A second additional course component may be instruction in a specific work or study content (for example, banking practices). A third possible component is the development of more generalisable skills, such as self-management and the ability to work effectively in teams, to equip students for a range of possible future jobs (Hare, 1992). Finally, short courses for students aiming to undertake studies in another country may provide study skills training.

The language syllabus is likely to be limited in some way, for example to oral skills only (Japanese for hotel employees), to particular topics, or to particular tasks (such as negotiating, or preparing research proposals). In the school or college situation, in particular, the syllabus may be geared to professional examinations.

## Methods and materials

In principle, any methodology may be used for LSP. In practice, there is usually a preference for activities which in some way mirror those of the target work or study situation. These are essentially task oriented and interactive, involving authentic material. Examples are role play and case studies. The broader category of 'project' can relate both to business and technical situations and to the needs of academic students. These might be derived from problems (for example: 'Design a low-cost recycling plant and suggest how the community could be encouraged to use it'), or involving the gathering and presentation of factual information (for example: 'Present a feasibility study of a region, with a view to developing its agriculture or industry'). On some courses, activities such as games and quizzes may be incorporated as a means of maintaining the momentum for participants attending class after a full day's work.

Commercially produced **TEXTBOOKS** focusing on a range of disciplines exist, along with videos and computer software material such as CD-ROMs. The need for authenticity at the workplace suggests, however, that locally produced materials be used, alongside non-pedagogical materials produced in the specialist area (for example, trade-promotional videos), together with off-air audio and video recordings.

## Issues

Several issues present themselves in relation to the teaching and learning of LSP. First, course designers and teachers need to decide how far they are teaching language, and how far language and content, whether this be directly work-related content or more general cultural content. This has implications for teacher training and development. For some companies and industries, a decision may need to be made as to whether it is more effective to recruit employees with good foreign language skills and then give them professional training, or to employ technically skilled staff and then offer them foreign language training.

The second issue concerns the relationship between the learning of LGP and LSP, a relationship which has been insufficiently researched. Course designers disagree as to whether learners need to study LGP before embarking on LSP. As Boehringer notes, complex topics (such as the legal aspects of business) or complex tasks (such as taking notes at meetings) may require at least an intermediate level of general competence in the language. However, there are business- or work-related topics and tasks which can be dealt with at a lower level of competence. He suggests that, for university language students, 'Although long-term instruction and a balanced curriculum will always remain a primary goal, it cannot necessarily be expected that students are willing to submit to two years of general college textbook German before topics with relevance to their future professions are addressed' (Boehringer, 1997: 4). In some cases, it seems, the LSP course serves to help students adapt their existing linguistic competence to new situations and tasks, rather than supplying them with new linguistic input.

A third issue, relating particularly to very short introductory courses, is the extent to which 'language-like behaviour' is being taught, rather than genuine linguistic competence. For example,

airline personnel (check-in staff or in-flight attendants) attending a one-day course may acquire a set of useful phrases but not be able to create novel utterances or respond to non-routine requests.

LSP presents a challenge to those involved in language teaching and **APPLIED LINGUISTICS**. Its very essence is language in use. As time and cost are very often at a premium, ways have to be found to equip learners with effective language as expeditiously as possible. Thus LSP provides a demanding testing ground for descriptions of language and for theories of learning and teaching. As yet, however, there has been insufficient basic research into the link between LSP and LGP, or into the efficacy of the descriptions of language, and methods of teaching and **ASSESSMENT** employed. The continued growth of LSP teaching suggests that it is now an accepted branch of foreign language provision, but the shortcomings in back-up research need to be rectified.

**See also:** Adult learners; Communicative language teaching; English for Specific Purposes; Genre; Higher education; Language across the curriculum; Needs analysis; Sociolinguistics

## References

Bloch, B.J. and Hahn, M. (1995) 'German as a business language', *The Journal of Language for International Business* 6, 2: 1–15.

Boehringer, M. (1997) ' "Von Anfang an": a new trend in German for business', *The Journal of Language for International Business* 8, 1: 1–18.

Hare, G.E. (1992) 'Transferable personal skills, communicative language and graduate employment prospects after 1992', in D. Staquet and R. Zeyringer (eds), *Les langues: pivot de nouvel espace economique Europeen* (*Languages: a key factor for the new Europe*), Association Internationale Langues et Economie (International Association Language and Business), Nottingham: Praetorius.

Johnson, E., Garner, M., Hick, S., Matthews, D. *et al.* (1993) *PoliceSpeak: Police communications and language and the Channel Tunnel*, a report, Cambridge: PoliceSpeak Publications.

Myles, S. (1994) 'Teaching foreign language skills for special purposes: French for engineers or engineering in French?', in G. Parker and C.

Reuben (eds), *Languages for the international scientist*, London: Association for French Language Studies in association with CILT.

## Further reading

Howard, R. and Brown, G. (1997) *Teacher education for LSP*, Clevedon: Multilingual Matters.

Parker, G. and Reuben, C. (eds) (1994) *Languages for the international scientist*, London: Association for French Language Studies in association with CILT.

Scott, W. and Muhlhaus, S. (eds) (1994) *Languages for specific purposes*, London: CILT/Kingston University.

Staquet, D. and Zeyringer, R. (eds) (1992) *Les langues: pivot de nouvel espace economique Europeen* (Languages: a key factor for the new Europe), Association Internationale Langues et Economie (International Association Language and Business), Nottingham: Praetorius.

PAULINE ROBINSON

# *Langue* and *parole*

Of the three aspects of **LINGUISTICS** which Saussure defines, *langue* is the most important one. Roughly speaking, it consists of the words and the grammatical rules of a (national) language. These are organised by syntagmatic and paradigmatic (associative) relations. *Langue* is made the norm of *parole*. Saussure's terms and their definitions became the common property of **STRUCTURALIST LINGUISTICS** and, thus, of the linguistic underpinning of language teaching. They lead to a didactic approach which centres around 'teaching rules' and 'application of rules in practice'. Criticism of this Saussurean framework has its repercussions for the practice of language teaching.

## *Langage, langue* and *parole*

In his *Cours de linguistique générale* (posthumously 1916, new French edn 1972, new English edn 1974; Harris, 1987), Ferdinand de **SAUSSURE** explains that in a discipline like linguistics the aspect chosen determines the object of reflections. Following this principle, he defines three terms which represent human language from three different aspects: *langage, langue* and *parole*. The first, *langage*, is the human faculty to create a system of signs representing various concepts of meaning. It is this psychological faculty, not the endowment with organs of speaking, that governs our handling of linguistic signs. The concrete shape of this abstract faculty is *langue*, a (national) language. It is the only means by which *langage* can be made an object of reflection. All members of an interacting group develop in their minds a number of almost identical *signifiants* with almost identical *signifiés*. (Saussure admits that these identities are never perfect.) They are a sort of social crystallisation, a common property used to the effect that speakers and listeners usually understand each other. A language consists of the hypothetical sum of all potential word-meanings stored in the minds of all its speakers, and moreover of the whole system of grammatical rules that is at their virtual disposal.

real in a *langue*, any *langue* can only become real in *parole*, i.e. in acts of speech (or writing). Speaking is performed by a psycho-physical mechanism; its linguistic quality, however, lies in the fact that it gives the system of *langue* a phonetic (or graphetic) expression. Contrary to *langue, parole* is individual. It is subject to the accidental circumstances of the act in time and space. However, it leaves speakers a certain liberty for their creative imagination. Acts of speech may contain elements which are not covered by the regularities of the language. Whereas *langue* represents the essential of language, which binds speakers by rules, *parole* represents the circumstantial. Both are dependent on each other. If there were no speech, no language would become real. If there was no language, speech would not be communicative, and would consequently not be speech.

## Syntagmatic and paradigmatic order

In spite of the fact that *langage, langue* and *parole* are simply three different aspects of the same thing, they are different objects of reflection in linguistics. Although all three objects are worthy of investigation, Saussure pays more attention to *langue* than to the other two because, for him, it gives the norm with which speech must be measured. Apart from its linguistic system, a language is also determined by its history. At a given moment in time, a language can be understood as the product of this history. However, this fact does not affect its synchronic system. A synchronic crosscut through a language is always artificial, because it ignores the changes which take place at every minute. In spite of this imprecision, synchrony is superior in linguistics to diachrony because the system effective at a given moment (or short period) in time is the only reality for language users.

In explaining the organisation of *langue*, Saussure focuses on words as semantic units (lexemes) and as types of grammatical behaviour (word-classes); and on types (structures) of sentences. He finds two kinds of order. The first is the syntagmatic one, a consequence of the linear character of signs. It determines the sequence of parts of words (morphemes, like 're-sist-ance') and of words in sentences. Thus it pertains to the rules of word-formation and of syntax. The second is the paradigmatic one, which Saussure calls 'associative'. It pertains both to meaning and to form. Paradigmatic relations of meaning exist between near-synonyms (like 'teaching, training, educating'), paradigmatic relations of form exist between words of analogous formation (like 'insistence, resistance, consistence'). Both kinds of order work together. Words related to each other paradigmatically can substitute in a syntagma. *V* + *tion*, for example, can appear as 'education, publication, vindication', etc. *N* + *V* + *Adv* can appear as 'Farmers work hard, Ostriches run fast, High-rises are modern', etc. When sentences are being formed, both orders are at work. Syntagmatic concatenation does not only move individual words, but whole systems of paradigmatically related ones, a fact which greatly enhances the potential of each syntagma.

Contrary to *parole*, the ordering systems of *langue* determine the stability, the order, the typical structure of language which speakers abiding by the rules – the majority – will use. But Saussure admits that there may also be creative elements in speech which are not covered by the rules of *langue* and yet are 'speech'. They are often the beginning of changes in the system.

## Criticisms

Saussure's ideas about *langage*, *langue* and *parole* were

a great success, in particular after 1945 when they started to conquer linguistic thinking in the whole world (Koerner, 1973). Before that date, Saussure's whole edifice of thoughts had largely been understood as a kind of formalisation of **HUMBOLDTEAN** ideas. The general success pertained, above all, to the synchronic study of *langue*. Language description according to structuralist principles, which was the linguistic underpinning of language teaching methodology after Saussure, thought of itself as the application of this Saussurean concept to one national language. One reason for this may be the fact that, in spite of his innovations, Saussure actually conforms in many respects to the status quo and to common experience. People have always looked at **DICTIONARIES** (words) and **GRAMMARS** (rules) as the two main repositories of the units of a language. Grammar has always been a crosscut of average usage, even if it was mostly related to the 'model' quality of those speakers who supposedly knew better than others. So linguists as well as the common teacher could in principle go on as before and yet follow Saussure.

Of course, there was (and still is) also criticism (Hartmann, 1998), in particular of *langue* as a hypothetical construct, because there is no such thing in reality as a collective brain or memory. If Saussure's construct is meant to explain why people who speak one language actually understand each other, a difficult philosophical problem was solved simply by presupposing what was to be proved. Indeed many philosophers paid attention to the problem without proposing such an easy solution (Taylor, 1992). In his dichotomy of **COMPETENCE AND PERFORMANCE**, Noam **CHOMSKY** tried to solve the same problem in his own way. What the hypothesised common property of *langue* is for Saussure, the genetic endowment of human competence is for Chomsky.

There were also linguistic observations which undermined the **VALIDITY** of the *langue*/*parole* dichotomy. The structural potential that develops out of the interplay between the syntagmatic and the paradigmatic orders is not realised in some cases because it violates some norm. Certain word-compounds, for example, could but do not exist (e.g. +*pocket-picker* [instead of 'pickpocket']). There is also a limit to the number of relative clauses within one sentence. The 'norms' that forbid such constructions can in many cases be described, but they are not covered by Saussure's understanding of *langue*. This is why the dichotomy was replaced by a tripartite framework which differentiated *langue*, *norme* and *parole*.

Furthermore, linguistic investigations into larger units than sentences found regularities of the syntagmatic as well as of the paradigmatic kind which had hardly been treated in grammar at all. **TEXT LINGUISTICS** deals with such issues of rules of anaphora and cataphora, of substitution and ellipsis, of pronominalisation and repetition, which are just as compelling as syntagmatic rules for sentences, and yet they are not usually subsumed under *langue*. Moreover, **DISCOURSE ANALYSIS** uncovered regularities of turntaking and turnyielding, of adjacency pairs, etc. They may ultimately be of a social rather than a linguistic nature, but they certainly have their repercussions in linguistic structures.

Such criticism can lead to quite different consequences. Either more and more phenomena of *parole* will be accepted as properly belonging to *langue*, which, in the long run, renders the two terms useless. Or the dichotomy is eventually given up altogether. Linguists following Ludwig Wittgenstein, for example, maintain that no hypothetical store of rules, no fixed yardsticks above daily language use, are needed in order to explain linguistic regularities. In what he calls 'games', it suffices to assume that people permanently and cooperatively evolve forms of linguistic behaviour, that they accept, criticise, negotiate, agree and disagree about how to use their language in the same way in which they do so in games or rituals. Although there are many similarities between *langue* and the 'language game' (Harris, 1988), speech would then not be a practice following a set of stable (or slowly changing) rules, it would be a practice which sets and discards its own rules by its very performance and, in order to do this, is in constant flux.

This consequence is rather of a theoretical (or philosophical) than a practical nature in linguistics. Yet, it has its impact on the classroom. Following the Saussurean model, language learning appears to be being taught a set of rules and applying these in practice. The stability of teaching and learning lies in grammar and word-meanings. Linguistic practice is measured by the fluency and, above all, the correctness with which these are realised in acts of speech. Following the post-Saussurean model, language learning appears as a practice of **SPEAKING** where the communicative effect matters more than the correctness of expression, where meaning is expressed by approaches and attempts, and where it is finally reached by a kind of negotiation. This difference may be more of a stylistic and attitudinal character for schools rather than fundamentally a question of curriculum. It will none the less affect the way in which a newly-learned language is handled.

**See also:** Competence and performance; History: the nineteenth century; Linguistics; Pragmatics; Saussure; Sociolinguistics; Structural linguistics

## References

Harris, R. (1987) *Reading Saussure. A critical commentary on the 'Cours de linguistique générale'*, London: Duckworth.

Harris, R. (1988) *Language, Saussure, and Wittgenstein. How to play games with words*, London: Routledge.

Hartmann, R.A. (1998) *Grundlagenprobleme der Sprachwissenschaft. Kritische Analyse und Abwägung der allgemeinen Ansichten über Sprache von Saussure, Chomsky und Piaget (Fundamental issues of linguistics. Critical analysis and consideration of Saussure's, Chomsky's and Piaget's general opinions on language)*, Konstanz: Hartung-Gorre.

Koerner, E.F.K. (1973) *Ferdinand de Saussure. Origin and development of his linguistic thought in Western studies of language*, Amsterdam: Benjamins.

Saussure, Ferdinand de (1972) *Cours de linguistique générale. Publié par Charles Bally et Albert Sechehaye. Avec la collaboration de Albert Riedlinge*, nouvelle edition, edition critique préparée par Tullio di Mauro, Paris: Payot.

Saussure, Ferdinand de (1974) *Course in general linguistics*, trans. Wade Baskin, London: Owen.

Taylor, T.J. (1992) *Mutual misunderstanding. Scepticism and the theorizing of language and interpretation*, Durham, NH and London: Duke University Press.

WERNER HÜLLEN

# Large classes

Large classes are widely considered to be problematic for language learning and yet some teachers effectively manage large classes in which students learn successfully. Class size in itself does not necessarily have a negative impact on the quality of teaching and learning. What matters is teachers' and students' perceptions and assumptions about large classes, the **TEACHER METHODS** and the ways of organising interaction, and giving attention to individual learners and adequately assessing students' work.

The notion of 'large' is relative. In different countries the average number of students in language classes can vary enormously. In Britain, a class of 30 to 40 students is considered large, while in **CHINA** average numbers can be 50 to 60. Attitudes to class size are greatly affected by the context. At national levels, in many developed countries educational policies are designed to reduce class sizes; in recent years average class sizes have become smaller and teachers want this to continue, yet funding arrangements may encourage larger classes (the more students, the more fees the school receives). In many developing countries, however, participation rates in schooling have increased dramatically. There may be teacher and accommodation shortages and therefore larger classes, but the popularity of foreign languages, notably English, has often meant high **MOTIVATION**.

At a personal level, concepts of 'large' depend on teachers' experience: the larger the class which teachers regularly teach, the larger their idea of what class numbers are intolerable, problematic or even ideal (The Lancaster–Leeds Project, 1989). At an institutional level, private language schools in many countries flourish because they are able to ensure small classes and this is desired by students or their parents. However, there is an interesting paradox in some of the same countries; a fast-track class or classes in a key school may be of larger-than-average size because students want to be placed in such a class since they believe it guarantees exam success for university entrance. The issue of class size is thus bound up with students' **NEEDS**, **ATTITUDES** and motivation, and perceptions of learning outcomes. In different situations, the effect of these factors can either reinforce or override the perceived difficulty concerning a large number of students, and this can also be greatly influenced by teaching methods.

The problems experienced in large classes include issues about management and classroom control, how to ensure student involvement in interaction for effective language learning, how to assess all individual learners, and affective consequences of classes of large numbers for teachers and students. There are a range of methods and strategies to help teachers handle these problems, but some of these will themselves be constrained by the fact that large classes are often found in circumstances which are difficult to teach in, quite apart from the matter of student numbers. Classroom control and management problems can be reduced by getting to know students' names rapidly (e.g. using seating plans and giving individual attention), by reducing noise levels (talking or whispering quietly in pairs, regulating activities by quick responses to teacher signals), by keeping activities brief, by ensuring that students know what to do and easing transitions from one task to another (using clear signals and instructions, demonstrations and examples). Student involvement in activities, particularly for oral **SKILLS**, can be facilitated by work in pairs or groups. This can be managed, despite the frequently encountered difficulties of lack of space and crowded fixed seating, by using short, purposeful activities with pre-organised pairs. Such activities may have a clear outcome and can be demonstrated in advance by the teacher (or by chosen pairs of learners) or prepared with silent planning or through homework. **ASSESSMENT** problems can be reduced by making notes on brief individual oral presentations to the class and by keeping **WRITING** tasks focused. In assessing writing, the teacher's marking load (which can be enormous in large classes) can be reduced by giving clear guidelines or models of writing, by limiting word length of assignments, encouraging student editing and redrafting, and using some peer marking or adopting a policy of selective marking (provided students and parents understand this).

Affective consequences of large classes include the threat to both teachers' and students' morale and **MOTIVATION**, the difficulties for the teacher to establish rapport with learners and to know them as individuals, and teachers' feelings of frustration, self-doubt and guilt about having to use teacher-led activities and limit more communicative, participatory kinds of interaction (the latter are often also constrained by limited resources and **MATERIALS**). Such feelings can be countered by a belief that success is possible (given hard work), by making strong efforts to know students, and by some willingness to use an eclectic mix of methods.

Research on successful language teaching in large classes in China (Jin and Cortazzi, 1998) shows that teachers practise combinations of the above points. In addition, they use whole-class interactive teaching; this means the teacher uses some choral activities but will also engage one or two students in sustained dialogues or talk about their reading while the others listen. It means that feedback on written work may involve several students in writing their work on different sections of the board or on wall posters to explain it to the class, or that groups will prepare oral presentations for the class. Such activities in which a few students talk at some length are successful because the classroom participants share a cultural belief that interaction is not only social but also cognitive, i.e. students understand that effective learning includes **LISTENING** with close attention and giving their mind both to the teacher and to each other. There are further key factors in this successful teaching. First, teachers train the students in the ways of learning which are encouraged. Second, lessons are taught with a wide variety of activities (some routine ones, some more innovatory), a smart pace and rapid transitions between tasks (this also saves time). And third, of critical importance, teachers are given adequate time for detailed preparation, marking of written work, and involvement in out-of-class language practice activities, such as language clubs or giving individual attention during breaks.

Educational research on large classes is often equivocal regarding learning outcomes; the results of some studies would favour reductions in class size, but there have been few longitudinal studies, few specific studies of language classrooms, and few international comparisons. Such research is complex since class size is inseparable from other constraining factors, especially in developing countries. Social and educational traditions and cultural attitudes and beliefs about learning and teaching

methods are part of this complexity but, as indicated above, there are situations where these can be key elements in successful teaching and learning of languages even when class numbers are apparently unacceptably high.

**See also:** Africa; China; Group work; Internet; Language laboratories; Linguistic imperialism; Questioning techniques; Skills and knowledge in language learning; Teaching methods; Visual aids

### References

Jin, L. and Cortazzi, M. (1998) 'Dimensions of dialogue: large classes in China', *International Journal of Educational Research* 29: 739–61.

The Lancaster–Leeds Project (1989) *Language learning in large classes* (12 research project reports including detailed studies of several countries), Leeds: University of Leeds.

### Further reading

Coleman, H. (1997) 'Teaching large classes and training for sustainability', in G. Abbott and M. Beaumont (eds), *The development of ELT*, Hemel Hempstead: Prentice Hall.

Nolasco, R. and Arthur, L. (1988) *Large classes*, London: Macmillan.

LIXIAN JIN AND MARTIN CORTAZZI

# Learning styles

Learning styles are cognitive differences in the ways in which individuals learn. A learning style is a relatively permanent, characteristic approach to a wide range of perceptual and intellectual activities, tasks and situations. Witkin *et al.* (1971) define what they call cognitive style as:

a characteristic, self-consistent mode of functioning which individuals show in their perceptual and intellectual activities ... it is a term used to describe individual differences in the way one habitually tends to perceive, organise, analyse or recall information and experience.

Although interest in learning style has a long history in **PSYCHOLOGY** and **ANTHROPOLOGY**, it was only in the 1960s that it became a topic of intensive research and speculation with particular reference to language teaching and learning. By the early 1970s some twenty-five different styles had been identified or at least suggested. Typically, learning styles have been investigated and described on the basis of polarities such as:

- field dependence and field independence
- holists and serialists (globalists and analysts)
- broad categorisers and narrow categorisers
- data gatherers and rule formers
- planners and correctors
- impulsivity and reflectivity
- levelling and sharpening

Although the **VALIDITY** of some of these distinctions, in particular field-dependence/independence, is now generally accepted, the proliferation of terms is indicative of a number of conceptual and methodological problems which continue to hamper research in this area. For instance, field dependence/independence as determined by the Embedded-Figures Test (Witkin et al., 1971) came under attack in the early 1990s (Griffiths and Sheen, 1992; Chapelle, 1992; Sheen, 1993). In addition to the sheer complexity of the issues and objects in question, these include the lack of an overall theoretical framework bringing together the psychological, linguistic and social aspects of 'learning' and the difficulty of designing instruments for collecting data and comparing results across individuals, groups and cultures. These are major objections, and explain to a considerable extent why, although the notion of learning style continues to fascinate teachers and learners alike – and with good reason, since it addresses matters which both experience and intuition show to be of real pedagogical relevance – there has been a distinct cooling-off of scientific enthusiasm in linguistic circles in recent years.

This article will look first at the historical background to the emergence of learning styles as a topic of interest in the field of language didactics, then review some of the main theories and approaches. It will also look at some of the objections which have been raised against them. Finally, there will be a discussion of a number of pedagogical applications and implications of this notion, including the relation of learning styles to a learner-centred pedagogy,

cultural variation, the so-called 'good' language learner (Naiman et al., 1975; Rubin, 1975).

## Historical development of interest in learning styles

The identification of the sources of individual and cultural variation in cognition, as opposed to the universal characteristics of the human mind, is a central and defining concern of modern psychology. The cognitive effects of cross-cultural differences have been of interest to anthropologists and psychologists since at least the nineteenth century. A long line of investigation can be traced from Herder and the German linguists, including Grimm and **HUMBOLDT**, through to Boas and the early twentieth-century American anthropologists in which the notions of cognitive relativity and determinism were debated and investigated. The **SAPIR–WHORF** hypothesis is a linguistic variant on this theme. In particular, the question of possible relationships between variations in language and behaviour and differences in perception has been the subject of numerous studies.

One of the aims of the Torres Straits Expedition of 1899 was to evaluate the perceptual capacities and proclivities of groups which were remote from Western civilisation, including hearing, smell, cutaneous sensitivity and discrimination of weight, reaction times, acuity of vision, and colour perception. Amongst the other factors which have been investigated since are: group maintenance structures (social, political: e.g. hunter-gatherers, agriculturalists, fisherfolk), economic and rearing practices, environmental and ecological features such as terrain and climate, shelter and architecture, and language. Witkin (Witkin and Goodenough, 1981), for example, has related child-rearing practices to the degree of field dependence shown by members of a culture, showing that those with higher levels of dependence have more difficulty in perceiving as discrete the constituent elements of a perceptual field than do those with lower levels.

Such work had little influence on education in general or on language didactics in particular until a number of contingencies obliged various actors in the field of education to rethink just what 'learning' is and how it is related to 'teaching'. Until the late 1950s, what passed for the study of learning was really the study of teaching, the investigation of the ways in which the behaviour of one person can influence the behaviour of a second person. This was particularly true of academic psychology, of course, with its **BEHAVIOURIST** bias, but in contemporary educational discourse the two terms were used as near synonyms, since approaches to both psychological and educational research were overwhelmingly teacher- and teaching-centred. Only as humanistic and learner-centred approaches developed did a redefinition of learning as a psychological process slowly emerge. Learning came to be seen as the extension of meanings of which the individual is capable and to be the fruit of a number of mechanisms, such as the assimilation of new information, decision taking and problem solving. This development was due to the limitations of academic psychology and its inability to respond to the interest in personal development and self-realisation which characterised the 1960s and to which the conditioned reflexes of pigeons pecking at popcorn seemed completely irrelevant.

It has also been suggested that the growing interest in learning styles, and the ways in which that interest was canalised, were directly related to the contemporary opposition in language teaching methodology between the **GRAMMAR–TRANSLATION** and the **AUDIOLINGUAL** approaches. It can be argued that any language teaching methodology is an attempt, however vague or unconscious, to encourage a given learning style and that the contrast between these two approaches in particular, because they imply learning styles which are so very different, served to bring out this fact, which in turn encouraged researchers to investigate, identify and describe the differences. The grammar–translation method concentrates on the language system and can therefore be seen as favouring learning styles that would later be dubbed 'field independent', 'sharpening', 'reflexive', 'rule-forming' and 'explicit'. The audiolingual method was largely based on a refusal to teach the system, and can be described, anachronistically, as 'field-dependent', 'data-gathering', 'encouraging impulsivity' and 'levelling'.

Amongst the most important contributions to the study of learning styles, and those to which linguists and didacticians tend to refer, are those of Pask (1976), Fischer and Fischer (1979), Letteri (1982) and Kolb (1984).

Pask (1976) proposes a taxonomy of 'styles and **STRATEGIES OF LEARNING**' which can be diagrammed and glossed as follows:

| | |
|---|---|
| **HOLIST** | *+ Global Learner*<br>gets an overall grasp before attending to details<br><br>*– Globetrotter*<br>superficial overgeneraliser |
| **GENERALIST** | a versatile learner, capable of metacognitive choice of learning approach |
| **SERIALIST** | *+ Operational learner*<br>step-by-step, analytical and methodical<br>*– Unreflecting learner*<br>Can't see the wood for the trees |

B. and L. Fischer (1979) suggest this list of 'learning styles':

1  The incremental learner
2  The intuitive learner

3  The 'specialist'
4  The 'all-rounder'

5  The involved learner
6  The uninvolved learner

7  The structure-dependent learner
8  The structure-independent learner

9  The eclectic learner

Letteri (1982) establishes 'cognitive profiles' along seven parameters:

| | | |
|---|---|---|
| 1 | Analytic . . . . . . . . . . | Global |
| 2 | Focused . . . . . . . . . . | Unfocused |
| 3 | Narrow . . . . . . . . . . | Broad |
| 4 | Complex . . . . . . . . . . | Simple |
| 5 | Reflective . . . . . . . . . | Impulsive |
| 6 | Sharpening . . . . . . . . | Levelling |
| 7 | Tolerant . . . . . . . . . . | Intolerant |

Although such models are all based on considerable amounts of empirical research, they are open in varying degrees to a number of criticisms. They are all based on binary oppositions, and on the assumption that learning styles are innate and unchanging, that one is born under the sign of a particular style and that nothing can be done about it. They all contain built-in value judgements and have little or no social or interactive component,

In many ways, Kolb's theory (1984) can be seen as a masterly synthesis of approaches like those outlined above, but it is also a largely successful attempt to deal with their limitations, particularly the social and interactive component. For Kolb, learning is seen essentially as a process of resolution of conflicts between dialectically opposed dimensions, the prehension dimension and the transformation dimension. *Prehension* refers to the way in which the individual grasps experience, and includes two modes of knowing: apprehension and comprehension. Apprehension is insight, instant and intuitive knowledge and understanding, without any need for logical processes, inquiry or analysis. Comprehension involves the introduction of conscious order into this flow of apprehended sensations. *Transformation* refers to the way in which experience is transformed or processed either by reflective observation or by active experimentation.

Since individuals emphasise or minimise the time and effort devoted to these different steps in the learning process, it is possible to establish four major categories of learner, or tendencies in learning approach, which Kolb describes as follows (Kolb, 1976):

1 The *Converger's* dominant learning abilities are abstract conceptualisation and active experimentation. This person's greatest strength lies in the practical application of ideas. A person with this style seems to do best in those situations like conventional intelligence tests where there is a single correct answer or solution to a question or problem. This person's knowledge is organised in such a way that, through hypothetical-deductive reasoning, this person can focus it on specific problems.

2 The *Diverger* has the opposite learning strengths to the Converger. This person is best in concrete experience and reflective observation. This person's greatest strength lies in imaginative ability. This person excels in the ability to view concrete situations from many perspectives. A person with this style performs better in situations that call for generation of ideas, such as a 'brainstorming' idea session.

3 The *Assimilator's* dominant learning abilities are abstract conceptualisation and reflective observation. This person's greatest strength lies in the ability to create theoretical models. This person excels in inductive reasoning and in assimilating disparate observations into an integrated explanation. This person, like the Converger, is less interested in people and more concerned with abstract concepts, but is less concerned with the practical use of theories. For this person it is more important that the theory be logically sound and precise; in a situation where a theory or plan does not fit the 'facts', the assimilator would be likely to disregard or re-examine the facts.

4 The *Accommodator* has the opposite learning strengths to the Assimilator. This person is best at concrete experience and active experimentation. This person's greatest strength lies in doing things – in carrying out plans and experiments – and involving oneself in new experience. S/he tends to excel in those situations where one must adapt oneself to specific immediate circumstances. In situations where a theory or plan does not fit the 'facts', this person will most likely discard the plan or theory. This person tends to solve prob-lems in an intuitive, trial-and-error manner, relying heavily on other people for information rather than on one's own analytic ability.

## Learning styles and language teaching

A number of attempts have been made to integrate research on learning styles into language teaching methodology, mostly in the context of learner-training activities where learners are being prepared for self-directed or **AUTONOMOUS** study. Two main approaches have developed. In the first, learners are invited to discover, reflect on and thereby optimise their own learning style. In the second, they are encouraged to become more flexible learners by widening their range of styles, so that they can make appropriate metacognitive choices when faced with particular tasks. In both cases, the methodology and aims have been strongly influenced by the work on **LANGUAGE AWARENESS** carried out by **HAWKINS** and colleagues in the 1970s and 1980s (Hawkins, 1984) and still very much alive as 'reflective learning'. Kohonen's work in the field of 'experiential learning' makes explicit use of Kolb's categories (Kohonen, 1990). In the United States, Dunn and Dunn (1979) have suggested that there are eighteen elements of learning style, whose relative importance will vary depending on whether the learners are tactual, kinaesthetic, auditory or visual: environmental elements (sound, light, temperature, design), emotional elements (**MOTIVATION**, persistence, responsibility, need for structure), sociological elements (working alone, with peers, with an adult, some combination), physical elements (perceptual strengths, intake, time of day, need for mobility). In **AUSTRALIA**, Willing (1989) has developed **MATERIALS** for 'teaching how to learn' which include a Learning Styles Inventory based on a quadripartite distinction: communicative/authority-oriented/concrete/analytical. In **FRANCE**, Narcy (1991) has devised self-**EVALUATION** questionnaires which include several binary distinctions, some of which have distinct psychological overtones: shy/extrovert; perfectionist/realist – clearly related to Hatch's (1974) distinction between 'rule-formers' and 'data-gatherers'; visual/audile; teacher-dependent/teacher-independent. In Britain, Ellis and Sinclair (1989) have produced learning-to-learn materials based in part on comparable questionnaires. Such materials and activities are being used and imitated worldwide in the language resource centres and autonomous or self-directed learning schemes which have followed on from the pioneering work carried out from the 1970s onwards by centres such as the **CRAPEL**, the Language Centre of the University of Cambridge and the Centre for Language and Communication Studies in Trinity College, Dublin.

**See also:** Autonomy and autonomous learners; Behaviourism; Cognitive code theory; Communicative language teaching; Cross-cultural psychology; Group work; Learning to learn; Second language acquisition theories; Strategies of language learning; Untutored language acquisition

## References

Chapelle, C.A. (1992) 'Disembedding "Disembedded figures in the landscape ..."': an appraisal of Griffith's and Sheen's "Reappraisal of L2 research on field dependence/independence" ', *Applied Linguistics* 13, 4: 375–84.

Dunn, R.S. and Dunn, K.J. (1979) 'Learning styles/teaching styles: should they ... can they ... be matched?', *Educational Leadership* (36), Association for Supervision and Curriculum Development.

Ellis, G. and Sinclair, B. (1989) *Learning to learn English*, Cambridge: Cambridge University Press.

Fischer, B. and Fischer, L. (1979) 'Styles in teaching and learning', *Educational Leadership* 36, 4: 245–54.

Griffiths, R. and Sheen, R. (1992) 'Disembedded figures in the landscape: a reappraisal of L2 research on field dependence/independence', *Applied Linguistics* 13, 2: 133–48.

Hatch, E. (1974) 'Second-language learning universals', *Working papers on bilingualism*, 3.

Hawkins, E. (1984) *Awareness of language*, Cambridge: Cambridge University Press.

Kohonen, V. (1990) 'Towards experiential learning in elementary foreign language education', in R. Duda and P. Riley (eds), *Learning styles*, Nancy: Presses Universitaires de Nancy.

Kolb, D. (1976) *Learning styles inventory*, Boston, MA: McBer and Company.

Kolb, D. (1984) *Experiential learning. Experience as the source of learning and development*, Englewood Cliffs, NJ: Prentice-Hall.

Letteri, C.A. (1982) 'Cognitive profile: relationship to achievement and development', in *Student learning styles and brain behaviour. Selected papers from the National Conference of Secondary School Principals*, Weston, VA.

Naiman, N., Frohlich, M., Stern, H. and Todesco, H. (1975) *The good language learner*, Toronto: Ontario Institute for Studies in Education.

Narcy, J.-P. (1991) *Comment mieux apprendre l'anglais (Improve the way you learn English)*, Paris: Editions d'Organisation.

Pask, G. (1976) 'Styles and strategies of learning', *British Journal of Educational Psychology* 46, 2: 128–48.

Rubin, J. (1975) 'What the "good language

learner" can teach us', *TESOL Quarterly* 9, 1: 41–51.

Sheen, R. (1993) 'A rebuttal to Chapelle's response to Griffiths and Sheen', *Applied Linguistics*, 14, 1: 98–100.

Willing, K. (1989) *Teaching how to learn*, NCELTR, Sydney: Macquarie University.

Witkin, H.A. and Goodenough, D.R. (1981) *Cognitive styles: essence and origins*, New York: International Universities Press.

Witkin, H.A., Oltman, P.K., Raskin, E. and Karp, S.A. (1971) *A manual for the embedded figures test*, Palo Alto: Consulting Psychologists Press.

## Further reading

Bickley, V. (ed.) (1989) *Language teaching and learning styles within and across cultures*, Hong Kong: Institute of Language in Education.

Naiman, N., Frohlich, M., Stern, H. and Todesco, H. (1975) *The good language learner*, Toronto: Ontario Institute for Studies in Education.

Reid, J.M. (ed.) (1995) *Learning styles in the ESL/EFL classroom*, New York: Heinle and Heinle.

RICHARD DUDA AND PHILIP RILEY

# Learning to learn

The term 'learning to learn' describes the process of acquiring those **SKILLS** that provide the learner with the possibility of understanding and mastering any area of knowledge at present or in the future. Learning to learn skills are transferable, inside and outside the classroom, and from one subject to another. Learning to learn can be carried out either by oneself as in independent study, or in learning with others as a social activity, with or without a teacher. It could be self-directed, group-directed in a collaborative context, or institutional.

Learners who have learned how to learn know how to take control of their own learning; how to develop a personal learning plan, to diagnose their strengths and weaknesses as learner, to chart a personal **LEARNING STYLE**, and to overcome personal blocks to learning. They know how to learn effectively in any situation, alone or with other people, and how to help others learn more effectively.

Skills of knowing how to learn involve three aspects: the conceptual understanding of the process of learning, a metalanguage, and a positive **ATTITUDE** to learning. The conceptual understanding of the process of learning implies having planning skills for deciding what, when, how and where to learn, setting realistic goals, finding learning resources, choosing and implementing learning strategies, estimating progress and assessing results. Metalanguage enables one to talk to oneself and to others about the learning process. A positive attitude towards learning new things in new contexts, and the ability to sustain **MOTIVATION**, are also necessary.

For learning to learn in a collaborative context, where leadership and participation are fundamental, members of a group need to learn to be adept at planning, conducting and evaluating their concerted efforts, to use the experience and expertise of all members to accomplish group tasks and goals, to utilise helping skills, and to be sensitive to the group process. Cooperative learning gives participants a positive experience of mutual support when faced with problems, helps to teach accountability for one's work, and develop social skills.

In the institutional mode, as in the workings of a school, college, or programme, the learner needs to learn how to study, take notes, write reports and essays, cope with taking examinations and satisfy the required criteria (for further information, see Smith, 1983).

Learning to learn includes the development of self-knowledge, i.e. the awareness of understanding self as learner. From practical experience and from exposure to theories of learning, in learning to learn one develops a sense of one's own learning style. Each person has their own unique way of learning and, through the process of learning to learn, an individual is empowered to understand, appreciate and use their own particular style. The learner will need to be exposed to a variety of learning styles so that they can choose the one that works best for them according to the particular task they want to do. Furthermore, identifying one's own learning style (Reid, 1995) becomes an opportunity to develop thinking skills.

Through preparing the mind for learning, the learner develops an understanding of a number of interacting processes, such as the affective (becoming motivated, reducing stress), the social (getting help, creating and using opportunities), the cognitive (a mental plan to understand knowledge), and the metacognitive (setting goals, plans, monitoring and evaluating learning), which work together to regulate how well the information being learned and expressed is being processed. Metacognition, knowledge about knowledge, or knowing what knowledge is like, how it works, and how it is acquired, plays a major role in a learner's success in learning. Metacognition includes affective factors, effective strategies, and knowledge of task demands such as the purpose and nature of tasks. A metacognitive strategy is a plan about how to organise and monitor cognitive strategies, e.g. the planning of subsequent mental actions to derive the meaning of an unknown text from the context (Westhoff, 1990).

Each learner may use one or more learning **STRATEGIES** at different times depending on a range of variables, such as the nature of the learning task, motivation levels and experience. The learner becomes aware of the factors that affect their learning both positively and negatively and, as a result, will recognise those learning strategies, situations, contexts and factors that suit them best, so that they may become more effective in learning. They will thus be able to make informed choices about what, how, why, when and where they want to learn.

The information that learners will look for to be able to make such choices is information about the nature of the subject itself, about learning techniques particular to the subject, and about themselves as learner. Learning to learn makes learning accessible to everyone, promotes **AUTONOMOUS LEARNING**, and implies the need for the availability of ample material and resources, as well as a new role for the teacher as a resource and support person.

The concept of learning to learn increasingly gained importance in the latter half of the twentieth century. John Dewey, the well-known American philosopher, proposed that schooling be evaluated by its success in creating in the learner the desire for 'continual growth' and for supplying them with the means for making that desire 'effective in fact' (Dewey, 1966). Smith (1983) outlines a number of factors that have contributed to the mounting concern with learning how to learn, such as the view of education as a lifelong process, the shift from a preoccupation with teaching to a preoccupation with learning, the interest in the notion of learning style, and the growing importance of **ADULT** education. The **COUNCIL OF EUROPE** has made a particularly significant contribution to a learning to learn approach in the field of modern language learning (see Holec, 1988; Holec and Huttunen, 1997). These works illustrate how the principles of learning to learn are applied to language learning.

The principles of learning to learn can be injected into the language **SYLLABUS**. Such a syllabus would be process- rather than product-oriented, and would take into consideration not only the declarative knowledge, but also the social skills, the existential competence (attitudes, values, motivation, beliefs), and the ability to learn (learning skills and strategies) that a learner needs to be able to communicate efficiently and effectively in the target language and culture (Newby, 1998).

In the classroom, learning to learn is enhanced through activities that encourage hypothetical thinking, the analysis of different points of view and the exploration of relationships. An example is an **EXERCISE** that looks into the effects of historical events, geographical features, population spread and density, and political systems, on peoples' attitudes, daily life, building structures and transport systems. Creativity is encouraged, for example, through the application of different symbol systems, such as the musical, the artistic, the graphical and even the mathematical in language learning (see Camilleri, 1998).

The following are ideas for use in the classroom to enhance the learning to learn process:

- Weekly tasksheets with a variety of exercises that allow for reflection, choice, decision making, **EVALUATION** of tasks and evaluation of attitude to work.
- Workshops that allow for individual work pace, for an awareness of personal learning strategies, capacities, **NEEDS**, motivation, and differentiation of level of difficulty.

- **GROUP WORK** that encourages cooperation among learners, and allows for choice and negotiation. The opportunity to present work in plenary sessions addresses creativity, self-confidence and presentation skills. The production of student and class magazines and project work allows for free choice of topics, for individual or group work, and for a space to address particular needs and interests (see Fleischmann, 1997).

**See also:** Autonomy and autonomous learners; Council of Europe Modern Languages Projects; Humanistic language teaching; Learning styles; Strategies of language learning; Untutored language acquisition

## References

Camilleri, A. (1998) 'The specification of objectives, resources and processes for learner autonomy', in A. Camilleri (ed.), *The specification of objectives for learner autonomy and cultural awareness within syllabus development at secondary level*, Graz: European Centre for Modern Languages, Council of Europe.

Dewey, J. (1966) *Democracy and education*, New York: Free Press.

Fleischmann, E. (1997) 'Attempts towards greater learner autonomy at GIBS seen in the context of a new development', in A. Camilleri (ed.), *Aspects of teaching methodology in bilingual classes at secondary school level*, Graz: European Centre for Modern Languages, Council of Europe.

Holec, H. (ed.) (1988) *Autonomy and self-directed learning: present fields of application*, Strasbourg: Council of Europe.

Holec, H. and Huttunen, I. (eds) (1997) *Learner autonomy in modern languages. Research and development*, Strasbourg: Council of Europe.

Newby, D. (1998) 'Approaches to syllabus design', in A. Camilleri (ed.), *Aspects of teaching methodology in bilingual classes at secondary school level*, Graz: European Centre for Modern Languages, Council of Europe.

Reid, J.M. (ed.) (1995) *Learning styles in the ESL/EFL classroom*, New York: Heinle and Heinle.

Smith, R.M. (1983) *Learning how to learn. Applied theory for adults*, Milton Keynes: Open University Press.

Westhoff, G. (1990) 'Strategies: some tentative definitions', *Learning to learn: investigating learner strategies and learner autonomy. Report on Workshop 2A, Uppsala, Sweden*, Strasbourg: Council of Europe.

## Further reading

Holec, H. (ed.) (1988) *Autonomy and self-directed learning: present fields of application*, Strasbourg: Council of Europe.

Holec, H. and Huttunen, I. (eds) (1997) *Learner autonomy in modern languages. Research and development*, Strasbourg: Council of Europe.

Smith, R.M. (1983) *Learning how to learn. Applied theory for adults*, Milton Keynes: Open University Press.

ANTOINETTE CAMILLERI GRIMA

# Le Français fondamental

*Le français fondamental (1er degré)* was developed between 1951 and 1954 by a team of **FRENCH** language researchers and teachers (M.A. Sauvageot, M.R. Michéa, M.G. Gougenheim, M.P. Rivenc and others) in order to make more effective the promotion of French as a foreign language. It consists of: (a) a number of *special lists* comprising certain structural words (such as articles, pronouns, conjunctions, etc.), interjections, counting words, indicators of quantity, chronology, points of the compass and relational terms; (b) an alphabetically ordered *general word list* of 1,445 items in all (1,176 lexical words and 269 grammatical words); and (c) recommendations for the selection and grading of various aspects of French **GRAMMAR** which are to be taught initially, whereas the treatment of other aspects is kept for a later point in time.

The selection of this basic **VOCABULARY** and grammar which is in principle open for further additions, was made first on the basis of the familiar criterion of frequency – which encompassed also the criterion of *range*, i.e. distribution across a variety of texts – and second on the basis of a new criterion of 'availability'. The investigation of frequency was founded – for the first time in the history of vocabulary statistics – on an *oral* language corpus of 312,135 words in total, consisting of transcribed tape recordings of 163 informal, spontaneous conversations about everyday topics with 275 speakers from all levels of society and from various regions of **FRANCE**.

Concrete nouns, whose value and usefulness do not correspond with their general level of frequency because they are highly context- and topic-specific, were not selected by the frequency criterion. In this case the criterion of availability was used. This criterion was developed largely by asking pupils to write for each of sixteen topic areas twenty nouns which they considered to be useful.

*Le Français fondamental 1er degré* was extended with a further 1,800 words of *Le Français fondamental 2ème degré* taken from a written corpus of newspapers and reviews.

*Le Français fondamental 1er degré* is still considered to be valid as a basis for the selection of vocabulary and grammar in **TEXTBOOKS** for the teaching of French. None the less a review of this pioneer work of the 1950s with equally careful and updated methods of investigation is urgently needed. The up-dating needed is particularly important not only for '*mots disponibles*' (available words) but also for the concept of the units investigated. A first step in going beyond the counting of individual words was made in the *Inventaire thématique et syntagmatique du français fondamental* (1971) by R. Galisson, in which collocations of nouns, verbs and adjectives were arranged under thematic headings. Unfortunately this was not developed any further. Larger lexico-grammatical units, which determine language use as *formulaic speech*, could be introduced instead of listings of individual words and grammatical structures. Furthermore the alphabetic ordering, which has no particular significance, could at least be complemented by a statement of frequency which would make transparent the distribution of different classes of words, of individual words within word classes (e.g. the most frequent verbs) and – in accord with a greater stress on language use – of the most frequent syntagms (such as *c'est*) with functional content.

An extension of listings of vocabulary and grammar with lists of speech intentions, topics, situations and **NOTIONS**, as is to be found in the curriculum documents of the **COUNCIL OF EUROPE**

(**THRESHOLD LEVEL**, *Niveau Seuil*) and in the *Volkshochschule*-Certificate or the ministerial guidelines of the Federal Republic of Germany, is not a solution to the problem of making a language inventory, created for teachers and textbook authors, directly applicable for use in the classroom.

**See also:** *Alliance française*; CIEP; CRÉDIF; Vocabulary

### Further reading

Chaurand, J. and Lerat, P. (1981) 'Français fondamental et français d'aujourd'hui', *Le Français dans le monde* 159: 20–5.

Gougenheim, M.G., Michéa, M.R., Rivenc, M.P., Sauvageot, M.A. (1967) *L'Élaboration du Français fondamental (1er degré). Etude sur l'établissement d'un vocabulaire et d'une grammaire de base*, Paris: Didier.

Michelini, L. (1988) 'Il "Français fondamental" 30 anni dopo', *Scuola e lingue moderne* 26: 268–78.

Ministère de l'Éducation Nationale (1958) *Le Français fondamental (1er degré)*, Paris: Institut National de Recherche et de Documentation Pédagogiques; (4th edn 1972).

Zeidler, H. (1980) *Das 'Français fondamental (1er degré)': Entstehung, linguistische Analyse und fremdsprachendidaktischer Standort*, Frankfurt a.M: Lang.

KRISTA SEGERMANN

# Lexicography and lexicology

Lexicography deals with the writing, compilation and editing of both general and specialised **DICTIONARIES**, while lexicology may be defined as the study of the stock of words in a given language, i.e. its **VOCABULARY** or lexicon. Both are derived from Greek *lexis* (word), *lexicos* (of/for words). They contribute knowledge to the production and use of dictionaries and to the teaching and learning of vocabulary.

### Lexicography

Lexicography may be viewed from at least three different standpoints: that of the profession of dictionary makers, the theory or set of principles involved, and the actual practice of dictionary making. All three standpoints are closely related.

As a profession, the focus is on the training, the job specification and career structure of professional lexicographers. As a theory, the accent is on the principles that underlie the process of compiling and editing a dictionary. Some of the principles are clearly of a lexical or lexicological nature, including the description of vocabulary as a whole and that of individual lexical items. Others stem from the domain of book production. Finally, as the practice of dictionary making, lexicography refers to the actual compiling and editing of dictionaries, with special emphasis on the various stages of dictionary making. It is assumed that the process of compilation and the principles underlying it cannot be separated. Consequently, the production of a dictionary is viewed as the sum total of a vast store of accumulated knowledge (Illson, 1986; Jackson, 1988).

The English lexicon received its first authoritative treatment in 1755 when Samuel Johnson compiled his *Dictionary of the English Language*. Although the book later received a great deal of criticism, 'the fact remains that Johnson's dictionary was the first attempt at a truly principled lexicography' (Crystal, 1995: 75). However, until the latter half of the twentieth century, lexicography maintained a tradition that was quite independent of developments in **LINGUISTICS**.

## Lexicology

As the study of a lexicon, lexicology first defines the word as a unit and studies its characteristics. Second, it investigates all the other aspects of words in a given language:

- their origin, discussing native as opposed to foreign words borrowed from other languages;
- the different types of words in the language and the kinds of meaning relations that may exist between them;
- the various processes of forming new words in the language, including how words become archaic or obsolete;
- words in use, viewing the vocabulary of the language as a package of subsets of words that are used in geographical, occupational, social and other contexts;

- the way words are treated in dictionaries, viewing the dictionary as the most systematic and comprehensive description of words;
- the use of computers for lexical research, including among others word frequencies, lexical patterns, collocation and style.

Lexicology deals not only with simple words in all their aspects, but also with compound and complex words. Since words must be analysed both in their form and in their meaning, lexicology relies on information derived from morphology, the study of the form of words and their components, and semantics, the study of their meanings. A third field which should be of particular interest in lexicological studies is etymology, the study of the origin of words.

## Lexicology as a level of language analysis

Lexicology is only one level of language analysis, the others being phonology, syntax and semantics. Although an attempt may be made at treating any of these levels in isolation, none of them can be studied successfully without reference to the others. All these levels of analysis interact with one another in various ways, and when we use language, we call on them simultaneously and unconsciously. For example, it may be thought at first sight that phonology does not interact with lexicology in any significant manner. But a close analysis will reveal that, in many cases, the difference between two otherwise identical lexical items can be reduced to a difference at the level of phonology. Compare for example the pairs of words toy and boy, feet and fit, pill and pin. They differ only in one sound unit (the position of which has been underlined in each word) and yet the difference has serious consequences at the level of lexicology.

## Lexicography as applied lexicology

Lexicography may be viewed as applied lexicology. In fact, lexicographers must operate with some notion of what a word (as lexical item) is, and what should be included in the description and definition of a word. Consequently it may be assumed that any lexicographical practice presupposes at least some implicit or explicit lexicological theory. For instance, lexicology pays special attention to homonymy (two words with the same meaning) and polysemy (one word with several meanings) which are also of great interest in lexicography. It is in this sense that lexicography may be regarded as applied lexicology.

As lexicology develops and lexicography takes its appropriate place in **APPLIED LINGUISTICS**, we may expect both of them to exert a greater influence on each other. In other words, while theoretical investigations will help improve practical applications, the latter will in turn help refine our theoretical framework. However, lexicology is not the only branch of **LINGUISTICS** which provides a theoretical framework for lexicography. For instance, **SOCIOLINGUISTICS** contributes not only in the study and selection of the language variety to be used in the dictionary, but also in the inclusion of information on style and registers (Gove, 1961/1976; Jackson, 1988; Crystal, 1995).

### Significance for language teaching and learning

Since lexicology deals with the study of the stock of words in a given language, it has a great deal to contribute to language teaching in general and the teaching and learning of vocabulary in particular. Knowledge gained from lexicology will be precious not only to curriculum designers but also to **TEXT-BOOK** writers. As for lexicography, its main impact on language teaching and learning lies in the use of dictionaries as didactic **MATERIALS**.

However, dictionary users should remember that, in addition to definitions, the dictionary supplies them with other types of information which are equally important. For instance, the dictionary gives not only the meaning of words but also information on phonology, the grammatical structure of the language, and the acceptability of words in different socio-cultural contexts. The dictionary is therefore the meeting point of all the linguistic and non-linguistic systems involved in the **SPEECH ACT**. Consequently it is an important but complex tool which must be used with care for maximum benefit, especially in the context of language teaching and learning.

**See also:** CRÉDIF; Dictionaries; *Le Français fondamental*; Linguistics; Mental lexicon; Pragmatics; Reference works; Text and corpus linguistics; Vocabulary

### References

Crystal, D. (1995) *The Cambridge Encyclopedia of English Language*, Cambridge: Cambridge University Press.

Gove, P.B. (1961/1976) *Webster's Third New International Dictionary*, Springfield, MA: Merriam.

Illson, R.F. (1986) *Lexicography: an emerging international profession*, Manchester: Manchester University Press.

Jackson, H. (1988) *Words and their meanings*, London: Longman.

### Further reading

Galisson, R. (1979) *Lexicologie et enseignement des langues (essais méthodologiques)* (Lexicology and language teaching; essays on methodology), Paris: Hachette.

Katamba, F. (1994) *English words*, London and New York: Routledge.

Wilkins, D.A. (1989) *Linguistics and language teaching*, London: Edward Arnold.

Yule, G. (1996) *The study of language*, Cambridge: Cambridge University Press.

ETIENNE ZÉ AMVELA

# Lingua franca

A language that is used as a medium of communication between people or groups of people each speaking a different native language is known as a lingua franca. The term lingua franca comes from Italian and means literally 'French' or 'Frankish language'. The first language to be so known originated in the Mediterranean area in the Middle Ages, and is linguistically based on Southern French and Italian mixed with elements of Greek and **ARABIC**.

Latin, associated with the rise of the Roman Empire, became the lingua franca of the Catholic Church and learning, while **FRENCH** used to be the language of international diplomacy, although it has largely been replaced by **ENGLISH**. In eastern and central **AFRICA**, Swahili serves as a lingua franca; in many parts of western Africa, this role is fulfilled by Hausa (Samarin, 1968). Being used in practically all spheres of international communication, i.e. politics, trade, industry, science, entertainment and the world-wide web, English is today the world's most widespread lingua franca.

A lingua franca can have different origins and forms. It can refer to a third *natural* language, as, for example, English in a communication between a Norwegian and a Chinese person; or it can be a *pidgin* language generally resulting from (restricted) business transactions in the East and West Indies and Africa, as well as North and South America. Pidgins are simplified communication systems generally based on English, French, **SPANISH** or Italian and one of the indigenous languages and are thus developed by speakers of mutually unintelligible speech communities. When a pidgin supersedes the original language of a speech community, it becomes a Creole. A further manifestation of a lingua franca is exemplified by *artificial* or *planned* languages such as **ESPERANTO**, Frater or Volapük.

In accordance with its historical origin, the concept of lingua franca is meant to describe communication exchanges between speakers of different **MOTHER TONGUES** by means of a third language, i.e. 'a medium of communication between people of different mother tongues, for whom it is a second language' (Samarin, 1987: 371). Failing to meet the criterion of third language for the use of the English language, e.g. between an Australian and a Bulgarian at an international meeting, would not fall within the scope of the preceding definition of lingua franca communication. However, most current conceptions of lingua franca include cases like the preceding one in their definitions, especially if the cause and topic of the communication are of a non-native nature and take place in neither of the communicators' country of origin, i.e. on 'neutral' territory.

## English as a lingua franca

Lingua franca is a functional concept in the sense that it refers to verbal communication between speakers of different languages irrespective of the number of speakers using a particular lingua franca, the range of use or the quality of communication, and it therefore must not be equated with an international language (Ammon, 1994). The use of Swahili as a lingua franca, for instance, is geographically restricted, whereas English has become not only an international lingua franca, but the first world language in human history. It is not so much the total of 400 million **NATIVE SPEAKERS** (**CHINESE** has one billion) that has made English a global language (Crystal, 1997), but the political, military and economic power behind the English language and the countries it is most associated with, above all the United States. The worldwide presence of English today originates historically from British colonialism (Pennycook, 1994; Phillipson, 1992), which from a linguo-political point of view helped English to become an official language in more than sixty countries.

Because of the very wide range of uses for which global English is employed, as well as its concomitant linguistic variability and instability, global English cannot be classified as a linguistic variety of English. Since it has no distinct phonological inventory, no specific lexis and no specific **GRAMMAR**, it does not affect the linguistic system of English. Thus, global English is not particularly a formal-linguistic phenomenon; instead it refers to contexts of use definable by extralinguistic factors such as the relationship between speaker and hearer, the time and place of communication, the purpose and topic of communication, etc. The use of English as an international lingua franca has a number of implications for the teaching or learning of English for such purposes (Gnutzmann, 1999).

It has been estimated that about 80 per cent of verbal exchanges in which English is used as a second or foreign language do not involve native speakers of English (Beneke, 1991; on the linguistic and intercultural characteristics of non-native/non-native discourse see Meierkord, 1996). As a result, when English is used as an international language, its use has become de-nationalised and is hardly connected any more with the values and assumptions of Anglo-American culture. The range of uses for which English as a global language can be employed may vary from extremely basic and rudimentary communication exchanges to very elaborate linguistic forms of expression practically indistinguishable from native speaker quality, e.g. in written academic discourse. To what extent a common cultural basis between the interlocutors needs to be negotiated will depend on the purpose and goal of an English-based lingua franca communication.

When used as a lingua franca, English is no longer founded on the linguistic and sociocultural norms of native English speakers and their respective countries and cultures. In principle, it is neutral with regard to the different cultural backgrounds of the interlocutors. As a consequence, in such lingua franca situations there is no need for non-native speakers to accommodate their identity and **ATTITUDES** to some kind of Anglo-American behavioural and cultural system. Depending on the length of the communication, the interlocutors, no matter whether they are native or non-native speakers, should work out some kind of common linguistic and intercultural basis for their communication.

Since English as lingua franca communication is not based on any particular national linguistic standard of English, relying on native speaker norms (or near-native speaker norms) does not necessarily guarantee that the communication will be successful. On the contrary, using elaborate linguistic structures or **VOCABULARY** may even be harmful to the success of the communication, if the participants do not share a similar linguistic repertoire. Thus, not only non-native but also native speakers of English need to become aware of the different attitude to and assumptions about English and apply this knowledge in order to adapt their verbal and **NON-VERBAL COMMUNICATION** behaviour to the particular circumstances. Native speakers should recognise that in lingua franca communication their 'native speakerism' does not entitle them to any feeling of linguistic or cultural superiority.

The increasing use of English as a global language, in particular its use as a means of communication among non-native speakers of English, makes it necessary to draw a distinction between English as a lingua franca and English as a Foreign Language. With regard to the use of English among non-native speakers it is important to remember that the way we perceive other people's acts of communication may to a large extent be determined by our own culture. In order to ensure a high degree of success in communication among non-native speakers of English through the **MEDIUM** of English, future teachers need to be made aware of the diversity of English(es) (Görlach, 1991; McArthur, 1998) and to learn how to recognise culture-induced misunderstandings and how to cope with them. For this reason, it seems essential for **TEACHER EDUCATION** that appropriate communication strategies and the general principles of **INTERCULTURAL COMPETENCE** should be dealt with. Examples of these include awareness of the culture-specific dependency of thought and behaviour; knowledge of general parameters such as religion or role of the sexes according to which cultures can be distinguished; interpersonal sensitivity – the ability to understand a person in his or her own right; cognitive flexibility – openness to new ideas and beliefs; behavioural flexibility – the ability to change one's behaviour patterns (Gnutzmann, 1997).

Since communication with native speakers will undoubtedly continue to be a major linguistic and cultural challenge for foreign learners of English and, due to the lack of a 'World Standard English' (Crystal, 1994), some kind of Anglo-American lexical and grammatical standard should remain the linguistic basis of English language teacher education. Due to the immense amount of phonetic variation of English and the waning influence of former standards such as *received pronunciation*, it is much more problematic to decide on a unified **PRONUNCIATION** teaching standard (Jenkins, 1998). As far as the non-language, i.e. the cultural, content of the classes teaching English as a lingua franca is concerned, topics of the native English cultures play only a minor role and should, to a great extent, be replaced by culture-general topics which account for the use of English globally. In view of the omnipresence of American politics and its value system, however, the preceding remark on the role of culture is more theoretical than practical in character. Although the use of English as a world language is sometimes regarded as **LINGUISTIC IMPERIALISM**, it would be rather narrow-minded, on the other hand, to ignore the function of English as a means of global communication and its potential for international understanding.

**See also:** Africa; China; Creoles; India; Lexicography and lexicology; Monolingual principle; Mother-tongue teaching; Native speaker; Non-native speaker teacher; Pidgins; Sociolinguistics; Standard language; Text and corpus linguistics

## References

Ammon, U. (1994) 'International languages', in R.E. Asher (ed.), *The encyclopaedia of language and linguistics*, Oxford: Pergamon Press.

Beneke, J. (1991) 'Englisch als *lingua franca* oder als Medium interkultureller Kommunikation? (English as a *lingua franca*, or as a medium of intercultural communication?)', in R. Grebing (ed.), *Grenzenloses Sprachenlernen. Festschrift für Reinhold Freudenstein (Learning languages without frontiers. A festschrift for Reinhold Freudenstein)*, Berlin: Cornelsen and Oxford University Press.

Crystal, D. (1994) 'Which English – or English *Which?*', in M. Hayhoe and S. Parker (eds), *Who owns English?*, Buckingham and Philadelphia: Open University Press.

Crystal, D. (1997) *English as a global language*, Cambridge: Cambridge University Press.

Gnutzmann, C. (1997) 'Multilingualism and language teaching: some pedagogical implications', *Fremdsprachen Lehren und Lernen (FLuL)* 26: 156–66.

Gnutzmann, C. (ed.) (1999) *Teaching and learning English as a global language: native and non-native perspectives*, Tübingen: Stauffenberg.

Görlach, M. (1991) *Englishes. Studies in varieties of English 1984–88*, Amsterdam: Benjamin.

Jenkins, J. (1998) 'Which pronunciation norms and models for English as an international language?' *ELT Journal* 52, 2: 119–26.

McArthur, T. (1998) *The English languages*, Cambridge: Cambridge University Press.

Meierkord, C. (1996) *Englisch als Medium der interkulturellen Kommunikation. Untersuchungen zum 'non-native/non-native speaker'-Diskurs (English as a medium of international communication. An investigation into non-native/non-native discourse)*, Frankfurt am Main: Lang.

Pennycook, A. (1994) *The cultural politics of English as an international language*, London: Longman.

Phillipson, R. (1992) *Linguistic imperialism*, Oxford: Oxford University Press.

Samarin, W.J. (1968) 'Lingua francas of the world', in J.A. Fishman (ed.), *Readings in the sociology of language*, The Hague and Paris: Mouton.

Samarin, W.J. (1987) 'Lingua franca', in U. Ammon (ed.), *Sociolinguistics: an international handbook of the science of language and society*, vol. 3. 1, Berlin: de Gruyter.

## Further reading

Cheshire, J. (ed.) (1991) *English around the world. Sociolinguistic perspectives*, Cambridge: Cambridge University Press.

de Jong, W. (1996) *Open frontiers. Teaching English in an intercultural context*, Oxford: Heinemann.

Trudgill, P. and Hannah, J. (1982/1994) *International English* (3rd edn), London: Edward Arnold.

CLAUS GNUTZMANN

# Linguapax

Linguapax is a UNESCO project which aims at promoting a culture of peace through multilingual education and respect for linguistic diversity. The concept of Linguapax originated in 1986 in the Ukrainian capital Kiev at an international conference on the contents and methods of foreign language and literature teaching as a contribution to international understanding and peace.

Linguapax's overall objective is to promote the teaching of **MOTHER TONGUES** and of national and foreign languages, and to provide a specific linguistic response to the problems raised by the search for peace, the defence of **HUMAN RIGHTS** and the development of true education for democracy.

The means used to achieve these aims are the identification of new language teaching syllabi based on tolerance and solidarity, and the development of **TEACHER METHODS** integrating the fundamental concepts of cooperation at the international level, while eliminating demeaning **STEREOTYPES** and prejudices. The approach consists in intervening directly, upon request, at the level of the education system's decision-making, executive and supervisory bodies in the following fields:

- **LANGUAGE PLANNING**;
- the preparation of syllabi for the teaching of mother tongues and foreign languages;
- the design, preparation and **EVALUATION** of teaching instruments which reflect these syllabi in the concrete reality of the classroom;
- the training of language and social science teachers assigned responsibility for using these **TEXTBOOKS** in the classroom.

Linguapax is intended primarily for countries in a pre- or post-conflict situation.

### Website

The Linguapax website is: http://www.linguapax-unesco.com

# Linguistic imperialism

The concept of linguistic imperialism (LI) was expounded by Phillipson (1992) in a book with the same title, although the term can be found before this (see, for example, Wolfson, 1989). LI offers an explanation for the continued global predominance of former colonial languages, especially **ENGLISH**. In Phillipson's words, it is 'a particular theory for analysing relations between dominant and dominated cultures, and specifically the way English language learning has been promoted' (1992: 15). He raises a number of questions relating to the use of English as a world language, including the role played by English Language Teaching (ELT) in general and its practitioners and experts. The notion of ideology is also central here, with the implication that the promotion and marketing of the English language is not value-free: it is linked in a variety of ways with the former colonial strength of Britain and in more recent decades the power of the **USA**. As Phillipson puts it, 'whereas Britannia ruled the waves, now it is English which rules them' (1992: 1).

The term could be equally applied to other colonial languages, such as French and **SPANISH**, but the emphasis is on English since this remains 'the international language par excellence' (Phillipson, 1992: 6). Phillipson also refers mostly to the postcolonial context, although we can recognise that policies of 'linguistic imposition have roots which go

further back than recorded history' (Wolfson, 1989: 265). In most historical periods, powerful nations extended their borders usually 'without regard for the rights or desires of the ethnolinguistic groups whose territories they took. Conquest was nearly always followed by some form of linguistic imperialism' (Wolfson, 1989: 265). In **AFRICA** and Southern America, various colonial powers settled and brought with them their own languages as well as territorial and imperialistic aims.

Wolfson points out how this often led to linguistic diversity in the conquered nations, but this view is not shared by those who see LI as a contributory factor in the decline of many languages. In the short term, or in certain cases, the language of the colonising nation or peoples may be an extra language being spoken, but LI describes the negative effects of this. Examples from former historical periods when mass illiteracy was the norm are perhaps not strictly comparable with the contemporary period of post-colonialism when literacy rates are higher and dominant languages such as English are positively marketed and sold. Pennycook (**HISTORY: AFTER 1945**) also points to present trends that are leading to fewer languages being spoken and used in the world but more people studying the dominant ones, especially English.

The undeniable widespread use of English can also be seen in political, economic, scientific and technological fields. People from hundreds of different linguistic communities learn English as a means to further their educational and professional lives as well as for travel and tourism. Why and how this has been a fact of life are central parts of the LI thesis and relate to more than just factors of language. Using straightforward logic, any other language could have become predominant, especially as Britain declined as a colonial power in the post-war period. English can be considered as no better or worse in fulfilling the functions of an international language in simple linguistic terms. When considering newly independent nations, such as in Africa after the demise of the British Empire, an indigenous language could have been specified as the **LINGUA FRANCA** in multilingual, multiethnic contexts. Although this was certainly the case in some states, others chose to continue with English even though it was linked to the former state of colonialism.

The rise in popularity of the English language is also seen largely as a result of active promotion through political and economic factors. 'The spread of English has not been left to chance' (Phillipson, 1992: 6). If it had been, then another colonial language may have assumed its predominant position, or indigenous languages may have been promoted more.

It can be said that English was already well positioned in the immediate post-war period due to the extent of the former British Empire which had often imposed the English language. But after this time, ELT became a large and expanding business, supported by academic and linguistic developments and also by governments and their agencies. Related to these were organisations such as the **BRITISH COUNCIL**, to which Phillipson (1992) pays some attention.

Without the LI analysis, it would appear that the transition from imposition to 'market demand' for English has been a naturally occurring one related to its innate properties and the common-sense of foreigners in recognising its inherent value. Phillipson explains, as part of the LI thesis, that this trend is not only part of the prevailing ideology but also relates to hegemony, and he cites Gramsci's work on this point (Phillipson 1992: 8). Ideas and beliefs which may seem common-sense and remain unquestioned are part of hegemonic power, with a dominant group retaining control in this way once they have gained the upper hand. The status quo seems acceptable, and there is no need, when hegemony functions properly, for the dominant group to exert power directly over the people they are subordinating. Gramsci had developed this theory to explain how capitalism persists as a socio-economic and political system in spite of its in-built and often glaringly wide inequalities.

This is not to say that people involved in ELT, such as classroom teachers and trainers, as well as **TEXTBOOK** writers and producers, are involved in some sort of conspiracy, but the ultimate implication would be along those lines. They may be oblivious to or only partly aware of the underlying political and economic imperatives that have created a worldwide, multimillion pound industry. They may have simply concerned themselves more

with the linguistic and literary matters to hand in their professional lives rather than be cognisant of the wider implications that ELT might have had if we accept the LI thesis. Their role in terms of assisting the development of certain political systems, especially Western democratic ones, free-market capitalist practices and associated cultural forms may not have been hidden. Perhaps only in times of crisis have ELT teachers questioned their presence and role in foreign countries. LI does not necessarily criticise such practitioners directly but places them within the realms of the hegemonic power relations that helped to put the English language in a key position. In one sense, they can be seen as 'pawns' in the game, purveying their unquestioning attitude in exchange for a job abroad and a chance to travel.

The idea of the new post-colonial imperialism is backed up by analogies made by a variety of commentators. 'Once we used to send gunboats and diplomats abroad; now we are sending English teachers' (International House brochure, 1979, cited in Phillipson, 1992: 80). Overall, there is an attempt to link the previous militaristic and political force of the British Empire with a new one, which supports the spread of the English language and its links with certain cultural forms and political processes. The new 'foot soldiers' in this push are ELT practitioners.

The rush to expand ELT in former African colonies as well as the Far East can be cited as part of the linguistic imperialist drive in the period from the 1950s to the 1980s. In more recent times, the overthrow of communism in Eastern and Central Europe has opened up new areas. One aim, according to the incumbent British Foreign Secretary in 1990, was to replace Russian with English as the second language throughout the region (Phillipson, 1992: 10). In line with this, many resources were placed in these countries in the immediate aftermath of the Cold War, and the region appeared as a priority. An unstated premise seems to be that if people speak and read English they become part of the wider democratic, capitalist Western community, and that language can somehow bind them into certain processes and structures in ways superior to former colonial ruling practices.

Whilst there are many uses of this thesis, especially in the way in which it brings together historical events and trends with linguistic ones, it has been heavily criticised. Davies attacks what he sees as two inherent 'cultures' of LI which relate, first, to 'guilt' over imperialism and colonialism and, second, to 'romantic despair', with an unstated desire to allow peoples to return to their 'innocence' (Davies, 1996: 485). He analyses some of the key constituent features of LI, particularly in terms of why English became so dominant. The first 'why' is that, in Phillipson's account, English actively promotes the foreign policies of the major English speaking states. Davies counters this by saying that most countries do this in various ways and it is not such a conspiracy after all. The second 'why' relates to the critique of foreign aid being linked to language and that, ultimately, aid may assist the donors more than the recipients. Davies points out that it is 'unremarkable' that aid is linked to demands for the purchase of donor countries' goods, although it would be 'uplifting' if this were not the case (1996: 487).

The third reason is related to 'the ideology transmitted with, in and through the English language' (Davies 1996: 487), as well as those involved in this, such as the teachers already mentioned above. The problems of employing Gramsci's notion of hegemonic power leave almost no room for contradictory arguments, let alone free choice, by the former colonised nations who have taken English as their main language. Davies points out that, in many such nations, there are indigenous inequalities and languages and the imposition of a local language, such as that of an elite group, could also be viewed as hegemonic. This is not to say that this should not be a valid option, but neither is it to support the view that many of the linguistic developments in the post-colonial period, particularly in the Third World, have been about the move from direct to indirect imposition of the English language, as the LI thesis implies. It devalues the notion of free choice by these nation states, and LI's use of ideology in this way can be viewed as yet another form of colonial patronage.

In a development of the thesis, Canagarajah (1999) points out that the macro-political perspective taken by Phillipson overlooks the micro-social processes happening in classrooms. Here, in his ethnographic study of teaching and learning in English classrooms in Sri Lanka, Canagarajah argues that learners 'resist' the impositions of LI and use English to their own ends, either surreptitiously in their responses to the teaching materials imported from the anglophone world, or in ways of writing – of 'writing back', as Pennycook (1994) would call it – to use English for their own purposes. Thus, Canagarajah draws upon critical pedagogy (Giroux, 1983) to argue that resistance is possible and can be developed in a systematic pedagogy.

**See also:** Africa; British Council; Central and Eastern Europe; Communicative language teaching; History: after 1945; India; Intercultural communication; Internationalisation; Lingua franca; Sociolinguistics

### References

Canagarajah, A.S. (1999) *Resisting linguistic imperialism in English teaching*, Oxford: Oxford University Press.

Davies, A. (1996) 'Ironising the myth of linguicism', *Journal of Multilingual and Multicultural Development* 17, 6: 485–96.

Giroux, H.A. (1983) *Critical theory and educational practice*, Victoria: Deakin University.

Pennycook, A. (1994) *The cultural politics of English as an international language*, London: Longman.

Pennycook, A. (this volume) 'History: after 1945'.

Phillipson, R. (1992) *Linguistic imperialism*, Oxford: Oxford University Press.

Wolfson, N. (1989) *Perspectives: sociolinguistics and TESOL*, New York: Newbury House.

### Further reading

Phillipson, R. (1998) 'Globalizing English: are linguistic human rights an alternative to linguistic imperialism?', *Language Sciences* 20, 1: 101–12.

Phillipson, R. and Davies, A. (1997) 'Realities and myths of linguistic imperialism', *Journal of Multilingual and Multicultural Development* 18, 3: 238–48.

RUTH CHERRINGTON

# Linguistic psychodramaturgy (LPD/PDL)

Linguistic psychodramaturgy is an alternative, **HUMANISTIC** method developed for intensive courses with **ADULT** learners as part of a 'pedagogy of being' formulated by Bernard Dufeu of Mainz University. LPD quotes as its main sources J. Moreno's psychodrama and dramaturgic action principles, combining some of their bases and techniques and adapting them to create a framework of settings specifically for foreign language **ACQUISITION**. The LPD approach emphasises an individualised learning process within a group. A coherent technical framework of **EXERCISES** allows the linguistic content to be left open to each participant's personal wishes for expression in a real or imaginary context. Instead of imposing a pre-selected programme of topics, structures and lexical items for study, the language trainers react to the learners' immediate individual **NEEDS**.

## Pedagogy of being

In 1977 Bernard Dufeu, a French language teacher and phonetician, took part with his wife Marie Dufeu in a two-week experiment with '*Expression Spontanée*', conducted by W. Urbain at Mainz University. This marks the beginning of their work at LPD. Since then the Dufeus have been developing and constantly refining the LPD method, also enlarging its scope to describe a complete pedagogical approach.

Going back to the basic view of human beings that seems also to determine ideas on the teaching, acquisition and learning process, Dufeu opposes the prevalent 'pedagogy of having' with his 'pedagogy of being'. In traditional teaching contexts, he argues, language learners experience a twofold alienation: they are supposed to communicate in a language which is alien to them with words that are not their own since they have been pre-determined by someone else, as have the topics to be discussed, too. The learners have no choice other than to follow the route which has been pre-selected by **TEXTBOOK** authors and language teachers – irrespective of whether or not it fits the individual and his or her specific needs and

wishes for expression at the given time. The language being studied is seen as knowledge to be transferred or transmitted to the learner, usually in two stages: learning *about* the language first, then trying to communicate in it.

In contrast, Dufeu views the **ACQUISITION** of a new language as a process of personal development which cannot be separated from the participants' lives:

Acquiring a language cannot be dissociated from the individual who is its subject. We cannot behave as though we were simply transferring content, and leave the participant's personality to one side on the pretext that he or she is 'in a learning situation'. What we do as teachers has an impact on the participants and therefore on their learning.

(Dufeu, 1994: 12)

The role of the teachers, traditionally hierarchical in nature in the teaching contexts described above, is dramatically different in LPD in that it reverses certain responsibilities in the teaching–learning process: it is not the learners' responsibility to understand the teachers' explanations and to reproduce correctly what they want them to say, but the trainers' task to empathise with the participants and thus help them to express themselves. In the absence of a textbook or a predetermined programme, the trainers create a framework of open exercises that allow the participants to experience the language directly in **AUTHENTIC** use. The goals of this kind of pedagogical action are not defined in terms of mastering certain linguistic structures but in enabling the participants to situate themselves in the context of a real encounter within the group, by offering and enlarging on whatever linguistic means the participants need for their ends at the given time ('pedagogy of proposition' versus 'pedagogy of imposition'; 'pedagogy of encounter and relationship'). Through authentic communication, participants thus acquire the language, rather than 'study' it.

The scope of the LPD approach to language teaching is expressed in Dufeu's determination of goals:

- 'Deep-level goals', aimed at developing behavioural **ATTITUDES** like receptivity and expressiveness.

- 'Surface goals', comprising the prosodic, structural, lexical, functional and **INTERCULTURAL** components of the target language.

## Setting and structure of an LPD seminar

LPD is intended for **BEGINNERS** as well as for advanced learners, with its techniques being adapted to each level. Originally, LPD seminars were designed as intensive courses with between three and six hours per day over one or several weeks or weekends, and involved a maximum of twelve to fourteen participants and two trainers. Subsequently, settings with one trainer have gradually been developed, mainly for reasons of practicability, even though the classical design is still considered ideal, due to the carefully tuned coherence of its activities which has proved highly efficient. Nevertheless, most activities can easily be transferred to different contexts. Work usually takes place on the floor allowing participants to determine their spatial needs freely in relation to the group but also for practical reasons in the course of the activities.

Typically an LPD day starts with a *relaxation exercise* which functions as a separation from the outside world, allows for a little private time to become aware of oneself before coming into contact with others, and stimulates receptivity on the sensorial and consequently also the emotional and intellectual levels. It also supports retention and, within the LPD system, provides the first pleasant contact with the new language, giving participants, together with instructions for the exercises, a core of lexical items as one of the starting points for their first steps in the foreign language through the 'sandwich method' (target language – first language **TRANSLATION** – target language). Next follows a *'warm-up' exercise*, usually some group activity which prepares the participants for the *'main exercises'* in which – only during the first three days – they work individually with the trainers. After two or three main exercises in which the trainers offer 'custom-made' language to one individual, *'intermediate exercises'* provide a dynamic element involving the whole group in activities which concentrate on the language's rhythm and melody. In later stages (after at least

one week of seminar work) mainly dramaturgically-based activities are used involving participants on an imaginary level as well as in real-life situations.

## Progression and comprehension

At the beginning of the acquisition process progression is mainly *relational*, not structural; in other words, activities of the first stage are directed towards an individual, then towards a meeting of two persons, subsequently towards the group as a whole and, later on, to the 'outside world' (see Figure 8).

In LPD the act of comprehension is directed more towards the person than the language, and stems from the empathetic relationship between trainers and participants on the one hand, and the close relationship between the language and the situation experienced in the here and now on the other: 'understanding the meaning of the message is easier because participants are experiencing its context' (Dufeu, 1994: 48). The intuitive, deductive approach to meaning, and consequently to structural and functional linguistic rules, means LPD learning is an 'acquisition process' rather than a 'learning process'. Concerning grammatical rules, trainers again try to react to demand, completing the participants' intuitive knowledge when asked or sometimes where considered necessary.

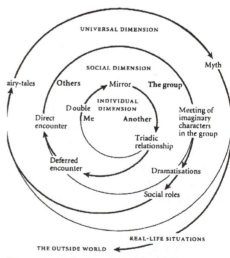

Figure 8   Spiral evolution in LPD

## Future developments

LPD, so far applied in Germany, Austria, **FRANCE**, Italy, Switzerland, Croatia and Turkey, is most widely used in **ADULT** education. Many trainers, however, have used certain techniques in school contexts and different versions of settings (e.g. for toddlers) are being developed.

**ASSESSMENT**

The reservations that some people have about LPD before they attend a seminar go back to misunderstandings concerning its psychodrama origins. Some people are afraid of receiving therapeutic treatment. Even though the authors of the method clearly recommend that trainers undergo some form of 'self awareness and human relations training' to be better prepared for the more intensive relational work, the method is quite obviously only pedagogically oriented. Many participants miss 'LPD-compatible' **SELF-ACCESS** study **MATERIALS** to bridge the gap between intensive workshops – a field for future work. LPD poses a challenge to many language teachers who are used to traditional teaching theories and practices, and it places heavy demands on the trainers' flexibility and their creative and spontaneous command of the target language. A truly person-centred approach, following LPD principles means renouncing the well-trodden paths of teacher-controlled, pre-determined processes and instead taking the role of companion on each individual learner's exciting journey into the language.

**See also:** Acquisition and teaching; Drama; Humanistic language teaching; Motivation; Neuro-linguistic programming; Silent Way; Suggestopedia; Teacher thinking; Teaching methods

## References

Dufeu, B. (1992) *Sur les chemins d'une pédagogie de l'être* (On the path to a pedagogy of being), Mainz: Editions Psychodramaturgie.
Dufeu, B. (1994) *Teaching myself*, Oxford: Oxford University Press.
Dufeu, B. (1996) *Les approches non conventionelles* (Unconventional approaches), Paris: Hachette.

Dufeu, B. (1999a) 'Les hypothèses fondamentales de la psychodramaturgie linguistique' (Fundamental hypotheses of linguistic psychodramaturgy), *Le Français dans le Monde – Recherche et Application* Apprendre les langues étrangères autrement, Janvier 1999: 112–24.
Dufeu, B. (in preparation) *Wege einer Pädagogik des Seins* (Paths to a pedagogy of being), Mainz: Editions Psychodramaturgie.

## Further reading

Moreno, J.L. (1953) *Who shall survive?* New York: Beacon.
Moreno, J.L. (1970) *Fondements de la sociométrie* (Fundamentals of sociometry), Paris: PUF.
Moreno, J.L. (1973) *The Theater of Spontaneity*, New York: Beacon.

MARTINA HUBER-KRIEGLER

# Linguistics

The use of teaching material is the distinguishing feature of language teaching as compared to **UN-TUTORED LANGUAGE ACQUISITION**. The writing of teaching material requires linguistic information from phonetics/phonology, **LEXICOLOGY** and semantics, **STYLISTICS** and idiom theory, syntax, **TEXT LINGUISTICS** and **CONVERSATION ANALYSIS**. Contrary to theoretical linguistics, this information must be rendered in a performance-oriented way, as the substance of procedural, not declarative knowledge, and coordinated with psychological and psycholinguistic information, with a didactic selection and marking of topics and with a consideration of the external conditions of classroom management. The resulting store of knowledge in **APPLIED LINGUISTICS** makes use of the achievements of traditional as well as of recent linguistics.

## Traditional and recent linguistics

'Linguistics' is a rather recent name for the scientific discipline whose representatives are concerned with the description and analysis of language in general and of national languages/dialects in particular. Unfortunately, the adjectival version of the term is ambiguous. It refers to 'language' in the more common sense (e.g. *linguistic atlas* = 'map showing the geographical distribution of languages') and also to the scientific methods of the academic discipline in its most recent version (e.g. *linguistic analysis* = analysis according to the methods of contemporary linguistics'). The meanings must be kept apart and properly understood. The OED Supplement gives as the first source for *linguistics* 'Webster 1847,' and then dates and names only from the twentieth century.

However, thinking about language has been a traditional element of European culture since the Classical Greek period (Lepschy, 1994). It covered themes which are today obsolete (e.g. 'the perfection of languages' or 'universal languages'), themes which are still topical today but not in the ancient contexts (e.g. 'the origin of languages' or 'the dependence of thinking on language'), and finally themes which enjoy an unbroken interest (e.g. grammar or style). As historical topics, they are usually called 'linguistic' in the more common sense of the word, e.g. in 'the history of linguistic ideas' or 'the history of linguistics' (Robins, 1990).

It is only since the end of World War Two that the narrower meaning of 'linguistics' has come into use. In the Anglo-Saxon and anglophone world, the seminal works for this development were Ferdinand de **SAUSSURE**'s *Cours de linguistique général* (1916) and Leonard **BLOOMFIELD**'s *Language* (1933). The paradigmatic features which evolved in the wake of these two books, after approximately 1950, and which at first were named '**STRUCTURAL LINGUISTICS**' – a term which has become somewhat archaic in the meantime – constituted a new disciplinary coherence and attracted the new meaning of the old name. This development was reinforced by the foundation of university chairs and institutes devoted to linguistics, and of journals, learned societies, etc., i.e. measures which give an academic discipline its institutional framework.

The focus of this new linguistics was at first on such features as syntax and structural semantics, but then widened more and more to include aspects of language use. Many of the traditional linguistic topics were resurrected in those branches of linguistics characteristically named with a qualifier, e.g. anthropological linguistics, psycholinguistics, **SOCIOLINGUISTICS**, ethnolinguistics, etc.

Only the term 'phonetics' was not drawn into this whirlpool of naming but, complemented with 'phonology', kept its stable meaning in the past and the present.

At first sight, it seems obvious that linguistics is the proper source discipline for language teaching. What else should be required for this activity other than a description and analysis of the teaching subject? However, the differentiations of the meanings of the lexeme 'linguistic(s)' already show that things are more complicated than that. A short summary of the writing of grammars, certainly a focal area of linguistics at any time, will show this.

It began with the *Techné grammatiké* of Dionysius Thrax (?170 BC–?90 BC) which established a century-long tradition expressing itself, above all, in a tightly knit set of grammatical terms (Michael, 1970; Padley, 1976). They dominated the teaching of Latin via Donatus (fourth cent. AD) and Priscian (sixth cent. AD) through the entire Middle Ages. At the beginning of the sixteenth century, an interest in vernaculars arose in Europe (Padley, 1985 and 1988). William Bullokar (?1520–90), for example, was the first to write a grammar of **ENGLISH** still entirely under the spell of Latin categories, as many grammarians after him would be, even if they intended to move away from them, as John Wallis (1616–1703) did. Since then there has been a continuous stream of grammars of English (and of all other European vernaculars in the respective countries) to the present day (Göbels, 1999). All too often the fact has been ignored that most authors of this century-long tradition saw themselves in a didactic context, first the teaching of Latin and then the teaching of English, mostly but not only as a foreign language. Most grammars which we today think to be landmarks of European grammatography were written as schoolbooks. This was also the case when the dominant works of Robert Lowth (1710–87, *A short introduction to English grammar with critical notes*, 1762) and Lindley Murray (1745–1826, *English grammar*, 1795, and *English exercises*, 1797) appeared, whose normative attitude established a direct connection between language description and norm-bound teaching. Between 1801 and 1900, no less than 856 grammars followed the two giants onto the market (Michael, 1991). They completed the move away from the Latin categories of description which centred around word-classes and inflectional paradigms, and favoured a phrase-and-clause approach, thus preparing the way for the generally accepted grammatical approach of today. Authors who did not write for the classroom were by far in the minority. Although Francis Bacon (1561–1616) had already spoken of a 'philosophical' and a 'literary' grammar – the one for the analysis of thinking, the other for learning a language – the difference between a 'practical' and a 'scientific' grammar hardly existed, although there were certainly works which proved more useful in one or the other role.

Leaving aside grammars on diachronic principles, like Otto **JESPERSEN**'s (1860–1943) seven-volume work, the dichotomy 'scientific versus practical' appeared sharply only with the methods of modern linguistics in the second half of the twentieth century. Now the conception and drafting of grammars grew into a highly abstract and formalised discipline with universalist but not with descriptive ambitions. A model-driven analytical way of treating language in general appeared, although mostly exemplified by English – at present the best-analysed language in the world. Its overriding aim is to make the system (or systems) of any language visible on its various levels, i.e. a philosophical grammar in Bacon's terminology.

Even where this is not the case, as in Quirk *et al.*'s descriptive *Comprehensive Grammar of the English Language* (1985), the systematic treatment of the English language grew to such a size that an adaptation for teaching purposes could only be done by much curtailing.

## Teaching material and linguistics

As a rule, the teaching of languages is done under formal conditions as they prevail in a classroom, in the presence of a teacher and with the use of teaching material. This represents the essential difference from what is called informal (or natural) language acquisition, which children undergo in and after their second year of life. There are so-called alternative **TEACHER METHODS**, e.g. **SUGGESTOPEDIA**, which avoid the conditions and routines of formal teaching, but measured against the general trend of language teaching they are exceptional.

Classroom procedures (e.g. **QUESTIONING TECHNIQUES** with exchanges frequently truncated by error correction) are just as alien to baby talk as information on the language to be learnt with the help of teaching material is. These aids appear in various kinds and sizes, as printed books and as audio-visual or computer-aided media (for **CALL – COMPUTER ASSISTED LANGUAGE LEARNING**), as integrated works, or as a set of specialised sources of information which complement each other. Irrespective of these differences, the aids for language teaching fulfil certain functions which are ultimately dictated by the nature of the language to be taught. Functionally, they consist of what used to be (and still is) a **TEXTBOOK**, a **GRAMMAR** and a **DICTIONARY**.

It is the function of textbooks to show the foreign language, above all, in written (printed) performance. Contrary to acoustic media, their opportunities of doing the same with oral performance are rather limited, yet they exist. The acoustic media are frequently added to the printed book. 'Showing the language' includes information on spelling and pronunciation (via phonetic script in the book, directly in the acoustic medium), information on style and idioms, and on the format of written as well as of spoken texts, e.g. letters or conversations. Of course, 'showing the language' also pertains to grammar and lexis, but both of these have their own text-independent order. Grammars (as books) give the rules of grammars (as structures) in their own system as a set of descriptive and normative statements, and frequently also examples. Information on style and idiomatic language use can be added by special rules or by the exemption from rules altogether. Dictionaries, finally, make lexis available, mostly – but not always – ordered according to the alphabet. This regularly includes information on spelling and meaning, and can include information on pronunciation, the grammatical behaviour of words, and special restrictions on use. In addition to the teaching aids, there is usually **EXERCISE** material of various types which serves potentially all the functions mentioned.

Obviously, the following subdisciplines of linguistics pertain to language teaching with the material used in the classroom:

- phonetics/phonology for the teaching of **PRO-NUNCIATION** and also, to a limited extent, of spelling;
- lexicology and semantics for the teaching of lexis;
- stylistics and idiom theory for the teaching of language performance;
- syntax for the teaching of grammar;
- text linguistics and conversation analysis for the teaching of text production and text reception.

All this linguistic information is regarded as being the substance of language teaching. But it is not intended that this substance be taught as such, i.e. as a corpus of statements and norms on a linguistic metalevel, but rather as the stimulation of the mechanism of mental decisions which we must make in correct language use, be it productive (**SPEAKING**, **WRITING**) or receptive (**LISTENING**, **READING**). This is the difference between what is usually called 'declarative knowledge' (know how) and 'procedural knowledge' (know that). The former is a store of descriptive statements on linguistic regularities, i.e. of rules, retrievable for application in language performance. The latter is the ability to produce or to understand these regularities without resorting to the rules (Anderson, 1990; Glover *et al.*, 1990). It is the common assumption of language teaching theory that, whereas children arrive at procedural knowledge without any declarative rule-formation, foreign language learners in the classroom cannot do without a certain amount of it, which will gradually be turned into the procedural faculty (Hüllen, 1987). It is the main function of the exercise material and also of language practice in the classroom without any printed or acoustic aids to achieve this goal.

## Applied linguistics

Those areas of traditional and recent linguistics which are a prerequisite for the writing of teaching material are usually called 'applied linguistics'. The term repeats the differentiation between theory and application as is to be found in many scientific disciplines, e.g. mathematics, musicology, the law, but also inside linguistics, e.g. lexicology (as opposed to lexicography), stylistics (theory versus practice), etc.

Seen against a universal theory of language and language use, the description of an individual language/dialect can be regarded as a first degree of application. Thus, a grammar of English, even if not planned as a teaching grammar, is an application of a set of theoretical presuppositions to one special case. However, as a theory of language can hardly ever be thought of without reference to languages, it seems feasible to define 'theoretical' (or 'pure') linguistics as embracing the categorial groundwork of the discipline as well as the description of a language, as long as the focus is on the language itself. In contrast, teaching **MATERIALS** are a true case of the application of linguistic insights to an area of interest which lies outside the language proper. It goes without saying that there are also such areas of interest outside the didactic one, like language acquisition, **TRANSLATION**, computer use, neurological applications, etc. The applicative transposition which leads from 'linguistics' to 'applied linguistics in a didactic perspective' is quite complex.

First, without any didactic perspective, linguistic information tends to be organised in modules of which there are simple ones (e.g. sounds, word-formation, linear order, or meanings corresponding to phonetics, morphology, syntax, or semantics) and complex ones (e.g. style and text-formats corresponding to stylistics and text linguistics). From a didactic perspective, however, linguistic information must be organised in a performance-oriented way. The difference between the one and the other is that the modular organisation of rules dissolves and rearranges itself in such a way that all modules become concomitant specialised parts of even the smallest utterance (Spillner, 1995).

Second, without any didactic perspective, performance-oriented linguistic information tends to appear as the contents of declarative knowledge. From a performance oriented, didactic perspective, however, linguistic knowledge, which is a stative aspect of the human mind, also dissolves and rearranges itself in such a way that all statements become concomitant specialised parts of even the smallest mental activity.

Third, the didactic perspective also comprises the learning aspect, i.e. the distance between 'not being able to' and 'being able to' with its many transitional phases (e.g. **INTERLANGUAGES**) in between. This entails an interdisciplinary matching of psychological knowledge about the nature of learning in general and of psycholinguistic knowledge about the nature of language learning in particular with the linguistic facts.

Fourth, it also entails a special selection and marking of the linguistic information available. There are insights which are too abstract or too subtle to be of interest to the average language learner. There are also insights which are too elementary to be of interest, because learners need not be taught how to speak. Didactic marking of linguistic insights also pertains to contrastive phenomena. Although the far-reaching expectations which were once attached to **CONTRASTIVE** linguistics have never been fulfilled, it is beyond doubt that the processes of learning a new language are inevitably influenced by the linguistic **COMPETENCE** already existing in the mind.

Fifth, and last, teaching under the formal conditions of classroom management is bound to the circumstances of time and place and to the availability of resources which are external to the phenomena of language and language learning and which, nevertheless, have their impact on the organisation of any sort of material.

It is probably futile to question whether applied linguistics is an academic discipline in its own right with its own subject, method, terms, aims (etc.) of investigation. Such (ultimately Cartesian) criteria are obviously hardly applicable to a field of scientific work between pure theory and the knowledge-driven activities in a classroom. The investigative principles of the disciplines which pool their stocks of knowledge in applied linguistics are too divergent ever to be unified in the strict sense. In fact, 'applied linguistics' is so unlike 'linguistics' in many respects that one could think of a separate name, like *Fremdsprachenforschung* or **FREMDSPRA- CHENDIDAKTIK** in German.

More important than naming is the fact that the integrative work which leads to applied linguistics is never a one-way process. Developments as they occurred in recent psycholinguistics or sociolinguistics, for example, should be taken into account, but they are not *per se* applicable to language teaching (Honey, 1997). New linguistic findings,

like those of **SPEECH ACT THEORY**, can, of course, initiate the reformulation of teaching aims; but teaching aims *per se* select and highlight certain linguistic phenomena and neglect others. Rules of **PEDAGOGICAL GRAMMARS** are certainly often the calques of rules which also appear in theoretical treatments of a language. But the twenty-five 'verb-patterns' in the preface of A.S. **HORNBY**'s *Advanced Learner's Dictionary of Current English* (1948), one-sidedly drawn from his experience of teaching English in **JAPAN**, antedated the later 'pattern practice' in the wake of structuralism by at least two decades. Far from being a one-way procedure, applied linguistics from the perspective of language teaching is like the demarcation of a domain from various directions where those involved need to be convinced that they must make every effort if they are to meet at all.

One consequence of all this is that, for example, grammars as teaching material show the same difference to linguistic grammars as applied linguistics does to theoretical linguistics. In fact these grammars work with a basic stock of terms (noun, verb, adjective, etc.) which is quite traditional and not too far removed from Latin grammar. Moreover, they employ a basic knowledge of phrases and clauses as sentence constituents in coordination or subordination as it evolved in the nineteenth century. From the more recent models it is only the central procedures, like segmentation, substitution, transposition, transformation, deletion and others, which are made use of mostly in the ways of presenting linguistic material in schoolbooks. Many attempts at using terms and more subtle arguments from recent linguistics were aborted as ineffective. This, however, does not preclude general approaches of very recent linguistic analysis from having a profiling effect on teaching. The so-called '**NOTIONS AND FUNCTIONS** approach', for example, was certainly stimulated by the shift from purely formal to more semantic models of explanations which occurred in the early 1970s. The mutual influences between theory and practice need not be systematic.

It is a prerequisite for the authors of teaching material of any kind that they be knowledgeable about the contents of and the interrelations between linguistics and applied linguistics, and that they have a good deal of practice in teaching itself. Moreover, it is highly advisable that teachers of foreign languages share this knowledge, at least to a certain extent, so that they need not blindly follow the teaching material, which after all is also a product of the market, but so that they can make their own decisions about the work in the classroom.

**See also:** Applied linguistics; Communicative language teaching; Grammar; Lexicography and lexicology; Notions and functions; Pedagogical grammar; Sociolinguistics; Speech act theory; Text and corpus linguistics

### References

Anderson, J.R. (1990) *Cognitive psychology and its implications* (3rd edn), New York: Freeman.

Glover, J.A., Ronning, R.R. and Bruning, R.H. (1990) *Cognitive psychology for teachers*, New York: Macmillan.

Göbels, A. (1999) *Die Tradition der Universalgrammatik im England des 17. und 18. Jahrhunderts (The tradition of universal grammar in 17th- and 18th-century England)*, Münster: Nodus.

Honey, J. (1997) *Language is power. The story of Standard English and its enemies*, London: Faber and Faber.

Hüllen, W. (1987) *Englisch als Fremdsprache (English as a foreign language)*, Tübingen: Francke.

Lepschy, G. (1994) *History of Linguistics*, 5 vols, London: Longman.

Michael, I. (1970) *English grammatical categories and the tradition to 1800*, Cambridge: Cambridge University Press.

Michael, I. (1991) 'More than enough English grammars', in G. Leitner (ed.), *English traditional grammars. An international perspective*, Amsterdam: Benjamins.

Padley, G.A. (1976, 1985, 1988) *Grammatical theory in Western Europe 1500–1700. The Latin tradition*, Cambridge: Cambridge University Press.

Quirk, R., Greenbaum, S., Leech, G. and Svartvik, J. (1985) *Comprehensive grammar of the English language*, London: Longman.

Robins, R.H. (1990) *A short history of linguistics*, London: Longman.

Spillner, B. (1995) 'Angewandte Linguistik (Applied linguistics)', in K.R. Bausch, H. Christ, W. Hüllen and H.J. Krumm (eds), *Handbuch Fremdsprachenunterricht (Handbook of foreign language teaching)* (3rd edn), Tübingen: Francke.

### Further reading

Caravolas, J.-A. (1994) *La didactique des langues. Précis d'histoire I: 1450–1700 (Teaching languages. Conspectus of history I: 1450–1700)*, Montreal: Les Presses de l'Université/Tübingen: Narr.

Caravolas, J.-A. (1994) *La didactique des langues. Anthologie I. À l'ombre de Quintilien (Teaching languages. Anthology I. In the shadow of Qulitilien)*, Montreal: Les Presses de l'Université/Tübingen: Narr.

Howatt, A.P.R. (1984) *The history of English language teaching*, Oxford: Oxford University Press.

Hüllen, W. (1976) *Linguistik und Englischunterricht 1 [and] 2 (Linguistics and the teaching of English 1 and 2)* (3rd edn), Heidelberg: Quelle and Meyer.

Kelly, L.G. (1969) *25 centuries of language teaching*, Rowley, MA: Newbury House.

Mackey, W.F. (1965) *Language teaching analysis*, London: Longman.

Sebeok, T.S. (ed.) (1975) *Current trends in linguistics. Vol. 13: History of linguistics*, The Hague and Paris: Mouton.

WERNER HÜLLEN

# Linguistique appliquée

Linguistics applied to language teaching (*linguistique appliquée*) began in **FRANCE** in the 1950s, influenced by work in North America. What is peculiar to France is the emphasis on one's own language taught as a foreign language and, from the 1970s, on creating an approach to language teaching (*DIDACTIQUE DES LANGUES*) which is not subordinate to **LINGUISTICS**. From the end of the 1980s, language teaching has drawn upon different disciplines – including linguistics – to define its issues and the term '*linguistique appliquée*' is now part of the past.

### From the 1950s to the early 1970s

The late arrival of **APPLIED LINGUISTICS** in France was due to a linguistic tradition which was not influenced from the other side of the Atlantic. French linguists were above all 'French-speaking', and French, together with **GERMAN**, was the most used language in European linguistics until the beginning of the 1950s. Unlike the United States, where linguists were interested in the teaching of foreign languages (German, Russian, Japanese, etc), in France efforts were devoted to the dissemination of the national language, **FRENCH**, abroad. It was French as a Foreign Language (abbreviated to FLE in the 1980s) which was a driving force in the development of methodologies and which was at the heart of applications of linguistics.

The development of *Linguistique appliquée* was linked to the policies put into place by France to renew its linguistic and cultural work after World War Two. The dissemination of French abroad was one of the key instruments of a policy whose aim was to re-affirm the position of France in international life. New constituencies were identified: foreign executives and technicians. New aims were defined: to focus on oral practices and to prove that French is a useful language. The efforts were focused primarily on the development of new methods and **TEXTBOOKS** based on data which were carefully selected and analysed. *Le FRANÇAIS FONDAMENTAL*, produced between 1951 and 1954, represents 'the first major work of *linguistique appliquée*', providing a lexis of 1445 words and a basic **GRAMMAR** from statistical studies of ordinary spoken language. This work informed 'Voix et Images de France', an **AUDIO-VISUAL** method produced for FLE which was 'the first product of modern methodology' (Galisson and Coste, 1976: 40). Having been trialled in 1958, this course was used in fifty-eight countries from 1962 and in 161 centres abroad, which demonstrates the extent of the dissemination of FLE. Another element of this French policy was the appearance in 1961 (with the support of the French Ministry of Foreign Affairs) of the first edition of *Le français dans le monde*, a review whose aim was to 'make French language and culture known throughout the world' (editorial of the first edition).

The applications of linguistics to the teaching of FLE, supported by official policies, coincided with a spectacular expansion of linguistics in France in the 1960s. Major reviews were founded: *Langages* in 1966, *Langue française* in 1969. Linguistics domi-nated the human sciences and it was the golden age of *Linguistique appliquée*. This success was evident in numerous ways. The first major centres of teaching and research devoted to French took the designation of *Linguistique appliquée* (Centre de Linguistique appliquée de Besançon, created in 1958; CLAD de Dakar in Senegal, created in 1963); the founding of the journal *Études de linguistique appliquée* in 1962; the first international conference on *Linguistique appliquée* took place in Nancy in 1964, marked by the creation of **AILA** (Association Internationale de Linguistique Appliquée) and of AFLA (Association Française de Linguistique Appliquée) whose presidents, B. Pottier and A. Culioli, were both linguists.

Reflecting the dominance of structuralism, the methods of FLE gave much emphasis to the notion of structure at the beginning of the 1970s. However, the applications of linguistics were different from the American case, as was illustrated by the audio-oral method. France has a particular methodological tradition in language teaching (including the **DIRECT METHOD**). The audio-visual method empha-sised the use of the language in communication situations and the importance of meaning. This led to criticism of the batteries of **EXERCISES** which were too focused on the manipulation of forms. Structural exercises were very successful in France but their role was generally limited to the reinforce-ment of constructions worked on in advance in context. Contrastive linguistics was also applied in a more limited way, used above all in the development of phonetic exercises. It was scarcely present in the textbooks produced for FLE in France. These were **MATERIALS** used in a policy of large-scale dissemina-tion throughout the world and had in fact a universalist aim, addressing an international public without distinguishing among their particular linguistic origins.

## The mid-1970s: a period of change

The changes which marked this period were not specific to France. What was in fact noticeable from the 1970s was the **INTERNATIONALISATION** of problems related to language teaching. Thus, in France as in other European countries, work was influenced by American thinking. First came the (belated) discovery of **CHOMSKY** (translated into

French in 1969) and his definition of learning as a creative act of the individual; then there was in 1975–76 the dissemination of the ethnography of communication by Hymes, who introduced the concept of communicative competence at the international level, and of the philosophy of language, with its key notion of the **SPEECH ACT**. It was the work of the psycholinguists (Jakobovits, Rivers and others) which emphasised subjective factors such as **MOTIVATION**, **ATTITUDES** and **STRATEGIES OF LEARNING**. Finally, it is important to take into account an important linguistic current in France, created by discourse linguistics which is interested in questions of meaning and the conditions of production of what is written or said.

Language pedagogy entered a period of change in the middle of the 1970s. What was a pedagogy of teaching gave way to a pedagogy centred on learning, and on the learner. Language teaching distanced itself from linguistics, considered to be too hegemonic, and turned towards other disciplines: sociology, **PSYCHOLOGY**, education and others. The challenge to *Linguistique appliquée* came from FLE specialists trained at institutions such as **CRÉDIF**, BELC (Bureau pour l'Enseignement de Langue et Culture Française) and the Centre International d'Études Pédagogiques de Sèvres, who took over from linguists and tried to take language teaching from under the dominance symbolised by *Linguistique appliquée*.

As a consequence, *Linguistique appliquée* and methodology, which had until then been seen as one, were defined as two complementary disciplines. The role of *Linguistique appliquée* was to help in the selection of linguistic elements for teaching and learning, from a perspective open to cultural and social dimensions. In this approach, the choice of contents was determined by the **NEEDS** of the learner. The new descriptions were developed in the context of the **COUNCIL OF EUROPE**'s **THRESHOLD LEVEL** (1975) and *Un niveau seuil* (1976). Methodology has a role to play at the level of 'how to teach and learn, to whom and why'. Its role was to develop techniques and pedagogical structures adapted to a specific public and its purposes in learning, by borrowing from a pluridisciplinary domain in which linguistics certainly had an important but not exclusive place. The day of direct application had gone; little by

little the languages domain became independent and constituted a discipline in its own right: language didactics (*didactique des langues*). There was in France much interest in sociolinguistic research and work on the varieties and uses of French, both in France and in the wider francophone world. This work stimulated passionate discussions on a very 'French' topic, the norm to be taught and attitudes towards 'local' varieties of French.

## From the end of the 1980s to the 1990s

With the development of research, notably in interactionism and cognitive sciences, two major orientations are characteristic of this period with respect to the relationships between 'language didactics' and 'language sciences', a term which covers linguistics and associated disciplines such as psycho- and sociolinguistics, ethnolinguistics, sociophonetics and others. The first of these involves studies on the acquisition of languages which emphasise the processes and the strategies of learning. The second involves an interactionist perspective which focuses on verbal and **NON-VERBAL** exchanges in the language class. Researchers describe such phenomena as the procedures of the negotiation of meaning, the strategies used to resolve problems of intercomprehension, the ways in which the learner 'grasps' linguistic information in interaction with partners.

The priority in language didactics has become that of seeking to understand better how teaching and learning a foreign language takes place in a given context and situation of learning. The complexity of the task requires interdisciplinary research that brings together, among others, linguists, psychologists, didacticians and specialists in educational technology. Is it, therefore, still possible to talk of *Linguistique appliquée*? In France, *Linguistique appliquée* remains associated with negative connotations (synonymous with dogmatism, with a dependency relationship of language pedagogy) and is scarcely still used. The history of the sometimes difficult relationships between linguistics and didactics is not finished, but from now on it will be as a function of the problems raised by the teaching and learning of languages that linguistics will be involved.

**See also:** Applied linguistics; *Didactique des langues*; France; French; Linguistics; Sociolinguistics; *Sprachlehrforschung*; Teaching methods

## Reference

Galisson, R. and Coste, D. (1976) *Dictionnaire de didactique des langues*, Paris: Hachette.

## Further reading

Coste, D. (1984) *Aspects d'une politique de diffusion de français langue étrangère depuis 1945*, Paris: Hatier.
Puren, C. (1988) *Histoire des méthodologies de l'enseignement des langues*, Paris: Nathan.

GISÈLE HOLTZER

# Listening

Listening involves processing phonetic language information and constructing a message from a stream of sounds, based on listeners' syntactic, phonetic and semantic knowledge of the language. That is, listeners can receive messages conveyed to their ears as sound waves pass through the medium of auditory organs. However, if they do not know the semiotic system of the language, even though a message is conveyed to the brain, listeners cannot decipher the message. Listeners cannot reconstruct speakers' messages and understand the messages until they come to possess a semiotic system like that contained in the speakers' language, with which to communicate mutually. In this way, listening is a very active behaviour, and is quite different from 'hearing', which is the activity of just receiving sound waves.

## Linguistic structures

The factors of which listening is composed include a knowledge of linguistic structures (syntactic structure, phonetic structure, etc.), prior knowledge, attention and memory. This can be illustrated from **ENGLISH** with respect to linguistic structures. English is an SVO (subject–verb–object) language. This means that, in the case of learners whose first language is an SOV (subject–object–verb) language, their knowledge of SOV word order can interfere with the processing of SVO linguistic information. In the case of learners who acquire a foreign language with a different structure from their **MOTHER TONGUE**, it is very important to have a knowledge of **GRAMMAR** to grasp the syntactic structure more precisely.

Second, when the numbers of vowel and consonant phonemes in a language are different from those of the learners' mother tongue (for example, Japanese has few vowel and consonant phonemes, compared with English), the difficulty in listening is partly caused by the number of phonemes. However, even though learners understand individual sounds, they cannot always pay attention to every sound. The sounds that we hear in **AUTHENTIC** situations are not determined by their presence in individual words, but by the speech which is created when words are connected. Words are individually pronounced differently than when used in speech. In speech, neighbouring sounds affect one another and their phonetic characteristics change. For example, in English there are phonetic phenomena such as liaison, glide, assimilation, the dropping of sounds, and weak forms, which affect pronunciation and therefore recognition of words.

The characteristics of rhythm are also different, depending on the language. In the rhythm of English, there is a tendency for stress to occur almost regularly regardless of the number of weak syllables interposed between other syllables. This is called stress-timed rhythm, and the characteristics of this rhythm are that stress controls time. Such a characteristic in English rhythm is the same as those in **GERMAN** and Russian. On the other hand, the rhythm of syllables that occurs regardless of stress, such as in Japanese, **FRENCH** and Tamil, is called syllable-timed rhythm. Thus, in listening to English, learners whose mother tongue is syllable-timed rhythm must identify linguistic information according to a stressed-timed rhythmic pattern. This difference can cause difficulty for some EFL learners.

Another factor is intonation, which reflects the speaker's mental attitude and is expressed in various forms, depending on the stream of discourse. Intonation, therefore, carries important semantic information and plays an important role in listening comprehension. Learners' understanding of intonation differs, according to their mother tongue. For example, as Ogata (1993) mentions, in the case of learners whose mother tongue, such as Japanese, tends to be constructed of monotonous intonation, it is not easy for them to get used to several kinds of rising intonation, such as in non-monotonous intonation patterns. Ogata gives examples on this point as indicated below:

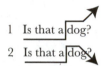

1   Is that a dog?
2   Is that a dog?

In comparing these examples, 1 is more difficult for the Japanese to listen to than 2.

## Prior knowledge

In comprehending speech, listeners compare and collate the speakers' linguistic information with their own structured knowledge, or prior knowledge. The linguistic information that can be collated with prior knowledge is integrated into the listeners' comprehension structures. In other words, those who cannot adapt their prior knowledge easily cannot understand speech properly. For example, when listening to difficult lectures involving complicated language, those listeners who know something about the content of the lecture beforehand and have prior knowledge of the subject find listening comprehension easier. They have existing schemata which help them to organise the information they are hearing and assimilate it to their prior knowledge.

## Attention and memory

In order to process phonetic language information that fades away instantly, much more attention is required than in **READING** comprehension. If listeners do not pay close attention to the speaker's utterance, they grasp only a slight amount of linguistic information, and have to infer the contents of the message just from this. As O'Malley *et al.* mention, 'effective listeners seemed to be aware when they stopped attending and made an effort to redirect their attention to the task' (1989: 428); thus

attention is one of the important factors necessary in order to listen to linguistic information.

There are short-term memory and long-term memory factors in listening comprehension. The former is the memory in which listeners catch and distinguish the speaker's utterance as linguistic information for only a few minutes, as a hypothesis about what is being said. On the other hand, the latter is memory organisation that memorises the content as a final conclusion for a long period of time. There is a rehearsal buffer between the short-term memory and the long-term memory, which utilises all the preconceived knowledge in long-term memory, ruminates on the meaning of the entire input product and transfers this information from the short-term memory to the long-term memory.

The relationship between listening comprehension and memory is complicated. There are some reports that consider the differences in the influence of short-term memory in listening comprehension by **NATIVE SPEAKERS** and non-native speakers. Conrad (1989) found, in work with non-native English speakers of high and medium skill levels listening to recorded sentences at different speaking rates, that non-native speakers tended to ignore information in the middle of sentences and tried to duplicate beginnings or ends of sentences. However, Dunkel *et al.* (1993), working with both native speakers and non-native speakers, presumably at high or advanced level, found that subjects with good short-term memory correctly recognised significant information and detailed information better than subjects with poor short-term memory.

It can be argued that differences of linguistic information processing cause the differences of memory capacity. As Richards (1987) suggests, 'spoken language is generally delivered one clause at a time'. His statement can be juxtaposed with Japanese characteristics in linguistic information processing – i.e. processing incoming discourse word by word; and 'back-to-front reading' (*kaeriyomi* in Japanese means an explication of an English sentence according to Japanese word order) – i.e. generally, from later sections to earlier sections. It is clear that these characteristics limit the quantity of linguistic information which can be processed at one time, which makes short-term memory capacity remarkably limited. As a result of listening to incoming discourse with an insufficient short-term memory capacity, learners come to listen to input separately, word by word, and infer the content of discourse, making it impossible to combine many pieces of information to construct a perfect understanding of the discourse.

As has been mentioned above, there are factors in listening which help in the construction of meaning. We now need to ask how human beings process linguistic information in listening comprehension. One view of the main points is as follows. First, speech conveyed as a wave of sounds makes the eardrum vibrate and is conveyed to the brain. Listeners comprehend the content of speech through the medium of phonetic, grammatical and semantic deciphering. These successive activities are instantly processed in the short-term memory and the processed information is stored there until the reconstruction of all the speech is achieved by integrating the incoming linguistic information. Stored messages are transferred to the long-term memory, coded again, and then stored in the long-term memory. In this way, listening comprehension is a complicated processing of phonetic language information which is influenced by various factors. There are various opinions concerning the mechanism in listening comprehension processing, and the definitive listening processing model has not yet been found. This concept needs further consideration by researchers in the field of listening comprehension processing from multiple perspectives.

The main point at issue in listening comprehension is that learners may decipher phonetic language information only imperfectly, because processing with respect to the syntactic structure is inadequate. If the deciphering is imperfect, it ends up causing trouble when the listener attempts to grasp the information in the message. Therefore, an important point in listening comprehension is how exactly learners grasp the characteristics of syntactic and phonetic structures of the target language, especially each sense group with stress-timed rhythm (Sakuma, 1998).

**See also:** Communicative language teaching; Intercultural communication; Language laboratories; Schema and script theory; Skills and knowledge; Speaking; Teaching methods

## References

Conrad, L. (1989) 'The effects of time-compressed speech on listening comprehension', *Studies in Second Language Acquisition* 11: 1–16.

Dunkel, P., Henning, G. and Chaudron, C. (1993) 'The assessment of a listening comprehension construct: a tentative model for test specifications and development', *Modern Language Journal* 77: 180–91.

Ogata, I. (1993) 'Hiaringu o kouseisuru Youso (Factors constructing listening)', in I. Koike (ed.), *Eigo no Hiaringu to Sono Shidou*, Tokyo: Taishukan Shoten.

O'Malley, J.M., Chamot, A.U. and Kupper, L. (1989) 'Listening comprehension strategies in second language acquisition', *Applied Linguistics* 10: 418–37.

Richards, J.C. (1987) 'Listening comprehension: approach, design, procedure', in M.H. Long and J.C. Richards (eds), *Methodology in TESOL: a book of readings*, New York: Heinle and Heinle.

Sakuma, Y. (1998) 'The role of sense groups in processing linguistic information in EFL listening comprehension', *Kenkyukiyou* 18: 34–47; Hirosaki, Japan: Tohoku English Language Education Society.

## Further reading

Flowerdew, J. (1994) *Academic listening – research perspectives*, New York: Cambridge University Press.

O'Malley, J.M. and Chamot, A.U. (1990) *Learning strategies in second language acquisition*, New York: Cambridge University Press/London: Longman.

Rost, M. (1990) *Listening in language learning*, London: Longman.

Underwood, M. (1989) *Teaching listening*, London: Longman.

Ur, P. (1984) *Teaching listening comprehension*, New York: Cambridge University Press.

YASUYUKI SAKUMA

# Literary texts

The use of literary texts in the foreign language classroom is disputed. Those who are interested in literature argue that literary texts should not simply be used as springboards for foreign language learning. In their opinion, foreign language learning should remain subordinated to the study of literature. For those primarily interested in learning foreign languages, literary texts are unsuitable for several reasons. First, the language of literary texts is not important for mastering practical situations in the foreign culture. Furthermore, the **READING** of literary texts is often class-related and thus presents a disadvantage for lower-class students. Finally, it is not motivating for foreign language learners to have to identify **STYLISTIC** and structural characteristics of literary texts. Yet, is such a critique of literary texts adequate? What is their potential for foreign language learning and education?

### Literary texts in the foreign language classroom

Before turning to the justifications, it might be necessary to say what is meant by literary texts. What is characteristic of them? What distinguishes them from other texts? There are critics who claim that literary texts are marked by a special use of language. Yet others argue that it is impossible to distinguish between literary and non-literary language (see Lott, 1988; Gilroy and Parkinson, 1997). Another attempt to distinguish literary from non-literary texts does not start with the text itself but with our **ATTITUDES** towards it. Sinclair distinguishes between a fictional and a nonfictional attitude. In nonfictional talk we assume 'that the speaker or writer vouches for the accuracy of what he utters, and that he is in a position to do so'. In fictional talk, however, the speaker or writer is free to arrange his or her world. From such a distinction we can infer the following consequences for reading literary texts: 'We are no longer concerned with absorbing and evaluating the individual statements in direct line with our experience, but instead are constantly placing ourselves in direct relation to the events portrayed, identifying with characters, reacting to what happens as if we ourselves might have been involved. We are not evaluating the truth or falsehood of the statements because they are offered to us as not factually relevant' (Sinclair, 1982: 18). We shall see below Rosenblatt's distinction between 'efferent' and

'aesthetic' reading, which is also based not on inherent characteristics of texts but on our attitude towards them.

It is difficult to come up with a general definition of literature if one considers the range of texts – from fables, fairy tales, short stories and poems, to plays and novels – and the various disciplines – **PSYCHOLOGY**, **ANTHROPOLOGY**, **LINGUISTICS**, literary history and literary criticism – which highlight different aspects of literary texts. The definition of what literature is and what it can achieve becomes further complicated when we take the learner's abilities into consideration. In the context of foreign language learning, four ways of justifying the use of literature are important.

### Contribution to foreign language learning

Literary texts in the foreign language classroom must contribute to language learning. Therefore the question of justification seems to be simple. If students enjoy reading literary texts and like to speak and write about them, they are justified. If there are other pedagogical goals involved in reading literature, they are welcome but not necessary. Duff and Maley seem to have such a justification in mind when they write in the introduction to *Literature*: 'The primary aim of our approach is quite simply to use literary texts as a resource ... for stimulating language activities ... What we are interested in is engaging the students interactively with the text, with fellow students, and with the teacher in the performance of tasks involving literary texts' (Duff and Maley, 1990: 5).

If emphasis is placed solely on practical situations such as buying a ticket, ordering a meal, or asking for directions, students will not be sufficiently motivated to learn a foreign language. They need interesting topics to read, write and talk about. Literary texts offer such topics. Yet it is not only the content of literary texts which makes them valuable for foreign language learning but the possibility they offer for developing a variety of tasks which also include creative **WRITING** in various forms. If literary texts play an important role in the foreign language classroom today, it is mainly due to the tasks which have been developed in connection with literary texts for **BEGINNERS** (Ellis and Brewster, 1991; Garvie, 1990) and

Wright, 1995, 1997), beginners and intermediate learners (Morgan and Rinvolucri, 1983) and intermediate and advanced learners (Carter and Long, 1991; Collie and Slater, 1987, 1994; Collie and Porter Ladousse, 1996; Duff and Maley, 1989, 1990; Lach-Newinsky and Seletzky, 1990; Lazar, 1993; and McRae and Boardman, 1984a, 1984b).

## Stylistic analysis of literary texts

Those who argue for a stylistic–linguistic analysis of literary texts question the belief that we learn foreign languages by reading and talking about interesting topics. We must gain an insight into the use of language if we want to improve the learner's 'expressive ability' (Sinclair, 1982: 19). A criticism expressed by Bernard Lott is that the teaching of literature often concentrates on the topics of literary texts and the biographical and historical background knowledge, but does not give a thorough analysis of its language: 'when the text itself is reached it is generally treated in a rather perfunctory way, and its distinctive nature as literature and as a display of language put to special uses, seems often to be lost sight of' (Lott, 1988: 9).

The stylistic analysis of literary texts can unite literary studies and foreign language learning: 'For teachers such methods may result in literature lessons which are also language lessons and language lessons which are almost indistinguishable from the study of literary texts' (Carter, 1982: 50). The stylistic analysis will also increase the learners' **MOTIVATION** because they will enjoy reading literary texts when they become aware of how language is used in them. This insight is an essential presupposition for appreciating literary texts.

Yet critics of the stylistic approach doubt that one will learn a foreign language by analysing the style of literary texts and that a stylistic analysis will be conducive to the learners' enjoyment of literary texts. Gower asserts that stylistic analysis turns the literary text into an object and reduces the distinction between analysis and reading: 'The impression is given of literature as an object, something inert, something you do something with, something that exemplifies the language system, to – well – analyse. What it *isn't*, is something you read and something which has an effect on you' (Gower, 1986: 126). Stylisticians have criticised

literary methods for being arbitrary and subjective. Fish, however, comes to the conclusion that such a critique does not take into account what is 'objectively true', namely that we create meaning in the interaction with the text and that it is therefore necessarily subjective: 'meaning is not the property of a timeless formalism, but something acquired in the context of an activity' (Fish, 1980: 89).

Yet one should not overlook what a stylistic analysis can achieve. It is often combined with the tasks mentioned in the previous section and uses justifications for reading literary texts discussed in the section that follows. Impressive examples of stylistic analysis are **WIDDOWSON**'s *Stylistics and the Teaching of Literature* and *Practical Stylistics: an approach to poetry*. **POETRY** demands from its readers special attention to the language, but this is only the first step in reading; the next one is that readers have 'to find relevance in the way language is textually patterned'. Since they have to 'make poems their own by individual response', the result is a variety of divergent interpretations (see Widdowson, 1992: 56). A variety of aspects which are relevant for teaching literature in the foreign language classroom are covered in the anthology *Literature and Language Teaching*, edited by Brumfit and Carter (1987).

## Aesthetic–pedagogical justifications

One form of justification can be called 'aesthetic–pedagogical' in order to indicate that it is not imposed on literary texts from the outside but is developed from an analysis of the aesthetic experience. Bleich (1975; 1978), Fish (1980), Iser (1987) and many others have described how readers are involved in making sense of the text. Reading as interaction stresses that the reader is not studying or analysing an object while he is reading, but is moving in the text. Sartre (1986) defines reading as 'guided creation' (création dirigée) and points out that readers put their prior experiences as well as their thoughts and feelings at the text's disposal. For Mukařovský and Dewey the literary text is only 'an artefact' or 'an art product' which needs the reader to turn it into an 'aesthetic object' or 'a work of art'. 'Without an act of recreation the object is not perceived as a work of art' (Dewey, 1958: 54; cf. Bredella, 1996). In a similar way, Bakhtin writes: 'One must enter as a creator into what is seen, heard, or pronounced' (Bakhtin, 1990: 305).

With reference to Dewey's aesthetics, Rosenblatt distinguishes between 'aesthetic' and 'efferent' reading. The latter mode directs our attention to the information given in a text. This is an important form of reading, but it ignores our interaction with the text. When we read aesthetically, however, we are attentive to what we experience while we are reading. As already indicated, aesthetic reading is not based on characteristics inherent in the text but on an attitude towards it. Each text can be read 'efferently' or 'aesthetically'. Yet literary texts merit aesthetic reading more than other texts do (see Rosenblatt, 1981). Aesthetic reading is pedagogically significant because it allows the learner to explore the thoughts and feelings elicited by the text. It comprises both involvement and detachment.

For Bruner, literary texts are important because they direct our attention to the 'narrative mode of thought' which is neglected in our culture. This narrative mode is comprised of 'the landscape of action', which includes 'agent, intention or goal, situation, instrument', and 'the landscape of consciousness', which highlights what 'those involved in the action know, think, or feel' (Bruner, 1986: 14). In stories our world is 'subjectivised' because the intentions, feelings and thoughts of the characters become important, and it is 'subjunctivised' because we experience the world from different perspectives so that we can no longer be so sure of what is right and wrong. When we read about the experiences of others, we may also ask ourselves what we might have felt, thought and done in their situation. Therefore the reading of literature can touch the deepest layers of our personality (see Mukařovský, 1979: 75). The emphasis on the significance of the experiences presented in literary texts for the learner's personality is important because texts used in foreign language classrooms are often shallow.

## The significance of literary texts for intercultural understanding

Literary texts are significant for intercultural understanding in a number of ways. They contribute to intercultural understanding because they encourage readers to imagine a world different from their own and to put themselves in the position of others. Being able to see things from the other's perspective comprises two aspects of intercultural understanding: first, we become aware of the relativity of our attitudes, values and world views; and then we transcend them when we extend our sympathies and become aware of the needs, hopes and fears of others.

Intercultural understanding may result in reducing members of the foreign culture to objects when we believe that we know what determines their behaviour. In reality, however, people are neither programmed by their culture nor are they mere products of their cultural condition. They are able to reflect on their situation, distance themselves to some extent from their culture, negotiate contradictory values and find creative solutions to their problems. In the aesthetic experience we regard characters not as objects but as subjects with whom we can identify.

Literary texts produce different readings with different readers. A conversation about such different readings in the foreign language classroom can make learners aware of their prior knowledge, their expectations and the **STEREO-TYPES** they bring to the text. Thus they can become conscious of what guides them in the background, a critical insight essential for intercultural understanding.

Literary texts depict, for example, what it means to be a child, a woman, or a member of a minority, and what it means to be in love or to experience death in the foreign culture. Such an understanding of literary texts opens up a new perspective for the relationship between literary texts and **CULTURAL STUDIES** or *Landeskunde*. Of special significance for **INTERCULTURAL** understanding are post-colonial and minority texts, because these often dramatise intercultural conflicts and reveal causes for misunderstanding and misrecognition of others.

## The reading of literary texts: between guidance and creativity

There are basically three different attitudes readers can take towards a literary text. Readers find meaning in the text (objective paradigm); create it under the guidance of the text (interactive paradigm); or create it according to their own needs (subjective paradigm). These attitudes have far-reaching consequences for determining what a good reader is and what the educational goals of reading are. According to the objective paradigm, the 'good reader' concentrates on what the text is saying and successfully fends off all other obtrusive thoughts and associations. According to the interactive paradigm, good readers activate their prior knowledge, follow associations and connotations, and formulate expectations and hypotheses. Whether prior knowledge, connotations, expectations and hypotheses prove to be misleading or fruitful can only be determined in and after the reading process. At any rate, they cannot be foregone. A text leaves a lot unsaid which the reader has to supplement. Our past experiences are necessary, but they will also be changed in the reading process

Yet both Bleich and Fish have criticised the interactive paradigm for epistemological, psychological and pedagogical reasons. Bleich argues that we should replace it with the subjective paradigm: 'To say that perceptual processes are different in each person is to say that reading is a wholly subjective process and that the nature of what is perceived is determined by the rules of the personality of the perceiver' (Bleich, 1975: 3). We may believe that we have created the meaning under the guidance of the text, but in reality we have created it in accordance with our needs. In a similar way, Fish argues that either everything or nothing is determined in a text, and favours the second possibility (see Fish, 1989). Yet, according to him, it is not the personality of the reader but the interpretive community which determines the meaning of the text. Feminist, Marxist, deconstructionist or other such communities define how a text should be read and what is important in it. For their members it does not matter whether they read a poem by Milton or by Eliot; what matters for them is that their basic presuppositions and interpretive strategies are confirmed. For Fish there are no specific texts: 'the notions of the "same" and "different" texts are fictions' (Fish, 1984: 181). Fish welcomes this freedom of the interpretive community pedagogically and politically because it liberates readers from the authority of the text.

Yet the objective paradigm as well as the subjunctive paradigm are problematic in educational terms. The first one reduces aesthetic reading to efferent reading, and the second one is in danger of becoming solipsistic when learners use literary texts only as a confirmation of their psychological needs and their interpretive strategies.

## Creative, text-based and response-based tasks

Creative tasks are important for improving reading competence because they activate the students' prior knowledge, which will help them to become familiar with the topic and to gain criteria for discussing and evaluating it (see Elliott, 1990).Yet they may result in using the text merely as a springboard, which will prevent them from becoming aware of the cultural differences and the specific world view of the text. Collie and Slater have developed a wide variety of creative tasks for Golding's *Lord of the Flies*. One of them is a role play: 'Imagine that on the way home, the Chief Officer decides to investigate what really happened on the island' (Collie and Slater, 1987: 161).

Kramsch criticises this role play because it is based on the assumption that the officer is interested in finding out the truth, whereas the ending of the novel suggests the opposite. The officer is not interested in finding out what happened on the island and is waiting for things to return to their proper order. For Kramsch the main justification for using literary texts in the foreign language classroom is 'literature's ability to represent the particular voice of a writer among the many voices of his or her community and thus to appeal to the particular in the reader'. Yet these creative tasks counteract rather than support such a goal (Kramsch, 1993: 131). Close reading and creative tasks, however, do not exclude each other if learners compare the message of the role play with that of the ending of the novel.

Besides text-based and creative tasks, we must

consider a third category: response-based tasks. It has often been stated that learners do not like poetry. There are several reasons for their dislike, but one is the result of our teaching methodology. Poems are difficult to understand. Their meanings are often considered to be 'elliptical and illusive' (Widdowson, 1992: 11). Yet instead of taking this illusiveness into consideration our methodology explains it away if we come up with only one correct interpretation. If the complex experience of making sense is not part of the meaning of the poem, then learners often feel frustrated and wonder why the poet did not tell them directly what he or she wanted to say. Another problematic approach is to ask learners what they think of the poem after the first reading. They need time to respond. Therefore Benton *et al.* (1988) invited learners to read a poem several times and make a note of associations and comments in each reading. In a next step they asked the students to talk about their 'story of reading'. From such a perspective the experience of making sense is no longer ignored but becomes part of the meaning of the poem.

Hirvela proceeds in a similar way. With reference to *This is just to say* by William Carlos Williams, he suggests the following questions: 'As you moved from one reading of the poem to another, how did your approach to reading it change? What did you do differently? And what did these changes in approach contribute to your understanding of the poem?' (Hirvela, 1996: 133). Hirvela rejects text-based tasks because they reduce aesthetic reading to efferent reading. We should no longer pay attention to 'the author's text' – this turns reading into 'a passive activity' – but regard only 'the reader's text' (Hirvela, 1996: 130). However, his approach is one-sided, for we must be attentive to the particularity of the author's text *and* to our responses to it. An important text-based question could be: How would you describe the relationship between the speaker and the person addressed? Hirvela separates what is related. Rosenblatt distinguishes between 'evocation' and 'response', and illustrates them with the following example: 'In our transaction with Dickens's text *Great Expectations*, we, for example, evoke the character of Pip and Joe. We participate in their relationship and at the same time we respond with approval or disapproval to their words and actions'

(Rosenblatt, 1985: 39). If we no longer considered the author's text but only the reader's, we would turn the interactive paradigm into the subjective paradigm with its problematic pedagogical implications.

Literary texts in the foreign language classroom are not only important for foreign language learning but also provide it with significant educational goals.

**See also:** Cultural studies; Drama; Literary theory; Literary texts and intercultural understanding; Poetry; Reading; Reading methods; Syllabus and curriculum design

### References

Bakhtin, M. (1990) *Art and answerability. Early philosophical essays by M.M. Bakhtin*, Austin: University of Texas Press.

Benton, M., Teasy, J., Bill, R. and Hurst, K. (1988) *Young readers responding to poems*, London and New York: Routledge.

Bleich, D. (1975) *Readings and feelings. An introduction to subjective criticism*, Urbana: National Council of Teachers of English.

Bleich, D. (1978) *Subjective criticism*, Baltimore and London: Johns Hopkins University Press.

Bredella, L. (1996) 'The anthropological and pedagogical significance of aesthetic reading in the foreign language classroom', in L. Bredella and W. Delanoy (eds), *Challenges of literary texts in the foreign language classroom*, Tübingen: Narr.

Brumfit, C. and Carter, R.(eds) (1987) *Literature and language teaching*, Oxford: Oxford University Press.

Bruner, J. (1986) *Actual minds, possible worlds*, Cambridge, MA and London: Harvard University Press.

Carter, R. (1982) 'Responses to language in poetry', in R. Carter and D. Burton (eds), *Literary text and language study*, London: Arnold.

Carter, R. and Long, M. (1991) *Teaching literature*, New York: Longman.

Collie, J. and Porter Ladousse, G. (1996) *Paths into poetry*, Oxford: Oxford University Press.

Collie, J. and Slater, S. (1987) *Literature in the language classroom. A resource book of ideas and activities*, Cambridge: Cambridge University Press.

Collie, J. and Slater, S. (1994) *Short stories for creative language classrooms*, Cambridge: Cambridge University Press.

Dewey, J. (1958) *Art as experience*, New York: Capricorn.

Duff, A. and Maley, A. (1989) *The inward ear. Poetry in the language classroom*, Cambridge: Cambridge University Press.

Duff, A. and Maley, A. (1990) *Literature*, Oxford: Oxford University Press.

Elliott, R. (1990) 'Encouraging reader-response to literature in ESL situations', *ELT Journal* 44, 3: 191–8.

Ellis, G. and Brewster, J. (eds) (1991) *The storytelling handbook. A guide for primary teachers of English*, London: Penguin.

Fish, S. (1980) *Is there a text in this class? The authority of interpretive communities*, Cambridge, MA: Harvard University Press.

Fish, S. (1984) 'Interpreting the *Variorum*', in J.P. Tompkins (ed.), *Reader-response criticism. From formalism to post-structuralism*, Baltimore and London: Johns Hopkins University Press.

Fish, S. (1989) 'Why no one's afraid of Wolfgang Iser', in S. Fish, *Doing what comes naturally*, Oxford: Clarendon Press.

Garvie, E. (1990) *Story as vehicle. Teaching English to young children*, Clevedon and Philadelphia: Multilingual Matters.

Gilroy, M. and Parkinson, B. (1997) 'Teaching Literature in a Foreign Language', *Language Teaching* 29, 4: 213–25.

Gower, R. (1986) 'Can stylistic analysis help the EFL learner to read literature?' *ELT Journal* 40, 2: 125–30.

Hirvela, A. (1996) 'Reader-response theory and ELT', *ELT Journal* 50, 2, 127–34.

Iser, W. (1987) *The act of reading. A theory of aesthetic response*, Baltimore: Johns Hopkins University Press.

Kramsch, C. (1993) *Context and culture in language teaching*, Oxford: Oxford University Press.

Lach-Newinsky, P. and Seletzky, M. (1990) *Working with poetry*, Bochum: Kamp.

Lazar, G. (1993) *Literature and language teaching. A guide for teachers and trainers*, Cambridge: Cambridge University Press.

Lott, B. (1988) 'Language and literature', *Language Teaching* 21, 1: 1–13.

McRae, J. and Boardman, R. (1984a) *Reading between the lines. Integrated language and literature activities*, Cambridge: Cambridge University Press.

McRae, J. and Boardman, R. (1984b) *Reading between the lines. Integrated language and literature activities*, Teacher's Book, Cambridge: Cambridge University Press.

Morgan, J. and Rinvolucri, M. (1983) *Once upon a time. Using stories in the language classroom*, Cambridge: Cambridge University Press,

Mukařovský, J. (1978) *Structure sign and function: selected essays*, New Haven and London: Yale University Press.

Mukařovský, J. (1979) *Aesthetic function, norm and value as social facts*, trans. and 'Afterword' M.E. Suino: Ann Arbor: University of Michigan Press.

Rorty, R. (1991) *Objectivity, relativism and truth*, Cambridge: Cambridge University Press.

Rorty, R. (1993) 'Human rights, rationality, and sentimentality', in S. Shute and S. Hurley (eds), *On human rights*, New York: Basic Books.

Rosenblatt, L.M. (1981) 'On the aesthetic as the basic model of the reading process', in H.R. Garvin (ed.), *Theories of reading, looking and listening*, Lewisburg: Bucknell University Press.

Rosenblatt, L.M. (1985) 'The transactional theory of the literary work. Implications for research', in C.R. Cooper (ed.), *Researching response to literature and the teaching of literature*, Norwood, NJ: Ablex.

Sartre, J.-P. (1986) *Qu'est-ce la littérature? (What is literature?)*, Paris: Gallimard.

Sinclair, J.McH. (1982) 'The Integration of language and literature in the English curriculum', in R. Carter and D. Burton (eds), *Literary texts and language study*, London: Arnold.

Widdowson, H.G. (1975) *Stylistics and the teaching of literature*, Harlow: Longman.

Widdowson, H.G. (1992) *Practical stylistics: an approach to poetry*, Oxford: Oxford University Press.

Wright, A. (1995) *Storytelling with children*, Oxford: Oxford University Press.

Wright, A. (1997) *Creating stories with children*, Oxford: Oxford University Press.

## Further reading

Bredella, L. and Delanoy, W. (eds) (1996) *Challenges of literary texts in the foreign language classroom*, Tübingen: Narr.

Brumfit, C. and Carter, R. (eds) (1987) *Literature and language teaching*, Oxford: Oxford University Press.

Collie, J. and Slater, S. (1994) *Short stories for creative language classrooms*, Cambridge: Cambridge University Press.

Duff, A. and Maley, A. (1990) *Literature*, Oxford: Oxford University Press.

Kramsch, C. (1993) *Context and culture in language teaching*, Oxford: Oxford University Press.

Widdowson, H.G. (1992) *Practical stylistics: an approach to poetry*, Oxford: Oxford University Press.

LOTHAR BREDELLA

# Literary texts and intercultural understanding

Literary texts from various cultures are read and enjoyed by readers from other cultures. One does not have to be English in order to understand plays, poems and novels by English authors. Literary texts can extend our sympathies, break down **STEREOTYPES** and prejudices and make us sensitive to the needs of others. In Rorty's opinion it is difficult to maintain the belief that others are inferior or inhuman if we see the world from their perspective and experience the fact that they suffer as we do when they are humiliated and treated unjustly. Thus literary texts can promote the respect and recognition of others (see Rorty, 1991: 204ff.; 1993). This general justification – literary texts contribute to intercultural understanding because they encourage us to put ourselves in the place of others and to see things from their perspective – is valid for all literary texts. In addition, certain texts offer more specific justifications than others. There are however some objections to literary texts.

## Stereotypes and other issues

Literary texts, it has been argued, do not break down stereotypes, they confirm them. Even great literary texts such as Shakespeare's *The Tempest*, Defoe's *Robinson Crusoe* and Conrad's *Heart of Darkness* have lately been accused of propagating degrading and contemptible images of Africans and Indians (Achebe, 1978; Bredella, 1996). A further objection says that it is problematic to expect literary texts to inform us about foreign cultures because this leads us to regard behaviours and events which are only meant to be idiosyncratic as typical of the foreign culture. We also have to take into consideration the fact that actions, events, places and entire cultures take on symbolic meaning in literary texts. **NATIVE SPEAKERS** will put them into their proper perspective, whereas foreign-language learners might take them literally (see Echeruo, 1978: 8). Often European novels, for example, use Oriental and African cultures to dramatise European conflicts. **AFRICA**, then, appears as the dark continent without history and culture in contrast to Europe, which stands for history, progress and civilisation. Such representations do not illuminate African cultures, they only indicate Europe's preoccupations. For Chinua Achebe it is an expression of arrogance and ethnocentrism when a whole continent is merely regarded as a stage for European conflicts (see Achebe, 1978: 13). Yet even these texts are important for intercultural understanding because they highlight how we often approach foreign cultures and how we can be made aware of the inherent problems in intercultural understanding. We regard as typical what is only accidental; we project aspects of our culture onto the foreign culture; we construct contrasts between them and us.

## Postcolonial and minority literature

Postcolonial and minority literature often depicts intercultural encounters. In *The Empire Writes Back*, Ashcroft *et al.* emphasise the importance of postcolonial literature for understanding our contemporary world:

More than three quarters of the people living in the world of today have had their lives shaped by the experience of colonialism. It is easy to see how important this has been in the political and economic spheres, but in general influence on the perceptual framework of contemporary peoples is often less evident. Literature offers one of the most important ways in which these new perceptions are expressed and it is in their writing … that the day-to-day realities experienced by colonised people have been most powerfully encoded and so profoundly influential.

(Ashcroft *et al.*, 1989: 1)

These words indicate that we can expect from postcolonial literary texts powerful descriptions of intercultural encounters which often lead to stereotyping and misunderstandings.

Of course, we have to realise that literary texts do not mirror the reality outside the text. Therefore students should not equate a literary text with the reality it explicitly or implicitly refers to but should rather direct their attention to the way reality is presented in the literary text. Such a critical faculty is also necessary for expository texts because they, too, do not represent reality as it is but select and combine things in certain ways. Yet literary texts, and in particular postcolonial and minority literary texts, do not only foreground their style and structure but also illuminate reality and cover a wide variety of aspects which are relevant for intercultural understanding.

One should avoid making general demands on literature. Nevertheless the following criteria for an award for children's literature set up by the Office of Multicultural Affairs in **AUSTRALIA** (quoted in Stephens, 1996: 2) states what we can find in many multicultural texts. It is said that the books should:

1 include insights into a non-Anglo culture within Australia;
2 present a comparison/contrast of an Anglo culture with another;
3 depict an active, conscious integration of cultures;
4 include insights into racism or clash of cultures;
5 include insights into issues of social justice/social harmony;
6 include insights into the immigration experience/loneliness/alienation.

An excellent book which won this award is James Maloney's *Gracey*.

The postcolonial discourse has sharpened our views for stereotypes in Western literature. For Yasmine Gooneratne, Cleopatra in Shakespeare's *Anthony and Cleopatra* 'represents all that is seductive, mysterious, cruel, impulsive – and Non-European … and the noble Marc Anthony's "weakness" is linked with his passion for the "Serpent of the Nile" and the East which she represents' (Gooneratne, 1994: 18). Postcolonial authors often rewrite these stereotypes. For example, Gooneratne believes that the Oriental or Asian woman in Australian fiction is still seen 'as beautiful, subservient, usually helpless and weak or childishly deceitful' and therefore she 'wanted to write about a normal, intelligent Asian woman's response to Australia' in her novel *A Change of Skies* (Gooneratne, 1994: 19). **READING** these texts in the foreign language classroom, learners can become aware of how the texts play with stereotypes and how they respond to such texts. This makes it possible for them to discuss their own process of understanding.

When foreign language learners read postcolonial and minority literature they are confronted with intercultural understanding on two levels. The texts themselves often deal with misrecognition of cultures and can make the learners aware of the complexity and significance of intercultural understanding. On another level the learners themselves have to practise intercultural understanding when they explore how they respond to these texts.

Reading postcolonial and minority literature also gives learners the opportunity to reflect on the function of literature in contemporary aesthetic and political struggles. What is expected from postcolonial and minority literature? For one group it should depict the achievements of the colonised and minority cultures in order to make their members proud of their culture and to refute the degrading stereotypes imposed on them. Yet writers often criticise their own culture and are therefore accused of betraying it and confirming the stereotypes of the dominant culture (see Bredella, 1997). Some writers explicitly refuse to praise their own culture. When film-writer Hanif Kureishi was asked 'Why don't you tell us good stories about ourselves, as well as good/bad stories? Why are your stories mixed about ourselves?', he said: 'There is sometimes too simple a demand for positive images. Positive images sometimes require cheering fictions – the writer as Public Relations Officer. And I'm glad to say that the more I looked at *My Beautiful Laundrette*, the less positive images I could see' (quoted in Hall, 1991: 60). The postcolonial and the minority discourse stress the social significance of literary texts. Writers are no longer lonely individuals but spokespersons for their groups. However, they also protest against this function. Hence students can learn to direct their attention to the functions literary texts are supposed to fulfil.

## Social criticism and intercultural understanding

Literary texts, including those of the dominant culture, often criticise their culture. This points to a general problem of intercultural understanding because, in the foreign language classroom, teachers want foreign language learners to have a positive image of the foreign culture. Does this not make literary texts inappropriate for intercultural understanding? It is true that they give us an insight into the values of the foreign culture, but they also highlight how problematic these values can be. Arthur Miller's *Death of a Salesman* makes learners aware of the importance placed on 'positive thinking', 'being popular' and 'being liked' in the American culture, but at the same time the play reveals how illusory and misleading these values are. Hence, irrespective of whether learners read a literary text by a mainstream writer such as Miller or one by a minority writer such as Toni Morrison or Maxine Hong Kingston, foreign language learners can use the literary text for rejecting the foreign culture and for justifying ethnocentric attitudes. One must acknowledge this possibility, although it is often a misuse of literary texts.

An ethnocentric reading ignores the fact that the literary text is also part of the culture it criticises and that it expects readers to relate it to their own world. Arthur Miller's *The Crucible*, which deals with events in the Salem of 1692, does not give an historical account but expects its readers and viewers to relate it to their own world. This could be the McCarthyite 1950s in the USA for an American audience, but it could also be the Nazi 1930s and 1940s in Germany for Germans (Bredella, 1992). Miller's *All My Sons* was a great success in CHINA in the 1980s, not because it says something about the United States, but because it says something about corruption in China to a Chinese audience. Such a use of literary texts has far-reaching consequences for the concept of intercultural understanding. It implies that we must read literary texts from two perspectives: what do they reveal about the reality they explicitly and implicitly refer to, and what do they reveal about the reader's own culture? Such readings prevent us from defining ourselves in contrast to the foreign culture but rather encourage us to discover *our own* problems in *their* culture and *their* problems in *ours*. This counteracts the tendency to project onto the foreign culture what is regarded as negative in our own culture.

## Collective and individual identity

Intercultural understanding must make learners aware of the differences between cultures. This is its essential goal. Yet such an approach is sometimes in danger of reducing others to their collective identity and ignoring that they are not only Chinese, German or English but have a personal history and can be fathers or mothers, sons or daughters, members of a party and a club, etc. Kwame Anthony Appiah points out that minorities must fight for the recognition of their collective identity, but they should not prescribe 'too tightly' what it means to be a member of this collective identity: 'It is at this point that someone who takes AUTONOMY seriously will want to ask whether we have not replaced one kind of tyranny with another. If I had to choose between Uncle Tom and Black Power, I would, of course, choose the latter. But I would like not to have to choose. I would like other options' (Appiah, 1996: 99).

Literary texts and feature films often explore this tension in the politics of identity. Stuart Hall says about Kureishi's *My Beautiful Laundrette*:

If you have seen *My Beautiful Laundrette* you will know that it is the most transgressive text there is. Anybody who is Black, who tries to identify with it, runs across the fact that the central characters of this narrative are two gay men. What is more, anyone who wants to separate the identities into their clearly separate points will discover that one of these Black gay men is white and the other of these Black gay men is brown.

(Hall, 1991: 60)

Intercultural learning must recognise that more and more people have bicultural as well as multicultural identities.

## Reflexivity and creativity

Literary texts can make learners aware that we should be careful with theories which explain why others behave as they do. In the short story 'The Discipline' by Austin Clarke, the protagonist, a Barbadian immigrant to Canada, is accused of child abuse. In court a social worker maintains that the immigrant's violent behaviour is a result of slavery. This explanation deeply hurts the protagonist because it ignores his individual life with its fears and hopes as well as the lives of his grandmother and mother (Clarke, 1996: 21). Ironically, the protagonist's outburst against such a degrading explanation of his behaviour is interpreted by the judge as a confirmation of the social worker's theory and has him removed from the courtroom.

The anthropologist Anthony P. Cohen sees the danger of **ANTHROPOLOGY** and sociology in reducing people to objects and ignoring their self-consciousness. Therefore he recommends approaching foreign cultures like a reader of literary texts who identifies with characters and uses their own experiences of the world to understand them: 'that is also how I begin to do fieldwork among others, others whom my own self-experience and introspection tell me cannot and must not be treated as mere ciphers of a collective and cultural condition' (Cohen, 1994: 188). This should lead us to reconsider our concepts of culture. Culture does not determine and programme people's actions but offers them a frame of reference in which they have to make their decisions and act.

The recognition of the other as an individual is necessary for intercultural understanding. In 'Chinese Talk', an episode from John Steinbeck's *East of Eden* (1995), Lee, a Chinese-American, who was born in the USA and attended the University of

California for several years, has to behave like an illiterate 'Chinaman' because Chinese-Americans are regarded as unassimilable. This episode between Lee and Samuel took place at the end of the nineteenth century. A hundred years later Maxine Hong Kingston comes to a similar conclusion when analysing reviews of her book *The Woman Warrior*. Many critics praised her book because it presented the unbridgeable gap between East and West and turned Chinese-Americans into exotic strangers. For Kingston such an emphasis on unbridgeable contrasts justifies stereotypes and ignores our common humanness: 'To say we are inscrutable, mysterious, exotic denies our common humanness, because it says that we are so different from a regular human being that we are by our nature intrinsically unknowable' (Kingston, 1982: 57). The dialectic between the recognition of differences and commonalties is also stressed by Bharati Mukherjee when she says that the one-sided emphasis on multicultural differences 'has often led to the dehumanisation of the different' (Mukherjee, 1997: 459).

## Literary texts and cultural knowledge

Literary texts can contribute to intercultural understanding, but learners also need cultural knowledge in order to understand them. When Delanoy read the short story 'Come to Mecca' with Austrian students, a great number of them could not make sense of what they were reading because of a lack of cultural knowledge. For him it is important that teachers become aware of the cultural, linguistic and aesthetic barriers that their learners will have to cope with (Delanoy, 1993). It is, however, difficult at times to decide whether learners' difficulties with literary texts are due to a lack of cultural knowledge or due to aesthetic barriers. When learners were asked what would have helped them to understand Maxine Hong Kingston's *The Woman Warrior* they replied 'knowledge about the Chinese culture'. At the same time it can be demonstrated that the reading difficulties are not so much due to a lack of cultural knowledge but rather to aesthetic challenges which reflect the book's protagonist's uncertainties about how to understand Chinese culture (Bredella, 1997). This becomes obvious when we compare *The Woman*

*Warrior* with Amy Tan's *The Joy Luck Club*. Both novels describe similar events, but in the case of the latter novel students rarely ask for cultural background knowledge.

Cultural background knowledge is important, but we should not overestimate it. As **WIDDOWSON** points out, 'there is always some disparity of realities in human communication of any kind. The meanings we achieve are always approximate and never complete'. More than this, in intercultural understanding we are always incompletely informed. Widdowson explicitly rejects the belief that we must provide students with the necessary cultural knowledge before reading a literary text: 'It is not a precondition but a consequence of interpretation' (Widdowson, 1992: 115). In a similar way, Barbara Herrnstein Smith argues that the provision of cultural knowledge will turn the literary text which is open to different interpretations into a 'determinate' one (Smith, 1978: 34ff). It could be a worthwhile experience for students to develop different interpretations and pursue how specific cultural knowledge changes their interpretations.

In *Teaching Multicultural Literature*, Reed Way Dasenbrock points out that we must learn to ask ourselves when reading multicultural texts why we are not told what certain things mean: 'In other words, the teacher leads the class through the experience of constructing a passing theory; to do otherwise, to annotate the unannotated text, would be to prevent the students from experiencing the meaning of the work. To reverse T.S. Eliot, they would have had the meaning but missed the experience' (Dasenbrock, 1992: 44). Yet we must also take into consideration that the foreign language learner might not know what authors themselves take for granted. Teachers must decide what cultural knowledge their students need for a fruitful interaction with the text. Therefore we should not play off literary understanding and cultural knowledge against each other but should explore how they can supplement one another.

**See also:** Acculturation; Cross-cultural psychology; Cultural studies; Intercultural competence; *Interkulturelle Didaktik*; Literary theory and literature teaching; Literary texts; Reading

## References

Achebe, C. (1978) 'An image of Africa', *Research in African Literatures* 9, 1: 1–15.

Appiah, K.A. (1996) 'Culture, identity: misunderstood connections', in K.A. Appiah and A. Gutman, *Color conscious*, Princeton: Princeton University Press.

Ashcroft, B., Griffiths G. and Tiffin, H. (1989) *The empire writes back*, London: Routledge.

Bredella, L. (1992) 'Understanding a foreign culture through assimilation and accommodation: Arthur Miller's *The Crucible* and its dual historical context', in R. Ahrens and H. Antor (eds), *Text – Culture – Reception. Cross cultural aspects of English Studies*, Heidelberg: Winter.

Bredella, L. (1996) 'Interkulturelle Begegnungen in literarischen Texten und Spielfilmen: Vorüberlegungen zu einer Didaktik des interkulturellen Verstehens (Intercultural encounters in literary texts and feature films: preliminary remarks on a pedagogy of intercultural understanding)', in L. Bredella and H. Christ (Hg.). *Begegnungen mit dem Fremden*, Gießen: Ferber.

Bredella, L. (1997) 'Involvement and detachment: how to read and teach Maxine Hong Kingston's *The Woman Warrior*', in G. Hoffmann and A. Hornung (eds), *Emotion in postmodernism*, Heidelberg: Winter.

Clarke, A. (1996) 'The Discipline', in B. Scheer-Schäzler (ed.), *Immigrant stories teacher's book*, Berlin: Cornelsen.

Cohen, A.P. (1994) *Self consciousness*, London: Routledge.

Dasenbrock, R.W. (1992) 'Teaching multicultural literature', in J. Trimmer and T. Warnock (eds), *Understanding others: cultural and cross-cultural studies and the teaching of literature*, Urbana: NCTE.

Delanoy, W. (1993) ' "Come to Mecca": assessing a literary text's potential for intercultural learning', in W. Delanoy, J. Köberl and H. Tschachler (eds), *Experiencing a foreign culture*, Tübingen: Narr.

Echeruo, M. (1978) *The conditioned imagination from Shakespeare to Conrad. Studies in exo-cultural stereotype*, London and Basingstoke: Macmillan.

Gooneratne, Y. (1994) 'An interview with Rudolf Bader', *Anglistik* 5, 1, 15–23.

Hall, S. (1991) 'The local and the global: globalization and ethnicity', in A.D. King (ed.),

*Culture globalization and the world system*, New York: Macmillan.

Kingston, M.H. (1982) 'Cultural mis-readings by American reviewers', in G. Amirthanayagam (ed.), *Asian and Western writers in dialogue. New cultural identities*, London: Macmillan.

Mukherjee, B. (1997) 'Beyond multiculturalism', in I. Reed (ed.), *Multicultural America: essays on cultural wars and cultural peace*, New York: Viking.

Rorty, R. (1991) *Objectivity, relativism and truth*, Cambridge: Cambridge University Press.

Rorty, R. (1993) 'Human rights, rationality, and sentimentality', in S. Shute and S. Hurley (eds), *On human rights* New York: Basic Books.

Smith, B.H. (1978) *On the margins of discourse: the relation of literature to language*, Chicago: University of Chicago Press.

Steinbeck, J. (1995) 'Chinese Talk', in R.F. Rau (ed.), *Great immigrant stories*, Stuttgart: Klett.

Stephens, J. (1996) 'Multiculturalism in recent Australian children's fiction: (Re-constructing selves through personal and national histories', in M. Machet, S. Olén and Th. van der Wuldt (eds), *Other worlds, other lives*, Pretoria: University of South Africa.

Widdowson, H.G. (1992) *Practical stylistics*, Oxford: Oxford University Press.

## Further reading

Ashcroft, B., Griffiths G. and Tiffin, H. (1989) *The empire writes back*, London: Routledge.

Delanoy, W., Köberl, J. and Tschachler, H. (eds 1993), *Experiencing a foreign culture*, Tübingen: Narr

Trimmer, J. and Warnock, T. (eds) (1992) *Understanding others: cultural and cross-cultural studies and the teaching of literature*, Urbana: NCTE.

LOTHAR BREDELLA

# Literary theory and literature teaching

Literary theories of the past forty years collectively have generated new definitions of the **LITERARY TEXT**. The first theoretical movements, often based on **LINGUISTICS**, established literary studies as separate from traditional philological studies and consequently language instruction. Since the late 1980s efforts have been made to integrate literary and language studies once again. Specifically, in their mature form, **STYLISTICS**, structuralism, feminist theory and reader response theories have liberated the literary text from the past. In addition, certain theories of language based on **METAPHOR** provide a more extensive definition and usage of the 'literary' in the classroom.

## Historical context

Before World War Two, **READING** and translating literary texts constituted a dominant approach to language instruction. After the war, literary studies on the upper levels ignored problems of language and treated literature as an isolated object of study. In **FRANCE** and other European countries, the *explication de texte*, or close, formalised analysis of the text, demanded a reader who was thoroughly knowledgeable in the language and who had a strong grounding in literary history. The practice of close reading also implied that the text had one meaning which the reader was expected to decode. 'New Criticism', as practised in the United States and Great Britain, also demanded sophisticated readers who would look upon the text as a 'well wrought urn' (the title of Cleanth Brooks's famous book of 1947), a precious object outside the realm of everyday experience. The canon guaranteed that literary works would be regarded as part of High Culture, separated from language instruction and popular forms of writing.

## Literary and linguistic theories

Although a number of origins might be found for the new literary paradigm, a logical place is in **STRUCTURAL LINGUISTIC** studies, not literature, and in the pioneering work of Roman Jakobson. Two of his articles have profoundly influenced literary thought over the past thirty years. In 'Linguistics and Poetics' (1960) Jakobson proposed that language was composed of six functions: referential, phatic (making contact, as in 'Lend me your ears!'), emotive, conative (the imperative, as in 'Get out!'), metalinguistic (commenting on language) and poetic. Jakobson defined the poetic as metaphor, parallels, repetition, and patterns of similar sounds, or phonetics, over meaning, as in **POETRY**. In other words, the poetic for Jakobson is found in those moments in poems, advertisements and everyday discussion where sound leads to meaning. It is significant that he selected examples from the world of everyday language. 'I Like Ike' and 'Oh, that horrible Harry!' stand out, because sounds determined the selection of words. For Jakobson, the poetic function is part of the real world. In the second article, 'Two Aspects of Language and Two Types of Aphasia' (1956), Jakobson was even bolder in his search for a global definition of language. Based on psychological studies (which today would be questioned by professional psychologists), he proposed that language is formed by two complementary processes: metaphor and metonymy. By metaphor, Jakobson meant relationships of resemblance, as well as mental processes of replacement. A banal example would be to refer to a 'bear' market, where the word 'bear' replaces a description of a falling stock market, where profits are devoured and an animalistic force takes over. By metonymy, Jakobson proposed contiguity, either spatial or causal. Spatially, he meant both syntax (the arrangement of words in a sentence) and semantics: the description of various rooms in a house, for example (spatial), or the causal chains that constitute a novel ('he shot the policeman, ran away in his car, was forced to rob a bank . . .'). Not content to limit himself to linguistics, Jakobson strongly suggested that various literary genres and film techniques are governed by the rules of metaphor and metonymy. Although criticised as an over-simplification (as is the theory of the binary brain), Jakobson's theory has become an integral part of literary and film studies, as well as significant linguistic research (see Lakoff and Johnson, 1980, and Lakoff, 1987).

One offshoot and direct reaction to Jakobson's theories was the so-called 'New Stylistics'. **STYLISTICS** as a practice had existed well before World War Two in various forms. Charles Bally in France, who studied the stylistic properties of language in general, and Leo Spitzer in Germany and later the United States, who concentrated on philological textual analysis, were representative names of two divergent yet over-lapping schools. But it was not until the publication of *Style and Structure in Literature*

in 1975 (edited by Roger Fowler) that the New Stylistics took shape. Bringing together critics from Great Britain and the United States, the authors set themselves apart from Jakobson by refusing to see literary studies as subordinate to linguistic studies. Instead, they sought to examine literary texts with 'concepts drawn from linguistics and from the linguistic-like sciences treating the structure of communicative systems' (Fowler, 1975: 5). They fully respected the uniqueness of literary texts and refused to create generalisations or abstractions.

Concurrent with the publication of *Style and Structure in Literature*, H.G. **WIDDOWSON** published *Stylistics and the Teaching of Literature*. The book stands as a felicitous marriage of theory and practice. Among various examples of possible **EXERCISES**, Widdowson juxtaposes different types of discourse (a person's vital statistics, adjectives describing a person, contrastive sets of adjectives) to teach students to infer from context and to analyse the uniqueness of each description. The aim is to prepare students to analyse literary texts in relation to other discourses. Thus the literary stands next to the linguistic, while retaining its individuality.

While the New Stylistics sought to retain the text as a unique object, the deconstruction and dismantling of the literary text as precious object occurred most notably in France after 1960 with the Structuralist triumph. Many names could be cited, but the career of Roland Barthes best describes the shift from literature as an isolated object to the study of literary texts as part of a more global sign system. After his first published work on Racine, the major classical French playwright, Barthes expanded his field of analysis to include almost all aspects of modern life, including automobiles, advertisements, fashion, and even wrestling in *Mythologies* (1986) and *Image, Music, Text* (1977). Recurring ideas in his work which have a direct impact on literature in the language classroom include:

- All encoded systems, whether verbal language, cinema, literature or fashion, are at the same time denotative and connotative. The word 'red' denotes a specific colour, while also connoting (suggesting) danger, passion or love. An advertisement for perfume denotes a specific brand of perfume, while the colour illustration and the words can connote a special world of sensuality and desire.

- No language system is 'natural', although the fashion world, advertisements and newspapers try to make it appear so. Even spoken language is not 'natural' because speakers know when to switch **VOCABULARY**, syntax, and rhythm as the situation demands. No one speaks the same way in a job interview and then with a friend over a beer. Thus the literary text, if studied next to other sign systems, is no more artificial or 'inauthentic' than the rest. For purposes of the classroom, it is as **AUTHENTIC** as any other discourse.

- Literary texts do not have one meaning intended by the author, as previous criticism declared. Literary texts have multiple meanings. The reader is confronted with a variety of avenues to follow and meanings to create. Rather than representing a Grecian urn, the literary text offers to the reader rhetorical avenues to follow.

- Reading is a process in which the reader engages with the text. The text itself is defined by its interaction with the reader, and, as Barthes declared, every detail has a meaning, or nothing has a meaning. Put into concrete terms of the classroom, the most insignificant questions are significant and can point to major aspects of the text.

- Reading is a pleasure. Until 1975, when Barthes published his slim volume *Le Plaisir du Texte* (The Pleasure of the Text), academics looked upon reading as a very serious business. Barthes recalled that literature has existed to be enjoyed and that reading should be a pleasure. By extension, as the Italian theoretician Gianni Rodari (1996) sought to show, literary texts are part of pleasurable games of the imagination, where children enjoy creating verbal associations which become the foundation for imaginary stories. The pleasure of reading is closely related to the pleasures of creating (for example, generating stories from associations created around the words 'pound', 'mound', 'sound' and 'found').

The Structuralists represented a major shift in literary theory, but they did not fully bridge the gap between literature and language within the aca-

demic hierarchy. While some texts by Barthes were intended for the general public, most of his contemporaries upheld the view that literary studies were for an élite. Finally, the structuralist movement was for the most part a male movement. While Barthes, Derrida (actually a post-structuralist) and others represented a revolution within the academy, they, like most of their colleagues in other countries, represented a male reading of texts and did not problematise the exclusion of women writers.

The feminist movement forced recognition of neglected women authors, and thus enlarged the corpus while radically shifting its focus. At the risk of over-simplifying, the feminists have made a major contribution to the redefinition of literature. First, they broke down the walls of the canon, which concentrated on male writers. By demanding that texts by women be taught, feminists demanded that the criteria for 'great literature' be rethought. A debate over 'feminine' writing has lead to the recognition that there is not one standard rule of excellence. In large part because of the initial feminist efforts, more marginalised literatures, such as French francophone writers (Africa and the Caribbean) as well as South American authors, have the audience they deserve in the academy.

However, one cannot really talk of a single feminist movement; rather, varieties of the same impulse grew up in the Western world. Catherine R. Stimpson outlines how these movements have redefined our reading practices. We are now sensitive to representations of **GENDER** and patterns of masculinity and femininity. Feminists have demanded that we be conscious of the 'patterns of masculine dominance' in literature and criticism, and that we redraw new 'maps' of female representation in texts (Stimpson, 1992: 251)

Reader response theory, as advocated by Iser and Jaus in Germany and Tompkins and Fish, among others, in the United States, was a final step in liberating the literary text from close, closed reading (see, e.g., Iser, 1978). Globally, reader response theory shifted emphasis from the text to the readers, who became the principal players in the dialectic between text and reader. Far from advocating a subjectivist theory of reading, reader response proposed focusing on how readers received and deciphered texts, without forcing a meaning on them. In other words, reception was more important than a hidden meaning in the text.

Finally, Deconstruction as articulated by Derrida (1976) argued that, historically, philosophy and more recently linguistics have privileged speech over writing and reading. According to Derrida, writing has been considered a supplement, an addition to speaking in major philosophical and linguistic works. According to him, writing was considered dangerous by thinkers from Plato to Rousseau, and Lévi-Strauss in our age. His work has revalorised writing, and by implication reading, so that they are not thought of as trivial or dangerous. If we accept Derrida, writing and reading hold places equal to speech in the classroom.

In *Literary Theory*, Eagleton (1983) summarised contemporary movements in literary theory around the practice of rhetoric, which, for him, explains and justifies modern theory:

> Rhetoric, which was the received form of critical analysis all the way from ancient society to the eighteenth century, examined the way discourses are constructed in order to achieve certain effects. It was not worried about whether its objects of enquiry were **SPEAKING** or writing, poetry or philosophy, fiction or historiography; its horizon was nothing less than the field of discursive practices in society as a whole, and its particular interest lay in grasping such practices as forms of power and performance ... Rhetoric, or discourse theory, shares with Formalism, Structuralism and semiotics an interest in the formal devices of language ... and its belief that discourse can be a humanly transformative affair shares a good deal with liberal humanism.
>
> (Eagleton, 1983: 205–6)

Unfortunately, Eagleton does not extend his concept of power and performance into the language classroom, but his synthesis set the stage for seeing how literary theory exists as a rich source for language instruction.

## Potential applications in the classroom

A fresh approach to literature in the foreign language classroom is now appearing. Literature finds a comfortable place in foreign language instruction because of the following theoretical insights:

- Because **WRITING** and reading are on an equal footing with speech, texts have an integral place in language classrooms.
- Because literary language is encoded in ways similar to advertisements, newspapers and everyday language, it can be taught along with other types of sign systems.
- Because the canon no longer exists, literary texts can be chosen not just because they are good but because students can actually understand and enjoy them. Texts need not be 'relevant', but challenging by their uniqueness and seductiveness.
- Because literature is no longer regarded as a closed world to be decoded by the reader, students may read in order to find their own meanings. They may also learn to play with the text.
- Because literature is as 'authentic' as any other type of discourse, it can be sought out as a source of different levels of expression. Poetry teaches the use of metaphor, which permeates all social discourse. Metonymy teaches narrative relationships, how to decipher a story, and implicitly how to tell a story, whether fictive or real.
- Because literature is basically connotative, in its suggestiveness, it teaches students implicitly that all utterances contain a connotative, or second, meaning. After having read a novel entitled *The Red and the Black*, students waken to the simple fact that colours have connotative meanings, whether in a novel or in real life.
- Because we are liberated from an antiquated canon, we can juxtapose texts by women (and other excluded groups) and men in order to teach the importance of gender.

## An outline of practice

As a result of these findings, literature in the foreign language classroom need not be separated from the instruction of 'normal' language. It is a part of other language systems, whether they be popular songs, advertisements, popular tales, short films or even letters. The theories outlined here provide numerous avenues for students to play with and write about texts. However, they do not include the basic approach of pre-reading (although reader response theory hints at it), which comes from practice in the classroom. Pre-reading might be regarded as the missing link between books and students' everyday lives. Traditional introductions to individual works included either historical or biographical information – important, to be sure, but preventing the student from situating their language and life in relationship to the text. Pre-reading exercises based on literary situations and the use of literary language are the valuable bridge between literature and students' language.

As an illustration of a move from theory to practice, let us imagine the study of a short poem where the poet describes spending an entire day walking across rough terrain to visit his daughter's tomb. Pre-reading exercises develop motifs and themes, as well as situations, that are encountered in the poem. Students are asked to write about a trip they once took which extended from dawn to dusk; they play associative games with key words found in the poem (dawn, dusk, mountains, the sea, seeing outside and 'seeing' within themselves); they describe different ways to walk to express sadness or joy. Questions on the text are open-ended and 'top-down' (global), to encourage students to establish traces or patterns (metaphors, causal chains or key oppositions) on their own. Their readings of the text, albeit far from exhaustive, give them the material to create their general reading or interpretation.

Pre-reading questions also establish the students' contexts and act as bridges between the language of their **TEXTBOOK** and literary conventions. Kramsch (1993) would argue that students create oppositional contexts in relationship to the text, when they position themselves in front of a text unlike them. But often in Western literature the distance between student and text is minimal and the two are complementary. In any case, by writing before reading, the students establish a strong linguistic and cultural base to lead into reading. In studying the text, the aim is not to account for every word to create a hermetic meaning; rather, students play with linguistic traces or patterns that they perceive in order to draw meanings which

they can justify. Readings are personal without being purely subjective, since they are based on specific features in the text (e.g., colour patterns, causal chains, repetitions).

While poetry would favour a metaphorical reading, many texts would also lend themselves to a narrative where students could start by retelling the story; about a voyage, for example. Along the same line of thought, prose narrative usually begins with retelling the story and noting causal links, but not excluding metaphorical relationships, such as resemblances between characters or décor (similar rooms, for example).

## The 'literary' in the language classroom

Recently critics have noted that, while literature is different from other discourses, it is so in degree, not in nature. Above all, literary theory of the past thirty years has taught us that we can distinguish between 'literature' and the 'literary'. Returning to Jakobson's original articles, the 'literary' permeates every aspect of human communication. The work by Lakoff and Johnson (1980) on metaphor and metonymy forcefully shows us that literary language is part of a much larger linguistic and cultural storehouse. In *Women, Fire, and Dangerous Things* (1987), Lakoff lists over a hundred ways to express anger, all of them 'literary' or 'poetic' according to Jakobson's definition. By contrast, foreign language textbooks usually teach as though there were just one standard way of expression and only one way to express an idea. There is no reason why semantic fields cannot be expanded as students progress in their instruction. Likewise, foreign language textbooks can be inspired by literature and teach different levels of language expression, such as irony, humour, narratives from daily life, and even hyperbole. If literature is to be a rich source for foreign language instruction, the most accessible texts can be models not just for reading but also for performing language.

**See also:** Cultural studies; Drama; Literary texts; Literary texts and intercultural understanding; Poetry; Stylistic variation; Teaching methods; Translation theory

## References

Barthes, R. (1975) *The pleasure of the text*, trans. Richard Miller, New York: Hill and Wang.

Barthes, R. (1977) *Image, music, text*, trans. Stephen Heath, New York: Hill and Wang.

Barthes, R. (1986) *Mythologies*, trans. Annette Lavers, New York: Hill and Wang.

Beri, K. and Giansiacusa, E.L. (1996) *In giro per la letteratura (Around literature)*, Boston: Heinle and Heinle.

Brooks, C. (1947) *The Well Wrought Urn*, New York: Neynal and Hitchock.

Derrida, J. (1976) *Of grammatology*, trans. Gayatri C. Spivak, Baltimore: Johns Hopkins University Press.

Eagleton, T. (1983) *Literary theory: an introduction*, Minneapolis: University of Minnesota Press.

Fowler, R. (ed.) (1975) *Style and structure in literature*, Oxford: Basil Blackwell.

Iser, W. (1978) *The act of reading: a theory of aesthetic response*, Baltimore: Johns Hopkins University Press.

Jakobson, R. (1956) 'Two aspects of language and two kinds of aphasia', in R. Jakobson and M. Hall, *Fundamentals of language*, The Hague: Mouton.

Jakobson, R. (1960) 'Linguistics and poetics', in T.A. Sebeok (ed.), *Style in language*, Cambridge: MIT Press.

Kramsch, C. (1993) *Context and culture in language teaching*, New York: Oxford University Press.

Lakoff, G. (1987) *Women, fire and dangerous things*, Chicago: The University of Chicago Press.

Lakoff, G. and Johnson, M. (1980) *Metaphors we live by*, Chicago: The University of Chicago Press.

Rodari, G. (1996) *The grammar of fantasy*, New York: Teachers and Writers Collaborative.

Stimpson, C R. (1992) 'Feminist criticism,' in S. Greenblatt and G. Gunn (eds), *Redrawing the boundaries*, New York: The Modern Language Association.

Widdowson, H.G. ( 1975) *Stylistics and the teaching of literature*, London: Longman.

## Further reading

Culler, J. (1992) 'Literary theory,' in J. Gibaldi (ed.), *Introduction to scholarship in modern languages and literatures*, New York: The Modern Language Association.

De George, R.T. (ed.) (1972) *The Structuralists from Marx to Levi-Strauss*, Garden City: Anchor Books.

Fowler, R. (1986) *Linguistic criticism*, New York: Oxford University Press.

Groden, M. and Kreiswirth, M. (eds) (1993) *The Johns Hopkins guide to literary theory and criticism*, Baltimore and London: The Johns Hopkins University Press.

Jardine, A. (1985) *Gynesis: configurations of women and modernity*, Ithaca: Cornell University Press.

Kramsch, C. (ed.) (1995) *Redefining the boundaries of language study*, Boston: Heinle and Heinle.

Marks, E. and de Courtivron, I. (eds) (1981) *French feminisms: an anthology*, New York: Schocken.

Miller, N.K. (1988) *Subject to change: reading feminist writing*, New York: Columbia University Press.

Schofer, P. and Rice, D. (1995) *Autour de la littérature (Around literature)*, Boston: Heinle and Heinle.

Swaffar, J.K., Arens, K. and Burns, H. (1991) *Reading for meaning: an integrated approach to language learning*, Englewood Cliffs: Prentice Hall.

PETER SCHOFER

# Lozanov, Georgi

b. 1926, Sofia

Lozanov studied medicine at the University of Sofia and then completed specialist training as a psychiatrist. In the 1960s he worked as a psychotherapist and psychiatrist. It was at this time that he began his investigations of suggestion which, in 1966, led to the founding of a state research centre on 'suggestology' in Sofia. Lozanov was the director and the centre remained until 1992 under the Ministry Of Education. In 1971 Lozanov wrote a doctoral thesis with the title 'Suggestology'. The text was also published in Bulgaria with the same title in the same year. This manuscript marked the founding of '**SUGGESTOPEDIA**', i.e. a *suggestive* pedagogy which was to use the elements of suggestion to develop optimum conditions for learning. Lozanov claimed to have found a method by which immeasurable 'reserve capacities of the brain' could be used. In 1978 there appeared in the West a somewhat altered version of the doctoral thesis with the title 'Suggestology and Outlines of Suggestopedy'. Because Lozanov had carried out his experiments in learning with foreign language **VOCABULARY**, and had apparently demonstrated learning achievements of an average of a hundred lexemes per day, which were retained over a long period, suggestopedia was hailed as a miracle method and was given in its Western commercialised form the name 'Superlearning'. However, the amazing Bulgarian results could not be replicated elsewhere, which justified doubts about the empirical **VALIDITY** of the Bulgarian experiments (see Schiffler, 1989; Baur, 1990). Despite this, suggestopedia has maintained a place as a so-called 'alternative method' of foreign language instruction, and with its processes and principles (Krashen, 1985) has influenced contemporary methodology.

The canonical sequence of the phases of learning prescribed by Lozanov are in three phases of presentation which, as a coherent complex period of (usually) four hours, make up the 'suggestopedic session' and the 'activation phases':

1  The first presentation of the text (which Lozanov calls the 'pre-session phase'): Learners have a dual-language text book in which on one page there is the target language text and on the other the translation in the learners' **MOTHER TONGUE**. The target language text is read aloud by the teacher and the **GRAMMAR** explained. The teacher reads aloud and explains, the learners follow, **READING** silently, or are asked by the teacher to read with him/her.

2  The second presentation: the 'active concert' is an emotional expressive reading of the text. The teacher reads the text aloud a second time whilst fitting his voice in terms of loudness, rhythm and intonation to an emotional expressive music which fills the room at a normal level of loudness; the teacher reads aloud, the learners follow in silence. The accompanying music used is the classical music of Beethoven, Brahms,

Haydn, Mozart and Tchaikovsky.

3  The third phase is called 'the passive concert' by Lozanov. Here the material is read against a background of slow, regular and relaxing baroque music (e.g. Bach, Corelli, Vivaldi). The learners sit in this phase in comfortable armchairs, close their eyes and are asked to relax and to concentrate on the text, which is read aloud with the background music; the teacher reads, the learners relax.

4  The activation phases, also called 'post-session phases' by Lozanov, usually include 6–8 lessons over the following two days. Usually there are **EXERCISES**, which are partly of a traditional kind and partly of a ludic nature and also involve role play. Often these are carried out with musical activities, including singing.

Lozanov published a Suggestopedic Manual with Evalina Gateva in 1981, which was translated into English in 1988.

**See also:** Humanistic language teaching; Silent Way; Suggestopedia

### References

Baur, R.S. (1990) *Superlearning und Suggestopädie*, Munich: Langenscheidt.

Krashen, S.D. (1985) *The input hypothesis. Issues and implications*, New York: Gordon and Breach.

Lozanov, G. (1978) *Suggestology and outlines of suggestopedy*, New York: Gordon and Breach.

Lozanov, G. and Gateva, E. (1988) *The foreign language teacher's suggestopedic manual*, New York: Gordon and Breach.

Schiffler, L. (1989) *Suggestopädie und Superlearning – empirisch geprüft*, Frankfurt: Diesterweg.

### Further reading

Lozanov, G. (1978) *Suggestology and outlines of suggestopedy*, New York: Gordon and Breach.

RUPPRECHT S. BAUR

# Materials and media

Throughout the history of foreign language teaching, theorists and practitioners have tried to support the language learning process as best they could (Frankenberg and Fuhr, 1997). To that end, foreign language teachers and materials developers have introduced a variety of aids, materials and media. Whatever supportive means are chosen, their conception and format to a large extent determine the layout of a foreign language course.

Developments in the understanding of what foreign language **COMPETENCE** implies and what is required to achieve it, combined with technological innovations and shifts in societal demands on education, have entailed changes in the way in which the foreign language teaching process is conceived and supported. Materials and media that were believed to be effective learning tools at one point in time are supplemented with or even supplanted by others, which may in their turn become marginalised.

The gradual increase in and diversification of teaching materials and media, with the ensuing danger of overburdening teaching with them for their sheer availability, makes it an absolute necessity that teachers are able to perceive both strengths and weaknesses of available teaching aids, and can make well-considered judgements as to when, how and to what end they can most effectively be harnessed to particular learning or teaching tasks. Often such decisions are influenced by considerations beyond the control of the course designers and producers. Questions of organisation, of coordination in any multimedia course, will play an important role. In addition, materials and media deliberations must be made with respect to the abilities and **NEEDS** of particular learner(s) groups.

## Definition and classifications

Materials and media are everything that can be used to support the foreign language learning process. In many foreign language classes today these aids will probably include the teacher's voice, a tape-recorder with cassettes, a writing board (black or white), the **TEXTBOOK** (textbooks), and a workbook (workbooks). Many teachers will use additional worksheets, sets of task cards and objects (props, pictures, posters, realia such as menus, food tins or labels, maps, wall charts and the like). Some teachers may also have an overhead projector (OHP) with transparencies or even a video player with videotapes or films at their disposal. In some language classrooms reference materials (reference books), such as **DICTIONARIES**, **GRAMMAR** or phrase books, may also be permanently available. Schools may have foreign newspapers, periodicals, magazines, cultural background books or supplementary readers in their library. The large majority of teachers may not yet consider computers with foreign language learning software, CD-ROMs, DVDs (digital versatile disks) or an **INTERNET** connection common teaching aids. A minority of often specialised language schools may have at their disposal a **SELF-ACCESS** centre, where a large variety of the above-mentioned media and materials are freely accessible to learners for (guided) self study (Sheerin, 1991). Still other materials and media which have at some point in time been introduced into foreign language teaching with more or less success could be mentioned here. They include the **LANGUAGE LABORATORY**, the flannel board, the epidiascope, the flipchart, **FLASHCARDS**, radio, television and even puppets.

This broad spectrum of teaching aids can be classified according to various perspectives. An obvious way to do so is to distinguish between *aural*, *visual* and *audio-visual* aids, with the last category having the advantage of combining sound and image. Another common way to classify materials and media is to do so according to their function. Thus a distinction can be made between *teaching* and *learning* materials, or between *data, instruction, process* and *reference* materials (Breen and Candlin, 1980). Data materials are chunks of language that are presented to learners for exploration; instruction materials typically include workbooks, exercise books and other materials designed for language practice; process materials are those parts of a language course that mediate to learners how the course is to proceed; reference materials include dictionaries, grammar books, spelling lists, thesauri, phrase books and the like. Third, materials and media may be referred to as either *basic* or *supplementary*, with the first category comprising materials and media that are considered essential parts of a particular language course, and the latter those aids that can but need not be used on top of the basic materials to assist students to meet the requirements of a particular course or to further improve their language competence. Whereas coursebooks, workbooks and course-related cassettes are now typically considered basic course materials, computer packages, slides and transparencies, videos, additional listening materials, sets of (card) games, simplified readers and the like, tend to be considered supplementary, although many multimedia courses attempt to integrate a large variety of different media and materials, and, consequently, might consider these aids to be basic, not supplementary. Fourth, materials may either be designed for use in the *classroom* or for *self study*. A final commonly used procedure is to classify materials and media according to the language components or **SKILLS** they aim to practise. Thus, listening materials are distinguished from, for example, **READING**, **WRITING**, *speaking* or *grammar*

*practice* materials. Some media are considered better suited to practise particular skills or deal with particular requirements of foreign language courses than others. Thus, learners' **LISTENING** skills may benefit most from aural aids, such as tapes, radio broadcasts or the teacher's voice. Cultural background information, on the contrary, may best be presented over video, television, films, transparencies, posters or pictures, or it may be taught via the internet or with the help of CD-ROMs.

## Materials and media in the history of foreign language education

When looking at the history of foreign language education from the point of view of materials, a number of evolutions in their selection and design are noticeable. At various stages in the development of foreign language teaching, new media and teaching aids have been introduced, of which some have managed to establish themselves firmly, and continue to be used to date, whereas others have become marginalised or seem to have gradually disappeared from mainstream teaching altogether. A diachronic analysis of teaching materials similarly reveals shifts in preference for particular task types, activities, ways of presentation and feedback, or for particular kinds of language data or contents (Klippel, 1994).

Shifts in the selection and conception of media and materials seem to have been dependent on a number of interrelated factors. Developments in the understanding of what competence in a foreign language entails and what is required to reach it, in theories about the nature of the language learning process and how it is best supported, combined with technological developments and the commercial exploitation of particular 'teaching and learning machines', have to a large extent determined the way in which materials and media have been used in foreign language instruction. Thus, whereas the need for the pupil to hear himself when practising **PRONUNCIATION** was recognised early (Kelly, 1969: 239) (audio-recording), no effective way of meeting the problem was found until the tape recorder was invented. The popularity of drill exercises (drills) in the **AUDIOLINGUAL** era of foreign language teaching can in part be explained by the commercialisation of a machine that was capable of doing these 'monotonous, unnatural and "inhuman" ' (Parker, 1962: 70) activities, i.e. the language laboratory. Television, and later video, were acclaimed by foreign language education theorists of the communicative era (communicative approach) for their capability of bringing 'real life' into the language learning classroom and of communicating the total situation of language to the learner (Council of Europe, 1979). Insights from cognitive **PSYCHOLOGY**, notably that people learn best when several senses (e.g. sight and hearing) are simultaneously addressed, triggered efforts of the teaching profession to introduce all kinds of visual, audio-visual and even tangible aids into foreign language teaching, so as to complement or replace the predominantly written and aural materials.

Teaching practice and teachers' and learners' experiences with particular materials and media, too, contributed to their refinement and adaptation to particular educational needs. Thus, following teachers' unsatisfactory experiences with films and videos which tended to be quite long when they were first introduced into the foreign language classroom, a clear evolution towards shorter films has been noticeable, replacing the input of large amounts of aural and visual data with shorter sequences, say of about four minutes, followed by careful (linguistic) exploitation. Learners' frustrating experiences with **MONOLINGUAL** dictionaries containing long entries formulated in a language too far above their level of competence incited publishers and researchers to develop learner dictionaries with clear definitions written in simple language, highlighting active words to be learnt first, providing study pages and grammar help boxes focusing on vital grammar points, building in a workbook section to develop students' dictionary skills, providing colourful illustrations with corresponding **VOCABULARY** practice exercises or usage notes designed to help learners avoid common errors.

Teacher frustration at the impracticability of certain media and materials proposed by theorists further determined their lifecycle. Whereas textbooks are very user-friendly 'packages' of materials – they are light, easily scanned, easily stacked and do not need hardware or electricity (Ur, 1996: 190)

– slide projectors or video machines are less so, also because in many institutions and schools the rooms where they are available have to be booked well in advance – which makes course planning more difficult. Some media can also be considered more flexible than others because they can be used for a variety of language practice activities, with various age groups and working arrangements. Thus, OHP transparencies can not only be used by the teacher to capture class attention, they may also be used by pupils to report on **GROUP WORK** results. They are easily wiped off and can be used in the context of almost any thinkable language practice activity. The language laboratory, on the contrary, appears more static and limited in use, seeming suitable foremost for individual pronunciation and drill practice, albeit that communicative group activities are not wholly excluded.

The selection of teaching materials and media is also partly dependent on the demands made by society at a given period in time. Computer literacy is now put forward as one of the aims which all teaching should pursue. In view of the explosion of knowledge and the fastness with which it is distributed, over the information highway and other (mass) media, society also demands that teachers and schools educate their children for independent, lifelong learning (**AUTONOMOUS LEARNING**), providing them with the skills to find and evaluate information next to passing a body of well-structured knowledge on to them which can serve as a guiding framework. Since computers use language, it would seem logical to take advantage of them for language learning. Computers, moreover, enable independent individual work, since learners can progress at their own pace and many programmes include a self-check facility, automatic contextualised feedback, the possibility to use reference materials on the screen, to listen to the spoken language, to watch pieces of video, to record one's own voice, or to interact in real time with **NATIVE SPEAKERS** of a foreign language, to name only a few advantages (Little, 1996). The fact that young and adolescent learners in particular find the use of computers attractive and motivating is an added benefit.

These societal demands urge a change in teachers' and learners' roles (Branson, 1991). Teachers have to become coaches rather than providers of information, since pupils can (learn to) find their own texts and language data. Coaching entails the need to redesign many of the materials that have been developed for teacher-guided instruction and to consider seriously how individual differences in **LEARNING STYLES**, needs, abilities and interests can best be catered for in integrated powerful multimedia learning environments (Collins, 1991).

## Debates and perspectives

With the boom of teaching media, interdisciplinary groups of social scientists, (cognitive) psychologists, educationists and technically oriented researchers started studying 'educational technology' (Ellington *et al.*, 1993). One of their major concerns was to investigate the possible surplus value of particular media over others in particular learning environments. A major problem facing this field of study is the fact that it is next to impossible to prove empirically the excess value of one medium over another, since each language learning situation is shaped by a complex whole of situational, relational, educational, cognitive and affective variables, which are hard to control and make a reliable comparison of two groups of learners – one working with a particular medium, the other without it – extremely difficult. Thus, recommendations to use particular media remain largely based on assumptions, not on generalisable facts. It follows that authors, course designers and teachers alike have very little evidence upon which they can base any improvements to existing media, materials or multimedia programmes, or suggestions for new approaches in new materials.

It seems that, partly as a consequence of this, teachers have become sceptical and critical toward the hyperbole created around new teaching media. They tend to prefer to stick to what is familiar and most practicable, being ill-disposed toward devoting energy to changing teaching approaches that may well not lead to more effective learning. The fact that theorists and researchers often overlook the practical institutional or organisational constraints every teacher has to live with may further undermine teachers' beliefs in proposals made by non-practitioners.

On top of this, teachers may be afraid that new media may come to replace them as teachers, and therefore prefer not to cooperate in what to them seems a self-destructive process. However, since it is only when media and materials are used in a meaningful and pedagogically well-considered manner that they may make the learning process more effective, and since the teacher best qualifies for designing appropriate learning environments, the chance that teachers will disappear altogether is small. Certainly, if learners are to be provided with a large variety of learning experiences that promote independent learning, teacher whole-class instruction time may well have to be reduced. Rather than supplanting the teacher (and the textbook), however, newer teaching aids will supplement and support them.

In view of the challenges that await teachers teacher training, institutions (**TEACHER EDUCATION**) have the responsibility to prepare teachers for an informed selection, adaptation and integration of available media and materials. It will be vital for teachers to perceive both the strengths and the weaknesses of teaching media and materials, and to find ways to overcome shortcomings. The dangers that threaten teachers are those of overburdening teaching with media for their sheer availability, and of falling prey to a naive belief in media's inherent capacities, without devoting sufficient attention to the quality of data input and instruction and process materials, or carefully considering learners' needs, learning styles, abilities, interests and levels of competence in designing learning environments.

**See also:** Dictionaries; Evaluation; Flashcard; Internet; Language laboratories; Media centres; Monolingual principle; Reference works; Syllabus and curriculum design; Teaching methods; Textbooks; Video

## References

Branson, R.K. (1991) 'The Schoolyear 2000 Concept', paper given at North-Western University, 7 March 1991.

Breen, M.P. and Candlin, C.N. (1980) 'The essentials of a communicative curriculum in language teaching', *Applied Linguistics* 1, 2: 89–112.

Collins, A. (1991) 'The role of computer technology

in restructuring schools', *Phi Delta Kappan* 73, 1: 28–36.

Comenius, J.A. and Rosenfeld, H. (1964) *Orbis sensualium pictus*, Neudruck von der Noribergae-Ausgabe 1658, Osnabrück: Zeller.

Council of Europe (1979) *A European unit/credit system for modern language learning by adults. Report of the Ludwigshafen Symposium*, Strasbourg: Council of Europe.

Ellington, H., Percival, F. and Race, P. (1993) *Handbook of educational technology* (3rd edn), London: Kogan Page.

Frankenberg, B. and Fuhr, L. (1997) *Visuelle Medien im Deutschunterricht. Erprobungsfassung 4/97* (Visual Media in German Language Teaching), Munich: Langenscheidt.

Kelly, L.G. (1969) *25 centuries of language teaching*, Rowley, MA: Newbury House.

Klippel, F. (1994) *Englischlernen im 18. und 19. Jahrhundert. Die Geschichte der Lehrbücher und Unterrichtsmethoden* (Learning English in the eighteenth and nineteenth century. The history of schoolbooks and teaching methods), Münster: Nodus Publikationen.

Little, D. (1996) 'Freedom to learn and compulsion to interact: promoting learner autonomy through the use of information systems and information technologies', in R. Pemberton, E. Li, W. Or and H. Pierson (eds), *Taking control. Autonomy in language learning*, Hong Kong: Hong Kong University Press.

Parker, W.R. (1962) *The national interest and foreign languages*, Washington: US Government Printing Office.

Sheerin, S. (1991) ' "Self-access". State of the art article', *Language Teaching* 24, 3: 143–57.

Ur, P. (1996) *A course in language teaching. Practice and theory*, Cambridge: Cambridge University Press.

### Further reading

Frankenberg, B. and Fuhr, L. (1997) *Visuelle Medien im Deutschunterricht. Erprobungsfassung 4/97* (Visual Media in German Language Teaching), Munich: Langenscheidt.

Jager, S.W. (ed.) (1998) *Language teaching and language technology*, Lisse: Swets en Zeitlinger.

Pemberton, R., Li, E., Or, W. and Pierson, H. (eds)

(1998) *Taking control. Autonomy in language learning*, Hong Kong: Hong Kong University Press.

Sheldon, L.E. (ed.) (1987) *ELT textbooks and materials: problems in evaluation and development*, London: Modern English Publications.

Wright, A. and Halcem, S. (1991) *Visuals for the language classroom*, London: Longman.

Yazdani, M. (ed.)(1993) *Multilingual multimedia: bridging the language barrier with intelligent systems*, Oxford: Intellect.

LIES SERCU

# Media centres

The evolution of the role of various media in language learning has been influenced both by the invention of new technologies and by innovative approaches to language learning and teaching. Media centres have grown out of language laboratories and have become part of the resources of **AUTONOMY** in language learning, with **SELF-ACCESS** being a significant purpose.

### Historical development

Media have played different roles in foreign language teaching, and have varied in form and function depending on the prevalent underlying didactic principles of the period, the language class or institution. In eras with a focus on formal **GRAMMAR** and literary **TRANSLATION**, with teachers checking on formal correctness rather than communicative effectiveness, media have turned out to be of minor importance. Occasional use of audio and video mainly served one aim: to support the reconstruction or production of primarily written, formally (i.e. grammatically and idiomatically) correct language. Blackboards – besides audio and video players – represent the major technical devices in such educational environments, sometimes supplemented by overhead projectors or pinboards.

The first language media centres in number were established in the 1970s. So-called **LANGUAGE LABORATORIES** in schools, universities and – above all – institutions of **ADULT** education had become irreplaceable to carry out the methodological steps of the structuralistic language teaching of the **AUDIOLINGUAL** and **AUDIO-VISUAL** approaches. The traditional set-up had learners sitting in isolated booths with headphones and microphones, repeating and (re)constructing situational dialogues. Certain control mechanisms allowed the teacher to listen in on the learners, to interrupt and correct them, or to communicate with all the group simultaneously.

An increased demand for more comprehensive, more flexible and versatile media has been manifest since the 1970s. Media have become an integral part of foreign language teaching and an important tool to meet the demands of new approaches developed on the basis of the major changes both didactics and society have undergone, such as:

- a focus on learner **NEEDS** and – consequently – a shift towards communication **SKILLS**, more 'realistic' themes and **AUTHENTIC MATERIALS**;
- an expansion of foreign language activities to professional, vocational and everyday topics;
- the modification of the term 'near nativeness' as the ultimate goal of language teaching and learning by focusing on principles such as '**INTERCULTURAL COMPETENCE**', 'language' and '**CULTURAL AWARENESS**' instead;
- the willingness for lifelong learning and the readiness of mobile employees to accept flexible work situations in a globalised business world.

Thus, within the concepts of the communicative and post-communicative periods, media nowadays have to serve different aims exceeding the mere **ACQUISITION** of basic language skills. Learners ought to be guided to develop key qualifications and core competencies such as strategic knowledge, team skills, ability to use primary and secondary sources, ability to act autonomously and independently, to take over responsibility and to organise one's own language learning process, and finally, to develop intercultural competence and **LANGUAGE AWARENESS** (Thume, 1998).

The unidimensional language laboratories of the 1970s had to give way to flexible, multidimensional, interactive learning centres that care for individuals as well as for groups of learners and which have their places within and outside organised language courses, promote autonomous forms of learning, provide (culturally relevant, topical, referential) information, as well as training grounds for active language use.

## Learners – materials – teachers

Language media centres facilitate individual training, **TANDEM LEARNING** as well as activities in small groups; they offer diagnostic instruments and self-**ASSESSMENT** tools (e.g. **DIALANG**) and provide the learners with expert advice in language learning matters. To fulfil these tasks, sets of materials of different kinds and qualities are usually provided:

- didactic materials and study programmes of traditional language courses or self-study packages, including course books, videos and CDs or audio tapes;
- authentic, topical, non-didactic materials for native speakers, such as TV and radio programmes, current news shows, on-line newspapers and magazines, documentaries and feature films;
- computer-assisted materials and digitised multimedia packages;
- secondary resources such as reference and grammar books, **DICTIONARIES**, encyclopedias, referential CD-ROMs.

Such materials integrate printed texts, audio and video elements, thus allowing an integrated (and also autonomous) training of the four language skills. Unlike traditional analogous technology, the digitised multimedia materials provided in modern language media centres allow for a never-before-known flexibility, enabling learners to decide about speed, time, form and order of the activities themselves. The full range of integrated technological devices of language media centres will expand the kind of activities carried out by the learners, and may include written authentic communication with native speakers or other learners through e-mail and **INTERNET**, as well as research tasks and field studies.

Language media centres require a new type of language teacher: they have to take over the tasks of advising learners and assisting them in planning their individual study paths rather than teaching traditional language courses. They are expected to help students select materials and train the acquisition of general study skills and techniques. Within this framework, and according to such changed teacher profiles, some language centres in institutions of higher education have started to organise international e-mail Tandems, networking learners around the globe (e.g., the universities of Bochum and Trier in Germany offer these services under http://www.slf.ruhr-uni-bochum.de and http://tandem.uni-trier.de).

## Organisation of media centres

In contrast to the language laboratories of the audio-visual/lingual periods, modern language media centres are usually organised into various 'study areas' and 'work stations' (German: '*Lerninseln*' – 'learning islands'), providing different media or a combination of them, offering places for groups or individuals – as the examples in Figure 9 demonstrate.

Such arrangements, combined with integrated digitised multimedia tools, access to primary and secondary information via CD-ROMs, the internet and traditional libraries, with e-mail hotlines to teacher-consultants, represent the new learning environment of modern multimedia centres.

## Perspectives and criticism

Being located on the crossroads of didactics, pedagogy and information science, language media centres show a high potential for developments in different directions, including the development of innovative multimedia materials, improvement and expansion of teacher training activities and delivering the foundations of further pedagogical research. The consumption of media alone, however, is no guarantee of any kind of pedagogical success. First of all, limitations are met in the technological field: if media centres are to fulfil all the above-mentioned criteria, the establishment of such centres will mean considerable financial investment. The technological equipment will have to meet the highest demands, but the lifecycles of hardware and software are quite short, so that high, regular consequential costs have to be taken into account.

On top of that, the number of adequate software and multimedia packages available is still limited:

didactics has not kept up with technological development – a situation which the international organisations of language centres CercleS and EUROCALL plan to alter by initiating further research, organising conferences and supporting material design.

**See also:** Beginner language learners; Group work; Internet; Language laboratories; Large classes; Learning styles; Learning to learn; Strategies of language learning; Task-based teaching and assessment; Video

## Reference

Thume, K.-H. (1998) 'Das elektronische Sprachlabor', *Zielsprache Englisch* 4: 25–34.

## Further reading

### Journals

*BJET (British Journal of Educational Technology)*: London.

*CAELL Journal (Computer Assisted English Language Learning)*: Oregon.

*The IALL Journal of Language Learning Technology (International Association for Learning Laboratories)*: Athens, GA.

### Books and articles

Boyle, R. (1995) 'Language teaching at a distance: from the first generation model to the third', *System* 3: 283–94.

Dickinson, L. (1995) 'Autonomy and motivation; a literature review', *System* 2: 165–74.

Levy, M. (1997) *Computer assisted language learning. Context and conceptualization*, Oxford: Clarendon Press.

Little, D. (1994) 'Learner autonomy: a theoretical construct and its practical application', *Die Neueren Sprachen* 93, 5: 430–42.

Rose, R.G. (1995) 'French satellite TV in the classroom', *Foreign Language Annals* 28, 4: 518–26.

ROLAND FISCHER

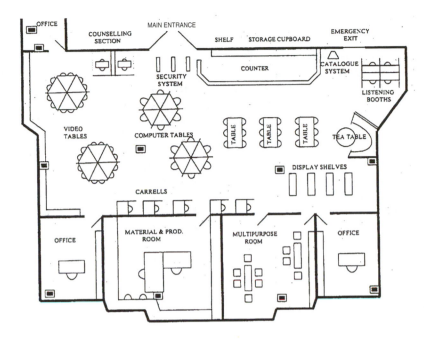

(a) Traditional language media centre

(b) Modern language media centre

Figure 9   Modern language media centres: (a) The Chinese University of Hong Kong; (b) the Self-Access
Centre of Hong Kong University of Science and Technology's Language Centre

# Medium of instruction

'Medium of instruction' refers to a means to
enhance levels of final attainment in language
**COMPETENCE** by using a second language to teach
non-language subjects like geography, history,
biology, etc. This form of language provision goes
under several names, including **BILINGUAL EDUCA-
TION**, immersion, **CONTENT-BASED INSTRUCTION**,
content and language integrated classrooms.
Although sharing many features with special
education provision for minority groups (sometimes known as language shelter or **HERITAGE
LANGUAGE** programmes), immigrant populations

(sometimes known as transitional bilingual pro-grammes), professional and vocational **NEEDS** (**LANGUAGES FOR SPECIFIC PURPOSES**), the target population is primarily conceived of as being the average schoolgoer operating in a **MONOLINGUAL** education environment. The role of the second language as a medium of instruction varies enormously according to the context in which the school operates, and there is no ideal model for universal application.

The use of a second language (whether indigenous or foreign, totally unknown or partially known by some of the pupils at the onset of schooling), for learning non-linguistic content-matter subjects has a longer history than is reflected by research. Throughout the ages, children with a different first language from that of the predominantly monolingual education systems of the world have received content-matter instruction through a different language, with varying degrees of success. Education through the medium of a second language only became a major focus of research interest when the inadequate results of second and foreign language instruction for majority children became apparent, leading to a quest for alternative paths towards higher second language proficiency among larger numbers of school-leavers. In spite of far-reaching shifts in language teaching, from the discredited **GRAMMAR–TRANSLATION** method, through a wide range of theoretically founded alternatives (**AUDIO-VISUAL**, pattern–drill, **COMMUNICATIVE LANGUAGE TEACHING**, **TOTAL PHYSICAL RESPONSE**, **NOTIONS AND FUNCTIONS** syllabus, etc.), for the majority of children receiving education in a monolingual school environment, levels of attainment in a second or foreign language are still poor and not commensurate with the time and effort devoted to language in the **SYLLABUS**.

## Immersion programmes

The growth and development of Canadian immersion programmes in the 1970s, under parental pressures, gave the impetus for a new approach to second or foreign language enhancement through education. Because of the increasing importance of **FRENCH** in **CANADA**, a group of anglophone parents in Montreal were worried that their English-speaking children might lose out in the job market where knowledge of both French and **ENGLISH** was required. They obtained support for an education system where initial learning would start in the unknown target language, French, with a gradual introduction of, and switch over to, predominantly English education as the children progressed into secondary school. This led to the development of early total immersion in French for anglophone children, where initial **READING** and **WRITING** and all other school activities except English lessons were taught through French. Hence, the content matter of primary school education, including the introduction to mathematics, elementary science, social studies and the standard primary syllabus, were taught through a different language. As the children progressed, subjects in English were introduced, in preparation for transfer to predominantly or totally English-medium secondary schooling. Alternative programmes were later developed, known as early partial immersion, where French was not the exclusive medium, and late immersion, where French was introduced for non-language subjects after the foundations of schooling had been encountered in English. Careful monitoring of results revealed that children compared well with English-speaking control groups on knowledge of English and on content-matter, e.g. mathematical skills, and fared far better on knowledge of French than those in English-medium schools who had only received French as a subject (Swain and Lapkin, 1982).

The impressive research on immersion led to adaptations in different parts of the world, often in circumstances totally different from the original Canadian context. At times the immersion model was misappropriated, when the methodological implementation of education through a second language was taken over, with insufficient awareness of the theoretical principles underlying the Canadian success story. This was particularly the case when foreign-speaking immigrant children were immersed in the host environment target language and did not obtain satisfactory outcome results, either on the target language or the content matter of the curriculum (Hernández-Chávez, 1984). The primary reason for failure in this misappropriation was neglect of the immigrant children's first language and an inadequate appraisal of the out-of-school environment (Skutnabb-Kangas, 1984; Cummins and Swain, 1986).

More successful adaptations were made in Catalonia and the Basque Country in attempts to promote bilingual proficiency in Castillian/Catalan and Castillian/Basque, by offering varied permutations of contact with the two languages important in their regions, both as subjects and as vehicles for non-linguistic content-matter (Artigal, 1993). Since the 1990s there has been an upsurge in movements towards the implementation of using a second/foreign language for teaching non-language subjects.

The major distinction between Canadian early total immersion programmes and content-based programmes lies in the fact that, in content-based second/foreign language teaching, there is no radical shift from the child's primary language to the use of a second for non-language subjects. In most cases the second language is first taught as a subject, as in traditional language lessons, before being used as the vehicle for other subjects like biology, geography or history. In most cases the switch to the use of a second/foreign language for content-matter occurs in **SECONDARY EDUCATION**, when the primary language has been well established and there is a sufficient foundation in the second language for rapid take-off and progress. In almost no cases does the second/foreign language take over as exclusive medium of instruction in the curriculum. Nor does the use of a second language for content-matter subjects imply that language teachers become redundant – on the contrary, most programmes maintain second/foreign language lessons in parallel to the use of the second language medium for content-matter lessons. This point is highly significant and accounts in part for the high levels of linguistic accuracy in productive **SKILLS** of **SPEAKING** and writing. In most cases there is some form of selection for pupils embarking on content-matter learning through a second/foreign language, either on a volunteer basis or via proficiency testing. In most cases final examinations are taken through the second/foreign language on the subjects that were taught through that medium.

### Variations and models in the European context

There are, however, many significant variations which can best be illustrated from concrete examples. Countries with the greatest experience in this area outside Canada are Germany and the Grand Duchy of Luxembourg. Luxembourg represents the most radical example, where all children start education in the national language, Luxemburgish, and gradually move to using **GERMAN**, followed by French, for different subjects.

The process operates on the principle of introducing the child to schooling in the home L1 (Luxemburgish), followed by a related, but distinct L2 (German) as a subject, but not a medium of instruction in grade 1. The L3 (French) is introduced as a subject in the second semester of the second year of **PRIMARY EDUCATION**, in preparation for its use as a medium in secondary education.

In primary education, teachers ensure that the switch from the exclusive use of Luxemburgish to the exclusive use of German occurs by the end of the cycle (except in language lessons), but are free to make the transition gradually. Writing is taught through German from the third year of primary education, but at this point in the curriculum more units are devoted to teaching French as a subject than German.

In secondary education most classes are taught through the medium of German in the first three grades, except for French as a subject, and mathematics, which is now taught through the medium of French. The further a pupil progresses in secondary education the more lessons are taught through the medium of French.

Three types of secondary programme account for differences in levels of proficiency attained in the three languages by the end of compulsory schooling. In technical secondary education the amount of time devoted to languages takes account of pupil capacities and needs according to the nature of the job being trained for. Hence, for technical education, languages as subjects take up one third of the curriculum in the first three years. However, in the fourth and fifth years the amount of language contact in the curriculum varies according to orientation. Pupils training for industrial jobs get up to 18 per cent of the programme devoted to language lessons, whereas those aiming for commercial and administrative jobs get up to 35 per cent of the curriculum devoted to language as a subject.

In non-technical secondary education the first three years devote between one third and one half of the curriculum to languages. From then on the weight of languages varies according to specialisation; in the last year for sciences, only six out of twenty-eight lessons are devoted to language learning, whereas in the humanities this may be in the proportion of ten out of twenty-eight. Bear in mind, however, that in secondary education, on top of the above distribution of language lessons, German or French are used as a medium for non-language subjects. For example, biology is taught through German in the early years and through French in the later years. Table 2 gives an overview of the distribution of languages as a subject and as a medium for other subjects throughout the curriculum.

In Germany, certain secondary schools have a so-called bilingual section where volunteers can follow three subjects, usually art, geography, history, politics or biology, through the medium of a foreign language (mainly English and French, but also Dutch, **SPANISH** and other languages, depending on location) from the middle of secondary education. Art is considered suitable, since it creates concrete situational functions where verbal communication is relatively free. Geography or biology carry a referential, information-giving function which allows for a fairly simple beginning phase in the second language. Politics, or civics, covers the partner-oriented and affective functions of language usage, with much greater linguistic subtleties.

Volunteers who opt for this programme receive two extra lessons of the target language as a subject for two years prior to entering the bilingual section. Usually one non-language subject is introduced for three hours per week in the seventh year of education, e.g. geography, followed by a second subject, e.g. politics, in the eighth year. The following year one of the subjects will be replaced by a new subject, e.g. history, to limit the use of a foreign language to two content-matter subjects. The German model explicitly takes into account the need for pupils to be capable of handling the content-matter in both the target language and German, particularly in terms of specialised lexis, and final examinations may be taken in either or both languages. On exit from the programme, inadequacies in knowledge of the content-matter will be sanctioned but not inadequacies in the use of the second language for the subject in question. On the other hand, high levels of competence in the second language will be credited with a 'bilingual mention' on the final diploma, where the fact of having followed a subject through the medium of a foreign language is seen as a plus-point (Mäsch, 1993; Christ, 1996).

Other countries have initiated similar variants of the German experience, though few have gone as far as Luxembourg. The European Schools (Swan, 1996) operate a model similar to that of Luxembourg, where the further a pupil progresses through secondary education the more contact hours are followed using a second or third language for non-language subjects (Baetens

*Table 2*   Number of contact hours per language for the entire curriculum in the Luxembourg system (non-technical secondary education)

| Subject | Primary | Secondary | Total |
| --- | --- | --- | --- |
| Luxemburgish as subject | 125 | – | 125 |
| Luxemburgish as medium | ? | ? | ? |
| German as subject | 1224 | 720–990 | 1944–2214 |
| German as medium | ? | 1331–2159 | ? |
| French as subject | 1080 | 954–1350 | 2034–2430 |
| French as medium | – | 2106–3744 | 2106–3744 |

*Source*: Lebrun and Baetens Beardsmore, 1993

*Note*: ? indicates it has not been possible to calculate the amount of time German and Luxemburgish have been used as a medium of instruction

Beardsmore, 1995). Austria, Finland, **FRANCE**, The Netherlands, Sweden and the UK are all increasing the availability of content-matter learning, partially through a foreign language (Fruhauf *et al.*, 1996). The videocassette 'Intertalk' (1997) is one of the best illustrations of varying practice and results in the use of a second language for content-matter subjects, across all age groups and from **VOCATIONAL** to academic orientations.

## Achievements and problems

Results on both language proficiency and knowledge of content-matter are striking. All programmes claim superior linguistic skills compared with those resulting from language courses alone. Although the majority of existing programmes have an element of pupil selection, which could account for these superior results, the case of the Grand Duchy of Luxembourg, where the entire school population undergoes content-learning through two foreign languages, reveals that selection is not a necessary criterion for success. In Luxembourg it is true that not all school-leavers attain the same levels of trilingual proficiency, but all achieve higher levels than in countries where foreign languages are taught solely as subjects.

Outcome achievements on language proficiency can be explained by a variety of factors. The amount of contact with a second or foreign language is considerably increased when used for content-matter lessons. The nature of linguistic activities becomes highly focused, depending on the subject being studied, and less artificial than in many, even the best designed language lessons, where **AUTHENTIC** materials rarely serve the natural function of language, i.e. to achieve some non-linguistic communicative goal. Teachers claim that using a second or foreign language for content-matter subjects enhances pupil concentration, which may well slow down the progress of lessons in initial stages but which is compensated for later. Teachers and pupils attest to the fact that having acquired high levels of proficiency in a second language through content-based lessons eases their acquisition of a third language (Mäsch, 1993; *Intertalk*, 1997). Follow-up studies of people who have gone through such programmes all reveal great satisfaction and ease at functioning professionally in more than one language.

Problems arising from the sudden expansion of programmes using a second language are manifold. The shortage of teachers proficient in a foreign language and with the specialist subject qualification is a major difficulty. Germany and Austria are fortunate in having teacher training programmes where candidates can obtain certification in both. Coordination between language teachers and subject teachers is important, yet insufficiently provided for in most teacher training courses, leading potentially to a lack of harmony in supplying the specific linguistic needs for the efficient exploitation of studying content-matter through a second language. Few programmes, apart from those developed in Germany, take sufficient account of the need to develop specialised linguistic skills (particularly in the lexis) in the first language, which may not have been used to cover significant parts of the curriculum. There is a dearth of suitable course **MATERIALS** in the second language which take into account the local syllabus and course content requirements, causing many teachers involved to improvise. Imported **TEXT-BOOKS** may have linguistic, cultural and content assumptions specific to the country in which they were produced but unsuitable for the needs of pupils studying for local examinations through a foreign language. Finally, examination criteria may constrain the expansion of the use of a second language for content-matter learning. Luxembourg has adapted its examination system to take the multilingual programme into account; Germany allows for double certification, which enables pupils to take German or foreign recognised examinations; in Britain, special dispensations have been negotiated to allow for secondary examinations to be taken through the foreign medium; while in The Netherlands, Dutch is the compulsory medium for final examinations, whatever the language of instruction.

In spite of such issues, the use of a second language for learning non-language subjects is gathering momentum, strongly supported by the European Commission, the **COUNCIL OF EUROPE** and many forward-looking education authorities.

**See also:** Bilingual education; Bilingualism;

Content-based instruction; Medium-oriented and message-oriented communication; Mother-tongue teaching; Second language acquisition theories

## References

Artigal, J.M. (1993) 'Catalan and Basque immersion programmes', in H. Baetens Beardsmore (ed.), *European models of bilingual education*, Clevedon, Multilingual Matters.

Baetens Beardsmore, H. (1995) 'The European School experience in multilingual education', in T. Skutnabb-Kangas (ed.), *Multilingualism for all*, Amsterdam: Lisse, Swets and Zeitlinger.

Christ, I. (1996) 'Bilingual teaching and learning in Germany', in G. Fruhauf, D. Coyle and I. Christ (eds), *Teaching content in a foreign language*, Alkmaar: Stichting Europees Platform voor het Nederlandse Onderwijs.

Cummins, J. and Swain, M. (1986) *Bilingualism in education*, London: Longman.

Fruhauf, G., Coyle, D. and Christ, I. (eds), (1996) *Teaching content in a foreign language*, Alkmaar: Stichting Europees Platform voor het Nederlandse Onderwijs.

Hernández-Chavéz, E. (1984) 'The inadequacy of English immersion education as an educational approach for language minority students', in California State Department of Education, *Studies on immersion education: a collection for United States educators*, Sacramento: CSDE.

*Intertalk: plurilingual education across Europe* (1997) Videocassette, Continuing Education Centre, University of Jyväskylä, Finland.

Lebrun, N. and Baetens Beardsmore H. (1993) Trilingual education in the Grand Duchy of Luxembourg, in H. Baetens Beardsmore (ed.), *European models of bilingual education*, Clevedon: Multilingual Matters.

Mäsch, N. (1993) 'The German model of bilingual education: an administrator's perspective', in H. Baetens Beardsmore (ed.), *European models of bilingual education*, Clevedon: Multilingual Matters.

Skutnabb-Kangas, T. (1984) *Bilingualism or not: the education of minorities*, Clevedon: Multilingual Matters.

Swain, M. and Lapkin, S. (1982) *Evaluating bilingual education: a Canadian case study*, Clevedon: Multilingual Matters.

Swan, D. (1996) *A singular pluralism: the European Schools 1984–1994*, Dublin: Institute of Public Administration.

## Further reading

California State Department of Education (1981) *Schooling and language minority students: a theoretical framework*, Los Angeles: Evaluation, Dissemination and Assessment Center, California State University.

Skutnabb-Kangas, T. (ed.) (1995) *Multilingualism for all*, Amsterdam: Lisse, Swets and Zeitlinger.

HUGO BAETENS BEARDSMORE

# Medium-oriented and message-oriented communication

This is a distinction between two main levels of communication in the foreign language classroom, both of which are necessary. In medium-oriented communication the focus is on form rather than on content. The underlying speech intention is for the teacher to give pupils an opportunity to build sentences, to show how they can handle the language, to demonstrate their verbal skills and to display their linguistic COMPETENCE. Pupils fill in gaps or give answers which the teacher knows already. Dictation, imitation, PRONUNCIATION and grammar drills as well as language corrections are usually unequivocal medium-oriented acts. Here the medium is the only message. However, when the speakers involved satisfy immediate non-linguistic NEEDS and really mean what they say – for instance: 'How can we prepare for the test tomorrow?' or 'In my view the British electoral system is undemocratic' – they transmit real messages, i.e. they are message-oriented. All classroom management is purely message-oriented (Butzkamm and Dodson, 1980).

Other terms for what is basically the same distinction are 'rehearsal language versus performance language' (Hawkins, 1981) and 'analytic versus experiential use of the language' (Stern, 1983). In Germany the distinction has become known as *sprachbezogene versus mitteilungsbezogene Kommunikation* (Black and Butzkamm, 1977). Since the same utterance may serve a variety of functions, many **SPEECH ACTS** in language lessons lie on a continuum between pure message-orientation and pure medium-orientation. Do the speakers take their utterances to be a real warning, a praise or promise, a real request for necessary information, etc., or are these functions merely incidental to the language-teaching function?

The distinction can be used to assess the communicative quality of classroom interactions. Both anecdotal and statistical evidence show that message-oriented communication is often conspicuously absent in the foreign language classroom. 'There is increasing evidence that in communicative classes interactions may, in fact, not be very communicative at all' (Nunan, 1987: 144). Mitchell (1988) found that a content vacuum was apparent in many lessons.

**See also:** Bilingual method; Content-based instruction; Medium of instruction; Monolingual principle; Reading; Syllabus and curriculum design; Teaching methods

### References

Black, C. and Butzkamm, W. (1977) *Klassengespräche. Kommunikativer Englischunterricht: Beispiel und Anleitung (Classroom conversations: a communicative approach to English teaching. Materials and strategies)*, Heidelberg: Quelle and Meyer.

Hawkins, E.W. (1981) *Modern languages in the curriculum*, Cambridge: Cambridge University Press.

Mitchell, R. (1988) *Communicative language teaching in practice*, London: Centre for Information on Language Teaching and Research (CILT).

Nunan, D. (1987) 'Communicative language teaching: making it work', *English Language Teaching Journal* 41: 136–45.

Stern, H.H. (1983) *Fundamental concepts of language teaching*, London: Oxford University Press.

### Further reading

Butzkamm, W. (1998) 'Communicative shifts in the regular FL-classroom and in the bilingual content classroom', *IRAL* 35, 3: 167–86.

Butzkamm, W. and Dodson, C.J. (1980) 'The teaching of communication from theory to practice', *IRAL* 4: 289–309.

Fazio, L. and Lyster, R. (1998) 'Immersion and submersion classrooms: a comparison of instructional practices in language arts', *Journal of Multilingual and Multicultural Development* 19, 4: 303–17.

WOLFGANG BUTZKAMM

# Mental lexicon

From the myriad of definitions of the lexicon in the literature, in this article the definition proposed by Eve Clark in her book on the lexicon in **ACQUISITION** is adopted: 'The lexicon of a language is the stock of established words speakers can draw on when they speak and have recourse to in understanding what they hear' (Clark, 1993: 2). The perspective taken here is a processing one, rather than a formal linguistic one, in which the lexicon is viewed as the stock of form/meaning complexes that are combined with grammatical rules to form syntactical structures. In various linguistic theories the role and function of the lexicon varies considerably. While in Lexical Functional Grammar the lexical–functional information is at the basis of syntactic structures, in various (now more dated) versions of generative **GRAMMAR**, phrase structure rules and the lexicon are clearly separated. In more recent versions of Chomsky's linguistic theories, in particular the minimalist approach, the lexicon has become more central again, and taken up much more of the syntactic information than before.

### The acquisition of lexical items

Serious word acquisition in the first language starts around **AGE** 2 and, by age 6, children have acquired about 14,000 words. This means that around 10 new words per day are acquired during those 4 years. Nagy and Herman (1987) estimate that children between 6 and 10 acquire about 3, 000 words a year, and from age 10–11 about 10, 000 new words a year. In later phases of acquisition children encounter an estimated 85,000 words, most of which they will acquire to a certain extent. Defining what it means to 'know a word' is notoriously difficult, as Nation (1993) points out. There are many facets of meaning, form and use that can be acquired, and there will be considerable variation with respect to the depth of knowledge of individual words.

In first language acquisition, children must first learn to identify words in the speech stream, which is quite a complicated task. Then they have to map meanings onto forms, i.e. they have to link words they hear with objects, actions and entities in their surroundings. Children start from the assumption that there is a one-to-one relation between forms and meanings, and will only gradually allow for multi-mappings. Clark (1993, 16) argues that 'Transparency, simplicity and productivity, in conjunction with conventionality and contrast ... account for when and how children build up a repertoire of word-formation devices for extending their **VOCABULARY**.'

## The lexicon in language processing

In Levelt's 'Speaking' model (Levelt, 1989; Levelt *et al.*, 1998), the mental lexicon is the storage of declarative knowledge about words, i.e. the meaning and syntactical properties of lexical items (the 'lemma') and formal properties (information about phonology and morphology). Words are retrieved from the lexicon on the basis of conceptual information, so the conceptual information 'young' + 'male' will lead to activation of the lemma-part of the lexical item 'boy'. The activation of a lemma on the basis of that conceptual specification also leads the activation of syntactic procedures that are part of the lemma (such as Verb Phrase for verbs), and the activation of the word form that is linked to the lemma. The word form is inserted in the grammatical structures that are generated by the coalition of lemmas of an utterance. A crucial aspect of this approach is that the syntactic structure is generated by the selection of lexical items. This is in marked contrast with other non-lexically-driven approaches in which the syntactic structure is generated first and lexical items are inserted in the end nodes of the structure.

## The bilingual lexicon

A lot of research has been done to answer the question of how the bilingual lexicon is organised ever since Kolers's work in the early sixties. For Kolers, the question was simply 'Are the words of two different languages stored in one big container or in two separate ones?' The answer to this question is not simply 'one' or 'two', because various factors appear to play a role in the way in which words are stored. Now the question is no longer whether the systems are separated or not, but under what conditions and for which parts of the lexicon they are separated. Based on neuro-linguistic research with bilinguals, Paradis (1987) proposes the 'Subset Hypothesis', which assumes the use of a single storage system where links between elements are strengthened through continued use. This implies that, in general, elements from one language will be more strongly linked to each other than to elements from another language, which results in the formation of subsets that appear to consist of elements from the same language, and that can be retrieved separately. At the same time links between elements in different languages will be just as strong as links between elements in one language in bilingual speakers who employ a 'code-switching mode', and who live in a community where code-switching is a normal conversational strategy.

## Word selection in processing

Oldfield (1963) estimates that average 18-year-olds in Great Britain have a passive lexicon of about 75,000 words at their disposal. Although the number of words we actively use is smaller, the active lexicon may still consist of about 30,000 words. The language user continually has to make the right choice from this enormous collection of words. When we consider that the average rate of speech is 150 words per minute, with peak rates of about 300 words per minute, this means that we have about 200 to 400 milliseconds to choose a word when we are speaking. In other words: two to five times a second we have to make the right choice from those 30,000 words. And usually we are successful; it is estimated that the chance of making the wrong choice is one in a thousand.

This is relevant for the hypothetical unilingual speaker. The situation is even more complex for the bilingual speaker. Even if we assume that the bilingual's lexicon is smaller for each language than the unilingual's lexicon, and that a proportion of the words are the same in different languages (cognates such as 'televisie' or 'multinational'), the total lexicon, even the active lexicon, could easily contain more than 60,000 elements. In order to get an idea of the complexity of the task, one might think of someone who has to find a specific marble of a particular colour in a container with 60,000 different marbles 2 to 5 times a second.

Obviously, it is not the case that for the word selection process each individual lexical item is looked at to see if it is suitable every time a choice has to be made. There is no doubt that our brain is a very powerful calculator, but this is probably too demanding a task. The lexicon must be organised in such a way that a choice can be made quickly and accurately. There is convincing evidence that words are ordered according to frequency, making highly frequent words easier to retrieve than less frequent ones. In order to achieve fast retrieval, irrelevant words or parts of the lexicon have to be eliminated as quickly as possible in the search process. One possibility is that, for the bilingual, the lexical items from one language can be retrieved as a separate set. The question is how this is achieved. A distinction is made between active and passive models. In active models the characteristics which words should comply with are defined, and subsequently the lexicon is scanned until the right candidate is found. An active retrieval process like this is very time-consuming because the entire lexicon has to be scanned. There are alternative versions of this active model, one, for example, being that words are ordered according to frequency of occurrence, or on the basis of semantic field characteristics. Such orderings make lexical searches far more efficient. After all, we usually use frequent words because we talk about a limited number of topics.

Yet these models do not seem very suitable because they are rather slow. A more promising type of model is the passive model. The workings of this type can be explained as follows. A lexical element has a number of characteristics and must reach a threshold level of activity before it can develop further to full activation. The lexical element has detectors for all these characteristics which continuously monitor to see if 'their'

characteristic is called for. If this is the case, the element is stimulated. As soon as a number of characteristics belonging to one element are asked for, it will become active: it will present itself as a candidate for a given slot. For example, suppose we are looking for the word SAMPAN. This word has many characteristics, such as 'inanimate', 'made of wood', 'ship', 'sailing the Sea of China', but for some people it is also 'one of those words they use in tip-of-the-tongue experiments'. If these characteristics are asked for, each characteristic stimulates a number of lexical items, but it is only when the number of characteristics is sufficiently large that the search is completed and SAMPAN is retrieved. As Green (1998) indicates, lexical selection is basically the outcome of lemma competition. In passive models, candidates automatically present themselves as a result of the information that is given. Passive models have an important advantage: they are extremely fast; by giving a number of characteristics, the number of possible candidates is narrowed down very quickly. Although this solution also presents some problems, it is by far the best model available at the moment.

The main questions to be answered with respect to bilingual processing in general and lexicon in particular is: 'How are the words from the right language selected?' Different tasks (**SPEAKING**, **READING**, **TRANSLATION**, code-switching) will entail different constraints in processing words. Green (1998) proposes a model in which a Supervisory Attentional System (SAS) controls the use of different languages in different tasks, controlling the selection of words from the right language for a given task. His model shares certain aspects with two of the other models that have been proposed: Grosjean's Bilingual Interactive Activation (BIMOLA) model (1998) which aims to explain bilingual auditory language perception, and Dijkstra and van Heuven's BIA (Bilingual Interactive Activation) model (1998).

## Learning and teaching words

No direct implications for teaching and learning can be drawn from the psycholinguistic knowledge that has accumulated so far, but those models do inform us about what it means to know words and how that knowledge is structured. It is obvious that 'knowing a word' is not a simple matter: knowing the translation of a word is only a part of what there is to be known. Both the semantic/conceptual part of a lexical item and the syntactic properties, the form-related characteristics, will gradually develop through extensive exposure, most of it through incidental rather than intentional learning. In early stages of L2 acquisition, learning of words in the L2 will proceed through mediation of the L1, but gradually it will diverge from that and the L2 lexicon will become an independent part of the cognitive system: for the incipient learner a 'jardin' may be the same as a 'garden', but the more advanced learner knows better.

While it takes time, and sometimes effort, to acquire new words in a second language, the bonus is that lexical knowledge appears to be very stable: research on long-term retention (de Bot and Stoessel 2000) has shown that a large part of our receptive vocabulary is still intact after decades of non-use.

**See also:** Applied linguistics; Bilingualism; Contrastive analysis; Disorders of language; Generative principle; Lexicography and lexicology; Linguistics; Native speaker; Neurolinguistics; Vocabulary

### References

Clark, E. (1993) *The lexicon in acquisition*, Cambridge: Cambridge University Press.

de Bot, K. and Stoessel, S. (2000) 'In search of yesterday's words: reactivating a long forgotten language', *Applied Linguistics* 21, 3: 364–88.

Dijkstra, T. and van Heuven, T. (1998) 'The BIA-model and bilingual word recognition', in J. Grainger and A. Jacobs (eds), *Localist connectionist approaches to human cognition*, Hillsdale, NJ: Lawrence Erlbaum.

Green, D. (1998) 'Mental control of the bilingual lexico–semantic system', *Bilingualism: Language and Cognition* 1, 2: 67–82.

Grosjean, F. (1997) 'Processing mixed language: issues, findings and models', in A. de Groot and J. Kroll (eds), *Tutorials in bilingualism: psycholinguistic perspectives*, Hillsdale, NJ: Lawrence Erlbaum.

Grosjean, F. (1998) 'Studying bilinguals: methodological and conceptual issues', *Bilingualism: Language and Cognition* 1, 2: 131–49.

Levelt, W.J.M. (1989) *Speaking. From intention to articulation*, Cambridge, MA: MIT Press.

Levelt, W., Roelofs, A. and Meyer, A. (1999) 'A theory of lexical access in speech production', *Behavioral and Brain Sciences* 22, 1: 1–38.

Nagy, W. and Herman, P. (1987) 'Breadth and depth of vocabulary knowledge: implications for acquisition and instruction', in M. McKeown and M. Curtis (eds), *The nature of vocabulary acquisition*, Hillsdale, NJ: Lawrence Erlbaum.

Nation, I.S.P. (1993) 'Vocabulary size, growth and use', in R. Schreuder and B. Weltens (eds), *The bilingual lexicon*, Amsterdam: Benjamins.

Oldfield, R. (1963) 'Individual vocabulary and semantic currency: a preliminary study', *British Journal of Social and Clinical Psychology* 2: 122–30.

Paradis, M. (1987) *The assessment of bilingual aphasia*, Hillsdale, NJ: Lawrence Erlbaum.

### Further reading

Clark, E. (1993) *The lexicon in acquisition*, Cambridge: Cambridge University Press.

Levelt, W.J.M. (1989) *Speaking. From intention to articulation*, Cambridge, MA: MIT Press.

Nagy, W. and Herman, P. (1987) 'Breadth and depth of vocabulary knowledge: Implications for acquisition and instruction', in M. McKeown and M. Curtis (eds), *The nature of vocabulary acquisition*, Hillsdale, NJ: Lawrence Erlbaum.

KEES DE BOT

# Metaphor

Metaphor involves the mapping of one domain of meaning onto a different one. For example, the statement 'Jenny is a rock' operates with two domains of meaning: that of Jenny, a female person, and that of 'rock', which in British English is a large stone, with the connotation of something stable and inert. To describe this statement we say rock is mapped onto Jenny, producing the meaning that Jenny is stable, strong and dependable.

Metaphor is a deviant or paradoxical use of

language that is meaningful while being logically meaningless. For example, 'Jenny is a rock' says something that appears false and true at the same time. Although we know that Jenny is a female person and not a type of stone, most of us would understand that the sentence is telling us that Jenny is mentally strong and dependable.

The most common analysis of a metaphor is as *topic*, or what the metaphor is about, and *the vehicle*, or the concept to which the *topic* is being compared. Thus, in 'Jenny is a rock', *the topic* is Jenny and the *vehicle* is rock. The vehicle can also be termed a *source domain*, as the source of the metaphor, and the topic *the target domain*, as the phenomenon onto which the metaphor is mapped.

Metaphors do not always occur in the very clear way expressed by this example. A text may build itself around an extended metaphor or have a meaning that is both literal and metaphorical. This is illustrated by the following: 'Then the bowman dropped into the water the light he held above his head and the darkness, rushing back at the boat, swallowed it with a loud angry hiss' (Conrad, 1950). Here, 'rushing back at' and 'swallowed' are clearly metaphorical because they represent actions of which 'darkness' is incapable. The topic or target domain is unstated and consists of 'a light going out'. The metaphor is therefore left to communicate this unstated meaning. The status of 'hiss' is interesting because, although darkness is literally always silent, water will extinguish a flame with exactly that sound, thus representing an action that could actually have occurred and confusing our ideas of what is literal or metaphorical.

One might think that metaphors entail unusual or literary language and have little interest for teachers, who should focus on normal usage. However, metaphor is now a topic of enormous and wide-ranging research interest. First, researchers would like to know how it is that we are able to find meaning in a statement that is demonstrably untrue. Our ability to produce one new, comprehensible meaning by blending two old ones may also tell us something larger about how we create and convey new ideas. Second, the current meanings of many words may arise from metaphorical extension. Thus, a current phrase such as 'focus on' (as in 'focus on normal usage' at the beginning of this paragraph) derives from the act of focusing an

optical instrument on an object to make it clear. Such metaphors are termed 'dead' because they are largely unrecognised even though they may account for much of our current meanings in language. Third, if metaphor creates new meanings, it may also play an even more fundamental role in how we grasp the world and reason about it, underlying the creation of most abstract meaning in language.

Language teachers might first consider how metaphors make a language what it is. For example, in English, the idea of 'up' may be a metaphor for stopping or for surrender as in the Elizabethan 'put up your swords'. Thus phrasal verbs that use the word 'up' are often about stopping or being stopped (e.g. hold up, give up, put up, shut up). Such knowledge can make an obscure area of language appear more comprehensible.

Yet the example of 'up is stopping' cannot be generalised beyond a set of difficult verbs. More interesting is an understanding of how metaphors organise the way a language expresses abstract meanings. For example, the modern founders of metaphor studies, Lakoff and Johnson (1980), have observed how our understanding of certain topics is expressed in language that is built out of certain base metaphors. Thus a metaphor such as 'life is a journey' will provide us with many of the expressions that we use to talk about life and death. Such expressions as 'I am coming to the end now; I've still got a long way to go; I will struggle on' all communicate the idea of a journey. Likewise 'time is space' means that time is very often expressed through spatial words and shows how spatial references help us to understand time. The pedagogical interest lies in providing students with themes around which they can gather the lexis they need to talk about the world.

If metaphor is fundamental to how we reason about the world, then it is also a useful way to focus discussion in the language classroom. Psychotherapists have noticed how metaphors can be used to trawl for thoughts which patients cannot admit even to themselves (Cox and Pines, 1987). This may be why many affective or **HUMANISTIC** classroom procedures use metaphors to provoke discussion (Moskowitz, 1978).

Finally, if languages are constantly being extended and recreated by new metaphors, a fully competent user of a language will feel that they have the freedom to participate in this process and allow their creativity full rein. Just as very young children experiment with language in order to name things for which they do not have words, so teenage and **ADULT** learners should perhaps be encouraged metaphorically to stretch their limited stock of language and express an experience for which they do not have the right term.

## Other figurative devices

Metaphor is one of a family of figurative devices or tropes that occur in language and is sometimes used loosely as a blanket term for all of such occurrences. Most discussed among these other devices are simile, analogy and metonymy.

Simile is signalled by the use of 'like', 'as', 'as … as' or 'as if'. Some have suggested that similes are in fact marked metaphors or that metaphors are elliptical similes. However, there are substantial reasons for not thinking this. Not least is the general view that similes are not as strong as metaphors. Thus, to say 'she is like a dog' has the sense of a state that is not irrevocable, while to say 'she is a dog' implies something more enduring. Equally the negatives, 'she is not a dog' and 'she is not like a dog' could have entirely different meanings, with the first possessing a literal sense.

In an analogy, the defining aspect is that the topic and the vehicle are not linked together by visual similarity or by how some of the properties of one are applicable to the other. The topic and vehicle are connected because they share logical structures. This can be made clear through the historical analogy: 'We cannot let this be another Munich'. Many historians agree that when the British Prime Minister, Chamberlain, agreed to let the German leader Hitler take much of Czechoslovakia at Munich in 1938, he precipitated World War Two. This was because Hitler was given reason to believe that the other European powers did not want to fight him. Since then, politicians have been motivated by a desire not to be like Chamberlain and not to give into tyrannical demands out of fear of war. In this desire, they are making an analogy between a past event and a present event. The analogy has the inference that if you do the same thing then the same events will unfold. This is because the events have the same structure but with different locations in times and space. This makes clear how inference is a key property of analogy. It also shows how analogies are essential to how we reason about the world (Holyoak and Thagard, 1995). Analogies are ubiquitous in education. They clarify abstract ideas – as when science teachers liken electricity to water. Also, in order to reason effectively about the world, we have to deal in analogical thought. Such thinking may require development by teachers.

Whereas a metaphor involves the mapping of one domain to another, metonymy entails mapping within a domain. Thus when we say 'a set of wheels' we are using a term from the domain of 'car' to refer to 'car.' Metonyms have this part/whole structure. Common also is for a place to represent its function, as when we use 'the White House' to refer to the US presidential administration.

Arguably, metonymy is essential to how we understand descriptive language. In description, we cannot generally represent every feature of a place or person. We evoke them through a few details, building the picture of a landscape from a tree, field and house, for example. From those details the reader or listener can often construct an impression of what is being conveyed. They are building a whole from its parts or interpreting an extended metonymy (Gibbs, 1994).

**See also:** Generative principle; Humanistic language teaching; Learning to learn; Literary texts; Poetry; Reading

## References

Conrad, J. (1950) *The rescue*, London: Penguin (first published 1920).

Cox, M. and Pines, M. (1987) *Mutative metaphors in psychotherapy*, London and New York: Tavistock.

Gibbs, R. (1994) *The poetics of mind*, Cambridge: Cambridge University Press.

Holyoak, J. and Thagard, P. (1995) *Mental leaps: analogy in creative thought*, Rowley, MA: MIT Press.

Lakoff, G. and Johnson, M. (1980) *The metaphors we live by*, Chicago: University of Chicago Press.

Moskowitz, G. (1978) *Caring and sharing in the language class*, Rowley MA: Newbury House.

## Further reading

Gibbs, R. (1994) *The poetics of mind*, Cambridge: Cambridge University Press.

Goatly, A. (1997) *The language of metaphors*, London and New York: Routledge.

Lakoff, G. and Johnson, M. (1980) *The metaphors we live by*, Chicago: University of Chicago Press.

Lakoff, G. and Turner, M. (1989) *More than cool reason*, Chicago: University of Chicago Press.

RANDAL HOLME

## Modern Language Aptitude Test (MLAT)

Professionally developed by John B. Carroll and Stanley M. Sapon, the MLAT is a prognostic measure, first copyrighted in 1955, designed to assess how well a native American English-speaking adult can learn a classical, or modern foreign language, in a typical foreign language programme.

The **ASSESSMENT** device itself, distributed until 1990 by The Psychological Corporation, but not available from 1999, consisted of 'a series of practice **EXERCISES** in learning various aspects of languages', and was administered with a tape recording in five parts: Number Learning (aural), Phonetic Script (audio-visual), Spelling Clues, Words in Sentences, and Paired Associates. The complete test, said to be suitable for Grades 9–12, college and adults, required about 60 minutes, and a short form (parts 3, 4 and 5) took 30 minutes.

Claimed as 'special features and benefits' of the MLAT in catalogue blurbs were that it offered practical measurement ('measures the student's "ear for languages" '), that it was only moderately related to general intelligence ('a better predictor of foreign language success than IQ tests') and that it was versatile ('applicable to classical as well as modern languages').

The significance of the MLAT, however, rests more with three of its attributes than with its actual use as a predictive measure. First, it represents an early, research-based, operationalisation of a high-

level construct, **APTITUDE** for language learning. Second, the MLAT has been used in a wide range of research studies which would define related constructs, their roles in language learning and **ACQUISITION**, the nature of these central constructs, or approach questions of social and educational significance (e.g. selectional procedures and ethics, **GENDER** and language learning, learning disabilities). Third, any appraisal of the MLAT must also consider Carroll's status during the past half-century as the leading – indeed, almost incomparable – expert in the area intersected by **LINGUISTICS**, cognitive **PSYCHOLOGY** and psychometrics.

**See also:** Aptitude tests; Assessment and testing; Attitudes and language learning

## Further reading

Bachman, L.F. (1990) *Fundamental considerations in language testing*, Oxford: Oxford University Press.

Carroll, J.B. (1981) 'Twenty-five years of research on foreign language aptitude', in K.C. Diller (ed.), *Individual differences and universals in language learning aptitude*, Rowley, MA: Newbury House.

Carroll, J.B. and Sapon, S.M. (1959) *Modern Language Aptitude Test manual*, New York: The Psychological Corporation.

Goodman, J.F., Freed, B. and McManus, W.J. (1990) 'Determining exemptions from foreign language requirements: use of the Modern Language Aptitude Test', *Contemporary Educational Psychology* 15: 131–41.

Sparks, R.L. and Ganschow, L. (1991) 'Foreign language learning differences: affective or native language aptitude differences?', *The Modern Language Journal* 75: 3–16.

DOUGLAS K. STEVENSON

## Monitor model

A monitor model is a model for second language learning advanced by Stephen Krashen in the late 1970s to account for problems that second language learners encounter in the formal classroom. Krashen made a strong distinction between language '**ACQUISITION**' and language '**LEARNING**', and argued that what is consciously 'learnt' is only available to learners as a means of monitoring, or checking on language which has already been 'acquired' through an unconscious process. Language that we pick up through the process of communication – language learnt unconsciously – can be *modified* by formally learnt knowledge, but the acquisition of the basic system does not benefit from conscious attempts to learn it. Thus the 'monitor' is only useful as a means of fine tuning what has already been acquired.

This view became very popular in the 1980s, partly because it seemed to offer an explanation of why language learners in formal classrooms so often fail to achieve fluency in the target language. It also reflects the trend associated with de-schooling movements in the 1970s of questioning the role of explicit teaching and an organised curriculum. Teachers, the model implied, did not help learning when they used long-established techniques such as formal presentation and correction. Much teaching could be regarded as negative interference in the natural process of language acquisition. At the same time, its emphasis on 'natural' procedures for learning linked it with the contemporary **COMMUNICATIVE LANGUAGE TEACHING** movement. (For basic exposition of his views, see Krashen, 1981, 1982.)

The 'monitor' was only one part of an ambitious attempt to build a theory of **SECOND LANGUAGE ACQUISITION**, but its influence was so great that it was often detached from other parts of the theory, and Krashen himself referred to the whole theory as the 'monitor model'. The model rests on five claims.

First, language which is acquired is stored in the brain separately from language which is consciously learnt. This claim is contentious, and from the beginning was challenged by psychologists who maintained that it could have no scientific status as it was impossible to test. It was also claimed that the model depended on a separation of conscious and unconscious language use which was unrealistic (as all language use involves a combination of these), and counter-intuitive (as many learners believe themselves to have benefited from conscious memorisation). Certainly the strong claim that 'learning cannot become acquisition' never achieved widespread acceptance among theorists (McLaughlin, 1978, provides early and cogent

criticism; McLaughlin, 1987, and Mitchell and Myles, 1998, provide more recent surveys, placing Krashen's work in the context of later ideas).

The second claim has also already been referred to: 'learning has only one function, and that is as a Monitor or editor' (Krashen, 1982: 15). Learning fine tunes what acquisition has already established.

The third claim is that the rules of language are acquired in a predictable order. This is less contentious, for there is empirical evidence for some degree of ordering of the acquisition of morpheme sequences, for example, and linguists who believe languages share a universal **GRAMMAR** have found regularities in the acquisition of syntactic patterns. But it is risky to present evidence from a limited number of studies as a justification for too strong a claim. Any language can be described by an enormous number of interacting rules. Only a few of these have been studied. And no studies have established that all rules can be fitted into a neat order. Indeed, there is evidence of some individual variation in the route of acquisition.

The fourth claim is that our language development is caused by 'comprehensible input', i.e. exposure to language which is a little beyond our current knowledge in its complexity. Again, critics feel that this formulation is unhelpful, because there is no mechanism for defining exactly what an individual's current level is, nor for determining what it means to provide language a little beyond that level. The statement is arguably true enough as common sense, but is impossible to test because the terms are indefinable.

Finally, the model depends upon the 'affective filter' hypothesis: learners have to be willing and able to allow comprehensible input to act on their minds. Learners may be mentally unable to respond to the language to which they are exposed, and this, Krashen suggests, accounts for why some learners fail to learn in spite of being in a satisfactory environment. This fifth claim, like its predecessor, makes general sense but proves difficult to formalise so that it can be explicitly tested or falsified.

Krashen was a persuasive communicator, and set himself the ambitious task of providing a comprehensive model of second language learning/acquisition. His five hypotheses were undoubtedly stimulating for language teachers, who often used them to devise activities and **MATERIALS** aimed at overcoming the affective filter, or providing appropriate comprehensible input, for example. He himself promoted a variety of pedagogic techniques drawn from his ideas, including a method, 'the natural approach', which he devised with Terrell as co-author (Krashen and Terrell, 1983). Overall, though, psycholinguists and pedagogic theorists remained cautious, feeling:

1 that too much of the model is either untestable in principle or falsified by empirical evidence;
2 that too much of the model is inexplicit or confusing (for example, on the definition of 'learning');
3 that it conflicts in crucial parts with the intuitions of successful language learners;
4 that it is often simply a description of teacher perceptions, with no explanatory powers.

Certainly, formal learning still retained its place in pedagogy long after the height of popularity of the monitor model.

**See also:** Acquisition and teaching; History: after 1945; Intercultural competence; Learning styles; Second language acquisition theories; Silent way; Speaking; Teaching methods; Untutored language acquisition

### References

Krashen, S. (1981) *Second language acquisition and second language learning*, Oxford: Pergamon.
Krashen, S. (1982) *Principles and practice in second language acquisition*, Oxford: Pergamon.
Krashen, S. and Terrell, T. (1983) *The natural approach: language acquisition in the classroom*, Oxford: Pergamon.
McLaughlin, B. (1978) *Second language acquisition in childhood*, Hillsdale, NJ: Lawrence Erlbaum.
McLaughlin, B. (1987) *Theories of second language learning*, London: Edward Arnold.
Mitchell, R.F. and Myles, F. (1998) *Second language learning theories*, London: Edward Arnold.

### Further reading

Barasch, R.M. and James, C.V. (eds.) (1994) *Beyond the monitor model*, Boston, MA: Heinle and Heinle.
Krashen, S. (1981) *Second language acquisition and second language learning*, Oxford: Pergamon.
Krashen, S. (1982) *Principles and practice in second language acquisition*, Oxford: Pergamon.

CHRISTOPHER BRUMFIT

# Monolingual principle

The monolingual principle espouses the exclusion of the native language (or other, previously acquired languages) from the classroom, the target language being both the object and the sole medium of teaching. In particular, it prescribes the strict avoidance of the **MOTHER TONGUE** for meaning conveyance and, less often, for explanation of grammatical rules. The use of **TRANSLATION** and **INTERPRETING** as valuable **SKILLS** in their own right is generally considered to be a separate issue. This article focuses on the acquisition of meaning.

Language is concerned with the communication of meanings, and it is meaning-conveyance that first comes to mind in any consideration of language teaching. On hearing an unfamiliar utterance, our first reaction is to wish to know what it means, and the most natural way to satisfy this desire would be through a mother-tongue version, unless, of course, we had already made much progress in the foreign language. Up to the second half of the nineteenth century, the mother tongue was generally seen as the most obvious and direct means for the transmission of meanings. It was an undisputed resource, and bilingual techniques for demonstrating meaning are usually identified as the oldest language teaching techniques. They include interlinear versions, translations in parallel columns, individual word glosses, and, later, bilingual **DICTIONARIES**. Modern bilingual phrase books for tourists and travellers may be added to the list.

On the other hand, it has always been understood that, quite apart from any consideration of how the meaning of new material is to be established, ample provision must be made for practice and communication without the intrusion of the mother tongue. The monolingual principle emphasises a general law of learning: we learn what we practise. So we should practise the precise function to be developed. If we do not practise conversing in the foreign language without native language support, we will never learn to do this. The monastery schools, while using translation in the classroom, stipulated that only Latin be used outside the classroom, and boys caught using the vernacular were punished.

Foreign language teachers have long been fascinated by the apparent ease with which children learn their mother tongue. Since there is no other language for them to fall back on, foreign languages should also be taught without recourse to another language. This point was forcefully made by the proponents of the **DIRECT METHOD** in the late nineteenth century. 'Direct' meant direct association between concepts and the new language, without interposition of the mother tongue. Even today, in the teaching guidelines issued by education authorities of many countries, there is a clear taboo against using the mother tongue – evidently an echo of the **REFORM MOVEMENT** of more than a hundred years ago.

However, it was soon pointed out by some of the reformers themselves (including, somewhat later, **PALMER**) that a distinction should be made between a quick, initial grasp of meaning and the subsequent acquisition of fluency in using the new language items, the latter requiring considerable time and effort. Among the terms used to characterise the distinction were *Verstehen* versus *Aneignung*, interpretation *versus* assimilation, identification *versus* fusion, recognition *versus* integration (Butzkamm 1973/1978). 'This important distinction was forgotten when the pendulum swung in the 1960s to **AUDIO-VISUAL** methods ... Insecure teachers, anxious to be in the fashion, were to be seen going through every kind of contortion ... trying to get precise meanings across to their class without letting slip a word of English' (Hawkins, 1981: 133).

A serious flaw in the direct method argument is that it uses first language acquisition as a point of reference. If it is true that language teaching should model itself as far as possible on learning in the nursery, then it should be the bilingual nursery that provides that model. This was self-evident to the great Czech reformer **COMENIUS**. When he discussed foreign language teaching, he referred to the development of natural bilinguals, not only

to infants learning their mother tongue. Modern studies in the bilingual upbringing of children all point to the fact that developing bilinguals use their dominant language as a point of reference through which they successfully extend their linguistic **COMPETENCE** in the weaker language. This natural strategy unfolds in several ways. Bilinguals ask for the equivalent expression in the language, which is not being used for communication at the time. They request translations from their interlocutor, to extricate themselves from a **VOCABULARY** problem or sometimes simply to satisfy their curiosity. They create clarity of meaning and order their linguistic worlds by contrasting equivalent expressions (Saunders, 1995).

Moreover, research has shown that good language learners cannot help but see the new in terms of the familiar. The new language must be firmly linked to the universe of things and events which learners have, for the most part, already experienced through the mother tongue. Their task is to establish new links and draw on their total language experience, not cut old links off. Successful learners capitalise on the vast amount of both linguistic skills and world knowledge they have already accumulated via the mother tongue. For the most part, they need not reconceptualise their world in the new language. 'Thousands of concepts, both simple (sweet/sour) and complex (true/untrue) already learned must be carried over into the new language, with any necessary cultural adjustment or refinement. At later stages of learning (assimilating, emancipating what has been presented) the mother tongue is rightly avoided...' (Hawkins, 1981: 175). It is hard to imagine how someone could comprehend the French *anniversaire* without making the connection – overtly or covertly – with birthday. Only students from cultures where birthdays are not celebrated would need additional explanations, and might even have to be taught the modern concept of the calendar. But most children today will have acquired a working concept of chronology in their mother tongue and be fully equipped to deal with such problems.

Foreign language explanations, demonstrations, actions, pictures and realia can enliven teaching, but can clarify meanings satisfactorily only if teaching texts are carefully graded and selected.

The danger of a content vacuum, especially in **BEGINNER** classes, is obvious (Mitchell *et al.* 1981: 66). Moreover, experiments have shown that the mother tongue generally is by far the quickest, safest and most precise means of getting the meaning across (Dodson, 1967/1972). Sometimes a combination of idiomatic and literal translation can be highly effective, as it clarifies both what is meant and how it is said:

Why have you marked this word wrong?
Warum hast du dieses Wort angestrichen? (clarifies the meaning)
Warum hast du dieses Wort falsch markiert? (renders the structure transparent)

This technique provides immediate access to a complete meaning. From the start, learners have a total survey and feel assured that they understand what they hear and know what they are talking about – and this may do much to maintain their confidence and self-esteem. They are now in a better position to practise the phrase (and its variations) and to try it out in personal communications.

From the second half of the nineteenth century to this day, the issue of the use of the mother tongue has been a veritable battleground. The mother tongue has mostly been portrayed as a hindrance, not as a help. Conventional wisdom has only managed to achieve a weak compromise: use the mother tongue as little as possible, usually only as a last resort. Translation is allowed when no easy alternative suggests itself. Instead, we have to re-define the functions of the native language as a major resource in foreign language learning and teaching.

The monolingual principle underlines the necessity of establishing the foreign language as the language of interaction for all classroom routines and activities. Teachers should not restrict the foreign language to the course book, but should also include informal social interactions with students as early and as far as possible. Teachers should be consistent in their use of the language and equip their students with the verbal means of reciprocating in the target language and of participating in classroom management. They should be able to anticipate their students' comprehension difficulties and employ a wide range of simplification techniques to forestall them. A positive target language working atmosphere must be sustained throughout.

Thus, the monolingual principle is best understood as a warning against the persistent temptation for pupils and (tired) teachers alike to fall back on their first language. And, admittedly, avoidance of indiscriminate use of the native language is a top priority. But a deliberate and well-calculated use of the mother tongue as a support is, in the final analysis, teaching from strength, not from weakness. Paradoxically, learners are best weaned from dependence on their first language not by the teacher ignoring it, but by using it. The native language, along with the concepts acquired through and in it, is the greatest resource a child brings to school.

**See also:** Bilingual method; Direct method; Generative principle; Grammar–translation method; History: the nineteenth century; Medium of instruction; Reform Movement; Speaking

### References

Butzkamm, W. (1973/1978) *Aufgeklärte Einsprachigkeit. Zur Entdogmatisierung der Methode im Fremdsprachenunterricht (The enlightened use of the mother tongue. Clearing methodological dogma from foreign language teaching)*, Heidelberg: Quelle and Meyer.
Dodson, C.J. (1967/1972) *Language teaching and the bilingual method*, London: Pitman.
Hawkins, E.W. (1981) *Modern languages in the curriculum*, Cambridge, MA: Cambridge University Press.
Mitchell, R., Parkinson, B. and Johnstone, R. (1981) *The foreign language classroom: an observational study*, Stirling Educational Monographs No. 9.
Saunders, G. (1995) *Bilingual children: from birth to teens* (2nd edn), Clevedon: Multilingual Matters.

### Further reading

Allen, W.S. (1948/49) 'In defence of the use of the vernacular and translating in class', *ELT Journal* 3: 33–9.
Butzkamm, W. (1998) 'Code-switching in a bilingual history lesson: the mother tongue as a

conversational lubricant', *International Journal of Bilingual Education and Bilingualism* 1, 2: 81–99.

Duff, A. (1989) *Translation*, Oxford: Oxford University Press.

Green, J.F. (1969) 'The use of the mother tongue and the teaching of translation', *ELT Journal* 24: 217–23.

WOLFGANG BUTZKAMM

# Mother tongue

The term 'mother tongue' has a number of different meanings. Historically it was used to refer to the first language acquired as a child. The origin of the term was based on the assumption that this first language would be the one spoken by the primary caregiver and this was assumed to be the mother. However, with changes and cultural differences in child-rearing practices, it cannot be assumed that the primary carer will always be the mother and there have been objections to this definition.

As a refinement of the original meaning, the following is suggested: the term *mother tongue* is the first language that the child learns, and inherent in this description is the assumption that the learning takes place in a naturalistic way, i.e. not through formal teaching. Synonyms for mother tongue include:

- *first language*, the first language the child learns to speak and understand;
- *home language*, the language used within the home for everyday interactions;
- *family language*, the language most frequently used within the family or the language used as a **LINGUA FRANCA** between family members;
- *HERITAGE LANGUAGE*, the language which is frequently a means of establishing and reaffirming consolidation with one's origins, though linguistic proficiency is not a prerequisite;
- *community language*, the language spoken by the immediate community, which may be identified as the mother tongue if the mother tongue is a vernacular and less widely used or perceived as of lower status.

These synonyms illustrate the range of meanings given to the term. It is important to emphasise that the mother tongue may not necessarily be a speaker's dominant language or the one most frequently used in everyday life. The mother tongue is the language on which the speaker relies for intuitive knowledge of language, its form, structure and meaning. In the case of bilinguals and multilinguals, the mother tongue is the language chosen for complex cognitive reasoning.

## Difficulties encountered in identifying the mother tongue

Irrespective of the definition adopted, identification of a person's mother tongue remains problematic. This may be due to a number of factors, which include an increase in individual geographical mobility, changes in social practices such as marriage and child-rearing, and the introduction of formal national **LANGUAGE PLANNING** policies in countries around the world. It is increasingly the case that many children learn more than one language simultaneously, even within the home, hence making the designation of just one language as the mother tongue difficult. There are two approaches to designation of a mother tongue: *self-ascription*, whereby an individual makes their own choice or, in the case of very young children, their family acts to do so on their behalf; and *official designation* when the choice is made by others. The Indian censuses are an example of the former, while Singapore policy is an example of the latter. Both approaches have faced difficulties that can lead to the imprecise labelling of individuals, and this in turn can distort large-scale national survey data.

To illustrate the kind of problems faced in the designation of a mother tongue, we can consider the following example. Child A's mother is a **NATIVE SPEAKER** of language *a*, and the father of language *b*. They live in Hong Kong with the parental grandmother, who speaks a dialect of language *b* and the maternal grandfather who speaks a dialect of language *a*. From birth, our imaginary child is looked after by a Filipino-speaking maid. If this child were required to identify one mother tongue for official purposes, the questions raised are:

1 Which language would the parents, jointly or individually, nominate for their child?

2 Which language would the child itself (eventually) choose?

3 Is the choice in any way related to the child's proficiency in the chosen language?

The imaginary situation is made yet more complex if we assume that the one child is in fact a twin who is also learning to communicate with its twin sibling.

It may be easy to dismiss this scenario as a hypotheses, but it is a linguistic sketch frequently found in multilingual societies. Difficulties arise because identification with a language is more than the ability to speak and understand that language, and yet the speaker's **COMPETENCE** and proficiency are rarely taken into account in the designation of the mother tongue. Affiliation with any language, including the mother tongue, is bound up with aspects of identity with or affinity to a particular group. This linguistic affiliation can be claimed through cultural, social or religious identity. This sense of solidarity or belonging to a group goes beyond an individual's linguistic competence. Indeed, the link between an individual's ability to speak and understand a language and their affinity with a particular ethnic group or mother tongue is tenuous.

For complex political and historical reasons, individuals may not always speak the language of the group with whom they claim close affinity and shared identity. Although second- or subsequent-generation migrants may no longer speak the language of their forebears, some would still claim that language as a heritage language, as a way of consolidating their sense of belonging to that group and as a way of reaffirming an element of their ethnicity. Under such circumstances the choice of mother tongue is a symbolic attachment closely linked to an individual's sense of identity and belonging. These factors complicate the identification of the mother tongue.

As populations change in composition, so, too, do their claims to linguistic and other heritage. For example, in the 1970 USA Census 33 million people (17 per cent of the population) claimed a mother tongue other than **ENGLISH**. This represented a 71 per cent increase since the 1960 census. This increase may be accounted for by changes within the population, but it is equally likely that people, when given the opportunity, will change their identity and with that the designation of their mother tongue. It may be that the longer migrants live away from their land or origin or homeland, the more likely they are to reinforce their sense of attachment to it through statements of symbolic identity, including the mother tongue. Language is just one facet in the complex infrastructure of individual identity.

If the choice of mother tongue is difficult for individuals, the dilemma encountered is multifold when compiling national data. Pattanayak (1998) chronicles some of the difficulties encountered with census surveys of mother tongues. These difficulties include political, pragmatic and philosophical dimensions which assume greater significance when the information gathered is to be used as the basis for the subsequent formulation of public policy, such as (mother tongue) education.

The twentieth century witnessed an unprecedented growth in geographical mobility. It can no longer be taken for granted that people will continue to live in the place of their birth throughout their lives. The degree of personal choice individuals can exercise in this cannot be taken for granted either. Natural disaster, political factors as well as individual aspiration are all influential factors. Geographical boundaries are created (e.g. partition of the Punjab region); re-created (e.g. Palestine and Kuwait); new nation states are established (e.g. Bangladesh and Slovakia); while established nations re-create themselves (e.g. the Russian Federation). The motives for mobility are complex. They include political and economic as well as personal factors. Such changes have brought about migration on a scale that ranges from the lone individual on the move to whole communities of peoples being displaced. Twentieth-century patterns of migration have precipitated governments to re-think public policy, not least in the field of the type of education they can provide. Changing populations have caused governments to consider alternatives to the monolingual, assimilationist approach to education as a means of achieving national unity and nation building. As a result, different forms of **MOTHER-TONGUE TEACHING** have been introduced.

**See also:** Bilingual education; Bilingualism; Heritage languages; Mother-tongue teaching; Native speaker; Neurolinguistics; Sociolinguistics; Standard language

### Reference

Pattanayak, D.P. (1998) 'Mother tongue: an Indian context', in R. Singh (ed.), *The native speaker: multilingual perspectives*, London: Sage Publications.

### Further reading

Herriman, M. and Burnaby B. (eds.) (1996) *Language policy in English-dominant countries*, Clevedon: Multilingual Matters.

Ho Wah Kam and Wong, R.Y.L. (eds.) (1998) *Language policies and language education in South East Asia*, Clevedon: Multilingual Matters.

Phillipson, R. (ed.) (1996) *Linguistic human rights*, Berlin and New York: Mouton de Gruyter.

Smolicz, J.J. (1987) 'National language policies in Australia and the Philippines: a comparative perspective', in A.H. Omar *National language and communication in multilingual societies*, Kuala Lumpur: Percetakan Dewan Bahasa dan Pustaka.

LINDA THOMPSON

# Mother-tongue teaching

The impetus for introducing mother-tongue teaching has come from sources as diverse as politicians, parents and educators. Support for the introduction of mother-tongue teaching in the initial stages of schooling is based on the assumption that providing some continuity of language experience facilitates the transition from the home to mainstream schooling and is therefore of educational, intellectual and emotional benefit to young learners. This is regarded as being particularly important for very young children who, in some countries, begin school when they are four years of age or even younger. However, research evidence (see Wells, 1984; Tizard and Hughes, 1984) does not necessarily support this motive. Rather, it suggests that the different styles or registers of

language used in the home and in the classroom, and the rules that govern interaction and social behaviour in school, also present difficulties for some monolingual children. Yet Willes (1983) found that monolingual children are very quickly socialised into new ways of behaving in school, and Thompson (1999) found similar patterns of enculturation for young bilingual pupils.

In some countries, including parts of the USA, programmes have been established to teach literacy in the home language as a bridge to learning to read and write in **ENGLISH**, the societal language. However, these programmes have been criticised because they do not rate the teaching of the **MOTHER TONGUE** as being of value in its own right.

### Influences on policy

Parental opinion has influenced mother-tongue teaching policy. As second- and third-generation migrants changed their status from temporary resident to permanent citizen, so too changed their educational aspirations for their children. Growing awareness of civil rights issues, equal opportunities and the economic potential of being bilingual, or even only monolingual in the dominant societal language, increased parents' demand for their children to be taught languages at school. However, consensus has not been established. Parental opinion varies between those in favour of mother-tongue teaching and those who believe that the best opportunities for their children lie within learning the mainstream, societal language and gaining academic qualifications in that way. The counter-argument is that mother-tongue teaching to the exclusion of the dominant societal language can leave some pupils marginalised, economically vulnerable and hence further disadvantaged.

Educational underachievement of pupils has also influenced the mother-tongue teaching debate. In the UK, the *Swann Report: Education For All* (Department for Education and Science, 1985) found that levels of educational underachievement as measured by success in public examinations, including levels of literacy and school dropout rates, to be highest among *some* black and ethnic minority pupils. Similar trends were noted in other contexts, notably the USA. One response to this was to introduce mother-tongue teaching in the belief that this would raise pupils' self-esteem and nurture a positive sense of identity, thereby improving success in school learning. These factors combined to add support for the introduction of mother-tongue teaching. In those contexts where it was decided to proceed, there remained a number of practicalities to be resolved.

In short, mother-tongue education is closely linked to economic, political and other social factors, and the range and types of mother-tongue teaching provision are not constant. They reflect the societies which they serve. Hence, as societies change, so too does their education provision. For example, in June 1998 the State of California in the USA decided by referendum to discontinue **BILINGUAL EDUCATION** programmes for Hispanic pupils after 18 years of provision.

## Issues in policy planning

The linguistic composition of a society is only one of the factors that influences policymakers and their decisions on mother-tongue teaching. Having decided to formulate a policy, the next step is to consider issues related to mother tongue teaching.

### Which language(s) should be taught as mother tongue(s)?

Societies with large populations, and small societies where several different languages are spoken, face this issue. For example, in the UK The Linguistic Minorities Project (1985) reported no fewer than 154 languages spoken in London primary schools. In formulating a policy it may not be possible to give all of the languages spoken equal recognition within the school system. This is a dilemma now being faced by the government of the new South Africa in formulating its education policy. It is an issue that is also under discussion within the European Union, as the number of member states, and hence languages, increases. How many languages can be recognised for official purposes, and which ones are these to be? Any selection will inevitably lead to some languages being excluded.

The result will be that, even with a mother-tongue teaching policy, not all languages (and hence the speakers of those languages) can be accorded equal status. Some mother tongues will not be taught. In those contexts consideration will need to be given to the question 'Is it better to have some rather than none, or is parity best achieved through teaching the official national language only?' Even in societies that aim for a policy that includes several languages, like Singapore for example, where there are four official languages, English, Malay, Mandarin and Tamil, this choice leaves other languages excluded. This is a particularly delicate issue when world languages – for example, **ARABIC**, English or **SPANISH** – are being considered alongside, lesser-spoken languages like Korean and Japanese. In July 1998 the government of Algeria legislated to make Arabic the official language in public life, leaving the indigenous Berber peoples (and others, including the older generation of French speakers) marginalised.

### The status of vernaculars and language varieties with no written form or orthography

An alternative way of asking which languages are to be included in a national policy for mother-tongue teaching is to consider which languages are to be excluded and why. Should only recognised languages be considered for inclusion, or should equal consideration be given to dialects, non-standard varieties of language and languages that have no standard written form? Recent discussions in the USA have explored issues relating to the introduction of ebonics in the school curriculum. Similar consideration has been given to **CREOLES**, **PIDGINS** and varieties that are still in the process of establishing an alphabet and an orthography. Such varieties are frequently perceived as low in status in comparison with already-established languages. Some argue that teaching the new varieties as school subjects cannot help pupils if it does not lead to better examination results and qualifications. Within the school curriculum, these newly introduced languages and varieties remain low in status in comparison with other school subjects, for example, mathematics or science, and languages that are already well established as part of the school curriculum (these are known as foreign languages). Parents who are themselves speakers of these varieties have been among those to express these concerns. This issue is closely linked to the centrality of literacy within education systems.

## Which language skills should be taught: speaking, listening, reading or writing?

Literacy is seen as central to the school curriculum. National standards of literacy are taken as measures of the relative success of government policy on education. The amount of time dedicated to mother-tongue teaching in the school curriculum determines what it is feasible to teach with limited time and teaching resources. If the emphasis of mother-tongue teaching is to be the teaching of literacy (or biliteracy), this will preclude some mother tongues that do not have a standard written form or orthography. Also, if mother tongues are to be taught for examination subjects, learning to read and to write the language will assume greater significance. If the school curriculum is to be expanded to include mother-tongue teaching, is this to be in addition to existing subjects or will it replace them; and how will this be decided? Much foreign language teaching within the school curriculum emphasises proficiency and **COMPETENCE** in the target languages. This ignores other aspects of education in these languages, including academic study of the language, i.e. a study of the structure, form and functions of the language; the literature written in the language; as well as cognitive language related skills, such as thinking in the language and using the language to perform complex cognitive reasoning. Language learning also demands learning appropriate cultural competence. All of these aspects need to be considered when designing a balanced mother-tongue teaching curriculum. Yet there are practicalities to be considered and a balance to be maintained within an already overcrowded school timetable limited by funding and time constraints.

## Are suitable curriculum materials available to support-mother tongue teaching?

Central to the teaching of all school subjects are quality teaching **MATERIALS** and resources. If the language to be taught as a mother tongue is not already being taught somewhere in the world, then suitable curriculum materials may not be readily available. Many materials produced by small printing companies or by classroom teachers may not be easily available to others. This will apply particularly to minority languages with small numbers of **NATIVE SPEAKERS**. For example, Frisian and Gaelic would fall within this category. Even if curriculum materials already exist in one country they may not be suitable for use in another context. When materials do not exist they will need to be produced, and this takes time. It is also important that the materials are perceived by pupils, parents and teachers as being of equal quality to the other curriculum materials that the children are using to study other subjects. If these already in use include audio-visual and electronic materials such as laser disks, CD-ROMs and the internet, for example, then pupils will expect no less for mother-tongue teaching classes. High-quality teaching materials are not only expensive to produce, they take time to develop and prepare. Publishing is a commercial enterprise and publishers may be reluctant to embark upon projects where demand for the products is limited to a specialist group, especially if that group has limited financial resources for their purchase. Mother-tongue teaching materials, when they are available, may be expensive.

## Where should mother-tongue teaching take place: the school or the community?

Not all teaching needs to take place in school, and not all learning does. In some instances mother-tongue teaching has been accommodated within the school curriculum, while in others pupils attend classes outside of school time, in the evenings, at weekends or at summer schools held during the school vacations. School premises, community halls or even local places of worship are all used as teaching venues. It is not just a question of where to hold these classes but who has control over the mother-tongue teaching provision. In some instances, for example, the teaching of Arabic for studying the Koran, the content and direction of the curriculum and mother-tongue provision has been assumed by parents and representatives of the community. When teaching takes place outside the school and of the control of education authorities and government, it is predictable that patterns of provision will remain uncoordinated. This devolution may make national provision less easy to achieve and to monitor. However, the results achieved by teachers in Saturday Clubs in the

United Kingdom with children of Caribbean heritage has surpassed those achieved via the traditional school route. There remains the possibility that **TEACHER METHODS** in the community may be at odds with the official school provision. Community teachers may or may not be trained professionals. This may lead to conflicts between the official and voluntary education providers.

## To examine or not?

Alongside issues of curriculum content and teaching materials comes the question of whether mother-tongue teaching should replicate approaches to other school subjects or should it be different. If the aim is to establish parity of status for the subject and recognition for the qualities of the pupils who have studied this subject, it is difficult to argue against examinations comparable with those for other curriculum subjects. The case may be clearer in primary schools where, in most countries, there is less emphasis on public examinations. However, **SECONDARY EDUCATION** is almost exclusively focused on preparing pupils for public examinations as a means of selection for entry to **HIGHER EDUCATION** and future employment.

## Teacher supply and training

Mother-tongue teaching is dependent on skilled and well-trained teachers who are proficient in the language, but is this enough? Teachers also need to be professionals who have undergone training and who hold qualifications. In some contexts, difficulties remain in finding and training adequate numbers of teachers to meet the local demand. Also, since training takes time, there is inevitably a discrepancy between the demand and the supply of suitably qualified mother-tongue teachers.

## Funding

Quality provision is dependent on adequate funding. Some mother-tongue teaching initiatives are provided for within the mainstream education budget – for example, in **CANADA** and Singapore; and the Languages Other Than English (LOTE) programmes in **AUSTRALIA**. However, this is not always the case. In the UK, for instance, funding has not been provided from the education budget but has come instead from Section 11 of the Local Government Act 1966. This enabled Local Education Authorities to claim a grant, at the rate of 75 per cent of the salary paid to each teacher employed. In retrospect this policy has been discriminatory in effect, if not in intent. Separate funding has led to separate provision, and this in turn has emphasised marginalisation and separation from mainstream provision for minority groups. The need for funding for mother-tongue teaching is self-evident, but the source of the funding is reflected in the status and stability of the provision. Variations in funding arrangements can in part account for the variability in the status and quality of provision of national mother-tongue teaching programmes.

## Current provision

From the range of education policies that exist, it is possible to identify five different approaches to education provision for teaching the mother tongue. They are ordered here in the degree of commitment demonstrated to the concept, and range from monolingual education systems through to bilingual, trilingual or multilingual education programmes.

1 *Monolingual education systems* where there is only one language recognised as the medium of instruction. This is usually the dominant societal language. In these systems other languages may be taught as part of the foreign language curriculum.

2 *Mother-tongue maintenance* aims to acknowledge the mother tongue(s) spoken by the pupils. However, there is no official recognition of these languages within the school curriculum. The use of the mother tongue(s) may be permitted in the school and even classrooms for informal interactions. In addition there may be library books in some or all of the mother tongue(s) spoken by the pupils. Mother-tongue maintenance aims to foster pupils' self-esteem and respect for the mother tongue(s) by allowing pupils to use the languages they know. However, in these contexts the mother tongue(s) are not used for any official

purposes, or for teaching, and since it is unlikely that there will be teachers who can speak and understand the languages, the pupils are unlikely to develop their competence in any way.

These programmes are frequently a pragmatic response to linguistic diversity amongst the school population. They are not dependent on additional resources and are rarely supported with formal policy statements. In some contexts the support is dependent upon non-teaching staff. These may range from voluntary workers to paid teaching assistants. They are essentially found as bridging programmes to help children through the transition from home to school or from one school to another. The pupils' mother tongue is used as a means of easing the transition to the official school language (Churchill, 1986).

3 *Mother-tongue support* programmes aim to provide opportunities for pupils to use their mother tongue(s) within the curriculum to support their learning. They go beyond merely allowing the use of the mother tongue in school. They encourage and promote the use of the mother tongue for a variety of purposes. The aim is not just to develop the children's proficiency in the mother tongue but actively to promote its use for informal and formal purposes in the classroom. Approaches vary, but are dependent upon having teachers or adult helpers who are sufficiently proficient in the mother tongue to provide the children with guidance and support in oral and written communication. However, since the mother tongue is not the language for teaching, these adults do not necessarily need to be qualified teachers. These programmes may rely on **TRANSLATION** as well as the use of the mother tongue for consolidating children's understanding. Frequently the mother tongue is the language of both informal and official communication between the pupils' homes and the school.

4 *Mother-tongue teaching* where one or more of the mother tongue(s) are taught within the school curriculum. In these situations the mother tongue(s) enjoy the same status as the other subjects of the curriculum. They will be taught by qualified teachers, with appropriate curriculum materials and **SYLLABUS** to inform the

teaching, as well as opportunities to take public examinations. In some contexts pupils may be able to continue to study the mother tongue(s) beyond secondary education at tertiary level, and thus earn high-status qualifications to specialised professions. The drawback to mother-tongue teaching is that the range of mother tongues being taught is restricted. Hence, not all of the mother tongue(s) spoken by the pupils may be offered within one school. This will be particularly true in those contexts where there are several languages spoken within the society and where pupils are speakers of a number of languages. In these circumstances pupils (and their families) will have to decide which of the mother tongue(s) they study. In contexts with few speakers of a particular language, pupils may find that their own particular mother tongue is not available. As Tollefson (1991) points out, in **PLANNING** language we may simply be planning inequality. Mother-tongue teaching does not necessarily lead to greater parity.

5 **BILINGUAL EDUCATION** is when the pupils' mother tongue(s) are both taught and used as a medium of instruction within the school. In these programmes pupils are expected to achieve a high level of proficiency in speaking, understanding, **READING** and **WRITING** the mother tongue as well as at least one other language. A number of established bilingual education programmes exist, each designed to meet local social and economic needs. These include Canadian second language immersion; European models of bilingual education; bilingual education in Wales (cf. García and Baker, 1995); and Singapore's national programme of English-knowing bilinguals (Goh, 1954). An overview of the language policies of thirteen countries in South East Asia is presented in Ho Wah Kam and Wong (1998).

**See also:** Australia; Bilingual education; Canada; Content-based instruction; Heritage languages; Medium of instruction; Medium-oriented and message-oriented communication; Mother tongue

## References

Churchill, S. (1986) *The education of linguistic and cultural minorities in OECD countries,* Clevedon: Multilingual Matters.

Department for Education and Science (1985) *Education for all (The Swann Report),* London: HMSO.

García, O. and Baker, C. (eds) (1995) *Policy and practice in bilingual education,* Clevedon: Multilingual Matters.

Goh Keng Swee (1954) *Report on the Ministry of Education (The Goh Report),* Singapore: Ministry of Education.

Ho Wah Kam and Wong, R.Y.L. (eds) (1998) *Language policies and language education in South East Asia,* Clevedon: Multilingual Matters.

Linguistic Minorities Project (1985) *The other languages of England,* London: Routledge and Kegan Paul.

Thompson, L. (1999) *Young bilingual learners in the nursery school,* Clevedon: Multilingual Matters.

Tizard, B. and Hughes, M. (1984) *Young children learning: talking and thinking at home and school,* London: Fontana.

Tollefson, J.W. (1991) *Planning language, planning inequality: language policy in the community,* London: Longman.

Tulasiewicz, W. and Admams, A. (eds) (1998) *Teaching the mother tongue in multilingual Europe,* London: Cassell.

Wells, C.G. (1984) *Language development in the pre-school years,* Cambridge: Cambridge University Press.

Willes, M. (1983) *Children into pupils,* London: Routledge.

## Further reading

Herriman, M. and Burnaby B. (eds) (1996) *Language policy in English-dominant countries,* Clevedon: Multilingual Matters.

Phillipson, R. (ed.) (1996) *Linguistic human rights,* Berlin and New York: Mouton de Gruyter.

Smolicz, J.J. (1987) 'National language policies in Australia and the Philippines: a comparative perspective', in A.H. Omar, *National language and communication in multilingual societies,* Kuala Lumpur: Percetakan Dewan Bahasa dan Pustaka.

LINDA THOMPSON

# Motivation

Motivation is one of the two key learner characteristics that determine the rate and the success of foreign language (L2) learning (the other being **APTITUDE**): motivation provides the primary impetus to embark upon learning, and later the driving force to sustain the long and often tedious learning process. Although the psychological literature contains a great number of different (and often contradictory) definitions and conceptualisations of human motivation (see **MOTIVATION THEORIES**), it is generally accepted that the concept has both a qualitative and a quantitative dimension. The former concerns the goal or the direction of learning, the latter the intensity of the effort invested. Thus, to provide a basic definition, motivation to learn a foreign language involves all those affects and cognitions that initiate language learning, determine language choice, and energise the language learning process. Due to the complex nature of language itself – it is at the same time a communication code, an integral part of the individual's identity, and the most important channel of social organisation – L2 motivation is a highly eclectic and multifaceted construct, consisting of a range of different motives associated with certain features of the L2 (e.g. various **ATTITUDES** towards the L2), the language learner (e.g. self confidence or need for achievement), and the learning situation (e.g. the appraisal of the L2 course or the teacher).

## The social psychological approach to L2 motivation

The systematic study of L2 motivation goes back to the late 1950s when two social psychologists in Canada, Robert Gardner and Wallace Lambert, launched a series of studies examining how language learners' attitudes towards the L2-speaking community affected their desire to learn the L2 (Gardner and Lambert, 1972). The researchers followed a social psychological approach, focusing on the influences of the social context and the relational patterns between the language communities, as measured by means of the individual's social attitudes. The original hypothesis that 'students' attitudes towards the specific language group are bound to influence how successful they will be in incorporating aspects of that language' (Gardner, 1985: 6) received ample empirical support in investigations carried out both by Gardner and his Canadian associates, and by other researchers in different parts of the world. It follows from this that L2 learning is not a socially neutral field and, therefore, the motivational basis of L2 attainment is not directly comparable to that of the mastery of other subject matters. Knowing an L2 also involves the development of some sort of 'L2 identity' which has a pronounced sociocultural angle and, therefore, in addition to the environmental and cognitive factors normally associated with learning motivation in current educational **PSYCHOLOGY**, L2 motivation also contains a featured social dimension. The significance of this dimension is underscored by the recollection that most nations in the world are multicultural and the majority of people in the world speak at least one second language.

As a result of the empirical investigations conducted, Gardner and his associates developed a comprehensive theory of L2 motivation, which features (a) a detailed analysis of what 'motivation' is and how the 'integrative motive' is made up; (b) a general learning model, labelled as the 'socio-educational model', which integrates motivation as a cornerstone; and (c) a standardised motivation test, the 'Attitude/Motivation Test Battery' (see Gardner, 1985: Appendix), which operationalises the various components of Gardner's theory.

According to Gardner (1985), motivation subsumes three components: motivational intensity, the desire to learn the language, and attitudes toward learning the language. Thus, in his view, 'motivation' refers to a kind of central mental 'engine' or 'energy-centre' that subsumes effort, want/will (cognition) and task-enjoyment (affect). This motivation engine can be switched on by a number of motivational stimuli such as a desire to communicate with members of the L2 community, the prospects of a good job that requires L2 proficiency, or, at school, a particular test to be taken or an involving instructional task. However, Gardner sees these 'triggers' as mere motivational antecedents rather than motivation itself – hence his objection to the common misinterpretation of his theory as consisting of a dichotomy of

'integrative motivation' (associated with a positive disposition toward the L2 group and the desire to interact with and even become similar to valued members of that community) and 'instrumental motivation' (related to the potential pragmatic gains of L2 proficiency, such as getting a better job or a higher salary). 'Motivation' in Gardner's theory does *not* contain any integrative or instrumental elements. There does exist an integrative/instrumental dichotomy in Gardner's model, but this is at the *orientation* (i.e. the goal) level, and, as such, is not part of the core motivation component. Rather, the function of the two orientations is merely to arouse motivation and direct it towards a set of goals, either with a strong interpersonal quality (integrative) or a strong practical quality (instrumental).

In Gardner's conceptualisation, the integrative motive is a composite construct made up of three main components, 'integrativeness' (subsuming integrative orientation, interest in foreign languages, and attitudes toward the L2 community), 'attitudes toward the learning situation', and 'motivation' (i.e. effort, desire, and attitude toward learning). The construct has received validation in numerous empirical studies, attesting to the fact that L2 motivation is generally associated with a positive outlook toward the L2 group and the values the L2 is linked with, regardless of the nature of the actual learning context.

The main importance of the socio-educational model (see Gardner and MacIntyre, 1993) lies in its clear separation of four distinct aspects of the second language **ACQUISITION** process: antecedent factors (which can be biological or experiential such as **GENDER**, **AGE** or learning history), individual difference (i.e. learner) variables, language acquisition contexts, and learning outcomes. The main learner variables covered by the model are intelligence, language aptitude, language learning **STRATEGIES**, language attitudes, motivation and language anxiety. These, in turn, affect L2 attainment in formal and informal learning contexts, resulting in both linguistic and non-linguistic learning outcomes. For an empirical validation of an extended version of the socio-educational model, see Gardner, Tremblay and Masgoret (1997).

Applying the social psychological approach, Gardner and his associates/followers did extensive research during the 1970s and 1980s on a variety of issues related to L2 learning and teaching, such as the effects of the social milieu, parental influence, language anxiety, the classroom environment, instructional techniques, and attitudes towards the language teacher and course (for reviews, see Gardner, 1985; Gardner and Clément, 1990; Gardner and MacIntyre, 1993). One particularly important addition to the social psychological paradigm was Richard Clément's (1980) conceptualisation of 'self confidence' as a powerful motivational process, mediating between the quality and quantity of past contact with L2 speakers (or with the L2 via the media), language anxiety, perceived L2 competence and motivational behaviour. Although linguistic self confidence, for Clément, is principally a socially determined construct, it bears a close resemblance to the cognitive concept of 'self efficacy,' which has come to be seen as one of the key motivational factors in mainstream psychology.

### New approaches in L2 motivation research in the 1990s

As discussed in the previous section, Gardner looked at L2 motivation from a social perspective, regarding it largely as a function of intergroup relations and a powerful factor to enhance or hinder **INTERCULTURAL COMMUNICATION** and affiliation. This socially grounded approach underlay most data-based studies examining the affective domain of L2 learning before the 1990s. However, by the 1990s, mainstream motivation psychology had developed a number of cognitive paradigms which had proven highly successful in investigating pedagogical issues in general educational contexts, but which had not been properly utilised in L2 research. Consequently, several researchers in various parts of the world felt that there was a growing gap between general and L2 motivational theories, and the desire for increased convergence engendered a flourish of both empirical research and theorising on motivation. In an overview of the 'new wave' of motivation research, Dörnyei (1998) reviewed over eighty relevant L2 studies from the 1990s, including more than ten newly designed L2 motivation constructs. In these studies, two general tendencies are clearly observable:

1 By paying more attention to motivational processes underlying instructed language learning (rather than L2 acquisition in natural contexts), researchers tried to make motivation research more 'education-friendly' and more relevant for classroom application.

2 There was a general endeavour to develop extended motivational paradigms by complementing the social psychological approach with a number of (mainly but not exclusively) cognitive concepts imported from mainstream psychology.

A prime example of the first trend is Crookes and Schmidt's (1991) pioneering study that distinguished between various levels of motivation and motivated learning (micro, classroom, **SYLLABUS**/curriculum, and extracurricular levels), and which set the tone for a number of further studies by explicitly calling for 'a program of research that will develop from, and be congruent with the concept of motivation that teachers are convinced is critical for SL [second language] success' (Crookes and Schmidt, 1991: 502). The cognitive shift is well represented by Tremblay and Gardner's (1995) model of L2 motivation, which integrated important cognitive concepts such as goal salience, valence (i.e. incentive value) and self-efficacy into Gardner's model as mediating variables between language attitudes and motivational behaviour, and which also subsumed attributions about past learning experiences (see Figure 10). Comparing this model with Gardner's earlier theory gives a clear indication of the extent of the changes that occurred in the 1990s.

The two most elaborate frameworks of L2 motivation to date have been offered by Dörnyei (1994) and Williams and Burden (1997), and are presented in Figures 11 and 12. Both contain an extensive list of motivational components, categorising them in broad clusters, without, however, defining directional relationships between them. This is, in fact, why they are referred to as frameworks rather than models proper. Dörnyei's construct synthesises many elements of Clément's (1980), Crookes and Schmidt's (1991) and Gardner's (1985) theories, and also elaborates on two aspects of L2 motivation that have received little attention in the past: teacher-specific and

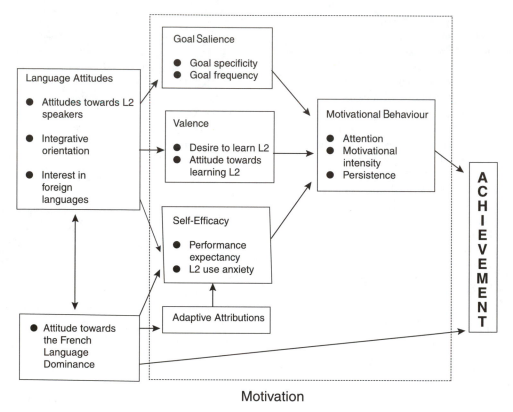

Motivation

Figure 10   Tremblay and Gardner's (1995) model of L2 motivation

group-specific motivational components. Drawing on various branches of psychology, Williams and Burden's list covers most of the relevant issues that have emerged in mainstream motivation research during the past fifteen years, which places their work very much in the forefront of the 'paradigm-seeking' movement of the 1990s.

In an attempt to integrate these and other conceptualisations of L2 motivation, Dörnyei (1998) presented a synthesis by tabulating the main motivational dimensions underlying thirteen different constructs (which included, in addition to the ones already mentioned, work by Clément, Dörnyei and Noels, 1994; Dörnyei, 1990; Julkunen, 1989; Laine, 1995; Oxford and Shearin, 1994; Schmidt, Boraie and Kassabgy, 1996; Schumann, 1998). Dörnyei found that most of the motivational constituents of the selected constructs could be classified into seven broad dimensions: affective/integrative; instrumental/pragmatic; macro-

context-related (i.e. multicultural, intergroup, ethnolinguistic relations); self-concept-related (i.e. personality factors such as self-confidence, anxiety, need for achievement); goal-related; educational context-related; and significant others-related (e.g. parents, friends).

In addition to the theories mentioned above, two further lines of research deserve special attention because of the novel insights they have offered: Schumann's neurobiological approach and Noels and her colleagues' integration of 'self-determination theory' in L2 motivation research. Based on a comprehensive overview of neurobiological research, Schumann (1998) has developed a model for the affective foundation of L2 acquisition that centres around a number of stimulus appraisal processes. He postulates five dimensions along which stimulus appraisals are made: novelty (degree of unexpectedness/familiarity), pleasantness (attractiveness), goal/need significance

LANGUAGE LEVEL                 Integrative motivational subsystem

                               Instrumental motivational subsystem

LEARNER LEVEL                  Need for achievement

                               Self-confidence

                               ● Language use anxiety
                               ● Perceived L2 competence
                               ● Causal attributions
                               ● Self-efficacy

LEARNING SITUATION LEVEL

*Course-specific*              Interest (in the course)
*Motivational Components*      Relevance (of the course to one's needs)
                               Expectancy (of success)
                               Satisfaction (one has in the outcome)

*Teacher-Specific*
*Motivational Components*      Affiliative motive
                               Authority type
                               Direct socialisation of motivation
                               ● Modelling
                               ● Task presentation
                               ● Feedback

*Group-Specific*               Goal-orientedness
*Motivational Components*      Norm and reward system
                               Group cohesiveness
                               Classroom goal structure

Figure 11   Dörnyei's (1994) framework of L2 motivation

(whether the stimulus is instrumental in satisfying **NEEDS** or achieving goals), coping potential (whether the individual expects to be able to cope with the event), and self and social image (whether the event is compatible with social norms and the individual's self-concept). Schumann argues that L2 motivation can be conceived as various permutations and patterns of these stimulus appraisal dimensions.

Noels, Clément, and Pelletier (1999) assert that the integration of Deci and Ryan's (1985) influential theory of intrinsic/extrinsic motivation (and the

subdivision of extrinsically regulated action on the basis of the extent of their self-determined and internalised nature) is potentially very fruitful for the L2 field. Self-determination theory provides a comprehensive framework within which a large number of L2 learning orientations can be organised systematically (on a continuum from intrinsic to extrinsic); the intrinsic/extrinsic paradigm also has a long tradition of being applied in classroom research, which can then be drawn on in examining instructed L2 learning. The authors found empirical evidence for several meaningful

INTERNAL FACTORS

Intrinsic interest of activity

- Arousal of curiosity
- Optimal degree of challenge

Percieved value of activity

- Personal relevance
- Anticipated value of outcomes
- Intrinsic value attributed to the activity

Sense of agency

- Locus of causality
- Locus of control RE process and outcomes
- Ability to set appropriate goals

Mastery

- Feelings of competence
- Awareness of developing skills and mastery in a chosen area
- Self-efficacy

Self-concept

- Realistic awareness of personal strengths and weaknesses in skills required
- Personal definitions and judgements of success and failure
- Self-worth concern
- Learned helplessness

Attitudes

- to language learning in general
- to the target language
- to the target language community and culture

Other affective states

- Confidence
- Anxiety, fear

Developmental age and stage

Gender

EXTERNAL FACTORS

Significant others

- Parents
- Teachers
- Peers

The nature of interaction with significant others

- Mediated learning experiences
- The nature and amount of feedback
- Rewards
- The nature and amount of appropriate praise
- Punishments, sanctions

The learning environment

- Comfort
- Resources
- Time of day, week, year
- Size of class and school
- Class and school ethos

The broader context

- Wider family networks
- The local education system
- Conflicting interests
- Cultural norms
- Societal expectations and attitudes

Figure 12   Williams and Burden's (1997) framework of L2 motivation

links between the relationship between students' intrinsic/extrinsic motivation to learn the L2 and their language teachers' communicative style, the most important being that a democratic (**AUTONOMY**-supporting) teaching style fosters intrinsic motivation.

## Pedagogical implications

Although motivation research in the period before the 1990s was not without any interest in specific classroom issues (for a review of relevant research, see Gardner, 1985), the educational shift described above placed the question of classroom relevance further into the limelight. This was an important development, because the amount of research devoted to understanding *how* to motivate learners rather than *what* L2 motivation is, had been rather meagre. As a result of this increased interest, a number of publications appeared that provided discussion of various motivational strategies (e.g. Brown, 1994; Dörnyei, 1994; Oxford and Shearin, 1994; Williams and Burden, 1997). However, a general shortcoming of the motivational techniques presented in these and other publications has been that they were not based on systematic L2 research and were somewhat *ad hoc*. Some empirical validation was offered by Dörnyei and Csizér (1998), who conducted a data-based study in which they asked a relatively large sample of practising L2 teachers working in a variety of teaching institutions to evaluate the classroom relevance of fifty-three motivational strategies. Based on the responses, the authors compiled a list of ten motivational macro-strategies, referred to as the 'Ten Commandments for Motivating Language Learners'.

---

**Dörnyei and Csizér's (1998) 'Ten Commandments for Motivating Language Learners'**

1 Set a personal example with your own behaviour.
2 Create a pleasant, relaxed atmosphere in the classroom.
3 Present the tasks properly.
4 Develop a good relationship with the learners.
5 Increase the learner's linguistic self-confidence.
6 Make the language classes interesting.
7 Promote learner autonomy.
8 Personalise the learning process.
9 Increase the learners' goal-orientedness.
10 Familiarise learners with the target language culture.

---

## Summary

In conclusion, it must be emphasised that L2 motivation is a multifaceted rather than a uniform factor, and no available theory has yet managed to represent it in its total complexity. The 1990s brought along the welcome tendency of incorporating contemporary theoretical concepts from mainstream psychology into established L2-specific frameworks and models, and, as a result, a number of novel theoretical constructs were put forward to describe L2 motivation. This paradigm-generating process is likely to continue, and it is hoped that future models of L2 motivation will demonstrate an increasingly elaborate synthesis of the numerous relevant factors, thereby achieving greater explanatory power and practical utility value in diverse contexts.

Besides striving for more precision, future L2 motivation theories will also need to address one particularly difficult issue: the question of time. The mastery of an L2 usually takes several years and is, very often, a lifelong process. It is not difficult to see that during such an extended period one's motivation does not remain constant but undergoes frequent changes. In fact, even within the duration of one language course, most learners experience that their enthusiasm and commitment tend to fluctuate. Thus, an adequate description of L2 motivation will need to include a temporal dimension, specifying patterns of motivational sequences, rather than merely assuming that motivation is simply the sum of a number of relatively stable components, as current motivation tests and frameworks suggest.

**See also:** Attitudes and language learning; Learning styles; Learning to learn; Motivation theories; Objectives in language teaching and learning; Psychology; Teacher education; Teacher thinking

## References

Brown, H.D. (1994) *Teaching by principles*, Englewood Cliffs, NJ: Prentice Hall.

Clément, R. (1980) 'Ethnicity, contact and communicative competence in a second language', in H. Giles, W.P. Robinson and P.M. Smith (eds),

*Language: social psychological perspectives*, Oxford: Pergamon.

Clément, R., Dörnyei, Z. and Noels, K.A. (1994) 'Motivation, self-confidence, and group cohesion in the foreign language classroom', *Language Learning* 44: 417–48.

Crookes, G. and Schmidt, R.W. (1991) 'Motivation: reopening the research agenda', *Language Learning* 41: 469–512.

Deci, E.L. and Ryan, R.M. (1985) *Intrinsic motivation and self-determination in human behaviour*, New York: Plenum.

Dörnyei, Z. (1990) 'Conceptualizing motivation in foreign-language learning', *Language Learning* 40: 45–78.

Dörnyei, Z. (1994) 'Motivation and motivating in the foreign language classroom', *Modern Language Journal* 78: 273–84.

Dörnyei, Z. (1998) 'Motivation in second and foreign language learning', *Language Teaching* 31:117–35.

Dörnyei, Z. and Csizér, K. (1998) 'Ten commandments for motivating language learners: results of an empirical study', *Language Teaching Research* 2: 203–29.

Gardner, R.C. (1985) *Social psychology and second language learning: the role of attitudes and motivation*, London: Edward Arnold.

Gardner, R.C. and Clément, R. (1990) 'Social psychological perspectives on second language acquisition', in H. Giles and W.P. Robinson (eds), *Handbook of language and social psychology*, London: John Wiley.

Gardner, R.C. and Lambert, W.E. (1972) *Attitudes and motivation in second language learning*, Rowley, MA: Newbury House.

Gardner, R.C. and MacIntyre, P.D. (1993) 'A student's contributions to second-language learning. Part II: Affective variables', *Language Teaching* 26: 1–11.

Gardner, R.C., Tremblay, P.F. and Masgoret, A.-M. (1997) 'Towards a full model of second language learning: an empirical investigation', *Modern Language Journal* 81: 344–62.

Julkunen, K. (1989) *Situation- and task-specific motivation in foreign-language learning and teaching*, Joensuu: University of Joensuu.

Laine, E.J. (1995) *Learning second national languages: a research report*, Frankfurt: Peter Lang.

Noels, K.A., Clément, R. and Pelletier, L.G. (1999) 'Perceptions of teachers' communicative style and students' intrinsic and extrinsic motivation', *Modern Language Journal* 83: 23–4.

Oxford, R.L. and Shearin, J. (1994) 'Language learning motivation: expanding the theoretical framework', *Modern Language Journal* 78: 12–28.

Schmidt, R., Boraie, D. and Kassabgy, O. (1996) 'Foreign language motivation: internal structure and external connections', in R.L. Oxford (ed.), *Language learning motivation: pathways to the new century*, Honolulu, HI: The University of Hawaii Press.

Schumann, J.H. (1998) *The neurobiology of affect in language*, Oxford: Blackwell.

Tremblay, P.F. and Gardner, R.C. (1995) 'Expanding the motivation construct in language learning', *Modern Language Journal* 79: 505–20.

Williams, M. and Burden, R. (1997) *Psychology for language teachers*, Cambridge: Cambridge University Press.

**Further reading**

Dörnyei, Z. (1998) 'Motivation in second and foreign language learning', *Language Teaching* 31: 117–35.

Gardner, R.C. (1985) *Social Psychology and Second Language Learning: The Role of Attitudes and Motivation*, London: Edward Arnold.

Gardner, R.C. and Clément, R. (1990) 'Social psychological perspectives on second language acquisition', in H. Giles and W.P. Robinson (eds), *Handbook of language and social psychology*, London: John Wiley.

Gardner, R.C. and MacIntyre, P.D. (1993) 'A student's contributions to second-language learning. Part II: Affective variables', *Language Teaching* 26: 1–11.

ZOLTÁN DÖRNYEI

# Motivation theories

Motivational psychologists have traditionally tried to understand why humans think and behave as they do. Little justification is needed as to why this issue is immensely complex and the number of potential determinants and influences of human behaviour is very large. Therefore, a substantial amount of effort in motivation research in various sub-fields of **PSYCHOLOGY** has been devoted to identifying a smaller set of key variables that would subsume or mediate other interrelated factors, thus explaining a great deal of the variance in people's behaviour. The endeavour can be compared metaphorically to lifting a large, loosely knit net: If you lift it up holding some of the knots, different shapes will emerge than if you lift it up holding others, even though the actual net is exactly the same. The question, then, is to decide which knots to grab (i.e. which factors to assign a key role to) and how to lift the net up in order to obtain a shape that makes most sense (i.e. what kind of relationships to specify between the selected factors).

Motivation theories have highlighted several different principal components as 'fundamental' to human behaviour and, if we look at the whole body of motivation literature in the twentieth century, it becomes clear that the number of motivational factors that are critical (in the sense that their absence can cancel or significantly weaken any other existing motives whereas their active presence can boost learning behaviour) is extremely extensive. There simply do not appear to exist any 'magic' variables that can universally overrule any other factors and which, therefore, could rightfully be considered the core motivational constituents (or the 'right' knots to grab, in the net metaphor). As a preliminary, therefore, we must note that none of the available theories in psychology offer a completely comprehensive overview of all the relevant motivational forces and conditions.

Although different conceptualisations of motivation show considerable variation, both in terms of their scope and their level of analysis, most researchers would agree that motivation theories in general attempt to explain three interrelated aspects of human behaviour: the *choice* of a particular action, *persistence* with it, and *effort* expended on it. That is, motivation is responsible for *why* people decide to do something, *how long* they are willing to sustain the activity, and *how hard* they are going to pursue it. The bulk of past research on motivation has focused on the 'choice'

or 'why' aspect, i.e. drawing up constructs and processes that affect decision-making and choice with respect to an individual's goals.

Looking at the different areas of psychology in which explaining human behaviour is a focal issue, we can identify two distinct research traditions:

- *motivational psychologists* tended to look for the *motors* of human behaviour in the *individual* rather than in the social being, focusing primarily on internal factors (e.g. drive, arousal, cognitive self-appraisal);
- *social psychologists* tended to see action as the function of the social context and the interpersonal/intergroup relational patterns, as measured by means of the individual's social attitudes.

The most influential approach in the social psychological tradition has been the theory of *reasoned action* and its extension, the theory of *planned behaviour* advocated by Ajzen and his colleagues (for reviews, see Ajzen, 1988; Eagly and Chaiken, 1993). According to these, the chief determinant of action is a person's *intention* to perform the particular behaviour, which is a function of two basic factors, the 'attitude towards the behaviour' and the 'subjective norm' (referring to the person's perception of the social pressures put on him/her to perform the behaviour in question). To these, a further crucial modifying component was added later: 'perceived behavioural control', which refers to the perceived ease or difficulty of performing the behaviour (e.g. perceptions of required resources and potential impediments or obstacles).

In motivational psychology there are currently three dominant approaches: *expectancy-value theories*, *goal theories* and *self-determination theory* (for comprehensive summaries from an educational perspective, see Pintrich and Schunk, 1996; Stipek, 1996; Wigfield, Eccles and Rodriguez, 1998).

Expectancy-value theories comprise a number of different constructs (beginning with Atkinson's classic achievement motivation theory; see, e.g., Atkinson and Raynor, 1974) that are based on the principle that motivation to perform various tasks is the product of two key factors: the individual's *expectancy of success* in a given task and the *value* the individual attaches to success at that task (Wigfield, 1994). Broadly speaking, if people perceive the task outcome to be valuable and feel that completing the task is within their abilities, they are likely to initiate action. The expectancy component is determined by multiple variables, and there are various subtheories that focus on these: *Attribution theory* (e.g. Weiner, 1992) is centred around the way individuals process past experiences (successes and failures); *Self-efficacy theory* (e.g. Bandura, 1993) analyses the causes and consequences of how people judge their own abilities and competence; *Self-worth theory* (Covington, 1992) focuses on how people attempt to maintain their self-esteem.

*Goal theories* are based on the assumption that human action is caused by purpose, and for action to take place, goals have to be set and pursued by choice. Therefore, the key component in these theories is the *goal* and its various properties. In *goal-setting theory* (Locke and Latham, 1990) the main goal variables include the specificity, difficulty and intensity of the goal, as well as goal commitment on the part of the individual. *Goal orientation theory* (Ames, 1992) is centred around two qualitative types of goal as defined by their success criteria: *mastery goals* (also labelled as task-involvement or learning goals) focus on learning the content, and *performance goals* (or ego-involvement goals) focus on demonstrating ability, getting good grades, or outdoing other students.

*Self-determination theory* (Deci and Ryan, 1985) was originally based on the well-known distinction of *intrinsic* versus *extrinsic motivation*. The first type of motivation deals with behaviour performed for its own sake. In order, for example, to experience pleasure or to satisfy one's curiosity. The second involves performing a behaviour as a means to an end, i.e. to receive some extrinsic reward (e.g. good grades) or to avoid punishment. Further research has found, however, that it is more appropriate to perceive internal and external regulation as a cline rather than a dichotomy, and therefore various types of motives were suggested along a continuum between self-determined and controlled forms of motivation (see Vallerand, 1997).

As was mentioned at the beginning, the primary concern of most theories of human motivation in the past has been the 'choice' or the 'why' aspect. However, from an educational perspective this is only of limited relevance, since in instructional contexts many of the decisions and goals are not really the learners' own products but are imposed on them by the system. In such contexts, the effort and persistence dimensions of motivation (the 'how hard' and 'how long' aspects) are more pertinent, with key motivational issues involving maintaining assigned goals, elaborating on subgoals, and exercising control over other thoughts and behaviours that are often more desirable than concentrating on academic work. Such 'volitional' or 'executive' issues have received increasing attention over the past decade (for reviews, see Corno and Kanfer, 1993; Snow, Corno and Jackson, 1996), mainly inspired by Heckhausen and Kuhl's *action control theory* (for a review, see Kuhl and Beckmann, 1994). A central theme within this approach is the analysis of various control strategies that the learner can apply in order to maintain, protect and enhance the initial motivational impetus – a topic that has considerable educational implications and that is closely related to the relatively new discipline of 'self-regulatory learning' within educational psychology.

**See also:** Attitudes and language learning; Autonomy and autonomous learners; Cross-cultural psychology; Motivation; Psychology; Strategies of language learning; Teaching methods

### References

Ajzen, I. (1988) *Attitudes, personality, and behaviour*, Chicago: Dorsey Press.

Ames, C. (1992) 'Classrooms, goals, structures, and student motivation', *Journal of Educational Psychology* 84: 267–71.

Atkinson, J.W. and Raynor, J.O. (eds) (1974). *Motivation and achievement*, Washington, DC: Winston and Sons.

Bandura, A. (1993) 'Perceived self-efficacy in cognitive development and functioning', *Educational Psychologist* 28: 117–48.

Corno, L. and Kanfer, R. (1993) 'The role of volition in learning and performance', *Review of Research in Education* 19: 301–41.

Covington, M.V. (1992) *Making the grade: a self-worth perspective on motivation and school reform*, Cambridge: Cambridge University Press.

Deci, E.L. and Ryan, R.M. (1985) *Intrinsic motivation*

*and self-determination in human behaviour*, New York: Plenum.

Eagly, A.H. and Chaiken, S. (1993) *The psychology of attitudes*, New York: Harcourt Brace.

Kuhl, J. and Beckmann, J. (eds) (1994) *Volition and personality: action versus state orientation*, Seattle: Hogrefe and Huber.

Locke, E.A. and Latham, G.P. (1990) *A theory of goal setting and task performance*, Englewood Cliffs, NJ: Prentice Hall.

Pintrich, P.L. and Schunk, D.H. (1996) *Motivation in education: theory, research, and applications*, Englewood Cliffs, NJ: Prentice Hall.

Snow, R.E., Corno, L. and Jackson, D. (1996) 'Individual differences in affective and conative functions', in D.C. Berliner and R.C. Calfee (eds), *Handbook of educational psychology*, New York: Macmillan.

Stipek, D.J. (1996) 'Motivation and instruction', in D.C. Berliner and R.C. Calfee (eds) *Handbook of educational psychology*, New York: Macmillan.

Vallerand, R.J. (1997) 'Toward a hierarchical model of intrinsic and extrinsic motivation', *Advances in Experimental Social Psychology* 29: 271–360.

Weiner, B. (1992) *Human motivation: metaphors, theories, and research*, Newbury Park: Sage.

Wigfield, A. (1994) 'Expectancy-value theory of achievement motivation: a developmental perspective', *Educational Psychology Review* 6: 49–78.

Wigfield, A., Eccles, J.S. and Rodriguez, D. (1998) 'The development of children's motivation in school contexts', *Review of Research in Education* 23: 73–118.

**Further reading**

Pintrich, P.L. and Schunk, D.H. (1996) *Motivation in education: theory, research, and applications*, Englewood Cliffs, NJ: Prentice Hall.

ZOLTÁN DÖRNYEI

# Native speaker

Native speakers can serve as a model for language learners only if their distinguishing features have been identified. Who, then, is a native speaker? A native speaker is traditionally defined as someone who speaks a language as their native language, also called '**MOTHER TONGUE**' or 'first language'. The trouble is that all the criteria for determining 'native speakerness' are fuzzy and controversial, including birth, the most oft-cited prerequisite (Davies, 1991; Medgyes, 1994; Stern, 1983). While it is generally true that a person who was born in an English-speaking country is a native speaker of English, this is not always the case. What about the girl, for example, who was born in the USA but at the age of one moved to Switzerland after she had been adopted by Swiss parents? Anyway, which countries belong to the English-speaking world? Can Pakistan or South Africa make that claim?

## The linguistic and sociolinguistic perspective

The case of **ENGLISH** is one of the most complex but also best-researched, and can be used here to identify the issues. Similar points could be made about other international and former colonial languages, particularly **FRENCH**. Recognising the difficulty of setting up a division line between English- and non-English-speaking countries, Kachru (1985) arranged countries into three concentric circles. The 'inner circle' includes nations where English is the primary language (e.g., UK, **USA, AUSTRALIA**). The countries in the 'outer circle' were historically affected by the spread of English,

often as colonies (e.g., **INDIA**, Uganda, Singapore); in these multilingual settings English is the second language, the major intranational means of communication. The 'expanding circle' involves nations which have accepted English as the most important international language of communication (e.g., **JAPAN**, Hungary, Argentina), and teach it as a foreign language. However, in Kachru's visual representation 'the distinctions are not watertight' (Crystal, 1995), and countries in each circle exhibit a great deal of variation and internal mobility.

It is on the basis of the three-circle model that Kachru (1985) went on to classify countries according to norms of English usage. The countries in the 'inner circle' use 'norm-providing' varieties. In the 'outer circle' are the 'norm-developing' varieties, which are not deficient but merely different or deviant from standard norms (Davies, 1989). The varieties in the 'expanding circle', however, are 'norm-dependent', in the sense that learners follow some norm-providing variety; they are, to use Kachru's metaphor, 'linguistic orphans in search of their parents' (1982: 50). These categories should not be viewed as closed sets, because under suitable conditions norm-developing countries can become norm-providing ones, and norm-dependent countries can turn into norm-developing ones.

Since the 1980s, the concept of a **STANDARD LANGUAGE** norm has come under repeated attack. The linguistic argument against it is that, as Ward succinctly put it, 'No one can define [Standard English], because such a thing does not exist' (cited in Kachru, 1982: 34). Standard English, British or any other, is an idealisation, an amalgam of assumptions about rules and norms to which learners attempt to adhere with varying degrees of success.

## The educational perspective

The native speaker model is not only the concern of linguists and sociolinguists but an issue which has fuelled debate among language educators as well. In countries where English is spoken as a first or second language, those who still favour the teaching of Standard British or American English for instruction have often been accused of **LINGUISTIC IMPERIALISM** (Phillipson, 1992), implying that the acceptance of any exclusive model would engender discrimination against those who come from non-standard backgrounds. In EFL contexts, on the other hand, the suggestion that Standard British and American should be superseded by English as an International Language (Smith, 1983) can be heard with increasing frequency. One argument for this suggestion is that the number of non-native speakers of English will soon exceed the number of native speakers (Graddol, 1997). In our age of globalisation, Fishman's remark that 'the sun never sets on the English language' (1982: 18) rings more true than ever: English is the unrivalled **LINGUA FRANCA** (Crystal, 1997), and as such its use is no longer the privilege of native speakers (Widdowson, 1994).

The controversy in ELT circles has become particularly acrimonious over the distinction between the native and the non-native speaker. As it was considered to be a useless binomial, new terms were recommended to replace it. For example, Edge (1988) offered 'accomplished users of English', Rampton (1990) coined 'expert speakers and affiliation', while Jenkins (1996) extended the traditional use of 'bilingual speakers' to include both natives fluent in another language and non-natives fluent in English (**BILINGUALISM**). In similar fashion, Kachru (1992) spoke of 'English-using speech fellowships' to stress 'WE-ness' instead of the 'us and them' division. The rancour of the polemic is well rendered by the title of Paikeday's (1985) book, 'The native speaker is dead!'

Although there are a number of persuasive arguments against the native/non-native separation, none of these alternative terms have stood the test of time. 'Native speaker' as opposed to 'non-native speaker' is as widely used in the jargon of both teachers and researchers today as ever. But why is this distinction so impervious? The handy, and somewhat cynical, answer is that the native speaker is a useful term, precisely because it cannot be closely defined (**HALLIDAY**, cited in Paikeday, 1985). Davies added: 'The native speaker is a fine myth: we need it as a model, a goal, almost an inspiration. But it is useless as a measure; it will not help us define our goals' (1995: 157).

Indeed, what are these goals? For the overwhelming majority of language learners the ultimate aim is an effective use of the target language. But can any learner hope to achieve full mastery of a language, with all its linguistic subtleties and cultural allusions? This is a question offering no easy solutions, as confirmed by all three full-length treatments of the native/non-native issue (Coulmas, 1981; Paikeday, 1985; Davies, 1991). Davies (1991) pointed out, with a degree of stoicism perhaps, that membership of one or the other category is not so much a privilege of birth or education as a matter of self-ascription. Kramsch, a non-native educator, agreed that anyone who claimed to be a native speaker was one, with the proviso that they were accepted 'by the group that created the distinction between native and non-native speakers ... More often than not, insiders do not want outsiders to become one of them, and even if given the choice, most language learners would not want to become one of them' (1997: 363f) – an argument echoed by Coulmas when he writes: 'The price of becoming "a facsimile of a native" is a change of one's personality. Everyone may not be ready to pay this price' (1981: 365). As a matter of fact, very few learners want and manage to metamorphose into native speakers of the language they are learning. After all, 'everyone is potentially, to a greater or lesser extent, a non-native speaker, and that position is a privilege' (Kramsch, 1997: 368).

**See also:** Cultural awareness; Intercultural

competence; Mother tongue; Non-native speaker teacher; Objectives in language teaching and learning; Reference works; Standard language

## References

Coulmas, F. (1981) 'Spies and native speakers', in F. Coulmas (ed.), *A festschrift for the native speaker*, The Hague/Paris: Mouton.

Crystal, D. (1995) *The Cambridge Encyclopedia of the English Language*, Cambridge: Cambridge University Press.

Crystal, D. (1997) *English as a global language*, Cambridge: Cambridge University Press.

Davies, A. (1989) 'Is international English an interlanguage?', *TESOL Quarterly* 23, 3: 447–67.

Davies, A. (1991) *The native speaker in applied linguistics*, Edinburgh: Edinburgh University Press.

Davies, A. (1995) 'Proficiency of the native speaker: what are we trying to achieve in ELT?', in G. Cook and B. Seidlhofer (eds), *Principle and practice in applied linguistics*, Oxford: Oxford University Press.

Edge, J. (1988) 'Natives, speakers, and models', *JALT Journal* 9, 2: 153–7.

Fishman, J.A. (1982) 'The sociology of English as an additional language', in B.B. Kachru (ed.), *The other tongue: English across cultures*, Oxford: Pergamon.

Graddol, D. (1997) *The future of English?*, London: The British Council.

Jenkins, J. (1996) 'Native speaker, non-native speaker and English as a foreign language: time for a change', *IATEFL Newsletter* 131: 10–11.

Kachru, B.B. (ed.) (1982) *The other tongue: English across cultures*, Oxford: Pergamon.

Kachru, B.B. (1985) 'Standards, codification and sociolinguistic realism: the English language in the outer circle', in R. Quirk and H.G. Widdowson (eds), *English in the world – teaching and learning the language and literature*, Cambridge: Cambridge University Press/The British Council.

Kachru, B.B. (1992) 'World Englishes: approaches, issues and resources', *Language Teaching* 25, 1: 1–14.

Kramsch, C. (1997) 'The privilege of the nonnative speaker', *Publications of the Modern Language Association of America* 112, 3: 359–69.

Medgyes, P. (1994) *The non-native teacher*, London: Macmillan.

Paikeday, T.M. (1985) *The native speaker is dead!*, Toronto: Paikeday Publishing Inc.

Phillipson, R. (1992) *Linguistic imperialism*, Oxford: Oxford University Press.

Rampton, M.B.H. (1990) 'Displacing the 'native speaker': expertise, affiliation, and inheritance', *English Language Teaching Journal* 45, 2: 97–101.

Smith, L.E. (1983) 'English as an international language: no room for linguistic chauvinism', in L.E. Smith (ed.), *Readings in English as an international language*, Oxford: Pergamon.

Stern, H.H. (1983) *Fundamental concepts of language teaching*, Oxford: Oxford University Press.

Widdowson, H.G. (1994) 'The ownership of English', *TESOL Quarterly* 28, 2: 377–89.

## Further reading

Corder, S.P. (1973) *Introducing applied linguistics*, Harmondsworth: Penguin.

Davies, A. (1991) *The native speaker in applied linguistics*, Edinburgh: Edinburgh University Press.

Graddol, D. (1997) *The future of English?*, London: The British Council.

Kramsch, C. (1993) *Context and culture in language teaching*, Oxford: Oxford University Press.

PÉTER MEDGYES

# Needs analysis

Needs analysis is the process of gathering and interpreting information on the uses to which language learners will put the target language (TL) following instruction; and what the learners will need to do in the learning situation in order to learn the TL. The results of needs analyses are used in language programme planning to make decisions about appropriate learning **OBJECTIVES**, **SYLLABUS** content, teaching and **ASSESSMENT** methods, learning **MATERIALS** and resources.

## Data collection

Needs analysis involves the collection before and during instruction of both *objective* information (relating to the learner's biographical data, learning purposes and language proficiency) and *subjective* information (relating to the learner's attitudes, preferences, wants and expectations).

A variety of procedures are used to collect information for needs analysis. These range from traditional research instruments to informal classroom methods, and include:

- questionnaires which may be administered to language learners themselves and/or to other people who are familiar with the context in which learners need to use the language;
- structured interviews (often used in conjunction with questionnaires) involving a series of set questions relating to needs;
- group discussions with learners;
- collection and linguistic analysis of **AUTHENTIC** spoken and written texts which are typically found in the future context of language use;
- language tests and assessments
- case studies of individual learners.

## Development of needs analysis

The concept of needs analysis in language learning came to prominence during the 1970s in the context of the **COUNCIL OF EUROPE'S MODERN LANGUAGES PROJECT** (Trim *et al*, 1973). This project was heavily influenced by philosophies of lifelong education which were based on the premise that instructional programmes would be more effective if they were centred around learners' individual needs and interests. The first model of needs analysis proposed by Richterich (1972) was based on a set of categories for establishing learners' communicative requirements in the future context of language use. Detailed information was sought on the settings in which learners would use the language, the people with whom they would interact and the language exponents (**NOTIONS AND FUNCTIONS**, syntax, lexis, etc.) they would need in order to communicate. This information was then used to define the content and objectives of the programme of instruction.

This type of needs analysis, known as 'target situation analysis' (TSA) (Chambers, 1980) was also closely identified with the **LANGUAGE FOR SPECIFIC PURPOSES** (LSP) movement which emerged during the 1960s and 1970s. Since LSP courses are usually set up in response to educational or occupational demands, the detailed specification of target language behaviour was seen as an essential first step in LSP syllabus design. The most influential model of TSA was John Munby's Communicative Needs Processor (Munby, 1978), a complex and very detailed analytic tool that allowed course planners to build up a profile of a learner's communication needs. These needs were then translated into a list of language **SKILLS** and micro-functions which formed the basis of the target syllabus specification.

During the 1970s and 1980s, the adequacy of the TSA model of needs analysis exemplified by the Munby instrument came under increasing challenge. Critics questioned the complex and time-consuming nature of the analysis involved, the lack of concrete information on how to translate the lists of micro-skills into actual discourse, and the failure of the model to take account of real-life constraints such as the availability of resources (West, 1994). It was also pointed out that, despite its concern with individual *language* needs, the Munby model ignored the *learning* needs of the learner since cognitive and affective variables such as the learner's attitudes, motivation and **LEARNING STYLE** were deliberately excluded from the analysis. This highlighted a major gap in content-oriented approaches such as Munby's: even though they were able to produce a detailed *target syllabus*, they did not provide an actual *teaching/learning syllabus*. Thus, even carefully designed courses could turn out to be pedagogically inappropriate (Brumfit, 1979).

Subsequent approaches to needs analysis have addressed many of the perceived deficiencies of the Munby model by broadening the focus of data collection to include not only objective data of the kind obtainable from TSA but also (Dudley-Evans and St John, 1998) information on:

- learners' current deficiencies;
- learners' preferred learning **STRATEGIES**;
- learners' wants and expectations of the course;

- the environment in which the course is to be conducted.

## Issues and problems

Although this expanded form of needs analysis enables course planners to build up a rich picture of the learners themselves, their language needs and the learning environment, it is obvious that the collection and analysis of such a wide range of information can be very time-consuming and expensive. Indeed, the process of needs analysis may raise false expectations and lead to frustration on the part of course participants if the information it provides cannot be acted upon due to a lack of resources. For this reason, commentators have emphasised the need for course planners to be clear about the purposes for data collection and how information derived from the analysis will be used (Dudley-Evans and St John, 1998). In addition, numerous writers have noted the importance of incorporating educational and institutional constraints into the needs assessment from the outset so as to provide courses that are appropriate for local conditions and deliverable with the resources available (see Berwick, 1989; Holliday, 1995).

Another potential problem in conducting needs analysis derives from the different perspectives of the various stakeholders in the programme concerning the goals, content and methods of instruction (Berwick, 1989). For example, a group of learners may feel that they need instruction in one area of language (e.g. **GRAMMAR**) whereas teachers may be of the view that their weaknesses lie elsewhere (e.g. **LISTENING** comprehension). Similarly, employers' perceptions of their employees' language needs may be at odds with the results of TSA. Even individuals within the same class will not have the same needs and priorities. This highlights the importance of discussion and negotiation between the various participants in the language programme in order to clarify the nature of the needs and to identify ways in which they can best be met (Brindley, 1989; Tudor, 1996).

Despite the potential difficulties involved in collecting and interpreting information on learner needs, the idea of using needs analysis as a basis for determining course content and methodology has met with wide acceptance, both in general language teaching and in LSP context. Needs-based approaches have had a major influence on other areas of **APPLIED LINGUISTICS** and language teaching, including materials design (Cunningsworth, 1983) and language test construction (Alderson and Clapham, 1992).

In line with developments in learner-centred instruction, contemporary approaches to needs analysis emphasise the active role of the learner in identifying needs. Thus, while TSA may be used to specify provisionally the language content of the course, the syllabus and methodology remain open to modification on the basis of ongoing negotiation and dialogue between the teacher and the learners. Used in this way, needs analysis can be seen as a way of raising learners' awareness of their own needs and goals and hence of developing their **AUTONOMY**.

**See also:** Adult language learning; Adult learners; English for Specific Purposes; Evaluation; Languages for specific purposes; Motivation; Sociolinguistics; Syllabus and curriculum design

## References

Alderson, J.C. and Clapham, C. (1992) 'Applied linguistics and language testing: a case study of the ELTS test', *Applied Linguistics* 13, 2: 149–67.

Berwick, R. (1989) 'Needs assessment in language programming: from theory to practice', in R.K. Johnson (ed.), *The second language curriculum*, Cambridge: Cambridge University Press.

Brindley, G. (1989) 'The role of needs analysis in adult ESL programme design', in R.K. Johnson (ed.), *The second language curriculum*, Cambridge: Cambridge University Press.

Brumfit, C.J. (1979) ' "Communicative language teaching": an educational perspective', in C.J. Brumfit and K. Johnson (eds), *The communicative approach to language teaching*, Oxford: Oxford University Press.

Chambers, F. (1980) 'A re-evaluation of needs analysis in ESP', *ESP Journal* 1, 1: 25–33.

Cunningsworth, A. (1983) 'Needs analysis – a review of the state of the art', *System* 11, 2: 149–54.

Dudley-Evans, T. and St John, M.J. (1998) *Devel-*

*opments in ESP*, Cambridge: Cambridge University Press.

Holliday, A. (1995) 'Assessing language needs within an institutional context: an ethnographic approach', *English for Specific Purposes*, 14: 115–26.

Munby, J. (1978) *Communicative syllabus design*, Cambridge: Cambridge University Press.

Richterich, R. (1972) *A model for the definition of language needs of adults learning a modern language*, Strasbourg: Council of Europe.

Trim, J.L.M., Richterich, R., van Ek, J. and Wilkins, D. (1973) *Systems development in adult language learning*, Strasbourg: Council of Europe.

Tudor, I. (1996) *Learner-centredness as language education*, Cambridge: Cambridge University Press.

West, R. (1994) 'Needs analysis in language teaching', *Language Teaching* 27: 1–19.

## Further reading

Hawkey, R. (1980) 'Needs analysis and syllabus design for specific purposes', in H.B. Altman, and C.V. James (eds) *Foreign language teaching: meeting individual needs*, Oxford: Pergamon.

Richterich, R. (ed.) (1983) *Case studies in identifying language needs*, Oxford: Pergamon.

Richterich, R. and Chancerel, J.-L. (1977) *Identifying the needs of adults learning a foreign language*, Strasbourg: Council of Europe.

Robinson, P. (1991) *ESP today: a practitioner's guide*, New York: Prentice Hall.

GEOFF BRINDLEY

# Neuro-linguistic programming

Neuro-linguistic programming (NLP) is about excellence, and how people act, interact and communicate. It is to do with how their brains work, the language they use and their ability to change, and as such it has a strong relevance to teaching and learning.

'Neuro' refers to the ways in which information is taken in through the five senses (referred to in NLP as VAKOG: Visual, Auditory, Kinaesthetic, Olfactory and Gustatory), and how it is processed by the brain. This processing is done through the internal senses (visualisation, the inner voice and feeling responses) and through 'filters' known as metaprograms. The premise is that every individual has a unique approach to the world – and to learning.

'Linguistic' clearly relates to language. The language people use, both to themselves and to others, reflects how they are thinking. Typically, they might use phrases such as 'that sounds right' or 'that rings a bell with me', if they are in auditory mode, or 'I can't get to grips with it' if they are in kinaesthetic mode, etc., where the verbal META-PHOR reflects the internal experience of the speaker. The precise language people use also affects how the intended message is received. If one uses 'artfully vague' metaphorical language, listeners will tend to understand very different things based on their own individual perception. Conversely, the choice of specific VOCABULARY or grammatical structures can have a very strong effect on the listener (or oneself): if you call something a 'problem', it immediately acquires negative connotations, while the same situation sounds much more appealing and open to resolution if described as a 'challenge'.

The word 'programming' implies flexibility and change. The brain works in certain ways, depending on one's predisposition and experience. NLP maintains that it is possible to 'reprogram' the brain's habitual responses, largely by manipulating the 'modalities', i.e. the inner pictures, sounds (e.g. the inner voice) and feelings that are involved in all decision-making. The manipulation involves changing the 'submodalities', which are the individual variations in each modality. When people visualise, for example, the internal pictures they see might be clear or foggy, in colour or black and white; they may see themselves from the outside (dissociated), or they may visualise from within (associated), etc. The inner voice and feelings can similarly be defined – and manipulated – very precisely. Simply changing the internal dialogue, from criticism and negativity to kind words spoken in a gentle, accepting tone, can make a profound difference to people's self-perception and self-confidence, and hence their ability to act effectively and successfully. Different people process things in different ways, and individuals may process things differently at different times – e.g. if they are thinking of a pleasant or unpleasant experience, the future or the past, etc.

NLP techniques and suggestions for action are based on a series of 'presuppositions' about the nature of human behaviour. It is not considered essential to believe them or believe in them. Simply acting as if they are true can affect behaviour. The presuppositions include:

- communication is **NON-VERBAL** as well as verbal;
- communication is non-conscious as well as conscious;
- mind and body are interconnected;
- the map is not the territory (we all have different perceptions of the world according to our inner 'maps').

The 'core concepts', also known as the 'four pillars' of NLP, are:

- rapport: successful communication or the possibility of influencing others depends on empathising with them;
- outcomes (goals): NLP is very much an achievement-oriented technology, based on the belief that knowing precisely what you want helps you to get it;
- sensory acuity: this involves using your senses to notice everything another person is communicating, often non-verbally and non-consciously; it means observing carefully, not making assumptions or judgements;
- flexibility: having a range of skills and techniques gives you choices and options in the way you act.

### History

NLP originated in the early 1970s. Two Americans, Richard Bandler (then a psychology student) and John Grinder (a professor of **LINGUISTICS**), started looking for 'the difference that makes the difference' between what people who are excellent in their chosen field do most of the time and what all of us are capable of doing, and are probably already doing, some of the time (Bandler and Grinder, 1979). By imitating excellent people (NLP calls it 'modelling'), anyone can learn to be excellent. As well as studying behaviour in relation to the chosen area of excellence, a full modelling

project might look at what the subject does in their spare time, what they eat for breakfast, how many hours a night they sleep – and other, more personal details. This may include their beliefs and values, how they use and understand language, how they 'talk to themselves', how they process information, and so on.

NLP has been developed by numerous practitioners, some of the most influential being Leslie Cameron-Bandler, Judith DeLozier, Steve and Connirae Andreas and Robert Dilts. It is still developing. Bandler himself has extended the 'programming' area of NLP into something he calls HDE (Human Design Engineering). Michael Grinder (brother of John) has worked specifically on NLP in education.

### Relevance to language teaching

NLP has direct relevance to education in general, and language teaching in particular, in the following respects:

- **LEARNING STYLES**: if both teachers and students are made aware of the range of different learning styles, both can play to their strengths and improve areas in which they are less strong; teachers can also make sure that they present and practise material to suit a range of learning styles;
- **LEARNING TO LEARN**: students can be taught those aspects of NLP which will help them learn more effectively;
- communication **SKILLS**: in addition to **GRAMMAR** and **VOCABULARY**, students can be taught the skills of effective communication, which will make them more effective users of the target language;
- approach to language: NLP adds other dimensions to language learning, by taking metaphorical meanings literally, and also focusing on the intention behind the words;
- teaching skills: the personal development aspect of NLP can be applied directly to enhancing the skills of teachers;
- NLP techniques: there are techniques and activities specific to NLP (e.g. the NLP spelling technique, which involves visualising words) which can enhance language learning.

**See also:** Acquisition and teaching; Humanistic language teaching; Learning styles; Metaphor; Motivation; Neurolinguistics; Silent way; Teacher thinking; Teaching methods

### Reference

Bandler, R. and Grinder, J. (1979) *Frogs into princes*, Moab, Utah: Real People Press.

### Further reading

Alder, H. (1994) *NLP: the new art and science of getting what you want*, London: Piatkus.

Beaver, D. (1994) *Lazy learning*, Shaftesbury: Element Books.

O'Connor, J. and McDermott, I. *Principles of NLP*, London: Thorsons.

Revell, J. and Norman, S. (1997) *In your hands: NLP in ELT*, London: Saffire Press.

SUSAN NORMAN

# Neurolinguistics

Neurolinguistics is an area of research that focuses on the neurological instantiation of language in the human brain. **LINGUISTICS**, cognitive **PSYCHOLOGY** and neuroscience contribute to an interdisciplinary approach to modelling language behaviour in relation to the brain functions, which subserve it. The underlying mechanisms of **LISTENING** and **SPEAKING**, and of language **ACQUISITION**, are investigated with reference to neurological **DISORDERS OF LANGUAGE**.

The goal of this area of research is to investigate the brain bases of language and speech. Research focuses on elucidating the neural and cognitive architecture underlying the **MENTAL LEXICON** (word processes) and **GRAMMAR** (phrase and sentence processes) for language comprehension (parsing) and production that allow humans to combine phonemes and morphemes to form words, and to combine words into larger words, phrases and sentences in a meaningful manner. Research interest extends from the auditory-verbal aspects of spoken language to the visual-gestural aspects of **SIGN LANGUAGES**, as well as the visual and motoric aspects of **READING** and **WRITING**. This analysis of input and output modalities allows for the possibility of analysing the linguistic processing components independent of speech to develop a richer view of human communication.

The neurological bases of lexicon and grammar are investigated by employing a range of methodological techniques and subjects:

1 developmental studies of language acquisition in normal and disordered children (e.g., specific language impairment, William's syndrome);
2 experimental psycholinguistic studies of language processing in normal adults, neurological studies of brain-damaged adults (e.g., aphasia, dementia);
3 electrophysiological recordings and functional brain imaging studies of normal adults (e.g., event related potentials, direct cortical recording and stimulation, and functional magnetic resonance imaging, positron emission tomography, magnetic stimulation).

The findings from these various neurolinguistic studies suggest that language processes function in a modular fashion and that the system in the brain processing linguistic behaviour is distinct from other cognitive processes.

Neurolinguistic research integrates knowledge of the structural properties of human language with the methods and models of cognitive neuroscience to develop an understanding of how linguistic behaviour arises neuropsychologically. Within the discipline of linguistics, the object of inquiry is seen as a particular kind of knowledge, an aspect of the organisation of the minds of speaker/hearers. The manner in which this knowledge is represented and utilised in the physical organisation and function of the brain is the theoretical goal. Neuropsychological studies of the relation between brain damage and the resulting functional deficits in linguistic capacity serve as evidence which bears on questions of the organisation of language (grammar) and speech (extralinguistic) and **NON-VERBAL COMMUNICATIVE** behaviours. Techniques which functionally map activity in the brain, are used to verify and support clinical studies of language disorders from the past two centuries. This evidence provides a basis for our understanding of the architecture of the underlying system of linguistic processing.

Within the broader domain of cognitive science, the pursuit of understanding general memory systems, perception and action has primarily relied upon experimentation with linguistic tasks. Language behaviour is amenable to observation, elicitation, experimental manipulation and analysis. Detailed and explicit linguistic theories exist at a variety of levels of abstraction. These are used to derive explanations at the physiological level of description, for developmental processes of acquisition, and for disordered behaviour. Cognitive neuroscientists have been attracted to the study of language, while at the same time linguists have pursued the neurological underpinnings of human language. The convergence of these two efforts has created the field of Neurolinguistics.

**See also:** Applied linguistics; Disorders of language; Grammar; Linguistics; Mental lexicon; Neuro-linguistic programming; Non-verbal communication; Psychology; Sign languages

### Further reading

Caplan, D. (1987) *Neurolinguistics and Linguistic Aphasiology*, Cambridge, UK: Cambridge University Press.

Caplan, D. (1992) *Language: structure, processing, and disorders*, Cambridge, MA: MIT Press.

Jackendoff, R. (1993) *Patterns in the mind: language and human nature*, New York: Harvester Wheatsheaf.

Jackendoff, R. (1997) *The architecture of the language faculty*, Cambridge, MA: MIT Press.

Nespoulous, J.-L. and Villiard, P. (eds) (1990) *Morphology, phonology and aphasia*, Berlin: Springer-Verlag.

Whitaker, H.A. (ed.) (1988) *Phonological processes and brain mechanisms*, Berlin: Springer-Verlag.

MARJORIE PERLMAN LORCH

# Non-native speaker teacher

A non-native speaker teacher is a foreign language teacher, for whom the foreign language they teach is not their **MOTHER TONGUE**; who usually works with monolingual groups of learners; whose mother tongue is usually the same as that of their students. To give an example, a Brazilian teacher of **FRENCH** who teaches French in Rio de Janeiro to a group of Brazilian school children is a non-native speaker teacher of French, just as their French colleague teaching French to the same group is a **NATIVE SPEAKER** teacher of French. They are often referred to as non-native and native teachers.

However, this definition has some flaws. First, non-native teachers do not always work with monolingual groups – there may be a few foreign students in the group. Second, the teacher may take up work abroad, in which case teacher and learners will not have the same mother tongue – the Brazilian teacher of French may move to work in Venezuela. Third, and most important, the existence of the term 'non-native teacher' is legitimate only if the existence of its superordinate, the 'non-native speaker', can be justified. In fact, the concept of dividing the world into native and non-native speakers has stirred heated debate amongst linguists, sociolinguists and educators alike.

Traditionally, the focus of educational research was on the native teacher. Most ELT studies, for example, on the prototypical English teacher analysed problems specific to the native teacher working in some private school of a country where **ENGLISH** was the primary language. Generally speaking, little attention was paid to state education, let alone state education in non-English-speaking countries. As for non-native teachers, the need to examine their distinguishing features was virtually overlooked. This neglect may be explained by financial constraints, as well as by the fact that most research was – and still is – carried out by researchers who were native speakers themselves (Holliday, 1994). Similar concerns were voiced by Phillipson in his seminal book, '**LINGUISTIC IMPERIALISM**' (1992a).

It was not until the late 1980s that this ethnocentric **ATTITUDE** began to change, and an interest in the non-native teacher gained momentum. This recognition was long overdue, especially since there are far more non-native teachers in the world than native teachers and the gap between the groups is rapidly growing (Norton, 1997; Widdowson, 1994). Nevertheless, apart from a number of articles and a collection of papers written on the non-native teacher (Braine, 1999), only one full-length book has been wholly devoted to an analysis of the features that distinguish native teachers from their non-native counterparts, with the emphasis placed on the latter group (Medgyes, 1994).

In 'The Non-native Teacher', Medgyes claims that native and non-native English-speaking teachers, or NESTs and non-NESTs as he calls them, are 'two different species' (1994: 27). This statement rests on four hypotheses:

- NESTs and non-NESTs differ in terms of their language proficiency;
- they differ in terms of their teaching behaviour;
- the discrepancy in language proficiency accounts for most of the differences found in their teaching behaviour;
- they can be equally good teachers in their own terms.

In an attempt to confirm these hypotheses, Medgyes conducted a series of surveys, including a total of 325 participating teachers from eleven countries. The results of these self-reports suggested that, indeed, native and non-native teachers differed in terms of both their language proficiency and their teaching behaviour and, furthermore, the relationship between these two variants proved to be significantly strong (Reves and Medgyes, 1994). The native teacher's linguistic superiority was offset by several weapons in the non-native teacher's arsenal – Medgyes identified six such competencies. Non-native teachers can:

- provide a good learner model for imitation (Edge, 1988; Ur, 1996);
- teach language learning **STRATEGIES** more effectively (Seidlhofer, 1996);
- supply learners with more information about the English language (Palfreyman, 1993; Widdowson, 1992);
- anticipate and prevent language difficulties better (Phillipson, 1992b);
- be more empathetic to the needs and problems of learners;
- make use of the learners' mother tongue (Atkinson, 1987; Hancock, 1997).

In comparing the results, neither group was found better in terms of teaching qualities; in the final analysis, their respective strengths and weaknesses balanced each other out. Hence the

conclusion that 'Different does not imply better or worse' (Medgyes, 1994: 76). This being the case, language teachers should be hired solely on the basis of their professional virtue, regardless of their language background. All other things being equal, the 'ideal' native teacher is the one who has achieved a fair degree of proficiency in the students' mother tongue, and the 'ideal' non-native teacher is the one who has achieved near-native proficiency in the target language.

This is in sharp contrast with two widely held views. On the one hand, many language schools are still in the habit of advertising teaching jobs for native English speakers only (Illés, 1991), in the face of clearcut anti-discriminatory recruitment policy statements issued by major ELT organisations such as **TESOL** and **IATEFL**. Similarly prejudiced is the contrary view which holds that 'the ideal foreign-language teacher is the trained non-native, speaking his/her variety of the foreign language' (van Essen, 1994), even if it is buttressed by such titans of the profession as **SWEET** and **PALMER**.

Medgyes's 'The Non-native Teacher' was criticised for overemphasising 'the linguistic deficit of nonnative professionals while neglecting other equally significant factors related to professionalism' (Samimy, 1997: 816), such as relevant teaching qualifications and length of experience. Seidlhofer reiterated this point: 'There has often been the danger of an automatic extrapolation from *competent speaker* to *competent teacher* based on linguistic grounds alone, without taking into consideration the criteria of cultural, social and pedagogic appropriacy' (1996: 69). Indeed, an issue waiting to be addressed is the complex relationship between different aspects of teachers' classroom practice. A further area may be the examination of matches and mismatches between perceived attitudes and actual practice through comparing questionnaire and interview data with video-recorded lessons (Árva and Medgyes, 2000). On the whole, the study of the non-native teacher remains a largely unexplored area in language education.

**See also:** Content-based instruction; Medium of instruction; Monolingual principle; Mother tongue; Native speaker; Teacher education; Teacher thinking; Teaching methods

## References

Árva, V. and Medgyes, P. (2000) 'Native and non-native teachers in the classroom', *System*, 24, 3: 1–18.

Atkinson, D. (1987) 'The mother tongue in the classroom: a neglected resource?' *English Language Teaching Journal* 41, 4: 241–7.

Braine, G. (ed.) (1999) *Non-native educators in English language teaching*, Hillsdale, NJ: Lawrence Erlbaum.

Edge, J. (1988) 'Natives, speakers, and models', *JALT Journal* 9, 2: 153–7.

Hancock, M. (1997) 'Behind classroom code switching: layering and language choice in L2 learner interaction', *TESOL Quarterly* 31, 2: 217–35.

Holliday, A. (1994) *Appropriate methodology and social context*, Cambridge: Cambridge University Press.

Illés, É. (1991) 'Correspondence', *English Language Teaching Journal* 45, 1: 87.

Medgyes, P. (1994) *The non-native teacher*, London: Macmillan.

Norton, B. (1997) 'Language, identity, and the ownership of English', *TESOL Quarterly* 31, 3: 409–29.

Palfreyman, D. (1993) ' "How I got it in my head": conceptual models of language and learning in native and non-native trainee EFL teachers', *Language Awareness* 2, 4: 209–23.

Phillipson, R. (1992a) *Linguistic imperialism*, Oxford: Oxford University Press.

Phillipson, R. (1992b) 'ELT: the native speaker's burden?', *English Language Teaching Journal* 46, 1: 12–18.

Reves, T. and Medgyes, P. (1994) 'The non-native English speaking EFL/ESL teacher's self-image: an international survey', *System* 22, 3: 353–67.

Samimy, K. (1997) 'A review on the non-native teacher', *TESOL Quarterly* 31, 4: 815–17.

Seidlhofer, B. (1996) ' "It is an undulating feeling". The importance of being a non-native teacher of English', *Views* 5, 3–4: 63–80.

Ur, P. (1996) *A course in language teaching*, Cambridge: Cambridge University Press.

van Essen, A. (1994) 'Language imperialism', *Plenary address*, Innsbruck: NELLE Conference.

Widdowson, H.G. (1992) 'ELT and EL teachers: matters arising', *English Language Teaching Journal* 4 , 4: 333–8.

Widdowson, H.G. (1994) 'The ownership of English', *TESOL Quarterly* 28, 2: 377–89.

## Further reading

Braine, G. (ed.) (1999) *Non-native educators in English language teaching*, Hillsdale, NJ: Lawrence Erlbaum.

Holliday, A. (1994) *Appropriate methodology and social context*, Cambridge: Cambridge University Press.

Medgyes, P. (1994) *The non-native teacher*, London: Macmillan.

Phillipson, R. (1992) *Linguistic imperialism*, Oxford: Oxford University Press.

PÉTER MEDGYES

# Non-verbal communication

Non-verbal communication can be defined as all the signs produced in interpersonal oral interaction except those which are explicitly verbal (words), and excluding the rules which govern these verbal signs – syntax, morphology, etc. Just like words, the voice (the way of pronouncing words and phrases, intonation and rhythm), gestures of various kinds, visual signs, posture, gaze, proxemic positioning and so on contain information which can be captured and used by the interlocutor in an appropriate and efficient manner, irrespective of the language and culture and in spite of certain quantitative and qualitative differences.

Such information is far from insignificant, and it has been shown (Mehrabian, 1972) that, as far as the emotional value of messages is concerned, only 7 per cent of information is transmitted by verbal means, the remainder being carried by the para-verbal (38 per cent largely by the voice and intonation) and the non-verbal (55 per cent largely due to gesture, posture, gaze and visual signs).

### Three principal modes of communication

The distinction between para-verbal and non-verbal is not always agreed on by those trying to describe what is happening beyond the words of a conversation, and it is in fact possible to make other distinctions in the totality of communication, either by simply making a distinction between the verbal and the non-verbal, or by a three-way distinction between verbal, vocal and gestural. This approach, the functional model of trimodal communication proposed by Guaïtella (1995), has the advantage of distinguishing clearly between vocal and verbal modes and the information they carry. Although the former often serves as a support to the latter, the information it carries is none the less different. Similarly, it would be reductionist to consider that voice and gesture simply augment or implicitly confirm what we are saying. On the contrary, the signals which are in the vocal or gestural mode may complement, confirm, throw doubt on or even negate what we are saying in words. We learn very early in life to take this information into account even if we are not usually consciously aware of it. When we notice irony or a lie, we are in fact noting the gap between at least two of the three principal modes of interpersonal communication, in other words between what we say, how we say it and what we are doing while we are saying it.

## Other modes of communication

In addition to these principal modes of communication, there are also other interrelationships which govern communicative space. We need to take into consideration other visual indices – which are often too readily reduced to the notion of 'context' – such as clothing, hairstyle, jewellery, etc., and also those which come from other sensory channels such as touch: physical contact in greetings for example; and olfactory: bodily odours and/or perfumes. All this influences or rather comprises communication.

This suggests, therefore, a fundamental principle: one cannot *not* communicate. Even if we attempt not to communicate, we communicate this intention itself, as every poker player would confirm. This does not, however, mean that we do or can do just anything with our voice and gestures. Communication comprises an integrated whole in which each participant, each mode and each parameter plays its part in an orchestra of communication. The 'musical communication' thus created, whether good or bad, is the result of this, being simultaneously multifarious and unique, codified but constantly renewed.

## Parameters of non-verbal communication

It is possible in general terms to distinguish different functions of the non-verbal elements of communication, each parameter or group of parameters being more or less adapted to these functions as a consequence of their nature – physiological constraints – or of local constraints, such as distance or noise. Non-verbal indicators may have a direct role in meaning by representing reality – miming an object, for example – or by referring to it – by pointing gestures. They also have value as structure-giving rhythm, where non-verbal elements are present as markers 'punctuating' the discourse. The structure of a dialogic exchange is also partly determined by the organisation of non-verbal parameters which have a back-channelling (feedback) function, especially with respect to turn-taking.

There are a number of misunderstandings current with respect to non-verbal communication, including the belief that vocal and gestural modes of communication are more ambiguous than what is contained in words, and therefore less reliable for the interlocutor, and less worthy of research. Yet we maintain that 'actions speak louder then words', and visual signs are considered more reliable than acoustic signs by interlocutors. Experiments have shown that, where there are conflicting indicators, acoustic and visual, with respect to a segment such as a consonant, it is the visual in the form of lip-reading which determines the choice made by the interlocutor. This phenomenon, called the 'McGurk effect' after one of the instigators of the first experiment, has led to theoretical and experimental developments which emphasise the multi-modal nature of vocal information, referring to sensory modes. In fact the voice itself is above all a gesture, a series of motor commands and actions. Acoustic indicators are only perceived by direct matching with the gestural articulations which create them.

This tendency to associate sounds – including sounds simulated internally – mental and physical images, and meanings is confirmed in many publications dealing with so-called 'phonetic symbolism'. We ought in fact to speak of inter-modal associations which create certain types of behaviour, including the McGurk effect, involving the construction of stable mental representations within a given sociolinguistic group. An example of this would be the subjective physical characteristics attributed to a person just by listening to their voice. Perception is above all a dynamic filter developed in and through the socialisation of the individual into a social group in which they grow up, and whose social representations they adopt or at least accept in an unconscious manner. In this case it is not surprising that the individual therefore considers indicators which are directly linked to their sociocultural experience as very strong.

Are vocal and gestural elements of communication produced more involuntarily than words? At first glance this might seem to be the case when certain items of information seem to derive from a reflex activity such as blushing, hoarse voice or nervous tic, but these cases are relatively marginal and, similarly, certain words seem to come out of our mouth involuntarily. Our gestures and voice do not betray us any more than the rest of our behaviour. It is perhaps the gap between what is produced in different modes of communication and/or the degree to which they conform to recognised modes of communicating that may create an awareness and a re-**EVALUATION** of the information received.

## Implications for language teaching

Argyle (1983) identifies four functions in which modes of non-verbal communication can operate:

- communicating interpersonal **ATTITUDES** and emotions;
- self-presentation;
- rituals;
- supporting verbal communication.

He points out that there is variation in non-verbal communication between cultures, and that 'when people from two different cultures meet, there is infinite scope for misunderstanding and confusion' (1983: 189). He deals briefly with the ways of overcoming such problems and suggests that language learning is a valuable but time-consuming approach to other cultures, as are modes of social skills learning which prepare people for contact with other cultures.

Poyatos (1992) addresses these issues from the perspective of the foreign language teacher, arguing that traditional foreign language teaching is too narrow in its concerns. Language teachers should be concerned with 'the triple reality of speech (language, paralanguage and kinesics)' and that these should be seen within a broader context of cultural signs of all kinds. He identifies ten dimensions of communication where the learner may meet problems, the first four of which are familiar to the language teacher, but are insufficient as a basis for **INTERCULTURAL COMMUNICATION**:

- phonetics/phonemics;
- morphology;
- syntax;
- **VOCABULARY**;
- paralanguage (e.g. tongue clicks, meaningful use of loudness and whispering);
- kinesics (e.g. communicative gestures, manners and postures);
- proxemics (e.g. personal or intimate distances between peers, parents, acquaintances);
- chemical/dermal (e.g. tear-shedding, blushing);
- body-adaptors/object-adaptors (e.g. cosmetics, clothes, occupational artefacts);
- built and modified environments (e.g. status objects such as homes and gardens).

Poyatos then proposes an approach to determining a **SYLLABUS** and a methodology for a course in non-verbal communication, dealing above all with the inter-relationships between language, paralanguage and kinesics. Unlike Argyle, who acknowledges the difficulty of acquiring the modes of non-verbal communication of other cultures, Poyatos assumes that they can in fact be taught, together with or separate from verbal communication. Argyle suggests the alternative of skills and sensitivity training in view of the difficulty. Argyle and Poyatos both assume the learner should attempt to acquire the non-verbal communication of a **NATIVE SPEAKER**. Poyatos sees the problems of learning as including the reduction of 'interference' from the learner's own non-verbal system in order to imitate the native speaker.

Yet precisely because many aspects of non-verbal communication, although learned within a given cultural environment, are unconscious, the language learner may not be able to control them, or wish to give up what feels like a part of their personality to acquire the non-verbal communication of others. The issues for language teaching have thus not yet been fully worked through.

**See also:** Communicative language teaching; Communicative strategies; Conversation analysis; Intercultural communication; Intercultural competence; Notions and functions; Speech act theory; Strategic competence

### References

Argyle, M. (1983) *The psychology of interpersonal behaviour* (4th edn), Harmondsworth: Penguin.

Guaïtella, I. (1995) 'Mélodie du geste, mimique vocale?', *Semiotica*, 3, 4, 103.

Mehrabian, A. (1972) *Nonverbal communication*, Chicago: Aldine-Atherton.

Poyatos, F. (1992) 'Non-verbal communication in foreign language teaching: theoretical and methodological perspectives', in A. Helbo (ed.), *Evaluation and language teaching*, Bern: Peter Lang.

Poyatos, F. (1993) *Paralanguage. A linguistic and interdisciplinary approach to interactive speech and sound*, Amsterdam: John Benjamins.

Santi, S., Guaïtella, I., Cavé, C. and Konopczynski, G. (eds) (1998) *Oralité et gestualité, communication multimodale, interaction*, Paris: l'Harmattan.

### Further reading

Poyatos, F. (1992) 'Non-verbal communication in foreign language teaching: theoretical and methodological perspectives', in A. Helbo (ed.) *Evaluation and language teaching*, Bern: Peter Lang.

Poyatos, F. (1993) *Paralanguage. A linguistic and interdisciplinary approach to interactive speech and sound*, Amsterdam: John Benjamins.

SERGE SANTI

# Notions and functions

A description of language in terms of its notions and functions derives from attempts to categorise language according to its meaning and use rather than through its forms or structures. These attempts comprise part of wider movements, both in **LINGUISTICS** and in language teaching, to take a broad view of language as a system of human communication. In linguistics this might be loosely termed a functional approach, in language teaching a communicative approach. Whilst among foreign language teaching methodologists there is general agreement on how the two terms are defined, in linguistics they may refer to different phenomena, which can sometimes be a cause of confusion.

### Definitions

The term *notion*, first used in connection with 'notional **GRAMMAR**', reflects a description of language based on various general concepts. In one use of the term, these concepts are of a grammatical nature, such as tense, mood, **GENDER**, etc., but more usually notions denote abstract concepts which reflect general, and possibly universal, categories of human experience, such as time, space, quantity, location, etc. It is in this sense that notions are defined in foreign language teaching.

As with notions, the term *function* also shows a meaning-based view of language, but while notions refer to categories of human thought and experience, functions are based on human behaviour. The various uses of the term all reflect the view that language is to be seen as a form of *action*, used to achieve a *communicative purpose* in *interaction* with other people. In its broadest sense, which has its roots in the works of British linguists such as J.R. Firth and M.A.K. **HALLIDAY**, a language function may be stipulated in terms of general functional domains, such as an 'instrumental function', 'regulatory function', 'representational function' (Halliday, 1973). However, in language teaching a more specific perspective is taken, which derives from linguistic theories of *speech acts*, formulated principally by J.L. Austin (1962) and J.R. Searle (1969), who provided a theoretical framework for analysing and categorising utterances as various types of action. One category of this framework is that of *illocutionary acts*, which can be defined as a speaker's (or writer's) purpose in making an utterance, including the effect that it is intended to have on the listener (or reader). This category has entered language teaching under the label of language or speech function, often shortened to 'function'. Functions are usually specified in English by a gerund phrase, or in other languages by an infinitive: 'greeting', 'offering help', 'accepting an invitation', etc. The corresponding words which can be used to express, or *realise*, the respective function – 'hello', 'shall I help you', 'I'd love to' etc. – are referred to as an *exponent* of the function. In a nutshell, it could be said that notions categorise *what* people can talk about in general; functions, *why* they say things in a particular context. In linguistics, this difference is reflected to an extent in the distinction between semantics and **PRAGMATICS**.

## Syllabus design

Since the mid-1970s, functions – and to a lesser extent notions – have represented an important category of **SYLLABUS** and **MATERIALS** design. The first attempts to provide a notional–functional description aimed at foreign language learners were made by **COUNCIL OF EUROPE** language experts in the early 1970s and subsequently developed, in particular by Wilkins in his *Notional Syllabuses* (1976), and in the **THRESHOLD LEVEL** (van Ek, 1975 and 1980; van Ek and Trim, 1991), though these influential publications used the terms in slightly different ways (see Johnson, 1982: 38). For Wilkins, 'notional' is an umbrella term for a semantic or **COMMUNICATIVE** approach to language description, which he further subdivides into three general categories: 'semantico-grammatical categories', 'categories of modal meaning' and 'categories of communicative function.' It was left to the Threshold Level to provide the clear distinction between, and definition of, notions and functions in the way that is now generally accepted in foreign language teaching.

In his introduction to the *Threshold Level*, van Ek distinguishes between 'language functions which he [*sic* – the learner] will have to fulfil', also defined as the 'purposes [for which] the learner will have to use the foreign language (1980: 7) and notions: 'he [the learner] will need to refer to things, to people, to events etc., and to talk about them. In order to do this he will be able to handle a large number of

*notions* in the foreign language' (1980: 8). A further distinction is made between *general notions*, which are general abstract categories such as 'identification', 'duration', 'shape', 'colour'; and *specific notions*, which are 'topic-related' and which can be of a lexical or a grammatical nature. Some specific examples corresponding to the general notions referred to in the last sentence are: 'name', 'length', 'round', 'red'.

There are various difficulties connected with this rather abstract form of notional categorisation. In some cases, there is no clear dividing line between them. For example, 'suasion' and other modal categories can be seen from a notional or a functional perspective. Also there is overlap between certain categories, such as 'specific notions' and 'topics'.

Following the publication of the *Threshold Level*, the concept of language functions found broad acceptance in syllabus and materials design and in foreign language teaching in general, which is confirmed by a glance at the contents pages of modern **TEXTBOOKS** and by many national syllabuses. Initial reservations that replacing grammatical structures with language functions would lead to a 'phrase-book' approach to language learning, in which the **GENERATIVE** base of language was denied to the learners, tended to fade with the realisation that functions could supplement existing categories rather than replace them. The communicative approach provided appropriate classroom techniques for learning language functions as well as grammatical categories.

As far as 'notions' are concerned, however, the influence on language teaching has been comparatively small. Whilst language functions represented a concept which can be easily understood by teachers and students and filled an obvious gap in language description, there proved to be various problems connected with taking and implementing a notional approach to syllabuses and materials. Principal among these was the fact that a notional approach sought to redefine lexical and grammatical categories. However, not only did lists and descriptions already exist for these, but since a notional specification had by necessity to be formulated in rather abstract and sometimes unwieldy terms, the resulting categorisation tended to be regarded as somewhat inaccessible to teachers and learners. For an international, multilingual organisation such as the Council of Europe, working from notional categories, which are non-language specific, has an obvious ideological appeal and practical application, as the many versions of Threshold Level have subsequently proved. However, for writers of materials and syllabuses in specific languages, it was convenient to by-pass a notional description and simply to work from checklists of vocabulary items or grammatical structures. Within the area of lexis, corpus analysis has, in the meantime, provided an alternative route to lexical specification and grading, which is arguably more scientific and more efficient than the 'brainstorming' approach of using notional checklists (Willis, 1990).

### Relationship with grammar

As far as grammar is concerned, notional descriptions did not fulfil their early promise and failed to provide the close and comprehensive specification of grammatical meaning that **PEDAGOGICAL GRAMMAR** requires. Some reference grammars (e.g. Leech and Svartvik, 1975) make use of general notional categories, but otherwise the influence has remained relatively small. As a result of these problems, the initial interest in the notional axis of the 'functional–notional approach' subsequently faded, and it was noticeable that textbooks soon tended to describe themselves as 'functional–structural' (see, e.g., Cunningsworth, 1995).

Perhaps the most important legacy of a functional–notional description of language is that, as part of a wider communicative approach to both language description and language learning, it helped methodologists and teachers to move away from a form-based view of language and to see it more in terms of a user-based communication system.

**See also:** Communicative language teaching; Competence and performance; Council of Europe Modern Languages Projects; Grammar; Pedagogical grammar; Syllabus and curriculum design; Text and corpus linguistics; Textbooks; Vocabulary

### References

Austin, J.R. (1962) *How to do things with words*, Oxford: Clarendon Press.

Cunningsworth, A. (1995) *Choosing your coursebook*, London: Heinemann.

Halliday, M.A.K. (1973) *Explorations in the functions of language*, London: Edward Arnold.

Johnson, K. (1982) *Communicative syllabus design and methodology*, Oxford: Pergamon Press.

Leech, G. and Svartvik, J. (1975) *A communicative grammar of English*, London: Longman.

Searle, J.R. (1969) *Speech acts*, Cambridge: Cambridge University Press.

van Ek, J.A. (1975) *The Threshold Level in a European unit/credit system for modern language learning by adults*, Strasbourg: Council of Europe.

van Ek, J.A. (1980) *Threshold Level English*, Oxford: Pergamon Press.

van Ek, J.A. and Trim, J.L.M. (1991) *Threshold Level 1990*, Strasbourg: Council of Europe.

Wilkins, D. (1976) *Notional syllabuses*, Oxford: Oxford University Press.

Willis, D. (1990) *The lexical syllabus*, London: Collins ELT.

### Further reading

van Ek, J.A. and Trim, J.L.M. (1991) *Threshold Level 1990*, Strasbourg: Council of Europe.

Wilkins, D. (1976) *Notional syllabuses*, Oxford: Oxford University Press.

DAVID NEWBY

# Objectives in language teaching and learning

Etymologically, 'objective' means that which is *placed in front*, towards which one moves, the purpose or the object which one plans to attain. In the field of pedagogy, teaching by objectives appeared in the USA in the mid-1950s, developed from two origins, that of organisation and efficiency in business on the one hand, and that of behavioural **PSYCHOLOGY** on the other. This inheritance helps to explain the ambiguity of the term which can mean the aims of a course and also a means of giving value to a personal journey towards **AUTONOMY**.

Defining objectives allows us to operationalise the aims and questions the presentation of the contents of a course, but the role of objectives in teaching and learning languages is greater than this, since the formulation of objectives, i.e. describing them and identifying one from another also means being able to determine what it means to have attained them. The relationship between objectives and **ASSESSMENT** is both determining and dynamic and seems to be at the heart of the teaching and learning of languages: there is no formative assessment without explicit formulation (and negotiation, as we shall see later) of objectives, and no formulation of objectives without taking into account the degree to which they can be realised.

Historically this relationship is part of a systems approach which developed in Europe in the 1970s. In a pedagogy by objectives, progression is organised in stages. These stages, which should ideally be apparent to all the partners involved, correspond to intermediate or operational objectives which are themselves defined in terms of behaviour-responses observable in the person being taught (Mager, 1962). It is precisely because the operational objective is an observable behaviour that it can be distinguished from aims and intentions (Bloom, 1956). The definition given by de Landesheere in 1975 emphasises this point: 'What observable behaviour will demonstrate that the objective has been attained, what will be the product of this behaviour, in what conditions will the behaviour have to take place?'

Finally, the formulation of objectives involves the analysis of a course. The famous taxonomy created by Bloom in 1956 by formulating **SKILLS** which are both capable of being isolated and placed in a hierarchy, and by identifying classes of objectives which are pedagogic but also cognitive (intellectual), psycho-motor, affective (emotional and moral), was a defining piece of research in the improvement of assessment. The aim was to restore a strict equivalence between the level of final requirements and that of learning (Hameline, 1979).

## Objectives and the learning process

In classroom practice, a close interaction of plans for activities/formative assessment/adaptation/new assessment can be developed and the circle is complete (Hameline, 1979). Teaching by objectives gives the teacher the means, at each stage, by intermediate objectives, of measuring the distance between actual behaviour and expected behaviour, and also the means of measuring the lasting and non-arbitrary change which appears in the person being taught, using appropriate procedures and in a given time and space. For the learner it is, or ought to be, an excellent tool for regulating their own learning process.

However, there is here a major contradiction in pedagogy. What in effect is learning unless it is to learn *simultaneously* both knowledge and the means of constructing this knowledge? The learning process is by definition unstable, uncertain and of varying speed, i.e. it is the permanent acceptance of new individual objectives. These objectives correspond to the 'logic' of learning and they are taken into account by a given learner at a particular moment and in particular strategies, and cannot correspond to the logic of presentation and the breakdown into intermediate objectives by 'experts'. It is no longer possible to talk about observable behaviours.

Furthermore, to what extent does the attainment of an objective, itself formulated in the most exact way possible, i.e. in terms of the realisation of the required task in a defined situation, signify the **ACQUISITION** of true constructed knowledge which is transferable to other situations?

The complexity of teaching by objectives is only one parameter of the necessary tension between teaching and learning. From this perspective, the role of the teacher-facilitator is both to formulate objectives, in order to define the criteria of success, and to take into account movement and uncertainty. From the notion of an explicit objective, we have moved to that of a negotiated objective, modified by the need to take into account the interactions between learner and environment.

## Objectives and needs in learning

Like objectives and assessment, there is also an inseparable relationship between objectives and **NEEDS**. As we have seen, the formulation of learning objectives is neither the establishment of a list of pre-determined contents nor the description of pedagogical aims, but rather the offer to all concerned of a tool which provides the best conditions for learning.

Every objective is in fact a learning objective. Its role is to help learning, and from this perspective,

contemporary language teaching has to adhere to a process of defining objectives no longer on the basis of proposals by experts but of the needs of learners. What kind of learner-oriented teaching would not take into account their needs? In a functional approach, every 'methodological preamble' involves the analysis of needs and of the learning public involved.

Needs analysis, which refers to the learners and the uses of language that these learners wish to make, should produce a flawless matching of the pedagogic material; in principle, it should lead to the definition of objectives. However, the notion of needs produces more problems than it resolves. The first is that of formulation: into what units should language needs be 'cut'? What, for example, is to be done about the **NON-VERBAL** dimension of interactions? Or the question of register? Second is the problem of knowing to what extent these needs are conscious. In a group of learners, it is those who best master their own learning **STRATEGIES** – for linguistic or social reasons, or both – who are able to express them. The third problem is to define the role of the institution, and how appropriate needs can be determined, which are both objective and appropriate for all, on the basis of individual requirements? Expectations and wants on the one hand may differ from perceptions on the other. As Besse and Galisson (1983) say: 'The analysis of needs includes what the learner wishes, what he is required to be able to do, and what he has to learn', and they then conclude by warning against the use of needs analysis. Since objectives cannot be defined once and for all, needs analysis is part of the decision about objectives but is not identical with it.

## Objectives and communicative competence

At the end of the 1970s, researchers working on the **THRESHOLD LEVEL** in the **COUNCIL OF EUROPE** defined unit-credits, of a functional nature, which themselves covered the abilities of learners to respond to defined situations of interaction. Coste (1979) defined functional learning objectives as those which are described in terms of communicative competence. In order to characterise learning objectives of this nature, it is possible to determine in which communication situations learners will need to function with the aid of a foreign language.

In the first **TEXTBOOKS** which made use of the research in concrete terms, learning was no longer defined in terms of the linguistic material presented by the teacher, the book or the institution, but in terms of the communicative competence to be achieved. Introducing the notion of communicative competence means considering the language less as a system, as pure linguistic **COMPETENCE** does, and more in terms of the use made of it. For the learner, the issue is thus no longer knowledge but skill (more precisely, the 'ability to do'), no longer knowing different forms of the past tense but being able to tell a story in the past. The teacher's job is also changed, from focus on language towards the capacity to teach the ability to communicate in the language. Form has to be made subservient to meaning, or, in other words, to move from concepts towards the forms of language which allow them to be realised.

In addition to linguistic competence and communicative competence, there was also sociocultural competence (which depends on factual knowledge) and social competence (which presupposes the ability to engage in interaction with the other), which are part of the specific objectives of language learning in contemporary approaches. Taking these into account was to change profoundly the choice of content and progression in the **MATERIALS** provided for teachers. Decisions have to be made about how the content should be presented, what criteria should be used, what order should be preferred.

Research in **PRAGMATICS** gave the didacticians in the Threshold Level team a first option and opened the way to productive theory based on the concept of the **SPEECH ACT**. For them, the notion of functional objective encapsulates that of the speech act, which has the advantage of representing a smaller unit of analysis. In textbooks, however, the unit of 'speech act' tended to be equated with the teaching unit. This relationship between the speech act and the teaching unit raises the question of progression: what are the criteria for suggesting one act before another? It also raises the question of the limits on **AUTHENTICITY**, for in an authentic situation every speech act is permanently linked to others and not isolated as it is in a teaching unit.

## Conclusion

In the *Dictionnaire de l'évaluation et de la recherche en éducation* (1979), de Landsheere provides thirty-nine different entries for the term 'objective'. The most important pairs have been presented here, but a final triad deserves to be noted: that which links communicative objective, linguistic objective and socio-linguistic objective, in the analysis of an authentic document – or of a credible document, of a unit of meaning, presented in a textbook. Let us hypothesise that, first, every language teaching and learning practitioner chooses their materials as a function of the negotiation between operational objectives and institutional progression, giving the maximum attention to the learning strategies at work. Second, the practitioner asks the three following questions: what communicative competence does this document allow learners to attain; what parts of the language does it allow them to acquire; what information on the culture in question does it allow them to discover? In other words, what are the three objectives for the class, and how are they related?

The search for the relationship between these three objectives is only an obligatory transition, one among many parameters in the pedagogical act. However, because this search is a concrete realisation of the learning process, it has the advantage of asking the teacher good questions, those concerned with guiding and with autonomy, those focusing on progression and content, those involving mediation and cognitive instruments.

Teaching by objectives, in so far as it is concerned with a focus on the learner, has a promising future.

**See also:** Assessment and testing; Communicative language teaching; Evaluation; Language planning; Needs analysis; Planning for foreign language teaching; Syllabus and curriculum design; Textbooks

## References

Besse, H. and Galisson, R. (1983) *Polémique en didactique, du renouveau en question*, Paris: Clé International.

Bloom, B.S. (1956) *Taxonomy of Educational Objectives.*

*Handbook I: Cognitive Domain*, New York: David McKay.

Coste, D. (1979) 'L'écrit et les écrits: considérations didactiques', in M. Martins-Baltar, M. Boutgain, D. Coste, V. Ferenzi and M.-A. Mochet (eds), *L'écrit et les écrits: problèmes d'analyse et considérations didactiques*, Strasbourg: Council of Europe.

Coste, D. and Galisson, R. (1976) *Dictionnaire de didactique des langues*, Paris: Hatier-Didier.

Hameline, D. (1979) 'L'entrée par la pédagogie par les objectifs', *Revue Française de Pédagogie* 46: 79–90.

de Landsheere, V. et de Landsheere, G. (1975) *Définir les objectifs de l'éducation*, Paris: PUF.

Mager, R.F. (1962) *Preparing objectives for programmed instruction*, Belmont: Fearon.

## Further reading

Coste, D. (1976) 'Décrire et enseigner une compétence de communication: remarques sur quelques solutions de continuités', *Bulletin C.I.L.A.* 24, Neuchâtel.

De Landsheere, V. et de Landsheere, G. (1975) *Définir les objectifs de l'éducation (Defining objectives in education)*, Paris: PUF.

Porcher, L. (1975) 'Questions sur les objectifs' *Le français dans le monde* 113: 9–12.

Richterich, R. (1985) *Besoins langagiers et objectifs d'apprentissage (Language needs and learning objectives)*, Paris: Collection F, recherches et applications.

CLAIRE-LISE DAUTRY

# OISE – Ontario Institute for Studies in Education; Modern Language Centre

The Modern Language Centre (MLC) was founded in 1968 within the Ontario Institute for Studies in Education of the University of Toronto (OISE/UT), CANADA's leading educational institution concerned with local, Canadian and international education. H.H. (David) STERN was the founding Director. The MLC addresses a broad spectrum of issues related to second and minority language education. Within this special field of interest, the MLC reflects the four functions of OISE/UT: (a) graduate studies, (b) TEACHER EDUCATION, (c) research and development, and (d) dissemination. The quality and range of the Centre's degree programmes, research and dissemination have brought it national and international recognition. For over thirty years, the work of the MLC has focused on language learning, teaching, curriculum and policy, covering many different areas, such as French immersion, ESL, HERITAGE LANGUAGES, bilingualism, curriculum development, testing and programme EVALUATION, education in indigenous languages, policy analyses and materials development.

## Graduate studies

Through its Second Language Education (SLE) programme, the MLC offers approximately twenty-five courses at Master and Doctoral levels. Examples of some of the fundamental courses in this programme are: Foundations of Bilingual and Multicultural Education, Methodology and Organisation of Second Language Teaching, Theory of Second Language Teaching, Descriptive and Educational Linguistics of ENGLISH, Second Language Learning, Second Language Assessment, LANGUAGE PLANNING and Policy, WRITING in a Second Language, and Research Themes in Canadian French as a Second Language Education. The SLE Programme, along with the varied academic programmes in the five other academic departments of OISE/UT, provide a wide array of options in graduate studies.

## Research and Development

The research undertaken by the MLC has been prompted by both the NEEDS arising in Canadian language education as well as the Centre's ASSESSMENT of the important issues in language pedagogy. With an overriding concern for relating theory to practice, the Centre has undertaken a considerable range of research and development projects, including work related to second language curriculum, materials development, second language teaching and learning, programme evaluation and test development, immigrant settlement, and heritage and aboriginal issues. Students are encouraged to participate in the Centre's research and development activities.

## Dissemination

The MLC provides consultation and information to individuals and organisations on questions related to second language pedagogy, **BILINGUAL** education and heritage language education. The Modern Language Centre collection in the OISE/UT Library is the most extensive resource for and about second and minority teaching and learning in Canada. It serves the graduate, pre-service and research programmes of OISE/UT, and second language teachers in Ontario, as well as nationally and internationally.

## Teacher education

The MLC offers pre-service teacher education courses in French as a second language and international languages (e.g. **GERMAN**, Italian, **SPANISH**) within the Bachelor of Education programme of OISE/UT. This programme qualifies candidates to teach in Ontario schools.

## Website

The centre's website is: http://www.oise.utoronto.ca/MLC

SHARON LAPKIN AND ALICE WEINRIB

# Overhead projector (OHP)

The Overhead projector (OHP) is a widely available piece of electronic equipment which uses a system involving an electric light, a lens and an adjustable mirror to project images on acetate transparencies onto a screen or wall.

There are two basic formats. The most common type has a metal box base which houses the lamp, and also usually a cooling fan, topped with a glass plate. The transparency with the image on it is placed on the glass plate and the light shines through it, up to a lens mounted on a vertical arm, with an angled, adjustable mirror which throws the image onto the screen or wall. The second type is usually portable, and consists of a flat base with a mirrored plate on it where the transparency is placed. The lamp is housed, along with the lens and adjustable mirror, at the top of the arm, so that the light shines down onto the transparency and is reflected back up through the lens and onto the mirror, from where it is projected onto the screen or wall. The former format is more usual as a fixed element in educational establishments, while the latter is useful for lecturers travelling from place to place and not sure if there is an OHP, or for use in temporary premises.

As a classroom tool, it has many advantages over the more traditional black/whiteboard:

1  it is clean to use, as the teacher writes on acetate with a coloured pen;
2  words and pictures can be produced with either temporary or permanent pens, so that transparencies can be either easily cleaned, or stored for use again;
3  when a teacher is using an OHP they can stand facing the class to write or discuss pre-drawn images;
4  the OHP allows the teacher to write in a natural way, both in class and when pre-preparing transparencies at home, in terms of size of both lettering and image, and in terms of angle (i.e. horizontal, not vertical); it is thus much easier to produce high-quality **MATERIALS** than on a board;
5  the teacher can use the technique of masking a transparency (picture or words) to hide what is coming, and then reveal it; and the technique of overlay, where one transparency is laid on top of another (for example, a photograph the teacher wishes to re-use is put underneath, and a blank transparency on top, on which to write **VOCABULARY** over the relevant parts of the picture);
6  One can take an OHP anywhere where there is an electricity supply and a surface which is light enough for images to show up on;
7  It is possible to produce images on transparencies through a photocopier (using the correct kind of transparency) and in colour, thus the teacher can bring any image into the classroom and show it large-scale to everyone;

8 Unlike a slide or a film projector, the image can be seen well without blacking out the classroom, except in extreme direct sunlight.

In terms of what one can project, there are many possibilities. One can project words, using the OHP as a continuous blackboard (with the advantage of being able to roll it back (with a continuous transparency roll system) or replace a transparency (with individual acetate sheets). One can project one's own drawings. One can project student words and drawings (it is easy to give groups an acetate to write ideas/draw pictures on at their desk, and then display them for the whole class to discuss). One can project colour and black-and-white photographs, pages from books, pages printed on the computer with words, charts, graphs and so on, which have been photocopied onto acetate. One can project silhouettes, because anything opaque placed on the base will not allow light through, so cardboard cut-outs or real objects can be made into a large screen/wall image. Equally, one can change the colour of the background by using different coloured acetates. There are endless ways of teaching language creatively using an OHP.

**See also:** Board drawing; Flashcard; Internet; Media centres; Teaching methods; Video; Visual aids

## Further reading

Jones, J.R.H. (1982) *Using the overhead projector*, London: Heinemann.

Wilkinson, J. (1979) *The overhead projector*, London: The British Council.

Wright, A. and Haleem, S. (1991) *Visuals for the language classroom*, Harlow: Longman.

DAVID A. HILL

# P

## Palmer, Harold Edward

b. 1877, London; d. 1949, Felbridge, UK

Language teaching theorist, phonetician, grammarian, lexicologist, materials writer

Harold E. Palmer worked tirelessly between the two World Wars to establish a principled basis for English language teaching (ELT). Given the subsequent influence of his ideas, he deserves greater recognition as the 'founding father' of (British) ELT. However, it is in Japan (where he spent the years 1922–36) that he is best remembered today.

Palmer first taught in Belgium, in a language school run along Berlitz lines. He then began to develop his own more systematic, less dogmatically monolingual version of **DIRECT METHOD** teaching, which he later termed the 'Oral Method' (Palmer, 1921b; see also Palmer and Palmer, 1925). He joined the **INTERNATIONAL PHONETIC ASSOCIATION** in 1907, and took on board the ideas of **REFORM MOVEMENT** theorists such as Henry **SWEET** and Otto **JESPERSEN**. In his subsequent work, Palmer brought together the direct method and Reform Movement traditions: his overall significance lies in the way he attempted systematically and consistently to relate practice to theory, thus foreshadowing **APPLIED LINGUISTICS** as constituted in the post-World War Two era (see in particular Palmer, 1917, 1921a, 1924a).

Palmer's best-known works on language teaching and learning theory were written during an extremely productive spell in Daniel Jones's Department of Phonetics at University College London (1915–21). There, Palmer also developed wider interests in English intonation and grammar, as reflected in a classic **PEDAGOGICAL GRAMMAR** (Palmer, 1924b) which he completed following his move to **JAPAN** in 1922.

Outside Japan, few teachers are aware of Palmer's achievements as 'linguistic adviser' to the Department of Education and founder of the Institute for Research in English Teaching (IRET), the first such centre in the world. However, Palmer's legacy continues to be valued by Japanese members of the Institute (now known as IRLT).

Palmer's output was considerable, and he devoted great energy to the provision of guides for teachers and innovative textbook materials (see IRLT, 1995; Smith, 1999). In the 1930s, he increasingly focused on issues of **VOCABULARY** control and text simplification, and his collaborative lexicological work with Michael West is relatively well-known internationally. After returning to England in 1936, he seems to have suffered from the absence of an organisation comparable to IRET, and it was largely due to the mediation of A.S. **HORNBY** (his successor as leader of research in Tokyo) that Palmer's ideas became influential as ELT established a base in post-war Britain.

## References

IRLT (eds) (1995) *The selected writings of Harold E. Palmer* (ten vols), Tokyo: Hon-no-Tomosha.

Palmer, H.E. (1917) *The scientific study and teaching of languages*, London: Harrap.

Palmer, H.E. (1921a) *The principles of language-study*, London: Harrap.

Palmer, H.E. (1921b) *The oral method of teaching languages*, Cambridge: Heffer.

Palmer, H.E. (1924a) *Memorandum on problems of English teaching*, Tokyo: IRET.

Palmer, H.E. (1924b) *A grammar of spoken English*, Cambridge: Heffer.

Palmer, H.E. and Palmer, D. (1925) *English through actions*, Tokyo: IRET.

Smith, R.C. (1999) *The writings of Harold E. Palmer: an overview*, Tokyo: Hon-no-Tomosha.

### Further reading

Anderson, D. (1969) 'Harold E. Palmer: a biographical essay', appendix to H.E. Palmer and H.V. Redman (1932/1969) *This language-learning business*, London: Oxford University Press.

IRLT (eds.) (1995) *The selected writings of Harold E. Palmer* (ten vols), Tokyo: Hon-no-Tomosha.

Smith, R.C. (1999) *The writings of Harold E. Palmer: an overview*, Tokyo: Hon-no-Tomosha.

RICHARD C. SMITH AND MOTOMICHI IMURA

# Pedagogical grammar

Pedagogical grammar, which we may define as a grammar developed for learners of a foreign language, draws on two separate but interrelated areas of theory. First, there are descriptive models of grammar, which can be incorporated into pedagogical reference grammars and teaching **MATERIALS** and formulated in ways which make the description accessible to the learner. Second, there are theories of **SECOND LANGUAGE ACQUISITION**, which will provide the basis for classroom methodology.

## Pedagogical and linguistic grammars

There has been considerable discussion (see Dirven, 1990; Chalker, 1994) about the differences between pedagogical and linguistic grammar, variously termed 'theoretical' or 'scientific', in particular concerning the extent to which a pedagogical description should have a theoretical

basis and what this basis should be. Despite the large number of reference grammars on the market and the important role which grammar rules play in many classrooms, there appears to be relatively little coherent theory underlying rule formulation. This is somewhat surprising since, as Dirven (1990) points out, 'learners can be and are misled into all kinds of wrong generalisations by the inaccurate rule formulations in their **TEXTBOOKS**'. Some grammarians have attempted to give a theoretical basis to their rules: for example, Leech and Svartvik (1975) draw on the linguistic model of functional/systemic grammar; Swan (1994) outlines his 'design criteria' for rule formulation; Newby (1989a) derives his rules from his own 'notional grammar' model (1989b). Yet on the whole the area of rule formulation is one that is relatively unexplored (see Westney, 1994).

Of the two theoretical areas that comprise pedagogical grammar – description and methodology – it is the latter that has been the main focus of attention and which has, at recurrent periods in the history of language teaching, represented a highly contentious topic. The main bones of contention concern:

- the aims of grammar teaching (knowing about grammar or using grammar; manipulating sentences or free production);
- the categorisation of grammar (form, meaning, use) into units which will form a **SYLLABUS** or teaching **OBJECTIVES**;
- the extent to which grammar should be dealt with separately from other aspects of language;
- the use of rules, in particular in how far a cognitive focus on grammar rules assists acquisition;
- the type of grammatical **EXERCISES** and activities which will lead to automatisation.

## Types of pedagogical grammars

In modern grammar teaching the influences of the following approaches are most strongly discernible or influential.

### *Traditional grammar*

Grammar is defined primarily as a set of forms and

structures, which comprise the main focus of the textbook syllabus. Whilst grammatical meaning plays an important role, it is dealt with in an unsystematic way. The sentence is the main unit of analysis, and emphasis is placed on the student's ability to form correct sentences. The usual classroom methodology is based on presentation, explanation, practice. Learning is seen largely as a conscious process and grammar rules are used deductively, i.e. they are explained by teacher or textbook prior to the practice stage. The most common forms of exercise type are gapped sentences, pattern drills and sentences for transformation, reflecting a form-based, rather uncontextualised view of grammar. Grammatical competence is measured according to the student's ability to manipulate sentences, rather than being performance-oriented.

## Communicative grammar

Here, language is seen not only as a formal system but also primarily as the process of communicating messages between human beings in actual contexts, grammar being a means of expressing meanings through grammatical forms. Attempts to recategorise grammatical meaning in terms of **NOTIONS AND FUNCTIONS** were only partly successful since they did not go very far in addressing the need for pedagogical grammar to give an accurate and systematic specification of meaning. Since, however, the focus of aims had shifted from formal correctness towards communicative effectiveness, the 'grammar vacuum' tended to go unnoticed or was patched up in textbooks by a structural–functional organisation or, in the case of the 'extremist fringe' of communicative teaching, grammar was dispensed with altogether. As far as grammatical rules were concerned, a distinction was made between knowing 'about' grammar and knowing 'how' to use it, referred to as declarative versus procedural knowledge (see Johnson, 1994), which led to a shift of focus from analysis to use. Rules tended to be dealt with inductively, i.e. understanding emerges from use, rather than the other way round. Various important features of communicative methodology can also be applied to grammar; in particular, a 'learning-by-doing' approach based on small-group oral activities

(information gap and similar communicative games), which is reflected in a number of grammar practice books (e.g. Ur, 1989). Whilst the communicative approach brought many benefits in the areas of methodology, its failure to integrate grammar in a coherent way led to the widespread but quite false 'grammar versus communication' dichotomy.

## Acquisition-based approaches to grammar

In the 1980s, various factors led some methodologists to take a quite different view of grammar. At the core of this movement was an increasing interest in the psychological processes underlying first language acquisition and the belief that many of these processes could apply to second languages if suitable learning environments and conditions were provided. The best-known proponent of this view was Krashen (1981), who distinguished between learning – with a conscious focus on grammar (explicit rules, terminology, etc.) and automatic, unconscious **ACQUISITION**. It was only through the latter that students could achieve communicative competence. The proposed method entailed providing learners with what he termed 'comprehensible input' and allowing the intake process to function automatically, following an innate acquisition order for which the learner's brain was already 'wired up' and which could not be influenced by structuring the input.

## Language awareness approaches to grammar

Another approach, taken particularly under the influence of educational psychologists, involves an interest in the special role of the learner in formal education in general and of the specific nature of various cognitive processes linked to learning a language in particular. Central to this view, which is part of a wider learner **AUTONOMY** credo, is the notion of **LANGUAGE AWARENESS** – that learners should be guided towards focusing on aspects of language and be encouraged to use various cognitive strategies to explore for themselves how language works. Teachers should not 'impose' their own grammatical knowledge on learners but should be facilitators of the learning process. Thus, grammar rules explained by the teacher give way to consciousness-raising or discovery techniques and tasks given to students (see Rutherford, 1987; Rutherford and Sharwood Smith, 1988; Bolitho and Tomlinson, 1995).

It would probably be true to say that many classrooms reflect a variety of approaches. Whilst there is almost uniform rejection of traditional grammar among methodologists, the security its structured practices offer to teachers and learners is obviously appealing. A traditional core, with bits of communicative methodology and awareness-raising activities superimposed, is not an uncommon classroom scenario.

**See also:** Communicative language teaching; Competence and performance; Grammar; Grammar–translation method; Language awareness; Monolingual principle; Objectives in language teaching and learning; Syllabus and curriculum design

### References

Bolitho, R. and Tomlinson, B. (1995) *Discover English*, Oxford: Heinemann.

Bygate, M., Tonkyn, A. and Williams, E. (eds) (1994) *Grammar and the language teacher*, Hemel Hempstead: Prentice Hall.

Chalker, S. (1994) 'Pedagogical grammar: principles and problems,' in M. Bygate *et al.* (eds), *Grammar and the language teacher*, Hemel Hempstead: Prentice Hall.

Dirven, R. (1990) 'Pedagogical grammar', *Language Teaching* 23, 1: 1–18.

Johnson, K. (1994) 'Teaching declarative and procedural knowledge', in M. Bygate *et al.* (eds), *Grammar and the language teacher*, Hemel Hempstead: Prentice Hall.

Krashen, S.D. (1981) *Second language acquisition and second language learning*, Oxford: Pergamon Press.

Leech, G. and Svartvik, J. (1975) *A communicative grammar of English*, London: Longman.

Newby, D. (1989a) *Grammar for communication*, Vienna: Österreichischer Bundesverlag.

Newby, D. (1989b) 'Towards a notional grammar of English', in B. Kettemann, P. Bierbaumer, A. Fill and A. Karpf (eds), *Englisch als Zweitsprache*

*(English as a second language)*, Tübingen: Gunter Narr Verlag.

Rutherford, W.E. (1987) *Second language grammar: learning and teaching*, London: Longman.

Rutherford, W.E. and Sharwood Smith, M. (1988) *Grammar and second language teaching*, Boston: Heinle and Heinle.

Swan, M. (1994) 'Design criteria for pedagogical grammars', in M. Bygate *et al.* (eds), *Grammar and the language teacher*, Hemel Hempstead: Prentice Hall.

Ur, P. (1989) *Grammar practice activities*, Cambridge: Cambridge University Press.

Westney, P. (1994) 'Rules and pedagogical grammar', in T. Odlin (ed.) *Perspectives on pedagogical grammar*, Cambridge: Cambridge University Press.

### Further reading

Batstone, R. (1994) *Grammar*, Oxford: Oxford University Press.

Bygate, M., Tonkyn, A. and Williams, E. (eds) (1994) *Grammar and the language teacher*, Hemel Hempstead: Prentice Hall.

Odlin, T. (ed.) (1994) *Perspectives on pedagogical grammar*, Cambridge: Cambridge University Press.

Rutherford, W.E. and Sharwood Smith, M. (1988) *Grammar and second language teaching*, Boston: Heinle and Heinle.

DAVID NEWBY

# Pidgins

A pidgin is a simple, auxiliary language that is a consequence of contacts between people who do not share a **MOTHER TONGUE**. It is often the result of trade and, since it is no-one's mother tongue, it tends to have a small **VOCABULARY** and a grammar that is sufficient for the expression of no more than simple commands and statements. Rudimentary pidgins are found throughout the world in contact situations where non-complex ideas are being exchanged. The speech is generally slow and supported by mime and gesture; the vocabulary is basic and taken mostly from the language of the dominant group; functional morphology is discarded; and the **GRAMMAR** has much in common with 'foreigner talk' and 'motherese'.

## Restricted pidgins

Restricted pidgins can develop rapidly when communication **NEEDS** arise between people who do not share a language. If a restricted pidgin proves useful, it tends to be elaborated and thus linguistically flexible. If it becomes a mother tongue, it is expanded to fulfil all its speakers' linguistic needs. Such mother tongues are known as '**CREOLES**'.

Restricted pidgins have developed on all of the world's trading routes and in the contacts brought about through war. Such pidgins developed in **JAPAN**, Korea and Vietnam between American soldiers and sections of the local populations. Elaborated pidgins are most likely to be found in multilingual communities where they serve an invaluable role as a **LINGUA FRANCA**. We find such pidgins in Papua New Guinea, for example, where there are over 700 languages for a population of under four million, and in West **AFRICA**, where as many as one fifth of the world's languages are found.

## Pidginisation

Pidgins are not a rare phenomenon, but the underlying principle of pidginisation is even more widespread. Pidginisation is a process of linguistic accommodation in which speakers utilise an innate ability to simplify their language or dialect in order to communicate with people who do not share their mother tongue. Each pidgin – like each language – is of course unique, but the majority of them share certain grammatical characteristics, including:

a fixed word order: → S P (O) (A)
little or no inflection: → *tu han* (two hands); *a go/i go* (I go/she goes)
a simple system of negation: → *No go* (Don't go); *yu no bin go* (you didn't go)
no irregular nouns: → *tu fut/man* (two feet/men)
no irregular verbs
no passives

no verb inflections; verbal nuances of time and aspect carried by small set of auxiliaries
small vocabulary but maximally used by exploiting:

1 multifunctionality, e.g. *bad* may function as adjective, adverb, noun and verb
2 reduplication, e.g. *ben* is 'bend'; *benben* is 'crooked'
3 semantic widening, e.g. *han* can be 'arm', 'hand', 'sleeve'

local idioms, **METAPHORS** and proverbs calqued from original mother tongues. Thus Atlantic pidgins and creoles have *big ai*, 'covetous', probably from Twi *ana uku* (eye big).

It seems likely that pidgins have existed as long as trade. Evidence suggests that there were pidginised versions of Latin that creolised into **FRENCH** and **SPANISH**, and there was certainly a medieval Lingua Franca in use between Muslims and Christians during the Crusades. Pidgins that derived from European languages developed extensively in the wake of maritime expansionism from the fifteenth century. Pidginised forms of **PORTUGUESE** and Spanish were the earliest to develop but were followed by pidginised forms of **ENGLISH**, French, Dutch and, to a lesser extent, Italian, Swedish and German.

Many theories have been advanced to explain the structural similarities of the world's pidgins. They have been regarded as the result of 'baby-talk'. They have been described as 'maritime media'. It has been suggested that the similarities can be explained because all pidgins with European lexicons result from the relexification of pidginised Portuguese. The most likely explanation is that pidginisation involves the utilisation of linguistic universals. In contact situations, where communication is essential, speakers intuitively make use of the linguistic programming that is part of every human being's biological blueprint.

The origin of the term *pidgin* is uncertain. There are a number of possibilities:

• It may come from a seventeenth-century reference to 'Pidian', meaning 'South American Indian'. In 1603, the English attempted to establish a colony on the northern coast of South America. The English of the Pidians would thus have been 'Pidian English'.

- It may be a Chinese modification of 'business'.
- It may be a form of Portuguese *pequeno*, meaning 'small'. Pidginised forms of Dutch and French have been called *baby hollands* and *petit nègre*.
- It may be derived from a Hebrew word *pidjom*, meaning 'barter'.

The lifecycle of a pidgin depends on sociological rather than linguistic factors. However, the following sequence is generally applicable:

- a marginal pidgin may develop within hours of contact. It is reinforced by gesture and mime; its vocabulary is drawn mainly from the dominant group; it survives as long as it serves a need.
- an elaborated pidgin may develop in a multilingual area to serve as a lingua franca. Such a pidgin may be linguistically sophisticated but tends to be no-one's mother tongue.
- a creole may develop out of necessity – as when millions of Africans were transported as slaves. They often had no option but to pass their pidgin on to their children, who creolised it. A creole may also come into being because of a pidgin's usefulness. Many urban dwellers in both Africa and Papua New Guinea use the local pidgin as a home language and children grow up speaking it as one of their mother tongues.
- a post-creole continuum may develop between the creole and the **STANDARD** form of the language, with speakers varying between basilectal, mesolectal and acrolectal variants. An example from West Africa may help to illustrate this. A speaker may say:

> *Mi, a di go mi fain dat ma man pikin dem.*
> *A di go luk my boys dem.*
> I'm going to find/look for my sons.

- the creole may merge with the metropolitan standard language.

Knowledge about pidgins can be of linguistic value in that they can shed light on language change, language loss and linguistic universals. They can be of assistance to the teacher, too, in that they may be regarded as examples of **INTER-LANGUAGES**.

Pidgins have proved useful in permitting communication where previously none existed; they have been found adequate for the writing of creative literature, parliamentary debates and for translations of Shakespeare and the Bible. If they develop into creoles, then they become as finely tuned to the needs of their speakers as any other mother tongue. If they die out, it is because they have outlived their social value, not because of any intrinsic linguistic weakness.

**See also:** Acculturation; Bilingualism; Creoles; Esperanto; Lingua franca; Mental lexicon; Mother tongue; Native speaker; Sociolinguistics; Universal grammar; Untutored language acquisition

### Further reading

Hancock, I. (1987) 'A preliminary classification of the anglophone Atlantic Creoles, with syntactic data from thirty-three representative dialects', in G. Gilbert (ed.) *Pidgin and creole languages: essays in memory of John E. Reinecke*, Honolulu: University of Hawaii Press.

Holm, J. (1988–89) *Pidgins and creoles* (vols 1 and 2), Cambridge: Cambridge University Press.

Romaine, S. (1988) *Pidgin and creole languages*, London: Longman.

Sebba, M. (1997) *Contact languages: pidgins and creoles*, Basingstoke: Macmillan.

Todd, L. (1990) *Pidgins and creoles*, London: Routledge.

LORETO TODD

# Placement tests

Placement tests aim to identify variations in students' abilities so that they can be grouped for teaching, either in terms of the level of difficulty of the course they attend or in terms of the general ability of the class in which they are placed. The content of these tests may be based on the **SYLLABUS** to be taught or on more general material. Some institutions assess the students' relative development in each skill and place them in different groups according to their abilities in these **SKILLS**. So, it is possible that a student might be in the top class for **READING** but a slower class for **SPEAKING** (or vice versa).

In order to make placement decisions it is important that the placement test spreads students out as much as possible across a range of scores so that distinctions can be made between them and decisions can be made more easily. Consequently, test writers attempt to include items across a wide range of difficulty. Placement tests differ from **ACHIEVEMENT** and **PROFICIENCY TESTS** in their use rather than in the language that they sample. They are usually considered to be low stakes tests because the students' test results do not have serious consequences for them, such as excluding them from a programme for which they have applied.

**See also:** Assessment and testing

**Further reading**

Alderson, J C., Clapham, C. and Wall, D. (1995) *Language test construction and evaluation*, Cambridge: Cambridge University Press.
Davies, A., Brown, A., Elder, C., Hill, K., Lumley, T. and McNamara, T. (1999) *Dictionary of language testing*, Cambridge: Cambridge University Press.

JAYANTI BANERJEE

# Planned languages

Planned languages are spoken or written languages that have evolved on the basis of written projects, usually with the goal of facilitating international communication. Such projects began to multiply in the second half of the nineteenth century and now number over a thousand, but very few have acquired a community of users. Planned languages in this sense are distinct from the philosophical language projects, whose history dates back to Descartes, and fantasy languages such as Tolkien's languages of Middle-Earth, although the three traditions share some common roots (Eco, 1995). Three classic sources are Couturat and Leau (1979, first published in 1903/1907), Haupenthal (1976, a collection of historical texts), and Blanke (1985, the most complete treatment to date); a readable popular treatment is Large (1985). More detailed works and articles are listed in the section 'Auxiliary languages. International languages' of the Modern

Language Association's International Bibliography of Books and Articles on the Modern Languages and Literatures.

By far the most widely learned and taught planned language is **ESPERANTO**, based on an 1887 project by L.L. Zamenhof. Although no other project has come close to this range of use, two can currently claim an international speech community: Ido, based on a 1907 project by Louis Couturat, which combines features of Esperanto with a number of radically different ideas; and Interlingua, based on a 1951 project of the International Auxiliary Language Association and intended as a compromise between the major European languages. Others with small groups of users and advocates include Glosa, based on a 1943 project by Lancelot Hogben, which combines a lexicon drawn from Classical Greek with many features of **ENGLISH** syntax, and Loglan/Lojban, two derivatives of a 1960 project by James Cooke Brown, intended to maximise logical consistency and linguistic neutrality and thereby to test the relationship between language, thought and culture. Projects of historical interest include Volapuk (1879), Latino sine Flexione (1903), Occidental/Interlingue (1922), Novial (1927) and Basic English (1935).

A wide range of claims have been made for various planned languages, including ease of **ACQUISITION**, logical structure, lack of ambiguity, suitability for human or machine **TRANSLATION**, internationality or neutrality, propaedeutic (or 'transfer of training') effects, broader effects on **LANGUAGE AWARENESS**, and so on. Evaluating these claims is one of the objectives of interlinguistics, a discipline dedicated to the study of planned languages and to the optimalisation of international linguistic communication in general. It investigates the design and function of international planned languages, and **LANGUAGE PLANNING** for international or **INTERCULTURAL COMMUNICATION**. Interlinguistics is thus unrelated to the concept of **INTERLANGUAGE**, although its field overlaps with second and foreign language studies in a number of ways, most evidently in the case of Esperanto. The two major orientations to interlinguistics are the semiotic, exemplified by Eco (1995) and Sakaguchi (1998), and the sociological, exemplified by Blanke (1985) and most of the contributions to Schubert (1989) and Tonkin

(1997). In practice, nearly all of the work in the sociological tradition has focused on Esperanto.

**See also:** BICS and CALP; Esperanto; Intercultural competence; Language planning; Lingua franca; Sign languages

### References

Blanke, D. (1985) *Internationale Plansprachen: Eine Einführung* (International planned languages: an introduction), Berlin: Akademie-Verlag.

Couturat, L. and Leau, L. (1979) *Histoire de la langue universelle. Les nouvelles langues internationales* (History of the universal language. The new international languages), Hildesheim and New York: Olms.

Eco, U. (1995) *The search for the perfect language*, Oxford: Blackwell.

Harrison, R. (1992–97) *Bibliography of planned languages (excluding Esperanto)*, http://www.geocities.com/Athens/5383/langlab/bibliog.html.

Haupenthal, R. (ed.) (1976) *Plansprachen. Beiträge zur Interlinguistik* (Planned languages: contributions to interlinguistics), Darmstadt: Wiss. Buchgesellschaft.

Large, J.A. (1985) *The artificial language movement*, Oxford: Blackwell.

Sakaguchi, A. (1998) *Interlinguistik: Gegenstand, Ziele, Aufgaben, Methoden* (Interlinguistics: topic, goals, functions, methods), Frankurt/M.: Peter Lang.

Schubert, K. (ed.) (1989) *Interlinguistics: aspects of the science of planned languages*, Berlin: Mouton de Gruyter.

Tonkin, H. (ed.) (1997) *Esperanto, interlinguistics, and planned language*, Lanham: University Press of America.

### Further reading

Blanke, D. (1985) *Internationale Plansprachen: Eine Einführung* (International planned languages: an introduction), Berlin: Akademie-Verlag.

Large, J.A. (1985) *The artificial language movement*, Oxford: Blackwell.

Tonkin, H. (ed.) (1997) *Esperanto, interlinguistics, and planned language*, Lanham: University Press of America.

MARK FETTES

# Planning for foreign language teaching

Language planning concerns the making of arrangements for the use of human language(s) in a number of different social domains of language use. Systematic attention for the planning of language teaching, in particular of foreign language teaching, is of fairly recent date. Planning of foreign language teaching requires careful consideration both of the planning objectives and of the many factors which are at play in the context of the planning process. Such factors are not only linguistic in kind, or psychological, sociological and educational, but they also pertain to the basic question with whom in each particular case the planning authority lies.

## General language planning

In planning for foreign language teaching, the concern is with educational arrangements for the learning and teaching of one or more foreign languages. Foreign language teaching planning is not the same as, although it may be included in, the **LANGUAGE PLANNING** by a country of the use of its language(s) or, for that matter, of its general approach to foreign languages. In such plans, for example, the use, the position or the preservation of a country's native and/or national and of its foreign languages are regulated and, possibly also, the rights of those citizens whose native language has not been designated one of the country's official languages.

In the general language planning literature, little separate attention is devoted to foreign language teaching planning, even when the focus is on a 'language policy for the European Community' (Coulmas, 1991). A specific and vivid interest in foreign language teaching planning arose in the early 1990s. International conferences specifically devoted to the topic were organised, a special issue of *The Annals* was devoted to it (Lambert, 1994), and a monograph on the subject appeared (Christ, 1991). A number of countries made notable progress, either in the awareness of the planning issue (for the **USA**, see, for example, Moore and Morfit 1993; Brecht *et al.*, 1995; for **FRANCE**, see

Arrouays, 1990), or in actually developing plans for foreign language teaching (for The Netherlands, see van Els and van Hest, 1990; Lambert, 1997).

Besides the term 'language planning' one often comes across 'language policy' or 'language policy-making'. There is a preference for 'language planning' over 'language policy-making', and for 'language policy' when reference is made to the outcome of the planning process.

## Planning for foreign languages

In all foreign language planning exercises there are a great many questions on which decisions have to be taken; all such questions must be clearly stated and defined beforehand. In essence, the questions can all be grouped under three major topics: 'what is to be learned/taught?'; 'how is it to be learned/taught?'; and 'what context-factors have to be taken into account?'

Of great importance, too, is another more or less preliminary point: the issue of 'who is to decide?' Decisions as to 'what?' and 'how?' and the context-factors need not all be taken by one and the same authority or person; they may lie at different levels. The planning authorities or persons may be the individual learners, their parents or the teachers involved; they may be the school board or the head of the school, but they may also be local or national or international bodies. The authority to plan is usually shared between these various 'levels', usually differently balanced for each specific case. Thus, the number of languages to be offered – and which exactly – and the number of languages each individual pupil is to learn, may be the prerogative of the central government to decide, but the decision as to which of these offered languages each individual pupil is to learn is often left to the pupils themselves. The resulting policy, which is only partly 'centralised' in the full sense of the word, may, on the other hand, still be said to be 'national'. A foreign language teaching policy is 'national' not because all decisions are taken at the national level, but when the policy covers all aspects of the planning process and, moreover, also holds a decision at what levels the authority lies to decide on the various relevant questions.

The scope of foreign language teaching policy statements tends to be limited, i.e. they often deal

with only a particular segment of the educational system. Many focus exclusively on (general) **SEC-ONDARY EDUCATION**, or they are restricted to the so-called lesser-taught languages. A truly national policy is national not only in the sense just indicated, but also sets out to be all-encompassing. It encompasses the full range of the demand for foreign languages, i.e. it deals with the need for foreign languages of all sub-sectors of the population and not only with the demand of, for instance, the academic world. It also encompasses the full supply range, which means that not only the facilities provided in secondary education are considered, but also the whole gamut of all educational sectors, including non-government-funded private language instruction.

In cases where a policy statement is restricted in scope, for example, to the sector of secondary education, a requirement is that it should also take into account how this particular sector is related to all other provisions. Otherwise the possibilities may be overlooked that other sectors hold for at least partly supplying to meet the demand in cases where an increase in demand surpasses the capacity of the secondary school timetables.

'Diversification' is a hotly debated issue in the discussions about what, how many and which foreign languages ought to be offered to, and/or should be chosen by, pupils in primary and especially secondary education. It is a big issue in many European countries (Arrouays, 1990: 15–16; Christ, 1991: 39–40; Phillips, 1989). 'Diversification' always refers to expanding the number of languages offered and generally implies extending the freedom of choice of the pupils. Diversification may apply to both the obligatory and the non-obligatory part of the foreign language curriculum. As for the former, in England and Wales, for example, there is an obligatory foreign language for every pupil, but a number of approximately 20 languages, i.e. all the national languages of the European Community and a number of 'languages of commercial and cultural importance', may be offered by schools for pupils to choose from.

In some countries the increasing demand for more foreign languages is translated into an expansion of the number of languages pupils are free to choose from for their first (obligatory) language. In other countries the policy is rather to extend the number of obligatory languages and, often in combination with that, to restrict the freedom of choice of the pupils with respect to the obligatory languages. In The Netherlands, for example, in general secondary education there is a fixed list of three obligatory languages for everyone (**FRENCH, GERMAN, ENGLISH**), and when in upper secondary education some freedom of choice is granted, the list of languages pupils may choose from is very limited (van Els, 1994: 39–40). There is little evidence to show, so far, that greater diversification has led to an increase – often hoped for – of the total foreign language competence of a country (Phillips, 1989: xi; Lambert, 1997: 82–4).

## Planning what to teach and learn

Foreign language teaching planning, even if, in principle, it covers the three major topics of 'what to learn/teach?', 'how to learn/teach?', and 'under what conditions to learn/teach?', usually restricts itself to policy statements with respect to 'what?'. Consideration of 'how?' very seldom leads to explicit policy statements on the topic, although, on the other hand, it regularly contributes to qualifying the choices made regarding the 'what?' topic. Thus, the respective (perceived) difficulty of learning and, therefore, of teaching different languages may lead to a well-reasoned choice of which languages to offer or of the sequence in which the languages are to be offered in the curriculum (Oud-de Glas, 1997).

The broad question 'what to learn/teach?' holds a number of sub-questions, the main ones of which are: 'what language(s) to learn/teach?'; 'to learn by/teach to whom?'; 'when to learn/teach?'; and 'what of the language(s) to learn/teach?'. The question of what particular situations and levels of language use the learner has to be prepared for is usually subsumed in policy statements on 'what to learn/teach?'. However, the more detailed aspects of the 'what?' topic are normally gone into in **SYLLABUS** and curriculum design, such as the specific **OBJECTIVES** to be achieved regarding communicative and sociocultural competence.

## Needs analysis

The analysis of the learner's foreign language needs plays an important role in finding answers to all the 'what?' questions. How needs can be investigated is dealt with under **NEEDS ANALYSIS**. Here their typology and, also, their weight in foreign language teaching planning will be discussed.

Arguments for the learning and teaching of foreign languages are of many different kinds, but in one way or another they are all statements of underlying needs. Surprisingly little principled discussion has been devoted to their typology so far (van Els, 1994: 37–9). It is not uncommon to divide needs into polar pairs, like 'individual' versus 'societal' or 'national'. But the opposition is hardly useful in a planning exercise, for it is evident that societal needs cannot be separated from individual needs: societal needs are always reducible to – i.e., they have been derived from – the individual needs of (a number of) members of that society. In essence, all needs are individual. On the other hand, not all individual needs are also societal. They only take on a societal dimension when society declares needs of (groups of) individuals important enough to take them into account when formulating a national policy for foreign language teaching.

Other such common polar oppositions one finds represented in 'non-utilitarian', 'cultural' or 'formative' versus 'utilitarian', 'directly useful' or 'capitalisable'. There is no clear-cut distinction between such pairs, in part also because there is no fundamental opposition between, for example, 'cultural' and 'directly useful'. Moreover, talking about the issues in these terms also leads people to carelessly equate 'utilitarian' with 'political' and 'practical'.

When needs have to be weighed one against the other with a view to formulating a foreign language teaching policy, the distinctions proposed so far are very inadequate. A more helpful criterion to distinguish needs for foreign language learning lies in the degree of communicative competence required to fulfil that need (van Els *et al.*, 1984: 162). On the basis of that criterion, three broad categories of needs can be distinguished:

1 *Communicative needs* one wants to be competent in a particular foreign language in order to be able to communicate effectively with speakers of that language.

2 *Language competence-related needs* one wants, for example, to become familiar with the culture, way of life, and, more specifically, the literature of another nation. **COMPETENCE** in the language in which that culture is embedded or the **LITERARY TEXTS** are written, is not a prerequisite to fulfil needs of this kind.

3 *Needs distantly, or not at all, related to language competence* one wants to develop particular social and/or intellectual **SKILLS** of a general nature. Such a general objective may be pursued through the learning/teaching of a variety of school subjects, among them foreign languages.

The relation between needs and foreign language competence becomes more indirect and diffuse as one proceeds down this list of three categories. With needs of the first category, there is no way around providing for the learning/teaching of the particular language(s) required. It is possible, however, to cater for some needs in the second category, such as a need for a better understanding of speakers of other languages in general, by providing for the learning/teaching of just one foreign language, no matter which, and even through the instruction of the native language. In the third category, the relation between needs and foreign language competence is even more tenuous.

The weight that these different categories of needs carry in foreign language teaching planning will differ from country to country. In a country like the **USA**, all arguments are equally valid or convincing: its inhabitants are in a position to use their native tongue in large parts of the world; when abroad, they are likely to cope without any competence in any other language. However, in most countries the question is not 'Should we learn a foreign language?', but rather 'Which languages, how many of them, and which skills should be learned to what levels of competence?' In such cases, where policy choices have to be made between the learning/teaching of a foreign language(s) and of other subjects, or for the learning/teaching of one foreign language against another,

arguments related to the first category of needs carry much more weight than those relating to the other two categories.

It should be noted that, when under those circumstances a choice for the learning/teaching of a particular language(s) is based on needs of category one, this fact as such does not require or for that matter justify that, in the actual learning/teaching of the language(s) chosen, needs of categories two and three should be overlooked.

## Other factors

Besides the obviously important needs factor, other factors have to be taken into account in foreign language teaching planning, either because they have an intrinsic value of their own or because they present some kind of obstacle or other to the achievement of a particular objective. These other factors are numerous and very diverse, but four broad categories may be distinguished:

### Psychological factors

Aspects of the processes of **BILINGUALISM** and foreign language learning may be decisive when decisions have to be taken regarding, for example, which language to learn/teach first, whether more foreign languages can be learnt/taught simultaneously – and, if so, how many – and what is the optimal **AGE** for starting learning/teaching. The inherent and/or perceived difficulty of a foreign language and all other **MOTIVATIONAL** considerations of learners are other such factors.

### Linguistic factors

The linguistic relations between the native language and the foreign language(s) to be learnt/taught on the one hand, and the relations between the foreign languages to be learnt/taught on the other, may justify the choice of one particular foreign language over another. For example, should there be room for (only) one more foreign language in the curriculum, a choice for French over Japanese might be argued for on the basis of the close relationship of French with other Romance languages (Italian, **SPANISH**) for which the learners might also feel some need. Another point to consider when little room for the learning/teaching of foreign languages can be claimed, is the possibility of opting for a **LINGUA FRANCA** or for one of the international languages like **ESPERANTO** (Christ, 1997: 130–2).

## Educational factors

Obvious educational factors that in foreign language planning have to be paid attention to are the restrictions of the timetable, and the availability of suitable teaching **MATERIALS** and adequately trained teachers. In many countries the foreign language needs cannot possibly all be satisfied in secondary education alone, and other sectors of the educational system will have to be considered to take their share.

The teaching of foreign languages cannot claim any special function when it comes to instilling into learners particular general educational objectives, such as '**LEARNING TO LEARN**' or **AUTONOMOUS LEARNING**. Claims for a special role are equally invalid when such attitudes are at stake as 'developing a stable system of ethical values' or 'accepting people with different social and ethnic backgrounds, avoiding rigidity and stereotyping' (Wilkins, 1987: 24). All the same, foreign language learning/teaching will have to make its contribution, together with other subjects, in realising objectives of a general educational nature.

## Language policy factors

The international situation of a country may make it desirable to make special provisions for the languages spoken in neighbouring countries, independent of the international status of those countries or of their languages (Christ, 1997: 132–4). Similarly, the international organisations a country belongs to and, in particular, the language policy pursued by those organisations may have to be taken into account. As for the internal language situation, a special case in point may be constituted by the country's policy regarding minority languages (Broeder and Extra, 1997).

**See also:** Evaluation; Languages for specific purposes; Language planning; Needs analysis;

Objectives in language teaching and learning; Syllabus and curriculum design

## References

Arrouays, M. (1990) 'Les finalités de l'enseignement des langues dans l'enseignement secondaire (The goals of foreign language teaching in secondary education)', *Les Langues Modernes* 84, 1: 7–29.

Brecht, R.D., Caemmerer, J. and Walton, A.R. (1995) *Russian in the United States: a case study of America's language needs and capacities*, Washington, DC: National Foreign Language Center.

Broeder, P. and Extra, G. (1997) 'Minority groups and minority languages in the Netherlands: empirical facts and educational policy', in Th. Bongaerts and K. de Bot (eds), *Perspectives on foreign-language policy*, Amsterdam/Philadelphia: John Benjamins.

Christ, H. (1991) *Fremdsprachenunterricht für das Jahr 2000. Sprachpolitische Betrachtungen zum Lehren und Lernen fremder Sprachen (Foreign language teaching for the year 2000. Language political observations on the teaching and learning of foreign languages)*, Tübingen: Gunter Narr Verlag.

Christ, H. (1997) 'Foreign-language policy from the grass roots', in Th. Bongaerts and K. de Bot (eds), *Perspectives on foreign-language policy*, Amsterdam/Philadelphia: John Benjamins.

Coulmas, F. (ed.) (1991) *A language policy for the European Community. Prospects and quandaries*, Berlin: Mouton de Gruyter.

Lambert, R.D. (ed.) (1994) *Foreign language policy: an agenda for change*, special issue of *The Annals of the American Academy of Political and Social Science*, vol. 532.

Lambert, R.D. (1997) 'Horizon taal and language planning in the United States', in Th. Bongaerts and K. de Bot (eds), *Perspectives on foreign-language policy*, Amsterdam/Philadelphia: John Benjamins.

Moore, S.J. and Morfit, C.A. (eds) (1993) *Language and international studies: a Richard Lambert perspective*, Washington, DC: National Foreign Language Center.

Oud-de Glas, M. (1997) 'The difficulty of Spanish for Dutch learners', in Th. Bongaerts and K. de

Bot (eds), *Perspectives on foreign-language policy*, Amsterdam/Philadelphia: John Benjamins.

Phillips, D. (ed.) (1989) *Which language? Diversification and the national curriculum*, London: Hodder and Stoughton.

van Els, T. (1994) 'Planning foreign language teaching in a small country', in R.D. Lambert (ed.), *Foreign language policy: an agenda for change*, special issue of *The Annals of the American Academy of Political and Social Science*, vol. 532.

van Els, T. and van Hest, E. (1990) 'Foreign language teaching policies and European unity: the Dutch national action programme', *Language, Culture and Curriculum* 3, 3: 199–211.

van Els, T., Bongaerts, Th., Extra, G., van Os, C. and Janssen-van Dieten, A. (1984) *Applied linguistics and the learning and teaching of foreign languages*, London/Baltimore: Edward Arnold.

Wilkins, D. (1987) *The value of foreign language learning*, Strasbourg: Council for Cultural Co-operation.

## Further reading

Corson, D. (1990) *Language policy across the curriculum*, Clevedon/Philadelphia: Multilingual Matters.

Lambert, R.D. (ed.) (1994) *Language planning around the world: contexts and systemic change*, Washington, DC: National Foreign Language Center.

Sajavaara, K., Lambert, R.D., Takala, S. and Morfit, C.A. (eds) (1993) *National foreign language planning: practices and prospects*, Jyväskylä: Institute for Educational Research.

Vandermeeren, S. (1998) *Fremdsprachen in Europäischen Unternehmen. Untersuchungen zu Bestand und Bedarf im Geschäftsalltag mit Empfehlungen für Sprachenpolitik und Sprachunterricht (Foreign languages in European enterprises. Investigations into uses and needs of day-to-day business practice, with recommendations for foreign language policy and language teaching)*, Waldsteinberg: Heidrun Popp Verlag.

THEO VAN ELS

# Poetry

Teaching poetry can take one of three forms: a **LITERARY** approach with a focus on accessing key cultural texts and acquiring literary competence; a linguistic approach using poetry as a language text; and a creative approach encouraging students to write their own poetry, where language is personally owned. Poetry offers an alternative language and discourse, often engaging learners' emotions, and encourages **LANGUAGE AWARENESS** and enhanced language memorisation contexts.

Three significant factors in the wider context are: the local/national teaching context; attitudes to 'poetry' in general; and priorities in foreign language teaching.

Local and national teaching contexts will influence the value in general placed on poetry and the age of the students (which in turn may affect attitudes to poetry). Adults are often the clients in an EFL context, where the use of poetry in the classroom can be welcomed. Another factor in a local context is **ASSESSMENT**, which can have a washback effect if poetry **SKILLS** are being tested. Students' existing constructs or images of poetry will affect their reactions to poetry in the foreign language classroom. Writers on **MOTHER-TONGUE TEACHING** (e.g. Andrews, 1991) have identified poetry-related problems: difficulties of meaning, **VOCABULARY**, metalanguage, allusion and image generally. Pupils' existing negative attitudes may then prove problematic. On the other hand, positive links to poetry exist in the enjoyment of rhythm in everyday life with advertising jingles, nursery rhymes, etc., and the turning to poetry for special occasions. In the classroom, making unexciting language items into raps or rhymed snippets can use this potential source of excitement to make learning more enjoyable and memorable for students.

Current priorities in foreign language teaching can also be influential. Poetry can be in conflict with a communicative **SYLLABUS** where the focus is on functional and utilitarian language, although discussions about poetry *can* be communicative. There may also be a similar discontinuity with a structural or grammatical syllabus.

### Poetry as part of a literary syllabus

Foreign language teachers may be required to teach poetry as part of their literature syllabus with sometimes little choice of text and probably with advanced learners. Many significant issues here relate to **LITERARY THEORY AND LITERATURE TEACHING** in general. Two key outcomes can be identified as important: access to an identified canon of important literature; and the development of literary competence.

Texts selected in a literary syllabus often represent key works in a culture. In studying these, students will be accessing the 'cultural capital' of a country (Bourdieu and Passeron, 1977) and thus can share some common reference points with target culture members. One can object that such a canon may not represent the diversity of cultures, present in the target country or sharing the target language.

The skill of literary competence has also been highlighted (Brumfit, 1991; Lazar, 1993). Lazar identifies two major skill areas: locating and analysing. Students may need to locate a text in terms of the writer's biography, the **GENRE**, the topic, any relevant literary movement, and its historical context. The particular focus will depend on the critical approach adopted by the teacher. Andrews (1991) identifies three main approaches to poetry: New Criticism, with the poem as object and a favoured interpretation reinforced by the teacher; a structuralist approach with no one text privileged but seen as a product of its historical context; and a post-structuralist approach focusing on the reader's interaction with the poem. The choice of approach will be affected by that favoured in assessment and/or by the teacher or foreign languages department. To attain literary competence, students will also need to hone or develop skills in appreciating features of an author's style, particularly the recognition of pattern, and in foreign language poems the understanding of the special cultural freight of symbols.

## Poetry as a language text

In the late 1980s and early 1990s there was a growth of interest in using literature texts, particularly for language purposes. With this approach, texts can be used with students of different ages; many different kinds of text can be used; and a teacher is also not restricted to choosing poems within a 'canon', since it is not the literary merits of the poem which are in question.

One important objection raised regarding the focusing on language in poetry (and this relates to poems in a literature syllabus as well), may be that the language of poetry is regarded as deviant (Lazar, 1993; Widdowson, 1984), offering pupils an unsuitable model. Several counter-suggestions have been identified to overcome this objection. Lazar suggests that deviance can itself become the focus of discussion (1993); Bassnett and Grundy reformulate the objection and present poetry as an example of 'highly skilful language usage ... [demonstrating] what language can do' (1993: 7). Pirrie points to positive aspects of a different form: 'Many ... pupils ... experience a relief that few words are required and welcome the security provided by pattern and structure' (1987: 80).

Other positive aspects also suggested include improvement of language awareness; engagement with students on an affective, personal level; improved memorisation of vocabulary; opportunities for performance and practical advantages. The latter relate to the brevity of most poetry texts, being well-suited to a single classroom lesson. The compactness of the poem means both that it is 'a self contained world' (Maley and Duff, 1989: 11) and that its 'compressed quality ... produces an unexpected density of meaning' (Collie and Slater, 1987: 5).

Poetry can aid language learning by increasing students' awareness of the 'vital areas of stress, rhythm and similarities of sound' (Collie and Slater, 1987: 226). The rhythms of the language used often provide 'a clear echo of ... everyday spoken language ... a kind of underlying heart beat' (Maley and Duff, 1989: 11). Maley and Duff also speak of poets 'stretching' language (1989), and **WIDDOWSON** talks of poetry as focusing attention particularly upon language itself (1984).

Another possible benefit for language learning is the enhanced context for memorisation. Maley and Duff suggest that particular rhythms or striking uses of language in poetry can fix language items securely in the memory (1989: 10–11). 'Sound' values of poetry can make it a suitable vehicle for choral or individual performance and thus help to develop students' **SPEAKING** skills.

A highly significant aspect is the involvement of learners' personal feelings. Poetry often deals with themes left untouched by other school texts (love, death, emotional experiences, and so on). These are not only non-trivial but can also engage learners and increase **MOTIVATION**. Poems can promote positive intercultural relationships by emphasising universal experiences, which can transcend cultures.

A wide range of different kinds of language activity can be used with poems: role-play, letters, guessing games, jigsaw tasks and so on, which will engage learners and capitalise on the benefits mentioned here. Poetry tasks can involve all four language learning skills and are particularly suited to collaborative learning with pair work or **GROUP WORK**.

## Teaching poetry-writing

The third way that poetry can be used in the classroom is by encouraging creative **WRITING**. This can be done either by using an existing text as a model, or by encouraging students to write 'poems' using a variety of stimuli, such as poems in particular forms or shapes or poetry written in response to pictures or music.

Benefits of creating poetry include facilitating **AUTHENTIC** discussions where students decide on suitable language formulations. It also offers the chance for students to own both the topic and the language of their communication, unlike many functional activities in a communicative syllabus; and, finally, it fosters student confidence in having produced 'poems', particularly where these are word-processed and/or accompanied by illustrations and then displayed. Students can pitch the writing at their own level and may experience a degree of distance and release which derives from writing in another language.

**See also:** Authenticity; Drama; Literary texts; Literary theory and literature teaching; Metaphor; Teaching methods; Translation theory

## References

Andrews, R (1991) *The problem with poetry*, Buckingham: Open University Press.

Bassnett, S. and Grundy, P. (1993) *Language through literature: creative language teaching through literature*, Harlow: Longman.

Bourdieu, P. and Passeron, J.-C. (1977) *Reproduction in education, society and culture*, (trans. R. Nice), London: Sage.

Brumfit, C. (ed.) (1991) *Assessment in literature teaching*, London: Macmillan, Modern English Publications.

Collie, J. and Slater, S. (1987) *Literature in the language classroom: a resource book of ideas and activities*, Cambridge: Cambridge University Press.

Lazar, G. (1993) *Literature and language teaching: a guide for teachers and trainers*, Cambridge: Cambridge University Press.

Maley, A. and Duff, A. (1989) *The inward ear: poetry in the classroom*, Cambridge: Cambridge University Press.

Pirrie, J. (1987) *On common ground: a programme for teaching poetry*, London: Hodder and Stoughton.

Widdowson, H. (1984) *Explorations in Applied Linguistics 2*, Oxford: Oxford University Press.

## Further reading

Thompson, L. (ed.) (1996) *Teaching poetry: European perspectives*, London: Cassell.

CAROL MORGAN

# Politeness

Linguistic politeness refers to language usage which enables smooth communication between conversational participants according to the norms of social interaction in a particular contextual situation within a given speech community. This is often achieved through the appropriate choice of verbal and **NON-VERBAL COMMUNICATION** strategies which allow the message to be conveyed in a manner favourable to the addressee in conformity with their expectations regarding communication norms. Linguistic politeness has traditionally been associated with indirectness in **SPEECH ACT** studies. The social indexing inherent in the use of honorifics is an aspect of linguistic politeness which has been examined within the field of **SOCIOLINGUISTICS**.

Principles of linguistic politeness have been developed by linguists working within the field of **PRAGMATICS**, most notably Lakoff (1973, 1975, 1989), Brown and Levinson (1978, 1987) and

Leech (1983). Claims regarding the universality of these principles have attracted attention within the field of cross-cultural pragmatics. Studies suggest that the universal concept of politeness results in pragmatic concerns to realise particular speech acts according to suitable levels of formality with regard to participant, situation and extent of imposition. Cross-linguistic equivalence in the realisation of particular speech acts in terms of form and usage, however, is shown to vary considerably. It is crucial for language learners to be made aware of this in order to minimise the likelihood of cross-cultural misunderstandings and to avoid incorrect judgements being formed concerning their communicative intent.

The most comprehensive theory of linguistic politeness is offered by Brown and Levinson (1978, 1987). Drawing upon Goffman's (1967) definition of 'face', their model describes how particular linguistic strategies are adopted to counteract the threats to face which particular speech acts, such as requesting or inviting, involve. Face is defined as the 'public self-image that every member wants to claim for himself' (Brown and Levinson, 1987: 61). It consists in two dimensions: 'positive face' and 'negative face'. The former is linked to the desire to be appreciated and win approval: 'the want of every member that his wants be desirable to at least some others' (1987: 62). Negative face is concerned with 'freedom of action and freedom from imposition' (1987: 61) – the want that one's actions be unimpeded by others. Maintaining face is perceived as a basic human desire which involves the employment of certain politeness strategies – the choice of which is contingent upon the estimated risk of face loss to the participants in the interaction. Factors such as Social Distance (D), Relative Power (P) between interlocutors and Absolute Ranking (R) of impositions within a particular culture are all said to contribute to the degree of threat posed by an 'FTA' – i.e., a 'face-threatening act' (1987: 60).

Brown and Levinson's framework has been criticised for several reasons. Ide (1989) claims that it fails to offer a precise definition of linguistic politeness which is necessary to allow more fruitful cross-cultural research. In addition, the universality of the proposed constituents of 'face' have been questioned with regard to non-Western contexts

(Mao, 1993) and, more specifically, with regard to the Japanese language and culture (Matsumoto, 1988). According to Mao (1993: 455), Brown and Levinson present face as 'an individualistic, "self"-oriented image'. Although this may be an accurate description of face in Western society where social interaction is based upon individualism, it is deemed problematic in non-Western contexts. Matsumoto (1988), for example, claims that it is the acknowledgement and maintenance of the relative position of others, rather than the pre-servation of an individual's 'proper territory' (1988: 405) which governs all social interaction in **JAPAN**. She illustrates this with reference to the expression '*doozo yoroshiku onegaisimasu*' (literally: 'I ask you to treat me well') which directly requests favourable treatment from the addressee, whilst functioning as a greeting in an initial encounter. Rather than signalling imposition and constituting a 'face-threatening act', Matsumoto (1988: 410) argues that 'deferent impositions' can enhance the face or good self-image of the addressee in Japan by elevating the recipient and revealing the speaker's humble position. Ide (1989: 241) similarly claims that, in societies such as Japan where group membership constitutes the basis of social interaction, the role or status defined in a particular situation through appropriate choice of linguistic form and behaviour is the key element in polite social interaction.

Despite the aforementioned deficiencies in Brown and Levinson's framework, their work has inspired considerable research into the use of politeness strategies which has implications for cross-cultural communication and language teaching. It has been recognised that some languages, such as Javanese, have complex systems of politeness which result in distinct speech styles being necessary in particular situations. Linguistic politeness may be encoded in formulaic expressions which occur in greetings, partings, pleas, thanks, excuses, apologies and smalltalk (Laver, 1981: 290), and in honorific forms which are essential for showing politeness in languages such as Japanese. The use of such expressions varies cross-culturally and, therefore, poses particular challenges for the language learner. Certain linguistic routines are culture specific. In Japanese, for example, it is customary to say *itadakimasu* (literally: 'I receive') before eating, whilst no corresponding expression exists in **ENGLISH**. According to Slama-Cazacu (1991: 400), such lack of correspondence between particular conversational routines may induce learner anxiety. It may be unclear to the language learner when it is appropriate to employ particular formulas. The scale of fixity of particular expressions may also prove troublesome. This certainly suggests that the impact of culture on this aspect of language usage should receive significant attention in the teaching of foreign languages.

The 1990 revision of **THRESHOLD LEVEL** has incorporated a section on politeness conventions due to their significance in the **ACQUISITION** of sociocultural competence. Learners are encouraged to adopt non-verbal politeness strategies, involving body language, facial expression and eye-contact, in accordance with target language norms because this may compensate for deficiencies in their linguistic repertoire with regard to politeness strategies. The revised edition also aims to raise learner awareness of general principles of politeness in the target language in the belief that this will aid language learners to make informed choices regarding appropriate linguistic expressions whilst taking into account contextual variables such as the age, status and relationship between the participants in the interaction. To facilitate this process, sub-maxims of politeness are offered, such as 'Do not be dogmatic' and 'Do not force the partner to act', and particular linguistic strategies are suggested, including 'add please', 'avoid imperatives' to mitigate imposition (van Ek and Trim, 1991: 105–6). Advice is also offered on how to decline invitations and how to apologise, and attention is directed to the crucial role which intonation plays in conveying a particular message.

**See also:** Competence and performance; Cross-cultural psychology; Culture shock; Discourse analysis; Intercultural communication; Non-verbal communication; Notions and functions; Objectives in language teaching and learning; Sociolinguistics; Speech act theory; Text and corpus linguistics

### References

Brown, P. and Levinson, S. (1978) 'Universals of language usage: politeness phenomena', in E. Goody (ed.), *Questions and politeness*, Cambridge: Cambridge University Press.

Brown, P. and Levinson, S. (1987) *Politeness*, Cambridge: Cambridge University Press.

Goffman, E. (1967) *Interaction ritual: essays on face to face behavior*, New York: Anchor.

Ide, S. (1989) 'Formal forms and discernment: two neglected aspects of universals of linguistic politeness', *Multilingua* 8, 2/3: 223–48.

Lakoff, R. (1973) 'The logic of politeness: or minding your p's and q's', *Papers from the Ninth Regional Meeting of the Chicago Linguistic Society*, 292–305. Chicago: Chicago Linguistic Society.

Lakoff, R. (1975) *Language and woman's place*, New York: Harper Row.

Lakoff, R. (1989) 'The limits of politeness: therapeutic and courtroom discourse', *Multilingua* 8, 2/3: 101–29.

Laver, J. (1981) 'Linguistic routines and politeness in greeting and parting' in F. Coulmas (ed.), *Conversational routine. Explorations in standardized communication situations and prepatterned speech*, The Hague: Mouton.

Leech, G.N. (1983) *Principles of pragmatics*, London: Longman.

Mao, L.R. (1993) 'Beyond politeness theory: 'face' revisited and renewed', *Journal of Pragmatics* 21: 451–86.

Matsumoto, Y. (1988) 'Reexamination of the universality of face: politeness phenomena in Japanese', *Journal of Pragmatics* 12: 403–26.

Slama-Cazacu, T. (1991) 'Politeness strategies and contrastive foreign language teaching', in V. Ivir and D. Kalogjera (eds), *Trends in linguistics. Studies and Monographs 54. Languages in contact and contrast. Essays in contact linguistics*. Berlin: Mouton de Gruyter.

van Ek, J.A. and Trim, J.L.M. (1991) *Threshold Level 1990*, Strasbourg: Council of Europe Press.

### Further reading

Brown, P. and Levinson, S. (1987) *Politeness*, Cambridge: Cambridge University Press.

Watts, R.J., Ide, S. and Ehlich, K. (eds) (1992) *Politeness in language studies in its history, theory and practice. Trends in linguistics. Studies and Monographs 59.* Berlin: Mouton de Gruyter.

JULIE NORTON

# Portuguese

The teaching of Portuguese as a foreign language (PLE: *Português como Língua Estrangeira*) has developed considerably in recent decades, although there is a tradition of imparting the Portuguese language abroad which goes back centuries to the court of Charles II and his Portuguese queen Catherine of Braganza. The language spread with the navigators of the fifteenth and sixteenth centuries, and was often learned by other nations in later eras to facilitate trade and commerce. The large numbers of immigrants or returning emigrants and their children to Portugal is another factor which influences the teaching of Portuguese within the country. Late-twentieth-century developments are largely due to increased interest in research into methodology and to the initiatives of teacher associations and the government, implemented to a large extent by the Camões Institute to promote its language and culture within Portugal, in other lusophone countries and across the world. In 1986 Portuguese became an official language of the European Union when Portugal joined the Common Market. In 1996 the Community of Portuguese-Speaking Countries (CPLP: *Comunidade de Países de Língua Portuguesa*) was formed to increase cooperation between Portugal and its former colonies and to facilitate cultural and linguistic exchange. With the **TRANSLATION** of theoretical texts in the late 1970s and 1980s, pedagogical research and interest in innovative methodology have flourished in Portugal. Increasing numbers of original **TEXTBOOKS** and multimedia packages are being published every year.

## Teaching methods and approaches

The first manuals designed for teaching PLE took a traditional grammatical approach. In the late 1980s more original textbooks and **AUDIO-VISUAL** packages began to be published, such as '*Vamos Aprender Português*', Jorge Dias de Silva *et al.* (Plátano,

Lisbon, 1988), '*Dia a Dia*', by Isabel Leiria *et al.* (Universidade Aberta, Lisbon, 1988), and '*Português Sem Fronteiras*', by Isabel Leite and Olga Coimbra (Lidel, Lisbon, 1989), marking interest in a more interactive teaching approach. These courses included audio-visual **MATERIALS**, books for teachers and pupils, cassettes and slides.

The 1990s has seen a huge growth in the publication of manuals and textbooks by a large number of the prominent Portuguese publishing houses such as Porto Editora and Lidel, but also from Brazil, Macau and from other European countries. Currently there is an extensive range of teaching materials available for teachers of Portuguese, from **GRAMMARS** and self-teaching texts to CD-ROMs and computer packages, all of which can be consulted in the pamphlet '*Materiais Didácticos*' published by the Association of Teachers of Portuguese (APP: *Associação de Professores de Português*).

## The establishment of state institutions

### The Camões Institute

The **CAMÕES INSTITUTE** was founded in 1992 with the aim of fulfilling two main objectives: to promote and disseminate the Portuguese language and culture, both in Portugal and on an international scale. These tasks are implemented in various ways: first, via a network of cultural centres; second, through the Institute's coordination of 160 leitores (language lecturers/assistants) working in colleges and universities in forty countries; and, finally, by the award of various grants to Portuguese and foreign students for undergraduate and postgraduate studies and the sponsorship and support of publications and cultural events.

### The Ministry of Education

The Bureau of European Affairs and International Relations (GAERI: *Gabinete de Assuntos Estrangeiros e Relações Internacionais*), a branch of the Ministry of Education, is involved in European Union initiatives and oversees the SOCRATES programme within Portugal. Another branch of the Ministry, the Institute for Educational Innovation (IIE: *Instituto de Inovação Educacional*), is involved in several

European projects including studies of the teaching and learning of foreign languages. It publishes works dedicated to educational research, and two journals: *Noesis* and *Inovação*.

### Diplomas in Portuguese as a Foreign Language

The Faculties of Arts at the Universities of Lisbon and Coimbra have courses which lead towards the awarding of a diploma in PLE, but the other universities which run similar language courses also grant PLE certificates.

The Camões Institute and representatives of the University of Lisbon have examinations to grant diplomas and certificates in the proficiency of Portuguese as a Foreign Language, in cooperation with the Association of Language Testers in Europe.

The Faculty of Arts at the University of Oporto organises a postgraduate diploma course designed mainly for foreigners (including students from Portuguese-speaking countries), intending to teach PLE. The course began in 1994 and has trained students from as far afield as JAPAN, Cuba, Hungary and Mozambique.

### The universities

The first university summer course for foreign students to learn Portuguese was inaugurated in 1934 in the Faculty of Arts of the University of Lisbon. Due to popular demand, a course to last the academic year was created in 1956, under the auspices of the Instituto de Alta Cultura.

Throughout the 1990s, with the investment in new universities and the creation of private universities, the teaching of PLE became a commonplace in HIGHER EDUCATION in Portugal. Almost all of these institutions run language courses, during the summer and the rest of the academic year, and most are also involved in the ERASMUS EXCHANGE programme.

Various Brazilian universities offer language courses for foreigners, including a PLE teacher training course at the Pontificia Universidade Católica (Catholic University) in Rio de Janeiro and a Masters course in PLE at the Universidade federal Fluminense (Fluminense federal University), also in Rio de Janeiro.

The Institute of Portuguese Studies at the University of Macau offers summer language courses and a teacher training course.

### Associations and conferences

The Calouste Gulbenkian Foundation provides grants for international exchange projects, and funds the publication of technical studies and theoretical texts.

The Association for Teachers of Portuguese (APP), an independent non-profit-making organisation, was formed in 1977. It develops training courses, coordinates research and resources, organises annual conferences and publishes texts and its own journal, *Palavras*. The APP is mainly involved with the teaching of Portuguese to nationals but is also concerned with PLE.

The newspaper *Jornal de Letras, Artes e Ideias* publishes a monthly education supplement which provides information on and debates about the education system in Portugal.

The International Society for the Teaching of Portuguese as a Foreign Language (SIPLE: *Sociedade Internacional de Português como Língua Estrangeira*) was formed in Brazil in 1992.

Since 1989, the Society for Language and Cultural Exchange (SILC: *Sociedade de Intercâmbio de Línguas e Culturas*) has organised the annual exhibition and conference EXPOLINGUA, which brings together people and institutions from the world of language teaching and learning.

**See also:** Africa; French; German; Language planning; Linguistic imperialism; Spanish; Syllabus and curriculum design; Teaching methods

### Websites

The Institute for Educational Innovation's website is: http://www.iie.min-edu.pt

The website of the Association for Teachers of Portuguese can be found at: http://www.app.pt

### Further reading

*Actas do Colóquio 'O ensino do Português nos países da C.E.' (Proceedings of the conference 'The teaching of*

*Portuguese in European Community countries')* (Lisbon: Universidade Aberta, 1994).

*Actas do Seminário Internacional 'Português como Língua Estrangeira' (Proceedings of the international seminar 'Portuguese as a Foreign Language')*, Macau, 1991 (Macau, Direcção dos Serviços de Educação Fundação Macau, 1991).

Fontoura, M.M. (1992) *Para a História do Ensino da Língua Portuguesa no Estrangeiro (Towards a history of the teaching of the Portuguese language abroad)*, Lisbon: Faculdade de Psicologia e Ciências da Educação da Universidade de Lisboa.

Leiria, I. (1989) 'O Ensino de Português a Estrangeiros na Faculdade de Letras de Lisboa (The teaching of Portuguese to foreigners at the Faculty of Arts in Lisbon)', *Seara Nova* 21.

'Português Língua Estrangeira já tem certificação (Certificates in Portuguese as a Foreign Language are now available)', *Camões*, supplement of *Jornal de Letras, Artes e Ideias*, 24 March 1999.

*Português Língua Estrangeira: Materiais Didácticos (Portuguese as a Foreign Language: teaching materials)* (Lisbon: Associação de Professores de Português/Instituto Camões, 1999).

CLAIRE WILLIAMS

# Pragmatics

A subfield of **LINGUISTICS** developed in the late 1970s, pragmatics studies how people comprehend and produce a communicative act or a speech act in a concrete speech situation which is usually a conversation (hence the term **CONVERSATION ANALYSIS**). It distinguishes two intents or meanings in each utterance or act of verbal communication. One is the informative intent or the sentence meaning, and the other the communicative intent or speaker meaning (Leech, 1983; Sperber and Wilson, 1986). The ability to comprehend and produce a communicative act is referred to as pragmatic competence (Kasper, 1999) which often includes one's knowledge about the social distance, social status between the speakers involved, the cultural knowledge such as **POLITENESS**, and the linguistic knowledge both explicit and implicit.

## Focus and content

Some of the aspects of language studied in pragmatics include:

- deixis: meaning 'pointing to' something. In verbal communication, however, deixis in its narrow sense refers to the contextual meaning of pronouns, and in its broad sense to what the speaker means by a particular utterance in a given speech context;
- presupposition: referring to the logical meaning of a sentence or meanings logically associated with or entailed by a sentence;
- performative: implying that by each utterance a speaker not only says something but also does certain things: giving information, stating a fact or hinting an attitude. The study of performatives led to the hypothesis of **SPEECH ACT THEORY** that holds that a speech event embodies three acts: a locutionary act, an illocutionary act and a perlocutionary act (Austin, 1962; Searle, 1969);
- implicature: referring to an indirect or implicit meaning of an utterance derived from context that is not present from its conventional use.

Pragmaticians are also keen on exploring why interlocutors can successfully converse with one another in a conversation. A basic idea is that interlocutors obey certain principles in their participation so as to sustain the conversation. One such principle is the cooperative principle, which assumes that interactants cooperate in the conversation by contributing to the ongoing speech event (Grice, 1975). Another assumption is the politeness principle (Leech, 1983), that maintains interlocutors behave politely to one another since people respect each other's 'face' (Brown and Levinson, 1978). A cognitive explanation to social interactive speech events was provided by Sperber and Wilson (1986), who hold that in verbal communication people try to be relevant to what they intend to say and to whom an utterance is intended – 'relevance theory'.

The pragmatic principles people abide by in one language are often different in another. Thus there has been a growing interest in how people in different languages observe a certain pragmatic principle. Cross-linguistic and cross-cultural studies reported that what is considered polite in one language is sometimes not polite in another. Contrastive pragmatics, however, is not confined to the study of certain pragmatic principles. Cultural breakdowns, pragmatic failure, among other things, are also components of cross-cultural pragmatics.

Another focus of research in pragmatics is learner language or **INTERLANGUAGE**. This interest eventually evolved into interlanguage pragmatics, a branch of pragmatics which specifically discusses how non-**NATIVE SPEAKERS** comprehend and produce a speech act in a target language and how their pragmatic competence develops over time (Kasper and Blum-Kulka, 1993; Kasper, 1995).

## History

Although pragmatics is a relatively new branch of linguistics, research on it can be dated back to ancient Greece and Rome where the term *pragmaticus* is found in late Latin and *pragmaticos* in Greek, both meaning 'of being practical'. Modern use and current practice of pragmatics is credited to the influence of the American philosophical doctrine of pragmatism. The pragmatic interpretation of semiotics and verbal communication studies in *Foundations of the Theory of Signs* by Charles Morris (1938), for instance, helped neatly expound the differences of mainstream enterprises in semiotics and linguistics. For Morris, pragmatics studies the 'relations of signs to interpreters', while semantics studies the 'relations of signs to the objects to which the signs are applicable' and syntactics studies the 'formal relations of signs to one another'. By elaborating the sense of pragmatism in his analysis of conversational meanings, Grice (1975) has enlightened modern treatment of meaning by distinguishing two kinds of meaning, natural and non-natural. Grice suggested that pragmatics should centre on the more practical dimension of meaning, namely the conversational meaning which was later formulated in a variety of ways (Levinson, 1983; Leech, 1983).

Practical concerns also helped shift pragmaticians' focus to explaining naturally occurring conversations, which resulted in hallmark discoveries of the cooperative principle by Grice (1975) and the politeness principle by Leech (1983).

Subsequently, Green (1989) explicitly defined pragmatics as natural language understanding. This was echoed by Blakemore (1990) in her *Understanding Utterances: The Pragmatics of Natural Language* and by Grundy (1995) in his *Doing Pragmatics*. The impact of pragmatism has led to crosslinguistic international studies of language use which resulted in, among other things, Sperber and Wilson's (1986) relevance theory which convincingly explains how people comprehend and utter a communicative act.

The Anglo-American tradition of pragmatic study has been tremendously expanded and enriched with the involvement of researchers, mainly from European countries such as the Netherlands, Denmark, Norway and Belgium. A symbol of this development was the establishment of the IPrA (the International Pragmatic Association) in Antwerp in 1987. In its Working Document, the IPrA proposed to consider pragmatics as a theory of linguistic adaptation and look into language use from all dimensions (Verschueren, 1987). Henceforward, pragmatics has been conceptualised so as to incorporate micro and macro components (Mey, 1993).

Throughout its development, pragmatics has been steered by the philosophical practice of pragmatism, evolving to maintain its independence as a linguistic subfield by keeping to its declared purpose of being practical in treating the everyday meaning.

## Criticisms

A longstanding criticism has been that pragmatics does not have a clear-cut focus, and in early studies there was a tendency to group those topics without a clear status in linguistics under pragmatics. Thus pragmatics came to be known as something of 'a garbage can' (Leech, 1983). Other complaints were that, unlike **GRAMMAR** which resorts to rules, the vague and fuzzy principles in pragmatics are not adequate in telling people what to choose in the face of a range of possible meanings for one single utterance in context. An extreme criticism from John Marshall (Shi, 1989) was that pragmatics is not eligible as an independent field of learning, since meaning is dealt with in semantics.

However, there is a consensus view that pragmatics as a separate study is more than necessary because it handles those meanings that semantics overlooks (Leech, 1983). This view has been reflected both in practice at large and in *Meaning in Interaction: An Introduction to Pragmatics* by Thomas (1995). Thus, in spite of the criticisms, the impact of pragmatics has been colossal and multifaceted. The study of speech acts, for instance, provided illuminating explanation into sociolinguistic conduct. The findings of the cooperative principle and the politeness principle also provided insights into person-to-person interaction. The choice of different linguistic means for a communicative act and the various interpretations for the same speech act elucidate human mentality in the relevance principle, which contributes to the study of communication in particular and cognition in general. Implications of pragmatic studies are also evident in language teaching practices. Deixis, for instance, is important in the teaching of **READING**. Speech acts are often helpful for improving translation and **WRITING**. Pragmatic principles are also finding their way into the study of literary works as well as language teaching classrooms.

**See also:** Communicative strategies; Conversation analysis; Cross-cultural psychology; Culture shock; Discourse analysis; Linguistics; Politeness; Speech act theory; Strategic competence; Text and corpus linguistics

### References

Austin, J.L. (1962) *How to do things with words*, New York: Oxford University Press.

Blakemore, D. (1990) *Understanding utterances: the pragmatics of natural language*, Oxford: Blackwell.

Brown, P. and Levinson, S. (1978) 'Universals in language use: politeness phenomena', in E. Goody (ed.), *Questions and politeness: strategies in social interaction*, Cambridge: Cambridge University Press.

Green, G. (1989) *Pragmatics and natural language understanding*, Mahwah, NJ: Lawrence Erlbaum.

Grice, H.P. (1975) 'Logic and conversation', in P. Cole, and J. Morgan (eds), *Syntax and semantics. Volume 3: Speech acts*, New York: Academic Press.

Grundy, P. (1995) *Doing pragmatics*, London: Edward Arnold.

Kasper, G. (1995) 'Interlanguage pragmatics', in J. Verschueren, J.-O. Östman and J. Blommaert (eds), *Handbook of pragmatics*, Amsterdam: John Benjamins.

Kasper, G. and Blum-Kulka, S. (eds) (1993) *Interlanguage pragmatics*, Oxford: Oxford University Press.

Leech, G. (1983) *Principles of pragmatics*, London: Longman.

Levinson, S. (1983) *Pragmatics*, Cambridge: Cambridge University Press.

Mey, J. (1993) *Pragmatics. An introduction*, Oxford: Blackwell.

Searle, J. (1969) *Speech acts*, Cambridge: Cambridge University Press.

Shi Cun (1989) 'Speeches at the IPrA Roundtable Conference', *Teaching Research* 2: 41–61.

Sperber, D. and Wilson, D. (1986) *Relevance: communication and cognition*, Oxford: Blackwell.

Thomas, J. (1995) *Meaning in interaction: an introduction to pragmatics*, London: Longman.

Verschueren, J. (1987) *Pragmatics as a theory of linguistic adaptation*, Working Document No. 1, Antwerp: International Pragmatics Association.

### Further reading

Blum-Kulka, S., Kasper, G. and House, J. (eds) (1989) *Cross-cultural pragmatics: requests and apologies*, Norwood, NJ: Ablex.

Davis, S. (ed.) (1991) *Pragmatics. A reader*, Oxford: Oxford University Press.

Kasper, G. and Blum-Kulka, S. (eds) (1993) *Interlanguage pragmatics*, Oxford: Oxford University Press.

SHAOZHONG LIU

# Primary education

The discussion of the purpose and practice of foreign language teaching in primary education has for a long time suffered from terminological confusion. Very often, the term *primary education* was used with varying meanings in different educational contexts. To avoid misunderstandings arising out of this variety, the **COUNCIL OF EUROPE** introduced, in its extensive Modern Languages Project (1989–97), a clear although somewhat arbitrary definition, namely: the school education of children from age 5/6 to 10/11. As a rule this education is practised without external differentiation and – as its main function – has to lay the foundation for all subsequent education in secondary schools. The definition has found many adherents and is also used in this article.

Since the 1960s an increasing number of educationists have demanded that primary education should include the teaching and learning of foreign languages. At first the arguments for such an inclusion were mainly taken from **PSYCHOLOGY** and psycholinguistics. The great flexibility of the human brain during childhood and the high **MOTIVATION** of young children to engage in verbal activities were seen as the main reasons for the introduction of primary foreign language teaching. However, the revival of systematic educational thinking at the end of the twentieth century led to a more genuinely pedagogical argumentation. The reasoning is as follows. If the central task of primary education is fundamental in the above-mentioned sense, then the foundations for all the main subject areas must be laid in it. Foreign language teaching and learning is one of these areas and should therefore become part of the core curriculum in the primary school.

The environment in which most children grow up today is no longer monocultural. They have contact with members of other cultures and direct experience of foreign influences from an early age onwards. Their local environment is often multicultural already; their peers come from different backgrounds; the objects which they work and play with come from distant places; the shop products which they see or buy are of foreign origin, etc. Therefore the old dichotomies of Here and There, of Near and Far, do not hold any more. If it is the purpose of all education to help the individual to function well in their society and, if this society is multicultural already, then such help cannot be postponed to the secondary level of education but must be given from the earliest stage of formal education, i.e. from the primary school onwards.

Many national governments have subscribed to this reasoning and have consequently introduced foreign languages in their primary school curricula. Of great help for the protagonists were the activities of the Council of Europe, which declared primary foreign language teaching to be one of its priority areas and conducted a considerable number of workshops for a clarification of the principal issues and for the appropriate preparation of teachers.

The question is no longer *whether*, but *how* foreign languages can be taught effectively at the primary level. The discussion concentrates on six issues that can be expressed in the form of dichotomies, each of which represents a theoretical opposition. In practice, teaching will often follow a path that lies somewhere between the opposing concepts; but the dichotomies can nevertheless serve as the cornerstones of a framework for the individual realisations and can help teachers in their orientation.

The six dichotomies are:

- Integration versus separate subject;
- Systematic course versus occasional teaching;
- Language learning versus linguistic and cultural awareness;
- Communicative competence versus sensitisation;
- Class teacher versus subject teacher;
- Part of the core curriculum versus optional activity.

### Integration versus separate subject

This first dichotomy refers to the *position* of the foreign language in the curriculum. Will it be integrated into the existing areas of the curriculum, or treated as a separate subject? The advantages of the latter solution are the better chances for a clearly definable linear teaching programme with its own body of contents and its own distinctive **OBJECTIVES**, but it has the definite disadvantage of separating the foreign language from all other areas of teaching and thus violating an important principle of primary education: the holistic approach to learning. The numerous adherents to this approach, therefore, favour the first solution, namely an integration that allows children to relate the foreign language to concepts about the world that they already possess or are actually acquiring through their **MOTHER TONGUE**. This solution enables the teacher to make various connections, those between the foreign language and practically all other fields of learning, whether in the area of mathematics, social and environmental studies, expressive arts or the study of the mother tongue. In its strongest version this teaching takes the form of *embedding*, where the foreign language is inserted in the traditional subjects whenever this is appropriate. Thus it is not taught as an additional subject, but as an added dimension of the existing ones.

## Systematic course versus occasional teaching

As to the *organisation*, there are two alternatives: either to proceed systematically from the basic language items to more special ones, from easy to difficult, from simple to complex; *or* to choose a more occasional approach and to teach the foreign language whenever the opportunity presents itself.

Embedding contains the danger that the language is taught systematically enough. The progression is topic-centred and the acquisition of the language can easily become a by-product. There is no predefined body of contents and no built-in progression of **VOCABULARY** and **GRAMMAR**. These important qualities can only be ensured in a systematic course, which provides repetition, consolidation and continuity in a coherent way. On the other hand the holistic organisation of teaching in the primary school is a definite asset and does not allow for a dominance of the principles of progression of one particular area of learning.

The obvious way out seems to be a compromise between the two alternatives. Although difficult to achieve, the best solution would be a coordination of **CONTENT-BASED** and language-based principles of progression. The experiences of **BILINGUAL EDUCATION** provide a good example, and certainly primary foreign language education (FLE) can profit from an application of the notional–functional approach proposed by the Council of Europe (van Ek, 1986) which attempts a logical deduction of the linguistic items to be learnt from the notions and functions that the learner has to acquire.

## Language learning versus linguistic and cultural awareness

The third dichotomy represents the *function* that FLE in the primary school is to fulfil. Should it be directed at language learning proper, or should it serve the purpose of acquiring linguistic and **CULTURAL AWARENESS**? The advocates of the first alternative argue that a concentration on the essential part of language education, namely the foreign language, would benefit the learners most. The adherents of the second alternative maintain that linguistic and cultural awareness must logically precede language learning, which they would therefore assign to **SECONDARY EDUCATION**.

In most European countries there is a tendency to combine the two functions and to avoid the promotion of one of the alternatives at the expense of the other. The experts seem to agree that the close relationship between language and culture forbids an exclusion of one of the two, and that, therefore, the function of FLE cannot be the furthering of linguistic **SKILLS** alone. It should try to contribute to the wider task of **INTERCULTURAL COMMUNICATIVE COMPETENCE**. This competence has at least three dimensions: pragmatic, cognitive and attitudinal. Byram and Zarate (1997) speak of

*savoir-faire* (skills)
*savoir* (knowledge) and
*savoir-être* (**ATTITUDES**)

and they suggest that any foreign language teaching should comprise these four dimensions. This general proposition applies naturally to FLE at the primary school in particular (Doyé, 1999). In the early projects, primary school teachers concentrated on enabling their children to gain linguistic competence. They aimed at a certain level of achievement in the basic skills such as **LISTENING** comprehension and **SPEAKING**, and at a later stage **READING** comprehension and **WRITING**; and if the children were able to produce well-formed utterances in the foreign language and to understand such utterances, this was regarded as satisfactory. Little or no attention was paid to the cognitive and attitudinal dimension. However, a better understanding of communicative competence and the changes in the political reality of our modern world have led to a different concept of the purpose of primary FLE.

For many young children, contact with members of other cultures is no longer an event that might occur in the distant future, but an immediate possibility in their present-day lives. They actually meet people of a foreign culture with a foreign language and consequently have to learn to cope with the situations arising out of such encounters. The task of the school and of FLE in particular is to help them in their learning, i.e. in the acquisition of the required skills, knowledge and attitudes. Only through this unified approach can primary school teachers make their contribution to the intercultural education of their pupils (see also *INTERKULTURELLE DIDAKTIK*).

## Communicative competence versus sensitisation

The *aims* of primary FLE must be seen in close connection with the accepted functions of this education. Two opposed options are discussed and practised in different educational systems: the promotion of communication competence up to a well-defined basic level; and the sensitisation for language in general and the language(s) to be studied in particular.

The advocates of the first option see primary FLE as the initial stage of a continuous process of learning, the purpose of which is to lay a solid basis for communicative competence. It profits from the readiness of young pupils to engage in various language activities and uses it for the establishment of a narrow solid foundation for future learning. Experiments have shown that – under favourable conditions – this approach can provide tangible results: the young learners acquires considerable basic communicative abilities in speaking and listening and thus gains a lasting superiority with regard to those of their peers who started their first foreign language in the secondary school. One of the conditions for this superiority is, of course, continuity. The teaching at the secondary level is to be conceived and practised as a second phase of instruction that builds on the achievements in the first. On no account must the pupils be treated as **BEGINNERS**. Wherever, in projects of the past, the primary linguistic experience of the learners was disregarded, this had a strong demotivating effect. Such an effect can only be avoided through the close cooperation of primary and secondary school teachers.

The need for continuity is much smaller with the second option. As the principal aim is to sensitise

children for the nature of language and linguistic phenomena in general and not yet to master basic representations in specific languages, there is no necessity for the secondary school to build on any previously acquired competence of the pupils.

The restriction to sensitisation and the avoidance of language learning proper, however, has serious disadvantages. It neglects the potential and the readiness of young children for linguistic learning and does not consider the societal desirability for many citizens to acquire early basic communicative competence in (at least) one foreign language.

## Class teacher versus subject teacher

In the primary school, a class (or form) teacher is an educator who is responsible for the education of a whole class of pupils and therefore teaches all subjects to them. To put this person in charge of foreign language teaching, too, has an obvious advantage: the class teacher can integrate the new area of learning much better into the curriculum than a subject teacher, who meets the children two or three times a week to teach them the foreign language and nothing else. The former model can realise the holistic approach to learning much more easily.

The reason why, in spite of all plausibility, many educational authorities hesitate to apply the class teacher model is that they consider foreign language teaching such a specialised subject that they do not want to entrust it to persons who might have a good general training but no special preparation for the highly complex requirements of FLE. Therefore it is common practice in a lot of countries to employ specialist teachers, often from secondary schools, to teach the foreign language. That most of them have no qualification for primary education is considered to be of less importance than the thorough preparation in their particular discipline, but in practice this is not the case. These specialists often find it difficult to communicate with young children appropriately and to 'make the match between the language and the children' (Curtain and Pesola, 1994). The obvious solution is to organise courses of studies that provide a combination of primary education with foreign language pedagogy. The need is for teachers who are well qualified in both fields. As primary school experts they are familiar with the conditions and the framework into which, as foreign language experts, they can integrate the language and culture of other countries.

However, a strict application of the class teacher model would mean that all primary school teachers would have to qualify for FLE as well, and serious doubts about the desirability of such an arrangement have been raised. These doubts have led some critics to the radical consequence of giving up the idea of an all-round teacher who is competent in all areas of teaching in the primary school and replace it by a more differentiated model. The concept of *moduli didattici* as practised in many Italian primary schools is the result of such reflections (Torchio, 1999). A *modulo didattico* consists of a group of three teachers who are assigned to two closely associated classes in which they work as a team. Besides establishing new social relationships between teachers (team teaching) and pupils and teachers (the children can refer to three educators instead of one), the new arrangement offers clear advantages in terms of teacher competence. It intelligently combines the positive qualities of the two original options: the pupils have close contact to a small group of 'significant others' who are together responsible for their educational progress *and* they profit from the united competence of three teachers who – having intensively studied two subjects each – provide the required expertise in six areas of teaching. In practice, this means that FLE can be introduced into the primary school, even if only one third of the teachers are qualified to teach the foreign language.

## Part of the core curriculum versus optional activity

The sixth dichotomy is the least controversial of all, as the case for including the foreign language(s) in the core curriculum is so strong: if FLE is of such great importance, as we have established, then it must become part of the core curriculum; if it offers one of the essential educational experiences of primary school children, then it has to be included in the obligatory course of studies of all pupils.

The English word 'core' is derived from the Latin word *cor* meaning 'heart'. Applied to the curriculum it means those types of experience that are thought to be at the heart of the learning of all children in order to develop the competencies required in their society. The logic is clear: intercultural communicative competence is needed for effective living in modern society. It can be acquired through foreign language education. Therefore this education has to become part of the core curriculum.

This logic is not new. It is inherent in the works of the protagonists of early foreign language learning from the beginning (e.g. Stern, 1969), and it is present in all the relevant documents of the 1990s (e.g. Felberbauer and Heindler, 1995). The only sustainable argument for making FLE an optional activity is that authorities of any democratic country should leave as many educational decisions to the discretion of the parents as possible. And if they make FLE part of the core curriculum, they – as a rule – also make it compulsory. Then there is no freedom of choice left for the parents. The children *have* to take part.

This argument deserves respect, but can also quite easily be contradicted. There is the danger that parents who underestimate the potential of their children shy away from any optional field of learning. They want their children to concentrate on the 'really important subjects' and, if FLE does not belong to them, these children do not get the chance to participate. Therefore education authorities who believe in the importance of foreign language education in primary schools will have to make this education part of the core curriculum of these schools.

**See also:** Bilingual education; Content-based instruction; Council of Europe Modern Languages Projects; Cultural awareness; Early language learning; Evaluation; *Interkulturelle Didaktik*; Mother-tongue teaching; Objectives in language teaching and learning; Syllabus and curriculum design

## References

Byram, M. and Zarate, G. (1997) 'Definitions, objectives and assessment of sociocultural competence', in *Sociocultural competence in language learning and teaching*, Strasbourg: Council of Europe.

Curtain, H. and Pesola, C.A. (1994) *Languages and children – making the match*, New York: Longman.

Doyé, P. (1999) *The intercultural dimension. Foreign language education in the primary school*, Berlin: Cornelsen.

Felberbauer, M. and Heindler, D. (1995) *Foreign language education in primary schools. Report on Workshop 8B*, Strasbourg: Council of Europe.

Stern, H.H. (ed.) (1969) *Languages and the young school child*, Oxford: Oxford University Press.

Torchio, L. (1999) 'Potenzialità educativo-didattiche dell' organizzazione della scuola elementare a moduli (Educational potential of elementary school organisation by modules)', in A. Riccò and U. Sandfuchs (eds), *Moduli didattici*, Bad Heilbrunn: Klinkhardt.

van Ek, J. (1986) *Objectives for foreign language learning. Volume I: Scope*, Strasbourg: Council of Europe.

### Further reading

Batley, E., Candelier, M., Hermann-Brennecke, G. and Szepe, G. (1993) *Language policies for the world of the twenty-first century, a report for UNESCO*, Paris: FIPLV.

Blondin, C., Candelier, M., Edelenbos, P., Johnstone, R., Kubanek-German, A. and Taeschner, T. (1998) *Foreign languages in primary and pre-school education: a review of recent research within the European Union*, London: CILT.

Doyé, P. (1999) *The intercultural dimension. Foreign language education in the primary school*, Berlin: Cornelsen.

Doyé, P. and Hurrell, A. (eds) (1997) *Foreign language learning in primary schools*, Strasbourg: Council of Europe.

Dunn, O. (1995) *Help your child with a foreign language*, London: Hodder and Stoughton.

Hagège, C. (1996) *L'enfant aux deux langues (The child with two languages)*, Paris: Odile Jacob.

Hellwig, K. (1995) *Fremdsprachen an Grundschulen als Spielen und Lernen (Language education in primary schools as playing and learning)*, Ismaning: Hueber Verlag.

PETER DOYÉ

# Proficiency movement

A combination of national, state, local and commercial initiatives to interpret, implement and institutionalise **COMMUNICATIVE LANGUAGE TEACHING** and **ASSESSMENT**, particularly of oral **SKILLS**, in foreign language classrooms in the USA, the proficiency movement began with the publication of the *ACTFL Provisional Proficiency Guidelines* in 1982. Federally funded workshops, designed to train university foreign language faculties to conduct and score oral proficiency interviews (OPIs), led to the widespread dissemination of the *Guidelines*, the design of language programmes and curricula, the development of pedagogical approaches and activities, and the publication of **TEXTBOOKS** purported to bring learners to functional or communicative language ability. Taken together, these activities constitute the proficiency movement in language teaching in the United States.

### Components

The proficiency movement includes the following elements:

- the *ACTFL Proficiency Guidelines*, adapted from scales of L2 proficiency used by US government agencies, which describe speech from Novice ('respond to simple questions on the most common features of daily life') to Superior ('participate fully and effectively in conversations in formal and informal setting'); although scales were initially developed for the four skills and for culture, at present only the **SPEAKING** scale is widely used;

- the oral proficiency interview (OPI), a face-to-face, interview-style performance test that elicits a speech sample that can be rated according to the levels of the *ACTFL Proficiency Guidelines*; adaptations have emerged in the last two decades, including the Modified Oral Proficiency Interview (MOPI), limited to the lower levels of the speaking scale and intended for early-stage language students; and the Simulated Oral Proficiency Interview (SOPI), a tape-mediated version suitable for large-scale testing;

- the popularisation through conference presentations, journal articles and methods texts of pedagogical activities claimed to enable students to develop communicative ability from the beginning stages of instruction, such as role plays and other pairwork or **GROUP WORK**, and **TASK-BASED** activities; these are intended strategically to transform teacher-centred classrooms into ones in which students assume a greater share of classroom talk;

- approaches to classroom testing, including oral testing, that aim to integrate linguistic knowledge with communicative skill; such instruments have been termed 'prochievement tests' (Gonzalez-Pino, 1989);
- **MATERIALS**, particularly commercially produced textbooks for the elementary and intermediate college market, that purport to lead students to communicative language ability; such textbooks are characterised by periodic reintroduction of grammatical structures for increasing control (termed 'recycling' or 'spiralling'), emphasis on high-frequency, everyday situations to develop **SOCIOLINGUISTIC COMPETENCE**, use of **AUTHENTIC** texts for **READING** and **LISTENING**, and activities that practise grammatical forms in communicative contexts (Hadley, 1993).

## Origins

The roots of the proficiency movement can be traced to US President Jimmy Carter's Commission on Foreign Language and International Studies, which recommended in its 1979 report the establishment of 'language proficiency achievement goals for the end of each year of study, with special attention to speaking proficiency' (p. 15). The *ACTFL Provisional Proficiency Guidelines* (1982) were developed in response to this recommendation. Intended for academic use, the *Guidelines* were based on the US government's Federal Interagency Language Roundtable (FILR) skill-level descriptions, which in turn were an outgrowth of the rating scale developed at the Foreign Service Institute of the US Department of State in the 1950s to measure whether US diplomatic personnel had attained a level of proficiency in a foreign language sufficient to handle routine representation requirements and professional discussions within one or more special fields. The *ACTFL*

*Guidelines* introduced modifications of the FILR rating scale: the expansion of the lower end of the scale to provide additional benchmarks to measure the proficiency attained by students in high school and college language classrooms, the reduction of performance distinctions at the upper end of the scale (the near-native range), and the coining of descriptive labels (Novice, Intermediate, Advanced, Superior) for the levels. Subsequent editions of the *Guidelines* (1986, 1999) have revised wording of some levels. In 1999, additional benchmarks were created within the Advanced level.

Workshops to train foreign language instructors to conduct and rate OPIs have been offered by ACTFL since 1982. ACTFL maintains a certification programme for OPI testers and trainers in commonly and uncommonly taught languages, as well as ESL. Language Testing International, the ACTFL testing office, conducts OPI tests for academic and commercial clients either face-to-face or by telephone. Since the late 1980s, ACTFL has offered workshops on curriculum and teaching approaches under the umbrella of the proficiency movement (www.actfl.org).

## Criticisms and developments

The proficiency movement was the subject of considerable controversy in the 1980s, much of it aimed at the *ACTFL Guidelines* and the OPI. In a 1989 article, Freed synthesised objections to the *ACTFL Guidelines*, the OPI and proficiency-oriented instruction. The *Guidelines* were criticised for lacking an empirical foundation, and for their failure to incorporate notions of communicative competence. Criticism was also directed at the wording of the *Guidelines* and the failure of promoters to define terms clearly, particularly the notion of the idealised educated **NATIVE SPEAKER**, conceived as the standard against which non-native speech was judged. The 'communicative competence' criticism – i.e., that the *Guidelines* represented a highly reduced and artificial type of speech – was paired with attacks on the **VALIDITY** of the *Guidelines* on psychometric grounds, namely that the OPI confounded the competence to be measured with the method of assessment. It was also argued that a single procedure, such as an oral interview, was insufficient to elicit a representational sample of an individual's language, and advocated the use of multiple oral interactions to assure valid test design.

On the teaching side, critics of the proficiency movement claimed that its emphasis on grammatical accuracy at early stages of instruction contradicted both SLA research findings and the movement's goal of encouraging spontaneous language use. At the other extreme, others criticised functional language proficiency for teaching mainly survival, tourist-type language to undergraduate students, at the expense of extended or abstract discourse. Critical discussions of proficiency-oriented instruction were clouded by confusion over interpretations of terms. An early article by Higgs and Clifford (1982) that aimed to differentiate 'proficiency' from 'communicative competence' led to polarisation and failure to recognise points of contact. Textbook publishers in search of market segmentation furthered this polarisation by publicity that sought to distance 'communicative' materials from 'proficiency-oriented' ones (Bachman, 1988; Bachman and Savignon, 1986; Barnwell, 1996; Lantolf and Frawley, 1985; Shohamy, 1988; VanPatten, 1985).

The impact of the proficiency movement on language teaching has been widespread. On a concrete level, respondents to a survey of secondary and college-level supervisors of foreign language programmes conducted by Birckbichler and Corl (1993) stated that the proficiency movement had greatly influenced their choice of classroom activities and **TEACHER METHODS**. When asked to indicate the degree to which particular activities and activity types reflected a proficiency orientation, the following surfaced as highest on the list: partner/small group activities; role plays/simulations; information gap activities; cooperative learning; free **WRITING**; and cultural units. On a more global scale, Swaffar, Arens and Byrnes assert that the *ACTFL Guidelines* and the OPI initiated a paradigm shift in language instruction. In the new model, the focus shifts away from linguistic accuracy as an independent goal and toward 'communicatively effective classrooms' in which student language production 'depends as much on ... cognition and communicative interaction as it does on language **COMPETENCE**' (1991: 9).

The proficiency movement has also inspired the *National Standards in Foreign Language Learning* (1996),

which are serving as the basis for a national-level foreign language assessment under the auspices of the National Assessment of Educational Progress (NAEP), as well as numerous state curriculum frameworks. The criticisms of the validity of the *Guidelines* and the OPI have inspired research on the validity and on the nature of learner language elicited in OPIs and other types of proficiency tests.

**See also:** Assessment and testing; Autonomy and autonomous learners; Communicative language teaching; Graded objectives; Motivation; Planning for foreign language teaching; Proficiency tests; Syllabus and curriculum design

### References

Bachman, L. (1988) 'Problems in examining the validity of the ACTFL oral proficiency interview', *Studies in Second Language Acquisition* 10: 149–64.

Bachman, L. and Savignon, S. (1986) 'The evaluation of communicative language proficiency: a critique of the ACTFL oral interview', *Modern Language Journal* 70: 380–90.

Barnwell, D.P. (1996) *A history of foreign language testing in the United States from its beginnings to the present*, Tempe, AZ: Bilingual Press.

Birckbichler, D.W. and Corl, K.A. (1993) 'Perspectives on proficiency: teachers, students, and the materials that they use', in J.K. Phillips (ed.), *Reflecting on proficiency from a classroom perspective*, Lincolnwood, IL: National Textbook Company.

Freed, B.F. (1989) 'Perspectives on the future of proficiency-based teaching and testing', *ADFL Bulletin* 20, 2: 52–7.

Gonzalez-Pino, B. (1989) 'Prochievement testing of speaking', *Foreign Language Annals* 22: 487–96.

Hadley, A.O. (1993) *Teaching language in context: proficiency-oriented instruction* (2nd edn), Boston: Heinle and Heinle.

Higgs, T.V. and Clifford, R. (1982) 'The push toward communication', in T.V. Higgs (ed.), *Curriculum, competence, and the foreign language teacher*, Lincolnwood, IL: National Textbook Company.

Lantolf, J.P. and Frawley, W. (1985) 'Oral proficiency testing: a critical analysis', *Modern Language Journal* 69: 337–45.

President's Commission on Foreign Language and

International Studies (1979) *Strength through wisdom: a critique of U.S. capability*, Washington, DC: Government Printing Office.

Shohamy, E. (1988) 'A proposed framework for testing the oral language of second/foreign language learners', *Studies in Second Language Acquisition* 10: 165–79.

Swaffar, J., Arens, K. and Byrnes, H. (1991) *Reading for meaning: an integrated approach to language learning*, Englewood Cliffs, NJ: Prentice Hall.

VanPatten, B. (1985) 'The ACTFL proficiency guidelines: implications for grammatical accuracy in the classroom', *Studies in Second Language Acquisition* 8: 56–7.

**Further reading**

Barnwell, D.P. (1996) *A history of foreign language testing in the United States from its beginnings to the present*, Tempe, AZ: Bilingual Press.

Hadley, A.O. (1993) *Teaching language in context: proficiency-oriented instruction* (2nd edn), Boston: Heinle and Heinle.

Swaffar, J., Arens, K. and Byrnes, H. (1991) *Reading for meaning: an integrated approach to language learning*. Englewood Cliffs, NJ: Prentice Hall.

JUDITH E. LISKIN-GASPARRO

# Proficiency tests

Like **ACHIEVEMENT TESTS**, proficiency tests are used for selection purposes such as the Test of English as a Foreign Language (TOEFL) that is taken primarily by students wishing to study in the United States. However, proficiency tests diverge from achievement tests in that the content of proficiency tests is not based on a prescribed curriculum. Instead they attempt to make global measures of language proficiency and to take a representative sample of the real language demands upon people, particularly in the contexts for which the test is used as a selection device. Proficiency tests are also similar to **PLACEMENT TESTS** in that they are designed to spread students out across a wide proficiency range. However, the stakes are much higher in the case of proficiency tests because placement tests simply assign students

to different levels of ability but do not exclude them from the teaching programme. The results of proficiency tests, however, are used to determine whether, based on the score they have received, students can be accepted onto programmes of study or employment.

A persistent problem, however, is deciding the cut-off score below which students cannot be accepted on the course they have applied for because they do not have an adequate language proficiency. Indeed, the relationship between test-takers' proficiency test scores and their eventual performance on the programmes to which they are admitted on the basis of those scores remains worryingly tenuous. Educational institutions such as universities, therefore, find it virtually impossible to establish a coherent admissions policy with respect to language proficiency scores.

**See also:** Assessment and testing; Proficiency movement

**Further reading**

Alderson, J.C., Clapham, C. and Wall, D. (1995) *Language test construction and evaluation*, Cambridge: Cambridge University Press.

Davies, A., Brown, A., Elder, C., Hill, K., Lumley, T. and McNamara, T. (1999) *Dictionary of language testing*, Cambridge: Cambridge University Press.

Henning, G. (1987) *A guide to language testing*, Boston, MA: Heinle and Heinle.

JAYANTI BANERJEE

# Progress tests

Since they are also based on a defined curriculum, these tests are very similar achievement tests. The difference between the two lies in the amount that is tested and in the stakes involved. Progress tests assess small amounts at a time. They are usually conducted as part of regular teaching, the purpose being to check how successfully a particular topic or section has been learned. This information is used to plan the next teaching phase. There is no risk to the students if they perform poorly on a progress test since the results are unlikely to be used to make decisions about their future. Consequently, progress tests are lower stakes than achievement tests.

**See also:** Assessment and testing

JAYANTI BANERJEE

# Pronunciation teaching

The aim of pronunciation teaching is to teach students to achieve meaning in contexts of language use through the production and perception of the sound patterns of the target language. These comprise segmental (i.e. individual) sounds, stressed and unstressed syllables, and the 'speech melody' or intonation. Other factors, such as voice quality, speech rate and overall loudness also influence the realisation of these sound patterns. Pronunciation teaching ranges from conscious analysis and practice of specific sounds to holistic approaches allowing learners to acquire sounds by use.

As **NATIVE SPEAKERS** of our first language(s) we have a predisposition for perceiving certain sounds – the distinctive sounds, or phonemes – as significant, and others as not. That is to say that we have acquired a kind of 'first language filter', which creates a problem for foreign language learning in that it predisposes us to hear other languages in terms of our own. While this tendency may not be an obstacle for some learners who are gifted mimics and do not need to analyse unfamiliar sounds in order to produce them, there are other learners (probably the majority) who feel unable to utter the sounds of the target language without consciously understanding how they are produced. For teachers to help such learners with pronunciation, some knowledge will be helpful of how we talk about the speech sounds we produce, and how we can compare the speech sounds of different languages. For this, a framework is needed which allows us to describe the systematic sound pattern of the (foreign) language we teach and, ideally, to contrast it with our students' first language(s). This entails understanding how these speech sounds are produced as physiological and acoustic events (the domain of phonetics) and how they are utilised, organised into a system of sounds in the particular language concerned (the domain of phonology) (see Roach, forthcoming).

Thus phonetics enables us to say, for instance, how vowels and consonants are produced. With consonants, where and how does the airstream get obstructed, and with how much energy is the sound produced? And with vowels, are the lips rounded or unrounded, and what is the position of the tongue? Phonology, on the other hand, enables us to describe the speech sounds of particular languages systematically, to say what the phonemes are that make up the sound pattern of a language, and how that system (say, of our L1) is different from another (say, that of the target language).

In any use of spoken language, all aspects of pronunciation are present simultaneously – even in minimal utterances such as 'yes'. In that sense, all teaching involving **LISTENING** and **SPEAKING** is also pronunciation teaching. Nevertheless, in its narrower sense of concentrating on speech sounds as we have defined it, pronunciation teaching has evolved as an area in its own right, its status and methodology varying across different overall approaches to language teaching. For **COMMUNICATIVE LANGUAGE TEACHING**, pronunciation presents something of a dilemma. On the one hand, intelligible pronunciation is recognised as a crucial component of communicative competence. On the other, the shift from drills to communicative activities based on meaningful interaction directs learners' attention away from language form and towards the messages they want to communicate. This is problematic since, for language items to be learnt, they have to be noticed and therefore highlighted, which, in turn, is difficult to do if the language used should be as communicatively **'AUTHENTIC'** as possible. This fundamental problem is one that communicative language teachers will have to confront when planning their pronunciation teaching, and for which there are no universal solutions.

## Methodological issues

The absence of one particular methodological orthodoxy can also be seen as an opportunity for teachers to make choices which are most appropriate for the specific learners they are working with, and it is probably no accident that the diversification of methodological options has coincided with a diversification of learning goals. The role of widely-used languages, notably **ENGLISH**, as **LINGUA FRANCAS**, and more positive **ATTITUDES** towards different native and non-native varieties, including accents, led to a reconsideration of what students are learning languages for, and what norms are appropriate to their purposes.

It is important to recognise that pronunciation plays an important role in our personal as well as our social lives: as individuals, we project our identity through the way we speak, and also indicate our membership of particular communities. At the same time, and sometimes even in conflict with this identity function, our pronunciation is also responsible for intelligibility – whether or not we can get our meaning across. The significance of success in L2 pronunciation learning is thus far-reaching, and matters are complicated by the fact that many of these things happen subconsciously and so are not readily accessible to conscious analysis and intervention.

Prior to any specific methodological decisions, then, there are large-scale issues that need to be considered, of which the questions of learner variables, learning purpose and setting are likely to be the most important ones. Celce-Murcia *et al.* (1996: ch. 2) summarise the most important learner variables and also offer suggestions for **NEEDS ANALYSIS** by means of student profile questionnaires. The factors they highlight are **AGE**, exposure to the target language, amount and type of prior pronunciation instruction, **APTITUDE**, attitude and **MOTIVATION**, and the role of the learner's first language. There are also issues relating to general learning theory which need to be taken into account, such as the tenet that perception needs to precede production, and achievability, i.e. success in little steps, is important to counter the insecurity that many learners feel when speaking another language.

## Teaching procedures

Actual teaching procedures can be arranged on a continuum from communication **TASKS** through analytic, cognitive **EXERCISES** to fairly mechanical practice. This continuum relates to the fundamental issues of 'communicating versus noticing' and 'innocence versus sophistication' in pronunciation teaching, as discussed in Dalton and Seidlhofer

(1994: ch. 10) and to **RIVERS** and Temperley's (1978) general distinction between 'skill-getting' and 'skill-using' activities.

## Pronunciation learning strategies

These involve learner training with the aim of fostering learner **AUTONOMY** and enabling students to develop **STRATEGIES** for coping on their own and for continuing to learn. Ways of working towards these goals include awareness-raising questionnaires (e.g. Kenworthy, 1987: 55f), learner diaries, recording of learners' production, dealing with incomprehensibility and employing metalinguistic strategies such as soliciting repetition, paraphrasing and monitoring feedback.

## Global, holistic activities

While many techniques can contain a game-like element, there are activities which are primarily focused on a particular communicative purpose or outcome, such as mini-plays whose interpretation depends entirely on the learners' use of voice quality and intonation (Dalton and Seidlhofer, 1994: 162), or many of the games in Hancock (1996). Whole-brain activities are intended to activate the right brain hemisphere and often involve music, **POETRY**, guided fantasies, relaxation techniques such as yoga breathing, and kinaesthetic experiences (e.g. Laroy, 1995).

## Cognitive analysis

Many learners, particularly more mature ones, welcome some overt explanation and analysis. There is a wide range of methodological options, such as:

- discussing stereotypic ideas about 'correct' and 'sloppy' speech for introducing assimilation and elision as features of connected speech;
- phonetic training: explanations of how particular sounds are articulated, with the help of head diagrams or videos, and conscious exploration by learners how they themselves articulate L1 and L2 sounds;
- teaching learners phonemic script: controversial, but appreciated by many students as it better

enables them to conceptualise the L2 sound system, to use pronunciation **DICTIONARIES**, to record pronunciation themselves, and to draw comparisons with their L1;

- giving rules;
- comparison of L1 and L2 sound systems: since learners tend to hear the sounds of a new language through the filter of their L1, it can be very helpful for them to be taught not only the articulation of the new sounds, but also the system of phonemes, i.e. the relevant oppositions;
- analysis of sounds in texts: for instance, dialogues not designed for pronunciation work can be used for awareness-raising of the functions of stress and intonation, e.g. pitch height for smooth turn-taking.

### Sounds for meaning contrasts

There are numerous ways in which otherwise drill-like exercises can be modified to make them more meaningful for the learner while retaining a focus on sounds. Most contemporary **TEXTBOOKS** offer such variations which endeavour to relate linguistic form to pragmatic meaning and action. This can be achieved through more active involvement on the part of the learner, a clear specification of purpose, and an element of choice. Minimal pairs (pairs of words distinguished by one phoneme only) can be embedded in sentences such as 'Please SIT in this SEAT.' The same principle can be applied for teaching how to employ pitch height for contrast. Similarly, chunking into meaning units can be practised with information gap activities such as arithmetic pair practice, where the correct answers depend on correct grouping, as in:

$$(2 + 3) \times 5 = 25 - \text{two plus three times five equals twenty-five}$$

versus

$$2 + (3 \times 5) = 17 - \text{two plus three times five equals seventeen}$$

(Gilbert, 1993: 109)

Peer **DICTATION** activities also challenge learners as both listeners and speakers.

### Ear training

Asking students to listen out for sound contrasts, e.g. by **READING** contrasting sounds or words aloud to a class and asking them to decide what has been uttered. This can take the form of a bingo-like game, as in Bowen and Marks's 'sound discrimination exercise' (1992: 36f) or Taylor's 'yes/no game' (1993: 87). An interesting variation of this, particularly suitable for monolingual classes, is 'bilingual minimal pairs' (Bowen and Marks, 1992: 21), which asks learners to listen out for differences in articulatory postures in lists of L1–L2 word pairs such as German 'Bild' and English 'build', or French 'flot' and German 'Floh'.

### Local, fairly mechanical exercises

'Listen and repeat' is a time-honoured technique in which learners imitate chunks of language provided by the teacher or a recording, still widely used in coursebooks accompanied by a tape, and particularly popular as a **LANGUAGE LABORATORY** exercise. Drills often practise sound patterns without apparent communicative reason and without offering learners an opportunity for making motivated choices of sounds, stress patterns, etc., such as manipulation of stress for prominence:

Would you like to go OUT with me tonight?
Would you like to go out with ME tonight?
Would you like to go out with me toNIGHT?

For individual sounds, tongue twisters of the 'she sells sea shells on the sea shore' kind have been proposed.

### Models for pronunciation

Though seldom explicitly addressed in textbooks, a crucial factor for any specific pronunciation **SYLLABUS** is whether it is designed for a foreign language or a second language setting. Apart from the obvious influence that the surrounding linguistic environment will have on teaching procedures, the whole complex question of target norms and intelligibility as an objective hinges upon the student's learning purpose and the setting. Thus many second language learners will strive to become comfortably intelligible to the **NATIVE**

**SPEAKERS** around them in order to integrate with the native speaker community. In contrast, in foreign language teaching the **OBJECTIVES** may be more varied: while some learners may wish to sound as similar as possible to native speakers, others – mainly in the case of languages with a fairly global spread, especially English – may primarily be interested in using the language as a **LINGUA FRANCA** for communication in international settings. This will often involve a variety of other non-native speakers, where sounding like a native speaker may actually be irrelevant and counter-productive. It is, therefore, essential for teachers to be familiar with the increasingly lively discussion about the range of different models for L2 pronunciation learning, and the socio-economic and socio-psychological factors which make intelligibility an inevitably relative notion (see Jenkins, 2000). Whatever the setting, social and situational appropriacy is likely to be a more valid criterion of success than 'correctness', and the overall 'philosophy' of pronunciation teaching is evolving from the concept of reduction or eradication of a foreign accent to the notion that learners can add an accent to their (L1-based) sound repertoire.

**See also:** Community language learning; Contrastive analysis; IPA; Linguistics; Listening; Native speaker; Non-native speaker teacher; Reform Movement; Silent way; Speaking

## References

Bowen, T. and Marks, J. (1992) *The pronunciation book. Student-centred activities for pronunciation work*, London: Longman.

Celce-Murcia, M., Brinton, D. and Goodwin, J. (1996) *Teaching pronunciation. A reference for teachers of English to speakers of other languages*, Cambridge: Cambridge University Press.

Dalton, C. and Seidlhofer, B. (1994) *Pronunciation (Language teaching: a scheme for teacher education)*, Oxford: Oxford University Press.

Gilbert, J.B. (1993) *Clear speech: pronunciation and listening comprehension in American English* (2nd edn), Cambridge: Cambridge University Press.

Hancock, M. (1996) *Pronunciation games*, Cambridge: Cambridge University Press.

Jenkins, J. (2000) *The phonology of English as an international language*, Oxford: Oxford University Press.

Kenworthy, J. (1987) *Teaching English pronunciation*, London: Longman.

Laroy, C. (1995) *Pronunciation (Resource books for teachers)*, Oxford: Oxford University Press.

Rivers, W. and Temperley, M. (1978) *A practical guide to the teaching of English as a second or foreign language*, New York: Cambridge University Press.

Roach, P. (forthcoming) *Phonetics (Oxford introductions to language study)*. Oxford: Oxford University Press.

Taylor, L. (1993) *Pronunciation in action*, Englewood Cliffs, NJ: Prentice Hall.

## Further reading

Bowen, T. and Marks, J. (1992) *The pronunciation book. Student-centred activities for pronunciation work*, London: Longman.

Celce-Murcia, M., Brinton, D. and Goodwin, J. (1996) *Teaching pronunciation. A reference for teachers of English to speakers of other languages*, Cambridge: Cambridge University Press.

Dalton, C. and Seidlhofer, B. (1994) *Pronunciation (Language teaching: a scheme for teacher education)*, Oxford: Oxford University Press.

Wells, J.C. (1990) *Longman pronunciation dictionary*, London: Longman.

BARBARA SEIDLHOFER

# Psychology

As a broad generalisation, one turns to **LINGUISTICS** for insights in describing the 'what' of language learning (the language itself) and to psychology for insights into the 'how' and the 'why' (ideas about learning and teaching, and **MOTIVATION**). However, when dealing with language, in contrast to learning most other **SKILLS** or areas of knowledge, the 'what' and the 'how' are interlinked in at least two ways. First, language is itself a crucial part of what defines us as humans, so the study of linguistics can and does claim to be a source of explanations about how the human mind works. Second, Chomskyan linguistic theory has developed to a point where identifying the universal rules that govern all languages is equated with a theory of acquiring language – any language – or at least the grammatical core of all languages. Thus, there are controversial advances in understanding **SECOND LANGUAGE ACQUISITION** from a number of traditionally independent points of view. These points of view – linguistic, psychological, socio-linguistic, social psychological, and also educational – have their own traditions of theory building, rules of evidence and methods of data gathering, so it is not surprising that there is lively debate between them as to where the truth lies, and that there is stiff competition for the attention of teachers of foreign languages.

Consequently, the role of psychology will be here given a deliberately wide interpretation, and presented under eight areas, together with a consideration of how we find out the relevant information.

In talking about language learning we should be careful not to assume that all learners are the same, or that all learning environments are the same. There is a danger of universalism: i.e., of assuming without evidence that every learner (young or old, learning their first or their tenth foreign language, learning where the language is spoken or thousands of miles away in a group who speak only their own language, learning by picking up the language 'naturally' or in a designed, instructed classroom environment) employs the same processes and performs in the same way. The fact that everybody grows up to be a **NATIVE SPEAKER** of some language (unless they are severely and tragically disabled from birth), whereas there is a wide range of achievement in learning a second language, should alert us to the dangers of universalism.

## The nature of second language learning

Views of how second languages are learned vary from general cognitive approaches based on the analogy between language and skill development, more specific cognitive approaches, including the notion of different kinds of strategy, and independent cognitive approaches involving linguistic theory.

General cognitive approaches tend to explain the internalisation of **GRAMMAR**, **VOCABULARY**,

**PRONUNCIATION** and social rules of language use essentially in information-processing terms usually used for learning to perform psychomotor skills. McLaughlin (1987: ch. 6) and Johnson (1995), in particular, have attempted to analyse and explain developmental patterns, error patterns, attention focus and cognitive load in these terms, drawing on the skill **ACQUISITION** literature. Thus they distinguish between declarative and procedural knowledge, automatic and controlled processes, discuss routinisation, and present a sequence of processes to explain various features of skilled performance, like smoothness, responsivity to feedback, release of attentional capacity, and speed with accuracy.

Specific cognitive approaches use much of the same general orientation but concentrate on **STRATEGIES** used by language learners to solve problems of language in use and understanding and remembering new features of the language that are encountered in classroom instruction, private language exposure, **DICTIONARY** look-up, **READING** and **LISTENING** (Cohen, 1998; McDonough, 1995; Oxford, 1996(b)). Much strategy research is directed at understanding how learners become **AUTONOMOUS** or can be empowered to be autonomous (Wenden, 1991).

Independent cognitive views see a significant part of language learning as having nothing to do with other kinds of skill learning but being driven by an independent language faculty, recapitulating in the second language case the interaction of exposure to language and maturation of innate language principles which is considered to produce native speakers. According to this approach, second language learning requires some kind of access – automatic access – to **UNIVERSAL GRAMMAR**, at least for the core principles, and information from language exposure about 'idiosyncrasies' of the new language (Cook, 1989; Gass and Schachter, 1989; Towell and Hawkins, 1994). A great deal of information from other sources about language use is also learned, but, according to the usual version of this view, is not relevant for the internalisation of the grammar of the language. An early and popular, but under-specified, version of this view was Krashen's **MONITOR MODEL** of 1981. An issue that divides the different cognitive approaches is the role of conscious awareness: much strategic behaviour seems to be conscious and voluntary, whereas the operation of the innate language faculty is assumed to be automatic and not available for conscious inspection. Schmidt (1995) has explored the implications of the voluntary mental acts of 'intention', 'attention', 'noticing' (awareness) and 'understanding' (control) for language learning, and there is a growing experimental literature on this topic (Hulstijn and Schmidt, 1994).

## Interactive learning

A further approach holds that second languages are learned particularly through interaction in the language, essentially a social psychological view. If communication is the primary use of language, then communication in ways that are most familiar to learners in their native languages may be the primary avenue for learning a new language. Allwright (1988) has traced the history of research on classroom interaction and produced his own interpretive model of some of the crucial dynamics. Pica and Doughty (1985) and Gass and Varonis (1985) have investigated the nature of **CLASSROOM LANGUAGE** use by learners in various kinds of interaction, comparing language used between groups of learners with that used between teachers and students. One abiding research issue here has been the 'naturalness' of classroom interaction, specifically concerning the use and benefits of display and referential questions (Pica and Doughty, 1985; Banbrook and Skehan, 1990). Another has been the attention paid to topics raised by different participants in 'uptake' (Slimani, 1989; Ellis, 1995). Williams and Burden (1997: ch. 9) have explored how theories of the structure and nature of the classroom environment from educational psychology can illuminate what goes on in language classrooms.

## Mediation

The general focus on the learner, the development of learner autonomy, and in particular the challenge of the universal grammar approach, have left language teachers to some extent wondering what their role is. If the teacher is not an instructor, then there are many other roles which, following Williams and Burden (1997),

might be subsumed under the heading of mediator. The teacher provides samples of the language, manages the interaction, gives advice on learning, helps the students to become autonomous, provides and manages the learning resources, offers feedback on their own performance. Studies of teachers and learners in classrooms have attempted to analyse many of these crucial aspects of the teacher's behaviour, in particular the teacher's modes of structuring the lessons, the provision of feedback and oral error correction, coaching in **WRITING**, writing feedback to students. Learning teaching has also been studied; the psychology of the trainee teacher is just as important as that of the novice bilingual.

## Differences in language learners

Language learners have classically been subcategorised by various test-oriented dimensions: intelligence, **APTITUDE**, cognitive style (or learning preference), personality, motivation. Skehan (1989) provided a book-length treatment of the whole issue and the difficulties inherent in the concept of individual differences. Gardner and Macintyre (1992, 1993a) present a review of the developments. Beyond the classical categories, modern work has unearthed consistent patterns of difference in modality preferences (Reid, 1987), classroom activities (Willing, 1985), beliefs about learning (Wenden 1987, Horwitz, 1987) and **AGE** (Harley, 1986). The significance of individual differences for teaching is probably obvious: different customers respond to different treatments, prefer different kinds of classroom activities, and different forms and levels of participation. **TEACHING METHODS** can be criticised on the grounds that they may not be flexible enough to cater for the variety of learners, as **AUDIOLINGUALISM** was by **RIVERS** (1964) and **COMMUNITY LANGUAGE LEARNING** by Brown (1977). Their significance for learning is less clear-cut. As Ellis (1994) pointed out, individual differences like these show up in difference of learning rate (either inhibiting or facilitating learning) but do not appear to affect basic processes and therefore the way in which people learn, the route of learning.

There is considerable literature on variability theory (for a succinct review and evaluation, see

Ellis, 1994: 363–9) which attempts to explain the considerable variability in learners' accuracy of performance on different occasions, mainly in syntax and phonology, but classical measures of individual difference do not relate to these indices of linguistic development. However, relevant individual differences warrant attention in investigating specific learning situations. An example is Carrell, Pharis and Liberto's (1989) study of pre-reading **EXERCISES**, which showed that the students who differed on a test of **LEARNING STYLE** (deep and shallow processing, and elaborative processes) responded differently to the two meta-cognitive strategy training methods employed ('semantic mapping' versus 'experience–text–relationship'). Finally, individual differences in learning are not set in stone, so theories of instruction have to allow for the twin facts that learners change as a result of their experiences, and that teachers also try to change their learners, sometimes successfully.

## Reasons for learning

An enduring interest in this field has been the reasons why people learn a foreign language and how those reasons, and the strength of feeling associated with them, affect the learning process and the level of achievement. Approaches to **MOTIVATION** were dominated for thirty years by the concept of 'orientation to language' introduced by Gardner and Lambert in 1959, contrasting instrumental and integrative orientations, of which the socio-cultural preference for integrating with the target speech community was originally shown to be the more effective for language learning in the majority of empirical studies. Recent results (Gardner and Macintyre, 1993b) have shown this to be false, or at least no longer true. This mainly factorial approach to motivation, involving large numbers of students answering questionnaires privately, was challenged but never rivalled by the beliefs about the cause of the differences. However, in the 1990s a fresh challenge to the statistical study of motivation has grown out of the work of Crookes and Schmidt (1991), to take into account how language teachers conceive of a 'well-motivated student' and how they are likely to participate in actual classroom work. Important work in this 'new

agenda' has been provided by Oxford (1996a) and Dörnyei (1994).

## Second language use

Crucially important in a comprehensive psychology of second languages is the issue of second language performance. How people actually use their second language has been investigated in various areas of L2 use since at least Tarone's (1977) initial opening-up of the question of how learners compensate for acknowledged, foreseen, or encountered failures of communication in conversations. There has been an explosion of research on language use strategies in all areas of language skill: **SPEAKING**, **READING**, writing, **LISTENING**, test-taking, classroom participation (Cohen, 1998; McDonough, 1995, 1999). At stake is detailed knowledge of how people function in a second language, to feed into theories of performance, to inform theories of learning (since in many cases there is a relationship between what people do and how they learn), and to inform theories of teaching (because one aim of teaching is to train learners to become **AUTONOMOUS LEARNERS** and users of two or more languages).

## Two or more languages

The theme of the previous section can be broadened to encompass the exciting question of the psychology of **BILINGUALISM** and multilingualism. There are many interesting questions to do with becoming and being bilingual, which focus on how the two languages interact with each other:

- How do we stay in one language and not flit between all available?
- What governs code-switching?
- How are the words stored – separately or together?
- Is there a limit on the number of languages we can learn?
- Is one language involved in the processing of the other?

on how the languages interact with cognition and thought:

- Is there a cognitive deficit or advantage in having two or more languages available?
- What language do bilinguals use to formulate thoughts in?

and how and why the users want the languages:

- To do specialised jobs (like **ENGLISH** for Air Traffic Control)
- To interact normally in a multilingual society (like Belgium or the Cameroons)
- To gain competitive advantage in international commerce

and so forth.

Cook (1991: ch. 7) expands on these and other themes, quoting international and national sources. Closer to the immediate concerns of the foreign language classroom, research has also investigated how (perhaps against the spirit of much teaching which insists on L2 use at all times) L2 users and learners use L1 when accomplishing tasks in the L2. For example, Cohen and Hawras have worked on L1 when reading in L2 (reported in Cohen, 1998: 179–86), and Cohen has worked on students doing maths problems in immersion L2 classes (1998: 186–210). In both cases the use of L1, for structuring comprehension and handling numbers respectively, followed consistent goals and contributed to smooth performance in L2. L1 use in planning writing in L2 has been investigated for compositions of particular types by Friedlander (1990), who found that writing was advantaged when the plans were drawn up in the language in which the topic was first encountered. Currently a great deal of research interest is devoted to the phenomenon of language thresholds in L2 reading. There exists the possibility that the skills and strategies for reading and writing which the learner commands in their L1 become available to them for use in the L2 when their level of L2 proficiency reaches a certain critical level (Hulstijn and Matter, 1991). When the nature of this threshold is understood, it may well be shown to exist in other skill areas as well, for instance writing and listening.

## Culture and context

An important aspect of the psychology of second languages, and one which shows the limits of the universalist approach mentioned at the beginning of this article, is the cultural dimension. We all belong to different cultures, indeed often to several, and while cultural boundaries are not the same as linguistic ones, the psychological effects of culture can be quite dramatic. Steffensen and Joag-Dev (1984), for instance, have highlighted the breakdown of comprehension caused by wrong beliefs about the significance of black and white for American and Indian readers (white being the colour of marriage in one culture and that of death in the other). Cultural misunderstandings like these are difficult to prepare for, because, unlike other kinds of communication breakdown, for which anticipation and repair strategies can be developed, the individual never knows when a cultural misunderstanding is going to happen, nor, often, that it has happened. Pritchard (1990) has shown how members of different cultures process their own languages differently in reading comprehension, and, more importantly, how cultural presuppositions and misunderstandings interfere with comprehension strategies. Readers reading about foreign cultural rituals (in his case, American and South Sea Islanders' funerals), even in their own language, failed to make connections between sentences and therefore failed to construct any kind of meaning for the passage as a whole.

Cultural presuppositions also affect the context of learning dramatically, both as a result of large-scale concerns, as in Schumann's **ACCULTURATION** theory (1978), and also in terms of traditions of classroom discourse, openness to innovation, distribution of power in the classroom, and preferred **LEARNING STYLES**. A dramatic illustration of the point was given by Politzer and MacGroarty (1985), who showed that notions of what 'good language learners' did to learn and behave inside and outside classrooms were heavily culture-bound, with many people from different cultures performing very well without doing the things expected by Western ideas of 'good language learners'. Another topical case in point is the argument about learner autonomy, which is widely regarded as a necessary stage in the pursuit of high achievement in the West but strongly questioned in the East, at least on the Western model (Aoki and Smith, 1996).

## The research base

It will be evident from the broad approach described above that, though strictly anchored in empirical data, the psychology of second language learning and use pursues a great variety of research types to obtain that data. Experiments, quasi-experiments, observations, surveys, case studies, action research, questionnaires, introspection, diary studies, using both quantitative and qualitative methods of analysis, all feature. This variety has developed because different kinds of problems require different kinds of attack. It is inadequate to argue that only one data source is legitimate with a subject matter as varied as this: no one method is employable in all situations. Since, however, **RESEARCH METHODS** tend to define fields as much as topics do, there have been several discussions of what is appropriate and what criteria of **VALIDITY**, generalisability, falsifiability, replication, etc., can be upheld (see, e.g., Johnson, 1992; McDonough and McDonough, 1997).

## Conclusions

This summary of eight areas of research and development in the psychology of second language learning and use has perhaps said enough to make the point that understanding how and why people learn and use a second language is

1 extremely interesting in its own right (it is, after all, about something that the majority of the world's population does, more or less successfully);
2 not always obvious and commonsensical (there are many challenges in the research results to traditional views); and
3 of great potential in informing language teaching practitioners. Of course, this potential needs to be carefully developed and evaluated: as in all applied sciences, it is inappropriate to transplant directly from 'the latest research' to innovations without careful development and evaluation in practice (Cohen, 1995; Ellis, 1997).

**See also:** Age factors; Attitudes and language learning; Autonomy and autonomous learners; Competence and performance; Disorders of language; Learning styles; Motivation theories; Neurolinguistics; Research methods; Second language acquisition theories

## References

Allwright, R.L. (1988) *Observation in the language classroom*, Harlow: Longman.

Aoki, N. and Smith, R.C. (1996) 'Autonomy in a cultural context: the case of Japan', in S. Cotteral and D. Crabbe (eds), *Learner autonomy in language learning: defining the field and effecting change*, Tübingen: Brockmeyer Verlag.

Banbrook, L. and Skehan, P. (1990) 'Classrooms and display questions', in C. Brumfit and R. Mitchell (eds), *Research in the language classroom*, ELT Docs 133, Macmillan Modern English Publications/British Council.

Brown, H.D. (1977) 'Some limitations of C-L.CLL models of second language teaching', *TESOL Quarterly* 11, 4: 365–72.

Carrell, P.L., Pharis, B.G. and Liberto, J.C. (1989) 'Metacognitive strategy training for ESL reading', *TESOL Quarterly* 23, 4: 647–78.

Cohen, A.D. (1995) 'SLA theory and pedagogy: some research issues', in F. Eckman, D. Highland, P. Lee, J. Milcham and R. Ruthkowski-Weber (eds), *Second language acquisition theory and pedagogy*, Mackworth, NJ: Lawrence Erlbaum.

Cohen, A.D. (1998) *Strategies in learning and using a second language*, New York and London: Longman.

Cook, V.J. (1989) 'Universal grammar theory and the classroom', *System* 17, 2: 169–82.

Cook, V.J. (1991) *Second language learning and language teaching*, London: Edward Arnold.

Crookes, G. and Schmidt, R. (1991) 'Motivation: reopening the research agenda', *Language Learning* 41, 4: 479–512.

Dörnyei, Z. (1994) 'Understanding L2 motivation. On with the challenge', *Modern Language Journal* 78, iv: 515–23.

Ellis, R. (1994) *The study of second language acquisition*, Oxford: Oxford University Press.

Ellis, R. (1995) 'Uptake as language awareness', *Language Awareness* 4, 4: 147–160.

Ellis, R. (1997) 'SLA and language pedagogy; an educational perspective', *Studies in Second Language Acquisition* 19: 69–92.

Friedlander, A. (1990) 'Composing in English:

effects of a first language on writing in English as a second language', in B. Kroll (ed.), *Second language writing*, Cambridge: Cambridge University Press.

Gardner, R.C. and Lambert, W.E. (1959) 'Motivational variables in second language acquisition', *Canadian Journal of Psychology* 13, 4: 266–72.

Gardner, R.C. and Macintyre, P.D. (1992) 'A student's contributions to second language learning. Part 1: Cognitive variables', *Language Teaching* 25: 211–20.

Gardner, R.C. and Macintyre, P.D. (1993a) 'A student's contributions to second language learning. Part 2 Affective variables', *Language Teaching* 26: 1–11.

Gardner, R.C. and Macintyre, P.D. (1993b) 'On the measurement of affective variables in second language learning', *Language Learning* 43: 157–94.

Gass, S.M. and Schachter, J. (eds) (1989) *Linguistic perspectives on second language acquisition*, Cambridge: Cambridge University Press.

Gass, S.M. and Varonis, E. (1985) 'Task variation and native/non-native negotiation of meaning', in S.M. Gass and C. Madden (eds), *Input in second language acquisition*, Rowley, MA: Newbury House.

Harley, B. (1986) *Age in second language acquisition*, Clevedon: Multilingual Matters.

Horwitz, E.K. (1987) 'Surveying student beliefs about language learning', in A. Wenden and J. Rubin (eds), *Learner strategies in language learning*, Hemel Hempstead: Prentice Hall.

Hulstijn, J.H. and Matter, J.H. (eds) (1991) 'Reading in 2 languages', *AILA Review* 8.

Hulstijn, J.H. and Schmidt, R. (eds) (1994) 'Consciousness in second language learning', *AILA Review* 11.

Johnson, D.M. (1992) *Approaches to research in second language learning*, New York and London: Longman.

Johnson, K. (1995) *Language teaching and skill learning*, Oxford: Blackwell.

Krashen, S. (1981) *Second language acquisition and second language learning*, Oxford: Pergamon.

McDonough, J.E. and McDonough, S.H. (1997) *Research methods for English language teachers*, London: Edward Arnold.

McDonough, S.H. (1995) *Strategy and skill in learning a foreign language*, London: Edward Arnold.

McDonough, S.H. (1999) 'Learner strategies', *Language Teaching* 22, 1: 1–18.

McLaughlin, B. (1987) *Theories of second language learning*, London: Edward Arnold.

Oxford, R.L. (ed.) (1996a) *Language learning motivation: pathways to the new century*, Technical Report 12, Manoa, HI: University of Hawaii Second Language Teaching and Curriculum Center.

Oxford, R.L. (ed.) (1996b) *Language learning strategies around the world: crosscultural perspectives*, Technical Report 13, Manoa, HI: University of Hawaii Second Language Teaching and Curriculum Center.

Pica, T. and Doughty, C. (1985) 'Input and interaction in the communicative language classroom: a comparison of teacher fronted and group activities', in S.M. Gass and C. Madden (eds), *Input in second language acquisition*, Rowley, MA: Newbury House.

Politzer, R.L. and MacGroarty, M. (1985) 'An exploratory study of learning behaviours and their relationship to gains in linguistic and communicative competence', *TESOL Quarterly* 12, 1: 103–23.

Pritchard, R. (1990) 'The effects of cultural schemata on reading processing strategies', *Reading Research Quarterly* 25: 273–95.

Reid, J. (1987) 'The learning style preferences of ESL students', *TESOL Quarterly* 21: 87–111.

Rivers, W. (1964) *The psychologist and the foreign language teacher*, Chicago: University of Chicago Press.

Schmidt, R. (1995) 'Consciousness and foreign language learning: a tutorial on the role of attention and awareness in learning', in R. Schmidt (ed.), *Attention and awareness in foreign language learning*, Technical Report 9, Honolulu, HI: University of Hawaii Second Language Teaching and Curriculum Center.

Schumann, J. (1978) *The pidginisation process: a model for second language acquisition*, Rowley, MA: Newbury House.

Skehan, P. (1989) *Individual differences in second language learning*, London: Edward Arnold.

Slimani, A. (1989) 'The role of topicalisation in classroom language learning', *System* 17: 223–34.

Steffensen, M.S. and Joag-Dev, C. (1984) 'Cultural knowledge and reading', in J.C. Alderson and

A.H. Urquart (eds), *Reading in a foreign language*, Harlow: Longman.

Tarone, E. (1977) 'Conscious communication strategies in interlanguage', in H.D. Brown, C.A. Yorio and R. Crymes (eds), *On TESOL 77: Teaching and learning ESL*, Washington, DC: TESOL.

Towell, R. and Hawkins, R. (1994) *Approaches to second language acquisition*, Clevedon: Multilingual Matters.

Wenden, A. (1987) 'How to be a successful language learner: insights and prescriptions for L2 learners', in A. Wenden and J. Rubin (eds), *Learner strategies in language learning*, Hemel Hempstead: Prentice Hall.

Wenden, A. (1991) *Learner strategies for learner autonomy*, New York: Prentice Hall.

Williams, M. and Burden, R. (1997) *Psychology for language teachers*, Cambridge: Cambridge University Press.

Willing, K. (1985) *Learning styles in adult migrant education*, Sydney: New South Wales Adult Migrant Education Service.

### Further reading

Cohen, A.D. (1998) *Strategies in learning and using a second language*, New York and London: Longman.

Cook, V.J. (1991) *Second language learning and language teaching*, London: Edward Arnold.

Ellis, R. (1994) *The study of second language acquisition*, Oxford: Oxford University Press.

Oxford, R.L. (ed.) (1996) *Language learning motivation: pathways to the new century*, Technical Report 12, Manoa, HI: University of Hawaii Second Language Teaching and Curriculum Center.

Towell, R. and Hawkins, R. (1994) *Approaches to second language acquisition*, Clevedon: Multilingual Matters.

STEVEN MCDONOUGH

# Pushkin Russian Language Institute

The Pushkin Russian Language Institute was founded in 1967, and since 1974 has been an independent state educational and scientific institution, which specialises in teaching Russian to foreigners, elaborating educational programmes, textbooks and educational materials for Russian as a foreign language.

The Institute offers doctorate, postgraduate and master's degree study. With more than 150 staff, there are about 1,000 students studying at the Institute at any one time. The educational process can be adjusted for individual students' NEEDS by organising practical studies, lectures, seminars.

### Website

The Institute's website is: http://www.academic.marist.edu/russia/pushkin.htm

# Q

## Quality management

Quality management is an approach developed in industrial contexts in the 1940s and 1950s and principally in the **USA** and **JAPAN**. It seeks to eliminate errors and defects in production processes by careful analysis of the function of individual elements, by attention to good design and, crucially, by giving responsibility for quality to the workers involved in production. One version of the approach is known as Total Quality Management or TQM, which introduced slogans such as 'zero defects', 'get it right the first time, all the time, every time'. When the approach is applied to service industries, where there is no tangible product, quality is frequently defined through customer or client charters or guarantees promising standards of service – such as the guaranteed punctuality of trains or the promise of prompt and courteous service in hotels. Quality management is divided into quality assurance – the steps taken to ensure quality in production processes or systems of providing services – and quality control – the verification, either internally in the organisation or by an external body, that standards are being kept.

### Applications to language teaching

The concepts and techniques of quality management have been explicitly applied to language teaching since the 1980s, though elements of both quality assurance and quality control have long been present in the activities of schools and institutions. The development of **CLASSROOM OBSERVATION SCHEMES** and **ACTION RESEARCH** are clearly concerned with the analysis of performance, and **NEEDS ANALYSIS** is a prerequisite for proper design of language learning activities. These are features of quality assurance. Quality control has been carried out by school inspectors since the nineteenth century and, specifically for private English language schools in the United Kingdom, through the inspection schemes of the Department of Education and Science and, after 1982, by the recognition scheme administered by the **BRITISH COUNCIL** at the request of ARELS. In this scheme, schools are inspected by external inspectors, usually on a two-day visit to the school, and must achieve satisfactory grades in categories such as Teaching, Teacher Qualifications, Management, Premises, Welfare, etc. The name of the scheme is now the English in Britain Accreditation Scheme and includes the institutions of BASELT (the British Association of State English Language Teaching) as well as private language schools.

In the 1990s there was considerable development in society in general of consumer awareness; that the customer has the right to receive well-made goods and services provided efficiently. In competitive markets, commercial organisations reacted to consumer demand by creating ways of labelling quality – the certificate of guaranteed verification that a product or service is meeting established and declared standards. This consumer awareness also affected the world of language education, most obviously in the competitive field of private language schools. The movement, however, has also influenced public institutions, which in many countries have obtained more autonomy with a concomitant requirement to be accountable to their 'clients' and to prove their quality by obtaining an externally validated certificate.

The best-known label is that of the International Standards Organisation (ISO) which gives a certificate, ISO 9001, for service organisations. The certification requires a considerable degree of self-evaluation and documentation, and concentrates on procedures such as ways of checking quality, of dealing with complaints and grievances. ISO certification is not product- or service-specific, so in the context of a language teaching organisation it would not inspect the teaching, but simply verify that there are systems for observing and evaluating teaching activities. A number of schools, both state and private, and university departments have obtained ISO 9001 certification.

There has, at the same time, been development of quality assurance and control systems more specifically directed towards language teaching and learning. A number of associations have been formed with the aim of promoting quality assurance and quality control. These are either national (such as SOUFFLE for French, IQ-Deutsch for German, CEELE for Spanish, QUEST for language schools in Romania) or international, for example, EAQUALS (the European Association for Quality Language Services). These associations typically have a Code of Practice that includes charters for learners and staff and describes fair and honest commercial practice. The respect of the code is verified by systems of inspection which include observation of the teaching and other services provided. Satisfactory verification of the respect of the code is then certified for a fixed period, frequently two or three years, and re-checked by a further inspection.

## 'Quality' in language teaching

All these systems can only function successfully if they have a clear concept of what they mean by 'quality' in language teaching. It is more difficult to define than in the case of an industrial product or many types of service, and is influenced by, among other things, educational values and principles, by the personal interrelational nature of teaching/learning activities, by issues related to intercultural communication. There are no recipes for good language teaching and no one methodological approach to suit all circumstances. The principles of good quality in general involve the requirement of clear definition of the activity and standards to be applied and verification of them – which can be defined as 'Say what you do. Do what you say you do. Check that you are doing what you say you are doing.' In other words, applying the principles of transparency of description and coherence of application. The **COMMON EUROPEAN FRAMEWORK** of the Council of Europe gives a description of the options which providers of language teaching services should take note of and the level descriptors in its Scale of Reference provide a common set of described objectives and a basis for coherent curriculum design.

Institutions wishing to implement quality in the provision of language teaching services will need to show a principled approach to the design and implementation of curriculum design, the choice of teaching methodologies, the application of valid and reliable **ASSESSMENT** of progress and achievement, and appropriate and fair certification of their courses. They will also typically need to prove that they have properly qualified staff, appropriate premises and resources, efficient systems for administration and for the provision of complementary services for learners – such as accommodation and leisure services.

Work has also been carried out in the definition of quality in the design of language teaching **MATERIALS** and programmes. Lasnier *et al.* (1999) have produced a quality guide which defines principles of quality – such as relevance, transparency, **RELIABILITY**, generativeness – and divide the process of producing quality into the three steps of design, implementation and outcome. ALTE (the Association of Language Testers in Europe) (1998) has similarly produced a code of practice defining principles and procedures for good practice in the field of assessment and testing.

The interest in quality management of language teaching and learning activities has provided a useful contribution to the development in the field. It is in a relatively early stage and still needs to develop fully efficient techniques for the standardisation and reliability of observation and evaluation of schools.

**See also:** Assessment and testing; Evaluation; Planning for foreign language teaching; Syllabus and curriculum design; Teacher thinking; Teaching methods

### References

ALTE (1998) *ALTE handbook of European language examinations and examinations systems,* Cambridge: ALTE.
Lasnier, J.-C, Morfeld, P., North, B., Borneto, C.S. and Späth, P. (1999) *A quality guide for the evaluation and design of language learning and teaching programmes and materials,* Brussels: European Commission.

### Further reading

Alderson, C. and Beretta, A. (eds) (1992) *Evaluating second language education,* Cambridge: Cambridge University Press.
British Council (1999 and published annually) *The English in Britain Accreditation Scheme Handbook,* Manchester: The British Council.
Deming, W.E. (1982) *Quality, productivity, and competitive position,* Cambridge, MA: MIT Press.
EAQUALS (1992) *A guide to the inspections scheme,* Trieste: EAQUALS.
Ishikawa, K. (1985) *What is total quality control? The Japanese way,* Englewood Cliffs, NJ: Prentice Hall.
Rea-Dickins, P. and Germaine, K.P. (1998) *Managing evaluation and innovation in language teaching,* London: Longman.

FRANK HEYWORTH

# Questioning techniques

The effective use of questioning techniques is important for classroom management, for developing students' skills in language and social interaction, and to extend students' thinking and cognitive involvement in the content of lessons. This topic is usually considered from the teacher's point of view but it is also important to develop students' questioning skills.

## Typology of questions

Teachers' questions can be classified by form or by function. According to their form they can be sequenced, from the generally more easily understood and easy-to-answer questions, to more complex types. Any of these can be language models for learners. Thus, in English one can ask *either–or* questions ('Did Kim go to the bank or to the hotel?') to which the answer is usually contained in the question itself; *yes–no,* or polar, questions ('Was Kim in the bank?'), which could be answered with a simple 'yes' or 'no'; *wh-* questions, which begin with such question words as 'Who', 'Where', 'What', etc. ('Why did Kim go to the bank?'); and *indirect* ('I wonder where Kim went?') and more complex questions ('If Kim had been in the bank at twelve, what would she have heard?'). However, a simple question can sometimes be hard to answer (for example, 'Why?'). According to their function, some teachers' questions may be social ('How are you today?'), or for classroom management and control, since they are intended partly to control participation and behaviour ('Are you listening, Kim?', 'Can you answer that question, Kim?'). As with rhetorical questions, the questioner does not expect an answer to these, but normally expects other behaviour in response.

Of course, teachers have to use language, including questions, to organise learning activities, and the frequency of management questions is one reason why teachers' questions predominate in classroom talk. Many teachers' questions are *display* questions, where the teacher already knows the answer but wishes the respondent to display language skill or knowledge. *Referential* questions, where the teacher does not know the answer, are rarer. They may be more personal to the student or involve opinions, and they may tend to lead to longer, more complex answers. Questions can be *open* (with a wide range of expected or possible answers) or, more commonly, *closed* (with a narrow range of expected answers), depending on the context. Teachers' questions can also make lesser or greater cognitive demands and are therefore powerful tools for developing students' thinking. Thus, in Bloom's taxonomy (1956), which has been widely applied to both oral classroom discourse and to **READING** comprehension, low-order or literal questions test learners' *knowledge* when relevant answers involve recognition or recall of ideas, or their *comprehension*, if answers emphasise the literal grasp of meaning and intent of material. These lower-order questions make lesser demands than higher-order questions. Higher-order questions involve drawing inferences through *application* to a new situation, *analysis, synthesis* or *EVALUATION* of content or language.

## Use of questions

Research studies have repeatedly shown that most teachers' questions tend to be lower-order questions that do not make high cognitive demands. This may be because the higher-order questions take more time to think of, and good, thought-provoking questions generally need to be prepared in advance. Since a teacher's questions not only focus attention on aspects of language and interaction but also promote different kinds of thinking and ways of working, effective questioners will ask a range of types of questions, deliberately including higher-order questions. For example, asking about time ('Did the task take longer than you expected?') or teamwork ('How can the **GROUP** work together better?') can help learners reflect on task organisation, learning and cooperation. Differentiating questions so that they are appropriate to individuals yet challenging enough to promote learning for all is difficult in mixed-ability classes.

Good questioning needs planning, awareness and reflection. The techniques of asking include distributing questions around the class so that as many learners as possible can be involved in answering, paying attention to the timing, pace and sequence of questions, and to prompting answers. Some students are rarely called upon to answer, perhaps because teachers may ask only those who seem to know or because the teacher is unwilling to pause or slow down the momentum of the class while waiting for an answer. However, studies have shown that slightly increasing the wait-time between a question and allowing a student to answer, or between the answer and the teacher's subsequent response, leads to better-quality answers from a wider range of students, probably because they are given more thinking time. The

teacher's responses usually evaluate answers, but they can also introduce conversational phrases ('I'm inclined to agree with you.').

Teachers can improve questioning techniques through observation, watching and listening to classroom recordings, analysing transcripts and reflecting on the purposes and effects of different types of questions on students' language, thinking and interaction. It is important to become aware of how questions are generally the leading element in the common, three-part language exchanges (e.g. question–answer–evaluation) which can dominate formal classroom talk. Such awareness can prevent exchanges from becoming routines and help teachers to use them appropriately and thoughtfully.

## Learners' questioning skills

Developing students' questioning skills is important as a way of improving their linguistic, cognitive and social skills. Moral aspects are also involved, for example, in asking politely, in learning from other peoples' questions and answers even when they have errors or are inappropriate, and in listening to others' contributions with respect and an open **ATTITUDE**. Students' questions can be developed in pairwork and role play, by writing and using questionnaires, by listing their own questions on a text, or by bringing prepared questions to class. A difficulty here is to develop the use of communicative or referential questions rather than only those which are for language skills practice. Like teachers' questions, those of students could be classified and discussed to promote **LANGUAGE AWARENESS** and to develop more critical thinking.

There are, however, cultural differences about asking questions. Some students are reluctant to ask questions of teachers in class because they are afraid of making mistakes or they do not want to interrupt the class. However, they may ask after the lesson. Others do not ask because they believe that asking shows disrespect for the teacher. Other students do not like to ask their peers because they believe that the teacher is in the best position to teach them. Many teachers and students, however, believe that questioning is a fundamental way of learning; learning how to ask is learning how to learn.

**See also:** Classroom research; Group work; Language laboratories; Large classes; Overhead projector; Teacher education; Teacher talk; Teaching methods

## Reference

Bloom, B.S. (1956) *The taxonomy of educational objectives. The classification of educational goals. Handbook 1: Cognitive Domain*, New York: David McKay.

## Further reading

Dillon, J.T. (1988) *Questioning and teaching: a manual of practice*, London: Croom Helm.
Morgan, N. and Saxton, J. (1991) *Teaching questioning and learning*, London: Routledge.

MARTIN CORTAZZI AND LIXIAN JIN

# R

## Reading

Some examinations allow learners to use **DICTION-ARIES** to solve reading comprehension tests in foreign languages. Examiners are confident that to understand the meaning of every word and phrase is not the same thing as being able to read. What, then, are the characteristics of reading? Besides the understanding of word and phrase meaning, the following can be regarded as some of the important factors: complexity of sentence structure, idea density, quantity and quality of illustrations, personal reference to the texts, and also legibility – for example type size or typeface. Traditionally, readability formulas have been based on the two main factors: difficulty of the words and phrases, and average sentence length. However, these formulas can be criticised from a schema theory perspective.

### Schema theory

Reading used to be regarded as giving information from texts to readers in a uni-directional sense. Thus, foreign language teachers made efforts to rephrase difficult expressions or grammatical items using plain words or structures. However, according to schema theory, readers acquire information from texts not passively but actively. They predict a certain development of a story, for example, with their prior knowledge of stories, and look for confirmation of their predictions. Effective reading requires both top-down and bottom-up processing. With over-reliance on bottom-up processing, readers can translate each word but may not grasp the overall structure of the passage. On the other hand, with an over-reliance on top-down processing, readers may make wrong predictions.

Reading comprehension can be likened to the process of driving a car. An incorrect prediction is dangerous. What is needed is a prediction which prepares for every possibility, with flexible amendment of a schema as required. This in turn means that the ability to monitor one's reading comprehension is required. Activating schemata is especially useful for foreign language learners. Most learners are old enough to have prior knowledge of many topics. Even poor readers of foreign languages have some schemata, and they can participate actively in lessons if their schemata are activated.

This theory has changed the view of reading from a passive to an active process. Readers' prior knowledge is far more important than the data they find in texts. The significance of the interaction between top-down and bottom-up processing has been brought to light by many studies.

However, schema theory is still too general to use in everyday foreign language classes. Giving a pictorial context, for example, proves to be effective when texts are particularly 'opaque', but we seldom come across such sentences. Furthermore, problems often arise with respect to schema activation, and pre-reading activities are needed to provide students with sufficient background knowledge of the texts. The purpose of pre-reading activities is to give students successful strategies. Most pre-reading activities have tried to give students related information. It is doubtful, however, whether this is sufficient for students to be able to access cues by themselves. To activate students' schemata, teachers need to evaluate first what students already know about the topic of the text and then provide the appropriate information.

## Reading problem or language problem

There are some good reading strategies common to all languages. Good readers do not look at or decode every word in the text. They pick up sufficient information for meaning and make maximum use of redundancy. Good reading strategies follow the same process, sampling information and confirming those predictions. These reading strategies can be called knowledge-based, conceptually driven processing.

Most foreign language learners are older than L1 learners when they begin learning to read. They have already acquired a certain amount of L1 reading ability. If good reading strategies are universal across different languages, good L1 readers have a much greater advantage in developing L2 reading abilities than poor L1 readers.

On the other hand, we have some evidence to support the hypothesis that L2 reading is a language problem. Beginning readers or poor readers are faced with more unknown **VOCABU-LARY** and structures than good readers. For them, L2 texts are something like worm-eaten historical documents. If their language proficiency is poor, readers are forced to use word-by-word decoding strategies. Data-driven processing or text-based processing are useful only when they are automatic.

It is clear, therefore, that both L1 reading ability and L2 language proficiency are factors of L2 reading ability, but the level of L2 language proficiency is significant. Good L1 reading ability can be transferred to L2 reading only after readers acquire a certain minimum amount of L2 language proficiency, a 'threshold'.

## Good reading strategies

The term 'strategy' is used to describe what is involved when we try to solve any problematic situation. In the interactive reading comprehension process, the readers' active role has been emphasised. Making guesses from the context, for example, is an effective strategy for reading. Good readers have a wide range of effective approaches to texts and they can choose a strategy suitable to a given text. One of the goals of foreign language reading instruction is to provide students with as many strategies as possible.

What are thought to be good reading strategies? Good readers can relate information which comes next in the text to previous information in the text. They can monitor accurately their comprehension ability. Then they can use their previous knowledge to predict the following story or to guess unknown words. Because they can distinguish between main points and supporting details of the passage, they can skip some words but can get the outline of the texts. Even when there are some parts that they cannot understand, good readers always try to get the outline of the texts, skipping some difficult parts.

Generally speaking, foreign language readers have trouble when they face unknown words. Good readers never give up even when they come across difficult unknown words. They manage to guess at word meaning, rereading a problematic part many times, whereas poor readers try to decode every word and phrase on the page. When poor readers come across difficult words, they do not find a way to overcome the problem. This means that foreign language teachers should discourage students from adopting a word-by-word strategy. They should show students that they do not have to decode every word and phrase in the text. Students should have training to realise there are important parts and not so important parts in a text. For example, showing students that they automatically skip some parts of the text written in their **MOTHER TONGUE** is an effective way of teaching this.

Good readers do not only depend on text information through bottom-up processing but also actively utilise top-down processing. They think that their guesses are often more correct than the information obtained from the text by translating. For example, they imagine what the characters in a story are thinking and also imagine how they would think or act if they were those characters. This vicarious reading is an effective strategy, and teachers should ask questions about this experience to get their students actively involved in stories.

Good readers have also been found to focus on changing their strategies or the aim of their reading according to the nature of the text, and to think about the main theme after reading. Teachers thus need to explain that there are different kinds of text and that the goals and strategies of reading should differ according to the kinds of text they are reading.

## Implications for teaching

On the basis of the above, the teaching of reading should have the following characteristics. First, we should teach not only the grammatical items or vocabulary but also reading strategies. Second, we should not check how students translate what they read but rather their ways of understanding the content or of extracting the information. Third, we should not give a definitive TRANSLATION but should instead show them how to extract the meaning. Fourth, we should have them focus on one or two strategies at a time by using easy passages. Fifth, we should have them read long passages and show them that, in doing so, they operate certain useful strategies unconsciously. Finally, we should make them realise that those strategies are really effective.

Teachers of reading should be making their students into risk-takers who read texts actively. Otherwise they will not give up the tendency towards word-by-word reading. Inference-type, generalisation-type and personal-involvement-type questions are needed to create good readers, rather than fact-finding questions which only make students scan the surface of the text.

**See also:** Audiolingual method; Literary texts; Literary texts and intercultural understanding; Reading methods; Schema and script theory; Skills and knowledge; Sociolinguistic competence; Teaching methods; Writing

## Further reading

Carrell, P.L., Devine, J. and Eskey, D.E. (eds) (1988) *Interactive approaches to second language reading*, Cambridge: Cambridge University Press.

Oxford, R.L. (1990) *Language learning strategies*, Boston: Heinle and Heinle.

Takanashi, T. and Ushiro, Y. (2000) *Eigo Reading Jiten (Encyclopedia of EFL Reading)*, Tokyo: Kenkyusha.

Ushiro, Y. (1995) 'Metacognitive difference in EFL reading strategies', *Tsukuba review of English language teaching* 16, 33–53.

YUJI USHIRO

# Reading methods

In Western societies the mastery of reading has become a powerful factor in social integration. The many forms of social exclusion are often linked to inadequate ability in reading. On the other hand, information technology requires specific reading competencies so that the computer is doubtless already modifying our reading practices.

As far as foreign language teaching is concerned, the communicative approach emphasised the fact that the written language, too, is a form of linguistic communication. Taking into account the specific NEEDS of certain learners led to the development of material to enhance reading comprehension in foreign languages. If it is desirable and necessary that there should be the best possible mastery of at least one foreign language, more limited OBJECTIVES, such as reading and/or aural comprehension, are quite reasonable when several foreign languages are to be acquired. Acquiring reading ability in a foreign language is a way for the learner of increasing the range of their linguistic capabilities, and is also a way of enhancing their reading ability in their own language.

## Teaching reading in the mother tongue

Three main types of method can be identified for teaching the interpretation of the graphic code:

- the 'synthetic': first the learning of the letters, then groups of graphemes corresponding to syllables, to words (depending on the combinations in the language in question) and to sentences;
- the 'analytic' proceeds in the opposite way to the synthetic: identifying words in a sentence, then syllables, then letters;

- the 'mixed' is between the two, though generally more analytic than synthetic.

There has been a long debate on the comparable effectiveness of these methods. Research suggests that the relationships between graphics and phonics play a significant role at the beginning of learning to read, and that phonological awareness developed in the reader is a determining factor. Phonological mediation seems in fact to serve as a support for the transitory processes of information handling in the working memory and it is on these that the process of understanding depends (Sprenger-Charolles, 1991: 80). In addition to these learning methods in the proper sense, there are also methods for accelerating the speed of reading (Richaudeau, 1983).

## Teaching reading in the foreign language

The problem of teaching reading in the foreign language varies according to the context:

- Adults not in education who are learning to read and write in a language different to the one(s) they speak. This is in essence an introduction to literacy.
- Children learning to read and write at school in a language other than the one through which they had their first experience of language (which we shall call their **MOTHER TONGUE**). In many educational contexts, an effort is made to initiate the child simultaneously into the written language of the mother tongue. This is considered to provide better support for the development of the written language in the foreign language.
- Early teaching of foreign languages (where children have already begun to learn to read and write in their mother tongue). There does not appear to be any specific pedagogy. The child is expected to learn to read by recognising and memorising words written down for them. The emphasis is on the lexis and on the basic morpho-syntactic forms. Apart from a few rhymes, songs and short poems, these methods do not really use texts. Nor are there any activities to raise children's awareness of the social functions of the written language, such as

can be found for example in **LANGUAGE AWARENESS** work (Haas, 1995).

- Methods for teaching reading in a foreign language to learners who are 'expert readers' in their mother tongue, where 'expert readers' does not signify a specific level in practical efficiency in reading, since we are all more or less 'experts' in our own language depending on the type of text, the contexts and the purposes etc for the reading.

There are then four aspects to consider:

- The question of decoding. There is no material designed to teach, for example, the graphic–phonic correspondences of French to speakers of **CHINESE**. The **AUDIO-VISUAL** structural-global methods of the 1960s suggested the following approach: entirely oral teaching at the beginning for approximately 60 hours, then the introduction of the written language by the use of **DICTATIONS**, with a basic progression based on the difficulties predicted in terms of the relationship between graphemes and phonemes. Nothing is proposed in the universalist methods claiming to be based on the communicative approach. The understanding of a text none the less implies that the learner has reached a certain degree of automaticity in decoding.
- The oralisation of reading. Purely visual reading, if it exists, is only possible for readers used to handling certain types of text. Yet for foreign language learners it is practically impossible. Oralisation is useful provided it is practised in a non-systematic way as a means of working on the meaning of the text.
- The (re)construction of meaning. The meaning of a text is not given, not simply transmitted from the author to the reader. The reader has to (re)construct it on the basis of the relationships they establish between the sender, the text and the receiver, and the reader is therefore not a passive agent. Previous knowledge relevant to the subject of the text plays a very important part. Such knowledge can be developed by establishing 'semantic maps' (Carrell, 1990: 16–29), by techniques of 'priming'. This is done by providing, in advance of reading the text, information which orients the reader towards a specific domain of knowledge. As for the

'discursive' and 'textual' dimension of the (re)construction of meaning, this can be approached either through textual schemas or through the process of identifying clues, as is suggested in the 'global approach' (Lehmann and Moirand, 1980: 72–9). There are several categories of clue to take into consideration: scriptual–visual clues which are related to the layout of the text on the page; clues which reveal the structure of the text at macro and micro levels; clues of enunciation which reveal the position taken by the writer on the issues in the text. From a more pragmatic perspective, the relationship between the sender and the receiver of the text can be taken into consideration, as can the effects of the text on the reader, on the reader as preconceived and implied in the text, and on the actual reader in practice.

- Meta-procedure. How the learner manages to understand the text in a foreign language. Is there **TRANSFER** of **SKILLS** acquired in the mother tongue? Some researchers believe that, in the foreign language, the reader is so overwhelmed by what is happening at the level of the graphic code (the lowest level) that they are not able to use the information provided by the text as a whole (the highest level), as they usually do in the mother tongue – the hypothesis of short-circuiting top-down processes (Gaonac'h, 1987: 164–7). It is for this reason that some teaching method theorists have recommended working on the verbalisation of reading strategies in order to make explicit and compare their degree of efficiency.

Whatever the pedagogical approach, it is desirable that reading in the foreign language class should be integrated into the work of the learner, that it should respond to their objectives, and as far as possible it should be a source of pleasure.

**See also:** Audio-visual language teaching; Communicative language teaching; Dictionaries; Exercise types and grading; Grammar–translation method; Languages for specific purposes; Reading; Stylistic variation; Textbooks; Writing

### References

Carrell, P.L. (1990) 'Rôle des schémas de contenu et des schémas formels', *Le français dans le monde/recherches et applications*, no. spécial 'Acquisition et utilisation d'une langue étrangère: 16–29.

Gaonac'h, D. (1987) *Théories d'apprentissage et acquisition d'une langue étrangère*, Paris: CREDIF-Hatier.

Haas, G. (1995) 'Qui ne connaît aucune écriture ne connaît pas la sienne au fond', in D. Moore (ed.), *L'éveil au langage. Notions en question 1*, Paris: Didier.

Hosenfeld, C. (1984) 'Case studies of ninth grade readers', in J.C. Alderson and A.H. Urquhart (eds), *Reading in a foreign language*, New York: Longman.

Lehmann, D. and Moirand, S. (1980) 'Une approche communicative de la lecture', *Le français dans le monde* 153: 72–9.

Richaudeau, F. (1983) *La lecture rapide*, Paris: Editions Retz.

Sprenger-Charolles, L. (1991) 'Premiers apprentissages de la lecture: 20 ans de recherches francophones', *Etudes de Linguistique Appliquée* 84: 65–83.

### Further reading

Coirier, P., Gaonac'h, D. and Passerault, J.M. (1996) *Psycholinguistique textuelle*, Paris: Armand Colin.

Giasson, J. (1990) *La compréhension en lecture*, Brussels: De Boeck-Wesmael.

MARC SOUCHON

# Reference works

A reference work is any database of information that can be accessed for a specific purpose. **DICTIONARIES**, glossaries and some kinds of **GRAMMAR** book are reference works containing linguistic information. Encyclopedias, atlases, almanacs, manuals and some kinds of **TEXTBOOK** are encyclopedic reference works, containing information about the world rather than about words and language. Timetables, telephone directories and catalogues can also be considered types of reference work, although they are not designed for teaching and learning.

The information in a reference work is usually presented visually, in the form of written text, diagrams, maps or tables. Reference works are not designed to be read in a linear way from beginning to end. Instead, each piece of information (or entry) in the reference work is designed to be accessed independently of the other entries. Within the same reference work, entries are often structured in a similar way; definitions within the same dictionary, for example, may have many features in common (Hoey 1986).

Printed reference works present entries in some kind of sequence, so that users can easily locate the information they need. Entries may be organised chronologically, spatially, thematically, alphabetically, numerically or according to any combination of these methods. For example, timetables and some history textbooks are chronologically ordered, atlases are spatially ordered, thesauruses are thematically ordered and telephone directories are alphabetically ordered (in countries where the writing system is alphabetical). In many cases there is also a secondary system of organisation: grammar books, textbooks, atlases and thesauruses often contain an alphabetical index to help users locate entries more easily, and although the entries in reference grammar books are often ordered numerically, they may also be sequenced according to the order in which the compilers believe the structures will be acquired, and/or they may be arranged thematically according to word classes or language notions.

Entries in reference works stored in electronic form, such as a CD-ROM or a website, do not need to be organised in a linear sequence, so the user often has a wider choice of search strategies. To find an entry in the *Encyclopaedia Britannica CD*, for example, the user can make natural language queries (in words, phrases or questions), set strict search parameters by using the Boolean operators AND, OR, NOT and ADJ (adjacency), click on time lines (for historical information), roll the cursor over a map (for geographical and statistical information), or browse an alphabetically ordered list of items within a given information category.

Reference works in electronic form sometimes combine a number of separate information sources, such as a reference grammar, a dictionary, a thesaurus, a collection of pictures, and audio and video files. This is the case, for example, with the *Longman Interactive English Dictionary* (1993) and the *Longman Interactive American Dictionary* (1997). Reference works can also exist in a combination of formats: some printed manuals and textbooks are packaged with additional reference material on CD-ROM, and some reference works on CD-ROM link directly to the World Wide Web. The World Wide Web can itself be regarded as 'the largest and most widely consultable work of reference that has ever existed' (McArthur, 1998: 217), because it integrates a huge number of reference sources around the world, such as library catalogues, instructional websites and language databanks.

Works of reference which integrate a number of information sources can be more flexible than single products because they are easier to change and supplement, but their loose structure may create access problems. The World Wide Web is often likened to a vast and continually expanding library without any catalogue system; it contains plenty of data, but it is sometimes difficult to locate specific pieces of information.

People have always felt the need to store and access information, and the use of reference works probably predates writing. Sticks, stones and bits of bones seem to have been used by cave dwellers for reference purposes (perhaps to keep tally of hunts, births and deaths, or astronomical cycles). Many of the earliest written documents in the world also functioned as works of reference; there are examples of bilingual wordlists, for example, dating from the second millennium BC. The Indian grammarian Pāṇini compiled grammar textbooks some time between the fifth and the seventh centuries BC, and a grammar of Greek was written in about 100 BC.

The forerunners of many of the dictionaries and encyclopedias available today were compiled in the eighteenth and nineteenth centuries; for example the *Encyclopaedia Britannica*, first published in three volumes in 1768 and 1771, and now available in thirty-two volumes or on CD-ROM; Löbel's *Konversationslexicon* (1808), which provided the model for the large family of subsequent Löbel-Brockhaus encyclopedias; Webster's *American Dictionary* (1828), which began the Merriam-Webster dictionary tradition; and Roget's *Thesaurus of English*

*Words and Phrases* (1852). We do not use updated versions of the 'traditional' grammar books popular in the eighteenth and nineteenth centuries, however, because attitudes towards grammar teaching changed in the twentieth century (although linguists still refer to the basic grammatical notions that were established by the ancient Indian and Greek grammarians). Traditional grammars had a prescriptive approach to language: only the standard variety used by the educated elite was considered 'correct' and worthy of study. Many modern grammars, on the other hand, are descriptive: they describe and analyse the forms found in all the varieties of language, including informal spoken varieties (see also **GRAMMAR**). As an aid to language description, modern compilers of dictionaries and grammar books refer to large corpora of naturally occurring spoken and written texts to check the frequency, range and behaviour of words and structures.

The use of reference works for language teaching and learning is especially associated with the **GRAMMAR–TRANSLATION** teaching method, which requires the learner to translate written passages with the aid of a grammar book and a dictionary. Although other **TEACHER METHODS** may place less emphasis on the use of reference works, grammars and dictionaries are consulted by most language learners, especially older children and adults who want to study independently.

Not all grammar books are intended for language teaching and learning, however. Theoretical grammars written for linguists or students of **LINGUISTICS** describe and evaluate a particular linguistic theory rather than the language itself (Corder, 1988). These are not really reference works, because they are not composed of independent entries. Instead, arguments and ideas are developed from chapter to chapter. Another type of grammar book, the large reference grammar, is intended as a record of the grammatical system, and tries to provide as comprehensive a picture of the language as possible. This type of work may be too complex and detailed for classroom use.

Grammars which are designed for teaching and learning a foreign language, or for developing awareness of the mother tongue, are known as **PEDAGOGICAL GRAMMARS**. Most are primarily intended to be used as reference works, although

some contain **EXERCISES** which may be treated like textbook material, just as some language teaching textbooks contain grammar sections and glossaries to be used as reference material.

Although dictionaries and grammar books are the two types of reference work most associated with language teaching and learning, other kinds of reference materials such as atlases, timetables, instruction manuals and catalogues may also be used in the language classroom. Tasks involving these types of reference work enable learners to practise handling information in the target language, for example by finding items in alphabetically ordered lists, relating written instructions to pictures and diagrams, and scanning for specific information.

**See also:** Exercise types and grading; Grammar; Internet; Lexicography and lexicology; Media centres; Pedagogical grammar; Text and corpus linguistics; Textbooks; Vocabulary

## References

Corder, S.P. (1988) 'Pedagogic grammars', in W. Rutherford and M. Sharwood Smith (eds), *Grammar and second language teaching: a book of readings*, New York: Newbury House.

Hoey, M.P. (1986) 'The discourse colony: a preliminary study of a neglected discourse type', in R.M. Coulthard (ed.), *Talking about text*, Discourse Analysis Monographs no 13. English Language Research, University of Birmingham.

McArthur, T. (1998) 'What then *is* reference science?', in T. McArthur (ed.), *Living words: language, lexicography and the knowledge revolution*, Exeter: Exeter University Press.

## Further reading

Hüllen, W. (1989) 'In the beginning was the gloss. Remarks on the historical emergence of lexicographical paradigms', in G. James (ed.), *Lexicographers and their works*, Exeter: University of Exeter Press.

McArthur, T. (1986) *Worlds of reference*, Cambridge: Cambridge University Press.

McArthur, T. (ed.) (1998) *Living words: language,*

*lexicography and the knowledge revolution*, Exeter: Exeter University Press.

HILARY NESI

# Reform Movement

The Reform Movement, which is usually connected with the development of modern language teaching principles during the last two decades of the nineteenth century, has to be seen as a reaction against the traditional **GRAMMAR–TRANSLATION METHOD**. Innovations were worked out especially with respect to the teaching of **PRONUNCIATION** and **GRAMMAR** as well as to methods and visual and aural **MATERIALS**.

First hints, which can be regarded as preliminary remarks for the Reform Movement, can be found in the 1860s and 1870s. In prefaces to **TEXTBOOKS**, for example, some authors supported the idea of modernising foreign language teaching by a more natural and pupil-centred approach. The most important impetus, however, was given by the German teacher and scholar Wilhelm **VIËTOR**, who published a famous and partially sarcastic pamphlet in 1882 entitled 'Language teaching must start afresh!' (*Der Sprachunterricht muß umkehren!*). 'Viëtor's appeal was heard all over Europe and also in America, especially after he started a review … that popularized the new approach' (Titone, 1968: 38). He denounced the defenders of the old grammar–translation method, which was connected with the teaching of Latin and had traditionally been transferred to the teaching of modern languages. The best-known innovation called for by Viëtor's essay was that of a **MONOLINGUAL PRINCIPLE** in foreign language teaching which led to the so-called **DIRECT METHOD**. Thus the foreign language as the normal means of classroom communication should provide the basis of instruction, and oral skills should enable the pupils to use the foreign language as a means of understanding and producing sentences in everyday situations.

Psychological principles of language **ACQUISITION** were derived from the common-sense psychology of those days, which was combined with the idea that the process of learning languages depended on the forming of associations. On the one hand pupils were supposed to acquire a foreign language similarly to the process of learning one's **MOTHER TONGUE**; on the other hand the monolingual method was thought to help pupils to associate words and structures with their meanings in a direct way (Franke, 1884; Sweet, 1899). Moreover, one could see the first signs that learner-oriented teaching had to deal with the fact that there were different types of learners, i.e. the visual, the aural, and the audio-visual type (Eggert, 1904).

A great number of the founders of the Reform Movement were linguists, who in the beginning gave priority to phonetics. The **INTERNATIONAL PHONETIC ASSOCIATION (IPA)** was founded in 1886 by a group of Frenchmen under the leadership of Paul Passy, who was soon joined by **JESPERSEN**, Viëtor, and **SWEET**. The international phonetic alphabet provided the basis not only for research work but also for the training of pronunciation in foreign language classes. Special courses were designed for the first weeks of language learning. The pupils should train their ears, their organs of speech, and undertake phonetic transcriptions. As teachers had to be well trained in phonetics, too, they were expected to have travelled to the foreign countries, and **NATIVE SPEAKERS** were asked to assist in foreign language classes.

> Great phoneticians have assisted in the improvement of FLT. The name of Henry Sweet (1845–1912) deserves to be mentioned in this connection. Besides a priority for phonetics Sweet repeatedly stresses the fact that every language has its own structure, and can therefore not be forced into the straitjacket of Latin grammar.
>
> (van Els *et al.*, 1984: 150)

The most significant change that was caused by the Reform Movement, however, was a new attitude towards the teaching of grammar. The reformers were convinced that there was a natural order in learning languages, namely **SPEAKING**, **READING**, **WRITING** and finally grammar. The old deductive way of learning grammar was now replaced by an inductive or analytic one. The basis for seeking, finding, describing and training rules was no longer single or disconnected sentences but texts that meant something. 'Gradually textbooks took a different pattern … The reading passages consisted mainly of simple modern prose designed to introduce the pupil to an understanding of the life and customs of the foreign people' (Titone, 1968: 38–9). Thus texts were fundamental in a double sense: pupils should get a general education by the contents, and they should comprehend grammar rules by analysing forms and functions. Written and oral dialogues and even conversational **EXERCISES** became important for applying and transferring the findings. Since then foreign language teaching has always also been direct language experience and the transfer of semantic concepts into forms of language.

The realistic approach to language learning led to a special use of visual and aural media. Wall pictures showing everyday scenes (e.g. in connection with the four seasons) were not only described in the foreign language classes but also exploited for the training of **VOCABULARY**, for the illustrating of grammar, and for inventing and constructing dialogues. The phonograph, or rather the gramophone, was used by the reformers initially for the purpose of experimental observation and description of phonological phenomena. From about 1905 onwards the production of special aural materials made it possible to use records for pronunciation exercises in foreign language classes. The particular advantage was the presentation of intonation patterns and literary scenes, which native speakers had recorded in studios.

It was obviously Viëtor's pamphlet in 1882 which attracted the greatest attention at the beginning of the Reform Movement, and it was Jespersen who, in his booklet 'How to Teach a Foreign Language' (1904), summarised the practical implications of the movement for classroom teachers. Even though the ideas of the reformers were put forward by several conferences and numerous publications, mostly in new journals and periodicals, the aims and methods were not always accepted peacefully. Various reasons and experiences gave rise to controversy (see Titone, 1968: 39; Schilder, 1985: 58–9). Consequently it became evident in the first decade of the twentieth century that compromises had to be found. Finally a combination or a mixture of the direct approach

and the traditional attitudes towards reading, learning grammar and translating developed.

Nevertheless it was the reformers who were most often referred to in the years to come. Their principles of the monolingual approach, the training of dialogues and conversation, and of pupil-centred activities were usually (and still are) mentioned when so-called new ways of foreign language teaching were (or are being) designed.

**See also:** Direct method; *Fremdsprachendidaktik*; History: the nineteenth century; Linguistics; Monolingual principle; Teaching methods

## References

Eggert, B. (1904) *Der psychologische Zusammenhang in der Didaktik des neusprachlichen Reformunterrichts* (The psychological context in the didactics of the reformed foreign language teaching), Berlin: von Reuther and Reichard.

Franke, F. (1884) *Die praktische Spracherlernung auf Grund der Psychologie und Physiologie der Sprache dargestellt* (Practical language learning described on the basis of the psychology and the physiology of language), Heilbronn: Henninger.

Jespersen, O. (1904) *How to teach a foreign language*, London: Allen and Unwin.

Schilder, H. (1985) *'Reformbestrebungen und Wendepunkte in den Grundlagen und Methoden des Fremdsprachenunterrichts'* (Reform efforts and turning points in the theories and methods of foreign language teaching), *Englisch Amerikanische Studien* 7, 1: 54–67.

Sweet, H. (1899) *The practical study of languages. A guide for teachers and learners*, London: Dent.

Titone, R. (1968) *Teaching foreign languages – an historical sketch*, Washington, DC: Georgetown University Press.

van Els, T., Bongaerts, T., Extra, G., von Os, C. and Janssen-van Dieten, A.-M. (1984) *Applied linguistics and the learning and teaching of foreign languages*, London: Edward Arnold.

Viëtor, W. (1882) *Der Sprachunterricht muß umkehren!*, Heilbronn: Henninger; reproduced in translation by A.P.R. Howatt as 'Language teaching must start afresh!', in A.P.R. Howatt (1984) *A history of English language teaching*, Oxford: Oxford University Press, 343–62.

## Further reading

Howatt, A.P.R. (1984) *A history of English language teaching*, Oxford: Oxford University Press.

Schilder, H. (1977) *Medien im neusprachlichen Unterricht seit 1880* (Materials and media in foreign Language teaching since 1880), Kronberg: Scriptor.

Sweet, H. (1877) *A handbook of phonetics, including a popular exposition of the principles of the spelling reform*, Oxford: Clarendon Press.

HANNO SCHILDER

# RELC – The Regional Language Centre

The Regional Language Centre, an educational project of the Southeast Asian Ministers of Education Organisation (SEAMEO), is located in Singapore. The members of SEAMEO are Brunei Darussalam, Cambodia, Indonesia, the Lao People's Democratic Republic, Malaysia, Myanmar, the Philippines, Singapore, Thailand and Vietnam. The main objective of SEAMEO is to provide constructive direction to the forces and challenges of change in the contemporary world through joint and cooperative efforts for regional educational development.

RELC was set up in 1968 to provide assistance to SEAMEO member countries in the area of language education. To achieve its purpose, the Centre conducts advanced training courses, produces publications and undertakes research and information dissemination and other activities related to the linguistic needs and problems of Southeast Asia.

The majority of those attending courses at RELC hold scholarships given by SEAMEO. There are two types of training course: Diploma in Applied Linguistics and Master of Arts in Applied Linguistics; and short-term specialist courses in practice-oriented language **TEACHER EDUCATION**. There are also distance education courses.

RELC publishes a journal twice per year, and occasional papers. It organises an international seminar each April bringing together leading language educators both from the region and from the West to discuss language teaching issues.

In addition to its regular courses at the Centre, RELC runs distance education courses in the region for language teachers. It manages a website for teachers to discuss language teaching issues; and another website for students to exchange ideas and to upload inputs about features of their countries such as transportation and sports. Both sites are accessible through the address given below.

RELC also runs proficiency courses in **ENGLISH** for both private and public officers from the region as well as courses on Southeast Asian languages.

## Website

The centre's website is: http://www.relc.org.sg

THOMAS KHNG

# Reliability

This is a statement of the accuracy, consistency and fairness of a measuring instrument and refers to the extent to which that instrument will give the same result each time it is applied. Consider the example of two different instruments for measuring the width of a sheet of paper: a standard ruler and an elastic tape measure. Regardless of the number of times the standard ruler were used to measure the width of the paper, it would give the same result. This ruler, therefore, is reliable, for it measures the trait concerned (in this case, length) consistently and accurately. An elastic tape measure, on the other hand, will give a different measurement of the paper depending on how much the elastic is stretched. It is, of course, possible to arrive at the correct measurement of the paper by chance/ accident, or by taking many repeated measurements of the paper and averaging them out. However, the elastic tape measure is considered unreliable because it is unlikely to give the same measurement each time it is used.

Applying this principle to the context of a language test, if a test is reliable it will give any single student the same result each time it is applied. Consequently, a reliable test is considered to be fairer than one that gives different and possibly misleading results for the same student. An unreliable test is considered to contain measurement errors that can be due to one or more of the following factors: the time at which the test is taken, the items in the test, and the scoring.

## Estimating reliability

In classical test theory, test reliability is estimated by comparing two sets of results from the same test and the same group of test-takers. This comparison is reported as a correlation and normally ranges from 0 to 1.0; the lower the correlation, the lower the reliability of the test. There are a number of ways of gathering these two sets of test results, each of which addresses different sources of measurement error.

### Test–retest reliability

Inconsistencies arising from the time at which the test is taken can be checked by using a test–retest procedure in which the test-takers take the same test at two different times (perhaps a week apart). The test-takers' scores on both occasions are then compared. This approach has the advantage of allowing clear comparisons to be made, because it provides two sets of scores on the same test items for the same set of test-takers. However, it is somewhat impractical because differences in the test-takers' performance need not necessarily be due to the different times at which the test is taken. Instead the differences might, arguably, be because the test-takers remember some or all of the test items, or are more familiar with the test method, or are bored by the exercise, or have learned more language in the period between the two administrations of the test.

### Parallel form reliability and Split-half reliability

These two approaches estimate inconsistencies arising from the items in the test and are most commonly used in relation to objective tests (tests with items that have a clearly specifiable correct answer). The parallel form approach involves the construction of two versions of the test, both of which are administered to the same group of students. This approach has the advantage of

providing information on the same group of students while avoiding the practice effect and/or boredom that could result from the test–retest approach. However, it is extremely difficult if not impossible to construct two genuinely parallel tests. It is also time consuming to administer two tests and the test-takers can become tired, particularly if the tests are administered consecutively. This fatigue is likely to have an adverse effect on their performance.

The split-half approach avoids these disadvantages because it takes the test and divides it into two halves, comparing the test-takers' performances on each half. The concern here is to ensure that each half contains equivalent items and this is difficult to ensure if only one 'cut' is made. Consequently, statistical procedures have been devised that estimate the split-half reliability for all possible divisions of a test.

### Intra-rater and inter-rater reliability

This approach estimates inconsistencies arising from the scoring of the test and is usually applied in the case of subjectively scored tests (in which there is no single specified answer and the score is partly dependent on the judgement of the examiner). Intra-rater reliability is typically measured by asking examiners to score each performance twice. Like the test–retest approach, however, the results of intra-rater reliability procedures can be affected by the familiarity of the examiner with the scripts he/she has marked, and by boredom with having to re-mark. Inter-rater reliability can be estimated if two or more raters are asked to independently assess the same set of test performances. These independent assessments are then compared for their consistency with each other.

## Factors affecting reliability

There are many factors that affect test reliability by causing deviations or fluctuations in the test-takers' performance and test scores.

### Test-taker characteristics

Test-takers' performance on tests are usually adversely affected by temporary personal factors such as whether the test-taker is tired or ill on the day of the test or whether they are unhappy or concerned either about the test or some other part of their life. Additional test-taker characteristics that can affect test reliability are the extent to which the test-takers are familiar with the test and have developed strategies based on this test-wiseness. The more familiar test-takers are with a test, the better their scores are likely to be. Finally, certain test-takers are also more inclined towards risk-taking than others and guess the answers to the test questions. The test-taker's scores might be boosted or depressed depending on the success of this strategy.

### Test characteristics

These include the number of items in the test and the speed at which it must be completed. If a test is particularly short (e.g. 15–20 items), its reliability is likely to be increased by the addition of more items. However, tests can also be too long (and can overtire the test-takers as a consequence). In such cases, a reduction in the number of items can increase the test's reliability. The reliability of a test can also be increased if test-takers are given more time. Like test length, however, it might be the case that the time allocated needs to be reduced.

Test reliability is also influenced by the extent to which the test items can discriminate/distinguish between high- and low-ability test-takers. The greater the test's ability to spread students out, the higher is its reliability likely to be. Interestingly, the more homogeneous the test items, i.e. the more similar they are to each other in content, the higher the reliability of the test, because such a test is taking repeated measures of the same traits.

### Features of test administration

These refer to the clarity of the instructions, the quality of the test papers and the test environment, the monitoring of cheating and the care with which test-takers are kept informed of time. If a test centre is poorly lit or if the examiners are not provided with microphones with which to make announcements in large rooms, then the reliability of the test is likely to be adversely affected. Similarly, poorly printed or photocopied test papers

and confusing or ambiguous instructions can reduce/impair the reliability of the test.

### The scoring procedure

Threats to reliability can occur both within a rater (intra-rater reliability) and between raters (inter-rater reliability). Intra-rater reliability is adversely affected by examiner fatigue or by idiosyncratic features such as a preference for neat handwriting. Additionally, less experienced raters are more likely to be inconsistent. Inter-rater reliability is limited by the extent to which the raters share the perspective with which they are judging the test performance.

Consequently, there are many ways of improving the reliability estimates for a test. These include standardising the test conditions (such as good quality test papers, clear and unambiguous instructions and guidelines for test administrators); standardising the scoring procedures (by providing well developed marking criteria and sufficient training for examiners); and conducting careful checks on test items before they are used in the test.

**See also:** Action research; Assessment and testing; Evaluation; Research methods; Validity

### Further reading

Davies, A., Brown, A., Elder, C., Hill, K., Lumley, T. and McNamara, T. (1999) *Dictionary of language testing*, Cambridge: Cambridge University Press.
Henning, G. (1987) *A guide to language testing*, Boston, MA: Heinle and Heinle.

JAYANTI BANERJEE

# Research methods

Research is a systematic process of formulating questions, collecting relevant data relating to such questions, analysing and interpreting the data, and making the results publicly accessible (Hatch and Farhady, 1982; Nunan, 1992). It is usually argued that, in order to count as research, data collection and analysis should be carried out following procedures to ensure reliability and validity. As with other social sciences, there is controversy within language teaching and learning as to the relative merits of qualitative as opposed to quantitative approaches to research (van Lier, 1988). The purpose of this entry is to provide an account of research methods for the study of teaching and learning. The first section deals with the distinction between quantitative and qualitative approaches. This is followed by sections covering the following key aspects of the research process: formulating questions, methods of data collection, and approaches to the analysis of data.

## Approaches to research

Within the social sciences, there are two competing research paradigms: the quantitative and the qualitative. Quantitative research is aimed at assessing the strength of relationships between variables, and is based on the experimental method which aims to control and manipulate. Qualitative research seeks understanding by observing phenomena in their natural settings. In recent years, increasing numbers of researchers have argued that the distinction between qualitative and quantitative research is simplistic and naive, and that the two traditions are indistinguishable in many respects. Nevertheless, the distinction continues to be observed and debated.

Among language researchers, there are some who argue that qualitative research is essentially a preliminary activity, carried out in order to identify possible causal relationships between variables that might be more rigorously investigated through quantitative research. Others argue that the nature of the type of questions being investigated should determine the research paradigm chosen. Yet others argue that the qualitative/quantitative distinction is oversimplistic, particularly once one looks at actual published research. Grotjahn (1987), for example, argues that one needs to distinguish between three different aspects of the research process:

1  the method of data collection (whether collected through an experiment, or non-experimentally);
2  the type of data (qualitative or quantitative);
3  the type of analysis (statistical or interpretative).

Grotjahn argues that there are two 'pure' research

paradigms, the 'analytical–nomological' in which quantitative data are collected experimentally and subjected to statistical analysis, and the 'exploratory–interpretative' in which qualitative data are collected non-experimentally and analysed interpretatively. In addition, however, there are hybrid paradigms in which the variables are mixed and matched.

In language research, it seems clear that at present the two traditions will continue to co-exist, and that both will add to our increasingly sophisticated understanding of the complex psychological and sociolinguistic factors at play in language learning and teaching.

## Formulating questions

In many ways, the most difficult aspect of the research process involves formulating a question or questions that are worth asking in the first place, and that are capable of being answered given the practicalities of data collection and analysis.

If one conducts an analysis of the questions that have been investigated over the last thirty years in the field of language education, one can see that the issue of what questions are worth asking is loaded with value judgements and assumptions about the nature of language and the language learning process. The questions that investigators have considered worth asking have, therefore, changed over time. At one time, foreign language teaching research was dominated by the so-called 'methods comparison studies' which were intended to settle debates over the relative superiority of competing classroom methods. These studies were costly and largely inconclusive, and did little to advance the cause of empiricism in the field (Ellis, 1995; Ritchie and Bhatia, 1996).

Within **SECOND LANGUAGE ACQUISITION** research, a distinction is drawn between research which investigates informal language acquisition in naturalistic environments, and that which looks at acquisition in tutored environments. Key questions posed by researchers working within second language acquisition include:

- Is learning a second language like learning a first? (Dulay and Burt, 1974a, 1974b).
- Is there a distinction between conscious learning

and subconscious acquisition? (Krashen, 1981, 1982).

- Why do some learners fail to acquire a second language successfully? (Schumann, 1978).
- How can we account for variation, (a) between learners and (b) within learners? (Labov, 1970, 1972; Ellis, 1985).
- What modes of classroom organisation, task types and input facilitate second language development? (Swain, 1997).

An analysis and review of research into these questions is provided in Nunan, 1996a.

## Data collection

The most commonly employed means of collecting data in language teaching are through observation, elicitation devices of various kinds including tests, questionnaires and interviews, and introspection. Each of these methods is more suited to the investigation of certain questions rather than others, and each has its own strength and weakness.

### *Observation*

Observation is employed in a wide range of language research into both instructed and naturalistic settings. Longitudinal case studies of children acquiring their first and second languages employ both observation and elicitation (see p. 518). It is now generally accepted that studies of language learning in instructed settings also need to employ an observational dimension, even when the study involves a formal experiment, because, without such observation, the quantitative data is often uninterpretable (Spada, 1990).

Observation is a basic data collection technique in ethnographic research, in which the researcher takes great pains not to intrude into or influence the behaviour of the individuals under study. However, observation, while the most 'natural' form of data collection, has several weaknesses. In the first place, it is an open question as to whether it is at all possible to obtain data through observation that have not been influenced in some way, either by the presence of the observer, or by the data collection procedures themselves. The

sociolinguist Labov has spoken of the 'observer's paradox', pointing out that the aim of much research is to find out how people behave when they are not being systematically observed, but that such data can only be obtained through systematic observation (Labov, 1972). Another weakness of observation is that the behaviour under investigation may not occur very frequently, thus necessitating many hours of data collection on the part of the observer.

In collecting observational data, the researcher is confronted with the issue of whether or not to engage in focused or unfocused observation. In unfocused observation, a type most often favoured by ethnographers, the researcher attempts to record everything that he or she observes, on the grounds that in limiting the focus of the observation the researcher might exclude potentially important or significant phenomena from later analysis. Unfocused observation can yield huge amounts of data which may be extremely difficult to quantify, and in which it is difficult to determine patterns and relationships. In recent years computer programs such as NUD.IST have begun to appear which were designed to assist in sorting and analysing large quantities of qualitative data. (NUD.IST enables the researcher to tag large quantities of text. The program then sorts and identifies patterns in the data.)

In focused observation the focus of attention is deliberately limited to prespecified phenomena. Such observations are generally conducted using observation checklists of various kinds which quantify the phenomena of interest. Observation checklists are particularly popular in classroom-based research, and in the last twenty years, over thirty such schemes have been developed and applied in language teaching and learning research. The first of these schemes were comparatively crude, with relatively few categories. More recently, they have become much more sophisticated, to the point where some require considerable training to use. The COLT (Communicative Orientation of Language Teaching) scheme, for example, deploys eighty-four different categories. (For further description and analysis of observation in language research, see Allwright, 1988; Spada and Frohlich, 1995.)

## Elicitation

Elicitation is a blanket term referring to a range of procedures for obtaining speech samples and other data from subjects. Devices include production tasks and standardised tests, interviews, surveys and questionnaires, and simulations and role-plays. A survey conducted some years ago revealed that elicitation was the most common of all the techniques used in language research (Nunan, 1991). The value of elicitation over straight observation is that it can yield large amounts of target language data in a relatively short space of time. This is a great advantage for researchers who are looking for the appearance of particular linguistic items that may occur only rarely in natural data.

Production tasks are used in research as an alternative to observation when the research wants to elicit target language items such as particular morphemes or grammatical structures. Such tasks became popular in the 1970s when researchers were interested in comparing the ACQUISITION of certain grammatical items in naturalistic and instructed settings. The aim of the research was to document the order in which these items appeared, and to study the effect of instruction and first language background on the order of acquisition. A device was developed called the Bilingual Syntax Measure. This consisted of a series of cartoon-like drawings which were designed to elicit the structures of interest to the researchers (Dulay and Burt, 1974b). There are two dangers in using devices such as this without collecting comparison data from other sources such as observation. First, because the researcher has determined the items of interest in advance, other potentially important items and phenomena might be overlooked; and second, the results obtained might be artefacts of the devices themselves (Ellis, 1985; Nunan, 1987). Some years later, Pienemann (1989) used a more sophisticated research methodology and also uncovered developmental stages in second language acquisition. He also proposed an explanatory model for these stages.

## Introspection

Introspection is the process of 'observing and reflecting on one's thoughts, feelings, motives,

reasoning processes and mental states with a view to determining the ways in which these processes and states determine or influence behaviour' (Nunan, 1992: 231). Introspection is widely employed in language research because it enables the researcher to obtain insights into aspects of language development that are otherwise unobservable. In research into teacher behaviour it has been used to obtain data on the relationships between teachers' belief systems and their classroom behaviour. Probably the most common type of introspective method is that involving the keeping of diaries, logs or journals. A diary study is 'a first-person account of a language learning or teaching experience, documented through regular, candid entries in a personal journal and then analysed for recurring patterns or salient events' (Bailey, 1990: 215). Such studies have been used to investigate second language acquisition (Schmidt and Frota, 1986), teacher–learner interaction (Nunan, 1996b), TEACHER EDUCATION (Bailey, 1990) and numerous other aspects of language teaching and learning. The major weakness of the technique is that it is virtually impossible to establish whether the verbal or written reports resulting from introspection accurately reflect the cognitive processes underlying the behaviour of interest. Despite this, there is little doubt that introspective techniques will continue to be employed in research that seeks to understand the relationships between behaviour and thought, because there is simply no other way at present of obtaining such data. (For further information, see Faerch and Kasper, 1987.)

## Data analysis

As already indicated, research data can be either quantitative or qualitative. Quantitative data is concerned with numbers, while qualitative data is concerned with meanings (Dey, 1993). In the initial section of this entry, we saw that experimental research can include qualitative as well as quantitative data. We also saw that naturalistic research can include quantitative as well as qualitative data. All qualitative data can, in fact, be quantified. When classroom researchers create observational checklists, and then check off and count the number of questions that are asked by the teacher, or the number of unsolicited bids by students, they are, in effect, quantifying qualitative data. The advantage of this quantification is that numbers are easier to manipulate, to group and to compare than meanings. It is easier to see patterns in numbers. And, of course, if one wants to compare two or more groups for making statistical inferences, then numbers are essential.

In many areas of language research, the researcher wants to work directly with the raw data. It is impossible to do morphological, syntactic or **DISCOURSE ANALYSIS** on sets of numbers, although it is possible, and sometimes desirable at some stage in the research process, to quantify the data one is working with. For example, one current line of research in instructed second language acquisition is investigating the relationship between instructional tasks and the negotiation of meaning. Data are collected from second language learners as they perform different types of task, the interactions are transcribed, and the researcher analyses the transcripts for instances of negotiation (where speakers and hearers check comprehension and request clarification to ensure that they are interpreting correctly and being interpreted accurately). Having identified instances of negotiation, the research can count these, and compare them across different task types to determine which types of task generate the greatest amount of negotiation.

Classroom transcripts and transcripts of naturally occurring conversations generate huge amounts of data, sometimes running to hundreds of pages. As already indicated, the large quantities of data can be difficult to analyse and quantify. However, there is also a line of research that carries out intensive analyses of relatively small samples of speech. This type of conversational analysis is known as ethnomethodology and ethnomethodologists can analyse two or three interactional turns, and their results sometimes run to many pages. The aim of ethnomethodology is to account for the ways in which mutual intelligibility is achieved in conversation. (For an introduction to this type of research, see Atkinson and Heritage, 1984.)

**See also:** Action research; Applied linguistics; Assessment and testing; Classroom observation schemes; Classroom research; Discourse analysis;

Evaluation; *Linguistique appliquée*; Reliability; *Sprachlehrforschung*; Validity

## References

Allwright, D. (1988) *Observation in the language classroom*, London: Longman.

Atkinson, J.M. and Heritage, J. (eds) (1984) *Structures of social action: studies in conversational analysis*, Cambridge: Cambridge University Press.

Bailey, K. (1990) 'The use of diary studies in teacher education programs', in J.C. Richards and D. Nunan (eds), *Second language teacher education*, Cambridge: Cambridge University Press.

Dey, I. (1993) *Qualitative data analysis*, London: Routledge.

Dulay, H. and Burt, M. (1974a) 'Natural sequences in child second language acquisition', *Language Learning* 24, 37–53.

Dulay, H. and Burt, M. (1974b) 'A new perspective on the creative construction process in child second language acquisition', *Language Learning* 24, 253–78.

Ellis, R. (1985) *Understanding second language acquisition*, Oxford: Oxford University Press.

Ellis, R. (1995) *The study of second language acquisition*, Oxford: Oxford University Press.

Faerch, C. and Kasper, G. (eds) (1987) *Introspection in second language research*, Clevedon: Multilingual Matters.

Grotjahn, R. (1987) 'On the methodological basis of introspective methods', in C. Faerch and G. Kasper (eds), *Introspection in second language research*, Clevedon: Multilingual Matters.

Hatch, E. and Farhady, H. (1982) *Research design and statistics for applied linguistics*, Rowley, MA: Newbury House.

Krashen, S. (1981) *Second language acquisition and second language learning*, Oxford: Pergamon.

Krashen, S. (1982) *Principles and practice in second language acquisition*, Oxford: Pergamon.

Labov, W. (1970) 'The study of language in its social context', *Studium Generale* 23, 30–87.

Labov, W. (1972) *Sociolinguistic patterns*, Oxford: Blackwell.

Nunan, D. (1987) 'Methodological issues in research', in D. Nunan (ed.), *Applying second language acquisition research*, Adelaide: National Curriculum Resource Centre.

Nunan, D. (1991) 'Methods in second language classroom oriented research', *Studies in Second Language Acquisition* 13, 2, 249–74.

Nunan, D. (1992) *Research methods in language learning*, Cambridge: Cambridge University Press.

Nunan, D. (1996a) 'Issues in second language acquisition research: examining substance and procedure', in W. Ritchie and T. Bhatia (eds), *Handbook of second language acquisition*, San Diego: Academic Press.

Nunan, D. (1996b) 'Hidden voices: insiders' perspectives on classroom interaction', in K. Bailey and D. Nunan (eds), *Voices from the language classroom*, Cambridge: Cambridge University Press.

Pienemann, M. (1989) 'Is language teachable?', *Applied Linguistics* 10, 1, 52–79.

Ritchie, W. and Bhatia, T. (eds) (1996) *Handbook of second language acquisition*, San Diego: Academic Press.

Schmidt, R. and Frota, S. (1986) 'Developing basic conversational ability in a second language: a case study of an adult learner of Portuguese', in R. Day (ed.), *Talking to learn: conversation in second language acquisition*, Rowley, MA: Newbury House.

Schumann, J. (1978) 'The acculturation model for second language acquisition', in R. Gingras (ed.), *Second language acquisition and foreign language teaching*, Arlington, VA: Center for Applied Linguistics.

Spada, N. (1990) 'Observing classroom behaviors and learning outcomes in different second language programs', in J.C. Richards and D. Nunan (eds), *Second language teacher education*, Cambridge: Cambridge University Press.

Spada, N. and Frohlich, M. (1995) *Communicative orientation of language teaching observation scheme: coding conventions and applications*, Sydney: National Centre for English Language Teaching and Research.

Swain, M. (1997) 'The output hypothesis, focus on form and second language learning', in V. Berry, B. Adamson and W. Littlewood (eds), *Applying linguistics*, Hong Kong: University of Hong Kong English Centre.

van Lier, L. (1988) *The classroom and the language learner: ethnography and second language classroom research*, London: Longman.

**Further reading**

Bailey, K. and Nunan, D. (eds) (1996) *Voices from the language classroom: qualitative research in second language education*, Cambridge: Cambridge University Press.

Freeman, D. (1998) *Teacher research*, Boston: Heinle and Heinle

Nunan, D. (1992) *Research methods in language learning*, Cambridge: Cambridge University Press.

DAVID NUNAN

# Rivers, Wilga Marie

b. 1919, Melbourne, Australia

Applied linguist, language and curriculum coordinator, educationist

Wilga Rivers became internationally recognised as a leader in the theory and practice of language teaching with the publication of *The Psychologist and the Foreign-Language Teacher* (1964). In this seminal work she turned away from the behaviourist model of language learning that underpinned the **AUDIO-LINGUAL METHOD** and showed how research in psycholinguistics could shape understanding of the processes of second language acquisition and guide classroom practice. In subsequent works, Rivers remained abreast of research in **LINGUISTICS**, **PSYCHOLOGY** and related fields to explore and explain this relationship.

Rivers began her career in language teaching in **AUSTRALIA**, where she taught **FRENCH** at the Melbourne Church of England Girls' Grammar School before leaving to work on her doctorate at the University of Illinois in Urbana-Champaign. In 1971 she was named language coordinator and teacher trainer at the University of Illinois. In 1973 she became Coordinator of Language Instruction in the Romance Languages at Harvard University, remaining there until her retirement in 1989.

Rivers's wide interests led to a broad range of professional activities. She served on bibliography and long-range **PLANNING** committees of the

Modern Language Association, the Linguistic Society of America, and the American Council on the Teaching of Foreign Languages, and on the Advisory Councils of the National Foreign Language Center (Washington, DC) and the Language Acquisition Resource Center (San Diego). She was Charter President of the American Association of Applied Linguistics and on the founding executive council of the American Association of University Supervisors and Coordinators of Language Programs.

In her 'Ten Principles of Interactive Language Teaching' (1991), Rivers presented the elements she believed essential to effective language learning and teaching in a communicative classroom, and succinctly defined her understanding of the necessary interaction between teaching and learning. This article underscored her lifelong commitment to encouraging language teachers to focus on the learner, to develop and use their own creativity, and to recognise the importance of taking a **HUMANISTIC** and humane approach to foreign language teaching.

Wilga Rivers brought to the international foreign language teaching community a heightened awareness of its role and a deep belief in the excitement of teaching languages. With clarity, intelligence and remarkable common sense, she helped language teachers gain an intellectual understanding and appreciation for their field and its complexities. Equally important, she taught that, while there is a common core to retain in the theory and practice of language teaching, each generation finds its own path to maintain the vitality of the foreign language classroom.

## Bibliography

Rivers, W.M. (1964) *The psychologist and the foreign-language teacher*, Chicago: University of Chicago Press.

Rivers, W.M. (1968) *Teaching foreign-language skills*, Chicago: University of Chicago Press.

Rivers, W.M. (1983) *Communicating naturally in a second language: theory and practice in language teaching*, Cambridge: Cambridge University Press.

Rivers, W.M. (1983) *Speaking in many tongues: essays in foreign-language teaching* (3rd edn), Cambridge: Cambridge University Press.

Rivers, W.M. (ed.) (1991) *Teaching languages in college: curriculum and content*, Lincolnwood, IL: National Textbook Company.

BERNICE MELVIN

# S

## Sapir–Whorf Hypothesis

The Sapir–Whorf Hypothesis (SWH) is particularly relevant in the discussion of linguistic relativity. It claims, in essence, that a language selects and isolates certain aspects of the 'kaleidoscopic flux of impressions' and thus structures reality for us. The following quotation from Edward Sapir (1884–1939) illustrates this assumption: 'Human beings do not live in the objective world alone, nor alone in the world of social activity as ordinarily understood, but are very much at the mercy of the particular language which has become the medium of expression for their society. It is quite an illusion to imagine that one adjusts to reality essentially without the use of language and that language is merely an incidental means of solving specific problems of communication or reflection' (Sapir, 1963: 162). Benjamin Lee Whorf (1897–1941), who was Sapir's student, found this concept of linguistic relativity confirmed when he studied Hopi and discovered that the grammatical categories of Hopi and those of European languages select and highlight different aspects of reality. From this insight he drew the conclusion that each language embodies a different world view:

> We dissect nature along lines laid down by our native languages. The categories and types that we isolate from the world of phenomena we do not find there because they stare every observer in the face; on the contrary, the world is presented in a kaleidoscopic flux of impressions which has to be organized by our minds – and

this means largely by the linguistic systems in our minds.

(Whorf, 1956: 213)

From the interpretations of Sapir's and Whorf's writings a strong and weak version of linguistic relativity was developed. The strong version says that we are imprisoned in our language and can only think what our language allows us to think. This claim was vigorously debated in various disciplines from **LINGUISTICS** to philosophy and **PSYCHOLOGY**. The philosopher Elmar Holenstein severely criticises the strong version of the SWH and uses the following example to refute it. When, for example, a language such as **CHINESE** does not possess the second conditional – 'If I had wings, I could fly' – the conclusion, according to the strong version, is that the Chinese are not capable of imagining unreal situations. Holenstein argues against this linguistic determinism and relativism by pointing out that one's linguistic competence not only makes it possible to say something in certain ways but also enables one to express the same thing by using metalinguistic and non-linguistic means (Holenstein, 1989: 44).

According to the strong version, language does not reflect reality but produces it. The weak version accepts the view that language is not a transparent window to reality but stresses that language itself is influenced by our natural, social and cultural environment. Language and reality are interdependent. This implies that reality is also reflected in the language. In her autobiography *Lost in Translation*, Eva Hoffman shows how in the North American context the terms 'friendship', 'kindness' and 'silliness' differ in meaning from their Polish equivalents and point to different world views. Therefore she is 'lost in translation' after her arrival in North America, but finally she is able to live in both worlds and can translate between them. The pedagogical implication of the weak version of the SWH for foreign language learning is that it is possible to understand different world views and become aware of one's own. Language shapes how we perceive the world, but we are not imprisoned by it.

The question of linguistic relativity also plays an important role in the debate about postcolonial literature. According to the strong version of the SWH, post-colonial authors should not write in colonial languages because they would otherwise take over the world view of the imperialists and betray their own. However, post-colonial authors who write in colonial languages stress that a language can embody many world views and that one can make the foreign language one's own. Chinua Achebe says about writing in English: 'And let no one be fooled by the fact we may write in English for we intend to do unheard things with it' (1975: 7). According to the weaker form of the SWH, there is a mutual dependence between biological, social and linguistic reality.

Sapir and Whorf stressed linguistic relativity in order to understand every language on its own terms and to respect the world view inherent in each. Sapir wrote: 'Many primitive languages have a formal richness, a latent luxuriance of expression, that eclipses anything known to the languages of modern civilization' (Sapir, 1921: 22). Whorf goes on to argue that we can only appreciate the achievements of each language when we transcend the language and look at it from the outside: 'The situation is somewhat analogous to that of not missing the water till the well runs dry, or not realizing that we need air till we are choking' (Whorf, 1956: 209). Hence translations are important. They defamiliarise the familiar: 'It was to me almost as enlightening to see English from the entirely new angle necessitated in order to translate it into Hopi as it was to discover the meanings of the Hopi forms themselves' (Whorf, 1956: 112f.).

These considerations can illustrate the relationship between relativism and universalism in the SWH. On the one hand Sapir and Whorf stress the relativity of languages: we must see them from within and not judge them from the outside. On the other hand, however, we can only appreciate their achievements when we transcend our own language and understand what different languages have in common. Whorf especially is interested in the basic structures of perception and thinking which all human beings share: 'My own studies suggest, to me, that language, for all its kingly role, is in some sense a superficial embroidery upon deeper processes of consciousness ...' (Whorf, 1956: 239). For Whorf it is 'a great fact of human brotherhood' that all human beings have an 'intellectual mind' which can 'systematize and mathematize on a scale and scope that no mathematician of the schools ever remotely approached' (Whorf, 1956: 257).

According to the SWH, learning and studying foreign languages does not only have an instrumental goal but also an important educational one. It can make us aware of the constraints of our language and world view and allows us to see what we have in common with other forms of speaking and thinking on deeper levels.

**See also:** Acculturation; *Civilisation*; Cultural studies; Intercultural competence; *Landeskunde*; Strategic competence; Teacher thinking; Translation theory

**References**

Achebe, C. (1975) *Morning yet on creation day*, London: Heinemann.

Holenstein, E. (1989) 'Europa und die Menschheit. Zu Husserls kulturphilosophischen Meditationen (Europe and mankind. About Husserl's reflections on culture)', in C. Janne and O. Pöggeler (eds), *Phänomenologie im Widerstreit. Zum 50. Todestag Edmund Husserls*, Frankfurt/M.: Suhrkamp.

Sapir, E. (1921) *Language. An introduction to the study of speech*, New York: Harcourt, Brace and World.

Sapir, E. (1963) *Selected writings of Edward Sapir in language, culture and personality* (edited by David G. Mandelbaum), Berkeley: University of California Press.

Whorf, B.L. (1956) *Language, thought, and reality:*

*selected writings of Benjamin Lee Whorf* (edited by John B. Carroll), Cambridge, MA: MIT Press.

### Further reading

Gumperz, J. and Levinson, S.C. (1996) *Rethinking linguistic relativity*, Cambridge: Cambridge University Press.

Lee, P. (1996) *The Whorf complex theory: a critical reconstruction*, Amsterdam and Philadelphia: John Benjamins.

Lehmann, B. (1998) *ROT ist nicht > rot < ist nicht [rot]. Eine Bilanz und Neuinterpretation der linguistischen Relativitätstheorie (RED is not > red < is not [red]. A history and new interpretation of linguistic relativity*, Tübingen: Gunter Narr.

LOTHAR BREDELLA AND ANNETTE RICHTER

## Saussure, Ferdinand de

b. 26 November 1857, Geneva, Switzerland; d. 22 February 1913, Geneva, Switzerland

1881–1891: teacher at the École des Hautes Études in Paris, then Professor of Linguistics at the University of Geneva

Above all, Saussure was a scholar of Indoeuropean languages and comparative philology. His fame, however, rests mainly on lecture courses pertaining to general **LINGUISTICS** given in 1907, 1908–09 and 1910–11 which were posthumously published from students' notes by C. Bally and A. Sechehaye under the title of *Cours de linguistique générale* (1916). This book made him the founder of the Geneva School of Linguistics, from where linguistic structuralism (and structuralism in other disciplines, e.g. **ANTHROPOLOGY**) originated and spread all over the world. More material pertaining to the *Cours* was published between 1957 and 1974.

Much of Saussure's seminal influence on linguistics stems from his dichotomic terminology. At a time when, for many linguists, historical studies were the only ones which could claim a scientific character, he defined synchronic versus diachronic linguistics each in its own right. For

Saussure, diachronic linguistics is devoted to phenomena in temporal succession which are not systematic in relation to each other and which the people of a speech community are not aware of collectively (i.e. language evolution and change). Synchronic linguistics is devoted to phenomena at a given point in time which are systematic in relation to each other and which the people of a speech community are collectively aware of (i.e. meaning, function and **GRAMMAR**). These phenomena are acoustic signs, as a rule without any natural relation to their meanings, i.e. they are arbitrary and accepted by convention. The signalling property of sounds (*signifiant*) as well as the signified section of reality (*signifié*) are constituted in the brains of speakers. This is probably the most revolutionary of Saussure's innovations. It does away with the idea that linguistic signs (words as names) are attached to objects of reality like labels. It makes the relation of *signifiant* and *signifié* a mental process. In the sign (*signe*) they belong to each other like the two sides of a coin.

The systematic character of linguistic phenomena is the real objective of linguistics. Saussure's comparison of linguistics with chess is famous as a means of explaining the systematic nature of language. In the same way in which the system of rules, represented in each figure, constitutes the game of chess, irrespective of for example the substance of the figures, the system of linguistic regularities constitutes language, irrespective of the substance of signs. The organisation of signs in this system becomes effective not by virtue of what they assert but by their difference from each other. The meaning of a word is defined by the meanings of its near-synonyms, and a syntactic structure, e.g. the present, functions by its difference to another syntactic structure, e.g. the past. The value (*valeur*) of each sign and each regular combination of signs (structure) is, thus, something positive, but the system as a whole comes into being only by differences, i.e. negatively. In order to understand an individual linguistic phenomenon one must understand other phenomena, and eventually even the whole.

These axiomatic statements on language and linguistics (and others pertaining to **LANGUE AND PAROLE**) have become the common property of **STRUCTURAL LINGUISTICS**. It had (and still has) a tremendous significance also for the theory of language teaching and its methodology, probably because many of its basic statements conform with observations to be made and difficulties to be encountered in the classroom. Teachers learn that their daily experience is of a scientifically valid nature: In language teaching historical information is of a different kind from information about current usage, information on the former is not useless but contributes something different to language teaching than information on the latter. The arbitrary nature of signs of a foreign language causes difficulties in relation to the first language of the learners, because any succeeding language remains foreign as compared to the first one. The way into a foreign language is didactically so difficult because definitions and explanations of rules always presuppose the knowledge of other rules, and so *ad infinitum*. The characterisation of such observations in terms of structural linguistics is purely descriptive, not explanatory. This may have the consequence that, after all, linguistic concepts do not help much to overcome the difficulties of daily practice. Indeed, the support that structural linguistics can give to the teaching of languages has for some time been overestimated. But at least it gives foreign language teachers the security that their activities are grounded in the basic observations of an undisputed academic discipline.

## Further reading

Amacker, R. and Engler, R. (eds) (1990) *Présence de Saussure*, Geneva: Dros.

Engler, R. (1975) 'European structuralism: Saussure', in T.A. Sebeok (ed.), *Common trends in linguistics*, vol. 13: *Historiography of linguistics*, The Hague: Mouton.

WERNER HÜLLEN

# Schema and script theory

Schema theory (also known as script theory) is a theory of the organisation of background knowledge in long-term memory and of its use in comprehension. Schemata are knowledge structures which contain generic information about aspects of the world, such as different types of objects, people, situations and texts. They arise from repeated exposure to similar experiences, and are used to make sense of new instances of such experiences. According to schema theory, comprehension involves an interaction between the (textual) input and the comprehender's existing knowledge, and successful understanding depends on the availability and activation of relevant schemata. Different responses to the same text or difficulties in comprehension can be related to variation in the range and content of the schemata different individuals possess, due to different life experiences or cultural backgrounds (Eysenck and Keane, 1995: 261ff.).

## Schemata in comprehension

The term 'schema' is widely accepted as the most general term for a generic knowledge structure in memory. Other terms, such as 'script', 'frame' or 'scenario', are sometimes used as alternatives to schema, or to refer to particular types of schemata. A schema is a structured bundle of knowledge, which consists of a set of slots and a set of relations. For example, a 'flight' schema will have slots for passenger/s, airline, place of departure, destination, etc., and will contain information about the relations that exist between the entities that correspond to different slots. When a schema is instantiated, i.e. applied to a particular experience, the slots will receive specific values (e.g. the destination slot may be filled in with the value 'Paris'). Slots carry constraints on what values can fill them (e.g. the captain of the aircraft has to be human) and are filled in by default values if no specific information is provided by the input (e.g. if food is mentioned, one will assume it was brought by cabin staff even if they are not explicitly referred to). Schemata can be embedded inside other schemata in a hierarchical structure (e.g. 'checking-in' is a sub-schema which is part of the 'flight' schema).

Schemata perform a range of functions in comprehension. Consider the following text:

I will never fly with that new airline again. They only had one check-in desk, so we were delayed. When I got on board, I had so little leg-room that I got backache. And when we finally arrived I discovered that my bags were missing!

The application of a 'flight' schema enables comprehenders

1  to disambiguate potentially ambiguous lexical items (e.g. deciding that here 'checking-in' involves showing tickets/passports and passing over luggage);
2  to infer implicit information (e.g. that the insufficient leg-room relates to the space between the seats of the aircraft);
3  to make predictions about what will happen next (e.g. that the missing bags will probably be returned).

All this is crucial for the perception of the text as coherent.

## Acquisition of schemata

Although it is generally claimed that schemata are formed by extracting common patterns from repeated experiences and that they need to be progressively updated, relatively little is known about the process of schema acquisition and change. A rare attempt to account for various types of learning from a schema theory perspective is provided by Rumelhart and Norman (1981). They envisage three different ways in which schemata may develop and change in the light of new experiences: accretion, tuning and restructuring. Accretion occurs when an existing schema can adequately account for a new instance of a familiar experience, so that the new experience simply reinforces the schema. Tuning occurs when a new experience causes a change in the values that can fill the slots of an existing schema or in what can count as default elements (e.g. after experiencing new low-price airlines, my 'flight' schema no longer includes fixed seat allocation and a 'free' meal as default elements). Restructuring occurs when new schemata are created, either by forming a totally new schema from experience, or by modelling a new schema on an old one.

## History

The notion of schema as a mental structure has

been traced back as far as Kant, and can be found in the work of the Gestalt psychologists during the 1920s. However, the birth of schema theory itself is usually identified in the work of the cognitive psychologist Bartlett (1932). Bartlett conducted a series of experiments which showed that comprehension and memory are largely shaped by people's existing knowledge and expectations. This persuaded him that new experiences are not stored separately in memory, but are assimilated to similar earlier experiences in generic structures which he referred to as 'schemata' (a term he borrowed from the neurophysiologist Henry Head). In the forty years that followed the publications of his findings, Bartlett's contribution was largely ignored, due to the dominance of **BEHAVIOURISM** and psychoanalysis. The 1970s, however, saw a resurgence of interest in the notion of schema, particularly due to the growth of Artificial Intelligence and the adoption of the computer as a **METAPHOR** for the mind in cognitive **PSYCHOLOGY**. During this period, some of the best-known versions of schema theory were developed. In his work on visual perception, Minsky (1975) introduced the notion of 'frame' to refer to knowledge relating to settings and visual scenes, such as different types of rooms. Schank and Abelson (1977) proposed a typology of schemata centring on the notion of 'script', a knowledge structure which relates to sequences of actions and events in everyday experiences. Their account of the roles, objects and actions which make up the 'restaurant' script is the best-known and most frequently cited exemplification of how a particular schema might be structured. Subsequently, Schank (1982) proposed a new, more dynamic version of schema theory, which tried to account more successfully for the flexible way in which background knowledge is used and adapted in everyday life.

## Critique

Although a wide range of empirical evidence has been provided for the existence of schema-type structures in memory, schema theory has often been criticised for being unprincipled and unconstrained (e.g. Eysenck and Keane, 1995: 264–5, 268–9). In attempting to deal with something as vast and varied as human knowledge in memory, schema theorists tend to be rather vague as to what can count as a schema, what exactly is contained within each schema, and how different schemata relate to each other. As a consequence, schema theory is ideal in providing *post hoc* explanations for specific findings, but has relatively little predictive power. The psychological reality of schemata as separate 'chunks' in memory has also been questioned. In particular, cognitive psychologists working within connectionist models of memory have suggested that knowledge is not stored in high-order complex chunks (e.g. the schema for kitchen), but in networks of interconnected units corresponding to low-level concepts (e.g. kitchen table, bread bin, coffee pot). Within this framework, schemata do not exist as separate entities but correspond to groups of units in knowledge networks which tend to be activated at the same time (e.g. the 'schema' for kitchen arises when needed from the simultaneous activation of the units corresponding to kitchen table, bread bin, coffee pot, etc.) (McClelland *et al.*, 1986).

In spite of these problems, schema theory has been successfully applied in a wide range of areas, including **ANTHROPOLOGY**, semantics, language **ACQUISITION**, **NEUROLINGUISTICS** and the analysis of **LITERARY TEXTS**. It has also been influential in work on **READING** comprehension and in the areas of second and foreign language teaching. Its appeal for those working in education lies in the fact that it provides a user-friendly framework within which to study the interaction between texts and readers, and within which to explain how differences in available background knowledge can result in differences and/or failures in comprehension.

**See also:** Acculturation; Intercultural communication; Intercultural training; Literary texts; Literary theory and literature teaching; Politeness; Reading; Reading methods; Sapir–Whorf Hypothesis

**References**

Bartlett, F.C. (1932) *Remembering: a study in experimental and social psychology*, Cambridge: Cambridge University Press.

Eysenck, M.W. and Keane, M.T. (1995) *Cognitive psychology: a student's handbook*, Hove: Erlbaum (UK), Taylor and Francis.

McClelland, J.L., Rumelhart, D.E. and the PDP Research Group (eds) (1986) *Parallel distributed processing: explorations in the microstructure of cognition*, vol. 2, Cambridge, MA: MIT Press.

Minsky, M. (1975) 'A framework for representing knowledge', in P.E. Winston (ed.), *The psychology of computer vision*, New York: McGraw-Hill.

Rumelhart, D.E. and Norman, D.A. (1981) 'Analogical processes in learning', in J.R. Anderson (ed.), *Cognitive skills and their acquisition*, Hillsdale, NJ: Lawrence Erlbaum.

Schank, R.C. (1982) *Dynamic memory: a theory of reminding and learning in computers and people*, Cambridge: Cambridge University Press.

Schank, R.C. and Abelson, R. (1977) *Scripts, plans, goals and understanding*, Hillsdale, NJ: Lawrence Erlbaum.

**Further reading**

Anderson, R.C. and Pearson, P.D. (1988) 'A schema-theoretic view of basic processes in reading comprehension', in P.L. Carrel, J. Devine and D. Eskey (eds), *Interactive approaches to second language reading*, Cambridge: Cambridge University Press.

Carrel, P.L. and Eisterhold, J.C. (1988) 'Schema theory and ESL pedagogy', in P.L. Carrel, J. Devine, and D. Eskey (eds) *Interactive Approaches to Second Language Reading*, Cambridge: Cambridge University Press.

Clapham, C.M. (1997) *The development of IELTS: a study of the effect of background knowledge on reading comprehension*, Cambridge: Cambridge University Press.

ELENA SEMINO

# Second language acquisition theories

Second language acquisition is a field of study which generates and tests theories concerning the acquisition of languages other than L1 in many different contexts, including – but not mainly – the foreign language classroom. Theories have a variety of origins and are of different kinds. They need to be evaluated.

While theories in a field differ substantively and in many other ways, at some level they are all *interim understandings* of how something works – in the case of SLA theories, interim understandings of how people learn second languages. Just as any understanding of how the human body works is likely to be relevant to medical practice at some level, so any theory of SLA is likely to be at least indirectly relevant to language teaching practice, in that SLA is the process language teaching is designed to facilitate.

## How SLA theories differ

SLA is a broad, expanding and diverse field. It encompasses, at the very least, the simultaneous and sequential learning and loss of second (third, fourth, etc.) languages and dialects, by children and adults, with differing **MOTIVATIONS**, abilities and purposes, as individuals or whole communities, with varying access to the L2, in formal, informal and mixed, foreign, second, and **LINGUA FRANCA** settings. By some accounts, and depending on what one counts, the literature offers as many as sixty theories, models, hypotheses and theoretical frameworks. These terms are often used non-technically in the literature (for a review, see Crookes, 1992) and, for reasons of space, in much of this article. Some view this situation as one of healthy, even inevitable, theoretical pluralism, others as indicative of pre-scientific chaos likely to obstruct progress as long as it lasts.

### Source

The first way in which SLA theories differ is by *source*, i.e., in their (primary) origins inside and/or outside the field. A number of theories have emerged, at least in part, from empirical research findings on second language learning. Examples include the ZIZA Group's Multidimensional Model (Meisel, Clahsen and Pienemann, 1981), Krashen's **MONITOR** Theory (Krashen, 1985), Schumann's **ACCULTURATION** Model (Schumann, 1986), Cummins's Linguistic Interdependence Hypothesis for bilingual proficiency (Cummins, 1991), and Ellis's Integrated Theory of Instructed

Second Language Acquisition (Ellis, 1990). Other theories have been imported ready-made from related areas of cognitive science, notably from **LINGUISTICS** and **PSYCHOLOGY**. Linguistic models tested as theories of SLA, or as parts of those theories, include Chomsky's and others' theories of **UNIVERSAL GRAMMAR** (e.g. White, 1996), Bickerton's Bioprogram Hypothesis (e.g. Huebner, 1983), Givon's Functional-Typological Model (e.g. Sato, 1990), O'Grady's general nativist theory (e.g. Wolfe-Quintero, 1992), and Bresnan's Lexical-Functional Grammar (e.g. Pienemann, 1998). Work introduced from psychology includes Giles's Accommodation Theory (e.g. Beebe and Giles, 1984), Bates and MacWhinney's Competition Model (e.g. Kilborn and Ito, 1989), several models based on Anderson's and others' distinction between declarative and procedural knowledge (e.g., Johnson, 1996), and various connectionist models (e.g. Gasser, 1990).

### Domain or scope

Theories also differ with respect to *domain*, or *scope*, i.e. as to what they purport to explain, or their 'coverage'. Most nativist theories, for example, focus primarily, or thus far even exclusively, on syntax and morphology, and at the level of form only, whereas some theories (e.g. Bates and MacWhinney, 1989; Givon, 1979) attempt to account for the acquisition of all levels of language and attribute a major role to communicative function in driving language acquisition. The acquisition type and context of interest – naturalistic or instructed, foreign or second, individual or community, etc. – also varies. The primary focus of Schumann's **ACCULTURATION** Model, for example, is naturalistic acquisition by learners as members of groups. Whereas the Acculturation Model speaks to naturalistic learning only and the domain of Ellis's theory, as its name implies, is the classroom, Krashen's Monitor Theory sets out to handle both naturalistic and instructed acquisition.

### Content

Theories differ with respect to *content*, i.e. in the variables, and kinds of variables, that make up their explanatory core, and at a broader level, the relative importance accorded internal or environmental factors. Theories such as Schumann's Acculturation Model and Gardner's Socio-Educational Model (Gardner, 1988) draw primarily on social and social-psychological variables for their accounts, attempting to predict *that* SLA will or will not occur, and the degree of likely success, mostly as a function of group membership and intra- and inter-group relations. White's Universal grammar-based theory and Eckman's functional-typological approach (Eckman, 1996a), on the other hand, invoke linguistic theory and related findings from studies of child language acquisition, first attempting to predict *how* acquisition will occur at the level of the individual, not the group, as an internal cognitive process, not a social one, mostly as a function of prior linguistic knowledge and L1–L2 relationships.

## Type

Schumann, Gardner and other theorists focus on SLA as a social process, and draw primarily on situational and social-psychological variables to explain success and failure at the level of whole communities, not just individuals. White, Eckman and others, conversely, emphasise SLA as a mental process, with the individual as the unit of analysis, and rely primarily on different kinds of linguistic theory to account for **INTERLANGUAGE** development. Most of these and many other models fall into one or other of two broad camps: nativist (special, general or hybrid), and empiricist.

- *Special nativist* SLA theories assume continued access by L2 acquirers, including adults, to genetically transmitted abilities specific to language learning – used for that, and nothing else – including innate knowledge of highly abstract syntactic principles and of the parameters along which languages can vary (universal grammar), or of a set of universal semantic distinctions (Bickerton, 1984), which are held to govern child L1A and **ADULT** SLA alike.
- *General nativist* proposals hold that SLA proceeds without universal grammar or any such language-specific innate knowledge and abilities, and is instead accomplished through use of modularised general cognitive mechanisms. In

O'Grady's (1996) formulation, there are five of these: perceptual, propositional, conceptual, computational and learning – innate mechanisms, which suffice *both* for language and other kinds of learning, although possibly supplemented by a few (non-syntactic) concepts used only for language.

- *Hybrid nativist* models (a term coined by Eckman, 1996b), such as those of Clahsen and Muysken (1986) and Bley-Vroman (1990 – his Fundamental Difference Hypothesis), are special nativist for L1 acquisition, usually holding it to be governed by universal grammar, but general nativist for SLA, proceeding via general problem-solving procedures of various kinds.

From a theory-construction point of view, while the success of particular exponents of these three general positions in predicting the facts about child and adult first and second language acquisition will ultimately determine their fate, general nativist theories have the initial advantage of being less 'powerful' than special nativist theories, because they set out to handle the same data without recourse to innate linguistic knowledge. Special nativist and general nativist theories, in turn, are less powerful than hybrid nativist theories, because they attempt to explain the data on both first and second language acquisition using only one set of innate abilities, whether language-specific or not, whereas hybrid theories assume both language-specific knowledge and general learning mechanisms.

In contrast to nativist theories, *empiricist* models are 'data-driven', with linguistic input acting on universal cognitive, not linguistic, mental mechanisms. They include a greater variety of theories than those in the nativist camp, ranging from functionalist linguistic accounts, through social-psychological models, to connectionism. Some empiricist positions are referred to as 'social-interactionist' (e.g. Gass, 1997) or 'cognitive-interactionist' (e.g. Andersen, 1989). Most theorists stress that the environmental factors they consider important interact with internal mental abilities – hence, 'interactionist' theories – and that their views by no means signal a return to behaviourism. In all cases, however, in combination with internal factors, the learners' or learner groups' linguistic *experience* is said to play a stronger determining role in acquisition than anything countenanced by nativists of whatever stripe.

'Experience' can refer to the amount and quality of contact with the target language and its speakers, as in the case of the Acculturation and Socio-Educational Models, and as in several 'skill-building' models of acquisition. The latter are usually based on variants of the idea from general cognitive psychology that learning (in the present context, language learning) is chiefly a matter of converting declarative knowledge (knowledge that) into procedural knowledge (knowledge how) through a process of automatisation (for a review, see Johnston, 1996: 77–151).

To illustrate, Hatch *et al.* (1986) claim that all linguistic knowledge (phonological, morphological, syntactic, semantic, pragmatic, etc.) can be accounted for in terms of the interaction of cognitive, social and linguistic systems, that 'language clarifies and organizes experience and, conversely, that language grows out of experience' (1986: 5). Elsewhere, following several child language acquisition researchers, Hatch had claimed that 'language learning evolves *out of* learning how to carry on conversations' (1978: 404), although she suspected that the process might not work as well for certain aspects of a new language. These hypotheses were borne out by the results of a longitudinal study (Sato, 1986, 1988, 1990) of two Vietnamese brothers, aged eight and ten at the beginning of the study, acquiring **ENGLISH** through submersion (not immersion) in state school classrooms in the USA. Sato concluded that conversation was *selectively facilitative* of development, a view since adopted by many social and cognitive-interactionists in SLA (for review, see Gass, 1997; Long, 1996).

While attributing far greater importance to the linguistic environment and to the social context for language acquisition, as noted above, empiricist models also assume considerable cognitive resources on the learner's part, including prior (but not innate) linguistic knowledge. The cognitive component of Andersen's cognitive-interactionist theory of SLA (Andersen, 1989), for example, includes two causal processes, 'nativisation' and 'denativisation', mental mechanisms which function in combination with (to date) twelve operating

principles as part of the learner's mental acquisition apparatus. Nativisation, according to Andersen, denotes 'a composite of (presumably universal) processes' by which, especially when access to the L2 is restricted, as in early stages of SLA or in pidginisation and creolisation, a learner 'creates an internal representation of the [target] language' (1989: 48), often resulting in a system very different from that of the input. Conversely, Andersen claims, where access to linguistic input is unrestricted, as in most advanced SLA, denativisation operates, and learners gradually restructure their initially idiosyncratic internal systems towards the target as a result of processing linguistic input, i.e. towards external, not internal, norms (1989: 49).

As each of these illustrations show, empiricist theories tend to be data-driven in a second sense, i.e. in often (though not always) having originally been derived inductively from empirical findings on interlanguage development. This is in contrast to most (not all) nativist models, which have usually been imported wholesale from outside the field, e.g. from linguistics, and then applied deductively in the design and interpretation of studies. An advantage most empiricist models share, as a result, is that they are often better supported empirically than many nativist models, especially during early stages in their development (which reveals the danger inherent in evaluating rival theories, especially early on, simply in terms of their empirical adequacy). Empiricist models tend to be pitched at a level closer to the data they set out to explain. While increasing the likelihood of their being 'correct', in a superficial sense, at any one time, the lower level of abstraction can also reduce their potential scope, and, hence, their interest.

### Form

SLA theories, like theories in general, also differ in *form*. In some cases, the theorist's interim explanation consists of little more or less than a collection of statements, based on repeated empirical observations of the phenomena of interest, observations that were consistent with *hypotheses* about those phenomena. The statements attempt to capture patterns in the findings, and take the form of *generalisations*. When the findings are repeated often enough, without exceptions, and with a consensus among researchers in the field as to what has been discovered, these generalisations may attain the status of *laws*. This form of theory is known as *set-of-laws* (cf. the law of gravity, or the laws of thermodynamics). There are very few, if any, laws in SLA as yet, but at least one theorist (Spolsky, 1989) has adopted this general approach to SLA theory construction, producing a listing, with brief surveys of supporting empirical findings, of over 100 statements of this kind, generalisations of greater or lesser certainty.

Theories cast in set-of-laws form are useful in that they provide a sort of stocktaking, a handy inventory of what (we think) we know about something. They are also limited. First, the statements they contain are often unrelated, usually having arisen from independent lines of inquiry. Testing any of them must generally be conducted separately. Second, since generalisations and laws started life as hypotheses, and since the hypotheses had to be operationalisable to be empirically testable, they, and the generalisations and laws to which some of them eventually gave rise, could not and cannot contain *constructs*: monitor, nativisation, learnability, teachability, and so on. Set-of-laws form theories stop at description, therefore, rarely providing anything more than implicit *explanations* for the phenomena they concern. Rather than constituting a theory of a process like SLA, theories in set-of-laws form are better seen as storehouses of information, repositories of the widely accepted facts (if facts they be) that an SLA theory needs to explain (Long, 1990). To be satisfactory, an SLA theory should be able to explain *why* younger starters do better, *why* developmental sequences are unaffected by instruction, and so on, not merely capture the observations themselves. To do this, they need to avail themselves of constructs, in the short term at least, and to posit explanatory *mechanisms* of some kind. And it is here that a second form of theory is more successful.

*Causal-process* theories (in some other fields, but not always in SLA, regrettably) contain definitions of their constructs and concepts, with operational definitions of at least some of the latter, existence statements, and deterministic and/or probabilistic causal statements, which are interrelated. Together, they specify how or why SLA will occur, not just

that or when it will. Chomsky's so-called 'Principles and Parameters' theory of the 1980s, as exemplified in the work of White (1996), Schwartz (1992) and others, O'Grady's (1996) and Wolfe-Quintero's (1996) general nativist models, and Pienemann's (1998) Processability Theory, are examples of causal-process theories in SLA.

## The evaluation of theories

Disciplines with much longer histories and far greater accomplishments than SLA have found it necessary to develop ways of evaluating theories, both in absolute terms and comparatively, i.e. relative to other theories. If theories represent researchers' interim understandings of the phenomena they are trying to understand, it follows that identifying faulty understandings, and culling the theories concerned, constitutes progress. Persistence of a plethora of theories, conversely, especially oppositional ones, obstructs progress (Beretta, 1991). Over the past forty years, various evaluation criteria have been formalised and themselves evaluated by philosophers of science (see, e.g., Cushing, 1989; Darden, 1991; Laudan, 1977; 1996; Riggs, 1992) and, while some observers consider it premature, discussions of possible approaches to evaluating SLA theories have begun to appear in the SLA literature.

In absolute terms, theories may be judged inadequate because they are too powerful, *ad hoc*, untestable, say nothing about relevant phenomena, and so on. In relative terms, they may be less adequate than rival theories of the same phenomena because they consistently make less accurate predictions, account for fewer data, require more mechanisms to handle the same data, etc. – and of particular importance, following Laudan (1977), in terms of their comparative ability to solve various kinds of differentially weighted empirical problems. Evaluation criteria which have evolved to achieve one or both of these two general goals include, but are not limited to: empirical adequacy, simplicity/ parsimony, generality, ability to explain phenomena different from those the theory was invented to account for, ability to make surprising novel predictions, continuity/rationality, problem-solving ability, fertility, explanatory power, consistency, and **GENERATIVE** potential (for review, see Long, 1993).

However acceptable (or accepted) a theory may be when evaluated by these and other standards, it is worth remembering that by definition, and for two reasons, even the 'best' theory can never be shown to be *true*. First, as rationalists, e.g. philosophical realists (but unlike postmodernists and relativists), most researchers in any scientific field believe that an objective reality exists independent of any individual's or group's (social) construction of it, i.e. that there are facts of the matter, even though that reality can never be fully comprehended. They also believe that, along with individual differences and particularities of time and place, there are universals, e.g. a universal law of gravity, supported by repeatedly attested phenomena. In SLA, most researchers believe that, while imperfect, the field's research methods permit theories to be evaluated, among other ways, by assessing the degree to which their predictions are borne out in nature. They believe it is possible to approximate the truth, in other words, without necessarily ever being able to be sure that a belief *is* the truth. The second reason a theory can never be true is simpler: if all the facts were in and agreed upon, and if a process like SLA were fully understood, and agreed to be understood, there would be no need for a theory about it.

**See also:** Acquisition and teaching; Learning styles; Monitor model; Mother tongue; Native speaker; Research methods; Self-access; Untutored language acquisition

## References

Andersen, R.W. (1989) 'The theoretical status of variation in interlanguage development', in S. Gass, C. Madden, D. Preston and L. Selinker (eds), *Variation in second language acquisition. Volume II: Psycholinguistic issues*, Philadelphia: Multilingual Matters.

Bates, E. and MacWhinney, B. (1989) 'Functionalism and the competition model', in B. MacWhinney and E. Bates (eds), *The cross-linguistic study of sentence processing*, Cambridge: Cambridge University Press.

Beebe, L. and Giles, H. (1984) 'Speech-accommodation theories: a discussion in terms of second language acquisition', *International Journal of the Sociology of Language* 46, 1: 1–32.

Beretta, A. (1991) 'Theory construction in SLA: complementarity and opposition', *Studies in Second Language Acquisition* 13, 4: 493–511.

Bickerton, D. (1984) 'The language bioprogram hypothesis', *The Behavioral and Brain Sciences* 7: 173–87.

Bley-Vroman, R. (1990) 'The logical problem of foreign language learning', *Linguistic Analysis* 20, 1–2: 3–49.

Bley-Vroman, R. (1997) 'Features and patterns in foreign language learning', plenary address to the Second Language Research Forum, East Lansing, MI: Michigan State University, October 17–19. (Available at time of publication at http://www.lll.hawaii.edu/bley-vroman/)

Clahsen, H. and Muysken, P. (1986) 'The availability of universal grammar to adult and child learners: the study of the acquisition of German word order', *Second Language Acquisition Research* 2: 93–119.

Crookes, G. (1992) 'Theory format and SLA theory', *Studies in Second Language Acquisition* 14, 4: 425–49.

Cummins, J. (1991) 'Interdependence of first and second language proficiency in bilingual children', in E. Bialystok (ed.), *Language processing in bilingual children*, Cambridge: Cambridge University Press.

Cushing, J.T. (1989) 'The justification and selection of scientific theories', *Synthese* 78: 1–24.

Darden, L. (1991) *Theory change in science: strategies from Mendelian genetics*, New York: Oxford University Press.

Eckman, F.R. (1996a) 'A functional-typological approach to second language acquisition theory', in W.C. Ritchie and T.K. Bhatia (eds), *Handbook of second language acquisition*, San Diego: Academic Press.

Eckman, F.R. (1996b) 'On evaluating arguments for special nativism in second language acquisition theory', *Second Language Research* 12, 4: 398–419.

Ellis, R. (1990) 'An integrated theory of instructed second language learning', in R. Ellis, *Instructed second language acquisition. Learning in the classroom*, Oxford: Blackwell.

Gardner, R. (1988) 'The socio-educational model

of second language learning: assumptions, findings, and issues', *Language Learning* 38, 1: 101–26.

Gass, S.M. (1997) *Input interaction and the second language learner*, Mahwah, NJ: Lawrence Erlbaum Associates.

Gasser, M. (1990) 'Connectionist models', *Studies in Second Language Acquisition* 12, 2: 179–99.

Givon, T. (1979) *On understanding grammar*, New York: Academic Press.

Hatch, E.M. (1978) 'Discourse analysis and second language acquisition', in E.M. Hatch (ed.), *Second language acquisition. A book of readings*, Rowley, MA: Newbury House.

Hatch, E., Flashner, V. and Hunt, L. (1986) 'The experience model and language teaching', in R.R. Day (ed.), *Talking to learn: Conversation in second language acquisition*, Rowley, MA: Newbury House.

Huebner, T. (1983) *A longitudinal analysis of the acquisition of English*, Ann Arbor: Karoma.

Johnson, K. (1996) *Language teaching and skill learning*, Oxford: Blackwell.

Kilborn, M. and Ito, K. (1989) 'Sentence-processing in Japanese–English and Dutch–English bilinguals', in B. MacWhinney and E. Bates (eds), *The crosslinguistic study of sentence processing*, Cambridge: Cambridge University Press.

Krashen, S.D. (1985) *The input hypothesis: issues and implications*, New York: Longman.

Krashen, S.D. and Terrell, T. (1983) *The natural approach: language acquisition in the classroom*, Oxford: Pergamon.

Laudan, L. (1977) *Progress and its problems: towards a theory of scientific growth*, Berkeley and Los Angeles: University of California Press.

Laudan, L. (1996) *Beyond positivism and relativism. Theory, method, and evidence*, Boulder, CO: Westview.

Long, M.H. (1990) 'The least a second language acquisition theory needs to explain', *TESOL Quarterly* 24: 649–66.

Long, M.H. (1993) 'Assessment strategies for second language acquisition theories', *Applied Linguistics* 14, 225–49.

Long, M.H. (1996) 'The role of the linguistic environment in second language acquisition', in W.C. Ritchie and T.K. Bhatia (eds), *Handbook of second language acquisition*, New York: Academic Press.

Meisel, J.M., Clahsen, H. and Pienemann, M. (1981) 'On determining developmental stages in natural second language acquisition', *Studies in Second Language Acquisition* 3, 2: 109–35.

O'Grady, W. (1996) 'Language acquisition without Universal Grammar: a general nativist proposal for L2 learning', *Second Language Research* 12, 4: 374–97.

Pienemann, M. (1998) *Language processing and second language development. Processability theory*, Amsterdam/New York: John Benjamins.

Riggs, P.J. (1992) *Whys and ways of science. Introducing philosophical and sociological theories of science*, Carlton, Victoria: Melbourne University Press.

Sato, C.J. (1986) 'Conversation and interlanguage development: rethinking the connection', in R.R. Day (ed.), *Talking to learn: conversation and second language acquisition*, Rowley, MA: Newbury House.

Sato, C.J. (1988) 'Origins of complex syntax in interlanguage development', *Studies in Second Language Acquisition* 10, 3: 371–95.

Sato, C.J. (1990) *The syntax of conversation in interlanguage development*, Tübingen: Gunter Narr.

Schumann, J.H. (1986) 'Research on the acculturation model for second language acquisition', *Journal of Multilingual and Multicultural Development* 7: 379–92.

Schwartz, B. (1992) 'Testing between UG-based and problem-solving models of L2A: developmental sequence data', *Language Acquisition* 2, 1: 1–19.

Spolsky, B. (1989) *Conditions for second language learning*, Oxford: Oxford University Press.

White, L. (1996) 'Universal grammar and second language acquisition: current trends and new directions', in W.C. Ritchie and T.K. Bhatia (eds), *Handbook of second language acquisition*, San Diego: Academic Press.

Wolfe-Quintero, K. (1992) 'Learnability and the extraction in relative clauses and wh-questions', *Studies in Second Language Acquisition* 14, 1: 39–70.

Wolfe-Quintero, K. (1996) 'Nativism does not equal Universal Grammar', *Second Language Research* 12, 4: 335–73.

## Further reading

Couvalis, G. (1997) *The philosophy of science. Science and objectivity*, London: Sage.

Doughty, C. and Williams, J. (eds) (1998) *Focus on form in classroom second language acquisition*, Cambridge: Cambridge University Press.

Gregg, K. (1996) 'The logical and developmental problems of second language acquisition,' in W.C. Ritchie and T.K. Bhatia (eds), *Handbook of second language acquisition*, San Diego: Academic Press.

Long, M.H. (1993) 'Assessment strategies for second language acquisition theories', *Applied Linguistics* 14: 225–49.

Riggs, P.J. (1992) *Whys and ways of science. Introducing philosophical and sociological theories of science*, Carlton, Victoria: Melbourne University Press.

MICHAEL LONG

# Secondary education

The reasons for the inclusion of a foreign language or even more than one foreign language, as a compulsory component, in the secondary school curriculum vary from society to society. Compulsory education in most societies has as its *raison d'être* the preparation of young people for adult life as well as a contribution to their personal, social, cultural, spiritual and physical development. Many societies deem foreign languages to have a central contribution to make in this respect. The relative importance of this contribution, however, varies, as do the status and the importance afforded to foreign languages as part of compulsory education. More often than not, foreign languages are a well established, integral part of the secondary school curriculum. In some instances, however, for example England and Wales, the existence of a requirement for all young people to study a foreign language during their compulsory schooling is rather recent and its necessity is still keenly debated – not to say questioned – by a number of policymakers, school managers and curriculum planners. This is despite the recognition by the European Commission of the need for European citizens to learn at least two foreign languages in order to become active citizens of a multilingual and multicultural Europe (European Commission, 1996: 45) and despite the fact that the world young people grow up in is increasingly characterised by the globalisation and internationalisation of their working as well as their personal lives.

## Educational purposes and societal needs

The nature and scope of foreign language provision tends to be determined by its underpinning rationale, and the time made available for foreign language study is often not only an indication of how seriously the need to know and to be able to use a foreign language is taken by a given society, but also of how proficient learners are likely to become in the foreign language. Over the years a broad international consensus on the aims and approaches to foreign language teaching around the notion of communicative competence, i.e. the ability to use the foreign language for the purpose of practical communication in everyday contexts, has emerged through **COMMUNICATIVE LANGUAGE TEACHING**. There remains, nevertheless, considerable diversity in the scope of foreign language learning and teaching in different countries, including what Eric **HAWKINS**, in his seminal treatment of the subject, called 'an apprenticeship in foreign language learning' (Hawkins, 1987: 282), i.e. the development in young people of a foundation for future foreign language learning. Then there is the suggestion, to be found in most curriculum statements, that foreign language learners should be exposed to new experiences and develop positive **ATTITUDES** to and insights into target cultures; also, the development of so-called transferable **SKILLS**, such as the ability to work with reference material; or the more ambitious, and – as some would argue (e.g. Byram, 1997) – misguided attempt to achieve near-native proficiency, given, for example, the limited time available for foreign language learning in secondary education or the implicit need for learners to give up their own language and identity. Any judgements of the effectiveness of foreign language provision in a given country or international comparisons, therefore, need to take into account the rationale for the inclusion of foreign languages in the secondary curriculum.

Different societies have different reasons for requiring their members to learn foreign languages, foreign language **NEEDS** will differ according to changing cultural, economic, political, educational and societal contexts, traditions and needs. The factors determining the choice of which foreign language(s) to offer are manifold and include:

- the importance of the language in terms of trade and industry;
- the number of speakers of the language (*native* and *non-native*);
- its usefulness for leisure purposes;
- its (perceived) level of difficulty;
- the attitudes of learners towards it;
- the availability of specialist teachers;
- the influence of the target culture(s) on the learner or the society they live in;
- its use as a medium for scientific discourse; or
- its significance in terms of output of works of a **LITERARY** or philosophical nature (Pachler and Field, 1997: 7–8).

As there is no one language that outperforms all the others on these criteria, as the foreign language needs of industry and the economy change over time, and as it is near to impossible to predict the foreign language needs of individuals in their adult lives, policymakers are well advised to ensure access to a diversified foreign language curriculum, despite the serious cost implications in terms of curriculum and teacher time.

## Methods of foreign language teaching in secondary education

The prevalent approach to foreign language teaching in secondary education since the late 1970s and early 1980s has been **COMMUNICATIVE LANGUAGE TEACHING** (CLT). Given its eclectic nature, it seems inappropriate to conceive of CLT as a method with universal applicability; instead, it is best thought of as an approach with many variants drawing on a range of ideas derived from a multidisciplinary perspective including, at least, **LINGUISTICS**, **PSYCHOLOGY**, philosophy, sociology and educational research, reflecting the realisation that the search for one definitive method of foreign language teaching is futile. Central is the development of 'communicative competence' in foreign language learners, based on a view of language as communication and a view of linguistic proficiency not as structural knowledge of language but as an understanding of and ability to use the functions linguistic items perform. The emphasis of CLT-

based foreign language teaching is on *meaning* rather than on *form*, and on the *ability to use* language rather than on *knowledge about* language.

In recent years, shortcomings of CLT have increasingly been identified. Important issues which remain to be resolved include:

- an overemphasis on transactional, topic-based situations/contexts and a lack of focus on the cultural dimension of language and language use, including **INTERCULTURAL COMPETENCE**;
- the tendency to underestimate the role of (explicit) grammatical knowledge; and
- an emphasis on teaching (and testing) in the target language (TL) without due recourse to the learners' L1.

Of particular importance in the development of CLT was the work of **VAN EK** (1975) on **THRESHOLD LEVELS** under the auspices of the **COUNCIL OF EUROPE**, designed for emigrant adult workers, as well as that of Wilkins (1976) on the functions language performs. Whilst important in moving the profession on from the by then outmoded **GRAMMAR–TRANSLATION METHOD**, the so-called notional–functional syllabuses developed as a result have tended to lead, in the United Kingdom at any rate, to a narrow transactional–functional orientation in which secondary school pupils are prepared for the linguistic (and non-linguistic) needs of tourists, with the emphasis on 'getting by' rather than an emphasis on understanding language and the ability to use it independently to express personal meaning. This approach tends to be characterised by a heavy emphasis on recall of often random lexical items and phrases derived from narrowly defined, idealised interactions and exchanges at the cost of transfer of knowledge, structures and skills across topics. More and more, though, there has been a move away from a notion of **AUTHENTICITY** which puts an emphasis on target language use in situations typically to be encountered in the target country and which require of learners the ability, and the willingness, to suspend disbelief. Instead, a recognition is developing of the importance, on the one hand, of tasks and situations which pupils are likely to encounter in their everyday lives, and, on the other, of situations which 'take account of the ways of living out of which others speak and write' (Byram, 1997: 4).

Furthermore, the importance of hypothesis-testing and of noticing new language and linguistic features – with reference to the grammatical system of the TL – and of comparing the TL ideal to their own TL production, i.e. of reflection on language use by others and on pupils' personal use of their first language – is being increasingly recognised. This is because it is thought that input becomes intake, i.e. part of the learner's short/medium-term memory, as a consequence of this hypothesis-testing and attention to new language. The need to move away from a limited notion of communicative competence akin to language contained in phrase books towards a broader interpretation is, therefore, being addressed. Nearly two decades after its publication, the conception of communicative competence advanced by Canale (1983) based on earlier work with Swain (Canale and Swain, 1980) is finally starting to find recognition and implementation in foreign language teaching in secondary education.

This comprises four interacting areas:

- grammatical competence;
- sociolinguistic competence;
- discourse competence; and
- strategic competence.

## Proficiency and skills attainable in secondary education

In recent years the question of what level of proficiency can be achieved by foreign language learners in secondary education has come into focus as education systems around the world are increasingly having to demonstrate value for tax payers' money, often in the context of establishing a culture of 'open' government which holds educators accountable and provides information to the public.

In order to make learners' achievements and proficiency more tangible to parents, to the wider public and of course to the learners themselves, policymakers in a number of countries have had national frameworks or curricula drawn up which describe the levels to be attained by learners. These documents, besides often specifying methods and content (e.g. topics, lexical items, functions, linguistic structures), tend to use the skill areas of LISTENING, SPEAKING, READING and WRITING as tools to conceptualise course requirements. Sometimes a hierarchy of skills is implied, but a number of national curriculum frameworks insist on a balanced approach by promoting mixed-skill tasks and activities. However, there are important questions about how accurately narrowly-conceived frameworks reflect overall proficiency in a foreign language; and legitimate concerns have been expressed about the effects of highly prescriptive curricula upon foreign language learning and teaching.

A keenly debated issue is the status of TRANSLATION and the use of reference material as distinct skill areas. Translation *can* have a valuable contribution to make to the communicative classroom, despite being 'viewed almost with hostility under certain interpretations of communicative approaches to foreign language learning' (Allford, 1999: 230). It can be used effectively – uses will vary according to context – to illustrate particular linguistic features or to explore differences in meaning. The ability to use reference materials effectively can also be seen as an authentic aspect of foreign language development and as essential in preparing learners to become independent of the teacher.

Depending on the nature and scope of foreign language provision, different levels of proficiency can be obtained. Outcomes of foreign language learning at secondary level tend to be assessed by way of traditional paper-and-pen tests as well as simulations, role-plays and information-gap activities.

At BEGINNER level, which in the context of this contribution can be taken as foreign language learning at ages 11 to 16, often only a rather limited linguistic proficiency can be achieved. Given the limitations imposed on learners by the ACQUISITION-poor nature of the classroom environment, expectations need to be realistic. Limitations include:

- the limited amount of curriculum time (often not more than 1–2 hours per week and 300–500 hours in total);
- the limited access to the undivided attention of the teacher;
- the lack of exposure to the target language; or

- the geographical and affectional distance from the countries and cultures where the TL is spoken (Pachler and Field, 1997: 51).

Learners at beginners level should be able to take part in simple transactions and conversations, often featuring simple and familiar language and contexts; their **PRONUNCIATION** will be intelligible, their knowledge of language forms limited and largely implicit; whilst able to communicate meaning, their ability to produce grammatically correct language will vary.

The transition from beginner to intermediate level (ages 16 to 18 or 19) tends to be characterised by an increase in focus on form rather than function/meaning, as well as by an increased emphasis on cultural and vocational components which, in turn, make increased reference to learners' developing world knowledge.

Progression is often built in by teachers in a multi-faceted manner, i.e. from

- pre-communicative → communicative activities;
- simple → complex language;
- short → longer spoken and written texts;
- implicit → explicit knowledge of **GRAMMAR**;
- scripted/didactically prepared (more salient) → authentic (less salient) language;
- known/familiar (e.g. classroom, self) → unknown/unfamiliar (world knowledge, target country) words and topics;
- teacher-led/aided (e.g. graded questions, examples) → independent (e.g. use of glossary, dictionary and other reference sources; pairwork, group work) interaction and working modes;
- concrete → abstract ideas;
- factual → non-factual/fictional spoken and written texts;
- predictable → unpredictable situations;
- less controversial → more controversial issues.

Different education systems approach the issue of systemic progression differently and require learners to specialise at different points in time. Compare, for example, the rather narrow focus of GCE A-level study in England and Wales with the much broader systems at 16–18/19 of the *Abitur* in Germany, the *Baccalauréat* in France or the *Matura* in Austria. Compulsion in relation to foreign language learning as well as the number of hours spent, therefore, can vary considerably.

## Unresolved issues

One of the questions facing policymakers in all countries is whether or not to have a national curriculum or national framework governing the teaching and learning of foreign languages. If so, how prescriptive should it be in terms of methods and content or how much should be left to the professional judgement of teachers? This decision will, to some extent, depend on the perceived status of teachers, the length and quality of their education and training as well as the locus of control of educational decision-making. Governments will allow schools and teachers more or less scope to develop and implement curricula or schemes of work and to assess and test foreign language skills, knowledge and understanding. Some systems rely heavily on formative and summative teacher **ASSESSMENT**, where the foreign language teacher decides what to teach and how to assess it; others favour statutory testing, where the proficiency and competence of learners in the TL is tested through a national exam. Both systems have advantages and disadvantages. Whilst there is a high degree of standardisation in systems with a national curriculum/framework and national tests, there can be a tendency to 'deliver' prescribed content and to 'teach to the test' rather than experiment with innovative methodology or to vary content according to the **NEEDS** of learners. In systems where foreign language teachers have a high degree of **AUTONOMY** there tends to be less standardisation but more scope for innovation, experimentation and focus on the needs of learners. There can, however, also be a tendency for certain course and text books to 'prescribe' covert curricula, which are followed more or less closely by foreign language teachers and supplemented more or less amply with additional material according to their level of expertise or the preparation time available.

Another fundamental question facing policymakers, educational managers and/or foreign language professionals is whether or not pupils should be taught in mixed-ability groupings or in sets or streams. Setting refers to pupils being grouped according to certain criteria but particularly their ability in individual subjects, and streaming to pupils being placed in a particular group in all or most subjects of the curriculum. In those systems, where mixed-ability teaching is widespread, the notion of differentiation within the group, which is based on the principle of helping individual pupils of all ability levels achieve the best they can taking into account their characteristics and prior learning, is very important. The teaching of mixed-ability groups presents a considerable challenge to even the most experienced teachers, as there is the danger, due to pressures of time, large class sizes and/or lack of resources, etc., of aiming at the middle, ignoring both the need of the less able for reinforcement and of the more able for extension work. However, it also presents methodological opportunities such as peer teaching and graded tasks and activities.

The ability to dispense increasingly with the teacher and to generate language of their own can be seen to be characteristic features of effective foreign language learners (Allford and Pachler, 1998: 1). Coupled with this is the length of time required for foreign language learning. Learner independence, therefore, becomes an important issue for foreign language teachers. As foreign language educators cannot assume that learners will necessarily bring with them the requisite skills to supplement what is on offer during contact time, there is a need to focus in foreign language teaching on opportunities for learners to learn how to become effective autonomous learners, and foreign language teachers need to gradually delegate responsibility for learning to learners. This implies the need for explicit coverage of learning **STRATEGIES** and learner training in foreign language teaching and requires important adjustments to foreign language teaching methodology.

Last, but by no means least, new technologies are starting to have a significant impact on foreign language teaching and learning. Although computer-assisted language learning (**CALL**) has been available to foreign language teachers for some time now, it has never really made a significant contribution to foreign language methodology due to, amongst other things, lack of hardware, cumbersome interfaces and unimaginative software very often drawing heavily on narrow **BEHAVIOUR-IST** concepts of learning. The increasing 'multi-modality' of **INTERNET**- and CD-ROM-based material, i.e. the combination of the written word, (moving) pictures and sound, as well as their increasing interactivity, affords foreign language educators access to a hitherto unimaginable wealth of attractive, up-to-the-minute, **AUTHENTIC** TL material. New technologies also enable asynchronous (delayed-time) and synchronous (real-time) computer-mediated communication (CMC) such as e-mail or video-conferencing. Whilst they present a considerable potential to foreign language learners, new technologies pose a significant challenge to foreign language teachers in so far as they require of them not only the requisite technical skills but also a whole new set of pedagogic and didactic skills. These are necessary to ensure effective **EVALUATION** of Information and Communication Technology-based material as well as their exploitation in the context of a social-interactivist learning paradigm, emphasising the social embeddedness of learning.

**See also:** Assessment and testing; Autonomy and autonomous learners; Graded objectives; Higher education; Objectives in language teaching and learning; Primary education

## References

Allford, D. (1999) 'Translation in the communicative classroom', in N. Pachler (ed.), *Teaching modern foreign languages at advanced level*, London: Routledge.

Allford, D. and Pachler, N. (1998) 'Learner autonomy, communication and discourse', *Proceedings of the Institution-Wide Language Programmes 7th National Conference*, Sheffield: Sheffield Hallam University.

Byram, M. (1997) *Teaching and assessing intercultural communicative competence*, Clevedon: Multilingual Matters.

Canale, M. (1983) 'From communicative competence to communicative language pedagogy', in J. Richards and R. Schmidt (eds), *Language and communication*, Harlow: Longman.

Canale, M. and Swain, M. (1980) 'Theoretical bases of communicative approaches to second language teaching and testing', *Applied Linguistics* 1, 1: 1–47.

European Commission (1996) *Teaching and learning: towards a learning society*, Brussels: Office for Official Publications of the European Communities.

Hawkins, E. (1987) *Modern languages in the curriculum*, Cambridge: Cambridge University Press.

Pachler, N. and Field, K. (1997) *Learning to teach modern foreign languages in the secondary school*, London: Routledge.

van Ek, J. (1975) *The threshold level in a European unit/credit system for modern language teaching by adults. Systems development in adult language learning*, Strasbourg: Council of Europe.

Wilkins, D. (1976) *Notional syllabuses*, Oxford: Oxford University Press.

## Further reading

Field, K. (forthcoming) *Issues in modern foreign language teaching*, London: Routledge.

Grauberg, W. (1997) *The elements of foreign language teaching*, Clevedon: Multilingual Matters.

Leask, M. and Pachler, N. (1999) *Learning to teach using ICT in the secondary school*, London: Routledge.

Pachler, N. (ed.) (1999) *Teaching modern foreign languages at advanced level*, London: Routledge.

Stern, H.H. (1983) *Fundamental concepts of language teaching*, Oxford: Oxford University Press.

Stern, H.H. (1992) *Issues and questions in language teaching*, Oxford: Oxford University Press.

Williams, M. and Burden, R. (1997) *Psychology for language teachers*, Cambridge: Cambridge University Press.

NORBERT PACHLER

# Self-access

'Self-access' refers to a mode of language learning in which learners work without direct teacher supervision, at their own pace, and often at times of their own choosing. Self-access learning may be undertaken to supplement a teacher-led course, or it may constitute a programme of learning in its own right. It usually takes place in a self-access centre, which provides learners with a library of language learning resources in various media and a range of technical facilities. Attempts to implement this mode of learning have been particularly widespread in **HIGHER** and **ADULT** education, where self-access has frequently been discussed in conjunction with **AUTONOMY** and **LEARNING STYLES**.

The notion of self-access arises from two ideas that are fundamental to education in general: that classroom contact between teachers and learners is not enough to achieve most formal learning goals – learners must also spend time learning on their own outside the classroom; and that worthwhile learning requires more resources than individual learners can be expected to acquire for themselves. This latter idea gains particular force when it is applied to adult learners who are responsible for directing their own learning. What distinguishes most self-access language learning centres from libraries is the central role played by the technologies associated with non-print media.

Self-access language learning first came to prominence in the 1970s. Its emergence was due partly to a concern to develop autonomous modes of learning in universities and adult education, and partly to the need to find a new role for **LANGUAGE LABORATORIES** following the widespread abandonment of the **AUDIOLINGUAL METHOD**. To begin with, most self-access centres comprised a language laboratory and a library of language learning **MATERIALS** in print and audio. But as the movement towards self-access gathered momentum, new technologies became available: first video and satellite television, then standalone computers, and after that multimedia computers and computer networks. The last of these developments represents a watershed in the history of self-access centres. Whereas the earliest centres necessarily focused on language learning rather than language use, the **INTERNET** enables learners to communicate directly with the target language community.

Educational policymakers have sometimes promoted self-access centres as a means of saving money: if teaching can be done by machines, they reason, it should be possible to employ fewer human teachers. But besides mistaking learning resources for teaching machines, this argument takes no account of the fact that learners do not necessarily know how to use a self-access centre. They need support, especially when they are following a programme of learning that does not include some form of classroom contact. The most common type of support is an advisory service that helps learners to clarify their learning aims, identify interim learning targets, select appropriate learning materials and activities, and gradually develop a capacity to monitor and evaluate their own learning (for examples, see Riley, 1985 and Esch, 1994). Learning contracts and learner journals are often used to stimulate and record these reflective activities, while learner support groups of various kinds may be formed in order to provide a social context for individual learning (see, e.g., Karlsson *et al.*, 1997). Self-access programmes that are organised in this way can lead to highly effective learning, but they are certainly no cheaper to provide than language classes.

The design of self-access centres and self-access language learning programmes is hampered by the fact that there has been relatively little principled discussion, either of the relation between media technologies, language use and language learning, or of the kinds of learning that the various uses of different technologies are apt to promote (but see Little, 1998). In the absence of clearly articulated principles, self-access learning has often been shaped by unexamined assumptions. For example, the audio-active-comparative language laboratory's focus on individual learning encouraged the belief that self-access learning is necessarily a matter of learners working on their own (the same mistake has been made in relation to autonomous learning). But human learning has its origins in social interaction, and it is therefore to be expected that self-access programmes will be strengthened rather than compromised if they provide learners with an opportunity to interact with **NATIVE SPEAKERS** of their target language or work collaboratively with other learners.

The need for appropriate theoretical underpinnings has become more rather than less urgent since the internet made it possible for self-access centres to put learners directly in touch with native speakers of their target language. For example, the potential of e-mail to support **TANDEM LEARNING** (partnerships between learners with different **MOTHER TONGUES** who are learning one another's language; see Little and Brammerts, 1996) can be fully exploited only if due account is taken of the psycholinguistic differences between oral and written, synchronous and asynchronous communication, and learners are supported accordingly.

By its very nature the language laboratory required a room of its own, which facilitated its evolution into the self-access language learning centre. In the subsequent history of language teaching, media technologies have been much more widely used in self-access centres than in classrooms. But the fact that the self-access centre has become a place where learners can make direct contact with the target language community is a consequence of the development of radically new channels and modes of communication. Arguably, the ability to engage in computer-mediated communication is now central to a general communicative repertoire in any language, and if language teaching follows where information systems are leading, language classrooms will necessarily begin to resemble self-access centres.

**See also:** Adult learners; Autonomy and autonomous learners; Distance learning; Internet; Language laboratories; Learning to learn; Media centres; Tandem learning; Task-based teaching and assessment; Video

### References

Esch, E. (ed.) (1994) *Self-access and the adult language learner*, London: Centre for Information on Language Teaching and Research.

Karlsson, L., Kjisik, F. and Nordlund, J. (1997) *From here to autonomy. A Helsinki University Language Centre autonomous learning project*, Helsinki: Yliopistopaino.

Little, D. (1998) *Technologies, media and foreign language learning*, Dublin: Authentik.

Little, D. and Brammerts, H. (eds) (1996) *A guide to language learning in tandem via the internet* (CLCS Occasional Paper No.46), Dublin: Trinity College, Centre for Language and Communication Studies.

Riley, P. (ed.) (1985) *Discourse and learning*, London and New York: Longman.

## Further reading

Esch, E. (ed.) (1994) *Self-access and the adult language learner*, London: Centre for Information on Language Teaching and Research.

Gardner, D. and Miller, L. (eds) (1999) *Establishing self-access: from theory to practice*, Cambridge: Cambridge University Press.

Karlsson, L., Kjisik, F. and Nordlund, J. (1997) *From here to autonomy. A Helsinki University Language Centre autonomous learning project*, Helsinki: Yliopistopaino.

Little, D. (ed.) (1989) *Self-access systems for language learning: a practical guide*, Dublin: Authentik.

Little, D. (1998) *Technologies, media and foreign language learning*, Dublin: Authentik.

DAVID LITTLE

# SIETAR

SIETAR was founded in the late 1960s by a group of cross-cultural trainers working mainly with the American Peace Corps. It is an interdisciplinary professional and service organisation whose purpose is to implement and promote cooperative interactions and effective communications among people of diverse cultures, races and ethnic groups. The **OBJECTIVES** are: to stimulate the growth of knowledge and **SKILLS** in the fields of international and intercultural relations; foster the professional development of theoreticians and practitioners in these and related fields; promote the effectiveness of the public, private and voluntary sectors for dealing positively with intercultural and related issues; disseminate and exchange information on concepts and methods related to intercultural and multicultural issues and practice. SIETAR publishes a journal, *The International Journal of Intercultural Relations*, and organises conferences, and in addition to the international society there are national branches in several countries linked in international and regional networks.

## Website

SIETAR's website is: http://www.sietarinternational. org

# Sign languages

Sign languages are human languages which are expressed primarily through the visual–gestural medium: they use movements of the hands and other bodily articulators, such as the eyes, mouth, head and shoulders, which are in turn perceived visually by the addressee. The impact of this visual–gestural modality on the nature and structure of language is the subject of considerable interest amongst linguists and those who teach and research human sign languages. While there is a general consensus that sign languages share the universal properties noted for spoken languages, there is some controversy as to whether they have specific characteristics which operate at both deep and surface levels.

While we can elaborate a range of characteristics of signed language, just as we can of spoken language, there are many individual sign languages in the world, just as there are many individual spoken languages. There is a general convention to name sign languages in relation to their geographical location – for example, Kenyan Sign Language, British Sign Language, American Sign Language and Hong Kong Sign Language – although, as with spoken languages, sign languages are not necessarily co-existent with national boundaries. Sign languages have developed primarily within Deaf communities. (Throughout this entry the convention of using 'Deaf' with a capital 'D' will be used to refer to persons with a hearing loss who are members of a community sharing a common sign language, a common cultural heritage, common life experiences and a common sense of identity. The use of 'deaf' with a lowercase 'd' will be used to refer to those persons who identify themselves or are identified as having a hearing loss.) However, visual–gestural communication systems have also evolved or been developed amongst hearing people. The precise linguistic status of such forms may vary. Amongst the most widely known of these signing systems are those used by the indigenous peoples of North America and **AUSTRALIA** and by Christian monastic orders such as the Cistercians. Monastic signing is probably the least complex linguistically, being essentially a set of **VOCABULARY** items usually produced by movements of the hands. The signing of the Plains Indians, as described in a range of North American accounts, and that of the Walpiri of Southern Australia, seem to exhibit certain grammatical features comparable to those found in Deaf sign languages.

## Sign languages used by Deaf people

### Manual and non-manual components

Early accounts of Deaf sign languages often used the term 'manual communication', and it was assumed that meaning was conveyed through movements of the hands. Whilst the hands do play an important role, later accounts have recognised the crucial importance of non-manual features, particularly with respect to syntax. These features play an important role in the expression of negation, questions and topic–comment focus. However, they also operate at the lexical level and as morphological adverbial and adjectival markers.

### The words of sign languages

The words of sign languages are typically referred to as signs. These are of three key types: manual, multi-channel and non-manual. The most common type, manual signs, involve actions of the hands; the second group, usually constituting a much smaller but frequently used sub-set of the vocabulary, involve movements of both the hands and some other bodily articulator(s); the third type, which usually make up a very small proportion of the overall lexical resources, make use only of non-manual features. However, non-manual signs seem to be used for very restricted linguistic purposes, such as 'back-channelling responses' with meanings such as 'That's right', 'Is that so?' 'You must be joking'.

Much of the 'lexical weight' within sign languages is carried by manual signs which may be one-handed or two-handed. Every manual sign can be described in terms of the handshape(s) used, the location of the hand(s) and the movements made by the hand(s). As with any other human language, sign languages exploit a small number of contrasting elements. One handshape may be distinguished from another by features such as

the extension, bending or spreading of the fingers and thumb.

Signs may be distinguished from each other simply by a small change in one of these contrasting elements. The sign SPEAK in British Sign Language (hereafter BSL) involves using a handshape in which the four fingers are held extended and together, and the hand is bent at the major knuckles with the thumb held parallel to the index finger. The hand is held so that the back of the hand is at the side of the mouth and the fingers and thumb make a repeated closing action. The sign BIRD uses exactly the same location, and repeated closing action, but the handshape involves the extension of only one finger (the index finger held parallel to the thumb) rather than four. Handshape, location and movement are regarded as the primary parameters of sign formation; three other parameters are also relevant: the orientation of the hands, the way the hands are placed in relation to each other in two handed signs, and the point and place of contact in signs where the two hands interact. Thus, in BSL DIFFICULT, the hands are held side by side and then the tip of the thumb of the dominant hand contacts the centre of the palm of the non-dominant hand.

## Morphology and syntax in sign languages

Sign linguists sometimes refer to spatial syntax. This term gives recognition to the fact that signing occurs in the space in front of the signer's body and this space is used in a highly structured way to express meaning. Signs are not simply produced at a central point in front of the signer's body, but are rather set up at different locations within the signing space. Such spatial patterning interacts with sequential patterning in the production of signed sentences and signed discourse. The signer is also simultaneously able to exploit a range of non-manual features: these play an important part in the expression of negation, questions and topic–comment forms.

The morphologies of all of the sign languages so far studied share a number of common features. All make use of so-called 'classifier' morphemes which play an important role in the expression of multi-morpheme verbs and in the creation of new lexical items. Classifiers are linguistic units which indicate what kind of group or category a particular referent belongs to. They indicate, for example, that an item belongs to the category of animate beings or the class of round objects or the category of vehicles. Classifiers are expressed in sign languages primarily by means of handshape: in American Sign Language (ASL), the handshape in which the thumb, index and middle finger are extended from the closed fist is a classifier for vehicles; in Thai Sign Language, the handshape in which the thumb and little finger are extended from a closed fist is used as a classifier for people; in Swedish Sign Language, the flat hand is used to refer to objects that are saliently two-dimensional.

Classifier forms are often used in multi-morphemic verbs of motion and location such as VEHICLE MOVING IN UPWARD DIREC-TION; PERSON LOCATED BESIDE VEHI-CLE; SMALL ANIMAL RUNNING IN A FORWARD DIRECTION. The signed context will usually allow a more specific meaning to be expressed by such forms. Thus, in context, we would know that the meanings above were more specifically: 'the car went up the hill'; 'the police-man was standing beside the motorbike' and 'the rabbit dashed off'. Often the signer will have supplied the more specific referents by the use of non-classifier forms.

Most of the sign languages so far analysed have complex inflectional morphologies. Thus the grammatical category of aspect is frequently expressed through changes in the movement parameter. In ASL, meanings such as 'wait for a long time', 'hit again and again', 'be about to start eating' are expressed through changes in the movements of the signs WAIT, HIT and EAT. Similarly, some verbs in sign languages show person and number agreement by the use of specific movements: in BSL I HELP YOU, the movement is made away from the body; in YOU HELP ME, the movement is made towards the body.

## Lip-patterns

Sign languages are characterised by the use of a range of lip-patterns. Certain lip-patterns are particular to sign languages whilst others have been borrowed from spoken languages (usually from the majority spoken language of the geographical area in which the sign language is used). Lip-patterns which are particular to sign languages include forms which mirror the action of the hands (e.g. the closing of the mouth and holding of the lips together as the dominant hand moves down to touch and maintain contact with the stationary hand in the BSL sign DEFINITE) and those used to provide an adverbial function or to convey degrees of intensity in relation to adjectives and classifiers. The following examples of adverbial or intensity lip-patterns are drawn from BSL, but equivalents may be found in other sign languages. The lip-patterns may involve the lips alone, as in the sign for SAUNTER in which the lips are closed and protrude slightly to convey that the action is done WITH EASE; or involve other parts of the mouth or face, as in a sign for PAIN in which the teeth are held together and the lips drawn back to convey INTENSITY, or in signs incorporating the sucking-in of the cheeks which creates a rounding of the lips conveying that the object is SMALL or THIN. Lip patterns of spoken language words may be used together with a sign to distinguish certain signs which are otherwise identical, e.g. the BSL signs JAM and MARMALADE. Signs created from the first fingerspelt letter of a spoken/written word are also usually produced with the lip-pattern of the spoken word, e.g. the BSL sign KITCHEN. (See p. 544 for an explanation of fingerspelling.)

As we have indicated, spoken language lip-patterns may accompany parts of the signed message. Thus we can have French information on the lips, whilst the rest of the message is exploiting the **GRAMMAR** of French Sign Language. However, if the signer were to use continuous French lip-patterns, then certain features of the French Sign Language grammar would be lost. It is simply not possible to mouth a spoken language and sign a sign language at the same time. Nevertheless, some spoken language lip-pattern is typical of sign language usage in a number of countries; in others, such patterns are minimal. Spoken language lip-patterning can be seen as comparable to fingerspelling, in that it allows spoken language elements to be borrowed into signed language. However, the fact that we can express elements of a spoken language 'on the lips' at the same time as using a primarily gestural language system does create a highly complex linguistic situation. This complexity may also be confusing for the uninformed observer whose primary language is a spoken language, since the observer may give sole attention to the lip pattern and (usually mistakenly) assume that they have understood the content of the message.

## Sign languages and fingerspelling

In many parts of the world, Deaf people make use of a manual alphabet which allows them to represent the written version of the spoken language used in their wider communities. This activity is known as fingerspelling. The manual alphabets used within sign languages vary from country to country. The majority of fingerspelling systems, including those within Irish Sign Language and American Sign Language, use one-handed manual alphabets, but some, like BSL, use a two-handed system. Sometimes non-sign language users assume that fingerspelling and signed language are one and the same. However, fingerspelling can be used independently of signing, but also as an integral part of a sign language. The extent to which fingerspelling is used in particular sign languages will vary from language to language and will depend upon specific sociolinguistic factors. Indeed the use of fingerspelling can vary across signers within a given linguistic community and even within the sign usage of an individual Deaf person. Given that fingerspelling evolved as a way of representing spoken languages, it plays an important part in those contact varieties of signing which have emerged as ways of communicating between Deaf and hearing people. Fingerspelt forms also allow the Deaf signer to borrow words from a spoken language for use within a sign language. Sometimes these forms become even more integrated into the particular sign language, losing the properties associated with the sequencing of individual representations of letters and looking more like the other signs of the sign language concerned. In Scotland, the BSL sign for the football team Celtic derives from the spelling out of the individual letters. However, while it is possible to recognise the letter 'c' configuration at the beginning and end of the sign, the intervening

letters have been reduced to a mere movement of the dominant hand.

## Visuality and signed language

One of the ongoing discussions within the field of sign linguistics is the extent to which the individual signs of sign languages, and indeed other aspects of their grammatical structure, can be regarded as 'iconic'. The term 'iconic' is usually used where the actual form of a linguistic expression itself provides an indication of its meaning. In many sign languages, the signs for animals are directly linked to some physical attribute of the animal: the trunk of an elephant; the mane of a lion; the shell of a turtle. Indeed it would be rather odd to find a sign language which did not have signs for animals which derive from such attributes. Many signs for objects may be regarded as iconic in this sense. However, these signs are expressed using the conventional formational properties of the particular sign language. Thus the different sign languages of the world may both focus on different physical features and express them through different handshapes, locations, etc. This means that even signs which are directly visually motivated may not be understood even by sign language users from other Deaf communities. The sign languages of the world are not mutually comprehensible. However, it is the case that, because visual motivation is a characteristic of human sign languages, when Deaf people from different countries come together, this aids their ability to communicate across sign language boundaries.

Visual motivation goes beyond the individual sign. Thus sign languages often make **METAPHO-RICAL** use of the signing space. Time in many sign languages is expressed through what have been termed 'timelines', such as an imaginary line running from behind the shoulder to approximately an arm's length in front of the body. The signer uses the area around the shoulder to indicate the present; behind the shoulder to indicate the past and in front of the shoulder to indicate the future. The signer can indicate future and past generally or mark out more specific periods. Some sign languages also use spatial metaphors such as the 'interaction' set of metaphors where the two hands interchange, for example, moving to and fro alternatively. This movement is used in such meanings as 'communicate', 'discuss', 'negotiate'. It is argued by some sign linguists that this choice of movement is motivated, not arbitrary.

The term 'visual encoding' refers to the tendency in signed language to incorporate real-world visual information as a matter of course. Thus, in most sign languages, if one were expressing information about opening a door, the signing itself would indicate physical information about the door – e.g. the type of handle, where it was located, whether one opened the door with a key, and so on. The signer's use of the signing space will typically provide visual information, such as that X was standing to the right of Y and the window was opposite to Y. In spoken languages we can, of course, provide such information if we wish; in signed language the actual grammatical and lexical resources of a specific language tend to ensure that such information is incorporated in a regular way.

## Sociolinguistic aspects of sign language usage

The sign languages of Deaf communities across the world have typically evolved and survived in the face of considerable odds. Transmission from generation to generation does not occur as in most spoken languages because the majority of deaf children – over 90 per cent – are born to hearing parents. Although some of these parents may learn a sign language, the majority of deaf children do not gain immediate access either to a sign language or to a Deaf community. The **AGE** of exposure to a sign language and subsequent acquisition can influence the nature of the signing used by Deaf adults. Thus some research suggests that those who develop a sign language after puberty, whilst they will be able to communicate competently, will nevertheless not be able to manipulate key areas of the grammar with the same ease and efficiency as early learners. In some countries, it is still the case that sign languages are not used either as the **MEDIUM OF INSTRUCTION** or even as one of the linguistic choices. Indeed there is a long history of suppression of sign languages. This situation has changed to some extent, partly through the impact of sign language research and the recognition by

Deaf people of their status as linguistic and cultural communities. A number of countries, such as Nicaragua and Sweden, now give formal recognition to their own sign languages with positive implications for the use of signing in education, the provision of spoken/signed language **INTER-PRETERS**, resources for the training of teachers of sign language and support for families of deaf children in learning to sign.

None of the sign languages so far studied has a well-established written form, although more recently there has been some experimentation with the creation of writing systems. This, combined with the low status of signed languages in some countries and their absence from educational contexts, sometimes contributes to a lack of standardisation. However, in those countries where the sign language is recognised and used in a range of educational and social contexts, standardised forms have emerged or are emerging. Internal variation with the usage of an individual sign language is influenced by many of the same factors as with spoken language. Thus, geographical location, the age, sex and social status of the signer, as well as situational factors such as status and audience, can all affect the variety used. However there are additional factors, such as whether the individual's parents are Deaf or hearing, the age of sign acquisition, and whether the individual is interacting with Deaf or hearing people. As sign linguists probe sign variation more fully, they have been able to discern the richness of sign variation and the complex interplay of a range of relevant sociolinguistic factors.

## Teaching Deaf sign languages

For many decades of the twentieth century, any hearing person wishing to learn to sign would most typically be taught by a hearing person. However, one of the effects of sign language research has been a recognition that Deaf people themselves have a central role to play in the teaching of their own native languages. Increasingly, especially in countries where sign language research has been established, Deaf people can undertake training to teach signed language. There has been a move towards teaching sign languages in their own terms, without reliance on spoken languages. This has resulted in Deaf people distinguishing between their sign languages and sign systems which involve the use of the signs of a sign language used in conjunction with, and as a support to, a spoken language. In teaching hearing people a sign language, Deaf teachers seek to enable hearing people to clue into the visual world of Deaf people. For Deaf people, gaining recognition for their sign languages is central to their campaign to achieve equality of opportunity with hearing people. The teaching of sign languages has an important contribution to make in achieving this end.

**See also:** Bilingualism; Creoles; Esperanto; Language planning; Linguistics; Native speaker; Pidgins; Planned languages; Pragmatics; Sociolinguistics; Standard language; Vocabulary

### Resources

For information on the sign language(s) of a particular country, contact the national association of Deaf people in that country. The addresses of national associations may be obtained from the World Federation of the Deaf, whose internet address is given below.

### Websites

The World Federation for the Deaf's website is: http://www.who.int/ina-ngo/ngo/ngo175.htm
The website of the Centre for German Sign Language and Communication of the Deaf at the University of Hamburg offers a range of bibliographical and other material: http://www.sign-lang.uni-hamburg.de/

### Further reading

Armstrong, D.F. (1999) *Original signs: gesture, sign and the sources of language*, Washington, DC: Gallaudet University Press.
Baker, C. and Cokely, D. (1980) *American Sign Language: a teacher's resource text on grammar and culture*, Silver Spring, MD: T.J. Publishers.
Brien, D. (ed.) (1992) *Dictionary of British Sign Language/English*, London: Faber and Faber.
Erting, C.J., Johnson, R.C., Smith, D.L. and Snider, B.D. (eds) (1994) *The Deaf way: perspectives from the International Conference on Deaf Culture*, Washington, DC: Gallaudet University Press.
Johnston, T. (ed.) (1998) *Signs of Australia on CD-ROM: A Dictionary of Auslan (Australian Sign Language)*, Parramatta, NSW: Royal Institute for Deaf and Blind Children.
Klima, E. and Bellugi, U. (1979) *The signs of language*, Cambridge, MA: Harvard University Press.
Stokoe, W.C. (1960) *Sign language structure: an outline of the visual communication of the American deaf.* Studies in Linguistics: Occasional Papers 8, Buffalo: University of Buffalo.
Sutton-Spence, R. and Woll, B. (1999) *The linguistics of British Sign Language: an introduction*, Cambridge: Cambridge University Press.

MARY BRENNAN AND DAVID BRIEN

# Silent Way

The Silent Way is usually considered to be one of the alternative or **HUMANISTIC** approaches to language teaching. It is the name given by Caleb Gattegno to the language teaching application of his general pedagogical approach. When Gattegno's approach is applied to other subjects such as reading or mathematics, it goes by other names. Caleb Gattegno based his whole approach on several general observations which underlie the Silent Way.

First, it is not because teachers teach that students learn. Therefore, if teachers want to know what they should be doing in the classroom, they need to study learning and the learners, and there is no better place to undertake such a study than on oneself as a learner. When Gattegno studied himself as a learner, he realised that only awareness can be educated in humans. His approach is therefore based on producing awarenesses rather than providing knowledge.

When he studied other learners, he saw them to be strong, independent and gifted people who bring to their learning their intelligence, a will, a need to know and a lifetime of success in mastering challenges more formidable than any found in a classroom. He saw this to be true whatever their age and even if they were perceived to be educationally subnormal or psychologically 'da-maged'. (For an account of Gattegno working with such learners, see Holt, 1982.) As a teacher, he saw that his way of being in the class and the activities he proposed could either promote this state of being or undermine it. Many of the techniques used in Silent Way classes grew out of this understanding, including the style of correction, and the silence of the teacher – though it should be said that a teacher can be silent without being mute. Simply, the teacher never models and doesn't give answers that students can find for themselves.

Second, language is often described as a tool for communication. While it may sometimes function this way, Gattegno observed that this is much less common than we might imagine, since it requires of speakers that they be sensitive to their audience and able to express their ideas adequately, and of listeners that they be willing to surrender to the message before responding. Working on this is largely outside the scope of a language classroom. On the other hand, language is almost always a vehicle for expression of thoughts and feelings, perceptions and opinions, and these can be worked on very effectively by students with their teacher.

Third, developing criteria is important to Gattegno's approach. To know is to have developed criteria for what is right or wrong, what is acceptable or unacceptable, adequate or inadequate. Developing criteria involves exploring the boundaries between the two. This in turn means that making mistakes is an essential part of learning. When teachers understand this because they have observed themselves living it in their own lives, they will properly view mistakes by students as 'gifts to the class', in Gattegno's words. This attitude towards mistakes frees the students to make bolder and more systematic explorations of how the new language functions. As this process gathers pace, the teacher's role becomes less that of an initiator, and more that of a source of instant and precise feedback to students trying out the language.

A fourth element which determines what teachers do in a Silent Way class is the fact that knowledge never spontaneously becomes know-how. This is obvious when one is learning to ski or to play the piano. It is skiing rather than learning the physics of turns or the chemistry of snow which makes one a skier. And this is just as true when one is learning a language. The only way to create a 'know-how to speak the language' is to speak the language.

Historically, the approach went through several stages. It came into being in the 1950s when Gattegno, a mathematician, encountered the Cuisenaire rods, small pieces of wood which vary in length and colour and are used in mathematics teaching. He soon became aware that the rods could also be used to create unambiguous and instantly apprehensible situations which would permit a teacher to give students step-by-step input as required by their learning. New words were introduced when necessary by being said once, and the students could explore the language using their natural gifts. The teacher could remain almost silent, giving the students the time and space necessary to practise the language, the teacher's silence indicating to the students this attitude to learning and the learners, and placing the onus for learning squarely on their shoulders.

Towards the end of the decade, Gattegno had the further idea of writing the functional **VOCABU-LARY** of the target language on wall charts, colouring the different letters so that each sound was always represented by the same colour. Using a pointer, the teacher indicated the words on the charts, and the students could work out their **PRONUNCIATION** by looking at the colours. The approach was given the name Silent Way at this time, referring of course to the teacher's silence.

A major advantage of this way of working is that using a pointer reproduces the inherently ephemeral nature of language. To indicate a phrase, the person pointing – teacher or student – must move the pointer from word to word, and the students have to hold the complete string in their minds as it is built from each written element. This leads to a greatly heightened level of retention.

Another advantage of using word charts is that they free the students from the need to rely on memorisation. They thus become more **AUTONO-MOUS**, and this in turn allows the teacher to devote more attention to being a sensitive source of feedback during the students' exploration of the language, indicating systematically when changes need to be made and finding the best way of inducing them. The teacher's feedback can be as simple as a slight movement of the hand indicating that the sentence needs to be modified somewhat, or more elaborate, if a word needs to be pointed on the charts or if a situation capable of illustrating the problem and allowing a solution to be found has to be created. The teacher's job is constantly subordinated to what the students are doing.

## Typical classes

A recurrent pattern in low-level Silent Way classes is the initial creation of a clear and unambiguous situation using the rods. This allows the students to work on the challenge of finding ways – as many as possible – of expressing the situation in the target language. The teacher is rather active, proposing small changes so that the students can practise the language generated, always scrupulously respecting the reality of what they see. They rapidly become more and more curious about the language and begin to explore it actively, proposing their own changes to find out whether they can say this or that, reinvesting what they have discovered in new sentences. The teacher can then gradually hand over the responsibility for the content of the course to the students, always furnishing the feedback necessary for the learning process. The content of the course then becomes whatever the students want it to be, usually an exploration of their own lives, their thoughts, feelings and opinions.

In more advanced courses, the basic way of functioning remains the same, although the class might look quite different to an inexperienced observer. The rods are seldom necessary and the word charts are used much less frequently, since the students can usually find their own mistakes once they become aware that there is a mistake to look for.

To learn to be a Silent Way teacher, it is of course necessary to know the position of the words on the charts and which colours correspond to which sounds. Only then does the real work begin. Silent Way teachers need to become aware of the role of awareness in their own learning in order to see the students' awarenesses more clearly. They need a strong commitment to self-exploration in order to develop an ever deeper awareness of themselves as people. They must develop a deep sense of the students' strengths and learn to have

confidence in them as people. They can then put into practice another important principle at the heart of the Silent Way – that, while the students work on the language, the teacher works on the students.

The Silent Way is used by a small but growing number of teachers around the world, often working in relatively extreme conditions – with illiterate refugees, for example, or in cases where speed of acquisition is important or accuracy is vital.

**See also:** Drama; *Handlungsorientierter Unterricht*; Humanistic language teaching; Linguistic psychodramaturgy; Medium-oriented and message-oriented communication; Monitor model; Suggestopedia; Teaching methods

### Bibliography

Holt, J. (1982) *How children fail* (revised edn), New York: Pelican Books.

Gattegno, C. (1976) *The common sense of teaching foreign languages*, New York: Educational Solutions.

Gattegno, C. (1987) *The science of education. Part 1: Theoretical considerations*, New York: Educational Solutions.

Stevick, E.W. (1990) *Humanism in language teaching*, Oxford: Oxford University Press.

ROSLYN YOUNG

# Skills and knowledge in language learning

Learning a language involves both getting to know how meanings are encoded in it, and being able to act upon this abstract knowledge to engage in actual behaviour. The relationship between abstraction and actuality is a problematic one and in linguistics has traditionally been avoided by imposing a clear distinction between them. Thus **SAUSSURE** proposed that *LANGUE*, a community's common knowledge of the encoded system, should be abstracted out of language as a whole (*langage*) as the object of linguistic description, leaving *parole*, actual language behaviour, out of account (Saussure, 1915/74). **CHOMSKY** followed suit by isolating **COMPETENCE**, knowledge of sentence encoding, as the proper concern of linguistic enquiry, and disregarding performance (Chomsky, 1965). Although it may be convenient for linguists to ignore behaviour and focus their attention exclusively on knowledge, it necessarily prevents any consideration of the interdependent *relationship* between the two. When we come to consider the use and learning of languages, however, it is this relationship which is crucial, and which is suggested, indeed, by the very term competence itself. For, in spite of Chomsky's use of the term, when we say somebody is competent in a language we do not mean that they know it as an abstract coding system, but that they are capable of doing things with it. We would not normally use the term competence in reference to knowledge that is not acted upon (even if we could identify it), nor to behaviour which we did not take as evidence of a more general and **GENERATIVE** knowledge of the language. When we seek to induce language learning by teaching, the central question is how this relationship is to be interdependently activated: what kinds of behaviour in class will lead to an internalisation of the requisite knowledge, and how learners can realise that knowledge as appropriate behaviour.

## The actualisation of knowledge

Knowledge of language, as of anything else, is abstract in that it is a cognitive abstraction from perceived experience. We acquire it by generalising from particular samples of behaviour, and these have to be actualised through the media of the perceiving senses. So we learn a language by producing and receiving instances of it in spoken or written form. We can therefore speak of language behaviour in terms of four skills:

|           | *Spoken*  | *Written* |
|-----------|-----------|-----------|
| *Producing* | Speaking  | Writing   |
| *Receiving* | Listening | Reading   |

One way of inducing language knowledge would be to get learners to abstract it from their own exercise of these skills. This is indeed the basic principle behind a **STRUCTURAL**/behaviourist ap-

proach to language pedagogy, whereby learners are required to produce and process instances of encoded language in the form of exemplary sentence patterns manifested in speech and writing. The assumption here is that the repetitive practice in giving behavioural substance to such encoded instances will result in their internalisation as abstract knowledge of the code, which can serve to inform subsequent behaviour.

What one needs to notice about this approach, however, is that the kind of behaviour directed at the internalisation of knowledge is entirely different from that which is normally realised from such knowledge in circumstances of natural use. When people use language, they do not *manifest* their knowledge of the code, they *realise* it in accordance with contextual requirements. They draw on the code as a communicative resource: they do not display it. So the oral and written processing of sentence patterns is an exercise of the language skills which has no parallel outside the classroom, and the learners are being required to behave in the foreign language in ways they would never do in their own. But to say that this is not language-using behaviour is not to say that it might not be effective as language-*learning* behaviour. Learners, one can reasonably argue, need to access the code of the language they are learning and need to be exposed to, and exercised in, the different ways it is made manifest in speech and writing as a precondition for subsequent, more user-like behaviour.

The crucial question, however, is whether, and to what extent, the exercise of manifesting skills in the classroom *is* in fact such a precondition, and does in effect provide for a transition to normal use. A distinction has been made between skill-getting and skill-using activities (Rivers and Temperley, 1978), and it seems obvious that to use a skill you have first to acquire it. But the skills the learners acquire in manifestation are not, as I have indicated, those that are called upon in realisation. They represent quite different ways of behaving.

## Medium and mode

The idea that language learning objectives are to be defined in terms of the four skills of **SPEAKING**, **LISTENING**, **READING** and **WRITING** is well-established in foreign language pedagogy. Whether it is well-founded is a different matter. As already indicated, these skills are defined in reference to what channel (aural or visual) is used in the transmission and reception of the linguistic signal. Since these physical signals are produced and apprehended physiologically by quite different motor-perceptive mechanisms, then we do clearly have four quite distinct kinds of behaviour here. But only in respect to the *medium* of manifestation. If we look at the way language is realised as use, the distinction no longer applies. Here, the code is only actualised when required by some factor in the context, and only in order to achieve a particular *mode* of communicative interaction. And there is no neat correspondence between medium and mode. Thus Halliday (in Halliday *et al.*, 1964 and elsewhere) identifies mode of discourse as one of the dimensions of register, and points out that we can have spoken language designed to be read, written language designed to be spoken, and so on. The factors that now come into consideration have to do not with the participants as physical producers and receivers, but with their interactant roles as social addressers and addressees. In considering language use, it is not medium as such that is of interest, but how it is relevant as a factor in creating conditions for different modes of communicative interaction. So it is that Halliday points out that written language is not more complex than spoken but that each typically has its own kind of complexity, writing being synoptic and speech dynamic in character, and they differ in degrees of lexical density in consequence (Halliday, 1989). But these differences are a function of how the media are used to produce different modes of communication. Similarly, the recent development of e-mail has created the possibility of new kinds of interaction between people. It is writing which has something of the immediacy of spoken dialogue.

Some scholars (e.g. Carter and McCarthy, 1995) have talked about the grammar of speech as distinct from that of writing. But the point to note is that these lexical and grammatical features are not intrinsic manifestations of the medium but consequent realisations of the fundamental features of orate as distinct from literate modes of communication, as discussed in Ong (1982) and elsewhere. A central point here is that, as these modes become conventionalised, they become

independent of the media through which they are actualised: you can, for example, talk like a book, or write in the manner of unscripted speech and simulate its spontaneity. Although modes develop to counter the constraints, and exploit the possibilities of media, once established they take on an independent life of their own.

What this means, of course, is that literacy is incorporated into cultural history, and members of a literate community will inevitably adopt certain literate modes of communication even if they find it hard to cope with the medium of writing. Being illiterate in an orate society is a totally different matter. By the same token, of course, you can learn how to cope with the medium of writing or speech, but this does not of itself provide for the ability to deal with the various modes of communication conventionalised within a particular community that the medium is commonly associated with. Thus literacy is not a matter of composing sentences in the graphological medium nor reading a matter of decomposing them, but of being able to act upon the conventions that define different kinds of written communication. And the same applies to oracy and the conventions associated with different modes of spoken interaction.

## Skills and abilities

If one defines the learning process as a matter of internalising knowledge of a code, then it makes sense to think of it as being achieved through the exercise of the four skills, the activity of encoding and deciphering linguistic signals as physically manifested in a particular medium. This is a structuralist/behaviourist view of the learning process, and of course it is one which has been extensively rejected over recent years in favour of a communicative approach, which seeks to bring learner behaviour into closer correspondence with user behaviour. What this should logically entail is a quite radical shift of focus away from these four skills as such to a consideration of how linguistic signals are realised to communicative effect in different modes of use. Curiously enough, even among those who firmly reject the approach that gives them warrant, the four skills continue to appear as the essential operational principles of language learning (see, e.g., Grabe, 1998; Hedge, 2000.)

Since the two ways of actualising linguistic knowledge, as I have described them here, are so essentially different, it seems sensible to use different terms in reference to them. The term skill we can retain as referring to manifestation in a medium and ability as referring to realisation in a mode of use (see Widdowson, 1978). The question now arises as to what the relationship between them might be. Can the exercise of language practice skills in the classroom contribute to the development of abilities in the use of language? Do they effectively lead to the internalisation of the code of the language, as they are designed to do, and if so, how is that internalised knowledge accessible for subsequent realisation as use if learners have not been expressly instructed in the ability to do so? The assumption of the proponents of skill-based teaching was that there is such a transfer: the current orthodoxy in language teaching pedagogy would, on the contrary, assert that there is not. Indeed, the argument for a communicative approach is based on the belief that there is no transfer from skill to ability, and that even if it is conceded that the linguistic code was, to some degree at least, internalised, it remained inert as useless knowledge which learners could not act upon when contexts of use called on them to do so. It was therefore proposed that communicative ability should be focused upon as the essential learning objective to be induced by teaching.

## Competence in language

Such a shift of focus necessarily involves a reconsideration of what it means to be competent in a language. As we have seen, Chomsky defined competence as knowledge of a linguistic code, and more specifically of the generative possibilities of its syntax. But in acting on such knowledge, as distinct from simply displaying it, it is obvious that other kinds of knowledge are implicated. In what was to become a key point of reference for language pedagogy, Hymes (1972) proposed that, to be communicatively competent in a language, one had to be capable of making four kinds of judgement about any instance of its occurrence:

1  Whether and to what degree it is possible.
2  Whether and to what degree it is feasible.
3  Whether and to what degree it is appropriate.
4  Whether and to what degree it is actually done (or attested).

Of these communicative conditions, only the first is accounted for by Chomsky's concept of competence (for further discussion of how the two concepts of competence relate, see Widdowson, 1989). The possible is a measure of conformity to the linguistic code, and particularly its syntax. Clearly it was this condition that structuralist teaching concentrated on. But since the abstract possible had to be internalised, it had also to be related to the second condition. Feasibility has to do with relative ease of processing. In structuralist teaching, the possible linguistic items to be made manifest through the exercise of the four skills were selected and ordered precisely so that they could be readily processed and internalised. The third and fourth conditions were made subservient to that purpose. Thus, the language produced and received in class was not, and not intended to be, appropriate to any contexts of 'real-life' use outside it. It was therefore not a matter of replicating such contexts of use, but of contriving whatever contexts were deemed appropriate for making the possible more feasible. In consequence, what was done in class, the language that was actually attested there, bore little resemblance to what speakers of that language actually produced.

If the objective of learning is redefined to incorporate competence in the language as evidenced by actual user behaviour, the dependency relations across these four conditions is reversed. Now it is the second two that are salient, and the first two subservient. Learning a language is now a matter of knowing not just the rules of its code but the conventions of its normal contextual use. And not only of *knowing* what these conventions are but of having the *ability* to act upon them to achieve communicate behaviour recognised as appropriate by particular communities of users.

Conceived of in this way, language learning becomes a much more complex process, of course, and poses a number of problems. With regard to the fourth of Hymes's conditions, for example, corpus descriptions have now made available a massive amount of factual evidence of what users of a particular language actually produce in naturally occurring contexts of use. With such findings at our disposal, we are now in a position to specify the objectives of learning in terms of the relative frequency of possible encoded features, lexical and grammatical, and their customary co-occurrence. Now we know what 'real' language looks like, it might seem, we no longer need to deal in contrivance. The obvious difficulty about this is that, in reality, the attested is always associated with the appropriate. The two conditions are interdependent. People only produce patterns of language in the process of using them in particular contexts. And such contexts are, of course, socio-culturally informed and presuppose all manner of shared knowledge, attitudes and values which are necessarily remote from the reality of learners as learners. The contextual appropriateness of the language in the original conditions of its use is something they are not yet in a position to realise, nor indeed may they ever be. The essential point is that the attested in isolation is just as much an analytic abstraction as is the possible in isolation. In both cases they can only be realised as communication in relation to contexts of use, and, to the extent that 'real' contexts cannot be replicated in classrooms, they have to be contrived.

## The language as subject

Learning a language means becoming competent in it, and competence means both knowing the possible as an encoded resource, and being able to act on this knowledge as appropriate to achieve communicative behaviour. The question then arises as to what is to be taught to induce such learning, in other words how the language subject is to be defined. It is obvious that the language subject that appears on the school timetable as part of the curriculum cannot be the same as the language experienced by users in naturally occurring social contexts of use. Even if learners might aspire eventually to arrive at a competence comparable with that of such users, they obviously have to go through a transitional process of learning to get there, and it is this process that the subject must be designed to induce. The

question is, what design is likely to be most effective as an investment for future use?

If the objective is to get learners to be competent in the language, the design of instruction cannot simply provide for the exercise of skills in manifesting the possible, but must also involve learners in activities whereby they will develop abilities to realise the possible in contextually appropriate ways. But, as pointed out earlier, the appropriateness conditions cannot replicate those that obtain in 'authentic' user contexts. They have to be contrived so as to engage the reality of the learners themselves while at the same time getting them to internalise the possibilities of the code as a communicative resource. Activities designed to meet these conditions have been widely proposed of late under the name of **TASK-BASED LEARNING** (see Nunan, 1989; Skehan, 1998; Willis, 1996). A task is different from an exercise, we may say, because whereas an exercise simply requires learners to manifest the possible by completing sentences, filling in the blanks and so on, the task requires them to realise the possible as appropriate to some contextual purpose. What needs to be noted, however, is that tasks are designed on the basis of a pedagogic re-interpretation of the Hymes conditions on communicative competence and their relationship. They no longer apply to what happens in the normal circumstances of language use, and indeed their effectiveness in engaging the learners in the process of learning depends on this dissociation from user reality. What this means, of course, is that what tasks do is not to rehearse learners in patterns of 'authentic' behaviour, but to develop general abilities for use, a capacity for communication.

Conceived of in this way, task-based teaching adheres to the same investment principle in defining the language subject that informed structuralist teaching. That is to say, both are based on the assumption that teaching cannot encompass everything that is to be learned, but can only provide learners with a capability for further learning. They differ, of course, in their notion of what that capability consists of. For structuralist teaching, it was the internalisation of the encoded possible through the exercise of the manifesting skills: once that was in place, it was assumed, then the realisation of that internalised knowledge as appropriate communicative behaviour could be left to the learner to achieve as and when occasion arose. In task-based teaching, the assumption is that this leaves too much to be learned and that abilities for realising language as appropriate communication need to be expressly taught.

But this still necessarily leaves much untaught, and yet to be learnt. Taking the appropriateness condition into account does not, as it is sometimes supposed, imply that learners have to be rehearsed in patterns of actual user behaviour. To do this is neither pedagogically effective, nor in fact feasible. A lot of time and effort can be fruitlessly expended in striving for authentic language in the classroom and trying to teach the unteachable. Effective pedagogy must be a matter of identifying what constitutes the best investment for future learning in terms of an ability to draw on the internalised knowledge of the language as a communicative resource. In this sense, one may say that language teaching is still what it essentially has always been: the art of the possible.

**See also:** Competence and performance; Language awareness; *Langue* and *parole*; Task-based teaching and assessment; Teaching methods; Text and corpus linguistics

### References

Carter, R. and McCarthy, M. (1995) 'Grammar and spoken language', *Applied Linguistics* 16. 2: 141–58.

Chomsky, N. (1965) *Aspects of the theory of syntax*, Cambridge, MA: MIT Press.

Grabe, W. (ed.) (1998) *Foundations of second language teaching (Annual Review of Applied Linguistics, Volume 18)*, Cambridge: Cambridge University Press.

Halliday, M.A.K. (1989) *Spoken and Written Language*, Oxford: Oxford University Press.

Halliday, M.A.K., McIntosh, A. and Strevens, P. (1964) *The linguistic sciences and language teaching*, London: Longman.

Hedge, T. (2000) *Teaching and learning in the language classroom*, Oxford: Oxford University Press.

Hymes, D.H. (1972) 'On communicative competence', in J. Pride and J. Holmes (eds), *Sociolinguistics: Selected readings*, Harmondsworth: Penguin.

Nunan, D. (1989) *Designing tasks for the communicative classroom*, Cambridge: Cambridge University Press.

Ong, W.J. (1982) *Orality and literacy: the technologizing of the word*, London: Methuen.

Rivers, W.M. and Temperley, M.S. (1978) *A practical guide to the teaching of English as a second or foreign language*, New York: Oxford University Press.

Saussure, F. de (1915/1974) *Course in general linguistics*, trans. Wade Baskin, London: Fontana.

Skehan, P. (1998) 'Task-based instruction', *Annual Review of Applied Linguistics* 18: 268–86.

Widdowson, H.G. (1978) *Teaching language as communication*, Oxford: Oxford University Press.

Widdowson, H.G. (1989) 'Knowledge of language and ability for use', *Applied Linguistics* 10. 2: 128–37.

Willis, J. (1996) *A framework for task-based learning*, London: Longman.

### Further reading

Annual Review of Applied Linguistics Volume 18 (1998): Foundations of Second Language Teaching.

Rivers, W.M. (1968) *Teaching foreign-language skills*, Chicago: University of Chicago Press.

Skehan, P. (1998) *A cognitive approach to language learning*, Oxford: Oxford University Press.

Widdowson, H.G. (1990) *Aspects of language teaching*, Oxford: Oxford University Press.

H.G. WIDDOWSON

# Sociolinguistic competence

Sociolinguistic competence refers to a speaker's (or writer's) knowledge of what constitutes an appropriate utterance according to a specific social context. This kind of knowledge about how language is used in social settings is widely accepted as a crucial element of the more general notion of communicative competence. The term 'communicative competence' was originally proposed to emphasise the importance of knowing the sociocultural appropriateness of an utterance in addition to knowing its grammaticality (Campbell and Wales, 1970; Hymes, 1972). A communicatively competent speaker, it is argued, not only knows the grammatical rules of a given language, but also knows a wide range of sociolinguistic phenomena: dialects, registers, collocations, figures of speech, etc. Applied linguists Canale and Swain (1980), Savignon (1983) and Bachman (1990) further refined the construct of sociolinguistic competence by elaborating its constituent parts and by examining its pedagogical implications. They argued that sociolinguistic rules of SPEAKING depend on dynamic, contextual factors such as the social status of the participants, and are therefore qualitatively different from the static, context-free rules of grammar found in most language TEXTBOOKS.

## Definition

According to Canale and Swain (1980) and Canale (1983), sociolinguistic competence may be sub-divided into two separate but related kinds of knowledge: knowledge about the appropriateness of form, and knowledge about the appropriateness of meaning. Appropriateness of form refers to the extent to which a given verbal or NON-VERBAL form appropriately conveys a meaning in a given context. For example, it would be a violation of the conditions on appropriateness of form if a waiter were to address a table of customers at an expensive restaurant with the question 'OK, what'll it be?' The question sounds rude because the waiter has chosen forms that are inappropriately informal. An example of a violation of the conditions on appropriateness of meaning would be if the waiter were to tell the customers what to eat instead of asking them what they would like to eat. In essence, appropriateness of meaning depends on knowing and respecting the rights and obligations of one's social role, such as 'waiter' or 'customer.'

Those working in the field of APPLIED LINGUISTICS have consistently pointed out that violations of sociolinguistic rules may actually cause more trouble for communication than grammatical errors. A good illustration is the misplacement of adverbs, a typical problem for many non-native speakers. A linguistic error concerning adverb placement would be the ungrammatical utterance 'I like really the cake.' While the error sounds

decidedly odd and foreign to most speakers of English, it is hardly offensive. On the other hand, the use of the first name to address someone of higher status, a violation of a sociolinguistic rule, is likely to cause much embarrassment or consternation (e.g., 'Thanks, Margaret', instead of 'Thank you, Mrs Thatcher'). Sociolinguists have argued that such errors, because they violate social convention, are frequently judged more harshly by NATIVE SPEAKERS than purely grammatical errors (Wolfson, 1983).

## Teaching sociolinguistic competence

Even though language educators now generally agree about the importance of developing students' sociolinguistic competence, there is still a tendency to give it short shrift in language programmes; i.e., to see it as less important than grammatical competence. Such an attitude is understandable given that the findings of sociolinguistic research are still relatively new and somewhat problematic. For example, despite the continued efforts of sociolinguists to discern actual language usage of native speakers in a variety of contexts, more descriptive work is required in order for educators to make informed decisions about how to teach most language forms (Sinclair, 1991). Moreover, valid questions remain about how to teach sociolinguistic competence, or whether it is teachable at all within the confines of the classroom (Valdman, 1992). Virtually all educators who have recognised the importance of contextual or situational factors in language learning argue for the importance of AUTHENTIC language texts in the language programme. However, no written text, regardless of authenticity, can be expected to exemplify the sociolinguistic patterns governing the spoken language. In fact, textbooks frequently fail even to mention constructions that are prevalent in the spoken language, a state of affairs due largely to a continued bias against orality within the profession (Valdman, 1992).

Compounding the specific problem of how to teach the spoken norm versus the written norm, there is the more general problem of how to facilitate sociolinguistic competence within the limited social context of the classroom. In essence, the challenge facing language educators is to figure out how to teach a socially constituted knowledge of language use based on an understanding of social factors that largely occur outside the formal setting of a classroom. As Kramsch and Andersen (1999) point out, 'the problem with learning a language from live context is that context itself cannot be learned, it can only be experienced, or apprenticed in' (1999: 33). They contend that the key to teaching language as a communicative practice embedded in a social setting is to capture real, interactional events on video and to turn them into multimedia 'texts' that can be easily objectified, annotated, explored and manipulated using current technology. In particular, multimedia technology appears to hold much promise in this regard by enabling students to control the viewing of live, unscripted videos, thereby experiencing the complex interplay between language and social context.

**See also:** Communicative language teaching; Grammar; Intercultural communication; Non-verbal communication; Sociolinguistics; Strategic competence; Strategies of language learning; Stylistic variation

### References

Bachman. L. (1990) *Fundamental considerations in language testing*, Oxford: Oxford University Press.

Campbell, R. and Wales, R. (1970) 'The study of language acquisition', in J. Lyons (ed.), *New horizons in linguistics*, Harmondsworth: Penguin.

Canale, M. (1983) 'From communicative competence to communicative language pedagogy', in J. Richards and R. Schmidt (eds), *Language and communication*, London and New York: Longman.

Canale, M. and Swain, M. (1980) 'Theoretical bases of communicative approaches to second language teaching and testing', *Applied Linguistics* 1: 1–47.

Hymes, D. (1972) 'On communicative competence,' in J. Pride and J. Holmes (eds), *Sociolinguistics*, Harmondsworth: Penguin.

Kramsch, C. and Andersen, R. (1999) 'Teaching text and context through multimedia', *Language Learning and Technology* 2, 2: 31–42; (available at time of publication at: http://polyglot.cal.mus.edu/llt/vol2num2article/index.html)

Savignon, S. (1983) *Communicative competence: theory and classroom practice*, Reading, MA: Addison-Wesley.

Sinclair, J. (1991) *Corpus, concordance, collocation*, Oxford: Oxford University Press.

Valdman, A. (1992) 'Authenticity, variation, and communication in the foreign language classroom', in C. Kramsch and S. McConnell-Ginet (eds), *Text and context: cross-disciplinary perspectives on language study*, Lexington, MA: D.C. Heath.

Wolfson, N. (1983) 'Rules of speaking', in J. Richards and R. Schmidt (eds), *Language and communication*, London: Longman.

### Further reading

Loveday, L. (1982) *The sociolinguistics of learning and using a non-native language*, Oxford: Pergamon.

CARL S. BLYTH

# Sociolinguistics

Sociolinguistics is an aspect of the exploration of the social influences on language and the role of language in society. A growth area of study since the late 1960s, it is concerned with linguistic variation within and across individuals and groups at the social, regional, national and international level with respect to such factors as age, **GENDER**, education, occupation, ethnicity and socio-economic status. From the study of the single sounds and **PRONUNCIATIONS** of individual speakers to the use of a world language for international communication, sociolinguistics draws from and contributes to a wide range of disciplines, including **ANTHROPOLOGY**, social **PSYCHOLOGY**, philosophy, education, political science and communication. Through investigation of such phenomena as social **ATTITUDES** to language, **STANDARD** and non-standard forms of language, patterns and needs of national language use, regional and social dialects, or language change and spread, socio-linguistic research sheds light on various social concerns; among them are language conflicts, language rights, literacy, language and disadvantage, the social bases of bilingualism and multilingualism, language and identity, and gender-based speech.

## Description

Sociolinguistics (also known as the sociology of language; see Fishman, 1972) aims to understand uses of language and the social structures in which the users of language function. Given its emphasis on social context, sociolinguists assume language cannot be studied in isolation from the communicative intentions of the users and the socio-cultural context in which a language or language variety is used.

A further assumption is that language is a communal possession that people use, and not an abstract, self-sufficient system. One especially relevant fact of language when viewed from this perspective is that no individual uses language the same way all the time. People constantly change styles, registers and dialects as well as languages depending upon their audience and purposes for **SPEAKING**. They use language differently whether speaking or **WRITING** to co-workers, neighbours and friends; interacting with clients, students or car mechanics; buying or selling a commodity, scolding or soothing a child; asking for help or giving an order; extending or declining an invitation; excluding someone from a conversation; or seeking identity with a speech community.

The variation represented by different speech or language varieties is highly structured and regulated. Thus, any variation associated with language use, whether pronunciation, intonation, **VOCABULARY**, rhetorical choices, or sentence and discourse structure, has limits. The group of people who speak this language, which is known as a speech community, determines the norms and rules defining the limits for use of the particular variety. To understand the structure of a text and the purpose it is intended to serve, it is necessary to refer to the norms and expectations and the social rules of use shared by this group. It is through members' interaction with one another that the communicative competence required to be identified with and become a member of that community is established. Such competence encompasses the ability to use the knowledge of the community's social and cultural values as well as the formal or structural features of its language variety.

Sociolinguistic research may be motivated by interest in the impact of linguistic variation on the social circumstances (e.g., educational failure or low socio-economic status) of individuals and groups (e.g., speakers of non-standard or minority languages) and ultimately on the improvement of the social conditions of the linguistically marginalised. Other motivations are interest in the avoidance or amelioration of language conflict, determination of national or regional languages, establishment of language standards, or improvement of both second and foreign language teaching.

Sociolinguistics is distinguished from general, theoretical **LINGUISTICS** by its emphasis on the social context of language use, i.e. the social influences on language and the role of language in society. Linguistics takes only the structure of language (phonology, morphology, syntax and semantics) into account, to the exclusion of the social contexts in which it is learned and used. For the sociolinguist, speech is social behaviour that serves as a means of self-identification for individuals as well as groups.

Data is collected by different methods of inquiry depending upon the relevant field of study, e.g. history, social psychology or gender studies. Methodological choices include, but are by no means limited to, ethnographic observation, statistical approaches, discourse studies, survey research and conversational or **DISCOURSE ANALYSIS**. The types of sociolinguistic investigation represent detailed investigation of speech events, e.g. differences in lexical choices, intonation patterns, or discourse strategies, the formal and functional characteristics of code-switching and code-mixing, and urban dialects; and more general investigation of the role of language in society, e.g. language policy and **PLANNING**, world languages, **LINGUISTIC IMPERIALISM**, standards of language, or language spread and death. These two broad approaches – detailed and general – are not discrete and mutually exclusive. In fact, meaningful investigation of some phenomena may benefit from and even require both types of analysis, e.g. the sociolinguistic study of a language that functions as a means of global communication.

One such phenomenon of contemporary interest is the worldwide spread and use of **ENGLISH**. Scholarship on this topic investigates the forms and varieties of English that develop in diverse cultural and sociolinguistic contexts. To meet the aim of understanding the nature of English and its numerous national, regional and international varieties, descriptive studies are conducted on the structural features of these varieties, e.g. their lexicon and **GRAMMAR**, and functional characteristics, e.g. the uses made of English for various purposes in particular domains of language use. **DISCOURSE** and **CONVERSATIONAL ANALYSES** investigate the practices and structures of making text through English and ways of speaking that may differ across contexts of use in such disparate locales as South Asia, Europe and the Middle East. Survey studies assess public attitudes toward the learning and use of English in countries and regions, and aid in language policy and planning. **LITERARY** analyses are appropriate in investigations of creative expression through the use of English in postcolonial literatures. Ethnographic methods are suited to the study of multiple cultural identities and traditions associated with English in non-Western contexts. By adopting various modes of inquiry, research into English as a world language has relevance for professionals whose work and livelihood depend upon its learning and use, e.g., lexicographers, **LANGUAGE PLANNERS** and policy-makers, creative writers, literary critics, linguists, language teachers, and **TEACHER EDUCATORS**.

While the existence of differing perspectives and interpretations may be viewed as problematic and as an obstacle to the study of language variation, diversity of approaches, models and methods is in fact a positive characteristic. Language and its use are highly complex, and limiting focus, investigative methods or approach would result in loss of important insights and findings on the interplay of language and society. No one theory or method can do everything sociolinguists want to do.

## History

In the late 1960s and early 1970s the field of linguistics was dominated by the theories and methodology of linguistic analysis associated with the American linguist Noam **CHOMSKY** (1965). His generative–transformation linguistics (later **UNIVERSAL GRAMMAR**) emphasised the decontextualised ideal **NATIVE SPEAKER** and restricted its attention to the sentence level and grammatical accuracy. This approach is too limited for researchers and scholars with an interest in the role of language in such social issues as access to educational and employment opportunities for minority populations who use a non-standard language variety, or the linguistic rights of indigenous and immigrant groups. Understanding the sources and effects of linguistic diversity on social status and mobility required a different approach to language. (See Giglioli, 1972, and Pride and Holmes, 1972, for early research that was influential in establishing and shaping the field.)

Sociolinguistics has its roots in European and American linguistics. The British linguistic tradition is an approach to linguistic analysis associated with J.R. Firth, British historian-turned-linguist, whose work, beginning in the 1930s, had a profound impact on developments in linguistic theory throughout the 1960s and 1970s. Firth's philosophy of language was based on the interdependence of language, culture and society and the belief that language needs to be studied as a social phenomenon. His notions of language varieties, social dialect and register, and functions of language, all have a place in contemporary sociolinguistic studies. Firth also acknowledged the role of language in a broader sense, e.g. as a means for international communication and for representing a particular culture and way of life. These realisations are echoed in subsequent sociolinguistic research.

In the late 1960s and early 1970s, M.A.K. **HALLIDAY** (1978) developed the sociological linguistics Firth advocated, particularly through investigation of the social functions of language. For Halliday, the best way to bring all the functions of language, and therefore all the components of meaning, into focus is through the description of written and spoken texts in the contexts of situation in which they occur. That is, it is necessary to take such environmental features into account as the people and their relationship to one another, their **NON-VERBAL** as well as verbal behaviour, and the effect of what is said or written. Such focus on the context is essential to understanding the meanings expressed, negotiated and interpreted by the users through the texts they create.

Parallel developments were also in progress in the USA around this time. Dell Hymes (1974), anthropologist and linguist, also critical of the notion that linguistic description could proceed without reference to context, proposed an ethnographic approach. It would take into account such various factors involved in speaking as the time and place of the interaction, the participants, the form and content of what is said, and the expected outcomes. Hymes was concerned with what a speaker knows with respect to appropriate use of language in interaction with other speakers. After all, learning a language also involves learning how to use it in order to get things done and interact with the people who speak that language, with members of the particular speech community. This attention to appropriateness evolved into the concept 'communicative competence', a specification of what it means to be a competent user of a particular language.

At least a century before Halliday and Hymes arrived on the scene, language scholars in Europe were researching language variation in the form of dialectology studies, which had as their focus the identification of regional differences in language form, particularly variations in pronunciation and vocabulary, and in determination of the geographic location of the pronunciations observed. In the 1960s, dialectology expanded to include class and ethnic urban dialects. William Labov's (1972) work in particular was influential in establishing investigations into the social dimensions of language variation as part of sociolinguistics. He also introduced an alternative, quantitative, research methodology. Trained as a chemist, Labov studied how pronunciation of certain sounds can change over time and across social groups by using precise techniques associated with the scientific approach of the natural sciences. Analyses of the frequency of particular speech patterns, e.g. the presence or absence of post-vocalic final 'r' in the speech of New Yorkers, were reported as percentages in tabular form.

The scope of sociolinguistic investigation continues to expand. For example it has opened to include the study of the relationship of language and sexism, gay and lesbian speech, and INTER-NET-user language. None the less, understanding meaning in variation continues to be the theme of the study of language and society.

## Conflicting views

Those who conduct sociolinguistic studies are not of a single mind on theoretical, methodological or empirical issues. Differences exist on such matters as theories of language, interpretations of what constitutes relevant data and valid evidence, formulations of research problems, beliefs about the generalisability of conclusions, and interpretations of both the theoretical and real world consequences of research.

A central disagreement among some sociolinguists is about the direction of influence between language and society. There are four basic positions. Some believe social structure – gender, regional origin or ethnicity – influences or determines linguistic structure or linguistic behaviour (the ways of speaking). Others maintain that linguistic structure influences social structure (it is not the speakers of a language who are sexist or racist, but the language). Still others take the view that the influence is bi-directional (speech behaviour and social behaviour are in a state of constant interaction). And finally, some question whether there is any relationship at all between linguistic and social structures (each is independent of the other).

The scope of sociolinguistics is also debated. While some (see Wardhaugh, 1992) argue that the field encompasses most research that is concerned with language and society – e.g. conversational and discourse analysis, SPEECH ACTS, BILINGUALISM, language standardisation, or language attitudes – others (see Trudgill, 1974/1983) accept as sociolinguistics only those studies with linguistic objectives, i.e. those that aim to improve linguistic theory and develop understanding of the nature of language. This more narrow view of the field admits studies of variation theory and language change – the relationship between language and social class – for the insight they provide into the nature of linguistic variability and the structure of linguistic systems. (See Hudson, 1996, and Romaine, 1994, for representations of a more inclusive view.)

## Significance for language teaching and learning

The significance of sociolinguistics for language teaching and learning manifests itself in first and second and foreign language teaching issues. Regardless of whether first or **SECOND LANGUAGE ACQUISITION** is the focus, in learning to speak everyone learns to communicate in those ways deemed appropriate by the speech community in which they are doing that learning or of which they desire membership. As ways of speaking differ from group to group and from language to language, new ways have to be learned in order for the learner to fit in. (See McKay and Hornberger, 1996, for a discussion of links between sociolinguistics and language teaching.)

In the setting of first language, the beginning of formal education may require learning a new way of speaking, that of the standard variety used by teachers and in **TEXTBOOKS** that identifies a speaker as 'educated'. It may be learning the language of a new professional group, e.g. lawyers and artists, or of a new **GENRE**, e.g. scholarly papers or speech writing. A topic of interest in sociolinguistics in the area of first language has been the relationship between the use of language and educational failure. In his research into urban and ethnic dialects, especially that of Black English Vernacular (BEV) speakers in urban contexts, Labov investigated the role of BEV, the primary language of communication at home, in the poor scholastic performance of children from families of lower socio-economic status. One key factor was the difference between the formal features of BEV and the standard English used by their teachers, who regarded BEV as ungrammatical and limited in syntax and vocabulary, and therefore illogical. These views influenced teachers' **ASSESSMENTS** of the children's intellectual capability and ability to participate and succeed in the educational process. This research and its findings have clear implications for the teaching of literacy, teacher education and standards and tools for language assessment.

In second and foreign language pedagogy, adoption of the notion of communicative competence has considerably influenced teaching theory and practice. Seeking alternatives to the form-focused instruction which characterised contemporary approaches, second language specialists in the 1970s found Hymes's attention to appropriateness in context, and Halliday's focus on meaning and function, valuable bases for reforming language teaching. While numerous functional and communication-based teaching models were subsequently proposed, it was not until the 1980s that a coherent and comprehensive theory was developed. In their theoretical framework for curriculum design and **EVALUATION** in second language programmes, Canale and Swain (1980; see also Canale, 1983) place linguistic competence squarely within the larger construct of communicative competence, where it is but one component with sociolinguistic, strategic and discourse competence. A similar perspective was taken by **VAN EK** (1986) and the development of the **THRESHOLD LEVEL**. Savignon's (1997) subsequent interpretation of this framework provided a pedagogical model that teachers could use in their own classrooms. A variety of innovations and initiatives in **COMMUNICATIVE LANGUAGE TEACHING** in diverse settings around the world demonstrated the relevance of social and cultural context to a range of theoretical and practical concerns. (See Savignon and Berns, 1984, 1987, for examples.)

Other relevant sociolinguistic constructs have proven useful in addressing essential concerns for language teaching in both second and foreign language contexts (Kachru, 1992). Notions of intelligibility, standard language and language norms highlight the key role of context as a central consideration in selecting classroom models, determining the communicative competence learners are to develop, and the level of intelligibility they are to achieve. Decisions on these matters directly impact pedagogical decisions in the areas of forms and standards for evaluation, **MATERIALS** design and selection, and teacher preparation.

**See also:** Communicative language teaching; Communicative strategies; Conversation analysis; Discourse analysis; Linguistics; Native speaker; Notions and functions; Politeness; Research methods; Sociolinguistic competence; Speech act theory; Text and corpus linguistics

## References

Canale, M. (1983) 'From communicative

competence to communicative language pedagogy', in J. Richards and R. Schmidt (eds), *Language and communication*, London: Longman.

Canale, M. and Swain, M. (1980) 'Theoretical bases of communicative approaches to second language teaching and testing', *Journal of Applied Linguistics* 1, 1–47.

Chomsky, N. (1965) *Aspects of the theory of syntax*, Cambridge, MA: MIT Press.

Fishman, J. (1972) *Sociology of language*, Rowley, MA: Newbury House.

Giglioli, P. (1972) *Language and social context*, Harmondsworth: Penguin.

Halliday, M.A.K. (1978) *Language as social semiotic, the social interpretation of language and meaning*, London: Edward Arnold.

Hudson, R.A. (1996) *Sociolinguistics: an introduction* (rev. edn), Cambridge: Cambridge University Press.

Hymes, D. (1974) *Foundations in sociolinguistics: an ethnographic approach*, Philadelphia: University of Pennsylvania Press.

Kachru, B. (ed.) (1992) *The other tongue: English across cultures* (2nd edn), Urbana, IL: University of Illinois Press.

Labov, W. (1972) *Sociolinguistic patterns*, Philadelphia: University of Pennsylvania Press.

McKay, S. and Hornberger, N. (eds) (1996) *Sociolinguistics and language teaching*, Cambridge: Cambridge University Press.

Pride, J.B. and Holmes, J. (eds) (1972) *Sociolinguistics*, Harmondsworth: Penguin.

Romaine, S. (1994) *Language in society: an introduction*, Oxford: Oxford University Press.

Savignon, S. (1997) *Communicative competence: theory and classroom practice* (2nd edn), New York: McGraw-Hill.

Savignon, S. and Berns, M. (1984) *Initiatives in communicative language teaching*, Reading, MA: Addison-Wesley.

Savignon, S. and Berns, M. (1987) *Initiatives in communicative language teaching II*, Reading, MA: Addison-Wesley.

Trudgill, W. (1983) *Sociolinguistics: an introduction to language and society* (rev. edn), Harmondsworth: Penguin.

van Ek, J. (1986) *Objectives for foreign language learning*, Strasbourg: Council of Europe.

Wardhaugh, R. (1992) *An introduction to sociolinguistics*, Oxford: Blackwell.

## Further reading

Berns, M. (1990) *Contexts of competence: social and cultural considerations in communicative language teaching*, New York: Plenum.

Grabe, W. (ed.) (1992) *Annual review of applied linguistics. Vol. 12: Literacy*, Cambridge: Cambridge University Press.

Kramsch, C. (1993) *Context and culture in language teaching*, Oxford: Oxford University Press.

Preston, D. (1989) *Sociolinguistics and second language acquisition*, Oxford: Blackwell.

Saville-Troike, M. (1989) *The ethnography of communication* (2nd edn), Oxford: Blackwell.

MARGIE BERNS

# Spanish

The teaching of Spanish as a foreign language (*Español como lengua extranjera* – ELE) has run along parallel lines with other European languages. In the last third of the twentieth century it underwent a considerable transformation in methodology. This has been accompanied by a growing number of institutional and professional initiatives: the founding of the Cervantes Institute, the creation of diplomas for Spanish as a Foreign Language, the publication of the multimedia course '*Viaje al Español*', the organisation of specialist courses in various universities and the publication of specialist journals.

It is essential to mention the *Gramática Castellana* by E. Antonio de Nebrija (1492), as this was the first codification of a modern language, or at least that is what the author intended when it was published. 'All those who have any intercourse and conversation in Spanish and need the language, if they do not learn it as children, will be able to do so more quickly with the assistance of my work', stated Nebrija in his introduction. Paradoxically, he did not have many followers, since, as Sánchez Pérez stated, 'most courses and materials used for teaching Spanish as a foreign language were published outside Spain until about the middle of the twentieth century' (Sánchez Pérez, 1992: 3). However, there has always been ELE, and it has seen a huge increase throughout the world, particularly in the **UNITED STATES OF AMERICA**.

## Methods and approaches

A review of the coursebooks which have been published for ELE teaching gives a good overview of the subject. According to Sánchez Pérez (1992: 369ff), the first to be published in Spain appeared towards the middle of the twentieth century, in response to the needs of the growing number of courses in ELE organised by Spanish universities. They were *Español para Extranjeros* by Martín Alonso (1949), and *Curso breve de español para extranjeros* (Frederico de Borja Moll, 1954). Both these courses were based on a grammatical framework, but they show an interesting variation on the strict grammatical approach in that they contain practical dialogues and speech forms which are designed to reflect Spanish customs and spoken usage. They had a huge distribution, and Moll's course had reached more than twenty editions by the 1970s.

In the middle of that decade two new courses were published which involved the introduction of the **AUDIOLINGUAL METHOD**. One was *Vida y diágolos de España* (A. Rojo Sastre, Salamanca), which was a faithful adaptation into Spanish of the SGAV methodology of the French school at Mons. The other, *Español en Directo* (Sánchez *et al.*) had more of a British influence, in that it was an eclectic combination of situational elements, the **DIRECT METHOD** and a strong grammatical basis with audiolingual principles.

The publication of *Un Nivel Umbral* (A Threshold Level: Slagter, 1979) coincided with the beginning of a period of complete transformation in ELE methodology. The twenty years between 1970 and 1990 saw the development of a series of important projects which were accompanied by a large number of manuals and supplementary **MATERIALS** for ELE teaching. These projects range from the most academic (masters' courses, doctorates, teacher-training days, and conferences) and the most professional (teachers' associations), through to state institutions (the Cervantes Institute, Diplomas de Español como Lengua Extranjera (DELE), *Viaje al Español*, and revitalisation of the

Language Attachés of overseas Spanish embassies). As far as publications were concerned, editorial offers flowed in, not only in quantity but also in diversity (there were various textbooks for teaching ELE in the world of commerce, there were materials for teaching the separate **SKILLS** and for teaching through tasks, etc.). One of the first courses of this period was *Para Empezar* (1980), which brings together a collection of innovative features such as the structuring of the learning content according to a series of notions and functions with their various linguistic components (inspired by the **THRESHOLD LEVEL**), differentiated treatment of oral and written usage, **LISTENING** comprehension activities (for the first time in an ELE textbook), etc. Towards the end of the 1990s a dozen more manuals came out, all with a notional–functional basis, ranging from the strictly linguistic early ones to the inclusion of elements which were nearer to the learning process (cognitive and constructivist) and which involved the student's participation (**AUTONOMY** and learning **STRATEGIES**). The influence of these later tendencies of communicative teaching, and in particular teaching through tasks, has become a prominent feature of some of these manuals.

In 1988 a group of teachers founded the journal *Cable*. Its publication came to an end in 1992, but the ten issues which appeared in those five years served as a good vehicle for innovation and communication within the profession. It was a platform for up-dating theory, spreading and applying new language-learning theory to language teaching, such as, for example, the autonomy of the learner and teaching though tasks, which are now part of most ELE teaching. Subsequently other journals have appeared, including *REALE, Frecuencia L, Carabela* etc.

## The establishment of state institutions

### The Cervantes Institute

The **CERVANTES INSTITUTE** was founded in 1991 for the promotion and international dissemination of the Spanish language, and by the mid-1990s there were thirty centres abroad offering around 2,000 language courses with a total registration of more than 20,000. In 1994 the Cervantes Institute published its curriculum, which was open, learner-centred, and which laid down a communicative **SYLLABUS** based on tasks. In 1997 the *Centro Virtual Cervantes* website was created. Among its contents are teaching materials, a discussion forum and a news bulletin.

### *The Ministry of Education and Science*

Within Spain there is a network of official public language schools for the specific purpose of teaching languages to adults, Las Escuelas Oficiales de Idiomas (EOI). The teachers in these centres are university graduates and civil servants. This is a very widespread network, and the largest of them include an ELE department. Spanish Embassies abroad have an Education Council, where one of the elements is the department of the Language Attaché, whose brief is the development of teaching and support for teachers of ELE. Its personnel is composed of specialist foreign language teachers. There is also a network of secondary schools which run courses following the Spanish system.

### Diplomas in Spanish as a Foreign Language

These diplomas in linguistic competence – *Los Diplomas de Español como Lengua Extranjera* (DELE) – were created by the Ministry of Education and Science in 1989. Subsequently an agreement was made with the University of Salamanca for the development and marking of the examinations, and with the Cervantes Institute for the organisation and administration of the tests in its centres throughout the world. There are two examinations each year, and by the mid-1990s the total number of annual candidates was about 10,000, in 150 towns and forty countries round the world.

### *Viaje al Español*

This multimedia course was published in 1992. It was designed to be broadcast on television and was a joint production between Radio-Televisión Española, the Ministry of Education and Science and the University of Salamanca.

### The universities

The Universidad Internacional Menéndez y Pelayo (UIMP) is a public university which has the special function of organising ELE summer courses in its centre at Santander. Among its programmes are courses designed for teacher development. Almost all the other Spanish universities organise ELE courses, both during the academic year and in the summer holidays. However, none of them grants qualifications related to ELE, except the Master's ELE postgraduate courses which are conferred by the universities of Alcalá de Henares, Barcelona, Complutense de Madrid, Granada and Salamanca, as well as the university institutes of Ortega y Gasset and Universitas Nebrissensis, both in Madrid. Some of these courses are organised by university departments which have research and doctorates in the acquisition of second languages, placing them not only in a professional but also in a research context.

### Associations and conferences

The oldest of these is the European Association of Teachers of Spanish (*Associación Europea de Profesores de Español* – AEPE). The Association for Teaching Spanish as a Foreign Language (Asociación para la Enseñanza del Español como Lengua Extranjera – ASELE) was founded in the 1980s. There is also the Spanish Association of Applied Linguistics (*Asociación Española de Lingüística Aplicada* – AESLA) which, although it includes teachers of other languages, does include in its conferences and publications themes related to ELE. All these associations organise annual conferences in a Spanish university. In the United States, The Association of Teachers of Spanish and Portuguese publishes the journal HISPANIA, which includes a section on ELE matters.

Finally, the *Fundación Actilibre* organises the annual EXPOLINGUA, an exhibition of teaching materials within the framework of which are days specialising in ELE methodology. The work done on these days is published by the same organisation in the collection *Cuadernos del Tiempo Libre*.

**See also:** Africa; Cervantes Institute; Creoles;

French; Lingua franca; Portuguese; Standard language

## Website

The website of the Cervantes Institute, *Centro Virtual Cervantes*, is: http://cvc.cervantes.es

## References

Sánchez Pérez, A. (1992) *Historia de la enseñanza del español como lengua extranjera*, Madrid: SGEL.
Slagter, P. (1979) *Un Nivel Umbral*, Strasbourg: Council of Europe.

ERNESTO MARTÍN-PERIS

# Speaking

Approaches to the teaching of speaking in a foreign language reflect understanding of at least two phenomena: the nature of speaking in a second language; and how people learn. Historically, the teaching of oral foreign language **SKILLS** developed under the following major assumptions: first, that speech is the fundamental mode of knowing a language; second, that speech is the same as written language except for being spoken; third, that language is learnt either **BEHAVIOURISTICALLY**, through imitation and repetition, or cognitively, through the study of rules and of **TRANSLATION** equivalents (Howatt, 1984). This set of basic assumptions meant that even those pedagogic traditions which made speaking central did so in ways which were incompatible with normal speech. Subsequently these assumptions were discarded. Rather, speech became seen as involving the speaker in a number of rapid decisions, taken within a changing context, with speech in a second language imposing additional problems (Scovel, 1998; Poulisse, 1997). Hence approaches to the teaching of speaking in a second language had to change in line with this changed understanding. In response, approaches came to highlight three areas for pedagogic attention: the students' exposure to the spoken language; the quality of the interaction between teacher and student; and the designing of

tasks capable of engaging students in appropriate processing of language.

## Approaches to teaching speaking

Early approaches to language teaching were based on assumptions about language and learning which largely ignored the particular patterns and processes of speech. The **GRAMMAR–TRANSLATION** approach defined language in terms of written texts, and saw the learning process as largely centred on establishing translation equivalents between the first and second language. Consequently this approach paid little attention to the forms of spoken language, or to the processes of using it (Howatt, 1984). In contrast, the **AUDIO-LINGUAL** approach advocated the development of speaking and **LISTENING** before that of **READING** and **WRITING**. Furthermore, its view that the learning process should consist largely or exclusively of developing rapid stimulus–response–feedback connections brought oral **EXERCISES** to centre stage (Fries, 1945; Lado and Fries, 1958; Lado, 1964). This view of the learning process, however, only focused on the processes of producing targeted structures within highly predictable initiation–response–follow-up exchange patterns. The approach did not require or enable students to develop the ability to process longer or more improvised patterns of interaction. Furthermore, the audiolingual view of language was largely defined in terms of the set of possible grammatical structures in the target language: it still largely failed to distinguish between written and spoken patterns of language. In contrast, the situational approach and the notional–functional approach introduced features of language reflecting more closely the particular uses to which it might be put (Wilkins, 1976). The situational approach saw the need to provide students with practice in the use of language appropriate to a range of typical situations, notably commonly occurring service encounters. The notional–functional approach introduced **SPEECH ACTS** into the repertoire of target language features. However, while these developments now began to address the nature of spoken language as product (a direction likely to be explored for some time: see Carter and McCarthy, 1997), they did not alter the types of exercises by which speaking was to be taught (Littlewood, 1981). Drills were still used, albeit now with functional or situational elements, and dialogues were used rather like extended drills (see, e.g., Abbs and Sexton, 1978). It was the advent of the communicative approach which helped change classroom activities, by focusing on the conditions of language use and language learning (Widdowson, 1978; Allwright, 1984; Brumfit, 1984). This movement insisted on the meaningful use of language within the learning process, both as a way of ensuring that students practise real communication, and as a means of language **ACQUISITION**. This view encouraged the use of information transfer or information gap activities, bringing with them techniques such as **GROUP WORK**, and the use of unscripted activities (Littlewood, 1981; Bygate, 1987). Spoken language could now be taught with due regard to its characteristics as both process and product.

## The nature of spoken language

Spoken language production (similar to the processing of written language) involves three main phases of language processing (Levelt, 1989; Poulisse, 1997; Scovel, 1998). The first is conceptualisation of the message content, whether in terms of the content of a short message or the content of a longer turn or sequence of turns. The second phase involves selecting an appropriate linguistic formulation for the message. The third phase involves articulation of the message. Normally the three phases operate smoothly and can often be hard to distinguish. However, there are times when each phase can cause problems. At the conceptualisation phase, a speaker can give someone an inappropriate message or convey an inappropriate intention. At the formulation phase, a speaker can choose the wrong word or expression to convey an appropriate intention. At the articulation phase, a speaker can mispronounce words. The fact that speakers routinely self-correct these different types of error implies that monitoring and self-correction must be further aspects of the production process. Finally, speaking involves adjusting one's speech to the interlocutor. This occurs in the patterns and types of turns that

speakers use, as well as in their phrases and **VOCABULARY**.

In second language speech, these processes can function differently from first language speech; they are commonly slower, and more prone to errors in all phases of the process, hence requiring more frequent self-correction. Speakers are also commonly unsure of what message to convey or how to convey it, giving rise to the use of communication strategies (Kasper and Kellerman, 1997) to improvise what to say and how to say it. Finally, it is common for second language speakers to have difficulty coping with the demands of managing social interaction. Here, too, in a second language, speakers find themselves having to improvise ways of communicating and of responding to their interlocutors. The pressure of managing the target language in speech is signalled by the relative degree of accuracy, fluency and complexity, measures used to assess speakers' levels of processing and proficiency (Skehan, 1998).

In terms of product, speech has been shown to differ from writing (Carter and McCarthy, 1997; Eggins and Slade, 1997; Biber, Conrad and Reppen, 1994). For one thing, there is much greater regional and social variation in speech than in writing, as well as a wider range in levels of formality. Further, the conditions and context of speech give rise to differences in the patterns of a number of features of language. Oral discourse patterns are generally dialogic rather than monologic, and involve not just turn-taking, but a variety of types of exchange, with their own range of patterns, including opening and closing sequences. Similarly, speech acts and lexico-grammar show a different frequency and range of features from those found in writing. Spoken language is far more likely to make reference to the temporal and spatial context in which communication occurs, significantly affecting the extent to which different parts of the lexico-grammar of a language will be used (Biber, Conrad and Reppen, 1994). Finally, spoken delivery requires the use of a range of fluency/disfluency features, which would not be countenanced in writing, such as silent and filled pauses, repetition and self-correction. Hence, both the processes and products of spoken language are distinct from those of written language. Both process and product will therefore require particular types of input and particular types of activity if their use is to be developed within the classroom context.

## Teaching speaking in a second language

Understandably in light of the above, the teaching of speaking in a second language focuses largely on four issues: what variety of spoken language to teach; what input to provide and how to provide it; how interaction between teacher and students can help the development of speaking; and the design and use of tasks. The problem of selecting a target variety of spoken language has no single solution. Options available to students will vary according to their context of learning or use (such as English as **MEDIUM OF INSTRUCTION** or English as a Foreign Language).

In terms of input, partly following the views of Krashen represented in his **MONITOR MODEL**, approaches agree on the need for students to listen meaningfully to extracts of the type of speech they are to acquire (Ellis, 1997). Course books include **AUTHENTIC**, largely unscripted taped material to be used for **LISTENING** comprehension, on the assumption that this exposure will assist students' speech production. **TEACHER TALK** is also seen as a valuable source of aural input, provided it is adjusted to the students' levels of comprehension and engages them in purposeful listening. However, speech cannot be mastered purely through exposure to comprehensible input: interaction has also been shown to contain features (such as lexico-grammatical prompts, turn-taking prompts, and clarification sequences such as paraphrases) which are likely to provide support for students' initially-tentative speech (Carter and McCarthy, 1997). Interactive teacher–class speech is therefore encouraged. The asymmetrical and often evaluative character of teacher–class interaction, however, can limit its effectiveness in developing students' ability to talk. A third element – unscripted oral tasks – is therefore needed in order to develop students' ability to initiate and sustain purposeful interactive speech (Bygate, 1987). Oral tasks consist of some aural, written or visual input with a goal to achieve (Nunan, 1989), and requiring students to perform a range of functions (such as brainstorming, listing, describing, comparing, recalling, re-

constructing, evaluating, narrating, persuading, arguing) in order jointly to achieve the goal (Ur, 1981; Riggenbach, 1999). This can often be associated with a related reading or writing task. In achieving the task goal, students need jointly to engage the speech production processes identified above, and, in so doing, to decide what messages need sending, and to work on ways of formulating and articulating those messages. An approach centred on the use of such tasks is known as a **TASK-BASED** approach (Willis, 1996; Willis and Willis, 1996; Skehan, 1998). Just as in other areas of the curriculum, it enables an important distinction to be drawn between the experience of practising the use of the whole skill, and practising 'part skills', such as **PRONUNCIATION**, grammatical accuracy, lexical fluency or the formulation of particular speech acts (Littlewood, 1981; Johnson, 1996). Part skills can then be practised through a range of exercises, some of them non-communicative such as the drills favoured in audiolingual approaches, in order to reduce the learning load and enable a focus on problematic parts of the skill. Task-based approaches thus attempt to ensure that both process and product of spoken language are fully integrated into the language classroom.

**See also:** Acquisition and teaching; Audiolingual method; Behaviourism; Communicative strategies; Direct method; Medium of instruction; Mental lexicon; Notions and functions; Skills and knowledge in language learning; Speech act theory; Strategic competence; Writing

## References

Abbs, B. and Sexton, M. (1978) *Challenges*, London: Longman.

Allwright, R.L. (1984) 'The importance of interaction in classroom language learning', *Applied Linguistics* 5: 156–71.

Biber, D., Conrad, S. and Reppen, R. (1994) 'Corpus-based approaches to issues in applied linguistics', *Applied Linguistics* 15, 2: 169–90.

Brown, G. and Yule, G. (1983) *Teaching the spoken language*, Cambridge: Cambridge University Press.

Brumfit, C.J. (1984) *Communicative methodology in*

language teaching, Cambridge: Cambridge University Press.

Bygate, M. (1987) *Speaking*, Oxford: Oxford University Press.

Carter, R. and McCarthy, M. (1997) *Exploring spoken English*, Cambridge: Cambridge University Press.

Crookes, G. and Gass, S. (eds) (1993a) *Tasks and language learning*, Clevedon: Multilingual Matters.

Crookes, G. and Gass, S. (eds) (1993b) *Tasks in a pedagogical context*, Clevedon: Multilingual Matters.

Eggins, S. and Slade, D. (1997) *Analysing casual conversation*, London: Cassell.

Ellis, R. (1997) *SLA research and language teaching*, Oxford: Oxford University Press.

Fries, C.C. (1945) *Teaching and learning English as a Foreign Language*, Ann Arbor: University of Michigan Press.

Galloway, C. and Richards, B.J. (1994) *Input and interaction in language acquisition*, Cambridge: Cambridge University Press.

Howatt, A.P.R. (1984) *A history of English language teaching*, Oxford: Oxford University Press.

Johnson, K. (1996) *Language teaching and skill learning*, Oxford: Blackwell.

Kasper, G. and Kellerman, E. (eds) (1997) *Communication strategies: psycholinguistic and sociolinguistic perspectives*, London: Longman.

Lado, R. (1964) *Language teaching: a scientific approach*, New York: McGraw Hill.

Lado, R. and Fries, C.C. (1958) *English sentence patterns. Understanding and producing English grammatical structures: an oral approach*, Ann Arbor: The University of Michigan.

Levelt, W.J.M. (1989) *Speaking: from intention to articulation*, Cambridge, MA: MIT Press.

Littlewood, W.J. (1981) *Communicative language teaching: an introduction*, Cambridge: Cambridge University Press.

Nunan, D. (1989) *Designing tasks for the communicative classroom*, Cambridge: Cambridge University Press.

Poulisse, N. (1997) 'Language production in bilinguals', in A.M.B. de Groot and J.F. Kroll (eds), *Tutorials in bilingualism: psycholinguistic perspectives*, Mahwah, NJ: Lawrence Erlbaum.

Riggenbach, H. (1999) *Discourse analysis in the language classroom. Volume 1: The spoken language*, Ann Arbor: The University of Michigan Press.

Scovel, T. (1998) *Psycholinguistics*, Oxford Introductions to Language Study, Oxford: Oxford University Press.

Skehan, P. (1998) *A cognitive approach to language learning*, Oxford: Oxford University Press.

Ur, P. (1981) *Discussions that work*, Cambridge: Cambridge University Press.

Ur, P. (1996) *A course in language teaching*, Cambridge: Cambridge University Press.

Widdowson, H.G. (1978) *Teaching language as communication*, Oxford: Oxford University Press.

Wilkins, D.A. (1976) *Notional syllabuses*, Oxford: Oxford University Press.

Willis, J. (1996) *A framework for task-based learning*, London: Longman.

Willis, J. and Willis, D. (eds) (1996) *Challenge and change in language teaching*, London: Heinemann.

Yule, G. (1997) *Referential communication tasks*, Mahwah, NJ: Lawrence Erlbaum.

## Further reading

Bygate, M. (1987) *Speaking*, Oxford: Oxford University Press.

Carter, R. and McCarthy, M. (1997) *Exploring spoken English*, Cambridge: Cambridge University Press.

Littlewood, W.J. (1992) *Teaching oral communication: a methodological framework*, Oxford: Blackwell.

Scovel, T. (1998) *Psycholinguistics*, Oxford Introductions to Language Study, Oxford: Oxford University Press.

Willis, J. and Willis, D. (eds) (1996) *Challenge and change in language teaching*, London: Heinemann.

MARTIN BYGATE

# Speech act theory

Pragmatic considerations are fundamental to any natural language system – more precisely to language in use – and therefore should influence linguistic analysis. It is not language as a system (*LANGUE*) but language as performance (*parole*) that should be the topic of research, especially where consequences for language **ACQUISITION** and teaching are concerned.

Speech act theory originated around movements such as American pragmatism and symbolic interactionism, the latter associated with G.H. Mead. More specifically, it derived from the so-called ordinary language philosophy of G.E. Moore and Ludwig Wittgenstein. Their main findings postulated that a good many philosophical (pseudo-)problems arise from linguistic causes: they are in reality a result of insufficient and vague formulations.

Speech act theory was first articulated in Austin's lectures (published posthumously as 'How to Do Things with Words', 1962) where a functional approach to the study of language was advocated. The Prague linguists had had similar ideas and were aware of the functional force of verbal structures. Grice (1975) and the ethno-methodologists (Hymes, 1972 *et passim*) had a similar outlook: how to analyse successful communication within certain speech communities. This approach matured in the late 1960s, hence language use is regarded as an essential element of social interaction (Halliday, 1978) and this is one reason why pragmalinguistic considerations influenced **SOCIOLINGUISTIC** research programmes as well.

The effect of these philosophical, sociological as well as linguistic considerations was a new approach to the analysis of communicative (and, in particular, verbal) acts whose communicative functions came into focus. The traditional approach had concerned itself mainly with the structural elements of language systems; in other words, with *langue* instead of *parole*. From the perspective of this novel kind of **LANGUAGE AWARE-NESS**, communication is visualised as the active handling of reality as well as dealing with one's partners, and communicative competence is predominantly oral, especially in face-to-face-interaction, i.e. oriented towards its actual communicative situation, and especially its participants.

The central idea of speech act theory is that verbal utterances effect and represent a lot more than what logicians acknowledge to be relevant, i.e. declarative speech acts which are either true or false with regard to a possible world. Language in use is designed to serve diverse intentions, or illocutions, i.e. **COMMUNICATIVE STRATEGIES**, such as those which start and close a conversation, greet or congratulate somebody, promise future activities, narrate and possibly evaluate past events, warn somebody of some danger, pronounce a threat or even try to hurt somebody's feelings by expressions that should not be used in a particular situation. Language can create both harm and pleasure.

A number of attempts at classification or categorisation of speech acts have been suggested, among which Searle's proposal seems the most prominent. He postulates, for example, the following categories: representatives (statements), directives (questions) and declaratives (naming, appointments). Habermas (1971) has different labels that cover approximately the same gamut of possible communicative actions: communicatives (say), constatives (describe), representatives (disclose) and regulatives (arrange, agree).

The aim of certain speech acts can be reached by explicit pronouncement, such as 'And herewith I pronounce you man and wife'. Specific performative formulas are used in this case. Some speech acts, on the other hand, cannot be announced, e.g. lying, but can nevertheless be described, meta-communicatively after the event.

Some speech acts cannot easily be misunderstood; others have to be decoded by the addressee, more often than not by examining their applicability to the actual situation, including the personal relationships of the interactants. This is obvious with deictic elements, e.g. ' . . . so we put it on top of the other one . . . ', and especially wherever personal concerns are involved: 'Considering our inveterate mutual friendly relations you should have been aware of the consequences . . . '.

Still others, for example indirect speech acts, although they seem to try to express a certain communicative intention, really mean something quite different: the meaning of the proposition does not fit with the illocution, e.g. threatening somebody by expressing a promise: 'If you do that again I promise you a sound hiding'. To distinguish direct from indirect speech acts, we also have to consider the social situation, because an indirect command or request may be regarded as being much more polite than a direct one; for example, 'It's cold in here' can mean 'Turn on the heating'. Austin argued that, although acts like promising or threatening cannot be judged according to their truth value, they can succeed or fail according to certain conditions that ought to be complied with.

Indirect speech acts are most easily misunderstood, and this may result in personal conflict. This is why they are regarded as a communicative skill to be acquired separately. It is noteworthy that, according to common pedagogical knowledge, children are unable to understand irony and easily fall victim to so-called double-bind actions. However, whereas indirectness is liable to misunderstanding, performatively realised direct speech acts may possibly appear impolite and can produce aggressive reactions. This has implications for the design of learning material, which usually tries to be simple and unmistakably direct and explicit.

The one communicative fact that is not dealt with – or only insufficiently so – in speech act theory is that every speech act is liable to meet with a response. The reaction of the recipient is the only reason why speech acts are realised at all. Thus, turn-taking and its rules and restrictions, as well as the sequentiality and the interdependence of speech events, identified in **DISCOURSE ANALYSIS**, should be regarded as important teaching goals.

Speech acts are inextricably connected with their situational setting. They cannot be used, decoded and reacted upon outside their situational surrounding and their intentional constellation. Failure in communication can be the result of a misapplication of linguistic devices to an interactional setting. Although **NON-VERBAL** signals contribute to the intelligibility of communicative interactions, disambiguate and supplement as well as clarify and intensify the verbal message, this dimension is usually neglected in language teaching, and, therefore, can also be responsible for misunderstanding.

Speech act theory has stimulated the teaching of pragmatic aspects of language, but it is insufficient as a base of a holistic didactic system, first because it concentrates on isolated communicative steps, and second because the important role of the interlocutor tends to be neglected. Being able to articulate a single illocution is not the same as being able to participate in a conversation. Communicative interaction is influenced by the hearer's or reader's presuppositions, cultural background and emotive attitude. These are elements that will most probably control their understanding and reaction to what the speaker is trying to do. In this respect it seems useful to distinguish between analogical and digital communicative elements. Digital elements carry the cognitive informational contents, whereas emotional and affective messages use different channels, e.g. non-verbal signals. If either of the two kinds of meaning apply, the result may be confusing, i.e. there is a discrepancy between what is being transmitted as referential information and what the recipient is expected to understand.

Affective attitudes result from role constellations and their modifications. These have a strong influence on conversational stages and procedures. Role constellations in the classroom (teacher-student) cannot easily be transferred to everyday interactions.

## Consequences for teaching

Emancipatory educational programmes try to reflect and consider the students' **NEEDS**, inclusive of their hopes, fears, expectations and dislikes, and implies that the teaching material should be appropriate to what students want to say and express. In fact, we do not know too much about these needs. To be able to realise just a few formulaic speech acts is not equivalent to communicative competence, i.e. the ability to participate in a conversation of any kind.

It is important to acknowledge that what speech acts aim at is the effect upon the recipients and the attempt to control their reactions, e.g. to impose some sort of obligation, to instigate an act of justification, etc. To understand an utterance and to react to it accordingly (in other words, being able to deal with the perlocution and the illocution) is probably one of the most challenging tasks to be performed for the learner of a foreign language. They have a variety of problems to overcome in trying to reach that goal. The difficulty of reacting in an appropriate way can be due to the relationship established between the speaker and the hearer, e.g. teacher-student, employer-employee, etc.

Language teaching can try to prepare students for situations where misunderstanding is possible by teaching techniques that help learners avoid and, where necessary, repair unfortunate interactions. Yet, teaching material often reduces its input to a sample of speech acts that can be simulated in classroom situations, excluding others that are, nevertheless, frequent in everyday interaction.

**See also:** Communicative language teaching; Communicative strategies; Competence and performance; Conversation analysis; Discourse analysis; Intercultural communication; *Langue* and *parole*; Notions and functions; Pragmatics; Speaking

### References

Austin, J.L. (1962) *How to do things with words*, Cambridge: Cambridge University Press.

Grice, H.P. (1975) 'Logic and conversation', in P. Cole, *Speech acts*, New York: Academic Press.

Habermas, J. (1971) 'Vorbereitende Bemerkungen zu einer Theorie der kommunikativen Kompetenz (Preliminary remarks towards a theory of communicative competence)', in J. Habermas and L. Luhmann, *Theorie der Gesellschaft oder Soziotechnologie. Was leistet die Systemforschung?*, Frankfurt/M.: Suhrkamp.

Halliday, M.A.K. (1978) *Language as social semiotic*, London, Edward Arnold.

Hymes D. (1972) 'Models of interaction of language and social life', in J.J. Gumperz and D. Hymes (eds), *Directions in Sociolinguistics*, New York: Holt, Rinehart and Winston.

Searle, J.R. (1969) *Speech acts. An essay in the philosophy of language*, Cambridge: Cambridge University Press.

### Further reading

Geis, M. (1988) *Speech acts and conversational interaction*, Cambridge: Cambridge University Press.

Levinson, S.C. (1983) *Pragmatics*, Cambridge: Cambridge University Press.

Meibauer, J. (1999) *Pragmatik (Pragmatics)*, Tübingen: Stauffenberg.

Searle, J.R. (1969) *Speech acts. An essay in the philosophy of language*, Cambridge: Cambridge University Press.

Verschueren, J. (1998) *Understanding pragmatics*, London: Arnold.

KARL SORNIG AND SILVIA HAUMANN

# Sprachlehrforschung

The term '*Sprachlehrforschung*' (literally: 'language teaching research), which is well established in Germany, is an abbreviation for '*Sprachlehr- und Sprachlernforschung*' (literally: language teaching and learning research) (also '*Sprachlehr- und -lernforschung*'). In a broad sense, it is a cover term for research in the area of teaching and learning of first, second or foreign languages in any teaching/ learning context. In a narrow sense, however, the term refers to a scientific discipline and institutionalised university subject area which was established in Germany at the beginning of the 1970s and has had a significant influence on both research and the training of foreign language teachers for schools and **ADULT** education. There exists an academic course of study leading to a Master's and a Doctorate at the Seminar für Sprachlehrforschung at the Ruhr University Bochum and at the Central Foreign Language Institute at the University of Hamburg, as well as a postgraduate course of study leading to doctorate at the Foreign Language Institute at the University of Münster.

*Sprachlehrforschung* as a scientific discipline can be more precisely described in terms of statements about its subject area, its epistemological interests and its research approach. The focus of *Sprachlehrforschung* as a discipline is on the teaching and learning of foreign languages taught in an institutional context. This definition of the subject area does not, however, exclude for example forms of **AUTONOMOUS** foreign language learning. It is assumed that the subject area comprises a large number of interdependent factors – a feature referred to as '*Faktorenkomplexion*' ('factor complexity'). The epistemological aims are both theoretical and practical. The theoretical aim is to understand the complexity of factors as far as possible in their entirety, and thereby also to establish cause–effect relationships. The practical aim is to make well-founded recommendations for action with respect to the teaching and learning of foreign languages which take into consideration the political and societal context. The research approach of *Sprachlehrforschung* is learner-oriented, integrative-interdisciplinary and empirical. 'Learner orientation' means that the focus is on the individual learner with their specific cognitive and affective characteristics. In this way, account is taken of the fact that teaching and learning are in a complex mutual relationship, and that well-founded statements about teaching ultimately are only possible on the basis of the understanding of individual learning processes and their specific preconditions. Unfortunately, the term '*Sprachlehrforschung*' does not adequately reflect this. 'Integrative' refers first to the fact that *Sprachlehrforschung* considers the object of research holistically and in its complete complexity. In this way it is distinguished from disciplines such as **LINGUISTICS**, psycholinguistics, pedagogy or **SOCIOLINGUISTICS**, which usually only focus on a partial dimension of the topic 'foreign language teaching and learning'. Furthermore, in the context of the requirement of interdisciplinarity, 'integrative' refers to the fact that, in contrast to an additive-interdisciplinary approach, insights and methods from other disciplines are analysed for their relevance for *Sprachlehrforschung* and, if appropriate, whilst avoiding discipline-specific reductions and making alterations appropriate to the object of research, they are integrated into the body of knowledge and methods in *Sprachlehrforschung*. The empirical dimension implies that hypotheses and findings must arise from the subject area itself or, if transferred from other disciplines, must be carefully checked (see Bausch, 1986; Bausch and Krumm, 1995; Edmondson and House, 1993: ch. 1; Königs, 1991; Koordinierungsgremium im DFG-Schwerpunkt 'Sprachlehrforschung', 1983).

The founding of the scientific subject '*Sprachlehrforschung*' in the Federal Republic of Germany is closely connected with the following events and dates in particular (see Bausch, 1996; Bausch, Königs and Kogelheide, 1986; Edmondson and House, 1993: ch. 1; Koordinierungsgremium im DFG-Schwerpunkt 'Sprachlehrforschung', 1983):

- At the beginning of the 1970s, development of the concept '*Sprachlehrforschung*' and a corresponding course of study at the (central) Language Institute of the Ruhr-University Bochum.
- In 1973, '*Sprachlehrforschung*' became an exam subject (MA, PhD) at the Ruhr-University Bochum.

- Also in 1973 the Deutsche Forschungsgemeinschaft (German Research Council) established a central research programme for the development of the discipline, to run until 1981. It was within this framework that fundamental conceptual work on the constitution of the discipline was done, as well as a number of projects being financed.
- In 1976 there followed the foundation of the *Seminar für Sprachlehrforschung* (previously the Central Foreign Language Institute) at the Ruhr-University Bochum.
- In 1978, another course of study entitled '*Sprachlehrforschung*' was introduced at the central Foreign Language Institute of the University of Hamburg.
- Since 1980, in cooperation with scholars from related disciplines, annual interdisciplinary 'Spring Conferences on Research into Foreign Language Teaching', each with a distinct theme, have been held and the proceedings published.

The foundation of the discipline in the 1970s and 1980s was characterised *inter alia* by a discussion about the distinction to be made between it and **FREMDSPRACHENDIDAKTIK**, **APPLIED LINGUISTICS** and **SECOND LANGUAGE ACQUISITION** research. It was argued, for example, from the viewpoint of *Sprachlehrforschung* and with respect to *Fremdsprachendidaktik*, that the latter focuses too much on the teaching perspective to the detriment of the learning perspective. The main objection to applied linguistics was that the latter on the whole focuses one-sidedly on language or, when it uses a multi-dimensional approach, usually works in an eclectic additive mode. Objections to second language acquisition research included the fact that the latter transferred findings from untutored second language acquisition to the teaching situation without sufficient testing. With this background, the establishment of *Sprachlehrforschung* can be seen, in terms of academic history, as a reaction against discipline-specific reductions of the object 'foreign language teaching and learning' (see, e.g., Bausch and Königs, 1983; Bausch and Krumm, 1995; Königs, 1991; Timm and Vollmer, 1993: 14ff). None the less, representatives of *Sprachlehrforschung* recognise that there are considerable affinities with German *Fremdsprachen-didaktik* in particular.

On the international level, too, there are a number of scientific concepts which are at least partially comparable with the concept of *Sprachlehrforschung* as explained here. This is, for example, the case with respect to specific versions of applied linguistics, or *'DIDACTIQUE DES LANGUES'* in **FRANCE** and glottodidactics in Poland (see Bausch, Christ and Krumm, 1995). There seems to be a major affinity with **CLASSROOM RESEARCH** in Britain or the **USA**. However, this research area does not have comparable status with German *Sprachlehrforschung* in the sense of being an academic discipline and university institution.

A large number of research projects have been carried out which can be classified under the concept of *Sprachlehrforschung* as described here. Sometimes the relationship is explicit and sometimes more implicit and more or less close. One example of a research project with an explicit and close link to the concept is Bahr *et al.* (1996).

Most research projects with allegiance to the concept of *Sprachlehrforschung* are in methodological terms qualitatively oriented. One characteristic *inter alia* is the partially innovative subject-specific adaptation of introspective methods for research into the mental processes and subjective theories involved in foreign language teaching and learning; another is the attempt at methodological triangulation (as, for example, in Bahr *et al.*, 1996).

Criticisms include the fact that, although the complexity of factors is a principal characteristic of the object of study, hitherto there have been only a few applications of multivariate statistical methods (Grotjahn, 1999).

**See also:** Applied linguistics; *Fremdsprachendidaktik*; Learning styles; Psychology; Reliability; Research methods; Second language acquisition theories; Untutored language acquisition; Validity

## References

Bahr, A., Bausch, K.-R., Helbig, B., Kleppin, K., Königs, F.G. and Tönshoff, W. (1996) *Forschungsgegenstand Tertiärsprachenunterricht: Ergebnisse eines empirischen Projekts*, Bochum: Brockmeyer.

Bausch, K.-R. (1986) 'Sprachlehrforschung revis-ited', in K.-R. Bausch and F. Königs (eds), *Sprachlehrforschung in der Diskussion. Methodologische Überlegungen zur Erforschung des Fremdsprachenunterrichts*, Tübingen: Narr.

Bausch, K.-R. (1996) 'Sprachlehrforschung: Eine Zwischenbilanz', in Bausch, K.-R., Christ, H., Königs, F.G. and Krumm, H.-J. (eds), *Erforschung des Lehrens und Lernens fremder Sprachen: Eine Zwischenbilanz. Arbeitspapiere der 16. Frühjahrskonferenz zur Erforschung des Fremdsprachenunterrichts*, Tübingen: Narr.

Bausch, K.-R., Christ, H. and Krumm, H.-J. (1995) 'Das Lehren und Lernen von fremden Sprachen: Wissenschaftskonzepte im internationalen Vergleich', in K.-R. Bausch, H. Christ and H.-J. Krumm (eds), *Handbuch Fremdsprachenunterricht* (3rd edn), Tübingen and Basel: Francke.

Bausch, K.-R. and Königs, F.G. (1983). ' "Lernt" oder "erwirbt" man Fremdsprachen im Unterricht? Zum Verhältnis von Sprachlehrforschung und Zweitsprachenerwerbsforschung', *Die Neueren Sprachen* 12: 308–36.

Bausch, K.-R., Königs, F.G. and Kogelheide, R. (1986) 'Sprachlehrforschung – Entwicklung einer Institution und konzeptuelle Skizze der Disziplin', in Seminar für Sprachlehrforschung der Ruhr-Universität Bochum (ed.), *Probleme und Perspektiven der Sprachlehrforschung*, Frankfurt/M.: Scriptor.

Bausch, K.-R. and Krumm, H.-J. (1995) 'Sprachlehrforschung', in K.-R. Bausch, H. Christ and H.-J. Krumm (eds), *Handbuch Fremdsprachenunterricht* (3rd edn), Tübingen and Basel: Francke.

Edmondson, W. and House, J. (1993) *Einführung in die Sprachlehrforschung*, Tübingen and Basel: Francke.

Grotjahn, R. (1999) 'Thesen zur empirischen Forschungsmethodologie', *Zeitschrift für Fremdsprachenforschung* 10. 1: 133–58.

Königs, F.G. (1991) 'Sprachlehrforschung: Konturen und Perspektiven', *Neusprachliche Mitteilungen aus Wissenschaft und Praxis* 44. 2: 75–83.

Koordinierungsgremium im DFG-Schwerpunkt 'Sprachlehrforschung' (ed.) (1983) *Sprachlehr- und Sprachlernforschung: Begründung einer Disziplin*, Tübingen: Narr.

Timm, J.-P. and Vollmer, H.J. (1993) 'Fremdsprachenforschung: Zur Konzeption und Perspektive eines Wissenschaftsbereichs', *Zeitschrift für Fremd-sprachenforschung* 4. 1: 1–47.

## Further reading

Bausch, K.-R., Christ, H. and Krumm, H.-J. (1995) 'Das Lehren und Lernen von fremden Sprachen: Wissenschaftskonzepte im internationalen Vergleich', in K.-R. Bausch, H. Christ and H.-J. Krumm (eds), *Handbuch Fremdsprachenunterricht* (3rd edn), Tübingen and Basel: Francke.

Bausch, K.-R. and Krumm, H.-J. (1995) 'Sprachlehrforschung', in K.-R. Bausch, H. Christ and H.-J. Krumm (eds), *Handbuch Fremdsprachenunterricht* (3rd edn), Tübingen and Basel: Francke.

Christ, H. and Hüllen, W. (1995) 'Fremdsprachendidaktik', in K.-R. Bausch, H. Christ and H.-J. Krumm (eds), *Handbuch Fremdsprachenunterricht* (3rd edn), Tübingen and Basel: Francke.

Edmondson, W. and House, J. (1993) *Einführung in die Sprachlehrforschung*, Tübingen and Basel: Francke.

Königs, F.G. (1991) 'Sprachlehrforschung: Konturen und Perspektiven', *Neusprachliche Mitteilungen aus Wissenschaft und Praxis* 44. 2: 75–83.

Koordinierungsgremium im DFG-Schwerpunkt 'Sprachlehrforschung' (ed.) (1983) *Sprachlehr- und Sprachlernforschung: Begründung einer Disziplin*, Tübingen: Narr.

RÜDIGER GROTJAHN

# Standard language

Standard language is a variety of language which incorporates a set of grammatical and other characteristics common to all or nearly all the varieties of a given language. It is a mode of expression used by speakers for communication beyond their immediate speech community. Standard language is also an ideal, a socially valued form which may never be perfectly realised. In language teaching and learning, opinion is divided on the exclusive use of the standard as opposed to the other varieties.

## Dialect, accent and standard language

Standard language may be defined in relation to the terms 'dialect' and 'accent'. Within a large speech community (e.g. that of the people who use **ENGLISH** all over the world), we can distinguish smaller communities, such as Britain, the **UNITED STATES OF AMERICA**, New Zealand, **INDIA**, West **AFRICA**, among others. Forms of language with community characteristics – which may be linguistic, geographical, social or a mixture of all three – are known as dialects and accents. Where the special identifying features are grammatical and/or lexical, the form is a dialect; where the identifying features are solely a matter of **PRONUNCIATION**, the form is an accent. In this context the standard language enjoys the widest range of acceptability within the community. For this reason, it may be referred to as a common core, a universal, non-regional dialect.

It follows from this view that every form of language, spoken or written by anyone anywhere in the world, can be identified as belonging to one dialect or another, and if spoken, as one accent or another. Such an assumption rejects the idea that a dialect is only anything that is not 'standard'. On the contrary, and as shown above, the standard language is also a dialect which may be spoken with one accent or another.

## Characteristics of standard language

It must be acknowledged that not all linguists adhere to the way we have defined standard language. For example, Abercrombie does not consider standard English as a dialect when he says:

> I have used the word dialect here to mean any form of English which differs from standard English in **GRAMMAR**, syntax, **VOCABULARY**, and, of course, **PRONUNCIATION** too, though a difference of pronunciation alone is not enough to make a different dialect.
>
> (Abercrombie, 1965: 11)

However, regardless of whether standard language is considered a dialect or not, it must have a number of inherent characteristics. Strevens (1977) identified six, while McArthur (1992) identified five main characteristics of standard English. From both discussions, we can extract six main characteristics of standard language:

- Whenever the standard language is used, it displays virtually no geographical or social variation; i.e. there is nothing in its grammar and vocabulary to tell us what part of the world it comes from.
- It may be spoken with an accent from any geographical locality or with a non-regional accent, and consequently does not refer to a type of pronunciation.
- It is the variety of language which carries most prestige within a community. 'Prestige' is a social concept whereby some people have high standing in the eyes of others. The language used by these people will generally become the standard within their community.
- It is recommended as a desirable educational target. It is used as the ideal, or the norm for communication by the community's leading institutions such as its government, law courts and the media. It is therefore the most widely disseminated variety among the public.
- Although the standard language is widely understood, it is not widely produced. Only a minority of people within a community (e.g. radio newscasters) actually use it when they talk. Most people use a regional variety of the language or a mixture of standard and regional varieties.
- Standard language is best manifested in print. It is the dialect of literature except for works that deliberately introduce or emphasise local features. It is also the variety which is most comprehensively described and studied.

A close examination of these characteristic features calls for the following three comments:

- First, as a descriptive term, 'standard' does not refer to a language that has been formally standardised by official action, as weights and measures are standardised. All it means is that it is used by the majority of the people concerned with education, educated usage, and literature.
- Second, the word 'standard' as used in the phrase 'standard language' does not mean 'better'. There is nothing inherently better in

the standard language – or in any other variety for that matter. But, for convenience, it is desirable to have one form which would be intelligible wherever the language is used. This is the role played by the standard language.

- Third, the existence of all these common features does not exclude the possibility of variation within the standard language. Such variation may occur at the level of spelling, accent (or pronunciation), vocabulary, and grammar.

Furthermore, the standard language may vary according to the user, which gives rise to geographical, educational and social varieties. Finally, it may vary according to differences in social relations between speaker and audience, thus giving rise to the formal/informal, polite/familiar, literary/elevated varieties, among others. The possibility of variation implies that there are in fact several standards rather than just one.

## Language teaching and learning

The concept of standard language is very useful in language teaching and learning. In order to avoid the confusion that may result from the use of conflicting models, it would be advisable for all teachers in a given language programme to teach the same variety of the language. This may be the standard language or a regional variety – for example, standard British English or standard Cameroonian English. In some contexts, teachers and students may be allowed to use two different varieties of the language, so long as they are consistent (e.g. either American or British English). In fact, some specialists share Trudgill and Hannah's view that 'it is not necessarily bad or confusing for school children to be exposed to more than one model' (1985: 3).

However, regardless of the attitude adopted, it is important for the teacher to be fully aware of the major differences between the standard language and the regional variety. Such an awareness has two major consequences. First, it makes it possible for the teacher to keep the two varieties separate when teaching, thus avoiding unnecessary confusion for the students. Second, it helps acquaint students with different varieties of the language, which is a good preparation for real-life situations where they will be confronted with many other varieties in addition to the standard language.

**See also:** Authenticity; French; Language awareness; *Le Français fondamental*; Linguistic imperialism; Mother tongue; Native speaker; Pedagogical grammar; Pronunciation teaching; Skills and knowledge in language learning; Vocabulary

### References

Abercrombie, D. (1965) *Studies in phonetics and linguistics*, London: Oxford University Press.

McArthur, T. (1992) *The Oxford Companion to the English Language*, Oxford: Oxford University Press.

Strevens, P. (1977) *New orientations in the teaching of English*, London: Oxford University Press.

Trudgill, P. and Hannah, J. (1995) *International English – a guide to varieties of Standard English* (3rd edn), London: Edward Arnold.

### Further reading

Aitchinson, J. (1994) *Language change: progress or decay* (2nd edn), Cambridge: Cambridge University Press.

Crystal, D. (1995) *The Cambridge Encyclopedia of English Language*, Cambridge: Cambridge University Press.

Milroy, J. and Milroy, L. (1985) *Authority in language: investigating language prescription and standardisation*, London: Routledge and Kegan Paul.

O'Donnell, W.R. and Todd, L. (1984) *Variety in contemporary English* (2nd edn), London: George Allen and Unwin.

ETIENNE ZÉ AMVELA

# Stereotypes

A stereotype is a view of an individual or a group of people held by others based on commonly held assumptions that may not be the result of direct, personal knowledge of those people. Stereotypes can act as filters through which we view other people, their way of life, cultural traits, values and so on. They may serve as summaries, offering a convenient way of dealing with the many social and cultural groups we may encounter in our everyday lives. Stereotypes are in evidence in most societies, and some even cross international boundaries. It will be emphasised that they are socially and culturally constructed and not immune to change and reworking. They frequently, but not always, contain negative content that can cause many difficulties for members of groups being judged by a stereotype rather than factual information.

The origins of the word come from Greek with '*stereos*' meaning solid and '*typos*' meaning mark. It entered more common social currency when considering reproduced ideas that are far removed from the original. The term is also used to refer to 'preconceived ideas about individuals, groups or objects, when these preconceptions are shared by members of particular groups or societies' (Mann, 1983: 378). In another definition, a stereotype is 'a label which involves a process of categorisation and evaluation. Although it may refer to situations or places, it is most often used in conjunction with representation of social groups. In its simplest terms, an easily grasped characteristic (usually negative) is presumed to belong to a whole group' (O' Sullivan *et al.* 1997: 126).

Problems arise when negative features of stereotypes prejudice views about people who we do not know. Stereotypes can also offer false justification of serious discrimination against different groups of people, such as foreigners and other minority groups, and lead to verbal and physical abuse, violence, murder and even genocide. This is because, in performing the function of providing shorthand information about a particular group, or acting as a measuring stick, false assumptions and preconceptions can take over from valid knowledge. Bigotry may take the place of reason. Derogatory ideas and beliefs, then, are often associated with the use of stereotypes. Stereotypes tend to be oversimplistic in content and unresponsive to evidence provided about the people being stereotyped which, if more rational criteria are used, indicates that the stereotype needs to be revised if not abandoned altogether.

Common stereotypes used by groups of people to judge others may be based on various notions of 'otherness' and difference, not only in terms of race and ethnicity but also **GENDER** and social class. Ideas about the 'typical woman', and what it is to be properly masculine or feminine, can often be heard (Abercrombie *et al.*, 1992: 224). There are sets of roles and related behaviours that are deemed suitable for each sex so that men and women become 'gendered subjects' (O'Sullivan *et al.*, 1997: 224). There are also clear stereotypes about ethnic groups, social class and geographical regions within a country – in England, for example, about 'cockneys' from London, or north-country people. Within most countries there are regional stereotypes, often based upon historical factors, competition for status and acceptance, even disputes, misunderstandings and possible enmity. There are also stereotypes of specific groups in society, such as professions like the police, lawyers, doctors and so on.

Stereotypes may include ideas not only about what people within a particular group may look like or how they talk but also about their general behaviour, traits, ways of thinking and even what type of food they may like. A stereotypical view might begin with the statement that all members of a particular group do or like something, which offers a very generalised set of ideas. Stereotypes can change, but some basic ideas may persist.

There are ideological functions to stereotypes, because they may be 'a means by which support is provided for one group's differential (often discriminatory) treatment of another' (O'Sullivan *et al.*, 1997: 127). It has been deemed acceptable in the past to treat people as slaves, to imprison and torture them, just because they have been members of a negatively stereotyped group. There are clear links to racist practices in this sense, just as sexism is supported by derogatory stereotypes about women. The use of extremely negative characteristics and features in political propaganda comes to mind here.

Ethnocentrism is also linked to this. Ethnocentrism involves members of one nationality viewing their own society and culture at the centre of the world and seeing them as more important than and superior to others. When nationalism and ethnocentrism go to the extreme, resulting in the unjustified hatred of other nations, we can talk of xenophobia.

We come in contact with stereotypes and internalise them during the process of socialisation as we grow up and learn about the society and culture around us. Stereotypes can be learned from others, such as immediate family members during primary socialisation, as well as through peer groups, education and the media during secondary socialisation. Patterns of behaviour are absorbed through the reading materials and playthings of children and the social roles they see acted out around them.

Various forms of media, such as advertisements, can reinforce certain stereotypes as well as confronting and perhaps changing others. The roles, behaviour, language and actions of characters in various television and radio programmes, advertisements and in print media can all be analysed in terms of the extent to which they conform to commonly held stereotypes. Children may be particularly sensitive to what is presented to them as they go through the socialisation process.

Educational practices may confront stereotypes learned at home and in the locality but they may also reinforce them. Stereotypes have appeared frequently in language teaching as a result of conscious intentions or unconscious reworking of commonly used social constructs. They can be considered as part of the cultural dimension of language learning. In the past there have been clear racial stereotypes used in the **MATERIALS AND MEDIA**, for example, about different groups of people as well as where they live and their ways of life. The 'typical' Englishman in his bowler hat in foggy London, and the kilted and parsimonious Scotsman, are two British examples. These have been reconsidered in more recent times with the advent of political correctness. Some have been viewed as relatively harmless or funny – although humorous stereotypes that mock or make fun of people can be viewed as a form of abuse. Jokes about ethnic groups are increasingly questioned, because they may help reproduce power inequalities and lead people to view those groups in derogatory terms.

Stereotypes in language learning materials may hinder rather than help learners of other languages, and this issue is one looked at more seriously now than in the past. No language materials are value-free and their cultural content can include whether or not stereotypes are evident, and how, if they are, they can affect the learner. **HUMAN RIGHTS** education would point out the dangers of stereotypes, and teaching involving empathy with minority groups in society can also be seen as ways to counteract negative effects upon learners.

Although stereotypes may appear as over-simplifications of social and cultural traits, Perkins (1997: 127) pointed out that it is not such a simple process. She identified shortcomings in the way that stereotyping is normally assumed to operate. It is not always negative nor always about minority groups or the less powerful in society. Stereotypes can also be held about one's own social group and not just the 'Other'. It has already been pointed out that they are neither constantly rigid nor un-changing, and sometimes they can be supported by empirical evidence. Perkins argued that stereotypes would not work culturally if they were merely simple and erroneous.

Stereotypes, then, are probably not going to disappear, because they can perform some useful functions if treated carefully. It is likely, however, that there will continue to be changes in existing stereotypes the world over. With increased **CUL-TURAL AWARENESS** and contacts, it is hoped that negative and untruthful aspects can be minimised so that people can judge for themselves the individual worth and merits of others rather than viewing whole groups in generalised and often prejudiced ways.

**See also:** Area studies; Attitudes and language learning; *Civilisation*; Cultural awareness; Exchanges; Global education; Human rights; Intercultural communication; Intercultural training; *Landeskunde*; Objectives in language teaching and learning; Study abroad

### References

Abercrombie, N., Warde, A., Soothill, K., Urry, J. and Walby, S. (1992) *Contemporary British society,* Cambridge: Polity Press.

Halsey, A.H.(1998) 'Stereotyping (sociology)', Microsoft Encarta 98 Encyclopedia .

Mann, M. (1983) *Student Encyclopedia of Sociology,* Basingstoke: Macmillan.

O'Sullivan, T.O., Dutton, B. and Rayner, P. (1997)

*Studying the media: an introduction*, London: Edward Arnold.

Perkins, T. (1997) 'Rethinking stereotypes', in T.O. O'Sullivan, B. Dutton and P. Rayner, *Studying the media: an introduction*, London: Edward Arnold.

### Further reading

Hart, A. (1991) *Understanding the media*, London: Routledge.

Young-Bruehl, E. (1996) *The anatomy of prejudice*, Harvard: Harvard University Press.

RUTH CHERRINGTON

# Stern, Hans Heinrich (David)

b. 1 June 1913, Kassel, Germany;
d. 2 August 1987, Toronto, Canada

H.H. (David) Stern was an influential theorist of foreign and second language teaching, whose thinking helped to shape policies for and research on language curriculum, instruction and **TEACHER EDUCATION**, particularly in North America and Europe from the 1960s to the 1990s. His major book, *Fundamental Concepts of Language Teaching* (1983), elaborated an analytic framework of fundamental concepts of which language teachers and policies should necessarily be cognisant: both to be aware of foundational theories and research and to guide their ongoing educational practices. These fundamental concepts include knowledge of one's own learning and teaching experiences, the history of language teaching, concepts of language, the role of language in societies, the **PSYCHOLOGY** of learning languages, and educational policies and theories. A later companion volume, (1992, edited posthumously by his colleagues Patrick Allen and Birgit Harley), presented a multidimensional curriculum framework that aimed to broaden the range of **OBJECTIVES** and content options conventional to language education while highlighting core issues in teaching, such as whether to present second languages in an intralingual mode (in reference to the second language and culture) or a crosslingual mode (in reference to the first language) and whether to approach language learning analytically or experientially (or both). These books, like Stern's numerous journal articles and contributed chapters, stressed the logical importance and **HUMANISTIC** value of closely interrelating language teaching practices, policies, theories and research.

Stern's career began in the 1930s as a teacher of **FRENCH** and **GERMAN** in Dorset. After completing an MA in 1948 at the University of London Institute of Education, Stern lectured at the University of Hull until 1965. During this time he completed a PhD at the University of London in 1956 and worked in the early 1960s as a research officer at the UNESCO Institute for Education in Hamburg on the IEA studies of educational achievement in twenty-two countries. The latter research led to two major books on language education in primary schools (1967, 1969). After a period as reader in **APPLIED LINGUISTICS** at the University of Essex, Stern moved in 1968 to Toronto, where he founded the Modern Language Centre of the Ontario Institute for Studies in Education, which he directed as professor until his retirement in 1981. He organised and inspired numerous projects on language teaching, particularly to enhance the teaching and learning of French in predominantly English-speaking regions of **CANADA**. Stern's professional contributions were warmly remembered by various educators in a festschrift honouring his retirement (Mollica, 1981).

## Bibliography

Mollica, A.S. (ed.) (1981) *In honour of H.H. Stern*, Special issue of *Canadian Modern Language Review* 37, 3.

Stern, H.H. (1967) *Foreign languages in primary education*, Oxford: Oxford University Press.

Stern, H.H. (ed.) (1969) *Languages and the young school child*, Oxford: Oxford University Press.

Stern, H.H. (1983) *Fundamental concepts of language teaching*, Oxford: Oxford University Press.

Stern, H.H. (1992) *Issues and options in language teaching*, ed. P. Allen and B. Harley, Oxford: Oxford University Press.

ALISTER CUMMING

# Strategic competence

In the literature on second language learning and use, the scope and function of strategic competence have been variously defined and interpreted. This is due partly to the variety of definitions of communicative competence, to which strategic competence is generally agreed to be indispensable, and partly to the problematic interface between implicit (unconscious) and explicit (conscious) mental processes. However, all definitions relate strategic competence to the fact that linguistic communication is one of the principal means by which we pursue our social purposes. Essentially, strategic competence is responsible for the plans, whether implicit or explicit, by which communication is shaped. The concept of strategic competence is fundamental to discussion of communicative approaches to language teaching, **COMMUNICATIVE STRATEGIES** and **STRATEGIES OF LANGUAGE LEARNING**, and centrally implicated in discussion of **AUTONOMOUS LEARNING** and **LEARNING STYLES**.

Among the most influential definitions of strategic competence is the one embedded in Canale and Swain's (1980) definition of communicative competence, which was an attempt to adapt Dell Hymes's (1972) concept to the second language learner/user. According to Canale and Swain (1980: 30), strategic competence is called into play 'to compensate for breakdowns in communication due to performance variables or to insufficient competence'. This definition coincides with one of the principal focuses of **INTERLANGUAGE** research in the 1970s and 1980s, the exploration of the ways in which language learners cope with the problems that arise when they are communicating in their target language (see, e.g., Selinker, 1972; Færch and Kasper, 1983); but it encourages a view of strategic competence as a capacity that is engaged only when things go wrong.

By contrast, Bachman (1990) has argued that strategic competence should be seen, not as a subordinate component of communicative competence, but as a more general cognitive capacity that underpins all problem-solving behaviour. According to this view, our strategic competence is obligatorily and continuously engaged in planning, monitoring and evaluating task performance; it is fundamental to the way in which we behave. When the task we are confronted with involves linguistic communication, some of the processes in which we engage are inaccessible to introspection and conscious manipulation (for example, those that have to do with phonological encoding; see Clark and Clark, 1977: 223), whereas others may operate either above or below the threshold of conscious awareness (for example, the selection of one phrase rather than another). When the task in question is one that we have performed many times before, these latter processes are likely to operate largely below the threshold of conscious awareness; whereas when the task is unfamiliar or presents us with some difficulty (the situation which Canale and Swain's 1980 definition addresses), some aspects of our assessment, planning and evaluation may become conscious and deliberate.

This view of strategic competence has three important consequences for foreign language teaching/learning. First, it entails that strategic competence is not something that language learners must develop anew with each new language: they already possess strategic competence by definition, though their explicit control of strategic processes is infinitely variable. At the same time, of course, the demands of learning and using another language should cause their strategic competence to grow both in its implicit and in its explicit dimension. Second, as a general cognitive capacity, strategic competence underlies social as well as linguistic **SKILLS**, and successful communication depends on interactional strategies as well as the strategies we use to overcome, say, gaps or temporary lapses in our lexical knowledge. Thus strategic competence must be seen in social-interactive as well as individual-cognitive terms (see Kasper and Kellerman, 1997). Third, although it may sometimes be possible to distinguish between communicative and learning strategies in terms of the language learner/user's focus and intention, in psychological terms the distinction cannot easily be maintained. Strategic control of communicative task performance and strategic control of aspects of the language learning process are underpinned by the same general cognitive

capacity. This argues for a close two-way relation between language learning and language use.

Perhaps the biggest obstacles to a straightforward understanding of strategic competence are the complex nature of consciousness (see Schmidt, 1994) and the problematic relation between implicit and explicit mental processes (see Morris, 1990). Much of the discussion of strategic competence, and especially of the role of strategies in second language learning and use, assumes continuity between conscious and unconscious mental operations. In many cases this is clearly justified. For example, when we compose a written text, the strategic processes of planning, monitoring and evaluation may sometimes present themselves to our conscious awareness, but they often proceed unconsciously. In other cases, however, and especially when our attempts to deploy communicative or learning strategies are guided by beliefs about aspects of cognition to which we have no introspective access, the matter is much less clear-cut: our minds do not necessarily work in the way we imagine they do.

Notwithstanding these difficulties, the development of explicit strategic control of communicative and learning task performance is necessarily a central concern of second language pedagogy, though how precisely this development should be achieved is likely to remain a matter of controversy.

**See also:** Communicative language teaching; Communicative strategies; Intercultural communication; Psychology; Second language acquisition theories; Speaking; Strategies of language learning

### References

Bachman, L.F. (1990) *Fundamental considerations in language testing*, Oxford: Oxford University Press.

Canale, M. and Swain, M. (1980) 'Theoretical bases of communicative approaches to second language teaching and testing', *Applied Linguistics* 1: 1–47.

Clark, H.H. and Clark, E.V. (1977) *Psychology and language. An introduction to psycholinguistics*, New York: Harcourt Brace Jovanovich.

Færch, C. and Kasper, G. (eds) (1983) *Strategies in*

*interlanguage communication*, London and New York: Longman.

Hymes, D. (1972) 'On communicative competence', in J.B. Pride and J. Holmes (eds), *Sociolinguistics*, Harmondsworth: Penguin.

Kasper, G. and Kellerman, E. (eds) (1997) *Communication strategies. Psycholinguistic and sociolinguistic perspectives*, London and New York: Longman.

Morris, P.E. (1990) 'Metacognition', in M.W. Eysenck (ed.), *The Blackwell Dictionary of Cognitive Psychology*, Oxford: Blackwell.

Schmidt, R. (1994) 'Deconstructing consciousness in search of useful definitions for applied linguistics', in J.H. Hulstijn and R. Schmidt (eds), *Consciousness in second language learning (AILA Review 11)*, 11–26.

Selinker, L. (1972) 'Interlanguage', *International Review of Applied Linguistics and Language Teaching (IRAL)* 10: 209–30.

## Further reading

Bachman, L.F. (1990) *Fundamental considerations in language testing*, Oxford: Oxford University Press.

Canale, M. and Swain, M. (1980) 'Theoretical bases of communicative approaches to second language teaching and testing', *Applied Linguistics* 1: 1–47.

Færch, C. and Kasper, G. (eds) (1983) *Strategies in interlanguage communication*, London and New York: Longman.

Kasper, G. and Kellerman, E. (eds) (1997) *Communication strategies. Psycholinguistic and sociolinguistic perspectives*, London and New York: Longman.

Little, D. (1996) 'Strategic competence considered in relation to strategic control of the language learning process', in H. Holec, D. Little and R. Richterich, *Strategies in language learning and use. Studies towards a common European framework of reference for language learning and teaching*, Strasbourg: Council of Europe.

DAVID LITTLE

# Strategies of language learning

A language learning strategy is any action that language learners perform in order to increase their target language proficiency. It may be focused on some quite specific task, for example, the learning of an item of **VOCABULARY** or the memorisation of a grammatical rule. Alternatively, it may have to do with the language learning process in general. For example, learners may decide to organise their vocabulary notes in a particular way, or to evaluate themselves at regular intervals in order to identify aspects of their proficiency that need special attention. Although learning strategies may begin as conscious actions, with frequent use they can become part of the learner's automatic learning behaviour. Research into successful learning has yielded taxonomies of learning strategies, which have been used to develop programmes of strategy training.

Among the most influential taxonomies of language learning strategies is the one elaborated by Oxford (1990: 14f.), who distinguishes between 'direct strategies for dealing with the new language' (subdivided into memory, cognitive and compensatory strategies) and 'indirect strategies for general management of learning' (subdivided into affective, social and metacognitive strategies). Although classifications of this kind are arguably helpful in providing both a map of the territory and a basis for pedagogical intervention, they can also be misleading: for one thing, they are not exclusive: behaviours described as language learning strategies are also deployed in language use (and in other domains too). For example, the affective strategies which learners employ to maintain positive self-perceptions may be called upon to manage **MOTIVATIONAL** aspects of the learning process, but they can also play a role in the management of interactions with **NATIVE SPEAKERS** of the target language. Similarly, metacognitive strategies (like consciously paying attention, or planning how to go about a particular task) are implicated in language use no less than in language learning. Taxonomies of language learning strategies can also mislead by seeming to propose clear-cut categories, whereas distinctions between strategy types are often fuzzy and difficult to maintain. In Oxford's taxonomy, for example, cognitive strategies are classified as 'direct' and metacognitive strategies as 'indirect', but in reality metacognition is part of cognition, and it is often impossible to draw a clear line between them.

The pedagogical move towards an explicit focus on strategies of language learning came from two impulses. The first was the interest in **COMMUNICATIVE STRATEGIES** that emerged from research into **INTERLANGUAGE** in the 1970s and 1980s (e.g. Færch and Kasper, 1983). Empirical explorations of the strategic behaviour of second language learners/users inevitably raised the question whether explicit instruction could enhance performance; and interest in explicit instruction gave rise to the idea that learners might also benefit from strategy training that focused on language learning rather than language use. Pedagogical measures that derive from this source tend to be strongly analytical and sharply focused (for practical examples, see Oxford, 1990).

The second impulse behind the pedagogical move towards an explicit focus on learning strategies was the growth of interest in **AUTONOMOUS LEARNING**. If learner autonomy arises from acceptance of responsibility for one's own learning (Holec, 1981), it follows that pedagogies oriented to the development of learner autonomy must be concerned to develop learners' explicit strategic control of the language learning process (cf. Little, 1996). While some of these pedagogies have followed the path of strategy training, others have been content to involve learners as fully as possible in the reflective processes of planning, monitoring and evaluating their own learning (see Dam, 1995), without attempting to distinguish clearly between strategy types or to focus learning activities on specific forms of strategic behaviour.

Strategy training is vulnerable to criticism on at least four grounds. First, 'it is not clear that what differentiates good and poor learners is the choice of strategy; it may simply be the range and amount of use of strategies' (McDonough, 1995: 83). Second, because most strategies can be deployed unconsciously as well as consciously, strategy training may simply make learners consciously aware of strategies they were already using unconsciously. Third, the existence of individual **LEARNING STYLES** casts some doubt on the extent to which all strategies are in principle equally accessible to all learners. Fourth, metacognition is by no means an infallible guide to cognition (see Morris, 1990), so that we can never be certain that what learners think they are doing corresponds to

underlying mental processes to which they have no introspective access. For all these reasons it is difficult to establish with certainty that strategy training is the best means of increasing learners' strategic control of the language learning process. It may be at least as effective to concentrate on helping them to engage as fully as possible in the reflective tasks of planning, monitoring and evaluating their own learning.

**See also:** Autonomy and autonomous learners; Communicative language teaching; Communicative strategies; Learning styles; Learning to learn; Motivation; Strategic competence

## References

Dam, L. (1995) *Learner autonomy 3: from theory to classroom practice*, Dublin: Authentik.

Færch, C. and Kasper, G. (1983) *Strategies in interlanguage communication*, London and New York: Longman.

Holec, H. (1981) *Autonomy and foreign language learning*, Oxford: Pergamon (first published 1979, Strasbourg: Council of Europe).

Little, D. (1996) 'Strategic competence considered in relation to strategic control of the language learning process', in H. Holec, D. Little and R. Richterich, *Strategies in language learning and use. Studies towards a common European framework of reference for language learning and teaching*, Strasbourg: Council of Europe.

McDonough, S.H. (1995) *Strategy and skill in learning a foreign language*, London: Arnold.

Morris, P.E. (1990) 'Metacognition', in M.W. Eysenck (ed.), *The Blackwell Dictionary of Cognitive Psychology*, Oxford: Blackwell.

Oxford, R. (1990) *Language learning strategies*, New York: Newbury House.

## Further reading

Little, D. (1996) 'Strategic competence considered in relation to strategic control of the language learning process', in H. Holec, D. Little and R. Richterich, *Strategies in language learning and use. Studies towards a common European framework of reference for language learning and teaching*, Strasbourg: Council of Europe.

McDonough, S.H. (1995) *Strategy and skill in learning a foreign language*, London: Arnold.

Oxford, R. (1990) *Language learning strategies*, New York: Newbury House.

Wenden, A. and Rubin, J. (1987) *Learner strategies in language learning*, Hemel Hempstead: Prentice Hall International.

DAVID LITTLE

# Structural linguistics

Structural linguistics has two different origins: one developed from the Prague School in Europe, and the other was related with the study and analysis of Indian languages in the United States of America. Because of its concern with the later flourish of Transformational Generative Grammar, as well as its influence on second language teaching in Japan and many other parts of the world, American structural linguistics is focused on in this section.

American structural linguistics (ASL) prospered mainly in the second quarter of the twentieth century, i.e. from the early 1930s to 1960. ASL differs from structuralism in Europe in that its originators were interested in describing the native American Indians' languages which had no writing system. The researchers relied solely on their auditory impressions to discover how the sound system of a given Indian language was phonologically and morpho-syntactically constructed. Kenneth L. Pike is well known for his fieldwork by his **MONOLINGUAL** demonstration – describing an unknown language only by talking to a native informant. The researchers avoided mixing linguistic levels, priority being given of course to the phonological description. Sticking to the phonology-first approach, pretending to know nothing about mental and semantic properties, reflects the **BLOOMFIELDIAN** concept that 'The only useful generalization about language is inductive generalization' (Bloomfield, 1933). Also C.C. Fries's emphasis on formal features of language is characteristic of ASL. In other words, some of the linguists in this tradition assumed that whatever is linguistically significant must be observed and that what is not observable should not be the research target because of its lack of observable

evidence. Second language teaching, based on the ASL tradition, aims for mastery of the sound system and grammatically observable features of arrangement. Fries's view was as follows:

> In learning a new language, the chief problem is not, at first, that of learning **VOCABULARY** items. It is first the mastery of the sound system – to understand the stream of speech, to hear the distinctive sound features and approximate their production. It is second the mastery of the features of arrangement that constitute the structure of the language.
>
> (Fries, 1945: 3)

This so-called oral approach formed the basis for foreign language teaching around the middle of the twentieth century. However, in 1957, Noam **CHOMSKY**, an initiator of transformational generative grammar, published *Syntactic Structures*, whose new concept fundamentally changed ASL-based teaching.

To summarise, the main problems he raised are as follows:

1 Stimulus–response theory (SR) only partially reflects what is happening in the mind. Bloomfield tried to describe language as objectively as possible, even to the avoidance of the concepts of the language user. As seen in Chomsky's critical review of Skinner's behaviourism, an animal's linguistic behaviour is clearly limited to the SR, while the use of the language by humans is free from SR, and is much more creative.

2 Structural differences do not always emerge. Although the following sentences (a) and (b) are structurally the same, the meaning is different: (a) John is easy to please; (b) John is eager to please. Sentence (a) means that John is a person who is easily pleased. On the other hand, sentence (b) means that John is the type of person who is eager to please people around him. As long as one sticks to the sentence observable on the surface, one cannot come up with the correct interpretation of sentences.

3 Ambiguity cannot be solved by formal features only. The sentence 'Who made her dress?' can be interpreted in two ways. One interpretation is 'Who made the dress she wore last night?', which is more or less the normal one. The other

is 'Who made her put on that dress she was wearing?'. On the surface there is no clue to which one to choose.

4   Language is internally rule-governed. What is observable on the surface, according to ASL, is the sole evidence which gives a clue to understanding the feature and structure of the language. On the other hand, transformational generative grammarians think that the string of speech on the surface is performance-related phenomena subject to false starts, rephrasing and careless mistakes, etc. Thus the deep structure and its transformation rules constitute the language, reflecting the competence of the language users.

5   The status of the phoneme is theoretically shaky. Consider the pair: (a) rider – ri[D]er ; (b) writer – wri[D]er. In the major dialect of American English, the intervocalics /t/ and /d/ are both realised as the same flap. As there is no phonetic difference between them, the phonetic symbol [D] is used to transcribe this common flap. Thus the question arises: Are 'rider' and 'writer' indistinguishable? The answer is no. The preceding diphthong /aɪ/ is lengthened before voiced sounds and shortened before voiceless sounds. And it is this vowel length that distinguishes (a) from (b). The Bloomfieldian concept of the phoneme was 'once a phoneme, everywhere a phoneme'. However, as the above example shows, the linear arrangement of phonemes was not always correct.

Although ASL's physicalism was severely criticised, the formal aspect of language should not be overlooked, particularly in foreign language teaching. Every language has its own phonological, morphological, syntactic and semantic systems differing in many respects from those of the language learner's **MOTHER TONGUE**. Unless the formal aspects of the target language are mastered, one cannot reach an advanced level. The mentalistic approach, if taken to the extreme, might be the return to the **GRAMMAR–TRANSLATION** method.

**See also:** Audio-visual language teaching; Grammar; *Langue* and *parole*; Linguistics; Notions and functions; Skills and knowledge in language learning; Text and corpus linguistics

## References

Bloomfield, L. (1933) *Language*, New York: Holt, Rinehart and Winston.

Chomsky, N. (1957) *Syntactic structures*, The Hague: Mouton.

Chomsky, N. (1959) 'A review of B.F. Skinner's "Verbal Behavior" ', *Language* 35: 26–58.

Fries, C.C. (1945) *Teaching and learning English as a foreign language*, Michigan: Ann Arbor.

Fries, C.C. (1952) *Structures of language: an introduction to the construction of English sentences*, New York: Harcourt, Brace and World.

## Further reading

Beebe, L. (ed.) (1987) *Issues in second language acquisition – multiple perspectives*, New York: Heinle and Heinle.

Hill, A. (1958) *Introduction to linguistic structure*, New York: Harcourt, Brace and World.

Pinker, S. (1994) *The language instinct – how the mind creates language*, New York: Harper Perennial.

TAKASHI SHIMAOKA

# Study abroad

Study abroad is often integrated into degrees in modern languages or other subjects in the belief that extended immersion in a society where the target language is used every day will enhance the learner's proficiency, especially oral-aural **SKILLS** and less formal registers. Improved linguistic skills are not the only gain: nor is improvement automatic. Because of the huge range of factors which come into play when a learner is abroad alone, the outcomes vary considerably from one individual to another.

## Origins

Several centuries ago, when Latin was the **LINGUA FRANCA** of educated people throughout the continent which invented universities – Europe – it was commonplace for teachers and students to move from one country to another. Erasmus (c.1466–1536), whose name was chosen in 1987 for a large-scale European programme promoting student mobility, was a native of Rotterdam whose academic life encompassed Paris and Basel, Cambridge and Turin. Today, many different models exist for students wishing to spend part of their degree course in another country (Parker and Rouxeville, 1995; Huebner, 1998). Some opt for a work placement in commerce, industry or education. Launched nearly a hundred years ago, the language assistant scheme provides mutual benefits: advanced students from one country teach their **MOTHER TONGUE** in schools in the country of their target language. But for the largest number of over a million students worldwide each year, 'study abroad' means precisely that – a period learning alongside native students at a foreign university.

The 100,000 Americans (Freed, 1999) who follow 'study abroad programs' often travel in cohesive groups for relatively short stays in another country, following courses at the local university without necessarily abandoning the academic structures and support systems of the home institution. The European model typically provides more autonomy, with individual students becoming immersed in the local community for a semester or a full year. The European Union's programmes – Joint Study Programmes 1976, ERASMUS 1987, SOCRATES 1995 – have now enabled half a million students to get credit at their home university for studying abroad.

## Research

Research into residence abroad has been hampered by the number of factors involved and the complexity of their interaction. In each individual case, biographical, affective, cognitive and circumstantial variables come into play, with students' previous language learning and **APTITUDE** impacted upon by their **MOTIVATION**, **ATTITUDES**, anxiety, **LEARNING STYLE** and **STRATEGIES**, as well as by unpredictable elements such as location, type of accommodation, and degree of contact with **NATIVE SPEAKERS**. All studies show high individual variation.

However, language research using questionnaires and proficiency tests (Coleman, 1996: 59–90, 1997; Dyson, 1988; Freed, 1995, 1998; Teichler, 1997; Willis *et al.*, 1977) suggests that overall proficiency typically does improve faster

through residence abroad than through tuition in the home country, especially for learners who are less proficient when they go abroad. Certain language skills improve more than others. On the one hand, there may be little or no morphosyntactic (**GRAMMAR**) gain, little improvement in **READING**, and still less in **WRITING**. On the other hand, **SOCIOLINGUISTIC COMPETENCE** can improve (Regan, 1995), **VOCABULARY** expands rapidly, and the greatest changes are observed in oral-aural domains – **SPEAKING** and **LISTENING** – and in fluency. Whatever measure of fluency is adopted – speed, self-correction, length of utterances, filled or reduced pauses, words per minute, accuracy of **PRONUNCIATION** and intonation, communication strategies – most students return from residence abroad speaking in ways which are closer to, and more acceptable to, native speakers, even if their other language skills have not progressed so quickly.

## Preparation for study abroad

As might be expected, what learners do when abroad affects their learning. The more they talk with locals, the more they improve. More advanced learners also benefit from receptive contact with the language, through radio and television, films, books and newspapers. But the false assumptions made by many students going abroad – that integration will be easy and that their language will improve automatically since they will be forced to use it all the time – need to be countered. Proper preparation at the home institution will include the development of **STRATEGIES OF LEARNING** appropriate to the extended period of **AUTONOMY**, and underlining the need to seek out interactive contact with native speakers. No longer described as a 'year out', study abroad is increasingly integrated into the degree programme, with appropriate preparation and follow-up, not least because proficiency starts to fall off on return unless actively maintained, for example by **TANDEM LEARNING** involving incoming **EXCHANGE** students.

Preparation (Coleman, 1998b) should also address potential problems such as **CULTURE SHOCK**, and other potential gains, since the positive outcomes of study abroad are not only linguistic. They may be personal (increased self-confidence and independence), professional (knowledge and experience of the world of work in another country) or academic (through courses not available at home). A deeper understanding of how the foreign society functions is also important, especially on **AREA STUDIES** courses. A further crucial objective is **INTERCULTURAL COMPETENCE**: an appreciation by the student of the relativity of all values, beliefs and behaviours, and a willingness and ability to observe objectively, to evaluate without applying narrowly ethnocentric criteria, and to adapt to local behaviour patterns – without necessarily adopting uncritically the attitudes embodied by the local culture. Disappointingly, residence abroad seems (Coleman, 1998a) to have little impact upon the national **STEREOTYPES** which students hold, and in a minority of cases results in a less positive attitude to speakers of the target language.

**See also:** Acquisition and teaching; Cross-cultural psychology; Culture shock; Exchanges; Intercultural training; Medium of instruction; Stereotypes; Untutored language acquisition

### References

Coleman, J.A. (1996) *Studying languages: a survey of British and European students. The proficiency, background, attitudes and motivations of students of foreign languages in the United Kingdom and Europe*, London: Centre for Information on Language Teaching and Research.

Coleman, J.A. (1997) 'Residence abroad within language study', *Language Teaching* 30, 1: 1–20.

Coleman, J.A. (1998a) 'Evolving intercultural perceptions among university language learners in Europe', in M. Byram and M. Fleming (eds), *Foreign language learning in intercultural perspective*, Cambridge: Cambridge University Press.

Coleman, J.A. (1998b) 'Student preparation for residence abroad: two stages in acquiring cross-cultural capability', in D. Killick and M. Parry (eds), *Cross-cultural capability: the why, the ways, the means – new theories and methodologies in language education*, Leeds: Leeds Metropolitan University.

Dyson, P. (1988) *The effect on linguistic competence of the year spent abroad by students studying French, German and Spanish at degree level*, Oxford: Oxford University Language Teaching Centre.

Freed, B.F. (ed.) (1995) *Second language acquisition in a study abroad context*, Amsterdam/Philadelphia: John Benjamins.

Freed, B.F. (ed.) (1998) Special issue of *Frontiers: the Interdisciplinary Journal of Study Abroad*, Fall 1998.

Freed, B.F. (1999) 'Study abroad and language learning', http://language.stanford.edu/about/conferencepapers/freedpaper.html

Huebner, T. (1998) 'Methodological considerations in data collection for language learning in a study abroad context', *Frontiers* Fall 1998: 1–30.

Parker, G. and Rouxeville, A. (eds) (1995) *'The year abroad'. Preparation, monitoring, assessment, current research and development*, London: AFLS/CILT.

Regan, V. (1995) 'The acquisition of sociolinguistic native speech norms: effects of a year abroad on L2 learners of French', in B.F. Freed (ed.), *Second language acquisition in a study abroad context*, Amsterdam/Philadelphia: John Benjamins.

Teichler, U. (1997) *The ERASMUS experience. Major findings of the ERASMUS evaluation research*, Luxembourg: Office for Official Publications of the European Communities.

Willis, F.M., Doble, G., Sankarayya, U. and Smithers, A. (1977) *Residence abroad and the student of modern languages: a preliminary survey*, Bradford: University of Bradford, Modern Languages Centre.

### Further reading

Coleman, J.A. (1997) 'Residence abroad within language study', *Language Teaching* 30, 1: 1–20.

Coleman, J.A. (1998) 'Language learning and study abroad: the European perspective', *Frontiers* Fall 1998: 167–203.

Parker, G. and Rouxeville, A. (eds) (1995)*'The year abroad'. Preparation, monitoring, assessment, current research and development*, London: AFLS/CILT.

JAMES A. COLEMAN

# Stylistic variation

There are always more than two or three alternatives in communicative actions; this is what we call stylistic variation. Anything that is being said can be said just as well in a different way, although probably with a different effect: a fact that has always been common knowledge to conversationalists and rhetoricians.

Linguistic variation is practised and functions in all kinds of human (perhaps even animal) interaction; it is an intrinsic and indispensable ingredient of communicative interaction. Anybody who tries to interact in a certain situation by expressing their opinion, assumptions, hopes or fears, and so on, must do this by making their choice from the repertoire of means of expression at their disposal.

## Dimensions of variation

The difference in situational components influences not so much the topic, i.e. what is going to be discussed, but rather the way in which it is or should be worded (its surface structures). It is by preference the lexical and syntactic area where such stylistic choice produces stylistic effects. This inevitable choice from among different structures, and its specific effect in and upon its recipient, depends on whether both the interlocutor and their partner use and master at least similar codes of expression, especially as far as connotative elements are concerned. Among the connotative elements, all kinds of associative, emotive and affective semantic features have a prominent role.

It is especially lexical variants and those on the textual level which play a considerable, if not exclusive, role among the stylistic means of influencing the recipient. Moreover, these lexical and some textual devices are also the elements that characterise various types of texts, such as bureaucratic, intimate, poetic, everyday smalltalk, etc. Their effects are evident above all in **SPEECH ACTS** with (per)suasive intentions. In particular, the connotational features of words, because of their potential to persuade and influence recipients of messages, are extremely problematic with respect to the effect they can have on the interlocutor, so much so that it seems advisable not to try to adopt either poetic language or slang terms as teaching **OBJECTIVES**. To use slang, for example, in order to signal intimacy can be a risky enterprise. However, because, as suggested above, stylistic choice is unavoidable and indispensable, there is no such thing as stylistically unmarked texts or language. A consequence for teaching is that the learner will always be confronted with formulations of a specific stylistic purport and character.

Texts in general are obviously considerably different, both in their lexical and syntactic as well as their phonological appearance and usage – not to mention regional variants. Moreover, there is of course historical variation among texts which is relevant for their acceptability, and **TEXTBOOKS** often contain items that would strike a **NATIVE SPEAKER** as at least old-fashioned. On the other hand, antiquated lexical elements have specific effects of their own, compared with new-fangled innovations or technical terms. There is any amount of specific technical **VOCABULARY** apart from continuously regenerated colloquialisms, only some of which will perhaps be acquired in language learning.

If the concept of stylistic variation is not restricted to poetic or experimental language products but is extended to everyday language use and its variation, it is obvious that the student of a foreign language will not be able to master more than two or three of these variants, e.g. writing a letter of application, an assignment, a personal season's greeting card, partaking in smalltalk, etc. What is offered in textbooks as representing the so-called 'normal' language use is, in reality, examples of specific stylistic variants.

## Consequences for teaching

The didactic consequences of an awareness of stylistic variation are varied. For example, **BEGINNERS** should not be faced with the diversified possibilities of saying the same thing in a different way and modified mood. On the other hand, if they are confronted with text examples of a drearily ordinary, even simplified, non-committal sort, this would not resemble communicative reality. This is the crucial decision for authors of teaching material: to choose examples that are as genuine as possible, without bordering on realms of communicative and associative elements that the learner cannot be expected to cope with.

Some of the aspects of stylistic variation that make teaching a foreign language difficult and need to be taken into consideration by the teachers are: the connotative elements of lexical and textual meaning (presuppositions as well as allusions, etc.), regional variation, obsolete usage, and – most difficult to handle – figurative language (**META-PHORS**, metonymy, etc.), and text fragments which are quotations (such as 'last but not least') with their specific literary associations.

**See also:** Authenticity; Discourse analysis; Materials and media; Metaphor; Poetry; Reading; Sociolinguistic competence; Speech act theory; Standard language; Textbooks

### Further reading

Haynes, J. (1993) *Introducing stylistics*, London: Unwin Hyman.

Sandig, B. (1986) *Stilistik der deutschen Sprache* (Stylistics of the German language), Berlin: de Gruyter.

Weber, J.J. (ed.) (1995) *The stylistics reader. From Roman Jakobson to the present*, London: Arnold.

Wright, L. and Hope, J. (1995) *Stylistics. A practical coursebook*, London: Routledge.

KARL SORNIG

# Suggestopedia

A method of language teaching developed by a Bulgarian medical doctor, Georgi **LOZANOV**, in the 1960s, and based on Indian yoga and Soviet **PSYCHOLOGY**, Suggestopedia attempts to accelerate learning through suggestion, relaxation and concentration, and emphasises that all students can be taught a foreign language at the same level of skill. It is also known as 'superlearning', especially in commercial literature.

### The method

The most conspicuous characteristics of Suggestopedia are 'the decoration, furniture, and arrangement of the classroom, the use of music, and the authoritative behaviour of the teacher' (Richards and Rodgers, 1986: 142). The procedures of a four-hour intensive Suggestopedic class involve a number of 'parts' and 'sessions'.

### The first part

This starts with a review of the previous day's lesson in the form of conversational exchange, songs, games, story-telling, sketches and plays. To help overcome inhibitions and to allow for more spontaneous expression, each student is given a new name and a new profession. Each 'foreign' identity assigned contains repetitions of one or more phonemes that students would find difficult to pronounce in the target language.

### The second part:

In the second part of the class, conscious analysis is realised in the form of **READING**, **GRAMMAR** and **TRANSLATION**. First, the teacher discusses the general content (not structure) of the material, which consists largely of real-life dialogues. The learners then receive the printed dialogue. The dialogues are originally arranged on the page in groups of three, each with five groups of three phrases or sentence fragments. The translation of each word-group is provided in a column at the right of the page. The teacher answers any questions of interest or concern about the dialogue.

### The third part (the seance)

The third part of the Suggestopedic language class, the *seance*, provides for memorisation of the new material at an unconscious level. Initially, at least for the 'concert' part of the seance, students recline comfortably in a specially constructed chair (with a long back on which there is a pillow or headrest) and listen to a second (the active session) and third (the passive session) readings of the dialogue by the teachers.

A *The active session*  The three words or phrases of each group are presented together, each with a different intonation or voice level, which corresponds to three forms of yoga suggestion. During the active session, the students look at the dialogue on the printed page and repeat to themselves the difficult foreign words and phrases.

B *The passive session (the concert session at which the unconscious learning system takes over)*  During the third reading the material is acted out by the teacher in a dramatic manner over a background of a special musical form (slow movements, usually sixty beats to a minute, of Baroque instrumental music).

B1  A two-minute introduction which serves as a 'countdown' (with baroque music as the background).

B2  A series of slow movements of baroque music, lasting some twenty minutes, over which the teacher acts out the lesson dialogue with an emotional or artistic intonation and during which the students, with eyes closed, meditate on the text.

B3  Fast, cheerful baroque music, lasting two minutes, which brings the students out of their deeply relaxed state.

## Origins and history

Suggestopedia, put together with **SILENT WAY**, **TOTAL PHYSICAL RESPONSE** and **COMMUNITY LANGUAGE LEARNING** under the title of **HUMANISTIC** methods, is a method developed by the Bulgarian psychiatrist–educator Georgi Lozanov. In the 1960s, Lozanov discovered that certain yogic techniques of physical and mental relaxation could be used to produce a state of analgesia, or relief from pain, on the one hand, and a state of hypermnesia, or greatly improved memory and concentration, on the other. One such report claimed that a yogi could repeat 1,000 phrases from memory after hearing them only once (Lozanov, 1992: 7). These findings were applied to the field of education. Suggestopedia is the product of his attempts to combine yoga relaxation and verbal suggestion with the **DIRECT METHOD** to produce a unique system of foreign language teaching (Bancroft, 1982). Suggestopedia is based on three assumptions: learning involves the unconscious and the conscious functions of the learner; people can learn much faster than they usually do; learning is interfered with by the norms and limitations which society has taught us, the lack of a harmonious, relaxed working together of all parts of the learner, and the consequent failure to make use of powers which lie idle in most people most of the time. In accordance with these assumptions, Suggestopedia aims at removing these limiting norms, inhibiting tensions and maximising learners' power of learning through the desuggestive–suggestive process. According to Richards and Rodgers (1986: 145), 'Desuggestion seems to involve unloading the memory bank, or reserves, of unwanted or blocking memories. Suggestion, then, involves loading the memory banks with desired and facilitating memories.'

## The process of desuggestion–suggestion

Lozanov (1992) lists six means of the desuggestive–suggestive process: authority, infantilisation, double-planeness, intonation, rhythm, and concert pseudopassiveness.

### Authority

People remember and are most influenced by information coming from an authoritative source. Lozanov dictates a variety of prescriptions and proscriptions aimed at having Suggestopedia students experience the educational establishment and the teacher as sources having great authority. Lozanov talks of choosing a 'ritual placebo system' that is most likely to be perceived of by students as having high authority (Lozanov, 1992: 267). He appears to believe that scientific-sounding language, highly positive experimental data, and true-believer teachers constitute a ritual placebo system that is authoritatively appealing to most learners. Well-publicised accounts of learning success lend the method and the institution authority, and commitment to the method, self-confidence, personal distance, acting ability and a highly positive attitude give an authoritative air to the teacher.

### Infantilisation

In a Suggestopedic classroom, students are expected to tolerate and in fact encourage their own infantilisation, which is thought to create a general atmosphere of easiness, spontaneity and absence of pressure. Infantilisation is accomplished in part by students' acknowledging the absolute authority of the teacher and in part by their taking part in role playing, games, songs and gymnastic exercises that help 'the older student regain the self-confidence, spontaneity and receptivity of the child' (Bancroft, 1982: 19).

### Double-planeness

The learner learns not only from the effect of direct instruction (the conscious level), but from the environment in which the instruction takes place (the unconscious level). The best learning takes place when what is happening on each of these two levels supports what is happening on the other. This is what Lozanov referred to as 'double planeness'.

Double-planeness comprises the enormous signalling stream of diverse stimuli which unconsciously, or semiconsciously, are emitted from or perceived by the personality. Usually this second plane in behaviour is the source of the intuitive impressions which form many of our attitudes toward persons and situations incomprehensible even to ourselves. A good knowledge of double-plane behaviour ensures creating conditions for the utilisation of the reserve capacities of paraconscious mental activity. In the Suggestopedic classroom, the bright decor of the room, the musical background, the shape of the chairs and the personality of the teacher are considered as the second plane which are as important in instruction as the form of the instructional material itself.

### Intonation, rhythm, and concert pseudo-passiveness

Varying the tone and rhythm of presented material helps both to avoid boredom through monotony of repetition and to dramatise, emotionalise and give meaning to linguistic materials. Lozanov recommends a moderately artistic intonation because it 'increases the information value of the material given, engages the emotional and double plane aspects of the communicative process more actively, and creates an atmosphere of acceptable significance' (1992: 196).

Suggestopedia uses an eight-second cycle for pacing out data at slow intervals. During the first four beats of the cycle there is silence. During the second four beats the teacher presents the material. Ostrander *et al.* (1979) present a variety of evidence on why this eight-second pacing to Baroque largo

music is so potent. They note that musical rhythms affect body rhythms, such as heartbeat, and that researchers have noted that 'with a slow heartbeat, mind efficiency takes a great leap forward' (1979: 63).

Both intonation and rhythm are coordinated with a musical background. The musical background helps to induce a relaxed attitude, which Lozanov refers to as concert pseudo-passiveness. This state is felt to be optimal for learning, in that anxieties and tension are relieved and power of concentration for new material is raised. Lozanov recommends a series of slow movements (sixty beats a minute, the ideal beat for meditation in Indian music) in 4/4 time for Baroque, strung together into about a half-hour concert. In such concerts, reported Ostrander, 'the body relaxed, the mind became alert' (Ostrander *et al.*, 1979: 74).

### Critique

The Lozanov method has gained attention in various parts of the world. In the United States, descriptions of the almost unbelievable successes of suggestology have appeared in *Psychology Today* (August, 1977), and in *Parade* magazine (March 12, 1978), a Sunday supplement that has an estimated readership in the United States of over thirty million. It has been popularised by Ostrander *et al.*'s book *Superlearning* (1979). However, Suggestopedia also received a scathing review in the *TESOL Quarterly*, a journal of somewhat more restricted circulation than *Parade* (Scovel, 1979). Scovel takes special issue with Lozanov's use (and misuse) of scholarly citations, jargon and experimental data and states that 'a careful reading of [Suggestology and Outlines of Suggestopedy] reveals that there is precious little in suggestology which is scientific' (1979: 257). He also notes that Lozanov is unequivocally opposed to any eclectic use of the techniques outside of the full panoply of Suggestopedic science. In the United States, the Society for Suggestive-Accelerative Learning and Teaching (SALT, a term used in the United States to refer to the Lozanov method) conducted experiments to study Suggestopedia.

**See also:** *Handlungsorientierter Unterricht*; Humanistic language teaching; Lozanov; Neuro-linguistic programming; Silent Way; Teaching methods

## References

Bancroft, W.J. (1982) 'Suggestopedia, sophrology and the traditional foreign-language class', *Foreign Language Annals* 15, 5: 373–9.

Lozanov, G. (1992) *Suggestology and outlines of suggestopedy*, Philadelphia: Gordon and Breach.

Ostrander, S., Schroeder, L. and Ostrander, N. (1979) *Superlearning*, New York: Dell.

Ramirez, S.Z. (1986) 'The effect of suggestopedia in teaching English vocabulary to Spanish-dominant chicano third graders', *The Elementary School Journal* 86, 3: 325–33.

Richards, J.C. and Rodgers, T.S. (1986) *Approaches and methods in language teaching*, New York: Cambridge University Press.

Scovel, T. (1979) 'Reviews of suggestology and outlines of suggestopedy', *TESOL Quarterly* 13, 2: 255–66.

Stevick, E. (1980) 'The work of Georgi Lozanov', in E. Stevick, *Teaching languages: a way and ways*, Rowley, MS: Newbury House.

## Further reading

Bancroft, W.J. (1972) 'The asychology of suggestopedia or learning without stress', *Educational Courier* February: 16–19.

Bancroft, W.J. (1978) 'The Lozanov method and its American adaptations', *Modern Language Journal* 62, 4: 167–75.

MENG-CHING HO

# Sweet, Henry

b. 1845, London; d. 1912, Oxford

Linguist

Henry Sweet, the irascible if genial phonetician and enemy of all woolly thinking in language learning methodology, was a pioneer in many areas of **LINGUISTICS**. His amusing critiques of contemporary 'methods' and **ATTITUDES** to language learning are well worth consideration today, with useful insights on the spoken language, the application of **GRAMMAR** rules, the selection and grading of **VOCABULARY**, and the **PSYCHOLOGY** of the learner.

As a descriptive linguist, Sweet published his highly regarded *New English Grammar* (1891) and short but pertinent descriptions of the phonology of many modern European languages (1877), presented in a 'Broad' (essentially phonemic) script that influenced the **INTERNATIONAL PHONETIC ASSOCIATION** (of which he became a member). As a philologist, he edited many Old English manuscripts for the first time and developed a rigorous approach to the design of the language **TEXTBOOK**. A related interest in the medieval history of language teaching seems also to have coloured his ideas on teaching through the 'natural sentence' and the dialogue.

Such experiences nourished his **APPLIED LINGUISTICS**. Thus the arrangement and methodology in his *Anglo-Saxon Reader* (1876) and *Primer* (1882) clearly led to the popular *Primer of Spoken English* (1885), remarkable for being both a textbook for learners of modern English and also a model of linguistic description.

His final word is the *The Practical Study of Languages* (1899/1964), a comprehensive work on the nature of language and languages (including Arabic and **CHINESE**), the preparation of **MATERIALS**, and the theory of teaching and self-study. Despite a bias towards a phonetic method in the early chapters, Sweet criticises practitioners of a single classroom technique, such as **GOUIN**, for their lack of 'general principles'. His solution is eclectic, combining his own emphasis on phonetics and collocation with new ideas from Hermann Paul (and Herbart) on patterns of association within the mind, the 'synthesis' of whole sentences, and language in context.

Sweet had links with the **REFORM MOVEMENT**, especially **JESPERSEN**, and he taught Daniel Jones. His writings influenced **PALMER**, and although Sweet was not a **BEHAVIOURIST**, some connections can be seen with **BLOOMFIELD**.

## Bibliography

Sweet, H. (1877) *Handbook of phonetics*, Oxford: Clarendon Press.

Sweet, H. (1885) *Elementarbuch des gesprochenen Englisch* (Primer of spoken English), Oxford: Clarendon Press; Leipzig: Weigel.

Sweet, H. (1891) *A new English grammar*, Oxford: Clarendon Press.

Sweet, H. (1964) *The practical study of languages*, London: Oxford University Press.

### Further reading

Atherton, M. (1995) 'Grasping sentences as wholes: Henry Sweet's idea of language study in the early middle ages', *Neuphilologische Mitteilungen* 96. 2: 177–85.

Atherton, M. (1996) 'Being scientific and relevant in the language textbook: Henry Sweet's primers for learning colloquial English', *Paradigm* 20: 1–20.

Atherton, M. (1996) 'Henry Sweet's psychology of language learning', in K.D. Dutz and H.-J. Niederehe (eds), *Theorie und Rekonstruktion*, Münster: Nodus.

Howatt, A.P.R. (1984) *A history of English language teaching*, Oxford: Oxford University Press.

Kelly, J. and Local, J. (1985) 'The modernity of Henry Sweet', *Revista Canaria De Estudios Ingleses* (Universidad de la Laguna) 10: 209–16.

MacMahon, M.K.C. (1994) 'Henry Sweet's linguistic scholarship: the German connection', *Anglistik* 5. 2: 91–101.

MARK ATHERTON

# Syllabus and curriculum design

A syllabus can be defined as the specification of aims and the selection and grading of content to be used as a basis for planning foreign language, or any other educational, courses. (It might be noted that the plural form 'syllabuses' is now usually preferred to 'syllabi'.) In English, though not in some other languages, a distinction is made between a *syllabus* and a *curriculum*. The narrower specification of a syllabus, which refers to the aims and content of a particular subject, can be seen as part of a wider and more general curriculum. This may go beyond specifying the content of a single subject and may include both organisational aspects and questions of overall policy or **LAN-**

**GUAGE PLANNING**, such as how many languages should be studied, at what ages, how many hours should be devoted to the study of a language, etc. It is the term 'syllabus' that is usually employed by applied linguists in discussions of foreign language, reflecting the tendency in foreign language methodology to separate foreign languages from the rest of the curriculum. However, when a broader perspective is taken – for example, in discussions of **LANGUAGE ACROSS THE CURRICULUM** or of how **CULTURAL AWARENESS**, information technology, etc., can be integrated into FL teaching – then the more general term may be preferred. Clearly, there is an area of overlap between the two concepts.

### Scope and significance of syllabus design

The scope of a syllabus can vary considerably. At one end of the scale it can be purely institutional – say, within a private language school – and specify the language content of a single specific course. At the other, it can be part of a national curriculum and take the form of a complex document drawn up by a ministry of education and incorporating components such as a 'teacher's handbook'. It is also common for examination boards to issue 'syllabuses', though it could be argued that this type of specification is an inventory rather than a coherent syllabus. A syllabus may be explicit – that is to say, it exists as a separate document, or it may be implicit – for example, in a **TEXTBOOK**, where it only becomes apparent by examining the categories in the table of contents.

In the last quarter of the twentieth century, syllabus design represented one of the central topics of **APPLIED LINGUISTICS** and educational policy, since the syllabus is seen as a means of positively influencing **MATERIALS** design and classroom practices. In respect of policy, its potential to provide a common basis for foreign language learning has both ideological and practical implications. This is apparent at national level in many countries, but it is also evident at an international level where considerable attention has been devoted to the issues by the **COUNCIL OF EUROPE**.

Syllabuses are necessary for three main reasons. The first, and least controversial, is transparency: a well-designed syllabus provides a framework for *clarifying* OBJECTIVES, content and methods for learners, teachers – and perhaps parents too. The second is that of *regularising* teaching and learning, which, particularly in the case of national syllabuses, may help to ensure uniformity of content, attainment standards, etc. The third is that of *guiding* the process of teaching and learning, in particular by specifying methodology. This represents a controversial aspect of syllabus design, since the dividing line between guiding and constraining can easily be overstepped. A syllabus that is prescriptive or too comprehensive in its specifications may be seen by teachers as forcing them into a straitjacket, and may result in the negative view that teachers sometimes have of the type of syllabus, referred to by van Lier (1996: 8) as 'disempowering', which seeks to impose content and methods on classroom teachers.

The degree of acceptance a syllabus enjoys amongst teachers and learners may be linked to factors such as: Who draws up the syllabus? Who is the intended reader? To what extent are teachers and learners consulted in the design process? How much scope does a syllabus leave for individual interpretation? One approach is to 'democratise' syllabus design procedures by including classroom teachers and students in the construction process, a *negotiated syllabus* (Nunan, 1988b), and by piloting it before it takes effect. Another interesting development in this connection is a type of syllabus designed to be read by the learners themselves rather than by teachers or textbook writers.

## Factors in designing syllabuses

The design of a syllabus may be a complex procedure, consisting of several stages: preparation; construction; implementation; and EVALUATION (Richards and Rogers, 1986: 159). An important part of the preparation stage is a NEEDS ANALYSIS, which has the function of determining the needs for which learners require a language. It might include aspects such as the situations or domains in which learners might use the foreign language, the topics which should form part of a course, the SKILLS required by the learner, their expected attainment levels, the methods by which they wish to be taught, their preferred LEARNING STYLES, etc.

The informants of a needs analysis are usually the students themselves, but may also be teachers or employers, and the analysis can take the form of a questionnaire, an interview, or some other piece of research. A second source of input which will determine the design of a syllabus will be theoretical aspects such as views of language learning held by the designers themselves, or current thinking in education or methodology, which will be reflected in the content specification.

The categories used in specifying content in foreign language syllabuses have expanded considerably from the traditional list of structures to a range of categories that incorporate not only language, but also learning and teaching as well as general educational aspects. The following types of categories are those most commonly found in modern syllabuses:

- Objectives of language learning, which might range in their definition from general aims or goals of foreign language learning (e.g. 'to be able to interact with NATIVE SPEAKERS in real situations') to more specific performance-based objectives (e.g. 'to be able to ask for and understand directions').

- Contextual categories which specify the type of domains in which students should be able to interact and which are therefore to be included in the foreign language programme. These include: settings (e.g. in a restaurant, church, school), topics (e.g. leisure activities, house and home), behavioural specifications, i.e. what learners should be able to do in communication (e.g. describing their own house, saying how they travel to school).

- Language items, which may be described in terms of grammatical forms or structures (e.g. present progressive, definite article); NOTIONS (e.g. size, time, frequency); functions (e.g. apologising, asking the way, greeting someone); lexical lists; the four skills – READING, WRITING, LISTENING, SPEAKING – and related sub-skills (e.g. listening for gist, scanning a text for specific information, note-taking); TEXT TYPES that students will be confronted with (e.g. a conversation, a newspaper advertisement); discourse categories (e.g. typical dialogue exchange patterns); compensation strategies to cope with language difficulties (e.g. asking for clarification, guessing from context).

- Teaching methodology, consisting of general pedagogical guidelines or specific examples of classroom tasks and activities.
- Learning **STRATEGIES**, usually examples of '**LEARNING TO LEARN**' techniques, ways of enhancing **AUTONOMOUS LEARNING**.
- Cultural awareness or sociocultural components, which may be: knowledge based (e.g. major national holidays), behavioural (e.g. interpreting body language, visiting rituals), or attitudinal (e.g. developing empathy towards otherness).
- Attainment levels, specified in terms of skill-based behaviour and corresponding degrees of proficiency, often defined as levels or bands (Carroll and West, 1989).

## Communicative syllabus design

Most differences between syllabuses – and controversies surrounding them – concern the specification of content, and run parallel to swings of the pendulum in linguistic and methodological approaches. Until the early 1970s, the main purpose of most syllabuses was seen as listing and grading the language content of courses, textbooks or examinations. In keeping with prevailing views of linguistic description, this took the form of lists of formal items to be mastered by students: the so-called structural syllabus. From the mid-1970s onwards a shift of emphasis in language description and corresponding changes in methodologies led to a broad acceptance of principles of **COMMUNICA-TIVE LANGUAGE TEACHING**, according to which language was to be seen in terms of 'acts of communication'. For syllabus designers, the nature of whose task requires them to think in categories, this necessitated a major re-orientation. First, this different approach required a broadening of categories beyond narrow linguistic units to incorporate use-based contextual and behavioural components, i.e. units of communication. Whilst this did not preclude the specification of language components, it became necessary to stipulate language categories based on the meanings that give rise to the forms, rather than the forms themselves, which in turn required new theories of

language meaning. The term 'notional–functional' reflects the two principal categories of meaning which found their way into communication syllabuses. Notions came to be used to refer to general existential concepts – possibly universal categories of human experience – such as time and space, whereas language functions can be defined as the purpose for which language is used, often specified as action-based or behavioural meaning, such as 'apologising' or 'asking for help'. Both the term *notional–functional syllabus* and *communicative syllabus* are used, and sometimes confused, in theoretical discussions. The former is a narrower term, referring to the semantically-oriented specification of language; the latter includes reference to aspects of language use (contextual features, skills, etc.) as well as to methodology.

One of the aims of communicative syllabus design was to take a broader 'top-down' entry point to categorisation, rather than the traditional 'bottom-up' view which begins with grammatical structures. To this end, Wilkins (1976) distinguished between a *synthetic* approach, in which language items are introduced separately and sequentially so that, as in a jigsaw puzzle, the student gradually builds up a picture of the whole structure, and an *analytic* approach, which involves a graduation based on broader units such as situations, texts, etc.

The practice of 'communicative' syllabus design was strongly influenced by two publications which attempted to provide communication-based descriptions in the form of comprehensive inventories, both of which appeared in the 1970s. These were Munby's *Communicative Syllabus Design* (1978) and the very influential Council of Europe publication, the **THRESHOLD LEVEL** (van Ek, 1975; van Ek and Trim, 1991) which, though an inventory rather than an actual graded syllabus, has served as the basis for the design of many European national syllabuses for a variety of different languages.

## Alternative designs

Although communicative or notional–functional syllabuses took a radically different approach, their primary task was nevertheless to categorise language, albeit from a user-based semantic, rather than formal, perspective. In the 1980s, following a general learner-centred view of foreign language learning, the attention of methodologists and applied linguists began to move away from the analysis of language use to focus more strongly on the process of **SECOND LANGUAGE ACQUISITION**. As a result, there was a shift in emphasis from *what* students should learn in the direction of *how* students do learn. As far as teachers were concerned, they came to be regarded less as 'managers of communication' and more as 'facilitators of acquisition'. This led to a distinction being made between *product-oriented* and *process-oriented* syllabuses (Nunan, 1988a; van Lier, 1996). 'Product' can refer to any kind of target knowledge, ability or other outcome of learning, be it linguistic, cultural or whatever, whereas 'process' refers to the means by which students gain this knowledge or develop these skills. This might be seen in terms of classroom activities or tasks – the *task-based* or *procedural* syllabus (see Johnson, 1982; Nunan, 1988b) – or at a more abstract, psychological level in terms of learning strategies or cognitive processes which learners employ to facilitate acquisition. A process approach, based on principles of learner autonomy, can represent a direct challenge to product-based syllabuses, as can be seen from the following quotation:

> [a curriculum] ... is process-oriented in the sense that pedagogical interaction is motivated by our understanding of learning rather than by a list of desired competencies, test scores, or other products. The settings of goals and objectives ... are themselves integral parts of the curriculum process, rather than pre-established constraints that are imposed on it from the outside.
>
> (van Lier, 1996: 3)

Despite its appeal to idealism, it is likely that both at an institutional, and more especially at a national, level a purely process-oriented approach will be difficult to implement, for, as Stoks (1996) points out, these pose a problem of accountability. It seems that governments, teachers and students alike feel a need for expected outcomes of learning to be stated at the outset of a course.

A further development is the outward expansion of the foreign language syllabus in the direction of a more general curriculum, in the sense that the two terms were distinguished above. One reason for this is the wish to locate language learning within more general educational aims, seen, for example, in the strong focus that is given to the category of **CULTURAL AWARENESS** or sociocultural competence, and another is a much broader view which is taken of learning. This trend can be seen by comparing the two major Council of Europe documents, the Threshold Level with its mainly language-based specification, and the **COMMON EUROPEAN FRAMEWORK** of Reference, whose categorisation reflects this broader perspective.

A further issue in syllabus design is the grading of content within a syllabus, with regard to both selection and organisation. In many syllabuses the criteria for selecting items of language (**GRAMMAR**, functions, **VOCABULARY**, etc.) are not made explicit but may be based on frequency of occurrence, usefulness to the learner or perceived difficulty or complexity of structure, content, task, etc. An interesting approach – the *lexical syllabus* – is taken by Willis (1990), who proposes as a basis for selection and grading the frequency of occurrence of lexical items in **AUTHENTIC** language. There are three significant features of this approach: first, Willis's data is based on a twenty-million-word corpus of authentic language (COBUILD): second, Willis not only incorporates lexical items but syntactic and discourse patterns too; and third, he proposes an analytic syllabus, i.e. that a syllabus should be based on texts rather than isolated lexical items of structures.

Another aspect of grading is the question of organisation. Most syllabuses take a linear approach. Each language item is specified only once to indicate when it is to be first introduced into a teaching programme. An alternative approach is offered by the *spiral* or *cyclical* syllabus (Corder, 1973: 297), which includes proposals for recycling various elements.

Every syllabus operates within certain contextual constraints and, as Johnson (1989: 18) says, one of the challenges of the syllabus designer is to reconcile 'what is desirable (policy) with what is acceptable and possible (**PRAGMATICS**)'. In addition, it is important to remember that a syllabus is only one element of an overall *operational framework*, which may begin with policy making, include materials development, and end up with what

Girard (Girard *et al.*, 1994: 108) in his model terms 'teaching and learning acts'. As van Lier says:

A map is not the territory. In a similar way, the syllabus is not the journey. Experience, appreciation, criticism, and so on, are not laid down in the syllabus, they are merely made available by it, and brought to it by the learners.

(van Lier, 1996: 20)

**See also:** Council of Europe Modern Languages Projects; Graded objectives; Notions and functions; Objectives in language teaching and learning; Planning for foreign language teaching; Proficiency movement; Teacher education; Textbooks

## References

Carroll, B.J. and West, R. (1989) *ESU framework*, London: Longman.

Corder, S.P. (1973) *Introducing applied linguistics*, Harmondsworth: Penguin.

Girard, D. (1994) *Selection and distribution of contents in language syllabus*, Strasbourg: Council of Europe.

Johnson, K. (1982) *Communicative syllabus design and methodology*, Oxford: Pergamon.

Johnson, R.K. (ed.) (1989) *The second language curriculum*, Cambridge: Cambridge University Press.

Munby, J. (1978) *Communicative syllabus design*, Cambridge: Cambridge University Press.

Nunan, D. (1988a) *Syllabus design*, Oxford: Oxford University Press.

Nunan, D. (1988b) *The learner-centred curriculum*, Cambridge: Cambridge University Press.

Richards, J.C. and Rodgers, T.S. (1986) *Approaches and methods in language learning*, Cambridge: Cambridge University Press.

Stoks, G.L.M. (1996) *Modern languages: learning, teaching, assessment. A common European framework of reference. Guide for curriculum developers*, Strasbourg: Council of Europe.

van Ek, J.A. (1975) *The Threshold Level in a European unit/credit system for modern language learning by adults*, Strasbourg: Council of Europe.

van Ek, J.A. and Trim, J.L.M. (1991) *Threshold Level 1990*, Strasbourg: Council of Europe.

van Lier, L. (1996) *Interaction in the language curriculum*, London: Longman.

Wilkins, D. (1976) *Notional syllabuses*, Oxford: Oxford University Press.

Willis, D. (1990) *The lexical syllabus*, London: Collins ELT.

## Further reading

Artal, A., Carrion, M.J. and Monros, G. (1997) 'Can a cultural syllabus be integrated into the general language syllabus?, in M. Byram and G. Zarate (eds), *The sociocultural and intercultural dimension of language learning and teaching*, Strasbourg: Council of Europe.

Council of Europe (1996) *Modern languages: learning, teaching, assessment. A common European framework of reference*, Strasbourg: Council of Europe.

Johnson, R.K. (ed.) (1989) *The second language curriculum*, Cambridge: Cambridge University Press.

Nunan, D. (1992) *Collaborative language learning and teaching*, Cambridge: Cambridge University Press.

Widdowson, H.G. (1990) *Aspects of language teaching*, Oxford: Oxford University Press.

DAVID NEWBY

# T

## Tandem learning

Based on the potent image of the concerted effort of tandem cyclists, tandem learning is a way of organising foreign language learning which brings together speakers of at least two different **MOTHER TONGUES** to learn and, to a certain degree, teach each others' languages and cultures reciprocally. Individual or group tandems constitute partly **AUTONOMOUS** learning contexts which are organised as face-to-face or virtual encounters that are usually binational. The growing importance of tandem learning in Europe during the last thirty years is a result of the development in foreign language teaching, from a narrow, **COMMUNICATIVE** approach to a growing integration of **INTERCULTURAL COMPETENCE** which sees a need for increased contact with **NATIVE SPEAKERS** and their cultures.

Precursors of today's individual tandems were tutorials and teaching one-to-one contexts in the nineteenth century. Since the 1960s, four different lines of development can be distinguished (Herfurth, 1993: 243–5).

The first time the tandem approach formed part of a teaching concept was in the binational holiday encounter programmes of the *Deutsch–Französisches Jugendwerk* (German–French youth organisation). From 1973 to 1983, Turkish immigrants and German workers participated in binational language classes in Munich to promote intercultural understanding as well as language learning. Based on individual Spanish–German tandems at the *Instituto Alemán* (German **GOETHE-INSTITUT**) in Madrid, Spain, various tandem initiatives were founded from 1979 onwards in a number of European cities. They eventually organised the 'tandem net' in which courses and **EXCHANGE** activities are coordinated. A fourth strand of tandem courses has grown at European universities since the 1980s. These binational language courses started between Spain and Germany and have since been established in many countries in Europe. Since 1989 the international tandem conference has taken place every two years, the major point of exchange on developments in the field.

Having started in out-of-school youth exchanges and forming part of university and **ADULT** education settings, as well as being used in the field of encounters between members of specific professions, the tandem idea has also been firmly established in many forms of exchange at the primary and secondary school level. From the project '*Lerne die Sprache des Nachbarn*' (learn the language of your neighbour), an intensive contact programme between primary students in the border area of France and Germany (Pelz, 1989), and the extensive field of student face-to-face exchanges worldwide, to the forms of class exchanges via correspondence, such as letter, audio-cassette, video or e-mail exchanges (Christian, 1997), the tandem approach has been used to prepare and structure encounters.

Mainly restricted to continental Europe during its pre-electronic phase, tandem learning has taken up a more global position since the advent of the **INTERNET** (Little and Brammerts, 1996: 1). This new form of communication extends the opportunities for tandem learning on the linguistic (access to more languages) as well as the thematic (access to more material) level, while also giving tandem learning a very distinctive new quality. New technologies change the learning arrangement. Not only are **READING** and **WRITING SKILLS** taking precedence over the other language skills, but asynchronous e-mail exchanges also allow ample space and time for editing and correcting letters, thus increasing time for engaging in meta-communication activities.

Tandems can be set up in special courses with external support from a teacher or counsellor, or they can function as additions to the traditional classroom situation. In a face-to-face encounter, individual or group tandems are set up, taking into account the possible differences in language proficiency of the various partners. In addition to being fundamentally **TASK-BASED**, the learning process moves between binational and mononational working phases. In the latter, participants have the opportunity to 'retreat' into a safe environment to work together.

Like any typical exchange situation facilitating natural, **AUTHENTIC** and spontaneous language contact, tandem learning functions on the principles of reciprocity and the responsibility of the learner. Both partners, being experts in their language and culture and depending on each other for mutual support, contribute and benefit equally in terms of their time, energy and interest. Reciprocity should also govern the choice of language and meeting place (in face-to-face encounters). Learners are responsible for their own learning process, planning and structuring the learning sessions, as well as collaborating on common products. To ensure mutual benefit, a contract between partners can form the basis of cooperation, regulating important aspects such as choice of language, turn-taking, forms of error correction, choice of texts or learning material. Since learners are usually not trained as teachers, they need help in identifying their goals, in applying the appropriate learning methods and strategies, and in critically evaluating the learning outcomes.

Tandem learning is thus characterised by the poles of traditional classroom learning and self-instruction. A balance is struck between the amount of external structuring and steering and the autonomy of the learners. In the classroom context, teachers give up some control over the learning situation for the benefit of increased learner's autonomy; i.e. they change from the sole person in charge and the only foreign language model in the classroom into a moderator who structures and guides the interaction. Apart from setting up and organising the exchange, the teacher is responsible for the development of target tasks to structure the collaborative work effort, and becomes a counsellor on the linguistic and thematic levels.

Tandem learning covers aspects of both language learning and intercultural learning. The foreign language is both content and **MEDIUM** of this process of linguistic and intercultural exchange. Agreement on the choice of language, various forms of clarification of words (**TRANSLATION**, code-switching) as well as different forms of error correction (how often and at which point in the discussion) are essential for successful interaction. Interaction between partners moves back and forth between content and form of language, incorporating phases of meta-communication about the language system, thus enhancing awareness of the language learning process. This can be supported by structured language **EXERCISES** as well as by advice on **COMMUNICATIVE STRATEGIES** (e.g. formulations for introducing a change of topic, for preventing and clarifying misunderstandings, for introducing repairs).

The tandem situation, structured thematically or by project-oriented tasks, allows for intensive negotiation of meanings. Partners bring different discourse patterns, cultural traditions and value systems, as well as different behaviours to the learning situations. Comparing experiences can lead to a process of negotiation of the two cultural reference systems, which in the long run might enhance changes in perspective and **ATTITUDE** towards the other culture, leading to a better understanding.

In addition to language skills, the tandem approach thus provides opportunities for learners to practise a number of transferable skills, such as 'organising themselves, their time and their work; managing their own learning; problem solving; obtaining and processing information; working as a member of a team; setting and meeting **OBJEC-TIVES**' (Little and Brammerts, 1996: 12).

Tandem learning increases contact time between non-native and native speakers, and, with the advent of electronic media, the financial problems of organising exchanges as well as the fear that languages such as **ENGLISH**, **SPANISH**, **FRENCH** and **GERMAN** might dominate the tandem market can be attenuated to a certain degree – notwithstanding the necessity of face-to-face encounters – since virtual connections allow for a cheaper connection and provide more access to lesser-taught languages.

Tandem learning not only increases motivation in language learning by creating a fear-free environment where making mistakes is seen as a natural part of the learning process, it also enhances awareness of the target language and culture, combines cognitive and affective learning modes, and allows for more conscious and effective language learning. The degree of external intervention in the learning process appears to play a crucial role as to the intensity and aims of the tandem situation. While a more thematically structured programme, for example, can enhance language learning as well as intercultural learning, more time and space for spontaneous developments in partner or group processes might lead to more intensive social and other forms of intercultural experience.

The advent of tandem learning has been seen in some quarters as forming a necessary and innovative antipode to traditional foreign language teaching (Künzle and Müller, 1990: 14–15; Pelz, 1995: 5–6), but the development in educational settings rather tends to point to a slow integration of tandem learning into existing, and thus evolving, language programmes.

**See also:** Autonomy and autonomous learners; CALL; Communicative strategies; Exchanges; Group work; Intercultural communication; Large classes; Learning to learn; Monolingual principle; Non-verbal communication; Study abroad

### References

Christian, S. (1997) *Exchanging lives: middle school writers online*, Urbana: NCTE.

Herfurth, H.-E. (1993) *Möglichkeiten und Grenzen des Fremdsprachenerwerbs in Begegnungssituationen (Possibilities and restrictions of foreign language acquisition in encounter situations)*, Munich: Iudicium.

Künzle, B. and Müller, M. (eds) (1990) *Sprachen Lernen im Tandem (Language learning in tandem)*, Freiburg, CH: Universitätsverlag.

Little, D. and Brammerts, H. (eds) (1996) *A guide to language learning in tandem via the internet*, Dublin: Trinity College.

Pelz, M. (ed.) (1989) *Lerne die Sprache des Nachbarn (Learn the language of your neighbour)*, Frankfurt/M.: Diesterweg.

Pelz, M. (ed.) (1995) *Tandem in der Lehrerbildung, Tandem und grenzüberschreitende Projekte (Tandem in teacher education, tandem and projects across borders)*, Frankfurt/M.: Verlag für Interkulturelle Kommunikation.

### Further reading

Little, D. and Brammerts, H. (eds) (1996) *A guide to language learning in tandem via the internet*, Dublin: Trinity College.

Rosanelli, M. (ed.) (1992) *Lingue in Tandem. Autonomie und Spracherwerb (Language in tandem. Autonomy and language acquisition)*, Merano: Alpha und Beta Verlag.

Rost-Roth, M. (1995) *Sprachenlernen im direkten Kontakt. Eine Fallstudie (Language learning in direct contact. A case study)*, Merano: Alpha und Beta Verlag.

Wolff, J. (1994) 'Ein TANDEM für jede Gelegenheit? Sprachlernen in verschiedenen Begegnungssituationen (A TANDEM for every opportunity? Language learning in different encounter situations)', *Die Neueren Sprachen* 93, 4: 374–85.

ANDREAS MÜLLER-HARTMANN

# Task-based teaching and assessment

Dissatisfaction with conventional linguistically-based **SYLLABUSES**, along with a growing understanding from research findings of how people learn second (including foreign) languages, has led since the 1980s to a number of proposals for various kinds of task-based alternatives. Examples include the procedural syllabus (Prabhu, 1987), the process syllabus (Breen, 1984), and the task syllabus (Long, 1985; Nunan, 1991; Robinson, in press; Skehan, 1998). In addition, there has been advocacy of 'task-based' approaches which in reality adhere to a linguistic syllabus of some kind, usually grammatical and/or lexical (see, e.g., Ellis, 1993), even if covert, as where tasks are employed in order to teach specific structures (e.g. Loschky and Bley-Vroman, 1993).

## A rationale for task-based language teaching

Most L2 syllabuses (and so-called language teaching 'methods') are built around one or more *linguistic* units of analysis, such as the word, grammatical structure, notion and function. Course design starts with the language to be taught, which the teacher or **TEXTBOOK** writer cuts up into small pieces for presentation to students in serial fashion (usually in violation of fairly well attested developmental sequences). The result is a 'grammatical' syllabus of some kind, overt or covert. Syllabus content is a series of linguistic forms. These are delivered via synthetic 'methods', (**GRAMMAR–TRANSLATION, AUDIOLINGUAL METHOD**, the **SILENT WAY, TOTAL PHYSICAL RESPONSE**, etc.) and such pedagogical devices as translation, explicit grammar rule explanation, pattern drills, 'error correction', and linguistically simplified graded readers. The forms become the major focus of classroom lessons – so-called *focus on forms* (Long, 1991; Long and Robinson, 1998). The learners' job, psycholinguistically ready or not, is to (try to) learn each item separately when it is presented, and then to synthesise the parts when they are needed for communication – hence, the term *synthetic* syllabuses (Wilkins, 1976).

There are numerous problems with focus on forms, including lack of a learner **NEEDS ANALYSIS**, the tendency of structurally graded **MATERIALS** to provide stilted language models, and resulting student boredom. While some learning takes place in such classrooms (probably despite, rather than because of, the approach used), results are generally poor and, unlike first language **ACQUISITION**, highly variable. Most serious of all is the fact

that synthetic syllabuses and synthetic language teaching 'methods' assume a model – an accumulation of isolated linguistic entities, each to near-native levels, one at a time – which is controverted by everything known about how people learn first or second languages. Far from mastering one word or structure at a time on demand, thirty years of **SECOND LANGUAGE ACQUISITION** research has shown that naturalistic, instructed and mixed learners all exhibit gradual approximation to target norms. Progress in a new language is non-linear, and rarely sudden and categorical. Learners pass through common (possibly universal) stages of seemingly immutable developmental sequences. Studies have found instruction capable of speeding up progress through sequences, among other things, but incapable of enabling learners to skip stages, e.g. to jump straight from zero knowledge of a structure to native-like use (a level very few learners ever attain). There is strong empirical evidence, and, more to the point, no counterevidence, for the idea that teachers can only teach what learners are ready to learn, i.e. are capable of processing. Acquisition sequences do not reflect the instructional sequences embodied in externally imposed grammatical syllabuses.

One response to recognition of the power of the learner's internal syllabus has been to abandon attempts to *teach* code features altogether, and instead, to try to recreate in the **ADULT** classroom the conditions under which children learned their native languages so successfully. Students are provided with holistic samples of target language use, and the teacher's job is to make the input comprehensible. Whatever remains of natural human language-learning abilities (innate or otherwise) is relied upon to allow students to induce the rules of the grammar through analysing the input – hence, the term *analytic* syllabuses (Wilkins, 1976). This approach has been called *focus on meaning* (Long, 1991; Long and Robinson, 1998), and it plays a role in a variety of foreign and second language programmes, including immersion education, the Natural Approach, 'sheltered' subject matter teaching, and some **CONTENT-BASED** courses. Syllabus and lesson content consists of general curricular subject matter or information about the foreign language culture and the people and societies using the language. Results from

EVALUATION studies of Canadian French immersion programmes are encouraging, if variable, with some students reaching very high levels of proficiency in receptive SKILLS, although only after several years of considerably more extensive exposure than is typically available for tertiary foreign language instruction. Speaking and writing tend to be fluent, but to remain far from native-like where grammatical accuracy is concerned.

The limitations of focus on forms and focus on meaning described above, together with theory and research findings on the importance of focal attention, and its facilitative role in language learning, triggered development of a third approach, known as *focus on form* (Doughty and Williams, 1998a; Long, 1991; Long and Robinson, 1998). Arguably a defensible orientation for the implementation of any analytic syllabus, focus on form explicitly constitutes a core *methodological principle* in Task-Based Language Teaching (see, e.g., Long, 1998). Focus on form refers to the use of a variety of pedagogic procedures designed to shift students' attention briefly to linguistic code features during an otherwise meaning-oriented lesson. The attentional shifts are triggered not by an externally imposed linguistic syllabus, as in focus on forms, but by perceived problems with comprehension or production that arise incidentally while students are engaged in pedagogic tasks, i.e. as prompted by the learner's internal syllabus.

Advantages of focus on form include the fact that attention to linguistic code features occurs just when their meaning and function are most likely to be evident to the learners concerned, at a moment when they have a perceived need for the new item, when they are attending, as a result, and when they are psycholinguistically ready to (begin to) learn the items. The precise pedagogic procedure used to achieve focus on form may vary from more implicit, e.g. input enhancement or corrective recasts, to more explicit, e.g. (reactive) use of the Garden Path technique (c.f. Doughty and Williams 1998b) or of simple PEDAGOGICAL GRAMMAR rules, with choices and the exact timing of the intervention indicated and determined locally by such matters as the sophistication of the learner and the difficulty of the code feature concerned (for detailed discussion, see Doughty, in press; Doughty and Williams, 1998b).

As noted by Doughty and Williams (1998a: 4), focus on form *entails* attention to formal elements of a language, whereas focus on forms is *limited* to such a focus, and focus on meaning *excludes* it. Focus on form allows teachers and students to complete interesting, motivating courses dealing with content they recognise as relevant to their needs, while still addressing language problems successfully (for reviews of empirical studies, see Long and Robinson, 1998; Norris and Ortega, 1999; Spada, 1997).

## Task-based language teaching

Task-based language teaching (TBLT), developed since the early 1980s (see, e.g., Long, 1985, forthcoming a; Long and Crookes, 1992; Robinson, in press; Skehan, 1998), is an attempt to harness the benefits of a focus on meaning via adoption of an *analytic* syllabus, while simultaneously, through use of *focus on form* (not forms), to deal with its known shortcomings, particularly rate of development and incompleteness where grammatical accuracy is concerned. There are six main steps in designing, implementing and evaluating a TBLT programme.

1 Through a task-based *needs analysis*, using multiple methods and sources (see Long, forthcoming a, b), learners' current or future communicative needs are identified in terms of *target tasks* (the real-world things people *do* in everyday life) for those learners, including related target discourse samples. Target tasks for tertiary foreign language learners about to start a study-abroad programme, for instance, might include: registering at a university, attending a lecture, reading an academic journal article, asking for street directions, and describing medical symptoms to a doctor.

2 In the interests of efficiency, and sometimes as a partial solution to the problem of heterogeneous needs within some learner groups, the target tasks identified via the needs analysis are classified into more abstract, superordinate *target task-types*. Such pre-boarding target tasks for airline flight attendants as checking lifejackets, oxygen bottles and air masks, might all be classified as 'inspecting emergency equipment'.

3  Target task-types are given flesh and blood as teaching/learning materials in the form of graded sequences of *pedagogic tasks*, initially simple approximations of gradually increasing task (not linguistic) complexity, developed to meet those needs. To illustrate, for the target task-type 'note-taking during academic lectures', students might initially complete a partly-finished set of notes while listening to a brief lecture in their subject area. Later, they might work on the same or longer lecturettes without an outline being provided, and so on.

4  Using a variety of non-linguistic criteria, e.g. number of steps, and time and space of event occurrence relative to the speaker (see Robinson, in press), the pedagogic tasks are sequenced to form a *task syllabus*.

5  The task syllabus is implemented in the classroom (**LANGUAGE LABORATORY**, computer laboratory, etc.) not via a brand-name language teaching 'method', or indeed by any one fixed 'method', but via appropriate *methodology* and *pedagogy*. Classroom methodology for TBLT has been designed to reflect (putatively universal) language-learning processes in the form of *methodological principles* (such as focus on form), but with the principles instantiated by rightfully particular *pedagogic procedures*, the purview of the classroom teacher (see Long, forthcoming a). Whereas the principles are universal, pedagogic procedures should vary systematically according to local conditions.

6  A task-based programme is *evaluated* by gathering formative, summative, process and product data, a central component being **ASSESSMENT** of student achievement. A complex and rapidly developing area in its own right, *task-based language assessment* is described in more detail in the next section.

## Task-based language assessment

Assessment associated with conventional linguistic syllabuses typically asks examinees to demonstrate knowledge about, rather than actual use of, the L2. A popular alternative is direct proficiency assessment, which requires performance of a range of tasks designed to elicit sufficient L2 data for the assignment, by trained raters, of holistic ratings according to global language proficiency scales (e.g. ACTFL, 1999). Neither of these approaches is appropriate for most assessment uses within task-based language programmes, where the goal is not to measure display of linguistic knowledge, nor to assign learners to broadly defined levels of language ability, but to ascertain whether students can use the L2 to accomplish target tasks.

As in task-based syllabus design and pedagogy, genuinely task-based language assessment takes the task itself as the fundamental unit of analysis, motivating item selection, test instrument construction and the rating of task performance. Task-based assessment (see, e.g., Norris *et al.*, 1998; Robinson and Ross, 1996) does not simply utilise the real-world task as a means of eliciting particular components of the language system which are then measured or evaluated; instead, the construct of interest is performance of the task itself. Language performance goals, such as accuracy, complexity and fluency (see Skehan, 1998), play a role in the evaluation of task-based performance only if inherently related to accomplishment of an assessment task.

There are six main steps in developing and implementing task-based assessment for task-based language programmes:

1  The *intended use(s)* for task-based assessment within the language programme must be specified, minimally addressing the following four issues: who uses information from the assessment? (e.g. teachers and students within a university-level **SPANISH** FL programme); what information is the assessment supposed to provide? (e.g. learners' abilities to use Spanish for placing a dinner order at a restaurant in Guadalajara); what are the purposes for the assessment? (e.g. as an end-of-unit assessment to inform teachers and students as to whether or not students have acquired sufficient ability for using L2 Spanish to accomplish relevant target tasks); and who or what is affected, and what are the consequences of the assessment? (e.g. based on assessment results, teachers and students decide either to review how to place dinner orders in Spanish or to move on to new target tasks). (For more on assessment use specification, see McNamara, 1996; Shepard, 1997).

2 Target tasks or task-types emerging from the needs analysis are analysed and classified according to a variety of *task features*. Analysis is undertaken in order to understand exactly what real-world conditions are associated with target tasks and should therefore be replicated under assessment conditions (e.g. setting, type and amount of L2 use involved, non-linguistic demands, number of steps involved, and sources of difficulty). Tasks may also be classified according to similarities or differences in such features, this classification forming the basis for estimating examinees' abilities with a range of related tasks. (For discussion of task features, see Bachman and Palmer, 1996; Norris *et al.*, 1998).

3 Based on information from the analysis of task features, *test and item specifications* are developed (see Lynch and Davidson, 1994). Specifications delineate the formats tests should take, procedures involved, tasks or task-types to be sampled, format for test tasks (items), and how performance on the task-based test should be evaluated. For example, a test specification for assessing the ability of an international teaching assistant to deliver a lecture on a field-specific topic might delineate: a general description of the assessment purpose and relationship to a course of study; instructions and input given the examinee; characteristics of the topic to be taught; task conditions to be replicated during performance assessment (time allowed for preparing the lecture, location and setting of the lecture, uncooperative students in the audience, etc.); and attributes of task performance to be evaluated.

4 Perhaps the most important stage in developing task-based language assessment is identification and specification of *rating criteria*, which form the basis for interpretations of examinee performance and task accomplishment (see Norris, forthcoming). Real-world criterial elements (aspects of task performance that will be evaluated) and levels (descriptions of what success looks like on these aspects of task performance) should be identified within initial needs analyses, with a view toward providing students and teachers with clear learning **OBJECTIVES**. For example, criterial elements for the task 'ordering a pizza' might be specified to include such aspects as greeting and leave-taking behaviour, placing the order (including size and ingredients of pizza), and responding to clarification questions from an employee. Criterial levels for each of these elements might specify minimal amount and type of greeting/leavetaking expected, minimal information about the pizza to be successfully communicated, and type of evidence in the performance reflecting minimal comprehension and response to clarification questions.

5 As with any assessment, task items, test instruments and procedures and rating criteria need to be *evaluated* (involving pilot-testing and revision) according to their efficiency, appropriacy and effectiveness with respect to the intended assessment uses.

6 Finally, task-based language assessment should incorporate procedures for systematic and on-going *validation* of its intended use within the language programme. Validation should minimally consider: to what extent test instruments and procedures are providing appropriate, trustworthy and useful information; to what extent particular uses for the assessment are warranted, based on the quality of information that they provide and the decisions or actions that they inform; and to what extent the consequences of assessment use can be justified, given the impact on students, teachers, language programmes and any other relevant stakeholders in the assessment process (see Messick, 1989).

**See also:** Assessment and testing; Medium-oriented and message-oriented communication; Second language acquisition theories; Syllabus and curriculum design; Teaching methods

## References

ACTFL (American Council on the Teaching of Foreign Languages) (1999) *ACTFL Proficiency Guidelines*, Hastings-on-Hudson, NY: ACTFL.

Bachman, L. and Palmer, A. (1996) *Language testing in practice*, Oxford: Oxford University Press.

Breen, M. (1984) 'Process syllabuses and the language classroom', in C. Brumfit (ed.), *General English syllabus design*, Oxford: Pergamon.

Doughty, C. (in press) 'Cognitive underpinnings of focus on form', in P. Robinson (ed.), *Cognition and second language instruction*, Cambridge: Cambridge University Press.

Doughty, C. and Williams, J. (1998a) 'Issues and terminology', in C. Doughty and J. Williams (eds), *Focus on form in classroom second language acquisition*, Cambridge: Cambridge University Press.

Doughty, C. and Williams, J. (1998b) 'Pedagogical choices in focus on form', in C. Doughty and J. Williams (eds), *Focus on form in classroom second language acquisition*, Cambridge: Cambridge University Press.

Ellis, R. (1993) 'The structural syllabus and second language acquisition', *TESOL Quarterly* 27, 1: 91–113.

Long, M.H. (1985) 'A role for instruction in second language acquisition: Task-based language teaching', in K. Hyltenstam and M. Pienemann (eds), *Modeling and assessing second language acquisition*, Clevedon: Multilingual Matters.

Long, M.H. (1991) 'Focus on form: a design feature in language teaching methodology', in K. de Bot, R. Ginsberg and C. Kramsch (eds), *Foreign language research in cross-cultural perspective*, Amsterdam/Philadelphia: John Benjamins.

Long, M.H. (1998) 'Focus on form in task-based language teaching', *University of Hawai'i Working Papers in ESL* 16, 2: 35–49.

Long, M.H. (forthcoming a) *Task-based language teaching*, Oxford: Blackwell.

Long, M.H. (forthcoming b) *Problems in SLA* in M.H. Long, Mahwah, NJ: Lawrence Erlbaum.

Long, M.H. and Crookes, G. (1992) 'Three approaches to task-based syllabus design', *TESOL Quarterly* 26, 1: 27–56.

Long, M.H. and Robinson, P. (1998) 'Focus on form: theory, research, and practice', in C. Doughty and J. Williams (eds), *Focus on form in classroom second language acquisition*, Cambridge: Cambridge University Press.

Loschky, L. and Bley-Vroman, R. (1993) 'Grammar and task-based methodology', in G. Crookes and S. Gass (eds), *Tasks and language learning: integrating theory and practice*, Clevedon: Multilingual Matters.

Lynch, A. and Davidson, F. (1994) 'Criterion-referenced language test development: linking curricula, teachers, and tests', *TESOL Quarterly* 28, 4: 727–43.

McNamara, T. (1996) *Measuring second language performance*, New York: Longman.

Messick, S. (1989) 'Validity', in R.L. Linn (ed.), *Educational measurement* (3rd edn), New York: American Council on Education/Macmillan.

Norris, J.M. (forthcoming) 'Identifying rating criteria for task-based EAP assessment', in T.D. Hudson and J.D. Brown (eds), *Processes in developing second language assessments: diverse applications*, Honolulu: University of Hawai'i, Second Language Teaching and Curriculum Center.

Norris, J. and Ortega, L. (1999) 'A meta-analysis of research on type of instruction: The case for focus on form', paper presented at the conference of the American Association for Applied Linguistics, Stamford, CT, March 6–9.

Norris, J., Brown, J., Hudson, T. and Yoshioka, J. (1998) *Designing second language performance assessments* (Technical Report #18), Honolulu: University of Hawai'i, Second Language Teaching and Curriculum Center.

Nunan, D. (1991) 'Communicative tasks and the language curriculum', *TESOL Quarterly* 25, 2: 279–95.

Prabhu, N.S. (1987) *Second language pedagogy*, Oxford: Oxford University Press.

Robinson, P. (in press) 'Task complexity, cognition and second language syllabus design: a triadic framework for examining task influences on SLA', in P. Robinson (ed.), *Cognition and second language instruction*, Cambridge: Cambridge University Press.

Robinson, P. and Ross, S. (1996) 'The development of task-based assessment in English for academic purposes programs', *Applied Linguistics* 17, 455–76.

Shepard, L. (1997) 'The centrality of test use and consequences for test validity', *Educational Measurement: Issues and Practice*, 16, 2: 5–13.

Skehan, P. (1998) *A cognitive approach to language learning*, Oxford: Oxford University Press.

Spada, N. (1997) 'Form-focussed instruction and second language acquisition: a review of classroom and laboratory research', *Language Teaching* 29, 1–15.

Wilkins, D. (1976) *Notional syllabuses*, Oxford: Oxford University Press.

## Further reading

Doughty, C. and Williams, J. (eds) (1998) *Focus on form in classroom second language acquisition*, Cambridge: Cambridge University Press.

Long, M.H. (forthcoming) *Task-based language teaching*, Oxford: Blackwell.

McNamara, T. (1996) *Measuring second language performance*, New York: Longman.

Norris, J., Brown, J., Hudson, T. and Yoshioka, J. (1998) *Designing second language performance assessments* (Technical Report #18), Honolulu: University of Hawai'i, Second Language Teaching and Curriculum Center.

Skehan, P. (1998) *A cognitive approach to language learning*, Oxford: Oxford University Press.

MICHAEL H. LONG AND JOHN M. NORRIS

# Teacher education

Language teacher education can be divided into *foreign* language teacher education and **MOTHER-TONGUE** or *national language* teacher education. Although, especially in multilingual classes, there is considerable overlap in sociolinguistic terms between the two, we shall focus in this contribution on foreign language teaching only. Foreign language teaching is to be distinguished from 'second language teaching', which takes place in the target language setting, thus offering the teacher and the learner opportunities for learning which are not available in a setting where the target language is foreign. The term 'education' for the schooling of foreign language teachers is used here instead of 'training', in keeping with the conviction that the latter term does not do justice to the complex process of helping teachers develop as reflective practitioners and true professionals (see Widdowson, 1987: 26).

## History

Foreign language teacher education does not have an impressively long history. When modern foreign languages came to be learned and studied in an institutional setting in the nineteenth century, side-by-side with the classical languages Latin and Greek, the main emphasis, by analogy with the study of the latter two since the Renaissance, lay on the **GRAMMAR** of the language. Teachers were required mainly to have a thorough insight into the way the language 'worked'. How communication worked was not yet thought to be of great importance. Foreign language teacher education consisted of a study of the target foreign language and its literature at university or comparable level. Starting teachers entered the profession with a minimum of methodological knowledge or experience, and they learned their trade while practising. The central activity in their lessons was based on the **GRAMMAR–TRANSLATION METHOD**, an approach which did not require a highly developed methodological 'know-how'.

In spite of protests as early as the beginning of the sixteenth century against a too-'mechanistic' view of the study of Latin as structure, it was not until well into the 1960s and 1970s that institutionalised modern foreign language teaching began to take into account that languages are means of (oral, and not primarily written) communication. The cross-cultural aspect of such communication only began to be recognised in the 1980s.

In the second half of the twentieth century, late-nineteenth-century ideas about language learning for oral communication, as realised, for example, in the **DIRECT METHOD**, were revived and a branch of **LINGUISTICS** termed **APPLIED LINGUISTICS** began to emerge. In the 1950s the need was felt in the USA to equip soldiers fighting communism in Korea with a working knowledge of the local language in a relatively short period of time. It seemed useful if they could communicate with the local population. Thus the question as to *how* languages are learned became urgent. A psychological approach to how human beings learn called **BEHAVIOURISM** became very influential. The spiritual father of behaviourism, B.F. Skinner, maintained that behaviour is learnt by going through a pedagogical stimulus–response–reward sequence. Language use was seen as a kind of behaviour and should therefore be learned according to this procedure (the **AMERICAN ARMY METHOD**).

Such emphasis on the **ACQUISITION** of a foreign language and its consequences for the teaching of it are behind a request for teacher qualifications other than the mastery of the grammar and lexis of the foreign language. Teachers had to be able to handle **AUDIO-VISUAL** aids and new inventions like the **LANGUAGE LABORATORY** efficiently and effectively. Even though it soon became evident that what seemed to work for soldiers in their particular training situation failed to work in classrooms, the idea had been revived that there had to be such a thing as an 'ideal' method for the teaching of foreign languages. Lado (1957) was the first to claim that we can 'predict and describe the patterns that will cause difficulty in learning'. To apply the method appropriately, teachers were offered extensive teacher guides accompanying **TEXTBOOKS**, which were often more voluminous than the textbooks themselves.

When results of the new method failed to emerge, empirical research was undertaken to ascertain why the method did not work. The research findings led to much more modest claims by applied linguists. They now claimed that applied linguistics had generated insights which *could* have important consequences for teaching. The teacher as a living agent acting as a source of inspiration between the learner and the language came (back) into view. So, for that matter, did the learner.

Questions had thus begun to be raised as to language acquisition processes. Psychologists of the new **COGNITIVE CODE** persuasion, rejecting Skinner's behaviourist approach, began to research the learner's language acquisition process, which led to a psychological branch of linguistics called 'psycholinguistics'. Some psycholinguists claimed, for example, that there is a set natural order for each language in which certain grammatical features are acquired, and that, consequently, following the traditional ordering of grammatical structures in textbooks might not be the most efficient way of teaching. Psycholinguists also claimed that languages are learned, like the mother tongue, by carrying on conversations (Vygotsky, 1962) in a motivating context. In addition, hypotheses were developed as to language acquisition, like Krashen's much-disputed input hypothesis and affective filter hypothesis (Krashen, 1982), and a polemic arose around the distinction between language learning and language acquisition in Krashen's **MONITOR MODEL**.

A decade earlier, in the wake of work done by the linguist Noam **CHOMSKY** in his theory of syntax

(1965), which gave rise to the study of generative grammar, the anthropologist Dell Hymes (1972) stressed the communicative use of language and coined the phrase 'communicative competence', parallel to Chomsky's 'linguistic competence'. Hymes insisted that it was not enough to know how to construct grammatically correct sentences in an ideal speaker–listener context: we also need to know how to use situationally appropriate utterances. The concept of 'communicative competence', although variously defined and interpreted, has become central to teacher education. The demand for **INTERCULTURAL COMMUNICA-TIVE COMPETENCE** has come to strengthen its position.

## Basic elements in a language teacher education curriculum

Clearly, for language teachers, whether in-service or pre-service, the various new fields of applied linguistic study are quarries in which to delve. Lack of theoretical grounding may lead to poor teaching. Indeed, after the demise of the **AUDIOLINGUAL** and **AUDIO-VISUAL** methods, the first critics had begun to make themselves heard. They compared language teachers who had adopted the new method to rainmakers performing ritual dances around the learner hoping that their rhythms would miraculously bring about the learner's communicative competence. For lack of insight into language acquisition they had 'gone back to the basics'. They had blithely misinterpreted the new cognitive-code approach as an argument to revert to the grammar–translation method. The insistence on the development of the learner's communicative **SKILLS**, however, as exemplified by the **COUNCIL OF EUROPE**'s publication of a unit-credit system for **ADULT** learners (Council of Europe, 1973) and the work done by **VAN EK** (1975) on the **THRESHOLD LEVEL** and by Wilkins on **NOTIONS AND FUNC-TIONS** (Wilkins, 1976), became a significant issue for language teacher educators. The new curricula that were developed clearly showed the influence of what was being achieved in applied linguistic study and research. For example, the efforts of a European working group of the Association for Teacher Education in Europe (ATEE) led eventually to the publication of attainment targets for foreign language teacher education (Willems, 1993). This booklet takes its inspiration from developments in applied linguistics and learning **PSYCHOLOGY**. The areas of study it builds on are:

- study of how languages are learned (psycholinguistics);
- study and practice of how to assess, select, design, sequence and exploit input **MATERIALS**, and how to manage a classroom;
- study of how language works (linguistics);
- study of how (intercultural) communication works (sociolinguistics).

The insight that language acquisition is basically skills acquisition deeply influences language teaching and teacher education. **LEARNING STYLES** (Duda and Riley, 1990), learning **STRATEGIES**, **ATTITUDES** (towards the target language and its culture), **MOTIVATION**, **APTITUDE** and social background play very important roles. Skills acquisition depends on action. We have to *do* something with the language, and have to do it in a meaningful context in order to begin to master it. Next, to help us along, it is beneficial to reflect on what we have done while communicating, whether our actions have been effective or ineffective, and why.

Learning **VOCABULARY**, **PRONUNCIATION** and functional grammar is invaluable for teacher and learner alike, but will, as such, never guarantee a fluent command of the language. To achieve that, language has to be used meaningfully, in situations where problem-solving and compensatory strategies are required.

In using language meaningfully, sociolinguistic rules of use in the target language community have to be observed and analysed. A special aspect of communication in a foreign language is that it is crosscultural. Side-by-side with the traditional dialogues between **NATIVE SPEAKER** (NS) and native speaker, as input in textbooks, therefore, input dialogues between native speakers (NSs) and non-native speakers (NNSs), and between NNSs, will also have to be offered to the learner (Dams *et al.*, 1998). And teachers and their educators will have to acquaint themselves with such dialogues and their analysis. The resulting **LANGUAGE AWARENESS**, i.e. the explicit knowledge about language (foreign and mother tongue), its learning and its communicative use, is the hallmark of the teacher's

professionalism. On the basis of such awareness, teachers know that to help their learners acquire a foreign language, their methodology will have to concentrate on the performance by the learner of meaningful tasks in a communicative classroom in which **GROUP WORK**, pair work and individual work are deployed according to the nature of the tasks, and in which there is ample time for reflection on learning and on communicative issues, by the teacher as well as the students.

Thus psycholinguistic, linguistic, sociolinguistic and psychological insights as well as pedagogical knowledge and skills are the essence of the language teacher's professionalism (see Stern, 1983: 520).

## The language teacher's education curriculum

The importance of teacher education, especially for the 10–16-year age range, has been increasingly recognised. This recognition has manifested itself in the establishment of teacher education institutions for secondary education in several European countries side-by-side with the much older colleges for the education of primary school teachers. The curricula of the new institutions usually run over a period of four years, teaching practice taking up a considerable percentage of the available time. In some countries, teaching practice is considered more important than professional studies. In **JAPAN**, however, it is comparatively limited in length and depth. University graduates in many countries receive their teacher education during only one year following their graduation. Clearly, uniformity in (language) teacher education is hard to find. The curriculum outline sketched in this section cannot, therefore, be offered in any specific detail as to its organisation over the available time but is to be taken as an indication of areas of attention that should be given explicit attention in the education of language teachers.

Language teachers have the task of helping their learners to master skills in the communicative use of the target language. As skills acquisition is an autonomous process, teachers need insight into the development of **AUTONOMOUS LEARNING**, and have to learn how to discuss and decide on attainment targets and practice and **ASSESSMENT** procedures with their learners. To that end, their education has to offer them a chance to develop a basic insight into learning styles and strategies, learner motivation, attitudes and aptitudes. Furthermore, they must have at their disposal a number of insights concerning the role of input materials, their selection, sequencing and use, and a large set of action parameters, in which the new communication media (e-mail and the **INTERNET**) play an important role. In order to put these insights into practice successfully, teachers also need to be skilful classroom managers.

Inevitably, a critical matter for language teachers as teachers is a fluent command of the target language, in terms of linguistic, pragmatic and discourse competence, and the strategic ability to negotiate meaning with their learners at an appropriate level. Therefore, a language teacher education curriculum contains a large component in which the student-teachers' linguistic pragmatic and strategic skills are trained in appropriate contexts. In order to prepare them for the guidance of their learners' acquisition processes and for their own continued professional development, they are encouraged to reflect on their own learning, their ability to formulate learning goals, assess their learning styles, their strategies, their motivation and attitudes, and, not least, their assessment of their own progress. In order to deal with assessment procedures of their own and their subsequent learners' level of command of the spoken and written language, they are familiar with what has appeared in the literature on all levels (e.g. van Ek, 1987; Trim *et al.*, 1998).

From a psycholinguistic point of view, teachers are aware that the acquisition of the foreign language by their learners follows more or less the same route, albeit that the speed and the rhythm in which it occurs, the distance covered and the pace may differ from one learner to the other. Teachers will bring this awareness to bear on the way they treat learner errors. Ideally, they should need to know at what stage of acquisition individual learners find themselves at particular points. The fact that the route followed may be more or less the same for all learners, however, does not signify that we have identified more than just a few scattered milestones on that route. This means that teachers will have to be eclectic in the selection and sequencing of the tasks they set their

learners. Against a basic knowledge of what reliable research has to offer the profession, language teachers should be able to adjust their methodology to meet their learners' **NEEDS**, i.e. to encourage the latter to reflect on their learning process and find their own routes, and to guide them on their (meta)cognitive way. In order to qualify for the latter requirement, teachers should be willing and able to do **ACTION RESEARCH** to discover what method produces the best results with a particular group of learners at a particular time.

As implied above, **TASK-BASED LEARNING**, in which learners have a chance to develop their skills at their own pace and at their own level, using their own strategies and appropriate media, has to be recognised by the language teacher as the best guarantee for learning in mixed-ability settings. Teachers face a major problem here, however, for more often than not the **TEXTBOOKS** at their disposal offer just one route to the desired goal. Therefore, teachers may have to develop their own materials and choose their own media. Consequently, they are to be educated to do so and to be critical users of textbooks and media, in the sense that they can distinguish between prescriptive input materials, which make a claim for general pedagogic effectiveness, and illustrative input materials of, for instance, an intercultural nature, which stimulate enquiry calling for appraisal (Widdowson, 1987: 26).

Sociolinguistically speaking, the language teacher's curriculum requirements are twofold. On the one hand, teachers need an adequate sociocultural knowledge of the target language community and a thorough command of the pragmatic rules of use of the foreign language in contexts that may be considered to belong to their professional sphere (e.g. staying with a foreign colleague to organise class **EXCHANGES** and/or e-mail contacts). They are also able to reflect on their pragmatic competence and to negotiate meaning where they sense cross-cultural misunderstanding. These insights enable them to assess input materials on their cross-cultural qualities and to guide their learners in analysing such input, comparing their own and the foreign culture (Dams *et al.*, 1998) while trying to identify latent prejudice, explain **CULTURE SHOCK** (Byram, 1995) and, hopefully, bridge gaps by the creation of what has come to be called a 'third culture', a safe place in which negotiation of meaning is accepted and promoted (Kramsch, 1993; Buffet and Willems, 1995).

On the other hand, teachers have also come to realise that cross-cultural communication comes in another guise as well: communication between interlocutors who *all* have to use a language foreign to them, a **LINGUA FRANCA**. Teachers realise how important input representing such discourse is in preparing learners for international communication. At the same time, they recognise such input for its moral and ethical potential. It is here that the true educational values of foreign language teaching are to be found: learners should learn to develop the insights, the skills and the willingness necessary to negotiate culturally different meaning. Cultural **ANTHROPOLOGY** has made us realise how cultural models (Holland and Quinn, 1987) differ and how they pervade our outlook on life and communication with others (Hofstede, 1991). The negotiation of such cultural models is of the utmost importance for the quality of global understanding. We are in need of Wilkins's 'divergent thinkers' (Wilkins, 1987), whose socio-cultural competence helps them approach what is different with an open and interested mind. Education needs language teachers who can realise language learning along these lines.

There is a long-standing dispute (cf. Phillipson, 1992) about which type of teacher or teacher educator is preferable: the native speaker of the target language or the teacher who shares his mother tongue with most of his learners. For a long time, the native speaker teacher was thought to be the ideal. This is no longer the case. A thorough education of the **NON-NATIVE SPEAKER TEACHER**, with an emphasis on the development of **SOCIO-LINGUISTIC COMPETENCE** in terms of the foregoing discussion, will make non-native speakers even better equipped, because they have access to two cultures. A well-prepared and prolonged stay in the target language culture is required, however, to ensure such access.

**See also:** Assessment and testing; Cross-cultural psychology; *Didactique des langues*; *Fremdsprachendidaktik*; Primary education; Secondary education; Teacher thinking

**References**

Buffet, F. and Willems, G.M. (1995) 'Communication interculturelle et "lingua franca" (Intercultural communication and a "lingua franca")', *Revue internationale d'éducation*, no. 6, June.

Byram, M. (1995) 'Acquiring intercultural competence', in L. Sercu (ed.), *Intercultural competence*, Aalborg: Aalborg University Press.

Chomsky, N. (1965) *Aspects of the theory of syntax*, Cambridge, MA: MIT Press.

Council of Europe (1973) *Systems development in adult language learning*, Strasbourg: Council of Europe.

Dams, A., Müller, L., Quartapelle, F. and Willems, G.M. (1998) 'The teaching of foreign languages for oral cross-cultural communication; towards the writing of new input materials', in G.M. Willems, F. Courtney, E. Aranda, M. Cain and J. Ritchie (eds), *Towards intercultural language teacher education*, Nijmegen: HAN Press.

Duda, R. and Riley, P. (eds) (1990) *Learning styles*, Nancy: Presses Universitaires de Nancy.

Hofstede, G. (1991) *Cultures and organisations. Software of the mind*, London: McGraw-Hill.

Holland, D. and Quinn, N. (eds) (1987) *Cultural models in language and thought*, Cambridge: Cambridge University Press.

Hymes, D. (1972) 'On communicative competence', in J.B. Pride and J. Holmes (eds), *Sociolinguistics*, Harmondsworth: Penguin.

Kramsch, C. (1993) *Context and culture in language teaching*, Oxford: Oxford University Press.

Krashen, S. (1982) *Principles and practice in second language acquisition*, Oxford: Pergamon.

Lado, R. (1957) *Linguistics across cultures. Applied linguistics for language teachers*, Ann Arbor: University of Michigan Press.

Phillipson, R. (1992) *Linguistic imperialism*, Oxford: Oxford University Press.

Stern, H.H. (1983) *Fundamental Concepts of Language Teaching*, Oxford: Oxford University Press.

Trim, J.L.M., Coste, D., North, D. and Shields, J. (prog. adviser) (1998) *Modern languages: learning, teaching, assessment. A common European framework of reference*, Strasbourg: Council of Europe.

van Ek, J. (1975) *The Threshold Level*, Strasbourg: Council of Europe.

van Ek, J. (1987) *Objectives for foreign language learning. Vol. II: Levels*, Strasbourg: Council of Europe.

Vygotsky, L.A. (1962) *Thought and language*, trans. E. Haufmann and G. Vakar, Cambridge, MA: MIT Press.

Widdowson, H. (1987) *A rationale for language teacher education*, Strasbourg: Council of Europe.

Wilkins, D. (1976) *Notional syllabuses*, Strasbourg: Council of Europe.

Wilkins, D. (1987) *The educational value of foreign language learning*, Strasbourg: Council for Cultural Cooperation.

Willems, G.M. (ed.) (1993) *Attainment targets for foreign language teacher education in Europe. A European view*, Brussels: ATEE (Cahier No. 5).

## Further reading

Chaudron, C. (1988) *Second language classrooms. Research on teaching and learning*, Cambridge: Cambridge University Press.

Ellis, G. and Sinclair, B. (1989) *Learning to learn English. A course in learner training*, Cambridge: Cambridge University Press.

Hubbard, P., Jones, H., Thornton, B. and Wheeler, R. (1983) *A training course in TEFL*, Oxford: Oxford University Press.

McArthur, T. (1983) *A foundation course for language teachers*, Cambridge: Cambridge University Press.

Willems, G.M., Courtney, F., Aranda, E., Cain, M. and Ritchie, J. (eds) (1998) *Towards intercultural language teacher education*, Nijmegen: HAN Press.

GERARD M. WILLEMS

# Teacher talk

Teacher talk refers to the type of speech used by language teachers to address classroom participants. It is generally grammatical and can include several modifications or adjustments such as simplifications, rephrasings, frequent pauses, etc. Teachers make these adjustments in their speech in order to facilitate L2 communication.

According to Ellis, 'the growth of interest in the analysis of teacher language and interaction has been stimulated by the rejection of language teaching method as the principal determinant of successful learning' (1985: 143). When in the late

1970s and early 1980s researchers began to stress the importance of comprehensible input (Krashen, 1981) and interaction (Long, 1983) for successful language **ACQUISITION**, teacher talk came into focus as a crucial source of input in the classroom. Some of the early work discussing teacher talk from this perspective was completed by Larsen-Freeman (1976) and Gaies (1977).

Although teachers generally seem to take their students' level of proficiency into account when addressing their classes (see, e.g., Håkansson, 1986), no clear guidelines exist for what constitutes appropriate or effective teacher talk. Ellis (1985) and Håkansson (1986) suggest that teachers address their speech to an 'average learner' (Håkansson, 1986: 96), i.e. to a construct based on the teachers' assessment of their learners' average level of proficiency. Since teachers are involved in classroom interactions with many interlocutors of varying levels of proficiency, the input they provide generally tends to be less finely-tuned than the input available in one-on-one interactions between language learner and **NATIVE SPEAKER**.

Lynch (1996) states that most studies on teacher talk are concerned with teachers who exhibit native or near-native **COMPETENCE** in the language taught. The aspects of teacher talk which have been investigated include amount of talking time, error treatment, input and interactional modifications, as well as teacher questions. As far as talking time is concerned, Chaudron (1988) observes that the studies he reviewed show a tendency of teachers to 'dominate classroom speech' (1988: 51; see also Allwright and Bailey, 1991). The amount of language which teachers produce is also related to factors such as teaching style, task type, student proficiency and **NEEDS**, as well as class level (Ellis, 1991).

Teachers' treatment of student error has received considerable attention from researchers. Several reviews (Allwright and Bailey, 1991; Chaudron, 1988; Ellis, 1994) provide a comprehensive survey of work which has been completed in this area. In general, studies on teacher treatment of error have identified the following main issues:

- the types of errors teachers choose to treat;

- who performs corrections;
- how and when corrections are accomplished.

Despite the large body of work which has focused on error treatment, the relationship between error correction and language acquisition remains unclear. As Ellis states: 'Probably the main finding of studies of error treatment is that it is an enormously complex process' (1994: 585).

Apart from the error treatment which teachers accomplish in their talk, researchers have also investigated interactional and input modifications which teachers make in order to facilitate L2 communication. These modifications include the following: 'exaggeration of pronunciation and facial expression; decreasing speech rate and increasing volume; frequent use of pause, gestures, graphic illustrations, questions, and dramatization; sentence expansion, rephrasing and simplification; prompting; and completing utterances made by the student' (Richard-Amato, 1996: 45; see also Chaudron, 1988, and Ellis, 1994, for a review of relevant studies). Long and Sato (1983) further observe that teacher talk generally refers to the here and now of the classroom situation.

Classroom interactions typically include a large number of questions posed by the teachers (see, e.g., Long and Sato, 1983; see also Chaudron, 1988). Teachers' tendency towards asking questions may be due to the asymmetrical distribution of roles in the classroom, with teachers as the source of knowledge and learners as its recipients. Furthermore, questions require answers and thus help involve learners in communicative interactions. The answers provided to questions also allow teachers insights into learners' comprehension of their teachers' talk. Summarising the literature on teacher questions, Ellis states that studies have been concerned with

> the frequency of the different types of questions, wait time (the length of time the teacher is prepared to wait for an answer), the nature of the learners' output when answering questions, the effect of the learners' level of proficiency on **QUESTIONING**, the possibility of training teachers to ask more 'communicative' questions, and the variation evident in teachers' questioning strategies.
>
> (Ellis, 1994: 589)

A somewhat wider perspective on teacher talk is offered by Johnson (1995). She distances herself from the more traditional discussions of teacher talk in terms of observable structural modifications. From her point of view, teachers' use of language is not solely related to the immediate classroom context. She argues that 'the ways in which teachers organize classroom communication tells us something about who these teachers are, what they know, what they believe, and how they think about teaching, teachers, students, and second language classrooms' (1995: 38). Teacher talk is considered here in the wider context of knowledge construction and established power structures. Teachers should realise, Johnson advises, that they are in control of classroom patterns of communication and have the power to decide when, how, and by whom language is used. She concludes that, even if these patterns of communication are only one in many factors contributing to our understanding of second language classroom communication, they might be of particular importance since it lies within the teachers' power actually to change these patterns 'as they see fit' (Johnson, 1995: 17).

**See also:** Classroom language; Classroom observation schemes; Communicative language teaching; Content-based instruction; Monitor model; Monolingual principle; Non-native speaker teacher; Teacher thinking

## References

Allwright, D. and Bailey, K. (1991) *Focus on the language classroom: an introduction to classroom research*, Cambridge: Cambridge University Press.

Chaudron, C. (1988) *Second language classrooms. Research on teaching and learning*, Cambridge: Cambridge University Press.

Ellis, R. (1985) *Understanding second language acquisition*, Oxford: Oxford University Press.

Ellis, R. (1991) *Instructed second language acquisition: learning in the classroom*, Oxford: Basil Blackwell.

Ellis, R. (1994) *The study of second language acquisition*, Oxford: Oxford University Press.

Gaies, S. (1977) 'The nature of linguistic input in formal second language learning: linguistic and communication strategies in ESL teachers' classroom language', in H.D. Brown, C.A. Yorio and R.H. Crymes (eds), *Teaching and learning English as a second language: trends in research and practice*, Washington, DC: TESOL.

Håkansson, G. (1986) 'Quantitative aspects of teacher talk', in G. Kasper (ed.), *Learning, teaching and communication in the foreign language class*, Aarhus: Aarhus University Press.

Johnson, K. (1995) *Understanding communication in second language classrooms*, Cambridge: Cambridge University Press.

Krashen, S. (1981) *Second language acquisition and second language learning*, Oxford: Pergamon.

Larsen-Freeman, D. (1976) 'Teacher speech as input to the ESL learner', *UCLA Workpapers on TESOL* 10: 45–9.

Long, M. (1983) 'Linguistic and conversational adjustments to nonnative speakers', *Studies in second language acquisition* 5: 177–93.

Long, M. and Sato, C. (1983) 'Classroom foreigner talk discourse: forms and functions of teachers' questions', in H. Seliger and M. Long, *Classroom oriented research in second language acquisition*, Rowley, MA: Newbury House.

Lynch, T. (1996) *Communication in the language classroom*, Oxford: Oxford University Press.

Richard-Amato, P. (1996) *Making it happen. Interaction in the second language classroom: from theory to practice*, White Plains, NY: Longman.

**Further reading**

Allwright, D. and Bailey, K. (1991) *Focus on the language classroom: an introduction to classroom research*, Cambridge: Cambridge University Press.

Chaudron, C. (1988) *Second language classrooms. Research on teaching and learning*, Cambridge: Cambridge University Press.

Ellis, R. (1994) *The study of second language acquisition*, Oxford: Oxford University Press.

Johnson, K. (1995) *Understanding communication in second language classrooms*, Cambridge: Cambridge University Press.

Lynch, T. (1996) *Communication in the language classroom*, Oxford: Oxford University Press.

BIRGIT MEERHOLZ-HÄRLE
AND ERWIN TSCHIRNER

# Teacher thinking

Teacher thinking is a field of research that studies the thinking of teachers about various aspects of teaching and learning. Included are perceptions, beliefs, thought processes and knowledge. This research looks for relationships between these perceptions and classroom teaching. Interest in the 'inner world' of teachers and their views of their profession was first seen in skill and content areas of education in general. In the 1970s and 1980s, studies searched for ways to predict and improve student achievement in content areas. The aim was to link teacher thinking to learning outcomes by means of following teachers' thoughts as they motivate teaching and influence student perceptions and actions. By studying the impact of these processes on each other, teaching could be related to learning. This became known as process-product research (Brophy and Good, 1986; Shulman, 1986a/b) because of the quantitative methods that were used.

Two seminal studies drew attention to in-depth description of teachers' cognitive worlds: Jackson's *Life in Classrooms* (1968) and Lortie's *Schoolteacher: A Sociological Study* (1975). Jackson studied elementary school teachers, drawing attention to the hidden aspects of teaching related to teacher thought processes. He extended the concern for predictability to the classroom as a social context. Lortie argued for recentring educational research on the classroom as the context of study that would help to understand teaching. These two studies led the way to studying teacher thinking, teacher thought processes, teacher learning and teacher knowledge, each having a cluster of separate research agendas.

Attention now was directed towards teachers' descriptions of how they construct the reality of the classroom. The aim was not so much to identity the effective teacher, but to understand and explain teaching processes, views, perceptions and understandings. (See the following literature reviews for an overview of the dimensions of teachers' inner worlds: Clark and Peterson, 1986; Fang, 1996; Shavelson and Stern, 1981).

In the field of foreign language study, teacher thinking research is often referred to as teacher belief research, building on the findings in the area of general education. Beliefs, assumptions and knowledge are studied in relation to how they interact, how they are used in the decision-making processes of teachers, and how they influence teachers' instruction (Woods, 1996). Exploratory, descriptive and interpretative ethnographic methods are used, drawing attention by the 1990s to the complexity of the social context of teachers and students.

## Beliefs and knowledge in education in general

Much debate has occurred about what is meant by teacher thinking, as well as about beliefs and the distinction between beliefs and knowledge. One view suggested by Pajares (1992) is that beliefs and knowledge are concepts that interweave along a spectrum of meaning. In this view, beliefs are often thought of as being a type of knowledge, and knowledge as a component of beliefs. Pajares sorted through the dilemma and distinguished beliefs as being based on **EVALUATION** and judgement and knowledge on objective fact.

Some general statements can be made about beliefs:

- Beliefs are evaluative, not factual, non-consensual. They often include anecdotal material, have different degrees of strength and unclear boundaries.
- They may be descriptive, prescriptive and have a cognitive component representing knowledge as an affective and a behavioural component.
- They are mental constructs of experience often condensed into schemata or concepts that guide behaviour.
- They are not observed or measured but inferred from what people say, intend or do.
- They make an assertion about some matter of fact or principle or law. They involve people manipulating knowledge for a particular purpose.
- They persist when they are no longer accurate representations of reality.
- They vary along a central–peripheral dimension (the more central, the more they will resist change).
- The earlier they are incorporated into the belief structure, the more difficult they are to alter.

Some find that the power of beliefs is drawn

from previous episodes or events (Goodman, 1988) and that teachers are influenced by 'guiding images' from past events that create 'intuitive screens' through which new information is filtered. Richly detailed episodic memory serves teachers as templates for their own teaching practice. Dewey (1933) argued that reflective thinking calls for careful examination of any beliefs to establish them upon a firm basis of evidence and rationality.

Distinctions have been drawn between teachers' educational beliefs and belief systems in general. Included in educational beliefs are: teachers' beliefs about their role in affecting student performance, the nature of knowledge, causes of teacher/student performance, self-concept, self-efficiency and beliefs about specific subjects or disciplines (reading instruction, whole language, for instance).

Belief systems take the form of beliefs about constructs, such as politics or art, for instance. They have been described as loosely-bound systems with no clear logical rules for determining the relevance of beliefs to real-world events and situations and with highly variable and uncertain linkages to events, situations and knowledge systems (Abelson, 1979). Linkages are tied to personal, episodic and emotional experiences of the believer (Nespor, 1987). Belief systems have an adaptive function in helping individuals define and understand the world and themselves.

Nespor (1987) looked at the structure and functions of teachers' beliefs about their roles, students, subject matter areas they teach and schools where they work. He sought in this body of field-based research on teacher thinking to present a theoretical model of belief systems in which he distinguished beliefs from knowledge by four features: existential presumption, alternativity, affective and effective loading and episodic structuring. Non-consensuality and unboundedness were included when beliefs were organised as systems.

In addition, Woods (1996) proposed a hypothetical concept representing an integrated network of beliefs, assumptions and knowledge (BAK) based on data collected from teachers' verbalisations over time.

## Beliefs and behaviour

Evidence pointing towards the idea of individuals'

beliefs strongly influencing behaviours (Abelson, 1979; Clark and Peterson, 1986; Nespor, 1987; Tabachnick and Zeichner, 1986) encouraged the study of teacher thought processes by exploring the relationship between the mental lives of teachers and their actions. This teacher/action research attempted to examine the mental constructs underlying behaviour before seeking to explain behaviour. Some disagreed about the separation of thought and action (see Elbaz, 1983, 1991), while others assumed a more dialectical relationship to exist in which thought and action are an inseparable part of the same event (see Tabachnick and Zeichner, 1986). Pajares (1992) strongly argued for firming up the terminology being used by members of the research community, the research constructs being followed, and the future directions of research. He synthesised primary findings in a comprehensive review of research on teachers' beliefs, and found problems stemming from the different understandings researchers had of what beliefs are. He also specified several important assumptions guiding research on beliefs; namely:

- Individuals develop a belief system that houses all the beliefs acquired through the process of cultural transmission.
- Knowledge and beliefs are inextricably intertwined, but the potent affective, evaluative and episodic nature of beliefs makes them filters through which new phenomena are interpreted.
- Thought processes may well be precursors to and creators of beliefs, but the filtering effect of belief structures ultimately screens, redefines, distorts and reshapes subsequent thinking and information processing (Pajares, 1992: 325–6).

Clark and Peterson saw the need to bring together the areas of research in a review of the literature on teacher thought and action. The result was a model that represented teachers' interactive thoughts during pre-active, interactive and post-active phases of teaching (1986: 257). In their model, the pre-active phases, for instance, included the thinking of teachers, their planning, thought processes and teacher–student interaction. Included were specific studies that found links between teacher planning and action in the classroom (Hill, Yinger and Robbins, 1989), as well as exploring further action with 'on-task'

(related to teaching) or 'off-task' (related to things outside the classroom or to personal life) (Peterson, Swing, Braveman and Buss, 1982). With this construct they could separate teachers' thought from language used to document those thoughts.

More recently, in the context of ethnographic research methodology, it has been argued by Freeman (1996) that accepting teachers at their word (a 'representational' approach to language data) fails to study language data for what it presents to the world. The 'presentational' approach extends methodologies to linguistic analysis, in particular that of **STRUCTURAL LINGUISTIC** analysis of language and to translinguistic analysis (Bakhtin, 1981). It approaches language as a social system in which individuals participate and through which they are defined.

A good illustration of the effective use of qualitative methods and procedures being used with teacher thinking in an area of general education is the study of Duschl and Wright (1989). In their study of mathematics and science teachers, they investigated perceptions about the nature of subject matter used in decision-making involving the planning and delivery of instructional tasks. In searching for the 'hidden meanings' of the social context of science teachers, they applied an ethnographic approach using Spradley's (1979, 1980) developmental research sequence (descriptive, selective and focused observations) and his levels of analysis (domain, taxonomic and componential). They found that teachers do not employ guidelines about the structure and role of scientific theories in their thinking about teaching, but instead their decision-making is dominated by considerations such as student development, curriculum guides, **OBJECTIVES** and pressures of accountability.

## Beliefs about foreign language learning

Research on foreign language teachers' beliefs began with interest about teachers' characteristics (such as personality, motivation, **LEARNING STYLES** and language **ATTITUDE**) and the relationship of these characteristics to language **ACQUISITION**. A primary aim was to determine what kinds of instructional environment best suit individual learners. Another was to identify learners' perceptions of what is involved in learning a foreign language to predict expectational conflicts that may contribute to student frustration, anxiety or lack of motivation.

Instruments used for eliciting beliefs include FLAS (Foreign Language Attitude Survey – De Garcia, Reynolds and Savignon, 1976) and BALLI (Beliefs about Language Learning Inventory – Horwitz, 1985, 1988). BALLI surveyed the difficulty of language learning, foreign language aptitude, the nature of language learning, **STRATEGIES** of communication and learning, and learner motivations and expectations. The FLAS was developed as a tool for helping teachers explore their own attitudes and assumptions concerning foreign language learning and teaching.

Horwitz and others have found conflicting instructional practices. At times beliefs coincided with communicative **TEACHER METHODS** (e.g. student willingness to guess), but other beliefs (such as the importance of correctness) may affect the level of comfort with communicative techniques and activities in class. Mismatches that occur between teachers' and students' beliefs about language learning are related to anxiety tensions.

The potential influence of teachers' beliefs on students' beliefs has been a primary concern of research. ('To what degree do foreign language students' beliefs about language learning correspond to those of their teachers?' 'What is the relationship?') Findings suggest that teachers' beliefs are one of many factors affecting students beliefs about language learning (Horwitz, 1985, 1988; Kern, 1995). The use of qualitative methods questions provided a means of studying in depth how teachers think about their profession, their role in teaching a language and its culture.

## Beliefs about culture and language

A major area of foreign language research involved in the study of language has been the study of the relationship of culture and language. Finding out teachers' beliefs about culture is preliminary to research goals. In the United States, Robinson (1985) studied a large population of foreign language teachers and their notions. Taking into account the **BEHAVIOURIST**, functional, cognitive and symbolic traditions related to culture, she grouped definitions of culture as 'observable' and 'non-observable'. In Mexico, Ryan (1994) worked with English university foreign language teachers in a long-term case study that traced teachers' definitions about the nature of culture to a model adapted from Kroeber and Kluckhohn (1952) and Keesing (1981) that had meaning categories such as adaptive systems (descriptive, historical and normative), cognitive and structural. In Europe, Byram and Risager (1999) explored foreign language teaching and its effect on secondary school students' perceptions of other cultures. They were interested in interpretation of the cultural dimension in language teaching. They traced and analysed definitions using a grid with two dimensions: thematic (such as a way of life/objective structure/norms and values/art, literature) and societal (such as international, national, group, individual).

In other international settings such as **CHINA**, teachers have been surveyed about their interpretations of culture teaching (Adamowski, 1991; Lessard-Clouston, 1996a). Both studies confirmed that teachers, when asked about culture and language, gave very broad definitions that included all aspects of daily life, and they said they taught culture both explicitly and implicitly in their classes.

A great lack of empirical research about sociocultural perceptions still exists. While attention has been drawn to this lack in the literature (Byram, Esarte-Sarries and Taylor, 1991; Lessard-Clouston, 1996b; Robinson, 1985; Ryan, 1994), very few studies of the 'inner world of teachers' have been carried out in foreign language settings, with some exceptions in China, Britain, Mexico and Morocco.

In Mexico during the 1990s, studies of teacher thinking about cultural aspects of language learning have looked at the sociocultural aspect of language learning in university settings. The route followed by the research started with teachers' beliefs about culture and the teaching of culture, and related these beliefs to classroom instruction and student perceptions of cultural aspects in their language classes.

The first long-term studies were aimed at **ENGLISH** as an international language, or **LINGUA FRANCA**, in the social context of urban universities.

In this setting the learning of English constitutes a special case in relation to other languages taught at the university level. English is an international language that university students feel obliged to study for professional and academic reasons. Tensions are created that can impede language acquisition and produce negative attitudes.

One of the first qualitative studies looked at the relationship between university English teachers' beliefs about the nature of culture and their classroom instruction (Ryan, 1994; 1997). For some teachers it was difficult to express their ideas and explain how they defined culture. Some were perplexed at first by the complexity of the abstraction and its elusive character. Their definitions were very broad, embracing many aspects of daily life, a finding noted in other research (see Adamowski, 1991; Robinson, 1985; Lessard-Clouston, 1996a, 1996b). Another pattern found was that teachers spontaneously used **METAPHORS** to capture their ideas as if they were photographic snapshots on which to hang their definitions of culture. The use of a metaphor conveyed the highly personal nature of the concept of culture.

Teachers perceived of students as having negative attitudes toward North Americans (Ryan, 1994). Ambivalent attitudes surfaced toward speakers of English when they were seen as an agent of English-speaking cultures trying to supplant their own culture. Moreover, stereotypes of North Americans ('cultural imperialists', 'cultural penetrators' and 'cultural interventionists') were observed as lateral results in a number of studies.

Students' attitudes were found to be complex and involve ambivalent feelings toward English and its speakers, especially North Americans. An illustration of students' perceptions is that they perceived of themselves as wearing a protective shield, one that developed as their home culture was threatened by the new ways of seeing the world brought from other cultures through language ('If I am seeing the world through a different set of eyes, where does my original point of view go?' 'Why do people want me to change what I have now, what I am proud of? Do I have to change?') (Ryan, Byer and Mestre, 1998; Ryan, 1998b). Strong defensiveness and monocultural tendencies were found present, along with a sense of national pride ('Don't touch my culture!' 'Don't teach culture', 'Learning

not losing'). At the same time, students recognised negative stereotypes and false images they held ('We have to get rid of myths by getting in contact with people. Both Mexicans and Americans have to do so.') Others were more positive ('I would be interested in learning about cultural aspects.' 'I would like a little more about the US in my English classes.')

A case study of a **NATIVE SPEAKER** of English and a native speaker of **SPANISH** followed teacher thinking into the classroom (Ryan, 1998a). When beliefs of teachers about culture and foreign language teaching are compared, beliefs are not dissimilar; that is, both teachers have goals in common for their students. When teachers are observed, knowledge about C1 (native culture) and C2 (English-speaking cultures) functions as a variable in the interaction of teachers, students and text, moderated by interest, memory and a desire to comment.

## Conclusion

Teacher thinking research has been driven by several different agendas and has generated a respectable corpus of findings that has input in teacher education. From its beginning in the field of general education, this research has been concerned with teacher accountability and student outcomes in various educational settings and subject areas. The primary aim was to improve student achievement. What was missing was discovered in later studies that focused on the social context of learning. The direction research took began to utilise the potential of qualitative techniques to study, in depth and over long periods of time, teacher beliefs about their subject matter and the process of learning. Beliefs were found to be very strong, and the earlier they were formed the stronger and more resistant to change they were. Their relationship to the classroom turned out to be extremely subtle.

With this foundation of research in general education, foreign language study became another of its subject areas. The first surveys confirmed the strong and resistant nature of beliefs, especially teacher beliefs about language and language learning, and their complex relationships to teaching. Qualitative data collected from interviews,

CLASSROOM OBSERVATION and institutional materials enable researchers to fine-tune teacher–student interaction in the classroom. One of the first areas of interest was culture in language teaching, where teachers' beliefs could be followed in great detail in teaching. Another area was READING instruction.

The future of this research lies in examining teacher identity, not only teachers of English but also of other foreign languages. In complex international settings, where attitudes can be very pronounced and perceptions play a prominent role in language learning, knowledge and insight into teacher–student thinking could provide essential input for teacher education.

**See also:** Cultural awareness; Language awareness; Metaphor; Non-native speaker teacher; Teacher education; Teaching methods

## References

Abelson, R. (1979) 'Differences between belief systems and knowledge systems', *Cognitive Science* 3: 355–66.

Adamowski, E. (1991) 'What does "teaching culture" mean?', in J. Sivell and L. Curtis (eds), *TESL '90: reading into the future*, Toronto: TESL Ontario.

Bakhtin, M. (1981) *The dialogic imagination*, Austin: University of Texas Press.

Brophy, J. and Good, T.L. (1986) 'Teacher behavior and student achievement', in M. Wittrock (ed.), *Handbook of research on teaching*, New York: Macmillan.

Byram, M. and Risager, K. (1999) *Language teachers, politics and cultures*, Clevedon: Multilingual Matters.

Byram, M., Esarte-Sarries, V. and Taylor, S. (1991) *Cultural studies and language teaching: a research report*, Clevedon: Multilingual Matters.

Clark, C.M. and Peterson, P.L. (1986) 'Teacher thought processes', in M.C. Wittrock (ed.), *Handbook of research on teaching* (3rd edn), New York: Macmillan.

De Garcia, R., Reynolds, S. and Savignon, S. (1976) 'Foreign language attitude survey', *The Canadian Modern Language Review* 32: 302–4.

Dewey, J. (1933). *How we think*, Boston, MA: Heath and Company.

Duschl, R.A. and Wright, E. (1989) 'A case study of high school teachers' decision making models for planning and teaching science', *Journal of Research in Science Teaching* 26, 6: 467–501.

Elbaz, F. (1983) *Teacher thinking: a study of practical knowledge*, New York: Nichol.

Elbaz, F. (1991) 'Research on teacher knowledge: the evolution of a discourse', *Journal of Curriculum Studies* 23, 1: 1–19.

Fang, Z. (1996) 'A review of research on teacher beliefs and practices', *Educational Research* 38, 1: 47–65.

Freeman, D. (1996) 'To take them at their word: language data in the study of teachers' knowledge', *Harvard Educational Review* 66, 4: 732–61.

Goodman, J. (1988) 'Constructing a personal philosophy of teaching: a study of preservice teachers' professional perspectives', *Teaching and Teacher Education* 4: 121–37.

Hill, J., Yinger, R.J. and Robbins, D. (1989) 'Instructional planning in a developmental preschool'. Paper presented at the annual meeting of the American Educational Research Association, Los Angeles.

Horwitz, E.K. (1985) 'Using student beliefs about language learning and teaching in the foreign language methods course', *Foreign Language Annals* 18, 4: 333–40.

Horwitz, E.K. (1988) 'The beliefs about language learning of beginning university foreign language students', *The Modern Language Journal* 72, iii: 283–94.

Jackson, P.W. (1968) *Life in classrooms*, New York: Holt, Rinehart and Winston.

Kagan, D.M. (1992) 'Implications of research on teacher beliefs', *Educational Psychologist* 27, 1: 65–90.

Keesing, R.M. (1981) 'Theories of culture', in R. Chasson (ed.), *Language, culture and cognition*, New York: Macmillan.

Kern, R.G. (1995) 'Students' and teachers' beliefs about language learning', *Foreign Language Annals* 28, 1: 71–92.

Kroeber, A.L. and Kluckhohn, C. (1952) *Culture, a critical review of concepts and definitions*, Cambridge, MA: Harvard University Press.

Lessard-Clouston, M. (1996a) 'Chinese teachers'

views of culture in their EFL learning and teaching', *Language, Culture and Curriculum* 9, 3: 197–223.

Lessard-Clouston, M. (1996b) 'Toward an understanding of culture in L2/FL education', *Ronko: K.G. Studies in English* 25: 131–50.

Lortie, D. (1975) *Schoolteacher: a sociological study,* Chicago: University of Chicago Press.

Nespor, J. (1987) 'The role of beliefs in the practice of teaching', *Journal of Curriculum Studies* 19, 4: 317–28.

Pajares, M.F. (1992) 'Teachers' beliefs and educational research cleaning up a messy construct', *Review of Educational Research* 62, 3: 307–32.

Peterson, P.L., Swing, S.R., Braverman, M.T. and Buss, R. (1982) 'Student attitudes and their reports of cognitive processes during direct instruction', *Journal of Educational Psychology* 74: 535–47.

Robinson, G.L.N. (1985) *Cross-cultural understanding, processes and approaches for foreign language, English as a second language, and bilingual educators,* New York: Pergamon.

Ryan, P. (1994) *Foreign language teachers' perceptions of culture and the classroom: a case study.* Doctoral Dissertation, Department of Educational Studies, University of Utah, Salt Lake City, Utah. (ERIC Document: ED 385 135, 1–25).

Ryan, P. (1997) 'Sociolinguistic goals for foreign language teaching and teachers' metaphorical images of culture', *Foreign Language Annals* 29, 4: 571–86.

Ryan, P. (1998a) 'Cultural knowledge and foreign language teachers: a case study of a native English speaker and a native Spanish speaker', *Language, Culture and Curriculum* 11, 2: 135–53.

Ryan, P. (1998b) 'Investigaciones sobre el papel de percepciones socioculturales y lingüísticas en la enseñanza de idiomas' (Research into the role of sociocultural and linguistic perceptions in the teaching of languages), *Estudios de Lingüística Aplicada* 17, 28: 101–12.

Ryan, P., Byer, B. and Mestre, R. (1998) 'Reconocimiento de Información Cultural en la Experiencia de Aprendizaje del Inglés' (The recogni-tion of cultural information in the experience of learning), *Antología, 10 Encuentro Nacional de Profesores de Lenguas* Mexico: CELE, UNAM.

Schulman, L.S. (1986a) *Paradigms and research programs in the study of teaching,* New York: Macmillan.

Schulman, L.S. (1986b) 'Those who understand: knowledge growth in teaching', *Educational Researcher* 15: 4–14.

Shavelson, R.J. and Stern, P. (1981) 'Research on teachers' pedagogical thoughts, judgements, decisions and behavior', *Review of Educational Research* 51: 455–98.

Spradley, J.P. (1979) *The ethnographic interview,* New York: Holt, Rinehart and Winston.

Spradley, J.P. (1980) *Participant observation,* New York: Holt, Rinehart and Winston.

Tabachnick, B. and Zeichner, F. (1986) 'Teacher beliefs and classroom behavior: some teachers responses to inconsistency', in M. Ben-Peretz, R. Bromme and R. Halkes (eds), *Advances of research on teacher thinking,* Lisse: Swets and Zeitlinger.

Woods, D. (1996) *Teacher cognition in language teaching. Beliefs, decision-making and classroom practice,* Cambridge: Cambridge University Press.

**Further reading**

Brown, R.W. (1990) 'The place of beliefs and of concept formation in a language teacher training theory', *System* 18, 1: 85–96.

Graden, E.C. (1996) 'How language teachers' beliefs about reading instruction are mediated by their beliefs about students', *Foreign Language Annals* 29, 3: 388–95.

Kern, R.G. (1995) 'Students' and teachers' beliefs about language learning', *Foreign Language Annals* 28, 1, 71–92.

Munby, H. (1987) 'Metaphors and teacher knowledge', *Research in the Teaching of English* 21, 4: 377–97.

Thornbury, S. (1991) 'Metaphors we work by: EFL and its metaphors', *ELT Journal* 45, 3: 193–9.

Woods, D. (1996) *Teacher cognition in language teaching. Beliefs, decision-making and classroom practice,* Cambridge: Cambridge University Press.

PHYLLIS RYAN

# Teaching methods

The question of method is one of the central issues of instruction. Despite this fact, method analysis has received far less attention in language education theory to date than one might imagine from the way different methods are promoted and advocated. Throughout the history of foreign language education, teachers and theorists have debated which methods are superior for certain goals (see Howatt, 1984). In the course of the development of foreign language teaching, the focus has shifted continuously between the key questions of what instruction should aim at (goals and **OBJECTIVES**), what should be taught in terms of language and subject matter (content), how foreign languages are learnt (learning process), and how they should be taught (teaching method). Of course, these issues are interrelated and, moreover, they are connected to a large number of subsidiary aspects, e.g. course structure, testing procedures, teaching **MATERIALS**, learner and teacher roles. Methods should also be seen in their cultural and social contexts (see Holliday, 1994) and as representations of underlying educational values, which are evident in society at large as well as in the daily practice of individual teachers.

## What is a method?

A method is a planned way of doing something. The original Greek word (*méthodos*) includes the idea of a series of steps leading towards a conceived goal. A method implies an orderly way of going about something, a certain degree of advance planning and of control, then; also, a process rather than a product. Thus the term 'method' may describe both the procedures used by a teacher to instruct learners in a language lesson and the steps and techniques adopted by the learners themselves in pre-planned phases of self-teaching. A method always is a means towards something, it is not an end in itself.

## Method analysis

In spite of the fact that the question of teaching method is a central aspect of language education, there have only been a few attempts to deal with method systematically. Mackey (1965) sees method analysis as distinct from teaching analysis. He states: 'The purpose of method analysis is to show how one method differs from another ... It is limited to the analysis of teaching materials

through which learners can study the language' (1965: 139). As he sees methods exemplified in **TEXTBOOKS**, his criteria for method analysis are based on material: 'All language-teaching methods, by their nature, are necessarily made up of a certain selection, gradation, presentation and repetition of the material' (1965: 157). For Mackey, method is closely linked to **SYLLABUS** and teaching procedures. Neither the roles of teachers and learners nor the underlying theories of language and language learning are part of his concept of method.

Anthony (1963) proposes a hierarchical model on three levels – approach, method, technique – which focuses on the relationship between the underlying theoretical principles (approach) and the classroom procedures derived from them (technique). He says: 'I view an approach – any approach – as a set of correlative assumptions dealing with the nature of language and the nature of language teaching and learning' (Anthony, 1963: 63f.). On the intermediate level of method the beliefs about language learning and teaching are put into practice through decisions regarding course content and goals. These decisions are then implemented by certain teaching procedures at the classroom level – technique.

Anthony's conceptualisation of method as being the intermediate stage between approach and technique is attractive in its simplicity. This view of method is less narrow than in Mackey's case and corresponds to that traditionally adopted in **GERMAN** foreign language education, where *Fremdsprachenmethodik* (foreign language teaching methodology) is concerned with principles, procedures and materials of foreign language learning in classrooms. In contrast, ***FREMDSPRACHENDIDAKTIK*** (foreign language education) refers to the whole field and includes those areas which Anthony (1963) subsumes under approach (Neuner, 1989: 145f.).

The most detailed discussion of the method concept is to be found in Richards and Rodgers (1986), who have extended and revised Anthony's proposal. Richards and Rodgers define method as comprising different areas. Anthony's hierarchy of levels is turned into a model constructed on parallel lines. 'Thus, a method is theoretically related to an approach, is organizationally determined by a design, and is practically realized in procedure'

(Richards and Rodgers, 1986: 16). Similar to Anthony, they regard approach as referring to 'theories about the nature of language and language learning that serve as the source of practices and principles in language teaching' (1986: 16). These theories have to be rendered practicable by using them to determine goals and syllabus, to guide the choice of task types which support the kind of learning which is being aimed for, to advocate particular roles for teachers and learners, and to describe the teaching materials. All these aspects belong to the field of 'design'. Finally, the range of actual tasks, the ways of presentation and feedback, the types of **EXERCISE** and activity favoured by a particular design, are analysed under the heading of 'procedure'.

Richards and Rodgers use their concept as an analytical tool to describe and compare a number of mainstream and so-called alternative or fringe methods. Their analyses provide valuable insights, both into the method concept itself and into the individual methods. Applying the same set of analytical questions to each method makes it obvious that, beneath the apparent differences, some methods share a common ground in their underlying theoretical assumptions. For example, two methods which seem very different in their classroom procedures, **COMMUNITY LANGUAGE LEARNING** (CLL) and **TOTAL PHYSICAL RESPONSE** (TPR), nevertheless share elements in their approach. 'Both TPR and CLL see stress, defensiveness and embarrassment as the major blocks to successful language learning ... They both view the stages of **ADULT** language learning as recapitulations of the stages of childhood learning, and both CLL and TPR consider mediation, memory and recall of linguistic elements to be central issues' (Richards and Rodgers, 1986: 155).

However, the reverse is also true. The same procedures may well be used for different methods and different purposes (Larsen-Freeman, 1986). This does not necessarily imply a shared approach or even – as Larsen-Freeman calls this level of design – shared principles. It is not easy, therefore, to draw clear distinctions between different methods without a thorough analysis; and some methods naturally share more principles or design features than others.

Concern with the general concept of method,

though not the discussion of individual methods or methodological questions, receded in the writing on foreign language education at the end of the twentieth century. Some scholars consider the concept of method obsolete or of doubtful value because of its underlying assumption that a single set of principles determines whether learning takes place or not (Nunan, 1991). These critics like to see the concept of method replaced with a range of options for content and teaching strategies (Savignon, 1983; Stern, 1992) or a set of principles (Brown, 1994). However, even if language teaching theory is not being pushed forward by a discussion of methods, for pre-service **TEACHER EDUCATION** a look at methods and their theoretical foundations may prove to be an important stage of orientation, when the complex structures of interrelated principles and options are too confusing for novices who have not yet had an extended period of teaching experience.

## Methods in the history of foreign language education

In the 1960s and 1970s the predominant view of the historical development of foreign language teaching was a linear one (e.g. Titone, 1968; Darian, 1972). The description of successive methods implied that foreign language education had made steady progress towards improvement. Historical references were often used to illustrate the superiority of informed contemporary practice over that of the unenlightened past. However, Kelly's (1969) extensive research into the history of foreign language teaching also showed that there are a number of recurrent themes and procedures, even if their concrete representations may have differed at various times.

More recent historical analyses (Howatt, 1984; Klippel, 1994; Musumeci, 1997) stress the fact that methods are embedded in the political, cultural and educational values of their respective times and cannot be evaluated outside this context. In addition, these studies include an analysis of teaching materials and real teaching practice, providing concrete examples of methods which were used at different times. When a variety of sources is examined, a much richer and more diverse past is revealed than was the case with method description based on the theoretical literature alone. It also becomes apparent that foreign language teaching before 1900 was not just the **GRAMMAR–TRANSLATION METHOD**, but included, among others, variations of the **DIRECT METHOD** (e.g. in the theoretical works and in the schools established by the educationists of the age of enlightenment in Germany) as well as inductive approaches (Klippel, 1994).

In the twentieth century, modified versions of the direct method first proposed by the **REFORM MOVEMENT**, e.g. **PALMER**'s Oral Method, have existed side-by-side with the grammar–translation method and more form-focused ways of teaching. After World War Two the **AUDIOLINGUAL METHOD** was widely propagated; in Europe – but not in the United States – it was largely replaced by the **AUDIO-VISUAL** method in the 1960s, which in turn became obsolete with the advent of the **COMMUNICATIVE** approach. This chain of development is reflected in the theoretical and practical publications of the English-speaking world and Western Europe. Method development in Eastern Europe was heavily influenced by the work of Russian psychologists and applied linguists. Unfortunately, research into the historical development of indigenous language teaching methods in other parts of the world has not been undertaken on a significant scale.

Historical research into foreign language teaching methods demonstrates clearly that methodological innovation is dependent not only on the propagation of theoretical advances but, more importantly, on the development of appropriate teaching materials and, more recently, on pre-service and in-service teacher training. This is because, at classroom level, methods have rarely been implemented in an unadulterated form. Research cX\o teachers' subjective theories has shown that methods are always adaptedm¼ by those who use them. Most teachers will pick and choose those procedures and proposals which are in tune with current educational values, which coincide with their subjective theories, which are supported by a wide variety of published materials, and, finally, which prove effective and easy to use.

## Method comparisons

Method comparisons are undertaken with two major goals. The first one is descriptive and seeks to increase our knowledge about foreign language teaching methods, classroom teaching and theory construction, as is the goal of Richards and Rodgers (1986), Larsen-Freeman (1986) and, less so, of Stevick (1998). The second goal is prescriptive, as it intends to prove that one method is better, i.e. more efficient, than another one. The implication is that the superior method should be used.

Descriptive method comparisons need to analyse methods using the same theoretical model or set of questions. What makes it difficult to compare methods using the three-tiered concept of Richards and Rodgers (1986) is the fact that at least some information on the three areas of analysis – approach, design, procedure – has to be inferred, because the proponents of each method do not always provide comprehensive outlines for the underlying theory and for all areas of practice. Therefore, determining some aspects may be a matter of interpretation of statements or materials and consequently carries the risk of misinterpretation. Pennycook (1989) considers this to be a major flaw of the Richards and Rodgers model.

Larsen-Freeman (1986) works with a list of ten questions which are applied to each method in turn. These questions cover much of the same ground as the method concept of Richards and Rodgers, namely goals, teacher and learner roles, characteristics of the teaching/learning process, student–teacher interaction, emphasis on certain **SKILLS** and areas of language, types of **EVALUATION**, teacher response to student errors, views of language (Larsen-Freeman, 1986: 2f.). Larsen-Freeman includes three further important aspects which are missing from the Richards and Rodgers concept: the affective domain ('How are the feelings of the students dealt with?'), the underlying concept of culture, and the role of the students' native language (Larsen-Freeman, 1986: 2f.). Both of these comparative studies have provided information on and detailed insights into the major current mainstream and fringe methods to help teachers make informed methodological decisions.

Interest in prescriptive method comparison reached a peak in the 1960s. One major large-scale quasi-experimental study with this aim was the Pennsylvania Project (Smith, 1970). However, taking method as the main category of comparison did not yield clear results. The superiority of one method over another could not be proved empirically, simply because the realisations of one method, in different settings with different groups of learners and by different teachers, turned out to be very diverse. In practice, foreign language classes are shaped by a complex network of situational, relational, educational, cognitive and affective factors, far too many to be controlled in an experimental study.

Although this experimental research did not fulfil expectations in terms of method comparison, it led to a more critical look at methods. 'It has also provided a sobering check on some of the claims, often extravagant ones, that innovators and advocators of different methods have been prone to make' (Stern, 1983: 492). And, of course, it has given us a more thorough understanding of the classroom situation, where learning processes and the interaction of teachers and learners may be more important than the method adopted. Unfortunately, disappointment with method research has also led to neglecting the teaching perspective for some time. At the end of the twentieth century, foreign language education theory was still primarily concerned with learning processes rather than teaching procedures, even though the teachers themselves, their education and reflective practice, are receiving more attention.

## Current methods

Historical research has shown that teaching methods at any given time are bound up in the web of educational thinking within a particular society. Teaching methods are part of the cultural context in which they exist. This partly explains why new teaching methods cannot easily be transferred from one cultural context to another. Method research has to take the cultural loading of methods into account (Holliday, 1994).

In Europe, and in 'core English-speaking countries' (Phillipson, 1992), the second half of the twentieth century produced foreign language teaching methods which may be linked to a number of ideas salient in educational thinking: individualism, learning by using as many senses as possible, the centrality of communication and the negotiation of meaning, the role of cognition. Apart from these general educational concepts, it was the development of **LINGUISTICS** which has shaped present-day teaching methods.

The communicative approach (**COMMUNICATIVE LANGUAGE TEACHING**) has been widely accepted and may be seen as an umbrella under which a number of methods have found their place: natural approach, **TASK-BASED** learning, community language learning, **HUMANISTIC** methods, **CONTENT-BASED INSTRUCTION**, **BILINGUAL METHOD** and, to a lesser degree, Total Physical response (TPR) and **SUGGESTOPEDIA**. The role of the senses in understanding and handling the foreign language is important in the audio-visual method, TPR, task-based learning and humanistic methods. A strong cognitive element is present in the **SILENT WAY** and the grammar–translation method. Cognitive learning does not play a big part in the audiolingual method or TPR. More than any other method, community language learning takes the **NEEDS** and the individuality of the learner as its focal point (Stevick, 1998). But the individual learner matters in all communicative methods. After all, the main objective of communicative language teaching is to enable the learner to express in the foreign language what he or she would like to express.

**See also:** Classroom research; Objectives in language teaching and learning; Planning for foreign language teaching; Pronunciation teaching; Research methods; Skills and knowledge; Teacher education

## References

Anthony, E.M. (1963) 'Approach, method, technique', *English Language Teaching* 17: 63–7.

Brown, H.D. (1994) *Principles of language learning and teaching*, (3rd edn), Englewood Cliffs, NJ: Prentice-Hall.

Darian, S.G. (1972) *English as a foreign language. History, development, and methods of teaching*, Norman: University of Oklahoma Press.

Holliday, A. (1994) *Appropriate methodology and social context*, Cambridge: Cambridge University Press.

Howatt, A.P.R. (1984) *A history of English language teaching*, Oxford: Oxford University Press.

Kelly, L.G. (1969) *25 centuries of language teaching*, Rowley, MA: Newbury House.

Klippel, F. (1994) *Englischlernen im 18. und 19. Jahrhundert. Die Geschichte der Lehrbücher und Unterrichtsmethoden (Learning English [in Germany] in the 18th and 19th centuries. A history of the textbooks and teaching methods)*, Münster: Nodus.

Larsen-Freeman, D. (1986) *Techniques and principles in language teaching*, Oxford: Oxford University Press.

Mackey, W.F. (1965) *Language teaching analysis*, London: Longman.

Musumeci, D. (1997) *Breaking tradition. An exploration of the historical relationship between theory and practice in second language teaching*, New York: McGraw-Hill.

Neuner, G. (1989) 'Methodik und Methoden: Überblick (Methodology and methods: a survey)', in K. Bausch, H. Christ, W. Hüllen and H. Krumm (eds), *Handbuch Fremdsprachenunterricht*, Tübingen: Francke.

Nunan, D. (1991) *Language teaching methodology*, New York: Prentice Hall.

Pennycook, A. (1989) 'The concept of method, interested knowledge, and the politics of language teaching', *TESOL Quarterly* 23, 4: 589–618.

Phillipson, R. (1992) *Linguistic imperialism*, Oxford: Oxford University Press.

Richards, J.C. and Rodgers, T.S. (1986) *Approaches and methods in language teaching*, Cambridge: Cambridge University Press.

Savignon, S.J. (1983) *Communicative competence: theory and classroom practice*, Reading: Addison-Wesley.

Smith, P.D. (1970) *A comparison of the cognitive and audiolingual approaches to foreign language instruction: the Pennsylvania foreign language project*, Philadelphia: Center for Curriculum Development.

Stern, H.H. (1983) *Fundamental concepts of language teaching*, Oxford: Oxford University Press.

Stern, H.H. (1992) *Issues and options in language teaching* (eds P. Allen and B. Harley), Oxford: Oxford University Press.

Stevick, E.W. (1998) *Working with teaching methods*, Boston: Heinle and Heinle.

Titone, R. (1968) *Teaching foreign languages. An historical sketch*, Washington, DC: Georgetown University Press.

## Further reading

Larsen-Freeman, D. (1986) *Techniques and principles in language teaching*, Oxford: Oxford University Press.

Mackey, W.F. (1965) *Language teaching analysis*, London: Longman.

Richards, J.C. and Rodgers, T.S. (1986) *Approaches and methods in language teaching*, Cambridge: Cambridge University Press.

Stern, H.H. (1983) *Fundamental concepts of language teaching*, Oxford: Oxford University Press.

FRIEDERIKE KLIPPEL

# TESOL – Teaching English to Speakers of Other Languages

TESOL is an international education association whose mission is to develop the expertise of its members and others involved in teaching **ENGLISH** to speakers of other languages, to help them foster effective communication in diverse settings while respecting individuals' language rights. To this end, TESOL articulates and advances standards for professional preparation and employment, continuing education and student programmes; links groups worldwide to enhance communication among language specialists; produces high quality programmes, services and products; and promotes advocacy to further the profession.

Membership comprises teachers, teachers-in-training, administrators, researchers, materials writers and curriculum developers. Members choose a primary interest section from a list of twenty and receive voting rights, periodic newsletters and access to the interest section listserver. They may also join a caucus that focuses on a social, cultural or demographic issue related to TESOL's mission.

TESOL publishes a newsletter and two journals, *TESOL Quarterly* and *TESOL Journal*, and organises annual conventions in North America.

## Website

TESOL's website is: www.tesol.edu

# Text and corpus linguistics

The intensive study of texts, for educational, religious and **LITERARY** purposes, has a very long history. For hundreds of years, concordances of major texts, such as the Bible and Shakespeare's works, have been used for detailed interpretation of word use and meaning. Since the 1890s, textual study has increasingly used quantitative methods, initially to study word frequency and later to study a wide range of language features. Such work became unfashionable in the 1960s, but has rapidly grown in influence again since the 1980s, when computer-assisted methods became widely available to study large text collections (corpora). These data and methods have had considerable influence on the design of **DICTIONARIES** and **GRAMMARS**.

## Text analysis

Text analysis assumes that the main unit of language in use is a text. A complete text can be very short ('Exit', 'Wet Paint', 'Closed for Lunch'). Longer texts (e.g. a newspaper editorial, short story, or school **TEXTBOOK**) have characteristic **VOCABULARY**, grammar and textual structure. It is natural to think initially of written examples, but the concept applies equally to purely spoken texts (e.g. a conversation or a transaction in a shop), or to mixed types (e.g. a lecture or a sermon). Whereas a sentence has a syntactic structure, a text has a semantic unity. It is 'about' some topic, with a coherent gist or a storyline which is not purely linguistic, but depends partly on everyday knowledge. There is also a close relation between many **TEXT TYPES** and social institutions: textbooks are used in schools, sermons are given in churches, cross-examinations occur in court-rooms, and so on.

Nevertheless, different linguistic features characterise different uses of language. Different topics require different words, and there are statistical preferences for using different vocabulary and grammar in different text types. Biber (1988) has used quantitative and distributional techniques to identify words and grammatical constructions which frequently co-occur (or never do) in text types (such as conversation, personal letters and science fiction), and to identify more general textual dimensions (such as informational, narrative and persuasive). (On textual cohesion, coherence and text structure, see Halliday and Hasan, 1976; Brown and Yule, 1983.)

Beyond the most elementary stages, language learners must be able to suit their language to different social contexts, and many adults learn **ENGLISH FOR SPECIFIC PURPOSES** (which are often academic). Materials should therefore embody accurate descriptions of the real language that they will have to cope with. Learners may, for example, need the features which characterise scientific and technical language, such as passives and nominalisations. Because of its social and intellectual importance, scientific language has been well researched: see Swales (1990) and Atkinson (1999) for just two such studies.

## Corpus analysis

In the 1890s, with the aim of improving court transcriptions, Kaeding (1898) used a corpus of eleven million running words to study word frequency in **GERMAN**. From the 1920s to the 1960s, Thorndike, Lorge, West and others calculated word frequencies in large English-language corpora, to set up wordlists for designing foreign language and literacy materials (see Howatt, 1984, for details). Largely under the influence of **CHOMSKY**'s theories, quantitative work went out of fashion, but the rapid development of computers, corpora and text-processing software from the 1980s has led to a renaissance of quantitative methods.

In the 1960s, the first computer-readable corpora consisted of just one million words of running text. By the late 1990s, the larger corpora consisted of hundreds of millions of words. A large general corpus is a text collection designed as a broad sample of language use: spoken and written, casual and formal, fiction and non-fiction, popular and technical, written for children and adults, and covering a wide range of subjects.

A significant indication of the influence of corpus linguistics is the publication in the mid-1990s of four major **MONOLINGUAL DICTIONARIES** of British English (CIDE 1995, COBUILD 1995, LDOCE 1995, OALD 1995), all aimed at advanced learners, and all based on detailed analyses of large text corpora. This involved wide-ranging changes in lexicographic practice, made possible by new technology. Corpus-based grammars have also appeared (e.g. COBUILD 1990).

The main research tool is the concordance. Computer software can search a corpus for examples of words or phrases, and display them within their co-text. This provides dozens or hundreds of attested examples from which the lexicographer or grammarian can accurately describe typical language use. The four dictionaries differ in their details, but all contain **AUTHENTIC** examples of current word usage. Indeed, only a corpus of contemporary language use can tell us which words are current, and which have dropped out of use. Other frequency information includes how often words occur, how often words with multiple meanings occur with their different meanings, and how often words are co-selected with other words (collocations) and grammatical constructions. Examples of real usage also provide information on the frequent evaluative connotations of words and their pragmatic force in different **SPEECH ACTS**.

By the late 1990s, the development of bilingual corpora and bilingual corpus-based dictionaries was also proceeding rapidly. This work has corresponding implications for the practice and theory of **TRANSLATION**.

Examples of patterns revealed by concordances and associated techniques can be found in Moon, 1998, Partington, 1998, Sinclair, 1991, Stubbs, 1996, and papers in Aijmer and Altenberg, 1991, and Thomas and Short, 1996. See Barnbrook, 1996, on general corpus methods, Sinclair, 1987, on lexicographic methods, and Willis, 1990, on applications to teaching **MATERIALS**.

## Outstanding issues

Because of their need to present 'general English', dictionaries and grammars can take only limited account of variation within the language. Whether varieties can be exhaustively classified is doubtful: apart from anything else, new text types are constantly arising. However, individual teachers or researchers can now easily set up their own smaller specialised corpora, in different languages, for learners with different specific purposes.

In addition, whether any corpus, however large, can truly represent a whole language is also doubtful. A language is continually growing and changing, and it is not theoretically possible to have a representative sample of a potentially infinite population. A general corpus must sample mainstream uses, such as quality newspapers, widely-read fiction and everyday conversation. But who is to say what would be appropriately-sized samples of more specialised text types such as research articles on bio-chemistry, business correspondence or television chat shows? A more modest aim is a balanced corpus which samples widely, is not biased towards data which are easy to collect (e.g. mass media texts), and does not under-represent data which are difficult to collect (casual conversation). The value of corpus data is not in doubt, but there is much debate on how to design the optimum corpus.

Although corpus work has profoundly influenced dictionaries and grammars, its influence on teaching materials has been more modest. There is often a lack of correspondence between traditional accounts of English usage and what **NATIVE SPEAKERS** actually say or write (as attested in corpora), but the exact place of findings from authentic data is disputed.

## Related areas and conclusions

The study of attested language use, in several branches of linguistics and the social sciences, has provided much of the theory behind **COMMUNICATIVE LANGUAGE TEACHING**. Approaches such as contrastive rhetoric, **CONVERSATIONAL ANALYSIS**, **DISCOURSE ANALYSIS**, **INTERCULTURAL COMMUNICATION** and **STYLISTICS** differ in their linguistic, sociological or literary focus, but they all investigate how language forms are used in real communication.

The technology underlying corpus linguistics has given access to new data, and opened up research topics which were previously inconceivable. We now have facts about language use which no amount of introspection or manual analysis could discover, but it will take time before this mass of new evidence is fully interpreted for its relevance to teaching materials and teaching practice.

**See also:** Authenticity; Conversation analysis; Discourse analysis; Grammar; Linguistics; Notions and functions; Pedagogical grammar; Schema and script theory; Stylistic variation; Vocabulary

**References**

Aijmer, K. and Altenberg, B. (eds) (1991) *English corpus linguistics*, London: Longman.

Atkinson, D. (1999) *Scientific discourse in sociohistorical context*, Mahwah, NJ: Lawrence Erlbaum.

Barnbrook, G. (1996) *Language and computers*, Edinburgh: Edinburgh University Press.

Biber, D. (1988) *Variation across speech and writing*, Cambridge: Cambridge University Press.

Brown, G. and Yule, G. (1983) *Discourse analysis*, Cambridge: Cambridge University Press.

CIDE (1995) *Cambridge International Dictionary of English*, (ed. P. Procter), Cambridge: Cambridge University Press.

COBUILD (1990) *Collins COBUILD English Grammar*, (ed. J. Sinclair), London: Harper Collins.

COBUILD (1995) *Collins COBUILD English Dictionary*, (ed. J. Sinclair), London: Harper Collins.

Halliday, M.A.K. and Hasan, R. (1976) *Cohesion in English*, London: Longman.

Howatt, A.P.R. (1984) *A history of English language teaching*, Oxford: Oxford University Press.

Kaeding, K. (1898) *Häufigkeitswörterbuch der deutschen Sprache* (Frequency Dictionary of the German Language), Steglitz.

LDOCE (1995) *Longman Dictionary of Contemporary English* (3rd edn), (ed. D. Summers), London: Longman.

Moon, R. (1998) *Fixed expressions and idioms in English*, Oxford: Clarendon Press.

OALD (1995) *Oxford Advanced Learner's Dictionary* (5th edn), (ed. J. Crowther), Oxford: Oxford University Press.

Partington, A. (1998) *Patterns and meanings: using corpora for English language research and teaching*, Amsterdam: Benjamins.

Sinclair, J.M. (ed.) (1987) *Looking up: an account of the COBUILD Project in lexical computing*, London: Collins.

Sinclair, J.M. (1991) *Corpus, concordance, collocation*, Oxford: Oxford University Press.

Stubbs, M. (1996) *Text and corpus analysis, computer-assisted studies in language and culture*, Oxford: Blackwell.

Swales, J. (1990) *Genre analysis: English in academic and research settings*, Cambridge: Cambridge University Press.

Thomas, J. and Short, M. (1996) *Using corpora for language research*, London: Longman.

Willis, J.D. (1990) *The lexical syllabus*, London: Collins.

**Further reading**

Biber, D. (1988) *Variation across speech and writing*, Cambridge: Cambridge University Press.

Partington, A. (1998) *Patterns and meanings: using corpora for English language research and teaching*, Amsterdam: Benjamins.

Sinclair, J.M. (1991) *Corpus, concordance, collocation*, Oxford: Oxford University Press.

Stubbs, M. (1996) *Text and corpus analysis, computer-assisted studies in language and culture*, Oxford: Blackwell.

MICHAEL STUBBS

# Text types and grading

Choosing the types of texts that go into a course and deciding on their sequencing can be guided by considering text types, topic types and readability. Texts provide opportunities for learners to meet language features and to become familiar with discourse structures. Research on text types thus has important implications for language curriculum design. The selection and grading of text types in language courses will directly affect what can be learned.

A major distinction in research on **READING** is between expository texts and narrative texts. An important grammatical distinction between these two text types lies in the types of conjunction relationships (Halliday and Hasan, 1976) that each typically contain. Narrative texts commonly involve conjunction relationships where all the sentences and clauses are of roughly equal value in terms of the message they express. That is, they express time sequence and inclusion relationships where each idea follows another in a steplike sequence. Expository texts, on the other hand, use a range of weighted relationships like cause and effect, generalisation and example, contrast, and summary, where one sentence or clause is given more importance than the other. Expository text thus requires more sophisticated **INTERPRETATION** skills.

Biber's (1989) corpus-based research has identified eight text types which differ from each other in the clusters of grammatical and lexical features they contain. These text types are intimate interpersonal interaction (telephone conversations, face-to-face conversations), informational interaction (business calls on the telephone, spontaneous speeches, interviews, personal letters), scientific exposition (academic prose, official documents), learned exposition (press reviews, popular magazines, academic prose), imaginative narrative (fiction, prepared speeches), general narrative exposition (newspaper reporting, non-sports broadcasts, humour), situated reportage (sports broadcasts), and involved persuasion (speeches, interviews, professional letters, magazines). Scientific exposition, for example, is characterised by use of the present tense, long words, nouns rather than pronouns, lexical variety, passives, relative clauses and adverbial subordination, etc.

Biber's research is significant for language teachers because it shows that, if language courses make use of a limited range of text types, learners will meet a limited range of grammatical and lexical features. If learners have special purposes, then the appropriate text types must be used. If learners have wide general purposes, then their course should include the full range of text types.

The selection of text types can be specified further by reference to Johns and Davies's (1983) topic types. A somewhat similar **GENRE**-based classification can be found in Derewianka (1990). Johns and Davies's topic types deal mainly with expository text. They include, for example, characteristics and physical structure texts which describe what things are like, instruction texts which tell the reader how to do things, process texts like lifecycles and descriptions of manufacturing processes which describe how things are formed, and state/situation texts like newspaper accounts and historical accounts which describe what happened. Texts which are of the same topic type

– for example, physical structure – can be on quite different topics – for example the structure of an ants' nest or the structure of a business organisation – and still share the same basic components of parts, location of the parts, characteristics of the parts, and function of the parts.

Although over a dozen topic types have been identified, typically only a small number of them are important for learners working within a particular subject area.

The choice and grading of the text types to include in a course will depend on **NEEDS ANALYSIS**, learners' proficiency level, and degree of background knowledge. Learners with academic purposes will need to work with the scientific exposition, learned exposition and informational interaction text types. Learners who need to use the target language as a second language in daily life will need to work with intimate interpersonal interaction, informational interaction, and involved persuasion text types.

An important factor in the choice and grading of texts is readability (Carrell, 1987), and **VOCABULARY** knowledge plays a very significant part in all readability measures. This importance is reflected in the central importance of vocabulary in graded reader schemes. Carrell argues that background knowledge should also play a significant role in the grading of texts for second language learners. This means that teachers should consider the amount of knowledge learners bring to the text when grading texts for difficulty. Successful comprehension of a text usually requires that learners bring substantial knowledge to the text.

Text types are an important consideration in the design of language courses, because familiarity with the important text types and the patterns that lie behind them will strongly affect the ease with which learners read and the skill with which they write.

**See also:** Authenticity; Beginner language learners; Exercise types and grading; Languages for specific purposes; Materials and media; Reading; Schema and script theory; Textbooks; Vocabulary

## References

Biber, D. (1989) 'A typology of English texts', *Linguistics* 27: 3–43.

Carrell, P. (1987) 'Readability in ESL', *Reading in a Foreign Language* 4: 21–40.

Derewianka, B. (1990) *Exploring how texts work*, Rozelle, NSW: Primary Teaching Association.

Halliday, M. and Hasan, R. (1976) *Cohesion in English*, London: Longman.

Johns, T. and Davies, F. (1983) 'Text as a vehicle for information: the classroom use of written texts in teaching reading in a foreign language', *Reading in a Foreign Language* 1, 1: 1–19.

## Further reading

Davies, F. and Greene, T. (1984) *Reading for learning in the sciences*, Edinburgh: Oliver and Boyd.

Derewianka, B. (1990) *Exploring how texts work*, Rozelle, NSW: Primary Teaching Association.

Johns, T. and Davies, F. (1983) 'Text as a vehicle for information: the classroom use of written texts in teaching reading in a foreign language', *Reading in a Foreign Language* 1, 1: 1–19.

I.S.P. NATION

# Textbooks

Textbooks are one particular resource amongst an increasingly wide and diverse range of teaching **MATERIALS**. They are bound collections of textual and visual material, designed for teaching and learning a particular subject and following particular methodological and didactical principles. Since the 1960s textbooks have been complemented with a wide range of supplementary materials, which together constitute a teaching course comprising at least a teacher's book and a workbook, and in many cases also reference materials (such as glossaries or **GRAMMAR** books), **AUDIO-VISUAL** materials (such as cassettes, videos, maps, slides, overhead sheets, photographs, etc.), and lately also additional practice materials on disk or CD-ROM. Textbook developments appear often to run parallel with developments in (language) learning theory and to be triggered by changes in society.

## History of textbooks

Like the history of textbooks for teaching other subjects, that of foreign language textbooks, too, reflects developments in the theory of (language) teaching and learning.

In Germany Götze (1994) distinguishes five generations of foreign language textbooks for teaching **GERMAN**. The first generation dominated the 1950s and, following the **GRAMMAR–TRANSLATION METHOD**, included language and grammar. The second dominated the 1960s, was influenced by linguistic structuralism and **BEHAVIOURISM** and was characterised by **MONOLINGUAL** approaches focusing on drilling spoken language patterns. The third generation developed from the 1970s onwards and was pragmatically and communicatively oriented. Valence theory and intercultural approaches characterised the fourth generation. The fifth generation currently attempts to integrate the four communicative skills, and is influenced by cognitive science (Götze, 1994: 29–30).

In other countries, similar developments could be observed, reflecting evolutions in the understanding of what it involves to acquire communicative competence in a foreign language, albeit that, depending on local traditions and circumstances, these developments may have occurred at different points in time, with different speeds and emphases. Whereas in some countries teachers may consider it self-evident that textbooks devote special attention to developing learners' **AUTONOMOUS LEARNING** skills, or to assisting them in the acquisition of **INTERCULTURAL COMMUNICATION** and **INTERCULTURAL COMPETENCE**, teachers in other countries may not.

Over the years the offer of textbooks became more diversified, in the sense that books were written which were geared towards specific learning groups, designed for learning **LANGUAGES FOR SPECIFIC PURPOSES**, for second language learning, or catering for specific differentiation needs.

## Textbooks: for and against

More than anything else textbooks continue to constitute the guiding principle of many foreign language courses throughout the world. Certainly at **BEGINNERS**' level, textbooks provide guidance with respect to grammatical and lexical progression. They translate the **OBJECTIVES** specified in the curricula into structured units, offering data materials, task sheets, reference, practice and sometimes also test materials. To a large extent textbooks determine the selection of texts, the choice of social work forms and audio-visual materials.

Despite their convenience, textbooks have often been criticised for being too rigid, not being able to cater for the needs of all pupils, not being effective in presenting multiple sides of any issue or in addressing timely and topical issues, imposing particular teaching styles onto teachers and **LEARNING STYLES** onto learners, allowing insufficient space for teacher or learner creativity, presenting a highly fragmented picture of the foreign culture and stereotypical tourist views of the target people. Other criticisms are typically levelled at the uninteresting selection of texts, the number and types of exercises on offer, the degree of variation in **TEXT TYPES** and **EXERCISE TYPES**, and the overall visual presentation.

Yet textbooks continue to have a presence in foreign language classrooms. In their article *What Textbooks Can – and Cannot – Do*, Christenbury and Kelly (1994) discuss other reasons, apart from linguistic progression, for which teachers may have to use textbooks in their classes, with time, money, convenience, reassurance and the school's desire to control teachers being the major reasons addressed.

Whereas some teachers pride themselves on rarely using textbooks and, when they do so, it is only as a resource for developing their own innovative plans, and some others may be found who insecurely clutch to the text and faithfully follow its sequence, questions and testing programmes, probably the majority of teachers use textbooks, supplementing them with materials of their own choice, adapted to their particular teaching circumstances and learning groups.

## Textbook analysis and textbook evaluation

With the exponential growth of the foreign language textbook market it became important to design instruments that were able to **EVALUATE** and compare textbooks in a systematic and objective way. To that end and from the 1960s onwards criteria lists were developed. These lists evolved with changes in textbooks' approaches to teaching foreign languages. On the basis of these lists, textbooks could be evaluated with respect to aspects as varied as design, content, structuring and sequencing, types of guidance offered, forms of interaction envisaged, grammatical and lexical progression, variety of text types, variety of exercise types, function of **AUDIO-VISUAL** materials, success in translation of curricular goals, etc. Examples of such lists are Engel *et al.* (1977a and b), Sheldon (1988), and Kast and Neuner (1994), providing criteria for evaluating the various aspects of textbooks mentioned above; or Sercu (1998) or Byram (1993), in which the focus is on one particular aspect, i.e. foreign language textbooks' success in integrating the teaching of language and culture.

Even though criteria lists can help to make the evaluation process transparent, it is important to realise that they cannot be considered wholly objective, since the selection and weighting of the different criteria may have been inspired by local considerations and circumstances. Textbook evaluations based on such lists, too, have to be understood as partially subjective and, perhaps, unbalanced because inspired by personal points of interest.

In all cases, it will be important to know who performed the analysis, why it was undertaken, what was analysed and how the analyst(s) proceeded. Analyses may have been performed by individuals or a team, by researchers or teachers, by textbook writers, publishers or education authorities. The procedures adopted may have been quantitative, qualitative or a combination of both. The function of the analysis may have been instrumental, giving jargon-free guidelines to publishers and authors as to how to design future textbooks, or to teachers, as to how to select one book from another.

## Textbook research

In the past, in the field of foreign language teaching as well as in that of other subjects such as social studies or history, three major approaches to researching textbooks have been developed:

*process-oriented*, *product-oriented* and *reception-oriented* (Weinbrenner, 1992: 23). Various authors regard process-oriented textbook research as being linked either to the life cycle of the textbooks (Weinbrenner, 1992: 23), or to the interaction triangle of teacher–textbook–pupil (Meijer and Tholey, 1997: 207). The product-oriented approach focuses on the textbook *per se*, i.e. as a teaching medium with particular contents, didactic features and visual characteristics. The reception-oriented or effect-oriented approaches examine textbooks from the point of view of the effects they have on the learning of pupils or the teaching of teachers.

As yet, there is no universally recognised theory of the textbook. Empirically, too little is known about how and when teachers and pupils use textbooks; how textbooks influence the learning process in comparison with other instructional materials; what research instruments are most reliable in the field of textbook research; how visual materials influence the learning process; how effective textbooks are in transmitting knowledge or promoting the acquisition of independent learning skills, to give but a few examples.

**See also:** Authenticity; Board drawing; Cultural studies; Internet; Literary texts; Materials and media; Syllabus and curriculum design; Text types and grading; Video

### References

Byram, M. (ed.) (1993) *Germany. Its representation in textbooks for teaching German in Great Britain*, Frankfurt/Main: Diesterweg and Georg-Eckert-Institut für Internationale Schulbuchforschung.

Christenbury, L. and Kelly, P.P. (1994) 'What textbooks can – and cannot – do', *English Journal* March: 76–80.

Engel, U., Halm, W. and Krumm, H.-J. (1977a) *Mannheimer Gutachten zu ausgewählten Lehrwerken Deutsch als Fremdsprache. Band 1 (Mannheim report on selected textbooks for teaching German as a foreign language. Volume 1)*, Heidelberg: Goos.

Engel, U., Krumm, H.-J. and Wierlacher, A., with von Ortmann, W.D. (1977b) *Mannheimer Gutachten zu ausgewählten Lehrwerken Deutsch als Fremdsprache. Band 2 (Mannheim report on selected textbooks for*

*teaching German as a foreign language. Volume 2)*, Heidelberg: Goos.

Götze, L. (1994) 'Fünf Lehrwerkgenerationen (Five textbook generations)', in B. Kast and G. Neuner (Hrsg.) *Zur Analyse, Begutachtung und Entwicklung von Lehrwerken für den fremdsprachlichen Deutschunterricht (On the analysis, approval and development of textbooks for teaching German as a foreign language)*, Berlin: Langenscheidt.

Kast, B. and Neuner, G. (eds) (1994) *Zur Analyse, Begutachtung und Entwicklung von Lehrwerken für den fremdsprachlichen Deutschunterricht (On the analysis, approval and development of textbooks for teaching German as a foreign language)*, Berlin: Langenscheidt.

Meijer, D. and Tholey, M. (1997) *Het Duitslandbeeld in Nederlandse leermiddelen (The image of Germany in Dutch teaching materials)*, Enschede: SLO.

Sercu, L. (1998) *Acquiring intercultural communicative competence from textbooks. The case of Flemish adolescent pupils learning German*, unpublished PhD thesis, Leuven: KULeuven, Departement Linguïstiek.

Sheldon, L.E. (1988) 'Evaluating ELT textbooks and materials', *ELT Journal* 42, 4: 237–46.

Weinbrenner, P. (1992) 'Methodologies of textbook analysis used to date', in H. Bourdillon (ed.), *History and social studies – methodologies of textbook analysis*, Amsterdam/Lisse: Swets and Zeitlinger.

### Further reading

Bourdillon, H. (ed.) (1992) *History and social studies – methodologies of textbook analysis*, Amsterdam/Lisse: Swets and Zeitlinger.

LIES SERCU

# Threshold Level

The Threshold Level is an objective for modern language learning and teaching designed on behalf of the **COUNCIL OF EUROPE** in the perspective of the Council's overall aim: to promote mutual understanding and collaboration among the inhabitants of its member states. The objective focuses on the ability to communicate with speakers of another language in such a way as to adequately transact the business of everyday life as well as to establish and maintain social contacts. It was assumed that such an objective would appeal to the large majority of potential foreign language learners and that it might induce many of them to undertake a pertinent language learning effort. For this effort to be successful it should be sustained long enough to enable the learners to reach their aim. It is essential for this that, throughout the learning process, the learners are aware of making progress in their **ACQUISITION** of the **SKILLS** required, and of doing this in a way which is both efficient and economical.

Considerations like the above led to the development of the Threshold Level as an objective for the acquisition of communicative ability and to the formulation of a set of principles that should determine the nature of the learning experiences to be proposed for leading up to it. The Threshold Level was thus deliberately designed as a point of orientation in the development of learning systems in which the features deemed relevant to language learning were to be meaningfully interrelated. The foundations for such systems, including those for the model used in the construction of the Threshold Level, were laid in the early 1970s by a group of experts convened by the Council of Europe to investigate ways and means of promoting language learning in Europe (Trim *et al.*, 1973). The elements proposed were brought together and further concretised in a model for the specification of behavioural objectives by **VAN EK**, who also undertook the first exemplification of the application of the model for the **ENGLISH** language, resulting in the first publication of the objective in 1975 (van Ek, 1975).

In a further study, van Ek expanded the original model into a more comprehensive one with special regard to the educational implications of learning a foreign language (van Ek, 1986). This expanded model was subsequently concretised for English (van Ek and Trim, 1991a).

## Components

In the Threshold Level, communicative ability is conceived as skill in functioning appropriately in a range of situations in which the learner is likely to need to use the foreign language. The first step towards defining the objective, therefore, is to describe these situations. This is done with special regard to such features as the *setting* in which the envisaged communication act takes place, the *transactions* the participants are likely to engage in, the *roles* they are likely to play, the *topics* they are likely to deal with, and the *communicative intentions*.

The next step is to indicate as explicitly as possible what learners might be expected to do in the various situations in which they are likely to find themselves and to analyse the skill involved in terms of the ability to fulfil certain language functions and to handle certain **NOTIONS**. The language functions denote what people are supposed to do by means of language (e.g. describing, inquiring, denying, apologising, etc.) and the notions stand for the concepts with regard to which people fulfil the language functions. Thus, if we say 'I'm sorry for being late' we fulfil the language function of *apologising* while referring to the concept of *lateness*. Among the notions, a distinction is made between *general* notions and *specific* notions. General notions are such as may be expressed in almost any situation, and specific notions are those which are likely to be expressed typically in particular situations only. In most situations the need may arise to refer to time, to place, to quantity or quality, to express relations between entities, etc. A notion, such as 'potatoes', on the other hand, is most likely to be expressed in connection with 'eating' or with 'agriculture'.

In order to give maximum guidance to users of the specification, each functional or notional item is provided with so-called 'exponents', i.e. actual language forms in the language concerned (words, structures, idioms) that may enable learners to meet their requirements both effectively and economically. These exponents are selected so as to ensure 'maximum efficacy with minimum means'. Together they represent a functional **GRAMMAR** core as well as a restricted though highly effective lexicon. The exponents are not meant, however, as anything like a prescribed grammar + vocabulary. They have the status of recommendations only, and how the individual learner is to fulfil the various functions and to handle the various notions is, in principle, left entirely open. Yet, they do provide guidance with regard to such matters as the overall range of linguistic ability expected of the learners at the level concerned, as well as the degree of formality/ informality envisaged, and they can be used as checklists (e.g. by course designers). Collectively, the exponents indicate the range of linguistic and, to a certain extent, that of **SOCIOLINGUISTIC COMPE-TENCE** expected of the learners.

In addition to this the latest version of the Threshold Level (van Ek and Trim, 1991a, *Threshold Level 1990*, re-issued in 1998 as *Threshold 1990*) deals with *discourse* competence, *sociocultural* competence and *compensatory* competence. Discourse competence is described as the ability to use appropriate strategies in the construction of texts, particularly those formed by stringing sentences together. It covers the ability to open a conversation and to end it, to contribute to the construction of a coherent dialogue, etc. It also covers such matters as the interpretation and processing of a written text, including the distinguishing, within a text, of more or less coherent parts, the establishment of links between these parts, the distinguishing between essential and non-essential information, etc.

Sociocultural competence is treated as 'awareness of the sociocultural context in which the language concerned is used by **NATIVE SPEAKERS** and of ways in which this context affects the choice and the communicative effect of particular language forms.' The distinction of this type of competence recognises the fact that the use of a particular language implies the use of a reference frame which is at least partly determined by the sociocultural context in which this language is used by native speakers. The Threshold Level describes sociocultural competence in systematically organised lists of 'what the learner at this level is supposed to be aware of or to be able to do' in using the foreign language.

Similarly it deals with *compensatory competence* as an essential component of communicative ability. This involves the use of strategies and techniques enabling the learners to cope with unpredicted demands as well as failures of recall. Again, the appropriate strategies and techniques are listed in terms of behavioural ability.

Finally, in recognition of the more general educational benefit learners may derive from 'learning for Threshold Level', the objective contains a component called **LEARNING TO LEARN**.

The behavioural ability specified in this component is meant to facilitate the achievement of Threshold Level on the one hand and further learning or learning in other directions (e.g. other languages) on the other.

## Target-groups and related objectives

Originally, the Threshold Level was developed as an objective for foreign language learning by adults wishing to acquire what might be regarded as a general communicative ability. It was not long, however, before its potential for school education was noted and van Ek was commissioned by the Council of Europe to develop a version for schools (van Ek, 1977). This adaptation to a different target group was readily made possible by the flexibility inherent in the objective, due to its systematic nature and its explicitness, which enables separate elements, sub-categories or even whole categories to be replaced by others to satisfy the requirements of diverse target groups. Meanwhile, in the most recent version of the Threshold Level (van Ek and Trim, 1991b), the flexibility has been increased to such an extent that it has become an integral element in the specification. Consequently, the distinction between versions for adults and for schools is no longer maintained.

Since 1975, the Threshold Level has been used on a large scale by the designers of **SYLLABUSES** of all kinds: for curriculum reform, for examination development, for **TEXTBOOK** writing and course design. As such it has become a powerful tool in the development of the prevalent communicative orientation of language teaching and learning. On the basis of the same model, a lower-level objective roughly halfway between zero and Threshold Level was developed and published as *Waystage* (van Ek *et al.*, 1977). Subsequently, *Waystage*, too, was revised on the basis of the expanded model and newly published as *Waystage 1990* (van Ek and Trim, 1991b). The most recent addition to the Council of Europe's objectives has been the development of an objective above Threshold Level, for which, again, the same model has proved to be suitable. Exemplified for the English language, it has been given the name of *Vantage Level* (van Ek and Trim: forthcoming). Waystage, Threshold Level and Vantage Level together form a system of flexible objectives ranging from a very elementary level to an advanced one, all described in terms of one and the same model of specification, and therefore suitable for the systematic planning of learning facilities for a very large and diverse section of the potential language learning public. Threshold Level may be regarded as the key element in the series, with Waystage as a reduced version and Vantage Level as an expanded one.

## Versions for other languages

Since Threshold Level is primarily specified in terms of what the learners can *do* in the foreign language rather than what they are supposed to *know* of the language, it is readily adaptable to other languages than English. Meanwhile, separate versions have been developed for over a score of European languages, including such diverse ones as Russian, Irish, Welsh, Norwegian, SPANISH, Maltese and Basque. These versions have not been mere translations. In each case account has been taken not only of the semantic categories obligatorily represented in the grammar of the language concerned, but also of the differences in the sociocultural context. Yet they are all strictly comparable in their common use of the original model underlying their specifications.

In many cases the versions for other languages than English have been developed by teams of leading researchers in the field from the countries involved. This has led to a strong consensus as to the major parameters to be distinguished in specifying objectives for modern language learning and teaching, as well as to procedures for treating them. The opportunities this offers for intensive collaboration, if not harmonisation, on an international scale have been only partly exploited so far and remain to be used to full advantage by interested individuals and institutions.

**See also:** Assessment and testing; Communicative language teaching; Council of Europe Modern Languages Projects; CRÉDIF; Notions and functions; Politeness; Vantage Level; Waystage

## References

Trim, J.L.M., Richterich, R., van Ek, J.A. and
Wilkins, D.A. (1973) *Systems development in adult language learning*, Strasbourg: Council of Europe; (1980) Oxford: Pergamon Press.

van Ek, J.A. (1975) *The Threshold Level*, Strasbourg: Council of Europe; re-issued as *Threshold Level English* (1980) Oxford: Pergamon Press.

van Ek, J.A. (1977) *The Threshold Level for Modern Language Learning in Schools*, London: Longman.

van Ek, J.A. (1986) *Objectives for foreign language learning*, vol. I: *Scope*, Strasbourg: Council of Europe.

van Ek, J.A., Alexander, L.G. and Fitzpatrick, M.A. (1977) *Waystage*, Strasbourg: Council of Europe; re-issued as *Waystage English* (1980) Oxford: Pergamon Press.

van Ek, J.A. and Trim, J.L.M. (1991a) *Threshold Level 1990*, Strasbourg: Council of Europe Press; re-issued as *Threshold 1990* (1998) Cambridge: Cambridge University Press.

van Ek, J.A. and Trim J.L.M. (1991b) *Waystage 1990*, Strasbourg: Council of Europe Press.

van Ek, J.A. and Trim, J.L.M. (forthcoming) *Vantage Level*, Cambridge: Cambridge University Press.

JAN VAN EK

# Total Physical Response

Total Physical Response, or TPR, is a language teaching method in which physical movement plays a central role. Linked initially to research into skills training, the method was developed by the research psychologist Professor James Asher of San Jose State College in California in the 1960s. The method aims to be stress-free and suitable for learners of all ages and abilities. Since its first introduction, TPR has spread worldwide, enjoying particular popularity with teachers of young learners. The approach is methodologically linked to the nineteenth-century work of François GOUIN (1894).

In a TPR language class, new language is introduced by the instructor in the form of commands or instructions accompanied by appropriate actions modelled by the instructor and a small group of four students who copy the actions observed by the rest of the class. The students do not repeat the commands. Subsequently all students are invited to model the particular action, both in groups and individually. The atmosphere in the class is always playful. The instructor attempts to ensure that students understand the commands before they are asked to model them. The point is never to catch a student out but rather to reinforce internalisation of language through watching others perform and performing oneself.

The TPR classroom is a sensory-rich environment of posters and teaching aids. Starting at **BEGINNERS'** level with a few simple props such as tables, chairs, books and windows, students learn classroom **VOCABULARY** following the instructor's commands, based initially on combinations of these objects with a series of common verbs such as walk, run, point, touch, turn, sit and stand. Commands such as 'walk to the door' form the principal basis of these early lessons. As students progress, new verbs, new nouns and more complex **GRAMMAR** forms are introduced. It is a central tenet of TPR that there is very little in language that cannot be presented through movement and commands, including complex grammar forms.

Since **SPEAKING** is allowed to emerge freely, when students feel ready, a 'silent period' is an integral part of the method. The research basis of the method suggests that speech will begin naturally when sufficient language has been internalised. In more advanced TPR classes, however, speech plays a regular role in classroom activities as students begin to give instructions to others as well as follow them.

TPR is rarely used in isolation; rather, the method is particularly favoured as a means of introducing new language. The model is that cognitive knowledge of the structures of a language should follow and is the result of acquisition or internalisation, not the cause of it.

The proponents of TPR argue that the method successfully harnesses the natural language acquisition mechanisms most usually observed in very small children by encouraging learners first to understand through observation, then to act in response to speech and, after language is internalised, to begin to speak. In Asher's view, this is the natural order for language acquisition in both children and adults. In using the term *acquisition* to describe this process, Asher, in common with Krashen's 'Natural Approach' (1989), identifies it

as a process of internalisation of language distinct from the cognitive learning of grammar and vocabulary and the conscious knowledge of such structures. Asher expressed the concept thus:

> A reasonable hypothesis is that the brain and the nervous system are biologically programmed to acquire language, either the first or the second in a particular sequence and in a particular mode. The sequence is **LISTENING** before speaking and the mode is to synchronise language with the individual's body.
> (Asher, 1996: 2–4)

In developing the theoretical basis of TPR, Asher spent much effort observing the behaviour of very small children as they interacted linguistically with parents and other adults. Most particularly he noted the key interaction in which adults spoke to an infant, encouraging the child to perform certain actions. These most usually took the form of commands such as 'look at me'. When the child performed the action they were rewarded with smiles and more attention. By the age of three, most children exhibit a very considerable ability to understand and act upon language whilst still being unable to speak more than comparatively few words. Asher called this condition 'comprehension fluency'. It is a central tenet of TPR that in language acquisition, by children or adults, comprehension fluency is both a precursor of fluent speech and also, importantly, its prerequisite. Asher argues that speech is the result of the acquisition of language, not the cause of it.

The experimental basis for TPR has been described in considerable detail, most particularly in Asher (1996: 18–34). As Asher wrote at the time, 'The Rosetta Stone of language acquisition was in the choreography of language and body movement. Nature had revealed, I believed, one of the great secrets of learning' (Asher 1996: 1–2).

A criticism commonly levelled at TPR is that it is suitable only for beginners. However, in recent years a number of publications have outlined strategies for using TPR with intermediate and advanced learners. Further, TPR does not attempt to teach speech. This has led to some criticism, especially emanating from those less familiar with the theoretical and experimental basis of the method. This basis predicates the notion that it is impossible for one person actively to teach another to speak because the brain is positively structured to acquire language in other ways, through observation and movement leading to comprehension fluency. In 1977 Asher published the first edition of his introduction to Total Physical Response under the title *Learning Another Language through Actions*, and it remains the key text.

**See also:** Direct method; Humanistic language teaching; Language awareness; Motivation; Neuro-linguistic programming; Suggestopedia; Teaching methods

## References

Asher, J. (1996) *Learning another language through actions* (5th edn), Los Gatos, CA: Sky Oaks Productions.
Gouin, F. (1894) *The art of teaching and studying languages*, London: George Philip and Son.
Krashen, S. (1989) *Language acquisition and language education*, London: Prentice Hall International.

ROBIN CAIN

# Transfer

Sometimes referred to as 'interference', this is the process whereby the learner transfers features of the first language (L1) into the target language (TL) during **SECOND LANGUAGE ACQUISITION** (SLA). This may be done either consciously or unconsciously, and the transfer items can range from **VOCABULARY** to **GRAMMAR** rules. The application of familiar rules, for example, to the TL may result in errors being made because new rules are required which are either partially known or incorrectly used. Transfer may also be positive, such as in cases where the languages have similarities which assist learning of the TL. Transfer is associated with **CONTRASTIVE ANALYSIS** where a study of first and second languages can reveal potential areas of difficulty for learners as a result of transfer. It is also closely linked with **ERROR ANALYSIS**, an applied linguistic methodology that draws upon the cognitive school, placing strong emphasis on universal and innate language learning abilities. The exact nature and role of transfer in SLA was debated a great deal in earlier decades by researchers in the

field, especially the extent to which it was a 'help or a hindrance in L2 learning' (Faerch, Haarstrup and Phillipson, 1984: 193).

Error analysis claimed that learners' errors were indicative of the underlying abilities and learning **STRATEGIES**, and not merely mistakes needing correction. Transfer can be seen in this perspective as part of learner hypothesis testing about the TL. Corder went so far as to say that 'the study of errors is part of an "experiment" to confirm or disprove the psycholinguistic theory of "transfer"' (1973: 266). Identifying and analysing interference was previously linked to the study of **BILINGUALISM** with intruding features affecting various aspects of speech (Richards and Rodgers, 1986: 172–88). Transfer theory is also related to **INTERLANGUAGE** (Selinker, 1972; 1992).

Transfer can be viewed, then, as the result of both similarities and differences between L1 and the language being learned. Learners transfer sounds, structures and usages from one language to the other with properties of L1 exercising an influence on the course of L2 learning. Where it is acceptable to use L1 habits in the L2, there is positive transfer, which is also described as 'facilitation' (Corder, 1973: 132). The application of familiar rules in new language situations can be beneficial, as also discovered by Faerch, Haarstrup and Phillipson (1984) in their comparative studies of Danish and English. The term 'interference' is 'negative transfer' when mistakes occur due to the inappropriateness of L1 rules or items or the use of 'false friends', such as words in L2 which seem very similar to L1 but have different meanings and are therefore used incorrectly.

There is general agreement that transfer is not a process of simple interference but that it operates in 'complex ways', especially with closely related languages (Faerch, Haarstrup and Phillipson, 1984: 135). It works at different levels and the different elements of language have to be considered separately. It may be more likely to occur with some elements than with others. This has led to some problems in studying it in practice. If we take errors as evidence of transfer, for example, there is a problem of attribution, i.e. to pinpoint exactly where errors emanate from because not all can be linked to negative transfer or interference from the **MOTHER TONGUE**. Dulay and Burt, for example, found as a result of their research 'that as many as 89 per cent of the errors committed by language learners could be accounted for without recourse to the notion of mother-tongue interference' (cited in Wilkins, 1990: 530). There may be interference from the target language itself, for example. Equating transfer with L1 interference is a 'convenient fiction' (Odlin, 1989: 27), since knowledge of both L1 and TL will affect the SLA process, and this has to be taken into consideration.

Odlin identified four main categories of the 'many theoretical and practical problems that attend the study of transfer' (1989: 25). These are, first, to do with problems of definition, or what exactly 'transfer' is. Since there is an element of controversy about the term, some scholars have suggested its abandonment altogether, or at least a more limited use. Second, there is the problem related to the systematic comparison of languages usually provided by contrastive analysis. It is not always easy in practice to produce rigorous and well-informed comparisons, and different elements may be contrasted rather than the same one in any given study. A related dimension here is that of comparing learners of one language who have different L1 backgrounds. The extent and similarities of their transfers would be illuminating but not always possible to identify, and a number of studies have come across this problem, with different conclusions.

The third category is that of prediction, which is also viewed as a weakness of contrastive analysis by those favouring error analysis. It is often the case that predictions of learner behaviour are usually descriptions of what has gone before.

Finally, there are problems of making generalisations about language transfer, since languages vary and what may be valid for some may be invalid for others, and language universals need to be discovered and proven beforehand. The extent to which generalisations can be made about transfer, therefore, is not an independent phenomenon but is closely related to applied linguistic theory.

There are many other potential factors involved in SLA other than transfer. Teaching materials and methods may be faulty or unsuitable; learners have different levels of **MOTIVATION** and intelligence as well as social background. It is not always possible

to separate the different variables causing errors in order to claim that transfer is a real process which actually occurs during SLA. Nevertheless, sufficient research in this field has indicated quite clearly that something of this nature does sometimes lead to incorrect L2 utterances and writing, as well as assisting in SLA in other cases.

Moving on from transfer as a process, there is then the problem of what it actually signifies. At the practical level, it can show areas of difficulty for learners, as suggested by the predictions of contrastive analysis. For error analysts, however, it indicates something more substantial, related to inherent language learning abilities as well as to what has been termed interlanguage. This is what learners develop sequentially, through a process of hypothesis formulation and testing, as they learn a second language.

The learner must be part of the equation, and a key strategy could ask what it is that determines whether learners decide to transfer or not and investigate their willingness to do so in certain circumstances. A close relationship between L1 and L2 does not necessarily mean that learners will automatically transfer. On the other hand, it cannot be assumed that where there is very little overlap between languages there will be little or no transfer. Studies have found variations in these situations. Learners assess L2 early on and perceive the distance or proximity to their own language at various linguistic levels, and this assessment will influence the amount of transfer which they will then be involved in. Faerch, Haarstrup and Phillipson point out that there are some areas of L1, such as idiomatic expressions, which learners are generally unwilling to transfer no matter how close the languages.

The notion of transfer offered useful explanatory powers and fitted in with the theories of the 1960s and 1970s, being linked to developments in theory and research at that time. The problem of generalisations as well as difficulties in identifying transfer as separate from other processes and factors did limit its explanatory powers, although it inspired much valuable research in the field. The interplay between L1 and L2 was put into focus, as well as how the learner actively approaches learning the new language and makes use of the linguistic knowledge they already possess.

See also: Acculturation; Contrastive analysis;
Error analysis; Fossilisation; Interlanguage;
Mental lexicon; Psychology; Speaking; Writing

## References

Corder, S.P. (1973) *Introducing applied linguistics*,
London: Penguin.
Ellis, R. (1994) *The study of second language acquisition*
Oxford: Oxford University Press.
Faerch, C., Haarstrup, K. and Phillipson, R. (1984)
*Learner language and language learning*, Clevedon:
Multilingual Matters.
Odlin, T. (1989) *Language transfer: cross-linguistic
influence in language learning*, Cambridge: Cam-
bridge University Press.
Richards, J.C. (1984) 'A non-contrastive approach
to error analysis', in J.C. Richards (ed.), *Error
analysis: perspectives on second language acquisition*,
Harlow: Longman.
Richards, J.C. and Rodgers, T.C. (1986) *Approaches
and methods in language teaching: a description and
analysis*, Cambridge: Cambridge University
Press.
Selinker, L. (1972) 'Interlanguage', *International
Review of Applied Linguistics* 10: 209–31.
Selinker, L. (1992) *Rediscovering interlanguage*, Harlow:
Longman.
Wilkins, D. (1990) 'Second languages: how they are
learned and taught', in N.E. Collinge (ed.), *An
encyclopedia of language*, London: Routledge.

## Further reading

James, C. (1980) *Contrastive analysis*, Harlow: Longman.

RUTH CHERRINGTON

# Translation

Translation and foreign language teaching are
historically and conceptually linked through their
common goal of communication, but also divided
through the different perspectives which each brings
to this goal. Translation is explicitly concerned with
mediating between two languages, usually both in
the written medium. In a professional context it
presupposes a high degree of proficiency in both
source language (SL) and target language (TL),
linguistically and culturally. Foreign language (FL)
teaching on the other hand aims to bring about
various degrees of proficiency in spoken and/or
written language and is only implicitly concerned
with mediation between languages and cultures in
so far as the learner is already proficient in at least
one natural language. The use of translation in the
FL classroom makes this relationship explicit, and
has been an aspect of FL pedagogy through the ages
(Kelly, 1969:171). From its mid-nineteenth-century
heyday in the form of the GRAMMAR–TRANSLATION
METHOD, translation was largely rejected as an FL
teaching method in the approaches which emerged
from the late nineteenth century and into the
twentieth century: naturalistic methods (REFORM
MOVEMENT; DIRECT METHOD), structuralist/BEHA-
VIOURIST methods (AUDIO-VISUAL and AUDIOLIN-
GUAL METHODS) and the COMMUNICATIVE
approach. However, while translation has continued
to be a feature of many traditional FL classrooms,
new ideas for exploiting the communicative potential of various types of translation began to emerge
during the 1990s, particularly in HIGHER EDUCA-
TION. This happened largely as a result of the
development of translation as an academic discipline and the growth of professionally-oriented
degree courses.

## The grammar–translation method

In the traditional grammar–translation method,
translation is used as a means of both practising
and testing knowledge of the language system. The
approach is deductive, typically starting from the
presentation of a rule, which is then practised by
the translation of sentences into the L2 on the basis
of a bilingual VOCABULARY list. At more advanced
stages, the translation of connected passages, often
of a LITERARY kind, may be required. Translation
into the L1 is typically used as a test of READING
comprehension, presupposing a close if not literal
translation strategy, and indicating, for instance,
that the learner has recognised certain structures in
the SL text such as passives, subordinate clauses
and particular vocabulary items. In other words,
the focus is on the form, not the message or the
sense, contrary to the practice of many literary

translators up to the beginning of the nineteenth century (see Newmark, 1988: 45) and beyond. The use of 'oral translation' by the teacher to explain the meaning of words and phrases is also a common pedagogic strategy. The grammar–translation method is still used with less commonly taught languages, in autodidactic courses, and in some universities.

The conception of translation as practised in the grammar–translation method is, however, a narrow one, based largely on the teaching of classical languages. Indeed, the focus is even narrower, since **STYLISTIC OBJECTIVES** – emulating authoritative L2 writers – receded over time from its Renaissance origins in favour of manipulating grammar and memorising vocabulary (Kelly, 1969: 173–6). Given its focus on the language system, such an approach tends to operate in a cultural and situational vacuum, ignoring questions such as the translation of institutional and administrative terms, numbers, the bridging of cultural gaps, the role of context, and the intended readership. These are all issues of relevance to the professional translator, normally engaged in non-literary translation, and to the development of what has become known as 'translational competence' (Campbell, 1998: 1–21), which is normally distinguished from linguistic competence.

## Professional translation

While translation in various forms has been an intermittent if controversial feature of language teaching through the ages, most courses in translation for professional purposes did not emerge until after World War Two, although translation as an 'administrative necessity' dates back 3,000 years (Kelly, 1969: 171). The post-war period saw a surge in the demand for non-literary translation for political, social and economic reasons and a concomitant growth in the number of institutions offering professionally-oriented courses. The teaching of translation for professional purposes is therefore much newer than the teaching of translation for language learning, and the role which language teaching plays in the development of translation competence is a relatively new topic (but see Malmkjær, 1998). The development of translation as an academic

discipline (variously known as translation studies, translatology, translation theory) has revealed a number of approaches – contrastive–linguistic, descriptive, functional – of which the contrastive–linguistic approach in particular shares common ground with translation for language learning.

Characteristic of the approach which developed in the 1960s (e.g. Catford, 1965; Vinay and Darbelnet, 1995) was the focus on solving structural translation problems. Solutions would often be presented, for instance, as a set of possible linguistic 'transpositions' or 'shifts' where the SL and TL differ: 'This text is intended for … / *Le présent manuel s'adresse à …*' (Vinay and Darbelnet, 1995: 97). Contrasting L1–L2 patterns were also used in the traditional **CONTRASTIVE ANALYSIS** method of language teaching, not as translation pairs, but rather as the basis for attempting to predict learning difficulties in order to target pedagogical attention in the form of L2 drills. In the 1980s, a revival of contrastive methods was proposed in a mentalist/deductive framework as a means of raising learners' awareness of particular features of L2 syntax. The use of contrastive patterns in the form of translation pairs is, however, still in use as a general method of language teaching in some universities (see, e.g., Sewell and Higgins, 1996: 45–65), following in the 'comparative stylistics' tradition of Vinay and Darbelnet.

## Literal versus free translation

One of the central issues in translation throughout the ages has been the 'literal versus free' debate. In language teaching the use of translation as a linguistic encoding or decoding **EXERCISE** requires a close, rather than a 'free', translation strategy. In L1–L2 translation, the L1 text or sentences are often constructed, or less obviously chosen, to 'force' the learner to use particular parts of the L2 language system. In such cases, the L1 text is simply a means of getting to the L2 and has no particular value of its own, and there is some burden on the learner to recognise what structure or vocabulary item is being prompted, like understanding the rules of a game. The texts used for L2–L1 translation are by contrast usually **AUTHENTIC** texts (possibly edited), but the focus is still on the learner showing, through the medium of the

L1, that the structures and vocabulary of the L2 have been understood.

While translation in language teaching is understandably characterised by an L2 orientation, regardless of whether the L2 is the SL or the TL in a translation exercise, in translation studies different approaches may be characterised as SL-oriented or TL-oriented. The contrastive–linguistic approach is generally characterised as source-text (ST) oriented in the sense that the function of the target text (TT) is assumed to be the same as that of the ST with the consequence that translation decisions naturally remain focused on linguistic rather than cultural or contextual issues. Later approaches, such as the functionalist view developed in Germany during the 1980s (see Kussmaul, 1995) are characterised by a TT orientation, in which translation decisions are taken in relation to the situation and purpose of the TT rather than that of the original. This includes decisions on whether to add or omit information, to make cultural adjustments according to the experience and knowledge of the target readership, or linguistic adjustments according to TL **GENRE** conventions. For instance, cultural conventions differ when indicating the size of a house or a flat: so, while translating 'How many bedrooms?' with '*Wieviele Schlafzimmer?*' is formally correct, it could be embarrassingly misleading in the target German culture if the question relates to the size of the accommodation (see Kussmaul, 1995: 94). It has, however, also been argued that an approach reflecting professional practice contributes to language learning in so far as it may improve passive knowledge of SL vocabulary and grammar (usually the L2), and focus attention on the different ways in which SL and TL fulfil their communicative purpose (see Sewell and Higgins, 1996: 121–34). Recent research using Think Aloud Protocols (TAPs) may also contribute to our understanding of translation competence.

During the period when translation has been developing as a subject concerned with producing a TT for a specific situation and purpose rather than as an exercise in formal transcoding, the teaching of translation, particularly in higher education, has often been marked by some confusion of purpose. There are, however, signs that synergies are now beginning to emerge and to be explicitly acknowledged, leading to more imaginative ways of integrating and adapting professional aspects of translation and even **INTER-PRETATION** (spoken–spoken communication) into language teaching. Two factors may be said to be supporting a return to favour for translation. First, some recent thinking on language learning has stressed the potential of translation as a means of language learning, if the process is regarded as the development of 'multi-linguistic competence' (reported in Malmkjær, 1998: 1). Second, translation as it is studied for professional purposes is not only in the ascendant as a university subject, it is also diversifying to include many different types of translation including the production of 'parallel' texts (tourist brochures, legislation), pre- and post-editing for machine translation, media translation (sur- and subtitling; voiceovers), websites, localisation and **DRAMA** (including adaptation). These 'modes' are beginning to serve as a rich source of innovative, communicatively-based ideas for the use of translation in language teaching (see, e.g., Sewell and Higgins, 1996; Malmkjær, 1998), although there is no empirical research base yet to support claims that such methods promote **ACQUISITION**.

**See also:** Contrastive analysis; Grammar–translation method; Higher education; Intercultural competence; Interpreting; Translation theory

## References

Campbell, S. (1998) *Translation into the second language*, London: Longman.

Catford, J.C. (1965) *A linguistic theory of translation. An essay in applied linguistics*, London: Longman.

Kelly, L.G. (1969) *25 Centuries of language teaching*, Rowley, MA: Newbury House.

Kussmaul, P. (1995) *Training the translator*, Amsterdam/Philadelphia: Benjamins.

Malmkjær, K. (ed.) (1998) *Translation and language teaching. Language teaching and translation*, Manchester: St Jerome.

Newmark, P.P. (1988) *A textbook of translation*, Hemel Hempstead: Prentice Hall.

Sewell, P. and Higgins, I. (eds) (1996) *Teaching translation in universities*, London: AFLS in association with CILT.

Vinay, J.P. and Darbelnet, J. (1995) *Comparative stylistics of French and English. A methodology for translation*, trans. J.C. Sager and M.-J. Hamel, Amsterdam/Philadelphia: Benjamins.

### Further reading

Howatt, A.P.R. (1984) *A history of English language teaching*, Oxford: Oxford University Press.
Newmark, P.P. (1991) 'Translation today: the wider aspects of translation', in P.P. Newmark, *About translation*, Clevedon: Multilingual Matters.
Stern, H.H. (1983) *Fundamental concepts of language teaching*, Oxford: Oxford University Press.

MARGARET ROGERS

# Translation theory

Translation is an ancient art, but the scientific study of translation is relatively recent. Translation Studies as a distinct discipline has been developing rapidly since the 1970s, and seeks to bridge the gap between the study of translation as a literary phenomenon and the study of translation as a branch of **APPLIED LINGUISTICS**. In the 1990s the emphasis has been increasingly on cultural aspects of translation, and earlier debates about problems of meaning and equivalence have been redefined.

### Defining translation

General assumptions about translation are based on the notion that a source language text can be rendered into the target language in such a way that the surface meaning of the two texts will be approximately the same and the structures of the source language will be preserved so far as is possible without seriously distorting the structures of the target language. To this end, the bilingual dictionary was developed.

The use of translation in language teaching is a long-established practice. Some of the earliest known bilingual texts are interlinear glosses, presumably created as a means of assisting readers with understanding a foreign text. The earliest vernacular writings in medieval Europe are mainly in the form of interlinear translations of Latin texts.

Later, with the development of systematic language teaching, translation came to occupy a central role.

Whilst in literary translation practice it is most common for the translation to be made into the translator's **MOTHER TONGUE**, in language learning translation is used in two quite different ways. A first level of language **COMPETENCE** can be tested by the use of translation *from* the foreign language. This process primarily involves **READING** and comprehension, combined with the ability to decode and then rephrase the syntactical structures of the foreign language in the learner's own language. The second stage involves translation *into* the foreign language, which demands a higher degree of active language knowledge, as demonstrated in the ability not only to read and understand in one's mother tongue, but then to restructure ideas and syntax in the language of study.

A central problem in the use of translation in language teaching concerns the question of the student's ability to demonstrate *faithfulness* to the source text. Whilst a literary or commercial translator will have few qualms about reshaping a text to suit the **NEEDS** of the target readers, the student may feel constrained by the syntax of the source text and by the need to demonstrate accuracy in comprehending the text. It is important that translation as a language learning strategy should be contextualised, and the issue of faithfulness broadened beyond the strictly semantic or syntactical.

Translation always, necessarily, involves both reading and writing. Most crucially, it requires an understanding not only of the elements of the text, but also of the circumstances surrounding the text. Context can be as significant for the translator as text, and this fact makes the use of translation as a means of monitoring language competence somewhat controversial. The translator has to read the source language text, which requires a high degree of analytical expertise, decode the text and then re-encode it in the target language. The process involved goes beyond the linguistic, as a simple example demonstrates. The French translation of the English greeting 'Good morning' is 'Bonjour'. The function of the greeting is the same, the use of the adjective 'bon' to translate 'good' is a straightforward lexical substitution, but the dictionary equivalent of 'morning' is 'matin', whilst 'jour' is given as 'day'. Strict linguistic equivalence here would result in an inaccurate translation. What has taken place is a complex process of decoding and recoding. The linguistic signs have been read in context, and a process of 'semiotic transformation' (Ludskanov, 1975) has taken place, as the linguistic signs encounter another set of signs from a different system, in this case the greeting systems operating in both source and target cultures.

## Equivalence

Defining equivalence is one of the most complex areas of translation studies. Distinctions have often been made between *linguistic* and *cultural* factors in translation, and different concepts of equivalence that result from such a distinction. Nida (1964) distinguishes between *formal* and *dynamic* equivalence, the former being a type of translation that seeks to match component parts of the text as closely as possible, the latter being formulated on the notion of equivalent effect. This, and similar endeavours to differentiate between categories of equivalence, are elaborations of St Jerome's famous distinction between word-for-word and sense-for-sense translation formulated in 384 AD, and which developed ideas articulated three centuries earlier by Cicero. Literary translators have always recognised that there are different categories of equivalence and have tended to favour a more flexible approach, that does not seek to define equivalence as sameness and recognises difference between languages. Jakobson claimed that full equivalence was impossible, and that only 'creative transposition' could be achieved (Jakobson, 1959). Today, that view is widely accepted, and equivalence is most often viewed as a dialectical relationship between the signs and structures both within and surrounding the source and target texts. Translators, whether literary, commercial or technical, tend to aim for equivalent effect, rather than for literal equivalence on the semantic or syntactic level. Where translators do not do this, and opt for semantic or **STYLISTIC** equivalence that ignores the conventions of the target system, the result is an inadequate translation of the kind that frequently occurs in guidebooks, menus or similar texts relating to the tourist trade that have been translated without due regard for the complexity of the transformation processes involved.

The problem of defining equivalence is directly linked to another major question in translation, the notion of translatability and untranslatability. Catford (1965) distinguishes between *linguistic* and *cultural* untranslatability, arguing that these categories present different kinds of translation difficulty. Linguistic untranslatability is inevitable, since no two languages have the same structures, and the problem of translating puns and wordplay highlights this fact. Cultural untranslatability derives from the different codes of behaviour and practice in different societies. Catford takes the example of different bathing practices in different cultures, pointing out that the term 'bathroom', although translatable between English, Japanese or Finnish, signifies quite different ritualised social behavioural practices. It could also be argued that the distinction between linguistic and cultural untranslatability is a false one, since translation always takes place in a context and therefore the cultural dimension is always present.

The basic activity of translation involves the transfer of texts across linguistic frontiers. But, in that process, all sorts of things happen to the text. Translation theorists have tended to focus unduly on the problem of loss in translation, but we could equally argue that, for every element that is lost, another is gained. It is important to remember that translation always involves change; the text that a source language reader reads cannot be the same as the text that a target language reader reads. Not only do lexical and syntactical aspects of language ensure that sameness is impossible, but it is also the case that different cultures interpret meaning in different ways. For example, the absence of consistency in defining colour across European languages has been pointed out frequently. Contemporary Irish, **ENGLISH** and **FRENCH** do not share terminology that covers the same interpretation of colours, and one solution to this problem is borrowing, hence the English terms *beige* or *ecru* to describe tonalities in the range from white to brown. Similarly, lexical items referring to food also vary widely, even within a relatively small geographical area. *Pastry*, *pasta* and *paté* have a common etymology, but have come to acquire completely different meanings and, as dining has become more international, have all become loan words, since any attempt to translate them would run into problems of transferable meaning.

## Translation and innovation

In translating any type of text, the translator has only two options: to take the text to the readers, or to take the readers to the text. Different translation strategies prioritise one or other of these options, which then tend to become conventionalised within a literary system. The strategy of making readers adapt to a new type of text, in either form or content, can lead to major literary innovations. The history of European poetry, for example, is full of innovations introduced through translation. The sonnet, which originated in Italy, spread across European literatures as a direct result of translations. Often the absence of a particular form in the target literature results in the translator introducing the original form as a literary innovation. The rapid spread of lyric poetry in medieval Europe is an example of the innovative power of translations, for the lyric effectively supplanted the epic that had previously been the dominant poetic form.

However, some cultures favour a different strategy, preferring to adapt the source language text into a known literary form in the target literature. In Britain and the United States, the most common tendency in translating for the past two hundred years has been towards **ACCULTURA-TION**, i.e. the rendering of foreign literature into forms and language immediately identifiable within the Anglo-Saxon tradition. Russian literature in English is a case of this acculturation process, and writers like Chechov or Dostoievski have entered the English canon. The tendency to acculturate texts in translation can result in resistance to any works that are not easily identifiable within the target system, which means that not all texts travel easily across literary frontiers.

## Translation studies

Recognition of the complexities of translation has led, in recent decades, to the development of a new inter-disciplinary field known as translation studies. The subject grew originally in the gaps between **LINGUISTICS** and literary studies, between translation theorists and practitioners. The goal of the discipline was first laid down in a manifesto by André Lefevere (Lefevere, 1978), which stated that there should be a comprehensive theory that could be used as a guideline for the production of translations. Theory and practice were therefore intimately linked from the outset, and translation studies scholars have endeavoured to avoid prescriptive theorising. The objects of study are the actual translations, and translation studies seeks to explore translation strategies through detailed analysis of what takes place during translation.

A key word in this investigation is *manipulation*. For the last twenty years, translation studies has seen the notion of textual manipulation as a central one. Given the impossibility of full equivalence, the translator is called upon to implement whatever strategies are deemed most appropriate for an adequate rendering of the source text in the target language, a process that inevitably involves decision-making, selection and other aspects of manipulatory activity. We need only look at instructions in various languages in public places to see the kind of manipulations that can occur. **POLITENESS** conventions in some languages may require phrasing of the 'passengers are kindly requested' variety, while other languages are content with direct imperatives. The choice of phrasing open to the translator will depend on the conventions operating in the target language, and the source text will be shaped accordingly.

Translation studies has developed in several ways since the early 1970s. In the early years, the emphasis was on challenging the notion of equivalence as sameness and on raising the status of translation as a textual activity. The expansion of research has led in two broadly distinctive directions: towards an examination of the norms governing translation in different contexts on the one hand, and towards an analysis of the history of translation practices through the ages on the other. Both translation history, which has shed light on the vastly different practices and theories obtaining at different moments in time, and translation theory, which has concerned itself with norms, have led to a change in perspectives on translation. Once seen as a secondary activity, something that could be practised by anyone with a minimal knowledge of another language, translation is now recognised as a highly complex activity that requires a range of **SKILLS** to be effective. The role of the translator is increasingly under scrutiny also, as it becomes clear that he or she plays a decisive role in determining what will reach the target language's readers. Debates have continued since the early 1990s about the *visibility* of the translator, led by Lefevere and Venuti in particular (Lefevere, 1992; Venuti, 1995).

The subject has also diversified in other ways. European translation studies has started to look at the ways in which translation practice reflects changes in a culture's poetics, focusing on questions of patronage and the power relations between original author, text, translator and mechanisms of production. More recently, post-colonial translation studies in such places as Brazil, **CANADA** and **INDIA** has started to examine ways in which the act of translation itself may be seen as directly linked to processes of colonisation, given that one of the things that translation does is to reinforce difference between cultures which may be interpreted to the detriment of one of the partners and to the advantage of the other. Here also, debates about equivalence have taken a new turn, for in positing the idea of equivalence as sameness, the underlying assumption was that textual transfer could take place between literary and cultural systems that were on equal terms. Revisiting the history of colonialism has meant that socio-cultural and textual relations have been viewed in a new light.

The most influential group in the new translation studies has been the *polysystems group*, led by Itamar Even-Zohar and Gideon Toury from Tel Aviv. Heavily influenced by formalist and structuralist models in their early years, the polysystems group began in the 1970s to investigate the role played by translated texts in other literatures. This trend, which was developed by José Lambert, James Holmes, Andrecaute; Lefevere, Theo Hermans, Susan Bassnett *et alia* shifted the focus of attention away from disputes about definitions of equivalence and away also from theories that privileged the source text. The polysystems group was concerned with broad questions about the role of translation in world literature, with how translations might be received at different moments, what contribution translations might make

to cultural development and why translation activity should vary so considerably. The group's work brought translation closer to **CULTURAL STUDIES** and social history, and one criticism of this approach was that it no longer prioritised linguistic questions.

However, recently there has been a rapprochement between applied linguistics and translation studies, as linguisticians have also begun to give greater attention to questions of language in context. Computer-assisted translation has also undergone great changes, and corpus language projects involving millions of words now form a substantial field of research within translation studies.

Translation has a long history, but the scientific study of translation is a recent phenomenon. It derives in part from developments in linguistics, literary studies and cultural studies, but also from the increased global use of English, which means that millions of people now use two or more languages in their daily lives. The importance of translation in global terms is a new phenomenon, but one that is set to continue. The rise of translation studies as a discipline is linked to this process, for, as translation becomes more visibly widespread, so it is important to understand what the activity of translation consists of, in order to train the translators of the future.

Translation studies underwent its 'cultural turn' in the 1980s, at the same time that other related disciplines were undergoing a similar process of change. The basic assumption about the interdependence of language and cultural context has become a fundamental element in translator and **INTERPRETER** training. In the commercial and business world, likewise, there is a growing interest in developing intercultural awareness, and the same holds true in tourism and the leisure industries. Translators in the new millennium are likely to have a broader training that stresses the importance of cultural background knowledge as well as linguistic competence.

**See also:** Cultural awareness; Grammar–translation method; Interpreting; Literary texts; Literary theory and literature teaching; Sapir–Whorf hypothesis; Translation

## References

Catford, J.C. (1965) *A linguistic theory of translation*, Oxford: Oxford University Press.

Jakobson, R. (1959) 'On linguistic aspects of translation', in R.A. Brower (ed.), *On translation*, Cambridge, MA: Harvard University Press.

Lefevere, A. (1978) 'Translation studies: the goal of the discipline', in J.S. Holmes, J. Lambert and R. van den Broeck (eds), *Literature and translation. New perspectives in literary studies*, Leuven: ACCO.

Lefevere, A. (1992) *Translation, rewriting and the manipulation of literary fame*, London: Routledge.

Ludskanov, A. (1975) 'A semiotic approach to the theory of translation', *Language Sciences* 35: 5–8.

Nida, E. (1964) *Toward a science of translating*, Leiden: E.J. Brill.

Venuti, L. (1995) *The translator's invisibility*, London: Routledge.

## Further reading

Alvarez, R. and Vidal, A. (eds) (1996) *Translation, power, subversion*, Clevedon: Multilingual Matters.

Bassnett, S. (1991) *Translation studies*, London: Routledge.

Bassnett, S. and Lefevere, A. (1998) *Constructing cultures*, Clevedon: Multilingual Matters.

Gentzler, E. (1993) *Contemporary translation theories*, London: Routledge.

Newmark, P. (1988) *A textbook of translation*, London: Prentice Hall.

Snell-Hornby, M. (1994) *Translation studies: an integrated approach*, Amsterdam: John Benjamins.

Toury, G. (1995) *Descriptive translation studies and beyond*, Philadelphia: John Benjamins.

Trosborg, A. (ed.) (1997) *Text typology and translation*, Amsterdam/ Philadelphia: John Benjamins.

SUSAN BASSNETT

# Trim, John Leslie Melville

b. 1924, London

Linguist, applied linguist, phonetician, journal editor, contributor to multi-media language courses

John Trim has been active in many fields of LINGUISTICS and APPLIED LINGUISTICS, though he is principally associated with the four COUNCIL OF EUROPE MODERN LANGUAGES PROJECTS which he directed from 1971 to 1997.

He started his academic career as Lecturer in Phonetics at University College, London (1949–58), and his first publications deal with phonetic features of GERMAN and ENGLISH. In 1958 he moved to the University of Cambridge, and in 1965 he became the first Head of the Department of Linguistics. It soon attracted a large number of postgraduate students, many of whom went on to staff linguistics departments in other universities. Applied linguistics flourished too, and with an international dimension. Trim's department at Cambridge hosted the second AILA Congress (1969) and held annual vacation courses in Linguistics and English Language. Trim himself worked on language testing and developed a lasting interest in the use of radio and television for adult language courses, which led to his becoming part author or consultant to several BBC courses, e.g. *Parliamo Italiano*, *Deutsch Direkt!* and *Follow Me*.

His association with the Council of Europe began in 1971, part-time at first, being combined until 1978 with his Cambridge post and from 1978 to 1987 with the Directorship of the Centre for Information on Language Teaching and Research (CILT), and then full-time from 1987 to 1997.

This long commitment to the Council of Europe Modern Languages Projects, with its round of conferences, workshops and report writing, may have prevented him from writing a substantial book of his own, yet it allowed him to devise and articulate a broad general framework for human communication. To the clarification of complex concepts and the drafting of concrete recommendations he brought an authoritative knowledge of the whole field of linguistics and language teaching, and great skill in coordinating the work of experts throughout Europe. He vigorously publicised the projects' contents and values.

Trim's contribution to language education, not only in these projects but also in various language associations and initiatives, and in the editorship of linguistics journals, has brought wide international recognition through a number of honorary doctorates and other academic distinctions.

## Bibliography

Trim, J.L.M. (with Kuna, F.) (1965) '*Komm mit!*: German by television. A course for beginners', London: BBC.

Trim, J.L.M. (1975) *English pronunciation illustrated* (2nd edn), drawings by P. Kneebone, Cambridge: Cambridge University Press.

Trim, J.L.M. (1980) *Developing a unit/credit scheme of adult language learning*, Oxford: Pergamon.

Trim, J.L.M. (with van Ek, J.A.) (1991) *The Threshold Level 1990*, Strasbourg: Council of Europe.

Trim, J.L.M. (1997) *Language learning for European citizenship: final report (1989–1996)*, Strasbourg: Council of Europe.

Trim, J.L.M. (with Coste, D., North, B. and Sheils, J.) (1998) 'Languages: learning, teaching, assessment. A Common European Framework of Reference', *Language Teaching* 31, 3: 136–51.

## Further reading

Brumfit, C. (ed.) (1994) 'The work of the Council of Europe and second language teaching', *Review of English Language Teaching* 4, 2 (special volume).

WALTER GRAUBERG

# United States of America

The different domains of language teaching and learning in the United States serve a variety of societal needs. These domains are:

1 the teaching of **ENGLISH** to **NATIVE SPEAKERS**;
2 language instruction for non-English speakers;
3 foreign language instruction in the formal education system; and
4 foreign language instruction for **VOCATIONAL** and other **ADULT** uses.

## Teaching and learning English

The vast majority of instruction in English is provided as part of the educational socialisation of native speakers, providing them with **SKILLS** in the use of the standard national language and its literature. Such instruction comprises the largest proportion of language teaching and learning within the formal education system. Over the past five decades a number of new curricular approaches – e.g., personal growth curricula, competency-based curricula, phase elective programmes – have been interspersed with recurrent 'back-to-basics' movements motivated by public dissatisfaction with the **READING**, **WRITING**, grammatical and spelling skills of students.

## Language instruction for non-English speakers

The United States has a large resource of language skills among its immigrant community. In the 1990 Census there were 15,430,804 people, or 6.2 per cent of the total population, who spoke a language other than English at home. While 50.8 per cent of these people spoke Hispanic languages, the Census reported speakers of sixty-three other languages who used those languages in their homes. This resource is largely underutilised, although it serves a few occupations where true native-speaker competencies are required, such as **INTERPRETERS**, translators, teachers of upper-skill-level classes, and various occupations that have need for native-level command of a language. Unlike in several European countries, there is no major government programme for teaching the standard language to adult immigrants, although as many as 3 million or 15 per cent report that they do not speak English well.

## Bilingual education

The United States has been more concerned with the influx of non-English-speaking children into the educational system which has resulted in the establishment of federal and state government-mandated **BILINGUAL EDUCATION** programmes to serve the special language needs of 'Limited English Proficient' (LEP) students, i.e. those students presumed to be unable to learn easily in English-only classrooms. There are approximately 3 million such students, 6.7 per cent of all students, and the number is growing rapidly. Three-quarters of LEP students speak **SPANISH** as their first language.

While all bilingual education programmes include some instruction in both the home language and English, the mix ranges from those that use both the home language and English throughout schooling, so-called additive bilingual education, to those where a full shift to English follows a brief initial period during which the home language is used and is seen as a transition stage on the way to a full mastery of English. Some of the leaders of the Hispanic community stress the continued use of the home language while the enabling legislation and the rest of the society, including several state governments, stress the latter.

Intergenerational linguistic and cultural continuity is fostered in several of the non-Hispanic ethnic communities in 'heritage schools' that provide home language instruction outside of the formal education system. For instance, in 1995 there were 82,675 Chinese and 80,012 Korean-origin students enrolled in such schools. One of the great, and largely unmet, challenges facing the American system of foreign language instruction is the accommodation of students with home language competencies other than English into the more general foreign language teaching system.

## Foreign languages in formal education

The bulk of foreign language instruction takes place within the formal educational system. There is a limited but expanding availability of foreign language instruction in elementary schools. About a third (31 per cent) of the elementary schools provide foreign language instruction, but only about 15 per cent of their students take it. Almost half (45 per cent) of elementary school foreign language instruction provides only a general exposure to a language and culture (FLEX programmes) rather than the acquisition of skill in a language. The majority (60 per cent) of elementary schools provide two hours or less per week of language instruction.

Secondary schools are much more likely (86 per cent) to provide foreign language instruction, usually for about five hours per week. However, some 40 per cent of secondary school students take no foreign language classes at all, and 80 per cent of those who do enrol take courses for two years or less. In fact, the organisation of secondary school foreign language instruction resembles a pyramid. The largest number of students are enrolled in first

year courses, then sharply diminishing numbers of students enrol in each of the advanced levels.

Language instruction at the college and university level has the same pyramidal shape. About 40 per cent of all students who receive undergraduate degrees have had no foreign language instruction, and there is a sharp drop-off in enrolments of almost 50 per cent after each year of instruction.

The educational focus at the various educational levels is somewhat different. In elementary school there is a heavy emphasis on exposure to a foreign language rather than skill ACQUISITION. In secondary schools, the emphasis is more clearly on the attainment of proficiency, and the tertiary level is divided between a substantial *ab initio*, skill-oriented language teaching in the first two years, followed by an emphasis on literature in advanced classes. As a result of the gaps between the twin pyramidal structure and the differences in focus at the various educational levels, the educational system has difficulty in articulating the various levels to give students a steady advance in foreign language skills.

Which languages are taught has varied considerably over the years. In 1890 and until World War One, Latin was the most commonly taught language, studied by between a third and a half of the enrolees in secondary schools. In 1998 only about 1 per cent of language enrolments were in Latin. In 1890 Spanish was not taught at all. Spanish is now taught in 79 per cent of the elementary schools, in secondary schools Spanish enrolments comprise about 65 per cent of all language enrolments, and in colleges and universities 55 per cent of enrolments. The next popular languages, FRENCH and GERMAN, began to attract students as Latin declined, fluctuating around 10 and 3 per cent respectively. Language enrolments are determined by a combination of staffing, reflected in which languages are offered, and student choice. Current trends are towards an increasing predominance of Spanish and a continuous decline in French and German. Shifts in student preferences among Spanish, French and German put great stress on the staffing of language instruction at all levels of the educational system.

Languages other than Spanish, French and German, often referred to as Less Commonly Taught Languages (LCTL), make up less than 2 per cent of enrolments in secondary school, but comprise 21 per cent of enrolments in colleges and universities. Russian enrolments in **HIGHER EDUCATION** at 2 per cent are declining, but Chinese enrolments at 2.4 per cent and Japanese enrolments at 3.6 per cent are expanding. The federal government supports advanced instruction at universities in more than a hundred languages.

At the primary and secondary school level, decisions about the organisation of the language programme and the teaching materials, and the pedagogical style to be used, are made at the level of the school, the school district, or the individual teacher. In higher education, such decisions are made by individual teachers. Some uniformity is introduced through the similarity of commercially available **TEXTBOOKS**, although increasingly teachers use teaching materials they prepare themselves. However, the almost complete dispersal of decision-making encourages frequent and widespread innovation and experimentation. Historically it has led to the seriatim introduction of radically different pedagogical paradigms: e.g. the Monitor Method, Total Physical Response, and the **SILENT WAY**. None of these methods has had a durable and system-wide impact. However, there has been a general shift in foreign language pedagogy from an earlier emphasis on **GRAMMAR**, **READING** and **WRITING** skills toward the current emphasis on the development of communicative competence in real-life situations. This trend has been accompanied by greater interaction between teacher and student in the classroom and an increased use of the language in the instructional process.

To the extent that there has been a national impetus to this change, it has come from the widespread adoption of a new **ASSESSMENT** strategy. Initially developed within government language teaching programmes – the Foreign Service Institute and the Interagency Language Roundtable – its non-governmental version was adopted by the American Council on the Teaching of Foreign Languages (ACTFL) as a scale to designate levels of oral proficiency from a 0 for novice level to 5 for native speaker proficiency, expanded by the use of pluses and minuses. More recently, ACTFL has developed a graduated set of standards to designate proficiency levels in Chi-

nese, Classical Languages, French, German, Italian, Japanese, Portuguese, Russian and Spanish. The widespread adoption of this scale with its emphasis on assessment through an oral interview has had a major impact on the character of language teaching more generally. More recently, a more general national standards setting movement (NAEP) has been developed for a substantial number of academic subjects, and will be incorporating standards for Spanish.

## Language education for use

One of the major problems in foreign language instruction in the United States is that there is so little use of foreign languages in the adult population in the United States, either occupationally or in people's private lives. Demand for foreign language use in American corporations and other vocational use is weak. To the extent that corporations seek foreign language education, they generally use one of the large number of proprietary schools that serve the more dispersed, largely recreational, adult **NEEDS**. There is, however, a substantial use-oriented foreign language educational system within the federal government to prepare its employees for diplomatic, military, intelligence or other governmental service. Neither the federal government nor the proprietary language education system is connected with the language system in schools and colleges.

**See also:** American Army Method; Bilingualism; Content-based instruction; France; India; Primary education; Proficiency movement; Secondary education; Spanish; US Standards for Foreign Language Learning

RICHARD D. LAMBERT

# Universal grammar

Since the 1950s the developing theories of Noam **CHOMSKY** have been a major inspiration for **LINGUISTICS**. The first version was known as 'transformational generative grammar' after two key concepts: language should be described in explicit formal rules (**GENERATIVE**) and these rules must be able to alter elements in the sentence in various ways (transformations). The later version became known as 'Universal Grammar' (UG) theory, after the central claim that language should be looked at in universal terms; then as 'principle and parameters' theory, after the way it described language through universal 'principles' that all languages obey and variable 'parameters' that change from one language to another. Then it became the 'Minimalist Program' after its quest to reduce all its apparatus to the basic minimum (Chomsky, 1995). Above all, the UG theory has integrated language acquisition with language description, seeing acquisition as setting the values for these parameters appropriately according to the examples of language the learner hears.

Chomsky (1986) set three main questions for linguistics:

1  What constitutes knowledge of language?
2  How is such knowledge acquired?
3  How is such knowledge put to use?

The starting point is what people know about language, their internal 'linguistic **COMPETENCE**', not their actual speech or use, their external 'performance', nor their purposes in using language, such as communication. This knowledge cannot be separated from how it comes into being; hence language description gets intertwined with theories of language **ACQUISITION**.

Universal Grammar is the distinct part of the mind common to all human beings that enables them to know and acquire languages. The language 'faculty' is a separate part of the mind, thus distinguishing UG theory from general psychological theories that see language and language learning as intrinsically no different from any other mental process. The stress on knowledge implicitly contradicts many approaches to language teaching, such as the social bias to the **COMMUNICATIVE** approach or the goal-based claims of **TASK-BASED TEACHING**; the emphasis on independence similarly goes against teaching methods that employ general ideas of learning, such as the habit formation concept integral to the **AUDIOLINGUAL METHOD**.

The form that this knowledge takes in the mind is necessarily complex and abstract since it has to be adaptable into all the myriad shapes that a human language can take. The nature of language is as difficult to state or to comprehend as other abstract theories such as quantum physics. The surface of the sentence is taken to be only a partial and inaccurate guide to the richness underneath. This insight was embodied in the difference between 'deep' and 'surface' structure. For example, the sentences 'John is eager to please' and 'John is easy to please' have the same surface structure but differ at deeper levels, because 'John' is the subject of 'eager to please' ( John pleases people) but the object of 'easy to please' (other people please John). Since the early 1990s, however, the UG theory no longer makes a technical difference between deep and surface structure.

The principles of Universal Grammar are part of the composition of the human mind. English questions, for example, are formed by a rule that moves the relevant elements to the front of the sentence; any speaker of English knows that in a sentence with a relative clause such as 'Sam is the cat that is black' you have to move the 'is' in the main clause to the front, yielding 'Is Sam the cat that is black', not the 'is' in the subordinate clause 'Is Sam is the cat that black?' It is the role of 'is' in the structure of the sentence that counts rather than simply finding an 'is'. This principle of structure-dependency compels all languages to move parts of the sentence around in accordance with its structure rather than just the sheer order of words. Even more general principles have been proposed, such as the principle of Economy that states that the only elements that can appear in a sentence are those that have to.

Structure-dependency could not be acquired by children from hearing sentences of the language; rather, it imposes itself on whatever language they encounter, just as in a sense the pitch range of the human ear restricts the sounds we can hear. Children do not have to learn these principles but apply them to any language they hear.

The parameters of Universal Grammar are the elements of language that have to be learnt. A much discussed example is the pro-drop parameter. Some languages such as Italian do not always require a subject in the sentence (pro-drop) 'Parla' (speaks). Others, such as English, require the subject always to be present (non-pro-drop) – 'He speaks', never 'Speaks' – even in sentences such as

'It's raining'. All human languages, therefore, have one or the other setting for this parameter. A small number of such parameters has knock-on consequences for the whole grammars of the languages. While the actual parameters are built in to children's minds, their values have to be set by the sentences they encounter. Children cannot choose any variation for the language they are creating in their minds but can only work within these pre-set limits. All the evidence they require to set the parameters must be available in the actual sentences they hear, called 'positive evidence', rather than through parents' corrections or explanation – 'negative evidence' – since this is the only type of input all children everywhere are known to receive. The pro-drop parameter could be set for English by hearing examples of sentences with dummy subjects such as 'There's a book on the table' or by noticing the type of inflections used in the present tense ('He likes' versus 'I/you/they/ we like'). Provided only that a child encounters a reasonable amount of normal speech, language acquisition will take place.

**SECOND LANGUAGE ACQUISITION**, however, might be different. Specific concentration of examples or grammatical explanation may be needed to get students through barriers that the child acquiring their first language (L1) does not encounter. The UG module may be no longer available for learning a second language (L2), whether because of the learner's **AGE** or because of the prior acquisition of the first language. Research suggests that, like L1 children, L2 learners know things they could not have learnt from language input, such as structure-dependency or indeed 'eager/easy to please', but these may be derived from the first language rather than from UG. The parameter values from the L1 **TRANSFER** to the L2; e.g. Spanish learners carry over their L1 pro-drop setting to English. But this is not always predictable; e.g. English learners do not carry over their non-pro-drop L1 setting to Spanish. The restriction to positive evidence in L1 acquisition may not apply to L2 learning: L2 learners can benefit from forms of negative evidence, such as correction, in ways unparalleled in L1 acquisition.

As the UG theory has developed, it has made a sharper distinction between the fixed properties of language called the 'computational system' with which all minds are equipped and the language-specific **VOCABULARY** that has to be used with these principles to get actual sentences of a language. To Chomsky himself, language acquisition is seen as chiefly a matter of acquiring idiosyncratic lexicon items: all variations, and hence all parameters, are part of the lexicon.

In itself this type of syntactic description could be a resource for language teaching in that it often covers basic issues that are important right from the first lesson of a course. Spanish differs from English in having no need for subjects; Japanese subject–object–verb word order differs from English SVO in almost every sentence. However, its abstractness of expression has led to few practical applications in **SYLLABUSES** and **TEXTBOOKS**. One tangential teaching use for a time was taking the descriptions as a basis for grammatical explanation techniques, called **COGNITIVE CODE THEORY**.

The general issues that UG theory has raised for language teaching are the idea that the crucial aspect of language is knowledge, not performance or function, the claim that acquisition depends on the language input setting certain parameter values in the mind, and the possibility that certain teaching methods such as grammatical explanation may after all be beneficial or indeed necessary.

**See also:** Acquisition and teaching; Chomsky; Competence and performance; Grammar; *Langue* and *parole*; Linguistics; Mental lexicon; Pedagogical grammar; Psychology; Second language acquisition theories

### References

Chomsky, N. (1986) *Knowledge of language: its nature, origin and use*, New York: Praeger.
Chomsky, N. (1995) *The minimalist program*, Cambridge, MA: MIT Press.

### Further reading

Cook, V.J. (1989) 'Universal grammar theory and the classroom', *System* 17, 2: 169–81.
Cook, V.J. and Newson, M. (1996) *Chomsky's universal grammar* (2nd edn), Oxford: Blackwell.

White, L. (1989) *Universal grammar and second language acquisition*, Amsterdam: John Benjamins.

VIVIAN COOK

# Untutored language acquisition

The systematic study of language **ACQUISITION** outside formal learning situations such as the classroom got under way in the early 1970s. In contrast to **BILINGUALISM**, where acquisition studies concentrate on the simultaneous or consecutive acquisition of two languages by children, informal language acquisition studies consider the **ADULT LEARNER**. The interest of such learners is that they are already cognitively mature speakers; they can draw on 'the **MOTHER TONGUE**, plus the entire experience of learning it' (Rutherford, 1989: 452). This allows research on language acquisition and use to rid itself of two major sources of interference: the stage of cognitive development of the learner and the effect of 'learned knowledge' on the acquisition process (rather than 'acquired knowledge' in Krashen's terms, see the **MONITOR MODEL**).

Research in this area has been overwhelmingly European, but undertaken from a variety of theoretical viewpoints. As in some other areas of linguistics, formal and functional approaches compete, with the result that most important questions are subject to controversy, as will be shown. There is, however, agreement on what these questions are:

- What is the amount and quality of linguistic knowledge available to the learner at the outset of acquisition (the 'initial state')?
- What is the path that acquisition takes (**DEVELOPMENTAL SEQUENCES**)?
- What pushes the learner along the path (communicative needs, **MOTIVATIONS** and **ATTITUDES**)?
- What shapes the path (**TRANSFER**, universal language constraints, processing complexity, and the type of input)?
- What causes acquisition to stop (**FOSSILISATION**) and why is this end-state subject to so much individual variation?

These questions will be reviewed after a brief historical and methodological description of the major empirical work, and a final paragraph will be devoted to the relevance of the findings to language pedagogy.

## Empirical research

The major empirical work of the 1970s was on the acquisition of **GERMAN** and, to a lesser extent, **ENGLISH** and Dutch. The methodology was almost always **CROSS-SECTIONAL**, with standard tape-recorded socio-linguistic interviews used as the main data collection technique. The Heidelberg project ('HPD': Klein and Dittmar, 1979) and the Wuppertal project ('ZISA': Meisel, Clahsen and Pienemann, 1981) each investigated the acquisition of German by more than forty Italian and Spanish adult immigrant workers. Both projects studied the development of syntax. HPD also analysed lexical development, communicative behaviour and the social correlates of acquisitional success, while ZISA analysed the role of socio-psychological factors explaining differences between learner types. In the so-called 'Harvard project', Schumann (1978) also correlated the (non-)acquisition of basic morpho-syntactic features of English with psychological and social variables in the elaboration of his pidginisation hypothesis. In Hawai'i, Huebner (1983) followed the development of one absolute **BEGINNER** over a period of twelve months. These latter studies are the first-published **LONGITUDINAL ANALYSES** of **SECOND LANGUAGE ACQUISITION**. Using a similar methodology to HPD's, Jansen, Lalleman and Muysken (1981) studied the effect of L1 knowledge on word order in the L2 Dutch of eight Turkish and eight Moroccan learners in their elaboration of the **ALTERNATION HYPOTHESIS**. This study was among the first-published explicitly **CROSS-LINGUISTIC ANALYSES**.

These early projects mostly restricted themselves to (morpho-) syntax, were concerned with the acquisition of one L2, and were only beginning to use a longitudinal methodology. Research in the 1980s went beyond these limitations in at least four ways, typified by:

- the range and type of data collection techniques used;

- the systematic adoption of longitudinal analyses;
- the number and range of L1s and L2s used in cross-linguistic comparisons;
- the range and type of linguistic phenomena investigated.

By far the most comprehensive investigation is the European Science Foundation's (ESF) Second Language Acquisition by Adult Immigrants reported in Perdue, 1993. This was a coordinated, comparative longitudinal study in five European countries (**FRANCE**, England, Germany, The Netherlands, Sweden). It followed the untutored language acquisition of groups of between four and eight immigrant beginners over a period of thirty months, using a shared data collection schedule. Ten different L1–L2 combinations were studied. Areas of investigation were, in language production, the development of syntax and lexicon in association with the means for referring to time and space, and, in native/non-native speaker interaction, the way mutual understanding was or was not achieved. Other projects of a similar functional-pragmatic orientation, and using similar methodologies, studied other linguistic cases of acquisition – that of Italian in particular (Giacalone-Ramat, 1995) – so that the linguistic development of six major European languages was relatively well described by the mid-1990s.

All these projects used recorded data, which were transcribed and stored on a computer. The ESF data form part of the worldwide 'databank' on language acquisition (CHILDES; see MacWhinney, 1991). The availability of these computerised data gave a new impulse to more formal (**UNIVERSAL GRAMMAR** inspired) research on untutored language acquisition. Up to the mid-1980s, generative research had concentrated on cross-sectional studies of university students of L2 English. These researchers were now able to test their theories on longitudinal data from relatively many languages. Thus Hilles (1986), for example, re-analysed the Harvard corpus (Schumann, 1978) to see whether learners with L1 Spanish – a language which allows omission of the grammatical subject – learning English – a language which does not – manage to master this typological difference (or 'parametric difference' in generative terminology) .

## Descriptive generalisations

All this empirical work resulted in a consensus on the descriptive generalisations across the languages studied. Lexical categories (nouns, verbs, adjectives) are acquired first and related to each other by simple juxtaposition. Then closed-class words (pronouns, prepositions, articles) are acquired. Acquisition of the L2 morphology comes last, and is not mastered by all the learners; subject–verb agreement is, for example, non-existent outside the very last stages of acquisition. The development of subordinate clauses (relatives, infinitives, etc.) is also very late. This development can be seen as a progression from the 'language-neutral' to the 'language-specific': whereas all languages have nouns and verbs, not all languages have prepositions or articles, and fewer still share the type of verb morphology shown by English (as learning difficulties with the progressive, for example, amply illustrate). It is this English-specific morphology which is acquired last. It can also be seen as gradually making the relations between items within an utterance, and relations between utterances, more explicit. A beginning learner of English who produces an utterance like 'Father, Rome' (the 'topic–comment' structure of the following paragraph) leaves a lot to be inferred by the interlocutor (Whose father? What is the relationship between father and Rome?). This relationship is made more explicit with the acquisition of determiners and prepositions: 'My father is from Rome'.

The developmental sequences towards individual L2s seem to be highly determined. Indeed, ZISA present their main results as an implicationally related sequence of developmental stages based on the re-ordering of utterance constituents from an underlying canonical word order. No learner was found to re-order the stages, and no learner missed out a stage. Bartning (1997) reviews the major findings and proposes the following general developmental sequence: a 'pre-basic' stage consisting of a restricted lexicon used in rudimentary topic–comment structures, then a 'basic' stage where utterances are structured around a non-finite verb form (the 'Basic Variety', Klein and Perdue, 1987); this is followed by intermediate stages characterised by the gradual development of closed-class words, a variable morphology and the beginnings of subordination, and an advanced stage where the morphology becomes systematic and the range of structures available to the learner increases. Finally, a minority of learners attain a near-native level where sentence-level GRAMMAR is mastered, although discourse organisational procedures and some grammatical intuitions remain non-native. Explanations for this developmental sequence are, however, very controversial, as a brief examination of the major research questions will show.

## Explanatory generalisations

Klein (1986) proposes three sets of factors determining the structure and success of the acquisition process: the initial cognitive/linguistic disposition of the adult speaker (1); exposure to the language (2); the speaker's propensity to acquire (3). These factors interact, and their relative weight changes throughout the acquisition process. All factors are taken into account in functionalist approaches, whereas more formal approaches are content to study the interaction of the learner's cognitive/linguistic disposition (1) and the L2 input (2).

1   The adult learner masters the L1, and this is the most straightforward way of defining the learner's 'initial state'. This incontrovertible fact gives rise, however, to widely differing interpretations. Researchers working within the generative paradigm analyse the similarities and differences between L1 and L2 in terms of 'parametric variation'. The human language faculty may be seen as consisting of universally valid principles and of areas subject to cross-linguistic variation – 'parameters' that have to be 'set' during L1 acquisition. The L1 grammar intervenes differently in L2 development, depending on whether the two languages have similar or different settings for these parameters. In the first case, acquisition is facilitated, whereas in the latter case acquisition is more difficult and more error-prone. This type of latter-day CONTRASTIVE ANALYSIS hypothesis leads, however, to different predictions. Some argue that it is impossible for the adult to recapitulate the 'parameter-setting' process of

L1 acquisition and that, although the universal principles are initially available (the learner's language is a natural language), the typological set of the L2 is inaccessible. Others argue that non-language-specific learning STRATEGIES available to the cognitively developed adult, but not to the child, compensate at least partly for this 'handicap'. A third position is that the language faculty remains intact in the adult learner, who is indeed capable of acquiring the parametric set of the L2, and, therefore, capable in principle of learning the L2 perfectly. The functionalist position is that such a debate, confined as it is to the core grammatical properties of a language, over-simplifies discussion of what is initially available to the learner: functionalists propose that those aspects of communicative competence which are most language-neutral comprise the initial learner hypotheses, in particular the adult speaker's fully transferable knowledge of how information is organised in discourse.

2   The learner needs exposure to the language. This incontrovertible fact is also interpreted differently following the theoretical bent of the researcher. The formalists adopt the computer metaphor of 'input', whereas the functionalists see the learner as essentially engaged in a process of learning by interaction with interlocutors. The generativists see the input as impoverished in many respects, a further mechanism is therefore needed to account for acquisition, namely the language faculty ('Universal Grammar' – UG – in generative terminology). UG provides further mechanisms to compensate for the poverty of the L2 stimulus. These mechanisms are, however, logico-deductive in nature, and say nothing of the actual perceptual mechanisms the learner relies on to analyse the input.

Functionalists working within the framework of the 'competition model' (Bates and MacWhinney, 1989) test the VALIDITY of certain perceptual cues – word order, morphology, semantic relations – in the interpretation of sentences in different languages. Their general hypothesis is that, initially, the learner will rely on the validity of the perceptual cues of the L1. For example, a speaker of English relies heavily on word order in interpreting an English sentence – subject is in initial position, etc. – so that when faced with German input, where initial position is frequently filled by non-subjects, this English learner must revise the word order strategy and pay more attention to morphology.

Other functionalists working in the tradition of linguistic interaction see the interlocutor as crucial in the intake of L2 material, and try therefore to theorise the relation between interaction and acquisition. Native/non-native interaction in fact throws a clearer light than native/native interaction on the **COMMUNICA-TIVE STRATEGIES** (Kasper and Kellerman, 1997) and on the work required to achieve mutual understanding (Bremer *et al.*, 1996) in any conversation. The sequences of turns which develop around communicative breakdowns turn out to be the most revealing of the learner's present difficulties. These analyses have given rise to the notion of 'sequences of potential acquisition' (SPA) (De Pietro, Matthey and Py, 1989): a difficulty occurs which hinders comprehension in some way, the native expert intervenes to clear up the difficulty, then the learner re-uses the native's intervention. We see, therefore, a pedagogical exchange, of a meta-linguistic nature, embedded in a conversation, and this exchange provides corrective feedback for the learner. There are, however, conditions to be met for this to succeed. First, the linguistic item under meta-linguistic scrutiny must be mutually recognised. Second, the learner must be 'ready', i.e. capable of integrating the item into the interim grammar, or, in other words, at the appropriate stage of a developmental sequence. This second condition is an instance of what Klein (1986) calls a 'critical rule': such a rule corresponds to a tentative hypothesis that the learner is presently working on, and which needs positive or negative confirmation. The SPA is a possible source of evidence.

3  The learner's propensity to acquire consists of the whole set of factors inciting the learner to apply his or her linguistic capacities to the L2 input: motivations, attitudes and communicative needs. This very extensive field of investigation will be illustrated by work from the large

empirical research programmes already mentioned (HPD, ZISA, ESF and the Harvard project). These factors may be divided into language-external and language-internal.

Bundles of *language-external* socio-biographic factors, such as the length of stay in the L2 environment, the type and amount of contact with native speakers, general educational level, instrumental or integrative motivation, attitude towards L2 speakers, etc., are correlated with linguistic factors defining the level of proficiency in the L2. HPD found, for example that the quantity of leisure-time contact with native speakers of the L2 was generally a good predictor. Schumann calculated from such factors a measure of socio-psychological distance of a learner from the L2 community which, in the case of his informant, was great, and had the consequence of restricting L2 contact to a necessary minimum, which in turn provoked early fossilisation.

*Language-internal* factors have to do with the way communicative needs may push acquisition along. Whatever the external circumstances of the learner (which can strongly affect the type of **VOCABULARY** acquired), certain communicative functions are recurrent, e.g. the necessity to express determination, or temporal, spatial or causal relations between items (Andersen, 1984: 79, terms these functions 'relational meanings'). There are many such functions and all are not equally important for the learner in communication, thus the order in which such functions receive linguistic expression over time reflects their communicative urgency.

The language-learning achievement of adults in an informal setting has thrown some light on the 'end-state': adult language acquisition not only often halts at a non-native mastery of the language, but the degree of inter-individual variation is great. Functional, grammatical and neurological reasons have been proposed as explanations. The functional approach to these problems holds that acquisition will cease when the communicative needs are met. In this respect, the Basic Variety (Klein and Perdue, 1987) can be seen as a first attempt at comprehensively describing a low level of potential fossilisation. Formal grammatical explanations for fossilisation were implicit in the discussion above of the initial state: if the adult has complete access to the acquisitional potential of the language faculty, then complete success is in principle possible, and grammatically non-relevant factors such as the external factors discussed above are responsible for lack of success. If, on the other hand, such access is no longer available, then ultimate success is in principle no longer possible. The neurological correlate of this latter position is of course the critical age hypothesis.

## Relevance for pedagogy

How does the type of work described here bear on language learning in the classroom? Although such a question is premature, there are two types of remark to be made. First, although the outcome of the process is variable, the path learners take towards a L2 is surprisingly highly determined, and the hypothesis to be entertained is that language pedagogy will be all the more successful – other things being equal – if it closely follows the reported developmental sequences. Pienemann (1985), for example, attempted to teach syntactic structures in a different order from the untutored developmental sequence first uncovered in the ZISA project, and found that pupils did not take into long-term memory pedagogical input for which their 'interim grammars' were not ready. All is, however, not equal, and the role of external (psycho-social) factors in determining the relative success of untutored language acquisition should be stressed. Corder's (1967) caveat for successful acquisition, 'given motivation', is, whatever the learning situation, of the essence.

**See also:** Acquisition and teaching; Adult language learning; Adult learners; Psychology; Research methods; Second language acquisition theories; Sociolinguistics

## References

Andersen, R. (1984) 'The one-to-one principle of interlanguage construction', *Language Learning* 34: 77–95.

Bartning, I. (1997) 'L'apprenant dit avancé et son acquisition d'une langue étrangère' (The so-called advanced learner and foreign language acquisition), *Acquisition et Interaction en Langue Etrangère* 9: 9–50.

Bates, E. and MacWhinney, B. (1989) 'Functionalism and the competition model', in B. MacWhinney and E. Bates (eds), *The cross-linguistic study of sentence processing*, Cambridge: Cambridge University Press.

Bremer, K., Roberts, C., Vasseur, M.-T., Simonot, M. and Broeder, P. (1996) *Achieving understanding. Discourse in inter-cultural encounters*, London: Longman.

Corder, S.P. (1967) 'The significance of learners' errors', *International Review of Applied Linguistics* IX, 2: 162–9.

De Pietro, J.-F., Matthey, M. and Py, B. (1989) 'Acquisition et contrat didactique: les séquences potentiellement acquisitionnelles de la conversation exolingue' (Acquisition and pedagogical contract: sequences of potential acquisition in inter-cultural conversations), in D. Weil and H. Fugier (eds), *Actes du Troisième Colloque Régional de Linguistique*, Strasbourg: The University Press.

Giacalone-Ramat, A. (1995) 'Function and form of modality in learner Italian', in A. Giacalone-Ramat and G. Galèas (eds), *From pragmatics to syntax*, Tübingen: Gunter Narr.

Hilles, S. (1986) 'Interlanguage and the pro-drop parameter', *Second Language Research* 2, 33–52.

Huebner, T. (1983) *Longitudinal analysis of the acquisition of English*, Ann Arbor: Karoma.

Jansen, B., Lalleman, J. and Muysken, P. (1981) 'The alternation hypothesis: acquisition of Dutch word order by Turkish and Moroccan foreign workers', *Language Learning* 31, 2: 315–36.

Kasper, G. and Kellerman, E. (eds) (1997) *Communication strategies*, London: Longman.

Klein, W. (1986) *Second language acquisition*, Cambridge: Cambridge University Press.

Klein, W. and Dittmar, N. (1979) *Developing grammars: the acquisition of German syntax by foreign workers*, Berlin: Springer.

Klein, W. and Perdue, C. (1987) 'The basic variety. Or: Couldn't natural languages be much simpler?', *Second Language Research* 13, 301–47.

MacWhinney, B. (1991) *The CHILDES project: tools for analyzing talk*, Hillsdale, NJ: Lawrence Erlbaum.

Meisel, J., Clahsen, H. and Pienemann, M. (1981)

'On determining developmental stages in natural second language acquisition', *Studies in Second Language Acquisition* 3, 2:109–35.

Perdue, C. (ed.) (1993) *Adult language acquisition: cross-linguistic perspectives*. Vol. 1: *Field methods*; Vol. 2: *The results*, Cambridge: Cambridge University Press.

Pienemann, M. (1985) 'Learnability and syllabus construction', in K. Hyltenstam and M. Pienemann (eds), *Modelling and assessing second language development*, Clevedon: Multilingual Matters.

Rutherford, W. (1989) 'Preemption and learning of L2 grammars', *Studies in Second Language Acquisition* 11: 441–58.

Schumann, J. (1978) *The pidginization process: a model for second language acquisition*, Rowley, MA: Newbury House.

### Further reading

Andersen, R. (ed.) (1990) 'Universals', *Studies in Second Language Acquisition* 12, 2.

Bartning, I. (ed.) (1997) 'Les Apprenants Avancés', *Acquisition et Interaction en Langue Etrangère* 9.

Bialystok, E. and Hakuta, K. (1994) *In other words: the science and psychology of second language acquisition*, New York: Basic Books.

Bremer, K., Roberts, C., Vasseur, M.-T., Simonot, M. and Broeder, P. (1996) *Achieving understanding. Discourse in intercultural encounters*, London: Longman.

Ellis, R. (1994) *The study of second language acquisition*, Oxford: Oxford University Press.

Kellerman, E. and Perdue, C. (eds) (1992) 'Cross-linguistic influence', *Second Language Research* 8, 3.

Perdue, C. (ed.) (1993) *Adult language acquisition: cross-linguistic perspectives*. Vol. 1: *Field methods*; Vol. 2: *The results*, Cambridge: Cambridge University Press.

CLIVE PERDUE

# US Standards for Foreign Language Learning

Standards for foreign language learning establish goals and expectations for learners by defining what students should know and be able to do as a result of language study. Standards designed by foreign language educators serve to raise student achievement levels, to provide a framework for curriculum design, and to improve instruction. They are closely tied to performance **ASSESSMENTS** in contrast to minimal standards set by nations or school systems that are measured by normative or standardised tests. In the United States, foreign language standards were developed simultaneously with standards in other disciplines as part of a federal initiative whose purpose was to influence the quality of instruction and student performance in the various states. In a similar vein, **AUSTRALIA** had developed guidelines (Scarino *et al.*, 1988) in the attempt to achieve consensus on outcomes for students in its diverse states.

The National Standards in Foreign Language Education Project in the United States (1996), a large-scale national effort, had reviewed standards in other nations as part of its development process, and *Standards for Foreign Language Learning: Preparing for the 21st Century* (SFLL) sets forth an agenda that is intentionally visionary and challenging for learners. The standards expand foreign language learning into goal areas beyond separate skills of **LISTENING**, **SPEAKING**, **READING** and **WRITING** and, although the standards build upon concepts embodied in the **COMMUNICATIVE** approach or the **PROFICIENCY MOVEMENT**, they attend to additional learning areas such as cultures, **CONTENT-BASED INSTRUCTION**, **INTERCULTURAL COMPETENCE** and **LANGUAGE FOR SPECIFIC PURPOSES**. No instructional approach is prescribed, yet the standards are founded upon relevant theories of **SECOND LANGUAGE ACQUISITION**, constructivism, and sociocultural/**SOCIOLINGUISTIC COMPETENCE**. The standards assume that '... ALL students are capable of learning other languages given opportunities for quality instruction' (National Standards in Foreign Language Education Project, 1996: 19) and, towards that end, the document advocates early language programmes and extended sequences of study.

The standards document is organised around five goal areas, within which are designated eleven standards:

*Communication* Communicate in languages other than English

- Standard 1.1. Interpersonal: students engage in conversations, provide and obtain information, express feelings and emotions, and exchange opinions.
- Standard 1.2. Interpretative: students understand and **INTERPRET** written and spoken languages on a variety of topics.
- Standard 1.3. Presentational: students present information, concepts and ideas to an audience of listeners or readers on a variety of topics.

*Cultures*  Gain knowledge and understanding of other cultures

- Standard 2.1. Cultural practices: students demonstrate an understanding of the relationship between the practices and perspectives of the cultures studied.
- Standard 2.2. Cultural products: students demonstrate an understanding of the relationship between the products and perspectives of the cultures studied.

*Connections*  Connect with other disciplines and acquire information

- Standard 3.1. Making connections: students reinforce and further their knowledge of other disciplines through the foreign language.
- Standard 3.2. Acquiring information: students acquire information and recognise the distinctive viewpoints that are only available through the foreign language and its cultures.

*Comparisons*  Develop insight into the nature of language and culture

- Standard 4.1. Language comparisons: students demonstrate understanding of the nature of language through comparisons of the language studied and their own.
- Standard 4.2. Cultural comparisons: students demonstrate understanding of the concept of culture through comparisons of the cultures studied and their own.

*Communities*  Participate in multilingual communities at home and around the world

- Standard 5.1. School and community: students use the language both within and beyond the school setting.
- Standard 5.2. Lifelong learning: students show

evidence of becoming lifelong learners by using the language for personal enjoyment and enrichment.

The standards are intended for all languages and for students from kindergarten through to secondary schools, but since their publication, many language organisations in the US have endorsed them as pertaining to undergraduate **HIGHER EDUCATION** as well. The standards are intentionally broad, are designed as 'content' standards (i.e. they address the question 'what should students know and be able to do?') and the determination of 'performance' expectations (that address the question 'how good is good enough?') is left to state and district authorities. These definitions of 'content' and 'performance' were in the federal legislation that supported standards development and reflect the federal and state separation of responsibilities in the US. The goals set forth are ambitious and meant to promote a higher quality of learning. The expectation of achievement is not immediate, and assessments aim at determining progress. In the publication *SFLL* (National Standards in Foreign Language Education Project, 1996), sample progress indicators demonstrate how a single standard would apply to students in US grades 4, 8 and 12 (and language-specific documents include higher education; NSFLE, 1999) as learners gain competencies over time. Learning scenarios describe students in classrooms where a standards orientation has been implemented.

The five goal areas and accompanying standards incorporate several frameworks that differentiate them from more traditional views of language learning. The most significant change involves a focus away from discussion of communication in terms of the four separate skills of listening, speaking, reading and writing. Borrowing from the structure of the discipline of communication, the standards are built on three modes of communication: the interpersonal, the interpretative and the presentational (National Standards in Foreign Language Education Project, 1996: 33). This schema recognises that language learners engage in different cognitive tasks and employ distinct strategies when, for example, they speak in an interpersonal mode or in a presentational one. In the former they negotiate meaning in two-way exchanges, whereas in the latter they must deliver their message to an audience where interaction is not assumed. Likewise, reading of a message in a letter or an e-mail can be clarified through correspondence with the writer, a condition not present for an interpretative task with a fixed text. Establishing standards around modes accommodates research and instructional variables more effectively and assesses student communicative performances more accurately.

Cultural learning is more fully integrated into all the standards, and adapts an **ANTHROPOLOGICAL** approach to foreign-language education whereby students understand the perspectives of the target culture through study of its practices and products. Such an orientation requires greater **PLANNING** for the development of **CULTURAL AWARENESS**, and encourages students to develop higher-level skills of cultural analysis and synthesis through observations, discussions and experiences (Lange, 1999). Furthermore, in the cultural comparisons standard (4.2), cross-cultural competence is sought as students gain insights into their own cultures through the study of another (Fantini, 1999).

The standards for the connections goal refer both to cross-disciplinary learning and **CONTENT-BASED INSTRUCTION**, which Met (1999) ties to constructivist theory and the role that meaning plays in learning. The pragmatic nature of the communities goal links directly to purposeful language learning and to the ultimate reasons today's students pursue language and cultural competencies.

The standards represent student performances or end results. The curricular means to those performances are described as a weave of processes, content areas and delivery systems (National Standards in Foreign Language Education Project, 1996: 2). Learners must develop process abilities in **COMMUNICATIVE STRATEGIES**, learning strategies and critical thinking skills. They must also learn to use the language system, acquire cultural knowledge, and bring their prior subject matter knowledge to the foreign language classroom. Finally, today's learners must be skilled users of technology to communicate and to access culturally authentic **MATERIALS**.

The impact of the US standards or the Australian guidelines has yet to be assessed. It will require years of professional development, changes in **TEACHER EDUCATION** programmes and the design of new performance-based assessments. In the US there is strong consensus around the standards and **CLASSROOM RESEARCH** projects are underway. The use of standards for multiple roles of improving student learning and advocacy for curriculum is a new and untried venture; standards are part of the educational reform movement in the US, and that carries political ramifications. At the same time, they were developed by professionals with strong bases in current theory and research models.

**See also:** Australia; Cross-cultural psychology; History: after 1945; Proficiency movement; Syllabus and curriculum design

## References

Fantini, A.E. (1999) 'Comparisons: toward the development of intercultural competence', in J.K. Phillips (ed.), *Foreign language standards: linking research, theories, and practices*, Lincolnwood, IL: National Textbook Company.

Lange, D.L. (1999) 'Planning for and using the new national culture standards', in J.K. Phillips (ed.), *Foreign language standards: linking research, theories, and practices*, Lincolnwood, IL: National Textbook Company.

Met, M. (1999) 'Making connections', in J.K. Phillips (ed.), *Foreign language standards: linking research, theories, and practices*, Lincolnwood, IL: National Textbook Company.

National Standards in Foreign Language Education Project (1996) *Standards for foreign language learning: preparing for the 21st century*, Lawrence, KS: Allen Press.

National Standards in Foreign Language Education Project (1999) *Standards for foreign language learning in the 21st century*, Lawrence, KS: Allen Press.

Scarino, A., Vale, D., McKay, P. and Clark, J. (1988) *Australian language levels (ALL) guidelines*, Canberra: Curriculum Development Centre.

## Further reading

Phillips, J.K. (ed.) (1997) *Collaborations: meeting new*

*goals, new realities*, Lincolnwood, IL: National Textbook Company.

Phillips, J.K. (ed.) (1999) *Foreign language standards: linking research, theories, and practices*, Lincolnwood, IL: National Textbook Company.

Phillips, J.K. and Draper, J.B. (1994) 'National standards and assessments: what does it mean for the study of second languages in the schools?', in G.K. Crouse (ed.), *Meeting new challenges in the foreign language classroom*, Lincolnwood, IL: National Textbook Company.

JUNE K. PHILLIPS

# Validity

Language test validity can be defined as the extent to which the test is testing what it claims to test. This is very important because it is necessary to be able to generalise from a student's test performance to describe what a student can and cannot do in the target language. For example, if a group of students were to take an **ACHIEVEMENT TEST**, it should be possible to explain their test results in terms of the aspects of the **SYLLABUS** that they have mastered. This can only be done if it is possible to be confident that the test is actually measuring the language abilities or features being described.

The term 'validity' is also traditionally linked to test purpose, for tests are not intrinsically valid. Rather, validity is a property of the context in which the test is used. It also follows that a test is not universally valid, i.e. there are degrees of validity, and tests can be more or less valid for their purposes.

## Information collection

Information about the validity of a test can be gathered in many ways. These include:

- Face validity: how acceptable the test is to the public. This is determined by conducting inter-views with or distributing questionnaires to test users (e.g. students, parents, admissions officers at educational institutions) to find out about their **ATTITUDES** and reactions to, and feelings about, a test they have just taken or looked at.
- Content validity: how representative the items

are of the content the test is expected to include and how adequately the expected content has been sampled. This is usually measured by asking expert judges to assess the content of the test by analysing the items and comparing this analysis either to the test specifications or to the syllabus on which the test is based. The judges may also be provided with a set of pre-determined criteria against which they judge/rate the test.

- Construct validity: how well the test measures the underlying theory upon which it is based. This is usually measured by comparing or correlating: the test-takers' performances on different sub-sections of the test; each sub-test with the whole test; the test-takers' scores with their biodata and psychological characteristics. It is often necessary to use statistical procedures such as factor analysis and multitrait–multimethod analysis in order to investigate the construct validity of a test. However, information about a test's construct validity can also be gathered qualitatively by asking test-takers how they have responded to specific test items. This data can be gathered either concurrently or retrospectively using think-aloud protocols or questionnaires, and it should throw light on what the test is actually testing, i.e. the language knowledge and/or skills that the test-takers actually use in order to complete each test question.
- Criterion-related validity: how well the test correlates with another measure of the students' abilities. This type of validity includes both concurrent validity and predictive validity.

'Concurrent validity' refers to how comparable the test-takers' performance on this test is with their performance on another measure. Typically, the test results are correlated with teachers' ratings of the students, the test-takers' self-assessments, the test-takers' performances on parallel versions of the same test, or their performances on a similar test, i.e. another test that is considered to test the same aspects of language. 'Predictive validity', on the other hand, refers to how well the test predicts the test-takers' future performance, and is measured by comparing (correlating) the test-takers' scores on this test with their scores in final exams or with other measures of their ability, such as teachers' ratings (collected at a future time).

## Recent developments

In recent years, however, there has been some concern that the concept of validity has become diffused and that test developers were in danger of forgetting that test scores are only an abstract representation of the test-takers' language ability. Therefore, a unified view of validity has developed that emphasises the inferences made from test scores and the consequences of those inferences. This unitary view of validity subsumes all validity considerations under construct validity, arguing that it is not possible to make a judgement of the quality of the inferences taken from test scores unless there is evidence of what the scores might mean.

So the way validity is approached has changed. First, researchers are encouraged to validate a test in as many different ways as possible, each method contributing to the picture of a test's validity. It is also clear that validation must be considered from the initial stages of test design onwards. Nor should validation be limited to a single study. Rather, multiple studies of a test are encouraged, across time and context, in order to ensure that the interpretations being made of test scores continue to be justified.

**See also:** Action research; Assessment and testing; Reliability; Research methods

## Further reading

Alderson, J.C., Clapham, C. and Wall, D. (1995) *Language test construction and evaluation*, Cambridge: Cambridge University Press.

Anastasi, A. (1988) *Psychological testing*, New York: Macmillan.

Cronbach, L.J. (1984) *Essentials of psychological testing*, New York: Harper and Row.

Henning, G. (1987) *A guide to language testing*, Boston, MA: Newbury House.

Hubley, A.M. and Zumbo, B.D. (1996) 'A dialectic on validity: where we have been and where we are going', *The Journal of General Psychology* 123. 3: 207–15.

Messick, S.A. (1988) 'The once and future uses of validity: assessing the meaning and consequences of measurement', in H. Wainer and H.I. Braun (eds), *Test validity*, Hillsdale, NJ: Lawrence Erlbaum.

JAYANTI BANERJEE

# van Ek, Jan Ate

b. 1925, Haarlem, The Netherlands

Applied linguist, Professor of English Language

Jan van Ek is best known for his work on English and **APPLIED LINGUISTICS**, and his involvement in the **COUNCIL OF EUROPE MODERN LANGUAGES PROJECTS**. His name is often associated with the **THRESHOLD LEVEL**, initially published for English in 1975 and revised and updated in 1991. The Threshold Level, together with **WAYSTAGE**, the lower level derived from it, constitutes one of the first attempts to formulate **OBJECTIVES** for modern languages in behavioural terms and has had a great influence on curriculum development for modern languages in Europe.

Van Ek studied English Language and Literature at the University of Amsterdam (1949–55). He taught English at secondary level before he was appointed staff member at the English Institute of the University of Groningen, where he obtained his PhD (cum laude) in 1966. He became director of the Institute for Applied Linguistics at the University of Utrecht (1966), but returned to Groningen to become reader (1971) and later full professor of English Language (1980–86).

Van Ek was president of AnéLA, the Association for Applied Linguistics in the Netherlands (1972–74), he was involved in curriculum reform committees for modern languages in the Netherlands, and gave numerous lectures both at home and abroad. He is honorary member of the Dutch Association of Teachers of Modern Languages.

Van Ek became associated with the work of the Council of Europe on Modern Languages in 1971, when he became member of the Modern Languages Project Group. He chaired the project group in a subsequent project. He retired from the University of Groningen in 1986, but continued his studies on objectives for modern languages for the Council of Europe (van Ek, 1986a, 1986b; van Ek and Trim forthcoming). In 1991, a revised and updated version of The Threshold Level (Threshold Level 1990), written together with John **TRIM**, was published to be followed by **VANTAGE LEVEL**, a specification of objectives above Threshold Level, also written with John Trim. Van Ek has been adviser to many authors of Threshold Levels for other languages, including those for Basque and Russian.

## Bibliography

van Ek, J.A. (1966) *Four complementary structures of predication in contemporary British English* (an inventory), Groningen: J.B. Wolters.

van Ek, J.A. (1975) *The Threshold Level*, Strasbourg: Council of Europe; re-issued (1980) as *Threshold Level English*, Oxford: Pergamon Press.

van Ek, J.A. (1986a) *Objectives for foreign language learning, Volume I: Scope*, Strasbourg: Council of Europe.

van Ek, J.A. (1986b) *Objectives for foreign language learning, Volume II: Levels*, Strasbourg: Council of Europe.

van Ek, J.A., Alexander, L.G. and Fitzpatrick, M.A. (1977) *Waystage*, Strasbourg: Council of Europe; re-issued (1980) as *Waystage English*, Oxford: Pergamon Press.

van Ek, J.A. and Robat, N. (1984) *The student's grammar of English*, Oxford: Basil Blackwell.

van Ek, J.A. and Trim, J.L.M. (1991) *Threshold Level 1990*, Strasbourg: Council of Europe.

van Ek, J.A. and Trim, J.L.M. (1991) *Waystage 1990*, Strasbourg: Council of Europe.

van Ek, J.A. and Trim, J.L.M. (forthcoming) *Vantage Level*, Cambridge: Cambridge University Press.

GÉ STOKS

# Vantage Level

Vantage Level is the highest level in a three-level system of specifications of learning **OBJECTIVES** developed within the **COUNCIL OF EUROPE**'s programme for the promotion of language learning in Europe. It has been designed to provide those learners who, having reached **THRESHOLD LEVEL** or a comparable level of communicative foreign language ability, wish to continue their learning to a higher stage with an enriched equipment adequate to deal effectively with the complexities and demands – seen and unforeseen – of daily living. Vantage Level is, in essence, an expansion of Threshold Level, characterised by a relaxation of the constraints still inherent in the circumscribed, though considerable, range of the earlier objective.

**See also:** Assessment and testing; Council of Europe Modern Languages Projects; European Language Portfolio; Threshold Level; Waystage

## Bibliography

van Ek, J.A. and Trim, J.L.M. (forthcoming) *Vantage Level*, Cambridge: Cambridge University Press.

JAN VAN EK

# Video

The serious use of projected images in language teaching can be traced back to the early work done by **CRÉDIF** with courses such as *Voix et Images de France* (1961) and *Bonjour Line* (1963). In their **AUDIOLINGUAL** approach, **TEXTBOOKS** without illustrations were used in conjunction with audio tapes and filmstrips.

Their techniques were influential in the format of Longman's *New Concept English* (1967), where the filmstrip pictures were transmuted into black-and-white line drawings in the textbooks; and were imitated by Oxford University Press in its *Access to English* course (1975 onwards). The CRÉDIF and OUP courses required highly accomplished technical **SKILLS** on the part of the teacher, with a filmstrip projector and a tape recorder to synchronise, as well as handling a class of students in the dark!

Undoubtedly there were teachers in the first two decades after World War Two who also used 8mm and 16mm film for language teaching. However, although plenty of film was produced for general educational purposes, little use was made of it for language teaching. A rare example is the Basic Films production *What's the Time?*, which was made for the **BRITISH COUNCIL** in 1962.

With the general access to TV that came in the 1960s, many television companies produced programmes for schools. These were tied to a timetable, which meant that classes had to be moved into and out of the TV room at set times during the day. A big problem with this for the teacher is the inability to control what goes on. There is no way, for example, of stopping or re-running a live TV programme broadcast in real time, in order to interact with students, check comprehension and so on.

The arrival of the video recorder on a general access commercial basis in the 1970s seemed to be the answer to every language teacher's dreams. Finally there would be dedicated, contextualised video-cassettes which the teacher could control. However, it wasn't so easy. Many institutions invested considerable sums of money in buying equipment:

> It seemed obvious to all of us that learning materials that added a moving visual element to sound could make language more alive and meaningful and could help to bring the real world into the classroom. Alas, a decade later much of this equipment sits collecting dust. It is perhaps used occasionally but more often it is referred to as the school's white elephant.
>
> (Geddes and Sturtridge, 1982: 6)

It really took until the 1980s for video to become a fact of life in language teaching, with many published language courses providing a video cassette or two to go with them, and teachers being familiar enough with the newer, simpler-to-use equipment they were often using in their own homes. This equipment was also considerably cheaper for institutions to buy, and the realisation that a wheeled trolley carrying a TV and video recorder is a far more flexible teaching tool than a specialist video laboratory finally dawned on many educational administrators.

The main concept that the 1980s gave the language teacher was that of 'active viewing'; i.e. the students interact with the video they are being shown, with the video film being used in short sections, rather than sitting the class in front of the screen for forty-five minutes non-stop. Writers such as McGovern (1983), Lavery (1984), Lonergan (1984) and Allen (1985) gave language teachers a wealth of ideas for using video in class. These books described what are now such common techniques as silent viewing to predict language used; **LISTENING** to the soundtrack and predicting character, action, setting, etc., and having it confirmed with viewing; action-predict techniques, where viewers watch part of a story, then predict the next piece of action; and much more. The possibility of using video cameras in language teaching has always been fraught with difficulties. The 1970s idea of specialised studios was intimidating and complicated. The 1980s brought more portable cameras, but ones which were still too heavy for long periods of use without a tripod, especially by younger learners, and then the 1990s brought 'handycam' machines which are cheap, light and simple to operate. This has opened up the possibility of classroom-based filming to all language teachers. Lavery (1984: 27–40) and Allen (1985: 75–81) touched on this with a few examples, but it took Cooper *et al.* (1991: 35–92) to give a systematic series of ideas for teachers to develop.

Since the 1990s, language teachers have much published video material at their disposal, either directly associated with a **TEXTBOOK** or for general use, as well as material for specific purposes (e.g. business), and cheap and easy-to-operate equipment which is readily available and affordable for many educational institutions.

**See also:** Board drawing; Internet; Materials and media; Media centres; Visual aids

## References

Allen, M. (1985) *Teaching English with video*, Harlow: Longman.

Cooper, R., Lavery, M. and Rinvolucri, M. (1991) *Video*, Oxford: Oxford University Press.

Geddes, M. and Sturtridge, G. (eds) (1982) *Video in the language classroom*, London: Heinemann.

Lavery, M. (1984) *Active viewing plus*, Oxford: Modern English Publications.

Lonergan, J. (1984) *Video in language teaching*, Cambridge: Cambridge University Press.

McGovern, J. (ed.) (1983) *Video applications in English language teaching*, Oxford: Pergamon Press/British Council.

## Further reading

Stempleski, S. and Tomalin, B. (1990) *Video in action*, Hemel Hempstead: Prentice-Hall International.

DAVID A. HILL

# Viëtor, Wilhelm

b. 25 December 1850, Kleeberg, Germany; d. 22 December 1918, Marburg

Professor of English Philology at the University of Marburg

Viëtor devoted his academic work mostly to phonetics. Previous to his university career, he was a teacher at a *Realgymnasium* in Silesia. He became interested in foreign language teaching there, but also in Britain during a stay as *Lektor* of German at the University College in Liverpool. His pamphlet *Der Sprachunterricht muß umkehren!* (Language teaching must start afresh) (1882), written during a holiday in Wales, became the opening trumpet call of the so-called **REFORM MOVEMENT**. For fear of the expected reactions in the academic world, he used as a pseudonym *Quousque tandem [abutere, Catilina, patientia nostra?]*, i.e.

the first words of Cicero's challenge against Catilina in front of the Senate. He declared himself as the author in the second edition in 1886.

In the nineteenth century, the teaching of (mostly) **FRENCH** and (a little) **ENGLISH** followed the ways of teaching Latin. The so-called **GRAMMAR–TRANSLATION METHOD** used semantically disconnected sentences, frequently taken from literature, for grammatical analysis and **TRANSLATION**. Towards the end of the century the foundation and growth of scientific phonetics, besides the general failure of the grammar–translation method, caused a demand for a Reform Movement which, like phonetics, arose simultaneously in Britain (Henry **SWEET**), Denmark (Otto **JESPERSEN**), **FRANCE** (Paul Édouard Passy, 1859–1940) and Germany (besides Viëtor, Hermann Klinghardt, 1847–1926).

Viëtor maintained that oral language had priority over the written one and that it had to be used in order to be learnt. He limited the value of **GRAMMAR** teaching to functional aspects and demanded that rules be found inductively from observation of speech. He disputed the value of translation for the learning process, looking at it as a special skill that the ordinary school was not concerned with. He encouraged oral methods of teaching, including the **MONOLINGUAL** explanation of word meanings. The primary aim of teaching was for him oral communication. All this included a sharp criticism, not only of conventional teaching habits but also of the knowledge of the average foreign language teacher who could, as a rule, speak English or French neither fluently nor phonetically correctly.

Viëtor's slim volume is written in a challenging style. He does not give arguments but postulates. Yet he obviously takes sides in some scientific controversies. For him, language is something sensual and empirical, a psychological process with communicative effects. It is not something logical and ideal, a system of formal rules. This issue between the sensualist and the rationalist approach to language created a long controversy among pedagogues. Viëtor's linguistic ideas also predetermined certain psychological ones. For him the human mind was dominated by experience and by associations which come from them, not by a general logical faculty which could be trained by any systematically organised subject. Again this psychological issue between a rationalist and an empirical approach to learning foreshadowed debates to come.

In the field of foreign language teaching, Viëtor initiated the rivalry between the traditional German humanistic *Gymnasien*, cultivating Greek and Latin, and new *Realschulen*, cultivating French and English. This meant a rivalry between the aims of a classical and general education in the liberal arts and more down-to-earth knowledge which even included practical skills. Besides such repercussions on the German pedagogical scene, Viëtor's short publication laid the ground for modern foreign language teaching in many European countries. If a teacher even today taught their class strictly according to Viëtor's rules, they would not be altogether wrong or outdated.

### Further reading

Howatt, A.P.R. (1984) *A history of English language teaching*, Oxford: Oxford University Press.
Hüllen, W. (1981) 'Dauer und Wechsel in 100 Jahren Fremdsprachenunterricht (Permanence and change in 100 years of foreign language teaching)', in F.-J. Zapp, A. Raasch and W. Hüllen (eds), *Kommunikation in Europa. Probleme der Fremdsprachendidaktik in Geschichte und Gegenwart (Communication in Europe. Issues of foreign language teaching methodology in past and present)*, Frankfurt: Diesterweg.

WERNER HÜLLEN

# Visual aids

Visual aids is a term used to cover an extremely flexible range of materials which can be tailored by the teacher to fit the exact requirements of a particular group of learners at a particular time in their development. They comprise any kind of visual classroom input which does not involve moving pictures (e.g. **VIDEO**).

The importance of the visual in language teaching was noted as long ago as 1658 in **COMENIUS**'s last book on language teaching, *Orbis Sensualium Pictis*. Visual aids probably became an institutionalised part of language teaching in the late nineteenth and early twentieth centuries. The **DIRECT METHOD** advocates that **VOCABULARY** be introduced through demonstration, objects and pictures. In the period 1920–60 the oral approach and situational language teaching both advocated that the teacher used **BOARD DRAWING** and **FLASH-CARDS** to make up for the distinct lack of illustrations in the **TEXTBOOKS** (e.g. Eckersley, 1955). The introduction of **AUDIO-VISUAL** courses by CRÉDIF in the early 1960s, where filmstrips and tapes were combined, led directly to the first fully illustrated language teaching books (e.g. Alexander, 1967). From then on illustration became an essential element of textbooks, increasing through the 'communicative revolution', and moving from the black-and-white line drawings of the 1960s and 1970s into the lavish productions with colour photographs which are today's basic products.

The general feeling of teachers is that, given the lack of reality involved in typical, textbook-based, general language learning, anything the teacher can do to bring the outside world into the classroom is likely to have a positive effect. To that end video, with its ability to present real-life contextualised language situations, is one of the best tools, audio tapes of others talking help, and written **INTERNET** exchanges such as those possible through so-called 'learning circles' are wonderful in that channel. The problem with the first two – especially pre-recorded, commercially-produced video and audio tapes, is that they are limited by what the author/tapemaker saw fit to put on them, and the activities invented to go with them in the textbook, workbook or by the teacher. Internet exchanges are limited by the channel and the people one has contact with. Visual aids, on the other hand, are often easy to produce (e.g. stick-figure board-drawing), easy to come by (e.g. magazine photographs), or readily available in teachers' rooms (e.g. wall pictures). In addition to outside aids such as these, there is often a great deal of excellent visual material which has now become an essential feature of basic coursebooks, and which is frequently underexploited in the coursebook itself or the accompanying teacher's book.

There are a number of types of visual aid which are open to teacher use, the most common of which are flashcards, board drawing, **OVERHEAD PROJECTORS** and wall pictures. Equally, there are a number of less-frequently encountered but valuable visual aids available such as flannelgraphs, plasti-graphs and magnetic boards. Each of them has its own particular attributes which the teacher needs to understand to be able to exploit them fully in the classroom. For example, there will be occasions when a board/OHP drawing – often a sponta-neous reaction to a classroom event – will be appropriate; on the other hand, there will be times when a carefully selected and prepared set of mounted, colour magazine photographs will be ideal. The competent language teacher needs to be able to handle all such aids in order to motivate students, give context to and offer a tangible point of reference for learning.

As with any kind of supplementary materials in language teaching, the teacher needs to build up a solid repertoire of behaviours to exploit visuals to maximum effect. The work of Wright (1984/1993) has shown the language teaching world that anyone can learn how to handle board/OHP drawing, and utilise it to great effect, whether with spontaneous classroom drawings to illustrate ob-jects or situations which occur in the lesson, pre-produced sets of drawings on cards, OHP trans-parencies for a game or discussion, or a planned set of drawings which are then reproduced in real time on the board/OHP in class to introduce (for example) a particular tense. Photographic flash-cards, with pictures taken from magazines, calen-dars and so on, require a little more preparation; the finding of suitable pictures to make into sets for classroom use and then mounting them on card can be a long-term occupation, but worth every hour of time spent given the resulting classwork. As with any other teaching apparatus, visual aids such as magnetboards require a little bit of practice beforehand to work out how to use them and to realise their full potential.

A key concept which teachers using any form of visual aid need to understand is the difference between talking *about* pictures and talking *through* pictures (thoroughly discussed by Corder, 1966). A simple example will clarify this. If the teacher holds up a picture of someone drinking a cup of tea, asks the class 'What did he do yesterday?' and gets the reply 'He drank a cup of tea', then the teacher and

the students are talking *about* the picture. This may be an extremely valuable means of checking **ACQUISITION** and ability to produce the formal aspects of the language system – tenses and vocabulary, for example. If, on the other hand, the teacher gives a set of action pictures to groups of four students, who then take it in turns to ask about the actions shown in relation to their own lives, we have a very different result. For example, when shown a picture of someone drinking tea, Student A begins by asking Student B a question: 'When did you last drink a cup of tea?'; and Student B replies truthfully: 'This morning at breakfast.' The other students then ask further questions related to this ('Who made the tea?', 'What kind of tea was it?' etc.), to which Student B replies truthfully. Here, the students are talking *through* the pictures. It is a very different activity, and is a moderately controlled practice activity where the students are involved in talking about their own realities. (For a full description of this activity, see Hill, 1990: 30.)

**See also:** Flashcard; Internet; Materials and media; Media centres; Video

## References

Alexander, L.G. (1967) *First things first*, Harlow: Longman.

Corder, S.P. (1966) *The visual element in language teaching*, Harlow: Longman.

Eckersley, C.E. (1955) *Essential English for foreign students*, Harlow: Longman.

Hill, D.A. (1990) *Visual impact*, Harlow: Longman.

Wright, A. (1984/1993) *1000+ pictures for teachers to copy*, Harlow: Addison Wesley Longman.

## Further reading

Bowen, B.M. (1982) *Look here! Visual aids in language teaching*, London: Macmillan.

Holden, S. (ed.) (1978) *Visual aids for classroom interaction*, Oxford: Modern English Publications.

McAlpin, J. (1980) *The magazine picture library*, London: George Allen and Unwin.

Wright, A. (1976) *Visual materials for the language teacher*, Harlow: Longman.

Wright, A. (1989) *Pictures for language learning*, Cambridge: Cambridge University Press.

Wright, A. and Haleem, S. (1991) *Visuals for the language classroom*, Harlow: Longman.

DAVID A. HILL

# Vocabulary

There are three major questions to consider when looking at the place of vocabulary in a language course. What vocabulary should be learned and in what order? What needs to be learned about particular words? How should vocabulary be learned?

## What vocabulary should be learned?

Corpus-based studies of vocabulary frequency have a very striking message for vocabulary learning. In terms of their frequency of occurrence in the language, all words are not created equal. A relatively small number of different words accounts for a very large proportion of the running words in written text or spoken language. The ten most frequent words account for 25 per cent of the words on any page and in any conversation. The 100 most frequent words account for 50 per cent, the 1,000 most frequent words for around 75 per cent, and the 2,000 most frequent for around 80–90 per cent. These 2,000 most frequent words, the high-frequency words, are useful no matter what use is made of the language, and they are essential for normal language use. They are the essential core of any language programme. Lists of these words for **ENGLISH** can be found in West (1953), Hindmarsh (1980), and the *Longman Dictionary of Contemporary English* (1995).

If learners intend to go on to academic study, their next vocabulary goal after the high-frequency words is the academic vocabulary (Nation, 1990; Coxhead, 1998). The most recent academic vocabulary list (Coxhead, 1998) contains 570 word families and covers between 8.5 per cent and 10 per cent of the running words in most kinds of academic text. It is useful for learners across a wide range of academic subject areas. It includes words like *analyse, data, function* and *legal*. For learners with

very special purposes, such as studying mathematics or working with computers, there is usually a technical vocabulary that they need to learn.

The remaining vocabulary is comprised of the low-frequency words of the language. There are thousands of these. For example, *Webster's Third New International Dictionary* (1961), the largest non-historical dictionary of English, contains 267,000 entries which consist of approximately 114,000 word families including proper words. A word family is a base word – e.g. *learn* – and its closely related inflected and derived forms – *learns, learned, learnt, learning, learner, learnable* (Bauer and Nation, 1993).

The high-frequency words of the language need to be learned first. They deserve a lot of attention and, because they are a relatively small group of words, they are a feasible goal for language learners. Learners will also get a good return for their learning effort. The low-frequency words do not deserve classroom time because there are so many of them and they are not frequent. However, learners need to learn them. Teachers can help learners with them by training them to use the strategies of guessing from context, direct learning, using word parts, and dictionary use.

## What needs to be learned about words?

There are many things to know about each word, and the learning of particular words is a long-term cumulative process. This process involves the strengthening and enriching of knowledge about the form, meaning and use of each word. This knowledge is both receptive (the knowledge needed for **LISTENING** and **READING**) and productive (**SPEAKING** and **WRITING**). Knowing the form of a word involves knowing its **PRONUNCIATION**, its spelling, and, if it is a complex or compound word, its word parts. Knowing the meaning of a word involves knowing the concept that lies behind the various uses of the word, the particular meanings it has in certain contexts, and its various associations, such as opposites, synonyms and members of the same lexical set. Knowing the use of a word involves knowing its **GRAMMAR**, its typical collocations (Sinclair, 1991), and the constraints on its use, such as German versus Austrian use for German, or French versus Canadian for French, formal and colloquial use, and so on. Words differ in the degree to which these various aspects are predictable from learners' knowledge of their first language, and from the regular patterns in the second language.

## How can vocabulary be learned?

Vocabulary can be learned incidentally or intentionally. Intentional learning is faster and more sure, but it is important to see the various ways of learning vocabulary as complementing each other. These include learning through input, learning through output, direct teaching and learning, and fluency development. The learning from these four strands overlaps, but each provides opportunities for learning and aspects of knowledge that are not easily provided in the other strands.

In order to learn vocabulary through meaning-focused listening and reading, learners need to know at least 95 per cent of the running words already. For many learners this will mean using simplified material. Fortunately, there are hundreds of graded readers at various levels (Day and Bamford, 1998) that can be used for extensive reading. Research on guessing words from context shows that small amounts of vocabulary learning can occur in this way. If learners read a lot, then these small amounts can become larger amounts (Nagy, Herman and Anderson, 1985). Research on vocabulary learning through listening to stories (Elley, 1989) shows that vocabulary learning is increased if the teacher draws the learners' attention to them without interrupting the story. Glossing words in written text also increases learning. The strategy of inferring words from context is the most important of all the vocabulary learning **STRATEGIES** and it is worth spending time training learners in its use. It is possible to design speaking and writing tasks so that learners pick up vocabulary as they do the task (Joe, Nation and Newton, 1996). It is also important to make sure that the high-frequency vocabulary and academic vocabulary are moved from receptive use to productive use.

Although teachers often feel that vocabulary needs to be learned in context, there is considerable research which shows that the direct study of words using word cards with translations is a very

effective way of quickly expanding vocabulary knowledge. Such learning needs to be supplemented by other strands of learning. Learners need to be trained in direct learning. This training should involve use of the keyword technique (Pressley, Levin and McDaniel, 1987), information about spacing repetitions, avoiding lexical sets (Tinkham, 1997), and the use of word part analysis. Learners can also benefit from training in dictionary use. When teachers deal directly with words, they need to decide if they should provide rich instruction (Graves, 1987) or deal with the word quickly. Rich instruction involves spending time on the word, focusing on its form, meaning and use, and involving learners in thoughtfully processing the word. A word deserves rich instruction if it is a high-frequency word and if the goal of the lesson is vocabulary learning. Intensive reading can provide useful opportunities for rich instruction.

Learners not only need to know vocabulary, they need to become fluent in its use, either receptively or receptively and productively. Fluency development activities should involve meaning-focused listening, speaking, reading and writing. They should involve no unknown vocabulary, and they should encourage learners to process the language faster then their normal speed.

Vocabulary learning can be maximised by giving careful consideration to what vocabulary to focus on, and how to focus on it.

**See also:** Dictionaries; Lexicography and lexicology; Linguistics; Mental lexicon; Pronunciation teaching; Silent Way; Speaking

## References

Bauer, L. and Nation, I.S.P. (1993) 'Word families', *International Journal of Lexicography* 6, 4: 253–79.
Coxhead, A. (1998) *An academic word list*, LALS occasional publication, Victoria University of Wellington, New Zealand.
Day, R.R. and Bamford, J. (1998) *Extensive reading in the second language classroom*, Cambridge: Cambridge University Press.
Elley, W.B. (1989) 'Vocabulary acquisition from listening to stories', *Reading Research Quarterly* 24, 2: 174–87.
Graves, M.F. (1987) 'The roles of instruction in

fostering vocabulary development', in M.G. McKeown and M.E. Curtis (eds), *The nature of vocabulary acquisition*, Hillsdale, NJ: Lawrence Erlbaum.

Hindmarsh, R. (1980) *Cambridge English lexicon*, Cambridge: Cambridge University Press.

Joe, A., Nation, P. and Newton, J. (1996) 'Speaking activities and vocabulary learning', *English Teaching Forum* 34, 1: 2–7.

Nagy, W.E., Herman, P. and Anderson, R.C. (1985) 'Learning words from context', *Reading Research Quarterly* 20: 233–53.

Nation, I.S.P. (1990) *Teaching and learning vocabulary*, New York: Newbury House.

Pressley, M., Levin, J.R. and McDaniel, M.A. (1987) 'Remembering versus inferring what a word means: mnemonic and contextual approaches', in M.G. McKeown and M.E. Curtis (eds), (1987) *The nature of vocabulary acquisition*, Hillsdale, NJ: Lawrence Erlbaum.

Sinclair, J. (1991) *Corpus, concordance, collocation*, Oxford: Oxford University Press.

Tinkham, T. (1997) 'The effects of semantic and thematic clustering on the learning of second language vocabulary', *Second Language Research* 13, 2: 138–63.

West, M. (1953) *A general service list of English words*, London: Longman, Green and Co.

**Further reading**

Coady, J. and Huckin, T. (eds) (1997) *Second language vocabulary acquisition*, Cambridge: Cambridge University Press.

McKeown, M.G. and Curtis, M.E. (eds) (1987) *The nature of vocabulary acquisition*, Hillsdale, NJ: Lawrence Erlbaum.

Schmitt, N. and McCarthy, M. (eds) (1997) *Vocabulary: description, acquisition and pedagogy*, Cambridge: Cambridge University Press.

I.S.P. NATION

# Vocational education and training

Situated between language learning for general purposes in schools and **LANGUAGES FOR SPECIFIC PURPOSES** in industry, language learning in vocational education and training (VET) covers the contribution languages make to the professional development and personal growth of (young) adults. It sees language learning as an important phase of a lifelong educational process and, at the same time, introduces work-related tasks which arise from the challenges of vocational qualification processes.

Language learning in VET is informed by recent changes in the structure of work, in new social and political developments and new self-concepts of young people. These challenges have changed attitudes and led to new methods of language learning which stress hands-on, project-based, cooperative forms of learning. This holistic approach tries to combine learners' needs and the demands of work, it leads to new delivery modes such as **DISTANCE LEARNING** and **CALL**, and it encourages flexible learning formats and different **LEARNING STYLES**.

Language learning in VET has long been seen as directed towards routine demands which trainees experience in their immediate work context, such as formulaic business letters or lists of lexical items in engineering. It is now increasingly seen as an important contribution to the professional growth of employees in which the communication aspects of work and life are linked to more specialised job-specific knowledge. Communicative competence is thus perceived as a key qualification which is central to the job prospects of learners.

The sometimes precarious balance between educational aspects (expressed in the wants of learners) and training aspects (expressed in the needs of industry) is reflected in the ways in which different countries set their priorities. In immigration societies such as the **USA** or **AUSTRALIA**, vocational language learning is predominantly regarded as a step into a new job market, with the language of work learned as a second language. In Europe, what is often called vocationally-oriented language learning (VOLL) is primarily a means to increase learners' job qualifications through competence in one or more foreign language.

## Language learning in VET in a world of economic and social change

Vocational language learning has to be discussed in the context of the far-reaching economic, social and cultural changes at the end of the twentieth century. Of particular importance in our context are the:

- **INTERNATIONALISATION** of economic activities;
- importance of information processes and information technology;
- changing character of work with its emphasis on teamwork and key qualifications;
- increasing number of internationally mobile workers;
- enlarged role of education in a world of lifelong learning;
- changing self-concepts of young people with new attitudes to work.

These new parameters have a direct influence on VET and the role and forms of language learning in a vocational context. The most important consequence is that the requirements of industry and the interests of employees are no longer opposed: the needs of industry and the wants of workers, professional qualification and personal growth complement each other. The common interest is to create a workforce consisting of people who can deal with new challenges. That is why communication processes are more and more regarded as central to modern work – and life. The consequences this has for language learning depend to a large extent on the role vocational education and training play in different countries.

## Vocational language learning in the USA and in Australia

The main function of vocational language learning in immigration countries such as the USA and Australia is to provide access to employment in the new country. In the USA, workplace literacy programmes used to offer short, intensive, immediately job-related language skills, often at beginners' level, designed to help recent immigrants to gain entry into the job market. These low-budget, low-skill programmes were aimed at easing the way for immigrants into mostly basic manufacturing

jobs. This approach has been criticised by Elsa Auerbach (Auerbach, 1992) as restricting learners to only those minimal language skills immediately relevant for their present menial jobs. Instead, she advocated linking workplace programmes to general literacy skills and education for citizenship, in order to integrate the immediate communication demands at work into the development of personal and social skills.

A second reason for opening up literacy programmes to wider aims came from the economic, technological and organisational changes which affected every workplace. Cooperative forms of production, new forms of decision-making, and multiple roles, even on the shopfloor, created new demands on the communicative competence of employees at all levels of industry. The teaching of skills required in the new high-performance workplace brought Vocational English as a Second Language (VESL) back into education: rather than merely providing immigrants with access to basic jobs, work-related language skills are now discussed in the wider context of educating the whole workforce for high power performances.

Australia, another major immigration country, provides the example of a society which from the outset saw workplace literacy in social and cultural terms. Every immigrant earned the right to **ENGLISH** language tuition financed by the government, which in turn stressed the dual emphasis of language provision: to help immigrants to find jobs they are qualified for, and to offer them access to the culture of their new country. The National Centre for English Language Teaching and Research (NCELTR) at Macquarie University in Sydney led the field in needs analysis and the development of teaching materials.

## Different traditions in European countries

Central and Northern European countries have long regarded vocational education as part of formal education, offering highly regulated, long-term training contracts where educational aspects are taught in vocational colleges and practical aspects are trained in companies. This 'dual system' seemed to offer a balance between education and training, between the interests of the individual and of society on the one hand and the interests of the companies on the other. Language learning in the dual system covered a wide range of options from a continuation of school-based learning to languages for special purposes.

The second tradition, perhaps best expressed in the UK, tended to see vocational training less as a responsibility of the state, but more that of the individual seeking entry into the job market. This approach led to short, modular courses immediately related to the needs of industry, which could react quickly to changes in the job market.

## European unification and its consequences for vocational language learning

Since its foundation in 1949, the common European cultural heritage has been the basis for the cultural work of the Council of Europe. Education for peace and democracy has always meant providing chances for citizens of different countries to meet and exchange views in the languages of their neighbours. Language learning in this view was no longer the privilege of an elite, but a basic social and political interest and instrument for everybody. After its early emphasis on general language ability, the work of the **COUNCIL OF EUROPE MODERN LANGUAGES PROJECT** soon included the politically sensitive group of young adults in vocational education and industrial training. These young people were seen as an underprivileged group which had often dropped out of language learning in general education. Their motivation for meaningful vocational language learning arose out of the new challenges of training and work. The language work of the Council of Europe consequently emphasised the dual aspect of VOLL as a combination of work-related language skills with personal growth and social awareness (Egloff and Fitzpatrick, 1997: 227).

In France and Germany, this political dimension of language learning was institutionalised in the vocational youth exchange programmes of the *Franco–German Youth Office*, a powerful instrument of intercultural cooperation between the two countries. The language of the neighbouring country has increasingly been learnt in an environment of joint action-oriented, work-related projects.

Vocational education and training soon became a top priority of the European Union (EU) in Brussels, which was expressed in the setting up of the European Centre for the Development of Vocational Training (CEDEFOP) in Thessaloniki, Greece. Research and development in youth exchange projects with a foreign language component were instituted on a large scale in the LEONARDO Programme, an ambitious long-term project of the fifteen EU member states and their Eastern European neighbours, informed by the overall vision of the future European society as a 'Learning Society' (European Commission, 1995). Foreign language learning and intercultural learning are again seen in both economic and political terms.

## Key issues in vocational language learning

A decisive factor for the present condition of language learning in VET is the fundamental change in foreign language teaching methodology from the communicative approach to pragmatist and constructivist views. They are expressed in the attempt to base foreign language learning on the experience and the interest of learners and to enable them gradually to take charge of their own learning through making learning:

- learner-centred
- content-based
- project-oriented
- reflective
- holistic
- intercultural.

Language learners start from their experience, choose methods and strategies together with their co-learners, involve teachers mainly as consultants, and take on responsibility for their own learning. They become aware of their learning strategies, and begin to evaluate their own progress. This vision of self-directed learners, which reflects recent developments in learning psychology, has fundamental implications for language learning in vocational education.

Learners, employers and the language teaching industry have identified as key issues in language learning in VET **NEEDS ANALYSIS**, the question of contents, intercultural learning, delivery modes,

**EVALUATION** and accreditation, and last but not least the training of trainers.

### Needs analysis

All stakeholders in VOLL agree on the necessity of data as a solid basis for developing foreign language courses in a vocational context. But, as Maggie Jo St John points out for the field of Business English, data are hard to come by, because most companies still consider information on their operations as confidential. 'Needs analysis is about understanding learners and also about understanding the communication events which the learners will participate in' (St John, 1996: 6). And even if a profile of the language skills needed at work has been established, the question remains how to prioritise and package them. Since the early 1990s, needs analysis has often been integrated into the more comprehensive framework of linguistic auditing, which offers methods for the systematic analysis of the entire communication needs and potentials within corporations (Reeves and Wright, 1996).

### Content-based language learning

The most striking advantage VOLL has compared to many other forms of language learning is its face **VALIDITY**. In a vocational setting, language tasks arise from the immediate work context, are immediately relevant for the completion of work, and engage the learners in meaningful activities. The demands of training and work thus constantly engage the learners in 'focused communication tasks' (Ellis, 1993) which lend themselves to a hands-on, team-oriented approach. Learners can see and experience the relevance of what they are learning.

Analyses of work-related language use have demonstrated that the domain extends far beyond its previous concentration on lexis, terminology and syntax. Genre research has so far been mainly based on written texts, because companies are still reluctant to disclose data on oral language use such as in meetings. What we know has established the importance of larger units such as moves and frames which distinguish the language of business and technology.

There is a shift from concentrating on language

systems to placing vocational language into the wider context of communication patterns which are often governed by social and cultural aspects such as power relationships, formality, strategies and negotiation.

### Intercultural learning

The importance of negotiations within teams as well as between businesses and clients has stressed the aspect of social and cultural relations in training and work contexts. It is no longer enough to know what to say, but it is more and more necessary to put linguistically correct utterances into a culturally appropriate context. Multicultural dimensions influence work performance from teamwork within small and medium-sized enterprises (SME) to customer orientation in a multinational company.

Multiculturality at a first level refers to work relations within companies. It concerns what is often called 'the culture of the workplace', the complex system of mostly unwritten rules which govern social interaction at work. At a second level it describes 'corporate culture', the ethos or mission that large companies try to foster as a unifying bond for their diverse workforce. It is only at a third level that interculturality refers to the sphere of multinational work contacts.

### Delivery modes

As new methods of transmitting information have changed the communication systems within industry, they have opened up new avenues for learning in a work context. The trend is toward flexible learning units on a modular basis, accessible from various entry points at or away from work. Forms of self-study, computer forums, **TANDEM LEARNING** partnerships and intensive contact sessions constitute multiple patterns which no longer demand class attendance. These forms of learning need self-directed learners who understand their learning styles and who can pace and monitor their own progress. The consequence for vocational language learning is to stress cognitive processing, procedural knowledge, **LANGUAGE AWARENESS** and transfer abilities.

## Evaluation and accreditation

Language learning in vocational education faces the challenge of providing data for assessing progress of linguistic performance in many specialist vocational domains. Work in this field explores means of process-oriented evaluation in an occupational context (Oscarsson, 1997: 55–65). The work of the *National Council of Vocational Qualifications* in the UK is one of the foremost attempts to set up standards in a national context.

The transnational dimension of assessment has informed the recent work within the Council of Europe in its attempt to develop a **COMMON EUROPEAN FRAMEWORK** for credits and credit transfer (Council of Europe, 1996). Rather than erecting a superstructure on top of different national (and often regional) systems, it suggests a graded model accommodating national qualifications, but making it possible to compare their respective standards. This process-oriented form of evaluation finds its expression in the portfolio approach, e.g. the **EUROPEAN LANGUAGE PORTFOLIO**. Learners can document their progress by collecting evidence of their language learning, which gives employers the chance to recognise the language profile of prospective employees.

## Training the (language) trainers

The stress is on trainers here, as opposed to teachers, indicating the growing feeling within the profession of occupying a space of their own in the language teaching community. Rather than seeing themselves as teachers, people working in language teaching in vocational education and training are becoming aware of their special contribution, the double mission of contributing to the educational formative process of their learners and of equipping them with tools for their professional career.

Vocational language trainers do not necessarily need a double qualification in language teaching and an industrial subject. What they need is openness to the world of work, and curiosity about how things work in industry, commerce and administration, which in many cases might imply the readiness to modify their world views. They need this openness to accept their new role as facilitators, acknowledging and making use of the competence their learners have in their specific fields of work. Language learning in a vocational context thus becomes a collaborative effort in which the exchange of information between trainer and learners provides the basis for authentic communication processes. The issue of trainer training for language learning in VET highlights the unique contribution it makes to language teaching. It offers chances for a new relationship between trainers and learners, for collaborative and self-directed learning, and for combining personal growth and professional qualification in the learning process.

**See also:** Adult learners; Autonomy and autonomous learners; Content-based instruction; Global education; *Handlungsorientierter Unterricht*; Intercultural training; Task-based teaching and assessment

## References

Auerbach, E.R. (1992) *Making meaning, making change: participatory curriculum development for adult ESL literacy*, McHenry, IL and Washington, DC: Delta Systems and Center for Applied Linguistics.

Council of Europe (1996) *Modern languages: learning, teaching, assessment. A Common European Framework of Reference*, Strasbourg: Council of Europe.

Egloff, G. and Fitzpatrick, A. (1997) 'Vocationally oriented language learning (VOLL)', *Language Teaching* 30, 4: 227–31.

Ellis, R. (1993) 'Focused communication tasks and second language acquisition', *ELT Journal* 47, 3: 203–10.

European Commission (1995) *White paper on education and training – teaching and learning – towards the learning society*, Brussels: European Commission.

Oscarsson, M. (1997) 'Conditions for assessment in vocationally oriented language learning', in G. Egloff and A. Fitzpatrick (eds), *Languages for work and life: the Council of Europe and vocationally oriented language learning*, Strasbourg: Council of Europe.

Reeves, N. and Wright, C. (1996) *Linguistic auditing: a guide to identifying foreign language communication needs in corporations*, Clevedon: Multilingual Matters.

St John, M.J. (1996) 'Business is booming: business English in the 1990s', *English for Specific Purposes* 15, 1: 3–18.

## Further reading

Dudley-Evans, T. and St John, M.J. (1998) *Developments in English for specific purposes. A multidisciplinary approach*, Cambridge: Cambridge University Press.

Egloff, G. and Fitzpatrick, A. (eds) (1997) *Languages for work and life: the Council of Europe and vocationally oriented language learning*, Strasbourg: Council of Europe.

Kramsch, C. (1993) *Context and culture in language teaching*, Oxford: Oxford University Press.

Legutke, M. and Thomas, H. (1991) *Process and experience in the language classroom*, London and New York: Longman.

Nunan, D. (1988) *The learner-centred curriculum*, Cambridge: Cambridge University Press.

Wenden, A. (1991) *Learner strategies for learner autonomy*, Hemel Hempstead: Prentice Hall.

GERD EGLOFF

# Waystage

An early-learning **OBJECTIVE** designed to provide learners with a broad range of resources at a very elementary level so as to enable them to cope, linguistically speaking, in temporary contacts with foreign language speakers in everyday situations. Waystage is the lowest level in a three-level system of behavioural objectives developed under the auspices of the Council of Europe. The central element in this system is the **THRESHOLD LEVEL**, from which Waystage was derived through a process of reduction. It contains what its authors considered to be the most basic categories within each of its parameters: the most essential situations, topics and functions, inescapable general **NOTIONS**, important specific notions, and their simplest and most basic lexical and grammatical exponents to enable the learners to cope at least minimally in those communicative situations which may be most directly relevant to them. Originally published as *Waystage* (1977), the objective has since been re-issued as *Waystage English* (1980) and revised (1991) on the basis of the expanded model of specification used in *Threshold Level 1990* as *Waystage 1990*.

**See also:** Assessment and testing; Council of Europe Modern Languages Projects; Threshold Level; Vantage Level

### References

van Ek, J.A. and Trim, J.L.M. (1991) *Waystage 1990*, Strasbourg: Council of Europe.
van Ek, J.A., Alexander, L.G. and Fitzpatrick, M.A. (1977) *Waystage*, Strasbourg: Council of Europe; re-issued as *Waystage English* (1980) Oxford: Pergamon Press.

JAN VAN EK

# Widdowson, Henry George

b. 1935, Leicester

Applied linguist.

Widdowson was educated at Alderman Newton's Boys' School, Leicester, and King's College Cambridge. From 1958 to 1961 he lectured at the University of Indonesia before joining the **BRITISH COUNCIL**, for whom he worked for six years, serving mainly in Sri Lanka and Bangladesh. In 1968 he joined the Department of Linguistics at the University of Edinburgh, where he took his PhD and worked for the next nine years. In 1976 he was appointed Professor of Education at the London University Institute of Education, following the retirement of Bruce Pattison, with specific responsibility for **ENGLISH** as a Foreign Language – later English for Speakers of Other Languages (ESOL). In the 1990s he combined this post with positions in the Universities of Essex and Vienna, holding a Chair in English Language at the latter from 1998. He served with distinction as one of the first editors of the journal *Applied Linguistics*, and chaired the British Council's English Teaching Advisory Committee from 1982 to 1991. In 1986–88 he was a member of the Kingman Committee of Inquiry into the Teaching of English Language, where his minority dissenting report, suggesting that the official findings lacked a clear basis in language **ACQUISITION** theory, was very influential.

Although Widdowson has carried out some empirical work, he has been mainly a theorist of language and language teaching; his extensive writings have addressed most significant areas in the field. They have been particularly notable in literature and **STYLISTICS**, **COMMUNICATIVE LANGUAGE TEACHING**, **ENGLISH FOR SPECIFIC PURPOSES** (ESP) and discourse, but he has also written on pedagogy, teacher training, critical linguistics, and **READING**. His approach has been distinctive and original, his works written in a style that is pungent, careful and occasionally polemical.

His most notable contribution to practice is probably an approach to stylistics and literature which has been adopted by both **MOTHER-TONGUE** and foreign language teachers. His 1975 book *Stylistics and the Teaching of Literature* typifies his procedure: texts, usually poems, are rewritten to reveal the effects of detailed lexical and syntactic changes, and thus to highlight the significance of the original form. In *Teaching Language as Communication* (1978) he examines the discourse bases of language in order to push towards a greater concern for genuine language use rather than the concentration on formal categories of earlier traditions. This is one of the most important texts of the communicative language teaching movement.

His later writing and editorial work develops these themes in volumes of essays and in monographs which extend his ideas in response to the changing scene in English language teaching. A key theme of his work has been the need for rigorous thinking and open debate; in his later years he has shown some impatience at what he perceived to be an unwillingness, particularly by critical discourse analysts, to recognise the limits of their procedures. Intolerant of obfuscation, Widdowson consistently defends clear-thinking and clear presentation of ideas. For international ESOL, he has probably been the most influential philosopher of the late twentieth century.

### Bibliography

Widdowson, H.G. (1978) *Teaching language as communication*, Oxford: Oxford University Press.

Widdowson, H.G. (1983) *Learning purpose and language use*, Oxford: Oxford University Press.

Widdowson, H.G. (1990) *Aspects of language teaching*, Oxford: Oxford University Press.

Widdowson, H.G. (1995) 'Discourse analysis: a critical view', *Language and Literature* 4, 3: 157–72.

Widdowson, H.G. (1998) 'The theory and practice of critical discourse analysis. A review article', *Applied Linguistics* 19, 1: 136–51.

### Further reading

Cook, G. and Seidlhofer, B. (eds) (1995) *Principle and practice in applied linguistics*, Oxford: Oxford University Press (Festschrift for HGW).

CHRISTOPHER BRUMFIT

# Writing

Initial composition studies were motivated by the question '*What* does the composing process look like?' The second question that emerged was '*Why* do writers make the decisions they make?' According to these two basic questions, text production is considered as a cognitive problem-solving process, but also as a form of social interaction in which the sociocultural context plays an important role. These two perspectives are the starting point for the following overview of research into, and the teaching of, L2 writing. First there are accounts of the process paradigm and cultural issues in research, and these are followed by an outline of four prominent approaches to instruction with the key words 'creativity', 'communication', 'cognition' and '**SKILLS**'.

### The process paradigm

Research into L2 writing is a rather young discipline. One of the first comprehensive collections to be devoted to research on this topic was published in 1990 (Kroll, 1990), and since 1992 the field has had a journal of its own (*Journal of Second Language Writing*). The investigation of the sociocultural and interactional aspects of writing characterises the state of the art of research into

L1 writing, but L2 research continues to be affected primarily by the process paradigm.

Due to the relatively narrow data basis and the lack of a comprehensive theory of the L2 writing process, the results of individual studies can only be generalised with significant restrictions. It is, however, possible to identify a few trends (see Krapels, 1990):

- L1 and L2 writing processes have similar basic structures, but they differ in frequency and the ways in which the individual processes are carried out. Writing strategies are also similar, but they are manipulated in different ways.
- Writing expertise and language proficiency are key factors, but they are independent of one another (Cumming, 1989). L2 proficiency has an effect on L2 writing *performance*, but writing strategies affect L2 writing *competence*.
- In L2 text production, not only content-planning features play an important role, but also realisation problems of a purely linguistic nature. Models of L2 writing processes thus often include a separate L2 problem-solving process (Krings, 1994) or make a distinction between a cognitive–strategic component and a semantic–linguistic text component (Whalen and Ménard, 1995).

With regard to individual aspects of L2 writing, the following trends are becoming discernible:

- Skilled writers plan more than unskilled writers. Skilled writers plan more at global levels, less-skilled writers plan almost only at local levels. In general, the initial hierarchical planning usually takes place in the mother tongue. When the planning has progressed further, L2 is used to translate the plan into text.
- The transfer of ideas into written language is more problematic in L2 than in L1, and is slower and more troublesome. Writers either write in L2 from the start, or they translate. The degree to which the mother tongue is used is dependent of how difficult the writing task is, and the use of L1 mainly helps the writers to retain thoughts for a short time.
- The revision patterns of L1 and L2 writers are quite similar. There is an interrelation between L2 proficiency and revision behaviour. Further-

more, during revision, experienced L2 writers focus more on the content than on parts of the text. They also revise at a level above that of words or phrases and revise in a more differentiated way than inexperienced writers.

- L1 writing strategies seem to play an important role in L2 writing. Writers with a considerable experience in L1 writing make use of their writing competence in relation to audience, writing strategies and planning patterns.
- Use of the mother tongue is a widespread strategy, but it varies considerably. This strategy uses L1 as a source for **VOCABULARY**; it also helps writers to find ideas, and sometimes it supports text organisation. The strategy is especially helpful for writers with a low level of L2 competence, but for more advanced learners it is quite counter-productive.
- When writing their own texts which are based on texts written by others, L2 writers adopt more material from the sources than L1 writers do. Whereas lower proficiency L2 writers integrate the material less well into their own texts, writers at a higher proficiency level are more capable of integrating it into their texts.

## Cultural issues

From a social perspective, the cultural technique 'writing' does not only take place in the minds of the writers. On the contrary, interactive, social and cultural factors shape both form and content of texts as well as the writers' ideas about the purpose and nature of writing.

Within discourse communities (Pogner, 1999) or cultures, there are conventions concerning how the production of knowledge and the negotiation of meaning 'usually' take place, and how the knowledge produced is passed on. Conventions place constraints on the individual writers, but they also provide the potential for producing knowledge and negotiating meaning in conjunction with others.

Since the 1960s, the study of Contrastive Rhetoric has been concerned with cultural issues. It interprets text organisations in different languages/cultures, either as an expression of thought patterns or as the result of rhetorical education. In the last decades, it has expanded its research subject area considerably with regard to the languages examined, and the **TEXT TYPES**, social contexts and discourse communities involved (Connor, 1996; González and Tanno, 2000). Thus, in his review, Huckin (1995/96) demonstrates that cultural issues play an important role in **GENRE** knowledge and in mastering genres. Some of the text features that can vary from culture to culture are:

- amount of personal information and degree of courtesy (request letters)
- level of formality (submission letters, academic essays)
- type of **POLITENESS** (apology letters, academic reports)
- point of view (academic essays)
- degree of self-reference (job letters)
- use of meta-text (academic reports).

## Teaching writing

The 'research space' described above can be summed up as a tension between the two approaches, 'writing as a cognitive problem-solving strategy', and 'writing as a culturally conditioned activity'. Which role do these two perspectives play in instruction?

Silva (1990) sums up the development of ESL writing instruction as follows. The concentration on lexical/syntactic features (controlled composition) was replaced by a focus on the discourse level (current–traditional rhetoric and Contrastive Rhetoric). The emphasis was then placed on the writer's composing behaviour (process approach) and finally on the genres in the academic discourse community (academic writing).

Silva criticises this state of affairs, as it seems to be characterised by an unproductive approach cycle. For this reason, the remainder of this entry will examine how this unproductivity can be overcome. For this purpose, four prominent approaches to writing instruction will be presented.

1 Expressive–creative writing promotes writing as an expression of self-realisation. Interest in and enjoyment of writing are to be encouraged by means of the playful use of language and active use of **LITERARY** forms. The Anglo-American concept of 'creative writing' is supported in Europe by approaches which also include the concept of the 'free text' in L2 teaching.

2 The communicative–functional approach gives particular emphasis to the functions of written texts. It focuses on the informative intention of writers and, in particular, on the adequacy of the 'communication offer' which the texts make to their readers. The communicative perspective is promoted by the increasing use of new communication technologies (computer, telefax, **INTERNET** and e-mail).

3 Writing is a complex cognitive process in which knowledge is organised hierarchically on the one hand and, on the other, is transformed into linear sentence chains, which in turn form a complex textual web. When writing goes beyond knowledge-telling, it can be of service for transforming or generating knowledge and thus promote intellectual development.

4 In order to make it easier for writers to manage their writing, they learn specific skills in order to obtain a better mastery of the individual processes involved. In teaching, different techniques are practised in order to supply contents, encourage planning behaviour, include the reader, and promote revising behaviour. Texts are rewritten and adapted to fit different rhetorical situations. The goal is to enable the writers to select their linguistic formulation as a result of conscious communicative choices. The learning of text conventions and genres is also significant in this context, because text production is constrained, but also made easier, by genre conventions.

The four approaches described above should not be considered as incompatible opposites. Instead, they can be combined or integrated, for example in the context of workshops in which a group of writers together goes through a complex writing process 'in slow motion'. In the collaborative production of a text, the writers can step out of the writing process in 'didactical loops' in order to reflect on their rhetorical choices – but also on their own writing processes. In this way, the linguistic knowledge and process awareness of the learners are both strengthened.

**See also:** Audiolingual method; Listening; Non-native speaker teacher; Pronunciation teaching;

Reading; Schema and script theory; Skills and knowledge; Speaking; Standard language

## References

Connor, U. (1996) *Contrastive rhetoric*, Cambridge: Cambridge University Press.

Cumming, A. (1989) 'Writing expertise and second-language proficiency', *Language Learning* 39, 1: 81–141.

González, R. and Tanno, D.V. (eds) (2000) *Rhetoric in intercultural contexts*, Thousand Oaks: Sage.

Huckin, T. (1995/96) 'Cultural aspects of genre knowledge', *AILA Review* 12: 68–78.

Krapels, A.R. (1990) 'An overview of second language writing process research', in B. Kroll (ed.), *Second language writing*, Cambridge: Cambridge University Press.

Krings, H.P. (1994) 'What do we know about writing processes in L2?', in K.-H. Pogner (ed.), *More about writing*, Odense: Odense University Institute of Language and Communication [ERIC ED 381811].

Kroll, B. (ed.) (1990) *Second language writing*, Cambridge: Cambridge University Press.

Pogner, K.-H. (1999) 'Discourse community, culture and interaction', in F. Bargiela-Chiappini and C. Nickerson (eds), *Writing business*, New York: Longman.

Silva, T. (1990) 'Second language composition instruction', in B. Kroll (ed.) *Second language writing*, Cambridge: Cambridge University Press.

Whalen, K. and Ménard, N. (1995) 'L1 and L2 writers' strategic and linguistic knowledge', *Language Learning* 45, 3: 381–418.

## Further reading

Ferris, D. and Hedgcock, J.S. (1998) *ESL composition*, Mahwah, NJ: Lawrence Erlbaum.

Grabe, W. and Kaplan, R.B. (1996) *Theory and practice of writing*, New York: Longman.

Pogner, K.-H. (ed.) (1997) *Text and interaction*, Odense: Odense University Institute of Language and Communication [ERIC ED 414583].

Rijlaarsdam, G., van den Bergh, H. and Couzijn, M. (eds) (1996) *Effective teaching and learning of writing*, Amsterdam: Amsterdam University Press.

KARL-HEINZ POGNER

# Index

Page numbers in **bold** indicate references for the main entry.